The Concise Encyclopedia of

GARDEN PLANTS

The Concise Encyclopedia of GARDEN PLANTS

Kenneth A. Beckett

ORBIS PUBLISHING · LONDON

First published in Great Britain by Orbis Publishing Limited, London 1983.
Reprinted 1984.

Printed in Yugoslavia.
ISBN 0-85613-534-8

Preceding pages:

Page 1 *Schizostylis coccinea* Mrs Hegarty
Page 2 *Viola × williamsii* Blue Heaven

Introduction

This important book is, though concise in descriptive text, probably the most comprehensive single volume work available which deals exclusively with plants to be grown outdoors in the garden.

The difference between this encyclopedia and other works is that it is able to concentrate on thousands of the excellent ornamental plants available rather than try and include as well those more suitable for greenhouses or eating. The benefit will hopefully bring more beauty into more gardens. Many, many more plants are now available than only a few years ago, especially for those wishing to try and raise them from seed. Besides the well known seed firms there are many more specialised concerns selling unusual and interesting perennial plants, including trees, shrubs, bulbs and herbaceous plants as well as annuals, and vegetables. Also included are a number of plants which are more tender but raised, usually annually, for their fine flowers or foliage, as bedding plants to be planted out in due course. These plants are often herbaceous perennials and grown as such in warmer climes, and include such types as the popular 'geraniums'. Some fruits, vegetables and herbs are included if their decorative potential is of as good or even greater standard than their culinary usage, such as borage.

Over 1600 of the thousands of species described are illustrated in colour and make this encyclopedia an astonishing reference work of hardy plant photographs. The accompanying text is concise yet precise and is arranged in the alphabetic order of the generic plant names and with A–Z cross references included. The main text therefore begins with Aaron's beard, which is cross-referred to the generic name of *Hypericum* and specific name of *calycinum*, while the next entry is the generic *Abelia*. Under each generic heading a brief description of the genus is given; how the genus name arose, the family group to which it belongs – such as *Rhododendron* being in the heather family, the Ericaceae; then follow details of how a typical plant in the genus may look and the typical cultivation requirements. Following this, the various species cultivated in each genus are described, giving the characteristics which distinguish them from each other, such as height, colour of flowers or foliage where this is part of their decorative garden value. For brevity, to fit so much information into the text, a few 'technical' terms are used to describe the shapes of such plant parts as leaves – ovate, lanceolate, cordate, and so forth. Most of these terms are 'botanic' in origin and are based on Latin for the most part. Often these words are very close to their English equivalents, ovate – egg shaped, lanceolate – lance shaped; cordate – heart shaped is of similar derivation to the English cordial – hearty, while sagittate – arrowhead shaped might most easily be understood by those familiar with the signs of the Zodiac. The glossary explains these terms and many more. A few, apparently arithmetic, symbols are also used. These are signs for different types of hybrid. For instance, the multiplication sign × before a plant's generic name means that it is a bigeneric hybrid – a cross between two plants of different genera, such as *Cupressus* and *Chamaecyparis* which gives rise to × *Cupressocyparis*, and × *Cupressocyparis leylandii* is a very popular plant; a × sign between a plants first two names means that two species of the same genus have been crossed to raise a new plant which remains within the same genus, and this gives rise to the largest group of hybrids to which so many of our finest garden plants owe their origin, such as *Abelia* × *grandiflora*; finally there is the plus sign + which indicates a hybrid plant resulting from a graft between two different genera, such as in + *Crataegomespilus*. The use of botanic names is to provide a name for a plant which will be understood throughout the world, each plant having at least two names, equivalent to a person's surname, the generic name, and a specific name equivalent to a Christian name; a plant's common name is similarly like a nickname, familiar but not understood generally. So, to take the first plant described in this encyclopedia, *Abelia* (surname/generic name) *chinensis* (Christian name/specific name) names a plant, unlike any other plant, which will be known by that name throughout the world. The names themselves might seem daunting at times but are also usually quite simple to understand, thus *Abelia chinensis* is just the Latinization of a Dr Abel, for the generic, and *chinensis*, the specific, from China.

Many of the plants described here will have more familiar names than *Abelia* perhaps, many will be rarer and less familiar plants but all have their decorative assets, some blatant, some subtle: enjoy this mine of information and growing some of the attractions mentioned.

Aaron's beard – see *Hypericum calycinum*.

Abelia

(named for Dr Clarke Abel, 1780–1826, botanist to Lord Amherst's embassy in China). CAPRIFOLIACEAE. A genus of 30 species of evergreen and deciduous shrubs from Asia and C.America, cultivated for their clusters of tubular, foxglove-like flowers. The small leaves are ovate and in pairs. They require well-drained soil and a sunny or partially-shaded site. Evergreen species need shelter from cold winds. Plant in autumn and spring. Pruning seldom required, but straggly stems and upper parts of flowered shoots may be removed in spring to maintain a shapely specimen. Propagate by cuttings with a heel from late summer to mid autumn.

Species cultivated: *A. chinensis*, China; 1–1·5m; leaves deciduous to 4cm; flowers fragrant, white, flushed purple with pink calyces, summer. *A.* × Edward Goucher (*A.* × *grandiflora* × *A. schumannii*), blends characters of parents; flowers lilac-pink. *A. floribunda*, Mexico; 1–2m; leaves semi-evergreen, glossy to 4cm; flowers pendulous, rose-red, to 5cm, summer. *A.* × *grandiflora* (*A. chinensis* × *A. uniflora*), popular hybrid resembling *A. chinensis* but leaves semi-deciduous and flowers in summer and autumn. *A.* × *g.* Variegata, yellow-variegated leaves. *A. schumannii*, China; 1–1·5m; leaves deciduous to 3cm; flowers rose-pink in summer. *A. triflora*, Himalaya; to 3m; leaves deciduous to 7cm; flowers fragrant, white, flushed pink, summer.

Abies

(from the Latin *abeo*, to rise – referring to height of some species). PINACEAE. A genus of 50 evergreen trees known as firs, from mountains, N.Hemisphere. They have central, erect trunks and whorls of branches in tiers, forming narrowly conical or columnar trees. The flower-spikes are known as strobili, the males catkin-like, the females like soft miniature cones. The ovoid to cigar-shaped cones stand erect on the branches and fall apart when ripe. The small leaves are blunt, needle-like, the stalk of each one forming a small disc of attachment (a distinguishing feature from the spruces – see *Picea*). Many species are valuable timber trees and several are grown for their imposing appearance. They need moist, but not waterlogged, soil, preferably acid to neutral, in sun or partial shade. Plant in autumn or spring. No pruning required. Propagate from seed in spring.

Species cultivated: *A. alba*, common or European silver fir; Europe; to 48m; leaves dark green, white-banded beneath. *A. balsamea*, balsam fir, balm of Gilead; N.America; to 25m in America but does not thrive in Britain. *A.b.* Hudsonia, low bush to 60cm, suitable for rock gardens. *A. concolor*, Colorado white fir; W.USA to Mexico; to 40m; leaves blue-grey. *A. c. lowiana*, midway between *A. concolor* and *A. grandis*. *A. delavayi forrestii* (*A. forrestii*), Forrest's fir; W.China; to 20m; leaves blue-green, white-banded beneath; young cones blue-purple. *A. grandis*, W. N. America; giant or grand fir; to 54m;, leaves aromatic, mid to yellow-green, silver-banded beneath. *A. g.* Violacea, leaves blue-grey. *A. koreana*, Korean fir; Korea, Quelpaert Is; to 10m; leaves dark green, white-banded beneath; young cones rich violet-blue slow-growing and ideal for the smaller garden. *A. nordmanniana*, Caucasian fir; W.Caucasus, Turkey; to 40m; leaves usually deep bright green, white-banded beneath. *A. pinsapo*, Spanish or hedgehog fir; S.Spain; to 33m; leaves grey-green with pale bands; male catkins red. *A. p* Glauca, leaves bright blue-grey. *A. procera*, Noble fir; W.USA; to 45m; leaves deep grey-green, banded pale grey beneath; male catkins crimson. *A. veitchii*, Veitch's silver fir; Japan; to 25m; leaves aromatic, dark glossy green, silver-banded beneath; male catkins orange-red; young cones blue purple gradually turning to brown.

Above: *Abelia grandiflora*
Right: *Abies grandis*
Below right: *Abies koreana*

Abutilon

(Arabic name for a type of mallow). MALVACEAE. A genus of about 100 evergreen shrubs, annuals and perennials mainly from the tropics and subtropics. They are grown for their pendulous, bell-shaped flowers and long-stalked, maple-like leaves. Except for a few species they need greenhouse treatment. The half-hardy sorts need well-drained soil and a sheltered, sunny wall; the tender species can be grown in pots of any commercial potting mixture or in the greenhouse border. Ventilate freely in summer and maintain a winter minimum temperature of 7–10°C. Repot, or pot on annually in spring, cutting the plants back hard at the same time, or grow annually from stem cuttings, spring, late summer.

Species cultivated: *A. darwinii*, Brazil; tender shrub to 2m or more; leaves velvety-downed, 10–15cm long, 3–7 lobed; flowers 5cm wide, orange-red, darker-veined, spring to summer. *A. globosum*, see the following: *A.* × *hybridum* (*A. globosum* of gardens), (hybrids between *A. darwinii*, *A. striatum* and other species), vigorous plants similar to *A. darwinii* with flowers in shades of red, orange, yellow and white; among those available are: *A.* × *h.* Ashford Red, crimson; *A.* × *h.* Boule de Neige, white; *A.* × *h.* Canary Bird, soft glossy yellow ageing reddish; *A.* × *h.* Firebell, orange-red; *A.* × *h.* Golden Fleece, golden-yellow; *A.* × *h.* Nabob, deep waxy crimson; *A.* × *h.* Orange Glow, orange-yellow; *A.* × *h.* Savitzii, small, slender growth, leaves heavily splashed with white; *A.* × *h.* Souvenir de Bon, pale orange-yellow veined light red-purple, leaves broadly margined creamy-yellow. *A. megapotamicum*, Brazil; half-hardy, slender-stemmed, pendulous shrub to 2m; crimson calyx and yellow petals. *A. m.* Variegatum, yellow-blotched leaves. *A. m.* Golden Fleece, orange-yellow petals and grey-red calyx. *A.* × *milleri*, hybrid of *A. megapotamicum* and similar to it. *A. ochsenii*, Chile; almost hardy shrub to 2m; leaves to 9cm long, 3-lobed; flowers saucer-shaped, 5–6cm wide, blue-purple, spring. *A.* × *suntense* (*A. ochsenii* × *A. vitifolium*), blends the characters of both parents equally but is hardier in gardens. *A.* × *s.* Jermyns, flowers violet-purple. *A. striatum*, Brazil; tender shrub to 3m or more; leaves 8–15cm long, 3–5 lobed; flowers 7–10cm long, red, veined orange, spring to autumn. *A. s.* Thompsonii, leaves smaller, yellow-mottled. *A. vitifolium*, Chile; almost hardy semi-evergreen shrub or small tree to 7m or more; leaves to 15cm long, 3–5 lobed; flowers saucer-shaped, 6–8cm wide, mauve-blue or white (*A. v.* Album). *A. v.* Veronica Tennant, large mauve flowers.

Acaena

(from the Greek *akaina*, a thorn – most species having spiny, bur-like fruit). New Zealand bur, bidi-bidi, piripiri. ROSACEAE. A genus of 100 species of low-growing, mainly evergreen perennials and sub-shrubs, chiefly from the S.Hemisphere. Several are grown as ground cover, having pleasing pinnate foliage, a few for their colourful seed burs. They require moist but well-drained soil and a sunny or partially-shaded site. Propagate by division or from

Top: *Abies pinsapo* Glauca
Above: *Abutilon × suntense*
Top centre: *Abutilon striatum* Thompsonii
Top right: *Abutilon × hybridum* Ashford Red
Centre right: *Acaena microphylla*
Bottom right: *Acantholimon glumaceum*

seed in spring.

Species cultivated: (the following are from New Zealand unless otherwise stated): *A. adscendens*, see *A. magellanica*. *A. anserinifolia* (*A. sanguisorbae*), vigorous, mat-forming; leaves 4·5–8cm long, bronze-flushed, sometimes silky-haired. *A. buchananii*, dense, mat-forming; leaves 2–5cm, often silky and somewhat blue-grey. *A.* Blue Haze (*A.* Pewter), of unknown origin, probably an unnamed species; loose mat-forming, stems red; leaves intense blue-green to 8cm long, burs reddish. *A. caesiiglauca* (*A. glauca* of gardens), vigorous, dense, mat-forming; leaves 3·5–5cm long, blue-grey, burs clear brown. *A. glaucophylla*, (S.America); like a blue-grey leaved *A. magellanica* (*A. adscendens*) and probably only form of that species. *A. inermis*, like *A. microphylla* but leaves blue-grey to bronze and seed-heads lacking spines. *A. magellanica*, S.America; the correct name for plants grown in gardens as *A. adscendens*; robust, prostrate to ascending, dark above, blue-green beneath, burs purplish. *A. microphylla*, very vigorous, mat-forming, stems creeping underground; leaves to 3cm or more with bronze sheen, burs scarlet, showy. *A. novae-zelandiae*, stems somewhat woody at base, prostrate to ascending; leaves 5–10cm long, rich bright green, burs purplish. *A. ovalifolia*, S.America; semi-evergreen, mat-forming; leaves 5–12cm long, bright, somewhat glossy green, burs reddish. *A. pusilla*, much like *A. anserinifolia* but smaller and more slender. *A. sanguisorbae*, see *A. anserinifolia*.

Acantholimon

(from the Greek *akanthos*, a spine, and *limon*, sea lavender). PLUMBAGINACEAE. A genus of 120 evergreen perennials from arid places and stony mountains, E.Mediterranean to C.Asia. They are mainly cushion-forming, thrift-like plants with tough, grassy, spiny-tipped leaves and spikes of small, 5-petalled flowers. Ideal for sunny, well-drained rock gardens or dry walls. Propagate from seed in spring, cuttings in a cold frame or alternatively by division in late summer.

Species cultivated: *A. androsaceum*, S.Europe; leaves rigid, sharp-spined, somewhat blue-grey; flowers red-purple, summer. *A. creticum*, Crete and Greece; probably only a more condensed version of: *A. glumaceum*, Turkey; dark green cushions; flowers pink, 12mm wide in 10cm long spikes, summer.

Acanthus

(from the Greek *akanthos*, a spine). Bear's breech. ACANTHACEAE. A genus of 50 species of perennials and shrubs from S.Europe, tropical and subtropical Africa and Asia. The hardy perennials are grown for their clumps of handsome foliage and flower-spikes. Flowers tubular, 1-lipped, and borne in the axils of spiny, overlapping bracts. Capsule explosive. They need a fertile, well-drained soil in sun or partial shade. Plant autumn or spring. Propagate by division at the same time, or from seed or root cuttings in spring.

Species cultivated: *A. balcanicus* (*A. longifolius*), Yugoslavia; 1–1·5m tall; leaves to 90cm sinuate; flowers rose-purple, summer. *A. dioscoridis*, Turkey to India; leaves spiny, about 30cm long, oblong-lanceolate sometimes with triangular lobes; flowers tubular, purple, in dense spikes to 25cm, summer. *A. mollis*, common bear's breech; S.Europe to Turkey; leaves obovate, deep-lobed, to 60cm long; flowers white or purple-flushed on 90–120cm stems, summer. *A. m. latifolius* is taller and more robust than type species. *A. spinosus*, Italy to Greece; similar to *A. mollis*, but leaves dark green, deeply cut into narrow, spiny lobes; flowers whitish, bracts sometimes purplish, summer. *A. spinosissimus*, a spinier form of *A. spinosus*.

Acer

Maple. ACERACEAE. A genus of 200 species, mainly deciduous trees but a few evergreen and shrubby, from northern temperate zone and tropical mountains, typified by palmate, 3–7 lobed leaves (with some exceptions) and fruit composed of pairs of winged nutlets (samaras). Maples are grown for their handsome foliage, often colouring brightly in autumn; some also have attractive flowers or bark. They require well-drained but moist soil in sun or partial shade. Some species, eg *A. japonicum*, *A. palmatum* and *A. pensylvanicum*, do best in neutral or acid soils. Plant from autumn to spring. Pruning should not be required. Propagate from seed sown when ripe.

Species cultivated: *A. campestre*, field maple; Europe, W.Asia, N.Africa; bushy tree, rarely to 26m; leaves 5-lobed to 12cm wide, rich yellow, flushed red or purple in autumn; flowers yellow-green, in panicles, late spring to early summer, wings of samaras horizontal. *A. capillipes*, red snake-bark maple; Japan; 10–15m; bark green, white-striped; leaves 3- lobed to 12cm long, yellow, orange, red in autumn; flowers yellow in 10–12cm pendant racemes early to mid summer; samaras angled. *A. cappadocicum*, Cappadocian maple; Caucasus, Himalaya to China; to 24m; leaves each 5–7 lobed, acuminate, 8–16cm wide, yellow in autumn; flowers yellow in panicles, early summer; samaras wide-angled. *A. c.* Aureum, young leaves pale yellow. *A. carpinifolium*, hornbeam maple; Japan; bushy tree to 10m; leaves unlobed, hornbeam-like, 7–17cm long, bright yellow in autumn, flowers green in pendant racemes, early summer; samaras incurved. *A. circinatum*, vine maple; W. N. America; shrub or small tree to 12m; leaves 7–9 lobed, circular, 7–12cm wide, red and orange in autumn; flowers purple and white in panicles, late spring; samaras horizontal. *A. davidii*, Père David's maple; China; to 16m; white-striped, olive- green bark; leaves ovate, shallowly or not lobed, 7–15cm long; flowers yellow-green in pendant racemes, early summer; samaras almost horizontal. *A. d.* Ernest Wilson, smaller, spreading tree, with bunched, yellow-green leaves, colouring orange in autumn. *A. d.* George Forrest, young stems dark red; leaves dark green, sometimes shallow-lobed, no autumn colour. *A. ginnala*, Amur maple; China, Japan; to 10m; leaves 3-lobed to 10cm long, crimson in autumn; flowers yellow-green in erect panicles, early summer; samaras almost horizontal. *A. griseum*, paper-bark maple; China; to 13m; bark peeling, reddish or coppery-brown, leaves trifoliate, irregular-toothed, centre leaflet 5–10cm long, red and orange in autumn; flowers greenish-yellow in hanging cymes, early summer; samaras downy, incurving (rarely fertile). *A. grosseri* see next entry. *A. hersii* (*A. grosseri hersii*), Hers's maple; China; to 15m; bark olive-green, white-striped; leaves broadly ovate usually with 3 small lobes, 5–12cm long, yellow to orange or red in autumn; flowers green in pendant racemes, spring; samaras large, pink- tinged. almost horizontal. *A. japonicum*, Japan; shrub or tree to 14m; leaves rounded, 7–11 lobed, 7–12cm long, crimson in

Top: *Acanthus mollis* flower spike tops
Above: *Acer cappadocicum* Aureum in autumn
Top right: *Acer palmatum* Dissectum
Right: *Acer griseum* peeling bark

autumn; flowers red-purple in pendant clusters, late spring; samaras almost horizontal. *A. j.* Aconitifolium (*A. j.* Laciniatum, *A. j.* Filicifolium), leaves deep-lobed and cut. *A. j.* Aureum, usually a shrub, leaves yellow. *A. j.* Vitifolium, large leaves with broad, deep lobes. *A.* × *lobelii*, hybrid resembling its dominant parent, *A. cappadocicum*, but of columnar habit. *A. macrophyllum*, Oregon or big-leaf maple; California to Alaska; to 25m; leaves, 5–7 deep, lobes, 15–30cm wide, pale brown to orange in autumn; flowers greenish- yellow, fragrant, in pendant racemes, late spring; samaras at about 90 degrees. *A. neglectum*, see *A.* × *zoeschense*. *A. negundo*, box elder or ash-leaved maple; N.America; to 15m; leaves to 20cm, of 3–7 ovate leaflets; flowers dioecious, yellow-green in pendant racemes before leaves, mid spring, samaras incurving at 60 degrees. *A. n.* Auratum, leaves yellow; *A. n.* Aureomarginatum, leaves variegated pale yellow; *A. n. californicum*, leaves downy; *A. n.* Elegans (*A. n.* Elegantissimum), leaves yellow-margined; *A. n.* Variegatum (*A. n.* Argenteo-variegatum), leaves broadly white-margined. *A. nikoense*, Nikko maple; China, Japan; to 13m; leaves trifoliate, centre leaflet elliptic to 10cm long, crimson in autumn; flowers yellow, in 3s, early summer; samaras at 90 degrees. *A. opalus*, Italian maple; C. and S.Europe; rather like *A. pseudoplatanus* but flowers large, petals yellow, showy, late spring. *A. palmatum*, Japanese maple; Japan, Korea; bush or tree to 15m; leaves 5–7 lobed, 5–10cm wide, lobes toothed, slender-pointed, scarlet in autumn; flowers purplish in erect corymbs, mid summer; samaras incurved, angled; many cultivars are known, the following being representative: *A. p.* Atropurpureum, leaves bronze-crimson to red-purple; *A. p.* Aureum, leaves soft yellow deepening with age; *A. p. coreanum*, leaves crimson in autumn; *A. p.* Dissectum, shrubby, leaves cut into 7–10 narrow, pinnatifid lobes; *A. p.* Dissectum Atropurpureum, leaves deep red-purple; *A. p.* Dissectum Flavescens, leaves yellow-green in spring; *A. p.* Heptalobum Septemlobum, leaves 7-lobed, larger than the type, broader than long; *A. p.* Heptalobum Elegans, leaves prominently toothed, green; *A. p.* Heptalobum Osakazuki, leaves pinkish-margined, intense scarlet in autumn; *A. p. koreanum*, see *A. p. coreanum*; *A. p.* Senkaki, coral bark maple, leaves yellow in autumn, twigs coral-red. (*A. pensylvanicum* (*A. striatum*), moosewood; E. N.America; to 12m or more; bark greenish to grey, striped white, leaves broadly ovate with 3 terminal lobes, to 20cm long, pale gold in autumn; flowers bell-shaped, yellow-green in racemes 10–15cm long, early summer, samaras forming a crescent. *A. p.* Erythrocladum, twigs crimson in winter. *A. platanoides*, Norway maple; Europe to Caucasus; to 27m or more; leaves 5-lobed with acuminate tips, to 18cm wide, yellow in autumn; flowers showy, bright green-yellow in erect corymbs

Top left: *Acer platanoides* autumn colour
Centre left: *Acer pseudoplatanus* Brilliantissimum summer colour
Below left: *Acer hersii* bark
Above: *Acer platanoides*

before leaves, late spring; samaras horizontal; nutlet very flat; among the several cultivars grown are: *A. p.* Columnare, columnar habit; *A. p.* Crimson King, leaves dark ruby-red; *A. p.* Cucullatum, columnar habit, leaves wrinkled, cupped or hooded; *A. p.* Drummondii, leaves white-margined; *A. p.* Faasen's Black, leaves black-purple; *A. p.* Goldsworth Purple, leaves dark red-purple, much confused with *A. p.* Crimson King and often sold for it; *A. p.* Schwedleri, rich crimson-purple. *A. pseudoplatanus*, sycamore maple, plane in Scotland; C. and S.Europe; to 35m; leaves 5-lobed, 10–25cm wide; flowers yellow-green in pendulous racemes, late spring; samaras at about 90 degrees; cultivars include: *A. p.* Atropurpureum, leaves deep purple beneath; *A. p.* Brilliantissimum, small, slow-growing, round-headed, young leaves change from pink to yellow to dark green, faintly marbled yellow; *A. p.* Corstophinense, smaller than type, young leaves yellow; *A. p.* Leopoldii, young leaves pinkish-yellow, then green, variegated yellow; *A. p. purpureum*, leaves flushed purple beneath; *A. p.* Purpureum Spaethii, the same as *A. p.* Atropurpureum; *A. p.* Worleei, leaves yellow-green to gold. *A. rubrum*, red, scarlet or swamp maple; E. N.America; to 23m or more; leaves 3-5 lobed, coarse-toothed, glaucous beneath, 8–11cm long, red when young, scarlet and yellow in autumn (not reliable everywhere); flowers red in small clusters before leaves in mid to late spring; samaras red, at about 60 degrees, ripening in summer. *A. r.* Columnare, columnar habit; *A. r.* Scanlon, conical habit, good autumn colour; *A. r.* Schlesingeri, autumn leaves rich scarlet. *A. rufinerve*, Japan; to 13m; similar to *A. pensylva-*

nicum but greyish bark with pink stripes or green with grey-white stripes; leaves 6–14cm long, orange to red in autumn; flowers yellow-green in erect racemes, late spring; samaras at 90–120 degrees. *A. r.* Albolimbatum, leaves flecked or margined white. *A. saccharinum* (*A. dasycarpum*), silver, white or river maple; E. and C. N.America; to 30m or more; leaves deeply 5-lobed, silvery-white beneath, 8–15cm long, yellow in autumn; flowers greenish-yellow or reddish, petalless, in small clusters before leaves, early to mid spring; samaras incurved, ripening in summer. *A. s.* Fastigiatum, see *A. s.* Pyramidale; *A. s.* Laciniatum, leaf-lobes sharply cut; *A. s.* Pyramidale, erect habit. *A. saccharum*, sugar maple; E. N. America; to 27m or more; leaves 5-lobed, the 3 central ones shallow-lobed again, to 18cm wide, red, orange and gold in autumn; does not always thrive; source of maple syrup. *A. s.* Temple's Upright, columnar, slow- growing. *A. velutinum vanvolxemii*, Van Volxem's maple; Caucasus; to 20m; leaves 5-lobed, like sycamore maple but yellow-green flowers in erect panicles, petalless, stamens white; samaras about 120 degrees, spring. *A. × zoeschense* (*A. campestre × A. × lobelii*), (*A. neglectum*), to 17m or more; leaves 5-lobed, each one acuminate, glossy deep green with red veins and stalk; flowers yellow-green in erect racemes, spring.

Achillea

(from the Greek hero Achilles, who reputedly used a species for healing wounds). COMPOSITAE. A genus of 200 species of perennial plants from northern temperate zone. Most are of tufted or low hummock-forming habit, often with deeply-lobed or dissected leaves. The tiny, daisy-like flower-heads are generally borne in clusters, creating a greater floral impact. All flower in summer unless otherwise stated. Several are grown in the herbaceous border or rock garden. They require well-drained soil and a sunny site. Plant autumn to spring. Propagate by division autumn or spring; cuttings or seed, spring.

Species cultivated: *A. ageratifolia*, Greece; 7–15cm tall; leaves lanceolate, grey-green; flowers solitary, daisy-like, yellow and white. *A. × argentea* (probably *A. clavenae × A. nana*), 15–23cm; leaves pinnate, grey-green; flower-heads in compact clusters, white, yellow and black. *A. aurea* of gardens – *A. chrysocoma*. *A. chrysocoma*, S.E.Europe; mat-forming, 10–15cm; leaves bi-pinnatisect, white-woollen; flower-heads in compact clusters, bright yellow. *A. clavenae*, E.Alps and Monte Generoso; 10–25cm; leaves narrowly spathulate, silvery silky hairs with 3–5 blunt lobes; flower-heads in loose clusters, white. *A. c. integrifolia*, Albania, Greece; similar to type but leaves almost unlobed. *A. clypeolata* (of gardens, origin uncertain; the true species from Greece appears not to be grown), clump-forming, 45–60cm; leaves bi-pinnatifid, grey; arching flower-heads in dense clusters, bright yellow. *A. decolorans*, see *A. serrata*. *A. eupatorium*, see next entry. *A. filipendulina* (*A. eupatorium*), Caucasus; clump-forming, 90–120cm; leaves pinnatisect, hairy; flower-heads in dense, plate-like clusters, bright yellow; several cultivars are known: *A. f.* Golden Plate, richer yellow, *A. f.* Cloth of Gold, and *A. f.* Coronation Gold (*A. filipendulina × A. clypeolata*), shorter, greyish foliage; *A.* Lye End Lemon, lemon-yellow, and *A.* Lye End Ivory, yellow-white, reputedly have the same parentage. *A. huteri*, Switzerland; 15cm; leaves pinnatifid, silvery; flower-heads white. *A. × jaborneggii* (*A. clavenae × A. moschata*), loose hummock, 10–15cm; leaves pinnatisect, grey-green; flower-heads in loose clusters. *A. × kellereri* (*A. clypeolata × A. aizoon*, or *A. pseudopectinata*), 6–9cm; leaves very slender, pinnatisect, grey-green; flower-heads in loose clusters, yellow and white. *A. × kolbiana* (*A. clavenae × A. umbellata*), intermediate between parents, 10–15cm. *A. × lewisii* King Edward (*A. clavenae × A. tomentosa*), loose mat-forming, 15–23cm; leaves pinnatisect, grey-green, woolly; flowerheads pale yellow. *A. millefolium*, yarrow; Europe, W. Asia; mat-forming, 30–90cm; leaves bi- or tri-pinnatisect; flower-heads in compact, flattened clusters, white or pinkish (a lawn weed). *A. m.* Cerise Queen, cerise-red; *A. m.* Fire King or *A. m.* Red Beauty, similar and darker red. *A. ptarmica*, sneezewort; Europe to Siberia; clump-forming, 45–60cm; leaves linear-lanceolate, serrulate; flowers in loose terminal clusters, white. *A. p.* The Pearl (*A. p.* Boule de Neige), double, button-like flower-heads; *A. p.* Perry's White, larger and whiter than *A. p.* The Pearl, but flops without support. Both *A. ptarmica*

Top: *Acer palmatum* Atropurpureum
Left above: *Achillea ptarmica* The Pearl
Left: *Achillea millefolium* Cerise Queen
Above: *Achillea filipendulina* Golden Plate

and the 2 cultivars described need a moist soil for best results. *A. rupestris*, S.Europe; mat-forming, 10–15cm; leaves spathulate, sometimes toothed; flower-heads in clusters, white, spring. *A. serrata* (*A. decolorans*), to 30cm; leaves linear, sharply-toothed; flower-heads in flattened clusters, yellow-white. *A. s.* W. B. Child, taller than type, flowers white. *A.* × *taygetea* (probably *A. clypeolata* of gardens and *A. millefolium*), similar to *A. clypeolata* but taller (60cm) and greener; flower-heads in flattened clusters, light yellow; *A.* × *t.* Schwefelblüte (*A.* × *t.* Flowers of Sulphur) is a brighter sulphur-yellow. *A. tomentosa*, mat-forming, 20–24cm; leaves bipinnatisect, woolly; flower-heads in flattened clusters, bright yellow. *A. t.* Maynard Gold, deep yellow. *A. umbellata*, Greece; 10–20cm; leaves simply pinnatisect, grey-green; flower-heads in compact umbels, yellow and white *A.* × *wilczekii* (*A. ageratifolia* × *A. lingulata*), 15–23cm; leaves spathulate to oblanceolate with overlapping, small-toothed lobes, white-haired; flower-heads in loose, flattish clusters, white.

Acidanthera – see *Gladiolus*.

Aciphylla

(from the Greek *akis*, a point, and *phyllon*, a leaf). Speargrass, wild Spaniard. UMBELLIFERAE. A genus of 42 species of very large to very small dioecious perennials from Australasia, mainly New Zealand. They are mostly tufted plants with leathery-textured, compound leaves, the lobes or leaflets sword or grass-like, spine-tipped. The tiny white to yellow flowers are borne in umbels that in turn may be carried in raceme-like spires or panicles. The small sorts are suitable for the rock garden, the large ones make interesting accent plants. They require moist but well-drained soil in a sunny or partially shaded site. Plant autumn or spring. Raise from seed sown in sandy soil.

Species cultivated (all come from New Zealand and flower in summer): *A. aurea*, golden Spaniard; about 1m tall; leaves to 70cm long, pinnate to bipinnate, spine-tipped, in dense tufts; flowers gold, in plume-like panicles. *A. crenulata*, to 60cm tall; leaves linear to 15cm, pinnate, spiny, veins red, in loose tufts; flowers in slender spires. *A. glaucescens*, feathery or blue Spaniard; to 50cm tall; leaves to 20cm long, bi- or tripinnate, bluish-green, spine-tipped, in grassy tufts; flowers in slender spires. *A. gracilis*, to 22cm tall; leaves bipinnate to 20cm, spiny, in loose rosettes; flowers in open panicles. *A. hectori*, about 25cm; leaves 6–12cm with 1 pair of rigid leaflets, spine-tipped, in tufts; flowers in panicles. *A. horrida*, horrid Spaniard; to 1m tall; leaves bi- or tripinnate to 80cm, rigid and spine-tipped; flowers white, in broad, conical panicles. *A. monroi*, pigmy speargrass; to 30cm; leaves pinnate to 10cm, flexible with firm tips; flowers white in open panicles. *A. scott-thomsonii*, giant Spaniard; to 3m tall; leaves pinnate or bipinnate, to 1·5m, blue-green, spiny; flowers yellow in robust spires – a statuesque plant. *A. similis*, to 40cm tall; leaves pinnate to 25cm, prickle-tipped, in neat tufts; flowers cream, in panicles. *A. squarrosa*, common speargrass, bayonet plant; to 1m tall; leaves tripinnate, 40–90cm, grey to bluish-green, spiny; flowers whitish, fragrant, in stiff spires. *A. sub-flabellata*, 1m or more; leaves bipinnate, 45cm, fan-like, spine-tipped in dense rosettes; flowers in spires.

Aconite, winter – see *Eranthis*.

Aconitum

(from the Greek *akoniton*, the ancient name for certain species in this genus). Monkshood, wolf bane. RANUNCULACEAE. A genus of 300 erect or climbing herbaceous perennials from northern temperate zone. They usually have deep-lobed, palmate leaves and racemes of hooded flowers. The latter are composed of 5 coloured sepals, the upper 1 large and narrowly helmet-shaped, 10–25mm tall; the 2–5 petals are reduced to stalked nectaries. All parts of the plants are poisonous. They need moist soil and a sunny or partially-shaded site. Plant from autumn to spring. Propagate by division at planting time or from seed when ripe, up to following spring.

Species cultivated: *A. amplexicaule*, Nepal; about 1m; leaves 3-lobed, large; flowers lustrous purple-blue in panicles, summer. *A. arendsii*, see *A. carmichaelii*. *A. bicolor*, see the following: *A.* × *cammarum* (*A. bicolor*), a group of hybrid plants blending the characters of *A. napellus* and *A. variegatum*, the parents, summer; *A.* × *c.* Blue Sceptre, 90cm tall, blue-purple and white; *A.* × *c.* Bressingham Spire, 90cm, violet-blue; *A.* × *c.* Bicolor (of gardens), 1·5m, blue-violet and white; *A.* × *c.* Sparks, 1·5m, intense blue-purple. *A. carmichaelii* (*A. fischeri*), Kamtschatka; to 1·2m; leaves 5–7 lobed; flowers in branched racemes, pale blue, late summer to autumn. *A.c.* Arendsii, darker blue than type; *A.c. wilsonii*, more robust, taller, to 1·8m; *A.c.w.* Barkers, a good selection; *A.c.w.* Kelmscott, violet-blue flowers. *A. lycoctonum*, see *A. vulparia*. *A. napellus*, Europe, Asia; 1–1·5m; leaves lobed; flowers purple-blue in erect racemes, sometimes with small side branches; a near-white *A.n.* Album and pink *A.n.* Carneum are known; several geographic forms are given specific rank, including the rare British *A. anglicum*, summer. *A. septentrionale*, Scandinavia, N. Russia; 90cm; leaves large, 4–6 trifid lobes; flowers purple in usually unbranched erect racemes, summer. *A.s.* Ivorine, ivory-white flowers (by some authorities placed under *A.* × *cammarum* (*A. bicolor*). *A. uncinatum*, E. USA; 60–80cm; stems need support; leaves 3–5 lobed; flowers blue in loose panicles of small clusters, summer. *A. variegatum*, E. Alps; 1·5–2m; stems somewhat zig-zag; leaves with 5 cleft lobes; flowers violet-blue or white in loose racemes, late summer. *A.v. bicolor*, shorter than type, purple-blue and white flowers. *A. volubile*, Altai Mountains; stems twining to 4m; leaves 5–7 lobed; flowers violet-purple, in short racemes, late summer to autumn. *A. vulparia* (*A. lycoctonum*), wolf bane; Europe, Asia; slender stems 1–1·5m; leaves with 5–7 deeply-trifid lobes; flowers cream to yellow with greatly elongated helmets in loose, branched racemes, summer; needs support. There are several closely allied species, some with blue-purple flowers (qv *A. septentrionale*). *A. wilsonii*, see *A. carmichaelii*.

Acorus

(from the Greek *akoron*, originally for the yellow flag iris but later applied to sweet flag). ARACEAE. A genus of 2 species of hardy evergreen perennials from northern temperate and subtropical zones. They have narrow, iris-like leaves and creeping

Left below: *Aciphylla scott-thomsonii*
Below: *Aconitum carmichaelii* Arendsii

rhizomes. The minute greenish flowers are borne in a spadix hidden by the foliage. Useful plants for moist or wet soils, the sweet flag growing well in water; sun or partial shade. Plant spring, propagate by division at planting time.
Species cultivated: *A. calamus*, sweet flag; Asia, N. America, naturalized in Europe; leaves sword-like, to 1m long, aromatic when crushed; spadix about 8cm, summer. *A.c.* Variegatus, leaves cream-striped. *A. gramineus*, India to Japan; leaves grassy, 30–50cm long; spadix slender, 5–10cm, spring. *A.g. pusillus*, smaller than type, tufted, useful as pot plant; somewhat smaller plants are sometimes listed as *A.g. pusillus minimus*. *A.g.* Variegatus, leaves cream-striped.

Acradenia

(from the Greek *akros*, upper or terminal, and *aden*, a gland – the young stems and upper leaf surfaces bear translucent oil glands). RUTACEAE. A genus of 1 species of shrub or small tree from Tasmania – *A. frankliniae*. It grows to 3m; leaves trifoliate, leaflets lanceolate, 2·5–7·5cm long; flowers white, 8mm wide, having 5–7 velvety-white petals, in terminal clusters (cymes), early summer. Needs a warm, sheltered site in moist, but well-drained soil.

Acroclinium – see *Helipterum*.

Actaea

(from the Greek *aktea*, elderberry – the leaves somewhat resembling those of elder). Baneberry. RANUNCULACEAE. A genus of 10 hardy herbaceous perennial species from northern temperate zone. They are clump-forming with elegant bi- or tri-ternate leaves, composed of ovate, toothed leaflets, short, fluffy spikes of cream flowers, and white, red or black, berry-like fruit. Ideal for shaded, informal areas, needing moist soil. Plant autumn to spring. Easily propagated by division of the roots at planting time or raised from seed sown outdoors when ripe. Dried seed usually takes a year or more to germinate.
Species cultivated: *A. alba* (*A. pachypoda*), white baneberry, doll's eyes; E. N. America; 60–90cm; flowers late spring; fruit white on thickened red stalks, late summer. *A. asiatica*, E. Asia; to 70cm; leaves sometimes 4 ternate, some leaflets may be lobed; flowers spring; fruit glossy black, 6mm across. *A. rubra*, red baneberry; N. America; like *A. alba*, but fruit glossy cherry-red. *A.r. neglecta*, fruit ivory-white on slender stalks. *A. spicata*, baneberry, herb Christopher; Europe, Asia; to 65cm; leaves bipinnate or biternate; flowers late spring; fruit shining black, ovoid.

Below: *Actaea rubra*
Bottom: *Actaea rubra neglecta*
Right above: *Acorus calamus*
Right: *Acradenia frankliniae*

Actinidia

(from the Greek *aktis*, a ray – referring to the styles that radiate like spokes of a wheel). ACTINIDIACEAE. A genus of 40 deciduous climbing shrubs from E. Asia. They have lanceolate to ovate, toothed leaves, often dioecious, 5-petalled, bowl-shaped flowers, and rounded-to-oblong edible berries. The taller-growing sorts look best rambling through a tree; the shorter ones are ideal for clothing walls, pergolas, and dead tree stumps. A support of vertical sticks, strings or wires is needed for the twining stems. Plant autumn to spring in any fertile, well-drained soil. Straggling or untidy stems may be cut back at any time. Propagate by cuttings, preferably with a heel in late summer with bottom heat.
Species cultivated: *A. arguta*, China, Japan, Korea; to 20m or more; leaves broadly ovate 7·5–12·5cm long; flowers white, fragrant, 2cm across, summer. *A. chinensis*, Chinese gooseberry, Kiwi fruit; China; to 10m; stems red-haired; leaves cordate, broadly-ovate, 12–20cm long; flowers cream to buff, 4cm across; fruit brown, hairy, oblong-ovoid, 5–8cm somewhat gooseberry-flavoured; grown commercially for fruit, particularly in New Zealand where several cultivars have been raised. *A. kolomikta*, China, Japan; to 7m; leaves ovate, 7·5–10cm long, the upper half more or less white or pink; flowers white, fragrant, 12mm across, mid summer; fruit yellowish, sweet, 2–3cm long; the plant is attractive to cats and may need protection while young. *A. polygama*, China, Japan; to 6m; leaves ovate-oblong, pointed, 7·5–12cm; flowers white, fragrant, 2cm wide, mid summer; fruit ovoid, beaked, yellow, 4cm long.

Adenocarpus

(from the Greek *aden*, a gland, and *karpos*, a fruit – the pods have sticky glands). LEGUMINOSAE. A genus of 20 species of evergreen and deciduous shrubs from the Mediterranean area and Canary Is that are allied to *Cytisus* (broom), with trifoliate leaves and pea-shaped flowers in dense racemes. Interesting, somewhat tender plants for well-drained soil and a sheltered, sunny site. Plant in late spring after fear of frost. Propagate from seed in late winter under glass, or late spring outside.
Species cultivated (all deciduous): *A. anagyrifolius*, Morocco; 1–2m; leaflets slightly blue-green; flowers rich yellow, summer. *A. complicatus*, Mediterranean; deciduous, to 4m; leaflets 1–4cm, often folded lengthwise; flowers orange-yellow, streaked red, 1–1·5cm long, from late spring to late summer. *A. decorticans*, Spain; to 3m or more; leaflets rolled lengthwise, to 2m long; flowers glossy yellow, late spring. *A. foliosus* (*Cytisus f.*), Canary Is; dense, evergreen shrub, 1–2m; leaflets small, hairy; flowers yellow, late spring.

Adenophora

(from the Greek *aden*, gland, *phoreo*, to bear – a gland girdles the style base). CAMPANULACEAE. A genus of 60 herbaceous perennial species from Europe and Asia, closely related to *Campanula*. They are tufted or clump-forming, with lanceolate to ovate leaves, and nodding, bell-shaped flowers in terminal racemes. Grow in moist but well-drained soil; sun or parial shade. Propagate seed in spring.
Species cultivated: *A. bulleyana*, China; to 1·2m tall; leaves oblong-ovate, 5–7·5cm; flowers pale blue, to 12mm long, in well-branched racemes, late summer. *A. potaninii*, Turkestan; 90–120cm; flowers violet-blue, in branched racemes, summer. *A. tashiroi*, also known as *A. polymorpha tashiroi*, Japan, Korea, Quelpaert; to 30cm; flowers blue to 2cm long in small terminal racemes, late summer.

Adiantum

(from the Greek *adiantos*, dry, unwetted – referring to the water-repelling nature of the leaf surface). Maidenhair. ADIANTACEAE. A genus of 200 species of herbaceous and evergreen ferns of cosmopolitan distribution, especially tropical America. In general they are typified by blackish, glossy leaf-stalks (stipes) and compound leaves that may be pinnate, bipinnate or multipinnate. Individual leaflets (pinnae or pinnules) vary from triangular or oblong, to fan-shaped, with a few rounded or other shapes, usually lobed. The spore-bearing sori are marginal. Some species are of tufted growth, others spread far by underground rhizomes. Some are winter-hardy, but most require greenhouse conditions. The hardy species need a moist but well-drained soil in dappled shade; plant in spring. Propagate all species by division or spores in spring.

Species cultivated: *A. pedatum*, N. America, Asia; tufted, fronds rounded in outline, pedate; each pinna pinnate; pinnules oblique-triangular, sometimes deeply-cleft, 1·5–2cm long; hardy. *A.p.* Imbricatum, pinnules shorter than type, broader, overlapping – confused in trade with *A.p. aleuticum*, that has fewer pinnae, and is pink-flushed when young, bluish-green later. *A. venustum*, Himalaya; rhizomatous; fronds triangular, 15–30cm long, 3–4 pinnate; pinnules rounded to oblong, to 10mm finely-toothed, hardy.

Adlumia

(for John Adlum, American horticulturist and amateur botanist, 1759–1836). FUMARIACEAE. A genus of 2 biennial climbing species from E. N. America and Korea. They have bi- to tripinnate leaves, the stalks of which act as tendrils, and inflated tubular flowers like slender hearts, in drooping panicles. A moist soil and a shaded site sheltered from wind are necessary, also the support by twiggy sticks, strings or a tall bush. Propagate from seed sown when ripe or in spring, transplanting seedlings to permanent site as soon as possible. The only species in cultivation is: *A. fungosa* (*A. cirrhosa*, *Corydalis fungosa*), climbing fumitory, mountain fringe; to 4m; flowers 12mm long, white, tinted green and purple, or pale pink, summer to autumn.

Adonis

(for the Greek god of plants). RANUNCULACEAE. A genus of 20 species of annuals and perennials from Europe and Asia. They have deeply-dissected, ferny leaves and buttercup-like flowers of 5–30 or more petals or petaloids. Grow in well-drained soil in a sunny site in early autumn or spring. Plant the perennials late summer or autumn. Propagate from seed when ripe or by division at planting time or after flowering.

Top left: *Adiantum pedatum*
Above: *Actinidia kolomikta*
Top right: *Actinidia chinensis* fruit
Right: *Adenocarpus decorticans*
Bottom right: *Adonis amurensis*

Species cultivated: *A. aestivalis*, S. Europe; much like *A. annua*, but petals spreading and ripe carpels (seed), 5–6mm long, larger than those of *A. annua* (3·5–5mm). *A. amurensis*, China, Japan; perennial, 10–30cm; leaf segments linear; flowers spreading flat in sun, 3–4cm wide, 20–30 yellow petals, late winter to spring. Several cultivars have arisen in Japan, among them *A.a.* Fukujukai with large golden-yellow flowers; *A.a.* Nadeshiku, satiny lime-yellow petals fringed; *A.a.* Pleniflora (*A.a.* Flore-pleno flowers double. *A. annua* (*A. autumnalis*), pheasants eye; Mediterranean, S. Europe, naturalized elsewhere; annual, 20–40cm tall; leaf segments thread-like; flowers cup-sahped, 15–25mm wide, 5–8 bright scarlet petals each with a dark basal spot, summer. *A. brevistyla*, Bhutan, Tibet, China; 20–30cm; flowers 3cm wide, 8 white petals, striped blue on the back, spring. *A. pyrenaica*, Pyrenees; 25–40cm; flowers 4–6cm wide, 12–20 golden-yellow petals, summer. *A. vernalis*, Europe; 10–40cm tall; leaf segments narrowly linear; flowers 4–8cm wide, 10–20 bright yellow petals, spring. *A. volgensis*, Russia; like *A. vernalis*, but leaf segments broader and toothed, stems more branched, flowers with more petals, spring.

Aegle – see *Poncirus*

Aegopodium

(Greek *aix*, a goat, and *podion*, a little foot). UMBELLIFERAE. A genus of 7 herbaceous perennial species from Europe and Asia. An ornamental-leaved variety of *A. podagraria*, *A.p.* Variegata, is sometimes cultivated. It has far-creeping rhizomes, ternate or biternate leaves to 20cm long, the ovate leaflets with creamy-white variegation and tiny white flowers in umbels on branched stems, 40–100cm tall. Both wild species and varieties are very invasive, the former being among the worst of perennial weeds found in the garden.

Aesculus

(Latin for a kind of oak). Horse chestnut, buckeye. HIPPOCASTANACEAE. A genus of 13 deciduous trees and shrubs from the N. Hemisphere. A number of the tree species make handsome flowering specimens. All are typified by digitate leaves composed of 5–7 usually obovate leaflets, and erect, narrow panicles (candles) of 4–5 petalled flowers in tubular calyces. Large, glossy-brown seeds (conkers) are borne in rounded, sometimes spiny fruits. Any moist but well-drained soil is suitable and a sunny or partly-shaded site. Plant autumn to spring. Pruning seldom necessary except for removing straggly branches or maintaining stem (trunk) when young;

winter. Propagate from seed when ripe and not later than early spring, or suckers autumn to spring.

Species cultivated: *A.* × *carnea* (*A. hippocastanum* × *A. pavia*), red horse chestnut; tetraploid, true-breeding hybrid, to 15m or more; leaflets to 15cm or more; flowers dull light red, yellow-eyed, candles to 20cm, early summer. *A.* × *c.* Briottii, superior to type

Above: *Aesculus indica*
Above right: *Aesculus hippocastanum* fruit
Above far right: *Aesculus* × *carnea*
Right: *Aesculus* × *carnea*
Below far right: *Aethionema* Warley Rose

with brighter flowers and compact growth; *A.* × *c.* Plantierensis (*A.* × *carnea* × *A. hippocastanum*), similar to latter parent but pink-flowered. *A. chinensis*, Chinese horse chestnut; N. China; to 25m (in wild), slow-growing, akin to *A. indica*; leaflets 12–20cm; flowers white, candles 20–30cm, early to mid summer. See also *A. wilsonii*. *A. flava*, see *A. octandra*. *A. hippocastanum*, common horse chestnut; Greece, Albania; to 30m or more; leaflets to 25cm; flowers white with yellow throat-spots turning crimson, late spring to early summer, fruit spiny. *A.h.* Baumannii (*A.h.* Flore Pleno, *A.h.* Albo-plena), flowers double, white, sterile. *A.* × *hybrida* (*A. flava* × *A. pavia*), 5–10m; leaflets 10–15cm; flowers yellow and/or red, candles 10–16cm, early to mid summer; a red-flowered form may be mistaken for *A. pavia*, but has bright red leaf-stalks (those of *A. pavia* are yellow, flushed pink). *A. indica*, Indian horse chestnut; N.W. Himalaya; to 20m or more; leaflets obovate to lanceolate, to 30cm; flowers white to pink, yellow blotches turning red, candles 13–30cm, mid to late summer. *A.i.* Sidney Pearce, flowers pink, blotched yellow, orange, red or purple. *A. neglecta*, S.E. USA; to 20m but often less, leaflets 10–16cm; flowers pale yellow, red-veined, candles 10–15cm, early to mid summer. *A.n.* Erythroblastos, sunrise horse chestnut; young leaves bright pink to reddish. *A.n. georgiana*, shrubby, flowers yellow and/or orange-red. *A. octandra* (*A. flava*), sweet buckeye; E. USA; to 20cm; leaflets elliptic, 7–15cm; flowers yellow, candles to 17cm, early to mid summer. *A. parviflora*, S.E. USA; wide-spreading, suckering shrub to 4m; leaflets 8–20cm; flowers white, stamens long, slender, pinkish, late summer to early autumn. *A. pavia*, red buckeye; E. USA; 6–18cm; leaflets 8–18cm; flowers crimson, candles to 16cm, mid summer. *A.p.* Atrosanguinea, richer red; *A.p.* Humilis, shrubby, spreading habit. *A. turbinata*, Japanese horse chestnut; Japan; 20–30cm; leaflets 20–40cm (largest in the genus); flowers white, red-spotted, candles 8–30cm, mid summer, fruit warty. *A. wilsonii*, W. China; much like *A. chinensis* and probably only a form of it, with pubescent stems and ovoid fruit, 3cm long. *A. chinensis* has smooth twigs and roundish fruit depressed at the top.

Aethionema

(uncertain, probably Greek *aitho*, to scorch, and *nema*, thread or filament – perhaps from the appearance of the stamens when dried). CRUCIFERAE. A genus of 70 mainly sub-shrubby and woody-based perennial species from the Mediterranean and W. Asia. Several species are suitable for the rock garden, forming low bushes, tufts or hummocks of small, grey to blue-green, somewhat fleshy leaves bearing numerous erect racemes of small, 4-petalled flowers in early summer. They need well-drained soil and a sunny site. Plant autumn or spring. Propagate by cuttings in summer, from seed in spring.

Species cultivated: *A. armenum*, Turkey to Anatolia; tufted perennial to 10cm; leaves linear, blue-grey; flowers pink, 6–10mm wide. *A. coridifolium*, Lebanon, Turkey; perennial, 15–20cm; leaves oblong-

linear, grey-green; flowers pink, 8–10mm wide. *A. grandiflorum* (*A. pulchellum*), Caucasus, Turkey to Iran; perennial, to 30cm; leaves narrowly-oblong; flowers rose-pink, 1–2cm wide. *A. iberideum*, Greece to Caucasus; sub-shrub, mat-forming, to 10cm high; leaves oblong to ovate, blue-grey; flowers white, fragrant, 1–1·5cm wide, late spring; sometimes grown as *A. theodorum*. *A. persicum*, an invalid name for a barely distinct form of *A. grandiflorum*. *A. schistosum*, Turkey to Taurus; perennial to 12cm; leaves linear, flowers pink, about 1cm wide, late spring. *A.* Warley Rose, uncertain origin, variously linked with *A. coridifolium*, *A. grandiflorum* and *A. armenum* – much like a rich pink form of latter; *A.* Warley Ruber; flowers crimson-magenta, a deeper coloured form of *A.* Warley Rose.

African corn lily – see *Ixia*.

African lily – see *Agapanthus*.

African marigold – see *Tagetes*.

Agapanthus

(Greek *agape*, love and *anthos*, a flower). African lily. ALLIACEAE. A genus of 5–12 species (depending on the classifier) from S. Africa. They are clump-forming evergreen or deciduous perennials with strap-shaped leaves and funnel-shaped, 6-sepalled flowers often in rounded umbels. All deciduous species and hybrids are fairly hardy and withstand moderate frosts, grown in sheltered, sunny sites in well-drained soil; the evergreen sorts need frost protection but can grow outside in warm areas. Or grow in large pots or tubs and bring into a cool greenhouse in autumn, or keep under glass all year. Repot ever other year in spring. Propagate from seed in spring.

Species cultivated: *A. africanus* (*A. umbellatus*), stems to 60cm; leaves evergreen, erect, to 35cm; flowers blue-purple, 3–5cm long, autumn; rare in cultivation; most plants under this name belong to the following (see also *A. praecox*): *A. campanulatus*, stems to 1m; deciduous leaves to 45cm, flowers mid blue or white, 3–4cm, late summer. *A.c. patens*, somewhat smaller and more slender, flowers with wide, spreading tepals in dense umbels; probably identical with *A. umbellatus globosus*, see also Headbourne Hybrids. *A. caulescens*, like *A. africanus*, but leaves arising from a stem-like base; flowering stem about 1m, flowers bright to deep blue, widely-expanded, early autumn. *A.c. gracilis*, plant more slender, tepals recurved. *A. comptonii*, evergreen; stem to 1m or more; leaves stiff, channelled to 60cm; flowers sky- to deep blue, narrow, bell-shaped; a dwarf form (30cm) is listed under this name but possibly derived from *A. praecox minimus*. *A. globosus*, see *A. campanulatus patens*. Headbourne Hybrids covers a group of cultivars derived mainly from *A. campanulatus*, with *A. inapertus* and possibly other species. They are robust, hardy plants, ranging from 60–120cm in a wide range of blues, blue-purples and whites. Plants raised from seed vary greatly; deep blues include Isis, Molly Howick, Midnight Blue, Dorothy Palmer, Cherry Holley (often producing a smaller second crop of blooms), Loch Hope (a magnificent cultivar to 1·2m, large heads late in the season). Light blues include Blue Moon (ice blue) and Luly (light blue). See also under *A. praecox praecox*. *A. inapertus*, deciduous, leaves blue-green to 60cm long, 2·5cm wide, springing from short stems; flowering stem to 1·8m, flowers tubular, flared at the mouth, pendant, violet-blue; needs a warm autumn to flower well outside. *A.i. intermedius*, varying in leaf width and shade of flowers, a white form is in cultivation; *A.i. pendulus* (*A.i. pendulinus* of gardens), leaves to 5cm wide; flowers narrowly-tubular, deep blue. *A. mooreanus*, an invalid name often used to cover hybrids derived from *A. campanulatus*. *A. orientalis*, see *A. praecox orientalis*. *A. patens*, see *A. campanulatus patens*. *A. pendulus*, see *A. inapertus pendulus*. *A. praecox* (*A. umbellatus*), stem 1m or more; evergreen; leaves to 90cm long, 6cm wide, arching; flowers to 7cm, opening widely in large umbels, summer and early autumn. *A.p. minimus*, much smaller, less than 60cm, with narrower leaves; *A.p. orientalis*, somewhat smaller, flowers to 5cm in dense umbels; *A.p. praecox* covers several variants formerly listed under *A. africanus* and *umbellatus*, among them *A.p.p.* Albus and *A.p.p.* Maximus Albus, both white; *A.p.p.* Aureovittatus, leaves yellow-striped; *A.p.p.* Giganteus, very large, dark blue; *A.p.p.* Maximus, very large, umbels bright blue; *A.p.p.* Monstrosus, very robust, leaves to 7·5cm wide. More recent cultivars, some of which may be of hybrid origin, are: *A.p.p.* Argenteo-Vittatus, leaves white striped; *A.p.p.* Blue Giant, large, rich blue; *A.p.p.* Blue Imp, to 75cm tall; *A.p.p.* Oxford, blue; *A.p.p.* Golden Rule, leaves gold-lined; *A.p.p.* Profusion, 90cm tall, vigorous, good mid blue; *A.p.p.* Flora Pleno, double flowers. *A. weillighii*, hybrid strain from *A. inapertus*; cultivars are best placed under *A.* Headbourne Hybrids.

Top left: *Agapanthus praecox praecox* Albus
Above left: *Agapanthus* Headbourne Hybrid
Top: *Agastache mexicana*
Above: *Ageratum houstonianum*

Agastache

(Greek *agan*, very much, *stachys*, an ear of wheat – referring to the likeness of the flower-spikes). LABIATAE. A genus of 30 perennial species from Asia and N. America (including Mexico). One widely cultivated species. *A. mexicana* (*Cedronella m.*, *Brittonastrum mexicanum*), Mexican giant hyssop; 75cm tall, clump-forming; leaves lanceolate to 6cm, glandular beneath; flowers red, tubular, 2-lipped and 2–3cm long, with several bracted whorls forming terminal spikes, summer. Grow in any well-drained soil in a sunny site. Plant autumn or spring. Propagate by division or from seed during spring.

Ageratum

(Greek *a*, not, and *geras*, old – presumably alluding to the comparative longevity of the flowers). COMPOSITAE. A genus of 60 species of mainly annual plants from tropical America. 1 half-hardy annual is a popular bedding plant. Any ordinary well-drained soil in a sunny state is suitable. Sow seed under glass in mid spring at a temperature of 15–18°C, and plant out in early summer or when fear of frost is over. *A. houstonianum* (*A. mexicanum*), Mexico; 15–60cm; leaves heart-shaped, in opposite pairs; flower-heads blue, rose, white, fluffy pompon-like, in terminal clusters to 10cm wide. Several cultivars are listed in seed catalogues, ranging through shades of blue-purple, pink and white, and varying in height from 13–60cm. Flowers in close spikes up to 4m, rarely found in cultivation; propagation from seeds only.

Agrostemma

(Greek *agros*, field, and *stemma*, a crown or garland). CARYOPHYLLACEAE. A genus of 3 closely-related annual species from the Mediterranean, S. Russia. They are slender plants with opposite pairs

of linear leaves and solitary, 5-petalled flowers with a tubular calyx topped by 5 slender lobes. Any well-drained soil in a sunny site. Sow mid to late spring, or mid autumn for early flowers.
Species cultivated: *A. coeli-rosa*, see *Silene coeli-rosa*. *A. coronaria*, see *Lychnis coronaria*. *A. githago*, corn cockle; Mediterranean; 45–100cm; flowers 3–5cm wide, red-purple, summer. *A.g.* Milas, flowers to 6cm, lilac-pink; *A.g.* Purple Queen, rose-purple.

Ailanthus

(Latinized version of Moluccan name meaning sky tree; hence, tree of heaven). SIMAROUBACEAE. A genus of 10 species of deciduous trees from Asia, N. Australia. They are tall, generally fast-growing trees with robust twigs, imparipinnate leaves and terminal panicles of tiny, 5–6 petalled flowers followed by winged fruit. Any moisture-retentive but well-drained soil and a sunny or partially-shaded site. Plant autumn to spring. Pruning seldom necessary. Propagate by suckers or root cuttings late winter to spring.
Species cultivated: *A. altissima* (*A. glandulosa*), tree of heaven; China; to 26m; leaves 30–60cm long, red-stalked, leaflets 13–25cm, oblong-lanceolate, 7–15cm long; panicles to 30 × 30cm; flowers yellow-green, late summer to early autumn; fruit flushed crimson. *A. giraldii*, China; like *A. altissima*, but leaves to 90cm long with up to 41 leaflets, hairy-veined beneath. *A. vilmoriniana*, W. China; like *A. altissima*, but mid-rib (rachis) and undersides of leaflets pubescent.

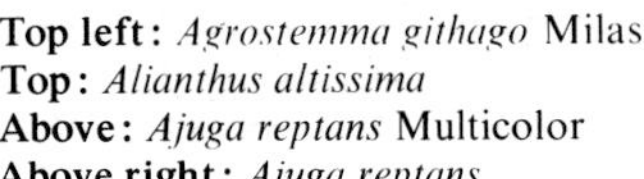

Top left: *Agrostemma githago* Milas
Top: *Alianthus altissima*
Above: *Ajuga reptans* Multicolor
Above right: *Ajuga reptans*

Ajuga

(origin obscure, perhaps derived from the old Latin name *abiga*). LABIATAE A genus of 40 annuals and perennials from temperate Europe, Asia. The species described form low mats or wide clumps of obovate leaves with erect stems bearing whorls of tubular flowers, each with a conspicuous, 3-lobed lower lip in the axils of purple or blue-tinted bracts. Any ordinary garden soil is suitable in sun or shade. Plant autumn to spring. Propagate from seed or by division in spring or after flowering.
Species cultivated: *A. genevensis*, Europe to S.W. Asia; stoloniferous; stems to 30cm; leaves 5–12cm, hairy; flowers bright blue, late spring to summer. *A.* Jungle Beauty, leaves glossy deep green; flowers deep bright blue (perhaps *A. genevensis* × *A. reptans*). *A. metallica*, see *A. pyramidalis* Crispa. *A. pyramidalis*, pyramidal bugle; Europe; rhizomatous; stem 10–30cm; leaves 4–11cm; flowers pale violet-blue, bracts deep purple or red-purple, spring to summer. *A.p.* Crispa (*A. metallica crispa*), leaves crinkly, metallic green-purple. *A. reptans*, common bugle; Europe to S.W. Asia; stoloniferous stem 10–30cm or more; leaves 4–7cm, more or less smooth; flowers blue, blue-purple, sometimes white or pink, spring to summer. *A.r.* Alba, flowers white; *A.r.* Atropurpurea (*A.r.* Purpurea), leaves glossy red-purple; *A.r.* Burgundy Glow, leaves wine-red; *A.r.* Delight leaves variegated silvery-white and pink; *A.r.* Multicolor (*A.r.* Rainbow), leaves green and bronze, mottled yellow, flushed pink; *A.r.* Pink Elf, stems to 10cm tall, flowers pink; *A.r.* Purpurea, see *A.r.* Atropurpurea; *A.r.* Variegata, leaves splashed grey-green and white.

Akebia

(Latinized version of the Japanese name *akebi*). LARDIZABALACEAE. A genus of 5 deciduous or partially evergreen, perennial climbing species from E. Asia. They are twining, woody-stemmed plants with palmate leaves of 3–5 leaflets and axillary

racemes of petalless flowers having 3 petaloid sepals; the fruit is a fleshy, sausage-shaped follicle. Any moisture-retentive but well-drained soil, thin, sandy or limy soils enriched with peat, leaf mould or compost. Strings, wires or sticks are required for the climbing stems. Propagate from seed when ripe, layering in spring, or cuttings in late summer.
Species cultivated: *A. lobata,* see *A. trifoliata. A. × pentaphylla* (*A. quinata × A. trifoliata*), much like *A. quinata,* but with flowers like *A. trifoliata. A. quinata,* China, Korea, Japan; semi-evergreen to deciduous, to 12m (in a tree); leaflets 5, oblong to obovate, entire, 3–5cm long; raceme pendant, flowers fragrant, chocolate-purple, females 2–3cm wide, males 12–16mm, spring; fruit dark purple, 5–10cm long. *A. trifoliata,* (*A. lobata*), Japan, China; to 9m (in a tree); leaflets 3, ovate, shallowly-lobed, 3–6cm long; raceme drooping, flowers dark purple, females 1·5–2cm wide, males 4–5mm, spring; fruit pale purple 7–13cm long.

Alcea – see *Althaea.*

Alchemilla

(Latinized version of the Arabic name, *alkemelych*). ROSACEAE. A genus of 250 species of herbaceous perennials mainly from northern temperate zone and tropical mountains. They are low, tufted, spreading plants with rounded, palmately lobed or digitate leaves and tiny, yellowish-green flowers in clusters or panicles. Easily grown in any ordinary garden soil in sun or shade; plant autumn to spring, propagate by division at planting time or from seed in spring. Good groundcover with attractive foliage.
Species cultivated: *A. alpina,* alpine lady's mantle; N. Europe to Greenland; stems 10–20cm; leaves deeply (5–7) lobed or digitate, 2–3·5cm wide, glossy dark green above, dense, silver, silken hairs beneath; flowers 3mm wide clustered in cymes, summer. *A. conjuncta,* Europe; a larger, finer version of *A. alpina* and often sold under that name. *A. erythropoda,* Balkans to Caucasus; leaves grey-green, broadly 5–7 lobed, deeply-toothed, soft-haired 3–6cm wide; flowers 4mm in dense clusters; rather like a neat, compact *A. mollis* but usually with reddish stems. *A. mollis,* Carpathians to Turkey; robust plant; stems 30–80cm; leaves with dense, soft hairs, broadly 9–11 lobed, boldly-toothed to 15cm wide; flowers lime-green, 3–5mm wide, in large panicles, summer. *A. splendens,* Alps, Jura; stems to 30cm long; leaves orbicular, smooth above, sometimes hairy on veins beneath, the 9–11 blunt lobes $\frac{1}{4}-\frac{1}{3}$ of leaf width, with distinct incisions and 7–9 small, sharp teeth.

Alisma

(classical Greek name for a member of this genus). Water plantain. ALISMATACEAE. A genus of 10 aquatic perennial species from northern temperate zone, Australia. They are hardy, tufted or rosette-forming plants with long-stalked, linear to ovate leaves and whorled panicles of 3-petalled flowers. Wet soil or shallow water and a sunny site are required. Plant spring or after flowering. Propagate by division when replanting or from seed in saturated compost, spring. Several species are now placed in allied genera (ie. *Luronium* and *Baldellia*).
Species cultivated: *A. natans* (*Elisma natans,* now *Luronium natans*), floating water plantain; Europe; stems slender, drifting or rooting at nodes, bearing ovate, floating, drifting leaves; lower leaves submerged, linear to spathulate, to 10cm; flowers white with yellow eye. 12–15mm wide, summer. *A. parviflora, see A. subcordatum. A. plantago-aquatica,* water plantain; northern temperate zone; leaf-blades ovate, boldly-ribbed, 8–20cm on erect stalks several times longer; flowering stems to 1m, flowers to 1cm wide, pale lilac, summer. *A. subcordatum,* (*A. parviflorum* and *A. plantago-aquatica parviflorum*), E. USA, Mexico; much like *A. plantago-aquatica,* but leaf-blades to 25cm; flowers white (rarely pink), to 3·5mm wide. *A. ranunculoides* (once *Echinodorus ranunculoides,* now *Baldellia r.*), lesser water plantain; Europe, N. Africa; leaf-blades linear to narrow lanceolate, stalk 2–4cm long; flowering stems 5–20cm, flowers to 15mm wide, pale rose-purple, late spring, summer.

Top: *Akebia quinata*
Above: *Alchemilla erythropoda*
Above right: *Alchemilla mollis*
Right: *Alisma plantago-aquatica*

Alkanet– see *Anchusa.*

Allium

(classical Latin name for garlic, *Allium sativum*) ALLIACEAE. A genus of 450 mainly bulbous perennial species from N. Hemisphere. They have linear, flattened, keeled or tubular leaves (a few lanceolate to elliptic), and umbels of 6-petalled, starry or bell-shaped flowers in terminal umbels (a few in tiered whorls). In some species the bulbs are not thickened and stem-like (a few rhizomatous). Most species smell of garlic or onion when bruised. Ordinary garden soil in a sunny or partially-shaded site. Plant bulbous species when dormant, the others from autumn to spring. Propagate by offsets or division when replanting, or from seed in spring. Alliums grown for culinary purposes, such as chives, garlic, leeks and onions, are not dealt with as vegetables or herbs in this work.

Species cultivated: *A. acuminatum,* W. N. America; stems to 30cm; leaves linear; flowers rosy-lilac to pink, 1–2cm wide, early summer. *A. albopilosum,* see *A. christophii, A. amabile,* China; bulbs barely thickened; stems 10–20cm; leaves filiform; flowers rose-red to magenta, bell-shaped, nodding, to 1·5cm long, late summer. *A. aflatunense,* China; stem 75–150cm; leaves strap-shaped, blue-green; flowers pale violet, starry, about 1·5cm wide in large, dense, spherical umbels, late spring. *A. beesianum,* China; stems 23–28cm; leaves linear; flowers blue, sometimes purple-blue, pendulous, 1·3–2cm long, late summer. *A. bidwelliae,* see *A. campanulatum. A. breweri,* see *A. falcifolium. A. callimischon,* Greece; stem to 15cm or more; leaves filiform, dying before flowering; flowers white or pink, bell-shaped, 9mm wide, late summer to autumn; a dwarf form, less than 10cm tall, represents this species in cultivation, with fragrant flowers, white with dark crimson freckles. *A. campanulatum* (*A. bidwelliae*), California, Oregon; stems 8–20cm; leaves linear; flowers pink, about 12mm wide, summer. *A. cernuum,* N. America; stems flattened; 20–75cm; leaves linear; flowers red-purple, pink or white, 5mm long, the whole umbel nodding, summer. *A. chamaemoly,* Mediterranean; stems below ground; leaves linear; pedicels 1·5–3·5cm long; flowers white, tepals with reddish central stripe, 8–15mm long, early spring. *A. christophii,* (*A. albopilosum*) stems 30–50cm; leaves narrowly lanceolate to strap-shaped; flowers metallic blue-purple, star-like, 3–4cm wide, in globose heads to 20cm wide, summer. *A. cowanii,* see *A. neapolitanum cowanii. A. cyaneum* (*A. purdomii*), W. China; virtually bulbless, tufted plant; stems to 15cm; leaves filiform; flowers deep blue, summer. *A. cyathophorum farreri,* also known as *A. farreri,* W. China; tufted, almost bulbless; stem winged or angled, about 25cm; leaves narrow-linear; flowers pendant, red-purple, 9mm long, early summer. *A. elatum,* Bokhara; stems to 90cm; leaves oblong; flowers glossy violet-purple, starry, in large globose heads, summer. *A. falcifolium,* California; stem to 12cm; leaves grey-green, linear, falcate; winged flowers pink to red-purple, 1·5–2cm wide, early summer. *A. flavum,* S. and E. Europe; stems to 30cm; leaves narrowly linear; flowers pale yellow, bell-shaped, about 5mm long, late summer; dwarf forms sometimes listed as *A.f. nanum, A.f. pumilum* or *A.f. minus. A. geyeri,* W. USA; stems 8–30cm; leaves linear; flowers pink, rarely white, about 1·5cm wide, summer. *A. giganteum,* Iran to C. Asia; stems 90–120cm; leaves blue-green, strap-shaped; flowers metallic-lilac, about 1cm wide, in spherical heads, to 10cm wide, summer. *A. glaucum,* see *A. senescens. A. kansuense,* China; much like *A. beesianum,* with smaller flowers in a more erect umbel. *A. karataviense,* Turkmenistan; stems 15cm; leaves broadly elliptic, grey-green and purple, handsome; flowers small, whitish or purplish, in spherical heads to 20cm wide, late spring. *A. macranthum,* Sikkim; somewhat rhizomatous; stems 60–90cm; leaves linear; flowers bright mauve-purple, bell-shaped, about 12mm long, summer. *A. mairei,* W. China; like *A. amabile,* but flowers pale pink or white, spotted pink. *A. moly,* S. W. Europe; stems 15–25cm; leaves grey-green, lanceolate; flowers bright yellow, to 1·5cm wide, summer. *A. murrayanum,* W. N. America; akin to *A. acuminatum,* but with broader, richer lilac-pink tepals. *A.*

Above: *Allium rosenbachianum*
Right: *Allium albopilosum*
Bottom right: *Allium moly*

narcissiflorum (*A. pedemontanum*), N.Italy, France; clump-forming, barely bulbous; stems 20–30cm; leaves grey-green, linear; flowers rich pink to rose-purple, bell-shaped, to 1·5cm long in pendant umbels. *A.n. insubricum* is the form in cultivation described here, with permanently pendant umbels. *A. neapolitanum,* S. Europe; stems 30cm; leaves linear, keeled; flowers glistening white, about 1·5cm wide, starry, spring. *A.n. cowanii,* large-flowered and more robust than type; not reliably hardy, sheltered, sunny border – good pot plant for a cool greenhouse. *A. odorum,* see *A. ramosum* and *A. tuberosum. A. oreophilum,* Caucasus, C. Asia; stems 10–15cm; leaves linear, channelled above; flowers reddish-purple, about 12mm wide, summer. *A.o. ostrowskianum,* leaves grey-green, flowers rose; *A.o.o.* Zwanenburg, carmine-rose. *A. pedemontanum,* see *A. narcissiflorum. A. pulchellum,* stems 30–60cm; leaves narrowly linear, dying before flowering; flowers bright red-purple, bell-shaped, 5cm long, late summer; white and dwarf forms are known, the latter allied to *A. flavum,* sometimes listed as *A. flavum pumilum roseum. A. purdomii,* see *A. cyaneum. A. pyrenaicum,* E. Pyrenees; stem 45–90cm; leaves lanceolate, tip-hooded; flowers pale pink, tepals with green keel, summer, *A. ramosum* (*A. odorum* in part), Asia; stems 25–50cm; leaves linear, hollow; flowers white, bell-shaped, 1cm long, summer. *A. rosenbachianum,* N. Afghanistan, USSR; stems to 1m; leaves lanceolate; flowers purple-violet, starry, 1·5cm wide, in dense, spherical umbels to 10cm wide, summer. *A. roseum,* S. Europe, N. Africa; stems 25–40cm; leaves linear-lanceolate; flowers pink, bell-shaped, 1–1·5cm wide, late spring; needs a sunny, sheltered site. *A. schubertii,* Syria, Israel; stems to 60cm; leaves strap-shaped; flowers pink, starry, about

1·5cm wide on pedicels of differing length forming rounded, sparkler-like heads to 25cm in diameter, late spring; needs a sunny, sheltered site. *A. senescens,* Europe to Siberia; stem 15–30cm; leaves narrowly linear, 5–12mm wide; flowers pink, in dense, 3–4cm wide umbels, summer. *A. montanum* (*A. glaucum*) very similar to *A. senescens,* and both hybridize in gardens, but leaves to 3cm wide. *A. siculum* (*Nectaroscordum s.*), S. France, Sicily, Italy; stems 60–90cm; leaves narrowly lanceolate, channelled above, keeled below; flowers pendant, broadly bell-shaped, each tepal maroon with a wide green stripe, 2cm long. *A.s. dioscoridis,* also known as *A. bulgaricum;* flowers white, tinged green and red; capsules erect with a 'dunce's cap' of hardened ivory-yellow tepals – good for winter flower arrangements. *A. sphaerocephalon* (*A. sphaerocephalum*), W. Europe to Iran; stems to 60cm; leaves narrow, half cylindrical; flowers dark red-purple, bell-shaped, 5mm long, in dense ovoid head, summer. *A. subhirsutum,* Mediterranean Europe; stems 20–50cm; leaves linear; flowers white, 1–1·5cm wide, late spring; needs a sheltered, sunny site. *A. sikkimense,* W. China; much like *A. beesianum,* but flowers smaller in an erect, tighter umbel. *A. stipitatum,* Turkestan; much like and confused with *A. rosenbachianum;* leaves hairy; flowers rose-purple, fragrant, late spring. *A. tricoccum,* E. N. America; rhizomatous and bulbous; stems to 40cm; leaves elliptic, dying before flowering; flowers creamy to greenish-white, cup-shaped, 6mm long, summer. *A. triquetrum,* W. Europe; stem triangular in section, to 20cm; leaves linear, channelled and keeled; flowers white, pendant, bell-shaped, fragrant, 1·5cm long, early summer; best in sheltered, shaded spot. *A. tuberosum, A. odorum* in part, Chinese chives; India to Japan; similar to *A. ramosum,* but leaves solid; flowers smaller with spreading tepals. *A. unifolium,* California; similar to *A. murrayanum* but more robust; flowers somewhat

Left: *Allium giganteum*
Top above: *Allium neapolitanum*
Centre above: *Allium narcissiflorum*
Above: *Allium oreophilum ostrowskianum*
Right above: *Allium murrayanum*
Right: *Alnus glutinosa* catkins

smaller and paler. *A. ursinum,* ramsons: Europe; stems to 30cm; leaves elliptic, glossy rich green; 3-angled; flowers white, starry, 1–1·5cm wide, spring. *A. victorialis,* Europe; stem 30–60cm; leaves oblong-lanceolate; flowers bell-shaped, greenish-white to yellowish, 6mm long, summer. *A. wallichii – A. wallichianum* of gardens – Himalaya; rhizomatous; stem 40–75cm; leaves linear; flowers purple, starry, in umbels 5–8cm wide, late summer.

Almond – see *prunus.*

Alnus

(classical Latin name for an alder). BETULACEAE. A genus of 35 deciduous tree and shrub species from northern temperate zone, Indochina, Andes. They have alternate, often ovate, toothed leaves; monoecious flowers in catkins, the females short and barrel-like, the males flexuous and slender; and fruiting clusters, cone-like and woody, bearing tiny, winged nutlets. Any ordinary garden soil, preferably moisture-retentive; some species thrive in wet places. Plant autumn to spring. Pruning seldom necessary except to remove unwanted shoots from the trunk or straggly branches; winter. Propagate from seed or by layering in spring, hardwood cuttings in autumn; cultivars usually grafted in spring.

Species cultivated: *A. cordata,* Italian alder; Corsica, Italy; conical tree to 27m; leaves dark glossy green, broadly ovate-cordate, 5–8cm long; male catkins pale purple, opening yellow, 7–10cm, winter to spring. *A. crispa,* see *A. viridis. A. glutinosa,* common alder; Europe to Siberia, N. Africa; broadly conical tree to 20m or more; leaves broadly obovate, dark, somewhat glossy green, to 9cm, male catkins dull purple, opening dark yellow, 5cm, late winter, spring. *A.g.* Laciniata, leaves with deep triangular lobes. *A.g.* Imperialis, small tree, leaves cut – sometimes almost to mid-rib – into slender tapered lobes; good for wet soils. *A. incana,* grey alder; Europe to Caucasus; somewhat conical tree to 25m; leaves ovate to broadly so, slightly lobed, dull green above, grey beneath, to 10cm; male catkins 5–10cm, late winter. *A.i.* Aurea, leaves golden-yellow; *A.i.* Laciniata (*A.i.* Acuminata, *A.i.* Incisa, *A.i.* Pinnatifida), leaves small, deeply cut into slender lobes; *A.i.* Pendula, weeping habit; *A.i.* Ramulis Coccineis, shoots orange-red, leaf and catkin bud scales bright red. *A. viridis,* green alder, Europe; large shrub to 3m; leaves ovate to broadly so, dark green above; male catkins 5–8cm long, spring. *A.v. crispa,* synonym of *A. crispa,* an allied species from E. N. America having crisped leaf margins and smaller male catkins.

Alonsoa

(for Alonzo Zanoni, Secretary of State for Colombia when it was a Spanish colony in the 18th century). SCROPHULARIACEAE. A genus of 6 species of sub-shrubs and perennials from S. America. 1 species is often grown as a half-hardy annual. It grows in any well-drained soil in sun or light shade. Sow seed under glass in mid spring at a temperature of 13–16°C and set out the resulting plants in early summer or when the fear of frost has passed. *A. warscewiczii* (*A. compacta*), mask flower; Peru; perennial, erect, bushy, 45–60cm tall; leaves cordate-lanceolate, double-toothed; flowers in racemes, scarlet, 2–3cm wide with five, broad, corolla lobes. Several dwarf cultivars are listed.

Alpine rose – see *Rhododendron ferrugineum*.

Alstroemeria

(for Baron Claus Alstroemer, 1736–94, friend of Linnaeus). ALSTROEMERIACEAE. A genus of 50 species of tuberous-rooted perennials from S. America. They are erect plants, the hardier sorts eventually forming large clumps or colonies; leaves usually lanceolate, borne upside-down owing to a twist in the stalk; flowers in terminal clusters, 6-tepalled, the 3 inner ones narrower, often blotched, streaked or suffused with a contrasting colour. Grow in well-drained soil in a sheltered, sunny site; tender species need a well-ventilated greenhouse with enough heat to keep out frost, either in a border or pots of a good commercial potting mixture. Plant in spring and protect the roots of the half-hardy kinds with a layer of peat or chopped bracken in autumn. Propagate from seed or division in spring. Sow seeds singly in small pots or prick out when small to avoid damaging the fleshy roots.

Species cultivated (all flower in summer): *A. aurantiaca*, Peruvian lily; Chile; hardy, to 90cm tall; leaves greyish beneath, 5–10cm; flowers bright orange, 2 upper tepals streaked red, about 4cm long. *A.a.* Aurea, golden-yellow; *A.a.* Dover Orange, rich orange; *A.a.* Lutea, yellow. *A. brasiliensis*, C. Brazil; hardy, to 1·2m; leaves linear, 6–10cm; flowers yellow, red-flushed, inner tepals brown-spotted, 4cm long. *A. gayana*, as named by Philippi; Chile; tender, 10–30cm tall; leaves somewhat fleshy; flowers to 6cm wide, rose-purple spotted crimson-purple, upper 2 tepals yellow at base. *A.g. humilis*, to 10cm in wild, forming dense hummocks of curled foliage but taller and looser in cultivation. *A. haemantha*, Chile; hardy, to 90cm; leaves 5–10cm long; flowers 5cm long, orange-red to yellow, inner tepals streaked purple-brown. *A. hookeri*, Chile; like *A. ligtu;* 30cm; flowers pink. *A. ligtu*, Chile; hardy, 60cm or more; leaves linear to 8cm; flowers about 4cm long, in shades of pale red to pink and white, inner tepals usually crimson-streaked, the upper ones splashed orange-yellow. *A.l. angustifolia*, flowers pink; *A.l. pulchra*, see *A. pulchra*. In cultivation *A.ligtu* is represented by *A.* Ligtu Hybrids, a strain evolved from crosses with *A. haemantha* and perhaps other species; the plants are taller than type, flowers pink to orange-red; several cultivars are listed. *A. pelegrina*, Chile; half-hardy, about 30cm; leaves to 5cm; flowers solitary or in small clusters, to 5cm wide, crimson to lilac-purple, upper petals paler to white, streaked dark crimson. *A.p.* Alba, lily of the Incas; flowers white. *A. pulchella* (*A. psittacina*), half-hardy, to 1m; leaves oblong-spathulate; flowers 4cm long, crimson, tipped green, the upper tepals brownish-red, spotted mahogany. *A. pulchra* or *A. ligtu pulchra* Chile; half-hardy, to 90cm; leaves narrowly ovate to lanceolate, waved, 4–8cm; flowers about 8cm wide, purple-flushed to white, upper tepals bright yellow, streaked and spotted crimson-purple. *A. sierrae*, as named by Muñoz; Chile; half-hardy; much like *A. pulchra*, but flowers bright rose-purple, the upper tepals yellow, heavily lined crimson-purple. *A. violacea*, Chile; 30–60cm; leaves 2–5cm; flowers mauve-purple, upper tepals darker-spotted, about 5cm wide.

Althaea

(Greek *althaia*, to cure – alluding to the medicinal properties of some species). MALVACEAE. A genus of 12 annual to perennial species from W. Europe to N.E. Siberia. They are generally erect plants with palmate, long-stalked leaves and terminal racemes of often showy, 5-petalled flowers. Grow in any ordinary, well-drained garden soil in a sunny site; the richer the soil the taller the plants. Propagate from seed sown in early summer where the plants are to flower, or in boxes and transplant as soon as possible. To grow as annuals, sow under glass in early spring at 13–16°C, prick off singly into 7·5cm pots and plants out in late spring. The species described are now included in *Alcea*.

Species cultivated: *A. ficifolia*, Siberia; biennial or short-lived perennial, to 2m or more; leaves deeply 7-lobed, fig-like; flowers to 10cm wide, usually yellow, orange or white, sometimes double; plants grown under this name are often hybrids with the following: *A. rosea*, hollyhock; China; woody-based perennial, to 3m or more; leaves 5–7, angled or shallowly-lobed; flowers pink or red, often fully double. Several cultivars listed in shades of red, pink, yellow or white are probably of hybrid origin.

Far left: *Alonsoa warscewiczii*
Left: *Alstroemeria* Ligtu Hybrids
Above: *Althaea ficifolia*

Alyssum

(Greek *a*, not, and *lyssa*, rage or madness – alluding to supposed medicinal properties against rabies). Madwort. CRUCIFERAE. A genus of 150 species of annuals, perennials and sub-shrubs from Mediterranean regions to Siberia. The species in cultivation are generally mat- or hummock-forming with obovate to spathulate or narrowly ovate, often grey or silvery, stellate, hairy leaves, and corymbs or racemes of 4-petalled, yellow or white flowers. Grow in any well-drained soil, preferably alkaline, in a sunny site. Plant autumn to spring. Propagate from seed in spring or cuttings in late summer in a cold frame.

Species cultivated (all late spring to summer): *A. argenteum*, Italy, S. Alps; erect, sub-shrubby, 15–40cm or more; leaves oblanceolate, grey beneath; flowers bright yellow, 5–8mm wide in corymbs. *A. cuneifolium*, mountains of S. Europe; grey-white, tufted perennial 5–15cm; leaves oblong-obovate; flowers yellow, about 10mm wide in dense, short racemes. *A. maritimum*, see *Lobularia*. *A. montanum*, Europe; a variable species represented in gardens by: *A.m.* Prostratum, mat-forming; leaves obovate to oblong, grey, hairy; flowers yellow in racemes to 8cm. *A. saxatile* (*Aurinia s.*), gold dust; C. and S.E. Europe; sub-shrubby, hummock-forming perennial, to 20cm or more; leaves obovate, grey-green; flowers yellow, about 5mm wide, abundantly borne in branched corymbs. *A.s.* Citrinum, bright lemon-yellow; *A.s.* Compactum, dwarf habit; *A.s.* Dudley Neville, biscuit-yellow; *A.s.* Plenum (*A.s.* Flore-pleno), flowers double. *A. serpyllifolium*, S.W. Europe; prostrate, sub-shrubby; leaves oblanceolate, grey-green above, white beneath; flowers 3–4mm wide, pale yellow in racemes. *A. spinosum* (*Ptilotrichum s.*) S.E. Europe; dense, somewhat spiny shrublet 8–15cm; leaves silver-grey, narrowly oblanceolate; flowers white, small, abundant in short corymbs. *A.s.* Roseum, flowers flushed pink. *A. troodii*, Cyprus; rounded sub-shrub, to 12cm; leaves small, silver-gey; flowers yellow, in corymbs. *A. wulfenianum*, S.E. Alps; in cultivation a mat-forming perennial; leaves oblong-obovate, silvery grey-green; flowers 6–10cm wide, golden-yellow, in racemes.

Amaranthus

(Greek *amarantos*, unfading – the flower clusters of some species retain their colour like everlastings). AMARANTHACEAE. A genus of 60 species of annuals from tropical and temperate regions. They are erect plants with lanceolate to ovate, alternate leaves, sometimes brightly-coloured, and tiny flowers in dense, spike-like clusters. Grow in any ordinary, well-drained soil, preferably enriched with manure or compost. The species described are half-hardy, raised from seed sown under glass in mid spring at a temperature of 15–18°C. Prick off the seedlings when large enough to handle and plant out when fear of frost has passed. Or sow outside then.

Species cultivated: *A. caudatus*, love-lies-bleeding; tropics; to 90cm or more; leaves ovate; flowers red, in clustered, pendant, catkin-like tails to 40cm or more long, summer and autumn. *A.c.* Viridis, flowers pale green; *A.c.* Green Balls, similar but flowers in ball-like clusters. *A. gangeticus*, see *A. tricolor*. *A. hypochondriacus*, prince's feather; tropical America; 1–1·5m, much like *A. caudatus*, but the flowering tails erect. *A. tricolor* (*A. gangeticus*) tropics; to 90cm; leaves to 20cm, ovate, flushed red, yellow, bronze; flowers red but hidden. *A.t.* Joseph's Coat, leaves patterned bronze, red, golden-yellow and deep green; *A.t.* Molten Fire, lower leaves copper, crimson, upper leaves scarlet; *A.t.* Salicifolius, 60cm, leaves lanceolate, drooping, orange-red and bronze.

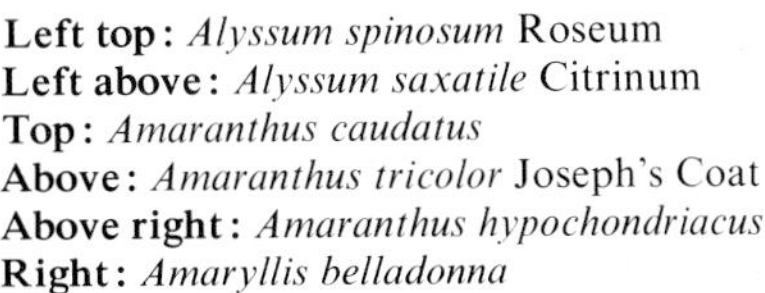

Left top: *Alyssum spinosum* Roseum
Left above: *Alyssum saxatile* Citrinum
Top: *Amaranthus caudatus*
Above: *Amaranthus tricolor* Joseph's Coat
Above right: *Amaranthus hypochondriacus*
Right: *Amaryllis belladonna*

Amaryllis

(after the beautiful Greek shepherdess of the same name). AMARYLLIDACEAE. A genus of 1 S. African bulbous species, *A. belladonna*, needing a sunny, sheltered site, preferably at the base of a wall or hedge in well-drained soil. Plant in summer while dormant. Propagate by offsets at planting time. This plant has long, strap-shaped leaves, dying in summer, followed by stout stems to 75cm, bearing 1–4 pink, trumpet-shaped flowers 10–15cm wide, late summer, autumn.

Amelanchier

(the French, Provencal, name *Amelancier* for *A. ovalis*). Juneberry, shadbush, snowy mespilus. ROSACEAE. A genus of 25 species of deciduous shrubs and trees from northern temperate zone (mainly N. America). They are bushy plants with ovate leaves that often colour well in autumn, and short racemes of white, 5-petalled flowers with young leaves in spring. The sweet, juicy, dark-purple, berry-like fruit of the species described is edible. Grow in any moisture-retentive soil in sun or partial shade; autumn colouring is best on acid or neutral soils. Plant autumn to early spring. Pruning seldom necessary. Propagate from seed sown when ripe or by layering in spring; some kinds by division or suckers at planting time; suckers from grafted trees will reproduce the stock not the scion.

Species cultivated: *A. canadensis* (*A. oblongifolia*), N.E. N. America; erect, suckering shrub, 3–8m tall; leaves 3–6cm long, oblong-oval to obovate, pale green and white-felted when unfolding; flowers 1·5–2cm wide. See also *A. laevis* and *A. lamarckii*. *A. × grandiflora*, see *A. lamarckii*. *A. laevis*, N.E. N. America; large, non-suckering shrub or small tree, to 10m or more; leaves 4–6cm, ovate-oblong, pointed, coppery-red and smooth when young; flowers 2–4cm wide. In cultivation, confused with *A. lamarckii* and *A. canadensis*. *A. lamarckii*, also known as *A.×grandiflora* and *A. confusa* (origin uncertain but naturalized in parts of N. Europe); non-suckering shrub or tree, to 10m; leaves 4·5–8·5cm long, oval to oblong, coppery-red and silken-haired when young flowers 2–3cm wide; much confused with *A. canadensis* and *A. laevis* in cultivation but separable on the young leaf characters. *A.l.* Rubescens, flowers pink-tinted. *A. ovalis*, snowy mespilus; C. and S. Europe; shrub to 3m; leaves 2·5–5cm long, oval to obovate; flowers 3–4cm wide; fruit blue-black.

Left: *Amelanchier canadensis* in autumn
Below: *Amelanchier canadensis* in spring

Above: *Ammobium alatum*

Ammobium

(Greek *ammos*, sand, and *bio*, to live – referring to native habitat). Winged everlasting. COMPOSITAE. A genus of 2 annual species from E. Australia, 1 grown for its everlasting flower-heads composed of chaffy, petal-like bracts: *A. alatum*, New South Wales; erect plant to 60cm; stems winged; flower-heads 2–3cm wide, silvery-white, central florets yellow, summer. *A.a.* Grandiflorum flower-heads to 4·5cm.

Ampelopsis

(Greek *ampelos*, a vine, and *opsis*, like – it is closely allied to grape vine). VITIDACEAE. A genus of about 20 species of deciduous climbing shrubs from C. and E. Asia, N. America. They have pinnate, palmate or simple leaves, twining tendrils, clusters of small, generally greenish flowers, and grape-like berries. Grow in moisture-retentive but well-drained soil and provide strings, wires or sticks for support; the larger species look well rambling through a tree or over a dead stump. Plant autumn to spring. Propagate by semi-hardwood cuttings in late summer, hardwood cuttings or layering in autumn and from seed when ripe. Many popular species formerly found here are now classified under *Parthenocissus*.

Species cultivated: *A. aconitifolia*, N. China; to 15m or more; leaves digitate, 3–5, lanceolate, leaflets 4–8cm long; fruit orange or yellow, sometimes bluish. *A. brevipedunculata* (*A. heterophylla*, *Vitis brevipedunculata*, *V. heterophylla*); N. E. Asia; to 10m or more; leaves broadly ovate-cordate, 3–5

Below: *Ampelopsis brevipedunculata* Elegans

lobed, 6–12cm long; fruit bright blue, but needs a warm summer to mature properly. *A.b.* Elegans (*A.b.* Tricolor, *A.b.* Variegata, *A. heterophylla* Elegans), leaves densely-mottled white, tinged pink; good pot plant. *A. hederacea,* see *Parthenocissus quinquefolia*. *A. heterophylla,* see *A. brevipedunculata*. *A. tricuspidata, A. veitchii,* see *Parthenocissus tricuspidata*. *A. quinquefolia* see *Parthenocissus q.*

Amsonia

(for Dr Charles Amson, a physician in Virginia, USA in the 18th century). APOCYNACEAE. A genus of 25 species of herbaceous perennials from N. America, Japan. 1 species is cultivated for its blue flowers, growing in well-drained but moisture-retentive soil in partial shade or sun. Plant autumn to spring. Propagate by division or from seed in the spring.
A. salicifolia, E. to C. USA; clump-forming; stems to 60cm or more; leaves narrowly lanceolate, in pairs, blue-grey beneath; flowers 10–15mm wide, starry with 5-pointed, blue-purple petal-lobes, in terminal, rounded cymes, summer. Sometimes confused with *A. tabernaemontana,* a more erect plant having ovate to oblong-lanceolate leaves, green beneath, flowers more blue. See also *Rhazya orientalis.*

Below: *Amsonia tabernaemontana*

Anacharis – see *Elodea.*

Anacyclus

(Greek *a,* without, *anthos,* flower, and *kuklos,* ring–referring to the ring of fertile florets around the periphery of the flower-head). COMPOSITAE. A genus of 25 species of annuals and perennials from

Below: *Anacyclus depressus*

Mediterranean regions, 1 or 2 of which are grown on the rock garden. They need sharply-drained soil and a sheltered, sunny site. Plant in spring. Propagate from seed or by cuttings in spring and summer. *A. depressus,* Morocco; prostrate perennial; stems to 15cm; leaves bi- or tripinnatisect, feathery; flower-heads daisy-like, disc yellow, ray florets white above, crimson beneath, late spring, summer. Plants listed as *A. atlanticus* and *A. maroccanus* are similar.

Anagallis

(perhaps from the Greek *anagelas,* to delight). PRIMULACEAE. A genus of 28 species of annuals and perennials from the tropics, S. America, W. Europe. They are mainly low-growing or prostrate with paired opposite or whorled leaves and 5-petalled red, blue or white flowers. With a few exceptions they need well-drained soil and a sunny position. The annuals should be grown *in situ* in autumn or spring. *A. monellii* and other short-lived perennials are best sown under glass in early spring and planted out when large enough. *A. tenella* needs moist soil and a sheltered site; propagate by cuttings or division in spring.
Species cultivated: *A. arvensis,* scarlet pimpernel, poor man's weather glass; cosmopolitan as a weed of cultivation; prostrate annual; stems 4-angled; leaves ovate, 15–28mm long; flowers to 14mm wide, red, pink, lilac, purple, blue. *A.a. foemina,* flowers always rich blue, petals margined with glandular hairs; this and *A.a.* Caerulea (without glandular hairs) are often cultivated. *A. linifolia,* see next species. *A. monellii* (*A. linifolia*), W. Mediterranean; short-lived perennial often grown as an annual; prostrate, woody-based; leaves linear-lanceolate; flowers to 1·5cm wide, gentian-blue, red in bud,

Left: *Anagallis monellii* Phillipsii
Left below: *Anagallis monellii collina*
Above: *Anaphalis triplinervis*

summer. *A.m. collina,* flowers red. *A.m.* Phillipsii flowers larger than type, deep blue. *A. tenella,* Europe, N. Africa; slender, creeping perennial; leaves ovate, 5mm long; flowers to 14mm wide, funnel-shaped, pnk to white, summer. *A.t.* Studland and *A.t.* Kinnadoohy, deeper pink than the type.

Anaphalis

(classical Greek name for a similar but now unidentifiable plant). Pearly everlasting. COMPOSITAE. A genus of 35 species of herbaceous perennials from temperate Europe, Asia, N. America. The plants form wide clumps with narrow, often grey or white, downy leaves, and terminal, corymbose clusters of generally white flower-head composed of chaffy, petal-like bracts surrounding yellow, tubular florets. Grow in any ordinary garden soil, planting autumn to spring. Propagate by division at planting time.
Species cultivated (all flowering late summer): *A. cinnamomea* (*A. yedoensis*), India, Burma; stems erect to 75cm; leaves 5–10cm long, lanceolate, taper-pointed, semi-amplexicaul, white-felted beneath and margined; flower-heads globose, 8mm wide. *A. margaritaceae,* N. America, E. Asia; stems to 60cm; leaves linear-lanceolate, 5–12cm long, grey down beneath; flower-heads pearly-white, to 1cm wide. *A. nubigena,* Tibet, China; tufted; stems to 20cm; leaves lanceolate, to 6cm, grey-felted beneath; flower-heads to 2cm wide in small clusters. *A. triplinervis,* Himalaya; tufted to clump-forming; stems 30–45cm; leaves obovate, tapered to winged stalk, grey-felted beneath, cottony above, 7–12cm long; flower-heads 1–2cm wide. *A.t.* Summer Snow, dwarfer than type, flowers whiter. *A. yedoensis,* see *A. cinnamomea.*

Anchusa

(Greek *ankousa,* alkanet – some species yield rouge). Alkanet. BORAGINACEAE. A genus of 50 species of annual and perennial plants from Europe, N. Africa, W. Asia. The species cultivated are tufted perennials with narrow, hispid leaves and tubular, bright blue flowers having 5 rounded petal-lobes in cymes. Grow in ordinary well-drained soil preferably enriched with compost or decayed manure. Plant autumn to spring. Propagate by division at planting time, root cuttings in winter or from seed in spring.
Species cultivated: *A. angustissima,* Turkey; stems 20–40cm tall; leaves linear, 5–11·5cm long; flowers 10–12mm wide in dense cymes, late spring, summer; confused in cultivation with *A. caespitosa*. *A. azurea* (*A. italica*) Caucasus; stems 90–150cm; leaves lanceolate, basal ones to 30cm or more long; flowers blue to purple-blue, early summer. Several cultivars are listed, among the best being *A.a.* Little John, to

Top far left: *Anchusa azurea*
Far left: *Andromeda polifolia*
Top left: *Androsace sarmentosa*
Left: *Androsace mucronifolia*
Above: *Androsace helvetica*

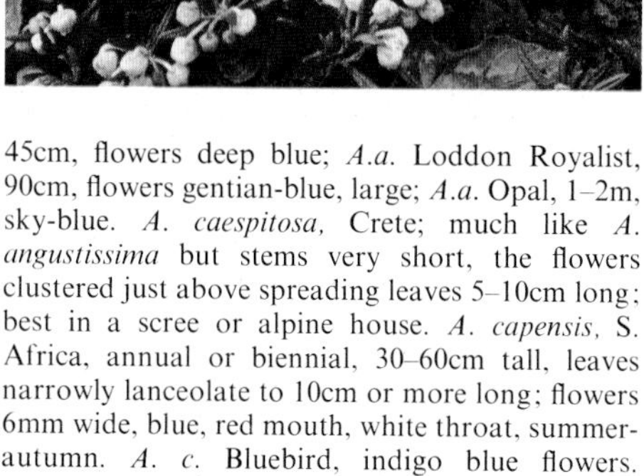

45cm, flowers deep blue; *A.a.* Loddon Royalist, 90cm, flowers gentian-blue, large; *A.a.* Opal, 1–2m, sky-blue. *A. caespitosa,* Crete; much like *A. angustissima* but stems very short, the flowers clustered just above spreading leaves 5–10cm long; best in a scree or alpine house. *A. capensis,* S. Africa, annual or biennial, 30–60cm tall, leaves narrowly lanceolate to 10cm or more long; flowers 6mm wide, blue, red mouth, white throat, summer-autumn. *A. c.* Bluebird, indigo blue flowers. *A. myosotidiflora* see *Brunnera macrophylla.*

Andromeda

(mythical Greek maiden offered as a sacrifice to a sea monster and rescued by Perseus). Bog rosemary. ERICACEAE. A genus of 2 species of evergreen shrubs from colder parts of N. Hemisphere. They are low-growing, wiry plants, spreading by rhizomes, with alternate, leathery, narrowly elliptic to lanceolate leaves and pendant, urn-shaped flowers, late spring, summer. Grow in acid, peaty soil in sun or light shade, planting autumn to spring. Propagate by division or from seed in spring, semi-hardwood cuttings with a heel late summer.

Species cultivated: *A. glaucophylla* (*A. angustifolia*), N.E. and N. America, much like *A. polifolia* and considered to be a form of it by some botanists; leaves larger, white tomentose beneath; stems to 70cm (rarely). *A. polifolia,* Europe, Asia; stems to 30cm; leaves glabrous, elliptic-linear; flowers globose, pink or white, 5–7mm long, late spring, summer. *A.p.* Alba, flowers white; *A.p.* Compacta, rounded, compact habit, to 20cm; *A.p.* Macrophylla, low, compact, broad dark green leaves, deep pink flowers; *A.p.* Major, larger than the type; *A.p.* Minima, almost prostrate, leaves linear, dark green; *A.p.* Nana, flowers bright pink. For species formerly included in this genus see *Cassiope, Pieris, Zenobia.*

Androsace

(Greek *aner,* man, and *sakos,* shield – said to allude to the shape of the anther, but name originally used by Dioscorides for a different plant). PRIMULACEAE. A genus of 100 species of perennials and annuals; mainly northern temperate zone alpines. They are tufted, mat- or cushion-forming, the individual shoots forming rosettes; flowers in terminal umbels on a slender, erect stem, tubular with 5 spreading petal-lobes, and a yellow eye. Grow in sharply-drained soil that does not dry out, in sun or partial shade. Plant autumn to spring; woolly-leaved kinds best protected from winter wet by sheet of glass. The tight, cushion-forming, high alpine species are best in pots of gritty soil in an alpine house, at least during the winter. Propagate by division after flowering, offsets or cuttings in summer, from seed when ripe or as soon as available.

Species cultivated (flowering mainly in summer): *A. albana,* Caucasus; annual; leaves spathulate, to 1·8cm long, in dense rosettes; flowers pink, 8mm wide, spring. *A. alpina* (*A. glacialis*), mat-forming; leaves glandular, hairy, grey-green, oblong-lanceolate, to 8mm long; flowers bright pink to white, 5mm wide, almost stemless. *A. arachnoidea* see *A. villosa. A.* × *aretioides,* Austria – natural hybrid; mat-forming; leaves oblong-lanceolate, 8mm long, stellate hairy; flowers pink, 5mm wide. *A. carnea,* Alps, Pyrenees; tufted; leaves 1–1·5cm, linear to awl-shaped; flowers pink or white. *A.c. halleri,* leaves and flowers larger than type, tufts loose; *A.c. laggeri,* leaves to 5mm, tufts dense. *A. chamaejasme,* N. Hemisphere; mat-forming, stoloniferous; leaves lanceolate, to 1cm long; flowers 7–10mm wide, white, pink-flushed with age, on tall stems to 6cm or more. *A. cylindrica,* Pyrenees; forming domed clumps 3–6cm high; leaves linear, downy, grey-green, 6mm long; flowers white or pale pink, 4–6mm wide. *A. glacialis,* see *A. alpina. A. hedraeantha,* Balkans; tufted, shortly rhizomatous; leaves lanceolate-oblong, leathery, 8mm long; glowers deep pink, 6–9mm wide. *A. helvetica,* Alps; cushion-forming; leaves downy, grey-green, narrowly lanceolate to spathulate, 2–6mm long; flowers solitary, white, 4–6mm wide. *A. imbricata,* see *A. vandellii. A. jacquemontii,* W. Himalaya; much like a blend of *A. sarmentosa* and *A. villosa;* leaves brown-haired; flowers white or lilac pink. *A. lactea,* Alps; mat-forming, bearing underground runners; leaves linear, 1–1·5cm; flowers milk-white with notched lobes, to 1cm wide on stems to 6cm or more tall. *A. lanuginosa,* Himalaya; non rosette-forming; stems trailing, 4–10cm; leaves lanceolate, to 2cm, silky, hairy; flowers 8–10mm wide, lilac-pink, eye yellow, ageing to crimson, *A.l. leichtlinii,* flowers white. *A. limprichtii* (*A. sarmentosa watkinsii*), N. W. China; much like *A. sarmentosa,* but smaller and more compact; flowers soft pink. *A. microphylla,* see *A. sempervivoides. A. mucronifolia,* Kashmir; cushion-forming, like *A. alpina;* flowers white to cerise-pink. *A. primuloides,* N.W. Himalaya; also known as *A. sarmentosa primuloides;* loosely mat-forming, woven together with stolons; summer leaves 3–7cm long, oblanceolate, silky-haired, winter leaves 5–15mm, densely white-haired; stems 5–10cm; flowers pink, 6–10mm wide. *A.p.* Brilliant, flowers deep pink; *A.p.* Chumbyi, smaller, more silky-haired than type, flowers larger, deeper pink. *A. pyrenaica,* Pyrenees; cushion-forming; almost stemless; leaves linear, keeled, hairy, 3–4mm long, dark green; flowers white, 4–5mm wide. *A. rotundifolia,* W.

Himalaya; tufted; stems 5–15cm tall; leaves round to kidney-shaped, 7-lobed, each lobe trifid; flowers pale rose-pink. *A. sarmentosa,* Himalaya, W. China; like *A. primuloides* in growth form but larger; flowering stems to 15cm, bracts beneath flowers linear, to 6mm long (those of *A. primuloides,* lanceolate, to 2cm). *A.s.* Salmon's, larger and stronger-growing than type; *A.s.* Sherriffii, like *A.s.* Salmon's but less hairy, stands winter wet well; *A.s.* Yunnanensis, smaller and more hairy than type, flowers deep rose. *A.s. watkinsii,* see *A. limprichtii. A. sempervivoides,* Kashmir, Tibet; mat-forming, stoloniferous; leaves 6mm long, spathulate, smooth, dark green; flowers pink, 5mm wide, late spring; sometimes wrongly listed as *A. microphylla. A. vandellii* (*A. imbricata*), Alps, Pyrenees, Sierra Nevada; cushion-forming, like *A. helvetica,* but leaves linear-lanceolate, hair dense white, stellate. *A. villosa,* Pyrenees, Alps, Appennines; tufted; stems 3cm or more tall; leaves 5mm, linear-lanceolate, silvery, silky-haired; flowers 6–10mm wide, white, ageing to pink. *A.v. arachnoidea* (*A. arachnoidea*), altogether neater in form and with leaves more woolly than the type *A. villosa;* commonest form in cultivation.

Anemone

(once said to be derived from Greek *anemos,* wind, but now considered to be Greek version of the Semetic Naamen, or Adonis, whose blood, legend says, produced *Anemone coronaria,* or *Adonis,* when he – Adonis – died in battle). RANUNCULACEAE. A genus of 150 perennial species of cosmopolitan distribution. They have a rhizomatous rootstock, either slender or erect, or irregularly tuber-like, lobed or compound leaves and erect stems bearing 1-to-several flowers. The latter are petalless, composed of 5–20, coloured, petaloid sepals, the stem bearing them carrying a characteristic whorl or involucre of 3–4, usually dissected, green bracts that may resemble leaves or true sepals. Grow in any ordinary, well-drained soil preferably enriched with leaf mould, peat or decayed compost, in sun or partial shade. Plant autumn; tufted perennials also in spring. Propagate by division at planting time, from seed when ripe or as soon as possible afterwards. Seed (achenes) often needs a cool winter period to germinate well.

Species cultivated: *A. alpina,* see *Pulsatilla alpina. A. angulosa,* see *Hepatica transsilvanica, A. apennina,* S. Europe; rhizome tuberous; stems to 15cm; leaves trifoliate, each leaflet stalked, deeply-lobed, hairy beneath; flowers solitary, 4cm wide, sepals 8–18, blue, spring. *A.a.* Alba, flowers white; *A.a.* Purpurea, reddish-purple. *A. baldensis,* Alps, Yugoslavia; rhizome tuberous; stems to 15cm; leaves biternate, leaflets lobed; flowers 2·5–4cm wide, sepals 6–10, white, late spring. *A. biflora,* Iran to Kashmir; tuberous; stem to 15cm; leaves trifoliate, cut into linear lobes; flowers globular, nodding, 2·5–3·5cm wide, sepals 5, red, yellow, coppery or white, spring. *A. blanda,* S.E. Europe, Turkey; much like *A. apennina,* but leaflets almost stalkless and hairless; flowers 10–20 sepals, blue, red, pink, purple; several cultivars are available. *A. coronaria,* poppy anemone; S. Europe, Turkey; tuberous; stems to 25cm or more; leaves trifoliate, deeply-lobed and toothed; flowers 3·5–6·5cm, tepals 5–8, red, blue, purple, pale yellow, late winter, spring; many cultivars are known, among them the De Caen and St Brigid races, robust plants of hybrid origin with *A. hortensis, A. pavonina* and *A. × fulgens* that can be flowered in winter under cloches and throughout the year if planted at intervals. *A. elegans,* see *A. × hybrida. A. × fulgens,* natural hybrid intermediate between parents (*A.*

Right: Japanese anemones

pavonina × *A. hortensis*), flowers of 15 narrow sepals, bright red. *A.* ×*f.* Annulata Grandiflora, flower yellow-centred; *A.* ×*f.* Multipetala, two rows of tepals. *A. halleri,* see *Pulsatilla halleri. A. hortensis* (*A. stellata*), Mediterranean; similar to *A. coronaria,* but leaves less divided and broader lobes or segments, involucre linear-lanceolate; flowers 3–4cm wide, tepals narrow, 12–19, pink, mauve, purple, spring. *A. hupehensis,* China; also known as *A. japonica hupehensis*; clump-forming; stems 60cm or more; leaves trifoliate, leaflets unequally 3-lobed, toothed: flowers 5cm wide, sepals 5, rounded, lilac-pink, crimson-flushed in bud, late summer. *A.h.*

Below: *Anemone coronaria*
Right: *Anemone pavonina*
Right centre below: *Anemone narcissiflora*
Right centre bottom: *Anemone blanda*
Bottom right: *Anemone* × *fulgens* Annulata Grandiflora

japonica, (*A. japonica* and *A. nipponica*), flowers a soft lilac-pink, sepals narrow, 20 or more. *A.* × *hybrida* (*A. elegans, A. japonica* of gardens) (*A. hupehensis japonica* × *A. vitifolia*), midway between parents; tepals 6–11, shades of pink to purple-red and white; several cultivars are available. *A. japonica,* see *A. hupehensis, A.* × *hybrida. A.* × *lesseri* (*A. multifida* × *A. sylvestris*), clump-forming; stems to 45cm; leaves palmate, usually 5-lobed, glossy green; flowers pink, purple, yellow, white, the form grown in gardens a deep rose-red, early summer. *A. multifida,* N. America; clump-forming, 15-30cm tall; leaves trifoliate, leaflets 3-lobed cut into many linear segments; flowers 2cm wide, sepals 5, silky, hairy, greenish, yellowish, purplish beneath, cream above. *A.m. sanguinea,* flowers bright red; *A.m. polysepala,* sepals to 16, red, summer. *A. narcissiflora,* C. and S. Europe, Asia; clump-forming; stems to 60cm; leaves palmate, 3–5 lobed, deeply-toothed flowers 3–4cm wide in umbels of 3–8, sepals 5–7, white, sometimes purple-flushed, summer. *A. nemorosa,* wood anemone; Europe; much like *A. apennina* but rhizome cylindrical, creeping; flowers 2–3cm wide, sepals 6, white, flushed pale purple beneath, spring. *A.n.* Alba-plena, double white; *A.n.* Allenii, large soft purple-blue flowers; *A.n.* Blue Bonnet, large pale blue; *A.n.* Rosea, strongly pink-flushed; *A.n.*

Robinsoniana, lavender-blue, large; *A.n.* Royal Blue, deep purple-blue; *A.n.* Vestal, centre of flower a boss of small petaloids. *A. palmata,* S.W. Europe; rhizome tuberous; stems to 15cm; leaves nearly round, 3–5 lobes, toothed; flowers 2·5–3·5cm wide, sepals 10–15, golden-yellow, spring. *A. patens,* see *Pulsatilla patens. A. pavonina,* C. and E. Mediterranean; like *A. coronaria* but flowers with a pale centre, sepals 8–12; St Bavo anemones are derived from this species. *A. pratensis,* see *Pulsatilla pratensis. A. pulsatilla,* see *Pulsatilla vulgaris. A. ranunculoides,* Europe; like *A. nemorosa;* flowers 1·5cm wide, sepals 5–6, yellow, spring. *A.r. wockeana,* plant small, forming dense colonies. *A. rivularis,* N. India; rhizome tuberous; stem 30–60cm; leaves trifoliate, leaflets trifid, sharply-toothed; flowers several to a stem, 4cm wide, sepals 5, white, tinged metallic-blue beneath, summer. *A. slavica,* see *Pulsatilla halleri slavica. A. stellata,* see *A. hortensis. A. sylvestris,* snowdrop windflower; Europe, W. Asia; clump-forming, spreading by suckers from the roots; stems to 45cm; leaves with 3–5 deep lobes, each deeply toothed; flowers fragrant, 4cm wide, sepals 5, silky, white. *A. vitifolia,* N. India, Burma, China; clump-forming; stems to 60cm; leaves large, cordate, 5-lobed; flowers to 5cm, sepals usually 5, white, late summer; a somewhat tender plant, often confused with the hardier. *A. tomentosa.*

Angelica tree – see *Aralia chinensis.*

Angels' tears – see *Narcissus triandrus.*

Anomatheca – see *Lapeirousia.*

Antennaria

(Latin *antenna* – the pappus of the seed fancifully resembles the antennae of a butterfly). Mountain everlasting, pussy's toes, cat's foot. COMPOSITAE. A genus of about 15 (100 by some authorities) species of evergreen perennials and low shrubs from arctic and alpine regions, mainly N. Hemisphere. The species described are mat-forming, with obovate to spathulate leaves, usually white, hairy – at least beneath – and erect, leafy stems bearing close, terminal umbels of small flower-heads, each having somewhat chaffy, petal-like bracts, white or pink. Grow in well-drained soil in a sunny site. Plant autumn to spring. Propagate by division after flowering, autumn or spring.

Species cultivated: *A. aprica,* N. America, N. Mexico; much like *A. dioica;* leaves 1–2cm long, densely silver-grey, hairy on both surfaces; flower-heads cream to white, summer. *A. chilensis,* Chile; much like *A. dioica;* leaves oblanceolate, 1–2cm long, white, hairy above and below; flower-heads small, whitish or pinkish, summer. *A. dioica,* N. and C. Europe, Siberia, N. America; densely mat-forming; leaves rosetted at ends of short stolons, obovate to oblanceolate, spathulate, 1–4cm long, smooth or sparsely cottony above, hairy and densely white beneath; flower-heads usually pale pink, summer. *A.d.* Minima, smaller silvery-white leaves about 1cm; *A.d.* Rosea, flowers good pink; *A.d.* Rubra, rose-red. *A. plantaginifolia,* N.E. USA; robust, loosely mat-forming; leaves prominently 3-veined, broadly obovate, to 6cm long, fine grey pubescence above; flower-heads white, florets sometimes red-tipped, spring to summer.

Anthemis

(Greek name for chamomile – *A. nobilis*). COMPOSITAE. A genus of 200 species of annuals and perennials from Europe, Mediterranean, Iran. They vary from mat- or cushion- to erect clump-forming, usually with feathery pinnate or bipinnate leaves

and daisy-like flower-heads with mainly white or yellow ray florets. Grow in well-drained soil in a sunny site. Plant autumn to spring. Propagate by division at planting time or from seed in spring.
Species cultivated: *A. biebersteiniana* (*A. beibersteinii* of gardens; *A. marschalliana*), Caucasus; 15cm or more tall, tufted to loosely mat-forming; leaves pinnate, leaflets cut into linear lobes, silky-white haired; flower-heads deep bright yellow, summer. *A. cupaniana*, Italy; mat- or low- cushion-forming; leaves bi- or pinnatipartite, silvery-grey haired; flower-heads white on stems to 15cm or more, summer to autumn. *A. frutescens*, see *Chrysanthemum frutescens*. *A. marschalliana*, the currently correct name for *A. biebersteiniana*, qv *A. nobilis*, see *Chamaemelum*. *A. rudolphiana*, resembling *A. biebersteinii* but probably only a form of that species; 15–25cm; leaves silvery-white; flowers golden-yellow, summer, early autumn. *A. sancti-johannis*, Bulgaria; to 60cm, clump-forming; leaves bi-or tripinnatisect, grey-haired; flower-heads bright orange to 5cm wide, summer; true species rare, most of the plants in cultivation being hybrids with the following: *A. tinctoria*, Europe; 60–90cm, clump-forming; leaves tripinnatified; flowers yellow, summer. The several cultivars offered under this name are hybrids with *A. sancti-johannis*, and recommended are: *A.t.* E. C. Buxton, lemon-yellow; *A.t.* Grallach Gold, vivid golden-orange; *A.t.* Wargrave, pale creamy-yellow.

Anthericum

(Greek name *antherikon* for asphodel). LILIACEAE. A genus of 300 species of perennial plants from Africa, Malagasy, Europe, E. Asia, America. They are tufted to clump-forming plants with thick, fleshy roots, slender, grass-like leaves, and starry, 6-petalled flowers in simple or branched racemes. Grow in fertile, well-drained soil in a sunny site. Plant autumn to spring. Propagate by division at planting time or from seed when ripe or in spring.
Species cultivated: *A. algeriense*, Algeria; 30–45cm, a tufted, slender plant much like *A. liliago*. In cultivation, a robust plant to 90cm that masquerades under this name is probably a fine form of *A. liliago*. *A. graminifolium*, see *A. ramosum*. *A. liliago*, St Bernard's lily; S. Europe to Turkey tufted to clump-forming; stems 45–60cm; leaves grey-green; flowers starry, white, 3–5cm wide, in usually simple racemes, early summer. *A. ramosum* (*A. graminifolium*), Europe; like *A. liliago* but flowers to 2·5cm in branched racemes; best in a sheltered site.

Top left: *Antennaria dioica*
Left: *Anthemis tinctoria* C.E. Buxton
Below left: *Anthemis cupaniana*
Below: *Anthericum liliago*
Below right: *Anthyllis montana*

Antholyza

(Greek *anthos*, flower, and *lyssa*, rage – the flowers fancifully resemble the open mouth of an enraged animal). IRIDACEAE. A genus of 1 species of cormous plants from S. Africa. *A. ringens* has ribbed, sword-shaped leaves, stems to 50cm, and spikes of zygomorphic, tubular red flowers, the 6 lobes of which are arranged like a slender, gaping mouth, summer. (For *A. paniculata*, see *Curtonus paniculatus*.) Grow in well-drained soil in a sheltered, sunny site, or in pots of any proprietary potting compost in a well-ventilated greenhouse. Plant spring. Propagate by offsets at planting time or from seed as soon as ripe, or spring.

Anthyllis

(ancient Greek name). LEGUMINOSAE. A genus of 50 species of annuals, perennials and shrubs from Europe, N. Africa, W. Asia. Variable in habit, they have trifoliate or imparipinnate leaves (sometimes of 1 leaflet) and dense clusters of yellow, red, purple or white, small pea-like flowers. Hardy species need well-drained, ordinary soil and a sunny site, the tender ones a well-ventilated greenhouse, minimum temperature 4°C in any proprietary potting compost, particularly the loam-based ones. The tender species mentioned here may be grown against a sheltered wall in mild districts, or stood outside in their pots late spring to autumn. Propagate by late summer cuttings with a heel (shrubs), division or from seed in spring.
Species cultivated: *A. barba-jovis*, Jupiter's beard; W. Mediterranean; tender evergreen shrub to 2m or more; leaves pinnate, leaflets 9–19, oblong-linear to 2·5cm, dense silver hair beneath; flowers pale yellow in globular heads 2–3cm wide, spring. *A. hermanniae*, Mediterranean region; hardy evergreen shrub to 1m or more; leaves tri- or unifoliate, leaflets oblong spathulate to 2·5cm long, glabrous or lightly silky-haired; flowers yellow, solitary or in forming an interrupted raceme, spring. *A.h.* Compacta, small, neat habit. *A. montana*, S. Europe mountains; hardy, woody based, mat-forming perennial; leaves pinnate, leaflets 17–41 narrowly obovate-oblong, pubescent, to 12mm long; flowers red to purple in paired dense heads on erect stems to 10cm tall. *A. vulneraria*, kidney vetch; Europe; very variable, tufted hardy perennial (sometimes biennial or annual); stems semi-prostrate; leaves pinnate, leaflets 1–13, ovate to linear-oblong, 1–4cm long; flowers in paired dense heads, calyx inflated, petals yellow, red, purple, orange or whitish; many sub-species and varieties of this species have been given individual names.

Antirrhinum

(Greek *anti*, like, and *rhin*, nose or snout – alluding to the appearance of the flowers, that resemble the snout of a dragon). SCROPHULARIACEAE. A genus of about 30 species of annuals, perennials and sub-shrubs from W. Mediterranean and W. N.America. They are prostrate to erect, with opposite paired to alternate, lanceolate to ovate leaves and racemes of tubular flowers, each one pinched together to form a closed mouth, then flaring into 5 waved lobes. Grow in well-drained soil in a sunny site. *A. majus*, common snapdragon, is grown annually from seed sown under glass early and mid spring in a minimum temperature of 15°C, the seedlings pricked off into boxes and later hardened off for planting out late spring to early summer. Alternatively, sow outside in late summer and set out the young plants in autumn for blooming the following spring. They can also be grown as pot plants for flowering during the winter to spring period under glass, provided temperatures do not drop below 7°C; sow for this purpose in summer. All the perennial species may also be propagated by cuttings of young shoots in spring or early autumn.
Species cultivated: *A. glutinosum*, see next species.

Aponogeton

(Latin *Aqui Aponi*, the healing springs now Bagni d'Abano, and *geiton*, neighbour; a name originally applied to a plant, horned pondweed, found there, but later used by Linnaeus's son for this genus). APONEGETONACEAE. A genus of 30 species of aquatic perennials from Africa, Malagasy, Asia, Australia. They have thickened rhizomes, floating leaves (in a few species submerged) and spikes of small flowers above the water. Grow the tender species in tanks or aquaria under glass in pots of loam-based mixture the water warmed to at least 15°C in good light. Grow the hardy sorts in ponds or slow streams planted in natural mud or baskets of loam and decayed manure or compost. Plant spring. Propagate by division at planting time.

Species cultivated: *A. distachyos*, Cape pondweed, water hawthorn; S. Africa; hardy; leaves oblong-elliptic, 7–15cm long; flowers fragrant, glistening white, having 1 'petal' (perianth segment), in dense, forked spikes, 5–10cm long, spring to late autumn. *A. fenestralis* (*Ouvirandra f.*), lattice-leaf; Malagasy; tender; leaves submerged, oblong-lanceolate, to 15cm long, much perforated, reduced to a network of veins; flower-spike forked, 5cm long. *A. kraussianus* (*A. desertorum*), S. Africa; much like *A. distachyos*, leaves narrower; flower-spikes creamy-yellow; best in shallow water.

Aquilegia

(Latin *aquila*, eagle – from the shape of the spurred petals). Columbine. RANUNCULACEAE. A genus of 100 species of perennials from N. Hemisphere. They are tufted or clump-forming with bi- or triternate leaves and usually nodding flowers in panicles or solitary, each one having 5 petaloid sepals and 5 spurred petals. Grow in well-drained, humus-rich

Above: *Antirrhinum* dwarf bedding form
Right: *Aponogeton distachyos*

A. hispanicum (*A. glutinosum*), S.E. Spain; mat-forming sub-shrub; leaves lanceolate to ovate, pubescent glands; 0·5–3·5cm long; flowers 2–2cm long, white to pale yellow with pale red or purplish striping sometimes suffused all over, summer. *A.h. mollissimum* (*A. molle*), leaves ovate to orbicular, large hairs on stems and leaves; not always reliably hardy. *A. majus*, S.W. Europe, naturalized elsewhere; erect, woody-based, short-lived perennial to 1·2m; leaves lanceolate to ovate, to 7cm long; flowers 3–4·5cm long, pink to red-purple; many cultivars are available including the very dwarf *A.m.* Tom Thumb and *A.m.* Magic Carpet, 10–15cm, and the tall, large-flowered *A.m.* Tetra Snaps; colours range from white, cream, yellow, pink, red and bronze; the mutant Penstemon-flowered strain has wide, open flowers. *A. molle*, see *A. hispanicum*. *A. sempervirens*, Pyrenees, E.C. Spain; prostrate sub-shrub; leaves oblong to elliptic, 1–3cm long; flowers white or cream, veined or lined purple with a violet splash on upper lip, summer; needs a protected and sheltered site.

Aphyllanthes

(Greek *a*, without, *phyllon*, leaf, and *anthos*, flower – the plant consists of green, rush-like stems). APHYLLANTHACEAE (LILIACEAE). A genus of 1 species of perennial from W. Mediterranean: *A. monspeliensis*, tufted evergreen; stems 10–25cm tall; leaves small, membranaceous at stem bases; flowers blue, 2·5cm wide, funnel-shaped with 6 spreading tepals, from terminal russet bracts, spring, summer. Grow in well-drained soil in a sheltered, sunny site. Plant spring. Propagate by division after flowering or spring, or from seed in spring or when ripe.

Top: *Aquilegia × hybrida*
Left: *Aquilegia canadensis*
Above: *Aquilegia fragrans*
Top right: *Aquilegia vulgaris*

soil in partial shade or sun. Plant autumn to spring. Propagate by division in spring or from seed when ripe or as soon afterwards as possible.

Species cultivated: *A. akitensis*, see *A. flabellata pumila*. *A. alpina*, Switzerland; to 30cm tall; leaflets deeply-lobed; flowers deep blue or blue and white, 5–7cm wide, early summer; *A.p.* Hensol Harebell, deep blue, hybrid with *A. vulgaris*. *A. amaliae (A. reginae-amaliae)*, Balkan Peninsula; 20–30cm tall; leaflets 2–3 cleft; flowers about 3cm long, sepals and spur pale violet-blue, petals white, early summer. *A. atrata*, C. Europe; much like *A. vulgaris*, but flowers dark violet-purple with longer stamens. *A. bertolonii*, S. E. France to Apennines; much like a smaller form of *A. pyrenaica*, but leaflets pilose beneath and sepals broader. *A. brevistyla*, Rocky Mountains, N. America; 30–60cm tall; leaves biternate; flower 2cm long, sepals blue, petals white, short spur blue, late spring to summer. *A. caerulea*, Rocky Mountains, N. America; 30–60cm; leaves biterante, leaflets 3-lobed; flowers erect, 5–7cm wide, sepals blue, petals white, spurs long (to 5cm), late spring and summer. *A. canadensis*, N. America; 30cm or more; leaves biternate; flowers 4cm wide, sepals yellow or red, petals lemon-yellow, spurs 2cm, late spring to summer. *A. chrysantha*, New Mexico, Arizona; 90–120cm tall; flowers 5–7cm wide, sepals pale, petals deep yellow, spurs to 5cm, slender, summer; 1 of the parents of the long-spurred hybrids. *A. clemataquila*, semi-double, flowered, spurless form of *A. vulgaris*. *A. clematiflora*, spurless mutant strain derived from *A. caerulea* Mrs Scott-Elliot. *A. discolor*, Spain; 10–15cm; leaves biternate; flowers 2·5–3·5cm long, sepals blue, petals white, spur 6–10mm long, spring to early summer; allied to *A. pyrenaica*. *A. einseleana*, Alps; to 45cm tall; leaflets shallowy 2–3 lobed; flowers blue-violet, 2·5–3cm long, spur 7–10mm, early summer. *A. flabellata*, Japan; 15–45cm; leaflets fan-shaped, 3-cleft, bluish grey-green; flowers white, tinted violet, 2–3cm long, late spring; *A.f.* Nana Alba, plant small, flowers white; *A.f.* Pumila *(A. akitensis, A. japonica)*, plant to 10cm tall, sepals violet, petals white. *A. formosa*, W. N.America; 60–90cm; leaflets cleft and lobed, blue-white beneath; flowers 2·5–4·5cm long, sepals red, petals small, yellow, spurs red 1–2cm long, summer; 1 of the parents of the long-spurred hybrids. *A. fragans*, Himalaya; 45–60cm; flowers pale claret-purple or white, 4–5·5cm long, fragrant, summer; needs a sheltered site. *A. glandulosa*, Altai Mountains, Mongolia; 20–30cm; leaflets narrow; flowers bright deep blue, 4cm wide, rather starry, late spring. *A.g. jucunda*, flowers broader white petals than type. *A. × hybrida*, a name covering hybrids between *A. chrysantha*, *A. formosa*, *A. caerulea*, and *A. vulgaris*, resulting in cultivar groups such as long-spurred Hybrids, short-spurred Hybrids – several named selections of which are available. *A. japonica*, see *A. flabellata pumila*. *A. jonesii*, Rocky Mountains, N. America; small, tufted; stem very short or to 8cm; leaflets small, crowded; flowers solitary, blue, to 4cm wide, summer. *A. kitaibelii*, N. E. Italy, Yugoslavia; 15–30cm tall; leaflets hairy; flowers red to blue-violet, 2–4cm long, late spring to summer. *A. longissima*, Texas to Mexico; 60–90cm; leaflets deep-lobed, bluish-white sheen; flowers pale yellow, sepals 2–3cm, spurs 10–15cm long, summer to autumn. *A. olympica*, Caucasus; like *A. vulgaris;* flowers claret-purple, sepals broader. *A. pyrenaica*, Pyrenees, N. Spain; 10–30cm; leaflets small, 2–3 lobed; flowers bright deep blue, petals sometimes white, to 4·5cm long, late spring to summer. *A. saximontana*, Colorado, USA; 12–15cm; flowers 5cm long, sepals blue, petals pale yellow, summer. *A. scopulorum*, S.W. USA; small, tufted; leaves blue-green; flowers to 7·5cm long, lavender to violet-purple, summer. *A. skinneri*, Mexico; 60cm tall; leaves blue-green, leaflets cordate; flowers to 5cm long, sepals green, petals orange-flushed, spur red, summer to autumn. *A. viridiflora*, Siberia, China;

30–40cm; flowers 3–5cm long, sepals green, petals yellow-green to purple, fragrant, summer. *A. vulgaris,* Europe; to 60cm or more, leaflets 2–3 lobed; flowers 3–5cm long, spur strongly-hooked, usually purple or shades of red, sometimes white. *A.v.* Flora Pleno, flowers double in various shades; *A.v.* Clemataquila, *A.v.* Clematiflora and *A.v.* Stellata are all spurless forms. Many strains or cultivars, some of hybrid origin, are available.

Arabis

(Latin, Arabs or Arabus, from Arabia, or perhaps a name for a kind of mustard). CRUCIFERAE. A genus of 120 species of perennial and annual plants from Europe, Asia, Mediterranean, tropical Africa mountains, N. America. They are mostly tufted or mat-forming with usually stellate, hairy, obovate to oblong-lanceolate leaves in rosettes and racemes of 4-petalled, white, sometimes pink or red, flowers. Grow in any well-drained soil in a sunny site; some species tolerate shade. Plant autumn to spring, propagate by division or from seed in spring, cuttings in summer.

Species cultivated: *A. albida,* see *A. caucasica. A × arendsii (A. caucasica × A. aubretioides),* intermediate between parents, flowers in shades of pink. *A.* × *a.* Rosabella and *A.* × *a.* Rosea *(A. caucasica* and *A. albida* Rosabella, *A. a.* Rosea), soft pink. *A. aubretioides,* Turkey; densely-tufted; leaves obovate, small, deeply-toothed; flowers purplish-pink, to 1·5cm wide in racemes 7–15cm high, summer. *A. blepharophylla,* California; loosely mat-forming; leaves obovate to oblanceolate, 2–8cm long; flowers red-purple, to 1·5cm wide, in racemes 7–20cm tall, spring, early summer; not reliably winter-hardy. *A. breweri,* California; tufted, from woody base; leaves broadly spathulate, 1–3cm long; flowers red-purple to pink, to 1cm wide, spring to summer. *A. bryoides,* Balkan Peninsula; densely-tufted; leaves small, densely pubescent, ovate, tapered to base; flowers white, 6–8mm wide, just above leaves, summer. *A. caucasica (A. albida),* mat-forming, vigorous; leaves grey-green, obovate, tapered to base or auriculate (sub-species *brevifolia),* shallowly-toothed; flowers white, fragrant, 1–1·5cm wide, spring, in racemes 15–25cm high. *A.c.* Plena *(A.c.* Flore-pleno of gardens), flowers double; *A.c.* Rosabella and *A.c.* Rosea, see *A.* × *arendsii. A.c.* Variegata, leaves yellow-variegated; several white-flowered cultivars are available. *A. cypria (A. albida billardieri),* Cyprus; tufted; leaves obovate-spathulate, margins waved or lobed, to 7·5cm long; flowers white to pink, to 1·5cm wide in racemes to 15cm; not fully hardy. *A. ferdinandi-coburgii,* Macedonia; low, cushion-forming; leaves narrowly oblong to lanceolate, long-stalked, pubescent; flowers white, about 1cm wide, spring. *A.f.-c.* Variegata, leaves white-variegated, sometimes flushed pink. *A.* × *kellereri (A. bryoides* × *A. ferdinandi-coburgii),* dense, cushion-forming; leaves lanceolate, thick grey-white hairs; flowers white, small, spring. *A. procurrens,* Carpathians, Balkan Peninsula; mat-forming with long stolons; leaves ovate to oblanceolate, acuminate, 2–3cm long; flowers white, about 1cm wide in racemes 10–30cm high, spring, early summer. *A.* × *sturii,* cushion-forming; leaves small, dark glossy green; flowers white in racemes to 10cm or so, spring. *A.* × *suendermannii (A. ferdinandi-coburgii* × *A. procurrens),* much like first parent, but leaves much larger, smooth and glossy above; flowers white, spring.

Aralia

(old French-Canadian name, aralie, in Latin form). ARALIACEAE. A genus of 35 species of trees, shrubs, herbaceous perennials from N. America, E. Asia, Indo-Malaysia. They have compound leaves, usually pinnate or bipinnate, and small, 5-petalled, green to purplish or white flowers in rounded umbels, that in turn are carried in branched racemes or panicles; fruit – a berry. The species described are hardy where temperatures stay above about −10°C. Grow in well-drained, humus-rich soil in light shade or sun. Plant autumn to spring. Propagate by suckers or root cuttings in late winter or from seed sown when ripe or as soon as possible.

Species cultivated: *A. chinensis,* angelica tree; N. E. Asia; deciduous, erect, suckering shrub or small tree

Far left: *Arabis caucasica* Plena
Far left below: *Arabis cypria*
Bottom far left: *Aralia elata* Aureovariegata
Below: *Araucaria araucana*
Right: *Arbutus andrachne* bark

to 10m or more; stems thick, spiny; leaves tripinnate, to 1·25m long; flowers white, umbels in large, branched racemes, late summer to autumn. *A. elata,* angelica tree; Japan; deciduous, usually a sparsely-branched, erect, suckering shrub to 4m or more; leaves bipinnate to 1m long, rosetted towards the stout, prickly stem tips; flowers like *A. chinensis*. *A.e.* Aureovariegata (*A.e.* Aureomarginata), leaflets irregularly bordered silvery-white; *A.e.* Variegata (*A.e.* Albovariegata), leaflets margined and splashed creamy-white, ageing to silvery-white. *A. japonica, A. moseri* and *A. sieboldii*, see *Fatsia*.

Araucaria

(from Arauco Province, Chile, named for the native Araucani Indians where the first species was found). ARAUCARIACEAE. A genus of 18 species of evergreen coniferous trees originating in S. America, Australia, Norfolk Is, New Guinea, New Caledonia and New Hebrides. They are erect trees with a central, spar-like trunk and horizontal branches usually in whorls; leaves leathery, spirally-arranged and overlapping, ovate or awl-shaped; male strobili (flowering cones) cylindrical, female ovoid to globose, the latter ripening in 2–3 years then falling apart. The single hardy species requires fertile, well-drained soil and a sunny site. Plant autumn or spring; propagate from seed when ripe or as soon afterwards as possible.

Species cultivated: *A. araucana (A. imbricata),* monkey puzzle, Chile pine; Chile, Argentina; 20–45m; leaves ovate, hard, glossy dark green, spine-tipped, to 5cm long, living 10–15 years; male and female strobili usually on different trees, male 7·5–12·5cm long, ripe cones globular, 10–18cm long; hardy.

Arbutus

(the old Latin name). Strawberry tree. ERICACEAE. A genus of 20 species of evergreen shrubs and trees from N. and C. America, W. Europe, Mediterranean, W. Asia. The species described are hardy, often with attractive, smooth, reddish to cinnamon, peeling bark; leaves leathery, alternate, ovate to lanceolate; flowers in panicles, urn-shaped, pendant; fruit spherical, red to orange, somewhat strawberry-like, insipid. Grow in well-drained, neutral to acid, humus-rich soil in a sunny site where frosts are not severe. Plant autumn or spring. Propagate from seed sown in well-drained pans of sandy peat in a cold frame when ripe or in spring, tip cuttings in a propagating case at 18–23°C in summer.

Species cultivated: *A. andrachne,* S. E. Europe,

Above: *Arbutus menziesii*
Left: *Arbutus unedo*
Top right: *Arcterica nana*

Turkey; large shrub, small tree to 12m; leaves ovate to oblong, sometimes serrate, 5–10cm long; flowers in compact terminal panicles, white, 6mm long, spring; fruit granular, orange, 12mm wide. *A* × *andrachnoides (A.* × *hybrida) (A. andrachne* × *A. unedo),* natural hybrid intermediate between its parents; bark a striking cinnamon-red; flowers ivory-white, autumn to winter; lime-tolerant. *A. menziesii,* madrona; California to British Columbia; tree to 15m or more; bark terracotta; leaves oval to oblong, 5–15cm long, dark glossy green above, bluish-white beneath; flowers in pyramidal panicles, white to pink, rounded to urn-shaped, 6–8mm long, spring; fruit orange-red to 12mm. *A. unedo,* Mediterranean to S. W. Ireland; lime-tolerant small tree to 10m; bark deep brown, shredding; leaves elliptic to obovate, 3–10cm long, serrate; flowers in pendant panicles, white to pink, 6mm long; fruit red, granular, 12–20mm. *A.n.* Rubra, flowers rich pink.

Arcterica

(Greek *arktikos,* northern, and *Erica*), ERICACEAE. A genus of one species of dwarf evergreen shrub from N. E. Asia, Japan, Sakhalin. *A. nana (Pieris nana, Andromeda nana),* low, cushion to mat-forming plant; leaves oblong-elliptic, 8–12mm, often in 3s; flowers white, rounded bell-shape, 5mm long, in short terminal racemes, autumn and spring; fruit a globose, dry capsule. Grow in acid, peaty but well-drained soil, in sun or partial shade. Plant autumn to spring. Propagate by cuttings with a heel, late summer, by division, or from seed in autumn or spring.

Arctostaphylos

(Greek *arktos,* a bear, and *staphyle,* a bunch of grapes – the fruit of some species is eaten by bears). ERICACEAE. A genus of 71 species of evergreen shrubs and small trees allied to *Arbutus* from W. N. and C. America, 1 circumpolar and northern temperate. They have leathery, elliptic or oblanceolate to ovate leaves, and pendant, urn-shaped flowers in terminal clusters; fruit a fleshy, 4–10 seeded, berry-like drupe. Culture as for *Arcterica.*
Species cultivated: *A. alpina,* circumpolar; now placed in the genus *Arctous,* but described here for convenience. Deciduous, mat-forming; leaves obovate to oblanceolate, 2–4cm long; flowers greenish-white to pinkish, 5mm long, spring to early summer; fruit glossy-black, broadly ovoid, to 1cm long. *A. manzanita,* California; erect, 2–4m tall; long, crooked branches, smooth red-brown bark; leaves oblong to broadly elliptic, bright green often glossy, 2·5–4·5cm long; flowers white to pink, 6–8mm long, spring; fruit deep red, 8–12mm wide. *A. myrtifolia,* California; semi-prostrate shrublet to 30cm or more; leaves narrowly ovate, 5–15mm long, pale shining green; flowers white to pinkish, 4mm long; fruit greenish. *A. nevadensis,* pine mat manzanita; W. USA; mat-forming shrub, sometimes semi-erect; leaves elliptic to oblanceolate, 2–3cm long; flowers white, 6–7mm long, spring; fruit flattened globose, carmine, 6mm wide. *A. pumila,* dune manzanita; California; mat- or low hummock-forming; leaves obovate, pubescent 1·5–2·5cm long; flowers white to pink, about 4mm long, spring; fruit red-brown 5–6mm wide. *A. tomentosa,* downy manzanita; California; shrub to 2m, twigs with dense white hairs; leaves oblong-ovate, 2·5–4·5cm long, hoary-tomentose beneath; flowers white, 5–6mm long, spring; fruit brown-red, 8–10mm wide. *A. uva-ursi,* bearberry; circumpolar, northern temperate; mat-forming, vigorous; leaves obovate, somewhat glossy, to 2·5cm long; flowers in small, pendant, terminal racemes white, flushed pink, 6mm long, spring; fruit bright red, globose, smooth 6–8mm wide.

Arctotis

(Greek *arktos,* a bear, and *otos,* an ear – the pappus scales on the 'seed' fancifully resemble a bear's ear). COMPOSITAE. A genus of 65 species of annuals, perennials and sub-shrubs from Africa and Australia. They have lanceolate to obovate leaves, often lobed or cut, and quite large, solitary, daisy-like flowers in shades of white, yellow, orange, red, purple. Grow in well-drained soil in a sunny, sheltered site. The perennials will need the protection of a cloche in winter, or in cold areas are best lifted, potted, and over-wintered in a well-ventilated, frost-free greenhouse. Alternatively, they may be grown for flowering as greenhouse pot plants. Propagate from seed sown in spring in a temperature of 18–21°C, or cuttings of perennials in late summer or early autumn. Young plants should not be planted out until fear of frost has passed in early summer.
Species cultivated: *A. acaulis (A. scapigera),* S.

Africa; perennial, tufted, from a woody base; leaves 15–20cm long, usually pinnately-lobed, white-woollen beneath; flower-heads to 9cm wide, ray florets yellow to red above, coppery or reddish beneath, summer. *A. breviscapa (A. speciosa)*, S. Africa; annual; 15cm or more tall; leaves oblong-lanceolate, variably pinnately-lobed, white-woollen beneath; flower-heads orange-yellow, summer. *A. fastuosa*, see *Venidium fastuosum*. *A.* × *hybrida*, see *Venidio-arctotis*. *A. stoechadifolia*, Africa; perennial; 60–90cm tall; leaves greyish-green, lanceolate, lobed; flower-heads to 7·5cm wide, ray florets white above, lavender-blue beneath, disc dark blue, summer to autumn. *A.s. grandis*, flowers larger than type, white to yellow. *A. venusta*, S. Africa; perennial, 30cm; leaves narrow; flower-heads pale blue, summer.

Arctous – see *Arctostaphylos alpina*.

Arenaria

(Latin *arena*, sand – many species are native to sandy soil). Sandwort. CARYOPHYLLACEAE. A genus of 250 species of annuals, perennials, rarely sub-shrubs, from northern temperate zone. They are mostly small, tufted, creeping or mat-forming plants with opposite pairs of filiform to linear-lanceolate or ovate leaves, and 5-petalled, white – rarely pink – flowers in panicles or solitary. Grow in well-drained, sandy or gritty soil in a sunny site. Plant autumn to spring. Propagate by division or from seed in spring. White flowered unless otherwise stated.

Species cultivated: *A. balearica*, W. Mediterranean Is; dense, filmy mats of interlacing stems; leaves ovate, 2–4mm long; flowers solitary, 5–6mm wide, spring to summer. *A. caespitosa* (of gardens), see *Sagina caespitosa*. *A. graminifolia*, see *A. procera*. *A. juniperina*, see *Minuartia j. A. laricifolia*, see *Minuartia l. A. ledebouriana*, Iran, Turkey; cushion-forming; leaves awl-shaped, spine-tipped, bluish-grey, to 10mm long; flowers, 8–12mm wide in 1–10 flowered panicles. *A. montana*, W. Europe; loosely mat-forming; leaves oblong-lanceolate, grey-green, hairy, 10–20mm long; flowers to 2cm wide, solitary or in cymes, spring to summer. *A. nevadensis*, S. Spain; annual; to 8cm tall; leaves 4–7mm, lower ovate, upper linear-lanceolate, glandules, hairy; flowers about 6mm wide, in more or less dense corymbs, summer. *A. norvegica*, N. W. Europe; tufted annual or perennial, 3–7cm tall; leaves oblanceolate; flowers 4–6mm wide, in 1–4 flowered cymes, summer. *A. purpurascens*, Pyrenees, Cordillera Cantabrica; mat-forming perennial; leaves elliptic to lanceolate; flowers pale purple or white, 1–2cm wide, in clusters of 1–4, late spring. *A. tetraquetra*, Pyrenees, mountains of S.E. Spain; perennial forming dense cushion; leaves grey-green, ovate, recurved, overlapping; flowers solitary, to 10mm or more wide, of 4 or 5 petals, summer.

Top left: *Arctotis stoechadifolia grandis*
Top: *Arctotis* species
Above: *Arenaria ledebouriana*
Above left: *Argemone munita*

Argemone

(*Argemon*, cataract, the Greek name for a poppy-like plant – not now identifiable – and reputedly curing cataract of the eye, taken up by Linnaeus for this genus). Prickly poppy. PAPAVERACEAE. A genus of 10 species of annuals and perennials from S. USA, Mexico, W. Indies. They are generally robust plants with more or less prickly stems, pinnately-lobed, prickly leaves, and poppy-like flowers with 4–6 petals. Grow in well-drained soil in a sunny, sheltered site. Sow seed *in situ* late spring or raise under glass earlier, pricking off seedlings as young as possible to small pots of a good commercial potting mixture. Perennials are not reliably hardy and best grown as annuals.

Species cultivated: *A. mexicana*, Mexico, C. America; annual stem prickly to 60cm; leaves blotched or shaded blue-white; flowers yellow or whitish to orange, 5–7cm wide, summer. *A. munita*

(*A. platyceras*), usually perennial; stems sparsely to thickly spined, 60cm or more tall; leaves glaucous; flowers white, 5–13cm wide, late summer; a variable plant in the wild, some sub-species being annual.

Arisaema

(Greek *aris* or *aron*, arum, and *haima*, blood – used in the sense of a blood relationship; the plants in this genus are much like arum). ARACEAE. A genus of 150 species of tuberous or rhizomatous perennials from E. Africa, E. N.America, Mexico, tropical Asia. Each plant has generally 1 or 2 long-stalked leaves, the blade pedately divided into 3–15 leaflets or lobes; flowers tiny, petalless, the males having 2–5 stamens, borne on a spadix surrounded by a spathe. Grow the hardy or almost hardy species in humus-rich soil in a sheltered, partially shaded site. The tender species need greenhouse treatment with a minimum temperature of 10°C. Plant in autumn, using any commercial potting mixture, preferably without lime. Pot-grown specimens benefit from liquid fertilizer given fortnightly or as soon as the leaves are expanded. Pot specimens should be kept almost dry when the foliage yellows in autumn; resume watering the following spring. Propagate by offsets at potting time or from seed when ripe.

Species cultivated: *A. atrorubens*, see *A. triphyllum*. *A. amurense*, see *A. robustum*. *A. candidissimum*, W. China; leaves trifoliate, solitary, stalk to 30cm or more, leaflets broadly ovate, 8–20cm long; spathes hooded, 7–10cm long, white, striped green without and pinkish within, early summer, maturing before leaf, hardy. *A. consanguineum*; E. Asia; leaves of 10–21 lanceolate-acuminate leaflets, stalk 45–90cm tall; spathes to 17·5cm long, green striped purple-brown within, white without, tip slender, tail-like, summer, almost hardy. *A. dracontium*, green dragon; E. N. America; leaves solitary, of 7–15 oblong to lanceolate-acuminate leaflets, stalk mottled, 30cm or more long; spathes slender, rolled, green, 5–9cm long, spadix yellow to 30cm, early summer, hardy. *A. flavum*, Himalaya; leaves in pairs, of 9–11, oblong-lanceolate leaflets, stalk to 36cm long; spathes 4cm long, purple, veined green, summer, almost hardy. *A. griffithii*, Sikkim, Himalaya; leaves in pairs, trifoliate, leaflets broadly ovate, 20–30cm long, stalk to 60cm; spathes to 23cm long, greenish, striped, netted and spotted violet-purple, late spring, hardy. *A. helleborifolium*, see *A. tortuosum*. *A. robustum* (*A. amurense*), leaves solitary, of 5 ovate leaflets, stalk to 30cm or more; spathes green, white-striped, about 10cm long, late spring. *A.r. atropurpureum*, spathes dark purple. *A. sikokianum*, Japan; leaves in pairs trifoliate, leaflets broadly ovate, to 15cm long, stalks 45cm; spathes waisted, 18–25cm long, brownish-purple, bearing green, purple-centred bands without, white-banded within, spadix white, bulbous, spring; hardy. *A. speciosum*, Himalaya; tuber rhizome-like; leaves solitary, trifoliate, leaflets oblong-lanceolate, 20–40cm long, red-margined, stalk brown-mottled, 60–90; spathes to 15cm or more, brownish-purple within, green-striped without, but lower part striped white or pale purple, spadix white, the glossy purple tip prolonged to a slender tail, to 50cm long, spring; needs a sheltered site or a frost-free greenhouse. *A. thunbergii*, Japan; leaves solitary, of 9–17 lanceolate-acuminate leaflets, stalk 30–60cm; spathe 8–10cm long, dark to reddish purple, spadix with tail-like appendage 30–50cm long, spring, hardy. *A.t. urashima*, see *A. urashima*. *A. tortuosum*, India; leaves 2 or 3, of 13–23 leaflets or lobes, stalks to 60cm long; spathes 7·5–17cm long, green and purple, with pale stripes, early summer; greenhouse. *A.t. helleborifolium* (*A. helleborifolium*), somewhat smaller than type, leaflets about 17. *A. triphyllum*, (*A. atrorubens*), jack-in-the-pulpit, USA; tubers bearing scaly rhizomes; leaves trifoliate, uniformly green on both surfaces, leaflets ovate-acuminate; spathes hooded, 5·5–9·5cm long, green or dark purple, pale-striped at the base, early summer. *A. t. triphyllum*, leaves glaucous beneath and the hood of the spathe reflexed. *A. t. stewardsonii*, darker green leaves, the hood of the spathe inrolled. *A. t.* Zebrinum, dark purple hood striped white within. *A. urushima* (*A. thunbergii urushima*), like *A. thunbergii*, but leaflets 11–15, spathe with tail-like tip, spadix appendage to 60cm long.

Arisarum

(Greek name *arisaron* for 1 of these plants). ARACEAE. A genus of 3 species of tuberous-rooted perennials from the Mediterranean region, allied to *Arum* and *Arisaema* and with similar flowering spathes. *A. proboscideum* needs woodland or shady conditions and a humus-rich soil. *A. vulgare* requires any well-drained soil in a sunny, sheltered site. Plant autumn. Propagate by division or offsets at planting time, or from seed sown when ripe or as soon afterwards as possible.

Species cultivated: *A. proboscideum*, Spain, Italy; tubers rhizome-like, creeping and forming colonies; leaves hastate, dark green, blade 7–10cm long; spathes 2–3cm long, oblong, whitish at base, maroon above, the tip prolonged into a slender tail to 15cm, spring; the spathes crouch beneath the leaves like tiny mice. *A. vulgare*, circum. Mediterranean; tubers slender to thick; leaves hastate, the basal lobes somewhat rounded, sometimes blotched, veined or marbled white; spathe 3–6cm long, hooded, palest green, striped darker green – ranging to purple-brown, striped whitish – spadix maroon, protruding and down-curving, winter to spring.

Below left: *Arisaema candidissimum*
Below: *Arisarum proboscideum*
Bottom: *Aristolochia sempervirens*

Aristolochia

(Greek *aristos*, best, and *locheia*, parturition – alluding to its supposed medicinal value). ARISTOLOCHIACEAE. A genus of 350 species of mainly deciduous and evergreen woody climbers or scramblers, some herbaceous perennials, from tropical and temperate regions of both hemispheres. They generally have rounded to ovate or triangular-cordate leaves and curious flowers formed of a straight or curved tubular perianth that may have a hooded, expanded funnel or dish-like mouth. Small flies enter the mouth attracted by the odour, down-pointing hairs preventing their return until the pollen is shed over them; the hairs then wither and the flies escape to visit another flower and effect pollination. Tender species need greenhouse treatment, grown in large pots of any commercial potting mixture or borders of humus-rich soil and given a support of strings or sticks. Hardy species need a sunny border outside. Plant autumn or spring Propagate from seed in spring, division at planting time or cuttings in a propagating frame with bottom heat of 21–23°C, in summer.

Species cultivated: *A. altissima*, see *A. sempervirens*. *A. clematitis*, birthwort; Europe; erect herbaceous rhizomatous perennial to 80cm; leaves ovate, 6–15cm long; flowers in small axillary clusters, tubular, dull yellow 2–3cm long, summer, autumn; *A. durior*, see *A. macrophylla*. *A. griffithii*, Nepal; climber to 6m or more; leaves cordate to 10cm or more; flowers euphonium-shaped to 7cm wide, dark red and papillose within, strongly curved basal tube, whitish, spring, summer; needs a frost-free greenhouse or very sheltered wall. *A. heterophylla*, China; climber to 5m; leave ovate-cordate, 5–13cm long, hairy; flowers curved, tubular, 3–4cm long, yellow and brown-purple, summer; hardy. *A. macrophylla* (*A. durior*, *A. sipho*), Dutchman's pipe; E. USA; vigorous deciduous climber to 9m; leaves heart- to kidney-shaped, 10–25cm long; flowers bent like a siphon, yellow-green expanding to a somewhat 3-lobed, flattened, purple-brown mouth 2cm wide, summer; hardy. *A. sempervirens* (*A. altissima*), C. S. Europe, Crete; climbing or trailing evergreen to 5cm, usually less, and often forming low mounds of interlacing stems; leaves glossy, triangular-ovate, 5–10cm long; flowers tubular, 2–5cm long, yellow, striped purple, late spring, summer; warm, sheltered site or frost-free greenhouse. *A. sipho*, see *A. macrophylla*. *A. tomentosa*, S. E. USA; like *A. macrophylla* but small and downy-hairy, flowers having a flared mouth of 3 yellow lobes.

Armeria

(Latinized old French name *armoires* for a cluster-headed pink – *Dianthus*). PLUMBAGINACEAE. A genus of 80 species of cushion- or mat-forming perennials from the sea coasts and mountains of the northern temperate zone and S. America. They generally have lanceolate to linear or grassy leaves and small, 5-petalled flowers in dense, spherical heads. Grow in well-drained soil in a sunny site. Plant autumn to spring. Propagate by division at planting time, cuttings taken in late summer or seed sown in spring.

Species cultivated: *A. alliacea* (*A. arenaria*, *A. plantaginea*), W. Europe tufted, stems 20–50cm; leaves lanceolate to linear; spathulate 5–13cm long, heads 1–2cm wide, red-purple, white, summer. *A. × caesalpina* (of gardens) (*A. juniperifolia* × *A. pocutica alpina*), midway between parents, dark green hummocks; stems 6-9cm; flowers soft pink, spring. *A. cespitosa* (*A. caespitosa* of gardens), see *A. juniperifolia*. *A. corsica*, see *A. maritima*. *A. juniperifolia* (*A. cespitosa*), C. Spain; hummock-forming; stems to 2·5cm; leaves linear, greyish-green, 4–15mm long; flower-head 1–1·7cm wide, flowers pink, late spring, *A.j.* Bevan's, possibly a hybrid, stems to 5cm, flowers deep rose; *A.j.* Beechwood, stems to 10cm, flowers deep pink; *A.j.* Six Hills, 10cm, pale pink. *A. maritima*, N. Hemisphere; very variable, usually mat-forming; stems 5–30cm; leaves somewhat fleshy, linear, 2–15cm long; flower-heads 1·5–2·5cm wide, flowers pink, red, white, spring, summer. Many geographic forms and cultivars are known, among them: *A.m.* Alba, white; *A.m.* Bloodstone blood-red; *A.m.* Corsica, a unique shade of brick red; *A.m.* Perfection, large heads, bright pink; *A.m.* Vindictive, deep pink. *A. plantaginea*, see *A. alliacea*. *A. pseudarmeria*, (*A. formosa* and *A. latifolia*), Portugal; tufted; stems 25–50cm; leaves obovate-lanceolate, 10–23cm long; heads 3–4cm wide, flowers usually white summer. *A.p.* Bees Ruby, bright ruby-red, and other colour forms are perhaps hybrids with *A. alliacea* and *A. maritima* Corsica.

Arnebia

(Latinized form of its Arabic name, *sagaret el arneb*). BORAGINACEAE. A genus of 25 species of perennials and annuals from Mediterranean, tropical Africa, Himalaya. 1 species is generally available, *A. echioides* (*Echioides longiflorum*), prohet flower; Armenia; perennial, 20–30cm tall; leaves narrowly oblong, rough, hairy; flowers in spike-like cymes, funnel-shaped with 5, rounded, primrose-yellow lobes, each with a basal black spot that fades as the flower ages, summer. Grow in well-drained soil in a sunny site. Plant autumn or spring. Propagate from seed in spring, root cuttings in winter, or stem cuttings with a heel, late summer.

Arnica

(perhaps from *arnakis*, lambskin – from the texture of the leaves of some species). COMPOSITAE. A genus of 32 species of perennials from northern temperate and arctic zones. 1 species is generally available: *A. montana*, mountain tobacco; mountains of Europe; tufted; stems 30–60cm; leaves oblong-lanceolate, 7–15cm long, aromatic, glandules hairy; flower-heads usually solitary, daisy-like, 7–8cm wide, orange-yellow, late spring, summer. Grow in any humus-rich soil in a sunny site. Plant autumn to spring. Propagate by division or from seed in spring.

Top far left: *Armeria maritima*
Top left: *Arnebia echioides*
Top: *Arnica montana*
Above: *Aronia melanocarpa* autumn leaves

Aronia

(derived from Greek *aria*, whitebeam, and formerly used as generic name for *Pyrus*, that in turn once embraced species now classified under *Aronia*,

Sorbus, etc). Chokeberry. ROSACEAE. A genus of 3 species of deciduous shrubs from E. N.America. They have elliptic to obovate leaves, 5-petalled flowers in small cymes, and red or black-purple, berry-like fruit. In autumn the foliage turns red and orange. Grow in acid or neutral, moisture-retentive soil, in sun or partial shade. Plant autumn to spring. Propagate from seed when ripe or soon afterwards, suckers or division at planting time.

Species cultivated: *A. arbutifolia (Pyrus a.* or *Sorbus a.)*, suckering shrub to 3m, rarely a small tree to 6m; leaves elliptic, oblong to obovate, 2–9cm long, toothed, grey and hairy beneath, dark green above; flowers 1cm wide, white or pink, spring; fruit 5–7mm across, usually bright red. *A. floribunda*, see *A. prunifolia*. *A. melanocarpa (Pyrus m.* or *Sorbus m.)*, shrub to 1m; leaves elliptic to oblanceolate, lustrous dark green, smooth on both sides, 2–6cm long; flowers 1cm wide, white, spring; fruit 6–8mm, glossy purple-black. *A. prunifolia (A. floribunda, Pyrus melanocarpa, Sorbus m.)*, shrub to 4m; much like *A. arbutifolia* with purple-black fruit.

Arrhenatherum

(Greek *arren*, male, and *anther*, awn or bristle – the staminate flowers bear awns). GRAMINEAE. A genus of 6 species of perennial grasses from Europe and the Mediterranean. The species described is a useful pasture grass but a weed equal to couch grass (with which it is often confused by gardeners) in gardens. *A. elatius*, false or tall oat grass; Europe to W. Asia, introduced and naturalized in other countries; erect, tufted plant to 1·5m, rhizomatous; leaves 10–40cm long, 4–10mm wide, flat, panicle usually loose, 10–30cm long; spikelets oblong, to gaping 7–11mm, pale green to purplish, lustrous, summer. *A.e. bulbosum*, onion couch; has basal internodes swollen and bulb-like. *A.e.b.* Variegatum has white-striped leaves. Grow in any soil that is not waterlogged, preferably in sun. Plant and propagate by division in spring.

Arrowhead – see *Sagittaria*.

Artemisia

(for the Greek goddess, Artemis). COMPOSITAE. A genus of 400 species of shrubs, sub-shrubs, perennials and annuals from northern temperate zone, S. America and S. Africa. They have generally small, alternate leaves, often pinnately-lobed or finely-dissected and covered with silky or woolly hairs. Flower-heads small to very small, composed of minute, tubular florets that are wind-pollinated. Many species are aromatic and several are used as culinary herbs or for flavouring liqueurs etc. Grow in any well-drained soil in a sunny site. Plant autumn to spring. Propagate by cuttings in late summer or by division in spring.

Species cultivated: *A. abrotanum*, southernwood, lad's love, old man; country of origin uncertain, naturalized E. C. S. Europe; sweetly aromatic shrub to 1m; leaves 2·5–6·5cm long, pinnate to tripinnate, lobes filiform, grey and hairy beneath; flower-heads yellowish, globose 3–4mm wide, in panicles. *A. absinthium*, common wormwood; Europe; woody-based perennial or sub-shrub to 90cm; leaves to 7·5cm long, bi- or tripinnate, lobes linear, blunt, silky-haired; flower-heads yellow, hemispherical, 3mm wide, in large, leafy panicles. *A.a.* Lambrook Silver, leaves bright silvery-grey. *A. afra*, Kenya; loose shrub to 2m; leaves bipinnate, lobes linear, grey-green; flower-heads small, yellow, in narrow panicles. *A. arborescens*, Mediterranean, S. Portugal; shrub to 1m or more; leaves to 7cm long, bipinnatisect, silvery-white hairs; flowers 6–7mm wide, hemispherical, in large panicles. *A. assoana*, see *A. pedemontana*. *A. baumgartenii*, see *A. eriantha*. *A. discolor*, W. N.America; suckering sub-shrub to 45cm; leaves pinnate or bipinnately lobed, white-haired, maturing smooth above; flower-heads, 4–5mm long, in slender, leafy panicles; can be invasive in some soils but very decorative. *A. dracunculus* (see Tarragon); S. and E. USSR; well-naturalized in Europe; aromatic glabrous perennial to 1·2m; leaves linear to lanceolate, to 7·5cm long, the lower one 3-toothed at apex; flower-heads nodding, globose, 2–3cm wide in loose panicles; a popular flavouring herb. *A. eriantha (A. baumgartenii)*, Pyrenees, Alps, Apennines, mountains of Balkan Peninsula, Carpathians; woody-based, tufted perennial, 7–10cm high; leaves biternate, lobes linear, pointed silky-haired; flower-heads, 7mm wide, hemispherical, in dense racemes to 25cm high. *A. glacialis*, S.W. Alps; densely-tufted, woody-based perennial, to 18cm high; leaves bipinnate, 1–3cm long, silver, silky-haired; flower-heads broadly hemispherical, 4–7mm wide, yellow, summer. *A. gnaphalodes*, see *A. ludoviciana gnaphalodes*. *A. lactiflora*, China, India, clump-forming perennial, to 1·8m; leaves to 10cm or more, pinnate, the lobes cut and toothed; flower-heads cream, 4mm wide in plume-like, terminal panicles, late summer; the only artemisia grown for its flowers alone. *A. lanata*, see *A. pedemontana*. *A. ludoviciana (A. purshiana)*, western mugwort, white sage; C. N.America, Mexico, naturalized E. USA; invasive, rhizomatous perennial, to 1·2m tall; leaves 2·5–10cm long, lanceolate to linear-oblong, sometimes with a few arching lobes or coarse teeth, densely white-felted beneath, grey-white haired above; flower-heads bell-shaped, 3–5mm long in narrow panicles (sometimes masquerades as *A. palmeri*, a smaller Californian species). *A.l. gnaphalodes*, leaves lanceolate to oblanceolate, sometimes toothed, plant usually smaller; *A.l.g.* Silver Queen, willow-shaped leaves, probably a selected clone of type species. *A. maritima*, sea wormwood; coasts W. and N. Europe; strongly aromatic, woody-based perennial or sub-shrub, 20–50cm tall; leaves 2–5cm, usually bipinnate, the lobes narrowly linear, white down on both surfaces; flower-heads ovoid, 3–6mm long, in narrow, leafy panicles. *A.m.* Nutans *(A. nutans* of gardens, not the species that follows), more slender and graceful than type. *A. nutans*, S.E. USSR; sub-shrub to 90cm; leaves 1–3cm, bi- or tripinnatisect, lobes linear; flower-heads hemispherical, pale yellow, 3–6mm wide, in a wide panicle; the true species is probably not in cultivation, see also *A. maritima* Nutans. *A. palmeri*, California; a somewhat woody-based perennial; stems wand-like, 50–80cm high; leaves 5–12cm, pinnately cut into 3–9 linear lobes, downy beneath; flower-heads hemispherical, 2·5–4mm long, in a broad panicle; confused with *A. ludoviciana*. *A. pedemontana (A. assoana, A. lanata)*, mat-forming; leaves bipinnatifid or twice trifid, 1–2cm long, silvery-white hair; flower-heads hemispherical, 4–6mm wide, in simple or branched racemes 20–30cm long. *A. pontica*, C. and E. Europe; aromatic rhizomatous perennial, 40–80cm tall; leaves 3–4cm long, pinnatifid or bipinnatifid, dense white down on both surfaces; flower-heads yellow, ovoid, 2–4mm wide, in narrow panicles. *A. purshiana*, now considered to be a variant of *A. ludoviciana*, but usually smaller; leaves ovate to lanceolate, white-woollen on both surfaces. *A. schmidtiana*, Japan, Kuriles, Sakhalin; aromatic, densely-tufted, woody-based perennial forming lacy mounds to 20cm or more; leaves 3–4·5cm long, bipinnate or bipalmate, lobes linear, blunt, dense silver down on both sides; flower-heads globose, 4–5mm wide in panicles. *A.s.* Nana, a little smaller than type. *A. splendens*, Turkey, Caucasus, Iran, Iraq; tufted to hummock-forming; leaves to 2cm long, bipinnatisect, with silvery, silky hair; flower-heads flattened, globose, 5–7mm wide, florets reddish, in a 1-sided raceme or narrow panicle 10–30cm tall. *A. stellerana*, beach worm-wood, dusty miller, old woman; N.E. Asia, naturalized N. Europe, N.E. N.America; rhizomatous perennial, 30–60cm high; leaves 5–10cm, pinnate or pinnatifid, densely white-felted; flower-heads broadly bell-shaped, 5–9mm wide in a slender panicle or raceme. *A. tridentata*, sage brush; N. America; evergreen shrub to 2m or more; leaves 1–4cm long, cuneate, tipped with 3 blunt teeth; flower-heads ovoid, 3–4mm long in stiff, slender panicles. *A. vallesiaca*, S.W. Switzerland, S.E. France, N.W. Italy; strongly aromatic, much-branched perennial with stout, woody base, to 50cm; leaves 3–4 times pinnatisect, to 4cm long, with linear lobes, dense white hair; flower-heads oblong to obovoid, 3–5mm long, in slender panicle.

Left above: *Arrhenatherum elatius bulbosum* Variegatum
Top: *Artemisia stellerana*
Above: *Artemisia arborescens*

Arum

(the Greek name *aron*, used by Theophrastus for some species in this genus). ARACEAE. A genus of 15 species of tuberous-rooted perennials from Europe and Mediterranean. They are like *Arisaema*, but have hastate or sagittate leaves, more convolute spathes, often club-shaped spadices and a zone of sterile flowers between the basal females and upper males. The expanded base of the spathe containing the flowers is closed by downward-pointing hairs (modified sterile male flowers). Pollinating flies attracted by the odour given off push past these hairs and cannot easily get out again until the hairs wither after pollen has been shed. The pollen-covered flies then escape and visit another newly-opened spathe, thus effecting cross-pollination. Generally hardy, growing in sun or partial shade in any humus-rich soil. Plant late summer to autumn. Propagate by detaching offsets when dormant, or from seed when ripe or soon afterwards.

Above: *Arum italicum* Pictum
Top right: *Arum creticum*
Right: *Aruncus dioicus*

Species cultivated: *A. creticum*, Crete, S. Greece; stems to 40cm; leaves 25–40cm tall; spathes 10–15cm long, pale yellow to white, spadix gold, spring; needs a mild area and best grown in a sheltered spot. *A. dioscoridis*, E. Mediterranean; leaves 30–60cm tall; spathe to 20cm long, pale green, spotted and marbled black-purple, spadix black, late spring. *A.d. smithii*, spathes pale green, internally marbled blackish. *A. dracunculus*, see *Dracunculus vulgaris*, known as dragon arum. *A. hygrophilum*, Syria; leaves 50–60cm tall; spathes 9cm long, whitish, flushed or margined metallic blue-purple, summer; not the hardiest. *A. italicum*, Mediterranean, S. to Sardinia and Cyprus, W. Europe; variable species; leaves narrow to broad, 30–60cm tall, sometimes veined yellow or white; spathe palest yellow, to 30cm or more, spadix darker, later spring. *A.i.* Marmoratum (of gardens), broad leaves marbled grey; *A.i.* Pictum (of gardens), narrow dark green leaves boldly white-veined. *A. maculatum*, lords and ladies, cuckoo pint, Adam and Eve; Europe to Black Sea; leaves 30–50cm tall, blade sometimes black-spotted; spathes 15–20cm long, pale green to yellowish or whitish and sometimes purple flushed, spadix purple or yellow, spring. *A. orientale*, Greece to Afghanistan; leaves about 30cm tall: spathe to 20cm or more long, black-purple, spring. *A.o. gratum* has a cream to yellow-green spathe and a bluish spadix; it needs a sheltered, warm site or frost-free greenhouse. *A. palaestinum*, Syria, Lebanon, Isreal; leaves 35–50cm tall; spathe 15–22cm long, yellow-green without, deep black-purple within, spring; it needs a warm spot or frost-free greenhouse.

Arum lily – see *Zantedeschia*.

Aruncus

(Latin *aruncus*, goat's beard). ROSACEAE. A genus of 12 species of perennials from N. Hemisphere, formerly included in *Spiraea*. 1 species is generally available: *A. dioicus (A. sylvester, A. vulgaris, Spiraea aruncus)*, N. Hemisphere; robust, clump-forming, woody-based herbaceous plant to 2m or so; leaves large, tripinnate or ternate, leaflets lanceolate to ovate, sharply-toothed, 3–12cm long; flowers very small, 5-petalled, creamy-white in dense, compound, plume-like panicles, summer. *A.*

d. Kneiffi, smaller than type, to 1m; curiously-reduced narrow leaflets; *A.d. triternatus*, Nepal; neat miniature version to 30cm. Grow in moisture-retentive soil in partial shade or sun. Plant autumn to spring. Propagation is done by division at planting time. Seed may be sown in spring but is slow to reach maturity.

Arundinaria

(Latin *arundo*, a reed or cane). GRAMINEAE. A genus of 150 species of bamboos mainly from the warmer regions of the world. They are clump-forming, some also spreading widely by rhizomes, with narrowly oblong leaves. The typically grass-like flowers are either rarely produced in cultivation or hidden by the leaves; generally they are produced only on long-established specimens. Grow the hardy species described here in moisture-retentive soil in partial shade or sun, sheltered from strong, cold winds. Plant and propagate by division in spring.

Species cultivated: *A. anceps*, N. W. Himalaya; rhizomatous canes to 3·5m or more, glossy deep green; leaves lustrous rich green, 10–15cm long; attractive but fast-spreading. *A. japonica (Bambusa metake, Pseudosasa japonica*, Japan; rhizomatous; canes olive-green, 3–6m tall; leaves 18–30cm, glossy, dark above, somewhat greyish beneath; often flowers; very hardy and vigorous, becoming a nuisance in rich, moist soils. *A. murielae (Sinoarundinaria m.)*, China; clump-forming to 3·5m or more; canes bright green when young, maturing yellow-green; leaves 6–10cm long, bright green; makes a fine specimen or accent plant. *A. nitida (Sinoarundinaria n.)*, China; much like *A. murieliae*, but canes purple-flushed. *A. pumila*, Japan; rhizomatous; canes to 80cm, very slender, dull purple; leaves 5–18cm long; fast-growing and useful as ground cover. *A. simonii (Pleioblastus s.)*, Japan; clump-forming, canes to 4·5m or more, olive-green bearing a waxy-white patina when young; leaves 7·5–30cm long, half of each under-surface greyish-green; flowers not infrequently. *A. variegata (A. fortunei, Pleiorblastus variegatus)*, Japan; rhizomatous; canes 80–120cm tall, pale green, somewhat zig-zag; leaves 5–20cm long, dark green, striped white, fading pale green. *A. viridistriata (A. auricoma, Pleioblastus viridistriata)*, Japan; rhizomatous; canes purple-green, to 2m, forming close colonies; leaves 7·5–20cm long, deep green, boldly-striped yellow; flowers not infrequently; may be cut back hard each winter to promote more bright young leaves.

Left below: *Arundinaria japonica*
Top: *Arundinaria viridistriata*
Above: *Arundo donax* Versicolor
Right top: *Asarum europaeum*

Arundo

(Latin *arundo*, a reed or cane. GRAMINEAE. A genus of mainly giant grasses from tropical and temperate regions. 1 species is generally available: *A. donax*, Mediterranean; clump-forming from a woody base; stems to 4m; leaves in alternate ranks, arching, grey-green, to 60cm long by 7cm wide; flowering spikelets reddish to whitish in dense, terminal panicles 30–60cm long, autumn, if they are produced. *A.d.* Macrophylla, leaves larger than type, more glaucous; *A.d.* Versicolor (*A.d.* Variegata), smaller-growing, leaves white-striped, less hardy. Grow in ordinary, humus-rich soil in a sheltered, sunny site. Where spring frosts are severe, protection will be needed, or else the plants should be grown in tubs and over-wintered in a frost-free greenhouse. Plant spring. Propagate by division in spring or cuttings of sideshoots in a propagating case in summer.

Asarabacca – see *Asarum europaeum*.

Asarum

(ancient Greek name, *asaron*, in Latin form). Wild ginger. ARISTOLOCHIACEAE. A genus of 70 species of evergreen perennials from northern temperate zone. They are low, tufted or carpeting plants with mainly heart- or kidney-shaped, long-stalked leaves, in some species flecked or marbled grey or white. The curious tubular or bell-shaped flowers have 3 perianth lobes triangular-ovate, 1·5–4cm long, at ground level. Grow in moisture-retentive but well-drained, humus-rich soil in shade or partial shade. Plant autumn to spring. Propagate by division at planting time, preferably autumn, or from seed when ripe.

Species cultivated: *A. acuminatum*, see following species. *A. canadense*, N. E. N.America; leaves kidney-shaped, often abruptly pointed, 5–20cm wide, hairy; flowers bell-shaped, brown-purple, the perianth lobes triangular-ovate, 1·5–4cm long. *A.c. acuminatum*, perianth lobes elongated, tail-like, spring. *A. caudatum*, W. N.America; leaves kidney-shaped, 2–10cm long, glossy above; flowers brownish-red, bell-shaped, perianth lobes, 2·5–8·5cm, often tapered and tail-like, late spring. *A. europaeum*, asarabacca; Europe, W. Siberia; leaves rounded to kidney-shaped, 2·5–10cm long, dark lustrous-green above; flowers brownish, tubular, about 1·5cm long, perianth lobes triangular with incurving points, spring, summer. *A. hartwegii*, California, Oregon; leaves ovate-cordate, 4–10cm long, pubescent beneath, glossy and mottled above; flowers brown-purple, hairy, bell-shaped, perianth lobes 2·5–6·5cm long, late spring. *A. shuttleworthii*, E. USA; leaves ovate-cordate to kidney-shaped, often mottled, 2·5–9·5cm or more long; flowers dark purple, broadly bell-shaped, 2·5–5cm long, perianth lobes triangular, to 1·5cm long, late spring to early summer.

Ash – see *Fraxinus*.
Aspen – see *Populus tremula*.

Asperula

(Latin *asper*, rough – referring to the roughish stems). RUBIACEAE. A genus of at least 200 species of small shrubs, perennials and annuals from Asia, Europe, E. Australia, Tasmania. They are mainly small plants, tufted to mat-forming, with square stems, narrow leaves in whorls, and slenderly tubular flowers with 4 corolla lobes. Grow in well-drained soil in sun; some of the Alpine species need scree conditions or pots of gritty soil in an alpine house. Plant autumn or spring. Propagate from seed or by division in spring, cuttings in summer.

Species cultivated (summer flowering): *A. arcadiensis*, mountains S. Greece; tufted, forming low hummocks; leaves broadly lanceolate, 8–10mm long, grey-woollen; flowers in terminal umbels to 1cm long, the lobes 2–3mm, spreading. Needs scree or alpine house treatment, confused in gardens with the easier to grow *A. suberosa*. *A. azurea*, see *A.*

orientalis. *A. gussonii*, mountains Sicily; tufted, numerous slender stems forming low hummocks; leaves narrowly elliptical to broadly linear, 4–9mm long; flowers 6–7mm long in umbels of 6–15, reddish-pink. *A. lilaciflora caespitosa*, E. Mediterranean; neatly mat-forming; leaves dark glossy green narrow; flowers carmine-pink. *A. nitida*, mountains C. Greece; densely tufted, forming low hummocks; leaves narrowly lanceolate to needle-like, 1–1·5cm long; flowers 5–8mm long, rose-purple, in elongated terminal clusters. *A. odorata*, see *Galium odoratum*. *A. orientalis* (*A. azurea* and *A.a. setosa*), Caucasus; annual, to 30cm or more; leaves bristly, lanceolate, about 8 in whorl; flowers fragrant, pale blue in dense clusters 2cm wide. *A. suberosa*, mountains N. Greece, S. W. Bulgaria; hummock-forming; leaves linear, 4–10mm long, silvery-haired; flowers 5–8mm long, in long clusters; best in scree or alpine house.

Asphodeline

(recording its close relationship to *Asphodelus*). LILIACEAE. A genus of 15 species of herbaceous perennials from the Mediterranean to Himalaya. They have tufts or clumps of erect stems bearing awl-shaped or grassy leaves and terminating in racemes of starry, 6-tepalled flowers. Grow in well-drained soil in a sunny, sheltered site. Plant autumn or spring. Propagate spring by seed or division.
Species cultivated: *A. liburnica* (S. E. Europe), like *A. lutea*, but somewhat smaller and more slender; stem with leafless zone before raceme begins; leaves rough-margined, to 1mm wide; flowers a little paler and later. *A. lutea* (*Asphodelus luteus*), yellow asphodel, king's spear; S. E. Europe, Algeria, Tunisia, Israel; stems clustered, stiffly erect to 90cm or more, densely leafy to raceme; leaves grey-green, 2mm wide, triangular in section, stiffly-pointed; flowers to 2·5cm wide, yellow, each tepal with green mid-vein, spring and summer; fruit an ovoid capsule, 10–15mm long.

Asphodelus

(ancient Greek name for the original asphodel). LILIACEAE. A genus of 12 species of annuals and perennials from the Mediterranean to the Himalaya. They are allied to *Asphodeline*, but have mainly basal leaves in tufts or clumps and white or pink flowers. Culture and propagation as for *Asphodeline*.
Species cultivated: *A. acaulis*, (Algeria); leaves linear, 15–30cm long, usually in a flattened rosette; flowers 2·5–4cm long, pink, in a stemless cluster in the centre of the plant, spring. *A. aestivus* (*A. microcarpus*, *A. ramosus*), asphodel; S. Europe; like *A. albus*, but flowers to 2cm wide, often pink-flushed, in pyramidal, branched racemes to 1·5m high. *A. albus*, white asphodel; S. Europe; robust perennial, stem to 60cm or more; leaves linear, keeled, to 60cm; flowers to 5cm wide, white (rarely pink-tinted), each tepal with a brown mid-vein, in a usually simple raceme, spring. *A. cerasiferus*, S. Europe; stem 1·2–1·5m; leaves sword-like, stiff, keeled, to 90cm; flowers white with a red-brown mid-vein, in branched racemes, summer. *A. luteus*, see *Asphodeline lutea*. *A. microcarpus* and *A. ramosus*, see *A. aestivus*.

Left above: *Asperula suberosa*
Top: *Asphodeline lutea*
Above: *Asphodelus albus*
Right: *Aster × frikartii*

Asplenium

(Greek *a*, not, and *splen*, the spleen – alluding to its supposed medicinal properties; also reputed to cause barrenness in women). ASPLENIACEAE. A genus of 650 species of ferns of cosmopolitan distribution from the tropics to cool, temperate climates. Generally tufted to shortly rhizomatous, they have simple, entire to tripinnatifid leaves with the oval to linear sori borne along the veins of the pinnae. Tender species require greenhouse treatment, minimum temperature 13–16°C, shading from direct sunlight spring to autumn, and humidity in summer. Grow in a peat mixture. The smaller, hardy species are ideal for the rock garden or dry walls, needing a well-drained, gritty soil with peat or leaf mould added. Plant spring. Propagate by division or spores, spring; plantlets summer.
Species cultivated: *A. adiantum-nigrum*, black spleenwort; Northern Hemisphere, S. Africa; hardy; fronds 10–50cm long, stalk blackish, blade triangular-ovate, bipinnate, pinnules lobed; sori 1–2mm long, linear-oblong. *A. dareoides*, S. S. America; hardy; fronds 8–10cm long, blade triangular-ovate, tripinnate, pinnules obovate, lobed, dense and overlapping, deep green, mossy; sori oval, 1–2mm. *A. marinum*, sea spleenwort; coasts W. Europe, N. Africa, Macronesia; hardy; fronds 15–30cm long, pinnate, pinnae triangular-ovate to oblong, crenate, 1–4cm long; sori linear, 3–5mm; best sheltered rock crevice or alpine house. *A. ruta-muraria*, wall rue; Europe; hardy; rhizomes tufted and sometimes creeping; frond 4–15cm long, blade ovate-lanceolate, bipinnate, pinnae 3–5 lobed and ultimate segments sometimes again lobed; sori linear, 2mm long. *A. scolopendrium* (*Phyllitis s.* and *Scolopendrium vulgare*), hart's tongue; S. W. and C. Europe; hardy, fronds 10–60cm, blade strap-shaped, entire, wavy-margined, cordate at base, glossy rich green; sori linear; very shade-tolerant. *A. trichomanes*, maidenhair spleenwort; northern and southern temperate zones, tropical mountains; hardy; fronds 4–20cm long, pinnate, stalk and mid-rib (rachis) dark red-brown, pinnae ovate to oblong, to 12mm long, sometimes crenate; sori linear, 1–2mm long. *A. viride*, green spleenwort; northern temperate zone; like *A. trichomanes*, but pinnae orbicular to broadly ovate, upper stalk and rachis green.

Aster

(Latin *aster*, a star – descriptive of the flower-heads of some species). COMPOSITAE. A genus of 500 species, mainly perennials from northern hemisphere and S. Africa. (For china aster see *Callistephus*). The species described are hardy herbaceous perennials unless otherwise stated, generally clump-forming with erect stems, narrow leaves and terminal clusters of daisy-like flower-heads. Grow in any ordinary soil that does not dry out excessively, in sun or partial shade. Propagate by division in spring. For best blooms split *Aster novi-belgii* annually into single-rooted shoots.

Species cultivated: *A. acris*, see *A. sedifolius*. *A. albescens* (*Microglossa a.*), Himalaya, W. China; shrubby, 1–2m; leaves elliptic, lanceolate to ovate, 2·5–10cm long, often hoary above, grey-white hairs beneath; flower-heads to 6mm wide, white, pale blue, purple-blue (the latter sometimes known as *A. harrowianus*), summer. *A.* × *alpellus* (*A. alpinus* × *A. amellus*), Triumph; compact, leafy plant to 23cm; flower-heads with blue ray florets and orange disc, summer. *A. alpinus*, Pyrenees, Alps, Apennines; tufted plant, to 15cm or more; basal leaves spathulate, stem leaves lanceolate; flower-heads solitary, 3·5–4·5cm wide, rays violet-purple, disc yellow, summer. White and pink-flowered forms are also grown. *A. amellus*, C. and S. Europe; stems rough, to 60cm; leaves oblong-lanceolate, rough, hoary; flower-heads solitary, 5–8cm wide, purple, late summer. *A.a.* Brilliant, bright pink; *A.a.* King George, violet-blue; other cultivars available. *A. cordifolius*, E. N. America; spreading by slender rhizomes; stems to 1·2m or more tall; leaves cordate-ovate, toothed; flower-heads to 2cm wide, rays pale violet-purple to white, in large terminal panicles, late summer. *A.c.* Silver Spray, flowers silvery-white. *A. corymbosus*, see next entry. *A. divaricatus* (*A. corymbosus*) E. N. America; clump-forming, stems slender often somewhat zig-zagged, dark purple; leaves thin-textured, cordate-ovate to lanceolate, sharply-toothed; flower-heads to 2cm wide, rays white, disc yellow, ageing purple, autumn. *A. dumosus*, E. N. America; to 90cm; leaves linear to narrowly oblong, 2·5–7·5cm long; flower-heads 6mm wide, ray florets pale lavender, bluish or white, disc yellow to brownish, autumn. *A. ericoides*, N. America; to 1m, much-branched; basal leaves spathulate, stem leaves linear, fine greyish hair; flower-heads 8–10mm wide, ray florets white-, pink- or blue-tinted, borne in profusion, autumn. *A.e.* Esther, 60cm, pink; *A.e.* Cinderella, blue; *A.e.* Ringdove, 90cm, rosy-mauve. *A. falconeri*, Kashmir, Nepal; to 45cm; basal leaves oblanceolate, 5–10cm long, toothed, stem leaves narrower, densely borne; flower-heads solitary, to 9cm wide, ray florets purple-blue, disc orange, early summer. *A. farreri*, W. China, Tibet; like *A. falconeri*, but basal leaves longer, few stem leaves; flower-heads to 7cm. *A. forrestii*, see *A. souliei*. *A.* × *frikartii* Mönch (*A. amellus* × *A. thomsonii*), midway between parents, combining their best characters; 80cm; flower-heads about 5cm, ray florets bright glossy purple-blue, disc orange-yellow, summer and autumn. *A. himalaicus*, Sikkim; to 30cm; basal leaves obovate-spathulate, to 5cm long, stem leaves oblong; flower-heads solitary, 4cm wide, purple-blue, summer. *A. horizontalis*, a form of *A. lateriflorus*. *A. laevis*, E. N. America; 1–1·2m; leaves narrowly lanceolate, 3–10cm long, somewhat fleshy; flower-heads about 2·5cm wide, rays pale violet to white, autumn; the old cultivar, Climax, may be a form or hybrid of this species with *A. novi-belgii*. *A. lateriflorus* (*A. 'laterifolius'* of some catalogues), 60–90cm, with wide-spreading branches; leaves broadly to narrowly lanceolate, 5–10cm long; flower-heads 6–12mm wide, rays white or pink-tinted, disc purple, autumn. *A.l.* Horizontalis (of gardens), slightly larger flowers than type, wider-spreading side-branches. *A. linosyris* (*Crinitaria l.* *Linosyris vulgaris*), goldilocks; S. and S. C. Europe; to 60cm; leaves linear, densely borne; flower-heads bright yellow without ray florets, late summer. *A. novae-angliae*, E. N. America; densely clump-forming; woody-based stems, 1·5–2m; leaves lanceolate, stem-clasping, hispid, to 10cm long; flower-heads 3–5cm wide, ray florets numerous, violet-purple to pink or white, autumn; of several fine cultivars, *A.n.-a.* Harrington's Pink, clear pink, *A.n.-a.* Lye End Beauty, phlox-purple, are recommended. *A. novi-belgii*, Michaelmas daisy; E. N. America – coastal strip to 100 miles inland; to 1·2m or more tall; leaves oblong to linear-lanceolate, somewhat stem-clasping, usually glabrous, to 12cm long; flower-heads 2·5–5cm wide, purple-blue, purple, red, pink, white, autumn; dozens of fine cultivars are available, many of hybrid origin with allied species, ranging in height from 25–150cm. *A. paniculatus* (*A. simplex*), N. E. N. America; to 1·2m; much like a larger form of *A. ericoides*, with white ray florets, autumn; often masquerades in gardens as *A. tradescantii*, a more slender plant to 60cm, flowering late summer. *A. pappei*, see *Felicia*. *A. sedifolius* (*A. acris*), S. and E. Europe; 60–90cm; leaves narrowly linear, scabrid; flower-heads to 2cm wide, borne in profusion, ray florets few, bright blue-mauve, late summer. *A. souliei* (*A. forrestii*), Tibet, N. W. Yunnan; leaves in rosettes from short rhizomes, obovate-lanceolate, 3–12cm long; flower-heads solitary on stems to 15cm, ray florets violet-

Top: *Aster cordifolius* Silver Spray
Left above: *Aster alpinus*
Left: *Aster ericoides*
Above: *Aster novi-belgii*

purple, disc orange, summer. *A. spectabilis*, E. USA; to 80cm or more; basal leaves ovate to lanceolate or spathulate; flower-heads 4–5cm wide, rays bright violet, autumn. *A. subcoeruleus*, see *A. tongolensis*. *A. tanacetifolius* (*Machaeranthera t.*), C. S. USA, Mexico; annual; to 40cm; leaves oblanceolate, pinnatifid to bipinnatifid; flower-heads 2·5–5cm wide, ray florets blue-purple, summer. *A. thomsonii*, W. Himalaya; 30–90cm; leaves broadly ovate, slender-pointed, toothed, stem-clasping; flower-heads few together, long-stalked to 6cm wide, rays lilac, late summer to autumn. *A.t.* Nanus, more compact than type to 45cm. *A. tibeticus*, Himalaya, Tibet; slender, to 30cm; leaves lanceolate, 2·5–5cm long; flower-heads to 5cm wide, rays bright blue, summer. *A. tongolensis* (*A. subcoeruleus*), mat-forming; leaves oblong; flower-heads solitary, 5cm or more wide, ray florets pale blue, disc orange-yellow, summer. *A.t.* Berggarten, 40–50cm tall, rays deep blue; *A.t.* Napsbury, rich purple-blue; *A.t.* Wendy, 30cm, pale rays, orange disc. *A. yunnanensis*, W. China, S. E. Tibet; variable species much confused with *A. tongolensis*, but distinct in having branched stems to 60cm or more, flower-heads to 6·5cm wide, mauve-blue; for *A.y.* Napsbury and other cultivars under this name, see *A. tongolensis*. *A. tradescantii* (of gardens), see *A. paniculatus*. *A. turbinellus*, E. USA; stems slender to 1m or more; leaves lanceolate, 6–12cm long; flower-heads 2·5cm wide, rays violet-blue, autumn.

Top left: *Aster novae-angliae* Harrington's Pink
Left above: *Aster yunnanensis*
Top centre: *Aster amellus* King George
Above: *Aster novi-belgii*
Top right: *Astilbe × crispa* Perkeo
Right centre: *Astilbe × arendsii*
Right: *Astilbe × atrorosea*

Astilbe

(Greek *a*, without, and *stilbe*, sheen – alluding to the dullness of the foliage of the original species compared with the goatsbeard that it resembles). False goatsbeard. SAXIFRAGACEAE. A genus of 25 species of herbaceous perennials from E. Asia and E. N. America. They are clump-forming or rhizomatous plants with bi- or triternate or pinnate leaves, and plume-like panicles of tiny 4–5 petalled flowers. Grow in moist soil in sun or shade. Plant autumn to spring. Propagate by division at planting time or from seed in spring (the latter is slow).

Species cultivated: *A. × arendsii*, hybrid group raised in Germany at the turn of the century, between *A. davidii*, *A. astilboides*, *A. japonica* and *A. thunbergii*, with often dark or coppery foliage and stems from 45–150cm, carrying plumes of white, pink, purple or red flowers in summer; many cultivars are listed, all very garden-worthy. *A. × atrorosea* (*A. simplicifolia × A. thunbergii*), like a more robust form of *A. simplicifolia* with glowing pink flowers. *A. chinensis* (*A. sinensis*), China; 40–90cm; leaves triternate, some pinnate; flowers white, flushed pink or purple, densely clustered, summer. *A.c. davidii* (*A. davidii*), taller than type, leaves more pinnately divided, flowers red-purple; *A.c.* Pumila, 30cm, mauve-pink, spreads widely by rhizomes. *A. × crispa*, group of hybrids similar to *A. chinensis* Pumila but with waved or crinkled leaves; *A. × c.* Perkeo, 15–25cm tall, leaves dark green, flowers pink; *A. × c.* Gnome, rose-pink; *A. × c.* Peter Pan, deep pink; all summer-flowering. *A. davidii*, see *A. chinensis davidii*. *A. glaberrima*, see *A. japonica terrestris*. *A. grandis*, China; 1·5m; leaves ternate and pinnate, downy; flowers white, in pyramidal panicle, 30–90cm long, summer. *A. japonica*, Japan; 50–80cm; leaves biternate, leaflets deeply toothed; flowers white, in dense panicles, to 20cm long, early summer. *A.j. terrestris* (*A. glaberrima*, *A. saxatilis*), dwarf, 10–15cm tall; leaves much-dissected, bronze-tinted; flowers white and pale pink, summer. *A. microphylla* (*A. chinensis japonica*), (Japan), 30cm or more; leaves to 4 times ternate, leaflets ovate to elliptic, sharply toothed, 1–5cm long; flowers pale rose in narrow panicle, summer; a plant under this name in gardens grows to 15cm and has white flowers. *A. rivularis*, Nepal; 1–1·5m or more; leaves biternate, yellow-white or red-tinted, late summer. *A. saxatilis*, see *A. japonica terrestris*. *A. simplicifolia*, Japan; tufted; stems 10–20cm, sometimes more; leaves simple, narrowly to broadly ovate, sharply toothed and sometimes shallowly lobed, lustrous, blade 3–8cm long; flowers white in loose panicle; a taller plant, to 30cm, with pink flowers, is sometimes offered as this plant – see *A. × atrorosea*. *A. sinensis*, see *A. chinensis*. *A. taquetii*, E. China; to 1·2m; leaves tripinnatisect, veins white-haired, flowers bright red-purple in panicles 30cm or more long, late summer; offered as *A.t.* Superba with purplish-tinted leaves and stems.

Astragalus

(Greek name for a now unidentifiable leguminous plant taken up by Linnaeus for this genus). LEGUMINOSAE. A genus of 2000 species of annuals, perennials and mainly small, often spiny shrubs of worldwide distribution except Australasia. They have pinnate leaves and pea-shaped flowers in racemes, spikes or umbels. The species described are hardy in any ordinary, well-drained soil in a sunny site. Plant spring or autumn, home-raised plants also in summer. Propagate from seed autumn or spring, potting the seedlings singly when young and planting out before they get pot-bound.

Species cultivated: *A. alopecuroides* (*A. narbonensis*), Spain, S. France; narrowly clump-forming perennial, to 75cm tall; leaves 15–20cm long, of 25–31 oblong leaflets, densely haired beneath; flowers 22–27mm long, pale yellow, in short, dense spikes, summer. *A. alpinus*, alpine milk vetch; C. and N. Europe; tufted, prostrate perennial; leaves 4–8cm long, of 15–25 lanceolate leaflets; flowers about 12mm long, pale blue, tipped purple, calyx densely haired in short racemes, summer. *A. angustifolius*, Balkan Peninsular, Crete, Turkey; cushion-forming, spiny shrub, 5–20cm long, of 12–20 linear to elliptic leaflets; flowers 13–23mm long, white, sometimes tinged blue or purple, or yellow, early summer. *A. danicus* (*A. hypoglottis*), purple milk vetch; N. Europe, Alps, Austria, Ukraine; tufted perennial; stems slender, ascending, 8–30cm long; leaves 4–10cm, of 15–25 oblong leaflets; flowers 15–18mm long, blue-violet, in ovoid to oblong racemes, summer. *A. monspessulanus*, S. Europe to W. Ukraine; tufted perennial; leaves 7–20cm long, of 21–41 ovate to oblong leaflets, hairy beneath; flowers 2cm long, rose-purple – in short, oblong racemes above leaves, summer. *A. onobrychis*, C. and S. Europe; woody-based tufted perennial; stem prostrate and ascending to 30cm or more; leaves 3–10cm long, of 17–31 elliptic lanceolate leaflets, hairy on both surfaces; flowers 1·5–3cm long, pale to dark violet, rarely white or yellowish, summer. *A. purshii*, California to British Columbia; tufted, white, hairy perennial; leaves to 13mm long of 7–11 ovate-elliptic leaflets; flowers 3–4cm long in head-like racemes, yellowish, purple-tipped (entirely pink or purple in *A.p. tinctus* and *A.p. longilobus*), spring and summer.

Astrantia

(perhaps from Latin *Magistrantia* – *magister* meaning master – or Greek *astron*, star). Masterwort. UMBELLIFERAE. A genus of 10 species of herbaceous perennials from C. and S. Europe to the Caucasus. They are erect plants, with palmately lobed or compound basal leaves and simple umbels of tiny, 5-petalled flowers surrounded by a ruff of petal-like bracteoles. Grow in moisture-retentive – but not waterlogged – humus-rich soil in sun or shade. Plant autumn to spring. Propagate by division at planting time, or from seed in spring.

Species cultivated: *A. biebersteinii* and *A. carinthiaca*, see *A. major*. *A. carniolica*, Austria, Italy, Yugoslavia; slender stems to 30cm or more; basal leaves of 5–7 ovate leaflets, the middle 3 united at their bases; flowers and bracteoles white- or pink-flushed, summer. *A.c.* Rubra, flowers and bracteoles red-purple. *A. helleborifolia*, see *A. maxima*. *A. involucrata*, see *A. major*. *A. major*, C. and E. Europe; stems 60–90cm; leaves of 3–7 obovate to lanceolate leaflets; flowers and bracteoles greenish-white, sometimes tinted pink or purplish. *A.m.*

Top right: *Astragalus danicus*
Centre right: *Astrantia major*
Right: *Atriplex hortensis* Rubra
Far right top: *Astrantia maxima*
Far right centre: *Athyrium felix-femina*

Rubra, flower-heads plum-red; *A.m.* Sunningdale Variegated, leaves splashed and striped yellow, best in sun; *A.m. biebersteinii*, bracteoles grey and green; *A.m. carinthiaca* (*A.m. involucrata* of gardens), bracteoles to twice as long as umbel – the white-bracteoled cultivar Shaggy is of the same origin and appearance. *A. maxima* (*A. helleborifolia*), Caucasus, Turkey; 40–60cm; leaves trifoliate, leaflets ovate-lanceolate, toothed; flowers and bracteoles rose-pink, summer.

Athyrium

(Greek *a*, without, and *thyrion*, a small door – referring to the indusium, a shield-like sorus cover that appears to be persistent). ATHYRIACEAE. A genus of 180 species of ferns of worldwide distribution. They may be tufted or clump-forming, some spreading by slender rhizomes with pinnate to tripinnate fronds; sori borne at the end of small branch veins. Species described are hardy. Grow in rich soil in partial shade. Plant and propagate by division autumn to spring or by spores in spring.

Species cultivated: *A felix-femina*, northern temperate zone, tropical mountains to S. S. America; clump-forming; fronds 30–100cm long, bi- or tripinnate, arching, pinnules oblong or oblong-lanceolate, 3–20mm, fertile ones bearing a double row of 1mm wide sori beneath; indusium persistent. Several forms or cultivars are known, varying in the size and shape of the pinnae and pinnules, in some cases creating crested or tasseled effect. *A. goeringianum* (*A. iseanum*), Japan; tufted; fronds 20–30cm or more long, arching, bipinnate, pinnules oblong to deltoid-ovate, 10–17mm long, irregularly lobed; sori 1–2mm covered by an indusium; *A.g.* Pictum, fronds with silvery-grey bands either side of mid-rib.

Atragene – see *Clematis alpina*.

Atriplex

(the ancient Greek name for orache, several allied species in this genus). CHENOPODIACEAE. A genus of 200 species of annuals, perennials and shrubs from northern and southern temperate and sub-tropical regions, often sea coasts and semi-deserts. They have opposite to alternate, obovate to triangular leaves and tiny, petalless, inconspicuous flowers. Grow in any well-drained soil in a sunny site. Propagate annuals from seed in spring, perennials and shrubs from seed or by division in spring, shrubs also by cuttings in late summer or autumn.

Species cultivated: *A. canescens*, W. N. America; much-branched semi-evergreen shrub 1–3m tall; leaves linear, spathulate to narrowly oblong, 1·5–5cm long, rather fleshy, grey-white; flowers in leafy, branched, spike-like panicles, summer. *A. halimus*, tree purslane; S. Europe; semi-evergreen shrub, 1–2m tall; leaves ovate to obovate, 1–6cm long, metallic silvery-grey; flowers in terminal panicles not always produced, summer. *A. hortensis*, orache; Europe, Asia; erect, branched annual to 2m; leaves triangular, to 10cm or more; flowers in large, leafy terminal panicles; fruit enclosed in glossy, circular, membraneous bracteoles. *A.h.* Rubra, leaves red, sometimes grown as a spinach substitute and should then be sown in humus-rich soil, thinned to 45cm apart in rows 60–75cm apart. *A. lentiformis*, S. W. USA; spreading, semi-evergreen shrub to 2m high, leaves oblong to ovate-triangular, 1·5–4cm long, grey scurfy; flowers in terminal panicles, summer; best in a sheltered spot, thrives in dry, alkaline soils.

Top right: *Aubrieta deltoidea*
Right: *Aucuba japonica*
Far right: *Azara serrata*

Aubrieta

(for Claude Aubriet 1668–1743, a French botanical artist). Aubretia. CRUCIFERAE. A genus of 15 species of evergreen trailing or mat-forming perennials from mountains of Italy to Iran. Grow in well drained, preferably alkaline, soil in sun. Plant autumn or spring. Propagate by division after flowering or seed in spring. 1 species and its many forms and cultivars is a popular rock garden plant: *A. deltoidea*, S. Greece, Aegean Is, Sicily; forms mat to low cushion shape; leaves spathulate to obovate with a few large teeth; flowers purple, to 2cm wide, of 4 rounded petals, in short racemes, spring; many named cultivars are available in shades of red, lilac, pink, purple and white. *A.d.* Argenteovariegata, flowers pale blue-purple, leaves variegated white; *A.d.* Aureovariegata, flowers lavender-blue, leaves variegated gold; *A.d.* Dr Mules, blue-purple; *A.d.* Leichtlinii, rose-pink; *A.d.* Red Carpet, port-red; *A.d.* Wanda, double-flowered, crimson.

Aucuba

(Latinized form of the Japanese vernacular name *ao-ki* or *aokiba*). AUCUBACEAE (CORNACEAE). A genus of 3–4 evergreen shrubs from Himalaya to Japan. They have opposite pairs of leathery, ovate to oblong leaves and insignificant, dioecious, 4-petalled flowers, the females followed by glossy red fruit. Grow in any moisture-retentive but well-drained soil in shade or partial shade. Male and female plants must be grown together if fruit is wanted, 1 male to several females is sufficient. Plant autumn to spring. Propagate from seed when ripe or by cuttings late summer, autumn.

Species cultivated: *A. chinensis*, China; 2–4m tall; leaves dark greyish-green, 8–20cm long; flowers in panicles to 10m long; fruit ovoid, berry-like, to 12mm long. *A. japonica*, Japan; 2–4m tall; leaves 8–20cm long, lustrous rich green on upper surface; flowers brownish to dark purple, about 7mm wide in panicles 7–10cm long, spring; fruit ovoid, 1·5–2cm long. Several cultivars are available, notably the yellow-freckled or spotted-leaved, virus-variegated ones such as *A.j.* Crotonifolia (male); *A.j.* Gold Dust (female); *A.j.* Speckles (male) and *A.j.* Variegata Maculata (female); *A.j.* Fructo-albo (female), leaves lightly spotted yellow, fruits ivory; *A.j.* Longifolia (female), very free fruiting, leaves long, lanceolate, bright and glossy green; *A.j.* Lance Leaf, like *A.j.* Longifolia but male.

Auricula – see *Primula auricula*.

Autumn crocus – see *Colchicum* and *Crocus*.

Avena candida – see *Helictotrichon sempervirens*.

Avens – see *Geum*.

Azalea – see *Rhododendron*.

Azara

(after N. Z. Azara, Spanish patron of the sciences, particularly botany). FLACOURTIACEAE. A genus of 11 species of evergreen shrubs from S. America and Juan Fernandez Island. They have leathery, alternate, obovate or ovate to lanceolate leaves, each with a pair of stipules, 1 or both of which are almost as big as the leaf, creating the appearance of an irregularly trifoliate leaf. Flowers small, petalless but conspicuous by having numerous yellow stamens and in being arranged in dense corymbs or spikes in the leaf-axils; red, purple or white berry

fruits are sometimes produced in mild areas. Grow in well-drained, humus-rich soil in sun or partial shade protected from cold winds. They are on the borderline of hardiness in the northern hemisphere and all but *A. microphylla* are best against a wall. Plant spring. Propagate by cuttings late summer.

Species cultivated (all from Chile): *A. dentata*, 2–3m tall; leaves 2·5–4cm long, ovate, deep lustrous green above, downy-felted beneath, toothed; flowers in corymbs, summer. *A. gilliesii*, see *A. petiolaris*. *A. integrifolia*, large shrub or small tree; leaves obovate to diamond-shaped, 2–4cm, usually glossy and toothless; flowers bright yellow, anthers dark, winter to spring. *A. lanceolata*, to 3m or more; leaves lanceolate to narrowly oval, 2–6·5cm long, coarsely-toothed, bright green; flowers soft yellow in small corymbs, spring. *A. microphylla*, to 4m or more; stems darkly pubescent; leaves obovate, 1–2·5cm long, more or less toothed, dark lustrous green; flowers very small, vanilla-scented, late winter to spring. *A.m.* Variegata, leaves cream-variegated. *A. petiolaris*, to 3m or more; leaves ovate to broadly lanceolate, 4–7·5cm long, widely-toothed, smooth rich green; flowers bright pale yellow, fragrant, late winter to spring; hardier than sometimes stated. *A. serrata*, to 3m, stems downy; leaves oval, 4–5cm long, toothed; flowers in stalked clusters, summer.

Azolla

(perhaps from Greek *azo*, to dry, and *olluo*, to kill alluding to the rapid death that follows drying) AZOLLACEAE. A genus of 6 species of small, floating aquatic plants, allied to the ferns, from tropical to warm temperate climates. 1 species is widely grown as an aquarium and pond plant: *A. caroliniana*, hairy moss, water fern; S.E. USA and widely naturalized elsewhere; moss-like, with minute overlapping leaves clothing forking stems, quickly spreading to form continuous carpets, pale green turning red in cooler weather outside. In northern temperate climates likely to be killed in winter, and some of the plants should be over-wintered in a tank in a light room or frost-free greenhouse. Plant outside when frosts are over. Propagate by division.

Babiana

(Latin form of Afrikaans word *babiaan*, baboon – reputed to eat the corms). Baboon-root. IRIDACEAE. A genus of 60 species of cormous plants from tropical and S. Africa, Socotra. They have flattened clusters of lanceolate, usually strongly pleated, leaves and short racemes of tubular or funnel-shaped, 6-tepalled flowers. Mainly tender, minimum temperature 7°C, sunny and well-ventilated. Grow in pots of any good potting soil. Pot late autumn, setting the corms about 5cm deep and apart each way and keep barely moist until leaves are several centimetres tall, then water more freely. When flower-spikes are visible commence liquid-feeding at 7 day intervals, ceasing when flowers fade. After flowering reduce watering but keep moist until leaves yellow, then dry off. Propagate from seed in autumn or spring, offsets, cormlets at potting time.
Species cultivated (all S. African): *B. ambigua* (*B. plicata*), 15cm or more tall; leaves lanceolate; flowers violet-blue or purple to reddish-purple, late spring. *B.* × *hybrida* (of gardens), race of named cultivars derived from *B. ambigua, B. stricta* and other species; flowers 4–5cm wide in shades of lavender and purple. *B. plicata*, see *B. ambigua*. *B. rubrocyanea*, see next species. *B. stricta*, to 30cm; leaves broadly lanceolate; flowers with 3 outer tepals white, 3 inner blue, late spring. *B.s. rubrocyanea*, winecups, flowers blue with rich crimson centres. *B. tubulosa tubiflora*, about 20cm; leaves narrowly lanceolate; flowers with long, slender tube, tepals reddish or purplish-pink, late spring, summer; can be grown outside in warm, sheltered sites.

Balloon flower – see *Platycodon*.

Ballota

(ancient Greek name for black horehound – *B. nigra* – an original species in this genus named by Linnaeus). LABIATAE. A genus of 35 species of perennials and sub-shrubs from Europe, W. Asia, Mediterranean. They have opposite pairs of hairy, generally ovate to rounded leaves and tubular, 2-lipped flowers, the upper lip hooded. The species described are grown for their foliage. Grow in any well-drained soil in a sunny site; partial shade is tolerated and hardy except where frosts are severe. Plant spring. Propagate by cuttings in spring or summer, perennial species also by division or from seed in spring.
Species cultivated: *B. acetabulosa*, Greece, Crete, Aegean; evergreen sub-shrub to 60cm or more, spreading; leaves 3–4cm wide, heart-shaped, crenate, white, woolly; flowers 15–18mm long, rose-purple and white, calyx salver-shaped, 10–15mm wide, summer; much confused with next species. *B. pseudodictamnus*, S. Aegean; smaller than *B. acetabulosa* and yellowish-woollen; leaves 1·5–2cm wide, calyx funnel-shaped, 7–8mm wide.

Far left below: *Babiana*, selection
Top left: *Ballota acetabulosa*
Above left: *Begonia* × *tuberhybrida* Camellia-flowered
Top: *Begonia semperflorens*
Above: *Begonia* × *tuberhybrida* Pendula

Balm – see: *Melissa*; **bastard balm** – see *Melittis*; **bee balm** – see *Monarda*.

Balsam fir – see *Abies balsamea*; **balsam poplar** – see *Populus balsamifera*.

Bambusa metake – see *Arundinaria japonica*.

Baneberry – see *Actaea*.

Baptisia

(Greek *bapto*, to dye – some of the species have been used as indigo substitutes). LEGUMINOSAE. A genus of 35 species of perennials from N. America. They are rhizomatous plants with usually erect stems, trifoliate leaves and terminal racemes of yellow, white or blue pea-like flowers. Grow in humus-rich soil (preferably moist for *B. australis* and *B. leucantha*) in sun or part shade. Plant and divide in autumn or spring. Sow seed in spring.
Species cultivated: *B. australis* (*B. exaltata*), false indigo; E. USA; about 1·2m tall; leaflets obovate, 4–8cm long; flowers 2–3cm long, soft indigo-blue, summer. *B. leucantha*, C. N. America; to 1·5m; leaflets oblong-cuneate, 3–6·5cm long; flowers white, 2–3cm long, summer. *B. tinctoria*, E. USA; 50–90cm tall; leaflets cuneate to oblanceolate, 6–18mm long, blue to grey-green; flowers 10–13mm long, yellow in branched racemes, summer, autumn.

Barberry – see *Berberis*.

Barrenwort – see *Epimedium*.

Bartonia – see *Mentzelia*.

Bastard balm – see *Melittis melissophyllum*.

Bay, sweet bay or **laurel** – see *Laurus nobilis*.

Bayberry – see *Myrica*.

Bead tree – see *Melia*.

Bearberry – see *Arctostaphylosuva-ursi*.

Bear's breech – see *Acanthus*.

Beauty bush – see *Kolkwitzia*.

Beech – *Fagus*.

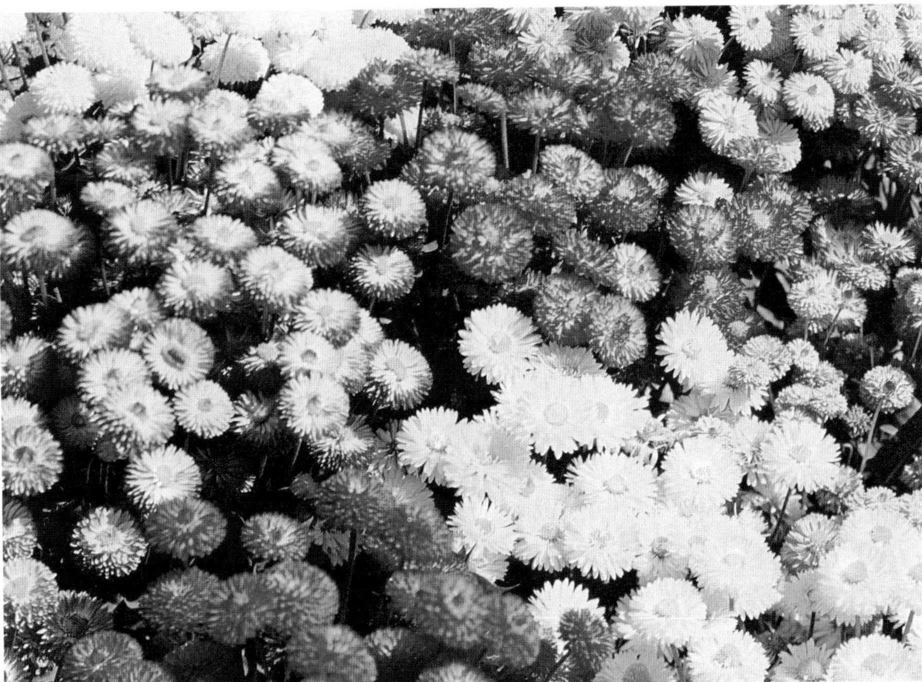

Begonia

(for Michel Bégon, 1638–1710, a French patron of botany and for a time Governor of French Canada). BEGONIACEAE. A genus of 900 species mainly of perennials, sub-shrubs and climbers from the tropics to warm temperate regions. Their main characteristics are the lopsided, ear-shaped leaves (there are a few exceptions) and clusters of dioecious, 4–5 (rarely 2) tepalled flowers, the females having winged or strongly angled ovaries. Among the perennial species, some are tufted or shrub-like with a fibrous root system, some are rhizomatous in varying degrees, others are tuberous. Apart from a few species, notably *B. evansiana* and *B. sutherlandii*, are moderately hardy in cool climates, all require greenhouse treatment, minimum temperature 7–10°C, and shade from direct sun in summer. Grow in any commercial potting mixture, particularly the all-peat types. A fortnightly application of liquid feed through the summer months is beneficial. Propagate by stem or leaf cuttings spring or summer, division of tuberous and rhizomatous species in spring or from seed late winter, early spring. Because of the wide diversity of species and their countries of origin, cultural requirements vary somewhat. Where necessary, special points will be mentioned under the descriptions of the species. Many more hybrids and cultivars are available than are described here; main flowering period is summer and early autumn unless otherwise stated.

Species cultivated: *B. evansiana*, E. Asia; tuberous, 30–60cm; leaves ovate-cordate, somewhat lobed, red purple beneath; flowers pink, 2–3cm wide; produces stem tubers; hardy in sheltered sites. *B. semperflorens*, wax begonia; Brazil; fibrous-rooted, bushy, 10–30cm or more tall; leaves somewhat fleshy and lustrous, rounded to broadly ovate, flowers pink or white, 2–3cm wide, in conspicuous clusters; a popular summer bedding plant with many cultivars in shades of red, pink, white, some doubles, and with bronze or purple leaves. *B. sutherlandii*, S. Africa; tuberous-rooted, to 15cm; stems low-arching; leaves ovate, to 8cm or more, shallowly lobed, pale green with red veins; flowers to 2cm wide, orange; hardy in sheltered spots. *B. × tuberhybrida*, the popular tuberous begonia derived from *B. boliviensis*, *B. pearcei*, *B. rosaeflora* and others; 2 main groups are recognized, Camellia-flowered and Pendula, the former having robust, erect, unbranched stems and large double flowers, the latter arching and pendulous, slimmer stems and smaller single or double flowers. Of similar origin to Camellia-flowered is the lesser-known Multiflora group, having much shorter, branched stems and a compact habit owed to the dwarf species *B. davisii*. All groups have a wide range of shades and colours including yellow, pink, red, orange, white, some picotees; *B. × tuberhybrida* is best grown by starting the tubers into growth laid on trays of moist peat at a temperature not less than 13°C. When shoots are 4–5cm high, place singly into 7·5–12·5cm pots, preferably of one of the all-peat composts, grow on in a frame or greenhouse at not less than 10°C night; harden off in early summer for bedding out mid summer. Good pot plants for a cool greenhouse; finish off in 18–20cm pots.

Belamcanda

(E. Asiatic vernacular name, *balamtandam*, in Latin form). IRIDACEAE. A genus of 2 species of perennials from E. Asia, 1 of which is generally available. *B. chinensis*, N. India to Japan; rhizomatous, iris-like leaves, sword-shaped, 30–50cm long, stem to 1m, usually less in gardens, bearing an open panicle of 6-tepalled, orange-red, purple-brown spotted flowers in summer; seed, shining black in a 3cm long obovoid capsule. Grow in well-drained, humus-rich soil in a sheltered, sunny or partially shaded site, with protection against severe frosts. Plant spring. Propagate by division or from seed in spring.

Bellflower – see *Campanula*.

Bellis

(Latin *bellus*, pretty). Daisy. COMPOSITAE. A genus of 15 species of perennials from Europe, Mediterranean. They are low-growing, clump-forming plants, with obovate to ovate leaves and daisy flower-heads borne solitarily. Grow in ordinary garden soil in sun or partial shade. Plant autumn to spring. Propagate by division at planting time or from seed in spring.

Top left: *Begonia × tuberhybrida* Pendula
Above: *Bellis perennis*

Species cultivated: *B. perennis*, common or lawn daisy, Europe to W. Asia; widely clump-forming evergreen perennial; stems 5–15cm; leaves obovate, 3–8cm long; flower-heads 2–3cm wide, ray florets white, often red beneath, spring, summer. There are 2 groups of cultivars: Monstrosa, with very large, usually double or semi-double blooms 5cm or more wide, and Miniature with small, double, pom-pom like heads of quilled florets 1–2cm wide. Both groups have white, pink or crimson blooms that come true from seed, but some miniatures, eg Dresden China (pink) and Rob Roy (red), are virtually sterile and must be propagated by division. *B. sylvestris*, S. Europe; similar to *B. perennis*, but leaves narrowly obovate to oblong; stems 10–45cm; flower-heads 2–4cm wide, ray florets white, tinged red-purple or entirely that colour, spring, summer.

Benthamia – see *Cornus*.

Left above: *Belamcanda chinensis*
Above: *Berberidopsis corallina*

Berberidopsis

(from *Berberis*, the barberry genus, and Greek *opsis*, like). FLACOURTIACEAE. A genus of 1 species of evergreen shrub from Chile, *B. corallina*. It has slender, wiry stems to 2m or more that will make low mounds or can be trained up a wall, trellis or old tree. Leaves to 8cm long, oblong-cordate, spiny-toothed but not sharply so; flowers in terminal racemes, rounded-bowl shaped, 1cm or more wide, of 9–15, crimson tepals. Grow in a humus-rich, preferably neutral to acid soil, in a sheltered, partially-shaded site. It is not fully hardy and in cold areas is best in a frost-free greenhouse. Propagate by cuttings or from seed in spring or layering in autumn.

Berberis

(Latinized form of the Arabic, *berberys* – after the edible fruit of some species). Barberry. BERBERIDACEAE. A genus of 450 species of evergreen and deciduous shrubs from Europe, Asia, N. Africa, America. Characteristic of the genus is the system of long and short shoots. The former extend the height and spread of the shrub, bearing alternate, 3-pronged spines derived from specially modified leaves. Within the axils of these spines are borne the short shoots, greatly condensed, lateral, spineless stems bearing 1 to several leaves in a rosette. The leaves vary from obovate to lanceolate and may be spiny-toothed. The short shoots bear umbels, panicles or racemes of bowl-shaped yellow, orange or reddish flowers. Each flower has 6 tepals, 6 nectaries, 6 stamens and 1 pistil. The stamens are sensitive: when touched at their bases by an insect probing for nectar they close inwards, quickly covering the visitor's head with pollen. The fruit is a globose to long, ovoid berry in shades of pink, red and black-purple, sometimes with a white, waxy patina. Unless otherwise stated, the species described are hardy except where frosts are very severe. Some half-hardy species may be cut back to ground level in bad winters but grow again from the base. Tender species need a warm sheltered site or a frost-free greenhouse. All need a well-drained soil in sun or light shade. Plant autumn to spring, the latter period only for the tender and half-hardy sorts. Propagate by cuttings with a heel, late summer, or from seed sown when ripe or spring. Well-suckered specimens may also be divided successfully.

Species cultivated (flowers in shades of yellow unless otherwise stated): *B. aggregata*, W. China; deciduous, densely branched, 1–1·5m; leaves obovate, 1–3cm long, grey-green beneath, 6mm wide, pale yellow, in dense panicles to 4cm; fruit sub-globose, red. *B. asiatica* Nepal, Bhutan, Assam; evergreen, half-hardy, to 2m; leaves to 7cm or more long, obovate, toothed, sea-green above, white beneath; flowers 12mm wide in umbel-like clusters; fruit ovoid, red to blue-black. *B. atrocarpa*, W. China; rather like *B. sargentiana* but with smaller leaves. *B.* Barbarossa, see *B.* × *carminea*. *B.* × *bristolensis* (*B. calliantha* × *B. verruculosa*), evergreen, dense, rounded habit, to 1m, blending characters of parents; leaves prickly, toothed. *B.* Buccaneer, see *B.* × *carminea*. *B. buxifolia* (*B. dulcis*), S. America Magellan Straits; semi-evergreen, to 2m; leaves obovate to elliptic, 1–2cm long, blue-grey beneath, spines 5–12mm long; flowers to 1cm wide; fruit globose, purple-blue. *B.b.* Nana, slow-growing, rounded habit, to 50cm. *B. calliantha*, S.E. Tibet; evergreen, compact habit, to 1m; leaves 2–6cm, elliptic, spiny-toothed, dark green with impressed vein pattern above, blue-white beneath; flowers about 2cm wide, in clusters of 1–3; fruit ovoid, black-purple. *B. candidula* (*B. hypoleuca* of gardens), W. China; evergreen, densely rounded to 60cm; leaves elliptic, 1·5–3cm long, lustrous dark green above, white beneath; flowers 10–15mm wide, solitary; fruit black-purple, waxy patina. *B.* × *carminea* (*B. aggregata* × *B. wilsoniae*), race of hybrid cultivars blending habits of parents with abundantly-borne berries in shades of red or pink. Best known are: *B.* × *c.* Barbarossa, 1·5–2m tall, berries red. *B.* × *c.* Buccaneer, erect habit, 1·5m or more, fruit large, deep red. *B.* × *c.* Pirate King, dense habit, to 1m; fruit bright orange-red. *B.* Chenaultii, see *B.* × *hybrido-gagnepainii*. *B. darwinii*, Chile; evergreen, to 3m or more; leaves obovate to oblong, spine-toothed, dark glossy green above, paler beneath; flowers bright orange-yellow tinged red, in abundantly-carried racemes, spring; fruit ovoid, purple-black with waxy patina; 1 of the finest species for floral display. *B.d.* Stapehillensis, more robust than type, with larger, brighter flowers, see also *B.* × *stenophylla*. *B. dictyophylla* (*B.d. albicaulis*), W. China; deciduous, erect habit to 2m, stems reddish, covered with white, waxy patina; leaves elliptic to obovate, 1–2·5cm long, bright green above, blue-white beneath; flowers 1·5cm wide, solitary; fruit ovoid, red. *B. dulcis*, see *B. buxifolia*. *B. empetrifolia*, Chile; evergreen arching stems, 60–90cm; leaves linear, somewhat hoary-green, 5–20mm long; flowers to 8mm wide, golden-yellow, solitary or in 2s, often freely-borne; fruit globose, black-purple, waxy patina. *B. gagnepainii*, W. China; evergreen, to 2m; leaves 3–10cm long, narrowly lanceolate with well-spaced, spiny teeth; flowers 1cm wide, in umbel-like clusters of 3–10; fruit ovoid, blue-black, waxy-white; the plant in cultivation is usually *B.g. lanceifolia* with longer leaves. *B. hookerii*, Himalaya;

Above: *Berberis linearifolia* Orange King

evergreen, dense habit to 1·5m; leaves elliptic to oblong-lanceolate, 2·5–7cm long, spiny-toothed, white beneath; flowers greenish-yellow, 12–18mm wide, in umbel-like clusters of 3–6; fruit oblongoid, black-purple. *B.h. viridis*, leaves green beneath; fruit black; the commonest form in cultivation. *B.* × *hybrido-gagnepainii* (*B. gagnepainii* × *B. verruculosa*), dense shrub, to 1m, blending characters of parents; leaves ovate. *B.* × *h.-g.* Chenaultii, similar to type, stems arching more strongly and leaves ovate-lanceolate; makes a good low hedge. *B. hypokerina*, Burma; akin to *B. hookerii* but generally smaller, stems purple; leaves to 10cm or more long; flowers in clusters of 6–10; fruit blue-violet. *B.* × *irwinii*, see *B.* × *stenophylla*. *B. jamesiana*, S.W. China; deciduous, to 3m; leaves obovate, 1–3cm long, entire or faintly spiny-toothed; flowers 6mm wide in pendant racemes to 10cm; fruit globose, translucent coral-red. *B. julianiae*, China; evergreen, to 3m; leaves to 6cm or more long, narrowly elliptic to oblanceolate, spiny-toothed; flowers to 1cm wide, in umbel-like clusters; fruit oblongoid, blue-black, with waxy patina; a good hedging plant with spines to 3cm long. *B. linearifolia*, Chile, Argentina; evergreen, erect habit to 2m, rather sparsely-branched; leaves linear-oblong, to 4cm or more long, dark green above, grey beneath; flowers about 1cm wide, orange to crimson, densely-borne, spring; fruit ovoid, blue-black. *B.l.* Orange King, flowers glowing, rich orange. *B.* × *lologensis* (*B. darwinii* × *B. linearifolia*), natural hybrid found in Argentina, blending characters of parents; flowers apricot-

Above: *Berberis* × *ottawensis* Purpurea

yellow; seedlings raised from it are variable but usually tend towards *B. darwinii*. *B.* × *ottawensis* (*B. thunbergii* × *B. vulgaris*), Canadian-raised hybrid rather like *B. vulgaris*, but leaves usually obovate, entire or somewhat serrulate, to 3cm long. *B.* × *o.* Purpurea, leaves red-purple. *B.* × Superba, leaves deep red-purple. *B.* × Parkjuweel (*B.* × Park Jewel), (*B.* × *hybrido-gagnepainii* Chenaultii × *thunbergii*), dense prickles, to 1m or so, blending parental characters; leaves obovate, sparingly-toothed,

Top: *Berberis darwinii* in fruit
Above: *Berberis × stenophylla*
Centre top: *Berberis darwinii*
Top right: *Berberis thunbergii* Rose Glow
Centre right: *Berberis wilsoniae* in fruit
Below right: *Berberis pruinosa* in fruit

colouring well and sometimes persisting through the winter. *B.* Pirate King, see *B.× arminea*. *B. polyantha*, W. China; deciduous, much like *B. aggregata*, but flowers to 1cm wide, deep yellow in loose, pendulous panicles, to 10cm or more long. *B. prattii*, W. China; much like *B. aggregata* but leaves to 3·5cm long; panicles to 6cm or more long; fruit ovoid, bright coral-pink, freely-borne. *B. pruinosa*, Yunnan; evergreen, to 2m or more; leaves rigid, obovate to elliptic-oblong, entire or coarsely-toothed, 2·5–5cm long, greyish to sea-green above, white beneath; flowers in umbel-like clusters of 8–25; fruit oblongoid, blue-black, heavy waxy-white patina. *B.× rubrostilla* (*B. aggregata × B. wilsoniae*), showy hybrid raised at RHS Gardens, Wisley, 1–1·5m; leaves oblanceolate, to 2·5cm long; flowers in umbels of 2–4; fruit inverted pear-shaped, to 1·5cm long, coral-red, among the largest in the genus; seedlings from this are variable, some with ovoid to sub-globose fruit; several cultivars are sometimes available. *B. sargentiana*, W. China; evergreen, to 2m or more, spines among the longest in the genus to 4cm; leaves elliptic-oblong to lanceolate, closely spiny-toothed, 4–10cm long; flowers 1cm wide in clusters; fruit oblongoid, blue-black. *B.* Stapehillensis (*B.* Stapehillii in some catalogues), see *B. darwinii*. *B.× stenophylla* (*B. darwinii × B. empetrifolia*), very variable group of cultivars combining the parent characters in various ways – the shrub under this name alone is best-known and recommended for hedging; to 3m, stems slender, arching, wand-like; leaves narrowly lanceolate, spine-tipped 1·5–2·5cm long; flowers light orange-yellow, to 1cm wide, in clusters of 2–6, freely-borne; fruit sub-globose, blue-black, waxy patina. *B.× s.* Coccinea (*B.× irwinii* Coccinea), to 1m; flowers orange, crimson in bud. *B.× s.*

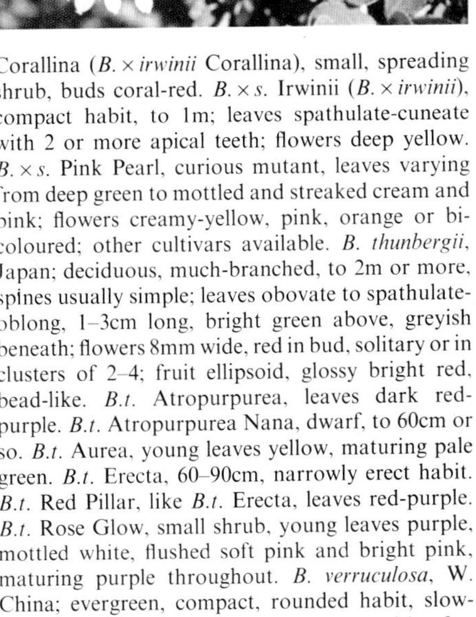

Corallina (*B.× irwinii* Corallina), small, spreading shrub, buds coral-red. *B.× s.* Irwinii (*B.× irwinii*), compact habit, to 1m; leaves spathulate-cuneate with 2 or more apical teeth; flowers deep yellow. *B.× s.* Pink Pearl, curious mutant, leaves varying from deep green to mottled and streaked cream and pink; flowers creamy-yellow, pink, orange or bi-coloured; other cultivars available. *B. thunbergii*, Japan; deciduous, much-branched, to 2m or more, spines usually simple; leaves obovate to spathulate-oblong, 1–3cm long, bright green above, greyish beneath; flowers 8mm wide, red in bud, solitary or in clusters of 2–4; fruit ellipsoid, glossy bright red, bead-like. *B.t.* Atropurpurea, leaves dark red-purple. *B.t.* Atropurpurea Nana, dwarf, to 60cm or so. *B.t.* Aurea, young leaves yellow, maturing pale green. *B.t.* Erecta, 60–90cm, narrowly erect habit. *B.t.* Red Pillar, like *B.t.* Erecta, leaves red-purple. *B.t.* Rose Glow, small shrub, young leaves purple, mottled white, flushed soft pink and bright pink, maturing purple throughout. *B. verruculosa*, W. China; evergreen, compact, rounded habit, slow-growing to 1·5m; leaves elliptic to ovate, with a few spiny teeth, 1·5–2·5cm long, lustrous above, blue-white beneath; flowers 1–1·5cm wide, in 1s and 2s; fruit ellipsoid, violet-black, waxy patina. *B. vulgaris*, common barberry; Europe to Caucasus; erect shrub to 2·5m, leaves obovate, 2–4cm long; flowers 6–8mm wide in pendulous racemes to 6cm; fruit oblongoid, red. *B.v.* Atropurpurea, leaves deep red-purple. *B. wilsoniae*, W. China; deciduous or partially evergreen, to 1m, stems arching; leaves oblanceolate, 6–20mm long, pale sea-green above, greyish beneath; flowers 7mm wide in short, dense panicles; fruit sub-globose, salmon to coral-red. *B.w. subcaulialata*, taller than type, 1·2–1·5m; shoots glabrous; leaves larger, up to 25mm long, may be toothed at apex; whitish beneath. *B.w.s.* Globosa, smaller, compact, rounded habit.

Bergamot – see *Monarda*.

Bergenia

(for Carl August von Bergen, 1704–60, German physician and botanist). (*Saxifraga*, *Megasea*). SAXIFRAGACEAE. A genus of 6 species of evergreen perennials from C. and E. Asia. They have stout, semi woody rhizomes and tufts of large, rounded to paddle-shaped, leathery leaves and panicles of somewhat bell-shaped flowers of 5 or more rounded petals. Grow in humus-rich soil in partial shade, preferably sheltered from strong winds. Plant autumn to spring. Propagate by division at planting time or from seed in spring. Makes good ground cover beneath trees.

Species cultivated: *B.* Abendglut, 1 of a group of 3 German hybrids of complex parentage, having obovate to broadly obovate leaves, often flushed red, and erect flowers in compact clusters. *B.* Abendglut (*B.* Evening Glow), flowers deep purple. *B.* Morgenrote (*B.* Morning Red), leaves more rounded; flowers red-purple. *B.* Silberlicht (*B.* Silver Light), calyx red-brown, petals white, ageing pinkish. *B.* Ballawley and *B. beesiana*, see *B. purpurascens*. *B. ciliata*, W. Himalaya; leaves to 25cm or more, broadly ovate to orbicular, hairy on both surfaces; flowers to 2·5cm or more long, sepals pinkish, petals white, ageing red-flushed, spring; liable to frost damage. *B.c. ligulata* (*B. ligulata*), leaves hairless except the margins; both it and *B. ciliata* are generally partially deciduous, overwintering with small, tougher leaves; frost-tender forms are in cultivation. *B. cordifolia*, Siberia; leaves orbicular, to 30cm long, rounded or cordate at base, crinkly-margined, somewhat puckered; flowers 1·5cm or more long, pale to deep rose-pink, in panicles to 40cm tall, spring. *B.c.* Purpurea, leaves flushed purple, particularly in winter; flowers rose-magenta. *B. crassifolia*, Siberia; leaves to 20cm, broadly oval to obovate, the base wedge-shaped to rounded or shallowly cordate (on the same plant); flowers more or less nodding, about 2cm long, rose-purple, in a somewhat 1-sided panicle, to 30cm tall, spring; see also *B.* × *schmidtii*. *B.c. pacifica*, flowers deep purple. *B. delavayi*, see *B. purpurascens*. *B. ligulata*, see *B. ciliata*. *B. purpurascens* (*B. delavayi*, *B. beesiana*), Himalaya, N. Burma, W. China; leaves to 20cm long, elliptic to ovate, usually convex and reddish-flushed; flowers nodding, to 3cm or more long, calyx purplish, petals bright pink to deep purple-red, in an open, purple-red stemmed panicle, to 40cm, spring. *B.p.* Ballawley (*B.p.* Delbees), very large and vigorous; leaves orbicular-cordate; flowers magenta. *B.* × *schmidtii* (*B. ciliata* × *B. crassifolia*), much like *B. crassifolia*, but leaf margins with short hairs and somewhat larger pink flowers, winter to spring, sometimes in late autumn; often grown as *B. crassifolia*. *B.* Silberlicht, see *B.* Abendglut. *B. smithii* (*B. cordifolia* × *B. purpurascens*), in general appearance rather like *B. cordifolia*; leaves reddish or purple-margined; flowers 2–3cm long. *B.s.* Bressingham Bountiful, fuchsia-pink. *B.s.* Margery Fish, glowing pink. *B.s.* Pugsley's Purple, to 60cm, fuchsia-purple. *B.s.* Sunningdale, deep purple. *B. stracheyi*, E. Afghanistan, W. Himalaya; leaves obovate to wedge-shaped, 10cm or more long, hairy-margined, carried more erectly than other species; flowers 1·5–2cm long, calyx pink-tinted, petals white, ageing pink-flushed; prone to frost damage; often represented in cultivation by a somewhat larger plant with brighter flowers in a hairy panicle – possibly of hybrid origin. *B.s.* Alba, flowers always white, leaves bronzy.

Top left: *Bergenia ciliata ligulata*
Left: *Bergenia purpurascens*
Below left: *Bergenia purpurascens* Ballawley
Above: *Beschorneria yuccoides*
Right: *Betula ermanii*
Bottom right: *Betula jacquemontii*

Berkheya

(for Jan Le Francq Berkhey, 1729–1812, Dutch botanist). COMPOSITAE. A genus of 90 species of shrubs and perennials from Africa. 1 hardy perennial species is generally available: *B. macrocephala*, S. Africa; clump-forming, to 90cm; leaves lanceolate, spiny-toothed, thistle-like; flowers bright yellow, daisy-like, surrounded by spiny bracts, summer. Grow in well-drained, humus-rich soil in a sunny site, preferably sheltered by hedge, fence or wall. Plant spring. Propagate by division or from seed in spring.

Beschorneria

(for Friedrich W.C. Beschorner, 1806–73, German amateur botanist). AGAVACEAE (AMARYLLIDACEAE). A genus of 10 species of evergreen perennials from Mexico. 1 species is generally available and fairly hardy in the south or where frosts are slight. *B. yuccoides*, rosette-forming stems red, to 1·2m or more tall, bearing large, rose-red bracts; leaves narrowly lanceolate, to 50cm long, greyish-green; flowers, pendant, tubular, green, 6-tepalled, about 2cm long, early summer. Sometimes confused with the taller *B. bracteata*, that has a branched flowering stem to 2m and longer, flowers ageing reddish. Grow in well-drained soil in a sunny, sheltered site. Plant spring. Propagate by removing the sucker-like offsets in late spring, or from seed in spring at 16–18°C.

Betonica, betony – see *Stachys*.

Betula

(ancient Latin name). Birch. BETULACEAE. A genus of 60 species of deciduous trees and shrubs from the cooler parts of northern temperate zone. They are generally graceful, slender-twigged trees, the bark peeling into papery strips; frequently white or reddish leaves, ovate to triangular, toothed; flowers tiny, petalless, dioecious; male catkins yellow, females much smaller and green, spring; seed (nutlets) small, winged. Can be grown in a wide range of soils, particularly the poorer acid, sandy ones, and will stand wet conditions during winter. Plant autumn to late winter. Propagate species from seed when ripe or in spring, sowing on the surface of sandy soil; cultivars by grafting onto the species, or *B. pendula*, early spring.

Species cultivated: *B. alba*, see *B. pendula*, *B. pubescens*. *B. albosinensis*, China; to 20m or more; bark orange, flaking reddish; leaves ovate, slender, pointed, 4–7cm long; male catkins to 6cm. *B.a. septentrionalis* is the most commonly cultivated form in Britain; bark duller; leaves to 17cm long. *B. ermanii*, N.E. Asia, Korea, Japan; to 20m; bark white at first, peeling to show pinkish under-bark; leaves triangular-ovate, 5–10cm long; female catkins barrel-shaped to 3cm. *B. jacquemontii*, W. Himalaya; to 14m or more; bark brilliant white in the best clones and the whitest of all birches; leaves ovate to broadly so, 4–7cm long, with 7–9 pairs of veins; see also *B. utilis*; known to hybridize with *B. pendula*, the progeny having grey and black patches in the bark. *B. japonica*, see *B. platyphylla*. *B. lutea*, yellow birch; E. N. America; to 16m or more; bark aromatic, yellow to silver-grey with pinkish or pale orange patches, often peeling shaggily; leaves ovate to oblong-ovate, 8–12cm long, rich yellow in autumn. *B. maximowicziana*, Japan; to 20m or more; bark white to grey and orange-brown; leaves broadly ovate, cordate, to 14cm long, the largest of all birches, clear yellow in autumn; male catkins 10–12cm long. *B. nana*, dwarf birch; circumpolar and mountains farther south; spreading shrub 60–120cm tall; leaves 5–15mm long, orbicular to broadly obovate, crenate; male catkins about 8mm long. *B. nigra*, black or river birch; E. USA; to 15m or more; bark reddish to black-brown, peeling in rolls and streamers, brighter on young trees; leaves diamond-ovate with small lobes on either side, 3–8cm or more long. *B. papyrifera*, canoe or paper birch; N. America; to 20m or more; bark usually white with pale orange to pinkish shading; leaves ovate, 4–10cm long, rich matt green; male catkins to 10cm. *B. pendula* (*B. alba* in part – see *B. pubescens*; *B. verrucosa*), silver birch; Europe to W. Siberia and W. Turkey, Morocco; to 30m; bark smooth and brown when young, then white with dark grey-brown patches, older trees with a dark diamond pattern, deeply-fissured, especially at base; twigs hairless, warted; leaves rounded-triangular, 3–7cm long, somewhat glossy; male catkins 3–6cm long. *B.p.* Dalecarlica, Swedish birch; leaves cut into slender lobes. *B.p.* Fastigiata, narrow, erect habit. *B.p.* Purpurea, leaves purple, slow-growing. *B.p.* Tristis, graceful tree with narrow head of pendulous branches. *B.p.* Youngii, weeping birch; small tree of vertically-weeping habit. *B. platyphylla* (*B. mandschurica*), N.E. Asia, Korea; to 15m or more; bark white, powdery; leaves ovate to diamond-ovate, 4–6cm long. *B.p. japonica* (*B. japonica*), Japanese white birch; leaves broadly ovate to 7·5cm long; male catkin to 7cm long. *B.p. szechuanica* (*B. mandschurica s.*), vigorous growth, bark chalk-white. *B. pubescens*, common or white birch; Europe to W. Turkey, north to Iceland, like *B. pendula* but twigs and leaves hairy, bark generally brown or grey, rarely white; hybridizes with *B. pendula*. *B. utilis*, Himalyan birch; Himalaya; to 17m; much like *B. jacquemontii* but leaves with 10–14 pairs of veins and bark white with greyish patches or, alternatively, glossy coppery-brown and grey. *B. verrucosa*, see *B. pendula*.

Big tree – see *Sequoiadendron*.

Bignonia

(for Abbé Jean Paul Bignon, 1662–1743, Librarian to Louis XIV of France). BIGNONIACEAE. A genus of 1 species of evergreen, woody climber (formerly 150 or more species, but these are now classified in several other genera; see *Campsis*.

Bilberry – see *Sequoiadendron*.

Bilderdykia – see *Polygonum aubertii* and *P. baldschuanicum*.

Billardiera

(for Jacques Julien de la Billardière, 1755–1834, French explorer and botanist). PITTOSPORACEAE. A genus of 9 species of evergreen climbers from Australia. They have twining, slender stems, alternate lanceolate leaves, 5-petalled, bell-shaped, nodding flowers, and berry-like edible fruit. Frost-free greenhouse or sheltered wall in the milder areas. Grow in well-drained, humus-rich soil. Plant or pot spring, providing supports for the stems. Propagate from seed sown in spring or cuttings inserted in sandy soil in late summer or early autumn with bottom heat 18–20°C.

Species cultivated: *B. longifolia*, Tasmania; to 2m; leaves lanceolate, 2–4cm long; flowers 2cm long, greenish-yellow, solitary in upper leaf-axils, summer; fruit deep blue, oblongoid, 2–2·5cm long. *B. scandens* (*B. angustifolia, B. mutabilis*), E. Australia; leaves oblong-lanceolate, 2–5cm long, wavy-margined and silky-haired; flowers green, 2cm long; fruit oblongoid, yellow-green or purple, downy.

Biota – see *Thuja*.

Birch – see *Betula*.

Bird cherry – see *Prunus padus*.

Bird's-foot trefoil – see *Lotus corniculatus*.

Birthwort – see *Aristolochia clematitis*.

Bistort – see *Polygonum bistorta*.

Bitter root – see *Lewisia rediviva*.

Bladder nut – see *Staphylea*.

Bladder senna – see *Colutea*.

Bladderwort – see *Utricularia*.

Blaeberry – see *Vaccinium myrtillus*.

Blanket flower – see *Gaillardia*.

Blazing star – see *Liatris*.

Blechnum

(classical Greek name for a fern, the identity of which is not known, taken up by Linnaeus for this genus). BLECHNACEAE (POLYPODIACEAE). A genus of 220 species of evergreen or partially deciduous ferns of world-wide distribution, mainly N. Hemisphere. They have pinnate or pinnately-lobed leaves in rosettes or tufts, some species having fast-growing rhizomes and forming mats. The sori are linear, carried either side of the pinnae mid-ribs, in some species on specially erect fronds with reduced pinnae. Grow the hardy species in well-drained soil enriched with peat or leaf mould, preferably in a sheltered, partially-shaded site (*B. spicant* will stand sun and exposed sites). Plant spring. Propagate by spores or division, spring.

Species cultivated: *B. pennamarina* (*Lomaria alpina*), southern temperate zone; fronds spreading, lanceolate to narrowly so, 5–20cm long, pinnate; pinnae linear-oblong (those of fertile fronds narrower and wider-spaced); a hardy mat-forming species that may get scorched during hard winters. *B. spicant*, northern temperate zone; like *B. pennamarina* but larger, more erect; forms have arisen with larger or crested pinnae.

Bleeding heart – see *Dicentra spectabilis*.

Bletia – see *Bletilla*.

Above: *Blechnum spicant*

Bletilla

(Latin diminutive of *Bletia*, a genus in which the species described here was formerly placed). ORCHIDACEAE. A genus of 9 species of terrestrial orchids from E. Asia, one of which is generally available: *B. striata* (*Bletia hyacinthina* of gardens), China, Japan; stems wiry, 30–60cm tall; pseudobulbs rounded, tuber-like, below ground; leaves narrowly oblanceolate, pleated, to 30cm or more long; raceme of 5–12 rose-purple flowers, each 3–5cm wide with a deep purple, keeled labellum, summer. *B. striata* Alba, tepals white with a tinge of rose, labellum pinkish. A hardy, clump-forming species suitable for sheltered sites in sun or partial shade, or may be grown in pots of peaty soil in a cool greenhouse. Repot or lift and divide only when congested. Propagate by division after flowering, or spring.

Blood root – see *Sanguinaria*.

Blue cupidone – see *Catananche caerulea*.

Blue poppy – see *Meconopsis betonicifolia, M. grandis*.

Bluebell – **1** common or English bluebell, see *Endymion*. **2** Scottish bluebell (harebell in England), see *Campanula rotundifolia*.

Blueberry – see *Vaccinium corymbosum* and *V. angustifolium*.

Blue-eyed grass – see *Sisyrinchium angustifolium* and allied species.

Bocconia – see *Macleaya*.

Bog bean – see *Menyanthes*.

Bog myrtle – see *Myrica gale*.

Bog violet – see *Pinguicula*.

Borago

(from medieval Latin *burra*, for a rough-haired material used for garments). BORAGINACEAE. A genus of 3 species of annuals and perennials from Europe, Mediterranean and Asia. They are rough-haired (scabrid) plants with lanceolate to ovate leaves, and nodding, 5-petalled, starry blue flowers. Grow in well-drained, humus-rich soil in sun or light

Above: *Bletilla striata*
Below: *Boykinia jamesii*

shade. Propagate from seed sown *in situ* autumn or spring.

Species cultivated: *B. laxiflora*, see *B. pygmaea*. *B. officinalis*, borage; a herb long grown for its cucumber-fragrant leaves and flowers used for flavouring and garnishing drinks, soups, stews, salads and for candying. It has the added advantage of being decorative enough to grow in the flower garden. A stout, bristle-haired annual from S. Europe, borage grows 30–70cm tall, has lanceolate to ovate leaves 10–20cm long, and 2·5cm wide, nodding, starry, bright blue flowers. Grow in well-drained, humus-rich soil, preferably in sun, although partial shade is tolerated. *B. pygmaea* (*B. laxiflora*), Corsica, Sardinia, Capri; rosette-forming perennial; leaves oblong to obovate, 5–20cm long; stem decumbent or trailing, 15–60cm long, branching, bearing small, stem-clasping leaves and 1·5–2cm wide, bright blue flowers through summer and autumn.

Bouncing bet – see *Saponaria officinalis*.

Box – see *Buxus*.

Box elder – see *Acer negundo*.

Boykinia

(for Dr Samuel Boykin, 1786–1846, American field botanist). SAXIFRAGACEAE. A genus of 8 species of perennials from Japan and N. America. They are rhizomatous plants, clump-forming to spreading,

with broadly ovate to kidney-shaped leaves and small, bell-shaped flowers with 5 petal-lobes in panicle-like clusters. Grow in humus-rich, moisture-retentive soil in partial shade or sun. Plant autumn to spring. Propagate from seed when ripe or in spring, or division after flowering or in spring.
Species cultivated: *B. aconitifolia*, E. USA; clump-forming; stems 30–60cm; leaves round to reniform, 5–15cm wide, palmately 5–7 lobed; flowers white, petals notched, summer. *B. jamesii* (*Telesonix j.*), Colorado, USA; tufted to small-clump forming; stems to 15cm; leaves reniform, toothed, to 2·5cm wide; flowers carmine-red, to 2cm wide, in racemes or narrow panicles, early summer. *B. tellimoides* (*Peltoboykinia t.*), Honshu, Japan; clump-forming; stems 30–60cm tall; leaves orbicular, peltate, cordate, 10–25cm wide, shallowly palmately-lobed, toothed; flowers creamy-white, about 1·5cm wide, summer. *B.t. watenabei* (*Peltoboykinia w.*), Kyushu, Shikoku; like *B. tellimoides* but leaves deeply 8–10 lobed and flowers pale yellow.

Brachycome

(Greek *brachys*, short, and *kome*, hair – alluding to hairy or bristle-like pappus crowning the 'seed' or fruit). COMPOSITAE. A genus of 75 species of annuals and perennials from N. America, Africa, Australia, New Zealand. The perennials are mainly of tufted growth, the annuals erect and branched, leaves linear often pinnately lobed, flower-heads daisy-like. Grow in well-drained soil in a sunny site. Plant perennials autumn or spring. Sow half-hardy annuals in spring at a temperature of 15–18°C, prick off the seedlings into boxes 4cm apart each way, harden off late spring to early summer, and plant out when fear of frost has passed. Propagate perennials by careful division or seed in spring.
Species cultivated: *B. iberidifolia*, Swan River daisy; West Australia; half-hardy annual 20–40cm tall; leaves pinnatifid with linear segments; flower-heads 2–3cm wide, ray florets blue-purple or white, summer, autumn. *B. nivalis*, S.E. Australia; densely tufted; stems to 15cm; leaves about 10cm long, glossy rich green, linear, some with a few linear lobes about the middle; flower-heads 3cm or more wide, rays white, summer. *B. rigidula*, S.E. Australia (Tasmania); tufted; stems 10–30cm tall; leaves glossy, finely pinnatisect; flower-heads 2–3cm wide, rays bluish or lavender, summer.

Brandy bottle – see *Nuphar*.

Brittonastrum – see *Agastache*.

Below: *Brachycome iberidifolia*
Centre right: *Briza maxima*
Far right: *Brunnera macrophylla* Variegata

Briza

(ancient Greek name for a grass – probably rye – taken up by Linnaeus for this genus). Quaking grass. GRAMINEAE. A genus of 20 species of annual and perennial grasses from northern temperate zone, S. America. They are tufted or rhizomatous plants with narrowly linear leaves and open panicles of pendant, rounded to ovoid spikelets composed of closely overlapping, membranaceous, helmet-shaped glumes. Grow in well-drained, fertile soil in a sunny site. Sow seed of annuals *in situ* autumn or spring, thinning seedlings 10cm apart. Plant and propagate perennials from seed or by division in spring.
Species cultivated: *B. maxima*, great quaking grass; Mediterranean; annual, 30–60cm tall; leaves 5–20cm long by 3–8mm wide; panicles to 10cm long, pale silvery-green or sometimes purple-flushed, summer. *B. media*, common quaking, totter or tottle grass; Europe, Asia; tufted perennial from shortly creeping rhizomes, 20–60cm tall; leaves 4–15cm long by 2–4mm wide; panicles 4–18cm long, spikelets broadly ovoid, 4–7mm long, often with a purple sheen, summer. *B. minor*, lesser quaking grass; Mediterranean; annual, 15–40cm or more tall; leaves 3–14cm long by 3–9mm wide; panicles 4–20cm long, spikelets triangular-ovoid to rounded, 3–5mm wide, usually shining green, summer to autumn.

Brodiaea

(for James Brodie, 1744–1824, Scottish botanist who specialized in the study of *Algae*). ALLIACEAE (LILIACEAE). A genus of 40 species of cormous plants from W. N. America and W. S. America. Some botanists have split the genus on small, mainly floral details into such genera as *Dichelostemma*, *Hookera*, *Triteleia*, but for convenience the species cultivated are all described here. They have narrowly linear leaves, often channelled; slender, erect, sometimes twining stems topped by rounded, often dense umbels of tubular to starry, 6-tepalled flowers in shades of white, yellow, purple, red; in some species 3 of the 6 stamens are transformed into staminodes. Grow in well-drained, fertile soil in a sheltered, sunny site at the base of a wall or fence, preferably with small, evergreen shrubs or other plants to provide some protection for the young leaves that, in some species, come up in autumn. Alternatively, grow in pots or pans of any commercial potting mixture in a sunny, well-ventilated, frost-free greenhouse. Pot or plant autumn. Propagate by separating cormlets or offsets at potting time or from seed in spring.

Species cultivated (all flowering late spring to summer, generally earlier under glass). *B. coccinea*, see *B. ida-maia*. *B. congesta* (*B. pulchella*, *Dichelostemma congesta*), leaves and stems 40cm or more; flowers tubular to 1cm long, constricted below the flared lobes, pale blue-violet, staminodes forked. *B. coronaria* (*B. grandiflora*, *Hookera coronaria*), California; stems to 25cm tall; leaves to 30cm; flowers tubular, to 2cm long, with flared, 1·3–2cm long, lobes, lilac to violet. *B.c. macropoda* (*B. terrestris*), stem very short, to 5cm tall. *B. grandiflora*, see *B. coronaria*. *B. hyacinthina* (species of many synonyms including *Hesperoscordum h.*, *Triteleia h.*, *Hookera h.* and *B. lactea*), W. USA; stems 30–60cm tall; leaves to 40cm long; flowers starry, 1·5–2·5cm wide, white with green mid-veins to the lobes. *B. hyacinthina* Lilacina, flowers pale bluish. *B. ida-maia* (*B. coccinea*, *Dichelostemma i.-m.*), fire cracker; California, Oregon; stems 30–90cm tall; leaves 30–50cm; flowers tubular, 2–4cm long, bright red – small, recurved lobes pale green. *B. ixioides*, see *B. lutea*. *B. lactea lilacina*, see *B. hyacinthina*. *B. laxa* (*Hookera l.*, *Triteleia l.* and *T. candida*), grass nut, Ithuriel's spear; California, Oregon; stems to 40cm or more; leaves 20–40cm; flowers tubular, 1–2·5cm long, with flared lobes 1–2cm long, purple-blue. *B. lutea* (*B. ixioides*, *Triteleia i.*, *Hookera i.*), California, Oregon; stems 30–50cm or more tall; leaves 20–40cm; flowers starry, 1·5–2cm wide, sometimes more, each segment with a deep purple mid-vein. *B. peduncularis* (*Hookera p.*, *Triteleia p.*), California; leaves and stems 20–40cm, the latter sometimes taller; flowers with funnel-shaped base, to 1cm long, spreading lobes 1–1·5cm long, white, sometimes flushed lilac. *B. terrestris*, see *B. coronaria*. *B.* × *tubergeniana* (*B. peduncularis* × *B. laxa*), hybrid nicely blending the characters of its parents, vigorous and very hardy. *B. uniflora*, see *Ipheion uniflorum*.

Broom – see *Cytisus*, *Sarothamnus*, *Spartium*.

Brunnera

(for Samuel Brunner, 1790–1844, Swiss botanist who collected in W. Africa, Crimea and Italy). BORAGINACEAE. A genus of 3 species of herbaceous perennials from S.W. Asia. 1 species is readily available: *B. macrophylla* (*Anchusa myosotidiflora*), W. Caucasus; clump-forming; basal leaves heart-shaped, 7–15cm wide; long-stalked flowering stems to 45cm tall, bearing 6–8mm wide, forget-me-not like flowers, spring, summer, sometimes again in autumn. *B.m.* Variegata, leaves margined creamy-white; forms are known with silvery-grey leaf markings; grow in any garden soil that does not dry

out rapidly, in sun or shade; plant autumn to spring; propagate by division at planting time.

Buckbean – see *Menyanthes*.

Buckeye – see *Aesculus*.

Buckler fern – see *Dryopteris*.

Buckthorn – see *Hippophae*.

Buddleja

(*Buddleia*). (for the Reverend Adam Buddle, 1660–1715, Vicar of Fambridge, Essex in England, a noted botanist of his day). BUDDLEJACEAE (LOGANIACEAE). A genus of 100 species of deciduous and evergreen shrubs and small trees from the tropics to temperate regions, particularly E. Asia. They have opposite pairs of oblong-ovate to lanceolate leaves and pyramidical panicles of small, tubular flowers with 4 petal-lobes; generally the fruit is a small, flattened capsule, but in a few cases it is a juicy berry. The hardy species require well-drained soil in a sunny site and will stand low temperatures. The tender ones a frost-free area or greenhouse, minimum temperature 7°C. Plant or pot autumn to spring. Propagate by cuttings, preferably with a heel, in late summer; *B. alternifolia* and *B. davidii* will root from nodal hard wood cuttings in autumn. Pruning consists of removing the previous season's flowering heads and several centimetres of stem each late winter to early spring (after flowering for *B. alternifolia*). *B. davidii* can be pollarded to near ground level, or on a leg of desired height if long, wand-like stems and massive flower-trusses are desired.

Species cultivated (all are hardy and deciduous unless otherwise stated): *B. alternifolia*, China; large shrub or small tree, to 8m or more, eventually of weeping or arching habit; leaves alternate, lanceolate, slender-pointed, 4–10cm long; flowers 6mm wide, rosy-lilac, in small, dense clusters all along the stems of the previous season, early summer. *B.a.* Argentea, leaves with silky, greyish hair, atypical of genus with its alternate leaves. *B. asiatica*, E. Indies; tender evergreen of slender habit, to 3m or more; leaves lanceolate, 10–20cm long, white-downed beneath; flowers white, fragrant, about 5mm wide in dense, terminal, narrowly-cylindrical panicles, to 15cm long, late winter, spring; best with a winter minimum of 10–13°C. *B. auriculata*, S. Africa; evergreen or semi-, half-hardy, requiring a warm, sheltered wall or greenhouse; 2–3m tall; leaves oblong-lanceolate, 5–10cm long, white-felted beneath; flowers 6–8mm long, white with yellow eye, in rounded terminal and axillary panicles, autumn, winter. *B. colvilei*, Himalaya; large shrub or small tree, to 10m; leaves ovate-lanceolate, 8–25cm long; flowers deep rose, to 2cm wide, in broad, drooping panicles, to 20cm long, summer; somewhat tender when young, but hardy when well-grown; the largest flowered species. *B.c.* Kewensis, flowers rich red. *B.crispa* (*B. paniculata*), white, woolly shrub, 2–4m; leaves ovate-lanceolate, 5–13cm long, cordate at base; flowers 8mm wide, lilac with white eye, fragrant, in 7–10cm long panicles, summer to early autumn. *B. davidii* (*B. variabilis*), butterfly bush; China; a variable shrub, 3–5m; leaves lanceolate, 10–25cm long, whitish-felted beneath; flowers 6mm wide, fragrant, lilac, purple or white with orange eye, in terminal panicles 25–40, or on pollarded specimens to 75cm long, summer, autumn; many cultivars have been raised, among them *B.d.* Black Night, deep violet; *B.d.* Empire Blue, violet-blue, orange eye; *B.d.* Facinating (*B.d.* Facination), bright violet-pink; *B.d.* Harlequin, red-purple, leaves variegated creamy-white; *B.d.* Peace, large white flowers in dense panicles; *B.d.* Royal Red, rich red-purple in large panicles; *B.d.* White Profusion, pure white, yellow eye, profusely-borne; *B.d. nanhoensis*, smaller, more elegant form from Kansu – *B.d.* Salicifolia is similar but more spreading. *B. fallowiana*, China; shrub, 2–3m; leaves lanceolate, slender-pointed, white-felted beneath, to 20cm or more long; flowers very fragrant, lavender, 8–10mm wide, in terminal panicles to 36cm long, summer. *B.f.* Alba milk-white, orange eye; best against a sunny wall. *B. globosa*, Chile, Peru; semi-evergreen shrub, 3–5m; leaves lanceolate, semi-lustrous and finely-corrugated above, tawny-felted beneath, 10–20cm long; flowers orange-yellow in globular heads, to 2cm wide, arranged in terminal panicles, to 20cm long, summer. *B.g.* Lemon Ball, flowers lemon-yellow, later than the type species, possibly of hybrid origin; cream to rich orange forms occur in the wild. *B.* × Lochinch (*B. davidii* × *B. fallowiana*), midway between the parents, bushy and compact, to 3m; flowers blue-violet with orange eye, fragrant; can be pruned hard like *B. davidii*. *B. officinalis*, China; half-hardy, semi-evergreen shrub to 3m; leaves narrowly lanceolate, slender, pointed, grey-woollen beneath; flowers fragrant, to 1cm long, pale lilac with yellow eye, in panicles 8–30cm long, autumn to winter; best under glass for its winter blossom. *B.* × *weyeriana* (*B. davidii* × *B. globosa*), shrub to 4m, in habit rather like *B. davidii*, with the ball-shaped flower clusters of *B. globosa*, in shades of creamy-orange to orange-yellow. *B.* Golden Glow, orange-yellow with purple shading; *B.* Moonlight, palest creamy-orange with purple shading.

Top left: *Brunnera macrophylla*
Above: *Buddleja alternifolia*
Right: *Buddleja globosa*
Far right: *Buddleja davidii*, two colour forms

Bugle – see *Ajuga*.

Bulbinella

(diminutive of *Bulbine*, an allied genus of less garden worth; Greek *bolbos*, a bulb – some bulbines having bulb-like tubers). LILIACEAE. A genus of 20 species of herbaceous perennials from S. Africa and New Zealand. They are tufted or clump-forming, with linear to strap-shaped, often channelled leaves, and erect racemes of usually starry, 6-tepalled flowers. 1 species is generally available: *B. hookeri* (*Chryobactron h.*), New Zealand; tufted to small clump-forming; stem 40–90cm tall; leaves to 30cm; flowers 12mm wide, bright yellow, in racemes to 15cm long, summer. Plant in warm areas in moisture-retentive, humus-rich soil, in sun or partial shade, in autumn or spring. Propagate by division or from seed in spring.

Bulbocodium

(Greek *bolbos*, bulb, and *kodion*, wool – there is a layer of hairs between the corm and its skin or tunic). LILIACEAE. A genus of 1 species, a cormous-rooted plant from the mountains of Europe. *B. vernum* (*Colchicum v.*), leaves 2–3, in a tuft, lanceolate to strap-shaped, somewhat channelled, to 15cm or more long; flowers like those of autumn crocus (*Colchicum*), but perianth segments not joined in a tube, 3–4cm wide, to 10cm tall, bright red-purple with white centre, spring, before leaves or while they are very short. Grow in any well-drained soil that does not dry out during the growing season. Plant autumn. Propagate by removing offset corms while dormant, or from seed when ripe.

Bulrush – see *Scirpus* and *Typha*.

Bunchberry – see *Cornus canadensis*.

Buphthalmum

(Greek *bous*, an ox, and *ophthalmos*, an eye – alluding to the shape of the flower-head). COMPOSITAE. A genus of 6 species of herbaceous perennials from Europe. They are clump-forming plants with lanceolate to ovate leaves and showy, daisy-like flower-heads. Grow in any humus-rich, moisture-retentive soil in sun or partial shade. Plant autumn to spring. Propagate from seed or by division, spring.

Species cultivated: *B. salicifolium*, yellow ox-eye; C. Europe; basal leaves lanceolate, about 10cm, often long-stalked; stems 30–70cm tall, sparingly branched with small, clasping leaves and solitary, 3–6cm wide, bright yellow flower-heads, summer. *B. speciosum* (*Telekia s.*), S.E. Europe; aromatic, basal leaves broadly ovate-cordate, coarsely toothed, hairy, to 30cm long; stems 1·5–2m tall, branched, with smaller sessile leaves; 5–6cm wide flower-heads, the rays deep yellow, disc brownish-yellow, summer.

Bupleurum

(ancient Greek name *boupleuros*, ox-rib, for a plant not now identifiable, taken up by Linnaeus for this genus). UMBELLIFERAE. A genus of 150 species of annuals, perennials and shrubs from Europe, Asia, N. America, Africa. They have alternate leaves, often distinctly parellel-veined, and umbels of tiny, 5-petalled, greenish-yellow, white or purplish flowers, in some species surrounded by petal-like bracteoles. Grow in any well-drained soil in a sunny site. Plant autumn to spring. Propagate from seed in spring, division of perennials autumn to spring, cuttings with a heel of shrubs late summer.

Species cultivated: *B. angulosum*, Pyrenees, S.E. Spain mountains; tufted perennial; basal leaves linear to lanceolate with winged stalks; stems 25–40cm tall, bearing ovate-cordate, stem-clasping leaves and umbels of creamy-green flowers surrounded by broadly-ovate, grey-green to yellowish bracteoles, summer. *B. falcatum*, sickle hare's ear; Europe; tufted perennial, very variable; basal leaves linear, elliptic or obovate; stems 15–100cm (usually about 30cm in cultivation), bearing semi-clasping, lanceolate to linear, often falcate leaves and umbels surrounded by yellow, linear-lanceolate bracteoles, late summer. *B. fruticosum*, shrubby hare's ear; S. Europe; evergreen shrub to 2m or more; leaves elliptic-oblong to obovate, bluish-green, somewhat glossy, 5–9cm long; flowers yellow, umbels 5–10cm wide, bracteoles small, soon falling, summer to autumn. A useful shrub for exposed seaside areas.

Burnet – see *Sanguisorba*.

Burning bush – see *Dictamnus* and *Kochia*.

Butchers broom – see *Ruscus*.

Butomus

(Greek *bous*, ox, and *temno*, to cut – the sharp leaf margins can cut the mouths of grazing animals). BUTOMACEAE. A genus of 1 species, a rush-like, aquatic perennial from temperate Europe and Asia: *B. umbellatus*, flowering rush; stoutly rhizomatous, eventually forming wide clumps; stems to 1·5m long; leaves erect, linear, triangular in cross-section, to same length as stems; terminal umbels of 2·5–3cm wide, 6-tepalled, pink flowers, summer, early autumn. Grow in wet soil or shallow water of pond or lake margins, preferably in a sunny site. If grown in an artificial pond, place in large pots or baskets of equal parts loam and decayed manure or compost. Plant and propagate by division in spring.

Butterbur – see *Petasites*.

Buttercup – see *Ranunculus*.

Butterfly bush – see *Buddleja davidii*.

Butterfly flower – see *Schizanthus*.

Butterwort – see *Pinguicula*.

Buttonwood – see *Platanus occidentalis*.

Buxus

(ancient Latin name taken up by Linnaeus). Box. BUXACEAE. A genus of 70 species of evergreen shrubs and trees from Europe, Africa, N. and S. America and Asia, including islands of S.E. Asia. They have opposite or alternate, generally small, oval to oblong leaves and clusters of inconspicuous, petalless, monoecious flowers, the males with 4 stamens in spring. The ovoid, horned capsules open explosively. Grow in any well-drained garden soil in sun or shade. The species described do well on chalky soil. Plant autumn to spring. Propagate by cuttings in late summer or from seed when ripe.

Species cultivated: *B. balearica*, S.W. Spain, Balearic

Below: *Buphthalmum speciosum*
Right below: *Bupleurum fruticosum*

Above: *Buxus sempervirens*
Top right: *Calamintha nepeta*
Above right: *Calandrinia umbellata*

Is; shrub or small tree up to 10m; leaves oval to ovate-oblong, 2–5cm long, leathery, bright glossy green; best in warm areas. *B. harlandii* (*B. chinensis*), China; compact, rounded shrub, to 60cm; leaves oblanceolate, bright green; the plant in cultivation under this name may not be the true species; fairly hardy. *B. japonica*, see next species. *B. microphylla*, China, Korea, Japan; twiggy shrub of dense habit to 1m; leaves obovate to lance-obovate, 8–15mm long. *B.m. japonica* (*B. japonica*), spreading habit, to 1·5m tall; *B.m. koreana*, of looser, more spreading habit, leaves often bronzy. *B. sempervirens*, common box or boxwood; S. Europe, W. Asia, N. Africa; variable species, 1–6m or more; leaves leathery, glossy dark green, ovate to oblong, 12–30mm long. *B.s.* Argentea, spreading habit; leaves margined creamy-white. *B.* Aureovariegata (*B.* Aurea Maculata), leaves mottled and splashed creamy-yellow. *B.* Elegantissima, slow-growing, dome-shaped habit; leaves having irregular creamy margin. *B.* Gold Tip, young shoots often yellow when young. *B.* Handsworthensis (*B.* Handsworthii), vigorous, erect habit; leaves rounded. *B.* Japonica Aurea, see next cultivar. *B.* Latifolia, dense, spreading habit, leaves large; *B.* Latifolia Macrophylla, leaves larger, broadly ovate; *B.* Latifolia Maculata (*B.* Japonica Aurea), to 1·5m or so, leaves irregularly blotched yellow, brightest in spring – listed in some catalogues as *B.* Latifolia Aurea. *B.* Suffruticosa, edging box; the familiar dwarf box used for parterres, standing close clipping well; leaves usually less than 2cm long.

Cabbage rose – see *Rosa centifolia*.
Cabbage tree – see *Cordyline australis*.
Cacalia – see *Emilia*.

Calamintha

(Greek *kalaminthe*, *kalos*, beautiful, and *minthe*, mint). Originally used for the closely allied savory, *Satureja*. LABIATAE. A genus of about 6 species of perennials and sub-shrubs from W. Europe to C. Asia. They have ovate to orbicular leaves in opposite pairs, and tubular, 5-lobed, 2-lipped flowers in axillary clusters forming leafy, tiered spikes. Grow in well-drained soil in sun. Plant autumn to spring. Propagate by division or seed, spring.

Species cultivated: *C. alpina* (*Acinos* and *Satureja alpina*), S. and C. Europe; tufted, spreading perennial, to 30cm or more; leaves elliptic to rounded, 6–20mm long; flowers 1–2cm long, violet with white markings on the lower lip, summer. *C. grandiflora* (*Satureja g.*), Spain to Turkey; tufted aromatic perennial with decumbent to ascending stems, 20–50cm long; leaves ovate to oblong, coarsely-toothed, 4–7cm long; flowers rose-purple 2·5–4cm long, summer, autumn. *C. nepeta* (*C. nepetoides*, *Satureja calamintha*), mountains S. and S. C. Europe; strongly aromatic, erect perennial, 40–80cm; leaves 1–3·5cm, ovate, toothed; flowers lilac or white, 1–1·5cm late summer, autumn.

Calandrinia

(for Jean Louis Calandrini, 1703–58, professor of mathematics and philosophy at Geneva). PORTULACACEAE. A genus of 150 species of annuals and perennials from W. N. America and W. S. America, and Australia. They are mainly low-growing, some softly sub-shrubby, often with fleshy, linear to obovate leaves, and flat, bowl-shaped, 5–7 petalled flowers in shades of pink to red-purple, borne in racemes or umbel-like clusters. The species described are half-hardy, generally grown as annuals, needing well-drained soil and a sheltered, sunny site. Sow seed in spring at a temperature of 15–18°C. Prick off the seedlings as soon as possible into a J.I. potting compost No 1 or equivalent, either in boxes at 3–4cm apart each way, or singly in 6–7cm pots. Harden off in late spring and plant out in early summer or when fear of frost has passed. They also make attractive pot plants for display in the cool greenhouse.

Species cultivated: *C. discolor*, Chile; leaves obovate, to 7cm or more, fleshy, purple beneath, pale-veined above; flowers 4–5cm wide, bowl-shaped, bright purple-red, summer. *C. crassifolia*, Chile; succulent sub-shrub to 25cm; leaves oblong-ovate to spathulate, thick and fleshy, usually grey-green, to 3cm or more long; flowers bowl-shaped, satiny red-purple, 3–4cm wide, summer; can be grown outside as a perennial where winter frosts are light. *C. umbellata*, Peru; trailing perennial with ascending flowering stems to 10cm or more; leaves linear, fleshy; flowers crimson-purple, about 2cm wide, in umbel-like clusters, summer; almost hardy in sheltered spots.

Top above: *Calceolaria integrifolia*
Centre above: *Calceolaria × herbeohybrida*
Above: *Calceolaria darwinii*
Right: *Calendula officinalis* Radio
Below right: *Calendula officinalis* Pink Magic

Calceolaria

(Latin *calceolus*, a little shoe or slipper – from the form of the flowers). Slipper-wort. SCROPHULARIACEAE. A genus of over 300 species of annuals, perennials, shrubs, from Mexico to S. America. They have broadly ovate to linear leaves in opposite pairs or whorls of 3, and curious, 2-lipped flowers, the lower lips of which are greatly inflated and pouched, or like the toe of a slipper. The alpine and a few of the annual and shrubby species are hardy or almost so; the remainder need greenhouse conditions, minimum temperature 7–10°C, at least in winter, with light shade from direct sun in summer. Plant the hardy sorts in well-drained but moisture-retentive soil in sun or partial shade in autumn or spring. Grow the tender species in pots of any of the commercial potting mixtures, the all-peat types being suitable with ¼-part coarse sand or grit added. Raise annuals either under glass in early spring at a temperature of 15–18°C, pricking off the seedlings into boxes and planting out in early summer; sow *in situ* late spring to early summer. The well-known, large-flowered group known as *C.* × *herbeohybrida* is usually treated as a pot-grown biennial. Sow seed in a cool greenhouse or frame in mid summer. Prick off seedlings as soon as large enough to handle into boxes 3–4cm apart each way, and as soon as the young plants are touching and just overlapping place in 7·5cm pots. From the time the seedlings are established in boxes they may be grown in a cold frame with top (lights) off, except in very wet or blustery weather. In mid autumn, pot on into 13–15cm pots, and as soon as nights get cool bring into a greenhouse or close the cold frames, keeping the temperature above 7°C at night, higher by day. Ventilate on all sunny or mild days. In late winter set in the final pots (18–20cm) for flowering. Alternatively the plants can be fed regularly at 7–10 day intervals and flowered in the 13–15cm pots. If plants are wanted for summer bedding, sow seed under glass and treat as annuals previously described; plant out when fear of frost has passed. The shrubby species are propagated by cuttings in late summer or spring, the subsequent plants potted on as above. Pinch out the tips of the young plants when about 10cm high and repeat later on the lateral shoots to promote bushiness. Plants needed for summer bedding should be hardened off during late spring and early summer, and planted outside when fear of frost has passed. The alpines are propagated from seed or by division in spring.

Species cultivated: *C. acutifolia*, Argentina, Chile; hardy perennial, creeping by slender rhizomes; leaves ovate-oblong to lanceolate, 3–8cm long; flowers solitary on erect 5cm stems, yellow, lower lip to 2cm long, red-freckled, early summer. *C. arachnoidea*, Chile; perennial, hardy in sheltered, sunny sites with sharply-drained soil; leaves oblong-spathulate, 3–10cm long, densely white-haired; flowers deep violet to almost black-purple, about 12mm wide, in small terminal panicles on leafy stems to 25cm, summer to autumn. *C. bicolor*, Peru; tender, slender-stemmed sub-shrub, to 90cm; leaves ovate-cordate, 5–8cm long, coarsely toothed; flowers canary-yellow and white, about 2cm long, in loose corymbs, summer, late autumn; of drooping habit and best grown in hanging baskets. *C. biflora* (*C. plantaginea*), Chile; hardy perennial, clump-forming; leaves ovate to rhomboid, 5–10cm or more long, bright green; flowers yellow, about 2cm long in a loose terminal corymb on a stem 10–30cm tall, summer. *C. darwinii*, Chile, Str of Magellan; hardy perennial, tufted; leaves oblong, 2·5–7cm long; flowers solitary to 3cm long, bright yellow freckled chestnut-red, thickly so at base of pouch and with a bold white cross-band, summer; much prone to slug damage. *C. falklandica*, Falkland Is; hardy perennial, rhizomatous and tufted; leaves 10–13cm long, oblong-spathulate; flowers pale yellow, spotted purple, about 12mm long on stem to 10cm, summer. *C. fothergillii*, Patagonia, Falkland Is; hardy perennial with shortly-creeping stems; leaves spathulate, 2–3cm long, crowded; flowers solitary, pale yellow, red-spotted, about 2cm long, on stems to 12cm tall, summer. *C.* × *herbeohybrida*, a race of giant-flowered strains largely derived from the Chilean *C. crenatiflora* and allied species; half-hardy but best treated as a biennial, plants to about 45cm tall; leaves ovate; flowers greatly inflated, to 6cm wide or more, in shades of yellow, orange and red, blotched and spotted in many combinations, borne in large, terminal trusses, late spring, summer; several strains are readily available in seed catalogues. *C. integrifolia* (*C. rugosa*), Chile, Chiloe; evergreen shrub to 1m or more, hardy in sheltered sites and much used for summer bedding; grown annually from cuttings or seed; leaves oblong-lanceolate to 5cm long, dark green and finely-wrinkled above, greyish to rusty-haired beneath; flowers yellow, about 12mm long, in densely-flowered corymbs, summer to autumn. *C.* × John Innes (*C. biflora* × *C. polyrrhiza*), much like the latter parent, but more vigorous and flowers to 4cm long, early summer. *C. mexicana*, Mexico; hardy annual to 24cm; leaves pinnate, to 7cm long, leaflets toothed; flowers pale yellow to 1cm long, in terminal corymbs, summer; will self-sow itself in some gardens. *C. plantaginea*, see *C. biflora*. *C. polyrrhiza*, Chile, Argentina; hardy rhizomatous perennial forming wide colonies; leaves lanceolate, to 5cm or more long; flowers yellow, spotted purple-red, 2·5–3cm long, solitary or several on stems to 15cm tall, summer. *C. scabiosifolia*, Peru; almost hardy annual to 45cm tall, much like a robust *C. mexicana*; leaves pinnate, to 15cm or more long, summer to autumn. *C. tenella*, Chile; hardy perennial, slender-stemmed and mat-forming; leaves broadly ovate, to 1cm long; flowers bright yellow, about 12mm long, in small clusters on stems to 10cm tall, early summer to autumn.

Calendula

(Latin *kalendae*, the first day of the month, and *kalendarium*, account – the almost perpetual flowering of this plant in its homeland was a constant reminder that interest was owed on the first day of each month). Marigold. COMPOSITAE. A genus of at least 20 species of annuals, perennials and sub-shrubs from Mediterranean regions as far east as Iran. They have alternate oblanceolate leaves and yellow or orange, daisy-like flower-heads. The roughly cylindrical 'seed' (achenes) are bow-shaped to almost circular, 2 or 3

distinct forms being found in each seed-head. 1 species and its several cultivars are commonly grown: *C. officinalis*, common or pot marigold; habitat unknown, perhaps derived from the smaller-flowered and very variable *C. arvensis* from S. Europe, locally naturalized in S. and W. Europe, much cultivated elsewhere; robust annual to short-lived, woody-based perennial, to 50cm; leaves 7–14cm long; flower-heads to 7cm wide, more in some cultivars, pale yellow to rich orange; several strains and cultivars, both single- and double-flowered, are available. Grow in well-drained soil in a sunny site. Sow seed *in situ* in spring or autumn. Flowers can be used to flavour soup.

Calico bush – see *Kalmia latifolia*.

California allspice – see *Calycanthus occidentalis*.

California bluebell – see *Phacelia*.

California laurel – see *Umbellularia*.

California lilac – see *Ceanothus*.

California poppy – see *Eschscholzia*.

Calla

(Greek *kallos*, beauty). ARACEAE. A genus of 1 aquatic perennial from northern temperate and subarctic regions. *C. palustris*, rhizomatous and wide-spreading; leaves broadly ovate-cordate, to 15cm or more long, carried on long stalks above the water; flowers tiny, petalless on a short, dense spadix surrounded by a widely-expanded white spathe to 7cm long, summer; fruit berry-like, red. Grow in permanently wet soil or shallow water. Plant the rhizomes in spring in natural pond mud or baskets of equal parts loam and decayed manure or compost. The site should be sunny or lightly-shaded. Propagate by division in spring.

Callicarpa

(Greek *kallos*, beauty, *carpos*, fruit – the berries are brightly-coloured). VERBENACEAE. A genus of 140 species of shrubs and trees mainly from the tropics and sub-tropics. They have opposite pairs of, generally, toothed, lanceolate to obovate leaves, axillary cymes of small, 4-lobed, tubular flowers, and small, rounded, berry-like fruit. Grow in any well-drained, humus-rich soil in a sheltered, sunny site, ideally against a hedge or wall. Plant autumn or spring. Propagate by cuttings late summer or from seed when ripe. The species described are hardy in all but very severe frosts, though soft shoot-tips may be frosted on occasions; this can be pruned away in late spring. If the shrub is killed to ground level it invariably grows again from the base. 1 or more specimens together, provided they are different clones, usually ensures a heavier fruit crop.

Species cultivated (all are deciduous): *C. bodinieri giraldii* (*C. giraldiana*), China; shrub to 2m or more; leaves lanceolate, 5–12cm long; flowers lilac in rounded clusters, summer; fruit glossy pale violet-purple, 3–4mm wide. *C. dichotoma* (*C. koreana* of gardens), China, Korea; compact shrub to 1·5m or more; leaves ovate to obovate; flowers pink, summer; fruit lilac-purple, 3–4mm wide. *C. giraldiana*, see *C. bodinieri*. *C. japonica*, China, Japan; shrub to 1·5m; leaves ovate to lanceolate, 6–12cm long; flowers whitish or pinkish, late summer; fruit violet, 4mm wide. *C.j. leucocarpa*, fruit white.

Callirrhoe

(for the daughter of Achelous, a minor Greek god). Poppy mallow. MALVACEAE. A genus of 10 species of annuals and perennials from N. America. 1 species is

Below: *Callicarpa bodinieri*
Above right: *Callirrhoe involucrata*
Right: *Callistephus* Starry Sky
Bottom right: *Callistephus* Fire Devil

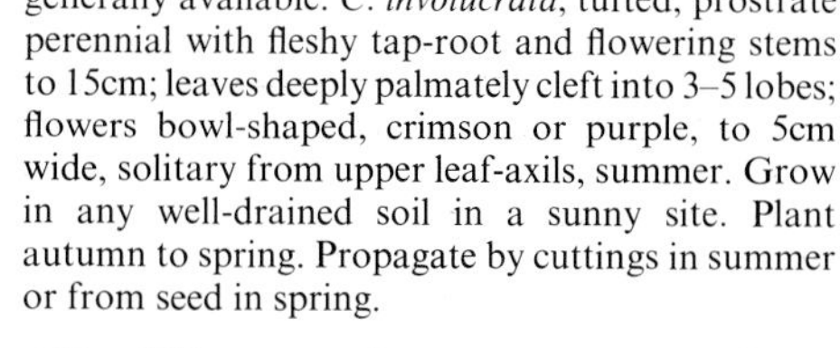

generally available: *C. involucrata*, tufted, prostrate perennial with fleshy tap-root and flowering stems to 15cm; leaves deeply palmately cleft into 3–5 lobes; flowers bowl-shaped, crimson or purple, to 5cm wide, solitary from upper leaf-axils, summer. Grow in any well-drained soil in a sunny site. Plant autumn to spring. Propagate by cuttings in summer or from seed in spring.

Callistephus

(Greek *kallos*, beauty, and *stephanos*, a crown – alluding to the large, colourful flower-heads). China aster. COMPOSITAE. A genus of 1 species, a half-hardy annual from China and Japan. *C. chinensis*, erect, branched plant to 60cm; leaves ovate, toothed, basal-stalked, upper ones sessile; flower-heads solitary or a few together, daisy-like, surrounded by a ruff of leafy bracts, ray florets deep purple, pink or white, disc yellow. Many mutants have arisen, each giving rise to named strains and cultivars, several of which are listed in seed

catalogues. For convenience they are classified according to flower-head shape: Ball – neat, rounded heads quilled; Chrysanthemum-flowered – chrysanthemum-like flowers, all florets strap-shaped; Ostrich Plume – large flower-heads with long, waved florets; Peony-flowered – compact, rounded heads with incurving florets; Pompon – dwarf plants to 30cm or more with many small, dense, rounded heads; Spider – florets long, slender, quilled. All these come in shades of red, purple and white, some including yellow and a few bicoloured. Grow in any well-drained, humus-rich soil in a sunny site. Sow the seed under glass in a temperature of 15–18°C. Prick off the seedlings into boxes of a commercial potting mixture at 4–5cm apart each way. Harden off late spring to early summer, and plant out when the fear of frost has passed.

Calluna

(Greek *kalluno*, to clean – alluding to its former use for making brooms). Heather or ling. ERICACEAE. A genus of 1 very variable species of low, evergreen shrub from Europe to Siberia, Iceland and the Azores. *C. vulgaris*, bushy, wiry-stemmed shrub, prostrate to erect, 3–60cm or more tall; leaves 1–2mm long, scale-like, with 2 pointed basal projections, overlapping on the lateral stems, smooth to densely grey-haired; flowers in narrow terminal racemes or panicles, bell-shaped, 4mm long, calyx and corolla deeply 4-lobed, the latter petaloid and larger, shades of purple and white, summer, autumn. *C.v. hirsuta*, foliage densely white-haired; numerous cultivars are available, many having arisen as natural mutations in the wild – others raised in gardens, some with yellow-, copper-, bronze- and red-tinted leaves: *C.v.* Alba Elata dense habit, white flowers, mid to late autumn (*C.v.* Alba Plena is a double-flowered form); *C.v.* Beoley, autumn; *C.v.* Blazeaway, foliage red and orange in winter, flowers lilac-mauve, early to mid autumn; *C.v.* Cuprea, young shoots yellow, reddish-bronze in winter, flowers pale mauve, early to mid autumn; *C.v.* C. W. Nix, flowers deep crimson, early to mid autumn; *C.v.* Elsie Purnell, flowers double, silvery- pink, mid to late autumn; *C.v.* Foxii Nana, tight, bun-shaped hummocks of bright green foliage to 7cm, flowers pale purple, sparse; *C.v.* Golden Carpet, prostrate, foliage yellow-, orange- and red-tinted in winter, flowers purple, early to mid autumn; *C.v.* Gold Haze, bright golden-yellow foliage, flowers white, early to mid autumn; *C.v.* H. E. Beale, one of the best double cultivars, flowers icing-pink, mid autumn to early winter; *C.v.* Tib, compact habit to 24cm, flowers cyclamen-purple, late summer to late autumn. Grow in acid, preferably peaty soil in a sunny site; some shade is tolerated. Plant from early autumn to late spring. Propagate by cuttings taken with a heel late summer. Lightly shearing off flower stems in late winter keeps the plants bushy and floriferous.

Calocedrus

(Greek *kalos*, beautiful, and *cedrus*, a cedar). CUPRESSACEAE. A genus of 3 species of evergreen coniferous trees from Burma to China, Taiwan, W. N. America. 1 species is generally available: *C. decurrens* (*Libocedrus d.*), incense cedar; W. USA, mountains Oregon, California, Baja C.; to 45m, of conical outline in the wild but represented in cultivation by the column-like *C.d.* Fastigiata (*C.d.* Columnaris): leaves slender, scale-like, closely overlapping in flattened, frond-like sprays, aromatic; cones narrowly ovoid, 2–2·5cm long, usually yellow-brown, with only 4, narrow, seed-bearing scales, the upper 2 fused together. *C.d.* Aureovariegata, scattered sprays of golden-yellow foliage. Grow in a well-drained but moisture-retentive, humus-rich soil in sun or partial shade. Plant autumn or spring. Propagate by cuttings with a heel early autumn, from seed in spring.

Far left below: *Calluna vulgaris* H. E. Beale
Far left bottom: *Calluna vulgaris* Gold Haze
Left: *Calocedrus decurrens*
Below: *Caltha palustris alba*
Bottom: *Caltha palustris*

Calonyction – see *Ipomoea bona-nox*.

Caltha

(old Latin for a yellow flower, probably calendula, used by Linnaeus for this genus). RANUNCULACEAE. A genus of about 30 species of herbaceous perennials from Arctic to northern temperate and southern cool temperate regions. They are mainly alpines or bog plants of tufted to clump-forming habit with long-stalked, oblong to orbicular, cordate leaves, and cup-shaped flowers, formed of 5 or more petaloid sepals in shades of yellow and white. Grow the bog species in wet ground or by the waterside; alpines in gritty but moist soil, both in sunny sites. Plant autumn or spring. Propagate by division in spring or after flowering or from seed.

Species cultivated: *C. biflora*, see *C. howellii*. *C. introloba*, S.E. Australia; tufted alpine; leaves usually long-stalked, the blades oblong-ovate with 2 slender basal lobes lying parallel and folded sharply forwards; flowers 2–3cm wide, sessile, white with 5–9 pointed petals usually having faint reddish lines from the base, late winter to spring. *C. howellii* (*C. biflora*), California, Oregon; clump-forming bog plant; leaf-blades rounded, 3–10cm wide; flowers white, to 3cm or more wide, usually solitary on stems to 30cm, spring to summer. *C. leptosepala*, N.W. N. America; much like the previous species and distinguished mainly by small botanical details; flower-buds often bluish. *C. minor* (*C. palustris minor*), N. Europe; much like a smaller version of *C. palustris* and varying from prostrate to semi-erect, the stems rooting at the nodes. *C.m. radicans* (*C. radicans*), prostrate stems; small, triangular-ovate leaves; solitary, 1·5–3cm wide flowers. *C. obtusa*, New Zealand; alpine; similar to *C. introloba*, but flowers on short stems and having 5, pure white, round-tipped sepals. *C. palustris*, marsh marigold, king cup; northern temperate and arctic zones; clump-forming bog species with stout, creeping rhizome; stems robust to 30cm, branched, leafy; leaves rounded to kidney or triangular-ovate, cordate, shining green to 10cm long; flowers 3–5cm wide, of 5–8 rich glossy yellow sepals, spring to summer. *C.p. alba*, flowers white; *C.p.* Flora-pleno, *C.p.* Multiplex, *C.p.* Monstrosa Plena (*C.p.* Plena), flowers fully double; *C.p.* Plurisepala (*C.p.* Semi-plena), semi – double. *C. polypetala*, Caucasus, Turkey; like a robust, far-spreading version of *C. palustris*, with stems to 60cm tall. *C. radicans*, see *C. minor*.

Calycanthus

(Greek *kalyx*, calyx, and *anthos*, a flower – the calyx is petal-like and coloured). CALYCANTHACEAE. A genus of 4 species of deciduous shrubs from S.E. and S.W. USA. They have opposite pairs of lanceolate to ovate leaves and terminal flowers composed of several narrow tepals of varying lengths; fruit is urn-shaped. The whole plant, including the wood, is pleasantly aromatic. Grow in any well-drained soil, preferably enriched with humus in a sunny site. Plant autumn to spring. Propagate from seed when ripe or spring, or layering spring or autumn.

Species cultivated: *C. fertilis*, S.E. USA; to 3m; leaves elliptic, oblong to ovate, 6–15cm long, dark shining green above, glaucous beneath; flowers crimson-brown, 3–5cm wide, summer. *C.f.* Purpureus, leaves purple-flushed beneath. *C. floridus*, Carolina allspice; S.E. USA; to 3m; leaves 5–12cm long, ovate to narrowly elliptic, grey-green, densely pubescent beneath; flowers about 5cm, brownish red-purple, fragrant, summer. *C. occidentalis*, California allspice; 3m; leaves 8–20cm long, ovate to oblong-lanceolate; flowers 5–7cm wide, brownish purple-red, summer. Less hardy.

Camassia

(the North American Indian name Quamash in Latin form). LILIACEAE. A genus of 5 species of bulbous plants from N. America. They have tufts of tapered, linear, arching leaves and wand-like racemes of 6-tepalled, star-like flowers in early summer. Grow in any moisture-retentive, humus-rich soil including the less-wet areas of a bog garden, in sun or shade. Plant autumn. Propagate from seed when ripe or spring, or removing offset bulbs at planting time.

Species cultivated: *C. cusickii*, N.W. USA; leaves to 36cm, greyish-green; flowers to 4cm wide, pale blue, in racemes to 90cm tall; often needs staking in shady or windy sites. *C.c.* Zwanenburg, more robust than type, deeper blue. *C. esculenta*, see *C. quamash*. *C. leichtlinii*, California to British Columbia; leaves to 60cm, rich green; flowers 4–8cm wide, violet to bright blue, rarely white, in racemes 90–120cm tall; *C.l. suksdorfii* covers the deeper blue and blue-purple forms in cultivation, notably *C.l.s.* Atroviolacea, *C.l.s.* Eve Price and *C.l.s.* Orion. *C.l.* Plena has rosette-like, double cream flowers. *C. quamash*, W. N. America; leaves to 50cm; flowers white to blue, 4–7cm wide in racemes to 90cm tall.

Left below: *Calycanthus floridus*
Above: *Camassia cusickii*

Camellia

(for Georg Josef Kamel, 1661–1706, Jesuit pharmacist (Czech) who botanized in Luzon Is, the Philippines and wrote about the flora. THEACEAE. A genus of 82 species of evergreen shrubs and trees from India to Indonesia, China and Japan. They have alternate, leathery, ovate to lanceolate leaves and rose-like, 5–7 petalled flowers; fruit a woody capsule with 1 to few large seeds. Grow the hardier species in partial shade sheltered from northerly winds, or on sheltered walls and the half-hardy sorts in a frost-free greenhouse, well-ventilated and shaded from direct sun. The soil or compost must be neutral to acid and humus-rich, consisting largely of peat and leaf mould, and coarse sand. Pot or plant autumn or spring. Propagate by stem or leaf-bud cuttings in late summer, layering in autumn, or from seed when ripe. All camellias, the cultivars of *C. japonica* in particular, make good pot plants for the cool greenhouse or room. Grow in 15–20cm pots and plunge outside after flowering, bringing in again in late autumn for flowering. Make sure they never dry out but avoid keeping the compost too wet. The temperature should not exceed 16°C during the late autumn period, otherwise the blooms may not develop properly or even fail to open. Application of a weak liquid fertilizer at fortnightly intervals will assist the plants when they are in full growth. Top dress or repot annually.

Species cultivated: *C. cuspidata*, W. China; hardy shrub to 2m or more; leaves lanceolate, 5–8cm long; flowers white, cup-shaped, to 3cm wide, usually profusely borne on well-established specimens; *C.* Cornish Snow (*C. cuspidata* × *C. saluenensis*), similar but more robust shrub with larger flowers. *C.* × Inspiration, see *C. reticulata*. *C. japonica*, Japan, Korea; hardy shrub or small tree to 9m; leaves broadly ovate, glossy, 6–12cm long; flowers very variable, in the wild type 6–8cm wide with 5 red petals, but many 100s of mutant cultivars in shades of red, pink and white, single and double occur, the largest to about 15cm wide, winter to spring; the following small selection can be recommended: *C.j.* Adolph Audusson, semi-double, blood-red, large; *C.j.* Alba Plena, fully double of formal shape, white; *C.j.* Alba Simplex, single white; *C.j.* Apollo, rose-red sometimes blotched white, semi-double, large; *C.j.* Drama Girl, deep salmon to rose-pink, semi-double, very large; *C.j.* Elegans, anemone-centred, bright rose-pink; *C.j.* Kimberley, single bright red with conspicuous yellow stamens; *C.j.* Magnoliaeflora, semi-double, pale shell-pink, somewhat magnolia-like; *C.j.* Nagasaki (*C.j.* Lady Buller), rose-pink, marbled white, large semi-double; *C.j.* Snowflake, medium white, single-flowered; *C.j.* Tomorrow, peony-shaped, semi-double, rose-pink, very large; *C.j.* Tricolor (*C.j.* Sieboldii), white, streaked carmine-red, medium semi-double. *C. reticulata*, W. China; shrub or small tree to 6m; leaves elliptic, distinctively net-veined, matt-green, to 10cm long; flowers funnel-shaped to widely spread, rose-pink, to 7cm wide; this wild type is hardier but rarer in cultivation than the several, more tender, Chinese cultivars with larger double to semi-double blooms; *C.r.* Buddha, semi-double, very large, with irregularly-waved petals; *C.r.* Captain Rawes (*C.r.* Semi-plena), carmine-pink, very large semi-double – the first *C. reticulata* to reach the west, introduced by Robert Fortune in 1820; *C.r.* Crimson Robe, carmine-red, semi-double with crinkled petals; *C.r.* Mary Williams, rose to crimson, large single; *C.r.* Shot Silk, bright pink, semi-double, waved petals. *C.* × Inspiration (*C. reticulata* × *C. saluenensis*), midway between parents with large, semi-double, deep pink flowers; *C.* × Salutation (same parentage) has large, soft, silvery-pink flowers; *C.* × Leonard Messel (*C. reticulata* × *C.* × *williamsii*), also akin to *C. reticulata*, with rich, clear pink flowers, large and semi-double. *C. saluenensis*, W.China; almost hardy shrub, to 5m; leaves oblong-ovate, blunt, shining dark green, to 6cm long; flowers carmine to pink or white, to 7cm wide. *C. sasanqua*, Japan; to 6m; leaves 3–7cm long, oblong-elliptic, blunt; flowers 4–5cm wide, pink or white, late autumn to spring; best on a sheltered wall because of its winter-flowering habit. *C.s.* Blanchette, single white; *C.s.* Briar Rose, soft pink single; *C.s.* Hiryu, deep crimson, double; *C.s.* Narumi-gata, creamy-white with pink shading *C.s.* Rosea Plena, double pink. *C. sinensis* (*C. thea, Thea sinensis*), tea – the commercial source of tea; Assam to China; almost hardy to half-hardy shrub, variable in stature and vigour, to 2m or more; leaves lanceolate, dull green, to 4cm long or more; flowers cup-shaped, white, 2·5–3·5cm wide, spring; best under glass, except in areas of light winter frosts. *C.* × *williamsii* (*C. japonica* × *C. saluenensis*), midway between parents, very free-flowering and a good garden plant; *C.* × *w.* Bow Bells, bright rose, semi-double; *C.* × *w.* Caerhays, lilac-rose, anemone-flowered; *C.* × *w.* Charles Michael, pale pink, semi-double; *C.* × *w.* Citation, silver-pink, semi-double; *C.* × *w.* Donation, orchid-pink, semi-double, vigorous growth; *C.* × *w.* Francis Hanger, white, single; *C.* × *w.* J.C. Williams, phlox-pink, single; *C.* × *w.* November Pink, like preceding but very early-flowering.

Campanula

(diminutive of Latin *campana*, a bell – in many species the flowers are bell-shaped). Bellflower. CAMPANULACEAE. A genus of 300 species of annuals, perennials and sub-shrubs from northern temperate zone and tropical mountains. Most of the species are

Top right: *Camellia japonica* Apollo
Centre: *Camellia japonica* Elegans
Right: *Camellia* × Inspiration
Top far right: *Camellia* × *williamsii* Donation

herbaceous perennials, many of dwarf stature and suitable for the rock garden and herbaceous bed or border. They are variable in foliage characters and the flowers range from wide, open stars to tubular bells, all with 5 prominent lobes, in shades of blue, pale yellow, white. Unless otherwise stated, all the species described are hardy, needing a well-drained soil and sun or light shade. Plant autumn to spring. Propagate from seed sown in sandy soil in a frame or outdoors in spring or by division at planting time which is from early autumn to late spring. Cuttings of young shoots can also be taken in late spring or summer. The less hardy species should be raised under the protection of a greenhouse.

Species cultivated: (bell-shaped unless otherwise stated) *C. alliarifolia*, Caucasus, Turkey; clump-forming; basal leaves ovate-cordate, long-stalked, white-haired beneath; flowers creamy-white, nodding, 3–4cm long in a 1-sided raceme 45–60cm tall, summer. *C. allionii* (*C. alpestris*), W. Alps; rhizomatous, tufted; leaves linear-lanceolate; flowers usually solitary, nodding, purple, 3–4·5cm long, summer to autumn, on stems to 10cm tall; needs scree conditions to thrive. *C. arvatica*, N. Spain; tufted, semi-prostrate; leaves ovate, toothed; flowers solitary or a few together, erect, widely funnel-shaped, 12–25mm wide, pale blue to violet, summer; needs a sheltered site or alpine house. *C.a.* Alba, flowers white. *C. aucheri*, Caucasus; tufted, dwarf; leaves oblong to ovate-spathulate; flowers solitary, violet-blue, large, on stem to 10cm, early summer. *C. barbata*, Europe; short-lived, rosetted perennial; leaves lanceolate; flowers pale blue, nodding, 2–3cm long, white-bearded within, in loose, 1-sided racemes 10–30cm tall, early summer. *C. betulaefolia*, Armenia; tufted; leaves ovate-cordate; flowers 2–3cm long, blue, on branched, reclining stems, to 15cm or more long; a white, pink-tinted form is listed as *C. finitima* in catalogues. *C.* Birch Hybrid (*C. portenschlagiana* × *C. poscharskyana*), midway between parents, with a profusion of rich purple-blue flowers. *C.* × *burghaltii* (*C. latifolia* × *C. punctata*), clump-forming to somewhat spreading; leaves ovate; flowers pendant, pale lavender, 6–8cm long, on stems to 60cm. *C. carpatica*, Carpathian mountains; clump-forming; lower leaves rounded to ovate-cordate, toothed; flowers blue, widely bell-shaped to 3cm wide, erect, solitary on stems 20–50cm or more tall, summer. *C.c.* Alba, flowers white; *C.c.* Turbinata (*C. turbinata*), dwarf, compact habit, to 15cm; other cultivars are available, varying in stature and in shades of blue to blue-purple and white. *C. cochlearfolia* (*C. bellardii*, *C. pumila*, *C. pusilla*), (mountains Europe); mat-forming by slender rhizomes; leaves rounded to oval, cordate, glossy; flowers lavender-blue, 13–16mm long, 2–6 on slender stems to 10cm tall, summer to autumn. *C.c.* Alba, flowers white. *C. collina*, Armenia; spreading by rhizomes; leaves ovate-cordate, long-pointed; flowers semi-pendant, rich purple-blue, funnel-shaped in 1-sided racemes, about 30cm, summer. *C. elatinoides*, Maritime Alps; tufted, prostrate; leaves ovate-cordate, sharply-toothed, grey-haired; flowers blue-purple, starry, 8mm wide, freely-borne, summer. *C. excisa*, Alps; spreading by rhizomes and forming small mats; leaves linear; flowers 2–2·5cm long, blue, with a punched-out hole between each of the lobes, solitary on stems to 10cm tall; needs acid scree conditions to thrive. *C. fenestrellata*, Yugoslavia, Albania, like a neat, compact *C. garganica*. *C. finitima*, see *C. betulaefolia*. *C. formanekiana*, N. Macedonia; monocarpic; leaves lyrate, grey-haired, in rosettes to 20cm wide; flowers blue or white, 4–4·5cm long, profusely-borne on a central, erect stem 30–40cm tall, and a ring of basal, prostrate laterals, summer; best in a dry wall or scree or given protection from winter wet. *C. fragilis*, Italy; allied to *C. isophylla*, but having firmer, almost fleshy, leaves, and longer, narrow, calyx segments. *C. garganica*, S.E. Italy, W. Greece; tufted, prostrate; leaves kidney- to heart-shaped, crenate; flowers blue with white centre, star-shaped 1–2cm wide, freely-borne, late spring to autumn. *C.g. hirsuta*, plant grey-haired; *C.g.h.* Alba, like type species but with white flowers. *C. glomerata*, Europe; clump-forming and spreading by rhizomes; leaves ovate, irregularly-toothed, hairy; flowers to 2–5cm long, funnel-shaped, violet-purple, in tight terminal clusters on stems to 80cm, late spring to autumn. *C.g.acaulis*, stem very short, or to 15cm; *C.g.a.* Nana, taller to 30cm; *C.g.a.* Nana Alba, white-flowered. *C.g. dahurica* (*C.g. speciosa*), robust; flowers rich violet-purple. *C.g.d.* Superba, similar but even more robust. *C.g.d.* Alba, flowers white. *C. grandis* (*C. latiloba*), Siberia; much like *C. persicifolia*, but flowers sessile, rigidly facing outwards on stiffer stems. *C.* × *hallii* (*C. cochlearifolia* × *C. portenschlagiana*), in habit a blend between the parents, with semi-erect, broad white bells generally solitary on 5cm stems. *C.* × *haylodgensis* (*C. cochlearifolia* × *C. carpatica*), much like the first parent, but flowers widely bell-shaped, double. *C. isophylla*, N.W. Italy; tufted; stems trailing, to 20cm or more; leaves rounded, cordate, toothed; flowers widely funnel-shaped, almost starry, lilac-blue, 1·5–2·5cm wide, late summer. *C.i.* Alba, flowers white; *C.i.* Mayi, leaves white-variegated, hairy, not reliably hardy and best in a dry wall or sheltered rock crevice – a good hanging-basket plant for the cool greenhouse or home. *C. kemulariae*, Transcaucasia; clump-forming, spreading by rhizomes; leaves broadly ovate-cordate, toothed; flowers bowl-shaped, to 4cm wide, violet to mauve-blue, in panicles on semi-prostrate stems to 30cm, summer. *C. lactiflora*, Caucasus; clump-forming; stems erect to 1·5m; leaves ovate-lanceolate, toothed; flowers widely funnel-shaped, 2–3cm wide, milky-blue in large terminal panicles, summer to autumn. Among cultivars: *C.l.* Alba, flowers white; *C.l.* Loddon Anna, lilac-pink; *C.l.* Pouffe, plant very compact 15–25cm tall; *C.l.* Prichard's, flowers violet-blue. *C. latifolia*, Europe; clump-forming; stem erect to 1·5m; leaves ovate-oblong, the basal cordate; flowers 4–5·5cm long, pale blue to violet-blue, pendant in terminal racemes, summer. Cultivars include *C.i.* Alba,

Top left: *Campanula carpatica*
Above: left: *Campanula persicifolia* Alba
Top: *Campanula glomerata*
Above: *Campanula isophylla* Star of Italy

flowers white; *C.l.* Brantwood, rich violet-purple; *C.l.* Macrantha, wider purple-blue bells. *C. latiloba*, see *C. grandis*. *C. medium*, Canterbury bell; N. and C. Italy, S.E. France; erect, hairy biennial to 90cm; leaves ovate-oblong to lanceolate, the basal ones forming a rosette to 30cm wide; flowers 5cm or more long, lilac-blue or white, summer. *C.m. calycanthema*, a mutant race with a saucer-like petaloid calyx; both this and the type are available in several strains from seedsmen, with flowers in shades of blue, pink, white, yellow. *C. nitida*, see next species. *C. persicifolia*, Europe, Asia; clump-forming, spreading by stolons; leaves lanceolate to spathulate; flowers blue, to 4cm wide, each on a slender stalk, in a few, flowered racemes to 90cm, summer to early autumn; several darker, white, and semi-double flowered forms are available, including *C.p.* Planiflora and *C.p.* P.Alba (white-flowered), (*C. nitida* and *C.n. alba*, *C. planiflora*, *C.p. alba*), a dwarf mutant of confused nomenclature, 23–30cm tall; *C.p.* Telham Beauty, more robust with rich purple-blue flowers. *C. pilosa*, Alaska to N. Japan; small mat-forming; leaves ovate to lanceolate-spathulate or linear; flowers deep purple to mauve, 3–4cm long, solitary or a few together on stems to 10cm, summer. *C. planiflora*, see *C. persicifolia*. *C. portenschlagiana* (*C. muralis*), W. Yugoslavia; widely clump-forming; leaves rounded-cordate, toothed; flowers 2cm long, lilac-blue, freely borne on semi-prostrate stems to 15cm long, summer, autumn. *C. poscharskyana*, W. Yugoslavia; clump-forming and spreading by stolons; leaves grey-haired when young, rounded-cordate, deeply-toothed; flowers starry, 2–2·5cm wide, lavender-blue, freely-borne on semi-prostrate stems to 30cm or more, summer to autumn. Cultivars: *C.p.* Alba, flowers white; *C.p.* E. H. Frost, milky-blue to white. *C. pulla*, N.E. Alps; rhizomatous, forming loose mats; leaves rounded to

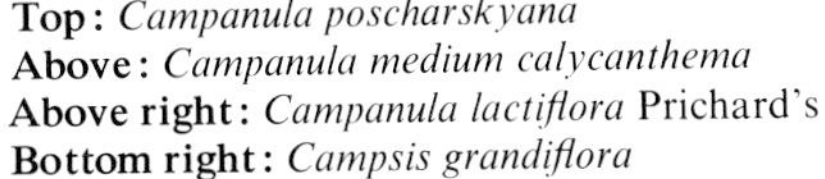

Top: *Campanula poscharskyana*
Above: *Campanula medium calycanthema*
Above right: *Campanula lactiflora* Prichard's
Bottom right: *Campsis grandiflora*

ovate; flowers nodding, solitary, 1·5–2·5cm long, rich purple-blue on slender stems 7–15cm tall, summer. *C.* × *pulloides* (*C. carpatica* Turbinata × *C. pulla*), having the running habit of *C. pulla*, but otherwise like the *C. carpatica* parent, with semi-erect *C. pulla*-like flowers. *C. punctata*, E. Siberia, N. Japan; clump-forming and speading by rhizomes; leaves ovate-cordate, coarsely-toothed; flowers pendant, tubular, creamy-white speckled purple within, to 5cm long, in a short raceme 20–30cm tall. *C. pyramidalis*, chimney bellflower; N. Italy, Yugoslavia, Albania; clump-forming, erect stems 1·5–2m tall; leaves ovate-oblong, subcordate to ovate-lanceolate; 3cm wide, starry, pale blue or white, on branches from leaf-axils forming large pyramidal panicles, summer; only hardy in a warm, sheltered spot; excellent as a large pot plant for the cool greenhouse and then best grown as a biennial from seed or offset rosettes rooted as cuttings. *C.raddeana*, Caucasus; clump-forming, rhizomatous; leaves triangular-ovate, cordate, sharply-toothed, glossy; flowers deep lustrous violet, nodding in loose panicles from erect stems to 30cm tall, summer. *C. raineri*, S.E. Alps, Italy; tufted, spreading by slender rhizomes; leaves obovate to ovate, grey-green; flowers broadly bell-shaped, blue or white, 3–4cm wide, erect on stems 5–10cm tall, summer; sometimes confused with *C.* × *pseudoraineri* (*C. carpatica* × *C. raineri*), a plant much like the first parent with a somewhat greyish leaf. *C. rapunculoides*, Europe; tufted, spreading widely by adventitious shoots from the roots; leaves ovate, slender-pointed, coarsely-toothed; flowers nodding, 2–3cm long, blue-violet, in erect branched racemes 30–90cm tall; an attractive but highly invasive plant, difficult to eradicate when well-established, sometimes masquerading under the names of more desirable species and brought into gardens from the wild. *C. rotundifolia*, harebell of England, bluebell of Scotland; N. Hemisphere; tufted, spreading by slender rhizomes; leaves rounded to kidney-shaped, subcordate, crenate; flowers 1–2cm or more long, blue or white, nodding to fully pendant, 1 to several on slender, mainly erect, stems, summer to autumn, varies much in stature, degree of branching, size of bell, and shades of blue to purple; named cultivars are sometimes offered. *C. sarmatica*, Caucasus; clump-forming; leaves oblong-ovate, cordate, downy grey-green; flowers velvety grey-blue, about 3cm long on 1-sided racemes to 30cm or more tall, summer. *C. saxifraga*, much like *C. tridentata*. *C.* × *stansfieldii* (probably *C. carpatica* × *C. tommasiniana*), slowly mat-forming with semi-pendant, violet, cup-shaped bells on stems to 13cm. *C.thyrsoides*, Jura, Alps, mountains of Balkan Peninsula; biennial or monocarpic; leaves oblong-lanceolate, somewhat wavy, forming a rosette; flowers 1·5–2cm long, yellow-white, hairy, in dense, unbranched spikes to 30cm or more tall, summer. *C. tommasiniana*, N.W. Yugoslavia; like *C. waldsteiniana* but flowers bell-shaped, tubular, pendant. *C. trachelium*, nettle-leaved bellflower; Europe, N. Africa, Siberia; clump-forming; leaves scabrid, broadly ovate-cordate, coarsely-toothed; flowers 2·5–3·5cm long, blue-purple, sub-erect or inclined in leafy panicles on erect, angled stems 50–100cm tall, summer to autumn. *C.t.* Bernice, flowers double. *C. tridentata*, Caucasus; tufted; leaves spathulate, toothed at the tip, in rosettes; flowers blue, white-centred, bell- to funnel-shaped, erect, solitary on stems to 10cm, usually less, summer; a variable species, the many variants of which have been given species names – in *C. saxifraga*, the leaves are longer and distinctly hairy; in *C. bellidioides*, the leaves lack teeth and are smooth etc. *C. turbinata*, see *C. carpatica* Turbinata. *C. waldsteiniana*, W. Yugoslavia mountains – tufted, shortly rhizomatous; leaves rounded to lanceolate; flowers 2cm wide, starry, erect, blue, in small panicles to 15cm tall, late summer; neat and floriferous. *C.* × Warley White (*C. warleyensis*), white-flowered seedling from *C.* × *haylodgensis*. *C.* × *wockii* Puck (probably *C. pulla* × *C. waldsteiniana*), low mounds of branched stems to 10cm or so with purple-blue flowers.

Campion – see *Silene* and *Lychnis coronaria*.

Campsis

(Greek *kampe*, bent or bending – alluding to the strongly-curved stamens). BIGNONIACEAE. A genus of 2 species of woody climbers from E. Asia and E. USA. They are deciduous, climbing by aerial roots, with pinnate leaves in opposite pairs and terminal clusters of tabular flowers with 5, rounded, petal-like lobes. Grow on sunny walls or over dead tree stumps in moisture-retentive but well-drained, humus-rich soil. Plant autumn or spring. Propagate from seed, layers or suckers in spring, cuttings with heel late summer. Overgrown specimens, or those that have filled their alloted space, may be pruned in spring, cutting back all the previous season's growth to 2 pairs of buds.

Species cultivated: *C. grandiflora* (*C. chinensis, Bignonia g., Tecoma g.*), China; to 10m; or more; leaflets 7–9, ovate, toothed, 4–7·5cm long; flowers 5–9cm long and wide, deep orange and red in terminal panicles, late summer to autumn; less hardy than *C. radicans*, needing a sheltered, warm wall and not reliable except in the south; also aerial roots rather sparse and needs some tying for support. *C.* × *tagliabuana* (*Tecoma grandiflora princei, T. hybrida*), (*C. grandiflora* × *C. radicans*), resembles *C. radicans*, with flowers midway between the parents. *C.* × *t.* Mme Galen, flowers salmon-red, hardier than the Chinese

parent. *C. radicans* (*Bignonia r.*, *Tecoma r.*) to 15m; leaflets 9–11, ovate, coarsely-toothed, 2–10cm long; flowers 5–8cm long, orange and scarlet, late summer to autumn. May need some means of support until fairly well established. Fairly hardy.

Canada rice – see *Zizania*.

Canadian pondweed – see *Elodea*.

Canary creeper – see *Tropaeolum peregrinum*.

Canary grass – see *Phalaris canariensis*.

Candytuft – see *Iberis amara*, *I.umbellata*.

Canna

(Greek *kanna*, a reed – some species are tall with reed-like stems). Indian shot. CANNACEAE. A genus of 55 species of perennials from tropical and subtropical America. They are clump-forming plants with fleshy, tuber-like rhizomes, erect, unbranched stems, and lanceolate to oblong-ovate leaves. The tubular flowers are borne in terminal racemes and have 3 petals and 1–5 petaloid stamens, 2 or 3 of which are coloured like petals, 1 forming the lower lip of the flower. The very hard seed borne in 3-celled capsules has been used as a substitute for shot. In areas where winter frosts are light, grow in well-drained, humus-rich soil in a sunny site, preferably against a south wall in the warmer areas. After the first autumn frost kills the foliage, place over each plant a mound of coarse sand, grit, chopped bracken or weathered boiler ash to a depth of about 10–15cm as protection for the rhizomes. Remove the covering about early summer or when fear of frost has passed. In the north lift the rhizomes before the first frosts fall and store in a frost free, dry place. Replant in the spring when fear of frost has passed. Generally, cannas are used as pot plants or for summer bedding. Start the rhizomes into growth in early to mid spring by just covering in moist peat and placing in a temperature of 15–18°C. When the leaves are 7–10cm tall, separate into single shoots each with a piece of rhizome, and pot into a 10cm container of a good commercial potting mixture. Keep moist and when the pots are full of roots pot on into 15–18cm pots, or larger if big specimens are required. Plants for bedding out can be started in mid spring and grown in 13cm pots, hardening off in early summer, ready for planting out when fear of frost has passed. Propagation as described, by division or from seed sown in a temperature of 21–25°C, soaking first for 24 hours in warm water. Germination is erratic and seedlings should be potted singly into 7·5cm pots as soon as 2 leaves show, potting on as required.

Species cultivated: *C. edulis*, S. America, W. Indies; stems to 2m or more; leaves ovate to oblong, 30–60cm; flowers to 4cm long, yellow and red, summer. *C.* × *generalis* (*C. hybrida* of gardens), race of hybrid cultivars derived from *C. flaccida*, *C. coccinea*, *C. indica*, and perhaps other species; stems 60–120cm tall; leaves ovate-lanceolate, bright green or purple-flushed; flowers 5–8cm wide in shades of orange, red, yellow, and bicoloured. The following cultivars are well-tried: *C.* × *g.* Bonfire, deep orange, 90cm; *C.* × *g.* Brilliant, bright red, 60cm; *C.* × *g.* Lucifer, bright red, edged yellow, 60cm; *C.* × *g.* President, vivid scarlet, 90cm; *C.* × *g.* R. Wallace, pale yellow, 90cm: all green-leaved. Purple-leaved cultivars: *C.* × *g.* America, deep red and one of the largest-flowered cultivars, 1m; *C.* × *g.* Di Bartolo, deep clear pink; *C.* × *g.* Feuerzauber, rich scarlet, 1m; *C.* × *g.* Verdi, deep orange, very dark foliage, 90cm; *C.* × *g.* Wyoming, bronzy-orange, handsome leaves, 1·3m. Variegated-leaved cultivars: *C.* × *g.* Striped Beauty, deep scarlet, leaves with a bold vein pattern of yellow to ivory-striped. *C. indica*, Indian shot; C. and S. America; stems 1–2m; leaves oblong-ovate, 30–45cm long; flowers pink and red, about 4–5cm long, summer. *C. iridiflora*, Peru; stems 2–3m tall; leaves oblong, 30–60cm long; flowers rose, nodding, slender, to 13cm long, early summer onwards; needs the protection of a frost-free greenhouse in cool temperate climes

Above: *Canna* × *generalis* Coq d'Or
Above right: *Canna* × *generalis* President
Right: *Capsicum annuum*

Canterbury bell – see *Campanula medium*.

Cape gooseberry – see *Physalis peruviana*.

Cape pondweed – see *Aponogeton distachyos*.

Caper spurge – see *Euphorbia lathyrus*.

Capsicum

(Greek *kapto*, to bite – from its hot taste). SOLANACEAE. A genus of 50 species of shrubs, sub-shrubs and annuals. They have ovate, oblong to lanceolate, alternate leaves, pendulous, 5-lobed flowers, each having a cone-shaped cluster of 5 stamens in the centre, and cylindrical, often twisted to oblong fruit – well-known as 'peppers'. The species described are grown as annuals either in pots under glass or planted out in a warm, sheltered spot when fear of frost has passed. Sow seed in a temperature of 16–18°C in mid spring, and prick off seedlings singly as soon as large enough to handle into 6·5–7·5cm pots of a commercial potting mixture. When the pots are well-filled with roots move on into 13cm containers. Some of the smaller-growing ornamental cultivars used for late autumn effect are best sown in late spring or early summer, pricked off into boxes at 3–4cm apart each way, then potted into 10–13cm pots for fruiting. All plants respond to liquid feed at 7–10 day intervals once they are well-rooted and until the fruit is well-grown. All plants may be stood in a sheltered, open frame for the summer. Those planted out need a well drained but rich soil.

Species cultivated: *C. annuum*, included here are cultivars of *C. annuum* with ornamental, mainly erect fruit, most of them probably being hybrids with the next species. The following can be recommended, all with erect fruit: *C.a.* Bonfire, fruit conical, yellow and red; *C.a.* Elf, pods long, slender, yellow changing to red; *C.a.* Fips, compact habit, fruit changes from creamy-green through orange to deep red; all the preceding are 18–20cm tall, suitable for small-pot culture. *C.a.* Friesdorfer Red and *C.a.* F. Yellow are both to 90 cm tall and suitable for cutting in mid winter. *C. frutescens*, short-lived sub-shrub to 1·5m, much like *C. annuum*, but fruit in pairs, erect, narrowly-conical, 1–2·5cm long, red or yellow, very hot-tasting. *C.f. baccatum*, berries globose, about 1cm wide.

Caragana

(Mongolian name *caragan* – for *C. arborescens* – in Latin form). LEGUMINOSAE. A genus of 80 species of deciduous shrubs and small trees from Himalaya, C. Asia, China. They have paripinnate alternate leaves and mainly yellow, pea-like flowers, borne – in the species mentioned here – in late spring. Grow in any well-drained soil in a sunny site. Plant autumn to spring. Propagate by cuttings with a heel late summer, from seed or by layering in spring.

Species cultivated: *C. arborescens*, pea tree; Mongolia, Siberia; eventually to 5m or more, erect to almost fastigiate; leaves 4–7·5cm long, leaflets 4–6 oval to obovate; flowers 1·5–2cm long, yellow, in clusters from buds of the previous year. Cultivars: *C.a.* Lorbegii, leaflets grassy, 1–2mm wide; *C.a.* Nana, a curious mutant forming a stunted, stiff-branched shrublet; *C.a.* Pendula, prostrate or forming a small, weeping tree if grafted onto a leg of the type species. *C. pygmaea*, Caucasus to Tibet; shrub to 1m or more with slender, pendulous to prostrate branches; leaves of 4, oblanceloate, 12mm long leaflets; flowers yellow, 2–2·5cm long, pendant and freely-borne.

Top: *Caragana arborescens* Nana
Left above: *Cardamine pratensis* Plena
Above: *Cardiocrinum giganteum*

Cardamine

(ancient Greek name, *kardamon*, for a kind of cress, taken up by Linnaeus for this genus). CRUCIFERAE. A genus of 160 species of annuals and perennials of cosmopolitan distribution mainly from temperate regions. The species described here are clump to mat-forming, with entire, imparipinnate or trifoliate leaves and erect racemes of white or coloured, 4-petalled flowers. Grow in moisture-retentive soil in sun or shade. Plant autumn to spring. Propagate by division at planting time or from seed in spring.
Species cultivated: *C. asarifolia*, Pyrenees, Alps, Apennines; stoloniferous, mat-forming perennial; leaves kidney-shaped, wavy, to 10cm or more wide, bright green; flowers white, to 1·5cm wide in racemes 20–40cm tall, early spring to summer, starting to flower with young leaves. *C. latifolia*, see *C. raphanifolia*. *C. pratensis*, cuckoo flower; Europe; clump-forming perennial; leaves pinnate, ovate/kidney-shaped leaflets; flowers 12–18mm wide, lilac, in racemes 30–55mm tall, spring. *C.p.* Flora Pleno (*C.p.* Plena), flowers double, longer-lasting; *C.p.* Bountiful, a more vigorous and floriferous form of the type plant. *C. raphanifolia* (*C. latifolia*), rhizomatous perennial forming mats; leaves pinnate, of 3–11 ovate to rounded leaflets, the terminal one largest, 3–7cm wide; flowers reddish-purple, 1·5–2cm wide, in robust racemes 30–60cm tall, late spring to summer. *C. trifolia*, C. Europe to C. Italy and C. Yugoslavia; rhizomatous, mat-forming perennial; leaves trifoliate, leaflets rhomboid to rounded, to 3cm long or more, dark green above, purplish beneath, dense; flowers white, sometimes pink, 1–1·5cm wide in racemes to 20cm, spring to summer.

Cardinal flower – see *Lobelia cardinalis*.

Cardiocrinum

(Greek *kardia*, heart, and *krinon*, a lily – alluding to the heart-shaped leaves). LILIACEAE. A genus of 3 species of bulbous plants from Himalaya and E. Asia. Apart from the large, heart-shaped basal leaves they resemble the true lilies (*Lilium*) and require the same conditions: partial shade, shelter from strong winds, and a moist, humus-rich soil. Plant in autumn, setting the bulb shallowly with the nose only just covered with soil. Propagate by separating at planting time the small offset bulbs that form around the base of flowered specimens or seed sown when ripe or in spring. Seedlings take 6–8 years to reach flowering size.
Species cultivated: *C. cordatum* (*Lilium c.*), heartleaf lily; Japan, Sakhalin, Kurile Is; stems 1·2–2m tall, naked for lower third then bearing a whorl of long-stalked, heart-shaped leaves to 30cm long, above which are scattered a few smaller leaves and a terminal raceme of 4–10 creamy-white, irregularly trumpet-shaped blooms each to 15cm long; liable to damage by spring frosts and best in a frost-free greenhouse in cold districts. *C. giganteum* (*Lilium g.*), giant lily; Himalaya; stems 1·8–3·8m; leaves forming a basal rosette, long-stalked, the heart-shaped blade to 45cm long, stem leaves smaller; raceme of up to 20 flowers, nodding, regularly funnel-shaped, fragrant, 15cm long, white, red-purple striped within, late summer.

Carex

(said to derive from the Greek *keirein*, to cut – alluding to the finely-spined, toothed leaves that can cut a finger drawn along them). CYPERACEAE. A genus of 1500–2000 species of sedges of cosmopolitan distribution, mainly from wet soils and temperate climates. They are tufted or rhizomatous and spreading, with linear, keeled, arching leaves, and slender flowering stems triangular in cross-section. The tiny, greenish or brownish, petalless flowers are unisexual, and arranged in dense, short, catkin-like spikes, often pendulous or inclined. Grow in moisture-retentive soil, by the waterside or in a bog garden. Plant spring or autumn. Propagate from seed or by division, spring (variegated-leaved cultivars by division only). Several species described here make good pot plants for cool or cold greenhouse and rooms.
Species cultivated: *C. brunnea*, China, Japan, Taiwan, Philippines; clump-forming; leaves 20–45cm or more long, stiff, bright green to yellowish; flowering stems 40–80cm, each carrying up to 10, nodding, 1–3cm long flowering spikes, late summer. *C.b.* Variegata, leaves bronze and gold variegated; best in well-drained soil – makes a good pot plant. *C. buchananii*, New Zealand; densely-tufted from an ascending rhizome; leaves stiff, erect, to 40cm or more, smooth, shining reddish-green beneath, matt creamy-green above; flowering stems to about 60cm, spikes 5–6, silvery, to 3cm long. *C. elata* (*C. stricta*), tufted sedge; Europe to Caucasus, N. Africa; clump-forming; leaves 40–100cm long,

3–6mm wide, arching; stems about as long as leaves; spikes 3–5, erect, 1·5–2cm long, the females purple-brown, early summer. *C.e.* Aurea (*C.e.* Bowles Golden), leaves golden-yellow when young, gradually changing green – sometimes listed under *C. riparia* in catalogues. *C. grayi*, E. N. America; robust, clump-forming; stems 30–90cm; leaves to 40cm long and 1cm wide, firm, arching, pale to grey-green; male spikes solitary, slender, females 1–2 spherical, 3–4cm wide, summer. *C. morrowii*, Japan; clump-forming, stems 20–40cm; leaves to 20cm or more long and 5–10mm wide, stiff, arching, deep green; spikes 4–6, erect, 2–4cm long, spring. *C.m.* Variegata, leaves white-striped; not fully hardy in cold areas – makes a good pot plant. *C. ornithopoda*, bird's foot sedge; Europe to Turkey; tufted; stems to 25cm; leaves 10–20cm, soft, arching; spikes 3–4, the females arching, 5–10mm long, orange-brown, spring. *C.o.* Variegata, leaves striped creamy-yellow. *C. pendula*, Europe, W. Asia, N. Africa; robust, clump-forming; stems to 1·5m; leaves to 1m long and 1·5–2cm wide, keeled, arching; spikes 5–6, the 4–5 females 7–16cm long, green, pendulous and catkin-like, early summer. *C. riparia*, greater pond sedge; Europe, N. Africa, W. Asia; rhizomatous, far-creeping; stems 1–1·6m; leaves to 1m or more long and 6–15mm wide, arching; spikes brown, 6–11, sub-erect to nodding, late spring. *C.r.* Variegata, leaves white-striped. *C. stricta*, see *C. elata*.

Carlina

(for Charlemagne – Carolinus or Carolus, Latin for Charles – who is said to have cured his army of the plague with a species of *Carlina*). COMPOSITAE. A genus of 20 species of annuals, biennials and perennials from the Mediterranean, Europe, Asia. They form rosettes of usually narrow, spiny, thistle-like leaves and bear terminal flower-heads of tubular florets surrounded by chaffy, petal-like bracts like an everlasting flower. Grow in a sunny site in well-drained soil. Plant autumn or spring. Propagate from seed sown when ripe or in spring.

Species cultivated: *C. acanthifolia*, Europe, Pyrenees to N. Greece; monocarpic; leaves ovate to oblong elliptic, pinnatifid to pinnatisect, spiny-toothed, velvety white-haired beneath and sometimes above, to 30cm long, in imposing flat rosettes; flower-heads lemon-yellow, 12–14cm wide, sessile in the centre of rosette, summer to autumn. *C. acaulis*, Europe; perennial, forming small clumps; leaves arching to prostrate, usually pinnatisect, spiny-toothed, 20–30cm long; flower-heads 5–10cm or more wide, florets often reddish, bracts silvery, summer to autumn. *C.a. acaulis*, flower-heads sessile or on stem to 15cm. *C.a. simplex* (*C.a.* Caulescens of gardens), stems 15–60cm tall, bearing 1–6 flower-heads.

Carmichaelia

(for Capt. Dugald Carmichael, 1722–1827, Scottish army officer who collected plants in India, S. Africa, Mauritius and Tristan da Cunha – but not New Zealand). LEGUMINOSAE. A genus of 38 species in New Zealand, 1 in Lord Howe Is. They are broom-like shrubs, leafless or sparsely pinnately-leaved, with small racemes or solitary pea flowers, often fragrant, followed by small, ovoid pods containing 1 to a few seeds. The species described are hardy in mild areas but need a sunny wall and well-drained, humus-rich soil to thrive. Plant spring. Propagate by cuttings with a heel late summer or from seed in spring.

Species cultivated: *C. australis* (of gardens), 1–4m tall, branchlets green, flattened, 2–4mm wide; leaves only on young plants, pinnate, with 3–5 small obcordate leaflets; racemes of 5 flowers, each one 4mm long, white, flushed and veined purple, summer, pods broadly ovoid to oblong with 1–2 orange-red, black-mottled seed; this plant is correctly *C. cunninghamii*, though 4 other species (*C. aligera*, *C. silvatica*, *C. solandri*, *C. egmontiana*) may all pass under the invalid *C. australis* name. *C. enysii*, tiny shrub to 5cm tall by up to 20cm wide; stems flattened, finely grooved; leafless when adult; racemes of 1–3 flowers, each one 5mm long, purple with darker veins, summer; a hardy alpine.

Carnation – see *Dianthus*.

Carolina allspice – see *Calycanthus floridus*.

Carpenteria

(for Professor William M. Carpenter, 1811–1848, an American doctor from Louisiana). PHILADELPHACEAE. A genus of 1 species of evergreen shrub from California, USA: *C. californica*, bushy habit, 2–3m or to 5m in favourable sites; leaves in

Top far left: *Carex elata* Aurea
Far left: *Carex acuta* Variegata
Bottom far left: *Carex riparia*
Left: *Carlina acanthifolia*
Left below: *Carlina acaulis* Caulescens
Below: *Carpenteria californica*

opposite pairs, lanceolate, 5–11cm long, leathery, smooth above, fine grey hairs beneath; flowers 5–7cm wide, saucer-shaped, with 5–7 broad white petals and a central boss of yellow stamens, carried in terminal clusters of 3–7 in summer. Not hardy in cold areas and the north. Grow in any well-drained soil in a sheltered, sunny site, best close to a wall except in the milder areas. In general it does not do well in areas of industrial air pollution. Plant spring. Propagate by layering or from seed in spring, or by cuttings with a heel in late summer in bottom heat 18–21°C, preferably under mist. Seedlings can be very variable, some having poor, narrow-petalled blooms.

Carpinus

(the ancient Latin name). Hornbeam. CARPINACEAE (BETULACEAE). A genus of about 35 species of deciduous trees from N. Hemisphere. They are mainly of small to medium size with somewhat zigzag twigs, alternate, conspicuously-veined, ovate to oblong leaves, and tiny, unisexual, petalless flowers in catkins. Fruit are small nuts each attached to a lobed, wing-like bract for dispersal by wind. They are carried in decoratively-pendant chains. The wood is of a bony hardness used for the internal parts of pianos, tool handles, wooden screws etc, and formerly for the cog wheels of mills. Grow in moisture-retentive, humus-rich soil, in sun or partial shade. Plant autumn to spring. Propagate from seed sown when ripe, cultivars by grafting in spring onto seedlings of the species. Pruning seldom required unless grown for hedging, when they should be sheared over in late summer.

Species cultivated: *C. betulus*, common hornbeam; Europe and W. Asia; 15–24m tall, or more when mature, branches spreading, trunk ridged or fluted, smooth, dark grey; leaves ovate, 4–10cm long, rounded or cordate at base, doubly-toothed, bright green, often yellow in autumn, male catkins yellow, 2·5–5cm long, females smaller, green, spring with young leaves; a good hedging plant, retaining russet-brown leaves all winter when regularly clipped. *C.b.* Columnaris, columnar when young but broadening with age; *C.b.* Fastigiata (*C.b.* Pyramidalis), narrowly pyramidal when young, broadening later; *C.b.* Incisa (*C.b.* Quercifolia), leaves smaller, deeply- and irregularly-toothed; *C.b.* Purpurea, young leaves purplish, soon turning green. *C. caroliniana*, American hornbeam, ironwood; E. N. America, Mexico; small, spreading tree to 10m or more, trunk ridged, smooth, dark, almost bluish-grey; leaves ovate to oblong, irregularly- and sharply-toothed. 3–8cm long, orange-yellow in autumn, male catkins to 4cm, spring; grows best in a moist or even wet soil.

Cartwheel flower – see *Heracleum mantegazzianum*.

Carya

(Greek *karya*, ancient name for a walnut tree – a similar and related genus). Hickory. JUGLANDACEAE. A genus of 25 species of handsome deciduous trees from E. N. America and E. Asia. They are ultimately of medium to large size, with pinnate leaves that generally turn bright yellow in autumn. The flowers are small, petalless, the males carried in branched, pendulous, greenish catkins, the females in spikes of 1–10, followed by green or yellowish, hard, plum-like fruit, the 'stone' of which is an oily nut – edible in some species. Grow in moisture-retentive, humus-rich soil in sun or partial shade. Plant autumn to spring. Propagate from seed sown when ripe or as soon afterwards as possible. They are best sown singly in 13–15cm pots of a good commercial potting mixture and plunged in a cold frame. The young plants resent root disturbance and are best planted out the following year. Pruning is seldom required.

Species cultivated: *C. cordiformis* (*C. amara*, *Juglans cordiformis*), bitternut, swamp hickory; E. USA; to 25m or more, of slender, conical habit; leaves to 25cm or more long, of 5–11 obovate leaflets, upper ones largest; male catkins in 3s, 5–7cm long, late spring; fruit in groups of 2–3, somewhat pear-shaped, yellowish, 2–4cm long; nut – sweetish to bitter. *C. glabra* (*C. porcina*, *Juglans glabra*), pignut, white hickory; E. N. America; to 22m or more, of broadly conical to oblong habit; bark purple-grey; leaves 20–30cm long, of 5–7, ovate-lanceolate to obovate, leaflets; catkins 7–13cm long, usually in 3s, late spring; fruit like those of *C. cordiformis*; nut – edible. *C. ovata* (*C. alba* in part, *Juglans ovata*), shagbark hickory; E. N. America; to 24m or more, oblong to rounded habit with comparatively few, irregularly disposed, branches; bark shaggy, pale grey; leaves 20–45cm or more long, of 5, rarely 3–7, obovate to ovate-lanceolate leaflets, upper 3 much larger; male catkins in 3s or 4s, early summer, 10–15cm long; fruit to 4cm long, obvoid, yellow-green; nut – sweet, edible. *C. tomentosa* (*C. alba* in part, *Juglans tomentosa*), mockernut; E. N. America; to 22m or more, slenderly conical, becoming broader and less regular with age, bark smooth, grey, ridged when old; leaves 30–50cm long, of 7, sometimes 5–9, obovate leaflets, somewhat aromatic when bruised; male catkins usually dull yellow in 3s, to 15cm long, early summer; fruit singly or in pairs, globose, to 4cm wide; nut – sweet, edible.

Caryopteris

(Greek *karyon*, a nut, and *pteron*, a wing – the tiny fruits are broadly-keeled). VERBENACEAE. A genus of 15 species of deciduous shrubs and sub-shrubs from Himalaya to Japan. They are mainly small in stature with opposite pairs of narrowly lanceolate to ovate leaves and usually profusely-borne axillary cymes of small, 5-lobed, tubular flowers from late summer to autumn. Grow in well-drained soil in a sunny site. Plant spring. Propagate by cuttings with a heel late summer, over-wintering the young plants in a cold frame or greenhouse. It is usual to cut back the previous season's stems of flowering-sized plants to about 2–3 pairs of buds in spring, the resulting new growth being strong and flowering well. Alternatively, remove the flowered tips only and treat as a true shrub.

Far left: *Carpinus betulus* fruit cluster
Above left: *Carya ovata* bark
Left: *Carya ovata* autumn foliage
Above: *Caryopteris × clandonensis* Kew Blue

Species cultivated: *C. × clandonensis* (*C. incana × C. mongolica*), to 1·5m if not pruned annually; leaves ovate-lanceolate, coarsely-toothed to entire, fine grey-silvery hairs beneath, 4–9cm long; flowers blue; *C. × c.* Arthur Simmonds, corolla lobes and anthers bright blue; *C. × c.* Ferndown, darker green leaves, deeper blue flowers; *C. × c.* Heavenly Blue, like *C. × c.* Arthur Simmonds, but habit erect and more compact; *C.×c.* Kew Blue, like *C.×c.* Arthur Simmonds, but flowers darker blue. *C. incana* (*C. mastacanthus*, *C. tangutica*), China, Japan, Korea, Taiwan; to 1m unpruned; leaves aromatic, ovate, 3–7cm long, grey-felted; flowers blue-purple, about 7mm long; *C.i. tangutica*, China; smaller leaves, less deeply-lobed corolla, hardier than type, that can be killed back to ground level in severe winters. *C. mongolica* (*C. mongholica*), China, Mongolia; 60–90cm tall; leaves linear-lanceolate, entire, 2·5–4·5cm long; flowers pale blue, about 1cm long; often short-lived; needs warm summers to do well.

Cassinia

(for Count Henri de Cassini, 1781–1832, French botanist who, in particular, studied the daisy family). COMPOSITAE. A genus of 28 species of evergreen shrubs from Africa, Australia and New Zealand. They are slender-stemmed and heath-like, with spirally-borne, small, linear to oblong-obovate leaves and clusters of tiny, daisy-like flower-heads lacking ray-florets. Grow in any well-drained soil in a sunny site. Plant autumn or spring. Propagate by cuttings with a heel late summer. The species described are generally hardy but can be browned or killed back to ground level during the severest winters; all are from New Zealand.

Species cultivated: *C. fulvida* (*Diplopappus chrysophyllus*), golden heather; to 2m tall, dense habit; leaves 4–8mm long, oblong-ovate, dark green above, yellow down beneath, sticky when young; flower-heads white-tipped, about 5mm long, in dense, terminal clusters, summer. *C. leptophylla*, much like *C. fulvida*, but with pale grey cast; leaves generally whitish-downed beneath, 2–4mm long; flower-heads 3–4mm long, summer to autumn. *C. vauvilliersii*, to 2m or more tall, erect stems yellowish-downed; leaves 5–12mm long, linear-spathulate to obovate, dark green above, yellowish down beneath; flower-heads white-tipped, about 4mm long, summer. *C.v. albida*, stems and leaves with dense white down.

Above: *Cassinia fulvida*
Left: *Cassiope* × Muirhead
Bottom left: *Cassiope fastigiata*

Cassiope

(for the wife of Cepheus, mother of Andromeda in Greek mythology). ERICACEAE. A genus of 12 species of very small evergreen shrubs from circumpolar regions and Himalaya. They have tiny, densely overlapping leaves, and pendant, dainty, white, bell-shaped flowers with 4–6 small lobes, borne singly on thread-like stalks, mainly in spring. Grow in acid, peaty soil that never dries out. A cool, partially-shaded site is necessary for success and they are not easy to keep in good health in some parts of S. England. Most species make satisfactory alpine-house plants in pans of peaty compost. Pot or plant autumn or spring. Propagate by cuttings or layering in late summer, from seed when ripe, autumn or spring.

Species cultivated: *C. fastigiata*, Himalaya; erect, tufted, densely-branched shrublet, 15–30cm tall; leaves lanceolate, 4–5mm long, edged with a silvery membrane and fine hairs; flowers widely bell-shaped, sometimes tinged pink, 8–10mm wide. *C. hypnoides* (*Harrimanella h.*), Arctic and sub-Arctic Europe, Asia, N. America and mountains farther south; mat-forming, to 7cm tall; leaves linear, about 3mm long; flowers 4–5cm long, calyx red, on arching, thread-like, red stalks, to 2cm long. *C. lycopodioides*, N.E. Asia, N.W. N. America; prostrate, mat-forming, interlacing stems; leaves 2–3mm long, ovate; flowers 5–6mm long on stalks to 2·5cm long. *C. mertensiana*, W. N. America; erect to spreading, 15–30cm tall; leaves about 5mm long; flowers widely bell-shaped, to 6mm wide, calyx often reddish. *C.m.* Gracilis, semi-prostrate, forming a low mound of paler green foliage. *C. selaginoides*, Himalaya, W. China; tufted, of mainly erect habit, 5–25cm tall; leaves 2–3mm long, lanceolate, downy-margined; flowers 6–9mm long, glistening white on hairy stalks to 2·5cm long. *C.s.* L.S.E. 13284, Bhutan; dwarfer, with larger flowers than type species. *C. tetragona*, Arctic and sub-Arctic; mainly erect, to 25cm tall; leaves 4–5mm long, ovate-lanceolate, closely-overlapping, the leafy stems having a 4-angled appearance; flowers to 6mm or more long, often red-tinged. *C.t. saximontana*, N.W. N. America; flowers short-stalked and borne close to the stems. *C. wardii*, E. Himalaya; allied to *C. fastigiata* but lacking the silvery-margined membrane, plant neater and more erect, rarely above 15–20cm. Several hybrids have been raised between some of the described species and generally are easier to grow; recommended are: Edinburgh (*C. tetragona* × *C. fastigiata*), that blends the parental characters and is very free-flowering, and Muirhead (*C. lycopodioides* × *C. wardii*), that resembles the first parent but is more erect and with larger flowers.

Castanea

(ancient Latin name). FAGACEAE. A genus of 12 species of deciduous trees and shrubs from N. Hemisphere. Grow in well-drained but moisture-retentive soil in sun or light shade, preferably sheltered from cold winds; does well in sandy soils enriched with humus. Plant early autumn to late spring. Propagate from seed sown in the open ground when ripe or not later than the following early spring, cultivars by grafting in spring.

Species cultivated: *C. mollissima*, Chinese chestnut;

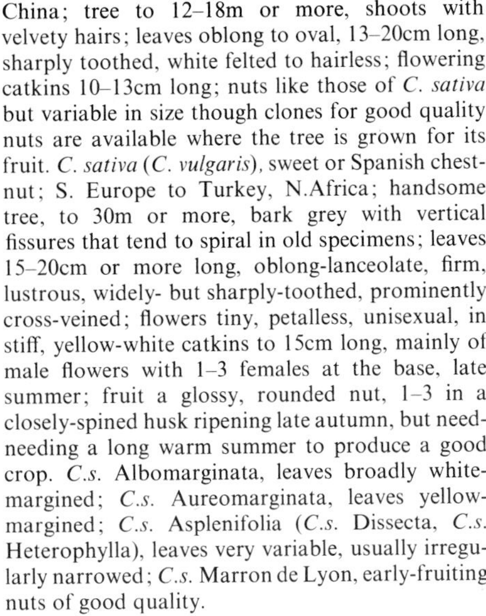

Left: *Castanea sativa* in fruit
Top: *Castanea sativa* ripe fruit
Above: *Catalpa bignonioides* in fruit

China; tree to 12–18m or more, shoots with velvety hairs; leaves oblong to oval, 13–20cm long, sharply toothed, white felted to hairless; flowering catkins 10–13cm long; nuts like those of *C. sativa* but variable in size though clones for good quality nuts are available where the tree is grown for its fruit. *C. sativa* (*C. vulgaris*), sweet or Spanish chestnut; S. Europe to Turkey, N.Africa; handsome tree, to 30m or more, bark grey with vertical fissures that tend to spiral in old specimens; leaves 15–20cm or more long, oblong-lanceolate, firm, lustrous, widely- but sharply-toothed, prominently cross-veined; flowers tiny, petalless, unisexual, in stiff, yellow-white catkins to 15cm long, mainly of male flowers with 1–3 females at the base, late summer; fruit a glossy, rounded nut, 1–3 in a closely-spined husk ripening late autumn, but need-needing a long warm summer to produce a good crop. *C.s.* Albomarginata, leaves broadly white-margined; *C.s.* Aureomarginata, leaves yellow-margined; *C.s.* Asplenifolia (*C.s.* Dissecta, *C.s.* Heterophylla), leaves very variable, usually irregularly narrowed; *C.s.* Marron de Lyon, early-fruiting nuts of good quality.

Castor-oil plant – see *Ricinus*.

Cat's foot – see *Antennaria*.

Cat-tail – see *Typha*.

Catalpa

(N. American Indian vernacular name in Latin form). BIGNONIACEAE. A genus of 11 species of deciduous and evergreen trees from America, W. Indies, E. Asia. They have opposite pairs of long-stalked ovate, usually cordate leaves and terminal panicles of tubular, 5-lobed, somewhat foxglove-like flowers followed by slender, bean-shaped fruit. Grow in humus-rich, well-drained soil in sunny site sheltered from strong, cold winds. Plant autumn to spring. Propagate from seed in spring or cuttings with a heel in a propagating case with bottom heat about 18–21°C, late summer, or from root cuttings in winter.

Species cultivated: *C. bignonioides*, Indian bean tree; S.E. USA; round-headed, deciduous tree 8–18m; leaf-blades rounded to shallowly cordate at base, 10–25cm long – larger in young or coppiced specimens – foetid when bruised; flowers to 4cm long, lobes frilled, white-, yellow- and purple-spotted within, borne in pyramidal clusters 20–25cm long, late summer; fruit pendulous, to 40cm long. *C.b.* Aurea, leaves soft yellow; variegated and dwarf forms are known. *C.* × *erubescens* (*C.* × *hybrida*), (*C. bignonioides* × *C. ovata*), blends parental characters; leaves 3-lobed and entire; flowers smaller than *C. bignonioides* but more prolific. *C. ovata* (*C. kaempferi*), China; to 10m, habit spreading; leaf-blades broadly ovate, usually 3-lobed, 12–25cm long; flowers 2–2·5cm long, white, flushed yellow and spotted red, in narrow panicles to 25cm long, late summer; fruit to 30cm. *C. speciosa*, C. USA; to 30m in its homeland, but rarely above 18m in Britain, crown usually conical; leaf-blades broadly ovate-cordate, long-pointed, to 30cm long, inodorous when bruised; flowers to 5cm long, lobes frilled, white-, yellow- and purple-spotted within, summer; fruit to 45cm.

Catananche

(Greek *katanangke*, meaning a strong incentive – the plant was formerly used in love potions). COMPOSITAE. A genus of 5 species of annuals and perennials from Mediterranean. They are of tufted habit with narrow, basal leaves and wiry stems bearing somewhat daisy-like flower-heads of ray-florets only, and surrounded by glossy, papery bracts like those of an everlasting flower. 1 perennial species is commonly grown: *C. caerulea*, blue cupidone; Portugal to Italy; leaves 10–30cm long, linear to narrowly lanceolate, often with a few, slender basal-lobes, stems branched, 50–80cm tall; flower-heads about 3cm wide, solitary, lavender-blue, summer. *C.c.* Bicolor, flowers white with blue centre; *C.c.* Major, flowers larger and brighter. Grow in any well-drained soil in a sunny site. Plant spring or autumn. Propagate from seed in spring or root cuttings late winter.

Catchfly – see *Silene* and *Lychnis*.

Catmint – see *Nepeta*.

Ceanothus

(Greek *keanothos* – a spiny plant and taken up by Linnaeus for this genus). California lilac. RHAMNACEAE. A genus of 55 species of shrubs and small trees from N. America, mainly California. Largely evergreen with alternate or opposite, ovate to linear-oblong leaves and axillary or terminal umbels or panicles of tiny, blue/purple/white/pink flowers often borne in profusion. Individual blooms have starry, almost petaloid calyces, with 5, broad, pointed lobes and 5, stalked (clawed), hooded, ladle-shaped petals. Grow in any well-drained soil in a sunny, sheltered site. Unless otherwise stated, the species and cultivars described are hardy in Britain if grown against walls, fences or in sunny shrub borders. Specimens of *C. americanus*, *C. coeruleus* and their hybrid cultivars (*C.* × *delilianus*) should be pruned hard in spring, cutting back all the previous season's stems to about 4 buds. The evergreen species are best when allowed to develop their natural habit of growth, though wall-trained specimens may need to have forward-growing

Left: *Catalpa bignonioides*
Bottom left: *Catananche caerulea*
Below: *Ceanothus* × Edinburgh

autumn. *C. cyaneus*, erect habit to 3m or more; leaves ovate-elliptic, 2·5–6cm long, lustrous above, dull beneath; flowers a clear bright blue in cylindrical panicles 5–13cm long. *C.* × *delilianus* (*C.* × *arnouldii*), (*C. americanus* × *C. coeruleus*), group of deciduous hybrid cultivars that may include some derived from *C. ovatus*, a species closely allied to *C. americanus*; 1–2m tall; leaves ovate, sometimes broadly heart-shaped, downy beneath, finely-toothed, 4–8cm long; flowers sky-blue in terminal panicles, summer to autumn. *C.* × *d.* Gloire de Versailles, large panicles of powder-blue flowers – the best-known cultivar; *C.* × *d.* Henri Defosse, similar to *C.* × *d.* Gloire de Versailles but flowers deep blue; *C.* × *d.* Indigo, very deep blue, but not quite as hardy as *C.* × *d.* Henri Defosse; *C.* × *d.* Marie Simon, flowers pink; *C.* × *d.* Perle Rose, carmine-pink; *C.* × *d.* Topaz, indigo-blue. *C. dentatus*, 1·5–2m tall; leaves 5–12mm long sometimes longer, linear-oblong to elliptic, appearing smaller because of inrolled margins (set with gland-tipped teeth), glossy deep green above, grey-felted beneath; flowers bright blue in small, rounded panicles. *C.d. floribundus* (*C. floribundus*), leaves broader and less rolled than type species, very profusely-blooming – sometimes confused in cultivation with *C.* × *lobbianus* and *C.* × *veitchianus*. *C.* × Edinburgh (*C.* × Edinensis) see next species. *C. foliosus* (*C. austromontanus*, *C. dentatus dickeyi*), spreading to semi-prostrate, 45–120cm tall; leaves generally 1-veined, glossy, oval to broadly-oblong, 6–20mm long, margins wavy, recurved, with gland-tipped teeth; flowers dark blue in rounded clusters to 2·5cm wide. *C.f. vineatus*, creeping, spreading habit; leaves larger than type species, broadly-elliptic – *C. austromontanus* of some catalogues belongs here. *C.f.* Italian Skies, more vigorous than type, to 1·5m tall by twice as wide; flowers brilliant blue. *C.* × Edinburgh (*C.* × Edinensis), hybrid with *C. griseus*, forming bushy shrub to 2m, pale blue flowers. *C. gloriosus* (*C. prostratus grandifolius*), prostrate or decumbent, 10–30cm tall by up to 3m wide; leaves 1–4cm long, elliptic to broadly-oblong, prominently sharply-toothed, dark glossy green; flowers deep purple-blue in umbels; in the wild an erect form (*C.g. exaltatus*), to 3m tall, is known. *C. griseus* (*C. thrysiflorus griseus*), rather like *C.*

Above: *Ceanothus* Delight
Right: *Ceanothus thyrsiflorus repens*

shoots spurred back after flowering. Plant spring. Propagate by soft-tip cuttings in spring or firmer shoots with a heel in summer, with bottom heat about 18°C. Seed may be sown under glass in spring but germinates erratically unless heat-treated, ie placed in a small cloth bag, and dropped into freshly-boiled water that is then allowed to cool and stand for up to 24 hours before sowing. Where convenient, layering may be carried out in spring.

Species cultivated (all from California and spring-flowering unless otherwise stated): *C. arboreus*, large shrub or bushy tree to 5m or more; leaves broadly-ovate, 2·5–8cm long; flowers pale blue, in axillary panicles 5–10cm or more long; one of the less hardy species best only in the milder climates or needing a large expanse of very sheltered wall. *C.a.* Trewithen Blue, flowers deep blue, lightly fragrant, probably marginally hardier. *C. azureus*, see *C. coeruleus*. *C. austromontanus*, see *C. foliosus*. *C.* × Autumnal Blue (*C.* × *delilianus* Indigo × *C. thyrsiflorus*), to 2m or more; leaves oval with 3 prominent veins, glossy above, greyish beneath, 1·5–4cm long; flowers mid-blue in panicles to 8cm long, summer to autumn. *C.* × Burkwoodii (*C. floribundus* of gardens, × *C.* × *delilianus* Indigo), similar to *C.* × Autumnal Blue, but leaves and panicles a little smaller and flowers a rich bright blue. *C.* Burtonensis, see *C. impressus*. *C.* Cascade, see *C. thyrsiflorus*. *C. coeruleus* (*C. azureus*), Mexico; deciduous, to 2m or more; leaves ovate, 2·5–6cm long, toothed, rusty-haired beneath; flowers deep blue in terminal and sub-terminal panicles 6–15cm long, summer to *thrysiflorus*, but leaves with fine grey hairs beneath and flowers violet-blue in smaller panicles; a prostrate form (*C.g. horizontalis*) is known in the wild. *C. impressus* (*C. dentatus impressus*), spreading habit, to 1·5m tall (double this on a wall); leaves 6–12mm long, elliptic to almost orbicular, the veins deeply-impressed, lustrous deep green, hairy, especially below, margins rolled; flowers rich mid-blue in clusters to 2·5cm long. *C.i.* Puget Blue, hybrid, more robust than type species; flowers deeper blue. *C.i.* Burtonensis is a vigorous hybrid, probably with *C. thyrsiflorus* as the other parent; leaves larger and more consistently-rounded. *C.* × *lobbianus* (*C. griseus* × *C. dentatus*), vigorous shrub to 3m or more; leaves 2–3cm long, elliptic-oblong with 3 main veins, dark – somewhat lustrous – green; flowers bright blue in ovoid clusters. *C.x.l.* Russellianus (*C. dentatus* Russellianus of gardens), leaves smaller and very glossy. *C. papillosus* (*C. dentatus p.*), spreading shrub 1·5–4·5m tall, young stems downy and roughish; leaves 1–5cm long, elliptic to linear with a blunt or truncated tip, lustrous green and glandular hairs above, felted beneath; flowers deep blue in racemes 1–5cm long. *C.p. roweanus*, low spreading habit; leaves narrower. *C. prostratus*, squaw carpet, mat-forming to 3m wide; leaves opposite, elliptic to spathulate with a few coarse teeth, 6–30mm long; flowers mid- to bright blue in umbels to 2·5cm wide; a variable species in the wild with both larger and smaller leaves. *C. rigidus*, spreading habit with a dense, intricate branch system, to 1·2m tall (more than twice this on a wall); leaves opposite, cuneate-obovate to narrowly-elliptic, toothed, dark glossy green, 3–12mm long; flowers purple-blue in umbels. *C.* Delight is a hybrid with *C. rigidus*, vigorous and hardy, with profuse, rich blue flowers. *C.* × Southmead, similar to *C.* × *lobbianus* and probably of the same parentage, of dense habit with bright blue flowers. *C. thrysiflorus*, blue blossom, large shrub or small tree to 9m; leaves ovate-oblong to broadly-elliptic, with 3 main veins, glandular-toothed, glossy rich green 2–5cm long; flowers pale blue in panicles to 7·5cm long. *C.t. repens*, creeping blue blossom, prostrate habit, forming low, wide mounds; *C.t.* Cascade, like the type species but with arching branches and powder-blue flowers. *C.* × *veitchianus* (*C.* × *v.* Brilliant), (probably *C. griseus* × *C. rigidus*), vigorous, to 3m; leaves obovate, glandular-toothed, glossy above, greyish beneath; flowers deep bright blue, in clusters to 5cm long, very hardy and free-flowering; regrettably, sometimes sold as *C. dentatus*, *C.d. floribundus* and *C.* × *lobbianus*.

Cedronella – see *Agastache*.

Cedrus

(Latin *cedrus*, Greek *kedros*, for a coniferous tree—probably a species of *Juniperus*, but taken up by C. J. Trew for this genus). PINACEAE. A genus of 3 or 4 species of evergreen coniferous trees from N. Africa, E. Mediterranean, Himalaya. They have needle-like leaves and are imposing, mainly large, trees, pyramidal when young, ultimately broad and flat-topped with layered, horizontal branches when old. The branchlets are of 2 kinds; leading or long ones that extend the size of the tree each year, bearing spirally-arranged leaves – and short spurs that grow very slowly and bear a terminal rosette of leaves. The latter sometimes grow out into long shoots and on mature trees produce flowers (strobili) in autumn. Male strobili are catkin-like, shedding abundant, pale yellow pollen when ripe; the females are like miniature versions of the erect, mature, barrel-shaped cones, green or purplish. Cones take 2 years to mature, then fall apart to release the winged seed. Grow in well-drained, moisture-retentive soil in a sunny site. Plant autumn or spring. Propagate from seed in spring. Cultivars, particularly the

Above and right: *Cedrus atlantica* Glauca Pendula
Far right: *Cedrus libani*

dwarf mutants, must be propagated by cuttings with a heel in late summer or grafted onto true species seedlings in a propagating case in early spring.

Species cultivated: *C. atlantica*, Atlas or Algerian cedar; mountains of Atlas in Algeria, Morocco; to 40m; leaves cylindrical, glossy deep green, 1–2·5cm long; male strobili tinted reddish, to 4cm long, mid autumn; mature cones to 8cm long, purplish to pale brown. *C. a. glauca*, leaves silvery to bright blue-grey, the commonest form in cultivation; *C.a.g.* Argentea has the most intense leaf coloration; *C.a.* Pendula and *C.a.* Glauca Pendula are low-growing, rarely to 10m, with branches and leader pendulous; *C.a.* Fastigiata, narrowly columnar; *C.a.* Aurea, foliage yellow, slow-growing and lacks vigour. *C. brevifolia*, see *C. libani*. *C. deodara*, deodar; Himalaya; to 36m cultivated (twice this height in the wild), elegantly pyramidal when young, with pendulous branchlet tips; leaves 2·5–4cm long or more, dark green, faintly grey-lined; male strobili 6–7cm, purple before shedding pollen in late autumn; cones to 14cm long. *C.d.* Aurea, leaves golden in spring, fading to greenish-yellow. *C. libani*, Cedar of Lebanon; S.E. Turkey, Syria; to 40m high, very broad-headed when mature; leaves 2–3cm long, dark green to grey or bluish; male strobili whitish-green to 5cm long, late autumn; cones 9–15cm long, greyish to pinkish-brown. *C.l. brevifolia* (*C. brevifolia*), Cyprus cedar; Cyprus; smaller and slower-growing, rarely to 18m; leaves 7–15mm long; cones cylindrical, to 12cm. *C.l.* Nana, dense, slow-growing, somewhat conical bush to 1·5m or so; *C.l.* Sargentii (*C.l.* Pendula Sargentii), small, slow-growing bush with down-curving branches and bluish-grey leaves.

Celandine – see *Ranunculus ficaria*.

Celandine poppy – see *Stylophorum*.

Celastrus

(Greek *kelastros*, for an unspecified evergreen tree, inappropriately used by Linnaeus for this genus). CELASTRACEAE. A genus of 30 species of shrubs and woody climbers mainly from the tropics and sub-tropics. They have alternate, elliptic to ovate leaves, axillary clusters of small, 5-petalled, greenish to yellowish flowers, and rounded capsules of small, 5-petalled, greenish to yellowish flowers, and rounded capsules that – when ripe – split open to show a coloured inner surface and seed covered with a fleshy, red aril. With 1 exception the species described are deciduous climbers. Grow in humus-rich, moisture-retentive soil in sun or partial shade, and provide support for the twining stems. Plant autumn to spring. Propagate from seed when ripe, or layering in spring. No pruning is required except

to limit growth where necessary, best done in late winter. Interesting plants for a tall, dead tree-stump or unwanted tree.

Species cultivated: *C. angulatus* (*C. latifolia*), China; strong-growing scrambling shrub to 3m tall by twice as wide; leaves broadly oval, 10–20cm long, shallowly-toothed; flowers greenish in panicles 10–15cm long; fruit 12mm wide, orange within. *C. articulatus*, see *C. orbiculatus*. *C. hypoleucus* (*C. hypoglaucus*), China; to 6m or more, shoots covered with a purplish, waxy patina; leaves oblong or obovate, 10–15cm long, dark green above, glaucous beneath; flowers yellowish in racemes; fruit like a large pea, yellowish within. *C. orbiculatus* (*C. articulatus*), N.E. Asia; vigorous, to 12m through a tree, stems spiny when young; leaves broadly-obovate to rounded, shallowly-toothed; flowers dioecious or bisexual in clusters of 2–4, green; fruit pea-like, opening glossy yellow with scarlet seed, autumn. *C. scandens*, staff tree; E. N. America; much like *C. orbiculatus*, but flowers yellow-white in racemes or panicles and inner surface of capsules orange; and male and female plants, must be grown together to get a crop of fruit.

Celmisia

(for *Celmisios*, in Greek mythology son of the nymph Alciope – for whom a related genus was named). COMPOSITAE. A genus of 65 species of evergreen perennials and sub-shrubs from New Zealand, Australia, Tasmania. They form tufted rosettes or mats of linear to obovate, often white-woollen leaves and solitary, white, daisy-like flower-heads. Grow in well-drained, lime-free soil, preferably largely of peat and granite or flint chips. Most species do well under scree conditions but must not become dry at the roots. Plant spring. Propagate from seed (often not fertile or of low viability) in spring, cuttings in spring or late summer, division (where possible) in spring.

Species cultivated (all from New Zealand and summer-flowering): *C. angustifolia*, small sub-shrub to 15cm or more tall; leaves 3–5cm long, linear, leathery, somewhat sticky – satiny, white, woolly beneath, lightly woolly above when young; flower-heads 2·5–4cm wide on sticky stalks to 15cm. *C. argentea*, sub-shrub forming hummocks to 15cm or more tall; leaves dense, 6–12mm long, linear, silvery-white woolly flower-heads sessile, 6-12cm wide. *C. bellidioides*, mat-forming; leaves 7–12mm long, spathulate, smooth, glossy, dark green; flower-heads to 2cm wide, spring to summer. *C. coriacea*, tufted or clump-forming; leaves lanceolate, 20–40cm long, covered with white, glistening, cottony hairs; flower-heads 4–7cm wide or more on stalks to 40cm tall. *C. hectori*, sub-shrub, forming low hummocks to 60cm wide; leaves in rosettes, 1–2cm long, linear to spathulate, white-haired, satiny beneath; flower-heads 1–2·5cm wide on stalks to 10cm. *C. incana*, mountain musk; mat-forming sub-shrub; leaves in rosettes, 2–4cm long, obovate-oblong, dense white wool; flower-heads 2·5–3·5cm wide on stems to 10cm. *C. ramulosa*, erect or semi-erect shrub to 30cm tall; leaves closely-packed, linear-oblong, pale green above, dense white wool beneath, margins rolled; flower-heads to 2·5cm wide on stalks to 4cm. *C. sessiliflora*, white cushion daisy; low sub-shrub forming mats or cushions to 10cm tall; leaves linear, 1·2cm long, rigid, in dense rosettes, with closely-pressed white hairs; flower-heads 1–2cm wide, almost stalkless. *C. spectabilis*, cotton daisy; tufted to wide clump-forming; leaves 10–15cm long, ovate to lance-oblong, shining green above, pale buff- or white-felted beneath; flower-heads to 5cm wide on hairy, cottony stalks 10–25cm tall. *C. traversii*, brown mountain daisy; tufted to clump-forming; leaves 15–25cm long, broadly oblong-lanceolate, leathery, rich green above, with brown, velvety, wool-like covering beneath; flower-heads 4–5cm wide, on brown, hairy stalks 20–30cm tall. *C. walkeri* (*C. webbii* of gardens), semi-prostrate shrub; stems 1–2cm long; leaves dense, 3·5cm long, oblong-lanceolate to obovate-oblong, somewhat sticky above, white-woollen beneath; flower-heads to 4cm wide, on hairy, glandular stalks to 15cm.

Celsia arcturus – see *Verbascum arcturus*.

Top left: *Celastrus orbiculatus*
Below: *Celmisia hectori*
Bottom: *Celmisia coriacea*
Right below: *Centaurea cineraria*
Right bottom: *Centaurea cyanus* Polka Dot

Centaurea

(centauros or centaur, in Greek mythology half man, half horse). COMPOSITAE. A genus of 600 species of annuals, biennials, perennials, sub-shrubs and shrubs from Europe, N. Africa to N. India and China, N. and S. America. They vary much in foliage and form but are typified by their flower-heads. These are composed of many tubular florets, each with a somewhat bell-shaped mouth and 5, slender lobes, the outer ring sometimes longer than the rest and equivalent to the ray florets of a usual daisy flower. The bracts that enclose the heads frequently have chaffy, fan-shaped tips, usually notched or fringed. Grow the species described in well-drained, fertile soil in a sunny site. The generally sub-shrubby, half-hardy to tender species grown as summer bedding plants need to be lifted in autumn, potted or boxed and kept in a frost-free greenhouse. Alternatively, cuttings can be taken and the old plants discarded. Propagate the annuals from seed in the early autumn or in spring, the perennials by division in the autumn or spring or from seed in spring, the sub-shrubs by cuttings in the late summer.

Species cultivated: *C. cana*, see *C. triumfetti*. *C. candidissima*, see *C. rutifolia*. *C. cineraria* (*C. gymnocarpa*), dusty miller; Italy to W. coast Sicily); somewhat tender sub-shrub to 80cm; leaves with dense, grey-white hairs, pinnatisect or bi-pinnatisect, often lyrate, long – arching to 30cm or more – having a fern-like quality; flower-heads 2–3cm, rose-purple, in clusters, late summer, rarely produced on plants grown annually for summer bedding schemes. *C. cyanus*, cornflower; S. E. Europe, naturalized elsewhere; hardy annual to

Top: *Centaurea macrocephala*
Above: *Centaurea montana*
Right: *Centranthus ruber*
Right below: *Cephalaria gigantea*
Far right: *Cephalotaxus harringtonia drupacea*

90cm tall, well-branched, particularly if autumn-sown; leaves lanceolate, usually remotely-toothed, sometimes narrowly-lobed; flower-heads solitary, 2·5–5cm wide, in shades of blue, purple, red, pink and white, summer. Several cultivars and strains are available, including dwarfs to 30cm, eg *C.c.* Polka Dot. *C. dealbata*, Caucasus; hardy, widely clump-forming perennial; stems 45–95cm; leaves pinnatisect, green above, grey-white hair beneath, long stalked; flower-heads 5–7cm wide, lilac-pink, summer. *C.d.* John Coutts, see *C. hypoleuca*; *C.d.* Steenbergii, rose-crimson, late summer, autumn. *C. gymnocarpa*, see *C. cineraria*. *C. hypoleuca*, Turkey, Iran, Transcaucasia; hardy perennial; stems 30–60cm tall; leaves lyrate-pinnate to pinnatipartite, green above, white-haired beneath; flower-heads 4–5cm wide, pink, summer, closely akin to *C. dealbata*. *C.h.* John Coutts, to 60cm tall; flower-heads deep rose – formerly mis-identified as form of *C. dealbata*. *C. imperialis*, see *C. moschata*. *C. macrocephala*, Caucasus; clump-forming hardy perennial; stems 90cm tall; leaves oblong-lanceolate, shortly-decurrent; flower-heads rich yellow, solitary, to 8cm or more wide, summer. *C. montana*, mountains of Europe; hardy rhizomatous perennial; stems winged, 40–60cm tall; leaves ovate to lanceolate, sometimes remotely toothed or lobed, woolly beneath; flower-heads 5–7cm wide, deep purple-blue, shaded reddish in centre, late spring to summer. *C.m.* Alba, flowers white; *C.m.* Rosea or *C.m.* Carnea, pink; *C.m.* Rubra, rose-red. *C. moschata* (*Amberboa moschata*), sweet sultan; S. W. Asia; hardy annual or biennial to 60cm tall; leaves greyish-green, entire, lanceolate to pinnately lobed or lyrate; flower-heads solitary, fragrant, white, yellow, red-purple to pink, 4–5cm wide, summer. *C.m. imperialis*, the commonest form, with flowers to 8cm wide. *C. pulcherrima* (*Aethiopappus p.*), Caucasus; stems 60–75cm tall; hardy perennial; leaves pinnate; flower-heads brilliant rose-pink, about 6cm wide, summer. *C. pulchra*, Kashmir; perennial; stems 30–40cm tall; leaves pinnate, the lobes linear; flower-heads purple-rose, about 4cm wide. *C.p. Major*, the commonest form in cultivation; stems to 60cm; flowers larger; not reliably hardy during the coldest winters. *C. ruthenica*, E. Europe; hardy perennial with woody rhizomes; stems to 1m or more; leaves to 25cm long, pinnatipartite to pinnate, lobes linear, toothed, deep green; flower-heads about 4cm wide, pale yellow, late summer. *C. rutifolia* (*C. candidissima* of gardens), S. E. Europe; somewhat tender evergreen perennial or sub-shrub; stems leafy, 20–80cm; leaves pinnatisect, velvety white hair; flower-heads 2–4cm wide, pink, late summer, but not commonly produced when grown annually as a bedding plant. *C. simplicicaulis*, Turkey; hardy perennial with spreading rhizomes; leaves lyrate to pinnatisect with broad segments, grey-white hair beneath; flower-heads rose-pink, 3–4cm wide on unbranched stems 20–30cm tall, summer.

Centranthus

(*Kentranthus*). (Greek *kentron*, a spur, and *anthos*, a flower – the flowers have a nectar-bearing spur). VALERIANACEAE. A genus of 12 species of annuals and perennials from Europe and Mediterranean. 1 species is generally available: *C. ruber*, C. and S. Europe, N. Africa, Turkey, naturalized elsewhere; bushy, woody-based perennial 40–90cm tall; leaves in opposite pairs, ovate to lanceolate, often somewhat glaucous, to 10cm long; flowers 8–10mm long, tubular with a slender basal spur and 5 oblong lobes, borne in a terminal panicle, red, pink or white, summer to autumn. Grow in any well-drained soil in a sunny site – it often becomes naturalized in old walls. Plant spring or summer. Propagate from seed when ripe or spring, or by cuttings of basal shoots in late spring.

Cephalaria

(Greek *kephale*, a head – the small flowers are arranged in a dense head, like those of scabious). DIPSACACEAE. A genus of 65 species of annuals and perennials from the Mediterranean to C. Asia and S. Africa. 1 species is generally available: *C. gigantea* (*C. tatarica* of gardens), giant or yellow scabious; Siberia; hardy, clump-forming perennial 1·5–2m tall; leaves pinnate, dark green; flower-heads solitary, 6–8cm wide, primrose-yellow, summer. Grow in humus-rich soil in a sunny site. Plant autumn or spring. Propagate from seed or division in spring.

Cephalotaxus

(Greek *kephale*, head, and *Taxus* yew – some of the species resemble common yew). CEPHALOTAXACEAE. A genus of 4–7 species of large, evergreen, coniferous shrubs or small trees from E. Asia. They have linear, pointed leaves in 2 opposite ranks, small, usually dioecious strobili composed of a cluster of bracts and ovules or stamens, and plum-like fruit formed from 1 ovule. Plant in humus-rich soil in sun or partial shade preferably sheltered from cold winds. The species described are hardy. They stand clipping and can be used for hedging. Propagate from seed in autumn or by cuttings with a heel late summer.

Species cultivated: *C. fortunei*, China; usually a large shrub 3–6m tall (to 12m in its homeland); leaves 5–9cm long, dark lustrous green above, pale beneath, the 2 ranks in 1 plane, male strobili globose, 5–6mm wide, spring; fruit ovoid, brownish-olive, 2·5–3cm long. *C. harringtonia* (*C. drupacea*, *C. pedunculata*, *Taxus harringtonia*), Korea, China,

Japan; spreading shrub 3–4m tall (to 12m in the wild); leaves 2–6·5cm long, mid to deep green above, having 2 glaucous bands beneath; fruit olive-green, 2–2·5cm long. *C.h. drupacea*, Japan; leaf ranks held in a V-formation, male strobili to 8mm wide – the commonest form in cultivation. *C.h.* Fastigiata, branches erect like those of Irish yew.

Cerastium

(Greek *keras*, horn – alluding to the shape of the curved seed capsules of many species). CARYOPHYLLACEAE. A genus of 60 species mainly of low-growing annuals and perennials from the temperate regions of both hemispheres. They have opposite pairs of ovate to linear leaves and terminal cymes of white flowers each having 5, notched to deeply cleft, petals. Grow in well-drained soil in a sunny site. Plant autumn to spring. Propagate from seed or by division in spring, or basal cuttings in spring or late summer.

Species cultivated: *C. alpinum lanatum*, Alpine mouse-ear chickweed; circumpolar, south to mountains of Europe, N. America, Asia; mat-forming perennial to 15cm wide; leaves 10–18mm long, oblanceolate to obovate, with covering of dense white wool; flowering stems ascending, 5–10cm or more long, flowers 1–4, about 10–12mm wide, summer; best in scree or gritty soil. *C. biebersteinii*, Russia to Crimea; mat-forming, rhizomatous and far-creeping; white, silky-woollen leaves 1–5cm long, lanceolate to linear; cymes of 3–15 flowers, each about 2cm wide, late spring to summer – see next species also. *C. tomentosum*, snow-in-summer, dusty miller; C. and S. Appenines, Sicily; much like *C. biebersteinii*, but more grey-white woollen and teeth of open seed capsule with rolled margins (those of *biebersteinii* being flat). *C.t. columnae* (*C. album*), leaves much whiter than type; crosses with *C. biebersteinii*, and hybrids often masquerade under the species names; both species and hybrids are very invasive and not suitable for the rock garden.

Cerasus – see *Prunus*.

Ceratostigma

(Greek *keras*, horn – from the horn-like outgrowths of the stigma). PLUMBAGINACEAE. A genus of 8 species of shrubs and perennials from E. Africa and Asia. The species described are deciduous with alternate lanceolate to obovate leaves, and dense head or spike-like terminal panicles of tubular blue flowers, each having 5 broad petal-lobes. Grow in well-drained soil in a sheltered, sunny site. Plant spring. Propagate the shrubs by cuttings with a heel late summer or careful division of well-suckered plants spring; the perennial also by division.

Species cultivated (all flowering summer to autumn):

Far left: *Cerastium tomentosum*
Bottom left: *Cercidiphyllum japonicum*
Above: *Ceratostigma plumbaginoides*
Below: *Cercis siliquastrum*

C. griffithii, E. Himalaya, China; spreading bushy shrub to 60cm or more, stems bristly; leaves obovate, pointed, 1–3cm long, turning red in autumn; flowers to 2cm wide in spiky clusters. Top growth may be cut during severe frosts. *C. plumbaginoides* (*Plumbago larpentae*), leadwort; China; hardy herbaceous perennial spreading underground and forming colonies; stems 30–45cm long, erect to reclining; leaves obovate, 2–5cm long, some turning red in autumn; flowers about 2cm wide in head-like clusters. *C. willmottianum*, W. China; shrub 60–120cm tall, stems bristly, often reddish; leaves lanceolate to diamond-shaped, 2–5cm long, some reddening in autumn; flowers about 2cm wide in compact ovoid heads. Best in the South.

Cercidiphyllum

(from *Cercis*, and Greek *phyllon*, a leaf – the leaves resemble a *Cercis* species). CERCIDIPHYLLACEAE. A genus of 1 species of deciduous hardy tree from China, Japan. *C. japonicum*, katsura; to more than 30m in the wild, seldom above 18m in Britain. bark fissured, sometimes spirally, finally peeling in shaggy strips, head conical to ovoid, the outer branches pendulous; leaves in opposite pairs, broadly ovate to rounded, shallowly-cordate and toothed to 8cm long, grey to sea-green above, glaucous beneath, coppery-pink when young, yellow to pink-flushed in autumn; flowers before leaves in late spring, dioecious, petalless, insignificant; fruit claw-like pods to 2cm long; seed winged. The young leaves of this tree are frequently killed by spring frosts but recovery is usually rapid and good growth is made each summer. *C.j. sinense* is the Chinese form but differs only in small and unreliable ways from the Japanese type: *C.j. magnificum*, Japan; bark smoother, leaves somewhat larger, more obviously cordate and toothed; seed longer. Grow in moisture-retentive, humus-rich soil in sun or partial shade sheltered from strong cold winds. Plant autumn to spring. Propagate from seed or layering in spring.

Cercis

(ancient Greek *kerkis* for the European species – and probably also poplar – taken up by Linnaeus). LEGUMINOSAE. A genus of 7 species of deciduous shrubs and trees from the N. Hemisphere. They have alternate, broadly ovate to rounded leaves, pea-like flowers often borne directly on the larger stems and branches (cauliflorous), and broad, flat, wing-like pods dispersed by wind. Grow in well-drained soil in a sunny site, preferably sheltered from strong northerly winds. Plant autumn or spring. Propagate from seed in spring, preferably under glass. Germination is erratic and may take several months or even years. Best in the south.

Species cultivated (all late-spring flowering): *C. canadensis*, redbud; E. and C. N. America; tree to 12m in the wild, often less and bushy in cultivation, leaves broadly heart-shaped, pointed, dull beneath, somewhat glaucous, 7–13cm wide; flowers pink, about 12mm long in clusters of 4–8. *C.c.* Alba, white flowered. *C. chinensis*, China; similar to *C. canadensis* but leaves a little larger and glossy below; not always successful in gardens and usually best on a sunny wall. *C. occidentalis*, western redbud; California; often a shrub in gardens, but a tree to 6m in its home environment; leaves rounded, cordate, often notched at tip; flowers rose-pink; rather more tender than the other species. *C. racemosa*, China; tree eventually to 12m; leaves heart-shaped, 6·5–13cm wide, smooth dark green above, paler and downy beneath; flowers pink in pendant racemes of 30–40; pod 7–13cm long. *C. siliquastrum*, Judas tree; S. E. Europe, Turkey, W. Syria; shrub or tree occasionally to 12m, head irregularly rounded; leaves rounded, cordate, sea-green or glaucous beneath, darker or yellowish above; flowers 2cm long, bright rose-purple, in clusters of 3–6; pods about 10cm long, red to red-brown. *C.s.* Alba, flowers white; several darker-flowered forms are known, including *C.s.* Bodnant, red-purple; of available *Cercis* species this is one of the best for gardens.

Chaenomeles

(Greek *chaino*, to gape, and *meles*, an apple – meaning not clear, probably alluding to the large hollow core of the fruit). ROSACEAE. A genus of 3 species of deciduous shrubs from China and Japan. Sometimes thorny, they have alternate obovate to lanceolate leaves with large stipules, cup-shaped 5-petalled flowers and quince-like aromatic fruit. Grow in humus-rich, well-drained soil in sun or partial shade, either as free-standing bushes, a hedge or trained to a wall. Plant autumn to spring. Propagate by layering in spring for the cultivars, from seed when ripe for the species.

Species cultivated: *C. cathayensis* (*C. lagenaria wilsonii*, *Cydonia cathayensis*), erect shrub to 3m or more, usually rather sparingly-branched with long thorns; leaves 7–13cm long, finely-toothed; flowers in small clusters, each about 4cm wide, white, flushed pink, spring; fruit 10–15cm long, roughly ovoid, yellow, inedible, even when cooked. *C.* × *californica* (*C. cathayensis* × *C.* × *superba*), much like the first parent but with large flowers to 5cm wide, in shades of pink and rose-red. *C.* × *c.* Enchantress, deep rose-pink is generally hardy in the south, unreliable elsewhere *C. japonica* (*Pyrus j.*, *P. maulei*, *Cydonia japonica*, *C. maulei*), Japan; suckering shrub, usually less than 1m tall; stems thorny, minutely-warted; leaves 2·5–5cm long, obovate to rounded, coarsely-toothed, stipules ovate, large, on young stems to 2cm wide; flowers 3–4cm wide, orange to blood-red, spring, usually freely borne; fruit rather apple-like, yellow, often red-flushed making a tasty conserve; long ago confused with the Chinese *C. speciosa*, that is still known as Japonica to many gardeners. *C.j. alpina*, much smaller with procumbent to ascending stems. *C. lagenaria*, see *C. cathayensis* and next species. *C. speciosa* (*C. lagenaria*, *Cydonia lagonaria*, and – in part – *Pyrus japonica*). Japonica of gardens, Japanese quince; China and long cultivated in Japan; spreading, somewhat rounded shrub to 2m or more; leaves oval, 4–9cm long, finely-toothed, glossy green above, stipules kidney-shaped to 4cm wide on vigorous young stems; flowers 3·5–4·5cm wide, scarlet, lightly-fragrant, winter to spring; fruit green-yellow, 5–7cm long, rounded to ovoid, good for conserves; introduced as *Pyrus* or *Cydonia japonica*, but later found to be the Chinese species (long cultivated in Japan). Several cultivars are grown, among the best being *C.s.* Cardinalis, crimson-scarlet; *C.s.* Falconnet Charlet, double salmon-pink; *C.s.* Moerloosii, white and pink; *C.s.* Nivalis; pure white; *C.s.* Simonii, low-growing, flowers semi-double deep red; *C.s.* Umbilicata, deep pink. *C.* × *superba* (*C. japonica* × *C. speciosa*), group of hybrid cultivars midway in stature and foliage between parents with flowers ranging from white to pink, orange and crimson. Among recommended cultivars are: *C.* × *s.* Boule de Feu, orange-red; *C.* × *s.* Crimson and Gold, crimson, prominent yellow anthers; *C.* × *s.* Hever Castle, shrimp-pink; *C.* × *s.* Knap Hill Scarlet, orange-scarlet, very free-flowering; *C.* × *s.* Pink Lady, rose-pink; *C.* × *s.* Rowallane, rich glowing crimson, spreading habit but good on walls.

Top: *Cercis siliquastrum*
Centre: *Chaenomeles speciosa* Apple Blossom
Above: *Chaenomeles speciosa* Simonii
Right: *Chamaecyparis obtusa* Crippsii

Chain fern – see *Woodwardia*.

Chalk plant – see *Gypsophila*.

Chamaecyparis

(Greek *chamai*, on the ground or dwarf, and *kuparissos*, Cypress – meaning rather obscure as the species are mainly large trees). False cypress. CUPRESSACEAE. A genus of 7 species of evergreen coniferous trees from N. America, Japan, Taiwan. They are pyramidal to columnar in outline with a single, erect, central trunk and many small branches generally at right angles. The tiny leaves are carried in opposite, overlapping pairs and clothe-flattened, frond-like branchlets. The leaves are scale-like, those of each other pair pressed flat to the stem (the median or facial leaves), those in between being folded, flattened and keeled. In the seedling stage, larger, linear or awl-shaped leaves are produced and in some cultivars these juvenile leaves persist throughout the life of the tree. The strobili are small, males ovoid, yellow, red or brown, the females globular usually green, followed by round cones composed of 6–12, peltate, woody scales each bearing 2–5 winged seeds. Grow in humus-rich soil in sun or shade, preferably the former for shapely specimens. Plant autumn or spring. Propagate from seed in spring, cuttings with a heel in late summer – the latter method for cultivars that seldom come true from seed.

Species cultivated: *C. lawsoniana* (*Cupressus l.*), Lawson cypress, Oregon cedar, Port Orfod cedar, white cedar; N. W. California, S. W. Oregon; to 60m tall in the wild, but more commonly only half or a bit more in cultivation; leaves 1·5–6mm long on vigorous shoots, somewhat glaucous, rich green, the median ones bearing a central, rounded, translucent gland; male strobili oblong-ovoid, pink to crimson often in abundance, spring cones globular about 8mm wide, pale brown; a very variable species and about 200 forms have been given cultivar names; the following is a selection of the best known: *C.l.* Allumii, broadly-columnar, foliage blue-grey in large sprays; *C.l.* Aurea Densa, small conical bush, eventually to 2m, foliage golden-yellow; *C.l.* Ellwoodii, slow-growing bush but eventually to several metres tall, juvenile foliage deep grey-green, bluish in winter; *C.l.* Ellwood's Gold, like *C.l.* Ellwoodii but foliage sprays yellow tinted; *C.l.* Erecta (*C.l.* Erecta Viridis), columnar, compact when young, rich bright green; *C.l.* Filiformis, broadly-conical, loose habit, to 6m or more, branchlets with 1 or more pendulous,

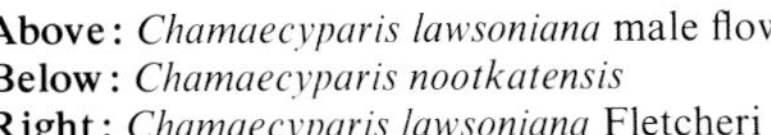

Above: *Chamaecyparis lawsoniana* male flowers
Below: *Chamaecyparis nootkatensis*
Right: *Chamaecyparis lawsoniana* Fletcheri

whip-like sprays; *C.l.* Fletcheri, dense, broad, columnar bush with bright blue-grey-green juvenile leaves, eventually to 10m or more; *C.l.* Gimbornii, dwarf dense globular bush, blue-green foliage with purple tints. *C.l. glauca*, blue-grey foliaged forms occur naturally in the wild – *C.l.g.* Blue Jacket, a good one; *C.l.* Green Hedger (*C.l.* Erecta Jackmanii), foliage bright green, good for hedging; *C.l.* Intertexta, very distinctive open habit with widely-dissected drooping branchlets; *C.l.* Kilmacurragh, very dense, narrow, columnar, dark green; *C.l.* Lanei, among the best of the yellow-foliaged cultivars; *C.l.* Lutea, golden-yellow foliage in large sprays, broad, columnar habit; *C.l.* Minima, slow-growing globular bush eventually to 2m; *C.l.* Minima Aurea, slow-growing (about 3cm a year) conical bush with golden-yellow foliage in vertical sprays; *C.l.* Nana, semi-globular bush eventually to 2m; *C.l.* Pottenii, columnar, dense habit, foliage sea-green in semi-erect feathery sprays; *C.l.* Stewartii, conical habit, foliage yellow to yellow-green in large sprays; *C.l.* Triomf van Boskoop, broad, conical, rather open habit, foliage bright blue-green; *C.l.* Wisselii, very distinctive, narrowly-conical, branches well-spaced, branchlets and shoots tufted – not flattened – dark bluish-green. *C. nootkatensis*, Nootka cypress, Alaska cedar, yellow cypress; N. California to Alaska; similar to Lawson cypress, but foliage sprays elegantly pendulous, narrower and more open; male strobili larger, yellow, cones 1cm wide, each scale with a pointed boss. *C.n.* Lutea (*C.n.* Aurea), young growth yellow, becoming yellow-green later; *C.n.* Glauca, leaves deep blue-green; *C.n.* Pendula, very pendulous the branchlets hanging in long streamers. *C. obtusa* (*Cupressus obtusa*, *Retinospora o. Thuja o.*), Hinoki cypress; Japan; to 36m in the wild, but often less in gardens; leaves blunt-tipped, 1–2mm long, glossy green above, white-lined beneath; male strobili dull yellow, very small, cones 8–10mm wide, orange-brown. Many cultivars are known, among the best being the following: *C.o.* Caespitosa (*C.o.* Nana Caespitosa), tiny, dense, bun-shaped bushlets to 10cm or so; *C.o.* Crippsii, loosely-conical to columnar habit, to 12m or so, foliage golden-yellow; *C.o.* Filicoides, fern spray cypress, irregular habit with pendant, fern-like leaf-sprays, slow-growing to 15m. *C.o. formosana*, Taiwan; smaller leaves and cones; *C.o.* Lycopodiodes, irregular habit, often sparsely-branched, foliage mossy and congested, dark blue-green, slow-growing (6–8cm a year); *C.o.* Minima (*C.o.* Nana Minima), dense, mossy cushion to 7cm or so; *C.o.* Nana, flat-topped bushlet with tiers of cupped, dark green branchlets, grows about 2cm a year; *C.o.* Nana Aurea, golden-yellow; *C.o.* Nana Gracilis, conical bush to 2m or more, foliage dark green in neat, rounded sprays; *C.o.* Pygmaea, dwarf, slow-growing bushlet to 60cm, rather wide-spreading, branchlets in tiers; *C.o.* Tetragona, irregular-habited bush or small tree, foliage sprays rather mossy and angular in outline; *C.o.* Tetragona Aurea, golden-yellow. *C. pisifera* (*Retinospora p. Cupressus p., Thuja p.*), Sawara cypress; Japan; to 30m or more in the wild, but often less in gardens leaves 3–5mm long with slender, spreading points, glossy green above, marked white below; male strobili pale brown, very small, cones about 6mm wide, pea-like. Many cultivars have arisen, some of the more important being: *C.p.* Boulevard (*C.p.* Cyanoviridis), conical bush to 6m with dense juvenile foliage tinted blue-grey to purple; *C.p.* Nana, dense, flat-topped hummock of dark green foliage, eventually to 60cm (at 2cm a year); *C.p.* Plumosa, large bush or small conical tree, juvenile leaves in plumy sprays; *C.p.* Plumosa Aurea, yellow-green, tinted bronze in winter; *C.p.* Plumosa Compressa, compact, bun-shaped bushlet with juvenile foliage; *C.p.* Pygmaea, conical bushlet with dense juvenile foliage; *C.p.* Squarrosa, broadly-conical tree to 20m with fluffy sprays of glaucous

leaves. *C. thyoides* (*Cupressus t.*, *Thuja t.*), white cypress, white cedar; E. USA; to 25m or more in the wild, often much less in gardens; leaves sharply-pointed, 2–2·5mm long, with white margins in small, fan-shaped sprays; male strobili minute, dark brown, cones about 6mm wide, reddish-brown; grows well in wet ground but sometimes short lived in gardens. *C.t.* Andelyensis, narrow, conical to columnar bush up to 6m; dark bluish-green juvenile foliage. *C.t.* Ericoides, small, dense, pyramidal bush to 1m or more with juvenile leaves, sea-green in summer, purple to bronze in winter.

Chamaecytisus – see *Cytisus*.

Chamaemelum

(Latin name for chamomile). COMPOSITAE. A genus of 2–3 species of perennials from W. and C. Europe, N. Africa. 1 species is widely cultivated: *C. nobile* (*Anthemis nobilis*), chamomile; W. Europe, N. Africa, Azores; sweetly aromatic, mat-forming; leaves 2–5cm long, bi- or tripinnate, the ultimate segments short, linear, sparsely-haired; flower-heads white, 18–25mm wide, on ascending stems to 10cm or more, summer. *C.n.* Plena, flower-heads double, pompon-like; *C.n.* Treneague, dense mossy foliage, practically non-flowering, the best for lawns. Grow in well-drained soil in a sunny site. For a chamomile lawn, space the plants about 20cm each way in spring. Propagate by cuttings in spring or summer, seed or division in spring.

Chamaepericlymenum – see *Cornus canadensis*.

Chamaespartium – see *Genista delphinensis*.

Chamomile – see *Chamaemelum*.

Chaste tree – see *Vitex agnus-castus*.

Checkerberry – see *Gaultheria procumbens*.

Top left: *Chamaecyparis pisifera* Boulevard
Left: *Chamaecyparis pisifera* Squarrosa Aurea Nana
Above: *Chamaemelum nobile* Plena
Below: *Cheiranthus cheiri* Harpur Crewe
Below right: *Cheiranthus cheiri* Eastern Queen

Cheiranthus

(origin doubtful, said to come from Greek *cheir*, a hand – alluding to the custom of carrying a bouquet of *C. cheiri* at certain ceremonies). Wallflower. CRUCIFERAE. A genus of 10 species of perennials and

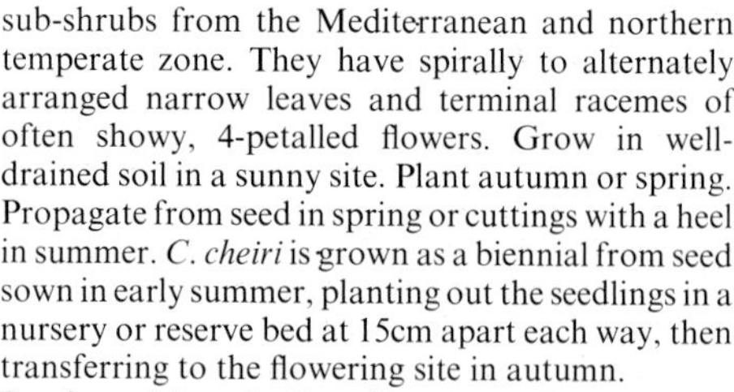

sub-shrubs from the Mediterranean and northern temperate zone. They have spirally to alternately arranged narrow leaves and terminal racemes of often showy, 4-petalled flowers. Grow in well-drained soil in a sunny site. Plant autumn or spring. Propagate from seed in spring or cuttings with a heel in summer. *C. cheiri* is grown as a biennial from seed sown in early summer, planting out the seedlings in a nursery or reserve bed at 15cm apart each way, then transferring to the flowering site in autumn.

Species cultivated: *C.* × *allionii*, see *Erysimum*. *C. alpinus*, see *Erysimum*. *C.* Bowles Mauve (*C.* Bowles Purple), similar to *C. mutabilis*, with greyish leaves and long racemes of rich, mauve-purple flowers off and on most of the year; not reliably hardy in exposed sites. *C. cheiri*, common wallflower; Europe; sub-shrubby perennial to 90cm (less as a biennial); leaves oblong-lanceolate, to 10cm long; flowers yellow, 2–4cm wide, spring, summer. Several cultivars in shades of red-brown, crimson, yellow, orange and ivory-white are available, including dwarf compact sorts: *C.c.* Harpur Crewe is a very old, fully-double yellow cultivar making bushlets to 25cm. *C. linifolius*, see *Erysimum*. *C. mutabilis* (sometimes erroneously described as a synonym of *C. semperflorens*), Canary Is, Madeira; well-branched shrub 60–90cm tall; leaves narrow, lanceolate, 4–8cm long; flowers 1·5–2cm wide, opening pale yellow, ageing lilac-purple, spring; needs a very sheltered site outside or a frost-free greenhouse. *C. semperflorens*, Morocco; sub-shrub to 60m; leaves narrow, lanceolate, greyish-green; flowers 1–1·5cm wide, sepals lilac, petals white; needs a sheltered site. *C.s.* Constant Cheer is a hybrid with *Erysimum* × *allionii*, forming compact mounds of dark green leaves and dusky-red to purple flowers in racemes to 24cm tall, summer.

Chelone

(Greek word for tortoise, the flowers fancifully resembling a reptilian head). Turtlehead. SCROPHULARIACEAE. A genus of 4 species of herbaceous perennials from E. USA. They are clump-forming plants with erect stems bearing opposite pairs of lanceolate leaves and terminal spikes of 2-lipped tubular flowers. Grow in moisture-retentive, humus-rich soil in partial shade or sun; suitable for a bog garden. Plant autumn to spring. Propagate by division at planting time or from seed in spring.

Species cultivated: *C. barbata*, see *Penstemon barbatus*. *C. glabra*, N.E. N.America; stems 60–90cm or more tall; leaves lanceolate to narrowly ovate, toothed; flowers 2·5–3·5cm long, white, flushed purple or deep rose, summer and autumn. *C. lyonii*, S.E. USA; similar to *C. obliqua*; leaves narrow, ovate; flowers sharply-ridged above, the lower lip with deep yellow beard, summer and autumn. *C. obliqua*, S.E. USA; to 1m tall; leaves lanceolate to elliptic; flowers about 3cm long, rose-purple with yellow beard, autumn.

Cherry – see *Prunus*.

Cherry laurel – see *Prunus laurocerasus*.

Cherry pie – see *Heliotropium*.

Cherry plum – see *Prunus cerasifera*.

Below: *Chelone obliqua*, close up and showing flowering spikes
Top right: *Chiastophyllum oppositifolium*
Right: *Chimonanthus praecox*
Below right: *Chimonanthus praecox* Luteus

Chestnut, horse – see *Aesculus*.

Chestnut, sweet – see *Castanea*.

Chiastophyllum

(Greek *chiastos*, diagonally borne, and *phyllon*, leaf – referring to the leaves arranged in opposite pairs). CRASSULACEAE. A genus of 1 species of evergreen perennial from the Caucasus: *C. oppositifolium* (*Cotyledon o.*, *Cotyledon simplicifolium* of gardens), small mats or colonies of erect stems to 5cm or more; leaves rounded to broadly ovate, fleshy, crenate, bright green, 5–10cm long; flowers tiny, 5-petalled, in branched, pendulous, catkin-like racemes to 15cm tall. Grow in well-drained soil in sun or partial shade, good for a dry wall and will tolerate more shade and moisture than most succulents. Plant autumn to spring. Propagate by division in autumn or spring or cuttings after flowering.

Chile pine – see *Araucaria araucana*.

Chilean crocus – see *Tecophilaea*.

Chilean fire-bush – see *Embothrium*.

Chimonanthus

(Greek *cheimon*, winter, and *anthos*, a flower). Wintersweet. CALYCANTHACEAE. A genus of 4 species of evergreen and deciduous shrubs from

China. 1 species is commonly grown: *C. praecox* (*C. fragrans*, *Calycanthus praecox*), well-branched shrub to 2·5m, more on a wall; leaves lanceolate, 5–13cm long, usually a rich, somewhat lustrous green; flowers stiffly-nodding, roughly bell-shaped, 2cm wide, the tepals variable in number and size, outer translucent dull yellow, the smaller, inner ones dark red-purple, very sweetly-fragrant, winter. *C.p.* Grandiflorus, flowers larger and a more definite shade of yellow; *C.p.* Luteus, flowers yellow throughout. Grow in moisture-retentive but well-drained, humus-rich soil in a sunny site preferably sheltered from the worst winter weather; makes a good wall shrub. Plant autumn or spring. Propagate from seed in spring, preferably in a cold frame or greenhouse, or layering in late winter.

China aster – see *Callistephus*.

China rose – see *Rosa chinensis*.

Chionanthus

(Greek *chion*, snow, and *anthos*, flower). OLEACEAE. A genus of 2 species of deciduous shrubs from N. America and E. Asia. They have opposite pairs of ovate to obovate leaves and snowy-white, 4-petalled, dioecious flowers in drooping panicles in summer. Fruit plum-like but not on solitary plants. Grow in moisture-retentive, humus-rich soil in a sunny site. Plant autumn to spring. Propagate from seed when ripe or layering in spring.

Species cultivated: *C. retusa*, Chinese fringe tree; China, Japan, Korea, Taiwan; in cultivation to 3m tall; leaves 4–10cm, broadly oval to obovate; flowers 2cm long, petals linear, in panicles to 10cm long; fruit egg-shaped, 12mm long, blue-purple. *C. virginica*, fringe-tree; E. USA; much like the previous species but finer and sometimes a tree to 10m tall; leaves 7–13cm or more long; flowers to 2·5cm long; fruit blue-purple.

Chionodoxa

(Greek *chion*, snow, *doxa*, glory of – in the wild they flower as the snow melts). LILIACEAE. A genus of 6 or 7 small bulbous plants from Alpine areas of Cyprus, Crete, Turkey. They are closely related to *Scilla* and included in that genus by some botanists, differing only in the flowers having a shortly tubular base and broad, flattened stamen filaments. The small, rounded bulbs produce 2–4 linear leaves and short racemes of starry blue, or blue and white, flowers in early spring. Grow in any well-drained soil in a sunny or lightly-shaded site. Plant autumn. Propagate by separating offset bulbs when dormant or from seed in autumn or spring.

Species cultivated (all from Turkey): *C. gigantea* (of gardens), largest-flowered species, individual blooms being to 3cm wide, lilac-blue with a small white eye in 1–3 flowered racemes to 20cm tall. *C.g.* Alba, flowers white; owing to previous confusion it is now considered that *C. luciliae* is the correct name for this species. *C. luciliae* (of gardens), flowers 2–2·5cm wide, deep blue with large white centre, in a rather 1-sided, 3–10 flowered raceme to 15cm tall. *C.l.* Rosea, flowers pink; *C.l.* Zwanenburg, large bright blue and white flowers; *C.l.* Pink Giant, large pink blooms. *C. sardensis*, leaves channelled; flowers to 2cm wide, clear deep blue, without or with a very small white eye. *C. tmolii*, much like *C. luciliae* (of gardens).

Choisya

(for Jacques Denis Choisy, Swiss professor of philosophy at Geneva and a noted botanist). RUTACEAE. A genus of 6 species of evergreen shrubs from S. USA, Mexico. 1 species is commonly grown: *C. ternata*, Mexican orange blossom; Mexico; bushy shrub 2–3m tall; leaves trifoliate in opposite pairs, leaflets obovate 4–7cm long, lustrous dark green, strongly-pungent when bruised; flowers white, 2·5–3cm wide, fragrant, in terminal clusters, mainly spring but usually a second flush in autumn with odd flower clusters at other times. Grow in well-drained soil in a sunny site, preferably sheltered from cold winds. Plant in spring. Propagate by cuttings with a heel late summer; sometimes suffers damage, particularly by wind frosts, but generally hardy in Britain.

Top: *Chionanthus virginica*
Top centre: *Chionodoxa luciliae*
Bottom centre: *Chionodoxa gigantea*
Above: *Choisya ternata*

Chokeberry – see *Aronia arbutifolia*.

Christmas rose – see *Helleborus niger*.

Chrysanthemum

(Greek *chrysos*, gold, and *anthos*, a flower – several species have yellow flower-heads). COMPOSITAE. A genus of 200 species of annuals, perennials and shrubs from northern temperate zone. Botanists have now split up the genus into a number of smaller genera, retaining only the annuals *C. segetum*, *C. coronarium*, and their allies, as true chrysanthemums, but this is unlikely ever to be wholly acceptable to gardeners. They have alternate, lanceolate to obovate leaves often lobed or more deeply-dissected, and terminal, daisy-like flower-heads in a wide range of colours and shades, often double or semi-double. Hardy species will grow in any well-drained, preferably humus-rich soil in a sunny site. The half-hardy *C. frutescens* requires pots of a good commercial potting mixture, in a greenhouse, minimum temperature 7–10°C well-ventilated and lightly-shaded from the hottest summer sun. Propagate from seed in spring, the annuals *in situ*, the perennials and shrubs under glass at 10–13°C; to 15°C for *C. frutescens*. The latter may be increased also by cuttings in spring or late summer and the hardy perennials by division in autumn or spring. For an account of the popular florists' chrysanthemums see section following 'Species cultivated'.

Species cultivated: *C. alpinum* (*Leucanthemopsis a.*), mountains of Europe; tufted to mat-forming hardy perennial; stems to 15cm tall; leaves ovate to spathulate, pinnately or palmately lobed, greyish-haired; flower-heads solitary, to 3cm or more wide, ray florets white, disc yellow, late summer. *C. argenteum*, see *Tanacetum a. C. balsamita* (*Balsamita major*), alecost, costmary; S.W. Asia; hardy herbaceous perennial to 90cm tall; leaves aromatic, oblong-elliptic with rounded teeth to 12cm or more long; flower-heads in terminal clusters each 1–1·6cm wide, yellow, with or without short, white, ray florets, autumn. *C. carinatum* (*C. tricolor*), N. Africa; hardy annual to 60cm; leaves bi-pinnatifid, somewhat fleshy; flower-heads to 5cm or more wide, disc purple, ray florets white with yellow base, in the garden cultivars variously banded red, maroon or purple, or wholly red, sometimes double, summer and autumn; mixed colour strains are available, those having yellow discs being hybrids with the next species, see *C.* × *spectabile*. *C. coronarium*, Mediterranean, Portugal; hardy annual 40–120cm tall; leaves bipinnatisect, stem clasping; flower-heads 4–5cm wide, discs yellow, ray florets broad golden-yellow to white, single to double; several cultivars are available. *C. corymbosum*, see *Tanacetum c. C. frutescens* (*Argyranthemum f.*), Canary Is; half-hardy, rounded shrub 30–80cm tall; leaves simple or bipinnatisect, glaucous and somewhat fleshy; flower-heads 2–3cm wide, disc yellow, rays white, off and on all year; the plants in cultivation (Paris daisies or marguerites) are larger and more vigorous with green leaves and flower-heads 5–10cm wide, perhaps hybrids with *C. coronopifolium*, an

Top left: *Chrysanthemum maximum*
Left: *Chrysanthemum hosmariense*
Above: *Chrysanthemum parthenium* Aureum

allied species from Tenerife – cultivars of the last-named, with compact anemone centres and pink or yellow ray florets, are grown. *C. haradjanii*, see *Tanacetum h. C. hosmariense* (*Leucanthemum h.*), Morocco; hardy, tufted, woody-based perennial with prostrate to ascending stems forming small mats; leaves singly or twice trifid, silvery-haired; flower-heads about 4cm wide, disc yellow, rays white, autumn to spring during mild winters. *C. leucanthemum* (*Leucanthemum vulgare*), ox eye or moon daisy, wild marguerite; Europe, much naturalized elsewhere; hardy perennial to 60cm or more; leaves obovate to oblong-ovate, crenate, stem leaves often lobed or pinnatifid; flower-heads 4cm or more wide, disc yellow, rays white; a common wild flower and sometimes listed by seedsmen; *C.l.* Silver Princess or *C.l.* Little Silver Princess is a hybrid with the next species. *C. maximum* (*Leucanthemum m.*), Shasta daisy; Pyrenees; hardy perennial 60–90cm, much like a robust *C. leucanthemum*, with almost fleshy, lanceolate, unlobed leaves and flower-heads 7·5cm wide; several cultivars are available with double- or anemone-centred blooms – *C.m.* Everest, *C.m.* Mayfield Giant and *C. m.* Wirral Supreme are well-tried. *C. multicaule* Algeria, hardy annual 15–30cm, well-branched from base; leaves spathulate, trifid or pinnatifid, somewhat fleshy, blue-grey; flower-heads 3–6cm wide, golden-yellow, late summer and autumn. *C. nipponicum* (*Leucanthemum n.*), Japan; like a sub-shrubby *C. leucanthemum*, with larger flower-heads having green-tinted discs, late autumn; not totally hardy. *C. parthenium* (*Leucanthemum p. Pyrethrum p., Tanacetum p.* – botanically the correct name – and *Matricaria eximia* – often under this latter name in seed catalogues), hardy, tufted, somewhat woody-based, short-lived aromatic perennial, often grown as an annual, 30–90cm tall; leaves pinnatisect, pale green; flower-heads to 2cm wide, disc yellow, rays short, white in large, terminal clusters, summer and autumn. *C.p.* Aureum, leaves bright green-gold, several compact cultivars 20–25cm tall are available, mainly with double, pompon-like blooms. *C. rubellum* (of gardens) (*C. erubescens*), hardy, rhizomatous perennial; stems to 90cm tall; leaves ovate, usually broadly pinnately lobed; flower-heads to 8cm wide, disc yellow, rays pink; once thought to be a hybrid, but in 'Flora of Japan' by Ohwi, equated with *C. zawadskii latilobum*; several hybrid cultivars are available. *C. segetum*, corn marigold; S.W. Asia, naturalized as a corn-field weed throughout Europe; much like *C. coronarium* but leaves more coarsely cut and blue-green, flowers smaller. *C.* × *spectabile* (*C. carinatum* × *C. coronarium*), hybrid race of annuals combining the characters of both parents but generally retaining the yellow disc florets of *C. coronarium*. *C. uliginosum* (*Tanacetum serotinum, Leucanthemella s.*), E. Europe; hardy perennial to 2m tall; leaves oblong-lanceolate to lanceolate, generally 2–4 lobed at base; flower-heads loosely-clustered, each to 7·5cm wide, autumn; good as a border or bog plant. *C. vulgare*. see *Tanacetum v.*

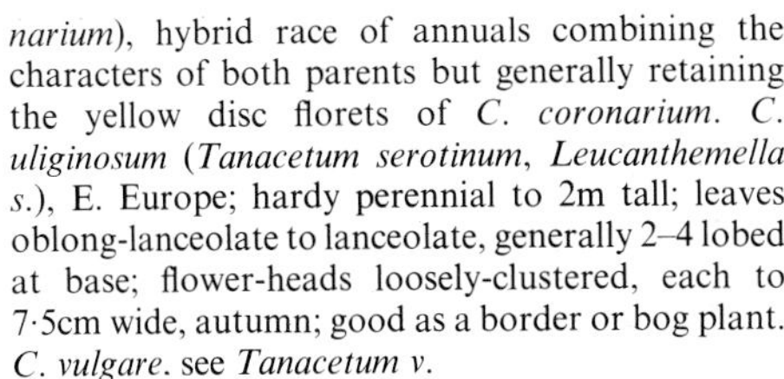

FLORISTS' CHRYSANTHEMUMS: race of very variable hybrid cultivars derived from *C. vestitum* (*C. morifolium*), *C. indicum* and probably other species. They originated in China before 500 BC, then were further developed by the Japanese from about AD 800 onwards. Chinese cultivars reached Britain via France in 1795 and Japanese cultivars arrived direct in 1861. Since then numerous cultivars have been bred in the western world and they have become one of the most popular of all temperate region flowers. With continuous hybridization and mutation, the chrysanthemum bloom has diversified in form in an astonishing way. This is largely shown in changes of size, shape and disposition of the florets in the flower. Except for the single or semi-double cultivars, the florets of all florists' chrysanthemums are strap-shaped, variously rolled and twisted. To bring some order to the chaos of cultivars, the English National Chrysanthemum Society has drawn up a classification based largely upon floral characters. There are 7 main groups, as follows: **1** Incurved: blooms globular, formed of firm-textured, incurving, overlapping florets. **2** Reflexed: blooms rounded, formed of florets that curve out and down, often with curl or sideways twist. **3** Intermediate: halfway between the previous groups, often with some incurving and some out-curving florets. **4** Single: daisylike blooms, having a flattened yellow disc and several

Below left: *Chrysanthemum rubellum*
Bottom left: *Chrysanthemum coronarium* cultivars
Below and bottom, florist's chrysanthemums: Marjorie Boden (1) and Honeyball (3)

radiating rows of ray florets. **5** Anemone-centred: basically daisy-like, but the disc formed of a cushion of elongated florets of a similar shade as the rays. **6** Pompon: small, cushion to globose-shaped blooms formed of numerous, short, broad, ray florets. **7** Miscellaneous: general category for the several small groups that do not fit into the previous 6, including Spider, with long-quilled florets, Spoon, similar but with the tips of the florets expanded, plus Spray, Charm and Cascade, with mainly small, single and semi-double blooms produced in profusion. Chrysanthemums are further divided by their season of blooming: Early-flowering, Late autumn flowering, and Late-flowering. Early-flowering cultivars bloom outside, the Lates under glass, with Late autumn sorts bridging the gap, either flowering outside or under glass, according to season and location. The plants on which these diverse blooms are carried are less variable, being clump-forming perennials, hardy or almost so, with erect, woody stems 60–150cm tall, and rough, ovate leaves variously lobed and somewhat oak-like, glossy rich green or greyish. The flower-heads are carried in branched terminal clusters known as sprays when not disbudded, as is the practice with most cultivar groups. Colours vary, ranging through shades of yellow, pink, red, bronze, purple and white. Chrysanthemums are known as short-day (more accurately long-night) plants, as they need nights of at least 9½–10 hours to initiate flower-buds. For this reason they bloom naturally from late summer onwards. However, by manipulating the length of day and night with artificial lighting and black-out equipment, plants may be had in bloom throughout the year. Pot-grown plants of this origin are now a feature of florists and supermarkets. If they are purchased, it is as well to realise that their dwarf stature and time of blooming have been artificially induced; traditionally-grown cuttings will be quite different. Although perennials, it is traditional to raise them annually from cuttings, some groups – notably Charm, Koreans, Cascades – also from seed. To obtain good-sized plants, seed is sown thinly in pots or boxes of a standard seed compost under glass from late winter to early spring at a temperature of 12–15°C. As soon as the first true leaf is well-grown, prick off the seedlings either directly into 7·5cm pots or 4cm apart in boxes of potting mix. Plants should be hardened off and planted out in the open in late spring or potted on as described for those raised from cuttings. To obtain cuttings, the previous season's plants (stools) should be brought into a greenhouse or frame heated to 7–10°C in late winter. Temperatures above this will induce thin, spindly shoots. As soon as young shoots are 5–7cm tall, take as cuttings, inserting into a seed mix or equal parts of peat and coarse sand at 4cm apart each way. Place in a propagating case or plastic bag and keep at a minimum of about 10°C. When rooted and just starting to grow, place singly into 7·5–9cm pots. Keep them growing in the same temperature with good ventilation on all mild days. Early and late autumn flowering cultivars are then hardened off in late spring and planted out late spring to early summer at 38–45cm apart each way. Unless the site is very sheltered, each plant should be tied to a stake, or if grown in rows, to wires between strong posts. When the plants are 15–20cm tall they must be stopped (the growing tips pinched out). With plants for garden decoration, all the shoots may be left but for flowers of large size and quality reduce the shoots to the 3 or 4 strongest before they are 10cm long. Apart from those cultivars grown as sprays and the Korean and Charm types, all chrysanthemums are disbudded to give larger blooms of better substance. When the bud clusters are clearly visible at the tips of the stems, carefully rub off or cut with fine, pointed scissors the several small buds that surround the main, large or crown bud. As many cultivars are not reliably hardy, it is general practice to lift the plants in late autumn or early winter, cut off the tops and place in boxes of potting mixture in a cold frame or greenhouse, well-ventilated on mild days. Late autumn flowering cultivars are usually lifted with a good root-ball in mid autumn and planted in a cool greenhouse border or into boxes, thereafter treating

Above, florist's chrysanthemums, **far left top:** Thora (5); **left top:** Mason's Bronze (4); **left above:** Tracey Waller (2); **top above:** Charm (7); **above:** Spoon-flowered Luyona (7); **top right:** Solley (6); **above right:** mixed single Spray (7); **far right top:** Korean group Salmon Pye (7); **far right above:** Spider-flowered White Spider (7)
Far left above: *Chrysanthemum carinatum* cultivars

as for Late-flowering cultivars. Flowering from late autumn to late winter, the Late-flowering group is grown in pots for its entire life. After the rooted cuttings are put in 7·5–9cm pots, they are grown on under glass as for Earlies, but instead of planting out they are potted on successively into 13–15cm, and then to 20, 23 or 25cm pots for flowering. Staking and stopping is the same for Earlies and in early summer the plants are usually stood outside in a sheltered spot, the stake in each pot tied to a post and wire support. The final potting should be into a potting mix with extra fertilizer. About 6 weeks later the plants should be given liquid feed at 7–10 day intervals until buds show colour. Some Late-flowering cultivars produce the best flowers from second crown buds and need stopping twice. In such cases the shoots resulting from the first stopping are themselves stopped when 6–10cm long. Cultivars with this requirement are generally listed in the nurseryman's catalogue with instructions when to stop. Pot-grown 'mums' must never be allowed to get dry and during hot weather may need watering once or even twice a day. When the plants have finished blooming cut back to about 15cm and keep almost dry in a frost-free frame or greenhouse until required for propagation. Among pests liable to attack chrysanthemums are aphids, capsids, earwigs, eelworms, leaf-miners, mites, thrips and whiteflies, while diseases include botrytis and mildew. Numerous cultivars of florists' 'mums' are listed by specialist nyrserymen and new ones are being raised annually. In their separate ways, all are good, and choice must be a personal one.

Chrysogonum

(Greek *chrysos*, gold, and *gonu*, knee or joint – referring to the yellow flowers and prominent stem joints). COMPOSITAE. A genus of 1 species of hardy perennial from E. USA. *C. virginianum*, clump-forming, semi-evergreen; leaves 3–7cm long, ovate, coarsely blunt-toothed, hairy; flower-heads 2–3cm wide with 5, broad, ovate, golden-yellow rays and a small disc, on leafy stems 10–30cm tall, spring to autumn. Grow in any humus-rich soil in sun or shade; the plant is a sun lover but does not appreciate too dry a position. Plant autumn to spring. Propagate by division at planting time.

Below: *Chrysogonum virginianum*
Right: *Cimicifuga simplex*
Far right: *Cirsium rivulare* Atropurpureum

Chufa, chuffa – see *Cyperus esculentus*.

Cimicifuga

(Latin *cimex*, a bug, and *fugo*, to drive away – *C. foetida* was formerly used as insect-repellent. Bugbane. RANUNCULACEAE. A genus of 15 species of herbaceous perennials from northern temperate zone. They are clump-forming with compound, bi- or triternate leaves, and fluffy wand-like racemes of small flowers each composed of up to 8 filiform petals or staminodes and numerous stamens. Grow in humus-rich soil preferably in partial shade, though sun is tolerated if the soil is moist. Plant autumn to spring. Propagate by division at planting time or from seed when ripe or soon afterwards.

Species cultivated: *C. americana*, bugbane; E. USA; stems leafy 1·5–2cm tall; leaves ternate with pinnate divisions, each leaflet ovate to oblong, lobed, toothed, pointed, the basal ones to 60cm long; flowers creamy-white, about 1cm wide, late summer; see *C. racemosa cordifolia* also. *C. cordifolia* – see *C. racemosa cordifolia*. *C. foetida*, N.E. Asia; stems to 1·5m; leaves biternate, leaflets ovate to narrowly so, irregularly sharply-toothed; flowers 1–1·5cm wide, greenish-white to almost yellow, several short, arching racemes forming an almost astilbe-like panicle. *C.f. intermedia*, see *C. simplex*, *C. racemosa*, black snakeroot, black cohosh; E.N. America; stems 1·5–2·5m tall; leaves bi- or triternate, some divisions with 5 leaflets, the latter ovate, tapered or subcordate at base, toothed and often lobed; flowers white 1cm or more wide, summer. *C.r. cordifolia* (*C. cordifolia*), leaflets fewer and larger, the terminal one at least deeply-lobed; flowers sometimes with a hint of green – sometimes confused with *C. americana*. *C. simplex* (*C. foetida simplex*, *C.f. intermedia* of gardens), smaller and neater than *C. foetida*, rarely above 1·2m tall, with dense, pure white, arching, bottle-brush like racemes, autumn; *C.s.* Elstead, flower-buds purplish, racemes strongly-arching; *C.s.* White Pearl, slender spikes, graceful habit; *C.s. ramosa* (*C. ramosa* of some catalogues), similar character to the original species, but to 2m tall with larger leaves.

Cineraria (of gardens) – see *Senecio hybridus*.

Cinquefoil – see *Potentilla*.

Cirsium

(Greek *kirsion*, for a kind of thistle taken up by Miller when he named this genus). COMPOSITAE. A genus of 150 species of annuals and perennials from the N. Hemisphere. They are clump-forming with basal tufts or rosettes of narrow, often lobed and spiny-margined leaves and terminal, thistle-like flower-heads formed of slender, tubular florets each with 5, narrow petal-lobes. Grow in any moisture-retentive soil in a sunny site. Plant autumn to spring. Propagate by division at planting time or from seed in spring.

Species cultivated: *C. japonicum* (*Cnicus j.*), Japan; stems to 1m, leafy; leaves obovate-oblong, toothed

to pinnately lobed, spiny-margined, loosely downy; flower-heads 3–5cm wide, pink to rose-purple, involucral bracts shortly spine-tipped, summer; more densely-spined and woolly-leaved forms occur and are occasionally cultivated. *C. rivulare*, C. Europe to W. USSR; colony-forming when established; stems 60–100cm tall, leafy only at the base; leaves elliptic to oblong-lanceolate, usually pinnately-lobed, to 15cm or more long, with small, weak spines; flower-heads purple, solitary or in small clusters about 3–4cm wide, summer. *C.r.* Atropurpureum (*Cnicus atropurpureus* of gardens), glowing crimson-purple.

Cistus

(ancient Greek *kistus* for several species). Sun roses. CISTACEAE. A genus of 20 species of evergreen shrubs from Canary Is, the Mediterranean to Caucasus. They have opposite pairs of linear to broadly-ovate leaves and terminal clusters of 5-petalled, rotate flowers like those of species roses in summer. Grow in well-drained soil in a sheltered, sunny site. Most of the species and hybrids described here are generally hardy in gardens if sited properly, but an extra severe winter or prolonged spell of non-stop freezing weather may kill back to ground level or completely. Plant spring. Propagate by cuttings taken with a heel in late summer using bottom heat of about 18°C, or from seed sown in spring under glass.

Species cultivated: *C.* × *aguilari* (*C. ladanifer* × *C. populifolius*), natural hybrid from Spain, Portugal, Morocco; to 2m or more; leaves lanceolate, 10cm long with finely-waved margins; flowers 10cm or more wide, white. *C.* × *a.* Maculatus, petals each with a basal crimson blotch. *C. albidus*, S.W. Europe to N. Africa; erect, bushy, to 1m; leaves oblong to elliptic, densely grey-white, downy; flowers 4–6cm wide, pale rose-purple. *C. clusii* (*C. rosmarinifolius* in part), erect, to 1m; leaves linear to 2·5cm long, dark green above, white-haired beneath; flowers in umbel-like clusters 2–3cm wide with yellow eye. *C. libanotis* is similar to *C. clusii*, but dwarfer and with reddish sepals. *C.* × *corbariensis* (*C. populifolius* × *C. salvifolius*), natural hybrid from Corbières, France; broad, bushy, 60–90cm tall; leaves 2–5cm long, ovate, often cordate, dark green above; flowers 4cm wide, white with yellow eye; one of the hardiest sun roses. *C. creticus* (*C. incanus*, *C. villosus*), S. Europe; bushy to 1m or more; stems and leaves covered with grey-white, star-shaped hairs, the latter ovate to obovate, 1·5–2·5cm long; flowers 4–6cm wide, purplish-pink. *C.c. corsicus*, leaves 2·5–5cm. *C.c. incanus*, sepals with many long, unbranched hairs. *C. crispus*, W. Mediterranean, Portugal; to 60cm tall, compact habit; leaves oblong to elliptic, 1–4cm long, grey-white hairs; flowers 3–4cm wide, purplish-red; confused with *C.* × *pulverulentus* in gardens. *C.c.* Sunset, see *C.* × *pulverulentus*. *C.* × *cyprius* (*C. ladanifer* × *C. laurifolius*), wild hybrid where the parents grow together, so not from Cyprus as name suggests; vigorous, bushy to 2m or more; leaves lanceolate to 10cm long, dark green above, grey beneath, mid-rib and stalk sticky; flowers 7–8cm wide, each white petal with blood-red basal blotch, in clusters of 3–6; among the hardiest of sun roses. *C.* × *c.* Albiflorus, flowers without blotches. *C.* × *florentinus*, (*C. monspeliensis* × *C. salvifolius*), leaves like those of first parent but a little broader, flowers similar to latter parent. *C. hirsutus* (*C. psilosepalus* now considered correct name), Portugal, Spain; well-branched, to 90cm tall; leaves ovate to narrowly oblong, 2–6cm long, downy; flowers 4–6cm wide, white with yellow eye, tepals shaggy white-haired; one of the hardiest. *C. incanus*, see *C. creticus*. *C. ladanifer* (*C. ladaniferus*), gum cistus; S. W. Europe; erect habit to 2m or more; leaves leathery, linear-lanceolate, sticky, dark green above to 10cm long; flowers solitary, 7–10cm wide, white with basal crimson blotch at each petal base.

C.l. Albiflorus, flowers pure white. *C. laurifolius*, S. W. Europe; erect, open habit, to 2m or more; leaves ovate to lanceolate, 3–8cm long, dark green above, white-downed beneath, slender-pointed, sticky; flowers 5–6cm wide, white in clusters of 4–8; the hardiest species. *C. libanotis*, see *C. clusii*. *C.* × *loretii* (*C. ladanifer* × *C. monspeliensis*), erect to 1·2m tall; leaves and flowers midway between parents; confused in cultivation with the following: *C.* × *lusitanicus* Decumbens (*C. hirsutus* × *C. ladanifer*), wide-spreading, 60cm tall by 1·2m or more;

Top left: *Cistus* × *pulverulentus* Sunset
Centre left: *Cistus* × *purpureus*
Above: *Cistus* × *salvifolius*
Top above: *Cistus crispus*
Centre above: *Cistus ladanifer*

leaves narrowly oblong-lanceolate, 2·5–6·5cm long, clammy, dark green above; flowers 6–7cm wide, white, petal bases crimson-blotched. *C. monspeliensis*, S. Europe, N. Africa; well-branched, 60–120cm tall; leaves narrowly-lanceolate to linear, margins inrolled, dark green, finely-wrinkled above, densely grey-downed beneath; flowers 2–3cm wide, white, very free-flowering. *C.* × *obtusifolius* (*C. hirsutus* × *C. salvifolius*), rounded, compact habit, 45–75cm tall; leaves oblong-ovate to obovate, 2·5–5cm long, grey-green; flowers 3–4cm wide, white with yellow eye; among the hardier sorts. *C.* × Paladin, see next species. *C. palhinhae* (*C. ladanifer latifolius*), Portugal; compact habit, to 50cm tall; leaves oblanceolate to spathulate, 2–6cm long; flowers pure white, 7–10cm wide. *C.p.* Paladin, hybrid with *C. ladanifer*, crimson-blotched flowers. *C.p.* Pat, same parentage as *C.* Paladin; rather like a low, bushy *C. ladanifer*. *C. parviflorus*, E. Mediterranean; compact habit, to 90cm; leaves ovate, 1–3cm long, grey-downed; flowers 2–3cm wide, clear rose-pink; some forms are remarkably hardy. *C. populifolius*, S. W. Europe; erect habit, 1·5–2m tall; leaves long-stalked, broadly ovate, cordate, 3–9cm long, prominently net-veined; flowers 4–6cm wide, white with yellow eye in clusters 2–6. *C.p. lasiocalyx* (*C.p. major*), larger flowers than type; strongly-waved leaves; among the hardier species. *C.* × *pulverulentus* (*C. albidus* × *C. crispus*), common wild hybrid, sometimes masquerading under the name of the latter parent and in the past known as *C. delilei* Roseus and *C.d.* Warley Rose; 60–90cm tall; leaves oblong-lanceolate, 4–5cm long, grey-downed; flowers rich cerise, 5cm wide. *C.* × *p.* Sunset, flowers glowing magenta-pink, usually about 45cm tall. *C.* × *purpureus* (*C. ladanifer* × *C. creticus*), rounded habit, 90–120cm tall; leaves oblong-lanceolate to obovate, to 5cm long, greyish-green; flowers 6–7·5cm wide, rose-crimson, each petal with a basal maroon blotch; popular and much

Above: *Cladanthus arabicus*

grown but not particularly hardy. *C.* × *p.* Betty Taudevin, leaves narrower than type; flowers brighter, hardier. *C. salvifolius*, S. Europe; compact habit, to 60cm tall; leaves ovate to elliptic, 1–4cm long, rough-textured, starry-downed; flowers 3–5cm wide, white with yellow eye. *C.s.* Prostratus, wide-spreading, to 30cm tall; leaves smaller, hardier than type. *C.* × Silver Pink, 60–75cm tall; leaves lanceolate, 2·5–7·5cm long, downy, dark grey-green above, paler beneath; flowers silvery-pink, 6–8cm wide; remarkably hardy if grown in a fertile soil, originated as a self-sown seedling at Hillier's Nursery (Britain) about 1910 and considered to be *C. laurifolius* × *C. creticus*. *C.* × *skanbergii* (*C. monspeliensis* × *C. parviflorus*), 1–1·5cm tall; stems with prominent white hairs; leaves linear-lanceolate to oblanceolate, 2·5–5cm long, silky, starry down beneath; flowers about 4cm wide, pale rose-pink, in clusters of up to 6; a rare natural hybrid from Greece. *C. symphytifolius* (*C. vaginatus*), Canary Is; open habit, to 2m tall; leaves ovate, 5–10cm long, dark green above, somewhat downy beneath with prominent veins; flowers 4–5cm wide, rose-purple; although from mountain regions rather tender in Britain. *C. villosus*, see *C. creticus*.

Cladanthus

(Greek *klados*, a branch, *anthos*, a flower – the flower-heads occur at the ends of the branches). COMPOSITAE. A genus of 4 species of annuals from S. Spain and N. Africa. 1 species is generally available: *C. arabicus*, S. Spain, N. Africa; bushy, aromatic plant 60–90cm tall; stems slender; leaves alternate, pinnatisect, the linear lobes often again lobed; flower-heads daisy-like, to 4cm wide, golden-yellow, summer to autumn; very distinctive in its habit of repeatedly branching just below each flower-head; grow in any well-drained soil in a sunny site, sowing seed *in situ* in spring.

Clarkia

(for Capt. William Clark, 1770–1838, co-leader with Capt. Meriwether Lewis of the first expedition to cross from St. Louis, Missouri, USA, to the mouth of the Columbia River, 1804–6). ONAGRACEAE. A genus of 36 species of annuals from W. N. America and Chile, including all the species formerly classified as *Godetia*. Plants generally slender, erect, branched, leaves alternate linear to lanceolate, flowers in terminal spikes, each of 4 petals, sometimes lobed. Grow in any well-drained, preferably humus-rich soil in a sunny site. Sow seed *in situ* in spring, or autumn in well-drained soil and a sheltered site. May also be grown as cool greenhouse pot plants, autumn-grown seedlings being placed singly in 13cm pots of commercial potting mixture in late autumn and kept at a minimum temperature of 7°C in winter with ventilation on all mild days. Flowering late winter, spring.

Species cultivated: *C. amoena* (*Godetia a. Oenothera a.*), California; to 60cm; leaves 1–6cm long, lanceolate; flowers 4–6cm wide, pink or lavender to white, summer. *C.a. whitneyi* (*C. grandiflora* of gardens), flowers larger than type with central red blotch; has given rise to several strains and cultivars with single and double flowers in shades of red, pink, lilac, white, and including dwarfs 20–24cm tall. *C. concinna* (*Eucharidium c.*, *E. grandiflorum*), red ribbons; California; 30–60cm; leaves lanceolate to ovate or elliptic, 1·5–5cm long; flowers deep bright pink, 2·5–4cm wide, petals slender, 3-lobed, the middle lobe longest. *C. elegans*, see *C. unguiculata*. *C. pulchella*, W. N. America; to 45cm tall; leaves lanceolate to linear; flowers to 4cm wide, lilac to white, summer, autumn; several strains are cultivated in shades of purple, pink, white, often semi-double. *C. unguiculata* (*C. elegans*, *Oenothera e.*); to 60cm or more, leaves lanceolate to ovate, 1–6cm long; flowers to 4cm wide, pale to deep red-purple, salmon, lavender or pale pink, summer, autumn; several mixed colour strains and single cultivars are available, mainly as double flowers.

Clary – see *Salvia sclarea*.

Clematis

(Greek name for several kinds of climbing plants and used by Linnaeus for this genus). RANUNCULACEAE. A genus of 250 species of woody and sub-shrubby climbers and herbaceous plants of cosmopolitan distribution, mainly temperate regions. They generally have opposite pairs of compound leaves that, in the climbing species, have twining stalks and mid-ribs that act as tendrils. The flowers are solitary or carried in panicles each having 4–6 or more petaloid sepals either partially closed and bell-like or of rotate form. The seed

Top: *Clarkia pulchella*
Centre: *Clarkia unguiculata*, double cultivars
Above: *Clarkia concinna*

(achenes) has long, feathery awns and is borne in rounded, sometimes decorative heads. Grow in humus-rich soil, moisture-retentive but well-drained, ideally with the root area in shade and the top in sun. The climbing species and more vigorous hybrids look well rambling through trees or over a tall, dead stump, and all can be grown on walls if trellis or wires are provided for support. Plant autumn or spring. Propagate by stem or leaf-bud cuttings in late summer. Species clematis do not need pruning except to thin out over-congested growth or to remove that which exceeds its allotted space. Cultivars derived from *C. viticella* and *C.* × *jackmanii* are best cut back to the lowest pair of buds on each previous year's stem, or if several stems arise from below the soil, right back to ground level. This should be done in winter and before end of mid spring. Pruning of the other hybrid groups is optional; leave unless allotted space is restricted.

Species cultivated (all climbing unless otherwise stated): *C. afoliata*, New Zealand; to 3m; stems dark

green, rush-like; leaves reduced to a mid-rib only or with 1 tiny leaflet; flowers bell-shaped, nodding, fragrant, green, tinted pale yellow, 2cm long, spring; an intriguing but not beautiful species, more trailing than climbing. *C. alpina* (*Atragene alpina*), N. Europe and mountains farther south; deciduous, to 2m; leaves biternate, leaflets ovate-lanceolate, coarsely-toothed, 2·5–5cm long; flowers solitary, pendant, bell-shaped, 2·5–4cm long, violet, appearing semi-double owing to petaloid stamens, spring; blue-, red- and pink-flowered cultivars are available. *C. armandii*, China; evergreen, to 6m or more; leaves trifoliate, leaflets ovate-lanceolate, 7–13cm long, dark glossy green; flowers 4–6cm wide, white, fragrant, in axillary clusters, spring. *C.a.* Apple Blossom, flowers pink-flushed; needs a sheltered wall. *C. buchananiana*, see *C. rehderiana*. *C. calycina*, see *C. cirrhosa*. *C. campaniflora*, Portugal, Spain; deciduous, to 7m; similar to *C. viticella* but flowers widely bell-shaped, white, tinged violet. *C. chrysocoma*, China; deciduous, to 6m or more; leaves trifoliate, leaflets ovate to obovate 2·5–5cm long, coarsely-toothed; flowers 4–5cm wide, pale pink in clusters of 1–3, spring and summer; not always reliably hardy. *C.c. sericea* (*C. spooneri*), flowers larger than type, hardier. *C. cirrhosa*, S. Europe; evergreen, to 4m; leaves ternate, biternate or simple, the latter usually 3-lobed or toothed, 2·5–5cm long; flowers nodding, 4–7cm wide, palest yellow, sometimes red-spotted within, winter. *C.c. balearica* (*C. balearica*, *C. calycina*), leaves much divided, almost fern-like, bronze-purple in winter; flowers invariably red-spotted within, autumn to spring; not reliably hardy in cold areas, needs a sunny south wall. *C. davidiana*, see *C. heracleifolia*. *C. flammula*, S. Europe; deciduous, to 5m; leaves bipinnate, leaflets narrowly oblong to rounded; flowers very fragrant, white, 2cm wide in panicles to 30cm long, autumn. *C. florida*, China; deciduous or partly evergreen, to 4m; leaves biternate, leaflets lanceolate to ovate, 2·5–5cm long; flowers solitary, 6·5–7·5cm wide, white with black-purple stamens, summer. *C.f.* Sieboldii (*C.f.* Bicolor), flowers with a rosette of purple, petaloid stamens. *C. heracleifolia*, China; deciduous sub-shrub, 60–90cm; leaves trifoliate, central leaflet much larger, ovate, to 13cm long; flowers 2–2·5cm long, fragrant, blue, the sepal tips recurved, in axillary panicles, autumn. *C.h. davidiana*, to 1m tall; flowers more spreading, sepal tips not recurved, deeper blue. *C.h.d.* Wyevale, flowers hyacinth-blue, larger; *C.h.d.* Crepuscule, hybrid with *C. stans*, vigorous and with larger flower clusters. *C. integrifolia*, C. and S. E. Europe to C. Asia; herbaceous perennial 90–120cm tall; leaves simple, ovate, pointed, to 9cm long; flowers nodding, usually solitary, 3–4cm long, violet-blue, summer. *C.i.* Hendersonii, flowers deep blue; *C.i.* Rosea, lavender-pink. *C.* × *jackmanii* (*C. lanuginosa* × *C. viticella*), deciduous, to 4m or more; leaves simple or trifoliate; flowers 10–13cm wide, of 4–6 rich violet-purple sepals, summer, autumn; horticulturally, this name now covers a wider hybrid group comprising most of the large-flowered cultivars, many dozens of which are grown by nurserymen, in a wide range of purples, reds, pinks, mauves and whites, some bicoloured, 10–25cm wide. *C.* × *jouiniana* (*C. heracleifolia davidiana* × *C. vitalba*), deciduous, to 3m; foliage midway between parents; flowers 2–3cm wide, pale lilac, in leafy panicles 30–60cm long, late summer, autumn. *C* × *j.* Campanile and *C.* × *j.* Cote d'Azur, flowers in deeper shades of lilac-blue than the type; both are seedlings from *C.* × *jouiniana* and much resemble *C. heracleifolia* in stature and general appearance. *C. lanuginosa*, China; deciduous, 2–3m, leaves simple or trifoliate, leaflets ovate-cordate, to 13cm long, grey-woollen beneath; flowers 10–15cm wide, sepals 6–8, white to pale lilac, summer, autumn. *C. macropetala* (*Atragene m.*), Siberia, China; de-

Top left: *Clematis alpina*
Left: *Clematis armandii*

ciduous, 2–4m; leaves mainly biternate, leaflets ovate to lanceolate, coarsely-toothed, pointed; flowers 6·5–10cm wide, solitary, nodding, appearing semi-double owing to several petaloid stamens, lavender-blue, white within, late spring, summer. *C.m.* Maidwell Hall, deeper, purer blue than type; *C.m.* Markham's Pink, lavender-pink. *C. montana*, Himalaya; deciduous, to 10m or more; leaves trifoliate, leaflets ovate to lanceolate, pointed, toothed, 5–10cm long; flowers 5–6cm wide, pure white in axillary clusters of 2–5, late spring, with stragglers until late autumn. *C.m. rubens*, China; flowers rose-pink, foliage purplish; *C.m.r.* Tetrarose, tetraploid form with larger, rose flowers, to 7·5cm wide. *C.m. wilsonii*, China, flowers smaller, white, but borne in greater profusion and fragrant; *C.m.* Grandiflora, flowers white, to 7·5cm wide. *C. orientalis*, N. Asia; deciduous, to 6m or more; leaves pinnate, the divisions often trifoliate, leaflets ovate to lanceolate, 2·5–5cm long, toothed and lobed, bluish-green; flowers nodding, to 5cm wide, yellow; seed-heads globular, silky-feathered; the commonest form in cultivation (collector's number L.S.E. 13372), from Himalaya, has very thick tepals likened to orange peel; see also

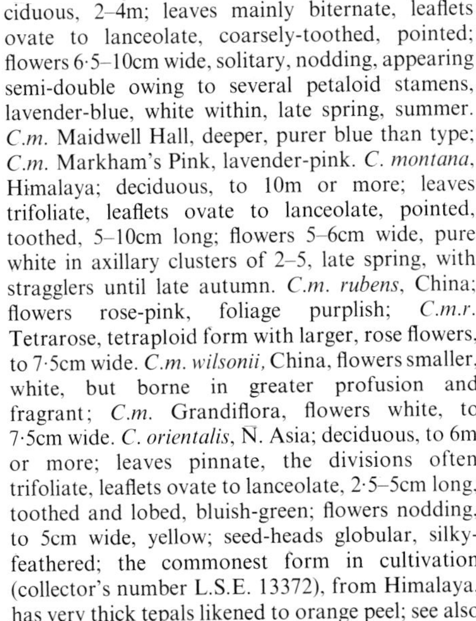

Top left: *Clematis orientalis*
Far left centre: *Clematis montana rubens*
Far left: *Clematis florida* Sieboldii
Left above: *Clematis* Vivyan Pennell
Left: *Clematis* Ville de Lyon
Top above: *Clematis* Countess of Onslow
Above: *Clematis integrifolia* Hendersonii

C. tangutica. *C. paniculata* (*C. indivisa*), New Zealand; evergreen, to 10m; leaves trifoliate, leaflets 3–10cm long, dark green, leathery, broadly ovate, sometimes cordate; flowers unisexual, males 5–10cm wide, females smaller, white, fragrant, in panicles to 30cm long; rather less than hardy and needs a very sunny, sheltered wall in all but milder areas; a deciduous species sometimes listed under this name is the Japanese *C. maximowicziana*, with white, hawthorn-scented flowers. *C. patens*, China or Japan; deciduous, to 4m, much like *C. florida* and considered by some authorities to be a form of that species, having leaves of 3–5 simple leaflets only, and no bracts on the flower-stalks. *C.p.* Fortunei, flowers double. *C. recta*, herbaceous perennial, to 1·5m; leaves pinnate, of 5–7 ovate, pointed leaflets, 2·5–6·5cm long; flowers white, about 2cm wide, fragrant, in terminal panicles; floppy habit, needing support. *C.r.* Purpurea, young foliage purple. *C. rehderiana* (*C. buchananiana*, *C. nutans*), China; deciduous, to 7m or more; leaves pinnate, primary divisions often trifoliate, leaflets ovate, toothed or lobed, 4–7cm long, light silk down; flowers fragrant, nodding, bell-shaped, about 2cm long, sepals pale yellow with sharply-recurved tips, panicles to 23cm long, autumn. *C. spooneri*, see *C. chrysocoma*. *C. tangutica*, N. W. China; much like *C. orientalis*; leaves sea-green; flowers lantern-shaped, 4–5cm long, the sepals slender-pointed. *C.t. obtusiuscula*, flowers about 3cm long, sepals blunt, silky seed-heads decorative. *C. texensis* (*C. coccinea*), Texas, USA; sub-shrubby climber dying back to near ground in cool areas; stems to 2m or more; leaves pinnate, glaucous, of 4–8 ovate leaflets, each one usually cordate, 3–7cm long; flowers solitary, nodding, pitcher-shaped, about 2·5cm long, light to deep crimson; not reliably hardy and needs a sunny, sheltered wall. *C.* × *vedrariensis* (*C. chryocoma* × *C. montana rubens*), much like latter parent but flowers larger and leaves downy. *C. vitalba*, travellers' joy, old man's beard; Europe to Caucasus, N. Africa; deciduous, to 15m; leaves pinnate, of 5, ovate to lanceolate, coarsely-toothed leaflets, each 3–10cm long; flowers greenish-white, about 2cm wide, in panicles 7–13cm long, summer and autumn, followed by decorative, fluffy seed-heads; rampant grower and best suited to the wild garden. *C. viticella*, virgin's bower; S. Europe; deciduous, somewhat sub-shrubby, to 4m; leaves pinnate with primary divisions trifoliate, each leaflet lanceolate to ovate, often lobed, 2–6·5cm long; flowers solitary or several together, nodding, about 4cm wide, reddish to purple-blue, summer and autumn. *C.v.* Alba Luxurians, white with dark anthers; *C.v.* Kermesina, crimson; *C.v.* Minuet, creamy-white, tipped mauve-purple.

Cleome

(name used by Theophrastus for a mustard-like plant, derivation unknown, later taken up by Linnaeus for this genus). CLEOMACEAE (CAPPARIDACEAE). Some 150 species of annuals and shrubs from the tropics and subtropics. 1 species is widely grown: *C. hasslerana* (*C. pungens*, *C. spinosa* of gardens); spider flower, W. Indies; annual, to 1m, erect, hairy sticky-glandular, aromatic; leaves digitate, leaflets oblong-lanceolate, 5–7, stipules at base of leaf-stalk spine-tipped; flowers white to pink, about 4cm with 4 petals so disposed as to give the impression of half a flower only, stamens to 5cm long, summer, early autumn; several cultivars are available in white or richer shades of pink to rose-purple and yellow. Grow in well-drained, humus-rich soil in a sheltered, sunny site. Sow seed in spring under glass at about 18°C, prick off seedlings as soon as the first true leaf is well developed, either into boxes at 4–5cm apart each way or singly into 7·5–9cm pots of a commercial potting mixture or its equivalent. Harden off the plant from the first week of early summer and plant out after frosts have finished.

Clethra

(Greek *klethra* for the alder tree – *Alnus* – certain species in each genus resembling each other somewhat). CLETHRACEAE. A genus of 68 species of deciduous and evergreen shrubs or trees from Asia, America and Madeira. They have alternate, oblong-ovate to elliptic, often prominently veined leaves and dense racemes of small, fragrant, 5-petalled flowers in late summer, autumn. Grow in a sheltered, sunny or partially-shaded site in a neutral to acid, humus-rich soil. *C. arborea* survives outside in only the mildest areas and needs the protection of a frost-free greenhouse elsewhere. Plant or pot spring. Propagate from seed or layering in spring, cuttings late summer, bottom heat about 18°C.

Bottom left and centre: *Cleome hasslerana* cultivars

Below: *Clethra alnifolia* Rosea

Species cultivated: *C. alnifolia*, sweet pepper bush; E. N. America; deciduous, 2–3m tall, generally erect, suckering habit; leaves obovate, toothed, 4–10cm long; flowers white, 1cm wide, in cylindrical racemes 5–15cm long. *C.a.* Paniculata, several racemes together forming terminal panicles; *C.a.* Rosea, buds deep pink, flowers paler than type. *C. arborea*, lily-of-the-valley tree; Madeira; small, evergreen tree, to 8m; leaves oblanceolate, finely-toothed, 7–15cm long, deep bright green above, paler beneath; flowers white, cup-shaped, about 8mm long in racemes to 15cm long, several borne together in terminal panicles; fine tub shrub for a large conservatory. *C. barbinervis*, Japan; deciduous, 2–3m tall, less erect and more bushy than *C. alnifolia*; leaves obovate to oval, 5–13cm long, toothed, hairy; flowers white, 8mm wide, in compact, terminal panicles; not fully hardy, but in gardens survives all but the hardest winters without damage.

Clover – see *Trifolium*.

Cobaea

(for the Spanish Jesuit Father Bernardo Cobo, 1572–1659, missionary and naturalist). COBAEACEAE. A genus of 18 species of climbing plants from tropical America. 1 species is readily available: *C. scandens*, cup and saucer creeper; cathedral bell; C. and S. America; woody climber to 10m or more; leaves pinnate, composed of 4–6 ovate or elliptic leaflets to 10cm long and branched, whip-like tendrils with minutely hooked tips; flowers broadly bell-shaped, 6–8cm long, yellow-green changing to purple, with a 5-lobed, saucer-like calyx, borne on long stalks from upper leaf-axils, spring to early winter. May be grown in a greenhouse border, but very vigorous and will rapidly outgrow its welcome without a regular pinching back. May be grown as a half-hardy annual, sowing seed singly in 7·5cm pots of good potting mixture, in mid spring at 18°C, potting on the young plants when about 30cm tall in to 13cm pots, hardening off and planting out latter part of early summer or when fear of frost has passed. Grown under glass it will survive temperatures down to 4°C.

Cocksfoot grass – see *Dactylis*.

Cockspur thorn – see *Crataegus crus-galli*.

Codonopsis

(Greek *kodon*, a bell, and *opsis*, like – referring to the flower shape). CAMPANULACEAE. A genus of 30 or more species of annuals and herbaceous perennials, some of the latter with twining, climbing stems, from Himalaya, Asia and Malaysia. The species described are hardy perennials, generally of tufted habit from fleshy or tuber-like roots, leaves lanceolate to ovate, alternate to almost opposite, flowers mainly bell-shaped, pendant, with 5 lobes but in some species they open out almost flat. Grow in well-drained, humus-rich soil in sun or partial shade. Provide the climbers with twiggy sticks for support or allow them to scramble through a shrub. Propagate from seed in spring or division if the plant has several crowns; cuttings of young basal shoots may also be taken in spring.

Species cultivated (all summer flowering): *C. clematidea*, mountains of Asia; erect to spreading; stems 40–100cm long; leaves ovate, slender-pointed;

flowers deeply bell-shaped, 3–4cm long, white, suffused blue with an intricate ring pattern of golden-brown at the base; needs planting on a bank so that the nodding flowers can be viewed properly. *C. convolvulacea*, Himalaya, W. China; stem climbing to 2m or so; leaves ovate, 2–5cm long; flowers rotate, up to 5cm wide, blue, with prominent petal-lobes. *C. ovata*, Himalaya; spreading habit, up to 30cm tall; leaves ovate, hairy, about 2cm long; flowers 2·5–3cm long, pale blue, flared at the mouth. *C. tangshen*, W. China; stem climbing to 3m or so; leaves ovate to lanceolate, 3–6·5cm long; flowers to 4cm long, bell-shaped with straight sides and flared lobes, pale green spotted and striped purple within. *C. vinciflora*, Tibet; stems climbing to 1·5m or more; leaves ovate to lanceolate, toothed; flowers rotate, periwinkle-like, purple to lilac-blue, 4–5cm wide; not always reliably hardy and best protected with a cloche in winter in cold areas; thrives best in acid soil.

Coix

(ancient Greek name for a reed-like plant, taken up by Linnaeus for this plant). GRAMINEAE. A genus of 5 species of grasses from Asia, 1 of which is commonly grown. *C. lacryma* (*C. lacryma-jobi*), Job's tears; tropical Asia and Africa; half-hardy annual 40–90cm tall; leaves linear, 1cm wide or more; flowering spikelets unisexual, in arching, leafy panicles, the females surrounded by a much enlarged bract sheath that matures to a 1cm long, woody, pear-shaped, smooth, pearly-grey bead-like fruit; forms are known with the ripe fruit ivory, blue, pink, brown and black; thin-shelled fruited cultivars are grown for food in S.E. Asia, known as Adlay in the Philippines and Ma-yuen in China. Grow in humus-rich soil in a sunny site. Sow seed singly in 7·5cm pots of any commercial potting mixture at about 16°C during mid spring. Harden off young plants in early summer and plant out when fear of frost has passed. Alternatively, sow outside *in situ* in late spring.

Colchicum

(from Colchis, eastern end of Black Sea). LILIACEAE. A genus of 65 species of cormous-rooted plants from Europe, Mediterranean to C. Asia and N. India. They have rounded to pear-shaped corms, each one producing a sheaf of 2–8 or more, lanceolate to ovate, often glossy and prominently-veined leaves. The flower has a long, stem-like, perianth tube that springs directly from the corm and 6 tepals or perianth lobes that open in the sun to a chalice or bowl shape, the narrow-lobed sorts having a starry appearance. In some species the ground colour is broken by a pale or dark tesselation or chequering. Many species produce their flowers in autumn before the leaves, like those of certain crocuses. They are readily separated from crocus by their generally large, broad leaves and flowers with 6 stamens (crocus has 3). Grow in any well-drained soil, preferably in a sunny site, although light shade is tolerated. Plant late summer for the autumn-flowering sorts, up to late autumn for the spring bloomers. Propagate from seed when ripe or separating offset corms when dormant.

Species cultivated: *C. agrippinum*, much like *C. variegatum* but more vigorous and flowering earlier (often second half early autumn onwards); probably of hybrid origin or perhaps a mutant clone. *C. autumnale*, popularly and confusingly known as autumn crocus and meadow saffron, both names more properly belonging to *Crocus*; Europe; leaves lanceolate, 15–30cm long; flowers 15–25cm tall, lobes 5cm, lilac-pink, sometimes lightly chequered, autumn. *C.a.* Album, white; *C.a.* Pleniflorum (*C.a.* Plenum, *C.a.* Roseum-plenum, *C.a.* Flore-Pleno) flowers fully double. Species closely allied to *C. autumnale* are: *C. alpinum*, smaller and neater but not easy to grow; and *C. neapolitanum*, Italy, Yugoslavia, paler with more obvious tesselation. *C. bivonae* (*C. bowlesianum*, *C. sibthorpii*), Italy, Greece, Yugoslavia, Turkey; leaves lanceolate to 30cm long; flowers to 15cm tall, lobes pointed to 7cm long, rose-purple with deeper chequering, autumn. *C. bornmuelleri*, see *C. speciosum*. *C. bowlesianum*, see *C. bivonae*. *C. byzantium*, see next species. *C. cilicicum*, Turkey, similar to *C. autumnale* but a deeper lilac-pink and more flowers per corm, opening over a longer period and more weather-resistant; *C. c. byzantium*, paler, earlier flowers than type, commencing in second half of early autumn in most years. *C. cretense*, Crete; not unlike *C.*

Left: *Cobaea scandens*
Below top: *Coix lacryma*
Below centre: *Colchicum agrippinum* (of gardens)
Bottom: *Colchicum speciosum*

Top: *Colchicum* Water lily
Above: *Colchicum* Lilac Wonder

hungaricum, with rosy-lilac, rather starry flowers, late autumn. *C. hungaricum*, Hungary to Greece; leaves 2–3, linear, channelled, to 10cm or so; flowers 3–6cm tall, lobes 2–2·5cm, white to lilac-pink, winter, with half-grown leaves; hardy but better appreciated in a cold greenhouse. *C. illyricum* (of gardens), see *C. speciosum bornmuelleri*. *C. laetum*, (of gardens), Caucasus, much like *C. autumnale*, the flowers generally paler and with narrow lobes giving them a starry appearance. *C. luteum*, N.W. India, W. Himalaya; leaves 2–5, narrowly linear; flowers to 8cm tall, the lobes about 2·5cm narrow, yellow, late winter, with young leaves; best in an alpine house. *C. neapolitanum*, see *C. autumnale*. *C. speciosum*, Caucasus, Turkey, Iran; leaves 4–6, oblong-elliptic, 30–40cm long, glossy; flowers 20–30cm tall, lobes 7–9cm long, pale lilac-rose to red-purple, autumn. *C.s.* Album, pure white flowers with greenish tube, of excellent form and substance; *C.s. bornmuelleri* (*C. bornmuelleri*), pale purple-rose with large white throat area (*C. illyricum* of gardens), is much like a smaller darker version of this, with generally more flowers per corm. Several hybrids have been raised between *C. speciosum* and other species, notably *C. bivonae;* among long-standing favourites are: *C.* Lilac Wonder, rosy-violet, lightly chequered, pointed lobes; *C.* The Giant, large, rose-lilac bloom on long tube with white throat and faintly chequered; *C.* Violet Queen, red-purple with white throat and moderate chequering, lobes pointed; *C.* Water Lily, fully double, rose-lilac, reputedly a hybrid from *C. autumnale* Plenflorum. *C. variegatum* (see *C. agrippinum*), Greece, Turkey; leaves 3–4, lanceolate to elliptic, undulate, 10–15cm long, somewhat bluish-green; flowers about 10cm tall, the spreading lobes 4–5cm long, pointed, lilac-purple, boldly and neatly chequered, autumn; not long-lived outside and best under glass.

Top and above: *Coleus blumei* hybrids
Below right: *Colletia cruciata*

Coleus

(Greek *koleos*, a sheath – the stamen filaments uniting and forming a tube around the style). LABIATAE. A genus of 150 species of perennials, annuals and sub-shrubs from tropical Africa and Asia. They have opposite pairs of ovate, stalked leaves and tubular, 2-lipped flowers in whorls forming spike or panicle-like inflorescences. Greenhouse, minimum temperature 13°C, well-ventilated and lightly shaded in summer. Grow in any good potting mixture or outdoors in summer. Propagate by cuttings in spring or late summer, from seed in spring. The species described are usually grown as annuals, but extra large plants can be obtained by potting on into larger containers each spring. Such plants are best pruned in late winter by cutting back the previous season's growth to 2–3 pairs of buds. Young plants from cuttings need stopping when 8–10cm tall and the sideshoots when of a similar size; *C. blumei* may need a 3rd pinching to promote a bushy plant. When in full growth in summer, apply liquid feed weekly.
Species cultivated: *C. blumei*, flame or painted nettle, known as 'the foliage plant' in USA; Java; to 60cm or more, of shrubby appearance; leaves broadly to narrowly ovate-cordate, coarsely toothed, yellow-green, suffused red or purple, 5–12cm long; flowers small, white and purple-blue in spike-like clusters, best removed when young to promote further leafy growth. *C.b. verschaffeltii*, leaves 10–13cm long, glowing crimson; numerous cultivars and several good mixed seed strains are available with leaves variously margined, blotched, marbled or veined in shades of yellow, pink, red, maroon and green, some with frilled edges.

Colletia

(for Philibert Collet, 1643–1718, French botanist). RHAMNACEAE. A genus of 17 species of shrubs from S. America. They have rigid green stems, opposite pairs of generally scale-like leaves that soon fall, and tiny, tubular, 5-lobed flowers often borne in profusion. The growth form is curious, 2 shoots arising in each leaf-axil, 1 becoming a thorn, the other a normal extension stem. The species described are hardy. Grow in well-drained soil in a sunny site. Plant spring or autumn. Propagate by cuttings with a heel in late summer, preferably with bottom heat 16–18°C, or from seed when ripe.
Species cultivated: *C. armata*, S. Chile; 2–4m tall, much branched and very thorny; flowers fragrant, waxy-white, 3–4mm long, autumn. *C.a.* Rosea, flowers pale pink. *C. cruciata*, Uruguay; 2–3m tall; twigs stout, dark green, well-spaced, bearing large, triangular, wing-like thorns in opposite pairs; flowers cream, 5–6mm long, singly or in small clusters at the base of the thorns, late summer, autumn; young plants, particularly seedlings, have bodkin-like thorns, and sometimes a juvenile shoot will appear on adult specimens.

Collinsia

(for Zaccheus Collins, 1764–1831, American botanist and Vice-President of the Philadelphia Academy of Natural Sciences). SCROPHULARIACEAE. A genus of 20 species of annuals from N. America, mainly W. coast. 1 species is generally available: *C. heterophylla (C. bicolor)*, Chinese houses; California; 30–50cm tall, erect, diffusely branched; leaves in opposite pairs, oblong-lanceolate, usually toothed, 2–7cm long; flowers 1·5–2cm long, tubular, 2-lipped, the upper lip white to pale lilac, the lower violet to rose-purple, borne in clusters in the upper

Above: *Collinsia heterophylla*
Right: *Convallaria majalis*
Right below: *Colutea × media*
Far right: *Convolvulus althaeoides*
Far right below: *Convolvulus cneorum*

axils and forming leafy spikes, summer, autumn. Grow in well-drained, fertile soil in a sunny or partially shaded site. Propagate from seed sown *in situ* in spring, or autumn in mild areas.

Columbine – see *Aquilegia*.

Colutea

(Greek *kolutea,* for common bladder senna). LEGUMINOSAE. A genus of 26 species of shrubs from S. Europe to Abyssinia, C. Asia and Himalaya. The species described have alternate pinnate leaves, pea-like blooms in small racemes, and curiously inflated, bladder-like pods. Grow in mild areas in well-drained soil in sun or partial shade. Plant autumn to spring. Propagate by cuttings with a heel in late summer or from seed in spring. May be hard-pruned each spring to maintain a small, neat specimen with fewer but larger clusters of flowers and pods.
Species cultivated: *C. arborescens*, common bladder senna; Mediterranean; vigorous, 3–4m tall; leaves of 9–13 elliptic to obovate leaflets having notched tips each to 2·5cm long; flowers to 2cm long, bright yellow, summer to autumn; pods 5–7cm long, often reddish-flushed. *C.* × *media* (*C. aborescens* × *C. orientalis*), similar to first parent but leaves grey-blue green and flowers flushed bronze. *C. orientalis*, Caucasus and area; to 2m tall; leaves glaucous, leaflets 7–9, obovate to rounded, each to 1·5cm long; flowers 1·5cm long, bronze to copper-red; pods 4cm or more long, often strongly red-flushed, open at the tip.

Comfrey – see *Symphytum*.
Compass plant – see *Silphium laciniatum*.
Cone-flower – see *Rudbeckia*.

Convallaria

(Latin *convallis,* a valley – in the wild they often grow in lowland or valley woods). LILIACEAE. A genus of 1 species of rhizomatous herbaceous perennial from northern temperate zone. *C. majalis* (including *C. montana* of E. N. America), lily-of-the-valley; rhizomes far-creeping, forming dense to scattered colonies; leaves in 2s or 3s, elliptic-lanceolate, deep green, 15-20cm long; flowers nodding, rounded bell shape, waxy white, sweetly and strongly fragrant, in 1-sided racemes the same height as the leaves or lower; fruit an orange-red berry. *C.m.* Major, *C.m.* Berlin Giant and *C.m.* Fortin's Giant have larger flowers on longer stems; *C.m.* Prolificans (*C.m.* Flore Pleno), flowers double; *C.m.* Rosea, pale pink, less vigorous. Grow in any humus-rich soil in partial shade. Plant after flowering or autumn. Propagate by division at planting time. Lily-of-the-valley may easily be forced into bloom from mid winter onwards. Ideally, plants should be specially grown for the purpose in well-manured land for at least 2 years, but any large colony may be dug up in autumn and the fattest budded crowns with 10-15cm of rhizome attached sorted out. Place these about 5cm apart, upright in 10-15cm pots or deep boxes of a peat compost, and place in a propagating frame with bottom heat 26-29°C. Batches treated in this way can be brought in at regular intervals of 1-2 weeks to provide a succession. Crowns waiting to be used are best stored at −2°C and may be kept in a retarded state to beyond their normal flowering time and brought into bloom in an ordinary cool greenhouse.

Convolvulus

(Latin *convolvo,* to roll or grow around – intertwine). CONVOLVULACEAE. A genus of 250 species of annuals, perennials, sub-shrubs and shrubs of cosmopolitan distribution. They have linear to ovate-cordate, sometimes palmately lobed leaves and funnel to trumpet-shaped flowers, solitary or in small clusters. The species described are hardy to half-hardy, all requiring well-drained soil and a sunny site, the less-hardy sorts shelter from cold winds and excessive frost. Plant the half-hardy species in spring when fear of severe frost has passed. Propagate from seed in spring for all groups, division at the same time for perennials, and cuttings with a heel in late summer for the shrubs.
Species cultivated: *C. althaeoides*, S. Europe; hardy, herbaceous perennial; stems twining or trailing; leaves triangular to ovate-cordate at the base, broader and pedately or pinnately lobed above, grey-green; flowers pink, 1-3 in leaf-axils, 2·5-4cm wide, summer, autumn. *C.a. tenuissimus* (*C. elegantissimus*), slender, densely silk-haired, upper leaves cut into deep, narrow lobes; when happily situated this species can be invasive. *C. cneorum*, W. and C. Mediterranean near the sea; half-hardy, spreading, evergreen shrub to 50cm tall; leaves linear to oblanceolate, 3-6cm long, silkily silver-haired; flowers white, 1·5-2·5cm wide, pink in bud, in terminal clusters late spring to autumn; only hardy where temperatures rarely fall below −5°C. *C. elegantissimus*, see *C. althaeoides tenuissimus*. *C. major*, see *Ipomoea purpurea*. *C. mauritanicus*, see *C. sabatius*. *C. minor*, see *C. tricolor*. *C. sabatius* (*C. mauritanicus*), half-hardy, woody-based perennial or sub-shrub; stems prostrate; leaves oblong-ovate to obovate, hairy; flowers to 2cm wide, silky purple-blue (pink forms are known), solitary in upper leaf-axils, summer, autumn. *C. tricolor*, Mediterranean, Portugal; hardy annual; stems erect to reclining,

Left above: *Convolvulus tricolor* Royal Ensign
Left: *Convolvulus sabatius*
Above: *Cordyline australis*
Right above: *Coreopsis verticillata*
Right: *Coreopsis auriculata* Superba
Right below: *Coreopsis tinctoria* dwarf strain

well-branched; leaves obovate to oblanceolate, 3-7cm long; flowers to 4cm wide, solitary, in the crowded upper leaf-axils, yellow, white, pink, red-purple, blue, usually with a white eye and sometimes zoned with a contrasting colour or shade, summer, autumn; several mixed colour strains and single colour cultivars are available.

Coral bells – see *Heuchera sanguinea*.

Coral berry – see *Symphoricarpos orbiculatus*.

Cordyline

(Greek *kordyle*, a club – probably alluding to the swollen stem bases of some species, rather like an inverted club). AGAVACEAE (LILIACEAE). A genus of 15 evergreen trees and shrubs from tropical and warm temperate regions, mainly S. Hemisphere. Confused with *Dracaena*, they have erect, usually sparingly branched or suckering stems, each tipped with a palm-like tuft of long, narrow leaves; flowers small with 6 perianth segments in often large terminal panicles; fruit a 3-seeded berry. Greenhouse, minimum temperature 5–7°C for New Zealand species, with good ventilation and very light shade in summer; 13–15°C for *C. terminalis* with humidity and moderate shade in summer. New Zealand species can be stood outside in summer in most areas and *C. australis* survives outside all year in areas of light or no winter frost or in sheltered sunny sites. It is often used as a dot plant in summer bedding schemes and grows to tree size in the mildest areas. Well-drained soil is essential. Pot in spring using any of the commercial potting mixtures; plant out when fear of frost has passed. Propagate from seed in spring under glass at 16–18°C; detach suckers in late spring and treat as cuttings until well-rooted; take 6cm-long cuttings of stem sections in early summer (from leggy specimens), and insert horizontally or vertically in equal parts peat and sand at 16–18°C for New Zealand species, 20–24°C for *C. terminalis*.

Species cultivated: *C. australis* (*Dracaena a.*), cabbage tree; New Zealand; tree to 8m or more tall (to 20m in the wild); stem usually unbranched for several years, but finally developing a crown; leaves dense, linear, 30–100cm long, drooping when old; flowers fragrant, white, 5–6mm wide, in broad panicles 60–120cm long, spring and summer; fruit white, 4mm wide. *C.a.* Purpurea, leaves suffused bronze to purple, some forms being darker than others, *C.a.* Rubra being red-bronze; good for the seaside. *C. banksii*, New Zealand; smaller than *C. australis*, 3–4m tall; suckering and eventually forming clumps; stems sparingly branched; leaves narrowly lanceolate, drooping at tips, to 1m or more long; flowers about 1cm long; fruit 4–5mm wide, white or bluish; stands more shade than *C. australis* but not so hardy. *C. indivisa* (*Dracaena i.*), New Zealand; robust; usually single-stemmed, 2–8m tall; leaves lanceolate, 1–2m long, often glaucous beneath and purple-flushed above, drooping with age; flowers white, 7–8mm long in compact panicle 60–120cm long; fruit 6mm, bluish; stands light shade but a little less hardy than *C. australis*. *C. terminalis* (*Dracaena t.*), ti tree; tropical Asia, Polynesia; stems 1–4m tall, erect, suckering, sparingly branched; leaves broadly lanceolate, 30–60cm long, distinctly stalked; flowers about 6mm long, white, reddish or purplish; fruit 8mm, red; generally known as dracaena to gardeners; represented in gardens by several colourful, variegated-leaved cultivars in shades of red, pink, yellow and white.

Coreopsis

Calliopsis. (Greek *koris*, a bug, and *opsis*, like – the 'seed' fancifully resembles a bug-like insect). COMPOSITAE. A genus of 120 species of annuals and perennials from America and Africa. Leaves in opposite pairs, usually pinnately lobed; flowers terminal, daisy-like with broad ray florets and comparatively small discs in those species cultivated; fruit (cypselas) often black, narrow and flattened with or without a pappus of scales or bristles. Grow in well-drained, humus-rich soil in a sunny site. Plant the perennial species spring or autumn, sow the annuals *in situ* in spring, or autumn in sheltered areas. Plants may be flowered in a cool greenhouse in late spring from a mid autumn sowing, over-wintering about 7°C. Propagate perennials by division at planting time, from seed or by cuttings in spring.

Species cultivated: *C. auriculata*, S.E. USA; perennial, clump-forming; stems to 80cm; lower leaves ovate to rounded, sometimes with small basal lobes; flower-heads to 5cm wide, rays yellow, maroon at base, summer. *C.a.* Superba and *C.a.* Astolat's, more robust with generally larger flower-heads; distinct in having almost leafless flower-stalks and good for cutting. *C. basalis* (*C. drummondii*), Texas; erect annual, 30–50cm; leaves bi- or tripinnatifid; flower-heads 3–5cm wide, ray florets rich yellow with a mahogany blotch at base, summer; several strains are available including double flowers and those with florets entirely chestnut-red, summer. *C. gigantea* (*Leptosyne g.*), California; half-hardy, sub-shrubby perennial, to 2m or more tall; stem stout, often unbranched, somewhat woody with a crown of 3–4 times pinnate leaves cut into filiform segments; flower-heads to 8cm wide, in cymose clusters, summer; needs a sheltered spot to survive the winter, or a frost-free greenhouse. *C. grandiflora*, S.E. USA; perennial, to 45cm tall; leaves lanceolate to oblanceolate, entire to 3–5 lobed; flower-heads to 5cm or more wide, bright yellow, ray florets deeply lobed at tips with small, brown-crimson spot at base, summer, autumn. *C.g.* Badengold, to 90cm tall; flowers larger than type; *C.g.* Mayfield Giant, 90cm, orange-yellow; *C.g.* Sunburst, to 75cm, double-flowered. *C. lanceolata*, E. N. America; much like *C. grandiflora* and perhaps confused with it in cultivation; leaves usually entire, linear to oblanceolate; flower-heads to 6cm or more wide, summer. *C. rosea*, N.E. N. America; perennial, to 60cm or more tall with slender, creeping rhizomes; leaves linear, sometimes lobed; flower-heads 2·5–4cm wide, ray florets 3-lobed at apex, deep to light rose-red, summer, autumn; good for moist soil; a white form is recorded. *C. tinctoria*, N. America; annual, to 60cm or more tall; leaves

often opposite, the basal ones pinnately cut into linear or narrowly lanceolate lobes; flower-heads to 4cm wide, rays 3-lobed at apex, yellow, purple-brown or parti-coloured, summer; several strains are listed by seedsmen including dwarfs to 23cm tall and double-flowered sorts. *C. verticillata*, S.E. USA; clump-forming perennial with many short rhizomes and slender, erect stems to 60cm or more; leaves in pairs, deeply palmately cut into several linear segments, appearing like a whorl of narrow separate leaves; flower-heads 3–4cm wide, rays bright yellow, summer, autumn. *C.v.* Grandiflora (*C.v.* Golden Shower), more robust with rays of a richer, more mellow hue.

Coriaria

(Latin *corium*, leather – some species are used in tanning). CORIARIACEAE. A genus of 15 species of herbaceous perennials, sub-shrubs, shrubs and trees from Mediterranean to Japan, Mexico to Chile and New Zealand. They have ovate to linear leaves in pairs or whorls borne on arching stems to form frond-like sprays. the small, 5-petalled, sometimes monoecious flowers in axillary or terminal racemes. The petals are persistent, becoming fleshy and covering the small fruit within, giving the appearance of a berry. In general, the genus is tender outside in gardens, but the species described here survive some frost if sited correctly, and the base of the plant is easily protected with straw or bracken held by chicken wire, or a heap of coarse sand or weathered ash. Grow in well-drained but moisture-retentive soil in sun or light shade in a sheltered position. Plant spring. Propagate from seed when ripe or in spring, or by cuttings with a heel in late summer.

Species cultivated: *C. angustissima*, New Zealand; woody-based rhizomatous herbaceous perennial, stems slender, erect to arching, plume-like; leaves linear, 7–10mm long; flowers to 4mm wide, with prominent red stigmas, summer; fruits globular, polished black; a hardy species but rarely available.

C. japonica, Japan; deciduous sub-shrub to 60cm or more; leaves ovate-lanceolate, slender-pointed 2·5–9cm long; racemes 6·5cm long, 2 or 3 together, laterally borne on previous year's stems, flowers green, the petals becoming red then purple-black in fruit, 5mm wide. *C. terminalis*, China, Sikkim, Tibet; suckering and rhizomatous deciduous sub-shrub to 1·2m tall; leaves ovate, 3–7·5cm long; racemes terminal on current season's stems, 15–20cm long, flowers greenish, becoming glossy black in fruit, 10–12mm wide. *C.t. fructu-rubro*, fruiting petals red: *C.t. xanthocarpa*, fruiting petals translucent yellow.

Left: *Coriaria terminalis*
Above: *Coriaria angustissima*
Right: *Cornus capitata*
Centre right: *Cornus florida* in autumn
Bottom right: *Cornus florida* Rubra

Cork oak – see *Quercus suber*.

Corn flag – see *Gladiolus segetum*.

Corn marigold – see *Chrysanthemum segetum*.

Cornel – see *Cornus*.

Cornelian cherry – see *Cornus mas*.

Cornflower – see *Centaurea cyanus*.

Cornus

(Latin name for Cornelian cherry, taken up by Linnaeus for the whole genus). CORNACEAE. A genus of 40 species of trees, shrubs and herbaceous perennials mainly from the N. Hemisphere. Botanists have now split the genus into 5 or 6 separate genera. With the possible exception of *Chamaepericlymenum* and *Swida* (*Thelycrania*), however, these new generic names are not familiar to gardeners and are unlikely to find favour for years to come. For this reason and also for convenience *Cornus* is treated in the broad sense (*sensu-lato*). They are mainly hardy and deciduous (1 partly or wholly evergreen) with leaves in opposite pairs (2 species alternate), and small, 4–5 petalled flowers in usually dense umbels or corymbs; in some species the flower clusters are surrounded by coloured bracts. In *C. mas* and its allies these bracts fall as the cluster expands, but in *C. florida*, *C. nuttallii* and others, they are large, persistent and petal-like. The fruit is a fleshy drupe or berry, in some species – *C. capitata* and *C. kousa* – fusing together to form a compound fruit or syncarp. Grow in humus-rich soil in sun or partial shade. Plant autumn to spring. Pruning is not generally necessary, but the coloured-twigged sorts, mainly *C. alba* Sibirica and *C. stolonifera*, may be stooled each spring to encourage lots of strong 1-year stems. Propagate from seed when ripe (sometimes taking 1 to several years to germinate), layering in spring, cuttings with heel in late summer; suckers or hard wood cuttings from the suckering species and division of the herbaceous sorts at planting time.

Species cultivated: *C. alba* (*Swida a., Thelycrania a.*), Siberia, China, Korea; suckering shrub, rarely to 3m; leaves 5–11cm long, oval to ovate, shortly pointed; flowers yellow-white, in cymes 4–5cm wide, early summer; fruit white- or blue-tinted, about 6mm wide. *C.a.* Elegantissima (*C.a.* Sibirica Variegata), leaves smaller than type, with creamy-white margin shaded grey-green in centre, twigs red in winter; *C.a.* Gouchaultii, much like *C.a.* Spaethii and probably confused with it in cultivation, generally duller with more green in the centre and stained light red; *C.a.* Sibirica, winter twigs glistening red, less vigorous than original species (*C.a.* Sibirica Westonbirt is the same, though at one time thought to be distinct); *C.a.* Spaethii, leaves margined bright yellow, twigs red, sometimes listed as *C.a.* Spaethii Aurea; *C.a.* Variegata, like a more vigorous *C.a.* Elegantissima. *C. alternifolia* (*Swida a.*), E. N. America; large shrub or small tree to 6m tall, with spreading habit; leaves alternate, ovate, tapered, often slender-pointed, 5–13cm long; flowers yellow-white in cymes 5–6·5cm wide, summer; fruit black with waxy-white patina, 6mm wide. *C.a.* Argentea, leaves smaller than type, with neat white margin, grey-green in centre. *C. amomum* (*Swida a.*), E. N. America deciduous shrub to 3m; leaves oval to ovate, abruptly short-pointed, silky-downed beneath, 5-10cm long; flowers cream, in cymes 4–6·5cm wide, summer; fruit 6mm wide, pale blue. *C. canadensis* (*Chamaepericlymenum canadense*), creeping dogwood, bunchberry; N. America, E. Asia, Korea, Japan; rhizomatous herbaceous perennial forming wide colonies; stems erect, rarely branched, 15–25cm tall; leaves ovate to obovate, 2–8cm long, crowded towards the top; flowers green or cream-white in terminal, rounded, umbel-like cymes, surrounded by 4, elliptic, petal-like bracts 1–2cm long, white, often tipped or flushed purple, summer; fruit 6mm wide, bright red. *C. capitata* (*Dendrobenthamia c., Benthamidia c., Benthamia fragifera*), Himalaya to China; eventually a tree to 12m or more, but damaged in areas of severe winter frost; leaves evergreen or partially so, elliptic, 5–10cm long, greyish-green; flowers very small, in hemispherical clusters to 1·5cm wide, surrounded by 4–6, pale yellow, obovate bracts 4–5cm long, summer; fruit crimson, strawberry-like syncarps 2·5–4cm wide; in Britain thrives well only in the south and west. *C. controversa* (*Swida c.*), Himalaya, China, Japan; eventually a tree to 15m but slow-growing, elegant habit with branches in horizontal tiers; leaves alternate, ovate, 5–12cm long; flowers white in flattened cymes 6–12cm wide; fruit 6mm, blue-black. *C.c.* Variegata, leaves smaller than type, lanceolate, somewhat irregular, boldly variegated creamy-white, sometimes called 'wedding cake tree'. *C. florida* (*Benthamidia f.*), flowering dogwood; E. USA; spreading deciduous shrub or small tree, 3–6m, sometimes much more in the wild; leaves broadly ovate, 7–15cm long, with short, abrupt, slender point, rich green above, pale, almost glaucous, beneath, colouring well in autumn; flowers in dense, rounded head 1–1·5cm wide, surrounded by 4, white, obovate bracts notched at the tips, 4–5cm long, late spring; fruit 1cm long, ovoid, dark red, in small clusters. *C.f.* Apple Blossom, bracts pale pink; *C.f.* Cherokee Chief, bracts rose-red; *C.f.* Rubra, rose-pink, young leaves reddish; *C.f.* Tricolor, leaves with creamy-white, pink-tinted margins; *C.f.* White Cloud, leaves bronze-tinted, bracts pure white, free-flowering. *C. kousa* (*Dendrobenthamia k., Benthamidia japonica, Benthamia j.*), Japan, Korea, China; large shrub or small tree 3–6m tall; leaves ovate, 4–7·5cm long; flower clusters like *C. florida*, but bracts lanceolate, slender-pointed to 4cm long, creamy-white, summer; fruit a red strawberry-like syncarp. *C.k. chinensis*, leaves and bracts somewhat larger, generally more free-flowering. *C. mas* (*Macrocarpium m.*), cornelian cherry; C. and S. Europe; large shrub or small tree to 7m, of rather open, twiggy habit; leaves ovate, 4–10cm long;

flowers yellow, 4-petalled, 3–4mm wide in umbels to 2cm wide, late winter, usually freely borne; fruit a polished oblong drupe about 1·5cm long, edible. *C.m.* Aurea Elegantissima (*C.m.* Tricolor), leaves widely bordered or entirely suffused yellow, some also pink-tinted; *C.m.* Macrocarpa, larger fruit than type; *C.m.* Variegata, leaves boldly margined creamy-white. *C. nuttallii* (*Benthamidia n.*), Pacific dogwood; W.N. America, large shrub in many gardens, but a tree to 18m and more in the wild; leaves oval to obovate, 7·5–13cm or more long;

Far left top: *Cornus alba* Sibirica
Far left: *Cornus alternifolia* Argentea
Left: *Cornus stolonifera* Flaviramea
Below left: *Cornus mas*
Below: *Cornus kousa*
Below centre: *Cornus nuttallii*
Bottom: *Cornus sanguinea* in fruit

flowers in dense, rounded head to 2cm wide surrounded by 4–8 (usually 6), oval to obovate bracts to 7·5cm long, creamy-white, flushed pink on ageing, late spring; fruit ovoid red drupes in clusters; short lived in some areas, but undoubtedly the finest of the bracted flowering' dogwoods and begins to bloom when quite young. *C. sanguinea* (*Swida s., Thelycrania s.*), common dogwood; Europe to S.W. Asia; generally suckering shrub, 2–4m tall, twigs purple-red; leaves oval to ovate, short-pointed, 4–8cm long; flowers dull white in flattened cymes 4–5cm wide; fruit glossy black, 6mm wide. *C. stolonifera* (*Swida s., Thelycrania s., T. sericea, Cornus s.*), vigorous suckering shrub to 2m or more, twigs purple-red; leaves oval to ovate-lanceolate, 5–12cm long; flowers dull white in corymbs to 5cm wide; fruit white, about 5mm wide. *C.s.* Flaviramea, winter twigs bright greenish-yellow.

Corokia

(Maori name in Latin form). CORNACEAE. A genus of 3 species of evergreen shrubs from New Zealand. They are much-branched, with slender, wiry stems; alternate, sometimes clustered, lanceolate to rounded leaves; starry, yellow, 5-petalled flowers; and ovoid, berry-like fruit. Grow in well-drained soil in a sunny, sheltered site. *C. buddleioides* and *C. macrocarpa* are half-hardy and not suitable in areas of hard winter frosts unless protected. Alternatively, grow in a frost-free greenhouse. Plant or pot spring. Propagate from seed when ripe or by cuttings with a heel in late summer, bottom heat about 18°C.

Species cultivated: *C. buddleioides*, New Zealand; to 2m tall; leaves usually narrowly lanceolate, 5–15cm long, leathery, dark green above, silvery-white felt beneath; flowers 7–10mm wide, bright yellow in small panicles, late spring; fruit 6–7mm long, red to black. *C. cotoneaster*, wire netting bush; rounded habit to 2m or more; stems very slender, zig-zagging and interlacing; leaves 4–15mm long broadly ovate to obovate, sometimes shallowly lobed, dark green above, white-felted beneath; flowers 5–8mm wide in axillary and terminal clusters of 2–4; fruit 5–8mm long, orange to red. *C. macrocarpa*, Chatham Is; akin to *C. buddleioides* but more tree-like, ultimately to 6m in wild; leaves broader, to elliptic-oblong; flowers to 1cm wide in axillary racemes to 4cm long; fruit to 1cm, red. *C.* × *virgata* (*C. cheesemanii*) (*C. buddleioides* × *C. cotoneaster*), this name covers the very variable swarms that occur in the wild where the 2 species grow together; in Britain the plant under this name is akin to *C. cotoneaster* but with stems less interlaced; leaves oblanceolate to spathulate, 6–45mm long; flowers 9–12mm wide; fruit bright orange; several plants of this parentage have been given cultivar names in New Zealand, some with bronze-flushed leaves and yellow to deep red fruit.

Coronilla

(diminutive of Latin *corona*, a crown – alluding to the often circular umbels of flowers). LEGUMINOSAE. A genus of 20 species of perennials, sub-shrubs and shrubs from Europe, Mediterranean. They have alternate, pinnate leaves, pea-shaped flowers in axillary or terminal umbels, and slender pods constricted between each seed (lomenta). Grow in well-drained soil in sun, the half-hardy species against sheltered walls or in a greenhouse. Plant hardy species autumn or spring, the half-hardies in spring when fear of severe frost has passed. Propagate from seed in spring for all species, cuttings of young shoots in spring of the perennials, cuttings with a heel in late summer for the shrubs. The half-hardy shrubs, particularly *C. glauca*, make good pot plants for a frost-free or cool greenhouse and grow readily in any commercial potting mixture.

Top: *Corokia* × *virgata*
Above: *Coronilla valentina glauca*
Above right: *Coronilla emerus*
Right: *Coronilla varia*

Species cultivated: *C. cappadocica* (*C. orientalis*), Turkey; hardy, tufted, herbaceous perennial with woody base; stems prostrate, 6–15cm long; leaves with 7–11 glaucous, oblong-cuneate leaflets; umbels 3–9 flowered, each 1–1·8cm long, yellow, late summer; good rock garden species. *C. emerus*, scorpion senna; Europe; hardy, deciduous shrub 1–2m tall; leaves of 5–9 obovate glaucous leaflets 1–2cm long; umbels 2–3 flowered, each 1·5–2cm long, pale yellow, late spring, autumn; pod like a scorpion's tail. *C. glauca*, see *C. valentina*. *C. iberica*, see *C. cappadocica*. *C. minima*, S.W. Europe; half-hardy shrub; stems procumbent or almost so, to 30cm or more long; leaves of 5–7 or more, elliptic to rounded leaflets 1–1·5cm long; umbels 7–10 flowered, each 5–8mm long, yellow, fragrant, summer; survives light frosts in a sheltered site. *C. montana* (*C. coronata*), S. Europe, Caucasus; half-hardy, sub-shrubby perennial, spreading or erect to 30cm or more; leaves of 7–13 elliptic to obovate leaflets, 1·5–3cm long; umbels 12–20 flowered, each 7–11mm long, yellow, late summer; survives light frost. *C. valentina*, S. Portugal, Mediterranean; half-hardy, evergreen shrub 1–1·5m tall; leaves bright green above, glaucous beneath; umbels 5–12 flowered, each 7–12mm long, yellow, smelling of ripe peaches, late spring, summer or later. *C.v. glauca* (*C. glauca*), leaves brightly glaucous on both surfaces: flowers rich yellow, appearing intermittently throughout the year under glass; needs a warm, sheltered site to thrive outside for long, makes a good patio plant in a tub, over-wintered under glass. *C. varia*, C. and S. Europe; hardy perennial; stems prostrate or decumbent, 20–120cm long; leaves of 11–25 oblong or elliptic leaflets 6–20cm long; umbels 10–20 flowered, each bloom 1–1·5cm long, white, pink or purple, summer, autumn; very vigorous and good as ground cover.

Cortaderia

(Argentinian name in Latin form for pampas grass). GRAMINEAE. A genus of 15 species of grasses from New Zealand and S. America. The species cultivated are densely tufted or clump-forming with arching leaves, and large, plume-like panicles of tiny spikelets. Grow in well-drained soil in a sunny site. Plant spring or early autumn. Propagate by division or from seed in spring. The old foliage may be burnt off in early spring, but it is best to pull away dead leaves with a gloved hand.

Species cultivated: *C. argentea*, see *C. selloana*. *C. conspicua*, see next species. *C. richardii* (*C. conspicua* and *Arundo c.* of gardens), toe-toe; New Zealand; stems 1·5–3m tall; leaves 60–120cm long; panicles

Above: *Cortaderia selloana* Sunningdale Silver
Right: *Corydalis cashmeriana*
Top far right: *Corydalis lutea*
Far right above: *Corydalis solida*

dense, 30–60cm long, spikelets silvery to creamy-white, summer. *C. selloana* (*C. argentea, Gynerium a., Arundo selloana*), pampas grass; temperate S. America; stems 1·5–3m tall; leaves 1–3m long, margins roughly scabrid, capable of cutting a finger if carelessly handled, more or less glaucous; panicles 45–120cm long, spikelets white, early autumn. *C.s.* Aureo-lineata, leaves yellow-striped; *C.s.* Monstrosa, to 3m tall, panicles spreading, large; *C.s.* Pumila, dwarf habit, to 1·5m tall, panicles dense, erect; *C.s.* Rendatleri, to 3m tall, panicles arching, large, tinted rose-purple; *C.s.* Sunningdale Silver, to 2m or more tall, panicles feathery, creamy-white, usually freely-borne.

Cortusa

(for Jacobi Antonio Cortusi, 1513–1593, Italian botanist and director of the Padua Botanic Garden). PRIMULACEAE. A genus of 2–10 species of herbaceous perennials from the mountains of C. Europe to Japan. They are separated from *Primula* by having the stamen filaments attached to the corolla base and by the apiculate-tipped anthers. The leaves are long-stalked, rounded and lobed, in basal tufts, the flowers bell-shaped with 5 spreading lobes borne in terminals umbels above them. Needs humusy soil, preferably in light shade. Plant autumn or spring. Propagate from seed when ripe or in spring; large plants may be divided after flowering or in spring.
Species cultivated: *C. matthioli*, C. Europe to Japan; stems 20–35cm tall; leaves rounded to kidney-shaped, cordate, palmately shallowly 7–9 lobed, the blades to 10cm long, stalks 8–12cm tall; flowers rose-purple, 1·5cm wide, pendant, 6 or more in each

umbel, late spring, summer. *C.m.* Alba, flowers white. *C.m. pekinensis* (*C. pekinensis*), China; leaves very hairy, lobes deep and pinnately divided; flowers usually darker. Plants encountered under the following names are now generally regarded as forms of this species: *C. brotheri, C. hirsuta, C. pubens, C. transylvanica.*

Corydalis

(Greek for 'crested lark' – the spurs of the flowers are likened to those of the bird). FUMARIACEAE. A genus of 320 species of mainly low-growing perennials from northern temperate zone. They are generally tufted plants, sometimes tuberous, with pinnately cut leaves often of fern-like delicacy, and terminal racemes of 4-petalled flowers, each flower upside-down appearing tubular and 2-lipped with a rear nectary spur uppermost. Fruits are oblong capsules containing arillate seed attractive to ants. Well-drained, moisture-retentive soil, partial shade or sun. Plant tuberous species autumn, others autumn or spring. Propagate by division or offsets at planting time, seed when ripe.
Species cultivated: *C. ambigua*, Japan, Sakhalin, Kuriles; tuberous; stems solitary, 10–30cm tall; leaves bi- or triternate, leaflets 1–3cm long, linear to broadly ovate, somewhat glaucous; racemes dense, erect, flowers 1·5–2·5cm long, blue-purple, spring. *C. bulbosa* (*C. cava*), Europe; tuberous; stems 10–30cm tall; grey-green, biternate leaves; racemes dense, of 10–20 flowers, each bloom 1·5–3cm long, rose-purple, spring. Confused in gardens with the less robust *C. solida*, that has an ovate scale on the stem below the lowest leaf (sometimes below ground level). *C. cashmeriana* (*C. kashmiriana, C. cachemiriana*), Kashmir to Bhutan; scaly-bulbous; stems 7–23cm tall; leaves long-stalked, bi- or triternate, bright green; racemes of 3–8 flowers closely set, each bloom sky-blue, 2–2·5cm long, late spring, summer; needs a cool site in a soil largely of humus; often short-lived. *C. cheilanthifolia*, China; leaves bronze-tinted in good light, bipinnate, fern-like, to 15cm long; racemes arching, just exceeding leaves, flowers pale yellow, about 1cm long, late spring to autumn. *C. diphylla*, W. Himalaya; tuberous; stem 7–15cm tall; leaves bi- or triternate, leaflets linear to oblanceolate, in opposite pairs on flowering stem (no basal leaves); racemes loose, flowers white, tipped red-purple, about 2cm long, early spring; usually seen at its best in an alpine house, but hardy. *C. lutea*, Europe: C. and E. Alps but widely naturalized elsewhere; densely tufted with brittle-branched stems 15–40cm tall; leaves bi- or tripinnate, leaflets obovate, glaucous beneath; racemes dense, or 6–16 flowers, each 12–20mm long, golden-yellow with darker tip, spring to autumn; excellent for old walls but rather invasive in the garden proper. *C. ochroleuca*, Italy, W. Balkans, naturalized elsewhere; much like *C. lutea*, but leaflets glaucous on both surfaces; flowers cream

with yellow tips, somewhat pendulous. *C. solida* (of gardens), see *C. bulbosa*. *C. wilsonii*, China; not unlike *C. cheilanthifolia*, but much finer; glaucous leaves; bright yellow flowers 2cm long. Less hardy.

Corylopsis

(Greek *korylos*, hazel nut, and *opsis*, like – referring to the general resemblances of leaf and habit of some species). HAMAMELIDACEAE. A genus of 20 species of deciduous shrubs or small trees from the Himalaya to Japan. They are generally slender-twigged and bushy, with alternate, prominently-veined, ovate-cordate leaves, and pendant, catkin-like racemes of small, 5-petalled, fragrant flowers. Plant in humus-rich, preferably acid or neutral soil in partial shade or sun, autumn to spring. Propagate from ripe seed cuttings with heel late summer, layering spring.

Species cultivated: *C. glabrescens*, Japan; wide-spreading shrub or small tree 2–5m tall; leaves 5–10cm long, ovate to rounded, bristle-toothed, somewhat glaucous beneath; racemes to 4cm long, flowers pale yellow, spring. *C. gotoana*, Japan; much like *C. glabrescens* and given by some botanists as a synonym for it; leaves obovate to rounded, more shortly bristle-toothed, blue-green above and whitish beneath. *C. pauciflora*, Japan; densely-branched, 1–2m tall; leaves 4–6cm long, ovate, sparingly bristle-toothed; racemes of 2–3 flowers, each about 1·5cm wide, primrose-yellow, spring. *C. platypetala*, W. China; spreading habit, 2–3m tall; twigs hairy, glandular when young; leaves ovate 5–10cm long, dark green above, somewhat glaucous beneath, bristle-like teeth small, racemes to 5cm long, of 8–20 pale yellow flowers, spring. *C. sinensis*, see *C. willmottiae*. *C. spicata*, Japan; wide-spreading, to 2m tall; leaves 5–10cm long, broadly ovate to rounded, shortly bristle-toothed, silky-downed and glaucous beneath, racemes of 6–12 bright yellow flowers, early spring. *C. veitchiana*, C. China; rounded habit, 1·5–2m tall; leaves oval or ovate, slender-pointed, 5–10cm long, somewhat glaucous; racemes to 4cm long, flowers primrose-yellow, densely-borne, spring. *C. willmottiae*, W. China; similar to *C. platypetala*, but leaves oval to obovate, downy beneath; flowers soft, somewhat greenish-yellow; sometimes confused with the rarer *C. sinensis*, China, that has downy branchlets and leaf-stalks, and lemon-yellow flowers.

Corylus

(Greek name for hazel, taken up by Linnaeus for this genus). CORYLACEAE. A genus of 15 species of deciduous trees and shrubs from northern temperate zone. They have alternate to obovate, toothed leaves, and monoecious flowers, the males in slender pendant catkins, the females bud-like with red stigmas. The fruit is an ovoid to oblong nut surrounded by prominent bracts and bracteoles (the husk). Grow in humus-rich soil in sun or light shade. Plant autumn and winter. Propagate from seed when ripe or by layers in spring, the latter method only for cultivars; suckers may also be used when convenient.

Species cultivated (all flowering before the leaves): *C. avellana*, hazel or cob-nut; Europe, W. Asia, N. Africa; 4–6m tall, suckering habit grown naturally; leaves rounded to obovate, cordate, cuspidate, 5–12cm long; male catkins to 8cm long, yellow, in clusters of 1–4, winter; nut ovoid-round, 1·5–2cm long, the surrounding husk is twice as long. *C.a.* Aurea, leaves yellow-green; weak-growing. *C.a.* Contorta, corkscrew hazel: twigs twisted and curled; curious mutant found in Gloucestershire hedgerow about 1863. *C.a.* Fusco-Rubra, leaves red-purple, lighter than the better known *C. maxima* Purpurea. *C.a.* Pendula, branches weeping – an interesting specimen tree for the smaller lawn. *C. colurna*, Turkish hazel; S.E. Europe, Turkey; tree eventually to 20m or more; bark fissured and oak-like when mature; head of branches broadly conical; leaves to 2·5cm long, irregularly rounded, short-pointed; male catkins 5–7cm long; nut about 1·5cm long in a deeply-lobed husk like a ragged fringe. *C. cornuta* (*C. rostrata*), beaked hazel; N. America; shrub 2–3m tall, like common hazel but male catkins shorter and nut closely enclosed in a tapered, beak-like, bristle-haired husk 3–4·5cm long. *C. maxima*, filbert; Balkan Peninsula, naturalized elsewhere; like common hazel but more robust, sometimes a small tree to 7m tall; leaves to 13cm long; nut longer, completely enclosed in a long, deeply-lobed husk; see also Hazel-nut. *C.m.* Purpurea, leaves dark purple, catkins purple-tinted.

Top: *Corydalis cheilanthifolia*
Above: *Corylopsis veitchiana*
Top right: *Corylopsis glabrescens*
Right top: *Corylus avellana* Contorta
Right: *Cosmos bipinnatus*
Far right top: *Cotinus coggygria purpureus*
Far right: *Corylus maxima* Purpurea

Cosmos

(Greek *kosmos*, beautiful). COMPOSITAE. A genus of 25 species of annuals and perennials from tropical and subtropical America including Mexico and W. Indies. They are mainly erect plants with pinnately dissected leaves in opposite pairs and terminal, daisy-like flower-heads having very broad ray florets. The species described are half-hardy annuals. Grow in most soils in a sunny site. Sow seed under glass in spring at 15°C; prick off seedlings about 4–5cm apart each way into boxes of a commercial potting mixture; harden off and plant out when fear of frost has passed in early summer. Seed may also be sown *in situ* in late spring to early summer. Support of twiggy sticks is advisable in windy sites.

Species cultivated: *C. bipinnatus*, Mexico; to 90cm or more; leaves bipinnate with linear segments; flower-heads on slender stems, 5–7cm or so wide, generally with 8 rose-purple ray florets, summer; several strains have been developed by seedsmen, with larger flower-heads in shades of purple, crimson, pink and white. *C. sulphureus*, Mexico; about 6cm tall; leaves bipinnatipartite, lobes lanceolate; flower-heads 4–5cm wide, ray florets yellow; cultivar strains with larger and semi-double flower-heads are available in shades of gold to orange-red.

Cotinus

(Greek *kotinos*, for the wild olive–seemingly of no relevance except that the twiggy grey bushes of olive also have a smoky appearance viewed *en masse*). ANACARDIACEAE. A genus of 2 deciduous shrubs or small trees from Europe and S.E. USA. They have alternate, obovate to rounded leaves and terminal panicles composed of many slender flower-stalks, a few smooth and bearing tiny, 5-petalled flowers, the remainder sterile and fine-haired, often pink- or red-tinted and creating a smoky effect. Grow in well-drained soil in a sunny site, although *C. obovatus* does well also in light shade. Plant autumn to spring. Propagate by cuttings with a heel in late summer, layering in spring.

Species cultivated: *C. coggygria* (*Rhus cotinus*), smoke tree, wig tree, Venetian sumach; C. S. Europe to China; shrub to 3m or so tall; leaves 4–7cm long, yellow to red in autumn; panicles to 15cm or more, pinkish-fawn, summer to autumn. *C.c.* Flame, orange-red foliage in autumn; *C.c.* Foliis Purpureis, leaves red-purple, brightest when young, panicles pink; *C.c.* Notcutts, darker, almost maroon leaves

and purplish-pink panicles; *C.c.* Royal Purple, even darker leaves; *C.c. purpureus*, panicles purplish-pink, leaves green. *C.* × *leschenaultii*, reputedly a hybrid between *C. coggygria* and *C. obovatus* and halfway between the 2, with good autumn colour. *C. obovatus* (*C. americanus*, *Rhus cotinoides*), S.E. USA; to 5m tall, double this in the wild; leaves 5–13cm long, bronze-pink when young, orange, scarlet and purple in autumn particularly on acid soils in sheltered sites; panicles 15–30cm long, rather sparse; inferior to *C. coggygria* in flower but a superb autumn foliage plant when well-suited.

Cotoneaster

(Latin *cotoneum*, quince, and *aster*, inferior or wild – the leaves of some species are somewhat quince-like). ROSACEAE. A genus of 50 species of mainly deciduous shrubs and trees from northern temperate zone. They have alternate leaves, small (8–10mm wide), white to pinkish, 5-petalled flowers, either solitary or in clusters, and berry-like pomes in shades of red and black, rarely yellow. Grow in any well-drained soil preferably in sun or light shade. Plant autumn to spring. Propagate by cuttings with a heel in late summer or from seed when ripe; the latter may take a year to germinate, particularly if allowed to dry out and sowing delayed to spring.

Species cultivated (deciduous unless stated otherwise): *C. acuminatus*, Himalaya; erect shrub 3–4m tall; leaves to 5cm long, ovate to lanceolate, long-pointed, dark green above, paler beneath, silky-haired when young; flowers pinkish in clusters of 2–5; fruit bright red, oblong-ovoid, 8mm long. *C. acutifolius* (*C. pekinensis*), spreading shrub to 2m or more; leaves oval to ovate-lanceolate, pointed; flowers white or pinkish, in clusters of 2–5; fruit black, ellipsoidal, about 1cm long. *C. adpressus*, China; rigid, wide-spreading shrub, to about 30cm tall; much like a smaller version of *C. horizontalis* and formerly classified as a variety of it; leaves 6–15mm long; fruit bright red, 6mm long. *C.a. praecox*, more vigorous than type species; to 60cm tall; larger leaves and fruit to 12mm. *C. affinis*, Himalaya; shrub to 5m; leaves 3–8cm long, obovate to elliptic, often in 2 parallel ranks; flowers white in cymose clusters 2·5–5cm wide; fruit rounded, purple-black. *C.a. bacillaris*, elegant, arching or pendulous habit. *C. bullatus*, Tibet, W. China; 3–4m tall, rather sparse, arching habit; leaves oblong-ovate, 4–9cm long, dark green and hairy above, paler and grey- or buff-felted beneath, somewhat bullate; flowers pinkish, in corymbs of 10–30; fruit rounded to obovoid, 8mm wide, bright red. *C. buxifolius*, N. India; evergreen shrub 30–60cm tall; leaves oval to obovate, 6–12mm long, tawny-felted below; flowers white in clusters of 2–7; fruit obovoid, 6mm long. *C.b. vellaeus* (*C. rockii*), China; prostrate, less hairy than type. The *C. buxifolius* of gardens is often *C. rotundifolius lanatus*. *C. congestus* (*C. microphyllus glacialis*, *C. pyrenaicus*), Himalaya; dense, compact, evergreen shrub 45–75cm tall, but wider and mound-like; leaves oval to obovate, about 8mm long, whitish beneath; flowers pinkish-white, solitary; fruit rounded, bright red, about 6mm wide. *C.c.* Nanus, prostrate and slow-growing, forming neat, small mats. *C. conspicuus* (*C.c. decorus*, *C. microphyllus decorus*, *C. permutatus*), evergreen, arching and spreading, to semi-erect, 2m or more tall; leaves ovate, oblanceolate to linear-obovate, 4–6mm long, dark green above, grey-woollen beneath; flowers white, to 12mm wide, solitary; fruit globose to obovoid, about 1cm long, bright scarlet. *C.c.* Decorus, low, arching habit, free-fruiting (although a synonym of the originally described species, *C.c.* Decorus is conveniently retained here to define the best-known, award-winning form). *C.* × Cornubia, see *C.* × *watereri*. *C. dammeri*, C. China; mat-forming evergreen; leaves oval to obovate, 2–3cm long, lustrous above; flowers white, solitary or in pairs; fruit broadly obovoid, about 6mm wide, bright red. *C.d. radicans*, confused with type and *C.d.* Major (larger leaves to 4cm long) in cultivation, although leaf- and flower-stalks longer. *C.d.* Skogholm, though probably a hybrid, is similar to *C.d. radicans* but more vigorous, sometimes with low, arching stems to 30cm tall. *C. dielsianus* (*C. applanatus*), C. China; deciduous twiggy shrub to 2m; young branchlets flattened like those of *C. horizontalis*; leaves ovate, 1–4cm long; flowers pinkish in clusters of 3–7; fruit rounded to pear-shaped, 6mm long, scarlet; usually has orange- to red-tinted foliage in autumn. *C. divaricatus*, China; spreading, deciduous shrub, to 2m tall; leaves rounded to oval or obovate, mucronate, 1–2·5cm long, dark glossy green; flowers bright pink, in clusters of 1–3; fruit red, obovoid, about 8mm long. *C.* × Exburyensis, see *C. watereri*. *C. foveolatus*, China; deciduous, 3–4m tall; leaves oval to ovate, slender-pointed, 4–10cm long, often somewhat bullate; flowers white, tinted pink, in clusters of 3–7; fruit red, changing to black, rounded, 6–8mm wide; autumn foliage orange to scarlet. *C. franchetii*, Tibet, W. China; evergreen shrub 2·5–3m tall; gracefully arching branches; leaves oval, 2–3cm long, lustrous above and hairy when young, buff-felted beneath; flowers white, tinted pink in bud, petals erect; fruit oblong-ovoid, 6–8mm long, orange-scarlet. *C.f. sternianus*, Burma; fruit globose to obovoid, frequently

Left: *Cotinus obovatus* in autumn
Bottom left: *Cotoneaster conspicuus*
Above: *Cotoneaster* × *watereri* Exburiensis
Right top: *Cotoneaster franchettii*
Right above: *Cotoneaster* × *watereri* Rothschildianus
Right: *Cotoneaster salicifolius rugosus*
Right bottom: *Cotula atrata*

masquerading as *C. wardii* in cultivation; see also *C. pannosus*. *C. frigidus*, Himalaya; deciduous large shrub or small tree to 7m; leaves narrowly obovate to oval, 7–13cm long, deep dull green above, pale and woolly beneath when young; flowers white, many in flattened corymbs 5cm or more wide; fruit bright red, globose, 5–6mm wide. *C.f.* Fructu-luteo (*C.f.* Xanthocarpus), fruit creamy-yellow. *C. glaucophyllus*, W. China; evergreen or partially so, to 3m or more; leaves oval or somewhat obovate, 4–6·5cm long, dark green above, glaucous beneath; flowers white in corymbs to 5cm wide, late summer; fruit crimson, globose, 6mm wide, late autumn. *C.g. vestitus*, leaves densely buff-downed beneath; the commonest form in gardens. *C.g. serotinus* (*C. serotinus*), more vigorous than type, to 9m tall; young shoots and leaf undersides white-downed; fruit obovoid. *C. henryanus* (*C. rugosus*), C. China; evergreen or partly so, 3–4m tall; leaves 5–12cm long, narrowly obovate to oblong-lanceolate, somewhat corrugated, dark green above, grey-haired beneath; flowers white, in corymbs 5–6·5cm wide; fruit dark crimson, ovoid, 6mm long; closely allied to *C. salicifolius* and by some considered only a form of it. *C. horizontalis*, China; deciduous, wide-spreading to several metres, about 60–90cm tall, unless trained up a wall when much more; twigs arranged in parallel ranks creating a fish-bone effect; leaves rounded, abruptly pointed, to 12mm long; flowers white and pink, singly or in pairs; fruit globose, bright red, about 5mm wide. *C.h. perpusillus*, dwarfer than type, with smaller leaves; *C.h.* Variegatus, leaves white-edged. *C.* × Hybridus Pendulus, prostrate, evergreen, blending the characters of *C. dammeri* and *C. salicifolius*, its probable parents; makes a small, weeping tree grafted to a stem of *C. frigidus* or *C. salicifolius*. *C. lacteus*, China; evergreen shrub, 2–4m tall; branchlets arching; leaves leathery, oval to obovate, dark green above, yellowish to greyish down beneath, to 6cm or more long; flowers white in corymbs to 7·5 cm wide, late summer; fruit ovoid, 5mm long, red, maturing late autumn; sometimes confused with *C. glaucophyllus serotinus*. *C. microphyllus*, Himalaya, S.W. China; evergreen, arching, spreading to prostrate; leaves 6–12mm long, ovate to obovate, glossy deep green above, grey-haired beneath; flowers white, usually solitary; fruit globose, scarlet, about 6mm wide; can be trained to cover a wall. *C.m. cochleatus*, prostrate, leaves wider than type and generally less glossy. *C.m. thymifolius*, much smaller than type, with narrower, paler green leaves. *C. multiflorus* (*C. reflexus*), Caucasus to China; deciduous, shrub or small tree to 4m; branchlets arching to pendulous; leaves ovate to rounded, 2–6·5cm long; flowers freely borne, white in clusters of 3–12; fruit globose to ovoid, red, 8mm wide. *C. pannosus*, China; evergreen, to 3m tall; similar superficially to *C. franchetti* and sometimes confused in gardens, but flowers white, petals spreading, fruit dull red, leaves matt green above, white-woollen beneath, to 2·5cm long. *C.* × Rothschildianus, see *C.* × *watereri*. *C. rotundifolius* (*C. prostratus*, *C. microphyllus uva-ursi*), semi-deciduous, prostrate, arching stems, sometimes to 1m or so tall; leaves obovate to rounded, 1–2cm long, dark green above; flowers white, 2 or 3 together; fruit rounded, about 6mm wide. *C.r. lanatus*, more vigorous than type; leaves densely haired beneath (the type is sparingly so); more flowers per cluster; can reach 2m tall; has also been named *C. buxifolius*, but quite different from that species. *C. salicifolius*, W. China; evergreen shrub or small tree to 5m tall; branches spreading; leaves elliptic to ovate-lanceolate, 4–9cm long, somewhat rugose, glaucous and downy beneath; flowers white in woolly corymbs to 5cm wide; fruit bright red, rounded, about 5mm wide. *C.s. floccosus*, leaves lanceolate, glossy above, to 6·5cm long, white-woollen beneath, freely fruiting on arching stems. *C.s. rugosus*, similar to *C.s. floccosus* but leaves and fruit larger and plant of coarser, more vigorous growth. *C.s.* Autumn Fire, almost pendulous habit and a profusion of orange-red fruit; *C.s.* Parkteppich, semi-prostrate; *C.s.* Repens (*C.s.* Avondrood), prostrate habit, leaves very narrow, good ground cover. *C. simonsii*, Assam-Khasi Hills; deciduous to semi-evergreen, erect habit, 2–3m tall; leaves in 2 parallel ranks 2–2·5cm long, oval, tapered to each end, dark glossy green above; flowers white in groups of 2–4; fruit 8–10mm long, ellipsoid to obovoid, scarlet. *C.* Skogholm, see *C. dammeri*. *C. wardii*, S.E. Tibet, much like *C. franchetti sternianus*, but probably not in cultivation, plants offered under this name probably being *C.f sternianus*. *C.* × *watereri*, a collective name covering hybrids between *C. frigidus*, *C. henryanus*, *C. salicifolius* and their forms; all are vigorous shrubs or small trees 3–5m tall, semi- or fully evergreen; leaves elliptic to lanceolate, 6–13cm long; flowers white in corymbs 3–5cm wide; fruit globose, about 6mm wide. *C.* × *w* Cornubia, semi-evergreen, to 6m tall, abundant red fruit; *C.* × *w.* Exburiensis (*C. frigidus* Fructu-luteo × *C. salicifolius* Fructu-luteo), evergreen, fruit apricot-yellow; *C.* × *w.* John Waterer, semi-evergreen, spreading habit, red fruit; *C.* × *w.* Rothschildianus, with creamy-yellow fruit.

Cotton grass, cotton sedge – see *Eriophorum*.

Cotton gum – see *Nyssa aquatica*.

Cottonwood – see *Populus*.

Cotula

(Greek *kotule*, a small cup – the stem-clasping leaf-bases of some species forming a cup). COMPOSITAE. A genus of 75 species of mainly small annual and perennial plants of almost cosmopolitan distribution particularly S. Hemisphere. Except for 1 tender annual, the species described are mainly prostrate, mat-forming or decumbent hardy plants with alternate, often pinnately cut leaves and button-like flower-heads composed of 4–lobed disc florets. Grow in any soil, preferably one that does not dry out unduly, in sun or light shade. Plant hardy species autumn to spring, half-hardy sorts when fear of frost has passed. Propagate from seed in spring or by division of the perennials late summer or spring. *C. barbata* can be sown *in situ* late spring to early summer, but is best sown under glass in early to mid spring at 15–18°C, the seedlings being pricked off into standard potting mixture at 3cm apart, hardened off and planted out early summer.

Species cultivated (all from New Zealand and summer-flowering unless otherwise stated): *C. atrata*, perennial, mat-forming, 20–30cm wide; leaves 1·5–3·5cm long, bipinnate, somewhat fleshy and flushed copper to purple; flower-heads 1·5–2cm wide, black-crimson with white, pin-like stigmas, spring and summer. *C.a. luteola*, florets burnt crimson in bud opening wine-red, fading pink, with very prominent creamy-white stigmas. *C. barbata* (*Cenia b.*, *Lancisia b.*), S. Africa; half-hardy annual, tufted, 8–20cm or more tall; leaves pinnatipartite, lobes linear, silky-haired; flower-heads to 2cm wide, yellow. *C. coronopifolia*, brass buttons; southern temperate zone; perennial; stems prostrate at base, then ascending 10–30cm tall; leaves linear-lanceolate, 1–5cm long, toothed or lobed; flower-heads bright yellow, 1·5cm wide. *C. potentillina* (*Leptinella p.*), perennial, mat-forming; leaf-blade 4–5cm or more long, pinnatisect to pinnatifid, the lobes serrate or crenate, long-stalked; flower-heads 1cm wide, yellowish; pleasing, mossy mats of foliage tinted purple-brown useful as ground cover for small bulbs. *C. pyrethrifolia*, mat-forming, to 1m wide, aromatic; leaf-blades to 1·5cm or more long, bright green, pinnate to pinnatisect, long-stalked; flower-heads yellow, 1–1·5cm wide. *C. sericea*, mat-forming, leaves 1–2cm long, pinnate to pinnatisect, silky-haired, grey-green, tinted purple-red; flower-heads 5–8cm wide, whitish. *C. squalida*, mat-forming, to 60cm or more wide; leaves bronzy-green, 2–7cm long, pinnatisect, lobes deeply-toothed; flower-heads to 5mm wide, yellowish-green; can be invasive in moist, fertile soils.

Cow parsnip – see *Heracleum*.

Cowberry – see *Vaccineum vitis-idaea*.

Cowslip – see *Primula veris*.

Crab or crab apple – see *Malus*.

Crambe

(Greek name for wild cabbage that vaguely resembles seakale, *C. maritima*, the original species so described by Linnaeus). CRUCIFERAE. A genus of 25 species of generally robust perennials from Europe, Africa, Macronesia, Asia. 1 species is generally grown as an ornamental: *C. cordifolia*, Caucasus; massive perennial; basal leaves somewhat fleshy, deep green, lobed and waved, to 1m long; stems to 2m or more tall, much branched, bearing numerous, small, white, 4-petalled flowers with a strong scent, creating the illusion of a giant gypsophila, summer. See also Seakale, that – though a vegetable – can be planted as an ornamental for its richly glaucous leaves. Grow in humus-rich soil in a sunny site. Plant autumn to spring. Propagate from seed, by division or root cuttings in spring.

Cranberry – see *Oxycoccus*.

Crane's bill – see *Geranium*.

+Crataegomespilus

(*Crataegus* + *Mespilus*). ROSACEAE. An interesting and curious asexual hybrid occurring as a chimaera at the graft union of hawthorn (*Crataegus monogyna*) and medlar (*Mespilus germanica*). + *C. dardarii*, Bronvaux medlar, Metz, France; much like a smaller, more twiggy medlar in all main characters but every now and then produces shoots of typical medlar and hawthorn. + *C.d.* Jules d'Asnieres, of the same origin but basically favours hawthorn except that young shoots are woolly and leaves vary from lobed to entire. For culture, see *Crataegus*; propagation only by grafting or layering.

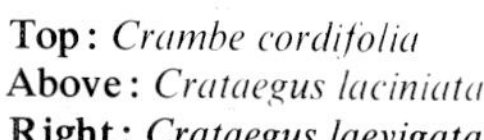

Top: *Crambe cordifolia*
Above: *Crataegus laciniata*
Right: *Crataegus laevigata*

Crataegus

(Greek name for hawthorn, from *kratos*, strength – the wood is hard and durable). ROSACEAE. A genus of about 200 clearly recognizable species of deciduous shrubs and small trees from northern temperate zone, although more than 1000 have been described, mainly from N. America, most of which appear to be natural hybrids. They are often spiny, with alternate, lobed or toothed leaves, corymbs of 5-petalled, white or pink flowers and berry-like haws (pomes) containing 1 or more seed (stones). The haws are often carried in large numbers and are generally red or orange in colour making a bright feature in autumn. Grow in any well-drained soil (although most species stand wet conditions in winter) in sun or light shade. Plant autumn to winter. Propagation in nurseries is often by grafting on to common hawthorn rootstocks and the resultant trees can be short-lived or unsatisfactory in other ways; layering may be used but is slow and not always successful. Seed provides the easiest and best method but germination does not take place until the second spring after ripening. Large quantities for hedging purposes may be stratified, small amounts sown in pots or pans in autumn and stored in a mouse-proof frame where the temperature drops to at least 5°C in winter to break the dormancy of the seed. Once sown the seed must not be allowed to dry out.

Species cultivated (white-flowered and early summer flowering unless stated otherwise): *C.* × *carrierei*, see *C.* × *lavallei*. *C. coccinea*, see *C. intricata* and *C. pedicillata*. *C. crus-galli*, cockspur thorn; E. and C. N. America; small, wide-spreading tree to about 7m; stems with thorns to about 8cm long; leaves obovate, tapered to base, 2·5–10cm long, dark glossy green, turning scarlet in autumn; flowers 1cm wide in corymbs to 7·5cm wide; haws globose, 1cm or more long, deep red, persisting all winter – birds permitting. *C. durobrivensis*, E. USA; shrub 3–4m tall; thorns 4–5cm long; leaves broadly ovate, to 7·5cm long, with several small triangular lobes and sharp teeth; flowers 2–2·5cm across; haws globose 1·5cm wide, deep glossy crimson, probably a natural hybrid. *C. flava*, yellow haw; S.E. USA; small tree to 7m or more; thorns about 2·5cm long; leaves 2·5–6·5cm long, obovate to diamond-shaped, usually with several small-pointed lobes and doubly-toothed; flowers to 1·7cm wide; haws oblong to ellipsoid, yellow 1·5cm long. *C.* × *grignonensis*, see *C.* × *lavallei*. *C. intricata* (*C. coccinea* in part), spreading shrub 2–4m tall; twigs somewhat zig-zagged; thorns about 4cm long; leaves ovate, 3–6cm long, sharply lobed and toothed; flowers 1·3–1·7cm wide, in clusters of 3–7; haws oblong to ellipsoid, to 1·5cm long, bronze-green to red-brown. *C. laciniata* (*C. orientalis*), almost thornless tree, 5–6m tall, with spreading, often somewhat pendulous-tipped branches; leaves 2·5–5cm triangular-ovate to obovate, pinnatifid with 5–9 narrow, oblong lobes, each sometimes toothed at apices, dark green and pubescent above, grey-downed beneath; flowers about 2cm wide; fruit globose, to 2cm long, downy, coral to orange-red. *C. laevigata* (*C. oxyacantha*, *C. oxyacanthoides*), Midland hawthorn; Europe; much like common hawthorn (*C. monogyna*), but leaves with 3–5 rounded, shallow lobes, slightly larger flowers with 2–3 styles, carried in smaller clusters. *C.l.* 'Paul's Scarlet (*C.l.* Coccinea Plena), flowers double, scarlet; *C.l.* Plena, double, white; *C.l.* Punicea, single, scarlet; *C.l.* Rosea, single, pink; *C.l.* Rosea Flore Pleno, double, pink. *C.* × *lavallei* (*C.* × *carrierei*) (probably *C. stipulacea* × *C. crus-galli*), Segrez Arboretum, France; tree 5–7m tall;

thorns few, 2·5–4cm long; leaves obovate or oval, tapered, 4–11cm long, coarsely toothed, glossy deep green above; flowers white, 2–2·5cm wide, in corymbs to 7·5cm wide; haws rounded to obovoid, 2cm wide, orange-red, long, persistent; this description refers to the plant long known as *C.* × *carrierei*, that arose via the same putative parents in the Jardins des Plantes, Paris, but was described later; to distinguish this well-known clone from true *C.* × *lavallei* it is best to retain the name as a cultivar, thus: *C.* × *l.* Carrierei; *C.* × *grigonensis* is another *C. stipulacea* hybrid that resembles *C.* × *lavallei* but has glabrous shoots (those of *C.* × *lavallei* are downy). *C. mollis*, red haw; E. USA; spreading tree 10–12m tall; sparingly thorny; leaves mainly ovate with several small, sharply-toothed triangular lobes; flowers 2cm or more wide in large corymbs; fruit rounded, bright red, to 1·8cm long, freely borne; among the finest fruiting thorns, but too large for small gardens. *C. monogyna*, common hawthorn; Europe to Afghanistan; shrub or small tree 2–10m tall, sharply-thorned; leaves 1·5–3·5cm long, ovate to obovate, deeply 3–7 lobed; flowers 1-styled, 1cm or more wide, to 16 or more in each corymb; fruit oblong-ovoid, deep red, 8–10mm long. *C.m.* Biflora (*C.m.* Praecox), Glastonbury thorn, scattered flowers during winter and again late spring; *C.m.* Fastigiata, see *C.m.* Stricta; *C.m.* Flexuosa, corkscrew-like branchlets; *C.m.* Pendula, arching or weeping habit; *C.m.* Praecox, see *C.m.* Biflora; *C.m.* Stricta, branchlets erect. *C. orientalis*, see *C. laciniata*. *C. oxyacantha* and *C. oxyacanthoides*, see *C. laevigata*. *C. pedicillata* (*C. coccinea* in part), N.E. N. America; thorny, spreading shrub or small tree 3–8m tall; leaves ovate, 7–10cm long, with 4–5 pairs of pointed, sharply-toothed lobes; flowers to 2cm wide in loose corymbs; fruit oblong to obovoid, 1cm or more long, bright scarlet; leaves often colour well in autumn. *C. phaenopyrum*, Washington thorn; S.E. USA; round-headed, to 9m; thorns to 7·5cm long; leaves broadly to triangular ovate, lustrous, 2·5–7·5cm long, sharply-toothed, prominently-lobed and somewhat maple-like, usually colouring well in autumn; flowers about 1cm wide, in corymbs to 7·5cm wide; fruit globular, 6mm wide, deep bright crimson. *C. prunifolia* (*C. crus-galli prunifolia*), not known wild and probably a hybrid between *C. crus-galli* and *C. macracantha* (the latter with very large thorns to 8cm long and elliptic to ovate leaves); small, broad-headed tree to 6m; sharply-thorned; leaves broadly ovate to obovate 4–9cm long, glossy dark green above, colouring well in autumn; flowers 2cm wide, in rounded corymbs; fruit globose 1·5cm long, deep red, falling with the leaves. *C. submollis*, N.E. N. America; similar to *C. mollis* and often grown under that name, but leaves smaller and fruit orange-red. *C. tanacetifolia*, Turkey, Syria; usually thornless tree to 10m or so, like *C. laciniata*, large stipules and deeply-cut mossy bracts at or near the bases of the fruit.

Creeping Jenny – see *Lysimachia nummularia*.

Left below: *Crataegus prunifolia*
Left bottom: *Crataegus monogyna*
Below: *Crataegus laevigata* Paul's Scarlet
Right: *Crepis incana*

Crepis

(Greek *krepis*, boot or footwear, but meaning obscure). COMPOSITAE. A genus of 200 species of annuals, biennials and perennials from the N. Hemisphere plus tropical S. Africa. They are rosetted or tufted plants with ovate or oblong to spathulate leaves, often deeply-lobed, and erect flowering stems, bearing 1 to many flower-heads composed entirely of ligulate florets rather like small

dandelions. Grow in any well-drained soil in a sunny site. Plant autumn or spring. Propagate from seed or division in spring.

Species cultivated: *C. aurea,* Alps, mountains of Italy, and Balkan Peninsula; perennialt basal leaves 1–10cm long, obovate to oblanceolate, pinnatifid or toothed, lustrous; flower-heads 2–3cm wide, usually solitary, yellow to orange, outer florets red beneath, autumn; the form in cultivation has coppery-orange flowers. *C. incana,* S. Greece; perennial; leaves 3–13cm long, oblanceolate, pinnatisect, somewhat hoary or grey-green; flower-heads pink, about 3cm wide, freely-borne, usually in small, open panicles to 15cm or more tall, summer. *C. pygmaea,* mountains S.W. Europe, S. Alps, S. Appenines; perennial; leaves 3–11cm, lyrate-pinnatifid, with large terminal leaflet; flower-heads 2cm wide, pale yellow, outer florets reddish-purple beneath, up to 8 in a panicle. *C.p. foliis-purpureis,* leaves purple-bronze; rosettes about 10cm wide; needs to be grown in a poor gritty soil – ideally in scree – to maintain its neat habit and leaf colour. *C. rubra,* S. Italy, Balkan Peninsula, Crete; annual; leaves to 15cm long, oblanceolate, dentate to runcinate-pinnatifid; flower-heads rose or white, 2·5–3·5cm wide, solitary or in 2s, summer and autumn.

× Crindonna

(*Crinodonna, Amarcrinum*). A bigeneric hybrid between *Amaryllis belladonna* and *Crinum moorei* raised independently by a Dr Ragioneri of Florence and a Mr Howard of Los Angeles. It has long, thick-necked bulbs, evergreen, strap-shaped, arching or recurved leaves to 60cm long, and funnel-shaped rose and white flowers, 7·5–10cm wide, in terminal umbels of 8–12 in autumn. See the *Crinum* parent for culture.

Crinitaria linosyris – see *Aster linosyris.*

Below: *Crinum moorei*
Bottom: *Crinum × powellii*
Right above: *Crinodendron hookerianum*

Crinodendron

(Greek *krinon,* lily, and *dendron,* tree – in allusion to the flowers). ELAEOCARPACEAE. A genus of 2 species of evergreen trees from Chile, with alternate leaves, and pendant, 5-petalled, bell-shaped flowers. Grow in a frost-free greenhouse in the coldest exposed areas, or on a sheltered but shaded wall where winter frosts are not severe. Suitable for light woodland in a humus-rich, neutral to acid soil. Plant or pot spring. Propagate by cuttings with a heel late summer.

Species cultivated: *C. hookerianum* (*Tricuspidaria lanceolata*), lantern tree; generally a shrub to 3m, but in favourable sites eventually a tree to 10m; leaves oblong-lanceolate, toothed, 5–13cm long, dark green above, paler beneath, hard-textured; flowers crimson, urn-shaped, 2·5–3cm long on long stalks from upper leaf-axils, late spring. *C. patagua* (*Tricuspidaria dependens, Crinodendron d.*), shrub or small tree to 10m; leaves ovate, 2·5–7·5cm long; flowers white, 2cm long, each petal 3-toothed at tip, late summer.

Crinum

(Greek *krinon,* lily – the flowers resemble those of the true lilies, *Lilium*). AMARYLLIDACEAE. A genus of 100 or more species of bulbous-rooted perennials from the tropics and subtropics, particularly sea coasts. They generally have large, long-necked bulbs, broad, strap-shaped, somewhat fleshy leaves, sometimes more or less in 2 ranks, and erect, leafless stems bearing umbels of funnel-shaped, lily-like blossoms. Greenhouse, minimum temperature 7–10°C. The few half-hardy to almost hardy species can be grown in well-drained soil in sunny, sheltered sites outside, making sure the bases of the bulbs are at least 30cm below the soil surface. In very cold areas even these will need a frost-free greenhouse. Plant or pot spring – large pots will be needed – and the bulbs are best set with their necks and upper $\frac{1}{3}$ above the soil to provide more root room. Any commercial potting mixture is suitable, particularly those which are loam-based. Provide humidity and light shade in summer. Apply liquid feed at fortnightly intervals once the foliage is growing well, keep barely moist in winter. Propagate by dividing large clumps or removing offsets in spring, or from seed sown as soon as ripe at 16–18°C (the large, fleshy seeds soon wither and lose their viability if stored dry).

Species cultivated: *C. asiaticum,* tropical Asia; stem to 60cm tall, 2-edged; leaves 90–120cm long in an arching rosette; flowers white, 14–18cm long in umbels of up to 20, off and on all year if minimum temperature at 15–16°C. *C. bulbispermum* (*C. capense, C. longifolium*), S. Africa; stems 30cm or more; leaves 60–90cm long, slender-pointed; flowers white, flushed red, to 15cm or more long in umbels of 6–12, autumn; the hardiest species. *C. capense,* see previous species. *C. macowanii,* S. Africa; stem 60–90cm tall; leaves 60–90cm long in arching rosette; flowers white, tinted purple, to 15cm or more long, in umbels of 10–15, late autumn; half-hardy. *C. moorei,* S. Africa; very similar to *C. bulbispermum,* but more leafy; flowering stems 45–60cm tall and starting to bloom in late summer. *C. × powellii* (*C. bulbispermum × C. moorei*), much like the latter parent but flowers more strongly rosy-purple to pink-flushed, more vigorous in growth and as hardy as *C. bulbispermum,* late summer and autumn; *C. × p.* Album, flowers pure white.

Crocosmia

(Greek *krokos,* saffron, and *osme,* smell – dried flowers of some species smell of saffron when placed in warm water). IRIDACEAE. A genus of 6 species of

cormous plants from southern and tropical Africa. They have flattened fans of sword-shaped leaves, and arching, branched spikes of obliquely funnel-shaped flowers in late summer. Grow in well-drained, humus-rich soil that does not dry out, in sun or light shade. Plant spring. Propagate by division, offsets or from seed spring.
Species cultivated (all South African): *C. aurea* (*Tritonia a.*), leaves and stems 60–90cm long; flowers about 5cm long, golden- to reddish-yellow with long, projecting stamens, somewhat nodding, half-hardy, the corms best lifted in very cold areas and over-wintered in pots of barely moist compost in a frost-free shed; rare in cultivation and sometimes usurped by 1 of its hybrids. *C.* × *crocosmiiflora* (*C. aurea* × *C. pottsii*), montbretia; range of cultivars combining the flower size and hues of *C. aurea* with the hardiness and vigour of *C. pottsii;* the original orange-red hybrid has become naturalized in many parts of the world, but only a few of the finer popular cultivars which were raised between 1880 and 1920 remain. The following are now commercially available again: *C.* × *c.* Citronella, 60cm, soft lemon-yellow, reasonably hardy; *C.* × *c.* Emily McKenzie, 60cm, dark orange and red, widely-expanded; *C.* × *c.* Jackanapes, 60cm, flowers dark red and yellow in startling contrast, hardy; *C.* × *c.* Solfatare, 60cm, leaves bronze, flowers pale apricot-yellow, not reliably hardy unless protected *in situ* or lifted. *C. masonorum*, leaves strongly pleated, to 1m; stems a little longer, the branched upper part arching downwards to display vermilion-orange, 3cm long flowers; hybrids between this and *Curtonus paniculatus* have recently been raised at Bressingham Gardens in Norfolk, England, combining the best characters of each species; selected cultivars available are: Bressingham Blaze, intense flame-red; Emberglow, burnt-orange, vigorous; Spitfire, like *C. masonorum*, but larger and brilliant orange-red. *C. pottsii*, to 90cm tall; stems less arching than other species; flowers erect, 2·5–3cm long, vermilion-red, yellow throat.

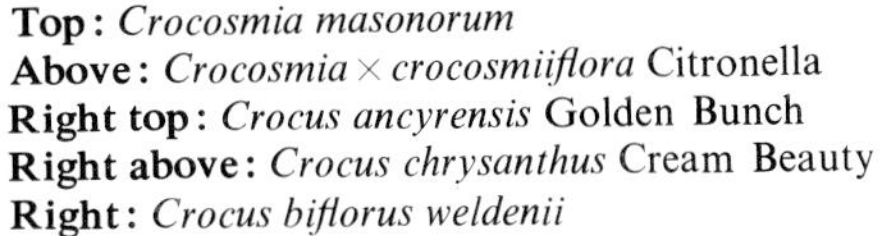
Top: *Crocosmia masonorum*
Above: *Crocosmia* × *crocosmiiflora* Citronella
Right top: *Crocus ancyrensis* Golden Bunch
Right above: *Crocus chrysanthus* Cream Beauty
Right: *Crocus biflorus weldenii*

Crocus

(Greek *krokos*, saffron – derived from the Semetic *karkom*, a yellow dye obtained from the stigmas of *C. sativus* and allied species). IRIDACEAE. A genus of about 75 species of cormous-rooted perennials from Europe, Mediterranean to C. Asia and W. Pakistan. In general they have grassy leaves with a white or silvery central stripe, and 6-tepalled, chalice-shaped blooms that expand widely in sun. Although the tepals are self-coloured within, they frequently bear a dark, lined or feathered pattern without, sometimes against a background suffusion of grey, buff or bronze. Each flower has 3 stamens only and a long, stalk-like tube with the ovary underground near the corm. Most of the autumn-flowering species bloom before the leaves, but the winter and spring sorts flower with the foliage. The corms are small, rounded and flattened to almost globular, bearing a distinctive skin or tunic much used as a character in classification. This tunic may be of parallel fibres, woven fibres, all-over shell-like, annulate (shell-like rings), coarsely- or finely-netted. After flowering, the leaves elongate greatly, and before they die away the seed capsules emerge above ground to ripen. Grow in any well-drained soil in a site that receives the low autumn to spring sun, otherwise the flowers will not open properly. Plant autumn-flowerers in late summer, the remainder in autumn. Propagate from seed sown when ripe or as soon afterwards as possible, offsets when dormant. All crocus make excellent plants for the cold greenhouse, and several species are best grown in this way in areas of wet summers or where the soil does not dry out. Plant in pans of a loam-based potting mixture, and keep just moist until leaves show, then water regularly. When the leaves start to yellow keep dry until repotting time.
Species cultivated (heights given are approximate flower-tube lengths above ground): *C. alatavicus*, USSR – Alatau mountains; leaves narrow, to 15 per corm; flowers 8cm, slender, basically white with a variable amount of bluish striping or freckling, late winter; probably best under glass. *C. albiflorus* (*C. vernus albiflorus*), mountains France to Yugoslavia; leaves 3–4 per corm; flowers 7cm, white, often suffused or veined purple, spring. *C. ancyrensis*, C. Turkey; leaves 3–4 per corm; flowers 7cm, rich orange-yellow, late winter. *C.a.* Golden Bunch, more flowers per corm. *C. angustifolius* (*C. susianus*), USSR – N. Black Sea, Crimea; leaves 5–6; flowers 6–7cm, orange-yellow, feathered bronze-brown without, late winter. *C. asturicus*, Spain; leaves 4–5 after blooming; flowers 10cm, lavender-purple, mid to late autumn. *C.a. atropurpureus*, deeper purple than type. *C. aureus*, see *C. flavus*. *C. balansae*, W. Turkey; leaves 1–3, broad (about 5mm), deep glossy green; flowers 4–5cm, deep yellow or orange, suffused or feathered bronze without, spring. *C. banaticus* (*C. byzantinus*, *C. iridiflorus*), Romania; leaves 2, very broad (about 8mm), spring; flowers 10–15cm, the 3 outer tepals clear purple, the 3 inner ones much smaller and paler, autumn; very distinctive species and surprisingly iris-like when outer tepals reflex back. *C. biflorus*, Italy to Caucasus and Iran; leaves somewhat greyish, 4–5; flowers 10cm, variable, white or blue with purple veining, often with yellow throats, spring. *C.b.* Alexandrei, outer tepals lustrous purple with white margins; *C.b.* Parkinsonii (*C.b.* Argenteus, *C.b.* Praecox), white, light buff with darker striping outside; *C.b. weldenii* (*C. weldenii*), white, freckled or suffused purple-blue; *C.b.w.* Albus, pure white; *C.b.w.* Fairy, white, tinted grey outside. *C. byzantinus*, see *C. banaticus*. *C. cancellatus*, Yugoslavia to Iran; leaves 4–5; flowers 8–10cm, white to pale blue, lined and feathered outside, early autumn, before or with very young foliage; needs sharply-drained soil or to be grown under glass. *C. candidus*, Asia Minor, white but rare in cultivation.

C. subflavus, W. Turkey; leaves 3–4, dark green; flowers 5cm, yellow, usually suffused or feathered purple outside, spring. *C. carpetanus*, Spain, Portugal; leaves 3–4, distinct in the genus by being semi-cylindrical in cross-section; flowers 7cm, whitish within, lilac-purple to pinkish outside; best under glass. *C. chrysanthus*, Yugoslavia to Turkey; leaves 5–7; flowers 5–7cm, orange, tepals broad, feathered outside, anther lobes black-tipped at base, late winter; many cultivars exist, most of them through hybridization with forms of *C. biflorus*; popular and well-tried are: Blue Pearl, pale blue; Cream Beauty, pale creamy-yellow; E. P. Bowles, deep butter-yellow, prominently feathered; Snow Bunting, white and cream, dark lilac feathering; Zwanenburg Bronze, deep orange, heavily suffused purple-brown without. *C. dalmaticus*, Yugoslavia; leaves narrow, 3–5; flowers 5–6cm, lilac, buff with dark feathering outside, late winter. *C. etruscus*, W. Italy; similar to *C. dalmaticus*, but leaves broad, dark green; tepals less feathered, spring; *C.e.* Zwanenburg, light blue-violet. *C. flavus* (*C. aureus*), Yugoslavia to Turkey; leaves 5–6; flowers 7–10cm, orange-yellow to lemon, winter to early spring; the very popular *C.f.* Dutch Yellow is a good, bright, orange-yellow clone. *C. fleischeri*, S. and C. Turkey; leaves 4–5; flowers slender, star-like when open, tepals narrow, white, striped purple at base outside, late winter. *C. goulimyi*, S. Greece; leaves 5, narrow; flowers 10cm, pale to deep lavender, before or with very young leaves, early autumn. *C. imperati*, Italy; leaves 5; flowers 7–10cm, satiny lilac-purple, light buff outside, variously lined or feathered, sometimes without, winter. *C. iridiflorus*, see *C. banaticus*. *C. karduchorum*, see *C. kotschyanus*, *C koralkowii*, Afghanistan and adjacent USSR; much like *C. alatavicus*, but flowers deep yellow, variously lined or stippled deep bronze outside, spring. *C. fleischeri*, S. and C. Turkey; leaves 4–5; flowers slender, star-like when open, tepals narrow, white, striped purple at base outside, late winter. *C. goulimyi*, S. Greece; leaves 5, narrow; flowers 10cm, pale to deep lavender, before or with very young leaves, early autumn. *C. imperati*, Italy; leaves 5; flowers 7–10cm, satiny lilac-purple, light buff outside, variously lined or feathered, sometimes without, winter. *C. iridiflorus*, see *C. banaticus*, *C. karduchorum*, see *C. kotschyanus*, *C koralkowii*, Afghanistan and adjacent USSR; much like *C. alatavicus*, but flowers deep yellow, variously lined or stippled deep bronze outside, spring. *C. kotschyanus* (*C. zonatus*), Turkey to Syria; leaves 5–7; flowers 6–8cm, lilac with ring of deep yellow spots in throat, early autumn before leaves. *C.k. leucopharynx*, white, unspotted throat, often masquerading as *C. karduchorum* in catalogues. *C. laevigatus*, Greece; leaves 4–5; flowers about 5cm, white to lilac, generally densely lined and feathered outside, occasionally unmarked or buff, winter. *C.l.* Fontenayi, clone with slightly larger, rosy-lilac, prominently feathered blooms. *C. longiflorus*, S. Italy, Sicily, Malta; leaves about 3; flowers 8–10cm, deep lilac-purple with orange throat sometimes feathered outside, fragrant, with young leaves, late autumn. *C. medius*, S. France, N. Italy; leaves 2–3; flowers 10–12cm, rich purple, before leaves, late autumn. *C. minimus*, Corsica, Sardinia; leaves 3; flowers 4–5cm, deep lavender-purple, lined or feathered dark purple outside, sometimes suffused purple or buff, spring. *C. napolitanus* (*C. vernus* in part), C. Italy to Yugoslavia; leaves 3–4; flowers 7–9cm, purple, spring, the primary ancestor of the Dutch crocuses, see *C. vernus*. *C. niveus*, S. Greece; leaves 5; flowers 7cm, white, rarely pale lilac, throat deep yellow, style scarlet, much branched, with young leaves late autumn, early winter. *C. nudiflorus*, autumnal crocus; Pyrenees; leaves 3–4; flowers 10–15cm, pale to deep purple, before leaves (early to late autumn), stoloniferous, spreading in moist soil and very tolerant of light shade. *C. ochroleucus*, Syria, Israel; leaves 4–6; flowers 7cm, slender, pale cream, throat deep-yellow, before or with very young leaves, late autumn. *C. pulchellus*, Yugoslavia to W. Turkey; leaves 4–5; flowers 10–12cm, pale blue-lilac with darker veining and pubescent, deep yellow throats, before leaves, early autumn. *C. salzmannii*, S. Spain, N. Africa; leaves 6–7; flowers 8–10cm, lilac, with leaves, late autumn; sometimes shy flowering, but otherwise vigorous. *C. sativus*, saffron crocus; Italy to Iran; leaves 6–8, narrow, usually greyish; flowers 10cm, purple with darker veining, autumn; the original clone grown in Europe for saffron is shy to flower in gardens and needs rich soil to do well. *C.s. cashmerianus*, large purple flowers freely-produced in ordinary soil; *C.s. cartwrightianus*, smaller than type in all its parts, with heavily-veined flowers. *C. sieberi*, Greece, Crete; leaves 5–7, broad, dark green; flowers 6–10cm, white to lavender-purple, large yellow throat, late winter. *C.s. atticus*, lavender-purple, the commonest form in cultivation; *C.s. tricolor*, upper halves of tepals lilac, lower yellow separated by a white zone; *C.s. sieberi* (*C.s. heterochromos* or *C.s. versicolor*), white, shaded or banded purple outside. *C.s.* Hubert Edelsten, outer tepals tipped and centrally splashed purple; *C.s.* Violet Queen, dark mauve. *C. speciosus*, W. Turkey to Caspian Sea; leaves 3–4; flowers 10–12cm, bright lilac to purple-blue with darker veining, before leaves or while they are very young, early autumn. *C.s.* Aitchisonii, large lavender-blue flowers; *C.s.* Albus, white; *C.s.* Oxonian, deep purple-blue. *C. stellaris* (not known wild, perhaps a selected clone of *C. angustifolius*), leaves 4; flowers 5–6cm, bright orange, bronze-lined without, late winter, spring;

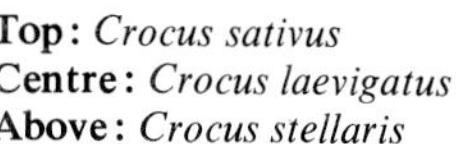

Top: *Crocus sativus*
Centre: *Crocus laevigatus*
Above: *Crocus stellaris*

Top: *Crocus* Vanguard
Centre: *Crocus speciosus* Oxonian
Above: *Crocus* Pickwick

Above: *Cryptomeria japonica*, young cones
Right: *Cryptomeria japonica*
Below right: *Cunninghamia lanceolata*

flowers sterile, the anthers and stigma imperfect. *C. susianus*, see *C. angustifolius*. *C. tomasinianus*, Yugoslavia; leaves 3–5; flowers 7cm, lilac to purple, the outer tepals silvery-buff outside, late winter. *C.t.* Whitewell Purple, flowers tipped red-purple; *C.t.* Ruby Giant even darker. *C. tournefortii*, Greek Is; leaves 4–6; flowers 8–10cm, pale violet-blue, throat yellow, remains open even in dull weather, unusual for a crocus, with young leaves, late autumn. *C. vernus*, a useful name for the several, large-flowered, so-called Dutch crocuses but now discarded by botanists, as it covered several disimilar plants now given separate names, notably *C. albiflorus* and *C. napolitanus* (qv.). The latter species, and hybrids with *C. albiflorus*, have provided many fine spring-flowering cultivars with larger flowers of good substance, among the best being: Jeanne d'Arc, pure white; Pickwick, white, striped deep purple; Purpureus Grandiflorus, large, purple-blue; Queen of the Blues, soft mauve-blue, very large; Vanguard, lilac-blue, silver buff outside. *C. versicolor*, S. France – Maritime Alps; leaves 4–5; flowers 10cm, slender, white to lilac, boldly-veined purple, late winter, spring. *C.v.* Picturatus, commonest clone.

Crowberry – see *Empetrum*.

Crowfoot – see *Ranunculus*.

Crown imperial – see *Fritillaria imperialis*.

Cryptomeria

(Greek *krypto*, to hide, and *meris*, a part – meaning obscure unless referring to the young female strobili that resemble terminal leaf rosettes and are not easy to distinguish). TAXODIACEAE. A genus of 1 species of evergreen conifer from China and Japan extensively grown in the latter country as a timber tree. Grow in humus-rich soil that does not dry out, in sheltered, sunny or partially-shaded sites; best growth occurs in areas of high rainfall. Plant autumn or spring. Propagate by cuttings with a heel in late summer, early autumn or from seed in spring (cultivars only by cuttings). *C. japonica*, Japanese cedar; pyramidal tree to more than 45m in Japan often less elsewhere, bark fibrous, red-brown; leaves awl-shaped, 6–12mm long, keeled, curving forwards and spirally arranged, male strobili 6–8mm long in clusters from leaf-axils, shedding pollen spring, female strobili solitary, green, cones globular to 2cm long; several mutant cultivars are grown, the best-known being: *C.j.* Bandai-sugi, slow-growing bush (to 1m or more after 30 years), shoots congested, mossy: *C.j.* Compressa, small, flat-topped, rounded bushlet similar to *C.j.* Vilmoriniana, reddish-bronze in winter; *C.j.* Elegans, a bushy tree with slender, 2–2.5cm long leaves on dense and drooping branchlets, juvenile leaves turning red-bronze in winter; *C.j.* Globosa (*C.j.* Globosa Nana), neat, domed-shaped bush 60–80cm tall in 15 years, reddish in winter; *C.j.* Knaptonensis, similar to the next, possibly more compact; *C.j.* Nana Albospica, slow-growing, flat-topped bush, young shoots creamy-white (sometimes browned by frost or hot sun); *C.j.* Spiralis, grannies' ringlets, spreading shrub or tree, slow-growing, leaves spirally twisted around the stems, bright green; *C.j.* Vilmoriniana, very slow-growing (60–100cm in 30 years), forming a dense, rigid globe.

Cuckoo flower – see *Cardamine*.

Cuckoo pint – see *Arum maculatum*.

Cunninghamia

(for James Cunningham, died 1709, East India Company surgeon in China who sent home to Britain large collections of plants and drawings between 1698 and 1702). TAXODIACEAE (PINACEAE). A genus of 3 species of evergreen coniferous trees

from China and Taiwan. 1 species is generally obtainable: *C. lanceolata* (*C. sinensis*), Chinese fir; conical to columnar tree, to 45m in the wild but often less in cultivation; rather gaunt and domed at the top when old; bark red-brown, fibrous; branches pendulous, at least at tips: leaves linear-lanceolate, 2·5–6cm long, lustrous deep green above, arranged in 2 parallel ranks; female strobili terminal, broadly ovoid with yellow, orange and pale green scales; cones rounded, 2–3cm long. Grow in humus-rich soil that does not dry out in a sheltered, sunny or partially-shaded site. Reasonably hardy but thrives best in a mild climate. Propagate from seed in spring or by cuttings with a heel, preferably from erect-growing stems, in late summer.

×Cupressocyparis

(*Cupressus* × *Chamaecyparis*). Bigeneric hybrids generally favouring the latter parent in foliage and general appearance, very vigorous and fast-growing. ×*C. leylandii* is suitable for large hedges and wind-breaks. Grow in any well-drained, preferably humus-rich soil in sun or light shade. Plant autumn or spring. Propagate by cuttings summer to autumn.

Species cultivated: × *C. leylandii* (*Cupressus macrocarpa* × *Chamaecyparis nootkatensis*), Leyland cypress; the best-known hybrid, occurring spontaneously at Leighton Hall near Welshpool (Montgomery, Wales) in 1888, seedlings being subsequently raised by C. J. Leyland at Haggerston Hall, Northumberland; columnar tree to 30m; leaves scale-like in flattened, drooping sprays, green to grey-green; cones intermediate between parents, about 1·5cm wide; severable clones are available: × *C.l.* Green Spire, narrow habit, bright green foliage; × *C.l.* Haggerston Grey, broad columns of somewhat grey-green foliage; × *C.l.* Leighton Green, like foregoing but leaves green; × *C.l.* Naylor's Blue, narrowly columnar, grey-green with bluish cast in winter. × *C. notabilis* (*Chamaecyparis nootkatensis* × *Cupressus glabra*), recent hybrid raised at the Forestry Commission Research Station, Alice Holt Lodge, Surrey, England, from seed collected at Leighton Hall, 1956; ultimate height not known, but favours the first parent, with dark green foliage. × *C. ovensii* (*Chamaecyparis nootkatensis* × *Cupressus lusitanica*), raised by Mr H. Ovens, nurseryman at Talybont, Cardiganshire, Wales in 1961; tree like first parent with drooping sprays of dark, glaucous-green leaves.

Cupressus

(Latin name for the Mediterranean or Italian cypress, *C. sempervirens*). CUPRESSACEAE. A genus of about 20 species of evergreen coniferous trees from Mediterranean region to Sahara, Asia, N. America to Mexico. They have tiny, scale-like, closely overlapping leaves arranged in plumy sprays, small, cylindrical male strobili, and rounded to ellipsoid female ones, cones woody, with angular, mushroom-shaped scales having a central boss or umbo and bearing several to many winged seeds. Grow in any well-drained, fertile soil, preferably in sun. Plant autumn or spring. Propagate from seed in spring or by cuttings with a heel late summer.

Species cultivated: *C. arizonica*, rough barked Arizona cypress; S.W. USA, Mexico; to 22m or more, with an ovoid head and greenish-brown, fissured, stringy bark; leaves 2mm long, sharply-pointed, usually grey-green but not invariably; cones globose; 1·5–2·5cm wide, often in clusters; generally hardy; sometimes confused with *C. glabra*. *C. cashmeriana*, Kashmir cypress; country of origin unknown though sometimes stated as Tibet, possibly only a fixed juvenile form of *C. torulosa;* conical, to 20m or more tall; leaves to 2mm long, slender-tipped, glaucous, arranged in pendulous, flattened, frond-like branchlets reminiscent of a chamaecyparis; cones globose, about 12mm wide; not generally hardy, though specimens survive in mild areas; makes a handsome pot plant for a frost-free greenhouse. *C. funebris* (*Chamaecyparis f.*), mourning or Chinese weeping cypress; China; similar to *C. cashmeriana* and even more like a chamaecyparis with pendant, flattened sprays of grey-green foliage; cones 8–12mm wide; needs a sheltered site in mild areas. *C. glabra* (*C. arizonica bonita*), smooth Arizona cypress; Arizona, USA; much like *C. arizonica*, but trunk smooth, purple, blistered, flaking to leave red and yellowish patches; leaves generally glaucous and at least grey-green. *C. goveniana*, Gowen cypress; California; much like a smaller version of *C. macrocarpa*, but foliage smelling of oil-of-citronella when crushed, and cones globose, 1·5–2cm wide. *C. lusitanica*, Mexican cypress or cedar of Goa; Mexico, mountains of Guatemala; broadly conical to dome-shaped, up to 30m or more tall; leaves 1–1·5mm long, tips pointed, spreading, particularly on vigorous shoots, dark

Left: × *Cupressocyparis leylandii*
Above: *Cupressus glabra* cones
Below: *Cupressus macrocarpa* Goldcrest
Bottom: *Curtonus paniculatus*

grey-green; cones globose 1·5cm wide, scales with small, sharp, curved boss; not unlike a darker version of the next species. *C. macrocarpa*, Monterey cypress; Monterey, California; columnar when young, broadly conical to flat-topped when mature, to 35m or more in cool climes – smaller and relatively wider-spreading in the wild; leaves 1–3mm long, blunt and slightly swollen at apex, dark to yellowish green with an aromatic, lemony aroma when crushed; cones rounded, 3–4cm long. *C.m.* Donard Gold, foliage deep golden-yellow; *C.m.* Goldcrest, juvenile rich yellow foliage; *C.m.* Lutea, foliage soft yellow, becoming green; *C.m.* Minima (*C.m.* Minimax), small, slow-growing bush of juvenile foliage; *C.m.* Pygmaea (*C.m.* Woking), dense shrublet to 15cm wide. *C. sempervirens*, Italian or Mediterranean cypress; Portugal to Syria, Mediterranean Islands, S.W. Russia; in Britain usually seen in its fastigiate or columnar form, *C.s. sempervirens* (*C.s. stricta*), to 18m or more tall (to 48m in the wild) but the wild type, *C.s. horizontalis*, becomes a spreading cedar-like tree when mature, leaves 1–2mm long, blunt, deep green, cones rounded to ovoid, 2·5–4cm long; confused with *C macrocarpa* but leaves lack the swollen tip of that species and are almost odourless when crushed; in addition the seeds are smooth (those of *C. macrocarpa* have small tubercles). *C. torulosa*, Bhutan or Himalayan cypress; Himalaya; dense, broadly conical tree to 26m or more (to 48m in the wild); leaves 1·5–2mm long, ovate, blunt, deep to bright yellow-green, arranged in flattened, pundulous sprays; juvenile foliage blue-green; cones globose, about 1cm wide, each scale with a small spine; not totally hardy and needs a mild climate to do well.

Curry plant – see *Helichrysum italicum*.

Curtonus

(Greek *kyrtos*, bent – alluding to the zig-zag nature of the flower-spikes). IRIDACEAE. A genus of 1 species of cormous-rooted perennial from S. Africa: *C. paniculatus*, clump-forming; stems to about 1·2m tall bearing stiff panicles made up of several zig-zag spikes; fans of pleated, sword-shaped leaves to 90cm long; flowers orange-red, trumpet-shaped with 6 oblong lobes, the uppermost longer like a hood, late summer. Grow in any well-drained soil in a sunny site. Plant autumn or spring. Propagate by division or separating offsets at planting time. For hybrids with *Crocosmia*, qv that genus.

Cyananthus

(Greek *kyanos*, blue, and *anthos*, flower – most species having blue or purple-blue flowers). CAMPANULACEAE. A genus of 30 species of herbaceous perennials from the Himalayas, Tibet, S.W. China. Mainly alpines, they have prostrate stems, alternate leaves, and upturned, tubular flowers with 5 broad petal-lobes and bell-shaped calyces. Grow in well-drained, neutral to acid soil with leaf mould or peat added, in a sunny site, preferably a rock garden or scree. Plant spring or autumn. Propagate from seed when ripe or spring, or by cuttings of young shoots in spring.

Species cultivated: *C. integer* (of gardens), see *C. microphyllus;* true *C. integer* differs in its larger, elliptic, basically tapered, white-haired leaves and the almost glabrous corolla, and probably still awaits introduction. *C. lobatus*, Himalaya; stems short, decumbent, the upturned ends to 10cm tall; leaves to 2cm long, obovate, shallowly lobed, somewhat fleshy; flowers erect, bright purple-blue, about 2·5cm wide, calyx inflated, black-haired, late summer, autumn. *C.l.* Albus, flowers pure white; *C.l. insignis*, larger flowers of deep Oxford-blue; *C.l.* Sherriff's, powder-blue. *C. microphyllus* (*C. integer* of gardens), Nepal, N. India; stems to 30cm long, branched, tips upturned; leaves about 1cm long, ovate to narrowly elliptic, rounded or cordate at base; flowers violet-blue, 2–3cm wide, autumn.

Cyathodes

(Greek *kyathodes*, cup-like – referring to the cup-shaped floral receptacle). EPACRIDACEAE. A genus of 15 species of evergreen shrubs from Australasia, W. Pacific Is, Polynesia. They are wiry-stemmed, with small, close-set leaves in spiral formation, tubular 5-lobed flowers, and berry-like fruit. 1 species is generally available: *C. colensoi*, New Zealand; prostrate or decumbent, forming mats to 60cm or more wide; leaves narrow-oblong, 5–9mm long, pinkish grey-green above, glaucous beneath; flowers about 7mm long, white, fragrant, in 3–5 flowered racemes, spring; fruit globose, 4–5mm wide, white to red. Not hardy where frosts are very severe.

Top left: *Cyananthus lobatus*
Above: *Cyclamen atkinsii* (*C. coum* of gardens)
Top: *Cyananthus microphyllus*

Grow in neutral to acid, preferably peaty soil, in a sunny site, though partial shade is tolerated. Plant autumn or spring. Propagate from seed when ripe or as soon afterwards as possible, by cuttings with a heel late summer or layering in spring.

Cyclamen

(Greek *kyklos*, circular – from the spiralling of the flowering stems after flowering). PRIMULACEAE. A genus of about 20 species of perennial plants from Europe, Mediterranean to Iran. They have rounded, flattened, somewhat woody corms, tufts of long-stalked, orbicular to ovate-cordate, sometimes lobed leaves, and solitary, pendant flowers with 5 sharply-reflexed petals in the form of a shuttlecock.

The flowering stem coils after fertilization and the globular seed capsules are pulled down to ground level where the sticky seed is dispersed by ants – and, as some authorities claim, by rooting wild pigs. Grow hardy species in humus-rich soil, preferably in light shade. They may also be grown in pans in a cool or frost-free greenhouse, especially those species that normally flower in the winter to early spring period. Plant or re-plant when dormant. Propagate from seed sown when ripe or spring. Grow tender species in a greenhouse at 7–10°C minimum, shaded from sun in summer and well ventilated. Propagate from seed in early autumn or late winter at 13–15°C. Prick off seedlings into 5cm pots when the second leaf is just visible and move on to 9cm, 13cm and 16cm pots for big plants. Spring-sown plants can be flowered in 9cm or 13cm pots. A mixture largely of peat and leaf mould is best and the all-peat mixes can be recommended. If plants are brought into the home, keep them as cool as possible, particularly at night – no more than 10°C if possible – or else the flowers will quickly fade and buds may fail to develop. When the leaves start to yellow in late spring, dry off and store in a cool, dry place. In late summer, remove the tuber (corm), shake off old soil, and repot, keeping just moist until the growth starts, then water more freely. It is usual to set the tubers with the upper part above the soil surface and to avoid pouring water into the centre of the growing plant, although in the wild the corms are buried.

Species cultivated: *C. africanum*, Algeria; in effect, a tetraploid N. African form of *C. hederifolium* (*C. neapolitanum*), having larger, somewhat fleshy and more sparingly silver-patterned leaves, and flowers with yellow anthers. *C. alpinum* and *C. atkinsii*, see *C. coum*. *C. balearicum*, Balearic Is; leaves ovate-cordate with rounded teeth, silvered above, reddish beneath; flowers small, white, fragrant, spring; not completely hardy, needing a sheltered spot or a frost-free greenhouse in cold areas. *C. cilicium*, Turkey; leaves orbicular to heart-shaped with a silvery zone above; flowers pale pink, each petal red-spotted at base, autumn, just before or with young foliage. *C. coum* (of gardens), E. Mediterranean to Iran; leaves orbicular, plain deep green; flowers squat, with broadly ovate petals, pale to deep purplish-pink, dark spotted at base, late winter, spring; the following are often listed as separate species but are now considered to be part of this 1 variable species: *C. alpinum*, Turkey, leaves ovate-cordate with rounded teeth and silver markings, petals spreading out almost horizontally, and *C. vernum* (including *C. atkinsii*, *C. hiemale*, *C. ibericum*, *C. orbiculatum*), leaves with a variable silver patterning, sometimes more oval than rounded, flowers in shades of pink and white. *C. creticum*, Crete; leaves ovate-cordate, dark green, spotted silvery-white, red beneath; flowers white or pink, fragrant, spring; not reliably hardy and best grown in a frost-free greenhouse – thrives best in shade. *C. cyprium*, Cyprus; leaves obcordate, broadly lobed and toothed; flowers fragrant, white, petals red-spotted at base, autumn; somewhat tender and best grown in a frost-free greenhouse. *C. europeum*, see *C. purpurascens*. *C. fratrense*, Slovakia; recently-described species much like *C. purpurascens* but with plain green leaves, red beneath, and carmine to purple flowers, summer to autumn. *C. graecum*, Greece to W. Turkey; leaves broadly heart-shaped, horny-margined, lustrous, almost unmarked to intricately silvery patterned or suffused; flowers pale to rich pink, usually darker at the mouth, autumn; selected forms have been given separate names, eg *C. pseudo-graecum* and *C. cypro-graecum*, but are only expressions of a variable species; needs a warm, sharply-drained site, ideally with the tuber set deeply at the base of a wall or rock. *C. hederifolium* (*C. neapolitanum*), sowbread; Italy to W. Turkey; leaves very variable in amount of lobing and silver patterning, from narrowly to broadly ovate, shallowly or deeply lobed and sometimes ivy-like; flowers in shades of pink to carmine, mauve and white, usually reddish around the mouth. *C.h.* Album, flowers of a pure white; peculiar in producing roots only from the top of the tuber, and benefitting from an annual mulch of leaf mould. *C. hiemale*, see *C. coum*. *C. ibericum*, see *C. coum*. *C. libanoticum*, Lebanon; leaves broadly ovate, sometimes lobed, deep green, with or without yellow-green blotches, sometimes silvery, red beneath; flowers large, pale salmon-pink, each broad petal paling to almost white at base with a contrasting crimson spot, spring; accepted by many as the most attractive of the wild species in bloom, but thrives outside only in mild areas and is best under glass. *C. mirabile*, Turkey; much like *C. cilicium* and distinguished only by a rather irregular toothing to the petals; at the most, probably only a sub-species or variety of *C. cilicium*. *C. neapolitanum*, see *C. hederifolium*. *C. orbiculatum*, see *C. coum*. *C. pseudibericum*, Turkey; much like *C. coum*, with silvered, heat-shaped leaves and much larger, red-purple, fragrant flowers. *C. purpurascens* (*C. europaeum*), S. Alps, Italy to Yugoslavia and Czechoslovakia; leaves rounded, cordate, the basal lobes touching or overlapping, usually variably patterned with silver, sometimes plain green; flowers pale to carmine pink, strongly fragrant, late summer and autumn; needs partial shade to thrive well. *C. repandum*, S. France to Greece and Aegean; leaves rounded, cordate, shallowly to prominently lobed and then ivy-like, usually patterned silvery, red-purple beneath; flowers fragrant, carmine in the commonly cultivated form but also in shades of pink and white, darker around the mouth, late spring; best in shade and needs a sheltered site. *C. vernum*, see *C. coum*.

Top left: *Cyclamen pseudibericum*
Above left: *Cyclamen vernum* (*C. coum* of gardens)
Left: *Cyclamen hederifolium*
Top above: *Cyclamen graecum*
Above: *Cyclamen repandum*

Cydonia – see *Chaenomeles* species.

Cymbalaria

(Latin *cymbalum*, Greek *kymbalon*, cymbal – referring to the shape of the leaves of some species). SCROPHULARIACEAE. A genus of 15 species of small perennials from W. Europe and Mediterranean, formerly included in *Linaria*. They are prostrate to decumbent, with alternate, orbicular to kidney-shaped, palmately-veined and sometimes lobed leaves. Flowers tubular with a rear nectary spur and a 5-lobed mouth compressed to form 2 lips, the lower with 3, the upper with 2 lobes. Grow in any well-drained soil in sun or shade, the less invasive species on the rock garden or in dry walls. Plant

autumn to spring. Propagate by division, cuttings and seed in spring.
Species cultivated: *C. muralis* (*Linaria cymbalaria*), ivy-leaved toad flax, Kenilworth ivy; S. Alps, W. Yugoslavia, Italy, Sicily, naturalized on old walls elsewhere; stems prostrate or trailing, 30–60cm long; leaves kidney-shaped, 1·5cm or more long, shallowly 5–9 lobed, dark lustrous green; flowers 9–15mm long, lilac to violet, yellow-mouthed, spur to 3mm long, solitary in upper leaf-axils, spring to late autumn; after flowering the stalks curve downwards thrusting the young capsules into crevices of the soil to mature; attractive on old walls or in hanging baskets, but invasive in the garden, the following cultivars excepted: *C.m.* Globosa Rosea, neat hummocks to 8cm wide, flowers pink; *C.m.* Nana Alba, tiny, creeping tufts to 15cm wide, flowers white with yellow throat. *C. pallida*, mountains of C. Italy; stems prostrate, to 20cm; leaves 2–3cm wide, entire to 5–lobed, pubescent; flowers 1·5–2·5cm long, pale lilac-blue, spur 6–9mm, summer and autumn.

Cynoglossum

(Greek *kyon* or *kynos*, dog, and *glossa*, tongue – alluding to the form and texture of the leaves of certain species). Hound's tongue. BORAGINACEAE. A genus of 50 or more species of perennials, biennials and annuals from the temperate to sub-tropical regions. They generally have erect, branched stems, lanceolate to oblong-ovate leaves, the basal ones largest, tufted or rosetted, and shortly tubular flowers with 5 rounded petal-lobes, arranged in bractless, monochasial cymes. The fruit consists of 4, flattened, oval to pear-shaped nutlets covered with hooks for animal dispersal. Grow in any well-drained soil in a sunny site. Plant perennials autumn or spring. Propagate perennials from seed in spring or by division at planting time; biennials from seed sown in a nursery plot late spring, early summer, pricking off seedlings at 15cm apart each way and

setting out in the flowering site in autumn. Biennials may also be grown as annuals by sowing under glass early spring at 13–15°C, pricking off into boxes of a commerical potting mixture at 4–5cm apart each way, hardening off and planting out early summer.
Species cultivated: *C. amabile*, China; biennial; 45–60cm tall; basal leaves lanceolate, up to 20cm long, greyish-green, soft-haired, stem with smaller leaves; flowers bright blue, about 1cm wide, in numerous terminal cymes, late summer to autumn. *C.a.* Blue Bird, sky-blue, sometimes listed as an annual in seed catalogues. *C. nervosum*, Himalaya; perennial, clump-forming, to 60cm tall; leaves narrowly lanceolate, to 20cm long, rough-haired; flowers about 1cm wide, intense blue, summer.

Cypella

(Greek *kypellon*, a goblet – referring to the bowl-shaped bases of the flowers). IRIDACEAE. A genus of 15 species of bulbous-rooted plants from Mexico to Argentina. They have tufts of narrowly lanceolate to linear leaves and solitary or corymbose clusters of iris-like flowers. Grow in sharply-drained soil in a sunny, sheltered site, or in pots of a commercial potting mixture in a frost-free greenhouse. Alternatively in colder areas the bulbs are best lifted in autumn and stored in dry peat or sand in a frost-free place until spring. Plant or pot spring. Keep potted bulbs dry when they yellow in autumn and repot annually. Propagate by separating offsets at potting or planting time, or from seed, preferably when ripe in a greenhouse at about 18°C.
Species cultivated: *C. herbertii*, Argentina, Uruguay; stems about 30–50cm tall, branched at top; leaves nearly same height as stems, linear-lanceolate; flowers 4–7cm wide, chrome to mustard-yellow, outer 3 segments or falls bearing a purple central line towards the base, inner 3 segments inrolled, thickly purple-spotted, late summer. *C. plumbea*, blue tiger lily; Brazil, Uruguay; stems to 75cm tall, not branched, terminating in spathe-like bracts; leaves sword-shaped, to 60cm or more long; flowers 6–8cm wide, mauve to light blue, spotted and flushed brown at the base, the 3 inner segments having central yellow zones, late summer to autumn; flowers last less than a day, but several are borne successionally from the spathes.

Cyperus

(Greek word for sedge, a term loosely applied to all members of the same family). CYPERACEAE. A genus of 550 species of mainly evergreen perennials (a few annuals) from tropical to warm temperate regions. They are often rhizomatous or stoloniferous, sometimes tuberous, with tapered, grass-like leaves and tiny, petaloid flowers composed of a single ovary and 1-3 stamens, arranged in flattened, grass-like spikelets that are in turn grouped in heads or umbels. Grow hardy species in moisture-retentive soil in a sunny site, tender species in a greenhouse, minimum temperature 10–13°C, in any commercial potting mixture. Plant or pot spring. Propagate by division or from seed, spring.
Species cultivated: *C. eragrostis* (*C. vegetus*), temperate S. America; hardy, clump-forming with short, thick rhizomes; leaves to 60cm or more, arching; stem 3-angled, 60–90cm tall bearing a head of smaller leaves, spikelets in compact globose head green to buff; seeds profusely. *C. esculentus sativus*, chufa, tiger nut; tropical Africa, Asia; tufted, stoloniferous; leaves slender, arching, to 30cm or so; spikelets yellowish, in terminal clusters rarely produced; of no great decorative value but grown for its small, oval, nut-like edible tubers, not fully hardy; the tubers are lifted in autumn and stored in a frost-free place until spring. *C. longus*, galingale; Mediterranean; hardy, shortly rhizomatous; stems erect to 1m, 3-angled; leaves arching, 50–100cm long, sharply keeled with rough cutting edges, glossy green; spikelets reddish-brown and green in loose, umbel-like clusters. *C. vegetus*, see *C. eragrostis*.

Cypress – see *Cupressus* and *Chamaecyparis*.

Cypripedium

(Greek *kypris*, Aphrodite – Venus – and *pedilon*, a slipper – incorrectly Latinized as 'pedium' by Linnaeus – referring to the shape of the labellum). Lady's slipper. ORCHIDACEAE. A genus of 50 species

Far left: *Cymbalaria muralis*
Bottom far left: *Cynoglossum nervosum*
Below: *Cypripedium reginae*
Below centre: *Cypripedium calceolus*
Bottom: *Cypripedium cordigerum*

of terrestrial orchids from northern temperate zone (not including the greenhouse cypripediums that are now separated under *Paphiopedilum*). Mostly hardy, fibrous-rooted, clump-forming; leaves deciduous, boldly-veined, generally hairy, lanceolate to ovate, several on short erect stems; flowers comparatively large, either solitary or in racemes. Basically, each bloom has 5, slender, often elegantly waved or twisted tepals, although in a number of species 2 of the outer ones – often referred to as sepals – are united into 1 broader segment, sometimes arching over the opening into the pouch-like labellum. The latter is large, rounded to oval, usually of a contrasting colour to the tepals. Grow in partial or dappled shade in a sheltered site in a neutral to acid rooting medium largely of peat and leaf-mould; the partly decomposed leaf litter beneath pine and other coniferous trees being used with great success for the N. American species in particular. Plant spring. Propagate by careful division in spring.

Species cultivated: *C. acaule*, moccasin flower, stemless or pink lady's slipper; N. America east of a line Alberta to Georgia; leaves 2 (rarely 3) downy, oblong to obovate-elliptic, 10–20cm long; flowers 5cm or more long, tepals yellow-green to olive, often with purplish streaks, labellum obovoid, velvety, pink-veined crimson (sometimes white), arching down from top of leafless, 20–35cm tall stem, late spring; distinct from other species described here in having leaves direct from rootstock. *C. arietinum*, ram's head; E. Canada, N.E. USA; stem to 30cm tall; leaves 3–5, ovate-lanceolate, bluish to deep green, 5–10cm long; flowers nodding, 2·5–3cm long, solitary, tepals greenish, flushed brownish-crimson, labellum avoid, with a down-pointing, nose-like tip, white to pink, heavily crimson-netted, early summer. *C. calceolus*, yellow or common lady's slipper; N. America, Europe, Asia; stem 30–60cm tall; leaves 3–6, ovate to lanceolate, pointed, 10–20cm long; flowers 1–3, tepals greenish-yellow to purple-brown, the lateral ones 5–9cm long, spirally twisted, the labellum 3–5cm long, glossy yellow, late spring. *C.c. parviflorum*, flowers somewhat smaller, but not invariably, tepals usually purple-brown; *C.a. pubescens*, tepals usually greenish-yellow. *C. californicum*, California, Oregon; stems 30–60cm tall; leaves to 5 or more, ovate, pleated, 7·5–16cm long; flowers 3–7 or more, each to 4cm long, outer tepals brownish-yellow, inner dull yellow, labellum white, sometimes pink-flushed and brown-dotted; some plants grown under this name have green tepals and white-tinted green labellums. *C. cordigerum*, Himalaya; like *C. calceolus*, labellum white and tepals greenish, yellowish or white. *C. himalaicum*, Himalaya; labellum purple-brown, tepals yellow to brownish. *C. macranthum*, N. Europe and Asia; stems 30–45cm; leaves lanceolate-elliptic, pointed, downy, 8–15cm long; flowers solitary or paired, 6–7cm long, deep or rose-purple to salmon-pink, summer. *C. montanum* (*C. occidentale*), N.W. N. America; stem 25–50cm tall; leaves 4–6, ovate to lanceolate, pleated, glandules hairy on veins; flowers 1–3, well-spaced, tepals brownish or greenish-purple, labellum globose, white, sometimes purple-tinted. *C. parviflorum* and *C. pubescens*, see *C. calceolus*. *C. reginae*, showy lady's slipper; N.E. N. America; stem 35–80cm tall; leaves 3–7, ovate downy, strongly ribbed, pleated; flowers solitary or paired (rarely 3–4) each to 5cm long, tepals white, broadly obovoid, labellum white, strongly flushed or banded pink, early summer.

Cystopteris

(Greek *kystis*, a bladder, *pteris*, fern – alluding to the globular sori). ATHYRIACEAE. A genus of 18 species of small ferns from arctic, temperate and subtropical regions, mainly from mountains in the warmer areas. They are tufted to rhizomatous, with 2–4 times pinnate leaves, the fertile pinnae bearing 2 rows of globular sori with hood-like indusia, either side of the mid-ribs. Grow in partial shade in well-drained but moisture-retentive, humus-rich soil. Plant autumn or spring, the latter for preference. Propagate by spores or division in spring.

Species cultivated: *C. bulbifera*, N. America; tufted, deciduous; fronds to 45cm or more tall, bipinnate, pinnules oblong; the sterile fronds are lanceolate in outline and shorter than the fertile ones, that have much-prolonged, slender, tapering tips and rounded bulbils beneath that soon fall and start new plants. *C. dickieana* (*C. fragilis d.*), arctic Asia and Europe; variable species difficult to separate from *C. fragilis*; plants in cultivation usually have overlapping pinnules that are crenate-toothed or shallowly-lobed. *C. fragilis* (including *C. alpina*, *C. regia*), brittle bladder fern (range of genus); deciduous, tufted, rhizome short and thick; frond 5–35cm tall (usually about 15cm in gardens), bi- sometimes tripinnate, individual pinnules 4–10mm long, ovate, lanceolate or oblong, toothed to deeply pinnatifid, generally not overlapping, though a few may do; plants under the names *C. alpina* and *C. regia* have even more dissected fronds but fit into the variability pattern of the main species. *C.f.* Cristata, fronds crested.

Top left: *Cystopteris bulbiferum*
Above: *Cytisus × beanii*
Top: *Cytisus battandieri*

Cytisus

(Greek *kytisos*, for several woody members of the pea family, used in this restricted generic sense by Linnaeus). LEGUMINOSAE. A genus of about 30 species of deciduous and evergreen shrubs and trees from Europe, Mediterranean, Canary Is to Azores, with alternate, simple or trifoliate leaves, often soon falling, green stems and racemes of pea-shaped flowers followed by flattened pods (legumes) Grow in well-drained soil in a sunny site. The few tender species need greenhouse treatment, minimum temperature 7°C, freely ventilated on all warm days. Grow in pots of any commercial potting mixture. Pot or repot spring. Propagate all species from seed in spring or cuttings with a heel in late summer, bottom heat for the tender sorts at about 18°C. Both rooted cuttings and seedlings should be grown singly in pots, the hardy sorts planted out directly into the flowering site, as they transplant

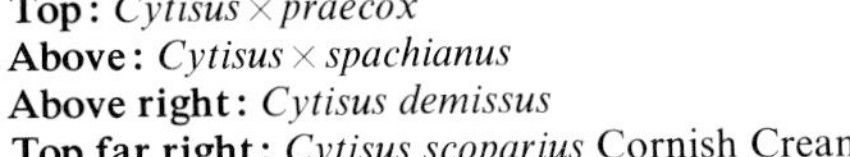

Top: *Cytisus × praecox*
Above: *Cytisus × spachianus*
Above right: *Cytisus demissus*
Top far right: *Cytisus scoparius* Cornish Cream

badly from the open ground.

Species cultivated: *C. albus*, see *C. leucanthus* and *C. multiflorus*. *C. ardoinii*, Maritime Alps; hardy, deciduous, mat-forming, rarely to 15cm or more tall; leaves trifoliate, leaflets narrowly oblong to obovate, appressed downy-haired, 4–10mm long; flowers about 12mm long, bright yellow in clusters of 1–3, spring. *C. battandieri*, Morocco – Atlas Mts; generally hardy, deciduous or semi-evergreen, to 4m or more; leaves trifoliate, silky white-haired, leaflets obovate 4–9cm long; flowers golden-yellow, pineapple scented, the standard petal to 12mm wide, in dense, erect racemes to 13cm long, summer *C. × beanii* (*C. ardoinii × C. purgans*), chance seedling raised at Kew Gardens, England, in 1900; spreading, hardy, dwarf deciduous shrub 15–45cm tall; leaves simple, linear, about 1cm long; flowers deep golden-yellow in profuse clusters of 1–3, late spring. *C. canariensis* (*Genista c.*, *Teline c.*), Canary Is; tender evergreen to 3m tall; leaves trifoliate, almost stalkless, leaflets obovate, 6–12mm long, appressed, with silky pubescence; flowers about 1cm long, yellow, fragrant, in short racemes, spring to summer. *C.c. ramosissimus*, racemes shorter, more dense and numerous, leaflets smaller – sometimes grown in pots as '*Genista fragrans*', but see *C. × spachianus;* may be grown outside in areas with mild winters. *C. decumbens*, S. Europe; hardy, prostrate, rarely above 10cm tall; leaves simple, 6–20mm long, obovate, hairy; flowers 1–1·5cm long, bright yellow in freely borne, 1–3 flowered clusters, early summer. *C. demissus* (*C. hirsutus d.*), Greece; hardy, prostrate, deciduous, to 10cm tall; leaves trifoliate, leaflets oval to obovate, hairy, 6–12mm long; flowers yellow, 2–3cm long in 2–3 flowered clusters, late spring. *C. fragrans* (of gardens), see *C. × spachianus*. *C. × kewensis* (*C. ardoinii × C. multiflorus*), hardy, deciduous, procumbent, eventually to about 30cm tall by 1–2m wide; leaves usually trifoliate, sometimes simple, soon falling; flowers about 12mm long, creamy-white to pale yellow, in profusely borne clusters of 1–3, late spring. *C. monspessulanus* (*C. candicans*, *Genista c.*), Montpelier broom; S. Europe to Syria, N. Africa; semi-evergreen, erect habit, to 2m or more tall; leaves trifoliate, leaflets obovate, abruptly pointed 1·2–2cm long, hairy beneath; flowers 12mm long, bright yellow in 3–9 flowered, umbel-like racemes, spring; not totally hardy and best against a wall. *C. multiflorus* (*C. albus*), deciduous, hardy, to 3m or more tall; leaves simple and trifoliate, leaflets silky hairy, linear, about 1cm long; flowers white, 8mm long, in clusters of 1–3, generally in abundance, late spring, must have neutral to acid soil. *C. nigricans* C. and S.E. Europe, USSR; hardy, deciduous, 1–1·5m tall; leaves trifoliate, leaflets ovate to oval, 1–2·5cm long; flowers 8–12mm long, yellow, in erect, slender racemes up to 30cm long, late summer. *C. × praecox* (*C. purgans × C. multiflorus*), habit of *C. multiflorus* but more dense; leaves mostly simple, soon falling; flowers sulphur-yellow, produced in great abundance late spring; this description refers to the original hybrid and should be known as *C. × p.* Warminster; seedlings of this have produced *C. × p.* Albus white, and *C. × p.* Allgold, deep yellow. *C. procumbens*, C. France to S. Italy and Albania; prostrate, hardy, deciduous, 10–30cm tall; leaves 8–20mm long, simple, narrowly oblong to oblanceolate or obovate, pubescent beneath; flowers in clusters of 1–3, bright yellow, about 1cm long, early summer. *C. purgans* (*Genista p.*), S.W. Europe; hardy, leafless to deciduous, dense and erect to 1m tall; leaves when produced simple or trifoliate, soon falling, oblanceolate 6–12mm long; flowers rich golden-yellow, about 12mm long, singly or in pairs, spring. *C. purpureus* (*Chamaecytisus p.*), S. and S.E. Alps, Albania, Yugoslavia; hardy, deciduous, spreading habit, to 30cm or more tall; leaves trifoliate, leaflets obovate 1–2·5cm long; flowers 2–3cm long, lilac-pink to purple, late spring. *C.f. albus*, flowers white; *C.p.* Atropurpureus, richer purple, late spring. *C. racemosus* (of gardens), see *C. × spachianus*. *C. scoparius* (*Sarothamnus s.*), common broom; W.S. and C. Europe; hardy, deciduous, erect, bushy, to 2m or much more in shade, but then rather gaunt; leaves mainly trifoliate, some simple, leaflets obovate, 6–15mm long; flowers rich, lustrous yellow, 2–2·5cm long, singly or in pairs, often in profusion, late spring; several cultivars are widely grown including: *C.s.* Andreanus, wing petals mahogany-red, standard flushed or lined a similar shade; *C.s.* Cornish Cream, creamy-yellow; *C.s.* Firefly, yellow, wings flushed bronze; *C.s. maritimus* (*C.s. prostratus*), naturally occurring sub-species with prostrate stems. *C. × spachianus* (*C. fragrans*, *C. racemosus*, *C. canariensis* – all of gardens – and *Teline × spachianus*), natural hybrid between *C. stenopetalus* and *C. canariensis*, originating in Tenerife about 1835; tender evergreen, eventually to 5m; leaves trifoliate on 6mm stalks, leaflets obovate, 1–2cm long, dark green above, appressed silky-downed beneath; flowers fragrant, rich yellow, about 12mm long, in slender, 5–10cm long racemes, winter to spring; flowers well when young and much used as a pot plant under the name '*Genista fragrans*'.

Top left: *Daboecia cantabrica*
Top: *Dactylis glomerata* Variegata
Centre above: *Dahlia* Nijinsky (Ba.)
Above: *Dahlia* Enfield Salmon (L.D.)

Daboecia

(for the Irish saint St Dabeoc). ERICACEAE. A genus of 2 species of dwarf evergreen shrubs from Atlantic Europe and Azores. They have alternate, narrowly lanceolate to broadly elliptic leaves, and erect racemes of pendant, urn-shaped flowers. Grow in acid to neutral, preferably peaty soil, in a sunny site, although part-shade is tolerated. Plant spring or autumn. Propagate from seed in spring, or cuttings with a heel in late summer.

Species cultivated: *D. azorica*, Azores; prostrate or decumbent, to about 15cm tall; leaves 5–8mm long, elliptic, dark glossy green above, white down beneath, margins rolled under; flowers broadly egg-shaped, 7–8mm long, in 3–7 flowered racemes, summer; not reliably hardy in cold winters and seldom available commercially but 1 parent of some hardier garden-worthy hybrids with the next species. *D. cantabrica*, W. Europe: W. Ireland to Portugal; erect to decumbent, 30–50cm or more tall; leaves narrowly lanceolate to ovate, lustrous dark green above, white-woollen beneath, 8–15mm long; flowers 9–14mm long, rose-purple, up to 9 in loose racemes, summer to autumn. *D.c* Alba, flowers white; *D.c.* Alba Globosa, dwarfer habit than type, flowers white, almost globular; *D.c.* Atropurpurea, deep rose-purple; *D.c.* Bicolor, some flowers white, others purple, and some bicoloured; *D.c.* Praegerae, deep clear pink, somewhat less vigorous. *D.* × *scotica* (*D. azorica* × *D. cantabrica*), represented in cultivation by *D.* × Jack Drake and *D.* × William Buchanan, dwarfer, bushier versions of *D. cantabrica* but with garnet to rose-red flowers.

Dactylis

(Greek *dactylos*, finger – from the stiff, somewhat fingered inflorescence). GRAMINEAE. A genus of 5 species of tufted perennial grasses from Europe, Mediterranean, temperate Asia. 1 species is an important pasture grass with ornamental variegated cultivars: *D. glomerata*, cocksfoot, orchard grass; Europe, Asia, N. Africa; densely tufted; leaves green to greyish-green, the linear blade 10–45cm long by up to 1cm wide; flowering panicles markedly 1-sided, usually with a few erect branches bearing several dense, rounded clusters of often purplish spikelets, summer to autumn. *D.g.* Aurea, leaves suffused yellow; *D.g.* Variegata, leaves white striped. The green-leaved wild type can be a nuisance in neglected lawns; the biggest plants are best removed by hand and regular close mowing eventually eliminates the rest.

Daffodil – see *Narcissus*.

Dahlia

(for Dr Anders Dahl, 1751–1789, Swedish botanist and a student of Linnaeus). COMPOSITAE. A genus of 27 species of tuberous-rooted perennials from Mexico and Guatemala. They have opposite pairs of pinnately-divided leaves and solitary, daisy-like flower-heads. All are half-hardy to tender perennials and can be grown outside in cool temperate climates only when fear of frost has passed. Grow in a well-drained, humus-rich soil that never dries out, in a sunny, preferably wind-sheltered site. Propagate by cuttings, from seed or by careful division of the tubers, making sure to retain a portion of the old stem with at least 1 good bud (individual root tubers are not capable of producing shoots). This is best done just before planting in early summer so that buds are clearly visible. To obtain cuttings, place the tubers in trays during early spring, barely cover with moist peat and place in a greenhouse or sunny window at 13–16°C (more by day and not less than 10°C at night). When shoots are 7–8cm long, remove with a sharp knife just below the lowest pair of recognizable leaves and insert singly in 5–6·5cm pots containing equal parts peat, potting mixture and coarse sand. Ideally, place these in a propagating frame with bottom heat at 16°C. When well-rooted and just starting to grow, pot on into 9 or 11·5cm pots of a commercial potting mixture. The young plants may now be acclimatized to cooler conditions with a night temperature of 7–10°C. By the middle of late spring no artificial heat should be required, although frames may need covering at night if frosts are forecast. Harden off in early summer and plant out during the first part of mid summer or when fear of frost has passed. Seed is generally sown towards the end of mid spring at 16°C; space it 3–4cm apart each way in boxes of a commercial potting mixture and cover thinly. When the seedlings have 2 pairs of true leaves and/or begin to overlap, transfer singly to 9cm pots and then treat as rooted cuttings. All except the dwarf bedding dahlias will need staking and it is best to insert these before planting to avoid root damage. Stop all young plants when 4–5 pairs of leaves have been formed to encourage shapely, bushy specimens. Larger cultivars will need disbudding as soon as flower-heads are large enough to handle. Make sure plants never lack for water and feed at 7–10 day intervals as soon as flower-buds are visible. If possible, apply a mulch of well-decayed manure or compost as well. Once frost has blackened the leaves in autumn, lift the tubers, cut stems back to 15cm or so and shake or wash away most or all of the soil. Dry off in an upside-down position for a few days, and then store in trays of dried peat in a cool but frost-free place.

Species cultivated: wild species are rarely obtainable, all the dahlias commonly available being cultivars originally derived from forms of *D. variabilis* (*D. coccinea*, *D. pinnata*, *D. rosea*) from the high plains of Mexico. These range from under 30cm to 1·5m tall, with erect, hollow stems and pinnate to bipinnate leaves, sometimes suffused coppery or dark purple-red. The flower-heads may be single, semi-double or double in shades of white, yellow, red, orange, purple with many bicolour combinations. Through continuous hybridization and mutation, dahlia blooms have diversified in form in a remarkable way. This has come about from changes of size, shape and disposition of the florets. These are basically broadly oval to elliptic, but by various degrees of shortening and rolling have assumed the forms of cups, horns, nibs and quills. These many mutations fall mostly into well-defined groups and provide the basis for a working classification of great value to amateurs and professionals alike, bringing some order to the chaos of thousands of cultivars. This classification is now generally used in catalogues and books, and has the added advantage of helping the potential buyer get a mental picture of any particular cultivar. It consists of 12 main groups, each divided according to bloom diameter; the generally approved abbreviations follow each heading in parenthesis: Group **1** – Single-flowered (Sin.), blooms of species formed with a ring of ray florets surrounding a central disc of small, yellow, tubular florets; mature heads to 10cm wide on plants 45–75cm tall. Group **2** – Anemone-flowered (Anem.), similar to Group 1, but with disc florets elongated to form a loose cushion, generally the same colour as the rays; mature heads to 7cm wide on plants 60–105cm tall. Group **3** – Collerette (Col.), basically like Group 1, but with a small collar of ray-like florets around the central disc, often a contrasting colour to the main rays; mature heads to 10cm wide on plants 75–120cm tall. Group **4** – Peony-flowered (Pe.), semi-double blooms with several rows of broad ray florets and a small irregular central disc visible when fully expanded; mature heads 10cm or more wide, on plants to 90cm tall. Groups **5-6** Decorative (D.), fully double blooms, the florets of which may be lightly waved or twisted and the margins somewhat folded; there are 5 divisions: Giant (G.D.), mature heads 25cm or more wide, plants 1·5m or more tall; Large (L.D.), heads 20–25cm wide, plants 1–1·5m tall; Medium (M.D.), heads 15–20cm wide, plants 1–1·2m tall; Small (S.D.), heads 10–15cm wide, plants 1–1·2m tall; Miniature (Min. D.), heads up to 10cm wide, plants 90–120cm tall. Group **7** – Ball (Ba.), fully double, ball-shaped blooms somewhat flattened at the top, composed of tightly borne short broad florets with inward curving margins; mature heads range from 10–15cm wide on plants 90–120cm tall. Miniature Ball (Min. Ba.), heads up to 10cm wide. Group **8** – Pompon (Pom.), basically like Ball, but heads up to 5cm wide. Groups **9-10** – Cactus (C.), fully double blooms, the florets rolled lengthwise into a quill; there are 5 divisions: Giant (G.C.), mature heads 25cm or more wide, plant to 1·5m tall; Large (L.C.), heads 20–25cm wide, plants 1·2–1·5m tall; Medium (M.C.), heads 15–20cm, plants 1–1·3m tall; Small (S.C.), heads 10–15cm wide, plants 1–1·2m tall; Miniature (Min. C.), heads to 10cm wide, plants 90–120cm tall; certain cultivars have the tips of the florets cut into slender teeth or threads and are known as Fimbriated (F.), the F. being added to the particular C. category. Group **11** Semi-cactus (S.C.), much like Cactus, but the florets only quilled for up to ½ their length from the tip downwards; the 5 categories are the same as Cactus, the abbreviations being G.S.C., L.S.C., M.S.C., S.S.C., Min. S.C. Group **12** – Any other. 100s of cultivars of dahlias are readily available, mostly clones, but some seed strains and mixtures, and new ones come on the market annually. In their separate ways all are good and choice must be a personal one.

Below: *Dahlia* Comet (Anem.)
Bottom: *Dahlia* Ruwenzori (Col.)
Centre below: *Dahlia* Gerrie Hoek (S.D.)
Centre bottom: *Dahlia* Lavendale (Min.D.)
Far right below: *Dahlia* Old Harry (Min. Ba.)
Far right bottom: *Dahlia* Rose Willo (Pom.)

Top: *Dahlia* Inca Breeder (M.S.C.)
Centre: *Dahlia* Hamari Bride (M.C.)
Above: *Dahlia* Doris Day (S.C.)

Top: *Dahlia* Wootton Monarch (G.S.C.)
Centre: *Dahlia* Pink Triumph (L.S.C.)
Above: *Dahlia* Highgate Torch (M.S.C.)

The illustrations above and on the previous pages will give some idea of this vast range and show the distinguishing characteristics of most of the groups.

Daisy – see *Bellis*.

Danaë

(for *Danae* – in Greek mythology daughter of Acrisius, King of Argos, who became mother of Perseus). RUSCACEAE (LILIACEAE). A genus of 1 species of evergreen shrub from Turkey to Persia: *D. racemosa* (*Ruscus r.*), Alexandrian laurel; clump-forming with slender, arching stems 60–120cm tall; bearing short lateral branches and bright green, oblong-lanceolate, leaf-like phylloclades 4–10cm long; flowers 6-tepalled, about 3mm long, bell-shaped, greenish-yellow, 4–6 in short racemes; fruit berry-like, 6mm wide, red. Grow in humus-rich soil in partial or full shade. Plant autumn or spring. Propagate from ripe seed or by division spring.

Daphne

(Greek name for bay tree – derived, according to mythology, from the nymph Daphne, who was turned into a bay tree to save her from the intentions of Apollo. Linnaeus appropriated the name for this unrelated genus). THYMELAEACEAE. A genus of 70 species of evergreen and deciduous shrubs from Europe, N. Africa, Asia, Pacific. They have mainly opposite, untoothed, oval to oblanceolate leaves, terminal to lateral clusters of tubular, often strongly fragrant flowers with 4 (rarely 5) petal-like lobes, and fruit of a berry-like, 1-seeded drupe. Grow in any well-drained soil that does not dry out, preferably enriched with leaf mould or peat, in sun or partial shade. Plant autumn or spring. Propagate by cuttings with a heel in late summer or from seed when ripe. Both rooted cuttings and seedlings should be grown on in pots and planted out young into the flowering site since they transplant badly from the open ground.

Species cultivated: *D. alpina*, European Alps; deciduous, 15–45cm tall; leaves oblanceolate 1·5–4·5cm long, often clustered towards the tip of the stems; flowers white, fragrant, 8mm long, lobes pointed, in terminal clusters early summer; fruit downy, ovoid reddish, quite hardy; *D. arbuscula*, E. Czechoslovakia – Carpathian Mts; evergreen bushlet to 15cm, occasionally more; leaves linear to oblanceolate, 1–2·5cm long, margins rolled under, dark lustrous green above; flowers about 1·5cm long, pink, in terminal clusters of 3–8, summer; by some authorities closely allied to *D. petraea*, by others to *D. cneorum*. *D. bholua* (*D. cannabina*), Himalaya; sparingly branched generally erect, evergreen or deciduous to 3m or so tall; leaves elliptic to oblanceolate, 5–10cm long; flowers fragrant, about 12mm long, reddish-mauve in bud, opening almost white, in terminal and axillary clusters, winter; fruit ovoid, black; has a wide altitudinal range in the wild, the higher ones being deciduous and fairly hardy, the lower evergreen and probably not fully hardy. *D. blagayana*, N. Greece, Yugoslavia, Bulgaria, Rumania; spreading evergreen to 30cm tall; leaves narrowly obovate, 2·5–4·5cm long, in almost rosette-like clusters at the tips of the twigs; flowers creamy-white, very fragrant, 1·5–2cm long in dense terminal clusters of 20–30, spring; of rather gawky habit and best if each stem is pegged or held down with a stone as soon as long enough, to create a low mound. *D.* × *burkwoodii* (*D. caucasica* × *D. cneorum*), semi-evergreen, quick growing, to about 1m tall, similar to *D. cneorum*, but with the bushy habit of *D. caucasica;* it should have the name Albert Burkwood (the raiser) to distinguish it from the almost identical but slightly more vigorous *D.* × *b.* Somerset, a sister seedling from the same cross. *D. cneorum*, garland flower; Spain to S.W. Russia; evergreen, decumbent, rarely above 15cm tall but spreading to 1m or more; leaves oblanceolate, 2–2·5cm long, dark green above, greyish beneath; flowers rich pink, fragrant, about 1cm long in dense, terminal clusters, early summer; fruit ovoid-oblong, orange to brown. *D.c.* Alba, flowers white; *D.c.* Eximia, flowers larger and deeper pink; *D.c.* Variegata, leaves margined cream, vigorous. *D. collina*, W. Italy and Crete to S. Turkey; evergreen 60–90cm tall, bushy habit; leaves obovate, 2–4·5cm

Above: *Daphne collina*

long, dark lustrous green above, pale and hairy beneath; flowers rose-purple, about 12mm long, fragrant, in terminal clusters of 10–15, early summer. *D. genkwa*, China; deciduous, erect, to 1m or more tall; leaves oval to lanceolate, 2·5–5cm long, silky-haired beneath, mostly opposite; flowers blue-lilac, about 1cm long in lateral clusters of 3–7 on the previous season's leafless stems, spring; not easy to establish and often short-lived, seeming to need warmer summers and abundant moisture at the root. *D. laureola*, spurge laurel; S. and W. Europe, N. Africa; evergreen, erect, to 1m or more tall; leaves oblanceolate, 4–11cm long, lustrous deep green, leathery; flowers bright yellow-green, fragrant at times – generally in quiet, mild, humid weather – about 8mm long in clusters of 3–8 from the axils of the upper leaves, winter, early spring; fruit ovoid, blue-black, poisonous. *D. mezereum*, mezereon; Europe, Asia; deciduous, erect, to 1·5m, occasionally more; leaves oblanceolate, 4–9cm long, somewhat greyish-green; flowers purple-red, fragrant, about 6mm long in clusters of 2–3 thickly wreathing the naked twigs late winter, early spring; fruit globose, scarlet, poisonous. *D.m. alba*, flowers dull white; fruit yellow – plants in cultivation under this name with pure white flowers should best be called Bowles White. *D.m.* Grandiflora (*D.m.* Autumnalis), larger flowers starting in autumn. *D. odora* (*D. japonica*), China, long cultivated in Japan; evergreen, bushy, 1–2m tall; leaves oblanceolate, 4–9cm long, somewhat leathery and lustrous; flowers very fragrant, red-purple in bud, paler within, up to 2cm long in dense terminal clusters, late winter to spring; fruit red, not reliably hardy. *D.o.* Alba, flowers white. *D.o.* Aureo-Marginata, leaves with narrow yellow margin, flowers very pale within; the commonest and hardiest form generally grown. *D. petraea* (*D. rupestris*), N. Italy; evergreen, gnarled bushling to 12cm tall, but usually less in cultivation; leaves linear-oblanceolate, 8–12mm long, dark green; flowers rich pink, about 1cm long in terminal clusters of 3–6, usually freely borne, early summer. *D.p.* Grandiflora, flowers larger; the best and most floriferous plants in cultivation are generally grafted on to *D. mezereum* or 1 of several evergreen species. *D. pontica*, S.E. Bulgaria, W. Turkey; evergreen, 1–1·5m tall; leaves obovate, 2·5–7·5cm long, rich glossy green; flowers yellow-green, fragrant, in pairs from bract-like leaves at the base of young shoots, spring; fruit ovoid, black; not unlike *D. laureola*, but of more spreading habit. *D. retusa*, W. China, E. Himalaya; evergreen, dense habit to 60cm tall; leaves oval to obovate, 2·5–5cm long, dark lustrous green, leathery; flower rose-purple in bud, white within, fragrant, about 1·5cm long in terminal clusters, late spring; fruit broadly oval, red. *D. tangutica*, W. China; evergreen, related to *D. retusa*, but taller, 1–1·5m, with longer leaves and smaller flower clusters, each blossom rosy-purple without, white stained purple within, spring.

Davidia

(for Père Armand David, 1826–1900, French missionary in China, 1862–73, primarily a zoologist but also an all-round naturalist with a keen interest in botany). A genus of 1 species of deciduous tree from S.W. China: *D. involucrata*, dove, ghost or handkerchief tree; conical habit, becoming more rounded with age, to 18m tall; bark purplish-brown, finely, vertically fissured and flaking; leaves broadly ovate-cordate, boldly and sharply toothed to 15cm or more long, usually rich, semi-lustrous green above, white-downed beneath; flowers unisexual, petalless, tiny, each inflorescence of 1 pendant female surrounded by a globular mass of purplish

Top: *Daphne × burkwoodii*
Above: *Daphne blagayana*

Top: *Daphne petraea* Grandiflora
Above: *Daphne mezereum alba*

Top: *Daphne retusa*
Above: *Daphne cneorum* Eximia

Above: *Davidia involucrata*
Below: *Decaisnea fargesii* in fruit

male flowers, in turn enclosed by 2 hanging white bracts of unequal size, the largest to 18cm long, late spring; fruit an oblate to ovoid drupe 2·5–4cm long, hard and greenish with a variable amount of russetting. *D.i. vilmoriniana*, leaves hairless beneath, sometimes semi-glaucous, fruit always ovoid. Grow in humus-rich soil that does not dry out, in sun or partial shade, preferably sheltered from strong, cold winds. Plant autumn to spring. Propagate by layering in spring, cuttings with a heel late summer, or from seed sown when ripe – the latter must be kept in a sheltered spot outside or in a cold frame, and takes $1\frac{1}{2}$–$3\frac{1}{2}$ years to germinate; 1 to several seedlings can result from each stone but overall viability is low.

Day-lily – see *Hemerocallis*.

Dead nettle – see *Lamium*.

Decaisnea

(for Joseph Decaisne, 1807–82, distinguished French botanist and horticulturist, and Director of the Jardin des Plantes, Paris). LARDIZABALACEAE. A genus of 2 species of deciduous shrubs from the Himalayas to China, 1 of which is generally available: *D. fargesii*, 3–5m tall, many-stemmed, clustering from ground level; leaves pinnate, 60cm or more long, leaflets 13–25, ovate, slender-pointed, glaucous beneath; flowers often unsexual, petalless, with 6 slender-pointed, yellow-green sepals 2·5–3cm long, in drooping panicles, summer; fruit 7–10cm, long, pendant, cylindrical, pod-like, but soft and fleshy with a dull, metallic purple-blue, finely-warted skin, edible. The other species, *D. insignis*, is virtually identical except for golden-yellow fruit, and some authorities make *D. fargesii* a variety of it. Grow in humus-rich soil in partial shade or sun preferably sheltered from strong, cold winds. Plant autumn to spring. Propagate from seed in a cold frame when ripe.

Deinanthe

(Greek *deinos*, strange or wondrous, and *anthos*, flower – at one time *Deinanthe* was considered to be a curiously atypical member of the Saxifrage family). HYDRANGEACEAE. A genus of 2 species of hardy perennials from China and Japan. They have opposite pairs of obovate to broadly elliptic leaves carried on erect, unbranched stems terminating in clusters of nodding sterile and fertile flowers, the latter with 5 petals and 5 or more broad petaloid calyx lobes, the former much smaller with 2 or 3 lobes. Grow in moist, peaty soil in partial shade sheltered from strong winds. Plant autumn or spring. Propagate by division or from seed in spring.
Species cultivated: *D. bifida*, Japan; rhizomatous, stems 40–70cm tall; leaves 10–20cm long, broadly obovate, toothed, notched or bilobed at tip, rough textured but rich green and lustrous; flowers white, the fertile ones 2–3cm wide, summer. *D. caerulea* China; clump-forming, rhizomatous; stems to 45cm or more; leaves 10–15c n or more long, broadly elliptic, toothed and pointed; flowers slaty violet-blue, of a curiously attractive shade, the fertile ones 3–4cm wide, summer.

Delphinium

(Greek *delphinion*, from *delphis*, a dolphin – alluding to the shape of the flower of certain annual species). RANUNCULACEAE. A genus of 250 species of annuals and herbaceous perennials from northern temperate zone and mountains farther south. They have erect stems, alternate, palmately or digitately lobed leaves, and terminal racemes of spurred flowers with 5 petaloid sepals and 2–4 much smaller, sometimes contrastingly coloured petals, 1 or 2 of them with nectiferous spurs inserted into the large sepal spur. The fruit consists of erect clusters of 1–3, sometimes to 5, cylindrical follicles. Grow in fertile, moisture-retentive but well-drained soil, enriched with compost or well-decayed manure for the Belladonna and Elatum hybrid cultivars. The site should be sunny and preferably sheltered from strong winds for both these hybrid groups. Plant autumn to spring. Propagate all by seed either as soon as ripe or the following spring, for they are short-lived. Hardy annuals can also be sown *in situ* in mid autumn for finer and earlier blooms the following year, but winter losses may occur on wet, heavy soils during severe weather. Propagate perennials by division or cuttings in early spring. Take cuttings just as the young leaves start to expand, severing below ground level close to the crown, discarding those with hollow centre. Place in a cold frame protected only from severe frosts. When well-rooted, harden off and plant out in nursery rows. Alternatively, place in 10cm pots of a good commercial potting mixture and grow on in a frame until roots mesh on the soil-ball before hardening off and planting out. The taller hybrid cultivars will require support and stakes should be put in position in spring.
Species cultivated: *D. ajacis*, see next species. *D. ambiguum*, rocket larkspur; Mediterranean region; annual, 45–100cm tall; basal leaves cut into oblong segments; racemes spire-like, flowers deep blue, 2–3·5cm wide, spur 13–18mm long, follicles 15–20mm long, summer; white-, pink- and purple-flowered cultivars or strains are grown, including the double 'Hyacinth-flowered'; some botanists now place this species in the genus *Consolida*. *D.* × *belladonna*, probably *D. elatum* × *D. grandiflorum* and not unlike the Elatum hybrids, but having the branched racemes and elegantly well-spaced flowers of *D. grandiflorum;* several cultivars are available, including a handful of well-tried ones raised pre-1940: *D.* × *b.* Blue Bees, light blue; *D.* × *b.* Lamartine, violet-blue; *D.* × *b.* Pink Sensation, see *D.* × *ruysii;* and *D.* × *b.* Wendy, gentian-blue, flaked purple. *D. brunonianum*, Afghanistan to W. China; perennial; stems 25cm or more; basal leaves 5-lobed, kidney-shaped, stem leaves deeply 3-lobed, both kinds hairy and somewhat musk-scented; flowers hooded, 2–3cm long, sepals blue, shaded purple, petals almost black, the lower ones golden-bearded, summer. *D. cardinale*, California, Mexico; tufted perennial, roots somewhat fleshy; stems to 1m or more tall; basal leaves deeply 5-lobed, each lobe shallowly to deeply 3-lobed, often withered at flowering time; flowers cupped, scarlet, 2–3cm wide, petals yellow, scarlet-tipped, late summer; will flower the first year if seed is sown under glass in early spring; often short-lived. *D. chinense*, see *D. grandiflorum*. *D. consolida*, see *D. regale*. *D. elatum*, Pyrenees to Mongolia; clump-forming perennial; stems 1–2m or more tall; basal leaves deeply 5–7 lobed, the lobes again cut; flowers deep blue, sometimes tinted violet, 2·5–4cm wide, petals blue to yellow or blackish-brown, summer; crossed with *D. exaltatum* and *D. formosum*, this species has given rise to 1000s of cultivars with single or double blooms in a wide range of blue, purple, pink, white and cream shades, and ranging in height from 1–2·5m; more recently the red species *D. cardinale* and *D. nudicaule* have been used and the University Hybrid group has evolved, some members of which are brilliant red. *D. grandiflorum*, Siberia, China; tufted perennial; stems 30–90cm tall; basal leaves long-stalked, divided into many linear segments; flowers up to 4cm wide, blue to violet, petals same colour to yellowish, summer. *D.g. chinense* (*D. chinense*), about 60cm tall; leaf segments narrower, 2–2·5mm wide; flowers about 4cm wide. *D.g.* Blue Butterfly, rarely above 30cm tall, bright blue, can be grown as an annual sown under glass in early spring. *D. menziesii*, California to Alaska; tuberous-rooted perennial; stems 15–45cm tall; basal leaves deeply 3–5 lobed, the lobes shallowly to deeply cleft; flowers rich deep blue, to 2cm wide, lower petals sometimes white-lined, upper petals paler blue, up to 10 in conical racemes, spring to summer. *D. muscosum*, Bhutan; tufted perennial; stems 10–15cm tall; leaves hairy, deeply linear-lobed; flowers about 3cm wide, deep violet-blue, on long stalks, late spring to summer. *D. nudicaule*, California, Oregon; tufted perennial; stems 25–50cm tall; basal leaves

Top right, right and far right: *Delphinium*, typical garden hybrids
Top far right: *Delphinium nudicaule*

Top left: *Delphinium* University Hybrid
Left, top centre and centre above: *Delphinium*, typical garden hybrids
Top: *Delphinium* × *ruysii* Pink Sensation
Above: *Dendromecon rigida*

deeply 3–5 lobed, each lobe shallowly rounded lobed; flowers deep red, cornucopia-shaped, 2·5–3·5cm long including spur, long-stalked in branched racemes, late spring to summer. *D.n. luteum* (*D. luteum*), sepals yellow, purple-tipped. *D. regale regale* (*D. consolida*), common larkspur; Europe; annual to 50cm tall, much like *D. ambiguum*, but basal leaf segments linear; floral spur 12–25mm long and ripe follicles 8–15mm long, racemes branched and panicle-like; several single and double-flowered strains and cultivars are available, some to 1·2m tall in shades of pink, carmine, blue, purple, white, including Giant Imperial with fully-double blooms in mixed or single colours; some botanists now place this species in the genus *Consolida*. *D.* × *ruysii* Pink Sensation (*D. elatum* × *D. nudicaule*, much like one of the Belladonna cultivars but flowers clear pink. *D. tatsienense*, China; much like *D. grandiflorum*, but plant hispidly hairy, leaf-lobes pinnately cut and floral spurs twice as long as sepals (same length as sepals in *D. grandiflorum*).

Dendromecon

(Greek *dendron*, tree, and *mekon*, poppy). PAPAVERACEAE. A genus of 2–3 species of evergreen shrubs from California and Mexico, 1 of which is generally available: *D. rigida*, tree poppy; California, Mexico; stiff, erect habit and rounded outline when grown away from a wall; leaves alternate, linear-lanceolate to lance-oblong, glaucous, somewhat leathery, 3–10cm long; flowers fragrant, 4-petalled, bright yellow, cup-shaped, eventually opening out almost flat, 4–6cm wide, summer to autumn. Grow in well-drained soil against a sunny, sheltered wall in all but the mildest areas. Liable to winter frost damage, best if at least the base is protected from late autumn. Or grow in borders or large pots in a frost-free greenhouse, or over-winter there, standing outside for the summer. Plant or pot spring using good potting mixture for the latter. Propagate from seed sown in spring or by cuttings taken in late summer or early autumn with bottom heat about 18–21°C.

Dentaria

(Latin *dens*, tooth – referring to the teeth-like scales on the rhizomes). Toothwort. CRUCIFERAE. A genus of 20 species of herbaceous perennials from Europe, Asia and Atlantic N. America. They are closely allied to *Cardamine* and are often included in that genus, but differ generally in having underground rhizomes and the pinnate leaves aggregated towards the top of the stems; flowers are 4-petalled in terminal racemes. Grow in humus-rich soil that does not dry out, in partial or dappled shade. Plant after

flowering or autumn to spring. Propagate by division at planting time or from seed in spring.

Species cultivated: *D. digitata*, see *D. pentaphylla*. *D. enneaphylla* (*Cardamine e.*), W. Carpathians, E. Alps to S. Italy and Macedonia; rhizomes bearing nodules; stems 20–30cm tall; leaves usually trifoliate in a terminal whorl, leaflets ovate-lanceolate, irregularly toothed; racemes usually pendant, flowers pale yellow or white, to 1·5cm long, somewhat bell-shaped, spring to summer. *D. heptaphylla* (*D. pinnata*, *Cardamine h.*), Pyrenees to S.E. Alps and N. Apennines; rhizomes with tiny, sickle-shaped scale leaves; stems 30–60cm tall; leaves pinnate; flowers similar to *D. pentaphylla*, but slightly smaller. *D. pentaphylla* (*D. digitata*, *Cardamine pentaphyllos*), Pyrenees to mountains of Yugoslavia; rhizomes with prominent, triangular, 3-lobed scale leaves 6–10mm long; stems 30–50cm tall; leaves pinnate but appearing digitate, with 3–5 or more, crowded, ovate-lanceolate toothed leaflets; racemes erect, flowers pale purple, pinkish or white, 1·5–2cm or more long, late spring to summer. *D. pinnata*, see *D. heptaphylla*.

Deodar – see *Cedrus deodara*.

Desfontainia

(for the French botanist, René Louiche Desfontaines, 1750–1833, professor at Jardin des Plantes, Paris). POTALIACEAE (LOGANIACEAE). A genus of 5 evergreen shrubs from S. America-Andes, 1 of which is generally available: *D. spinosa* (*D.s.*

Left below: *Dentaria pentaphylla*
Above: *Desfontainea spinosa*
Top right: *Deutzia corymbosa*
Below right: *Deutzia × hybrida* Mont Rose

hookeri), bushy, rounded shrub, eventually to 2m or more in favoured areas; leaves opposite, 2·5–6·5cm long, dark glossy green, rather like those of holly but flatter, the spines less sharp; flowers pendant, solitary, tubular, scarlet, 4cm long, expanded towards the yellow, shallowly 5-lobed mouth, summer to autumn. *D.s.* Harold Comber, flowers to 5cm long, vermilion shading to orient-red. Grow in humus-rich, neutral to acid soil in a sheltered but cool, preferably partially shaded site; in areas of mild winters it can be grown as a free-standing specimen. Plant spring. Propagate by tip cuttings in early autumn with bottom heat about 18°C, from seed (when available) or by layering in spring.

Desmodium

(Greek *desmos*, a band or chain – alluding to the united stamens). LEGUMINOSAE. A genus of 450 species mainly of perennials, sub-shrubs and shrubs from the tropics to temperate regions. They have alternate, trifoliate leaves, and pea-shaped flowers, usually in terminal or lateral racemes, followed by jointed, flattened pods. The hardy species need well-drained soil and a sunny position. Pot, repot or plant spring or autumn. Propagate from seed in spring.

Species cultivated: *D. spicatum*, China; hardy, deciduous sub-shrub to 2m or more, laxly-branched; terminal leaflet largest to 5cm long, broadly ovate, dark green, hairy above, softly grey-downed beneath; racemes to 15cm long, terminal, flowers 1·5cm long, rosy-carmine, autumn; the stems are usually of annual duration dying back to a woody base. *D. tiliifolium*, Himalaya; hardy sub-shrub 60–120cm tall; terminal leaflet broadly obovate, 5–10cm long, almost hairless in cultivated plants but can be downy beneath; flowers 12mm long, lilac to pink in branched, panicle-like racemes, 20–30cm long, late summer to autumn; in wet, cold seasons and areas fresh flowers may not open properly and the stems die back annually.

Deutzia

(for Johan van der Deutz, 1743–88, Dutch patron and friend of the botanist Carl Thunberg who named the genus after him). PHILADELPHACEAE. A genus of 50 species of deciduous shrubs mainly from Himalaya to E. Asia and Philippines with a few in Mexico. They are allied to *Philadelphus*, with opposite pairs of leaves, toothed, ovate to lanceolate bearing scurfy or starry hairs and starry, 5-petalled flowers in corymbose panicles or, less commonly, in racemes. Grow in any fertile, well-drained soil in sun or light shade. Although all are hardy, certain species mentioned in the descriptions are prone to late spring frosts and should have a sheltered site, preferably against a wall or just beneath a high tree canopy. Plant autumn to spring. Propagate by cuttings in summer with bottom heat 15–18°C, or hardwood cuttings in autumn – either in a cold frame or sheltered nursery bed.

Species cultivated: *D. corymbosa*, Himalaya; of vigorous growth, 2–3m tall; leaves 5–10cm long, ovate, slender-pointed; flowers pure white, 1·5cm wide in crowded corymbs, mid summer. *D. discolor*, China; 1·5–2m tall; leaves narrowly ovate-oblong, 4–11cm long; flowers 1·5–2cm wide, white, pink-tinted in bud carried in 7–8cm wide corymbs. *D.c.* Major, flowers 2·5cm wide; sometimes confused in gardens and nurseries with *D.* × *elegantissima* and *D.* × *rosea*. *D.* × *elegantissima* (*D. discolor elegantissima* of garden), hybrid group derived from *D. purpurascens* and *D. sieboldiana*, generally like the first parent but longer-pointed leaves; *D.* × *e.* Fasciculata, flower-bud rose-pink, paler within than type; *D* × *e.* Rosealind, deep carmine-pink. *D. gracilis*, Japan; erect habit, to 2m tall; leaves 3–7·5cm long, lanceolate, slender-pointed; flowers 1·5–2cm wide, pure white, in erect racemes or panicles to 8cm long, mid summer; liable to late frost injury. *D.* × *hybrida*, name covering a group of very garden-worthy cultivars derived from *D. longifolia* and probably *D. purpurascens* or *D.* × *elegantissima*, although *D. discolor* is usually given as the other parent. Typical of the *D.* × *hybrida* group is *D.* × *h.* Mont Rose, 1·5–2m or more tall; leaves to 9cm long, narrowly ovate, hsarply-toothed-flowers rose-purple in freely borne panicles, mid summer. *D.* × *h.* Contraste is similar to *D.* × *h.* Mont Rose but has an arching habit and a darker stripe on the back of each petal. *D.* × *kalmiiflora* (*D. purpurascens* × *D. parviflora*), much like first parent but flowers slightly larger, pale rose-pink, darker in bud. *D. longifolia*, W. China; 1·5–2m tall; leaves narrowly oval-lanceolate, slender-pointed, 5–13cm long, grey-green above, grey-white felted beneath; flowers about 2·5cm wide, pale rose-purple to white, in corymbs, mid summer. *D.* × *magnifica* (*D. scabra* × *D. vilmoriniae*), vigorous group of cultivars much like *D. scabra*, but with broader, denser panicles; best known is *D.* × *m.* Magnifica (*D. crenata magnifica*), having large panicles of double white flowers; *D.* × *m.* Eburnea, single white flowers in loose panicles; *D.* × *m.* Longipetala, flowers white, long-petalled. *D. monbeigii*, China; to 1·5m or more tall; leaves 1·5–2·5cm long, ovate-lanceolate, minutely toothed, whitened beneath with starry hairs; flowers glistening white, 2cm wide in corymbs of 7–15, late summer. *D. pulchra*, Taiwan, Philippines (Luzon); 2–3m tall; leaves deep green, 4–10cm long, lanceolate, slender-pointed, starry hairy particularly beneath; flowers somewhat bell-shaped, pendulous, to 1·5cm long, white, tinged pink, in panicles 5–10cm long; distinctive in its lily-of-the-valley like floral effect, but not quite as hardy as most species, needing a sheltered site. *D. purpurascens*, China; to 2m or more; leaves 5–7·5cm long, ovate-lanceolate, slender-pointed; flowers 2cm wide, white, tinted crimson-purple, in freely borne small corymbs, mid summer. *D.* × *rosea* (*D. gracilis* × *D. purpurascens*), group of generally spreading cultivars up to 1m tall; leaves ovate-lanceolate to oblong, about 5cm long; flowers pink, to 2cm wide in short, broad panicles, early to mid summer. *D.* × *r.* Campanulata, erect habit, flowers white, semi bell-shaped with purple calyces; *D.* × *r.* Carminea, flowers flushed crimson. *D. scabra* (*D. crenata*), China, Japan; erect habit to 3m or more; leaves ovate to ovate-lanceolate, slender-pointed to 10cm long; flowers bell-shaped 1·2–2cm long, white, often tinged pink beneath, in erect, cylindrical panicles 7–15cm long, mid to late summer. *D.s.* Candidissima, flowers double, pure white; *D.s.* Flore Pleno (*D.s.* Plena, *D.s.* Rosea Plena), white, tinged rose-purple, double (the commonest *Deutzia* in British gardens, introduced by Robert Fortune in 1861 from Chinese gardens); *D.s.* Pride of Rochester much like *D.s.* Flore Pleno, but pink-tinted. *D. setchuenensis corymbiflora*, China; to 2m tall; leaves oval-lanceolate, slender-pointed, 5–11cm long, grey starry hairy beneath; flowers glistening white, 1·5cm wide, in corymbs to 10cm wide, mid to late summer; not totally hardy and prone to spring frost damage.

Above: *Deutzia* × *elegantissimia* Fasciculata

Devil-in-the-bush – see *Nigella damascena*.

Devil's bit – see *Succisa pratensis*.

Dianthus

(Greek *di*, of Jove or Zeus, and *anthos*, flower – literally flower of the gods, sometimes translated as divine flower). CARYOPHYLLACEAE. A genus of 300 species of annuals, evergreen perennials and sub-shrubs from Europe, Asia, Africa, particularly Mediterranean region. They have opposite pairs of linear, often grey-green leaves and widely expanded, 5-petalled flowers from tubular calyces, the bases of which are enclosed by 2–3 pairs of bracts, a diagnostic character of the genus. Grow in any well-drained soil in a sunny site, preferably on rock gardens, dry walls, raised or scree beds; but see notes on pinks and carnations below. Plant autumn to spring. Propagate by cuttings in summer and early autumn or from seed spring to early summer, either outside or in a cold frame admitting plenty of light and air once rooting or germination has taken place; pinks and carnations may also be layered in summer. Pinks and carnations, as 2 great cultivar groups of ancient garden lineage, have somewhat more specialized requirements if the best is to be had from them.

GARDEN PINKS. It is believed that garden pinks are largely derived from *D. plumarius* with certain characters from other species via hybridization. They have single or double flowers up to 5cm wide, and can for convenience be placed into 4 groups according to colour and patterning of the petals: **1** Selfs, of 1 colour throughout; **2** Bicolours, largely of 1 colour with a basal blotch of contrasting tint; **3** Laced, the basal blotch extending as a thick or thin band around the entire petal margin; **4** Fancies, irregularly marked. These petal patterns are found in the so-called Old-fashioned and Modern pinks. The latter group are more vigorous and generally somewhat larger in all their parts, a characteristic derived from crossing Old-fashioned with Perpetual carnations. They are also more free-flowering, giving a main display in summer and a lesser one in autumn. On the debit side, however, they deteriorate more rapidly and need to be regularly propagated, ideally every 2nd or 3rd year. When setting out young plants in autumn, first rake in a dressing of bonemeal at 120g per sq m. The following spring apply 60g of sulphate of potash per sq m and pinch out flowering stems, to build up bushy plants. They seldom come true from seed and must be propagated by cuttings or layering.

CARNATIONS. These are largely derived from *D. caryophyllus*, and tend sometimes to be short-lived outside, mainly owing to wet, sunless winters rather than extreme cold. 3 main cultivar groups are available as a result of centuries of selection and breeding. **1** Annual carnations, perennials grown as annuals from a sowing under glass in late winter at about 15°C, the seedlings pricked off at about 5cm apart each way into boxes of good potting mixture, hardened off in late spring and planted out in early summer. **2** Border carnations, hardy perennials but often short-lived and best propagated by cuttings or layering every second year, the soil being prepared as for modern garden pinks; staking and disbudding is required for quality blooms. **3** Perpetual carnations, somewhat less hardy perennials grown under glass where – if a minimum temperature of 7–10°C can be maintained – they will flower in winter. It is usual to root cuttings in late winter at 16–18°C, potting singly when rooted into 6·5cm containers of good potting mixture, moving on into 10cm and then 15cm pots, the final potting into a richer mix. Stakes are required for support and head room to glass of at least 1m as the plants get tall. When they have made about 10–12 pairs of leaves pinch out the growing point.

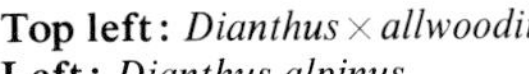

Top left: *Dianthus × allwoodii*
Left: *Dianthus alpinus*
Above: *Dianthus*, a Modern border pink
Top right: *Dianthus barbatus*
Right: *Dianthus chinensis*
Below right: *Dianthus chinensis heddewigii*
Bottom right: *Dianthus deltoides* in the wild

Later, stop the resulting lateral stems that form at 5–7 leaf pairs. A third stopping before the middle of mid summer will ensure autumn flowers; stopping between the middle of mid summer and the middle of late summer will give winter flowers, and a middle of late summer to end of early autumn stopping will give an early spring display. To have flowers continuously from autumn to spring therefore, 3 batches of young plants are required. From the time the first flower-buds show, apply liquid feed at 7–10 day intervals. Disbudding is required to get quality blooms. In the spring of the second year, pot on into 20cm pots, support with longer stakes and place on the floor to give greater head room. Plants become ungainly after 2 years and are discarded. Where greenhouse space is at a premium, plants may be grown annually from cuttings or layers. Like the pinks all carnations can be roughly classified according to petal colour and patterning, all being double-flowered: **1** Selfs; **2** Fancies; **3** Picotees, petals of 1 colour with a narrow edge of a contrasting shade. 100s of cultivars of pinks and carnations are listed by specialist nurserymen. All are good and selection is a matter of personal choice. **Species cultivated** (all summer flowering unless stated otherwise): *D.* × *allwoodii* (*D. caryophyllus* cultivars × *D. plumarius*), see Garden Pinks (Modern), already described. *D. alpinus*, E. Alps – Austria, Italy, Yugoslavia; mat-forming; leaves oblanceolate, glossy green; stems to 10cm, usually 1-flowered, blooms 2·5–4cm wide, pale rosy-purple to purple-red with a central ring of purple spots surrounding a pale eye. *D.a.* Albus, flowers white. *D. arenarius*, E.Europe; densely mat-forming; stems 20–30cm tall, simply or branched; leaves linear, green to grey-green; flowers fragrant, 2·5cm wide, white with green eye, petals fringed to at least halfway. *D.* × *arvernensis* (*D. monspessulanus* × *D. sylvaticus*), loosely mat-forming; stems 30–50cm tall, flowers purplish-pink; leaves linear; rarely cultivated, the plant listed in catalogues under this

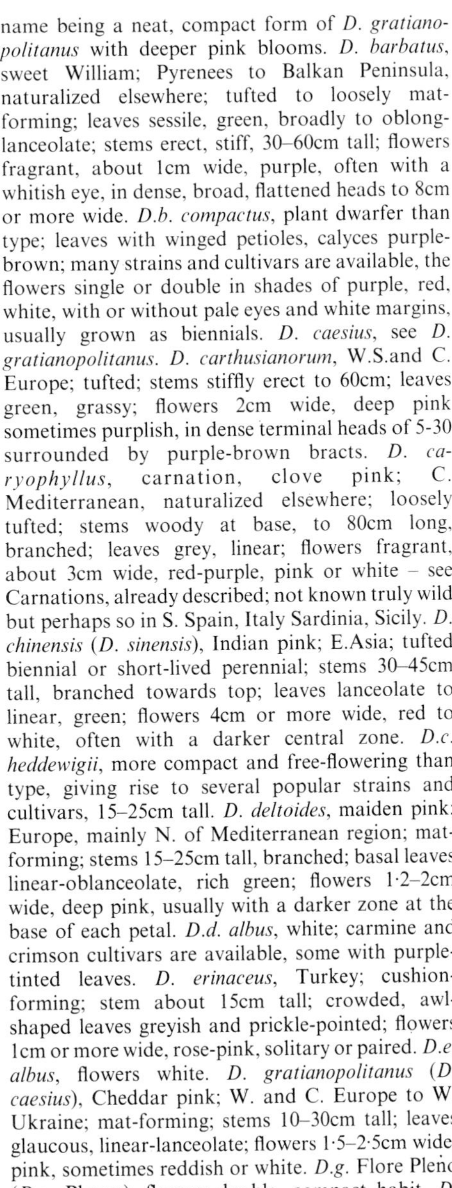

name being a neat, compact form of *D. gratianopolitanus* with deeper pink blooms. *D. barbatus*, sweet William; Pyrenees to Balkan Peninsula, naturalized elsewhere; tufted to loosely mat-forming; leaves sessile, green, broadly to oblong-lanceolate; stems erect, stiff, 30–60cm tall; flowers fragrant, about 1cm wide, purple, often with a whitish eye, in dense, broad, flattened heads to 8cm or more wide. *D.b. compactus*, plant dwarfer than type; leaves with winged petioles, calyces purple-brown; many strains and cultivars are available, the flowers single or double in shades of purple, red, white, with or without pale eyes and white margins, usually grown as biennials. *D. caesius*, see *D. gratianopolitanus*. *D. carthusianorum*, W.S.and C. Europe; tufted; stems stiffly erect to 60cm; leaves green, grassy; flowers 2cm wide, deep pink sometimes purplish, in dense terminal heads of 5-30 surrounded by purple-brown bracts. *D. caryophyllus*, carnation, clove pink; C. Mediterranean, naturalized elsewhere; loosely tufted; stems woody at base, to 80cm long, branched; leaves grey, linear; flowers fragrant, about 3cm wide, red-purple, pink or white – see Carnations, already described; not known truly wild but perhaps so in S. Spain, Italy Sardinia, Sicily. *D. chinensis* (*D. sinensis*), Indian pink; E.Asia; tufted biennial or short-lived perennial; stems 30–45cm tall, branched towards top; leaves lanceolate to linear, green; flowers 4cm or more wide, red to white, often with a darker central zone. *D.c. heddewigii*, more compact and free-flowering than type, giving rise to several popular strains and cultivars, 15–25cm tall. *D. deltoides*, maiden pink; Europe, mainly N. of Mediterranean region; mat-forming; stems 15–25cm tall, branched; basal leaves linear-oblanceolate, rich green; flowers 1·2–2cm wide, deep pink, usually with a darker zone at the base of each petal. *D.d. albus*, white; carmine and crimson cultivars are available, some with purple-tinted leaves. *D. erinaceus*, Turkey; cushion-forming; stem about 15cm tall; crowded, awl-shaped leaves greyish and prickle-pointed; flowers 1cm or more wide, rose-pink, solitary or paired. *D.e. albus*, flowers white. *D. gratianopolitanus* (*D. caesius*), Cheddar pink; W. and C. Europe to W. Ukraine; mat-forming; stems 10–30cm tall; leaves glaucous, linear-lanceolate; flowers 1·5–2·5cm wide, pink, sometimes reddish or white. *D.g.* Flore Pleno (*D.g.* Plenus), flowers double, compact habit. *D.*

haematocalyx, Yugoslavia, Albania, Greece; cushion-forming; stems to 15cm or more; leaves linear, grey-green; flowers about 2cm wide, petals rose-purple above, yellow beneath, calyx purple-red. *D.h. pindicola* (*D.h. alpinus* of gardens), Greece, Albania; flowering stems about 5cm tall. *D. knappii*, W. Yugoslavia; tufted; stems 30cm or more tall; leaves linear-lanceolate, pale to greyish-green; flowers sulphur-yellow, about 1·5cm wide in head-like clusters. *D. microlepsis*, mountains of Bulgaria; small, tufted, cushion-forming; leaves blunt; flowers rose-pink, about 1cm wide, almost stemless. *D. myrtinervis*, Macedonia – Yugoslavia, Greece; mat-forming; stems 10–15cm long, semi-prostrate, branched; leaves small, elliptic, dense; flowers up to 1cm wide, deep pink. *D. neglectus*, S. W. Europe; tufted to small cushion-forming; stems 10–23cm; leaves linear-lanceolate, usually green; flowers 2–3cm wide, petals pink to crimson above, buff beneath; very variable species, some forms very poor; now relegated by botanists to a form of *D.*

Left top: *Dianthus neglectus*
Left centre: *Dianthus gratianopolitanus*, red form
Left above: *Dianthus*, old fashioned pink
Top: *Dianthus*, free-flowering Modern pink
Centre: *Diascia cordata*
Above: *Dicentra spectabilis*

seguieri, an even more variable entity. *D. pindicola*, see *D. haematocalyx*. *D. plumarius*, common pink; E. C. Europe; much like *D. gratianopolitanus*, but generally more robust with stems up to 40cm long and flowers up to 3cm or more wide, the petals cut to halfway into narrow lobes giving a fringed appearance, probably the main parents of the Old-fashioned and Modern pinks, see previous description. *D. squarrosus*, USSR – Ukraine to W. Tazakhstan; rather like a smaller version of *D. arenarius* and sometimes confused with it; stems 15–30cm; flowers 1·5cm wide. *D. superbus*, Europe, Asia; loosely tufted, woody-based; stems erect to decumbent, to 60cm or so; leaves linear-lanceolate, usually green; flowers fragrant, 3–6cm wide, but appearing less, as petals with deep-hanging fringe, lilac to rose-purple; better known as a parent of the Loveliness strain (*D.* × . *allwoodii* × *D. superbus*), dwarfer plants in a range of red, pink, purple, and white shades, best grown as biennials.

Diascia

(Greek *di*, and *askos*, a sac, alluding to the 2 nectary spurs). SCROPHULARIACEAE. A genus of 42 species of annuals and perennials from S. Africa. They vary from erect to prostrate, with ovate leaves and erect racemes of 5-petalled, 2-spurred flowers. Grow in well-drained humus-rich soil in a sheltered, sunny site. The species described are half-hardy and in cold areas the perennials may need protection, or cuttings taken and young plants over-wintered in a frost-free frame. Propagate the annual from seed sown under glass in spring at about 16°C, pricking off seedlings 4 cm apart in boxes of good potting mixture, hardening off and planting out in early summer or when fear of frost has passed, Propagate the perennial by cuttings in spring or late summer, or from seed in spring.

Species cultivated: *D. barbarae*, erect, well-branched annual 30–45cm tall; leaves toothed; flowers 1·5–2cm wide, rose-pink with green-spotted throats, summer; makes a good pot plant for a cool greenhouse and may be sown in late summer for spring flowering. *D. cordata*, Lesotho; almost hardy, mat-forming perennial; leaves broadly ovate, 1–2cm long, dark green, somewhat glossy; flowers terracotta-pink, up to 1·5cm wide in racemes to 15cm tall, summer to early autumn.

Dicentra

Dielytra. (Greek *dis*, twice, and *kentron*, a spur – the flowers have 2 nectaries that in some species are spur-like). FUMARIACEAE. A genus of 20 species of herbaceous perennials from W. Himalaya to E. Siberia and N. America. They are clump-forming to rhizomatous, the latter in some species swollen at intervals like a chain of bulbs, leaves much dissected and fern-like, flowers mainly in arching panicles or racemes, each bloom pendant, 4-petalled, the outer 2 pouched and spurred. Grow in humus-rich soil in sun or shade. Plant autumn to spring. Propagate by division at planting time or root cuttings in late winter in a cold frame. *D. spectabilis* makes an attractive, cool, greenhouse plant if roots are potted in autumn and brought into a temperature of 10–13°C from mid winter onwards.

Species cultivated: *D. cucullaria*, Dutchman's breeches; N. America; rootstock a crowded mass of grain-like scales; leaves glaucous, tri-ternate, ultimate segments linear; flowers white, tipped yellow, spurs prominent, straight and diverging, in 4–10 flowered racemes 8–13cm tall, late spring. *D. eximia*, E. USA; rhizomatous; leaves long-stalked, ternate, leaflets much divided; stems to 30cm or so tall, tipped by compact nodding panicles of rose-red, narrowly heart-shaped flowers 1·5–2cm long, spurs prominent, incurving, the reflexed part of petal tips 5–8mm long, late spring to autumn. *D.e.* Alba, flowers white; confused in gardens with the next species. *D. formosa*, mountains of California, Oregon; much like *D. eximia* but inflorescences often larger and more diffuse; flowers pink to red and reflexed part of petal-tips 3–5mm long. *D.f. oregana*, leaves glaucous on both surfaces; flowers pale yellow, pink-tipped. The following cultivars are often listed under *D. eximia:* Adrian Bloom, crimson; Bountiful, glaucous leaves, flowers deep red; Spring Morning, light pink flowers, glaucous foliage. *D. oregana*, see *D. formosa*. *D. spectabilis*, bleeding heart; Japan, Korea, China; clump-forming; leaves long-stalked, biternate, the leaflets

Top: *Dictamnus albus*
Centre: *Dictamnus albus purpureus*
Above: *Dierama pulcherrimum*

3–5 lobed, somewhat glaucous; stems 40–60cm tall, branched, leafy; flowers 2·5–3cm or more long, flattened, heart-shaped, rose-crimson, white-tipped in long, arching racemes, spring.

Dichelostemma – see *Brodiaea*.

Dictamnus

(Greek name for Cretan dittany – *Origanum dictamnus* – transferred by Linnaeus to this genus). RUTACEAE. A genus of 6 species of herbaceous perennials from C. and S. Europe to China and Siberia. 1 species is generally available: *D. albus* (*D. fraxinella*), burning bush; Italy to Greece, and N. to E. Russia; clump-forming from a somewhat woody root-stock; stems 40–80cm tall; leaves pinnate, of 7–13 ovate to lanceolate, glandular, aromatic leaflets that, especially during hot still weather, give off a volatile oil which can be ignited with a light. Flowers in stiff, terminal racemes each 3·5–4·5cm wide, composed of 5, lanceolate, stalked petals, the lowest thrust forwards like a labellum, purple-pink, darker-veined (*D.a. purpureus*) or white, summer, seed capsule 5-lobed, explosive. Grow in fertile, well-drained soil in full sun, although partial shade tolerated. Plant autumn or spring. Propagate from seed sown when ripe – if left until spring they usually take a year to germinate. May also be divided in spring but take some time to re-establish.

Didiscus – see *Trachymene*.

Dielytra – see *Dicentra*.

Dierama

(Greek for funnel, the shape of the flowers). IRIDACEAE. A genus of 25 species of evergreen cormous plants from tropical and S. Africa. The species described are clump-forming, each corm producing a slim fan of leathery, narrowly sword-shaped leaves and a wiry arching stem bearing thread-like branches and pendant, 6-tepalled flowers. Grow in fertile, well-drained but moisture-retentive soil, preferably in a sheltered, sunny site. Not completely hardy but may be grown under protection in cooler areas. Plant spring. Propagate by division of congested clumps or from seed in a frame or greenhouse in spring.

Species cultivated: *D. pendulum*, S. Africa; stem to 90cm or over; leaves to 50cm or more long; flowers pink to purple or white, 3cm long from brownish or striped, papery bracts, summer. *D. pulcherrimum*, S. Africa; much like *D. pendulum*, but more robust; stems to 2m tall; flowers purple to dark red from almost white bracts; several fine hybrid cultivars have been raised between these 2 species in shades of pink, violet-purple and wine-red, some with bird names e.g. Blackbird, Jay and Kingfisher.

Diervilla – see *Weigela*.

Digitalis

(Latin *digitus*, a finger – the flowers fancifully being likened to the fingers of a glove). SCROPHULARIACEAE. A genus of about 26 species of biennials, perennials and shrubs from Europe, Mediterranean and W. Asia. They have solitary or clumps of basal rosettes of lanceolate to ovate leaves and erect, leafy stems bearing terminal, 1-sided racemes of nodding, somewhat flattened, thimble-shaped flowers with 5 rounded lobes, the lowest 1 largest. Grow in humus-rich soil in sun or shade. Propagate from seed in late spring, pricking off the seedlings 15–20cm apart in nursery rows and subsequently planting into permanent sites in autumn or spring. Clump-forming perennials may also be divided in spring.

Species cultivated (all summer flowering): *D. ambigua*, see *D. grandiflora*. *D. ferruginea*, S. Europe – Italy eastwards; perennial, sometimes biennial; stems 60–120cm tall; leaves lanceolate; racemes long, dense, flowers 2·5–3·5cm long, yellowish or reddish-brown with a network of darker veins, lower lobe 2–4 times longer than the others. *D. dubia*, Balearic Is; not unlike a small, neat version of *D. purpurea*, and allied to that species; perennial; stems 15–25cm tall, sometimes to 50cm; leaves oblong-lanceolate, mostly basal, white-haired beneath; racemes loose, few-flowered, blooms 3–4cm long, pale purple-rose, dark spotted within, summer to autumn; not reliably hardy in cold areas. *D. grandiflora* (*D. ambigua*), biennial to perennial; stems 60–100cm tall; leaves ovate-lanceolate, finely toothed, lustrous above; flowers 4–5cm long, soft yellow, marked brown within. *D. lutea*, W. and W. C. Europe; perennial; like *D. grandiflora* in habit, but flowers paler, 1·5–2·5cm long, with a pointed, tongue-like lower lobe. *D.* × *mertonensis* (*D. grandiflora* × *D. purpurea*), true, breeding, tetraploid hybrid produced at the John Innes Institute (then at Merton, Surrey, in England), much like *D. purpurea* but more compact; stems 60–90cm; flowers 5cm long, crushed strawberry-pink. *D. purpurea*, foxglove; S. W. Europe; biennial or short-lived perennial; stems 1–1·5m tall; leaves ovate, somewhat corrugated; racemes dense, long, flowers 4–5cm long, rose or red-purple, maroon-spotted within. *D.p. alba*, flowers white; *D.p.* Excelsior, robust strain 1·5–2m tall, with flowers

Above: *Digitalis grandiflora*

Above: *Digitalis dubia*

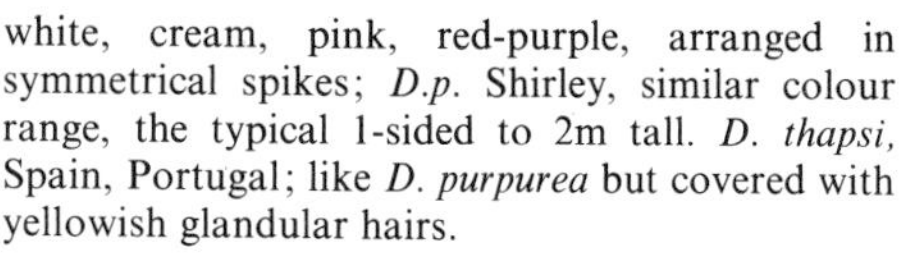

white, cream, pink, red-purple, arranged in symmetrical spikes; *D.p.* Shirley, similar colour range, the typical 1-sided to 2m tall. *D. thapsi*, Spain, Portugal; like *D. purpurea* but covered with yellowish glandular hairs.

Top: *Digitalis purpurea* Excelsior
Left above: *Digitalis lutea*
Centre and above: *Dimorphotheca aurantiaca* cultivars
Right above: *Dipelta floribunda*

Dimorphotheca

(Greek *dis*, twice, *morphe*, form or shape, and *theka*, fruit – referring to the 2 different cypsela – seed – shapes in each head). COMPOSITAE. A genus of about 20 species of annuals, evergreen perennials, sub-shrubs from S. Africa. They are mainly of spreading growth with narrowly oblong to lanceolate leaves and solitary, daisy-like flower-heads. They are not hardy generally, although a few – mentioned here – survive outside unless winters are severe. Grow in well-drained soil in a sunny, preferably sheltered site. Propagate from seed in spring at 16–18°C, pricking off seedlings into any commercial potting mixture at 4–5cm apart each way, hardening off and planting out in early summer. Alternatively, take cuttings in late summer and over-winter young plants in pots at 5°C.

Species cultivated: *D. annua* (*D. pluvialis*), annual, spreading or erect; to 30cm tall; leaves hairy, narrowly obovate-oblong; flower-heads 5–6cm wide, ray florets white above, purple beneath, disc golden-brown, summer to autumn. *D. aurantiaca*, shrubby perennial grown as an annual, spreading habit; 30–45cm tall; leaves linear-oblong to spathulate; flowers 5–6·5cm wide, ray florets bright orange, disc golden-brown, dotted metallic-blue, summer to autumn; see also *D. calendulacea;* several hybrid cultivars are available with ray florets from white to salmon-orange. *D. barbariae* (*Osteospermum b.*), spreading, shrubby perennial; to 45cm or so tall; leaves oblong-lanceolate; flower-heads about 5cm wide, rays rose-purple above, dull purple beneath, late spring to autumn. *D.b.* Compacta, plant prostrate with erect flowering stems to 15cm, hardy. *D. calendulacea*, well-branched annual; to 30cm tall; leaves linear-oblong, glandules downy; flower-heads 6–7cm wide, rays yellow to white, discs steely-blue, summer to autumn. *D. ecklonis* (*Osteospermum e.*), sub-shrub; to 60cm tall; leaves lanceolate to narrowly so; flowers 6·5–7·5cm wide, rays white above, blue-purple at base, purple beneath, summer to autumn. *D.e.* Prostrata, plant prostrate; flowering stems to 23cm tall; outside needs warm, sheltered sites.

Dipelta

(Greek *di*, 2, and *pelte*, a shield – alluding to the bracts at the base of each flower). CAPRIFOLIACEAE. A genus of 4 species of deciduous shrubs from

China. They have opposite pairs of ovate to lanceolate leaves, lateral clusters of foxglove-like flowers and small seed capsules attached to rounded wing-like bracts. Grow in any well-drained soil, preferably humus-enriched in sun or partial shade.

Plant autumn to spring. Propagate by cuttings with a heel in late summer.
Species cultivated: *D. floribunda*, to 3m or more; bark of older stems peels in papery strips and flakes; leaves ovate to narrowly so, slender-pointed, downy when young, 5–10cm long; flowers 2·5–3cm long, pink with yellow-flushed throat, often in profusion, late spring. *D. yunnanensis*, 2–3m tall, spreading habit; young stems 4-angled; leaves ovate-lanceolate, slender-pointed, downy, 6–13cm long, dark glossy green above; flowers 2–2·5cm long, creamy-white, often tinted pink, throat orange, late spring.

Diplopappus – see *Cassinia*.

Disanthus

(Greek *dis*, twice, and *anthos*, flower – the flowers are carried in pairs). HAMAMELIDACEAE. A genus of 1 species of deciduous shrub from China, Japan: *D. cercidifolius*, to 3m high and wide, usually less; leaves alternate, 5–11cm long, broadly ovate to rounded, sometimes with a heart-shaped base, smooth bluish-green, rather like those of *Cercis siliquastrum* (Judas tree), turning to shades of red, orange and purple in autumn; flowers 12mm wide in back-to-back pairs, each one starry, with 5, dark purple, linear-lanceolate petals, autumn. Grow in moisture-retentive, neutral to acid, humus-rich soil in shelter, partial shade or sun. Plant autumn to spring. Propagate by cuttings with a heel in late summer, bottom heat about 18°C.

Disporum

(Greek *dis*, twice, and *spora*, a seed – the ovaries of some species contain only 2 ovules). LILIACEAE. A genus of 20 species of perennials from N. America and Asia, 1 of which is generally available: *D. smithii* (*D. oreganum*, *Prosartes o.*, *P. menziesii*), fairy bells; California to British Columbia; rhizomatous, forming clumps or colonies of erect, branched stems to 15cm tall or more; leaves alternate, sessile, ovate to lance-ovate, slender pointed, 4–10cm long; flowers 1·5–2·5cm long, greenish-white, narrowly bell-shaped, of 6 tepals, pendant in clusters of 1–5; fruit an obovoid pale orange berry 1·2–1·5cm long. Grow in peaty or leafy, moisture-retentive soil, preferably in partial shade. Plant autumn to spring. Propagate from seed when ripe or by division in spring.

Dodecatheon

(Greek *dodeka*, 12, and *theos*, god – ancient Greek name for a flower – possibly a primrose – under the special care of their 12 main gods, but used by Linnaeus for this genus reputedly because it means 12, and the original species, *D. meadia*, often has umbels of 12 flowers). Shooting stars. PRIMULACEAE. A genus of 14–52 species (depending on the classifier) mainly from N. America, 1 only from N. E. Asia. They are tufted herbaceous perennials with basal rosettes of oblanceolate or obovate to oblong-elliptic leaves and slender, leafless flowering stems bearing umbels of nodding, cyclamen-like flowers, the 4–5 petals sharply reflexed and stamens exserted. Grow in moisture-retentive, humus-rich soil in sun or partial shade. Plant after flowering or autumn to spring. Propagate from seed sown when ripe or early spring, or by division when possible – in spring or after flowering. Some species produce rice-grain-like bulblets at the root bases, and these can be carefully detached when the plants die down and treated as seed.
Species cultivated (all late-spring blooming): *D. alpinum*, California, Oregon, Nevada; stem to 14cm tall; leaves 2–6cm long, linear-lanceolate; umbels 1–3 flowered, each bloom 4-petalled, 1·2–1·7cm long, lavender to magenta. *D.a. majus*, stems 14–30cm tall; leaves 6–16cm long; flowers 1·5–2·2cm long. *D. clevelandii*, California, stems 18–40cm tall; leaves 5–11cm long, spathulate to oblanceolate; umbels 5–16 flowered, each bloom up to 2·5cm long, magenta to white, maroon and yellow at base. *D. dentatum*, Oregon to B. Columbia and Idaho; stems 15cm tall; leaves ovate, toothed, to 10cm long; umbels few-flowered, each bloom about 2cm long, white, dark maroon at base. *D. hendersonii* (*D. integrifolium latifolium*), stems 12–48cm tall; leaves 5–15cm long, spathulate to elliptic; umbels up to 17 flowered, each bloom to 2cm or more long, magenta to deep lavender or white, maroon and yellow at base; bulblets at flowering time. *D. jeffreyi* (*D. tetrandrum*), California to Alaska; stems 15–60cm tall; leaves 9–50cm long, oblanceolate; umbels up to 18 flowered, each bloom 4- or 5-petalled, 2–3cm long, magenta to lavender or white, maroon and yellow at base. *D. latifolium*, see *D. hendersonii*. *D. meadia* (*D. pauciflorum*), E. USA; stems 15–50cm tall; leaves oblanceolate to elliptic-oblong, 5–15cm long; umbels 4–40 flowered, often about 12 and rarely to 100 or more, each bloom 2–2·5cm long, pink to lilac. *D.m.* Album, flowers white; much confused with the similar *D. pulchellum*, but distinguished by tough-walled seed capsules (those of *pulchellum* being thin) and flower pedicels 3–7cm long (those of *D. pulchellum* only 1·5cm long). *D. pauciflorum*, see *D. meadia*. *D. pulchellum* (*D. radicatum*, *D. pauciflorum*, etc), W. USA; stems 10–50cm tall; leaves 5–25cm long, oblanceolate to ovate; umbels up to 25-flowered, each bloom 1·2–2·5cm long, magenta to lavender, base maroon and yellow; a very variable species, red- and white-flowered cultivars are available.

Dog's tooth violet – see *Erythronium*.

Dogwood – see *Cornus*.

Dondia – see *Hacquetia*.

Doronicum

(Arabic name *doronigi* in Latin form). COMPOSITAE. A genus of 35 species of herbaceous perennials from Europe, N. Africa and Asia. They are clump-forming with stalked, reniform to ovate basal leaves, stems erect, and usually narrow stem leaves, either sessile or with winged stalks, branched or not, bearing terminal, bright yellow daisy flowers. Grow in any well-drained but moisture-retentive soil in sun or light shade. Plant autumn to spring. Propagate by division at planting time or from seed in spring.
Species cultivated (all spring-flowering): *D. austriacum*, mountains C. and S. Europe; basal leaves 9–13cm long, ovate, somewhat cordate; stems to 45cm or more tall, bearing 5–12 flower-heads each up to 6cm wide. *D. caucasicum*, see *D. orientale*. *D. columnae* (*D. cordatum* of gardens), E. Alps, Apennines; mountains of Rumania and Balkan Peninsula; stems 15–30cm tall; basal leaves 3–7cm long, ovate-orbicular or cordate, round-toothed; flower-heads 3–5cm wide. *D. cordatum* (of gardens), see *D. columnae*. *D.* × Miss Mason, probably a hybrid between *D. orientale* and *D. austriacum*, and much like a vigorous, free-flowering version of the latter. *D. orientale*, S.E. Europe; similar to *D. columnae*, but rhizomes with conspicuous tufts of silky hairs and generally taller stems to 30cm or

Top: *Disanthus cercidifolius* in autumn
Above: *Disporum smithii*
Top right: *Dodecatheon meadia*
Above right: *Dodecatheon alpinum*

Above: *Doronicum orientale* Spring Beauty
Right above: *Doronicum plantagineum*

more. *D.o.* Spring Beauty, double flower-heads of good substance; perhaps of hybrid origin. *D. pardalianches*, leopard's bane; W. Europe to S.E. Germany and Italy; basal leaves 7–12cm long, broadly ovate-cordate, toothed to almost entire; stems to 90cm tall bearing 2–6 or more 3–5cm wide flower-heads; inclined to be invasive and now seldom listed in catalogues. *D. plantagineum*, plantain-leaved leopard's bane; W. Europe to N. France; basal leaves 5–11cm long, ovate-elliptic, narrowed to base; stems to 80cm tall, usually with 1 flower-head about 5cm wide. *D.p.* Harpur Crewe (*D.p.* Excelsum), taller to 1·5m with 3–4 larger flowers per stem.

Dorotheanthus

(for Dorothea, mother of Professor G. Schwantes, a specialist in succulent plants, particularly *Mesembryanthemum* and its allies). AIZOACEAE. A genus of about 10 species of succulent annuals from S. Africa, 1 is readily available: *D. bellidiformis* (*Mesembryanthemum criniflorum*, *M. cuneifolium*), Livingstone daisy, ice plant; Saldanha Bay area; prostrate, mat-forming, to 30cm or more wide; leaves alternate, obovate, almost cylindrical, 2·5–7cm long, covered with small, glistening papillae like sugar grains; flowers daisy-like, 3–4cm wide in shades of red, pink, white or bicoloured with dark centres, summer. Grow in well-drained soil in a sunny site. Sow seed thinly *in situ* in late spring, or, for a longer display, early to mid spring under glass at 15–18°C, prick off seedlings at 3–4cm apart each way into boxes of a good commercial potting mixture, and plant out in early summer after the likelihood of frost has passed.

Dorycnium

(Ancient Greek, *doryknion*, for a kind of convolvulus, used when describing this genus by the horticulturist and botanist Philip Miller). LEGUMINOSAE. A genus of 15 shrubs and perennials from the Mediterranean region and Portugal, 1 of which is generally available: *D. hirsutum* (range of genus), shrub or sub-shrub; 25–50cm tall; branches erect, often dying back to a woody base each winter; leaves trifoliate with 2 basal stipules, leaflets and stipules similar, obovate, 1–2·5cm long, white-haired; flowers pea-like, 1·5cm long, white, flushed pink, 4–10 in compact rounded heads from the upper leaf-axils, spring, summer and autumn; pods reddish, narrowly oblong, 6–12mm long. Grow in any well-drained soil in a sunny site. Plant autumn to spring. Propagate from seed in spring.

Douglasia

(for David Douglas, 1798–1834, Scottish horticulturist and plant collector). PRIMULACEAE. A genus of about 8 species of alpines from arctic N. America and mountains farther south and from Europe. They are tufted perennials forming low hummocks or mats of small rosettes each composed of linear leaves and bearing small, bracted umbels of androsace-like, but longer-tubed flowers. Grow in well-drained but moisture-retentive soil ideally composed of humus and grit. Plant autumn or spring. Propagate from seed when ripe or as soon afterwards as possible, or by careful division after flowering.

Species cultivated: *D. laevigata*, N. W. USA; eventually mat-forming; leaves oblong-lanceolate, 1cm long, grey-green; flowers crimson to rose, about 8mm wide, 2–4 on stems to 4cm tall, spring, sometimes later *D. vitaliana* (*Androsace v.*, *Primula v.*, *Vitaliana primuliflora*), S. and W.C. Europe to S.E. Alps and C. Appenines; cushion- or mat-forming; leaves linear to oblong-lanceolate, 4–12mm long; flowers solitary, 1–1.15mm wide, yellow; several sub-species are known, varying in density of habit, greyness of foliage and size of flower, the most readily available being *D.v. praetutiana*, with grey-green cushions and freely produced flowers; botanists currently place this in the genus *Vitaliana*.

Draba

(ancient Greek name *drabe*, probably for hoary cress – *Cardaria draba* – but used for this genus by Linnaeus). CRUCIFERAE. A genus of 300 species of

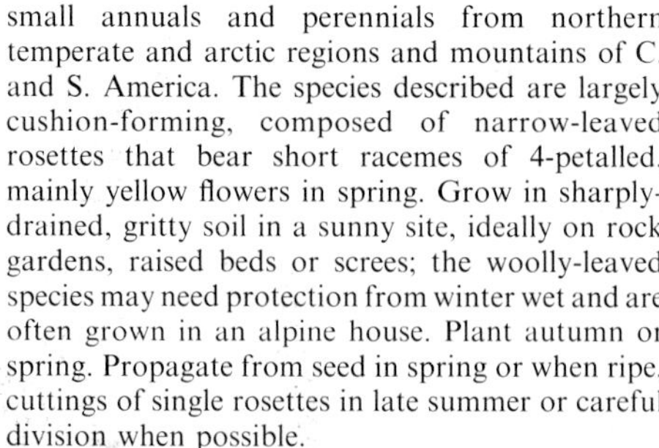

small annuals and perennials from northern temperate and arctic regions and mountains of C. and S. America. The species described are largely cushion-forming, composed of narrow-leaved rosettes that bear short racemes of 4-petalled, mainly yellow flowers in spring. Grow in sharply-drained, gritty soil in a sunny site, ideally on rock gardens, raised beds or screes; the woolly-leaved species may need protection from winter wet and are often grown in an alpine house. Plant autumn or spring. Propagate from seed in spring or when ripe, cuttings of single rosettes in late summer or careful division when possible.

Species cultivated: *D. aizoides*, Pyrenees to Carpathians; leaves 1–1·5cm long, linear, tipped and margined with bristle-like hairs; racemes 5–10cm tall, flowers up to 1cm wide. *D. aizoon*, see *D. lasiocarpa*. *D. athoa*, Greece, Balkan Peninsula; similar to *D. lasiocarpa* but more robust with leaves to 2cm long and longer petals. *D. borealis*, Arctic; tufted; leaves narrowly obovate to spathulate, 1–3cm long, starry hairy above; racemes 5–20cm tall, flowers white, about 5mm wide. *D. bruniifolia*, Caucasus to Turkey; leaves linear, bristly-margined, pale green, about 5mm long; racemes 4–10cm tall, flowers golden, 5mm or more wide. *D. bryoides* (*D. rigida b.*), Caucasus; densely cushion-forming, rarely more than 7cm wide; leaves oblong, about 3mm long; racemes very slender, to 5cm tall, flowers about 5mm wide; *D.b. imbricata* (*D. imbricata*), plant smaller and more compact than type, to 3cm wide. *D. dedeana*, mountains N. and E. Spain; densely cushion-forming from woody base; leaves broadly linear, about 5mm long; racemes to 7cm tall, flowers about 5mm wide, white, tinted purple.

Left below: *Dorotheanthus bellidiformis*
Below: *Dorycnium hirsutum*
Bottom: *Draba aizoides*

D. imbricata, see *D. bryoides*. *D. lasiocarpa* (*D. aizoon*), mountains E. Austria to Balkan Peninsula; not unlike *D. aizoides* but more robust; leaves linear-lanceolate; racemes to 15cm or more tall, flowers sulphur-yellow, about 5mm wide. *D. mollissima*, Caucasus; densely hummock-forming, downy, pale grey-green; racemes slender, 4cm tall, flowers about 1cm wide. *D. polytricha*, Turkey; densely cushion-forming; leaves about 5mm long, narrowly obovate, white-haired margins; racemes to 4cm tall, flowers 5mm wide. *D. rigida*, Turkey; tufted; leaves rigid, linear to linear-obovate with stiff, marginal hairs, to 6mm long; racemes 5–10cm tall, flowers 4–5mm wide. *D.r. bryoides*, see *D. bryoides*. *D. rosularis*, Turkey; tufted; leaves narrowly elliptic, grey-green with starry hairs, 8–20mm long; racemes to 10cm tall, flowers 4–5mm wide.

Dracocephalum

(Greek *drako*, dragon, and *kephale*, a head, alluding – somewhat fancifully – to the shape of the flowers). LABIATAE. A genus of 45 species of annuals and perennials from C. Europe to Asia, 1 in N. America, allied to *Nepeta*. They have opposite pairs of lanceolate to broadly ovate, toothed or lobed leaves, and terminal spires of whorled, tubular flowers that are markedly 2-lipped and resemble a gaping mouth; fruit is a group of 1–4 nutlets. Grow in any well-drained, preferably humus-rich soil in sun. Plant autumn to spring. Propagate perennials by division at planting time or cuttings in spring; annuals and perennials from seed in spring, the annuals *in situ*.

Species cultivated: *D. argunense*, see *D. ruyschiana*. *D. grandiflorum*, Siberia; clump-forming perennial; basal leaves long-stalked, the blades oblong-cordate, deep green; stems 20–30cm tall with short-stalked leaves and dark violet-blue flowers to 3·5cm long, summer. *D. moldavica*, Himalaya to E. Siberia; erect, branched annual; 40–60cm tall; leaves lanceolate, deeply crenate-dentate; flowers lavender-blue, to 2cm long, in leafy spires, late summer. *D. prattii* (of gardens), see *D. sibiricum*. *D. ruyschiana*, Pyrenees to mountains of USSR; clump-forming perennial; stems to 60cm tall; leaves 2–7cm long, narrowly lanceolate, margins entire and rolled under, the basal ones short-stalked, upper sessile; flowers 2–2·8cm long, usually purple-blue, sometimes violet, pink or white, in dense spires, summer; *D.r. speciosum* (*D. argunense*), N.E. Asia; leaves longer than type, to 7·5cm; flowers larger, 3–3·5cm long. *D. sibiricum* (*D. prattii*, *Nepeta macrantha*, *N. sibirica*), clump-forming perennial; stems erect, branched above, up to 1m tall; leaves 8–12cm long, lanceolate often cordate, boldly toothed; flowers lavender blue, 1·5–2cm long, late summer. *D. tanguticum*, China; clump-forming; stems 20–40cm tall; leaves to 5cm or more long, deeply cut into 3–5 or more narrow lobes, white-haired and aromatic; flowers 2·5–3cm long, rich blue in short, dense spires, late summer; best in partial shade.

Dracunculus

(Latin for little dragon; originally used by Pliny for a plant of now doubtful identity, later taken up for this genus by Philip Miller). ARACEAE. A genus of 2 species of tuberous-rooted perennials from the Mediterranean and Canary Is. They are much like *Arum*, but the leaves are deeply pedately lobed and the spadix tip is much elongated. Culture as for *Arum*, preferably in sun. Generally available is *D. vulgaris* (*Arum dracunculus*), Mediterranean; to 1m tall; several long, flattened leaf-stalks wrapped around each other form a pseudo stem, whitish with prominent green mottling; leaf-blade fan-like, of 11–15 lanceolate leaflets, the largest 15–20cm long; spathes chocolate-purple, 25–35cm long, wavy-margined, spadix tip often as long as spathe and the same colour, foetid, summer. The rarely seen *D. canariensis* has leaves with 5–7 leaflets and greenish-white to cream spathes, requiring cool greenhouse treatment in all but the mildest areas.

Far left above: *Draba rigida*
Left above: *Dracocephalum sibiricum*
Above: *Dracunculus vulgaris*

Drimys

(Greek for acrid, the taste of the bark of *D. winteri* – winter's bark – once used as a stimulant and to alleviate indigestion, colic etc); WINTERACEAE (MAGNOLIACEAE). A genus of about 65 species of mainly tender evergreen trees and shrubs from S.

Below: *Drimys winteri latifolia*

America and Australasia to Borneo. The species described have alternate, lanceolate to ovate or oblong leaves, and 5–20 petalled flowers in umbel-like clusters followed by fleshy capsules or berries. Grow in well-drained, humus-rich soil in a sheltered site, preferably against a S. or W. wall in light shade or sun. *D. colorata* needs a frost-free greenhouse in all but the warmest areas. Pot or plant spring. Propagate by cuttings with a heel in late summer or from seed sown as soon as possible in a frost-free greenhouse.

Species cultivated: *D. aromatica*, see *D. lanceolata*. *D. colorata* (*Wintera c.*), pepper tree; New Zealand; shrub to 2m tall; leaves elliptic to obovate, to about 6cm long, red-blotched above, glaucous beneath; flowers 5–6 petalled, greenish-yellow, about 1cm wide in axillary clusters of 2–5; fruit a red to black, barely fleshy berry; whole plant aromatic; now classified as *Pseudowintera c.* but retained here for convenience. *D. lanceolata* (*D. aromatica*, *Winterania lanceolata*, *Tasmannia aromatica*),mountain pepper; S. E. Australia, Tasmania; dense shrub or small tree to 5m in the wild; young stems crimson; leaves elliptic or oblanceolate, very variable in length but generally about 5–8cm; flowers 1·5–2cm wide, dioecious, with up to 8 white petals, solitary in terminal leaf-axils and appearing as umbels; fruit black; male flowers have up to 25 buff-pink stamens rendering a bush in full bloom a conspicuous sight; the form often seen in cultivation has a broadly columnar habit, leaves about 4–5cm long, and appearing to be hardier. *D. winteri* (*Wintera aromatica*), winter's bark; in the broad sense (*sensu lato*) a very variable species ranging from Mexico to Tierra del Fuego, but in the currently accepted narrow sense, a less variable large shrub or tree to 5m tall from C. Chile and adjacent Argentina southwards; leaves oblong-elliptic to oblanceolate, up to 20cm long, glossy above, glaucous beneath; flowers fragrant, white to creamy, 3–4cm wide, composed of 5–20 petals, solitary or in clusters; fruit compound of up to 10 berry-like sections. *D.w. chilensis*, has umbels of 4–7 flowers, each bloom with 6–14 petals; habit many-stemmed from base, conical to columnar. *D.w. latifolia* (of gardens), a name used for the hardier more tree-like forms which may reach 15m, sometimes with broader, longer leaves than type. *D.w. andina*, low bushy variety rarely above 1·5m tall and more hardy; fruit narrowly egg-shaped, olive-white, speckled and blotched maroon, 9mm long.

Dropwort – see *Filipendula*.

Drosera

(Greek *droseros*, dewy – the glandular hairs on the leaves bear dew-like droplets). DROSERACEAE. A genus of 100 species of deciduous and evergreen carnivorous perennials from the tropics to temperate regions, especially from Australia and S. Africa. They are rosette-forming, either solitary or in tufts, the leaves orbicular to linear, covered with prominent, red-stalked hairs (tentacles) that secrete a glistening, sticky fluid; flies and other small creatures mistake the fluid for nectar and get stuck to it. The struggling of the prey causes the other tentacles to bend towards it, smothering and pushing it down to the leaf surface, where a digestive enzyme breaks down the animal protein ready to be absorbed by the plant. 5 to 8 petalled flowers are carried in racemes well above the leaves. Grow hardy species outside in a bog garden in a sunny site. The hardy species make interesting specimen plants for a cold greenhouse. Grow in pans of 1 part good peat mixed with 2 parts sphagnum moss, ideally topping the pans with living-moss tips. Pot or repot spring, standing the completed pans in permanent saucers of water Propagate by division or from seed in spring; *D. binata* also by root cuttings.

Species cultivated: *D. anglica*, great sundew; Europe to N. Asia; leaves more or less erect, long-stalked, the blades to 3cm long; flowers 5mm wide with 5–8 white petals, summer. *D. binata*, New Zealand, S. E. Australia including Tasmania; leaves long-stalked, mainly erect, the blade usually with 2 linear lobes 7–15cm long and resembling the prongs of a hayfork, but sometimes with 4 or more lobes; flowers white, 1·5–2cm wide, in corymbose racemes 30–50cm tall, summer. *D. rotundifolia*, common sundew; temperate zone; rosettes flattened; leaf-blades orbicular, to 1cm wide; flowers about 5mm wide with usually 6 white petals, summer. *D. spathulata*, New Zealand, S. E. Australia; leaves spreading, flat to semi-erect, blades oval-obovate, to 5mm long, but tapering gradually into a broad, reddish stalk and appearing larger; flowers about 1 cm wide, white or pink, summer.

Dryas

(Greek for a wood nymph or dryad, particularly associated with oak – the leaves of *D. octopetala* are somewhat oak-like). ROSACEAE. A genus of 2 species of evergreen, prostrate shrubs from arctic and northern Europe, Asia and N. America and mountains farther south. They have elliptic to ovate-oblong leaves and solitary, 8–10 petalled flowers. Grow in well-drained, preferably limy and gritty soil in a sunny site. Plant autumn to spring. Propagate from seed when ripe, cuttings with a heel late summer or layering in spring.

Species cultivated: *D. drummondii*, Canada N. W. USA; leaves 1–4·5cm long, elliptic to narrowly obovate, leathery, with rounded, lobe-like teeth, smooth above, white-downed beneath; flowers nodding and bell-shaped, of 8–10 orange-yellow petals, summer; fruit a head of achenes with feathery, white to buff plumes 3·5–5·5cm long. *D.d.* Grandiflora, free-flowering clone. *D. integrifolia*, see *D. octopetala*. *D. octopetala*, Arctic, mountains of south to northern temperate zones; leaves 1–2·5cm long, deeply crenate, usually dark green, somewhat glossy above and white-downed beneath; flowers erect, white, 3–4cm wide, usually of 8, spreading petals, summer, achenes with whitish plumes 2–3cm long. *D.o. tenella* (*D.o. integrifolia*), leaves entire or with a few basal teeth only, flowers smaller than type; *D.o. lanata*, leaves grey-downed, smaller than type; *D.o. minor*, leaves and flowers about half the size of type. *D. × suendermannii* (*D. drummondii × D. octopetala*), similar to latter parent, but flowers somewhat nodding, yellow in bud, opening creamy-white. *D. tenella*, see *D. octopetala tenella*.

Dryopteris

(Greek *drys*, oak, and *pteris*, a fern – suggestive of the habitat of these ferns, but not restricted to oak woods). ASPIDIACEAE (POLYPODIACEAE). A genus of about 150 species of evergreen and deciduous ferns of cosmopolitan distribution. They have thick, short rhizomes, sometimes ascending and erect to arching rosettes of generally bi- or tripinnate fronds carried on stalks chaffy-brown scales; the fertile pinnules bear comparatively large, rounded sori covered by kidney-shaped epidermal tissue (indusia). Many species are of tropical origin, but are now seldom grown, all those described being hardy, requiring a humus-rich soil in shade or sun, preferably sheltered from strong winds. Plant autumn to spring. Propagate plants with 2 or more crowns by division at planting time or by spores in spring.

Species cultivated (all formerly classified in other

Top: *Drimys lanceolata*
Centre top: *Drosera spathulata*
Centre bottom: *Drosera rotundifolia*
Left: *Dryas octopetala*

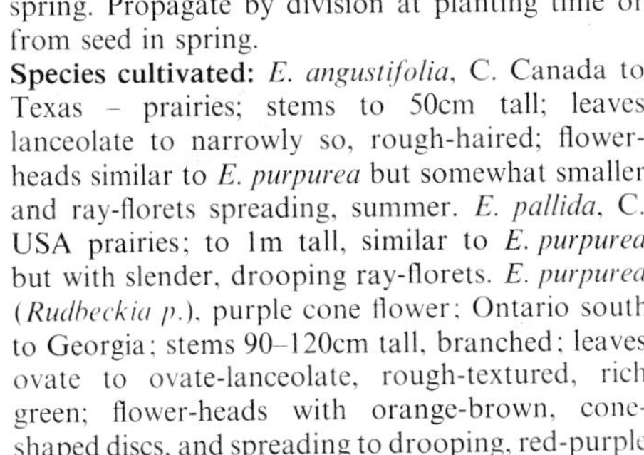

Top: *Dryopteris pseudo-mas*
Above: *Dryopteris filix-mas*, sori
Right top: *Dryopteris pseudo-mas*, opening fronds
Right centre: *Eccremocarpus scaber*
Far right: *Echinacea purpurea* Robert Bloom

genera, mainly *Aspidium* and *Lastrea*): *D. borreri*, see *D. pseudo-mas*. *D. carthusiana* (*D. lanceolatocristata*, *D. spinulosa*), narrow buckler fern; northern temperate zone; fronds deciduous, 30–120cm tall, long-stalked, blades lanceolate, bipinnate, with 30–50 pinnae; pinnules pinnately lobed, pale to yellow-green; suitable for bog and waterside planting. *D. cristata*, crested buckler; Europe to S. C. USSR; frond deciduous, of 2 kinds, short-stalked, sterile, outer ones to 30cm long, and long-stalked, fertile, inner fronds 60–100cm long, blades pinnate or bipinnate, oblong-lanceolate; suitable for bog and waterside. *D. dilatata* (*D. austriaca*), broad buckler; Europe, temperate Asia; deciduous; fronds 30–150cm long, blades tripinnate, triangular-ovate to lanceolate, usually dark green. *D.d.* Lepidota Cristata, pinnae narrow, frond tips crested. *D. erythrosora*, China, Japan; evergreen in sheltered sites; fronds 30–60cm or more long, blades ovate-bipinnate, flushed coppery-red when young; immature sori bright red. *D. filix-mas*, male fern; northern temperate zone and mountains south to Peru, Malagasy, Java, Hawaii; semi-evergreen to deciduous; fronds 30–130cm tall, blades oblong to elliptic-lanceolate, pinnate, linear pinnae deeply pinnatifid; pinnules irregularly toothed, rich green. *D.f.-m.* Decompositum, fronds smaller and more finely cut than type; *D.f.-m.* Decompositum Cristatum, like preceeding but frond tips crested; *D.f.-m.* Linearis, pinnae slender and fronds more elegant; *D.f.-m.* Polydactyla, frond and pinnae tips crested. *D. goldieana*, Goldie's or giant wood fern; E. N. America; fronds 40–120cm long, blades ovate to ovate-oblong, pinnate, the pinnae broadly lanceolate, deeply pinnatifid; much like a bolder version of *D. filix-mas*. *D. pseudo-mas* (*D. borreri*, *D. filix-mas paleacea*), usually evergreen until at least late winter; frond much like thicker-textured *D. filix-mas*, but densely rusty scaly and pinnules with a few blunt teeth at apex only.

Duchesnia – see *Fragaria*.

Dyer's greenweed – see *Genista tinctoria*.

Eccremocarpus

(Greek *ekkremes*, hanging or pendant, and *karpos*, fruit). BIGNONIACEAE. A genus of 5 species of evergreen climbers from W. S. America. 1 species is generally available: *E. scaber*, Chile; to 4m or more; stems 4-angled; leaves bipinnate, the terminal pair of pinnae transformed into tendrils, leaflets 1–2cm long, obliquely ovate-cordate; flowers 2–3cm long, obliquely bottle-shaped, constricted at base and mouth, orange-red to scarlet, in lateral racemes opposite leaves; fruit an ovoid-oblong capsule 2–4cm long; seed disc-like with membraneous, circular wing. *E.s aureus*, flowers yellow. Grow in well-drained soil against a sheltered wall or through a tall hedge or shrub. Generally a short-lived perennal and unreliably hardy, but easily raised from seed and worth growing as a half-hardy annual. Sow seed in a temperature of 15–18°C in early spring, pricking off seedlings into 5–6·5cm pots of a commercial potting mixture, later potting on into 10cm containers, hardening off and planting out latter half of early summer. Support for the tendrils is necessary at all stages of growth.

Echinacea

(Greek *echinos*, a hedgehog, alluding to the prickly-scaly receptacle, best seen after the seeds, (cypselas), have fallen). COMPOSITAE. A genus of 3 or more species of herbaceous perennials from E. N. America. They are clump-forming, with edible roots, long-stalked, ovate to lanceolate basal leaves, erect leafy stems and large, daisy-like flower-heads with spreading, drooping or down-curving ray florets. Grow in a humus-rich, well-drained but moisture-retentive soil in a sunny site. Plant in early spring. Propagate by division at planting time or from seed in spring.

Species cultivated: *E. angustifolia*, C. Canada to Texas – prairies; stems to 50cm tall; leaves lanceolate to narrowly so, rough-haired; flower-heads similar to *E. purpurea* but somewhat smaller and ray-florets spreading, summer. *E. pallida*, C. USA prairies; to 1m tall, similar to *E. purpurea* but with slender, drooping ray-florets. *E. purpurea* (*Rudbeckia p.*), purple cone flower; Ontario south to Georgia; stems 90–120cm tall, branched; leaves ovate to ovate-lanceolate, rough-textured, rich green; flower-heads with orange-brown, cone-shaped discs, and spreading to drooping, red-purple rays 3–5cm or more long, late summer to autumn. *E.p.* Robert Bloom, ray florets cerise-mauve-crimson, spreading; *E.p.* The King, crimson-pink, drooping rays; *E.p.* White Lustre, warm white.

Echinops

(Greek *echinos*, hedgehog, alluding to the somewhat spiky flower-heads). Globe thistle. COMPOSITAE. A genus of 100 species of annual and perennial plants from E. Europe, Asia and Africa. Those described are clump-forming herbaceous perennials with prickly, pinnately lobed leaves and erect, almost woody-branched stems bearing globular flower-heads. The latter are unique in being composed of numerous small, slender flowers each having an involucre of bracts and 1 tubular, 5-lobed floret. Grow in any well-drained soil in sun. Plant autumn to spring. Propagate by division at planting time or from seed in spring. There is some confusion over the naming of these plants in cultivation.

Species cultivated (all flowering late summer): *E. bannaticus*, S. E. Europe; stems to 1·5m tall; leaves bipinnatisect to pinnatifid, white-downed beneath, somewhat cobwebby above, lobes triangular, with a few spines; flower-heads 3–5cm wide, florets grey-blue. *E. commutatus*, see next species. *E. exaltatus* (*E. commutatus*), E. C. Europe to Italy and Balkan Peninsula; stems to 1·5m tall, branched; leaves pinnatifid to bipinnatifid, lightly bristle-haired above, downy beneath, lobes triangular with a few short spines; flower-heads 3·5–6cm wide, florets white to palest blue-grey. *E. humilis*, Asia; as seen in gardens, similar to *E. ritro*, but leaves almost spineless, wavy-margined and stems to 1·2m tall. *E.h.* Taplow Blue, about 2m tall; flowers bright blue, possibly of hybrid origin. *E. nivalis* or *E.niveus* (of gardens), see *E. sphaerocephalus*. *E. ritro*, E. Europe – W. Asia; stems to 60cm tall; leaves bipinnatisect, white-downed beneath, with a few hairs or slightly cobwebby above, lobes linear to oblong-lanceolate,

Top: *Echinops humilis*
Above: *Echinops sphaerocephalus*
Top right: *Echium fastuosum*
Right: *Echium lycopsis* Dwarf Bedding Mixed

4mm or more wide, spiny; flower-heads 3·5–4·5cm wide, bracts deep metallic-blue, florets blue (*E.r.* Veitch's Blue, richer flower colour); the *E. ritro* of gardens generally grows to 1·2m. *E.r. ruthenicus* (*E. ruthenicus*), leaves deeply and narrowly pinnatifid, the lobes to 2mm wide. *E. ruthenicus*, see *E. ritro ruthenicus*. *E. sphaerocephalus*, C. Europe, W. Asia; similar to *E. exaltatus*, but leaves stem-clasping, glandular, hairy above and with revolute margins; stems 1·5–2m tall; often listed under the invalid names '*E. nivalis*' and '*E. niveus*'.

Echioides longiflorum – see *Arnebia echioides*.

Echium

(Greek *echion*, for viper's bugloss). BORAGINACEAE. A genus of 40 species of annuals, biennials, perennials and shrubs from Europe to W. Asia, Canary Is, Mediterranean, N. and S. Africa. They have spirally arranged, lanceolate to ovate or oblong leaves, generally covered with coarse, bulbous-based hairs, and erect stems bearing simple or forked cymes of narrowly to broadly obliquely funnel-shaped flowers, 5-lobed at the mouths, many together in spikes or panicle-like clusters. Frost-free, well-ventilated, sunny greenhouse or sheltered sites outside in areas of mild winters for half-hardy species, sunny borders or beds for the hardy sorts; well-drained soil for both. Ideally for greenhouse culture use a loam-based commerical compost mixture. Propagate hardy biennials from seed *in situ* in late summer or grow as annuals, sowing under glass in early spring at 13–16°C. Prick off seedlings at 5cm apart each way into boxes, harden off and plant out in early summer. Propagate half-hardy species from seed in late spring at 16–18°C, prick off seedlings singly when first rough leaf is well-developed, into 7·5cm pots of potting mixture. Pot on successively when soil-ball becomes enmeshed with roots, either planting out between the latter half of early summer and mid summer or finishing off in 25–30cm pots or small tubs, ideally stood outside in summer.

Species cultivated: *E. bourgaeanum*, see *E. wildpretii*. *E. callithyrsum*, Gran Canaria; half-hardy evergreen shrub to 1m or more; leaves lanceolate to ovate, to 15cm or more long; inflorescences usually less than 15cm long, flowers deep blue, late spring. *E. fastuosum*, Canary Is; half-hardy sub-shrub to 1·2m; leaves oblong-lanceolate, taper-pointed, white-haired; flowers deep blue in dense panicles, spring to summer. *E. lycopsis* (*E. plantagineum*), purple viper's bugloss; S. and W. Europe; hardy biennial or annual branching from base; leaves ovate at base, upper ones oblong to lanceolate, softly-haired 5–14cm long; flowers pink, purple, blue, in spike-like clusters, summer to early autumn; several cultivar strains are available, including carmine and mauve shades, eg *E.l.* Dwarf Bedding Mixed, 30cm. *E. pininiana*, La Palma, Canary Is; half-hardy, woody-stemmed, monocarpic perennial to 3m; leaves elliptic lanceolate, to 30cm or more long, forming elongated rosettes on stems to 1m or so; flowers blue in tapered spires to 2m long, summer. *E. plantagineum*, see *E. lycopsis*. *E. rubrum*, see next species. *E. russicum* (*E. rubrum*), E. Europe to C. USSR; hardy biennial close to *E. lycopsis*; leaves lanceolate, 5–10cm long; flowers red in spike-like clusters to 50cm tall. *E.r.* Burgundy, dark red flowers, summer, early autumn. *E. vulgare*, viper's bugloss; Europe to Ural mountains and Turkey; hardy biennial or short-lived perennial; stems erect, leafy; leaves lanceolate to oblong, 5–15cm long; flowers blue or blue-purple in a spire-like panicle, summer to autumn; a good bee plant. *E. wildpretii* (*E. bourgaeanum*), Canary Is; half-hardy, monocarpic perennial to 2·5m or so tall; leaves linear-lanceolate, silvery-grey haired, 30cm or more long, forming basal rosettes; flowers red in long, spire-like clusters, late spring to summer.

Edelweiss – see *Leontopodium*.

Edgeworthia

(for Michael Pakenham Edgeworth, 1812–81, British amateur botanist who collected plants in India, many of them new to science). THYMELAEACEAE. A genus of 2 species of shrubs from the Himalayas and China. They are allied to, and similar to, *Daphne*, but the flowers are densely borne in pendant, rounded, umbel-like clusters. Culture as for *Daphne*, but the species described is not totally hardy and is best in a frost-free greenhouse in colder areas. Plant outside in spring only. 1 species is sometimes available: *E. chrysantha* (*E. papyrifera*), China, much cultivated in Japan for high-quality paper-making; deciduous shrub 1–2m tall (occasionally more); stem erect, repeatedly branching in 3s; leaves lanceolate to broadly so, silky-haired beneath, 8–15cm long; flowers tubular, 1–1·5cm long with 4 short lobes, silky-haired outside, deep yellow within, lightly fragrant, 20–50, in close, terminal clusters, early spring before leaves. Fruit a small drupe surrounded by the slightly fleshy perianth tube. Propagate by cuttings taken in summer.

Edraianthus

(Greek *hedraios*, sitting or sessile, and *anthos*, flower – alluding to the sessile flowers). CAMPANULACEAE. A genus of 10 species of small, perennial plants closely allied to *Wahlenbergia* from S. E. Europe to the Caucasus. They are tufted in habit with mainly grassy leaves and erect to decumbent stems bearing solitary or small, terminal umbels of stalkless bellflowers in summer. Grow in sharply-drained soil in a sunny site. Plant autumn or spring. Propagate from seed sown in spring, or cuttings of basal shoots inserted into coarse sand in a cold frame in spring.

Species cultivated: *E. dalmaticus*, W. Yugoslavia; stems 3–7cm long, erect to ascending; basal leaves 3–5cm long; flowers blue-violet, 1·5–2cm long in clusters of 4–10. *E. dinaricus*, W. and C. Yugoslavia; like *E. pumilio*, but flowering stems 2–6cm tall, sparsely-leaved above; leaves 2·5–3·5cm long and flowers 1–1·5cm long. *E. graminifolius* (*Wahlenbergia g.*), Balkan Peninsula to S. and C. Italy, and W. C. Romania; stems ascending or erect, 5–10cm long or more; basal leaves 3–10cm long; flowers purple, 1·2–2cm long in clusters of 3–8. *E. pumilio* (*Wahlenbergia p.*), W. Yugoslavia, densely tufted, forming small, low hummocks; stems 1–3cm long, ascending to erect, densely leafy; basal leaves 8–20cm long with rolled margins, greyish-green; flowers 1·4–1·8cm or more long, blue-purple, solitary. *E. serpyllifolius* (*Wahlenbergia s.*). N. Albania, W. Yugoslavia; stems 2–5cm or more long, procumbent to ascending, sparsely-leaved, arising from a thick, woody rhizome; basal leaves spathulate, 7–20mm long; flowers 1·5cm long, deep violet-purple, solitary.

Top: *Edraianthus pumilio*
Above: *Edraianthus serpyllifolius*
Below: *Edgworthia chrysantha*

Edwardsia – see *Sophora*.

Egeria – see *Elodea*.

Elaeagnus

(name given by Theophrastus to the sallow, *Salix caprea*, but used by Linnaeus for this genus; usually stated to be from Greek *elaia*, olive tree, and *agnos*, the chaste tree, *Vitex*, but probably *heleagnos*, from *helodes*, marshy, and *hagnos*, pure, referring to the habitat and white, fluffy, seeding masses of the sallow). ELAEAGNACEAE. A genus of 45 species of evergreen and deciduous shrubs and trees from the northern temperate zone. They have often spiny stems, alternate, lanceolate to ovate or oblong leaves, and pendant, axillary clusters of small flowers formed of tubular or bell-shaped, 4-lobed, petaloid calyces. The fleshy, 1-seeded berries (pseudo-drupes) are edible. Grow in any well-drained soil, preferably in sun, but evergreen species will stand partial shade. All species grow well near the sea. Plant autumn to spring, preferably 1 or the other for the evergreens. Propagate by cuttings with a heel in late summer, or from seed when ripe, or in autumn. The latter sometimes takes 18 months to germinate but results in more vigorous plants of the deciduous species; cultivars must be raised vegetatively.

Species cultivated: *E. angustifolia* (*E. argentea*), oleaster; W. Asia, naturalized S. E. Europe; deciduous shrub or tree to 12m tall; stems sometimes spiny, covered with silvery scales when young; leaves narrowly oblong to lanceolate, 3–8cm long, silvery-scaled beneath; flowers fragrant, 8–10mm long, bell-shaped, yellow within, silvery-scaled without, in clusters of 1–3, early summer; fruit ellipsoid, 1–1·5cm long, yellowish-silvery scaled, sweet, succulent. *E. argentea*, a synonym used by different botanists for the previous and following species. *E. commutata* (*E. argentea*), silverberry; Canada to C. USA; deciduous suckering shrub 4m tall, otherwise similar to *E. angustifolia*, but leaves silvery on both surfaces and fruit mealy. *E.* × *ebbingei* (*E.* × *submacrophylla*), (*E. macrophylla* × *E. pungens*), vigorous evergreen shrub to 4m or more, similar to *E. macrophylla* but leaves smaller; good for large hedges and shelter belts. *E. glabra*, China, Japan; similar to *E. pungens* but of semi-climbing habit when well-established; up to 6m or so; leaves glossy metallic-brown beneath. *E. macrophylla*, Japan, Korea; spreading evergreen shrub to 3m or more, often wider than tall; young stems silvery-white scaled; leaves ovate to broadly so, 5–12cm long, silvery-white scaled when young, rich lustrous green above when mature; flowers fragrant, bell-shaped, about 1·2cm long, silver and brown scaled, in clusters of 4–6, late autumn; fruit ovoid, red, scaly, about 1·5cm long. *E. multiflora* (*E. edulis*, *E. longipes*), China, Japan; deciduous (sometimes partially evergreen) shrub to 3m or more; young stems red-brown scaled; leaves obovate-oblong to ovate or elliptic, 3–10cm long, the undersides densely covered with silvery-white and larger brown scales; flowers usually solitary, fragrant, bell-shaped, 1·5cm long, coloured like the leaf undersides, spring; fruit oblong-ovoid, 1·5cm long, orange and scaly, on slender pedicels 1·5–5cm long. *E. pungens*, Japan; evergreen shrub to 4m or more, more or less spiny; young stems brown-scaled; leaves oval to oblong, 4–8cm long, leathery, margins wavy, lustrous rich green above, densely whitish and brown-scaled beneath; flowers bell-shaped, about 12mm long, silvery-white, fragrant, in 2s and 3s, late autumn. *E.p.* Aurea, leaves margined deep yellow; *E.p.* Dicksonii is similar but with a broader margin; *E.p.* Fredericii, leaves smaller and narrower than type, pale yellow with narrow dark green border; *E.p.* Maculata (*E.p.* Aureo-Maculata, *E.p.* Aureo Variegata), leaves with a bold central yellow splash; *E.p.* Variegata, similar to *E.p.* Aurea but paler yellow. *E. umbellata*, China, Japan, Himalaya; deciduous shrub or small tree, 4–10m tall, often spiny; leaves narrowly oval to oblong-lanceolate, 4–10cm long, densely silvery-white scaled beneath; flowers in clusters of 1–3, funnel-shaped, about 12mm long, white-scaled outside, creamy-white within, early summer; fruit rounded to broadly ellipsoid, silvery-scaled, red, 6–8mm long. *E.u. parvifolia*, Himalaya; young stems silvery-scaled; young leaves starry-hairy above; near to, or identical with, Japanese plants (formerly known as *E.u. typica*).

Left: *Elaeagnus pungens* Dicksonii
Left below: *Elaeagnus macrophylla*
Below: *Elaeagnus pungens* Maculata

Elder – see *Sambucus*; **box elder** – see *Acer negundo*.

Elecampane – see *Inula*.

Elephant's ear – see *Begonia*.

Elm – see *Ulmus*.

Elodea

(Greek *helodes*, marsh or bog-loving). HYDROCHARITACEAE. A genus of 10 species of aquatic perennials from temperate N. and S. America. They grow submerged, with slender, flexuous, branched stems bearing small, narrow, semi-translucent leaves in whorls, and unisexual, often dioecious, 3-petalled flowers. The female flowers of some species float on the surface attached to the plant by thread-like perianth tubes; the males break off when mature buds, and float to the surface where they open and shed pollen that drifts to trailing stigmas. Grow in ponds or aquaria, preferably with a mud base or set in containers of loam or potting mixture, although the plants can also live as free-floating masses provided the water is not totally lacking in nutrients. Plant spring. Propagate by division or cuttings in spring.

Species cultivated: *E. canadensis* (*Anacharis c.*), Canadian pondweed; N. America; plants rooted in mud, spreading by thread-like stolons; stems to 50cm or more, brittle, fast-growing; leaves oblong-lanceolate, 6–13mm long, firm-textured, dark green, minutely toothed, arching back, in crowded whorls of 3; flowers 5mm wide, greenish-purple, rarely produced in Britain and then usually female only. *E. crispa* (*Anacharis c.*, *Lagarosiphon major*), S. Africa; much like *E. densa*, but with leaves rolled back in rings. *E. densa* (*Egeria d.*, *Anacharis d.*), Brazilian pondweed; S. America, mainly Argentina; much like a robust *E. canadensis;* leaves 2–3cm long, mostly in whorls of 4; flowers white, about 1cm wide.

Elsholtzia

(for Johann Sigismund Elsholtz, 1623–1688, German doctor and naturalist). LABIATAE. A genus of 35 species of sub-shrubs and perennials from Europe, Asia, Abyssinia. 1 species is fairly widely available: *E. stauntonii*, China; deciduous sub-shrub to 1·5m, much of the current season's growth dying back in winter, hardy except in far north; leaves in opposite pairs, lanceolate, coarsely toothed, 5–10cm or more long, smelling of mint when bruised; flowers tubular, 2-lipped, lilac-purple, in terminal, spike-like panicles 10–20cm long, autumn. Grow in well-drained, humus-rich soil in a sunny site. Plant autumn or spring. Propagate by cuttings in summer.

Below: *Elodea canadensis*
Centre below: *Elsholtzia stauntonii*
Bottom: *Elymus arenarius*
Right below: *Embothrium coccineum*

Elymus

(Greek *elymos*, for a kind of millet – used by Linnaeus for this genus). GRAMINEAE. A genus of 70 species of perennial grasses from northern temperate zone and S. America. A species is generally cultivated: *E. arenarius*, lyme grass: northern temperate zone; robust, rhizomatous grass forming extensive colonies; leaves linear, to 60cm or so long by 8–20mm wide, bright blue-grey; flowering stems 60–200cm tall, spikelets 2–3cm long, wedge-shaped, in close-set pairs forming wheat-like spikes 15–35cm long, summer. Lyme grass inhabits sand dunes in the wild and has been used as a sand binder. It is an effective foliage plant in the garden but apt to be invasive in light soils. Grow in any well-drained soil in sun. Plant spring or autumn. Propagate by division at planting time.

Embothrium

(Greek *en*, in, and *bothrion*, a little pit, referring to the siting of the stamens). PROTEACEAE. A genus of 8 species (or according to some botanists 1 only) of semi-evergreen and evergreen trees or shrubs from Chile, Argentina, New Guinea and Australia. 1 species is generally available: *E. coccineum* (*E. lanceolatum*, *E. longifolium*, *E. valdivianum*, *E.*

gilliesii), Chilean fire-bush; Chile and borders with Argentina; semi- to almost evergreen tree or large shrub, 6–15m in cultivation, much more in the wild although dwarf deciduous forms occur in the mountains; leaves alternate, lanceolate, oblong-elliptic to obovate, 6–15cm long, deep, somewhat lustrous green; flowers tubular, splitting to form 4, spoon-shaped, perianth segments, the head of each concave and bearing a stamen, crimson to orange-scarlet, often in great profusion. *E.c. lanceolatum*, barely semi-evergreen; leaves linear-lanceolate, the hardiest of the tree-sized forms, represented in gardens by *E.c.l.* Norquinco Valley. *E.c. longifolium*, long-leaved almost evergreen form; yellow-flowered mutants occur in the wild. Best in the south and west.

Emilia

(probably commemorative, but of whom, history does not relate). COMPOSITAE. A genus of 30 species of annual and perennial plants from the tropics. 1 species is generally available: *E. flammea* (*Cacalia coccinea*), tassel flower; tropical America; erect annual, 30–60cm tall; leaves oblong-lanceolate; flower-heads small, composed of tiny, tubular, 5-lobed, scarlet florets carried in showy, long-stalked, flattened clusters, summer to autumn; orange-scarlet and yellow forms are known; leaves edible. Grow in well-drained, fertile soil in a sunny site. Sow seed *in situ* in late spring, or under glass in early spring at 15–18°C, pricking off seedlings at 4–5cm apart each way in boxes of a commercial potting mixture, later hardening off and planting out in early summer.

Below: *Emilia flammea*
Bottom: *Empetrum nigrum*
Bottom right: *Endymion hispanicus × nonscriptus*

Empetrum

(Greek *empetron*, growing on rock – used by Dioscorides for another plant and taken up for this genus by Linnaeus). EMPETRACEAE. A genus comprising 2 or about 16 species (depending on the classifier) of small evergreen shrubs from northern temperate and Arctic regions, S. Andes, Falkland Is, Tristan da Cunha. They are small and heath-like, with wiry stems, linear-oblong leaves in whorls, tiny flowers with 4–6 perianth segments, and berry-like drupes. Grow in acid to neutral, preferably peaty soil in a sunny site in cool areas. Plant autumn to spring. Propagate by cuttings in late summer.

Species cultivated: *E. hermaphroditum*, crowberry; N. Europe and mountains south, arctic Siberia, W. Greenland, Canada; similar to *E. nigrum*, but stems more or less erect; young twigs green, becoming brown; leaves broader; flowers hermaphrodite. *E. nigrum*, crowberry; northern temperate zone and Arctic; 15–45cm tall; tufted habit with many prostrate and ascending stems; young twigs reddish, becoming brownish; leaves linear-oblong, 4–6mm long; flowers dioecious, 1–2mm wide, pinkish to purplish, summer; drupes 5mm wide, flattened globose, glossy black.

Endymion

(in mythology, the handsome Greek youth beloved by Juno). LILIACEAE. A genus of 10 species of bulbous perennials from W. Europe. Formerly in *Scilla* but now placed in *Hyacinthoides* by some. They have strap-shaped, almost succulent leaves, and erect, leafless racemes of 6-tepalled, bell-shaped flowers. Grow in any soil that is not waterlogged, in partial shade or sun. Plant late summer to autumn. Propagate by separating offsets or dividing clumps while dormant or from seed when ripe or autumn.

Species cultivated: *E. hispanicus* (*Scilla h.*, *S. campanulata*), Spanish bluebell; C. and N. Italy, W. France, Spain, Portugal, N. Africa; similar to the next species but leaves 1–3·5cm wide; flowers facing outwards or upwards and more widely bell-shaped; most, if not all, of the cultivars offered under this name are hybrids with *E. nonscriptus*, having all or at least the lower flowers pendulous, the following being readily available: Blue Queen, light blue, late-flowering; Excelsior, large deep blue bells; Rose Queen, lilac pink; Alba Maxima, white. *E. nonscriptus* (*Scilla nonscripta*, *S. nutans*), bluebell, wild hyacinth; Scotland; stems 20–25cm tall; leaves 20–45cm long by 7–15mm wide; racemes nodding at tips, flowers pendant, narrowly bell-shaped, 1·5–2cm long, violet-blue, spring to early summer; white and pink forms occur naturally and are sometimes commercially available.

Above: *Enkianthus campanulatus*
Right: *Enkianthus campanulatus* in autumn

Enkianthus

(Greek *enkyos*, pregnant or swollen, and *anthos*, flowers, alluding to the pouched base of the flowers of some species). ERICACEAE. A genus of 10 species of mainly deciduous shrubs from the Himalayas to Japan. They are bushy in habit with slender, whorled branchlets, similarly arranged, or alternate, obovate to elliptic leaves, and pendant, urn or bell-shaped, 5-lobed flowers in small, umbel-like racemes. Although attractive in bloom, most of the species are even more colourful when the leaves turn to bright shades of yellow and red in autumn. Grow in lime-free, loamy or peaty soils that are well-drained but moisture-retentive, in partial shade or sun in the open or light woodland. Plant autumn to spring. Propagate from seed in spring or cuttings with a heel in late summer.

Species cultivated (all deciduous): *E. campanulatus*, Japan; eventually 4–5m tall but taking many years to reach half this; leaves 3–7cm long, obovate-elliptic, serrulate; flowers bell-shaped, 8–12mm long, straw-yellow with dark red striping, in 5–15 flowered racemes, late spring. *E. cernuus*, Japan; 1·5–3m tall; leaves 2–5cm long, obovate, serrulate; flowers broadly bell-shaped, 6–8mm long, white. *E.c. rubens*, flowers deep red; leaves usually relatively shorter and wider. *E. chinensis*, W. China, N. Burma; 2–4m tall; leaves 5–8cm long, lanceolate, oblong or oval, shallowly toothed; flowers 1cm long, bell-shaped, straw-yellow, pink-striped, in racemes 7–13cm long. *E. japonicus*, see next species. *E. perulatus* (*E. japonicus*), Japan; 1–2m tall; leaves 2–4cm long, obovate to elliptic-ovate, finely toothed and pointed; flowers broadly urn-shaped, about 8mm long, white to palest jade-green, in clusters of 3–10, spring.

Eomecon

(Greek *eos*, dawn – the east – and *mekon*, a poppy – alluding to the homeland of the genus). PAPAVERACEAE. A genus of 1 species of herbaceous perennial from E. China: *E. chionanthum*, snow poppy; far-spreading by slender but fleshy rhizomes; leaves in small tufts, long-stalked, the blade glaucous, cordate kidney-shaped, up to 10cm wide; flowers 4-petalled, white, about 4cm wide, 1 to several on erect stems 20–40cm tall, summer. Grow in humus-rich soil composed largely of leaf mould or peat, in light shade or sun. Plant autumn or spring. Propagate by division or removing the wandering rhizomes in spring.

Epilobium

(Greek *epi*, upon, and *lobos*, a pod – ovary; the petals, sepals, stigma and stamens are carried above, or at the tip of, the ovary). Willow herb. ONAGRACEAE. A genus of 215 species of perennials and sub-shrubs from temperate and cold regions of both hemispheres. They have alternate or opposite pairs of lanceolate to ovate leaves on prostrate to erect stems, and 4-petalled flowers generally in racemes, but sometimes solitary. Grow in sun in any well-drained soil that is moderately moisture-retentive. Plant autumn to spring. Propagate by division or from seed sown in shade outdoors or a cold frame. New Zealand species may not be fully hardy.

Species cultivated: *E. chloraefolium*, New Zealand; tufted; stems ascending, often much branched, 15–45cm tall; leaves opposite at base, alternate above, broadly ovate to oblong, subcordate, remotely and coarsely toothed, 8–20cm long, usually pinkish-brown flushed; flowers white or pink, 8–12mm wide, summer. *E.c. kaikourense* (often misspelt as *E.c. kaikoense*), more robust than type, flowers 2–3cm wide, cream to ivory. *E. crassum*, New Zealand; tufted; stems prostrate, rooting, 5–15cm long; leaves arching to erect, obovate, 2–4cm long, somewhat fleshy, glossy, tinged or edged red or purple-red; flowers pink or white, 8–10mm wide from terminal leaf-axils, summer. *E. dodonaei* (*Chamaenerion d., C. angustissimum, E. rosmarinifolium*), C. France to W. Ukraine; tufted; stems erect, 20–100cm tall; leaves linear, 2–2·5cm long; flowers about 2–2·5cm wide, bright pink with dark sepals and a style 7–15mm long, summer; plants in cultivation under this name with shorter, decumbent stems, narrowly lanceolate leaves, and flowers with styles 3·5–5mm, belong to the closely allied *E. fleischeri*. *E. glabellum*, New Zealand; tufted; stems decumbent at base, then erect, 15–30cm tall; leaves opposite at base, narrowly ovate to elliptic-oblong, 8–20mm long, often bronze-flushed; flowers to 1cm wide, white to cream (sometimes pink in wild) in short racemes. *E.g.* Sulphureum, flowers soft sulphur-yellow; hybrids between this and *E. chloraefolium kaikourense* have been raised at the Broadwell Nursery (Stow-in-the-Wold, Gloucestershire), 1 being sold as Broadwell Hybrid, having stems to 15cm and creamy-pink flowers. *E. obcordatum*, W. USA, Sierra Nevada; tufted, from a woody base; stems decumbent, to 15cm long; leaves opposite, ovate, glaucous, 6–12mm long; flowers 2–3cm wide, the rose-purple petals broadly obcordate, summer to early autumn; hardy, but best in a scree or over-wintered with a pane of glass overhead.

Epigaea

(Greek *epi*, upon, and *gaia*, the earth – alluding to the habit of growth). ERICACEAE. A genus of 3 species of prostrate evergreen shrubs from E. USA, Caucasus to E. Turkey and Japan. They have alternate, ovate to oblong, bristly-haired, leathery leaves, and short racemes of tubular to bell-shaped, 5-lobed flowers in spring. Grow in acid soil largely composed of leaf mould or peat, in partial shade with shelter from strong winds. Plant autumn or spring. Propagate by cuttings with a heel in late summer, layering and from seed in spring.

Species cultivated: *E. asiatica*, Japan; stems 10–25cm long, bearing coarse brown, gland-tipped hairs; leaves 4–10cm long, lustrous; flowers tubular, 1cm long, palest pink with darker lobes; fruit rounded, fleshy, edible capsules 1cm wide; hybrid cultivars have been raised with the next species (*E. × intertexta* Aurora and *E. × i.* Apple Blossom), but are rarely commercially available. *E. repens*, mayflower, trailing arbutus; E. Canada, USA; stems 15–30cm long; leaves rough-textured, wavy, 2–8cm long; flowers tubular, white to pink, larger lobed than *E. asiatica*, 12–15mm wide scented.

Below left: *Epigaea asiatica*
Below: *Epilobium glabellum*

Epimedium

(old Greek name *epimedion*, for a plant not now indentifiable, taken up by Linnaeus for this genus). BERBERIDACEAE. A genus of 21 species of evergreen and deciduous perennials from N. Italy to the Caspian, W. Himalaya, N.E. Asia including Japan and N. Africa. They are rhizomatous, forming clumps and colonies, with long-stalked, mainly trifoliate or biternate leaves, particularly attractive in spring when tinted or flushed in shades of pink, copper or red, and arching, leafless panicles or racemes of 4-petalled, pendant flowers with nectary pouches or spurs. Grow in humus-rich soil in partial shade or sun. Plant after flowering or autumn to spring. Propagate by division at planting time or from ripe seed, seed may take 1½ years to germinate.

Species cultivated (all spring-blooming): *E. alpinum*, barrenwort; N. and C. Italy to Albania; deciduous; rhizomes slender and extensive; leaves bi- or triternate to 30cm tall, leaflets heart-shaped, toothed; flowers 9–13mm wide, dark red, each with 4 bright yellow, slipper-shaped nectaries. *E.*

colchicum, see *E. pinnatum*. *E. grandiflorum* (*E. macranthum*), Japan; deciduous; clump-forming; leaves 2–4 times ternate, 20–40cm tall, leaflets triangular, ovate to ovate-cordate, toothed, 3–6cm long; flowers deep rose to violet or white, with slender nectary spurs, to 1cm or so. *E.g.* Rose Queen, flowers crimson-pink; *E.g.* White Queen,

white; *E.g.* Violaceum, deep lilac. *E. macranthum*, see previous species, *E.* × *perralchicum* (*E.* × *percolchicum* of some catalogues), name covering hybrids between *E. pinnatum colchicum* × *E. perralderanum* and blending their similar characters in various ways. *E. perralderanum*, Algeria; evergreen, forming colonies; similar to *E. pinnatum*, but leaflets usually 3, cordate-ovate, 5–7·5cm long, lustrous bright green; flowers bright yellow with brown spurs. *E. pinnatum*, Iran; almost evergreen, forming colonies; leaves more or less biternate, about 30cm tall, leaflets ovate; flowers in arching racemes largely hidden by previous season's leaves, bright yellow with very short, brown spurs. *E.p. colchicum*, Caucasus, Georgia, USSR; somewhat taller than type; leaflets 3–5, larger. *E. pubigerum*, Caucasus, Turkey, Balkan Peninsula; clump-forming; leaves to 45cm tall, of 3–5 broadly ovate-cordate leaflets, lustrous green above, white-downed beneath; flowers about 1cm or more wide, pale yellow and pink or white. *E.* × *rubrum* (*E alpinum* × *E.* × *grandiflorum*), much like first parent but more robust; leaves between bi- and triternate, leaflets strongly tinted red when young; flowers red with white spurs; sometimes listed as *E. alpinum rubrum*. *E.* × *versicolor* (*E. grandiflorum* × *E. pinnatum colchicum*), deciduous; leaves to 30cm tall with 5–9 leaflets; flowers similar to *E. grandiflorum*, about 2cm wide, yellow and pink with red-tinted spurs. *E.* × *v.* Sulphureum, flowers pale yellow. *E.* × *warleyense* (probably *E. alpinum* × *E. pinnatum colchicum*), rhizomes long; leaves to 30cm tall,

Left: *Epimedium* × *rubrum*
Below left: *Epimedium* × *youngianum* Niveum
Bottom left: *Epimedium* × *perralchicum*
Below: *Eranthis cilicus*

usually of 5–9 leaflets, sometimes only 3; flowers 1·5cm wide, coppery-red (appearing orange) and yellow, spurs blunt, sometimes red-streaked. *E.* × *youngianum* (*E. diphyllum* × *E. grandiflorum*), deciduous; clump-forming; leaves 15–25cm tall, biternate; flowers 1·5–2cm wide, with short, slender spurs or none, white, tinted green. *E.* × *y.* Niveum, to 15cm tall, compact, flowers white.

Eranthis

(Greek *er*, spring, and *anthos*, a flower – the plants bloom early). Winter aconite. RANUNCULACEAE. A genus of 7 species of perennials from Europe and Asia. The leaves and flowering stems grow directly from tuber-like rhizomes; the leaves are umbrella-like, usually cut into 3 lobes or leaflets, each of which is deeply divided; flowering stems similar, with solitary, buttercup-like blooms of 5–8 petal-like sepals surrounded by a ruff-like involucre of bracts resembling a more coarsely lobed leaf. Grow in humus-rich soil in sun or shade. Plant in early autumn or as soon afterwards as possible. Propagate by separating offsets when dormant or division of clumps at flowering time.

Species cultivated: *E. cilicicus*, Greece to Syria; similar to *E. hyemalis*, but flowers slightly deeper yellow, later-opening, involucre smaller and more deeply divided, bronze-flushed at flowering time; some botanists merge it with *E. hyemalis* as intermediary forms unite the 2 in S.E. Europe. *E. hyemalis*, S.E. France to Bulgaria; clump-forming; stems 5–10cm tall; leaf-blades rounded, about 8cm wide when mature, of 3 overlapping, wedge-shaped leaflets, each deeply divided; flowers 2–3cm wide, usually of 6 bright yellow tepals, buttercup-like, each one surrounded by a more coarsely lobed but leaf-like ruff. *E.* × *tubergenii* (*E. cilicicus* × *E. hyemalis*), more robust and larger flowered than either parent, generally favouring *E. cilicicus* and often bronze-flushed at flowering time; *E.* × *t.* Guinea Gold is the best named clone.

Eremurus

(Greek *eremia*, desert, and *oura*, tail – alluding to shape of the flower-spikes and the desert-like steppe habitat of many species). LILIACEAE. A genus of 50 species of herbaceous perennials from W. and C. Asia. They are mainly clump-forming with stout, fleshy roots, strap-shaped leaves, and long, tapered racemes of starry, 6-tepalled flowers fancifully reminiscent of a fox's tail – hence the vernacular name foxtail lily. Grow in fertile, well-drained soil in a sunny site but preferably sheltered from early morning sun as the young leaves can be damaged by spring frosts. Plant or replant in autumn, damaging the roots as little as possible. An annual mulch of

Above: *Eremurus stenophyllus*

decayed manure or compost in spring will maintain vigorous growth. Propagate by careful division at planting time or from seed when ripe (seedlings usually take 5 years or more to reach flowering size).

Species cultivated: *E. aitchisonii*, see *E. robustus elwesii*. *E. bungei*, see *E. stenophyllus*. *E. elwesii*, see *E. robustus elwesii*. *E. himalaicus*, N.W. Himalaya to Nuristan; stems 75–150cm tall; leaves 30cm or more long, to 4cm or more wide; flowers 2–3cm wide, white, densely borne, late spring; one of the easiest to grow. *E. olgae*, Iran, N. Afghanistan; similar in effect to *E. himalaicus*, but leaves longer and narrower, to 1·5cm wide; stems 70–100cm tall; flowers white, rarely pink, summer. *E. robustus*, Turkestan; stems 1·5–3m tall; leaves 75–120cm long by 10cm wide, bright bluish-green; flowers peach-pink, in long racemes, summer. *E.r. elwesii*, flowers pink, late spring to early summer, possibly the same as *E. aitchisonii*. *E.* × Shelford (*E. olgae* × *E. stenophyllus*), a range of hybrid cultivars and their un-named seedlings variously combining parental characters; flowers yellow to orange-buff, pink and white, summer. *E. stenophyllus*, Iran and adjacent USSR; stems 60–120cm tall; leaves about 30cm long by 12mm wide; flowers bright yellow, 1–2cm wide, densely borne, summer.

Erica

(Greek *ereike*, Latin *erice*, for the tree heath – *E. arborea*). ERICACEAE. A genus of about 600 species of evergreen shrubs or small trees, mostly from S.

Africa, but also Canary Is to Azores, N. Africa, Europe to Turkey and Syria. They are wiry-stemmed with small, linear to oblong leaves, usually with rolled-under margins, often in whorls or spiralled, and small, bell to urn-shaped flowers often carried in profusion. The plants live in association with a fungus that permeates the whole plant, particularly the roots (endotrophic mycorrhiza). Most of the fungal partners need acid conditions, hence all but a few erica species need acid-peaty soil to thrive. Grow the hardy species in a sunny site, the tender species under glass, minimum temperature 7–10°C with good ventilation. Plant hardy species in autumn or spring. Pot or repot greenhouse sorts after flowering or spring, using one of the acid, all-peat composts. Propagate by cuttings with a heel, late summer for hardy sorts, spring for tender species. All may be raised from seed in spring at about 15–16°C. Hardy ericas benefit from shearing over after flowering or spring, and greenhouse sorts should have all spent flower-spikes and a few centimetres of stem below removed when flowers fade. Pot-grown plants may with advantage receive a few applications of liquid feed at 2–3 weekly intervals during summer.

Species cultivated (all hardy unless stated otherwise): *E. arborea*, tree heath; Mediterranean, S.W. Europe, Canary Is; large tree or shrub to 7m, bushy and erect; leaves dense, 3–5mm long, linear, in whorls of 3–4; flowers broadly bell-shaped, fragrant, white, 2·4–4mm wide in leafy panicles 20–45cm long, spring; lime-tolerant, not reliably hardy in very severe winters. *E.a. alpina*, hardier, rarely above 2·5m tall. *E. australis*, Spanish heath; W. Spain, Portugal; slender, erect, to 2m tall; leaves 3·5–6mm long, linear, in whorls of 4; flowers tubular, fragrant, 6–9mm long, pink to red-purple, in umbel-like clusters, spring to early summer; sometimes damaged in very cold winters. *E.a.* Mr Robert, somewhat more tender and taller than type, flowers white; *E.a.* Riverslea, flowers fuchsia-purple. *E. carnea*, see *E. herbacea*. *E. ciliaris*, Dorset heath; W. Europe, N.W. Morocco; stems erect from a decumbent base, 30cm or more tall; leaves 3–4mm long, ovate to oblong-lanceolate with ciliate margins, in whorls of 3, sometimes 4; flowers urn-shaped, somewhat curved-down, 8–10mm long, reddish-pink, in terminal racemes, summer to autumn; can be cut back in severe winters. *E.c.* Camla, hardier, rose-pink flowers; *E.c.* David McClintock, flowers white, pink-tipped; *E.c.* Globosa, vigorous, taller than type, flowers large, pink, more rounded; *E.c.* Maweana, stiff habit, flowers larger than type, pink; *E.c.* Mrs C. H. Gill, dark green foliage, red flowers; *E.c.* Stoborough, tall, 60cm or so, flowers pearly-white. *E. cinerea*, bell heather; W. Europe east to Norway and N. Italy; spreading to semi-erect; stems 15–60cm long; leaves linear, 4–6mm long; flowers ovoid to urn-shaped, 4–7mm long, rose-purple, in racemes, summer to autumn; stands dry conditions well; dozens of cultivars are known, many very similar – recommended are: *E.c.* Alba Minor, very compact and free-blooming, white; *E.c.* Atrorubens, prolific ruby-red flowers; *E.c.* C. D. Eason, dark green foliage, glowing pink flowers; *E.c.* Cevennes, erect habit, lavender-pink flowers; *E.c.* Coccinea, bright deep red; *E.c.* Eden Valley, lilac-pink; *E.c.* Foxhollow Mahogany, dark green leaves, mahogany flowers; *E.c.* Golden Drop, low-growing, almost prostrate, leaves coppery-yellow, rusty-red in winter, pink flowers seldom borne; *E.c.* Golden Hue, erect habit, leaves coppery-yellow in summer, red-flushed in winter, flowers pink; *E.c.* Hookstone White, long racemes of large white flowers; *E.c.* John Eason, like *E.c.* Golden Hue but flowers salmon-pink; *E.c.* Mrs Dill, dwarf to 10cm tall, deep glowing pink: *E.c.* Polypetala, see *E.c.* Schizopetala; *E.c.* P. S. Patrick, bright purple; *E.c.* Schizopetala, pale purple, the corolla split into 4 petal-like lobes once considered a hybrid between *Erica* and *Calluna* more interesting than attractive. *E.* × *darleyensis* (*E. erigena* × *E. herbacea*), a name covering several clonal cultivars, basically like a taller (to 45cm), spreading *E. herbacea* with profusely borne flowers; the original plant under this name (a chance seedling at Darley Dale at the end of last century) is now called *E.* × *d.* Darley Dale and has pale mauve-pink flowers, winter to spring; *E.* × *d.* Alba, see *E.* × *d.* Silberschmelze; *E.* × *d.* Arthur Johnson (*E.* × *d.* A. T. Johnson), deep pink flowers in long racemes; *E.* × *d.* George Rendall, deep pink, autumn to spring; *E.* × *d.* Silberschmelze (*E.* × *d.* Molten Silver, *E.* × *d.* Silberlachs, *E.* × *d.* Silver Bells, *E.* × *d.* White Form), flowers white, scented, winter to spring: *E. erigena* (*E. mediterranea*, *E. hibernica*), Irish or Mediterranean heath; W. Ireland to N. Portugal and Spain and W. France; erect and of dense habit, 60–250cm tall; leaves 5–8mm long, linear, dark green; flowers urn-shaped, 5–7mm long, purplish-pink or red, scented in racemes or leafy panicles, early spring to early summer; lime-tolerant. *E.e.* Brightness, slow-growing to 1m, flowers bronze in bud, opening bright pinkish red; *E.e.* Coccinea, similar to *E.e.* Brightness but bright rose-purple from darker buds; *E.e.* W. T. Rackliff, compact, to 60cm tall, flowers white. *E. gracilis*, S. Africa; tender, well-branched to 45cm or more; leaves linear, 3–5mm long in whorls of 4 or more; flowers globose, 3–4mm long, rose-purple, autumn to winter; *E.g.* Alba (*E. nivalis*), white. *E. herbacea* (*E.

Left: *Eremurus robustus elwesii*
Below: *Erica australis*

Top left: *Erica arborea alpina*
Left: *Erica erigena* W. T. Rackliff
Top: *Erica × darleyensis*
Above: *Erica cinerea* Cevennes

carnea), winter or mountain heath; Alps to E.C. Germany and Austria, S. to C. Italy and Greece; decumbent to semi-erect, to 25cm tall; leaves linear, 5–8mm long; flowers narrowly urn-shaped, 5–6mm long and rosy-red, in dense racemes, autumn to spring; very lime-tolerant. *E.h.* Aurea, foliage golden, particularly spring to early summer; *E.h.* Eileen Porter, carmine-red, from late autumn to late spring; *E.h.* King George, deep rose, compact habit, winter to spring, often sold as *E.h.* Winter Beauty; *E.h.* Praecox Rubra, prostrate, flowers deep rose-red, winter to spring; *E.h.* Snow Queen, large white flowers well above the main foliage; *E.h.* Springwood Pink, vigorous trailing habit, rose-pink; *E.h.* Springwood White, like preceeding but flowers white, winter to spring; *E.h.* Startler, pale coral-pink; *E.h.* Vivellii, bronze-green foliage in winter, bright carmine flowers; *E.h.* Winter Beauty, much confused with *E.h.* King George but less robust and rarely grown. *E. lusitanica*, Portuguese heath; W. France, Spain, Portugal; similar to *E. arborea* but more erect habit; 2–4m tall; leaves 5–7 mm long; flowers narrower than *E. arborea*, 4–5mm long, white, tinged pink, spring (late winter in warm sites); lime-tolerant and hardy in all but the hardest winters. *E. mackaiana* (*E. mackaii*), W. Ireland. N.W. Spain; similar to *E. tetralix*, but of denser habit and spreading widely when old; 15–45cm tall; leaves 2–4·5mm wide, oblong-lanceolate, ciliate, dark green above, white beneath, in whorls of 4; flowers urn-shaped, 5–7mm long, bright deep pink in terminal umbels, summer to autumn; *E.m.* Plena (*E.m.* Flore-pleno, *E.m.* Pleniflora), flowers double, more vigorous and floriferous. *E. mediterranea*, see *E. erigena*. *E. pageana*. S. Africa; half-hardy, erect, bushy, 30–90cm tall; leaves linear, about 6mm long, in whorls of 4; flowers bell-shaped, 6mm long, rich yellow, in small clusters forming narrow, leafy panicles, spring, summer; needs warm sheltered site outside or a frost free greenhouse where it makes an unusual pot plant. *E.* × *praegeri* Connemara, (*E. mackaiana* × *E. tetralix*) similar to *E. mackaiana* with pale pink flowers having downy sepals. *E. scoparia*, besom heath; S.W. Europe, Canary Is east to C. Italy and Tunisia; erect, open habit, to 3m or more; leaves linear, 4–7mm long in whorls of 3–4; flowers globular or broadly bell-shaped, greenish, some-times red-tinted, in racemes or panicles, early summer or later. *E.s.* Minima (*E.s.* Compacta, *E.s.* Pumila, *E.s.* Nana), dense habit to 60cm tall; foliage light glossy green; flowers greenish-white. *E. terminalis*, Corsican heath; S. Spain, Morocco, Corsica, Sardinia and S. Italy; stiff, erect, usually bushy, 1–2·5m tall; leaves linear, 3–5·5mm long in whorls of 4, sometimes to 6; flowers 5–7mm long, rose-pink, urn-shaped, in terminal umbels, summer

Top left: *Erica cinerea*
Left: *Erica herbacea* cultivars
Top centre: *Erica tetralix* Alba Mollis
Top right: *Erica vagans* Mrs D. F. Maxwell
Above: *Erica* × *watsonii* Dawn

to autumn; lime-tolerant. *E. tetralix*, cross-leaved heath; W. and N. Europe to Iceland and Finland; erect when young, spreading later, 15–40cm tall; leaves 3–6mm long, linear-oblong to lanceolate, dark green above, white beneath; flowers cylindrical to urn-shaped, 5–9mm long, pale pink, in terminal umbels, summer to autumn. *E.t.* Alba Mollis, leaves silvery-grey haired, white flowers; *E.t.* Con Underwood, greyish foliage, crimson flowers; *E.t.* L. E. Underwood, grey foliage, pink flowers from apricot buds. *E. umbellata*, Spanish heath; W. Spain, Portugal; erect, 20–80cm tall; leaves 3–4mm long, linear in whorls of 3; flowers broadly bell-shaped to ovoid, 3·5–5·5mm long, purplish-pink to cerise, in terminal umbels, early summer; lime-tolerant. *E. vagans*, Cornish heath; C. Spain and Portugal, W. France and S.W. England; spreading to ascending, 30–60cm tall; leaves linear, 6–11mm long in whorls of 4–5; flowers broadly bell-shaped, to 3·5mm long, lilac-pink to purple, in dense racemes, summer to autumn. *E.v.* Cream (*E.v.* Alba Superba Darleyensis), vigorous, dark green foliage, cream-white flowers; *E.v.* Grandiflora, rose-pink, in long racemes; *E.v.* Lyonesse, pure white; *E.v.* Mrs D. F. Maxwell, deep cerise; *E.v.* Rubra, deep purple-red; *E.v.* St. Keverne (*E.v. kevernensis*), clear rose-pink, flowers in profusion, *E.* × *veitchii* (*E. arborea* × *E. lusitanica*), similar to the latter parent but

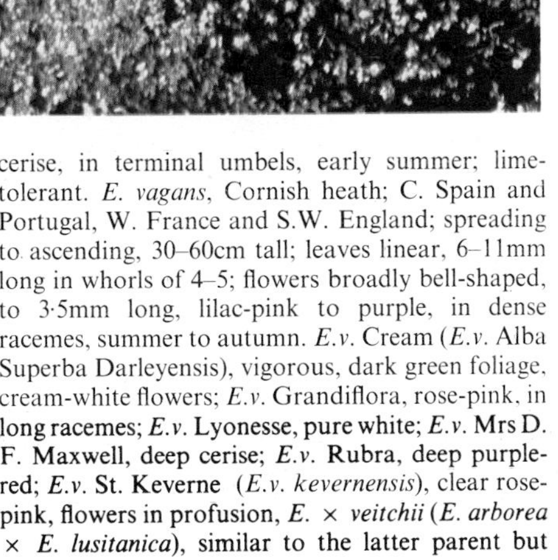

much more floriferous, vigorous and hardy; represented in cultivation mainly by *E.* × *v.* Exeter. *E.* × *watsonii* (*E. ciliaris* × *E. tetralix*), original clone now known as *E.* × *w.* Truro of spreading habit with large, pink to crimson flowers favouring the *E. tetralix* parent. *E.* × *w.* Dawn favours *E. ciliaris*, with rich rose-pink flowers and young foliage yellow to orange. *E.* × *williamsii* (*E. tetralix* × *E. vagans*), the following clones are roughly intermediate between the parents with yellowish young foliage: *E.* × *w.* Gwavas, flowers pale pink; *E.* × *w.* P. D. Williams, rose-pink, generally in racemes, the leaves bronzing in winter.

Erigeron

(Greek *eri*, early, and *geron*, old man, an ancient name given to an early-flowering member of the daisy family, with hoary-downy leaves, taken up for this genus by Linnaeus). Fleabane. COMPOSITAE. A genus of at least 200 species of annuals and perennials of worldwide occurrence but mainly N. America. They are mainly erect, the perennials tufted to clump-forming, with alternate oblong, lanceolate, ovate or spathulate leaves and daisy-like flower-heads. The latter resemble those of *Aster*, but have rather more, narrower ray florets. Grow in

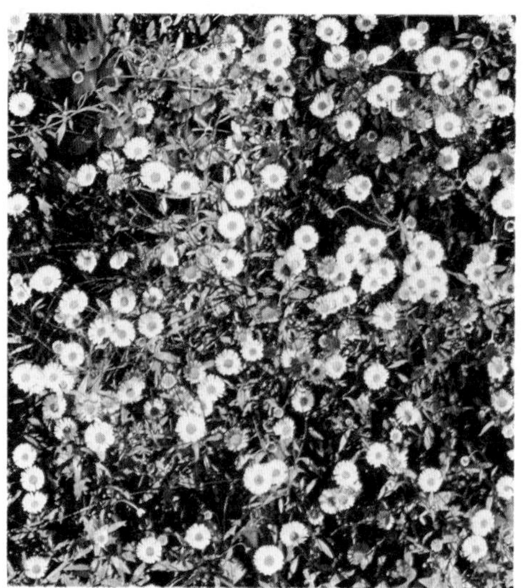

well-drained, fertile soil in a sunny site. Plant autumn to spring. Propagate by division at planting time or from seed in spring.

Species cultivated (all perennial): *E. alpinus*, Alpine fleabane; Pyrenees, Alps, Apennines; tufted; stems leafy, to 20cm or more; basal leaves spathulate, coarsely haired, 3–8cm long; flower-heads 2–3cm wide, rays lilac-purple to reddish, solitary or in 2s or 3s, late summer. *E. aurantiacus*, Turkestan; clump-forming; stems leafy, to 30cm tall; basal leaves oblong to lanceolate, to 8cm long or more; flower-heads about 5cm wide, rays bright orange, solitary. *E.a. sulphureus*, rays yellow. *E. aureus*, W. N. America; tufted to clump-forming; stems leafy 6–8cm tall; basal leaves spathulate; flower-heads to 2cm wide, rays deep yellow, comparatively broad, summer. *E. compositus* (*E. multifidus*), W. USA to Alaska; tufted; stems 5–15cm tall; leaves 2–6cm long, long-stalked, the blade fan-shaped, deeply bi- or triternately lobed; flower-heads 2·5–3cm wide, rays white, bluish or purplish, sometimes lacking, spring to summer. *E.c. trifidus*, more congested habit with trifid leaves, generally white-haired. *E. glaucus*, seaside daisy; California, Oregon; evergreen, low mound to hummock-forming, almost sub-shrubby; leaves broadly spathulate to obovate, 3–10cm long, more or less glaucous; flower-heads solitary, 4–8cm wide, summer to autumn. *E. leiomerus*, W. USA alpine; tufted; stems to 10cm; leaves spathulate, to about 2·5cm long; flower-heads solitary, 2cm wide, rays violet to purple-blue, summer. *E. macranthus* and *E. mesa-grandis*, see *E. speciosus*. *E. mucronatus* (*E. karwinskianus*), Mexico; rhizomatous, forming tufts and mats; stems 10–25cm tall, twiggy, branched; upper leaves linear-lanceolate; flower-heads 1·5cm wide, rays white above, purple-red beneath, summer to autumn, best in mild areas as sometimes cut back in severe winters but seldom killed; good for dry walls, occasionally invasive. *E. multifidus*, see *E. compositus*. *E. simplex* (*E. uniflorus*), W. USA alpine; tufted; stems 5–20cm tall; leaves mostly basal, oblanceolate, white or purplish-haired, 1–4cm long; flower-heads solitary, about 3cm wide, rays white to purple, summer. *E. trifidus*, see *E. compositus*. *E. speciosus*, W. N. America; clump-forming; stems 45–60cm tall, branched; basal leaves oblanceolate, ciliate, 5–10cm long; flower-heads 3–10, each one about 5cm wide, rays lilac to violet, varying in shade and width, summer. *E.s. macranthus* (*E. macranthus*, *E. mesa-grandis*), usually 3–5 heads per stem, ray florets purple to bluish, usually slightly longer than type. *E. speciosus* has given rise to several cultivars, many of hybrid origin, including the once popular *E.s.* Quakeress, with lilac-pink rays; crossed with such species as *E. glaucus*, *E. aurantiacus* and *E.s. macranthus*, it has also given rise to many fine, modern cultivars, the flower-heads often having several rows of ray florets and appearing semi-double – recommended are: Charity, pink; Darkest of All, deep violet-blue; Dignity, mauve-blue deepening with age; Gaiety, to 80cm tall, deep pink; Serenity, to 80cm, deep violet; Foerster's Leibling, very semi-double, deep pink; Dimity, very dwarf, pink rays, orange-tinted in bud.

Erinacea

(Latin *erinaceus*, a hedgehog, alluding to the outward pointing spines). LEGUMINOSAE. A genus of 1 species of dwarf shrub from Spain, France, Algeria, Tunisia. *E. anthyllis* (*E. pungens*, *Anthyllis erinacea*), hedgehog broom, blue broom; stiff, hummock-forming shrub to 30cm tall; branchlets green, silvery-haired, sharply spine-tipped; leaves in opposite pairs or alternate, 5mm long, narrowly oblanceolate, of brief duration; flowers pea-shaped, blue-violet, 1·5–1·8cm long, emerging from silky-haired, inflated calyces carried in short, terminal racemes, late spring to summer. Grow in any well-drained soil in mild areas. Plant autumn or spring.

Above, from left to right: *Erigeron* Foerster's Liebling, *E.* Gaiety and *E. mucronatus*.

Propagate from seed in spring in a cold frame or greenhouse, the seedlings pricked off when still in the cotyledon stage into small pots and planted out later direct into flowering site; cuttings with a heel may be rooted in late summer and grown as above.

Erinus

(ancient Greek name probably used for a basil-like plant, and taken up for this genus by Linnaeus). SCROPHULARIACEAE. A genus of 1 species of small, evergreen perennial from the Alps and Pyrenees: *E. alpinus*, fairy foxglove; tufted, with many rosettes of obovate to spathulate toothed leaves, 2–4cm long; stems 5–15cm tall, erect, bearing racemes of tubular, 1cm wide flowers having 5 oblong, notched, tipped, rose-purple petal-lobes. *E.a. albus*, flowers white; *E.a.* Dr Hanaele, carmine; *E.a.* Mrs Boyle, soft pink. Spring, summer. Grow in sharply drained soil in a sunny site. Plant autumn or spring. Propagate from seed when ripe or spring. Ideal for retaining walls and will naturalize on any well-creviced old wall.

Eriobotrya

(Greek *erion*, wool, and *botrys*, a cluster of grapes – flower clusters are woolly). ROSACEAE. A genus of 30 species of evergreen trees and shrubs from the Himalayas to Japan, S.E. Asia, W. Malaysia. 1 species is generally available: *E. japonica*, loquat; China, Japan; large shrub or small tree, 4–10m tall; young stems stout, woolly; leaves alternate, oblong-

Left: *Erinacea anthyllis*
Below left: *Erinus alpinus*
Below: *Eriobotrya japonica*

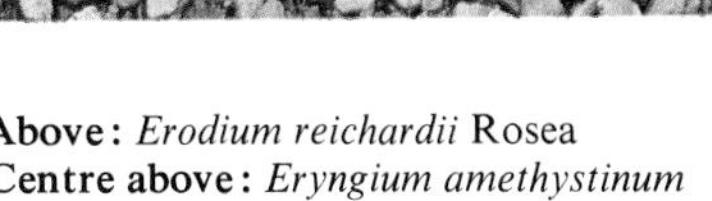

Above: *Erodium reichardii* Rosea
Centre above: *Eryngium amethystinum*
Far right above: *Eryngium proteiflorum*

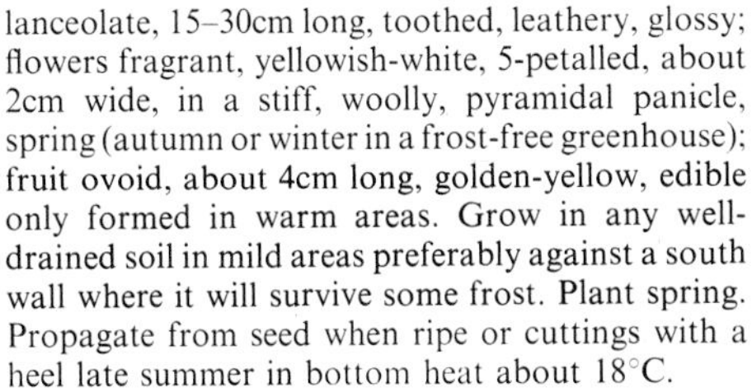

lanceolate, 15–30cm long, toothed, leathery, glossy; flowers fragrant, yellowish-white, 5-petalled, about 2cm wide, in a stiff, woolly, pyramidal panicle, spring (autumn or winter in a frost-free greenhouse); fruit ovoid, about 4cm long, golden-yellow, edible only formed in warm areas. Grow in any well-drained soil in mild areas preferably against a south wall where it will survive some frost. Plant spring. Propagate from seed when ripe or cuttings with a heel late summer in bottom heat about 18°C.

Erodium

(Greek *erodios*, a heron – the fruit is beaked, resembling a heron's bill). Stork's bill. GERANIACEAE. A genus of 90 species of annuals, perennials and sub-shrubs from Europe, Mediterranean to C. Asia, S. America, Australia. They are allied to *Geranium* and *Pelargonium*, having alternate, simple to bi-pinnatisect leaves and 5-petalled flowers, solitary or in umbels. The fruit is formed of 5 'seeds' (carpels) attached to the base of the enlarged style. On ripening the seed springs off with a tail split from the style. This tail is hygroscopic, expanding when damp, twisting spirally when dry. By such alternate movements the pointed seed may be driven into the soil. Grow in any well-drained soil in a sunny site. Plant autumn or spring. Propagate by division, cuttings of roots or basal shoots, or from seed in spring.

Species cultivated: *E. chamaedryoides*, see *E. reichardii*. *E. chrysanthum*, mountains of S. and C. Greece; tufted; stems 10–15cm tall; leaves 3cm or more long, pinnate, the leaflets pinnatisect, silvery-white haired; flowers 1·5–2cm wide, pale yellow, in umbels, summer. *E. corsicum*, Corsica, Sardinia; tufted to mat-forming, with prostrate stems to 25cm long; leaves grey-green, rounded to oblong-ovate, sometimes pinnatifid, blunt-toothed, downy, 1–2·5cm long; flowers white or pink, 1–2cm wide, solitary or in umbels of 2–3, about 6–8cm tall, summer; needs a sheltered site. *E. daucoides*, mountains of Spain; tufted; stems to 15cm tall; leaves to 8cm long, pinnate, leaflets ovate to lanceolate, toothed or pinnatifid; flowers lilac to rose-purple, up to 2cm wide, the upper 2 petals with basal, dark purple blotches, in umbels of 1–7, summer. *E. guttatum*, S. Spain, N. Africa; tufted to mat-forming with prostrate, almost woody stems; leaves to 2·5cm long, triangular to broadly ovate, the upper ones deeply 3-lobed; flowers deep violet to white, about 2cm wide, the upper 2 petals with black basal spots, in umbels of 2–3, about 10–15cm tall; sometimes mis-identified with other species in gardens; needs a sheltered site. *E.* × *hybridum* (*E. daucoides* × *E. manescavii*), similar to the latter parent with more deeply dissected leaves and paler, rosy flowers; also sometimes used for *E.reichardii* Roseum. *E.macradenum*, see *E.petraeum glandulosum*. *E.manescavii*, W. and C. Pyrenees; tufted at first, later mat-forming with almost woody, prostrate stems; leaves 15–30cm long, pinnate, leaflets ovate, deeply pinnatifid; flowers about 3cm wide, carmine to purple-red in umbels to 30cm or more tall, late summer. *E.pelargoniiflorum*, Turkey; tufted, with prostrate, woody stems; leaves ovate, shortly 3–5 lobed, crenate to dentate; flowers to 2cm wide, white, purple-veined, in umbels 12–30cm tall, late spring to autumn outside in mild areas, all-the-year-round in a cool greenhouse. *E. petraeum*, Spain, S. W. France; tufted to mat-forming, with prostrate almost woody stems very variable in leaf and flower size, several sub-species being recognized; leaves 1–7cm long, bi-pinnate, white-haired, ultimate lobes again deeply cut; flowers 1·5–2·5cm wide, pale purple to pink, or white, the 2 upper petals sometimes with blackish basal patches, summer. *E.p. crispum*, leaves densely haired; flowers white, pink or lilac, veined red or purple, with blackish-purple basal patches – *E. supracanum* (of gardens) fits in here, having white flowers with large, blackish blotches, small leaves and a dwarf habit. *E.p. glandulosum* (*E. macradenum*), leaves glandular-pubescent; flowers pale violet with darker veins and blotches on stems to 15cm tall. *E. reichardii* (*E. chamaedryoides*), Balearic Is; similar to *E. corsicum* but more compact; leaves 5–15mm long, sparsely haired; flowers always solitary, just above the leaves, white with purple veins, summer. *E.r.* Roseum, flowers pink, red-veined; may be killed back in severe winters but usually grows again from the roots. *E. supracanum*, see *E. petraeum crispum*.

Eryngium

(Greek *eryggion* for field eryngo, *E. campestre*, used for the whole genus by Linnaeus). UMBELLIFERAE. A genus of 230 species of mainly herbaceous and evergreen perennials from temperate to subtropical regions, excluding tropical to S. Africa. They are erect, tufted to clump-forming, with sword, or strap to heart-shaped leaves, often deeply lobed and spiny toothed. The tiny, purple to blue, whitish or greenish flowers are carried in dense, hemispherical to conical heads surrounded by an involucre of narrow, spiny, coloured bracts. Grow in well-drained soil in a sunny site. Plant early autumn or spring. Propagate from seed when ripe, or by careful division when possible in spring, or root cuttings late winter.

Species cultivated (all summer-flowering): *E. agavifolium*, Argentina; evergreen; stems to 1·5m tall; loose rosettes of sword-shaped, spiny-toothed leaves to 45cm or more long; flower-heads thimble-shaped, about 5cm long, greenish, bracts tapered from a broad base, not or barely spiny, greenish. *E. alpinum*, Jura, Alps and mountains W. and C. Yugoslavia; clump-forming; basal leaves persistent, long-stalked, the blades broadly ovate to triangular-cordate, 8–15cm long, irregularly toothed; stems to about 70cm tall, bearing palmate leaves; flower-heads cone-shaped, to 4cm long, blue, surrounded by many longer, deeply divided, spiny, feathery bracts of metallic blue. *E. amethystinum*, Italy, Sicily, Balkan Peninsula; stems 40–60cm tall; basal leaves usually persistent, leathery, blades 10–15cm long, obovate, spiny toothed, with pinnatisect bases and palmate tips; flower-heads globose to ovoid, 1–2cm long, blue, bracts spiny, linear-lanceolate, 2–5cm long, amethyst; confused in gardens with hybrids akin to *E. tripartitum*. *E. bourgatii*, Pyrenees; stems to 60cm tall; basal leaves persistent, 3–7cm long, rounded, 3-lobed, each lobe pinnatifid or bi-pinnatifid, spiny toothed, waved and angled, grey-green, white-veined; flower-heads broadly ovoid, 1·5–2·5cm long, bracts linear-lanceolate, 2–5cm long, spiny toothed or not, blue-green. *E. bromeliifolium*, see next species. *E. eburneum* (*E. paniculatum*, *E. balansae*), S. America; stems to 1·5m tall; dense evergreen rosettes of arching, narrow, almost grassy leaves, 30–60cm long with slender, marginal prickles; flower-heads greenish with white stamens, bracts slender, green; grown in gardens as *E. bromeliifolium*, the true species being a stiffer, half-hardy Mexican. *E. decaisneana* (*E. pandanifolium*), S. America; evergreen; stems to 2·4m or more tall, bearing large panicles of pea-sized, brownish-purple flower-heads; leaves narrowly sword-shaped, spiny margined, 1–1·8m long. *E. giganteum*, Caucasus; monocarpic, usually biennial; stems 1m or more; leaves in rosettes, long-stalked, the blades ovate-cordate, crenate, to 10cm long; flower-heads thimble-shaped, 3–5cm long, bluish, bracts ovate-lanceolate, spine toothed, bluish. *E.g.* Miss Willmott's Ghost, flowers greenish, bracts gleaming ivory-white. *E. maritimum*, sea holly; Europe, coastal sands; deciduous; basal leaves blue-grey, white-veined, rounded, often cordate, 4–10cm long, 3–5 lobed with coarse, spiny teeth; stems to 30cm tall, widely branched bearing hard-textured, stem-clasping leaves and rounded, blue flower-heads 1·5–3cm long, bracts ovate, like the leaves or more bluish. *E.* × *oliveranum* (*E. oliverianum*), garden-worthy hybrid of uncertain parentage, perhaps from *E. alpinum* and *E. amethystinum*; not unlike *E. alpinum*, but heads smaller and bracts stiffer and broader, rich steely-blue. *E. planum*, C. and S.E. Europe; stems 60–90cm tall; basal leaves persistent, blades 5–10cm long, oblong to ovate, cordate, serrate; flower-heads ovoid to globose, 1–2cm long, light blue, bracts linear-lanceolate,

spiny toothed, to 2·5cm long, greenish-blue. *E. pandanifolium*, see *E. decaisneana*. *E. proteiflorum*, Mexico; evergreen, clump-forming; stems to 90cm tall; leaves sword-shaped, marginal spines sometimes 3 pronged; flower-heads cone-shaped, to 5cm long, bracts lanceolate, irregularly toothed, longer than head, spreading, shining steely-white; often erroneously listed under the name of the botanist who first described the plant (Delaroux). *E. serra*, Brazil; similar to *E. agavifolium* and sometimes confused with it, but leaves broader and doubly toothed; flower-heads smaller and more rounded. *E. tripartitum* (of gardens), provenance unknown, probably a hybrid, perhaps from *E. planum*, which it most resembles; basal leaves obovate-oblong, 3-lobed, stems to 75cm tall with many slender branches bearing heads smaller than those of *E. planum* with deep blue bracts. *E. variifolium*, Morocco; evergreen; stems 40–50cm tall; basal leaves rounded to heart-shaped, 5–10cm long, deep glossy green, conspicuously white-veined, in flat rosettes when young; flower-heads rounded, 1–2cm long, grey-blue, bracts longer than heads, lanceolate, white. *E.* × *zabelii*, strictly a name to cover the hybrids between *E. alpinum* and *E. bourgatii*, but also used to cover other named hybrids.

Erysimum

(Greek *erysimon*, possibly from *eryomai*, to help or save, because of supposed medicinal properties; alternatively from *eryo*, to draw up, some species allegedly causing blisters). CRUCIFERAE. A genus of about 100 species of annuals, biennials and perennials from Mediterranean, Europe, Asia, N. America. They resemble *Cheiranthus*, differing in small botanical details, eg nectaries at the bases of all 6 stamens (only of the outer 2 in *Cheiranthus*). Culture as for *Cheiranthus*.

Above, left to right: *Eryngium alpinum* and *E. variifolium*

Species cultivated: *E.* × *allionii* (*Cheiranthus allionii*), Siberian wallflower; probably a hybrid between the Caucasian annual *E. perovskianum* and the perennial *E. decumbens* (*E. dubium*, *E. ochroleucum*); short-lived perennial best grown as a biennial, with erect stems to 30cm or more tall; leaves lanceolate, 5–8cm long; flowers bright orange about 1·5cm wide, spring to summer. *E. alpestre*, Turkey; tufted perennial; stems 5–15cm tall; basal leaves hoary, oblanceolate to spathulate, in rosettes; stem leaves narrower, scattered; flowers pale bright yellow, 1–1·5cm wide; probably the same as *E. rupestre* (of gardens). *E. alpinum* (*Cheiranthus alpinus*) (of gardens), Scandinavia(?); low hummock-forming, to 15cm tall; leaves lanceolate, about 3cm long; flowers fragrant, sulphur-yellow, 1·2–1·5cm wide, late spring. *E.a.* Moonlight, flowers primrose-yellow. *E. linifolium*, Spain, Portugal; tufted; stems 15–30cm tall or so; leaves linear-lanceolate; flowers lilac-purple to violet, about 1·5cm or or more wide, spring to autumn; less hardy. *E.l.* Variegatum, leaves striped with creamy-white. *E. pumilum* (*E. helveticum*), Pyrenees, Alps, Balkan Peninsula; tufted; stems to 15cm tall; leaves linear-lanceolate; flowers yellow 1·5cm–2cm wide, fragrant, late summer. *E.p.* Golden Gem, flowers deep golden-yellow. *E. rupestre*, see *E. alpestre*.

Erythrina

(Greek *erythros*, red – the colour of the flowers). Coral tree. LEGUMINOSAE. A genus of 100 species mainly of trees and shrubs from the tropics and subtropics. They have alternate trifoliate leaves and terminal racemes of basically pea-shaped flowers with small or vestigial wing petals, followed by knobbly pods containing hard, often red seed. 1 half-hardy, sub-shrubby species is generally available: *E. crista-galli*, common coral-tree; Brazil; stem robust, erect, thorny, 1–2m or more tall, often unbranched; leaves somewhat glaucous, leathery, with prickly stalks; flowers rich bright scarlet, 5cm long in dense terminal racemes, summer. Grow in a warm site at the foot of a south wall in well-drained, humus-rich soil and protect the woody crown from late autumn to spring. May also be grown in pots in a frost-free greenhouse. Pot or plant spring. Cut

Far left bottom: *Erysimum* × *allionii*
Left below: *Erysimum linifolium*
Left bottom: *Erysimum pumilum* Golden Gem
Below: *Erythrina crista-galli*
Bottom: *Erythronium californicum*

Top far left: *Erythronium dens-canis*
Above far left: *Erythronium* Pagoda
Top centre: *Erythronium revolutum* Pink Beauty
Above centre: *Erythronium oregonum* White Beauty
Top: *Escallonia* × *rigida* Glory of Donard
Above: *Escallonia* × *rigida* Apple Blossom

back previous season's stems to within a few centimetres of the base in spring when young shoots appear there. Plants grown in pots are best kept almost dry in winter. Propagate from seed or by soft cuttings with a heel in spring, the latter with bottom heat about 21°C.

Erythronium

(Greek *erythronion*, from *erythros*, red – originally applied to a now unidentifiable plant, used for this genus by Linnaeus). LILIACEAE. A genus of 25 species of herbaceous perennials from Europe, temperate Asia and N. America (mostly from the latter). They have usually deeply buried, elongated corms (by some authorities considered to be solid-scaled bulbs), giving rise to 2, ovate to lanceolate, rarely cordate leaves, usually glossy and in several species attractively mottled and/or marbled; flowers solitary or in small racemes, pendulous, the 6 narrow tepals reflexed, opening in spring. Grow in humus-rich soil, preferably beneath the shade of trees or large shrubs. Plant autumn, the earlier the better. Propagate from seed when ripe or as soon afterwards as possible – if kept until spring they usually take 12 months to germinate – also by removing offsets when dormant.

Species cultivated: *E. albidum*, N. America, Ontario to Texas; leaves 10–15cm long, rarely mottled; flowers solitary, white, sometimes pinkish- or bluish-tinted, yellow-centred, about 4cm wide on stems to 20cm or so tall; produces offsets or stolons. *E. americanum* trout lily, yellow adder's tongue; E. N. America; similar to *E. albidum* but leaves mottled reddish-brown; flowers yellow-spotted within; often shy flowering, needing a moist soil to do well. *E. californicum*, California; leaves lanceolate to oblong-ovate, 10–15cm long, dark green, strongly mottled; flowers white to cream with a ring of yellow-orange or brownish markings within, usually 1–3 (rarely to 10 or more) on stems to 25cm or more. *E. dens-canis*, dog's tooth violet; Europe to Japan; leaves broadly oval to elliptic, somewhat glaucous, variably blotched and suffused purple-brown; flowers to 5cm wide, pink to deep rose-purple, having white, yellowish or brownish centres ringed with dark orange or purplish marks, solitary on stems to 15cm tall. *E.d.-c. japonicum*, flowers to 7·5cm wide, violet-purple; several cultivars are available in shades of pink, red-purple and white. *E. giganteum*, invalid name formly used for *E. grandiflorum* and *E. oregonum*. *E. grandiflorum*, glacier lily; W. N. America; leaves plain green, oblong-lanceolate, 8–15cm long; flowers bright yellow, to 5cm wide, 1–5 on stems 15–30cm long; not always easy and needs moist soil; much like the similar *E. tuolumnense* but having a trilobed stigma. *E. hendersonii*, California, Oregon; leaves oblong-lanceolate, heavily mottled purplish-brown with a marbling of pale veins; flowers pale lilac with dark purple centres, 3–4cm wide, 1–4 or more on stems to 30cm tall. *E. howellii*, California, Oregon; leaves lanceolate, 8–15cm long, mottled; flowers creamy-white, yellow-barred or orange-centred, sometimes tinged pink on fading, 1–4 on stems to 20cm tall, similar to *E. californicum*. *E. japonicum*, see *E. dens-canis japonicum*. *E. klamathense*, Oregon, California; leaves lanceolate, yellow-green, 7–15cm long; flowers about 3cm wide, basal half of tepals yellow, upper white 1–3 or more on stems up to 20cm tall. *E. oregonum*, W. N. America; similar to *E. revolutum* but leaves usually more richly mottled and flowers cream or white (at least in cultivation) with a yellow centre outlined in deep orange-brown. *E.o.* White Beauty, larger white flowers having reddish-brown markings, possibly of hybrid origin. *E. revolutum*, pink trout lily; W. N. America; leaves 15–20cm long; ovate-lanceolate mottled purple-brown and marbled with whitish veins; flowers deep pink with yellow basal bands, 5–7cm wide, 1–3 or more stems 15–30cm or more tall. *E.r.* Pink Beauty, robust, rich pink flowers; *E. r.* White Beauty, see *E. oregonum*. *E. tuolumnense*, California; leaves yellow-green, 20–30cm long; flowers deep yellow with a pale greenish eye, 3–6cm wide, 2–4 or more on stems to 30cm tall; several hybrids possibly with *E. californicum* or *E. oregonum* are available: Kondo, flowers primrose-yellow, darker-centred; Pagoda, leaves marbled, flowers deep yellow.

Escallonia

(for Señor Escallon, Spaniard who travelled in S. America). ESCALLONIACEAE (SAXIFRAGACEAE). A genus of about 60 species of shrubs and small trees from S. America, chiefly the Andes region. They are mainly evergreen with alternate, oval to obovate, finely-toothed leaves, often appearing to be in clusters but actually very condensed shoots in the main axils; flowers 5-petalled, tubular-based with spreading rounded lobes, in terminal and axillary panicles. Most of the species are tender or half-hardy, but those described below are hardy except in severe frost and long hard winters unless otherwise stated. Grow in well-drained soil in a sunny site, the less hardy sorts against a wall or wind break; all do well near the sea. Plant spring. Propagate by cuttings with a heel in late summer or from seed under glass in spring.

Species cultivated: *E. bifida* (*E. montevidensis*), S. Brazil, Uruguay; large shrub or rarely small tree 3–5m tall; leaves 4–7·5cm long, obovate, deep lustrous green; flowers pure white, 1·2–2cm wide, late summer, autumn; fairly hardy but needs a wall in colder areas. *E.* × Edinensis, see *E.* × *rigida*. *E.* × *exoniensis* (*E. rosea* × *E. rubra*), vigorous shrub 2–4m tall, similar to *E. rubra* but flowers white to blush. *E. floribunda* (of gardens), a barely distinguishable form of *E. bifida*. *E.* × Ingramii, see *E. rubra*. *E.* × *iveyi*, assumed to be *E. bifida* × *E.* × *exoniensis* and much like the first parent, with highly lustrous, deep green leaves and somewhat smaller white flowers; somewhat hardier. *E. macrantha*, see *E. rubra*. *E. montividensis*, see *E. bifida*. *E. punctata*, see *E. rubra*. *E.* × *rigida* (*E.* × *langleyensis*), group name for cultivars derived from *E. rubra* × *E. virgata* and covering most of the popular escallonias largely raised at the Donard Nursery, Ireland; they are evergreen or almost so, to 2m or more tall, often with the arching habit, narrow leaves and profuse blooming of *E. virgata;* among the best are: *E.* × *r.* Apple Blossom, about 1·5m tall, pink and white; *E.* × *r.* Crimson Spire, erect habit to 2m tall, crimson, good for hedging; *E.* × *r.* Donard Gem, compact habit, leaves small, flowers large, pink, fragrant; *E.* × *r.* Donard Radiance, compact habit to 1·5m tall, dark pink; *E.* × *r.* Donard Seedling, vigorous grower to 2m or more tall, flowers white, pink in bud; *E.* × *r.* Donard Star, compact, erect habit 1·5–2m tall, flowers large, deep rose pink; *E.* × *r.* Edinensis, similar to *E.* × *r.* Langleyensis but less pendant and flowers paler; *E.* × *r.* Gwendolyn Anley, deciduous, very hardy, 1–1·2m tall, spreading more widely, flowers white, pink in bud; *E.* × *r.* Langleyensis, to 2m or more tall, stems pendulous, flowers carmine-pink; *E.* × *r.* Peach Blossom, like *E.* × *r.* Apple Blossom but a darker shade of pink; *E.* × *r.* Slieve Donard, similar to *E.* × *r.* Langleyensis but paler flowers with carmine markings, very hardy. *E. rubra*, C. to S. Chile, adjacent Argentina; 1·5–3m tall, sometimes more; leaves lanceolate to obovate, 2–5cm long, glossy; flowers pink to crimson, about 1cm long in panicles 3–10cm long, summer to early autumn. *E.r.* Ingramii, intermediate between *E. rubra* and *E.r. macrantha* and probably a hybrid of these parents. *E.r. macrantha* (*E. macrantha*), Chiloë, of denser habit than type, to 4m tall; leaves larger, glossier; flowers rose-red, 1·5cm long; excellent near the sea in milder areas, inland best against a wall or fence. C. F. Ball is a form or hybrid of *E.r. macrantha* with glowing crimson flowers. *E.r.* Pygmaea, see next cultivar. *E.r.* Woodside (*E.r.* Pygmaea), dwarf compact mutant to 60cm tall, originating as a witch's broom, with smaller leaves and light crimson flowers – rather apt to revert to typical *E. rubra* and all strong growing shoots should be cut out. *E. virgata* (*E. philippiana*, *Stereoxylum virgatum*), Chile, Argentina; deciduous, to 2m or more tall; stems arching; leaves narrowly obovate, 1–2cm long; flowers pure white, to 1cm wide, the petals spreading and not forming a tube as in other species, summer; rare in cultivation, but parent of many cultivars.

Above: *Escallonia* × *iveyi*

Eschscholzia

(*Eschscholtzia*, *Escholtzia*). (for Johann Friedrich Eschscholz, 1793–1831, Russian doctor and naturalist of German extraction who, in the early 1800s, accompanied 2 Russian scientific expeditions to the N.E. Pacific). California poppies. PAPAVERACEAE. A genus of about 10 species of annuals or perennials from Mexico to Washington State, USA. They are tufted in habit, with alternate, deeply, several times ternately, dissected leaves, and 4-petalled, poppy-like flowers followed by long, slender, pod-like seed capsules. Grow in any well-drained soil in full sun. Propagate from seed sown *in situ* in spring or autumn.

Species cultivated: *E. caespitosa* (*E. tenuifolia*), California; stems 10–30cm tall, usually about 15–20cm in cultivation; leaves cut into almost thread-like, somewhat glaucous segments; flowers bright yellow, 2·5–4cm wide, summer; the cultivars such as Miniature Primrose and Sundew, with primrose-yellow flowers on 12–15cm stems are probably derived from this species. *E. californica*, California to Washington State; short-lived perennial or annual; very variable in the wild: from erect to prostrate, glaucous to grey-leaved, deep orange to light yellow flowers; in cultivation, stems 20–40cm or more tall, leaves glaucous, cut into many narrow segments, flowers lustrous orange-yellow, 4–6cm wide, summer and autumn; several mixed colour strains and single colour cultivars, some with double flowers are available: *E.c.* Ballerina, semi-double with fluted petals in shades of yellow, orange, pink, carmine, crimson-scarlet; *E.c.* Alba, creamy-white; *E.c.* Aurantiaca (*E.c.* Orange King), orange; *E.c.* Carmine King, deep rose-pink; *E.c.* Mikado, mahogany-red; *E.c.* Monarch Art Shades, semi-double in shades of yellow and orange to pink, purple and white.

Eucalyptus

(Greek *eu*, well, and *kalypto*, to cover: the united sepal lobes and petals form a cap that is shed when the flower opens). Gum tree. MYRTACEAE. A genus

Left below: *Eschscholzia californica* Ballerina
Below: *Eschscholzia californica* Monarch Art Shades

of 500–600 species of evergreen trees and shrubs, mainly from Australia with a few in Indomalaysia. On young plants, they have opposite pairs of leaves (juvenile foliage) that often differ in shape from the adult ones; in extreme cases they are rounded, sometimes perfoliate and richly glaucous. The adult leaves are basically linear to lanceolate, sometimes falcate, and arranged alternately. The flowers are borne in axillary clusters or solitarily, the showy part being the crown of numerous stamens followed by woody, disc-, button-, cup- or top-shaped fruit formed of the hollowed floral receptacles. Grow in a well-drained, moderately fertile soil that does not dry out excessively, in a sunny site. Plant out in summer. Unless otherwise stated, the species described here are reasonably hardy, but more frost-susceptible when very young. For this reason it is best to protect their bases the first winter by mounding around with either sand or dry leaves in a collar of chicken wire. Do not cover the foliage. If a severe winter kills the tops the protected bases will usually sprout again with vigour from a swollen area known as a lignotuber. Propagate from seed sown under glass in early spring at about 15°C. If possible, obtain seed from locally-grown specimens that have withstood hard winters, or from the wild at the upper limit of its altitudinal range. Prick off seedlings once the true leaves are clearly visible, singly into 7·5–10cm pots, preferably the deep, so-called long-toms. Use a good commercial mixture or make an all-peat one with ¼-part grit added. By mid or late summer the plants will be 15cm or more tall and ready for planting out. If plants are allowed to become starved and root-bound they never recover properly and are usually weak at the base, always needing a stake. Eucalypts may be grown as bush or small standard trees by annual pollarding in early summer. This results in a continuation of the juvenile type foliage that is often more decorative than the adult. In exposed sites young trees may need staking for the first 2–3 years until wind-firm, using a method that allows movement of the main stem, see Staking. Some of the more tender species make good pot plants for a few years, being over-wintered in a frost-free greenhouse. Certain species with bold blue-white juvenile leaves are regularly used to enhance summer bedding schemes, notably *E. globulus*. They are then grown as half-hardy annuals, sown in early spring and potted on into 13cm pots 4–6 weeks before being planted out when frosts have finished in summer.

Species cultivated: *E. citriodora*, lemon-scented gum; Queensland, Australia; to 45m in the wild; grey-white or pinkish bark; juvenile leaves rough-textured, hairy, oblong-lanceolate, 8–15cm long, adult leaves smooth, both fragrant with oil of citronella; flowers white; tender, grown as a foliage pot plant and for its lemon scent. *E. coccifera*, Tasmanian snow gum; Tasmania; to 40m, growing about 1m a year; bark white to grey; juvenile leaves elliptic, sometimes cordate, blue-green or green, to 4·5cm long; flowers white, early summer; wind-resistant; when sown, seed needs several weeks at low temperatures (3–5°C) to break dormancy. *E. coriacea*, see *E. pauciflora*. *E. dalrympleana*, mountain white gum; Tasmania, S.E. Australia; to 40m tall, growing 1m or more a year; bark white and pink or brown; juvenile leaves broadly ovate to almost round, more or less cordate, dark or blue-green, 4–6cm long, adult leaves lanceolate, 10–18cm long, glossy green; flowers white, autumn. *E. divaricata*, see *E. gunnii*. *E. glaucescens*, tingiringi gum; Victoria, New South Wales; very hardy and vigorous, growing 1m or more a year; bark red-brown to white; juvenile leaves rounded, about 4cm long, brightly glaucous, adult lanceolate to oblong, somewhat falcate, to 15cm long; flowers white, autumn; sown seed must be kept cool as for *E. coccifera*. *E. globulus*, Tasmanian blue gum; Tasmania and Victoria; to 60m, growing 1–2m a year, but tender except in the south and usually grown as a bedding or pot plant; juvenile leaves ovate-cordate, sessile, brightly glaucous, 7–16cm long, adult stalked, lanceolate-falcate, 10–30cm long; flowers cream-white, spring. *E. gunnii* (*E. divaricata*), cider gum; Tasmania; to 20m tall, growing about 1·5m or more a year; bark smooth, green to cream, ageing grey-brown; juvenile leaves amost orbicular to broadly elliptic, to 5cm or more wide, blue-white to green, adult leaves ovate to lanceolate, to 8cm long; flowers white, summer. *E. nicholii*, New South Wales; slender, elegant, non-eucalyptus looking tree growing 1–1·5m in a year; juvenile leaves linear, 4–5cm long, usually glaucous, adult to 10cm long, deep green; best grown as an annually stooled shrub. *E. niphophila*, see next entry. *E. pauciflora* (*E. coriacea*), cabbage gum, white sallee; S.E. Australia, Tasmania; to 20m tall; bark smooth, white darkening to grey; twigs glossy deep red (at least in some cultivated material); juvenile leaves few, ovate to rounded, grey-green, adult broadly lanceolate, 6–15cm long, bright glossy green; flowers white, summer; one of the hardier species. *E.p. alpina* (*E. niphophila*), snow gum; to 10m or more; bark blue-white streaked sienna and dull yellow; young twigs, buds and leaves silvery-glaucous; adult leaves to 8cm long, glossy green or glaucous; the hardiest and most wind-resistant of all eucalypts. *E. perriniana*, round-leaved snow or spinning gum; Tasmania, S.E. Australia; to 6m in the wild, taller in cultivation, growing up to 2m a year when young; juvenile leaves united, disc-like, usually brightly glaucous surrounding the stem (perfoliate), adult leaves lanceolate to falcate, glaucous 7–12cm long; flowers white, late summer; best grown as a stooled bush or pollard to maintain the unique juvenile foliage. *E. polyanthemos*, red box; Victoria, New South Wales; to 15m, fast-growing when young; juvenile leaves rounded, glaucous, to 5cm or more wide, adult narrowly to broadly lanceolate, to 15cm long; flowers white, spring to autumn. *E. pulverulenta*, to 10m or more, very vigorous, growing 1·5m or more a year; juvenile leaves oval, sessile, to 7cm long, usually brightly glaucous; flowers cream, spring. *E. urnigera*, urn or urn-fruited gum, Tasmania; 15–45m tall, growing to 1·5m a year; bark smooth, white, blotched green and orange-brown; juvenile leaves sessile, orbicular to broadly elliptic, dark green to glaucous, 3–6cm long, adult leaves narrowly lanceolate to ovate, glossy dark green, to 12cm long; flowers cream, late summer; *E.u. glauca* covers forms with glaucous juvenile leaves.

Below: *Eucalyptus gunnii* juvenile
Right: *Eucalyptus pauciflora alpina* bark
Right below: *Eucalyptus pauciflora alpina* in flower
Far right below: *Eucalyptus perriniana* juvenile

Eucharidium – see *Clarkia*.

Eucomis

(Greek *eu*, good, and *kome*, hair, in the sense of a head of, – the flower-spike bears a terminal tuft of narrow, leaf-like bracts). Pineapple flower. LILIACEAE. A genus of 14 species of bulbous perennials from tropical and S. Africa. They have bulbs with enlarged, sometimes almost stem-like

Eucryphia

(Greek *eu*, well, and *kryphios*, covered: alluding to the sepals that are united at their tips, forming a cap). EUCRYPHIACEAE. A genus of 5 species of evergreen and deciduous trees and shrubs from S.E. Australia (including Tasmania) and Chile. They have simple or pinnate leaves in pairs, and handsome, 4-petalled, multi-stamened white flowers from late summer to autumn. They need sheltered sites in sun or light shade, and preferably neutral to acid soil that does not dry out rapidly. Plant spring, the hardier sorts also in autumn. Propagate by layering in spring, cuttings with a heel in late summer, bottom heat 16–18°C.

Species cultivated: *E. billardieri*, see *E. lucida*. *E. cordifolia*, Chile; evergreen tree; to 20m in the wild, rarely half this in cultivation; leaves oblong-cordate, 4–7·5cm long, wavy-margined – on young plants larger and toothed; flowers 5cm wide, solitary. *E. cordifolia* × *E. lucida* resembles the latter parent, but with larger, wavy-edged leaves and larger flowers. *E. glutinosa*, Chile; deciduous or partially evergreen; often a small tree to 6m or more (to 15m or more in the wild); leaves pinnate, leaflets 3–5, ovate, 4–6·5cm long, toothed, rich lustrous green; flowers to 6·5cm wide, singly or in pairs; the hardiest and most tolerant species growing where moderate frosts occur if sheltered, and on my limy soils if enriched with humus. *E.* × *intermedia* Rostrevor (*E. glutinosa* × *E. lucida*), blends characters of parents, with both simple and trifoliate leaves, rather glaucous beneath; flowers to 5cm wide, singly or in pairs; a vigorous and floriferous hybrid of neat, columnar form. *E. lucida*, Tasmania; slender evergreen tree; 6–12m (to 30m in the wild); leaves oblong to lanceolate-elliptic, to 4·5cm long, lustrous deep green above, whitish to glaucous beneath; flowers solitary, 3–5cm wide; reasonably hardy in sheltered

Above: *Eucomis comosa*
Right: *Eucryphia glutinosa*

base plates, strap-shaped, somewhat fleshy-textured leaves, and erect, dense racemes of star-shaped, 6-tepalled flowers usually in shades of green or white. Grow in well-drained soil in warm areas or in sheltered sites, preferably at the base of a sunny wall. Plant spring or autumn – if the latter, protecting the first winter at least with a mound of weathered boiler ash or coarse sand. Where moderate frosts occur, this must be a regular operation each late autumn. All species make good pot plants for a frost-free greenhouse in pots or pans of a proprietary compost, repotting annually in early spring and applying liquid feed at fortnightly intervals during the main growing season until flowers are visible. Little watering is necessary during the winter months. Propagate by offsets planted 12–15cm deep, spring or autumn, or from seed sown in spring under glass at about 15°C.

Species cultivated: *E. autumnalis* (*E. undulata*), S. Africa; leaves ovate-oblong, wavy-margined, up to 60cm long; racemes about 45cm tall, flowers 1–1·5cm wide, greenish or white, late summer to autumn. *E. bicolor*, S. Africa: Natal; similar to *E. autumnalis*, but flowers pale green, the tepals purple-margined, in somewhat shorter racemes; less hardy. *E. comosa* (*E. punctata*), S. Africa; leaves lanceolate, to 60cm long; racemes to 90cm tall, the stem boldly purple-spotted, flowers to 1·5cm wide, yellow-green to whitish, sometimes tinged purplish and with a dark purple ovary, fragrant, early autumn, although sometimes starting in late summer. *E. pole-evansii*, giant pineapple flower; S. Africa: Transvaal, Swaziland; leaves to 60cm or more long; racemes 1–1·5m or more tall, flowers greenish-white, late summer; suitable only for the mildest areas, generally best under glass. *E. punctata*, see *E.comosa*.

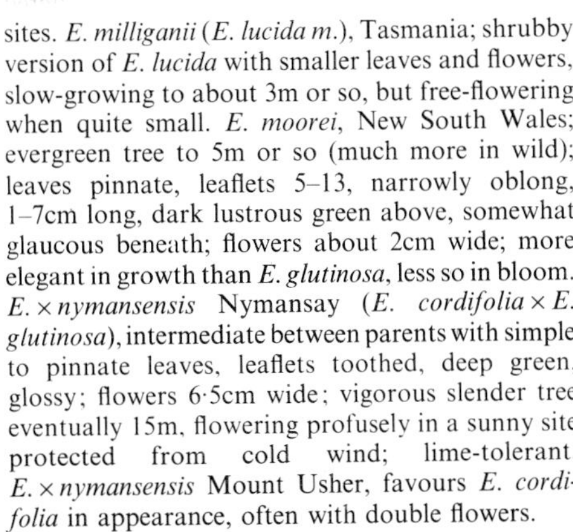

sites. *E. milliganii* (*E. lucida m.*), Tasmania; shrubby version of *E. lucida* with smaller leaves and flowers, slow-growing to about 3m or so, but free-flowering when quite small. *E. moorei*, New South Wales; evergreen tree to 5m or so (much more in wild); leaves pinnate, leaflets 5–13, narrowly oblong, 1–7cm long, dark lustrous green above, somewhat glaucous beneath; flowers about 2cm wide; more elegant in growth than *E. glutinosa*, less so in bloom. *E.* × *nymansensis* Nymansay (*E. cordifolia* × *E. glutinosa*), intermediate between parents with simple to pinnate leaves, leaflets toothed, deep green, glossy; flowers 6·5cm wide; vigorous slender tree eventually 15m, flowering profusely in a sunny site protected from cold wind; lime-tolerant. *E.* × *nymansensis* Mount Usher, favours *E. cordifolia* in appearance, often with double flowers.

Euonymus

(ironical Latin name derived from Greek *euonymon dendron*, meaning 'of good name' – although many of the species are poisonous to livestock). Spindle. CELASTRACEAE. A genus of 176 species of deciduous evergreen trees and shrubs of almost cosmopolitan distribution but mainly from Himalaya to Japan. They have opposite pairs of narrowly lanceolate to ovate or elliptic leaves, and small cymes of generally insignificant, whitish-, greenish- or purplish-tinted flowers with 4 or 5 petals. The seed capsules are mainly 4–5 angled, sometimes with wing-like flanges or horns, and contain comparatively large seed, each surrounded by a fleshy, yellow to scarlet coat or aril. Grow in any well-drained soil in sun or partial shade. Plant autumn to spring. Pruning is generally unnecessary but the evergreen species stand clipping well and *E. japonicus* makes a good hedge, especially near the sea. Propagate from seed when ripe (about 18 months to germinate), by cuttings with a heel in late spring or late summer, or layering in spring.

Species cultivated: *E. alatus*, China, Japan; deciduous shrub; of stiff habit, 1–2m tall by more in width; twigs with distinctive corky wings; leaves narrowly oval to obovate, 2·5–7·5cm long, turning to shades of pink and crimson in autumn; flowers yellowish, about 6mm wide; fruit purplish, to 8mm long; seed scarlet. *E.a. apterus*, stems wingless or almost so, of looser habit than the type. *E. europaeus*, common spindle; Europe; deciduous shrub or small tree 3–8m tall; leaves ovate to oblong-lanceolate, minutely-toothed, 3–8cm or more long; flowers yellow-green, about 1cm wide; fruit 1–1·5cm wide, 4-lobed, pink; seed bright orange. *E.e.* Atropurpureus, leaves dull purple, bright red in autumn; *E.e.* Red Cascade, fruit rosy-red, in abundance if pollinated by another clone. *E. fortunei* (*E. japonicus acutus*, *E. radicans acutus*), China, Japan, Korea; evergreen; stems climbing by aerial roots like ivy, or prostrate if not supported, to 6m long; like ivy, the climbing or trailing stems are juvenile; greenish-white flowers and 8mm-wide, rounded, pinkish fruit with pale orange seed are carried on the upper, branching, non-clinging, adult stems; leaves elliptic to 6cm long. *E.f. radicans*, leaves elliptic to oblong-ovate, to 4cm long; *E.f.r.* Argenteo-marginata, see *E.f.r.* Variegatus. *E.f.r.* Carrierei, shrub to 2m tall, of non-climbing, adult growth only; *E.f.r.* Colorata, climbing to 8m, leaves red-purple on winter; *E.f.r.* Kewensis, miniature mutant from Japan with minutely warted stems and rounded to oblong leaves with pale veins, 7–10mm or so long, forming mats or low mounds, but climbing if support is available and sometimes developing into typical *E.f. radicans*. *E.f.r.* Emerald n'Gold, leaves yellow-margined, sometimes flushed pink winter; *E.f.r.* Gracilis, see *E.f.r.* Variegatus; *E.f.r.* Minimus, like *E.f.r.* Kewensis but larger leaves; *E.f.r.* Silver Queen, compact shrub to 1m or so, can be much taller and sometimes climbing

Top left: *Euonymus europaeus* Red Cascade
Above left: *Euonymus japonicus* Microphyllus Variegatus
Top: *Euonymus alatus* in autumn
Above: *Euonymus fortunei radicans* Emerald 'n Gold

against a wall, leaves irregularly margined creamy-yellow; *E.f.r.* Variegatus (*E.f.r.* Argenteo-marginata, *E.f.r.* Gracilis), climbing or trailing, leaves larger than type, margined white, often pink-tinted. *E. hamiltonianus*, Himalaya to Japan; similar to *E. europaeus* but variable, often semi-evergreen and larger. *E.h. sieboldianus* (*E. semiexsertus*, *E. yedoensis*), Japan, Korea, China, Sakhalin; leaves obovate to elliptic, up to 13cm long, yellow-pink and red in autumn; fruit deeply 4-lobed, pinkish; seed orange, the aril sometimes split. *E. japonicus*, Japan; evergreen; large shrub or small tree to 7m (more trained to a wall); leaves elliptic to obovate, thick-textured, glossy, 3–8cm long; flowers whitish-green, 5mm wide; fruit rounded, 7mm wide, greenish or pinkish; seed orange-yellow; not reliably hardy during very cold winters. *E.j.* Albomarginatus, leaves narrowly white-margined; *E.j.* Aureopictus (*E.j.* Aureus), leaves having central gold blotch; *E.j.* Latifolius, like *E.j.* Macrophyllus; *E.j.* Macrophyllus, leaves larger than type, elliptic; *E.j.* Microphyllus (*E.j.* Myrtifolius), dense, small shrub to 1m tall, leaves crowded, 1–2·5cm long (*E.j.* Microphyllus Pulchellus, leaves gold, variegated; *E.j.* Microphyllus Variegatus, leaves white-margined); *E.j.* Ovatus Aureus, leaves oval with rich yellow margin, requires sunny site for good colour. *E. latifolius planipes* see *E. planipes*. *E. oxyphyllus*, Japan, Korea; deciduous; small tree to 7m or so; leaves ovate to oblong, toothed, 4–9cm long, red and purple in autumn; flowers about 1cm wide, greenish-purple; fruit to 12cm wide, rounded, ribbed, deep pink; seed scarlet, hanging on long, wiry stalks. *E. phellomanus*, China; deciduous; 3–5m tall, spreading habit; stems like those of *E. alatus* with 4 corky wings; leaves oval to obovate, slender-pointed, finely toothed, 5–11cm long; flowers about 1cm wide, yellow-green; fruit 12mm wide, 4-angled and lobed, deep pink; seed deep red. *E. planipes* (*E. sachalinensis* in part; *E. latifolius planipes*), Japan, China, Korea; deciduous shrub or small tree; to 3m or more, with spreading, open habit; leaves oval or oblong to obovate, coarsely toothed, 7–13cm long; flowers about 1cm wide, pale to whitish-green; fruit long-stalked, pendulous, 1–2cm wide, rounded with 5 narrow wings, deep pink; seed orange. *E. radicans acutus* see *E. fortunei*. *E. sachalinensis*, N.E. Asia; much like *E. planipes*, but flowers purple to dark reddish in smaller clusters, confused with *E. planipes* in cultivation. *E. semiexsertus* see *E. hamiltonianus sieboldianus*. *E. yedoensis*, see *E. hamiltonianus sieboldianus*.

Eupatorium

(for Mithridates Eupator, King of Pontus, who reputedly found that 1 species acted as an antidote to poison). COMPOSITAE. A genus of 1200 species, largely of shrubs and herbaceous perennials, mainly from the Americas but also Africa, Asia and Europe. They have opposite pairs of simple, rarely deeply lobed leaves, and often large, terminal corymbs of small, groundsel-like flower-heads. The greenhouse shrubby species are now rarely available and those described here are hardy or half-hardy. Grow in any well-drained but moisture-retentive soil in sun or light shade. Plant hardy species autumn to spring, half-hardy in spring. Propagate herbaceous perennials by division at planting time, the shrubs by cuttings in spring or summer; both from seed in spring.

Species cultivated: *E. micranthum* (*E. weinmannianum*), Mexico; half-hardy shrub to 2m or more in mild areas; leaves elliptic to lanceolate, 5–10cm long; flowers white, sometimes pink-tinted, in corymbs to 20cm wide, autumn; in all but the most sheltered sites the stems are frosted, and best cut back hard in spring. *E. purpureum*, joe-pye-weed; E. USA; hardy perennial 2–3m tall; leaves in pairs or whorls of 3–5, ovate to lanceolate, toothed; flower-heads purplish-rose to magenta-crimson on purple stalks, autumn.

Euphorbia

(reputedly for Euphorbus, doctor to the King of Mauretania). Spurge. EUPHORBIACEAE. A genus of 2000 species of annuals, perennials, shrubs and succulents of cosmopolitan distribution, but mainly from subtropic to warm temperate zones. They differ enormously in form and are best recognized by floral characters. What appears to be an individual flower is a cyathium: a tiny, cup-shaped whorl of fused bracts, containing several male flowers reduced to 1 stamen each and a single female reduced to a 3-lobed ovary. The tips of the cyathical bracts may bear crescent-shaped, nectar-bearing glands, or petal-like structures. In many species the cyathia are arranged in dichasial cymes, the stalks of which are known as rays and grouped into umbel-like clusters (pseudumbels) at the stem tips. At the bases of the cyathia are pairs of bracts known as raylet leaves, and at the base of each pseudumbel a ring of larger bracts, sometimes coloured, called pseudumbel leaves. The fruit are 3-lobed capsules that explode when ripe, and the leaves are carried alternately. Grow the hardy and half-hardy species in any well-drained soil, preferably in a sunny site (a few mentioned here thrive in shade or moist conditions). Plant autumn to spring. Sow hardy annuals *in situ* in spring, half-hardy species under glass at about 16°C, pricking off seedlings at 4–5cm apart each way and hardening off in early summer. Propagate from seed, by division where possible or by cuttings of basal shoots, all in spring.

Species cultivated: *E. amygdaloides*, wood spurge; Europe, S.W. Asia, N. Africa; hardy evergreen perennial, 30–80cm tall; stems biennial, erect, seldom branched; leaves oblanceolate, dark green, 3–8cm long, pseudumbels to 12cm or more wide, raylet leaves yellow-green, fused in cup-shaped pairs, spring. *E.a.* Purpurea, leaves purplish; good for moist, shady sites. *E. biglandulosa*, see *E. rigida*. *E. capitulata*, Balkan Peninsula; hardy, rhizomatous, mat-forming perennial; stems to 10cm long; leaves obovate, to 1cm long, grey-green, dense, cyathium solitary, purplish. *E. characias*, Portugal, Mediterranean; hardy, evergreen, sub-shrubby

Above: *Eupatorium purpureum*
Right: *Euphorbia characias wulfenii*

Top left: *Euphorbia characias*
Centre left: *Euphorbia epithymoides*
Left: *Euphorbia griffithii*
Top: *Euphorbia marginata*
Above: *Euphorbia myrsinites*
Right: *Euryops acraeus*

perennial; stems biennial, erect, 60–180cm tall; leaves 3–13cm long, oblanceolate to linear, greyish-green, pseudumbels tiered, forming broad columns to 15cm or more long, raylet leaves yellow-green, cyathial nectar glands reddish-brown, spring. *E.c. wulfenii* (*E. veneta, E. wulfenii*), E. Mediterranean; more robust than type, leaves brighter grey-green, raylet leaves bright greenish-yellow. *E. cyparissias*, Europe; hardy, rhizomatous, herbaceous perennial, 20–50cm tall; leaves linear, 1–4cm long, grey-green turning reddish in autumn, raylet leaves greenish-yellow, not always freely produced; rather invasive and may become a weed, especially on sandy soils. *E. epithymoides* (*E. polychroma*), C. and S. Europe; hardy, clump-forming, herbaceous perennial; stems about 30cm at flowering time, elongating to 60cm later; leaves oblong to lanceolate, softly-hairy 2–5cm long, pseudumbels to 8cm or more wide, raylet leaves chrome-yellow, spring to summer. *E. griffithii*, Himalaya; hardy, rhizomatous, herbaceous perennial forming clumps or colonies; stems to 1m tall; leaves lanceolate with reddish mid-ribs, raylet leaves light red. *E.g.* Fireglow, bright brick-red. *E. heterophylla*, painted spurge; E. USA, much naturalized elsewhere; hardy annual; 30–90cm tall; leaves ovate to fiddle-shaped, sometimes variegated, the pseudumbel and raylet ones scarlet or partly so, summer. *E. lathyris*, caper spurge; Europe; hardy annual or biennial; 60–180cm tall; lower stem leaves opposite, narrowly oblong, somewhat bluish-green 7–10cm long, raylet leaves green to yellow-green, summer. *E. marginata*, snow-on-the-mountain; N. America; hardy annual; 30–100cm tall; leaves broadly oblong to ovate, pale green to 8cm long, the upper ones pseudumbel and raylet leaves broadly white-margined. *E. mellifera*, Madeira, Canary Is; half-hardy evergreen shrub; to 5m (15m in wild); leaves narrowly lanceolate, dark green, raylet leaves reddish-brown, cyathia honey-scented, late spring; best in a frost-free greenhouse in cold areas. *E. myrsinites*, S. Europe to W. Turkey; hardy, evergreen, tufted perennial; stems prostrate, to 40cm or more long, unbranched, leaves crowded, obovate to rounded, mucronate, brightly glaucous, pseudumbels to 10cm wide, raylet leaves chrome-yellow, spring. *E. nicaeensis*, Europe; hardy, evergreen, tufted perennial; stems 50–80cm long, ascending to erect, reddish; leaves 2–7·5cm long, lanceolate, blunt-tipped, bright glaucous, raylet leaves greenish-yellow, spring to summer. *E. niciciana*, see *E. seguierana niciciana*. *E. obesa*, S. Africa; succulent, stem-ball to broadly pear-shaped; 8–12cm tall; finely ribbed longitudinally, light grey-green with a criss-cross network of reddish lines; cyathia dioecious, small and greenish. *E. palustris*, Europe; hardy herbaceous perennial, wide clump-forming; stems erect, to 1m or more; leaves lanceolate to narrowly oblong, 2–6cm long, grey-green, often purple-red in autumn, pseudumbels large, raylet leaves yellow, late spring to summer; good for wet soils. *E. polychroma*, see *E. epithymoides*. *E. rigida* (*E. biglandulosa*), S. Europe; akin to *E. myrsinites*, but stems ascending and leaves lanceolate. *E. robbiae*, N. W. Turkey; hardy evergreen perennial, soon forming wide colonies by shooting adventitiously from the roots; leaves obovate, deep lustrous green, raylet leaves bright yellow-green, spring to summer. *E. seguierana*, Europe, S.W. Asia; hardy tufted perennial; stems ascending, to 60cm tall; leaves glaucous, linear to elliptic-oblong, up to 3·5cm long, pointed, raylet leaves sulphur-green, spring to summer. *E.s. niciciana* (*E. niciciana*), Balkan Peninsula; somewhat more robust than type, with larger flowering clusters: the form generally cultivated. *E. sikkimensis*, E. Himalaya; akin to *E. griffithii* but young shoots glossy red, mature leaves white-veined and raylet leaves greenish-yellow. *E. venta* and *E. wulfenii*, see *E. characias wulfenii*.

Euryops

(Greek for large eyes – alluding to the comparatively large flowers of some species). COMPOSITAE. A genus of 70 species of evergreen shrubs from S. Africa, Socotra, Arabia. 1 species is widely available: *E. acraeus* (*E. evansii*), S. Africa: Drakensberg mountains: fairly hardy shrublet to 30cm or so; leaves alternate, oblong, silvery-grey hairy, 1–2cm long; flower-heads solitary, daisy-like, canary-yellow, 2–3cm wide, late spring to summer. Grow in well-drained soil in a mild, sunny site autumn to spring. Propagate by cuttings spring, summer.

Exacum

(derived from the Gallic, *exacon*, a vernacular name for *Centaurium* and used by Linnaeus for this genus). GENTIANACEAE. A genus of 40 species of annuals, biennials and perennials from India and tropical Asia. 1 species is generally available: *E. affine*, Socotra; bushy annual or biennial; to 15–25cm tall; leaves opposite, broadly ovate, lustrous; flowers 1·5–2cm wide, rotate, 5-petalled, bluish-purple with a central cone of yellow stamens, summer to autumn. Greenhouse, minimum temperature 13°C, light shade and good ventilation in summer. Sow seed in spring at 18°C, pricking off the seedlings at 4cm apart each way into boxes of any proprietary potting compost, then singly into 10 or 13cm pots or bedded out. May also be sown in autumn for larger, earlier-flowering specimens the

following year provided a minimum of 16°C can be maintained.

Exochorda

(Greek *exo*, outside, and *chorde*, cord – referring to fibres around the placenta within the ovary). ROSACEAE. A genus of 4 species of large deciduous shrubs from N. Asia. They have alternate, oblong to ovate or obovate leaves, and racemes of 5-petalled, white flowers in early summer. Grow in any well-drained, fertile soil in a sunny site. Plant autumn to spring. Propagate from seed when ripe or by layering in spring; suckers may also be detached at planting time.

Species cultivated: *E. giraldii*, N.W. China; vigorous, spreading shrub to 3m or more tall; leaves ovate to oblong, 4–6·5cm long with a pinkish stalk and veins; flowers about 4cm wide, 6–8 per raceme. *E.* × *macrantha* (*E. korolkowii* × *E. racemosa*), similar to *E.* racemosa with spreading habit, very floriferous; *E.* × *m.* The Bride, low arching habit. *E. racemosa*, N. China; to 3m or more tall, of

dense, rounded habit; leaves narrowly obovate, 4–7·5cm long; flowers 3–4cm wide, up to 10 per raceme.

Fabiana

(for Francisco Fabian y Fuero, 1719–1801, Spanish archbishop and patron of botanists). SOLANACEAE. A genus of 25 species of evergreen shrubs from S. America. 1 species is generally available: *F. imbricata*, Bolivia, Chile, Argentina; heath-like, erect to spreading shrub up to 2m or more; leaves triangular, densely overlapping, 2–3mm long; flowers slenderly trumpet-shaped, 1·5–2cm long, pure white, summer. *F.i.* Prostrata, forming low mounds, flowers pale mauve, hardier than type. *F.i. violacea*, flowers mayve-blue. Generally hardy where frost is light but liable to damage during severe winters. Grow in any well-drained soil in sheltered, sunny sites. Plant spring. Propagate by cuttings, preferably with a heel, in late summer.

Top left: *Exacum affine*
Above left: *Fabiana imbricata*

Top: *Exochorda* × *macrantha* The Bride
Above: *Fagus sylvatica* Pendula

Fagus

(the ancient Latin name). Beech. FAGACEAE. A genus of 10 species of deciduous trees from northern temperate zone and Mexico. 1 species is widely in cultivation: *F. sylvatica*, European common beech; Europe; imposing, broad-headed tree to 30m, rarely to 40m tall; trunk bearing smooth, grey bark; winter buds cigar-shaped, pointed; leaves alternate, 4–9cm long, ovate-elliptic, obscurely toothed and fringed with silky hairs. Flowers in spring, unisexual, petalless, males in tassel-like clusters on slender, pendant stalks, females on short, stiff stalks in pairs surrounded by 4 bracts that later become brown and woody, forming a capsule or husk containing 2, triangular, polished, red-brown nuts (beech mast). Grow in fertile, well-drained but moisture-retentive soil in sun or partial shade. Frost pockets should be avoided as the young leaves are tender and quickly brown. Plant autumn to spring. Propagate from seed as soon as ripe, protecting from mice; cultivars must be grafted on to 1- or 2-year-old seedlings in spring. Several forms and mutants have arisen, among the best-known being: *F.s.* Aspleniifolia, see *F.s. heterophylla*; *F.s.* Atropurpurea, see *F.s.* Riversii; *F.s.* Cuprea, see *F.s. purpurea*; *F.s.* Dawyck (*F.s.* Fastigiata), narrow, columnar habit; *F.s. heterophylla*, fern or cut-leaved beech, leaves narrow, variously cut or lobed – several cultivars are known, including *F.s.h.* Asplenifolia and *F.s.h.* Laciniata; *F.s.* Pendula, large, weeping tree with pendulous branchlets; *F.s. purpurea*, purple and copper beech, name covering plants with leaves purple or coppery-red, eg *F.s.* Cuprea; *F. s.* Purpurea Pendula, weeping purple beech, usually small and slow growing though a tall growing form is also found, leaves deep purple; *F.s.* Riversii, purple beech, leaves very dark purple; *F.s.* Rotundifolia, branches strongly ascending, leaves small, rounded.

Fair Maids of France – see *Ranunculus aconitifolius* and *Saxifraga granulata*.

Fair Maids of Kent – see *Ranunculus aconitifolius*.

False acacia – see *Robinia pseudoacacia*.

× Fatshedera

(bigeneric hybrid combining *Fatsia* and *Hedera*). ARALIACEAE. 1 clone of evergreen shrub raised by the French nursery firm, Lizé Frères of Nantes, in 1910: × *F. lizei* (*Fatsia japonica* Moseri × *Hedera helix hibernica*), semi-climber or shrub to 3m; leaves alternate, 10–25cm wide, palmately 5-lobed, leathery, lustrous dark green; flowers starry with 5 pale green petals arranged in rounded umbels, these in turn carried in terminal panicles, sterile, late autumn. × *F.l.* Variegata, leaves irregularly white-margined; very tolerant of environmental defects and makes an excellent house plant. Grow in any well-drained soil or commercial potting mixture in sun or shade. Plant or pot autumn or spring. Propagate by cuttings from summer to autumn. Best grown trained to a wall or tree trunk, or as ground cover, but reasonably bushy, free-flowering specimens will result if repeatedly pinched when young.

Fatsia

(Latinized version of *fatsi*, said to be an obsolete or misrendered Japanese name). ARALIACEAE. A genus of 1 or 2 species of evergreen shrubs from Japan, Korea, Taiwan. 1 species is commonly grown as a garden and house plant: *F. japonica* (*Aralia j.*, *A. sieboldii*), Japan, S. Korea; shrub or small tree to 5m; sparsely branched, robust stems covered with prominent, crescent-shaped leaf scars; leaves 20–40cm wide, palmately 5–9 lobed, wavy-margined, leathery, lustrous; flowers milky-white, 5-petalled, starry, 5mm wide, in rounded umbels that in turn are carried in terminal panicles, late autumn; berries glossy black, globose, 5mm wide. *F.j.* Moseri, leaves larger than type, more compact habit; *F.j.* Variegata, leaves white-margined. Grow in mild areas in well-drained, humus-rich soil in sun or shade, or grow as a pot or tub specimen in any commercial potting mixture. Plant or pot autumn or spring. Propagate from seed in spring at 10–13°C, by cuttings in late summer or air layering in spring.

Feijoa

(for Don de Silva Feijo, 19th century Brazilian botanist). MYRTACEAE. A genus of 2 species of evergreen shrubs from S. America, but some botanists now combine it with the allied genera, *Acca* or *Psidium*. 1 species is generally available: *F. sellowiana* Brazil, Uruguay; shrub or small tree to 6m or so; leaves in opposite pairs, oval to ovate, dark, lustrous green above, whitish-felted beneath, 3–7·5cm long; flowers solitary from leaf-axils, 3–4cm wide, the 4 petals oval, concave at first, then reflexed, red in the centre, fading to almost white at the margins, stamens crimson in a central, brush-like cluster; fruit an egg-shaped berry, to 5cm long with an aromatic flavour. Not fully hardy and outside the milder areas needs the protection of a sunny south wall or growing in a greenhouse. Any well-drained, fertile soil is suitable. Plant spring after fear of frost has passed. Propagate by cuttings of young growth, taken with a heel in summer and rooted in a propagator, with bottom heat 18–21°C.

Felicia

(for Herr Felix, died 1846, German official of Regensburg). COMPOSITAE. A genus of 60 species, mainly of dwarf sub-shrubs and annuals, from tropical and S. Africa. They have alternate or opposite, linear to ovate leaves, and daisy-like flower-heads, often profusely borne. Grow the half-hardy species mentioned here in well-drained soil in a sunny, sheltered site. Plant in spring when fear of frost has passed. In subsequent winters protect perennials and sub-shrubs with open-ended cloches in all but the mildest areas. Propagate perennials and sub-shrubs by cuttings in summer, the annuals from seed in early to mid spring at about 16°C. Prick off the seedlings about 4–5cm apart each way into boxes of a commercial potting mixture, and harden off before planting out. All the species mentioned make good pot plants for a cool greenhouse, potting on rooted cuttings or seedlings into 10–15cm pots of a good commercial potting mixture for flowering.

Species cultivated: *F. amelloides* (*Agathaea coelestis*), blue daisy or marguerite; S. Africa; tufted perennial 30–45cm tall; leaves often opposite, broadly ovate; flower-heads sky-blue, about 4cm wide, summer, opening only in sun; often grown as an annual. *F. bergeriana*, kingfisher daisy; S. Africa; annual; 10–15cm tall; leaves lanceolate to narrowly oblong, hairy; flower-heads 2–3cm wide, deep electric-blue, summer to autumn if regularly dead-

Left below: × *Fatshedera lizei* Variegata
Left bottom: *Fatsia japonica*
Below: *Feijoa sellowiana*
Bottom: *Felicia bergeriana*

headed. *F. pappei* (*Aster p.*), S. Africa; sub-shrub; 25–35cm tall; leaves opposite and alternate, linear to narrowly spathulate, 2–3cm long, somewhat fleshy; flower-heads 2–3cm wide, china blue, summer to autumn, or later under glass.

Fescue grass – see *Festuca*.

Festuca

(Latin name for grass stem). GRAMINEAE. A genus of 80 or more species of perennial grasses, cosmopolitan in temperate climates. They are tufted, sometimes rhizomatous or stoloniferous, with evergreen linear leaves, often very narrow and rolling lengthwise in dry conditions. The spikelets are generally small and flattened, arranged (with some exceptions) in narrow, erect panicles. Several fescues are important constitutuents of fine lawns and bowling greens, others are grown for their ornamental appearance. Grow in any well-drained soil in sunny sites. Plant ornamentals and lay turf autumn to spring. Propagate from seed or by division autumn or spring.

Species cultivated: *F. glacialis* (*F. ovina frigida*), Alps, Pyrenees; similar to *F. ovina* but smaller and more densely tufted; stems to 15cm; leaves filiform, somewhat glaucous; panicles very short, dense, spikelets usually violet-flushed. *F. glauca* (*F. ovina glauca*), blue fescue; Europe; similar to *F. ovina* but more robust; leaves longer and strongly blue-grey; spikelets bluish-green. *F. ovina*, sheep's fescue; northern temperate zone; densely tufted; leaves green or greyish, bristle-like, the blade inrolled, up to 25cm long but usually less; flowering stems 15–60cm tall, panicles narrow, erect, 3–12cm long, spikelets sometimes purplish; a hardy and drought-resistant lawn grass. *F. punctoria* (*F. acerosa*), mountains of W. Turkey; densely tufted; stems to 30cm; leaves 6–8cm long, bristle-like, prickle-tipped, glistening grey-green; spikelets greyish in narrow panicles to 5cm long. *F. rubra*, red or creeping fescue; northern temperate zone; rhizomatous, forming loose to dense colonies; leaves and spikelets similar to *F. ovina* but spikelets often reddish- or purplish-tinted; valuable lawn and pasture grass. *F.r. commutata*, chewing's fescue; densely tufted, lacking rhizomes – extensively grown as a lawn grass.

Feverfew – see *Chrysanthemum parthenium*.

Ficaria – see *Ranunculus ficaria*.

Figwort – see *Scrophularia*.

Filipendula

(Latin *filum*, thread, and *pendulus*, hanging – alluding to the root tubers of some species, which are attached to slender roots). ROSACEAE. A genus of 10 species of herbaceous perennials from northern temperate zone. They have alternate pinnate leaves and erect stems bearing large, terminal, panicle-like clusters of tiny, 5-petalled flowers with prominent stamens. Grow in any moisture-retentive soil, all but *F. vulgaris* thriving best in a bog or by the waterside. Plant autumn to spring. Propagate by division at planting time or from seed in spring, preferably under glass.

Species cultivated (all summer-flowering): *F. camtschatica*, see *F. kamtschatica*. *F. digitata*, see *F. palmata*. *F. hexapetala*, see F. *vulgaris*. *F. kamtschatica* (*Spiraea k.*, *S. gigantea*), Kamchatka to N. Japan; stems 1·2–2m or more tall; leaves having palmate, usually 5-lobed, terminal leaflets 15–25cm wide, doubly toothed, lateral leaflets few and small; inflorescence large, flowers white- or pink-tinted. *F.k.* Elegantissima Rosea, flowers satin-pink; *F.k.* Rosea, flowers blush-pink. *F. palmata* (now correctly reclassified as *F. multijuga*), stems about 1m tall; leaves with large, 1–7 lobed, palmate, terminal leaflets, and usually 3-lobed lateral ones; flowers pink. *F.p.* Nana (*Spiraea digitata* Nana), dwarf and compact, 30–45cm tall; *F. palmata* in gardens is frequently confused with the next species. *F. purpurea*, Japan, but not known

Far left: *Festuca glauca*
Above left: *Filipendula palmata*
Left: *Filipendula vulgaris* Plena
Above: *Filipendula ulmaria* Aurea

wild; possibly a hybrid between *F. palmata* and the allied *F. auriculata*; stems 1–1·5m tall; leaves similar to *F. palmata* but lateral leaflets few or none; flowers cerise, in large, flattened heads. *F. rubra* (*Spiraea lobata*, *S. venusta*), queen-of-the-prairie; E. USA; stems 1·5–2m; leaves with large, palmate, 7–9 lobed terminal leaflets, and 3–5 lobed lateral ones; flowers rich peach-pink. *F.r.* Venusta, flowers deep pink in very large clusters. *F. ulmaria* (*Spiraea ulmaria*), meadow sweet; Europe, W. Asia; stems 90–120cm tall; leaves 30cm or more long, leaflets ovate, sharply doubly toothed, terminal leaflet larger, 3-lobed; flowers creamy-white. *F.u.* Aurea, leaves golden-green to yellow when young; *F.u.* Variegata, leaves striped and blotched yellow. *F. vulgaris* (*F. hexapetala*, *Spiraea filipendula*), dropwort; Europe to Siberia and N. Africa; roots bearing small, ovoid tubers; stems to 60cm or more tall; leaves 10–25cm long, leaflets oblong, deeply lobed and toothed, the largest lateral ones larger than the terminal; flowers creamy-white, flushed reddish in bud. *F.v.* Grandiflora, larger than type in all its parts; *F.v.* Plena, flowers double, longer-lasting, but plants will often need the support of stakes in wet or windy weather.

Fir – see *Abies*.

Firethorn – see *Pyracantha*.

Flax – see *Linum*.

Foam flower – see *Tiarella cordifolia*.

Forget-me-not – see *Myosotis*.

Forsythia

(for William Forsyth, 1737–1804, Scottish superintendent of the Royal Gardens, Kensington Palace,

author of a popular book on fruit-growing and inventor of a highly controversial 'plaister', plaster, claimed to renovate decaying trees). OLEACEAE. A genus of 6 or 7 species of deciduous shrubs from S.E. Europe to E. Asia. They have opposite pairs of simple or 3-cleft leaves and yellow, 4-lobed, bell-like flowers before the leaves unfurl. Grow in any well-drained garden soil, preferably in sun, although shade is tolerated. Plant autumn to spring. Propagate by tip cuttings in summer or hard wood cuttings in autumn; seed may also be sown when ripe or in spring.
Species cultivated: *F.* × Arnold Dwarf (*F.* × *intermedia* × *F. japonica saxatilis*), low, arching shrub to 60cm or more tall with a spread of 2–3m; leaves 2–5cm long, ovate, boldly toothed; flowers pale yellow, often sparingly produced; sometimes remains disarmingly neat and small for several years, then ramps. *F. giraldiana*, N.W. China; to 4m or more, habit loose but graceful; young stems shaded black-purple; leaves narrowly ovate, rarely toothed, 5–10cm long; flowers solitary, soft pale yellow, 2·5–3·5cm wide, late winter, early spring. *F.* × *intermedia* (*F. suspensa* × *F. viridissima*), variable group of hybrid cultivars of erect or arching habit, 2–4m tall; *F.* × *i.* Lynwood, like *F* × *i.* Spectabilis but flowers richer yellow, lobes broader and less spreading; most commonly grown is *F.* × *i.* Spectabilis, vigorous shrub to 3m or more, leaves ovate-lanceolate, 7–10cm long, flowers bright deep yellow, 2–3cm wide, profusely borne; *F.* × *i.* Spring Glory, less vigorous, to 2m tall, flowers bright sulphur-yellow. The following cultivars are of the same *F.* × *intermedia* parentage but are tetraploid with larger, thicker-textured leaves and more robust stems: *F.* × *i.* Beatrix Farrand, very vigorous, eventually to 4m or more, leaves coarsely toothed, flowers deep canary-yellow with a darker striped throat and very broad lobes – when first raised, originally at the Arnold Aboretum, USA, this cultivar was stated to be a triploid but subsequent investigation proved it tetraploid and it may be that the plant we call Beatrix Farrand is not the original seedling; *F.* × *i.* Karl Sax, similar to *F.* × *i.* Beatrix Farrand and confused with it, although usually less vigorous, more bushy and slightly deeper yellow. *F. ovata*, Korean forsythia, Korea; 1·2–1·5m tall; leaves 4–9cm long, broadly ovate, coarsely few to many toothed; flowers bright, almost amber-yellow, 2cm wide, mid spring; *F.o.* Tetragold, compact, sturdy habit, deep yellow flowers, tetraploid. *F. suspensa*, China; to 3m or more tall, much higher trained to a wall, untidily pendulous; leaves 5–10cm long, ovate, trifoliate or 3-lobed on vigorous shoots, coarsely toothed; flowers 2–3cm wide, golden-yellow, often in clusters, spring; strictly, this description refers to *F.s. sieboldii* which is the most commonly seen form. *F.s. fortunei*, of stiffer habit than type with arching to erect stems; however, there are intermediates between this and *F.s. sieboldii*. *F.s. atrocaulis*, young stems shaded black-purple; flowers lemon-yellow, sometimes confused with *F. giraldiana*. *F. viridissima*, E. China; 1·5–2·5m tall, erect, almost fastigiate habit with angular stems staying green for 2 years; leaves lanceolate, 6–12cm long, entire or toothed in upper half; flowers bright yellow, 2–3cm wide, later than other species, usually starting half way through late spring. *F.v.* Bronxensis, pygmy mutant rarely exceeding 30cm tall; leaves ovate, 2–4·5cm long; flowers primrose-yellow, shy-flowering unless in a warm, sunny site.

Fothergilla

(for Dr John Fothergill, 1712–80, English Quaker doctor who specialized in growing American plants). HAMAMELIDACEAE. A genus of 2 species of deciduous shrubs from E. N. America. They have alternate, oval to obovate, coarsely toothed leaves colouring well in autumn, and short, terminal, bottle-brush like spikes of small, petalless flowers with long white stamens. Grow in moist but well-drained, lime-free, preferably peaty soil in sun or light shade. Plant autumn to spring. Propagate from seed when ripe (usually taking 18 months to germinate), layering or suckers in spring, cuttings with a heel in latish summer, and with bottom heat of about 18°C.
Species cultivated: *F. alnifolia*, see next species. *F. gardenii*, S.E. USA; to 1m or so; branches spreading, slender; leaves 2·5–6·5cm long, oval to obovate-cordate, downy; flower-spikes fragrant, up to 4cm long, before the leaves, spring. *F. major* (*F. monticola*), E. USA – Allegheny mountains; 1·5–2·5m tall, rounded habit; young stems starry white-hairy; leaves 5–10cm long, broadly oval or ovate, dark glossy green above, somewhat glaucous beneath with starry hairs; flower-spikes fragrant, to 5cm long, the stamen filaments often pink-tinted, with young leaves late spring; plants grown as *F. monticola* may be less hairy, or shorter and more spreading in habit, but are merely expressions of a variable species propagated clonally.

Four o'clock – see *Mirabilis*.

Foxglove – see *Digitalis purpurea*.

Fragaria

(Latin *fraga*, for strawberry, derived from *fragrans*, referring to the fragrant fruit). ROSACEAE. A genus of 15 species of evergreen perennials from northern temperate zone and temperate S. America. They are rosette-forming to tufted, spreading by runners, with trifoliate leaves and 5-petalled, rotate flowers followed by rounded to conical fruit that is actually swollen, juicy receptacles bearing achenes (tiny, seed-like true fruits). Grow in any well-drained fertile soil in sun or light shade. Plant autumn to spring. Propagate from seed when ripe or spring, or by detaching rooted runners.
Species cultivated: *F.* × *ananassa* (*F. grandiflora*), (*F. chiloensis* Chilean form × *F. virginiana*), cultivated or garden strawberry, similar to *F. chiloensis* but more robust, with larger leaves, flowers and fruit; *F.* × *a.* Variegata, leaves white-variegated; useful ground cover. *F. californica*, California; loosely tufted; leaflets broadly obovate, the central one to 5cm long, coarsely toothed, silky-hairy beneath; flowers 1·5–2cm wide; fruit rounded, 1–1·5cm wide; sometimes confused in gardens with next species. *F. chiloensis*, W. N. and S. America, mainly coastal; densely tufted; leaflets thick-textured, broadly obovate 2–5cm long, deep glossy green above, densely downy beneath; flowers

Far left above: *Forsythia suspensa atrocaulis*
Left: *Fothergilla gardenii*
Below left: *Fothergilla major* in autumn
Below: *Fragaria vesca*

2–3cm wide; fruit 1·5–2cm wide. *F. indica* (*Duchesnea i.*), Afghanistan to Japan; mat-forming; leaflets ovate, 3–7cm long, rich green, hairy; flowers 1·5–2·5cm wide, yellow, solitary; fruit rounded, about 1cm wide, insipid; flowering and fruiting from late spring to autumn, useful as ground cover. *F. vesca*, wild strawberry; temperate zone – scattered; loosely tufted, rather erect, 5–30cm tall; leaflets 1–6cm long, oblong to obovate, coarsely toothed, somewhat hairy, glaucous beneath; flowers 1·2–1·8cm wide in small, erect cymes; fruit pendulous, rounded to ovoid, red, sometimes white. *F.v. monophylla*, 1-leaved strawberry, leaves of 1 leaflet only; *F.v. semperflorens*, alpine strawberry, flowering and fruiting from late spring to autumn. *F. virginiana*, scarlet strawberry; E. N. America; similar to *F. vesca* but plant less erect, leaflets obovate, firm-textured when mature; flowers dioecious, females smaller, 6–25cm wide; fruit rounded, 1–2cm wide.

Francoa

(for Francisco Franco, 16th century Spanish doctor). FRANCOACEAE (SAXIFRAGACEAE). A genus of 1 variable species of evergreen perennial from Chile. *F. appendiculata* (*F. ramosa*, *F. sonchifolia*), bridal wreath; rhizomatous, clump-forming; leaves mostly basal, rosetted, erect, pinnate, 15–30cm long, the terminal leaflet ovate-cordate, somewhat lobed and waved, far exceeding the laterals in size; flowers 5-petalled, bell-shaped, white, pink or red, darker-spotted at base, in simple or branched erect racemes 60–90cm tall, summer. *F.a. ramosa*, flowers white in much-branched racemes (panicles); *F.a. sonchifolia*, flowers pink in loose racemes. Not reliably hardy in colder parts though it makes a good pot plant for a cool greenhouse. Plant in spring in moisture-retentive but well-drained soil in sheltered, sunny or lightly shaded sites. Propagate from seed in spring at 10–13°C, by division or cuttings late spring.

Frankenia

(for Johan Frankenius, 1590–1661, professor of anatomy and botany at Uppsala, Sweden). FRANKENIACEAE. A genus of 80 species of evergreen perennials and sub-shrubs from temperate and tropical sea coasts and salt deserts. 1 species is readily available: *F. thymifolia*, Spanish sea heath; Spain; mat-forming sub-shrub 30cm or more wide; leaves in opposite pairs with short shoots in their axils giving the appearance of whorls, 2–3·5mm long, ovate, with strongly rolled margins, grey-green, dotted or completely covered with a white encrustation, reddish in summer and autumn; flowers 5-petalled, pale rose to purple, 5–7mm wide, singly and in small, nodding clusters forming terminal, leafy spikes, summer; sometimes confused with *F. laevis*, sea heath, that has leaves to 5m and more scattered flowers, never in nodding clusters. Grow in any well-drained soil in a sunny site. Plant autumn to spring. Propagate by division or cuttings in spring.

Fraxinus

(ancient Latin name for the ash tree). OLEACEAE. A genus of 70 species of deciduous trees and shrubs from N. Hemisphere. The genus is divisible into 2 groups on flower characters: *Ornus* (flowering ashes), flowers with white, linear petals in often large, terminal panicles with young leaves; and *Fraxinaster* (true ashes), flowers without petals in small, lateral panicles before the leaves. Both groups have pinnate leaves in opposite pairs and narrow winged fruit called samaras. Grow in any well-drained, fertile soil, although moister and clay soils are tolerated, preferably in sunny sites. Plant autumn to spring. Propagate from seed when ripe – they often take 18 months to germinate – or by grafting cultivars on to the original species.

Top: *Francoa appendiculata sonchifolia*
Above: *Fraxinus ornus*

Species cultivated: *F. americana*, white ash; E. N. America; to 26m tall; bark grey, evenly fissured; crown somewhat domed, of well-spaced branches; winter buds brown; leaves to 35cm or more long, leaflets 5–9, each one oblong-lanceolate, 5–13cm long, silvery beneath, sometimes purple or yellow in autumn; flowers petalless. *F. excelsior*, common ash; Europe east to Caucasus; to 35m (occasionally 45m or more), bark pale grey, smooth then fissured; crown domed, open, upper branches steeply ascending; winter buds black; leaves 20–30cm long, leaflets usually 9–11, oblong-lanceolate, 5–11·5cm long; flowers petalless. *F.e.* Aurea, see *F.e.* Jaspidea; *F.e.* Aurea Pendula, small, weeping tree, young shoots yellow; *F.e.* Jaspidea, vigorous tree, young shoots golden-yellow, older stems yellowish, conspicuous in winter – has been confused with the true *F.e.* Aurea, a rare, slow-growing, bushy tree; *F.e.* Diversifolia (*F.e.* Monophylla), leaves reduced to 1 leaflet; *F.e.* Pendula, weeping ash, pendulous, strong-growing. *F. ornus*, manna ash; S. Europe to Turkey; to 24m; bark dark grey, smooth; crown rounded; leaves 20–30cm long, leaflets 5–9, oblong-ovate to 10cm long; flowers with petals, creamy-white, fragrant, in dense, conical panicles, early summer. *F. oxycarpa*, S. E. Europe, Turkey, Caucasus; to 20m or more; bark pale grey, smooth; crown narrowly domed; leaves 15-25cm long, leaflets 3–7, lanceolate, 4–6·5cm long; flowers petalless. *F.o.* Raywood, very vigorous, leaves plum-purple in autumn; by some botanists classified as a sub-species of *F. angustifolia*. *F. pennsylvanica*, red ash; E. N. America, W. to Rocky Mountains; similar to *F. americana*, but young shoots pubescent; leaf undersides green and leaflet stalks darkly hairy; grows best in moist soil. *F.p.* Variegata, leaves greyish, margined and mottled white.

Fremontia – *Fremontodendron*

Fremontodendron

(*Fremontia*). (for Major Gen. J. C. Frémont, 1813–1890, explorer and amateur botanist). STERCULIACEAE. A genus of 2 species of evergreen shrubs from S. W. USA and Mexico. They have alternate, ovate-cordate, 3–7 lobed leaves with a scurfy covering of starry hairs and bowl-shaped flowers composed of 5, glossy yellow, petal-like sepals. They are hardy only in warm areas and rather short-lived, but very fast-growing and flower young. Grow in well-drained, preferably poorish soil training the branches flat if grown on a wall. Plant out in spring when fear of frost has passed. Propagate from seed or by cuttings under glass in late spring at about 16°C. Prick off the seedlings when cotyledons fully expanded into 10cm pots of a commerical potting mixture. Stand outside for the summer, potting on if necessary, over-winter in a frost-free greenhouse and plant out the following spring. Alternatively sow earlier, set out young plants in permanent sites when about 30cm tall, and protect with plsstic or glass the first winter. Winter-hardiness can often be increased by the application of sulphate of potash at 30g per sq m in late summer.

Species cultivated: *F. californicum*, California, Arizona; 2–9m tall; leaves 5–10cm long, usually 3-lobed, sometimes entire, felted pale brown beneath, thin-textured; flowers widely cup-shaped to almost flat, to 5cm or more wide, golden-yellow, late spring; capsules ovoid, with rounded or shortly-pointed tip; seed dull brown or black, pubescent; many plants under this name are hybrids with the next species. *F. mexicanum*, S. and Baja California; similar to *F. californicum*, but leaves generally 5-lobed, somewhat wider and thicker-textured; flowers larger, to 7cm wide, but more starry in appearance, usually more orange-yellow, spring to autumn; capsules slender-pointed; seed glossy black, smooth; plants under this name in gardens are often of hybrid origin.

Below: *Fremontodendron californicum*

Fritillaria

(Latin *fritillus*, dicebox – alluding to chequered markings on the flowers of some species). Fritillary. LILIACEAE. A genus of about 85 species of bulbous plants from northern temperate zone. They have

Top and above: *Fritillaria imperialis* cultivars
Top right: *Fritillaria persica*
Above right: *Fritillaria meleagris* cultivars

erect, unbranched stems, alternate, ovate to linear leaves, and 6-tepalled, nodding, bell-shaped flowers either solitary or in few to many flowered racemes. Grow in well-drained soil in sheltered, sunny sites, the less hardy species in a frost-free greenhouse in pots of any commercial potting mixture (the peat ones with ⅓-grit or coarse sand added). Under glass ventilate whenever possible even during the winter. Repot, pot or plant in autumn. Water potted bulbs very sparingly until growth is well up, then water freely but allow the soil almost to dry out each time. Apply liquid fertilizer at 2–3 weekly intervals once the flower-buds show until just after flowering. When leaves yellow, dry off but do not allow to remain dust-dry until repotting time. Propagate from seed when ripe or in spring, or by offsets and bulblets removed when repotting and potted up.

Species cultivated: *F. acmopetala*, Cyprus, Syria, Turkey; 30–40cm tall; leaves linear, grey-green; flowers 1–3, jade-green and maroon, 3–4cm long, 2–3cm wide, spring. *F. assyriaca*, Iraq, W. Iran; to 20cm or more tall; leaves lanceolate or broader, green or greyish; flowers solitary, maroon with waxy-greyish patina and yellow tips; vigorous and worth trying outside where frosts are not severe but often grown under glass. *F. camtschatcensis* (*Sarana c.*), N. E. Asia, N. W. N. America; 30–40cm tall; leaves narrowly lanceolate, glaucous to glossy green, usually in whorls; flowers 1–4, dark chocolate or maroon-purple, to 3cm long, early summer; grows well outside in cool, peaty soils. *F. cirrhosa*, Himalaya; 20–60cm or more tall; leaves narrowly lanceolate, the upper ones at least with an apical tendril; flowers 1–3, pale green with brown chequering or the reverse, about 4cm long; unreliable outside. *F. imperialis*, crown imperial; Iran, W. Himalaya; robust, 75–120cm tall; leaves dense, lanceolate, bright glossy green; flowers 6 or more in terminal umbel just below a terminal tuft of leafy bracts, 5–6·5cm long, red or yellow, spring. *F.i.* Aurora, deep reddish-orange; *F.i.* Lutea Maxima, deep lemon-yellow; *F.i.* Rubra Maxima, shades of red and dusky orange. *F. lanceolata*, checker lily; W. N. America; 30–80cm tall; leaves in whorls, ovate to narrowly lanceolate; flowers 1–4 or more, brown-purple mottled with yellow or the reverse, 2–4cm long. *F. meleagris*, snake's-head fritillary; C. Europe to Scandinavia; to 30cm tall; leaves narrowly lanceolate, grey-green, scattered; flowers solitary or in 2s, shades of red-purple with darker chequering, about 4cm long; thrives best in moist soils; several cultivars are available in shades of dusky purple to purple-rose, or white. *F. pallidiflora*, USSR to Tien Shan and Ala-Tau mountains; 20–50cm tall, leaves opposite or alternate, broadly lanceolate, glaucous; flowers 1–4, about 4cm long by 3cm wide, pale yellow; very hardy and easily grown outside. *F. persica* (*F. libanotica*), Cyprus, Turkey, Iran; robust, 30–100cm tall; leaves dense, lanceolate, grey-green; flowers up to 30 in a terminal, bractless raceme, each one usually deep maroon-purple with grey patina, but sometimes dark red or greenish, flushed purple, spring. *F.p.* Adijaman, flowers deep plum-purple, foliage plain green. *F pontica*, Bulgaria, Greece, Turkey; 15–35cm tall; leaves lanceolate, greyish, scattered; flowers 1–3, pale or yellow-green, each tepal margined and tipped brownish-purple, 3–5cm long; grows well outside, best in light shade. *F. pudica*, W. N. America; 10–20cm tall; leaves linear, mainly at base of stem; flowers usually solitary, 1·5–2·5cm long, bright yellow, sometimes with an orange suffusion. *F. pyrenaica*, Pyrenees; to 30cm or more; leaves lanceolate, greyish-green; flowers usually solitary, to 4cm long, purplish-brown, usually chequered deeper crimson-purple, glossy yellow-green within; hardy and easily grown outside. *F. recurva*, scarlet fritillary; California, Nevada, Oregon; 30–40cm tall; leaves narrowly lanceolate in whorls; flowers 1–4 or more, narrowly bell-shaped, to 3cm long, scarlet, chequered yellow, the scarlet darkening with age, tepal tips sharply recurved.

Fuchsia

(for Leonhart Fuchs, 1501–66, German doctor and herbalist who wrote a herbal with very fine woodcut illustrations). ONAGRACEAE. A genus of about 100 species of shrubs and small trees from Mexico to S. America, New Zealand and other Pacific Is. They have opposite pairs or whorls of oblong to elliptic, usually toothed leaves, and pendant flowers composed of a short to long, perianth tube, 4, spreading, coloured sepals, and 4, sometimes contrastingly coloured, down-pointing petals forming a bell. The fruit are oblong-ovoid to rounded, often purplish berries, edible but generally rather insipid. The species and hybrid cultivars in cultivation are mostly half-hardy and grown as greenhouse or house pot plants, minimum temperature 4°C, with good ventilation and light shading in summer. However, in mild areas most of these can be grown outside with winter protection and several are hardy in all but the severest winters. Any well-drained, fertile soil is suitable, preferably in sun, although light shade is tolerated. Plant outside when fear of frost has passed. In cold areas in early winter mound weathered ashes, coarse sand or peat around the base of each plant to 10–15cm deep. In spring clear this hard material away and cut back to remove all dead and frosted stems. In very cold areas lift the plant in late autumn, pot or box and place in a frost-free frame or greenhouse. Under glass, repot or pot on annually in spring, using a commercial potting mixture cutting back the previous season's growth to a few cms and raising the minimum temperature to 10°C. Apply liquid fertilizer at fortnightly intervals during the summer. Propagate by cuttings in spring to late summer at about 16°C, or from seed in spring. Autumn-rooted cuttings are best grown on during the winter at 10–13°C minimum. Place rooted cuttings into 7·5–10cm pots, and pinch out the tip when about 10–15cm tall if required for a bush or pyramid-trained specimen. For bush plants pinch again when the laterals are about 10cm long, repeating once more if necessary to build up a well-branched specimens. Pyramids require a good stake 1–1·5m tall. When lateral growths have appeared after the first pinching, select the strongest and tie to the cane. When this is 15cm long, pinch out the tip and again tie in the strongest sideshoot that forms. Repeat this until the desired height is reached. Cultivars used for hanging baskets usually need 2 pinchings as for bushes. Standards also need a strong stake for support. Ideally, select only the strongest-growing rooted cuttings for this method of training. Tie to the stake at 15cm intervals and remove all sideshoots until 3–4 leaf pairs above the desired stem height. Pinch out the tip and repeat again later on the laterals that grow out from the top buds.

Species cultivated: *F. austromontana* (*F. serratifolia*), Peru; tender, eventually to 3m tall, bushy; leaves in pairs or whorls, narrowly oblong, distinctly toothed, 3–7cm long; flowers red, 4–5cm long, summer. *F. corymbiflora*, Ecuador, Peru; tender, loose or scrambling shrub to 3m or more, with slender, arching stems; leaves 7–13cm long, oblong-lanceolate, pubescent; flowers deep red with long, slender tubes 4–6·5cm long, in terminal drooping clusters, summer. *F.c.* Alba, white-flowered. *F. excorticata*, New Zealand; shrub or small tree to 6m (to 12m in the wild); leaves oblong-lanceolate to ovate, 3–10cm long, silvery beneath;

flowers about 3cm long, tube and sepals green flushed red-purple, petals dark purple, spring; hardy in mild areas and on sheltered walls. *F. fulgens*, Mexico; tender shrub 1–2m tall; leaves ovate-cordate to 7cm or more long; flowers scarlet with long, slender tubes 5–7·5cm long, sepals green-tipped, in terminal leafy clusters, summer. *F.* × *hybrida*, invalid but useful gardener's name covering all the many 100s of hybrid cultivars derived mainly from *F. magellanica* and *F. fulgens*, but probably other species as well. They favour the first parent in general appearance but have larger, often broader leaves, and much larger flowers in shades of red, pink, orange, purple and white, many strikingly bicoloured. There are 100s of cultivars commercially available, some hardier than others, and full descriptions are to be found in the catalogues of specialist nurserymen. *F. magellanica*, Chile, Argentina; deciduous shrub to 4m; leaves lanceolate to ovate, sometimes in whorls of 3; flowers 4–5cm long, tube short, deep red like sepals, petals purple, summer to autumn; the hardiest species. *F.m.* Alba, see *F.m. molinae*. *F.m. gracilis* (*F.m. macrostemma*), graceful habit; narrow leaves and slender flowers – *F.m.g.* Variegata is a form with cream, flushed pink, leaf margins (*F.m.g.* Tricolor is very similar), and *F.m.g.* Versicolor another variant with grey leaves pink-tinted when young and white-variegated when mature; *F.m. molinae* (*F.m.g.* Alba), flowers like those of *F. magellanica*, but rose-white; *F.m.* Pumila, very dwarf habit with small, narrow leaves and half-sized flowers; *F.m.* Riccartonii, much like type species but even hardier, more vigorous, the sepals darker and petals broader. *F. microphylla*, Mexico; tender twiggy shrub 1–2m tall; leaves crowded, 6–20mm long, oblong-lanceolate to obovate; flowers deep red, about 1cm long, petals small, paler, toothed, autumn; confused in gardens with *F. thymifolia*. *F. procumbens*, New Zealand; prostrate, almost hardy, deciduous outside; leaves rounded 6–20mm long; flowers upright, 1·2–2cm long, tube light orange-yellow, sepals green tipped purple, petals lacking; fruit to 2cm long, red. *F. serratifolia*, see *F. austromontana*. *F. thymifolia*, Mexico; similar to *F. microphylla* but to 1m tall, leaves somewhat larger, flowers pink or white, petals not toothed. *F. triphylla*, Haiti, Santo Domingo; tender shrub or sub-shrub 30–60cm tall; leaves 4–10cm long in pairs or whorls, lanceolate, purple beneath; flowers orange-scarlet, 4cm long, tube slender, tapered, petals small, in dense terminal clusters, summer to autumn.

Below: *Fuchsia procumbens*
Centre: *Fuchsia fulgens*
Bottom: *Fuchsia magellanica molinae*

Below: *Fuchsia* Mission Bells
Centre: *Fuchsia* Southgate
Bottom: *Fuchsia* Cascade

Funkia – see *Hosta*.

Gaillardia

(for Gaillard de Charentonneau, pre-1780, French magistrate and patron of botany). Blanket flower. COMPOSITAE. A genus of 28 species of annuals and perennials from temperate N. and S. America. They are tufted with lanceolate to spathulate, basal and stem leaves, and daisy-like flower-heads with broad, 3-lobed ray florets. Grow in any well-drained soil in a sunny site. Sow seed *in situ* in spring for annual species; perennials are best sown in nursery rows in

Below: *Gaillardia* hybrid cultivar
Bottom: *Gaillardia aristata* Dazzler

summer, thinned or transplanted to about 15cm apart and placed in permanent sites early autumn or the following spring. Perennials sown early will often flower in same season.
Species cultivated: *G. aristata*, N.C. and N.W. N. America; perennial, 40–60m tall; leaves oblanceolate, greyish downy, sometimes lobed or pinnatifid, alternate on stems; flower-heads 6–7cm wide, ray florets yellow, sometimes purple-red at base, disc florets purple. *G.a.* Dazzler, rays bright orange-yellow; other cultivars offered with rays largely red or purple-red are hybrids with *G. pulchella*. *G.* × *grandiflora*, name covering known hybrids between *G. aristata* × *G. pulchella*. *G. pulchella*, C. and S. USA, Mexico; 35–45cm tall, similar to *G. aristata* but ray florets red-purple with or without small yellow tips; several cultivars are offered in shades of yellow, bronze and red, some of which are hybrids with *G. aristata*.

Galanthus

(Greek *gala*, milk, and *anthos*, flower – the flowers of all species are mainly white). Snowdrop. AMARYLLIDACEAE. A genus of about 20 species of bulbous perennials from Europe to W. Asia. Each bulb has 2 narrow leaves (sometimes 3), and the way these are folded together in the emerging shoot is an aid to identification. They may be convolute (rolled together 1 inside the other), eg *G. elwesii*, or applanate (pressed flat together), either with the margins flat, eg *G. nivalis*, or plicate (sharply reflexed), eg *G. plicatus*. The solitary flowers are composed of 6 tepals, the 3 outer ones long, spreading and pure white, the inner ones short, notched, green-tipped and forming a cup. Grow in any well-drained but moisture-retentive soil, preferably humus-rich. There must be adequate

Above: *Galanthus ikariae*

water during the winter to spring growing period for good establishment and increase. Plant autumn as early as possible, or in spring when in bloom or immediately the flowers fade. Propagate by offsets removed at planting time or from seed as soon as ripe; old or dried seed will take 1 year or so to germinate.
Species cultivated: *G. caucasicus*, Caucasus, Iran; stems to 14cm tall; leaves convolute, broad, glaucous; flowers 4–4·5cm wide, early spring. *G.c. hiemalis*, flowering mid winter. *G. elwesii*, Turkey; stems to 15cm; leaves convolute, broad, glaucous; flowers 4·5–5cm wide, inner tepals with basal and apical green blotches, usually early spring, sometimes earlier or later. *G.e. maxima*, leaves twisted, usually narrower than type; *G.e. whittallii*, more robust, larger flowered. *G. ikariae*, Grecian island of Ikaria; stems about 15cm tall; leaves convolute, rich bright glossy green; flowers about 4·5cm wide, outer tepals about 2·4cm long by 1·2cm wide, mid to late spring. *G.i.latifolius* (*G. latifolius*, *G. platyphyllus*), Caucasus, Turkey; like the type species but outer tepals about 2·7cm long by 7mm wide; although

Top: *Galanthus nivalis* Plena
Above: *Galanthus nivalis*

treated as a sub-species because of botanical rules of priority, this is the widely distributed mainland population, *G. ikariae ikariae* being the true geographical variant. *G. nivalis*, common snowdrop; Europe; stems 10cm or more tall; leaves applanate, flat, grey-green; flowers 2–3cm wide, late winter to early spring; a variable species sometimes with green marking on the outer tepals, or yellow instead of green on the inner ones. *G.n.* Plena, flowers double; *G.n.* Scharlokii, donkey's ears snowdrop, has 2, long, erect, green spathe segments at the base of the flower and green tips to the outer tepals. *G.n. reginae-olgae* (*G. octobrensis*), Greece; flowers in late autumn before the leaves; several named cultivars are available, mostly of hybrid origin with *G. plicatus*, notably the massive Samuel Arnott and Atkinsii. *G. plicatus*, Rumania, Crimea; stems 16–20cm tall; leaves plicate, green with a central glaucous zone; flowers 4–5cm wide, mid to late spring; *G.p.* Warham, a fine robust form.

Galax

(Greek *gala*, milk – presumably alluding to the colour of flowers). DIAPENSIACEAE. A genus of 1 evergreen perennial from E. USA: *G. aphylla*, rhizomatous, forming dense clumps or colonies; leaves long-stalked, all basal, the blades 3–16cm wide, rounded, cordate, crenate-toothed, leathery, lustrous deep green; flowers small, white, 5-petalled, in dense, spike-like racemes to 60cm or more tall. Grow in humus-rich, neutral to acid soil preferably in light shade. Plant autumn to spring. Propagate by division at planting time or from seed when ripe or in spring.

Top right: *Galega officinalis* Lady Wilson
Right: *Galega orientalis*

Galega

(Greek *gala*, milk, a reference to the formerly held belief that goats and cows fed on the foliage would yield more milk). LEGUMINOSAE. A genus of 2–3 species of herbaceous perennials from S. Europe to W. Asia. They are clump- or colony-forming with erect stems, pinnate leaves and racemes of small pea flowers. Grow in any well-drained but moisture-retentive soil in sunny sites. Plant autumn to spring. Propagate by division at planting, seed spring.
Species cultivated: *G. officinalis* (including *G. patula*), goat's rue (range of genus); 1–1·5m tall, clump-forming; leaves of 9–17 oblong to elliptic leaflets, 1·5–5cm long; flowers 1–1·5cm long, white to pale purple-blue, sometimes lilac or pink, in dense lateral and terminal racemes; hybrids between the type species and *G. patula* (now considered only a variant) = *G. hartlandii*, the origin of several named cultivars including *G.o.* Lady Wilson, with mauve-pink flowers. *G. orientalis*, Caucasus; similar to *G. officinalis* but rhizomatous and wider-spreading, leaflets 3–6cm long, flowers blue-violet.

Galeobdolon – see *Lamiastrum*.

Galingale – see *Cyperus longus*.

Galium

(Greek *gala*, milk; *G. verum*, lady's bedstraw, was formerly used to curdle milk for cheese-making).

RUBIACEAE. A genus of 400 species of annuals and perennials of cosmopolitan distribution. 1 species is generally available: *G. odoratum* (*Asperula odorata*), sweet woodruff; Europe, N. Africa, Siberia; perennial, rhizomatous, forming large patches; stems slender, 4-angled, erect, to 15cm or more tall; leaves lanceolate, 2–4cm long, in whorls of 6–9; flowers white, 4–6mm long, tubular, with 4, spreading, narrow lobes, fragrant, in small, terminal, umbel-like clusters, early summer. Grow in any well-drained but moisture-retentive soil in sun or shade. Plant autumn to spring. Propagate by division at planting time.

Galtonia

(for Sir Francis Galton, 1822–1911, anthropologist, geneticist, meteorologist and distinguished all-round scientist). LILIACEAE. A genus of 4 species of bulbous plants from S. Africa. They have erect to arching, strap-shaped leaves in rosettes and leafless stems bearing racemes of pendant, 6-lobed, bell-shaped flowers. Grow in any well-drained, humus-rich soil in sunny, sheltered sites. Plant autumn in mild areas, spring in colder areas, setting each bulb about 15cm deep. In very cold areas lift the bulbs in autumn and store in pots of barely moist soil in a frost-free shed or room. May also be grown in large pots for cool greenhouse or conservatory decoration. Propagate from seed in spring or by removing offsets from the mother bulb when planting or lift already planted bulbs and treat in the same way.

Left above: *Galium odoratum*
Left below: *Galtonia candicans*
Above: *Garrya elliptica*
Right below: × *Gaulnettya wisleyensis*

Species cultivated: *G. candicans*, summer hyacinth; leaves to 60cm or so long, stems overtopping leaves, bearing about 15, somewhat fragrant white flowers, each about 4cm long, summer. *G. princeps*, akin to *G. candicans* but smaller, the flowers palest green, usually more widely expanded.

Garrya

(for Nicholas Garry, Secretary of the Hudson Bay Co). GARRYACEAE. A genus of 15 species of evergreen trees and shrubs from W. USA, Mexico, W. Indies. 1 hardy species is readily available: *G. elliptica*, silk tassel bush; California, Oregon; vigorous large shrub or small tree 4–8m tall; leaves oval to elliptic, 6–8cm long, wavy-margined, deep, somewhat lustrous green above, grey-woolly beneath; flowers dioecious, petalless, in pendant grey catkins 10–20cm long, carried in terminal clusters, late winter; the male form is commonly cultivated, the female rarely – if both are together, strings of purple-brown berries result. *G.e.* James Roof, male catkins to 35cm long. Grow in any well-drained soil, preferably in full sun although some shade is tolerated; best on a south wall in very cold areas. Plant autumn or spring. Propagate by cuttings in late summer, bottom heat about 18°C, or from ripe seed in a cold frame.

× Gaulnettya

(*Gaultheria* × *Pernettya*). Name for all hybrids between various species of the 2 genera. Only 1 is generally available: × *G. wisleyensis* (× *Gaulthettia w.*) (*G. shallon* × *P. mucronata*), bushy, evergreen suckering shrub to 1m or more; leaves alternate, elliptic, 2–4cm or more long, prominently net-veined, leathery; flowers urn-shaped, white, in clustered racemes, early summer; fruit 6mm wide, held in enlarged, fleshy calyces. × *G.w.* Ruby, fruit

ruby-red; × *G.w.* Wisley Pearl, fruit deep red-purple. Grow in acid, preferably peaty soil, well-drained but moist, in sun or partial shade. Plant autumn or spring. Propagate by division, rooted suckers or cuttings with a heel in late summer or early autumn.

Gaultheria

(for Jean Francois Gaultier, or Gaulthier, c1708–1756, French-Canadian doctor and botanist). ERICACEAE. A genus of 200 species of evergreen shrubs from countries around the Pacific, plus Himalaya, E. N. America, E. Brazil. They are often rhizomatous and low-growing with alternate, lanceolate to oval or obovate leaves, nodding, bell or urn-shaped, white flowers in racemes, and dry, capsular fruit with or without a fleshy, coloured calyx. Culture as for × *Gaulnettya;* propagation also from seed when ripe, or spring.

Species cultivated: *G. adenothrix*, Japan; 10–30cm tall, wide-spreading; leaves 1·5–3cm long, broadly ovate, dark glossy green; flowers solitary, bell-shaped, 7–8mm long, late spring; fruit red, 8mm wide. *G. cuneata*, W. China; 30–45cm tall, compact habit; leaves 1–2cm long, 6–12mm wide, oblanceolate to obovate, dark lustrous green; flowers urn-shaped, 6mm long in clustered racemes, summer; fruit white, globose, to 1cm wide. *G. hispida*, Tasmania; 60–90cm tall, rarely to 2m; stems reddish-bristly; leaves 2·5–5·5cm long, oblong to narrowly lanceolate; flowers broadly urn-shaped, 4mm long, in clustered racemes; fruit white, to 1·2cm wide. *G. itoana*, Taiwan; closely related and similar to *G. cuneata*, but dwarfer and leaves narrower (3–6mm wide). *G. miqueliana*, Japan; 20–30cm tall, wide-spreading, sparingly branched; leaves oval, 1–3cm long; flowers broadly urn-shaped, 6mm long, in racemes of 2–6, sometimes solitary; fruit white, 6mm wide. *G. nummularioides*, Himalaya to Java, Sumatra; prostrate to 15cm tall, wide-spreading; stems slender, wiry, bristly; leaves heart-shaped, 6–15mm long, in 2 opposite ranks; flowers solitary, urn-shaped, to 6mm long, sometimes pink-tinged, late summer; fruit blue-black, seldom produced in Britain. *G. procumbens*, wintergreen, checkerberry; USA; 5–15cm tall, extensively creeping underground and forming carpets; leaves obovate, dark glossy green, 2–4cm long, aromatic when bruised; flowers urn-shaped, 6mm long, white or pinkish, in small terminal groups, summer; fruit bright red, about 8mm wide; good ground cover beneath trees. *G. shallon*, salal or shallon; W. N. America; 1·5–2m tall, forming dense thickets; leaves 4–10cm long, broadly ovate, bristle-toothed; flowers urn-shaped, to 1cm long, pink-tinted, early summer; fruit hairy, dark to black-purple, to 1cm wide, pleasantly tasting. *G. trichophylla*, Himalaya to Burma; 7–15cm tall, spreading widely; stems wiry, bristly-haired; leaves 6–12mm long, elliptic oblong to lanceolate; flowers bell-shaped, pink, 4mm long, solitary; fruit ovoid, to 1cm or more long, clear blue, but not always freely borne.

Left: *Gaultheria cuneata*
Left below: *Gaultheria procumbens*
Above: *Gazania* hybrids
Below: *Gaultheria shallon*

Gaura

(Greek *gauros*, superb – referring to flowers of some species). ONAGRACEAE. A genus of 18 species, mainly of annuals and perennials from N. America, Mexico and Argentina. 1 species is generally available: *G. lindheimeri*, Texas, Mexico; tufted habit; stems 90–120cm tall, branched; leaves lanceolate, toothed, to 9cm long at base; flowers in branched racemes, 4-petalled, 3–4cm wide, white, ageing pink, summer. Grow in well-drained, humus-rich soil in sunny sites. Sow seed in a nursery bed in spring, thin to 10cm apart and plant in permanent sites when leaves touch. Alternatively, sow under glass early spring at 10–13 C, prick off at 4–5cm apart each way and plant out in early summer. Either way, the plants usually flower the first year.

Gaya – see *Hoheria*.

Gazania

(for Theodore of Gaza, 1398–1478, translator into Latin of the botanical works of Theophrastus). COMPOSITAE. A genus of 40 species of evergreen perennials from tropical and S. Africa. In gardens the genus is largely represented by hybrids, both seed strains and named cultivars, the wild species being seldom offered. They are prostrate or semi-

Left: *Genista cinerea*
Above: *Genista hispanica*

prostrate, with lanceolate to spathulate, sometimes pinnately lobed leaves that may be dark green above and grey-white felted beneath or grey-downy all over, flowers daisy-like, 6–8cm wide, shades of orange, red, yellow, the bases of the ray florets sometimes patterned black-brown and white or olive green. Species known to have given rise to these hybrids are: *G. bracteata*, *G. pavonia*, *G. pinnata* (*G. krebsiana*), *G. ringens*, *G. uniflora* and named hybrid *G.* × *splendens*. Grow in any well-drained soil in a sunny, sheltered site. They sometimes survive the winter in dry walls or warm borders, but are generally grown as half-hardy annuals. Sow seed in early spring at 18°C; prick off seedlings 5cm apart each way into boxes of J. I. potting compost No 2 or singly into 7·5 or 9cm pots, harden off and plant out when fear of frost has passed. Cuttings may be taken late summer, potted when rooted and over-wintered at 7°C with good ventilation. Alternatively, trim and pot or box whole plants in autumn, over-winter and take cuttings early spring.

Gean – see *Prunus avium*.

Genista

(ancient Latin name, perhaps derived from the Celtic *gen*, a little bush). Broom, gorse. LEGUMINOSAE. A genus of about 75 species of deciduous shrubs and small trees from Europe, N. Africa, W. Asia. They are closely allied to, and like, *Cytisus*, although some species are spiny, with short-lived leaves, green twigs and pea flowers, generally in racemes. For culture and propagation see *Cytisus*.
Species cultivated: *G. aetnensis*, Mount Etna broom, Sicily, Sardinia; to 5m or more usually with 1 main trunk; branchlets pendulous when young; leaves sparse, linear, to 1cm long; flowers solitary, 1cm or more wide, bright golden-yellow, produced in profusion, summer. *G. cinerea*, S.W. Europe; 2–4m tall, branchlets long, slender, silky-hairy when young; leaves narrowly lanceolate, to 1cm long, grey-green; flowers bright yellow, 1cm or more long, in small, profusely borne clusters, summer. *G. delphinensis* (*Genistella d.*), S. France, E. Pyrenees; in effect a diminutive *G. sagittalis* and by some botanists made a sub-species of that species. *G. fragrans* (of gardens), see *Cytisus* × *spachianus*. *G. hispanica*, Spanish gorse; S.W. Europe; 40–60cm tall, forming dense, even hummocks; stems interlacing, bearing branched spines and linear-lanceolate leaves to 8mm long, on flowering twigs only; flowers bright golden-yellow, 8mm long in rounded clusters of up to 12, early summer. *G. humifusa*, confused name used as synonym for *G. pulchella* and probably the same as *G. tinctoria prostrata*. *G. lydia*, E. Balkans, W. Turkey; about 60cm tall and eventually 90cm or so wide, forming mounds of slender, pendulous branchlets; leaves linear, to 1cm long; flowers 1cm long, bright yellow, in profusely carried clusters of 3–4, early summer. *G. pilosa*, Europe; prostrate to semi-erect, to 45cm (exceptionally to 1·5m); almost evergreen; leaves oblanceolate, 5–12mm long; flowers 1–1.5cm long, in racemes, early summer. *G.p.* Procumbens, always prostrate; leaves smaller than type. *G. pulchella* (*G. villarsii*, *G. humifusa* of gardens), S.E. France, W. Balkans; miniature shrub to 10cm tall; leaves linear, hairy, about 6mm long; flowers solitary, yellow, 8mm long, late spring. *G. sagittalis* (*Chamaespartium s.*, *Genistella s.*), C. and S.E. Europe; mat-forming; stems broadly green-winged and appearing leaf-like; true leaves sparse, oval, 1–2cm long, hairy; flowers 1cm long, yellow, in short, erect racemes, early summer. *G. tinctoria*, dyers' greenweed; Mediterranean, Europe to Caucasus and W. Turkey; variable in habit, usually erect or ascending to 60cm, sometimes much more; leaves oblong-lanceolate, to 3cm long; flowers 1·5cm long, bright yellow, in terminal racemes, sometimes clustered to form panicles, summer to autumn. *G.t.* Plena, flowers double, semi-prostrate; *G.t. prostrata*, totally prostrate habit. *G. villarsii*, see *G. pulchella*.

Genistella – see *Genista delphinensis*, *G. sagittalis*.

Gentiana

(for King Gentius of Illyria – present day W. Yugoslavia – who reputedly discovered the medicinal properties of gentian-root, *G. lutea*, around 500 BC). Gentian. GENTIANACEAE. A genus of 350–400 species of annuals and perennials from the temperate and alpine regions of the world except Africa. They are usually tufted with opposite pairs of linear to ovate leaves, and funnel- or bell-shaped, 5-lobed flowers generally carried erect. Grow in well-drained but moisture-retentive, humus-rich soil – that for certain species noted here must be acid – in sunny sites, although some species stand partial shade. Plant spring. Propagate by careful division at planting time or basal cuttings in spring, and from seed when ripe, older seed may take a year or more to germinate.
Species cultivated: *G. acaulis* (*G. excisa*, *G. kochiana*), trumpet gentian; Alps, Carpathians to N.E. Spain, C. Italy, C. Yugoslavia; shoots rosetted, many forming small mats; leaves elliptic to oval, 4–6cm or more long; flowers solitary, 5–7cm long, deep blue, the throat spotted green, spring; there are 6 other species closely allied to *G. acaulis*, some of which pass under this name in gardens, see *G. angustifolia* and *G. clusii*. *G. angulosa*, see *G. verna*. *G. angustifolia*, W. Alps, Pyrenees; much like *G. acaulis* but leaves narrowly lanceolate, to 5cm long. *G. asclepiadea*, willow gentian; Alps, N. Apennines; herbaceous; stems to 60cm or more tall, gracefully

Top left: *Gentiana clusii*
Left: *Gentiana asclepiadea*
Below left: *Gentiana lutea*
Bottom left: *Gentiana verna*
Above: *Gentiana sino-ornata*
Top right: *Geranium dalmaticum*
Right: *Geranium macrorrhizum*

arching; leaves lanceolate, 4–8cm long; flowers deep blue, paler-striped in terminal leafy racemes, summer to autumn. *G.a. alba*, flowers white. *G. clusii*, mountains of C. and S. Europe; much like *G. acaulis* but leaves elliptic-lanceolate and calyx lobes straight and sharp-pointed, equal to length of tube; those of *G. angustifolia* are shorter than tube, and *G. acaulis* spreading and leaf-like. *G. farreri*, N.W. China; stems to 20cm long, prostrate; leaves linear-lanceolate, 1–4cm long; flowers solitary, terminal, Cambridge blue, banded and spotted greenish-blue, 5–6·5cm long, late summer; acid soil. *G. gracilipes* (*G. purdomii* of gardens), N.W. China; stems decumbent, to 25cm long; leaves lanceolate, the basal ones to 15cm long; flowers solitary, 4cm long, deep purple-blue, the tube greenish, late summer. *G.* × Inverleith (*G. farreri* × *G. veitchiorum*), like a more robust *G. farreri* with deeper-blue flowers, early autumn; acid soil. *G. kochiana*, see *G. acaulis*. *G. lagodechiana*, E. Caucasus; prostrate stems to 35cm or so; leaves ovate to heart-shaped, 1–2·5cm long; flowers solitary, deep blue, paler without, green-spotted, 4cm long, autumn. *G. lutea*, great yellow gentian; mountains of C. and S. Europe; stems robust, erect, 50–120cm tall; leaves to 20cm or more, lanceolate to ovate, the stem ones paired or in whorls; flowers unlike gentian, yellow, short-tubed, long-lobed, to 2·5cm long, in clusters in upper leaf-axils forming tiered spikes, summer; yields the gentian root of commerce. *G.* × *macaulayi* (*G. farreri* × *G. sino-ornata*), habit of *G. farreri*, somewhat more robust, flowers deep blue, autumn; acid soil. *G. purdomii* (of gardens), see *G. gracilipes*. *G. saxosa*, New Zealand; small, hummock-forming; stems about 10cm tall; leaves spathulate, 2–4cm long, somewhat fleshy, often bronze-tinted, in rosettes; flowers solitary or in small cymes, white, short-tubed, large-lobed, cup-shaped, about 2cm wide, summer to autumn. *G. septemfida*, Turkey to Iran; stems ascending to decumbent, 15–30cm long; leaves ovate, 2·5–4cm long; flowers purple-blue, paler-spotted within, to 4·5cm long, usually in terminal clusters to 7 or more, summer. *G. sino-ornata*, W. China, Tibet; prostrate; stems to 30cm or more; leaves linear-lanceolate, 1–4cm long; flowers solitary, 6cm long, rich bright blue, the tube striped deep purple and yellow-green, autumn; must have acid soil, then easy to grow. *G. verna*, spring gentian; Europe to Arctic Russia; rosettes in small clusters; leaves lanceolate to ovate, 1–2cm long; flowers solitary, rotate, deep brilliant blue, to 2cm wide, on stems 3–10cm tall, spring; white, pale blue, purple and pinkish forms exist. *G.v. angulosa*, more robust, flowers larger, calyx somewhat inflated, prominently winged.

Geranium

(Greek *geranus*, a crane – referring to the beaked fruit). Crane's bill. GERANIACEAE. A genus of 300–400 species, mainly of annuals and perennials, of cosmopolitan distribution. They are tufted, clump-forming or wide-spreading by rhizomes, with long-stalked, rounded leaves, usually palmately lobed. The 5-petalled flowers may be bowl or saucer-shaped, flattened or reflexed, and are followed by long-beaked fruit that split suddenly when ripe, catapulting out the 1–5 seeds. For the familiar pot and bedding geraniums, see the allied genus *Pelargonium*. Grow in any well-drained garden soil, preferably in a sunny site, although some species stand partial shade. Plant autumn to spring. Propagation: division at planting, seed in spring.

Species cultivated: *G. armenum*, see *G. psilostemon*. *G. cinereum*, Pyrenees; tufted, to 15cm tall; leaf-blades to 3cm wide, 5–7 lobed, each lobe with 3 teeth or segments, pubescent; flowers 3–3·5cm wide, lilac to pink, darker-veined, late spring. *G.c.* Ballerina, flowers white, heavily feathered crimson-purple; *G.c.* Album, flowers white. *G.* × Claridge Druce (*G. endressii* × *G. versicolor*), similar to first parent but taller, more robust, flowers larger, purplish-pink. *G. dalmaticum*, S.W. Yugoslavia, N. Albania; rhizomatous, forming mats; stems to 12cm tall; leaves to 3cm or more wide, 5-lobed, often red in autumn; flowers 2·5cm wide, rich, clear pink, summer. *G.d.* Album, petals white. *G. endressii*, S.W. France and adjacent Spain; rhizomatous, forming clumps or colonies; stems 30–50cm tall; leaves 5–8cm wide, deeply 5-lobed and toothed; flowers about 3cm wide, pale pink, summer to autumn. *G.e.* A. T.

Left above: *Geranium cinereum* Ballerina
Above: *Geranium himalayense*
Right above: *Geranium psilostemon*
Right: *Geranium renardii*
Right below: *Geranium wallichianum*

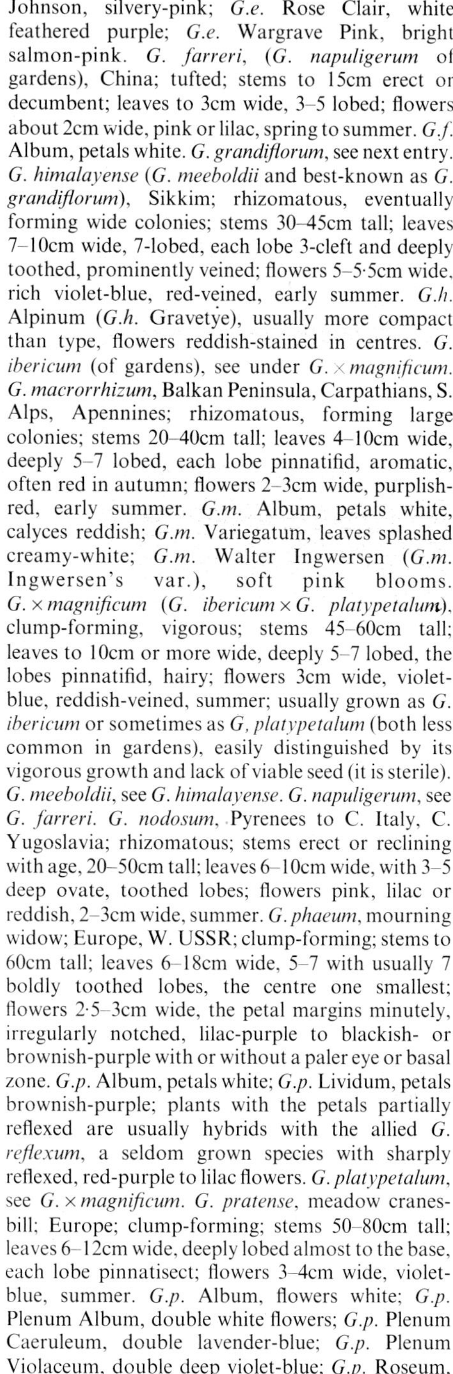

Johnson, silvery-pink; *G.e.* Rose Clair, white feathered purple; *G.e.* Wargrave Pink, bright salmon-pink. *G. farreri*, (*G. napuligerum* of gardens), China; tufted; stems to 15cm erect or decumbent; leaves to 3cm wide, 3–5 lobed; flowers about 2cm wide, pink or lilac, spring to summer. *G.f.* Album, petals white. *G. grandiflorum*, see next entry. *G. himalayense* (*G. meeboldii* and best-known as *G. grandiflorum*), Sikkim; rhizomatous, eventually forming wide colonies; stems 30–45cm tall; leaves 7–10cm wide, 7-lobed, each lobe 3-cleft and deeply toothed, prominently veined; flowers 5–5·5cm wide, rich violet-blue, red-veined, early summer. *G.h.* Alpinum (*G.h.* Gravetye), usually more compact than type, flowers reddish-stained in centres. *G. ibericum* (of gardens), see under *G. × magnificum*. *G. macrorrhizum*, Balkan Peninsula, Carpathians, S. Alps, Apennines; rhizomatous, forming large colonies; stems 20–40cm tall; leaves 4–10cm wide, deeply 5–7 lobed, each lobe pinnatifid, aromatic, often red in autumn; flowers 2–3cm wide, purplish-red, early summer. *G.m.* Album, petals white, calyces reddish; *G.m.* Variegatum, leaves splashed creamy-white; *G.m.* Walter Ingwersen (*G.m.* Ingwersen's var.), soft pink blooms. *G. × magnificum* (*G. ibericum × G. platypetalum*), clump-forming, vigorous; stems 45–60cm tall; leaves to 10cm or more wide, deeply 5–7 lobed, the lobes pinnatifid, hairy; flowers 3cm wide, violet-blue, reddish-veined, summer; usually grown as *G. ibericum* or sometimes as *G, platypetalum* (both less common in gardens), easily distinguished by its vigorous growth and lack of viable seed (it is sterile). *G. meeboldii*, see *G. himalayense*. *G. napuligerum*, see *G. farreri*. *G. nodosum*, Pyrenees to C. Italy, C. Yugoslavia; rhizomatous; stems erect or reclining with age, 20–50cm tall; leaves 6–10cm wide, with 3–5 deep ovate, toothed lobes; flowers pink, lilac or reddish, 2–3cm wide, summer. *G. phaeum*, mourning widow; Europe, W. USSR; clump-forming; stems to 60cm tall; leaves 6–18cm wide, 5–7 with usually 7 boldly toothed lobes, the centre one smallest; flowers 2·5–3cm wide, the petal margins minutely, irregularly notched, lilac-purple to blackish- or brownish-purple with or without a paler eye or basal zone. *G.p.* Album, petals white; *G.p.* Lividum, petals brownish-purple; plants with the petals partially reflexed are usually hybrids with the allied *G. reflexum*, a seldom grown species with sharply reflexed, red-purple to lilac flowers. *G. platypetalum*, see *G. × magnificum*. *G. pratense*, meadow cranesbill; Europe; clump-forming; stems 50–80cm tall; leaves 6–12cm wide, deeply lobed almost to the base, each lobe pinnatisect; flowers 3–4cm wide, violet-blue, summer. *G.p.* Album, flowers white; *G.p.* Plenum Album, double white flowers; *G.p.* Plenum Caeruleum, double lavender-blue; *G.p.* Plenum Violaceum, double deep violet-blue; *G.p.* Roseum, pink, darker-veined; *G.p.* Striatum (*G.p.* Bicolor), petals erratically white-striped or sectioned, sometimes white with purple flecks – a curious sectional chimaera; *G.p.* Johnson's Blue, probably a hybrid with *G. himalayense*, rarely above 30cm tall with large, lavender-blue, darker-veined flowers; *G. rectum album* (of gardens), Kashmir; in effect, a form of *G. pratense* and best considered a subspecies of it, having a running habit and large white flowers with fine purple veins. *G. psilostemon* (*G. armenum*), USSR – Armenia; clump-forming, robust; stems 75–120cm tall; leaves 10–20cm wide, 5-lobed, deeply toothed, often turning red in autumn; flowers about 4cm wide, crimson-magenta with black eye, summer. *G. pylzowianum*, China; spreading underground by slender rhizomes having enlarged, tuber-like nodes; stems up to 30cm tall; leaves to 5cm wide, 5-lobed almost to the base, each lobe trifid; flowers about 3cm wide, purple, summer. *G. rectum album*, see *G. pratense*. *G. renardii*, Caucasus; clump-forming, making neat mounds; leaves 5–6cm wide, broadly 5–7 lobed, sage-green, finely wrinkled above, felted beneath; flowers 4–4·5cm wide, white, heavily veined purple, on stems 20–30cm tall, early summer. *G.* × Russell Prichard (*G. endressii × G. traversii*), favours the latter parent, with silvery leaves but larger flowers of rose-magenta, summer to autumn. *G. sanguineum*, Europe, W. Asia; rhizomatous; stems usually decumbent, forming wide mats to 30cm tall; leaves 3–5cm wide, deeply divided into 3–7 pinnatisect lobes; flowers 2–2·5cm wide, red-purple, early to late summer. *G.s.* Album, taller than type, flowers white; *G.s. lancastrense* (not *G.s. lancastriense* as so often listed), plant prostrate; leaves smaller than type; flowers pale pink, red-veined. *G.s.* Prostratum, almost prostrate, flowers rich red-purple. *G. sessiliflorum*, Australia, New Zealand; tufted, forming low hummocks; leaves bright green, 5–7 lobed, 3–4cm wide; flowers white, 1–1·5cm wide, often rather hidden by leaves, summer. *G.s. nigricans*, leaves suffused purple-brown. *G. stapfianum roseum* (of gardens), akin to *G. pylzowianum*, spreading into mats by beaded rhizomes; stems 10–15cm tall; leaves 4–6cm, with 5–7 narrow lobes cut almost to base, each lobe again deeply cleft, often tipped or margined dull red-purple; flowers about 3cm wide, bright lilac-pink, early summer. *G. subcaulescens*, C., S. Italy, S., W. Balkan Peninsula; like *G. cinereum*, but segments of leaf-lobes to 5mm long (those of *G. cinereum* about 2mm); flowers red-purple; confused in gardens with *G. cinereum*, but flowers lacking the dark veining of that species. *G.s.* Splendens, flowers bright carmine-pink. *G. sylvaticum*, Europe to Siberia; clump-forming; stems to 60cm or more tall, branched above; leaves 5–12cm wide, deeply divided into 5–7 toothed or pinnatisect lobes; flowers about 3cm wide, bluish-purple, late spring to summer. *G.s.* Album, petals white; *G.s.* Mayflower, rich violet-blue; *G.s.* Roseum and *G.s.* Wanneri, shades of pink. *G. tuberosum*, S. Europe; tufted habit, from rounded tuber; stems 30–60cm tall; leaves divided almost to base into 5–7 pinnatisect lobes; flowers 2·5–3cm wide, pale pinkish-purple, early summer. *G. traversii*, Chatham

Is, New Zealand; tufted; forming 15cm mounds of silvery grey-green 5–7 lobed leaves, each 2–5cm wide; flowers to 2·5cm wide, pink, sometimes white, summer to autumn; not reliably hardy, although survives most winters in Britain. *G.t.* Elegans, petals shell-pink, darker-veined. *G. wallichianum*, Himalaya; tufted; stems prostrate or decumbent, to 60cm or more long; leaves 5-lobed, deeply toothed; flowers 3·5–4cm wide, violet-blue, late summer to autumn. *G.w.* Buxton's Blue, flowers bluer with prominent white eye. *G. wlassovianum*, N.E. China, Siberia; clump-forming; stems about 60cm tall; leaves 3–5 lobed, velvety dark green; flowers deep violet with darker veins, 3–4cm wide, early summer onwards.

Geum

(ancient Latin name). ROSACEAE. A genus of 40 species of herbaceous and evergreen perennials from northern and southern temperate zones and arctic. They are tufted to clump-forming, with usually pinnate basal leaves and 5-petalled flowers, nodding and bell-like to erect and widely expanded. Grow in any well-drained but moisture-retentive soil in sun or light shade. Plant autumn to spring. Propagate by division at planting time, from seed when ripe, or spring.

Species cultivated: *G.* × *borisii* (reputedly *G. reptans* × *G. bulgaricum*, but evidence suggests that the true red-flowered *G. coccineum* from the Balkan Peninsula is the second parent, it and *G. bulgaricum* being confused in cultivation), clump-forming; stems 30cm tall; leaves pinnate, to 15cm or more long; flowers about 2·5cm wide, bright clear orange,

Left above: *Geum chiloense* Prince of Orange
Above: *Geum montanum*
Right: *Gilia capitata*

early summer. *G. chiloense* (*G. coccineum* of gardens), Chile, Chiloe; clump-forming; stems to 60cm tall; leaves pinnate, 20cm or more long, terminal leaflet large, cordate; flowers about 3cm wide, scarlet, early summer; usually represented in gardens by larger, double-flowered cultivars, notably *G.c.* Fire Opal, rich bronze-scarlet, *G.c.* Lady Stratheden, yellow, *G.c.* Mrs Bradshaw, bright brick-red, *G.c.* Prince of Orange, rich bronze-scarlet; the name *G. chiloense* has no botanical standing, the correct name being *G. quellyon*. *G. coccineum*, see *G. chiloense*. *G.* × *intermedium* (*G. rivale* × *G. urbanum*), see *G. rivale*. *G. montanum* (*Sieversia m.*), alpine avens; mountains of S. and C. Europe; rhizomatous, stems to 15cm tall; forming mats; pinnate leaves, the terminal leaflets large, to 6cm long; flowers solitary, golden-yellow, 2·5–4cm wide; best in peaty, gritty soil. *G. quellyon* see *G. chiloense*. *G. reptans*, (*Sieversia r.*), creeping avens; Alps, Carpathians to S.W. Bulgaria; rhizomatous and stoloniferous, forming mats; stems 10–15cm tall; leaves pinnate, the segments deeply toothed; flowers solitary, bright yellow, 3–4cm wide; best in peaty, gritty soil. *G. rivale*, water avens; N. Hemisphere; clump-forming; stems 30–40cm tall; leaves pinnate, 20cm or more long, terminal leaflets largest, rounded, lobed, toothed; flowers bell-shaped, nodding, calyx purple, petals to 1·5cm long, orange-pink, early summer to autumn; although basically like *G. rivale*, the following cultivars are of hybrid origin with *G. urbanum* (herb bennet or wood avens): *G.* × Lionel Cox, petals yellow, *G.* × Leonard's Variety, petals coppery-pink.

Gilia

(for Filippo Luigi Gilii, 1756–1821, Italian astronomer). POLEMONIACEAE. A genus of annuals, biennials and perennials from N. and S. America; depending on the taxonomic treatment, there are between 20 and 120 species. 1 hardy annual is widely available in cultivation: *G. capitata*, W. N. America, to 50cm or more, erect, slender-branched; leaves to 10cm long, bi- to tripinnate, segments linear; flowers 6–8mm long, tubular with 5 linear lobes, lavender-blue, 50–100 packed into terminal rounded heads, summer to autumn. For *G. coronopifolia* and *G. rubra*, see *Ipomopsis*; for *G. lutea*, see *Linanthus androsaceus*. Grow in well-drained, preferably humus-rich soil in a sunny site. Sow seed *in situ*, early autumn or spring, thinning seedlings to 20cm apart each way; twiggy sticks will be needed for support in exposed areas. Autumn-sown plants may also be grown in pots in a cool greenhouse for a spring display.

Gillenia

(for Arnold Gillen, Latinized Gillenius, 17th century German physician and botanist). ROSACEAE. A genus of 2 species of herbaceous perennials from E. N. America, 1 of which is generally available. *G. trifoliata* (*Porteranthus t.*), Indian physic; clump-forming, to 1·2m tall; stems reddish; leaves trifoliate, leaflets ovate-oblong, toothed; flowers 5-petalled, starry, white, 2·5–4cm wide, summer; after flowering, the calyces remain and turn red. Grow in humus-rich, moist soil preferably in partial shade. Plant autumn to spring. Propagate by division at planting time, from seed in spring. This is an easily raised plant.

Left: *Gillenia trifoliata*
Above: *Ginkgo biloba*
Top right: *Gladiolus byzantinus*
Right: *Gladiolus* Greenbird (Miniature)
Below right: *Gladiolus* Oscar (Large-flowered)

Ginkgo

(Latinization of the ancient Japanese *gin-kyo*, now obsolete, meaning silver apricot). GINKGOACEAE. A genus of 1 hardy deciduous tree from China, formerly classified among the Conifers but now considered to be the last surviving member of an even more ancient order. *G. biloba* (*Salisburia adiantifolia*), maidenhair tree; probably extinct in the wild in China, but much cultivated there and in Japan and Korea; to 25m tall; bark brownish to dull grey with a network of ridges and wide fissures, sometimes fluted. Often erect and sparsely branched when young, later becoming columnar and pyramidal or much-branched and round to oval-headed; leaves alternate, fan-shaped, deeply cleft in the middle, irregularly margined, 5–8cm long; flowers dioecious, the males in catkins to 3cm long, the females of 1 or 2 naked ovules like minute acorns. The fruit is plum-like, to 4cm long, yellow-green, falling when ripe and giving off a smell of rancid butter; seed nut-like, edible. *G.b.* Fastigiata, variable but generally of columnar habit; *G. b.* Laciniata, has leaves more deeply divided; *G. b.* Pendula, has weeping branches. Grow in any well-drained but moisture-retentive soil, preferably humus-enriched, in sunny sites. Plant autumn or spring. Propagate from seed when ripe or as soon afterwards as possible. Not always easily established, of erratic growth; in some years little or no increment is made, in others stems up to 60cm long develop rapidly.

Gladiolus

(Latin for small sword, referring to the shape of the leaves). IRIDACEAE. A genus of 200 species of cormous-rooted plants from W. and C. Europe, Mediterranean to S.W. and C. Asia, tropical and S. Africa. They have rounded to flattened corms, narrow to broadly sword-shaped leaves in fan-like tufts and 1-sided spikes of widely funnel-shaped flowers. Each bloom has a short, curving tube and 6 petal-like lobes, the 3 upper ones usually larger, the 3 lower ones often blotched or patterned. Comparatively few species are generally grown, the genus being represented in gardens mainly by many 100s of half-hardy hybrid cultivars derived from such S. African species as *G. cardinalis*, *G. carneus*, *G. natalensis* (including *G. primulinus*), *G. oppositiflorus*, *G. saundersii* and *G. papilio*. They come in practically every colour except true blue, and in a wide range of sizes and forms. Several named groups are recognized, in particular the popular Large-flowered (Exhibition), with massive spikes of large blooms; the Miniatures, smaller and neater and including the Butterfly strain with blooms startlingly blotched; and Primulinus, with well-spaced flowers having the characteristic hooded upper petal. Like all the other popular garden flowers, eg Chrysanthemum, Dahlia, Rose, where new cultivars are continually appearing and ousting older ones, choice is very much a personal matter and catalogues of bulb specialists the best source of up-to-date information. Grow in well-drained, humus-rich soil in sunny sites. Plant half-hardy hybrid cultivar corms usually in mid to late spring, although in mild areas early spring would not be too soon. If a succession of bloom is required, plant batches of corms at 3-weekly intervals until early summer. Set corms 7–10cm deep, 10cm or more on light, sandy soils. In windy sites the large-flowered, taller cultivars usually need a cane support. 6–8 weeks after the last flower has faded, lift the plants, cut off foliage about 5cm above the corm, and dry off as rapidly as possible, ideally not less than 24°C for the first 3 days, then 13–15°C for the following 10 days. Clean off the withered previous season's corms and the spawn (tiny cormlets), and store at not less than 10–13°C until next planting season. Hardy species and hybrids may be planted in autumn and left *in situ* until they become crowded. Tender species and hybrids are grown under glass, minimum temperature 5–7°C.

Grow in pots of a commercial potting mix or its equivalent; all-peat types are good with $\frac{1}{3}$-part coarse sand or grit. Set the corms about 5cm apart and deep in late autumn, water well, then very sparingly until shoots appear. Thereafter keep moist, but do not overwater. Ventilate on all mild days. Apply liquid feed at fortnightly intervals once the flower-spike is visible and continue until the flowers fade. Hybrid cultivars may also be grown in this way for early blooms, particularly the smaller-flowered sorts such as Nanus and Primulinus. Propagate from seed in spring, offsets and spawn at the usual planting time; plants take up to 3 years to flower.

Top: *Gladiolus × colvillei*
Above: *Gladiolus* Columbine (Primulinus)
Top right: *Gladiolus italicus*
Above right: *Gladiolus* Melodie (Butterfly)

Species cultivated: *G. blandus*, see *G. carneus*. *G. byzantinus*, throughout the Mediterranean region; half-hardy, to 75cm tall; flowers 5cm long, tepals touching or overlapping, rose-purple to magenta, early summer. *G.b. albus*, flowers white. *G. callianthus* (*Acidanthera bicolor*, *A.b. murielae*), Ethiopia, Malawi, Tanzania; half-hardy, to 90cm tall; flowers 4–6, long-tubed, 6–8cm wide, white, blotched maroon within, fragrant, autumn; *G. carneus* (*G. blandus*), painted lady; S. Africa; tender, 30–60cm tall; flowers widely expanded, about 5–6cm wide, pink-mauve or cream, usually with red, purple or yellow, hastate or v-shaped markings on the lower 3 petals, spring. *G.* × Christobel (*G. tristis concolor* × *G. virescens* (*G. bicolor*)), similar to *G. tristis* but flowers slightly hooded, primrose-yellow, upper tepals heavily veined and shaded purple, fragrant, spring; greenhouse plant in all but the warmest spots. *G.* × *colvillei* (*G. tristis* × *G. cardinalis*), and *G.* × *nanus* (*G. carneus* × *G. cardinalis*), almost hardy, to 45cm tall; flowers scarlet, almost erect, tepals pointed, the lower ones marked yellow within. *G.* × *c.* The Bride (*G.* × *c.* Albus), flowers white; 1 of the first gladiolus hybrids and original parent of the modern Nanus group. *G. imbricatus*, E. Europe, Turkey; half-hardy, to 60cm tall; flowers widely funnel-shaped, shades of purple-red, summer. *G. papilio* (*G. purpureo-auratus*), S. Africa; hardy, stoloniferous; stems 50–90cm tall; leaves grey-green; flowers 4–5·5cm long, arching, narrow, the 3 upper tepals forming a hood, bright to dull yellow or variously tinged or heavily suffused mauve to purple as in the form originally called *G. purpureo-auratus*, autumn; spreads widely in light soils and can be a nuisance. *G. italicus* (*G. segetum*), Mediterranean; similar to *G. byzantinus*, but flowers rose-purple, more expanded, the upper tepals oblong and open at the base, very unusual pellet seeds, early summer. *G. tristis*, S. Africa; tender, to 45cm tall; leaves narrow, rush-like; flowers funnel-shaped, erect, to 7cm wide, sulphur-yellow, shaded red without, fragrant, late spring. *G.t. concolor*, flowers entirely yellow, slightly larger than type, plant somewhat hardier; can be grown outside in mild areas, although leaves may suffer damage from winter weather.

Left below: *Glaucium flavum*
Below: *Glaucium corniculatum*

Glastonbury thorn – see *Crataegus monogyna* Biflora.

Glaucium

(Greek *glaukos*, grey or bluish-green – referring to the leaf colour). PAPAVERACEAE. A genus of 25 species of annuals, biennials and perennials from Europe and Asia. They have rosettes of grey-green, ovate to oblong, pinnatifid leaves, and 4-petalled, poppy-like flowers followed by slender, horn-like pods. Grow in any well-drained soil in a sunny site. Sow seed *in situ* in spring, thinning seedlings 20–30cm apart.

Species cultivated: *G. corniculatum* (*G. phoeniceum*), red horned-poppy; S. Europe to Hungary, S.C. USSR; annual; stems 30–60cm tall, branched; basal leaves lyrate pinnatifid; flowers scarlet or orange, 3–5cm wide, summer. *G. flavum*, yellow horned or sea poppy; S. and W. Europe, mainly sea coasts but naturalized inland; stems branched, 30–90cm tall; basal leaves pinnately lobed, 15–35cm long; flowers yellow, 6–8cm wide, summer to autumn. *G. phoeniceum*, see *G. corniculatum*.

Glechoma

(Greek *glechon*, for a kind of mint). LABIATAE. A genus of 10–12 species of perennials from temperate Europe, Asia. The variegated cultivar of 1 species is grown for its ornamental foliage and as ground-cover: *G. hederacea* (*Nepeta h.*, *Nepeta glechoma*), ground ivy; Europe, Asia; prostrate; stems rooting at nodes, forming extensive mats; leaves in opposite pairs, rounded to broadly ovate-cordate, crenate, softly hairy, 1–3cm wide; flowers violet, 1·5–2cm long, tubular, 2-lipped, in whorls in upper leaf-axils, spring. *G.h.* Variegata, leaves splashed white. Grow in any well-drained soil in sun or shade. Plant autumn to spring. Propagate by division in spring, cuttings spring to autumn. Grows well under glass and useful in hanging baskets.

Gleditsia

(*Gleditschia*). (for Johann Gottlieb Gleditsch, 1714–1786, professor of botany and Director of the Berlin Botanic Garden). LEGUMINOSAE. A genus of 11 species of deciduous, generally spiny trees from N. America, Asia, W. tropical Africa. 1 species is generally available: *G. triacanthos*, honey locust; E. N.America; to 20m in Britain, to 45m in native habitat, with eventually a broad, spreading head; trunk dark purplish-grey, bearing clusters of sharp branched spines; leaves alternate, pinnate and bipinnate, 10–20cm long, leaflets oblong-lanceolate, 2–4cm long: flowers unisexual, pale yellow, about 5mm long, with 5, tiny petals and a bell-shaped calyx in racemes 5–12cm long, summer; fruit flattened, usually spirally twisted pods to 25cm or more long. *G.t.* Sunburst, young leaves rich yellow, ageing yellow-green. Grow in any well-drained but fertile, moisture-retentive soil. Plant autumn to spring. Propagate from seed in spring; they may germinate erratically and are best heat-treated, that is dropped into a small quantity of freshly boiled hot water and allowed to cool and left to stand for 24 hours before they are sown. *G t.* Sunburst is budded onto seedlings of the original species, *G. triacanthos*.

Globe flower – see *Trollius*.

Globe thistle – see *Echinops*.

Globularia

(Latin *globulus*, a small ball – referring to the flower-heads). GLOBULARIACEAE. A genus of 28 species of shrubs, sub-shrubs and evergreen (sometimes deciduous) perennials from S. Europe to W. Asia, Canary and Cape Verde Is. The species described are tufted, sometimes mat-forming, with obovate to wedge-shaped leaves and compact heads of many, tiny, tubular, 5-lobed, 2-lipped flowers in shades of blue. Grow in well-drained soil in a sunny site. Plant autumn or spring. Propagate from seed or by careful division – where possible – in spring, or by cuttings of non-flowering shoots late summer.

Species cultivated: *G. aphyllanthes*, see *G. punctata*. *G. bellidifolia*, see *G. meridionalis*. *G. cordifolia*, N.E. Spain to mountains of S. Bulgaria; creeping shrub, forming mats to 30cm or more wide; leaves spathulate, to 2·5cm long, usually notch-tipped,

Left: *Gleditsia triacanthos* Sunburst
Above: *Globularia incanescens*

deep green; flower-heads 1–2cm wide, greyish-blue, on erect, almost leafless stems 5–10cm tall, summer. *G.c. bellidifolia*, see *G. meridionalis*. *G. incanescens*, N. Apennines, Appian Alps; deciduous, rhizomatous, mat-forming; leaves long-stalked, rounded to lanceolate, about 1·7cm wide, with a grey-blue patina; flower-heads about 1·5cm wide, pale blue, summer. *G. meridionalis* (*G. bellidifolia*, *G. cordifolia b.*), S.E. Alps, Apennines, Balkan Peninsula; similar to *G. cordifolia* but more robust; leaves 2–9cm long, lanceolate to oblanceolate. *G. punctata* (*G. aphyllanthes*, *G. willkommii*), similar to *G. trichosantha* but tufted and lacking stolons; stem leaves lanceolate, 1·5–2·5cm long, basal leaves 2–3cm wide; flower-heads 1·5cm wide. *G. trichosantha*, E. Balkan Peninsula; stoloniferous; leaves rosetted, long-stalked, obovate; stems to 20cm tall, bearing elliptic leaves and light blue flower-heads to 2·5cm wide, summer. *G. willkommii*, see *G. punctata*.

Gloriosa daisy – see *Rudbeckia*.

Glory of the snow – see *Chionodoxa*.

Glyceria

(Greek *glykys*, sweet – the seed or grain of some species being sweet). GRAMINEAE. A genus of 20 species of perennial wetland grasses from temperate regions of both hemispheres. 1 species is grown for its ornamental foliage: *G. maxima* (*Poa aquatica*), reed sweet, or reed meadow grass; Europe, Asia; rhizomatous, forming clumps and colonies; stems 1–2m or more tall; leaves 30–60cm long by 8–20mm wide, arching; spikelets oblong to 1cm or more long, green to purplish in graceful, much-branched panicles 15–45cm long, late summer; *G.m.* Variegata (*G. aquatica* Variegata or *G.a.* Foliis-variegatis of gardens), leaves boldly white or cream-striped, sometimes pinkish-flushed when young. Grow in any moisture-retentive soil in sunny sites – the wetter the soil the more vigorous the growth. Plant in spring or autumn. Propagate by division during spring.

Goat willow – see *Salix caprea*.

Goat's rue – see *Galega*.

Goatweed – see *Aegopodium*.

Godetia – see *Clarkia*.

Golden chain – see *Laburnum anagyroides*.

Golden club – see *Orontium*.

Golden rain – see *Koelreuteria paniculata* and *Laburnum anagyroides*.

Griselinia

(for Francesco Griselini, 1717–83, Italian naturalist). GRISELINIACEAE (CORNACEAE). A genus of 6 species of evergreen shrubs and trees from New Zealand, Chile, S.E. Brazil. They have alternate, ovate-oblong or obovate leaves, and tiny, dioecious, 5-petalled, greenish flowers in axillary panicles followed by fleshy, berry-like fruit. Grow in well-drained, humus-rich soil in sun or light shade, preferably by the sea or in mild areas. *G. lucida* is best grown under glass in the colder areas, minimum temperature 5°C, or grown in pots or tubs outside in summer and over-wintered frost-free. Commercial potting mixture is suitable. Pot or plant spring. Propagate by cuttings, preferably with a heel in late summer, over-wintering the young plants under glass, or from seed in spring.

Species cultivated: *G. littoralis*, New Zealand; shrub or eventually a tree to 10m or more; leaves broadly ovate to oblong, 3–10cm long, lustrous, often yellowish-green; fruit 5–10mm long, purple. *G.l.* Variegata, leaves splashed white; hardy in mild areas, although liable to damage or poor growth in some cold inland areas. *G. lucida*, New Zealand; usually a shrub 2–3m tall, but sometimes a tree to 8m in the wild, often epiphytic; leaves 10–18cm long, obliquely broadly ovate, rich green, very glossy; fruit 6–10mm long, purple; variegated-leaved forms are sometimes available; rather tender and best under glass or over-wintered there except in the mildest areas.

Golden feather – see *Chrysanthemum parthenium* Aureum.

Golden rod – see *Solidago*.

Gomphrena

(Latin for a sort of amaranth). AMARANTHACEAE. A genus of 100 species of annuals, biennials and perennials from C. and S. America, S.E. Asia, Australia. 1 species is generally available: *G. globosa*, globe amaranth; tropical Asia; half-hardy annual to 45cm tall, erect, branched; leaves opposite, oblong to elliptic, to 10cm long; flowers tiny, each with a 5-lobed perianth almost hidden by chaffy, purple, pink, white, yellow or orange bracts, forming terminal ovoid heads, 2·5–4cm long, summer; a dwarf strain to 15cm or so tall is often grown. If cut when the heads are fully developed they dry and retain their colour well like other everlastings. Sow seed under glass in mid spring at 15–18°C, prick off seedlings into boxes of a commercial potting mixture, at 4–5cm apart each way, harden off in late spring, and plant out in a warm, sunny position when fear of frost has passed. A useful bedding plant.

Top left: *Glyceria maxima* Variegata
Left: *Gomphrena globosa*
Top: *Grevillea rosmarinifolia*
Above: *Grevillea sulphurea*
Above right: *Griselinia littoralis*

Gorse – see *Ulex*.

Grape hyacinth – see *Muscari*.

Grevillea

(for Charles Francis Greville, 1749–1809, founder of the Horticultural Society of London). PROTEACEAE. A genus of 190 species of evergreen trees and shrubs from Australia, New Caledonia to E. Malaysia. They have alternate, simple to pinnately compound leaves, and racemes of petalless flowers each formed of a coloured calyx (or perianth) tube that splits down 1 side and from which a prominent coloured style protrudes. Greenhouse, although some may be grown outside in mild areas or sheltered sunny corners. Under glass maintain minimum temperature 5–7°C, well-ventilated on all sunny days. Grow in a neutral to acid soil. Pot or plant spring. Propagate from seed in spring or cuttings with a heel in summer, bottom heat 18°C.

Species cultivated: *G. alpina* (*G. alpestris*), mountains of S.E. Australia; low, bushy shrub usually less than 60cm tall; leaves narrowly oblong to oval, sometimes rounded, dark green, silky-haired beneath, 8–25mm long; flowers red, 1–2cm long, spring to summer; fairly hardy and worth trying outside in sheltered places. *G. juniperina*, see *G. sulphurea*. *G. robusta*, silky oak; Queensland, New South Wales; tree to 30m in the wild, 2–3m as a pot plant; leaves bipinnately lobed and up to 45cm long on young plants, fern-like, pinnate and much smaller on sizeable trees, rich green above, silky beneath; flowers yellow in dense, 1-sided racemes (not on pot-grown specimens). *G. rosmarinifolia*, S.E. Australia; shrub to 2m, of loose habit; leaves linear, 3–4cm long, dark grey-green above, silvery-haired beneath; flowers rosy-red to pink, 2–3cm long, summer; will survive some light frost. *G. sulphurea* (*G. juniperina*), New South Wales; shrub to 2m tall; leaves linear, 1–2·5cm long, prickle-tipped, pale-downed beneath; flowers pale yellow, 1–2·5cm long, spring to summer; almost hardy in sheltered sites.

Ground elder – see *Aegopodium*.

Ground ivy – see *Glechoma*.

Guelder rose – see *Viburnum opulus*.

Guernsey lily – see *Vallota*.

Gum tree – see *Eucalyptus* and *Nyssa*.

Gunnera

(for Ernst Gunnerus, 1718–1773, Norwegian bishop and botanist). GUNNERACEAE (HALORAGIDACEAE). A genus of 50 species of evergreen and deciduous perennials from the S. Hemisphere, Malaysia to Hawaii and Mexico. They are rhizomatous to clump-forming, with ovate to palmate leaves in tufts or rosettes; flowers are sometimes unisexual, very small, petals 2 or none, usually greenish, in spikes or dense, cone-shaped panicles; fruit is berry-like. Grow in moist to wet, humus-rich soil in sun or light shade. Plant spring. Propagate from seed when ripe or by division at planting time.

Species cultivated: *G. chilensis*, see *G. tinctoria*. *G.*

Left above: *Gunnera manicata*
Top: *Gyposphila paniculata* Bristol Fairy
Above: *Gypsophila repens*
Below: *Haberlea rhodopensis*

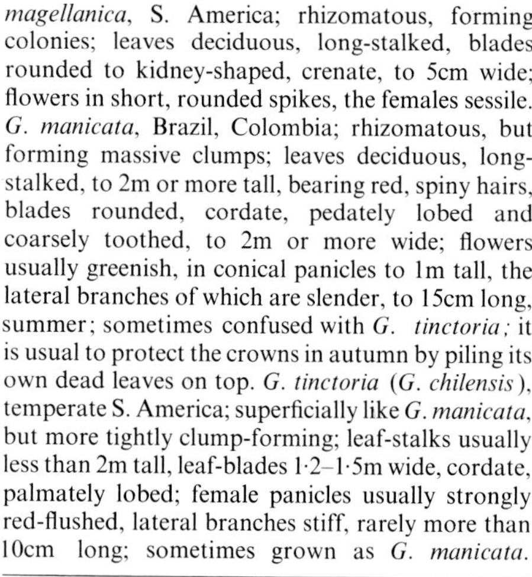

magellanica, S. America; rhizomatous, forming colonies; leaves deciduous, long-stalked, blades rounded to kidney-shaped, crenate, to 5cm wide; flowers in short, rounded spikes, the females sessile. *G. manicata*, Brazil, Colombia; rhizomatous, but forming massive clumps; leaves deciduous, long-stalked, to 2m or more tall, bearing red, spiny hairs, blades rounded, cordate, pedately lobed and coarsely toothed, to 2m or more wide; flowers usually greenish, in conical panicles to 1m tall, the lateral branches of which are slender, to 15cm long, summer; sometimes confused with *G. tinctoria;* it is usual to protect the crowns in autumn by piling its own dead leaves on top. *G. tinctoria* (*G. chilensis*), temperate S. America; superficially like *G. manicata*, but more tightly clump-forming; leaf-stalks usually less than 2m tall, leaf-blades 1·2–1·5m wide, cordate, palmately lobed; female panicles usually strongly red-flushed, lateral branches stiff, rarely more than 10cm long; sometimes grown as *G. manicata*.

Gynerium – see *Cortaderia*.

Gypsophila

(Greek *gypsos*, gypsum, and *philos*, loving: several species grow among gypsum rocks or limestone in the wild). CARYOPHYLLACEAE. A genus of 125 species of perennials and annuals mainly from the Mediterranean region, Europe and Asia. They are erect, prostrate or cushion-forming with opposite pairs of linear to lanceolate leaves, 5-petalled flowers white to rose-pink, usually in dichasial or panicled cymes. Grow in sunny sites in well-drained soil. Plant perennials autumn or spring. Sow seed of annuals *in situ* in spring, or autumn in sheltered areas on light soils. Propagate perennials from seed, root or stem cuttings in spring; the sterile, double-flowered border cultivars may also be grafted onto roots of wild species in a shaded frame in spring.

Species cultivated: *G. cerastioides*, Himalaya; tufted, basal leaves stalked, spathulate to oval, 1·5–5cm long, greyish-green; stems to 10cm tall, branched; flowers about 1cm wide, white, veined red-purple, early summer-autumn. *G. dubia*, see *G. repens*. *G. elegans*, Iran, Turkey, Caucasus; annual, 30–50cm tall; stems much branched; leaves oblong-spathulate to linear-lanceolate; flowers about 1cm wide, white or pink, summer to autumn. *G.e.* Paris Market, flowers white, smaller than type but very profuse; *G.e.* Covent Garden, flowers white, large; *G.e.* Grandiflora Alba, large white, much like *G.e.* Covent Garden; pink and carmine strains are often available. *G. fratensis*, see *G. repens*. *G. paniculata*, baby's breath, chalk plant; C. Europe to C. Asia; clump-forming perennial 90–120cm tall; leaves lanceolate, to 7cm long; flowers about 5mm wide, white to pink, in large, cloud-like panicles, summer. *G.p.* Bristol Fairy, pure white double flowers; *G.p.* Flamingo, double pale pink; *G.p.* Rosy Veil (*G.p.* Rosenschleier), 30–40cm tall, double rose-pink. *G.repens* (*G.dubia*, *G.prostrata fratensis*), C. and S. Europe – mountains; stems forming low mounds, arching to prostrate, to 60cm wide; leaves 1–3cm long, linear, usually glaucous; inflorescences corymbose, to 20cm tall; flowers 5–30, about 1cm wide, white to lilac or pale purple, summer.

Haberlea

(for Carl Constantin Haberle, 1764–1832, professor of botany at Budapest). GESNERIACEAE. A genus of 1 species of evergreen perennial from Bulgaria and Greek mountains: *H. rhodopensis*, rosette-forming; stems 10–13cm tall; leaves 3–8cm long, obovate to ovate-oblong, coarsely toothed, softly hairy, deep green; flowers 1–5, lilac, tubular with 5 broad-spreading, waved lobes, about 2·5cm wide, spring. *H.r. ferdinandi-coburgii*, somewhat larger in all its parts than type, leaves hairless above; *H.r.* Virginalis, flowers pure white. Grow in humus-rich, well-drained soil in partial shade, preferably north-facing rock crevices or banks. Plant autumn or spring. Propagate from seed when ripe or in spring in a cold frame, or alternatively take leaf cuttings in the summer.

Hacquetia

(for Balthasar Hacquet, 1740–1815, Austrian writer and alpine plant enthusiast). UMBELLIFERAE. A genus of 1 species of herbaceous perennial from C. Europe. *H. epipactis* (*Dondia e.*), small, to about 10–18cm high, clump-forming; leaves long-stalked, trifoliate leaflets 2–3 lobed, bright green; flowers 5-petalled, tiny, in small, compact umbels surround-by 5-6 petal-like, greenish-yellow bracteoles, each 1–2cm long, opening before and with the young leaves, late winter to spring. Grow in a moist, but not boggy, cool situation, and in partial shade, but one not obscured by taller plants, preferably in heavy loam or clay soil, or one enriched with humus. Plant spring, as leaf growth starts. Propagate by careful division at planting time in spring or from seed when ripe.

Hakonechloa

(Hakone, an area in Honshu, Japan, and Greek *chloa*, grass). GRAMINEAE. A genus of 1 species of perennial grass formerly classified as a reed (*Phragmites*): *H. macra*, rhizomatous, forming colonies; stems erect or spreading, 30–50cm long; leaves linear, 10–25cm long, slender-pointed; panicles ovoid, nodding, 9–18cm long, spikelets pale green, narrowly oblong, 2–4cm long. *H.m.* Albo-aurea, white and yellow variegated, often with an overall bronze hue; *H.m.* Albo-variegata, green with white lines; *H.m.* Aureola, leaves yellow with green lines. Grow in any well-drained but not dry soil, preferably in partial shade. Plant and propagate by division in spring.

Halesia

(for the Reverend Stephen Hales, 1677–1761, inventor, physiologist and chemist, and author of 'Vegetable Staticks'). Silver bell or snowdrop tree. STYRACACEAE. A genus of 5 or 6 species of deciduous trees and shrubs from E. Asia and E. USA with alternate, elliptic to obovate leaves, pendant, 4-petalled, white bell flowers and woody winged fruit. Grow in humus-rich, moisture-retentive soil, preferably neutral to acid, in sun or dappled shade. Plant autumn to spring. Propagate from seed when ripe – it may take 18 months to germinate – and layering in spring.

Species cultivated: *H. carolina* (*H. tetraptera*), S. E. USA; large shrub or tree to 9m tall, or more in the wild, leaves ovate to elliptic; 5–13cm long; flowers to 2cm long, early summer; fruit narrowly pear-shaped, 4-winged nearly 4cm long, a beautiful flowering tree. *H. monticola*, mountain snowdrop tree; S. E. USA; much like *H. carolina*, but a tree in the wild, 16–33m tall; leaves to 18cm long; flowers 2·5cm long; fruit 4-winged, about 2·5cm wide and to 5cm long; a fine, fast growing tree which flowers when comparatively young, of spreading habit. *H.m.* Rosea, flowers flushed pink. *H. tetraptera*, see *H. carolina*.

Top left: *Hacquetia epipactis*
Left: *Hakonechloa macra* Aureola
Top: *Halesia carolina* fruits
Above: *Halesia monticola*
Top right: × *Halimiocistus wintonensis*
Above right: *Halimium ocymoides*

× Halimiocistus

(hybrids between the genera *Halimium* and *Cistus*). The plants blend characters of both with an overall tendency towards *Halimium*. Culture as for *Cistus* but propagation only by cuttings.

Hybrid species cultivated: × *H. ingwersenii*, believed to be *H. umbellatum* × *C. hirsutus*; found wild in Portugal; hardy, wide-spreading, 30–45cm tall; leaves linear-lanceolate, 2–4cm long, dark green above, densely starry-downy beneath; flowers white, 2·5–3cm wide. × *H. sahucii* (*H. umbellatum* × *C. salviifolius*); found wild in France; hardy, spreading but dense habit, 35–45cm tall; leaves linear, 1·5–4cm long; flowers white, 2·5–3cm wide. × *H. wintonensis*, believed to be *H. ocymoides* × *C. salviifolius*; raised at Hillier's Nursery, Winchester in England; almost hardy, of bushy, spreading habit, 45–60cm tall; leaves elliptic-lanceolate, 2–5cm long, white-woolly when young; flowers about 5cm wide, white, yellow and crimson-maroon centre.

Halimium

(Greek *halimos* – *Atriplex halimus* – alluding to the similar foliage of some species). CISTACEAE. A genus of 14 species of evergreen shrubs from Portugal and the Mediterranean region. They are much like *Cistus*, but are botanically more akin to *Helianthemum* and have formerly been classified in both genera. Culture as for *Cistus*.

Species cultivated (all summer-flowering): *H. halimifolium*, Portugal to S. E. Italy and N. Africa;

half-hardy, dense, erect habit, 1·5–2m tall; leaves 2–4·5cm long, narrowly obovate to elliptic, white-woolly when young; flowers 4cm wide, yellow, with or without small, crimson spots. *H. lasianthum*, S. Portugal; this species is represented in cultivation by *H.l. formosum* (*Cistus formosus*), having larger, more boldly blotched flowers; hardy, wide-spreading, to 90cm tall; leaves oblong to obovate, 1–4cm long, white-haired; flowers 4cm wide, bright yellow, each petal having a purple-brown basal blotch. *H. ocymoides*, Portugal and Spain; hardy, erect habit 60–90cm tall; leaves obovate to oblanceolate, 1·5–3cm long, white-downy; flowers 2·5–3cm wide, deep yellow, each petal with a basal, purple-black blotch. *H.o.* Concolor, petals unblotched; a prostrate form is known. *H. umbellatum*, Mediterranean region; erect, open habit to 45cm tall; leaves 1–3cm long, linear, sticky when young, dark, glossy green above, white-felted beneath; flowers 2cm wide, white, yellow-centred.

Hamamelis

(Greek for a plant with pear-shaped fruit, perhaps the medlar; name taken for this genus by Linnaeus). Witch-hazel. HAMAMELIDACEAE. A genus of 6 species of deciduous shrubs and small trees from E. Asia and E. N. America. They have alternate, oval to obovate leaves and clusters of small flowers having 4 slenderly strap-shaped petals in the form of a cross, which open from autumn to early spring. The small, oval, rather woody pods open explosively. Grow in sun or partial shade in humus-rich soil that does not dry out. Plant autumn to spring. Propagate by layering in spring or from seed when ripe, usually taking 1½ or 2½ years to germinate; commercially, they are often grafted onto seedling *H. virginiana* in spring under glass at 14–16°C; cuttings with a heel may be taken in late summer, but are not easy to root, even under mist, without special wounding pre-treatment.

Species cultivated: *H.* × *intermedia* (*H. japonica* × *H. mollis*), blending characters of the parents, but often inclining towards *H. japonica*; the following cultivars are vigorous and free-flowering: *H.* × *i.* Jelena, good autumn foliage colour, petals rust-red and yellow-ochre, the overall effect being copper-orange; *H.* × *i.* Ruby Glow, petals copper, suffused red, good autumn colour; *H.* × *i.* Winter Beauty, deep yellow, free-flowering even when quite young. *H. japonica*, Japanese witch hazel; Japan; large shrub or small tree to 7m or more; leaves ovate to obovate, elliptic to rhomboid, shallowly toothed, 5–9cm or more long; flowers bright yellow, petals 1–1·8cm long, crimped and twisted, calyx red-purple within, lightly fragrant, winter; some forms have good autumn leaf colour. *H.j. arborea*, scarcely distinct from type species but seeming to flower a little later and with wide-spreading branches; *H.j. flavopurpurascens* (*H.j. rubra*), parent of the reddish *H.* × *intermedia* cultivars, petals sulphur-yellow, shaded red in lower half; *H.j.* Zuccariniana, petals pale yellow, inside of calyx greenish. *H. mollis*, Chinese witch hazel; W. and W. C. China; large shrub to 3m or so; leaves broadly obovate to elliptic, obliquely cordate, often greyish-green, downy, densely so beneath; flowers golden-yellow, flushed red at base, petals 1·5cm or more long, flat, but somewhat rolled, fragrant, latter half of mid winter onwards. *H.m.* Brevipetala, petals shorter than type, less spreading, buttercup-yellow; *H.m.* Pallida, flowers profusely borne, petals soft pale yellow. *H. virginiana*, Virginian witch hazel; E. N. America; large shrub or small tree to 6m or more; leaves broadly ovate to obovate, 8–15cm long, crenate in upper half, turning clear yellow in autumn; flowers faintly fragrant, golden-yellow, petals 1–1·7cm long, crimped, twisted, often lost among leaves, autumn.

Harebell – see *Campanula rotundifolia*.

Above: *Hamamelis* × *intermedia*
Left: *Hamamelis japonica* Zuccariniana

Harrimanella – see *Cassiope hypnoides*.

Hart's-tongue fern – see *Asplenium scolopendrium*.

Hawkweed – see *Hieracium*.

Hawthorn – see *Crataegus laevigata*, and *C. monogyna*.

Heartsease – see *Viola tricolor*.

Heath – see *Erica*.

Heather – see *Calluna*.

Hebe

(for the Greek goddess of youth and cup-bearer to the gods, who married Hercules). Shrubby Veronica. SCROPHULARIACEAE. A genus of 100 species or more of evergreen shrubs and trees mainly from New Zealand, but also S.E. Australia including Tasmania, New Guinea, S. S.America and Falkland Is. They have opposite pairs of rarely toothed leaves and mostly small, tubular-based flowers with 4 sub-equal spreading lobes, mainly in axillary racemes or panicles. The genus falls easily into 2 groups, those with normal elliptic, oblong-elliptic to lanceolate and linear leaves, and those with tiny scale leaves closely pressed to the stem and often overlapping, resembling a cupressus, known as whipcord or cupressoid Veronicas. The genus has a reputation for tenderness and some of the more popular cultivars derived from lowland or North Island (New Zealand) species will not stand prolonged freezing weather without protection. Most of the species and cultivars described here are hardy except in areas of prolonged winter cold, the sub-alpine sorts being the hardiest. Grow in any ordinary, well-drained soil, preferably humus-rich in sunny sites, the half-hardy sorts against walls or in sheltered places; light shade is tolerated by the larger-leaved species and cultivars. Plant autumn or spring. Propagate by cuttings of non-flowering shoots any time from late spring to autumn. Seed may be sown in spring under glass, but as the species hybridize freely plants may not come true.

Species cultivated (mainly summer flowering; all from New Zealand): *H. albicans*, spreading, rounded habit 60–120cm tall; leaves sessile, crowded, ovate-oblong, to 3cm long, very glaucous, straight; flowers white, in 3–6cm long, cylindrical axillary racemes; greener and narrower-leaved forms are probably hybrids. *H.* × Alicia Amhurst, see *H. speciosa*. *H.* × *andersonii* (*H. speciosa* × *H. salicifolia* or the allied *H. stricta*), similar to first parent, but leaves oblong-lanceolate to 11cm long;

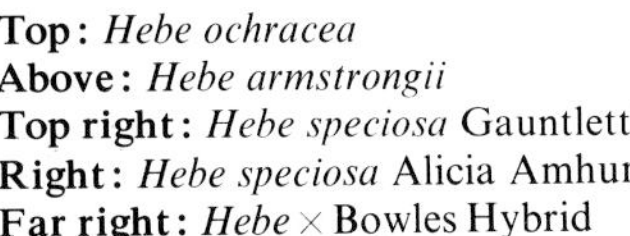

Top: *Hebe ochracea*
Above: *Hebe armstrongii*
Top right: *Hebe speciosa* Gauntlettii
Right: *Hebe speciosa* Alicia Amhurst
Far right: *Hebe* × Bowles Hybrid

flowers violet, fading white, in racemes 10–15cm long. *H.*×*a.* Midsummer Beauty, leaves flushed red-purple beneath, at least when young; flowers lavender-purple, summer to late autumn. *H.*×*a.* Variegata, leaves in shades of grey-green, margined creamy-white, smaller than type. *H. armstrongii*, whipcord; erect, much-branched, eventually to about 1m; stems and 1mm long leaves matt yellow-green; flowers white, 2–6 in terminal spikes; much confused with *H. ochracea* in gardens (qv). *H.*× Autumn Glory (*H.*× Autumn Beauty), popular hybrid, exact parentage unknown (possibly *H. albicans*, *H. pimeleoides* and *H.*×*franciscana* are involved); erect to somewhat spreading when old, about 60cm tall; stems dark red-purple; leaves 2–2·5cm long, obovate, dark glossy green with glaucous hue; flowers violet in 3–4·5cm long racemes, summer to early winter. *H.*× Bowles Hybrid, of uncertain parentage, perhaps *H. diosmifolia* or *H. parviflora* is 1 parent; to 60cm tall; leaves narrowly elliptic, to 2·5cm long; flowers pale lavender-purple in 7–10cm long panicles. *H. brachysiphon* (*H. traversii* of gardens), 1–2m tall, rounded habit; leaves elliptic to lanceolate, 1·5–2·5cm long, more or less erect, densely arranged; flowers white in racemes to 4cm long, sometimes branched; not to be confused with the rarely seen true *H. traversii*, that has narrowly oblong, spreading leaves. *H.b.* White Gem, compact, to 75cm tall, very free-flowering. *H. buchananii*, much-branched, rounded, to 20cm or more tall; leaves 5–7mm long, broadly ovate, usually concave, somewhat glaucous; flowers white in racemes to 1·5cm long. *H.b.* Minor, miniature version usually less than 10cm tall. *H. buxifolia*, see *H. odora*. *H.*×

Carl Teschner, reputedly *H. elliptica* × *H. pimeleoides*, semi-prostrate, spreading, eventually to 20cm or so in the centre; stems black-purple; leaves elliptic, about 1cm long; flowers violet, in racemes to 3cm or more long. *H. carnosula*, see *H. pinguifolia*. *H. cupressoides*, whipcord; dense, rounded habit, to 1m or more; stems and 1–1·5mm long leaves green to grey-green, often somewhat purplish in winter; flowers pale bluish-purple, 5–8 in terminal spikes. *H. darwiniana*, see *H. glaucophylla*. *H.* × Edinensis, believed to be *H. hectori* or *H. lycopodioides* × *H. odora*; decumbent, spreading habit, 15–30cm tall; leaves dense, sessile, 5–7mm long, oblong-ovate, arching outwards, keeled beneath, glossy deep green above; flowers white, sparingly produced; there appear to be 2 or more plants in cultivation under this name, 1 with smaller, obovate leaves. *H. elliptica* (*H. decussata*), New Zealand, Falkland Is, S. S.America; erect, to 2m or more in milder areas; leaves elliptic to oblong-obovate, 1·5–4cm long, glossy above; flowers white or palest violet; rarely cultivated, the plant under this name in gardens being frequently *H.* × *franciscana*. *H. epacridea*, mat-forming, stem tips erect; leaves rigid, stem-clasping, spreading and recurved, broadly ovate-oblong, keeled, to 7mm long; flowers white, in several short spikes forming a compact terminal head. *H.* × *franciscana* Blue Gem (*H. speciosa* × *H. elliptica*), dense, rounded habit, 1–1·5m or sometimes more; leaves 3–6·5cm long, elliptic to obovate, somewhat fleshy, glossy; flowers violet, in dense racemes 3–6cm long, summer to autumn; a good seaside and mild area plant, not reliably hardy *H.* × *f.* Variegata, leaves broadly margined creamy-white; self-sown seedlings of *H.* × *franciscana* tend to produce plants nearer to *H. elliptica*, with smaller leaves and paler or white flowers. *H.* × Gauntlettii, see *H. speciosa*. *H. glaucophylla* (*H. darwiniana* of gardens), erect, bushy habit to 1m; stems slender, purple-brown; leaves lanceolate, 1–1·5cm long, grey-green; flowers white in racemes 2–4cm long. *H.g.* Variegata (*H. darwiniana* Variegata), leaves irregularly cream-margined; plants in cultivation in Britain tend to have longer, narrower leaves (to 20 × 4mm); in addition the name is sometimes mistakenly used by nurserymen for forms of *H. albicans* and *H. pinguifolia*. *H.* × Great Orme, probably derived from *H. speciosa* and 1 or more other species; much-branched, spreading habit, to 1m or more tall; leaves 3–7·5cm long, oblong-elliptic, reddish-tinted, glossy flowers pink, fading white, in racemes to 10cm or so long, summer to autumn. *H. hectori*, whipcord; erect, rather rigid habit, 20–70cm tall; stems and 2–2·5mm long leaves yellowish-brown to deep yellow-green; flowers white, sometimes pink-tinted in spikes of up to 15. *H. hulkeana*, of open habit, sometimes rather gaunt, to 60cm or more; leaves 3–7cm long (including winged stalk), broadly ovate to oblong-elliptic, toothed, glossy; flowers lavender to lilac, 6–8mm wide in terminal panicles 15–30cm or more long; among the most distinctive and beautiful of hebes, best at the foot of a sunny wall, and hardier than often stated. *H.* La Seduisante, see *H. speciosa*. *H. macrantha*, usually erect, sometimes decumbent, rather straggly when old; leaves 1·5–3cm long, elliptic to obovate, toothed; flowers white, to 3cm wide, in 2–6 flowered racemes from upper leaf-axils, often abundantly; the largest-flowered species. *H.* × Midsummer Beauty, derived from *H. salicifolia* and probably another hybrid involving *H. speciosa*; leaves oblong-lanceolate, slender-pointed, up to 10cm long, purple-flushed when young; flowers lavender-purple, in racemes to 13cm long. *H. ochracea*, whipcord; similar to, and confused with, *H armstrongii* in gardens, but rarely above 60cm tall and usually with arching, frond-like branches creating a flat-topped appearance; shoot-tips ochre-

Top: *Hebe* × Carl Teschner
Right: *Hebe brachysiphon*
Far right: *Hebe* × *andersonii* Variegata

yellow imparting an almost bronze-yellow hue to the whole plant; flowers white in spikes of up to 10. *H. odora* (*H. buxifolia* of gardens), variable habit, generally bushy and rounded to 1·5m or more tall; leaves elliptic-ovate, 1–1·5cm long, sometimes more, dark lustrous green above, margins bevelled; flowers white, in 3–5 terminal clustered spikes. *H. pinguifolia* (*H. carnosula*), variable habit, but in gardens usually spreading, decumbent, to 23cm tall; leaves more or less spreading, broadly ovate, concave, 1–1·5cm long, matt-glaucous; flowers white in dense, branched spikes 2–5cm long, several at stem tips; the plant known as *H. carnosula* tends to have broader, obovate leaves. *H.p.* Pagei (*H. pageana*), leaves intensely glaucous, oblong-elliptic; doubtless of hybrid origin. *H. propinqua*, much like a more compact, green-leaved *H. cupressoides* with white flowers. *H. rakaiensis*, dense, rounded habit to 1m, but slow-growing; leaves 1·2–2cm long, elliptic to obovate, bright, somewhat glossy green; flowers white in 3–5cm long racemes; much confused with *H. subalpina* in British gardens. *H. recurva*, akin to *H. albicans*, but the type plant has leaves narrowly lanceolate, spreading to reflexed, more or less glaucous and racemes tapered; this should be distinguished by the cultivar name *H.r.* Aoira (a misspelling of Aoere, the river beside which it was collected) to differentiate between it and broader-leaved, perhaps hybrid forms. *H. salicifolia*, vigorous, bushy, 2–4m tall; leaves 5–15cm long, lanceolate to oblong-lanceolate, slender-pointed, usually spreading; flowers white in racemes to 15cm or more long; the parent of many, usually large-leaved hardy hybrids. *H.* × Simon Delaux, see next entry. *H. speciosa*, rounded habit, 1–2m tall in warm areas; leaves broadly elliptic to obovate-oblong, to 10cm long, dark glossy green; flowers red-purple in racemes to 10cm or more long; not reliably hardy and best in warm areas or over-wintered under glass in areas of hard frost; the parent of all the large-leaved, coloured-flowered cultivars; the type plant is rare in gardens, being represented by hybrid cultivars such as *H.s.* Alicia Amhurst (*H.s.* Royal Purple, *H.s.* Veitchii), deep purple-blue; *H.s.* Gauntlettii, salmon-pink; *H.s.* La Seduisante, magenta-purple; *H.s.* Simon Delaux, crimson. *H. subalpina* (*H. montana*, *H. monticola*), rounded, dense habit, 1–2m tall; leaves lanceolate, 2·5–4cm long, glossy; flowers white in racemes 2–3cm long; plants under this name in gardens are often *H. rakaiensis*. *H. traversii*, see *H. brachysiphon*.

Hedera

(Latin for ivy). ARALIACEAE. A genus of 5–15 species of evergreen climbers from W. and C. Europe, Mediterranean to Caucasus, Himalaya to Japan. They have climbing sterile or juvenile, and non-climbing fertile or adult stems, the former bearing pads of short adhesive roots and alternate, ovate, often palmately lobed leaves, the latter usually with smaller, narrower, unlobed leaves and terminal umbels of small, greenish, 5-petalled flowers followed by globular, blackish berries. Grow in any well-drained soil in sun or shade, providing support for the climbing stems, ideally on trees or walls; without support, ivy forms good ground cover in sites too shady for most other plants. Cuttings rooted from fertile stems form non-climbing bushes known as tree ivies. All ivies make good pot plants for the home. Plant autumn or spring. Propagate by cuttings spring to early autumn or from ripe seed.
Species cultivated: *H. amurensis*, see *H. colchica* Amurensis. *H. canariensis* (*H. helix c.*), Canary Is to Azores, N.W. Africa; stems often purple-red; leaves on juvenile shoots broadly ovate-cordate, shallowly 3–5 lobed, to 15cm or more wide, dark glossy green; not totally hardy and outside needs a sheltered wall. *H.c.* Gloire de Marengo, leaves mostly unlobed, green and grey-green with an irregular, creamy-white margin. *H. colchica* (*H. helix c.*), Persian ivy; Caucasus to N. Iran; robust and vigorous; leaves ovate, heart-shaped, to 25cm long by 18cm wide, dark glossy green, leathery, sometimes irregularly toothed. *H.c.* Amurensis, leaves to 30cm or more with tiny pointed teeth, origin obscure but not from Amur, USSR; *H.c.* Dentata, leaves smaller, paler and less glossy, distantly toothed; *H.c.* Dentata Variegata, green and grey-green with irregular, creamy-yellow margins. *H. helix*, common or English ivy; Europe to the Caucasus; stems to 30cm tall on trees; leaves broadly ovate, 3–5 lobed, dark glossy green, 3–10cm wide, those on fertile stems ovate to almost diamond-shaped; a very variable species, frequently producing mutants, the leaves of which vary enormously in size, shape, number and depth of lobes and shades of green, several being variegated in various ways; the following is a selection of well-tried sorts: *H.h.* Buttercup, leaves bluntly 3–5 lobed, cordate, golden-yellow, ageing yellow-green; *H.h.* Conglomerata Erecta, perpetually juvenile, non-climbing, stems erect to decumbent to 60cm or more long; leaves very small, closely packed in 2 parallel ranks; *H.h.* Glacier, leaves small, 3-lobed, green, mottled grey, irregularly margined white; *H.h.* Goldheart (*H.h.* Jubilee), leaves small, dark, with central, bright yellow blotch; *H.h.* Green Ripple, matt dark green, lobes slender, the middle one much longer. *H.h. hibernica*, Irish ivy, now known as a distinct and naturally occurring race of common ivy from Ireland, W. Britain, N. and N.W. France; commercial clone, best designated as a cultivar, *H.h.* Hibernica, has larger, usually 5-lobed leaves wider than long, to 15cm by 10cm long, bright green, those on fertile stems being broader and cordate; *H.h.* Marginata, leaves small, scarcely lobed, margined white, often suffused pink in winter: also listed as *H.h.* Marginata Rubra, *H.h.* M. Tricolor, *H.h.* M. Elegantissima; *H.h.* Sagittifolia, leaves 5-lobed, central one very much larger, triangular.

Helenium

(Greek *helenion*, for a plant named after Helen of Troy, used by Linnaeus for this genus). Sneezeweed. COMPOSITAE. A genus of about 40 species of annuals and herbaceous perennials from N. and S. America. 1 species and its hybrid cultivars is generally available: *H. autumnale*, N. America; herbaceous, clump-forming perennial to 1·5m tall; stems

Top left: *Hedera helix* Goldheart
Top: *Hedera colchica* Dentata Variegata
Centre above: *Helenium* Coppelia
Above: *Helenium autumnale*

Above: *Helenium* Wyndley
Centre right: *Helianthemum oerlandicum alpestre* Serpyllifolium
Far right: *Helianthus × multiflorus* Triomphe de Gard
Below right: *Helianthus annuus*

branched above, erect, leafy; leaves 5–15cm long, elliptic to linear-lanceolate, broader at base; flowerheads yellow, 5cm or more wide, the discs almost globose, late summer; most of the cultivars are of hybrid origin with several other allied species, notably the similar *H. bigelovii* from W. USA, some forms of which have orange-yellow rays and soft brown disc florets: *H.* Bruno, 1m tall, mahogany-red; *H.* Butterpat, 90–100cm tall, rich yellow; *H.* Coppelia, 90cm tall, coppery-orange; *H.* Pumilum Magnificum, 75–80cm tall, clear yellow, summer to late autumn; *H.* Wyndley, 65–90cm tall, yellow, flecked orange-brown. Grow in well-drained but moisture-retentive soil in sunny site. Plant autumn to spring. Propagate by division at planting time.

Helianthemum

(Greek *helios*, sun, and *anthemum*, a flower). Sun or rock rose. CISTACEAE. A genus of about 100 species of annuals, perennials and small shrubs from Europe, Mediterranean, Canary Is to Azores, N. Africa to Iran and C. Asia. They have alternate, ovate, to oblong, lanceolate or linear leaves, and 5-petalled, widely expanded flowers, like small, single roses, in terminal racemes. Grow in any well-drained soil in a sunny site. Plant spring or autumn. Propagate by cuttings with a heel in summer, pot when rooted and over-winter in a cold frame, or seed in spring.

Species cultivated: *H. alpestre*, see *H. oelandicum*. *H. apenninum* (*H. polifolium*), S. and W. Europe including S. England, W. Germany; similar to *H. nummularium*, but leaves narrower and grey to white-felted; flowers white, rarely pink, summer; probably 1 parent of some of the grey-leaved cultivars listed under *H. nummularium*. *H. chamaecistus*, see *H. nummularium*. *H. lunulatum*, Italian Maritime Alps; small, tufted, more or less erect shrub to 15cm or more tall; leaves to 1cm long, elliptic-oblong to lanceolate; flowers 1cm or more wide, the petals yellow with basal orange blotch, summer. *H. nummularium* (*H. chamaecistus*, *H. vulgare*), common sun or rock rose; Europe; mat-forming; stems prostrate to ascending; leaves ovate to oblong or lanceolate, downy beneath; flowers 2·5–3·5cm wide, golden-yellow, some sub-species cream, white, pink, orange. *H.n. pyrenaicum*, Pyrenees; leaves felted beneath, flowers pink, the main parent of many garden cultivars: *H.* Ben Hope, leaves grey-green, flowers carmine with orange centre; *H.* Jubilee, flowers double, primrose-yellow; *H.* Mrs C. W. Earle (*H.* Fireball), double scarlet; *H.* Rhodanthe Carneum, foliage silvery-grey, flowers pink with orange centre (perhaps a form of *H. apenninum*); *H.* Wisley Primrose, leaves grey-green, flowers single, primrose-yellow with deeper eye; *H.* Wisley White, white. *H. polifolium*, see *H. apenninum*. *H. oelandicum* (*H. alpestre*), spreading habit, to 20cm tall; leaves elliptic to linear-lanceolate, 1–1·5cm long; flowers 1cm or more wide, yellow, summer. *H.o. alpestre*, prostrate habit, flowers 2cm wide; *H.o. alpestre* Serpyllifolium, leaves smaller than type, grey-green. *H. serpyllifolium*, see previous entry. *H. vulgare*, see *H. nummularium*.

Helianthus

(Greek *helios*, sun, and *anthos*, flower). Sunflower. COMPOSITAE. A genus of 110–150 species of annuals and herbaceous perennials from N. and S. America. The perennial species may be fibrous-rooted, tuberous or rhizomatous, forming clumps or

colonies of erect, branched stems bearing ovate to lanceolate leaves and several daisy-like flower-heads, usually with ray florets in shades of yellow. Grow in any well-drained but not dry soil in a sunny site. Plant perennials autumn to spring, propagating by division at the same time. Sow seed of annuals *in situ* in spring, in humus-rich soil for big plants.

Species cultivated: *H. annuus*, N. America, Mexico; annual to 3m or more; leaves ovate, to 30cm long; flower-heads to 30cm wide, ray florets orange-yellow, rarely purple-red. *H.a.* Californicus, 2m tall, yellow heads double. *H. atrorubens* (*H. sparsifolius*), E. USA; 1·5–2m tall; leaves ovate, rough-haired, to 18cm long; flower-heads about 5cm wide, rays rich yellow, disc purple-black. *H.a.* Monarch, flower-heads semi-double, much larger than type. *H. debilis* (*H. cucumerifolius*), S. USA; annual to 2m; leaves triangular-ovate to lanceolate, 4–8cm long; flower-heads to 7·5cm wide, rays yellow, sometimes purple, summer to autumn; crossed with *H. annuus* to create more robust, taller plants with ray florets in shades of yellow, red, purple, bronze, eg *H.* Excelsior. *H. decapetalus*, E. USA; 1–1·5m tall; leaves lanceolate to ovate, to 20cm long; flower-heads 5–7·5cm wide, rays pale yellow; represented in gardens by its hybrid *H.×multiflorus* (*H. decapetalus×H. annuus*), that is somewhat larger and more robust; cultivars are: *H.×m.* Capenoch Star, light yellow; *H.×m.* Loddon Gold, double rich yellow; *H. × m.* Triomphe de Gard, semi-double clear yellow. *H. orgyalis*, see next species. *H. salicifolius* (*H. orgyalis*), S.E. USA; stems 1–2m tall; leaves narrowly lanceolate, to 20cm long; flower-heads 5cm wide, rays yellow, disc purple-brown, early autumn. *H. sparsifolius*, see *H. atrorubens*. *H. tuberosus*, Jerusalem artichoke, grown for its roots.

Helichrysum

(Greek *helios*, sun, *chrysos*, golden; after flower-heads of some species). Everlasting, immortelle. COMPOSITAE. A genus of 300–500 species of annuals, perennials, sub-shrubs and shrubs from Europe, Africa, S. India, Sri Lanka, Australasia. They may be tufted or clump-forming, with alternate, ovate to linear, usually hairy leaves. The flower-heads are entirely composed of disc florets, but the surrounding bracts (involucre) are chaffy, sometimes coloured and petal-like. Species in the latter group, eg *H. bracteatum*, are dried and used for winter flower arrangements. All the species described are hardy or half-hardy. Grow in well-drained soil in a sunny site, the half-hardy ones in sheltered places or over-wintered in a frost-free greenhouse. Plant spring, the hardy kinds also in autumn. Propagate shrubby and perennial sorts by cuttings from late spring to late summer, clump-formers also by division at planting time; all species from seed under glass in spring. The annual *H. bracteatum* is best sown in mid spring at 18°C, the seedlings pricked off into boxes at 5cm apart in good potting soil, harden off and plant out early summer.

Species cultivated: *H. alveolatum*, see *H. splendidum*. *H. anatolicum*, see *H. plicatum*. *H. angustifolium*, see *H. italicum*, *H.i. serotinum*. *H. bellidioides*, New Zealand; mat-forming, soft, evergreen shrub; leaves to 6mm or more long, ovate, dark green above, white-felted beneath; flower-heads solitary, bracts white; plants from lowland provenances are not reliably hardy everywhere. *H. bracteatum* (*H. macranthum*), Australia; half-hardy annual, 75–120cm tall; leaves oblong-lanceolate, to 13cm long; flower-heads to 5cm, the spreading, petal-like bracts red, orange, pink, yellow, white, summer to early autumn; the species rarely seen, being represented by *H.b.* Monstrosum, having larger heads with more bracts; several strains are available including *H.b.* Nanum, to 30cm or more. *H. coralloides*, New Zealand; erect shrublet to 30cm (sometimes twice this in the wild); leaves 5mm long, scale-like, overlapping, white-woolly; flower-heads solitary, to 6mm wide; rare in cultivation, needs sheltered scree or dry wall or alpine house. *H. italicum* (*H. angustifolium*, *H. serotinum*), curry plant; S. Europe; sub-shrub, to 60m when in bloom; pungently aromatic; leaves linear, 1–3cm long, thinly white-felted; flower-heads 2–3mm wide, yellow, in dense terminal clusters, summer; *H.i. serotinum* (*H. angustifolium*), longest leaves to 4cm long, flower-heads 3–4mm. *H. macranthum*, see *H. bracteatum* *H. marginatum* (of gardens), see next species. *H. milfordiae* (*H. marginatum*), Basutoland, mountains of Natal; cushion-forming; leaves 8–12mm long, obovate to lanceolate, silvery-haired, in rosettes; flower-heads to 2·5cm wide, bracts white, sometimes tipped crimson, solitary on stems to about 10cm tall, early summer; alpine house or scree. *H. orientale*, S.E. Europe; sub-shrub, to 40cm tall; leaves obovate, to 7cm long, grey-felted; flower-heads about 1cm wide, straw-yellow, in terminal clusters, early autumn. *H. petiolatum*, S. Africa; as seen in British gardens, trailing shrub, eventually forming wide carpets; leaves broadly ovate, heart-shaped, to 4cm long, white-felted; flower-heads small, creamy-white to biscuit-coloured in terminal heads, not often seen on young plants; usually grown as a summer bedding plant but sometimes survives the winter outside in mild dry areas. *H. plicatum* (*H. anatolicum*), S. E. Europe, W. Asia; woody-based perennial about 40cm tall; leaves linear, 1–10cm long, grey-downy; flower-heads to 1cm wide, yellow, in dense terminal clusters, summer. *H. rosmarinifolium* (*Ozothamnus r.*), S. E. Australia; erect shrub to 2m or more; stems grey-white; leaves linear, 1·5–4cm long, dark green above, white-felted beneath; flower-heads white, 3–5mm long, in dense clusters, summer; needs a sheltered site, but much hardier than sometimes supposed. *H. selago*, New Zealand; dense shrublet 15–30cm tall; leaves 3–4mm long, scale-like, overlapping, glossy outside, woolly within; flower-heads solitary, dull white, 6mm wide, summer alpine house, dry wall, scree, *H. serotinum*, see *H. italicum*. *H. sibthorpii* (*H. virgineum*), N. E. Greece; tufted, woody-based perennial to 10cm or more tall; leaves oblong to narrowly spathulate, white-woolly, 1·5–6cm long; flower-heads white, 1·5cm wide, in clusters of 1–3, late spring; best in alpine house or scree. *H. splendidum* (*H. alveolatum*, *H. trilineatum*), S.

Left above: *Helichrysum bracteatum*
Top: *Helichrysum italicum*
Centre: *Helichrysum milfordiae*
Above: *Helichrysum bellidioides*

Africa; small, spreading shrub with erect stems to 30cm or more; leaves silvery-woolly, oblong, prominently 3-veined to 2cm long; flower-heads tiny, yellow, in rounded terminal clusters, late summer. *H. trilineatum*, see *H. splendidum*. *H. virgineum*, see *H. sibthorpii*.

Helictotrichon

(Greek *helictos*, twisted, and *trichon*, a hair – alluding to the basally twisted awns in the spikelet). GRAMINEAE. A genus of about 90 species of grasses, mainly from Europe, Africa, Asia. 1 species is generally available: *H. sempervirens* (*Avena s.*, *Avena candida*), S.W. Europe; densely clump-forming; leaves up to 45cm long, arching, grey-green; flowering stems 60–120cm tall, panicles nodding, loose, 5–20cm long, usually purple-tinted, summer. Grow in any well-drained soil, preferably in sun, although light shade is tolerated. Plant and propagate by division in spring.

Heliopsis

(Greek *helios*, sun, and *opsis*, like – alluding to the likeness to sunflower). COMPOSITAE. A genus of 12 species of annuals and perennials from N. America. 1 species, its forms and cultivars, is generally available: *H. helianthoides*, E. N.America; clump-forming, to 1·5m tall; leaves in opposite pairs, lanceolate to oblong-ovate, slender-pointed, toothed; flower-heads yellow, to 6·5cm wide, autumn; represented in gardens largely by *H.h. scabra* (*H. scabra*), leaves rounded at base, rough-textured. *H.h.s.* Gigantea, larger than type, deep yellow; *H.h.s.* Golden Plume, double, orange-yellow, 1m tall; *H.h.s.* Goldgreenheart, double, chrome-yellow, greenish-centred; *H.h.s.* Incomparabilis, almost fully double, orange, zinnia-like. Culture as for *Helianthus*.

Heliotropium

(Greek *helios*, sun, and *tropé*, turning – referring to the now disproved notion that the flowers turned with the sun). Heliotrope, cherry pie. BORAGINACEAE. A genus of about 250 species of annuals, sub-shrubs and shrubs from the tropics to warm temperate regions. The species generally grown are tender shrubs, having alternate oblong-lanceolate leaves and small, salver-shaped, 5-lobed, very fragrant flowers in monochasial cymes. Greenhouse, minimum temperature 7–10°C, well-ventilated and lightly shaded in summer, or then

Top left: *Helictotrichon sempervirens*
Left: *Heliopsis helianthoides scabra* Golden Plume
Below: *Heliotropium arborescens*

stood or planted out. Pot or repot in any standard potting mixture, spring. Cut back previous season's growth by ⅔ in late winter. Harden off in early summer and plant out when fear of frost has passed or pot on and flower under glass. Plants lifted from open ground in autumn should have all current season's stems cut back by ½ and be kept only just moist during the winter. Propagate by cuttings from cut-back plants in spring, or more mature growth in late summer. Seed may also be sown in late winter at about 18°C, the seedlings pricked off about 5cm apart each way, then singly into 9cm pots.
Species cultivated: *H. arborescens* (*H. peruvianum*), common heliotrope; Peru; shrub to 2m tall; leaves to 7·5cm long, deep green and finely wrinkled; flowers to 6mm long, violet or lilac, in branched cymes to 7cm or more wide, late spring to autumn. *H. corymbosum*, Peru; shrub to 1·2m tall; similar to *H. arborescens*, leaves narrower, flowers to twice as large; garden cultivars are reputedly hybrids between this and *H. arborescens*, and often listed as *H.* × *hybridum* (although the name has no botanical standing), having flowers in shades of deep violet-purple to white. *H. peruvianum*, see *H. arborescens*.

Helipterum

(Greek *helios*, sun, and *pteron*, a wing – the pappus on the fruit – seed – is composed of radiating plumose bristles like a diagramatic sun). Everlasting. COMPOSITAE. A genus of 60–90 species of annuals, perennials, sub-shrubs and shrubs from S. Africa and Australia. They have alternate simple leaves and flower-heads of similar structure to those of *Helichrysum*. The perennial species described here are hardy in sharply drained soil or scree in a sunny site. Plant perennials in spring or autumn. Sow annuals *in situ* in ordinary soil towards the end of spring or raise under glass in mid spring at about 16°C, planting out in early summer.
Species cultivated: *H. albicans*, S.E. Australia including mountains of Tasmania; tufted perennial; leaves mostly basal obovate-oblong to linear, white-woolly; flower-heads golden-yellow, 2·5–3·5cm wide, solitary on stems to 20cm tall, summer. *H. anthemoides*, S.E. Australia; tufted, no basal leaves; stems erect, to 30cm tall, clad with grey-green linear leaves to 1cm long; flower-heads solitary, white, 2–3cm wide, summer. *H. roseum* (*Acroclinium r.*), W. Australia; annual, to 40cm; leaves linear to lanceolate, about 6cm long; flower-heads solitary, to 5cm wide, pink to white, summer to autumn.

Left: *Helipterum albicans*
Above: *Helleborus orientalis* hybrid
Right: *Helleborus lividus corsicus*

Helleborus

(ancient Greek name *helleboros* for *H. orientalis*). RANUNCULACEAE. A genus of 20 species of evergreen and deciduous perennials from Europe and Mediterranean to Caucasus – 1 in China. There are 2 distinct groups: **1** clump-forming, most of the leaves springing from ground level; **2** tufted, shrub-like plants, all the leaves borne on erect biennial stems. Leaves palmate or pedate, deeply cut into 3–11 lobes or leaflets, more in a few species; flowers bowl-shaped or flat, of 5–6, broad, petal-like sepals, the petals transformed into nectaries (honey leaves). Grow in any well-drained, limy, preferably humus-rich soil in sun or light shade. Plant autumn or after flowering. Propagate by careful division immediately after flowering or from seed as soon as ripe. Dried seed may take up to 18 months or more to germinate. Seedlings take 2–3 years to flower.
Species cultivated: *H. argutifolius*, see *H. lividus corsicus*. *H. atrorubens* (of gardens), group 1; leaves pedate, to 30cm wide, leaflets about 9, broadly lanceolate; flowers bowl-shaped, up to 5cm wide, nodding, red-purple, shaded green, winter. *H. corsicus*, see *H. lividus corsicus*. *H. cyclophyllus*, see note under *H. orientalis*. *H. foetidus*, stinking hellebore; W. Europe; group 2; stems 30–80cm tall; leaves pedate, about 23cm wide, leaflets 7–11, narrowly lanceolate, toothed; flowers nodding, cup-shaped, 1–3cm wide, pale green, edged brownish-purple, winter to spring. *H. lividus*, Majorca; group 2; stems to 30cm, sometimes more; leaves trifoliate, leaflets unequally ovate-lanceolate, entire to irregularly toothed, deep glossy green marbled with white veins above, purplish beneath; flowers bowl-shaped, yellow-green, flushed purplish-pink, spring; not reliably hardy and needs a warm corner or frost-free greenhouse. *H.l. corsicus* (*H. corsicus*, *H. argutifolius*), robust, to 60cm or more tall; leaflets clear glossy green, regularly spiny-toothed; flowers brighter yellow-green than type, larger, without purple flush. *H.l.* Sternii (*H.l. lividus* × *H.l. corsicus*), group of hybrids intermediate between the parents, very variable in the degree of leaf marbling, toothing and flower colour. *H. niger*, Christmas rose; E. Alps, Apennines: group **1**, leaves to 30cm wide, leaflets 7–9, ovate, irregularly toothed, dark green; flowers bowl-shaped, 5–10cm wide, usually pure white but sometimes green or pink-tinged, on stems 15–30cm tall, winter, usually starting the end of mid winter, sometimes before. *H.n.* Potters Wheel, flowers 10cm or more wide. *H. orientalis*, Greece, Turkey; leaves palmate to pedate, 30–40cm wide, leaflets 5–11, broadly lanceolate,

doubly toothed; flowers bowl-shaped, to 7·5cm wide, creamy-white, sometimes tinged pink, on stems 60cm tall, spring. There are many hybrids in gardens under the name *H. orientalis*, some with cultivar names, derived from *H. cyclophyllus* (similar bright yellow-green flowered species), *H. abschasicus* (deep red-purple), *H. guttatus* (much like *H. orientalis* but red-purple spotted within), and possibly *H. purpurascens* (deep purple with a bluish sheen); the cultivars range from white, through shades of pink, red-purple, to almost black. *H.* × *sternii*, see *H. lividus* Sternii. *H. viridis*, green hellebore; W. and N.W. Europe; group 1; leaves palmate to pedate, to 23cm wide, leaflets 7–13 broadly lanceolate, very coarsely toothed; flowers 4–5cm wide, deep green with greyish sheen, winter to spring. *H.v. occidentalis*, leaves larger than type; flowers 4cm, dark green; stands deep shade.

Helxine – see *Soleirolia.*

Hemerocallis

(Greek *hemera*, day, and *kallos*, beauty – the flowers last a day only). LILIACEAE. A genus of 15–20 species of herbaceous perennials from C. Europe to E. Asia. They are clump-forming, with arching, linear, keeled leaves and lily-like, 6-tepalled, funnel-shaped flowers in terminal branched clusters. Grow in any ordinary soil, preferably humus-rich and moisture-retentive, in sunny sites. Most species succeed well near water. Plant autumn or spring. Propagate by division at planting time or from seed sown when ripe or during the spring.

Species cultivated: *H. disticha* Flore Pleno, see *H. fulva* Kwanso. *H. flava*, see *H. lilioasphodelus*. *H. fulva*, Europe to Siberia; stems 80–100cm tall; leaves 40–60cm long; flowers about 10cm long, buff-orange, summer. *H.f.* Kwanso (*H. disticha* Flore Pleno), flowers double, tinted red and copper. *H. lilioasphodelus* (*H. flava*), S. E. Europe to Siberia; stems 60–90cm tall; leaves to 60cm long; flowers to 10cm long, clear yellow, fragrant, spring. *H. middendorffii*, E. Asia, including Korea, Japan; leaves 40–60cm long; flowers to 7cm long, orange-yellow from brown-tipped buds, fragrant, tightly clustered on stems 30cm or more tall, early summer. *H. minor*, E. Asia; stems to 45cm tall; leaves grassy, 40–50cm long; flowers to 10cm long, clear yellow, brown-tinted in bud, spring; among several species being used to create smaller garden hybrids. *H. nana*, China; stems to 45cm tall; leaves to 35cm long, strongly recurved; flowers to 7cm long, orange, often reddish-brown in bud, fragrant, summer.

Hybrid cultivars: dozens of cultivars, raised in Britain and the USA, are available. They usually have larger flowers in a wide range of colours and all are easy to grow.

Hemlock spruce – see *Tsuga.*

Hepatica

(Greek *hepar*, the liver; at one time the leaves were thought to be good for liver complaints). Liverwort. RANUNCULACEAE. A genus of about 10 species of tufted perennials from the N. Hemisphere. They are closely related to *Anemone*, but differ in having small, calyx-like bracts on the flowering stems and long-stalked, 3–5 lobed, evergreen leaves. Culture as for *Anemone*, all species mentioned here thriving well in shade.

Species cultivated: *H. angulosa*, see *H. transsilvanica*. *H. nobilis* (*H. triloba*, *Anemone hepatica*), Europe; leaf-blades cordate with 3 ovate lobes; flowers 1·5–2·5cm wide with 6–10 blue-violet, pink or white sepals, on stems to 10cm tall, early spring. *H. transsilvanica*, C. Romania; similar to *H. nobilis* but less densely tufted, leaf-blades larger, 3–5 lobed; flowers 2·5–4cm wide, usually light violet or white.

Left: *Hemerocallis fulva*
Top left: *Hemerocallis* Golden Chimes
Above: *Hemerocallis* Stafford

Far left above: *Hepatica transsilvanica*
Above: *Heracleum mantegazzianum*
Left: *Hesperis matronalis*

Heracleum

(Greek *Herakleion* or *Herakles* for Hercules). Cow parsnip, hogweed. UMBELLIFERAE. A genus of 70 species of biennials and perennials from northern temperate zone and tropical mountains. They have tufts or rosettes of long-stalked, pinnately lobed leaves and erect stems bearing 1 to several flat-topped umbels of tiny, 5-petalled flowers. Some of the large species make statuesque garden plants but if the juice from the stems get onto skin exposed to strong sunlight severe blistering results. Grow in any ordinary garden soil in sun or partial shade. Plant autumn or spring. Propagate from seed when ripe or spring, the biennials sown *in situ* or transplanted to the permanent site while small. Perennials may be carefully divided in spring.
Species cultivated: *H. mantegazzianum*, cartwheel flower or giant hogweed; S.W. Asia, naturalized Europe; biennial, monocarpic or short-lived hairy perennial; stems ridged, robust, red-spotted, 2–4m tall, branched above, bearing several umbels to 15cm wide; leaves up to 1m long, arching; flowers white, to 2cm wide, summer. *H. minimum*, mountains of S.E. France; rhizomatous perennial; stems 15–25cm tall; leaves bipinnatisect, leaflets oblanceolate, to 1cm long, glossy; umbels about 6cm wide, flowers white. *H.m. roseum*, flowers pink, summer.

Herb Christopher – see *Actaea*.

Herb paris – see *Paris*.

Hermodactylus – see *Iris tuberosa*.

Heron's bill – see *Erodium*.

Hesperis

(Greek *hespera*, evening, the time when some species become fragrant). CRUCIFERAE. A genus of about 30 species of biennials and perennials from Europe, Mediterranean to Iran, W. China. 1 species is generally available and a popular cottage garden plant: *H. matronalis*, Dame's violet, sweet rocket; Europe, Asia; perennial, 70–120cm tall; leaves alternate, ovate to lanceolate, 10–20cm long, hispid; flowers lilac-purple, 4-petalled, 3–3·5cm wide, in long, terminal, stock-like racemes, fragrant in evening, summer. *H.m.* Candidissima (*H.m.* Nivea), flowers white; double-flowered forms in white and purple occur, but are seldom available. Grow in any well-drained, preferably humus-rich and limy soil in sun or light shade. Plant autumn or spring. Propagate from seed when ripe or spring, the doubles by cuttings or careful division in spring.

Heuchera

(for Johann Heinrich von Heucher, 1677–1747, German professor of medicine). SAXIFRAGACEAE. A genus of 30–50 species of evergreen perennials from N. America. They have tufts of long-stalked, rounded, cordate leaves from somewhat woody rhizomes, and slender, mainly leafless stems, bearing narrow panicles of small, 5-petalled flowers with saucer to urn-shaped calyx tubes well above the leaves. Grow in any well-drained, humus-rich soil in sun or light shade. Plant after flowering, autumn or spring. Propagate by division at planting time or from seed in spring.
Species cultivated: *H. americana*, alum root, rock geranium; stems to 45cm long; leaves 4–15cm long, with 5–9 rounded lobes, blunt-toothed, usually dark green and glistening, flushed and veined coppery-brown when young; flowers greenish or red-tinged, early summer. *H.* × *brizoides*, a group of hybrids between *H. sanguinea*, *H. micrantha* and perhaps *H. americana*, somewhat resembling the first parent with elegant panicles of small flowers ranging from near white (*H.* × *b.* Pearl Drops), light crimson (*H.* × *b.* Coral Cloud) to salmon-scarlet with bronzy foliage (*H.* × *b.* Splendour). *H. cylindrica*, N.W. N. America; stems to 75cm; leaves lobed and scalloped, to 6·5cm or so long; flowers greenish-yellow to cream, in spikes, summer. *H.c.* Greenfinch, flowers greenish-sulphur. *H. micrantha*, California, Oregon; stems 30–70cm tall; leaves 3–8cm long, 5–7 lobed, with pointed teeth; flowers glandular downy, calyx greenish or purple-tinted, petals white, early

summer. *H. sanguinea*, coral bells; S.W. USA, mountains of Mexico; stems 30–60cm tall; leaves 5–7 lobed, toothed, ciliate, somewhat marbled; flowers bell-shaped, crimson to scarlet, early summer; several good named cultivars are available, including: *H.s.* Shere, intense scarlet, to 45cm. *H. villosa*, E. N.America; stems to 60cm or more tall; leaves 10–30cm long, angular-lobed and toothed, downy beneath, coarsely-hairy above; flowers with white to pinkish petals, latish summer.

× Heucherella

(*Heuchera* × *Tiarella*). Hybrids blending the characters of the parents and requiring the same conditions as *Heuchera*, but more shade-tolerant. **Hybrids cultivated:** × *H. alba* Bridget Bloom (*H.* × *brizoides* × *T. wherryi*), clump-former favouring the heuchera parent with dainty panicles of light pink flowers to 45cm tall. × *H. tiarelloides* (*H.* × *brizoides* × *T. cordifolia*), spreading plant, but less vigorous than the *Tiarella* parent, bearing 30cm tall panicles of tiny, salmon-pink bells, early summer.

Hibiscus

(Greek name for mallow, *Malva*, used by Linnaeus for this closely allied genus). MALVACEAE. A genus of 250–300 species of annuals, perennials, shrubs and trees from the tropics and subtropics. They have alternate, ovate to palmate, often deeply lobed leaves, and solitary, 5-petalled, widely funnel-shaped flowers in upper leaf-axils. Grow the hardy shrubs, perennials and half-hardy annuals in well-drained soil in a sunny, preferably sheltered site. Grow the tender shrubs under glass, minimum temperature 8–10°C, humidity and light shade in summer. Plant hardy shrubs and perennials in autumn or spring. Propagate hardy shrubs by cuttings with a heel in late summer, bottom heat about 16°C, and hardy perennials by division or seed in spring. Propagate half-hardy annuals from seed sown in mid spring in a temperature of 15–18°C,

Above: *Heuchera* Red Spangles
Right: × *Heucherella alba* Bridget Bloom
Below right: *Hibiscus syriacus* Blue Bird

pricking off seedlings into a proprietary compst and planting out in early summer. *H. trionum* may also be sown *in situ* towards end of spring.

Species cultivated: *H. grandiflorus*, see next species. *H. moscheutos*, common rose mallow; E. USA; hardy perennial 1–2m; leaves to 20cm long, lanceolate to broadly ovate, often shallowly 3–5 lobed, white downy beneath; flowers 15–20cm wide, white, pink or rose-red with crimson centre, summer; needs a rich soil that never dries out to do well; can be grown as a half-hardy annual; *H. grandiflorus* generally covers hybrids with the allied *H. militaris* and more tender, deep red *H. coccineus*, *H.* Southern Belle being an F_1 strain of this origin with flowers to 28cm wide. *H. sinosyriacus*, C. China; much like the next species, but leaves broadly ovate, to 10cm long, and flowers larger. *H.s.* Lilac Queen, lilac-flushed, red-centred flowers; *H.s.* Ruby Glow, white, cerise-centred flowers. *H. syriacus*, E. Asia; deciduous hardy shrub to 2m or more tall; leaves up to 7cm long, triangular-ovate, mostly deeply 3 lobed; flowers 5–7·5cm wide in shades of pink, red, purple and violet-blue, late summer to autumn. *H.s.* Blue Bird, violet-blue, darker eye than type; *H.s.* Coelestis, pale violet-blue, reddish eye; *H.s.* Duc de Brabant, dark rose-purple,double; *H.s.* Monstrosus, white, maroon eye; *H.s.* Snowdrift, pure white – *H.s.* Totus Albus is virtually the same; *H.s.* Violaceus Plenus (*H.s.* Violet Clair Double), wine-purple, double – *H.s.* Puniceus Plenus and *H.s.* Roseus Plenus are scarcely distinguishable; *H.s.* Woodbridge, rich rose-piük, carmine eye. *H. trionum*, flower-of-an-hour; Africa and Asia; half-hardy annual to 60cm or more tall; leaves to 7cm long, palmately 3–5 lobed, the mid-lobe largest; flowers in terminal racemes, 3–6cm wide, ivory to primrose-yellow with brown-crimson eye, calyx hairy, inflated, purple-veined, summer; may need staking.

Hickory – see *Carya*.

Hieracium

(ancient Greek name *hierakion*, for various yellow-flowered composites, chosen by Linnaeus for this genus). Hawkweeds. COMPOSITAE. A genus of 700–1000 species of perennials from temperate regions, mainly N. Hemisphere. They are tufted or stoloniferous, with lanceolate to obovate leaves and flower-heads entirely of ligulate (ray) florets in corymbs or panicles – sometimes solitary. Many species are weedy and invasive and are best dead-headed to prevent seeding. Grow in any well- drained soil in a sunny site. Propagate from seed or by division in spring.

Species cultivated: *H. aurantiacum* (*H. brunneocroceum*), Grim the collier, fox and cubs; mountains of N. and E. Europe, naturalized elsewhere; stoloniferous, forming mats; leaves lanceolate to oblanceolate, 6–15cm or more long, hairy, pale to glaucous green; stems to 50cm tall with 1–4 smaller leaves, bearing dark, glandular hairs; flower-heads clustered, covered with long, dark hairs, florets orange to reddish, summer to autumn; can be invasive. *H. maculatum*, W. and C. Europe; tufted; stems to 50cm tall; leaves lanceolate to ovate, toothed, hairy, 5–15cm long, spotted and blotched brownish-purple; flower-heads glandular hairy, florets yellow, summer to autumn. *H. pilosella*, mouse-ear hawkweed; Europe; stoloniferous, forming mats; leaves spathulate to elliptic, white-hairy; flower-heads solitary, 2·5cm wide, florets pale yellow, red-striped beneath, on stems 10–20cm tall, early summer. *H. villosum*, mountains of Europe; tufted; stems to 30cm; leaves deciduous, oblong to ovate or oblanceolate, fluffy white hairy, to 10cm long; flower-heads 4–5cm wide, white-woolly, rays rich yellow, summer. *H. welwitchii*, name of no standing, origin unknown; tufted; stems to 50cm; leaves deciduous, ovate, grey-white felted, 8–12cm long; flower-heads thinly felted, rays yellow.

Top left: *Hibiscus trionum*
Left: *Hieracium villosum*
Above: *Hippophae rhamnoides*

Hippophae

(ancient Greek, probably for prickly spurge, but taken up by Linnaeus for this genus). ELAEAGNACEAE. A genus of 2 species of dioecious deciduous spiny shrubs from Europe and Asia, 1 of which is generally available: *H. rhamnoides*, sea buckthorn (range of genus mainly coastal); suckering shrub to 2m or more, sometimes a tree to 10m; leaves alternate, linear, 2–8cm long, silvery-scaled; flowers tiny, petalless, in small clusters, spring; fruit bright orange, rounded, 6–8mm long, often in abundance provided male and female plants are together. Grow in any well-drained soil in sunny sites. Plant autumn to spring. Propagate by suckers preferably in autumn, or from seed sown when ripe. The latter take 18 months or so to germinate, although up to 5 per cent may germinate the first spring, and large amounts are best stratified. Male plants generally have larger winter buds than the female plants.

Hoheria

(from the Maori *houhere*). MALVACEAE. A genus of 5 species of deciduous and evergreen trees and shrubs from New Zealand. They have alternate, lanceolate to ovate, coarsely toothed leaves and small, axillary cymes of 5-petalled, white, somewhat mallow-like flowers. Grow in well-drained, preferably humus-rich soil in a sheltered site, the evergreens against a wall in all but the mildest areas with little frost; the deciduous species are hardier. All species are subject to damage during severe winters. Plant spring. Propagate from seed or by layering in spring, or by cuttings with a heel late summer. Seed-raised plants pass through a juvenile phase when they are densely twiggy and bear much smaller, differently shaped leaves.

Species cultivated: *H. angustifolia* (*H. populnea a.*), evergreen, slender tree 5–10m tall under favourable conditions; leaves 2–3cm long, oblong to oblanceolate, coarsely, almost spiny-toothed; flowers to 1·5cm wide, late summer. *H. glabrata* (*H. lyallii g.*), like *H. lyallii* but stems and leaves glabrous or almost so, leaves greener, margins not lobed, sometimes more shrubby and flowering a little earlier. *H. lyallii* (*Plagianthus l.*), deciduous large shrub or small tree to 6m; leaves 5–10cm long, broadly ovate, margins incised into small lobes, grey-green with hoary down; flowers 2·5–4cm wide, latish summer. *H. populnea*, evergreen tree 5–10m or more tall; leaves broadly ovate to elliptic, 7–15cm long; flowers 2·5cm wide, late summer to autumn; variegated and purple-leaved forms are known. *H.p.* Sinclairii, more robust than type, larger leaves and flowers. *H. sexstylosa* (*H.p. lanceolata*), evergreen shrub or small tree to 6m tall; leaves 5–12cm long, lanceolate to narrowly ovate; flowers 2cm wide, late summer. *H.s.* Pendula, neat weeping habit; *H.s.* Glory of Amlwch, evergreen or almost so, leaves ovate, pale green, flowers to 4cm wide, in abundance, probably a hybrid with *H. glabrata*.

Holly – see *Ilex*.

Hollyhock – see *Althaea*

Left: *Hoheria glabrata*
Above: *Holodiscus discolor*

Holodiscus

(Greek *holo*, whole, *diskos*, disc – the base or disc of the flower is unlobed). ROSACEAE. A genus of 8 species of deciduous shrubs from W. N.America, 1 of which is generally cultivated: *H. discolor* (*Spiraea d.*, *S. ariaefolia*), ocean spray; California, S. Oregon; to 3m or more tall; branches gracefully arching; leaves 5–9cm long, broadly ovate, margins cut into small, toothed lobes, undersides villous or tomentose; flowers tiny, 5-petalled, creamy-white, about 4mm wide, carried in pendant, plume-like panicles 10–30cm long, summer. *H.d. delnortensis*, leaves white tomentose beneath, common garden form. Grow in any well-drained soil in sun or light shade. Plant autumn to spring. Propagate by semi-hard cuttings in late summer or hardwood cuttings in sheltered site in autumn.

Honesty – see *Lunaria*.

Honey locust – see *Gleditsia*.

Honeysuckle – see *Lonicera*.

Hop – see *Humulus*.

Hordeum

(old Latin name for barley). GRAMINEAE. A genus of about 20 species of annual and perennial grasses from northern temperate zone and S. America. 1 species is grown for its ornamental flower-spikes: *H. jubatum*, fox-tail barley, squirrel-tail grass; northern temperate zone; short-lived perennial or annual, tufted; leaves linear, to 15cm long by 3mm wide, rough; stems 30–60cm tall; spikes 7–13cm long, flattened, arching and plume-like, each spikelet with green to purple awns up to 7cm long, summer to autumn. Sow thinly *in situ* in spring.

Above: *Hordeum jubatum*
Top right: *Hosta* Thomas Hogg
Right: *Hosta fortunei* Aurea

Horminum

(ancient Greek for sage, transferred to this genus by Linnaeus). LABIATAE. A genus of 1 species of evergreen perennial closely allied to *Salvia*, but flowering stems usually leafless and upper lip of flower straight, more or less erect: *H. pyrenaicum*, dragon's mouth; C. Pyrenees, Alps; tufted; stems 10–30cm tall; leaves 3–7cm long, ovate to rounded or elliptic, dark green in rosettes reminiscent of *Ramonda*; flowers tubular, 2-lipped, 1·5–2cm long, dark bluish-violet or rose-purple in whorled spikes, summer. Grow in any well-drained soil in sun or light shade. Plant spring or autumn. Propagate from seed when ripe or spring, or by division at planting time.

Hornbeam – see *Carpinus*.

Horned poppy – see *Glaucium*.

Horse chestnut – see *Aesculus*.

Hortensia – see *Hydrangea macrophylla*.

Hosta

(*Funkia*). (for Nicholas Tomas Host, 1761–1834, Austrian botanist and doctor). Plantain lilies. LILIACEAE. A genus of about 40 species of herbaceous perennials from E. Asia, mainly Japan. They are clump-forming with long-stalked, lanceolate to ovate basal leaves and racemes of nodding, tubular, somewhat lily-like flowers. Grow in moisture-retentive, preferably humus-rich soil in light shade or sun. Plant autumn to spring. Propagate by division at planting time or from seed

in spring. Seed from garden sources seldom comes true to type.
Species cultivated (from Japan unless stated otherwise): *H. albomarginata*, leaf-blades to 15cm long, ovate-elliptic to narrowly lanceolate, narrowly white-bordered, sometimes plain green; racemes to 60cm tall, flowers about 5cm long, pale violet with deeper stripes, late summer; some botanists now call this *H. sieboldii* but there is risk of confusion with *H. sieboldiana* from a gardener's point of view. *H. crispula*, leaf-stalks short, blades ovate-lanceolate to elliptic, to 20cm long, margins strongly waved and broadly white-banded; racemes 50–80cm tall, flowers 4–5cm long, lavender, late summer to autumn; sometimes confused with *H. albomarginata*. *H. elata*, leaf-blades to 30cm long, ovate-elliptic, somewhat wavy; racemes to 90cm tall, flowers 5–6cm long, pale bluish-violet, summer; sometimes grown as *H. sieboldiana*, but deep, somewhat glossy green leaves distinguish it. *H. fortunei*, leaf-blades ovate-cordate, to 13cm long; racemes to 90cm tall, flowers dense, lilac to violet, about 4cm long, summer. *H.f.* Albopicta, leaves yellow with green border when young; *H.f.* Aurea, (*H.f.* Aurea-marginata), leaves all yellow when young; *H.f. hyacinthina*, leaves glaucous, flowers somewhat reddish-violet. *H. glauca*, see *H. sieboldiana*. *H.* × Honey Bells (reputedly *H. plantaginea* × *H. lancifolia*), much like *H. plantaginea* but more robust, racemes 1m or more tall, flowers white with purple lines, fragrant. *H. lancifolia*, leaf-blades to 18cm long, ovate-lanceolate, slender-pointed, glossy, strongly arching; racemes 40–60cm tall, flowers 4cm long, deep purple, late summer. *H.l. albomarginata*, see *H. albomarginata*. *H. plantaginea*, China; leaf-blades to 25cm long, ovate-cordate, lustrous pale green; racemes 60–75cm tall, flowers pure white, fragrant, 10–12cm long, late summer to autumn. *H.p. grandiflora*, perianth lobes longer than wide (broadly ovate in type species), leaves more elongated than type – an excellent garden form *H. rectifolia* (*H. longipes* of gardens), leaf-blades broadly lanceolate, up to 15cm long, dark green; racemes 60–90cm tall, flowers 5cm long, violet with darker lines, late summer. *H. sieboldiana* (*H. glauca*, *Funkia sieboldii*, not to be confused with *H. sieboldii* – see *H. albomarginata*), the most robust species; leaf-blades 25–38cm long, ovate, glaucous, thick-textured; racemes to 60cm or so, barely above foliage; flowers 4cm long, pale lilac, summer. *H.s. elegans*, leaves more intensely glaucous than type, somewhat corrugated; variegated forms are sometimes available. *H. sieboldii*, see *H. albomarginata*. *H. tardiflora* (*H. lancifolia t.*, *H. sparsa*), leaf-blades lanceolate, long-tipped, deep glossy green, to 15cm long; racemes 60cm tall, flowers 4–5cm long, pale lavender, autumn. *H.* Thomas Hogg, similar to *H. crispula*, but leaves less waved and pointed; also confused in gardens with *H. undulata* Albomarginata. *H. undulata* (*H. lancifolia u.*), leaf-blades to 15cm long, elliptic to ovate, strongly waved, with a central area of white; racemes up to 90cm tall, flowers 5cm long, pale violet to lavender, late summer. Several clones of *H. undulata* are in cultivation, differing in the amount of white in the leaves, *H.u. univittata* having a white central stripe only and less-waved leaves. *H.u.* Albomarginata, leaves green, narrowly white margined; *H.u. erromena*, pure green and only slightly waved foliage larger and more robust than type – presumably the original wild kind. *H. ventricosa*, leaf-blades broadly ovate-cordate, to 24cm long, deep, somewhat glossy green; racemes to 90cm tall, flowers about 5cm long, deep violet, late summer. *H.v.* Aureomaculata, leaves yellow-centred; *H.v.* Variegata, leaves yellow-margined.

Houseleek – see *Sempervivum*.

Houstonia

(for William Houstoun, 1695-1733, Scottish doctor and botanist who collected in C. America). Bluets. RUBIACEAE. A genus of 50 species of small annuals and perennials from USA and Mexico; by some botanists united with *Hedyotis* to form a 400 species genus also from Asia. The hardy species described here are tufted and spreading with slender stems, linear to rounded leaves, and tubular, 4-lobed flowers. Grow in moisture-retentive soil in light shade. Plant and propagate by division in spring.
Species cultivated: *H. caerulea*, E. N.America; annual or perennial; stems 5–20cm tall; leaves oblong-spathulate, 1-1·5cm long; flowers lilac to pale blue with a yellow eye, to 1cm long, spring to summer; often confused with next species. *H. michauxii* (*H. serpyllifolia*), E. USA; mat-forming; stem prostrate and rooting, then erect; leaves ovate to rounded to 1cm long; flowers milky-blue to violet, 9–13mm long, spring to summer; *H.m.* Fred Mullard (*H.m.* Mullards Variety), flowers clear blue.

Far left: *Hosta sieboldiana elegans*
Far left below: *Hosta fortunei hyacinthina*
Top left: *Hosta plantaginea*
Left: *Hosta ventricosa* Variegata
Below left: *Hosta undulata univittata*
Below: *Houstonia michauxii*

Houttuynia

(for Martin Houttuyn, 1720–94, Dutch naturalist). SAURURACEAE. A genus of 1 species of herbaceous perennial from Himalaya to Japan: *H. cordata*, rhizomatous, widely creeping, forming extensive colonies, may become invasive; stems 15–60cm tall, erect to decumbent, branched; leaves 5–7cm long, ovate-cordate, red-flushed when young, later somewhat glaucous and when grown in sunny places becoming richly coloured in autumn, pungent orange scent; flowers tiny, petalless, in dense, 2–3cm long spikes surrounded by 4 white, petal-like ovate bracts. *H.c.* Plena, flower-spikes composed of numerous small white bracts, summer to autumn. Grow in moist soil or by water in sunny sheltered sites. Plant and propagate by division in spring.

Humulus

(Low German name for hop in Latin form). Hop. CANNABIDACEAE (CANNABACEAE). A genus of 2 twining herbaceous perennials from the N. Hemisphere. They have opposite pairs of broad, palmately lobed leaves, and small, petalless, dioecious flowers, the males in loose panicles, the females in cone-like clusters of green bracts. The latter are used to flavour and assist the brewing processes of beer. Grow in any fertile, well-drained but not dry soil in sun or partial shade, providing support for the climbing stems. Plant autumn or spring. Propagate from seed in spring in a cold frame or by division at planting time. Cuttings of young shoots in spring. Sowings under glass in early spring at 13–16°C, can be grown as annuals.

Species cultivated: *H. japonicus*, Japanese hop; temperate E. Asia; to 6m or more tall, stems branched, scabrous; leaves long-stalked, 5–7 lobed, toothed, 5–12cm long and wide; male flowers in erect to arching panicles, 15–25cm long, females ovoid, 7–10mm long, late summer: *H.j.* Variegatus, leaves splashed and streaked white. *H.lupulus* (*H.americanus*), common or European hop; northern temperate zone; much like *H.japonicus* but leaves somewhat longer, 3–5 lobed; female flower clusters 1·5–2cm long, enlarging to 5cm as seed mature; *H.l.* Aureus, leaves flushed golden-yellow.

Hutchinsia

(for Ellen Hutchins, 1785–1815, Irish botanist). CRUCIFERAE. A genus of 1 species of evergreen perennial from Europe: *H. alpina*, mountains of S. and C. Europe; densely tufted; leaves pinnatisect with 3–7 segments; flowers white, 4-petalled, 6–9mm wide, in short racemes on leafless stems to 10cm tall, late spring to summer. *H.a. brevicaulis*, flowering stems to 5cm; *H.a. auerswaldii*, stems leafy, to 15cm long. Grow in well-drained, preferably sandy or gritty soil in sunny sites. Plant autumn or spring. Propagate from seed when ripe or spring, or by division in spring.

Hyacinthella – see *Pseudomuscari*.

Hyacinthus

(traditionally for *Hyakinthos*, a Greek youth accidentally killed by Apollo with a discus, but actually derived from an earlier non-Greek language – Thraco-pelasgian – and relating to the reflected blue of water). LILIACEAE. A genus of 1 species of bulbous plant, others formerly included in the genus being transferred to other genera, ie *Bellevalia*, *Brimeura*, *Hyacinthella* and *Pseudomuscari*. *H. azureus*, see *Pseudomuscari*. *H. candicans*, see *Galtonia*. *H. orientalis*, C. and E. Mediterranean; stem erect, robust, 20–30cm tall; leaves strap-shaped, channelled, 25–35cm long, in a basal cluster; flowers 2–3cm long, bell-shaped, with 6 mauve-purple to blue, recurved tepals, fragrant, in dense racemes opening with short young leaves, spring. *H.o. albulus*, Roman hyacinth; S. France; each bulb producing several smaller stems with

Left: *Houttuynia cordata* Plena
Bottom: *Humulus japonicus* Variegatus
Below: *Hyacinthus* Salmonette

loose racemes of white flowers – much like the original wild species. Many cultivars of *H. orientalis* are available, most more robust with very dense racemes in shades of red, pink, purple, blue, white and yellow. Grow in any well-drained, humus-rich soil in a sunny site. Plant autumn. Propagate by removing offsets when dormant or from seed when ripe. Seed from named cultivars seldom comes true to type. Plants may also be grown in pots or bowls for home, cool or cold greenhouse decoration. Pot bulbs as soon as available, setting them in fibre or commercial potting mixture the nose just above the surface. Put in a cool place, preferably plunged in peat, sand or weathered ashes outside, or in a cellar until well-rooted and with shoots 4–5cm tall; then bring into room or greenhouse at a temperature not above 15–18°C. Higher temperatures will result in erratic growth and poor-quality flowers. If flowers are wanted early to mid winter, specially prepared bulbs must be obtained or the smaller-spiked Roman hyacinths grown.

Hydrangea

(Greek *hydor*, water, and *aggos*, a jar – alluding to the tiny, cup-shaped seed capsules). HYDRANGEACEAE (SAXIFRAGACEAE). A genus of 23–80 species (depending on the authority) of evergreen and deciduous shrubs, small trees and climbers from northern temperate zone, C. and S. America. They have opposite pairs of lanceolate to oblong or ovate, toothed leaves and terminal corymbs or panicles of small flowers of 2 distinct types: normal or fertile with 4–5 petals, and sterile with 4–5, very much larger, petal-like sepals. Grow in well-drained but moisture-retentive soil enriched with humus, in partial shade or sun. Plant autumn or spring. Pruning is seldom required by most species, but *H. arborescens*, *H. macrophylla* and *H. paniculata* benefit from having 3-year-old stems removed near the base annually in early spring. Propagate from seed in spring under glass or cuttings in late summer, ideally with bottom heat about 15–18°C, also by layering in spring. *H. macrophylla* is frequently grown as a pot plant. For large specimens, take cuttings in spring, potting when rooted into 9cm pots of potting mixture and pinching out the tips at 3–4 pairs of leaves. Pot on successively in 13, 18 or 20cm containers and grow outside in a sheltered spot. Over-winter in a well-ventilated cold frame, and if early flowers are required bring into a minimum temperature of 7–10°C from the start of early spring onwards. Apply liquid feed at 2-weekly intervals when flower-

Far left: *Hyacinthus* Ostara
Far left below: *Hydrangea macrophylla* Blue Wave
Left: *Hydrangea macrophylla* Deutschland
Below: *Hydrangea paniculata*
Bottom: *Hydrangea quercifolia*

bud clusters show. Plants may be cut back to 10cm after flowering, repotted and grown on for another 1 to several years. Small plants with 1 good flower cluster will result from early to mid autumn rooted cuttings placed in 10–13cm pots and left unpinched. **Species cultivated:** *H. acuminata*, see *H. macrophylla serrata*. *H. anomala*, Himalaya, China; deciduous, self-clinging climber to 15m tall or more; stems clinging like ivy; leaves to 13cm or more long, ovate; corymbs 15–20cm wide, slightly convex, mainly of yellow-white fertile flowers, petals united and falling as cap, sterile flowers white, marginal, summer. *H.a. petiolaris*, climbing hydrangea; Japan, Sakhalin, Korea, Taiwan; leaves somewhat smaller than type and finely toothed; corymbs flatter, whiter. *H. arborescens*, S.E. USA; deciduous, well-branched shrub to 1·2m or more; leaves broadly ovate, 7–15cm long; corymbs 10–15cm wide, white, with a few marginal sterile flowers; summer to autumn; usually represented in gardens by *H.a.* Grandiflora, having all-sterile flowers. *H. aspera* (*H. villosa*, *H. strigosa*), E. Asia; deciduous, wide-spreading shrub 2–4m tall; leaves 10–25cm long, lanceolate to ovate, white-haired, densely so beneath; corymbs to 25cm wide, fertile flowers white to purplish, with conspicuous blue stamens, sterile ones white to lilac-pink (or blue-purple in some clones formerly called *H. villosa*). *H.a. sargentiana*, Hupeh, China; twigs thicker than type, bristly-haired, leaves ovate, to 30cm long; fertile flowers bluish to lilac, sterile ones white or pink-tinted. *H. bretschneideri*, see *H. heteromalla* Bretschneideri. *H. heteromalla*, Himalaya to China; deciduous shrub 2–3m tall; leaves 8–20cm long, ovate, densely to sparsely pubescent; corymbs white, to 30cm wide, with large, marginal, sterile flowers, summer. *H.h.* Bretschneideri, hardy in full exposure and with peeling bark. *H.hortensis*, see next species. *H. macrophylla* (*H. hortensis*), Japan; deciduous shrub to 2m; leaves broadly ovate to obovate, 10–15cm long; corymbs white, pink, purple, blue, 15–25cm wide, summer to autumn. *H.m. macrophylla* (*H.m. hortensia*, *H. hortensis*), corymbs entirely of sterile flowers or with a few fertile ones hidden beneath – many cultivars, known as Hortensias, are available; *H.m. normalis*, the wild type, having flat corymbs of fertile flowers ringed with large sterile ones – cultivars of this form, often with a few extra sterile flowers, are known as lacecaps; *H.m. serrata* (*H. acuminata*, *H. thunbergii*), 90–120cm tall, leaves narrower than type, more pointed, corymbs like *H.m. normalis* but smaller, sterile florets sometimes notched or toothed, hardier. Among several clones available are: *H.m.s.* Rosalba, sterile flowers white, blotched crimson; *H.m.s.* Grayswood, fertile flowers blue, sterile white, ageing pink to red; apart from these 2 cultivars and a few others, most forms of *H. macrophylla* vary in flower colour, depending on soil acidity and amount of aluminium present. Cultivars catalogued as blue will only be so on acid soils, ranging from purple to pink as the lime-content increases. Red or pink cultivars will take on purple or bluish tones on acid soils. Proprietary bluing compounds can be obtained, but are not always very effective on chalky soils. *H. paniculata*, China and Japan; large shrub or small tree if grown unpruned, but easily kept to 2m tall; leaves ovate, 7–15cm long; flowers creamy-white in pyramidal panicles 15–25cm long, sterile ones to the outside, late summer to autumn. *H.p.* Grandiflora, flowers mainly sterile, ageing pinkish; *H.p.* Praecox, panicles smaller than type but opening earlier, very hardy. *H. petiolaris*, see *H. anomala*. *H. quercifolia*, Oak-leaved hydrangea; S.E. USA; deciduous shrub, to 2m tall but often less, leaves broadly ovate with 5–7 triangular lobes, 8–20cm or more long, colouring in autumn; panicles bluntly pyramidal, 10–25cm long, of white fertile and sterile flowers, the latter ageing purplish. *H. sargentiana*, see *H. aspera*. *H. serrata*, see *H. macrophylla s.*

Right: *Hypericum polyphyllum*

Hypericum

(Greek *hypereikon*, for St John's wort; *hyper*, above, and *eikon*, picture: somewhat obscure reference to folklore notion that St John's wort keeps the Devil at bay). St John's wort. HYPERICACEAE (GUTTIFERAE). A genus of 300–400 species, mainly of perennials, sub-shrubs, shrubs and small trees, from temperate regions and tropical mountains. They have opposite pairs of rounded to linear leaves, often with pellucid or black dots, and terminal cymes or panicles of 5-petalled flowers, each with a prominent boss of strong, slender stamens. Grow in well-drained soil in a sunny site, although some species mentioned here thrive in shade. Plant autumn to spring. Propagate shrubs by cuttings in late summer, division, when possible, at planting time, and from seed in spring, perennials by division, cuttings and from seed, spring.

Species cultivated: *H. androsaemum*, tutsan; Europe to W. Asia, N. Africa; deciduous shrub 60–90cm tall; leaves 7–10cm long, ovate-cordate, sessile; flowers light yellow, about 2cm wide in cymes of 3–5, summer to autumn, followed by red to black, berry-like fruit; very shade-tolerant. *H. balearicum*, Balearic Is; evergreen shrub to 60cm tall; stems winged and warted; leaves to 1cm long, ovate to oblong, waved and curiously warty-corrugated; flowers solitary, fragrant, 3–4cm wide, petals narrow, yellow, summer to autumn; not hardy in cold winter areas, needing a sunny, sheltered site. *H. beanii*, similar to *H. pseudohenryi* and *H. forrestii* but stems slightly flattened and 4-lined towards the tips and just beneath the flowers; leaves blunt-tipped, sepals ovate, pointed or acuminate. *H.b.* Gold Cup, probably of hybrid origin, leaves lanceolate, pale red in autumn; flowers bright yellow, cup-shaped, to 6cm wide. *H. calycinum*, rose of Sharon, Aaron's beard, S.E. Bulgaria, Turkey; rhizomatous evergreen shrub 30–60cm tall, forming wide, dense colonies; leaves 4·5–8·5cm long, oblong to narrowly ovate; flowers usually solitary, bright yellow, 6–9cm wide, summer to autumn; excellent ground cover for partial shade but can be very invasive. *H. cerastoides* (*H. rhodoppeum* – 'rhodopeum' of catalogues), Balkan Peninsula; tufted perennial; stems prostrate to decumbent, forming mats; leaves oblong to ovate, 8–30mm long, grey-haired; flowers 2–4cm wide, bright yellow, summer. *H. coris*, Switzerland to N. and C. Italy, S.E. France; evergreen shrub or sub-shrub; stems 10–40cm long, prostrate or decumbent; leaves 4–18mm long, linear, usually in whorls of 4; flowers in pyramidal panicles to 12cm long, each one golden-yellow, streaked red, about 2cm wide, late summer. *H. elatum*, see *H.* × *inodorum*, *H. empetrifolium*, Greece, N. Albania; evergreen shrublet 30–50cm tall; stems slender, erect; leaves linear, 6–12mm long, in whorls of 3; flowers in panicles, 1–1·5cm wide, pale gold, late summer to autumn. *H. fragile*, Greece; tufted, woody-based perennial; leaves 2–7mm long, ovate to broadly oblong, glaucous; flowers solitary or in corymbs of up to 8, each about 2·5cm wide, yellow, tinged red, late summer; plants under this name in gardens are often *H. olympicum*. *H. forrestii* (*H. patulum forrestii*), Assam Himalaya to China; deciduous, spreading shrub to 1·5m or more tall; stems somewhat flattened at tips, but not lined or edged; leaves 2–4·5cm long, lanceolate to ovate, mucronate; flowers golden-yellow, saucer-shaped, 4–6·5cm wide, stamens ½ as long as petals, solitary or in 3s, summer to autumn; leaves persist until early winter and colour well; confused in gardens with *H. pseudohenryi*. *H.* Hidcote (possibly *H. forrestii* × *H. calycinum*), almost evergreen shrub, to 1·5m tall; leaves lanceolate, rich green above, pale and net-

veined beneath; flowers to 7cm wide, saucer-shaped, golden-yellow, summer to autumn. *H.* × *inodorum* (*H. elatum*), (*H. androsaemum* × *H. hircinum*), semi-evergreen shrub to 1·5cm tall; leaves 4–9cm long, broadly ovate to oblong-lanceolate, sessile, variably aromatic when bruised; flowers 1·5–3cm wide, yellow, profusely borne in terminal cymes; fruit ellipsoid, about 1cm long, reddish, then black. *H.* × *inodorum*, usually represented in gardens by *H.* × *i.* Elstead (*H. elatum* Elstead), fruit ripening salmon-red. *H.* × *moseranum* (*H. patulum* × *H. calycinum*), blends characters of parents – deciduous, weakly rhizomatous; flowers in small cymes, golden-yellow with reddish anthers, 5–6·5cm wide, summer to autumn; sometimes cut back to ground level in hard winters but soon regenerates from base. *H.* × *m.* Tricolor, leaves edged white, flushed pink. *H. olympicum*, Balkan Peninsula; tufted, woody-based perennial; stems decumbent to semi-erect, 15–36cm long; leaves 6–30mm long; lanceolate to narrowly oblong, glaucous; flowers bright yellow, 3–6cm wide, in small cymes, summer; much confused in past with *H. fragile*. *H. patulum*, S.W. China, naturalized Japan; semi or evergreen shrub to 1m tall; stem tips strongly flattened and 2–4 lined; leaves ovate to lanceolate-oblong, 2·5–6·5cm long, blunt and apiculate, dark green above, glaucous beneath; flowers about 5cm wide, cup-shaped, golden-yellow, singly or in small cymes; not always reliably hardy and rarely cultivated, but described here to distinguish it from the several different shrubs still grown under its name: *H.p. forrestii*, see *H. forrestii*, *H.p. henryi*, see *H. pseudohenryi*, *H.p.* Hidcote see *H.* Hidcote. *H. polyphyllum*, W. Turkey; allied and similar to *H. olympicum*, but sepals and petals usually black-dotted and sepals apiculate or acute (in *H. olympicum* they are acuminate). *H. pseudohenryi*

(*H. patulum henryi*), similar to – and confused in gardens with – *H. forrestii*, but stem tips much flattened and 4-lined, gradually becoming 2-lined, then terete; flowers with stamens at least ¾ as long as petals. *H. reptans*, Himalaya; mat-forming, deciduous shrub; leaves 6–20mm long, oblong-oval, usually overlapping; flowers solitary, golden-yellow, to 4·5cm wide, summer to autumn. *H. rhodoppeum* (of gardens), see *H. cerastoides*. *H. trichocaulon*, Crete; tufted evergreen perennial; stem usually prostrate, forming mats; leaves 5–11mm long, ovate-oblong to linear; flowers 3cm wide, soft yellow from red buds, summer; not reliably hardy, best in a sunny scree or alpine house.

Hypsela

(Greek *hypselos*, high, presumably referring to the mountain habitat of the type species). LOBELIACEAE (CAMPANULACEAE). A genus of 4–5 species of creeping perennials from S. America, Australia and New Zealand, 1 of which is generally available: *H. reniformis* (*H. longifolia*), S. America; mat-forming; stems slender; leaves rounded, somewhat folded along mid-rib, about 1cm long; flowers 1cm long, tubular with 5 pointed lobes, white or pale pink with darker veins and yellow-spotted throat, summer; fruit a greenish berry; confused in British gardens with *Selliera radicans*. Grow in moist soil in sheltered sites shaded from hot sun. Plant and propagate by division, cuttings or seed in spring.

Left: *Hypericum androsaemum*
Below left: *Hypericum calycinum*
Above: *Hypsela reniformis*
Top right: *Iberis amara* cultivar
Above right: *Iberis umbellata* mixed hybrids

Iberis

(from Iberia – Spain, Portugal – where many species are native). CRUCIFERAE. A genus of 30 species of annuals, perennials and sub-shrubs from Europe, Mediterranean, W. Asia. They have alternate, linear to spathulate or obovate leaves and corymbs or racemes of flowers with 4 petals, 2 longer than the rest. Grow in any well-drained soil in a sunny site. Plant autumn or spring. Propagate from seed, that of annuals *in situ* in late summer or spring; sub-shrubs also by cuttings in spring or late summer.

Species cultivated: *I. amara* (*I. coronaria* of gardens), candytuft; W. Europe; annual, 15–40cm tall; leaves spathulate to oblanceolate, widely pinnatifid or toothed; flowers to 8mm wide, white to purple, fragrant in corymbs expanding to racemes, summer; several cultivars and strains are available, some of them probably hybrids with *I. umbellata*. *I. gibraltarica*, Gibraltar candytuft; Gibraltar, S. Spain, Morocco; tufted, woody-based perennial forming hummocks; stems 15–30cm tall; leaves broadly spathulate, up to 2·5cm, somewhat fleshy, deep green; flowers to 2cm wide, reddish-lilac, in corymbs late spring to summer; not reliably hardy in cold areas. *I. saxatilis*, S. Europe; evergreen semi-procumbent sub-shrub; leaves linear, semi-cylindrical, to 2cm long; flowering stem erect, 7–15cm tall, flowers white, often purple-tinged, in corymbs, summer. *I. sempervirens*, Mediterranean; evergreen semi-procumbent sub-shrub to 20cm or so high and much wider; leaves oblong-spathulate, 2–4cm long; flowers pure white racemes to 10cm or more, spring to summer (occasionally confused with the similar but somewhat tender *I. semperflorens*, which flowers from autumn to spring in mild weather). *I.s.* Little Gem, smaller than type, to 15cm tall, more erect and neat habit; *I.s.* Snowflake, similar habit but larger. *I. umbellata*, Mediterranean; erect annual 15–40cm tall; leaves linear-lanceolate, acuminate, 3–7cm long, the lower ones sometimes with a few obscure teeth; flowers pink, red, purple, white, in corymbs; the common candytuft of gardens, although some of the cultivars may be hybrids with the species *I. amara*.

Ice plant – see *Mesembryanthemum crystallinum*, *Dorotheanthus bellidiflorus* and *Sedum spectabile*.

Ilex

(Latin name for holm oak taken by Linnaeus for this genus). Holly. AQUIFOLIACEAE. A genus of 400 species of evergreen and deciduous trees and shrubs of world-wide distribution, but mainly N. and S. America, Asia. They have alternate, rounded to narrowly oblong leaves, and axillary clusters of small, 4–6 petalled, white or greenish, often unisexual flowers followed by usually red berries. Grow in well-drained, moisture-retentive soil in sun or light shade. Plant autumn or spring. Propagate by cuttings with a heel in late summer or from seed when ripe (it often takes 18 months to germinate).

Species cultivated (all evergreen; male: m, female: f): *I.* × *altaclarensis* (*I. aquifolium* × *I. perado*), group of hybrid cultivars largely derived from back-crosses of this hybrid to English holly, and much resembling robust forms of it. *I.* × *a.* Camelliifolia, f; leaves mainly without spines, oblong, up to 13cm long, dark lustrous green; berries large, dark red. *I.* × *a.* Golden King, f; leaves oblong-elliptic, margined golden-yellow; fruit large but not freely produced. *I.* × *a.* Lawsoniana, f; leaves with central yellow splash. *I. aquifolium*, English or common holly; Europe to W. Asia, N. Africa; tree to 20m or more, but usually much less, pyramidal when

young; bark grey, smooth; leaves 5–12cm long, ovate, spine-tipped, wavy-margined, and spine-toothed on young trees and lower branches of old ones; flowers dioecious, white, 8mm wide, spring; berries 8–10mm wide, bright red; many cultivars varying in leaf size, shape, colour and berry colour have arisen, some of the best known being: *I. a.* Angustifolia, m or f, narrow habit, slow-growing, leaves lanceolate to 4cm long, weakly spined; *I. a.* Argenteo-marginata, m or f, a name covering several similar clones with silvery-white margined leaves; *I. a.* Aureo-marginata, several clones with yellow-margined leaves; *I.a.* Bacciflava (*I.a.* Fructuluteo), f, berries yellow; *I.a.* Ferox, hedgehog holly, m, leaves with spines also on upper surface; *I.a.* Golden King, see *I.* × *altaclarensis*; *I.a.* Pendula, f, weeping habit; *I.a.* Pyramidalis, f, extra shapely pyramidal habit, free-fruiting; *I.a.* Silver Queen, m, reddish stems, leaves grey-mottled and white-margined. *I. cornuta*, horned holly; China, Korea; shrub, to 3m tall, rounded habit; leaves 4–10cm long, more or less sharply oblong with a spine at each corner and a spined tip, sometimes with extra smaller spines, glossy green; flowers dull white, spring; fruit red, to 1cm diameter. *I.c.* Burfordii, f; leaves ovate, spine-tipped only; free-fruiting. *I. crenata*, Japanese or box-leaved holly; Japan; slow-growing shrub, eventually to 4m or so; small leaves elliptic to obovate, 1–2cm long; flowers dull white, females solitary, males in clusters; berries black. *I.c.* Convexa, f; 90cm tall; leaves convex, glossy, bushy habit. *I.c.* Golden Gem, to 45cm tall, compact habit, flattened top; leaves yellow. *I.c.* Mariesii (*I.c.* Nummularia), f; very dwarf, slow-growing; leaves crowded, rounded. *I. perado*, Azores or Madeira holly; Canary Is, Azores; similar to *I. aquifolium*, but leaves elliptic oblong to rounded, to 6cm long, entire or with a few spines; not reliably hardy in cool areas. *I.p. platyphylla*, Madeira, Canary Is; leaves to 15cm or more long, the variety most likely to be seen in cultivation but confused with a form of *I.* × *altaclarensis* which has broadly ovate, short-spined leaves. *I. pernyi*, C. and W. China; shrub or small tree, to 9m tall; leaves dense, similar to those of *I. cornuta* but smaller (1·5–5cm long) and with a more tapered tip; flowers pale yellow; fruit deep red, to 6mm wide. *I.p. veitchii* (*I. bioritensis*, *I. veitchii*), leaves larger than type, with an extra pair of spines.

Impatiens

(Latin impatient, alluding to the seed capsules that explode violently when touched). Balsam. BALSAMINACEAE. A genus of about 500 species of annuals, perennials and soft shrubs mainly from the warmer parts of Africa, Asia, Europe; a few in the Americas. They usually have fleshy stems, alternate or opposite, ovate to lanceolate leaves and unique, often hooded flowers. The latter occur in the upper leaf-axils and have 3–5 small sepals, 1 petaloid

Top far left: *Ilex* × *altaclarensis* Camelliifolia
Far left: *Ilex aquifolium* Argenteo-marginata
Below far left: *Ilex crenata* Golden Gem
Top left: *Ilex* × *altaclarensis* Lawsoniana
Left: *Ilex aquifolium* Bacciflava
Below: *Impatiens wallerana* Mixed Imp

and spurred, and 5 petals, the upper (standard) one sometimes helmet-shaped, the remaining 4 more or less united in pairs (wings). Sow seed of half-hardy annuals and tender perennials used for summer bedding in mid spring at 16–18°C, prick off seedlings at 5cm apart each way, harden off in early summer and plant out when fear of frost has passed. Grow hardy annuals in moisture-retentive soil in a sunny site and propagate by sowing seed *in situ* in spring.
Species cultivated: *I. balsamina*, balsam; India, China, Malay Peninsula; half-hardy annual, erect, usually sparingly branched, 45–75cm tall; leaves 7–15cm long, narrowly to broadly lanceolate, acuminate, toothed; flowers to 4cm wide, in shades of red, pink, purple, yellow, white, summer; almost entirely represented in gardens by the larger double or rose-flowered form, of which there are several cultivars including *I.b.* Camellia-flowered, to 45cm tall, and *I.b.* Tom Thumb, 25–30cm. *I. glandulifera* (*I. roylei*), Indian balsam, policeman's helmet; Himalaya; hardy annual, to 2m or more tall; leaves in pairs or whorls of 3, ovate, sharply toothed, to 15cm long; flowers 3cm long, pale to deep rose-purple or white, summer to autumn; apt to be invasive unless surplus self-sown seedlings are kept in check. *I. holstii*, see *I. wallerana*. *I. petersiana*, see *I. wallerana*. *I. sultanii*, see next species. *I. wallerana* (*I. holstii, I. sultanii*), busy Lizzie; Tanzania, Mozambique; shrubby greenhouse perennial, to 60cm or more tall; leaves lanceolate to ovate, 4–10cm long; flowers scarlet, orange, purple, carmine or white, flat-faced and almost pansy-like, 3–5cm wide, spur to 4cm long, almost all year if minimum temperature above 13°C; may be used for summer bedding in sheltered areas. *I.w. petersiana*, somewhat taller than type, leaves longer, strongly suffused bronze-red.

Incarvillea

(for Pierre Nicholas le Chéron D'Incarville, 1706–57, Jesuit missionary and probably the first trained western botanist to collect in China). BIGNONIACEAE. A genus of 10 or more species of perennials and annuals from Asia. They are tufted to clump-forming, some species with most leaves basal, others having erect, leafy stems. Leaves are alternate or opposite, pinnate of pinnatifid; flowers are in racemes, funnel-shaped with 5 broad lobes. Grow in well-drained, humus-rich soil in sun or light shade (the perennials described here are usually hardy, some others need winter protection). Plant spring. Propagate from seed under glass in spring, or by division. Seedlings take 2–4 years to flower.
Species cultivated (all perennials): *I. delavayi*, China; leaves basal, to 30cm long, leaflets 12–23, lanceolate; racemes 40–60cm tall, flowers to 7cm wide, bright purple-rose with yellow throat, early summer. *I. grandiflora*, see next species. *I. mairei* (*I. grandiflora brevipes*), Nepal and Tibet to China; leaves basal, to 16cm long, leaflets 5–9, ovate to oblong, to 4cm long, terminal one larger; racemes 20–30cm tall, flowers to 10cm wide, bright purple-crimson with yellow or white throat, early summer. *I.m. grandiflora*, leaflets 1–5; *I.m.g.* Frank Ludlow, flowers crimson-pink, racemes 10cm; *I.m.g.* Nyoto Sama, bright pink racemes, 15cm.

Indian corn – see *Zea*.

Indian cress – see *Tropaeolum majus*.

Indian shot – see *Canna*.

Indigofera

(from *indigo*, the blue dye, and Latin *fero*, to bear).

Far left below: *Incarvillea delavayi*
Above: *Inula hookeri*
Left below: *Indigofera amblyantha*

Indigo. LEGUMINOSAE. A genus of 700 species of perennials and shrubs from tropical to warm temperate zones. The shrubs described have alternate, pinnate leaves and axillary racemes of small pea-flowers. Grow in well-drained soil in a sunny, sheltered site. Plant spring or autumn. May be pruned almost to ground level annually in spring if desired. Propagate from seed under glass in spring or cuttings with a heel in late summer, bottom heat 15–18°C. Both seedlings and rooted cuttings are best over-wintered in a frame in all but the mildest areas.
Species cultivated: *I. amblyantha*, China; deciduous, 1·5–2m tall; leaves 10–13cm long, leaflets 7–11, narrowly oval; flowers pale to deep clear pink, 6mm long in dense racemes 7–11·5cm long, summer to autumn; see also comments under *I. potaninii*. *I. gerardiana*, see next species. *I. heterantha* (*I. gerardiana*), N. W. Himalaya; deciduous, to 3m tall on a wall or sheltered site, about 1m if cut back by frost; leaves 5–10cm long, leaflets 13–20, oval to obovate, finely grey-downy; flowers 1cm long, rose-purple, in racemes 7–13cm long, summer to autumn. *I. potaninii*, China; similar to *I. amblyantha* and confused with it in gardens; leaves 4–5cm long, often fewer leaflets; racemes longer than leaves.

Inula

(old Latin name). COMPOSITAE. A genus of 100–200 species of annuals and perennials from Europe, Asia, Africa. The perennial species described here are clump-forming, mostly with erect stems bearing broadly ovate-cordate to narrowly lanceolate leaves, and daisy-like flower-heads with numerous, very slender, yellow ray-florets. Grow in moisture-retentive but well-drained soil, preferably humus-enriched. Plant autumn to spring. Propagate by

Top: *Ionopsidium acaule*
Above: *Ipheion uniflorum*
Top right: *Ipomoea nil* Scarlett O'Hara
Above right: *Ipomoea acuminata*

division and from seed in spring.

Species cultivated (all flowering late summer): *I. acaulis*, Turkey; leaves to 4cm long, oblong-spathulate, all basal; flower-heads 5cm wide, sessile. *I. ensifolia*, E. and C. Europe to Caucasus; to 30cm tall; leaves linear-lanceolate, 4–9cm long, upper ones sessile; flower-heads 4cm, usually solitary. *I. glandulosa*, see *I. orientalis*. *I. helenium*, elecampane; probably C. Asia to S.E. Europe but much naturalized elsewhere; to 2m or more tall; leaves ovate, 40–70cm long, the basal ones long-stalked; flower-heads 7–8cm wide, bright yellow; roots formerly used medicinally for coughs and lung complaints. *I. hookeri*, Himalaya; to 60cm or more tall; leaves oblong-lanceolate to 10cm long; flower-heads 7–9cm wide, light yellow with a hint of green *I. magnifica*, Caucasus; to 2m tall; leaves ovate, to 30cm long; flower-heads 13–15cm wide, deep bright yellow. *I. orientalis* (*I. glandulosa*), Caucasus; to 50cm tall; leaves oblong, sessile, to 15cm long; flower-heads solitary, to 7cm wide, orange-yellow, summer onwards. *I. royleana*, Himalaya; 60cm tall; leaves ovate, narrowed to winged stalk; flower-heads solitary, 10cm wide, orange-yellow, summer.

Ionopsidium

(Greek *ion*, violet, and *opsis*, like). CRUCIFERAE. A genus of 1 annual from Portugal: *I. acaule*, violet cress or diamond flower; almost stemless; leaves dense, long-stalked, to 5cm or more tall, the blades rounded, 8–12mm wide; flowers 4-petalled, about 1cm wide, lilac to white, violet-tinted, solitary from leaf-axils but freely borne above foliage, summer to winter. Grow in well-drained but moisture-retentive soil in partial shade. Sow seed *in situ*, spring for summer blooming, summer for autumn flowering, autumn for a spring display. Will flower in winter if grown in pans in a cool greenhouse.

Ipheion

(derivation unknown). LILIACEAE (AMARYLLIDACEAE of some botanists). A genus of several species of bulbs from S. America, 1 being generally available: *I. uniflorum* (*Brodiaea uniflora*, *Tristagma u.*, *Triteleia u.*), Argentina, Uruguay; leaves tufted, basal, linear, pale to greyish-green, to 20cm or so long, smelling of onions when bruised; flowers solitary, on stems to 15cm tall, tubular, with 6 pointed sepals forming a star, to 4cm wide, milky-blue, spring. *I.u.* Wisley Blue, purple-blue. Grow in any well-drained soil in a sunny site. Plant autumn. Propagate by separating the freely produced offsets when dormant, or from seed in spring.

Ipomoea

(Greek *ips*, a worm, and *homoios*, similar to – alluding to the twining stem tips). Morning glory. CONVOLVULACEAE. A genus of about 500 species of climbing and erect annuals, perennials and shrubs from tropical to warm temperate zones. The species described are twining climbers with ovate-cordate, sometimes lobed leaves, and tubular to funnel-shaped flowers. All can be grown outside in summer in humus-rich, sunny, sheltered sites or under glass, minimum temperature 13–16°C. Sow seed (pre-soaked in tepid water for 12 hours) in spring, ideally singly in 6·5–7·5cm pots of a proprietary potting compost at 18–21°C (to 24°C or more for *I. nil* and *I. tricolor* if possible). When seedlings show first true leaf, temperature should be reduced to about 15°C minimum. Support with sticks, and pot into 10cm pots when well-rooted. Harden off in early summer and plant out when fear of frost has passed. If kept under glass pot on into 20–25cm pots of a good commercial potting mixture, or set in greenhouse border. Apply liquid feed to pot plants at fortnightly intervals once flower-buds show.

Species cultivated (all flowering summer to autumn): *I. acuminata* (*I. learii*, *Pharbitis l.*), blue dawn flower; tropical America, much grown and naturalized in warm countries; perennial to 6m or more; leaves 10–20cm long, broadly ovate to rounded, sometimes 3-lobed; flowers 6–10cm wide or more, rich purple-blue, ageing reddish-pink. *I. bona-nox* (*I. noctiflora*, *Calonyction aculeatum*), moonflower; probably tropical America but much naturalized in tropics; vigorous perennial to 4m tall; leaves sometimes 3-lobed, to 20cm long; flowers to 15cm long and wide; white with green tube, fragrant, opening at night. *I. coccinea* (*Quamoclit c.*), S.E. USA; annual to 3m tall; leaves to 15cm long, sometimes toothed; flowers to 4cm long, scarlet with yellow throat, in small clusters. *I. hederacea* (*Pharbitis h.*), similar to and much confused with *I. nil*, but sepals contracted to linear, spreading or recurved tips. *I. learii*, see *I. acuminata*. *I. nil*, tropics; similar to *I. purpurea*, but sepals lanceolate, to 2·5cm long; flowers about 5cm long, violet-purple, pink, blue; *I.n.* Scarlett O'Hara, flowers crimson; the large and often double-flowered Japanese Imperial morning glory (*I. imperialis* of gardens) is derived from this species. *I. purpurea* (*Pharbitis p.*), common morning glory; tropical America; annual, to 3m; leaves broadly ovate, to 13cm long; flowers 7cm long, purple, blue, pink, sepals oblong, short-pointed. *I. quamoclit* (*Quamoclit pennata*), cypress vine; tropical America; annual, 2–6m tall; leaves pinnately cut into thread-like segments; flowers about 4cm long, scarlet, narrowly funnel-shaped and unlike most morning glories. *I. rubrocaerulea*, see next species. *I. tricolor* (*I. rubrocaerulea*), tropical America; perennial, 2–4m tall; leaves rounded to broadly ovate, 15–25cm wide; flowers to 10cm long and wide, tube white, lobes red, maturing purple-blue; several cultivars are available in shades of blue, lavender and white: *I.t.* Heavenly Blue, rich sky-blue, *I.t.* Flying Saucers, blue and white striped.

Iresine

(Greek *eiros*, wool – the flowers are woolly). AMARANTHACEAE. A genus of 70–80 species of perennials and sub-shrubs, some climbing, from tropical and warm temperate regions. A few species are grown as greenhouse and house plants and for summer bedding. They have opposite pairs of coloured, ovate to lanceolate leaves, and tiny, insignificant, white or greenish flowers usually removed to promote more leafy growth. Greenhouse, minimum temperature 13°C, light

Below: *Iresine herbstii* Aureo-reticulata

Above: *Iresine lindenii*

shade and humidity in summer. Pot or repot spring, or autumn if bedded outside. Propagate by cuttings in spring at 18–20°C, potted when rooted into 9cm containers of commercial potting mix. Pot on when necessary or harden off in early summer.
Species cultivated: *I. herbstii*, beefsteak plant; S. America; about 45cm tall if grown annually but eventually to 2m in large containers; stems bright carmine; leaves ovate, notched at tip, to 13cm long, deep red-purple with paler veins. *I.h.* Aureo-reticulata, leaves green, veined or blotched yellow. *I. lindenii*, blood leaf; Ecuador; to 60cm tall, often less; leaves narrowly lanceolate, pointed, 5–7·5cm long, deep blood-red; needs frequent pinching when young to get a good bushy specimen.

Iris

(for the Greek rainbow goddess). IRIDACEAE. A genus of up to 300 species of rhizomatous and bulbous perennials from northern temperate zone. They are tufted or clump-forming with mainly basal, ensiform (sword-like) or linear leaves, usually 2-ranked in fan formation, and showy, 6-tepalled, tubular-based, solitary or clustered flowers. The latter have a highly distinctive form. The 3 outer and generally larger tepals are formed of flattened stalks or hafts and petal-like tips, often arching or hanging down, known as falls. The 3 inner tepals are known as standards and may be erect, arch inwards, spread out, or – rarely – droop. Alternating with the standards are 3-winged styles known as the style branches or arms, each sheltering a stamen; in some species the tubular base is much elongated, appearing like a stalk, eg *I. reticulata*. The fruits are ovoid to narrowly oblong capsules containing spherical to flattened seed adapted for distribution by water, wind or animals.

The genus splits naturally into 2 divisions (or sub-genera) on rootstock character: *Iris*, with rhizomes (**R**), and *Xiphium*, with bulbs (**B**). Within these divisions are a number of groups each having characters in common: *Pogon* (1), rhizomatous, falls bearded; 3 sub-groups are recognized, all having seed with whitish arils: *Regalia* (1a), standards and falls bearded, rhizomes producing stolons, *Pseudoregalia* (1b), falls only bearded, no stolons, and *Oncocyclus* (1c), falls with scattered hairs, rhizomes red-skinned and producing stolons. *Evansia* (2), rhizomatous, falls bearing a ridge or cockscomb-like crest. *Apogon* (3), rhizomatous, falls smooth, without beard or crest. *Xiphium* (4), bulbous, standards large, erect. *Scorpiris* (*Juno*) (5), bulbous, each bulb with 1 to several, fleshy, radish-like store roots, standards very small, spreading or hanging. The letters and numbers in brackets are used at the start of each of the following species descriptions. In general, irises thrive in ordinary soil in sunny or lightly shaded sites; any special cultural requirements are mentioned after the individual description. Plant rhizomatous species autumn to spring, the bearded types ideally after flowering; bulbous sorts in early autumn. All the smaller irises make good pot plants for the alpine or cool greenhouse, particularly those that flower in winter and are best kept on the dry side when they die down. Propagate from seed when ripe, during autumn or spring, and by division or offsets at planting time.
Species cultivated: *I. attica*, see *I. pumila* *I. bakerana*, Turkey, Iraq; **B**4; leaves cylindrical, 8-ribbed, to 30cm when mature; flowers solitary, almost stemless, long-tubed, falls deep blue-violet, blotched white and purple, sometimes yellow-crested, fragrant, winter. *I. bucharica*, Uzbek and Turkestan (USSR); **B**5; leaves narrowly lanceolate, deeply channelled, glossy, 20–30cm long; flowers 5–7 in upper leaf-axils, 6·5cm long, falls rounded, golden-yellow, standards small, spreading, lanceolate, white, spring; best at the foot of a sunny wall; when lifting and dividing it is essential to retain the store roots. *I. chamaeiris* (*I. lutescens*), S. Europe; **R**1; much like *I. pumila*, but flowers on a distinct stem 3–25cm tall. *I. chrysographes*, W. China; **R**3; clump-forming; stems to 45cm long; leaves narrowly ensiform, to 50cm long; flowers several, outer tepals to 5·5cm long, falls velvety violet-purple with golden veins, standards narrow, somewhat spreading, violet, summer. *I.c.* Rubella, flowers wine-red without yellow veins. *I. clarkei*, Himalaya; **R**3; clump-forming; stems to 90cm tall, branched; leaves narrowly ensiform, to 60cm long, glossy; flowers several, outer tepals 3·5cm long, falls violet-purple with white centre and yellow base, standards erect, narrower, violet, summer. *I. cristata*, S.E. USA; **R**2; stem 2·5–10cm tall; leaves ensiform, to 20cm long; flowers 2 or more, outer tepals to 4cm long, falls purple to lilac-white and yellow at base, late spring; see also *I. lacustris*. *I. danfordiae*, Turkey; **B**4; leaves cylindrical, 4-angled, to 30cm long; flowers to 5cm wide, stemless, solitary, before or with very young leaves, bright yellow, falls spotted olive-green, winter; bulbs break up after flowering into several varying-sized bulblets that take 1–3 years to reach maturity. *I. douglasiana*, California, Oregon; **R**3; stems to 30cm or more; leaves to 40cm or more long, narrowly ensiform, deep green, reddish at base; flowers several, red-purple to lilac or white, outer tepals to 9cm long, early summer. *I. foetidissima*, gladwin; W. Europe to N. Africa; **R**1; stems to 40cm or more; leaves narrowly ensiform, to 60cm long; flowers several, purplish-grey to mauve or yellowish, outer tepals obovate, to 5cm long; seed bright orange-red, remaining attached to widely gaping capsules, showy in autumn to winter, thrives in quite deep shade. *I.f.* Variegata, leaves white-edged. *I. forrestii*, W. China; **R**3; stems to 45cm tall; leaves to 38cm long, narrowly ensiform; flowers several, outer tepals 5cm long, falls oblong-ovate, yellow, veined brown-purple, early summer. *I. germanica*, S. Europe; **R**1; stems to 75cm or more tall; leaves ensiform, stiff, to 45cm or more long, glaucous; flowers several, outer tepals 7–8cm long, falls obovate, deep purple with yellow beard, early summer; probably of hybrid origin and not known truly wild – the name is sometimes (incorrectly) given to the large-flowered complex hybrid group of bearded iris cultivars, see entry. *I. gracilipes*, Japan; **R**2; stems 20–25cm; leaves narrowly ensiform, 20–30cm long; flowers several, lilac, outer tepals to 2·5cm long, falls bearing a wavy orange crest, early summer; needs leafy or peaty soil in partial shade. *I. graminea*, Europe; **R**3; densely clump-forming; stems to 23cm tall; leaves grassy, 50–90cm long;

Top right: *Iris danfordiae*
Centre right: *Iris foetidissima* in fruit
Right: *Iris innominata*

flowers 4–5cm wide in pairs, blue-violet, falls rounded with yellowish purple-veined patch, style arms pinkish-purple, fragrant of ripe plums, early summer. *I. histrio*, Turkey to Israel; B4; leaves cylindrical, 4-angled, to 30cm long when mature; flowers solitary, stemless, with young leaves, outer tepals to 5·5cm long, falls palest blue-purple with darker veining and flecking and yellow crest, winter; better appreciated in an alpine house. *I.h. aintabensis*, flowers smaller than type, leaves shorter at flowering time, more weather-resistant. *I. histrioides*, C. Turkey; **B**4; not unlike a larger, squat version of *I. histrio*, but deep purple-blue with an orange crest, opening before the leaves appear, winter; very weather-resistant. *I.h.* Major, the richly coloured clone in general cultivation. *I. hoogiana*, Turkestan; **R**1a; rhizomes underground; stems 45–75cm tall; leaves ensiform, somewhat glaucous, to 45cm long; flowers several, to 13cm long, lavender-blue, golden-bearded, early summer. *I. innominata*, Oregon, California; **R**3; stems to 20cm tall; leaves narrowly ensiform, to 35cm long; flowers several, outer tepals 5–6cm long, golden to pale yellow, often veined light brown, sometimes lavender to deep purple, summer. *I. kaempferi*, Japan; **R**3; stems to 60cm or more; leaves to same length, ensiform; flowers several, outer tepals to 7·5cm long, falls elliptic to obovate, deep red-purple, summer; several cultivars in shades of white, blue, red and purple (some double) are available; best in acid soil by the waterside. *I. kamaonensis*, Himalaya; **R**1b; stems 6–10cm; leaves grassy, to 45cm long; flowers with young leaves, purple, mottled lilac, falls oblong-ovate, white-bearded, late spring. *I. kernerana*, Turkey, Armenia; **R**3; dense clump-forming; spirally twisted stems to 30cm tall; leaves 45cm long, narrowly ensiform; flowers several, yellow, outer tepals 6·5cm long, slender and widely arching, standards erect, somewhat twisted, early summer. *I. kumaonensis*, see *I. kamaonensis*. *I. lacustris*, N.E. N.America; **R**2; like a smaller and neater version of *I. cristata;* inhabits stony lake shores in the wild. *I. laevigata*, E. Asia; **R**3; stems 50–60cm tall; leaves ensiform, to 60cm long, somewhat glaucous; flowers several, clear blue, outer tepals 6–7cm long, standards erect, about 6cm summer; several cultivars are sometimes available, from white to deep blue or bicoloured, best in shallow water or a bog. *I. lutescens*, see *I. chamaeiris*. *I. missouriensis*, C. and W. N.America; **R**3; stems to 60cm tall; leaves narrowly ensiform, glaucous, to 45cm long; flowers several, pale lilac to white, veined purple, outer tepals to 6cm long, summer. *I.m.* Alba, flowers white. *I. ochroleuca*, see next species. *I. orientalis* (*I. spuria ochroleuca*, see also *I. sanguinea* for what was formerly known as *I. orientalis*), W. Turkey; **R**3; stems 90cm or more tall; leaves ensiform, 60–90cm tall, dark green; flowers several, white, outer tepals slender, the rounded falls blotched or flushed yellow. *I. pallida*, S.E. Europe; **R**1, much like *I. germanica*, but flowers lavender-blue, fragrant, the spathes protecting the flower-buds dry and silvery at flowering time. *I.p. dalmatica*, flowers larger than type, lavender-blue, leaves very glaucous; *I.p.d.* Aurea-variegata, leaves striped yellow; *I.p.d.* Variegata, leaves striped creamy-white. *I. pseudacorus*, yellow flag, yellow iris; Europe, W. Asia, N. Africa; **R**3, leaves ensiform, 1–1·5m tall, stems the same height; flowers several, bright yellow, outer tepals 5cm long, falls ovate to obovate, often purple veined and with a basal orange spot, summer. *I.p.* Bastardii, flowers creamy-yellow; *I.p.* Variegata, leaves yellow-striped. *I. pumila* (*I. attica*), C. Europe to S. USSR and Turkey; **R**1; leaves ensiform, to 20cm long; flowers solitary, stemless with short young foliage, straw-yellow, outer tepals to 5cm long, falls oblong, bearing central brownish spot, bearded; several colour forms occur wild and are often available, with flowers from deep to pale yellow and in shades of purple and blue. *I.* × *regelio-cyclus*, a group of cultivars derived from crossing members of sub-groups **R**1a and **R**1c

Top: *Iris pseudacorus* Variegata
Centre: *Iris pumila* Blue Denim
Above: *Iris pumila* Pogo
Top right: *Iris gracilipes*
Centre right, top: *Iris kaempferi* cultivar
Centre right, bottom: *Iris laevigata* cultivar
Right: *Iris reticulata*

and combining the characters from both; stems 36–45cm tall; leaves ensiform; flowers with large arching standards, summer. *I.* × *r.-c.* Chione, white, standards veined blue, falls veined and spotted blackish-brown; *I.* × *r.-c.* Thor, pearly-grey, boldy veined purple, bright purple blotch on falls. *I. reticulata*, C. Turkey to Caucasus, Iran, Iraq; **B**4; leaves cylindrical, 4-angled, to 40cm or so long; flowers solitary, sessile with short leaves, pale blue to purple, sometimes 2-toned, outer tepals to 7cm long, the ovate falls bearing orange-yellow, white-bordered crests, fragrant, late winter, early spring. *I.r.* J. S. Dijt, flowers red-purple; *I.r.* Cantab, pale blue; several other cultivars are available, some derived from crosses with *I. histrioides*. *I. ruthenica*, E. Europe to China, Korea; **R**3; stems to 20cm tall; leaves grassy, to 30cm long; flowers several, outer tepals to 4cm long, falls creamy-white with blue veins, standards deep violet, erect, early summer. *I. sanguinea* (*I. orientalis*, *I. sibirica o.*), Manchuria, Japan; **R**3; like *I. sibirica*, but leaves and stems about 45cm tall; flowers somewhat larger. *I. setosa*, Alaska, N.E. Asia; **R**3; stems to 60cm long; leaves same length as stems, ensiform; flowers several, outer tepals 4–5cm long, falls rounded, to 2·5cm wide, deep blue-purple with paler streaks and white basal blotch, standards erect, 1·5cm tall, pointed, summer; a variable species. *I.s. canadensis*, dwarfer than type, with somewhat smaller flowers. *I. sibirica* (see *I. sanguinea*), C. Europe to Russia; **R**3; stems to 1m or more; leaves ensiform, to 75cm long; flowers several, outer tepals 3–4cm long, falls rounded, to 2cm wide, lilac-blue to blue-purple with purple veined white basal patch, summer. *I.s.* Caesar, deep violet-purple; *I.s.* Mrs Rowe, pearly-grey; *I.s.* Perry's Blue, sky-blue, large flowers; *I.s.* Snow Queen, pure white. *I. spuria*, butterfly iris; C. Europe to Iran, N. Africa; **R**3; stems 30–60cm tall; leaves narrowly ensiform, to 30cm long; flowers several, blue-purple to lilac, outer tepals to 5cm long, haft yellow, falls rounded, 2cm wide, standards lilac, summer; a variable species; several larger and more colourful cultivars are sometimes available. *I. spuria ochroleuca*, see *I. orientalis*. *I. stylosa*, see *I. unguicularis*. *I. tectorum*, Japanese roof iris; China, much and long grown in Japan; **R**2; stems 30–50cm tall; leaves broadly ensiform, pale green, 30–60cm long; flowers several, deep lilac to blue-purple, spotted and veined darker, outer tepals to 5cm long, falls rounded, waved with white crest, early summer. *I. tenax*, N. California, Oregon, Washington; **R**3; stems slender, 20–35cm tall; leaves grassy, light green, to 20cm long; flowers solitary, sometimes in pairs, lavender, blue, purple, yellow, rarely white, outer tepals to 5cm long, falls ovate, 3cm long, early summer. *I. tuberosa* (now classified as *Hermodactylus tuberosus*, but included here for convenience), snake's head iris; S. France to E. Mediterranean; rootstock tuberous, finger-like;

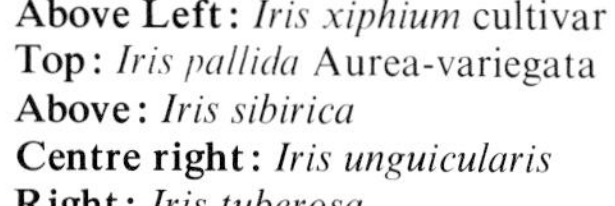

Above Left: *Iris xiphium* cultivar
Top: *Iris pallida* Aurea-variegata
Above: *Iris sibirica*
Centre right: *Iris unguicularis*
Right: *Iris tuberosa*

stems to 30cm or more; leaves cylindrical, 4-angled, to 60cm long, glaucous; flowers solitary, outer tepals semi-erect, to 5cm long, greenish-yellow, falls 1–2cm wide, rounded, velvety deep plum-purple, late spring. *I. unguicularis* (*I. stylosa*), Algerian or winter iris; Greece and Algeria east to Syria; **R**3; leaves narrowly ensiform, to 60cm long; flowers sessile, solitary, bright deep lilac, fragrant, perianth tube to 20cm or more, outer tepals 7cm or more, semi-erect, falls rounded, recurved, white, veined purple at base, late autumn to spring during mild spells; several forms are sometimes available with darker, larger or smaller flowers and leaves. *I.u.* Alba, flowers white. *I. vartanii*, Israel; **B**4; leaves

Below: *Iris* Buttercup Bower
Centre below: *Iris* Alcazar
Bottom: *Iris* Wild Apache

cylindrical, 4-angled, to 45cm long; flowers solitary, sessile, with short young foliage, slaty-lilac to blue or creamy-white, outer tepals 5cm long, falls lanceolate, darker veined, haft with yellow ridge, almond-scented, winter; best in alpine house; bulbs split up like those of *I. danfordiae* after flowering. *I. verna*, E. USA; **R**3; similar to *I. pumila* but falls without beard, tepals violet-blue, haft yellow to orange; leaves narrow, elongating after flowering. *I. versicolor*, E. N.America; **R**3; stems 60–90cm tall; leaves ensiform, 50–90cm long; flowers several, lavender, blue to red-purple, occasionally white, outer tepals to 7·5cm long, falls oval often with a greenish basal spot, standards erect, to 4cm, early summer. *I.v.* Kermesina, flowers glowing violet-crimson. *I. winogradowii*, Caucasus; **B**4; much like a pale yellow *I. histrioides*. *I. xiphioides*, English iris; Pyrenees, N.W. Spain; **B**4; stems 45–60cm tall; leaves linear, channelled, arching, to 45cm long; flowers several, deep purple-blue, outer tepals 6–8cm long, falls orbicular with golden blotch, summer; does best in moist rich soil; several cultivars, some of hybrid origin, are available in shades of blue, purple, white. *I. xiphium*, Spain, Portugal, S. France, N. Africa; similar to *I. xiphioides* but more slender in leaf and stem; flowers a little smaller and 2–4 weeks earlier, the primary parent of the popular Dutch iris, many cultivars of which are readily available in shades of yellow, white, bronze, purple, blue and mauve, some bicoloured. All make good ornamental pot plants for the cool greenhouse.

BEARDED HYBRIDS: the most popular and well-known of all irises comprising a vast complex group of cultivars derived from several bearded (**R**1) species and embracing all the colours of the rainbow. There are 3 divisions based on height: Tall, with stems above 85cm tall; Intermediate or Median, stems 25–65cm tall; Dwarf, stems up to 23cm tall. The Tall bearded group has *I. pallida*, *I. mesopotamica*, *I. trojana*, *I. variegata* among its parent species and takes its general appearance from the first; the Dwarf group derives from *I. chamaeiris*, *I. pumila*, *I. flavescens*, and the Intermediates have arisen as crosses between the two. For ease of description a 6-category colour code has been devised: *Amoena*, standards white or almost so, falls coloured; *Bicolor*, flowers 1 colour, but the standards a lighter shade; *Blend*, several colours in various combinations, including a yellow base tone; *Plicata*, white or yellow ground colour stippled, speckled or feathered around the margins with other colours; *Self*, standards and falls of the same colour; *Variegata*, standards yellow, gold or orange, falls a contrasting colour, either pure or veined, generally a shade of brown or red. Many cultivars are available and new ones are marketed annually. All are good garden plants in their various ways and choice is a personal one.

Isolepis – see *Scirpus*.

Itea

(Greek name for willow used for this genus by Linnaeus). ITEACEAE (ESCALLONIACEAE, SAXIFRAGACEAE). A genus of 10–15 species of evergreen and deciduous shrubs from tropical and temperate Asia, 1 from E. USA. They have alternate, ovate, sometimes spiny leaves and racemes or panicles of tiny, 5-petalled flowers. Grow in humus-rich soil, well-drained for the evergreen species, moisture-retentive for the deciduous, in sun or partial light shade. Site evergreens in sheltered corners or against walls in all but the milder areas. Plant autumn or spring. Propagate by cuttings with a heel in late summer, bottom heat at about 18°C, or layering in spring.

Species cultivated: *I. ilicifolia*, W. China; evergreen,

Top: *Itea ilicifolia*
Above: *Itea virginica*

2–4m tall, well-branched; leaves 5–10cm long, broadly oval, soft spine-toothed, deep lustrous green; flowers white, tinted green in dense, pendulous, catkin-like racemes 15–30cm long, late summer. *I. virginica*, Virginia willow; E. USA; deciduous, to 1·5m tall (double this in wild); leaves narrowly oval to oblong, tapered, finely toothed, bright green, 4–9cm long; flowers fragrant, creamy-white in semi-erect racemes 7–15cm long, summer; leaves do not fall until early winter and then sometimes turn red. *I. yunnanensis*, China, evergreen, much like *I. ilicifolia*, but leaves often narrower and less spiny; flowers dull white, racemes to 18cm long, summer.

Ithuriel's spear – see *Brodiaea laxa*.

Ivy – see *Hedera*.

Ixia

(Greek for bird lime, referring to the sticky sap). African corn lily. IRIDACEAE. A genus of 30–40 species of cormous plants from S. Africa. Each corm produces a narrow fan of sword-shaped leaves and a wiry stem topped by a raceme of 6-tepalled, somewhat crocus-like flowers. Grow outside in well-drained soil in a sheltered sunny border or in pots under glass, minimum temperature 5–7°C. Plant corms in late autumn, those outside protected by cloches, coarse sand or bracken in cold areas; alternatively, delay planting until spring. Under glass, place about 5 corms in a 13cm pot of any commercial potting mixture and keep barely moist until growth appears. For early (spring) flowering, maintain a minimum temperature of 13°C. Water freely when in full growth but allow the soil almost to dry each time. Apply liquid feed at fortnightly intervals when leaves are full-sized and

until flowers fade. Dry off when leaves yellow. Propagate from seed in spring or by separating corms when dormant.

Species cultivated: *I. maculata*, stem to 50cm; leaves to 30cm long by 6mm wide; flowers about 4cm wide, yellow to white, with prominent black-purple eye, in dense racemes, early summer; this species is probably the main parent, perhaps crossed with *I. patens* (pink to light red) and/or *I. speciosa* (crimson) and others, to produce the many cultivars now available in shades of white, yellow, orange, red, purple. *I. viridiflora*, much like *I. maculata*, but flowers luminescent blue-green with an almost black eye; best grown under glass.

Ixiolirion

(*Ixia*, and Greek, *leirion*, a lily – alluding to the similarity). AMARYLLIDACEAE. A genus of 3 species of bulbous plants from W. and C. Asia, 1 of which is generally available: *I. tataricum* (*I. ledebourii*, *I. montanum*), C. Siberia to Turkey, Persia, Afghanistan; stems 30–45cm tall; leaves tufted,

linear, grassy; flowers in umbels, 6-tepalled, trumpet-shaped, 4cm long, deep to pale blue, sometimes purple-suffused, early summer. *I.t. pallasii*, flowers rose-purple, opening later than type. Grow in well-drained soil in a sunny sheltered site. Plant autumn, or, in cold areas, store frost-free but cool, and plant early spring. May also be grown in pots in a cool greenhouse.

Jacob's ladder – see *Polemonium*.

Japonica – see *Chaenomeles*.

Jasminum

(Iranian name *Yasmin* in Latin form). Jasmine or jessamine. OLEACEAE. A genus of 200–300 species of deciduous and mainly tropical evergreen shrubs and climbers from Africa, Asia, Australia. They have opposite pairs of pinnate, trifoliate or simple leaves and terminal or axillary cymose clusters of tubular flowers with 4–9 (usually 6) petal-like lobes spread out flat; fruit a black berry. Grow in well-drained but moisture-retentive soil in sun or light shade. *J. mesnyi* and *J. polyanthum* need a frost-free greenhouse in all but the mildest areas. Plant autumn or spring and provide support for the twining species. Propagate by cuttings in late summer or early autumn.

Species cultivated: *J. beesianum*, China; slender deciduous climber to 3m or more; leaves simple, ovate-lanceolate, tapered, to 5cm long, dark green; flowers deep velvety-red, fragrant, 1–1·5cm long, early summer; fruit about 1cm wide, glossy black, sometimes in abundance. *J. humile* (*J. farreri*, *J. revolutum*), yellow or Italian jasmine; Afghanistan to W. China; semi-evergreen shrub, usually of loose or semi-scandent habit; leaves pinnate, leaflets 3–7, ovate, the terminal one to 5cm long; flowers bright yellow, to 1·5cm wide, sometimes fragrant, summer to autumn; a variable species with several forms known; usually represented in cultivation by *J.h.* Revolutum (*J. reevesii*, *J. triumphans*), that is more robust, leaves larger, terminal leaflets to 7cm long, flowers to 2cm wide, fragrant, not reliably hardy in severe winters. *J. mesnyi* (*J. primulinum*), primrose jasmine; W. China; evergreen, scrambling but not twining shrub, 3–4m high; leaves trifoliate, leaflets oblong to lanceolate 3–7cm long; flowers 4cm wide, bright yellow, often semi-double with 6–10 lobes, in leaf-axils, spring to summer. *J. nudiflorum*, winter jasmine; China; deciduous, scrambling habit but not twining shrub, 3–5m high; stems green; leaves trifoliate, leaflets 1·5–2·5cm long, deep green; flowers 2–2·5cm wide, bright yellow from leafless nodes, late autumn to spring; very hardy and will flower on a north wall. *J. officinale*, common jasmine, jessamine; Caucasus, Himalaya to W. China; vigorous, twining, deciduous climber to 10m; leaves pinnate, leaflets 5–9, ovate, 2·5–6·5cm long, terminal, largest slender-pointed; flowers white, about 2cm wide, sweetly fragrant, in terminal

Top left: *Ixia viridiflora*
Below left: *Ixiolirion tataricum*
Below: *Jasminum polyanthum*
Top: *Jasminum officinale*
Above: *Jasminum mesnyi*

clusters, summer to autumn. *J.o. affine*, flowers pink in bud; *J.o.* Aureovariegatum (*J.o.* Aureum), leaves and shoots irregularly yellow-blotched. *J. parkeri*, Himalaya–N.W. India; hummock-forming evergreen bushlet to 30cm tall; leaves alternate, pinnate, leaflets 3–5, ovate, to 1cm long; flowers yellow, 1cm or more wide, solitary, summer. *J. polyanthum*, W. China; evergreen or semi-deciduous twiner, much like *J. officinale* but flowers more plentifully borne, pink in bud, very fragrant, spring to summer (earlier under glass); best under glass, but in mild areas worth trying on a sheltered wall. *J. primulinum*, see *J. mesnyi*. *J.* × *stephanense* (*J. beesianum* × *J. officinale*), raised intentionally in France before 1921 but also found in the wild; midway between parents; some leaves simple but most pinnate with 3–5 leaflets; flowers soft pink, 1cm or more wide.

Jerusalem sage – see *Phlomis*.

Job's tears – see *Coix*.

Joe pye weed – see *Eupatorium purpureum*.

Jonquil – see *Narcissus jonquilla*.

Joseph's coat – see *Amaranthus tricolor*.

Jovellana

(for Gaspar Melchor de Jovellanos, a patron of Peruvian botany in the 18th century). SCROPHULARIACEAE. A genus of 7 species of perennials and sub-shrubs from New Zealand and Chile. They are very closely allied to *Calceolaria* but have helmet or bell-like, 2-lipped flowers lacking the pouch. 1 species is generally available: *J. violacea*, Chile; sub-shrub, to 2m under glass or in mild areas, but cut back in winter outside elsewhere, behaving as a herbaceous perennial to about 60cm tall; leaves ovate, to 3cm long, coarsely and irregularly toothed or lobed; flowers 1cm or more wide, pale violet-purple, spotted purple within, throat bright yellow, in terminal corymbs, summer; best under glass in cold areas. Culture as for *Calceolaria*; outside at the foot of a sheltered wall.

Above: *Jovellana violacea*
Right: *Juniperus* × *media* Pfitzerana Aurea

Jovibarba – see *Sempervivum*.

Juglans

(Latin *jovis*, of Jupiter, and *glans*, acorn). JUGLANDACEAE. A genus of 15–20 species of deciduous trees from N. and S. America, S.E. Europe to E. Asia. They have alternate, pinnate leaves and petalless, unisexual flowers, males in catkins, females naked ovaries, solitary or in small groups. The fruit are thin-fleshed, green, plum-like drupes, each with a single seed (nut). Grow in fertile, moisture-retentive but well-drained soil in a sunny site, preferably with a southern exposure. Plant autumn to spring. Propagate from seed when ripe, sown singly in 13cm pots, in a cold frame; cultivars are grafted on to seedlings of the wild species.

Species cultivated: *J. nigra*, black walnut; E. N.America; to 45m in wild, rarely to 30m in Britain; bark dark brown to black, narrowly and thickly ridged; leaves to 45cm or more, leaflets 11–23, sometimes without terminal leaflet, ovate-oblong; catkins 5–12cm long, females in clusters of 2–5; fruit globose, 4–5cm long; nuts very thick-shelled; grows best in moist soils. *J. regia*, common walnut; S.E. Europe, China; grown in Britain at least since the 15th century and probably before. Its large size makes it prohibitive for the smaller garden, but where room allows it serves the dual purpose of enhancing the landscape and providing tasty nuts. Walnuts require deep or at least humus-rich, well-drained but moisture-retentive soil in sun. Ideally the site should be sheltered from cold winds and away from frost pockets, as the unfurling foliage and tiny female flowers are not fully hardy. Plant autumn to spring, ideally choosing 1–3 year old plants, for they replant badly when older. If more than 1 tree is to be planted set them at least 13m apart, preferably 20–25m. Once the desired stem height is attained, cut out the top and allow the top 3–5 buds to grow out to form the main branches. Thereafter no pruning is necessary except to remove crossing branches or to thin crowded ones, and remove dead wood. Seedling trees seldom start to crop before they are 10–15 years old, but grafted ones may start at about 7 years. Propagation is from seed of selected parent trees known to crop well, or by whip-grafting named cultivars onto seedling *J. nigra*, *J. regia* or *J. californica* in spring. In the main areas of commercial walnut orchards, dozens of cultivars are known but few are obtainable elsewhere.

Juniperus

(Latin name for juniper). Juniper. CUPRESSACEAE. A genus of 60–70 species of evergreen coniferous trees and shrubs from N. Hemisphere. They have needle- or awl-like leaves in pairs or whorls of 3 when young, but when mature, some species produce smaller, closely overlapping pairs of scale leaves; male flowers small, ovoid to columnar catkins, females like tiny cones, the scales becoming fleshy and fusing together to form a berry-like fruit. The fruit of some species are dried and used for culinary purposes. Grow in well-drained soil in a sunny site. Plant autumn or spring. Particularly for named cultivars, propagate by cuttings of young shoots with a heel in a cold propagating frame late summer to autumn; cultivars can also be grafted onto established stock of their respective type; seed may be sown when ripe, best extracted from berries – can take 18 months to germinate.

Species cultivated: *J. chinensis*, Chinese juniper; China, Japan; conical or columnar tree, to 18m or smaller and shrubby; adult scale and juvenile, awl-shaped leaves are found together even on mature specimens, the juvenile ones to 8mm or so long, spiny-pointed with 2 glaucous bands above; berries rounded, to 8mm wide, glaucous-brown; several cultivars in a variety of forms are known, among them: *J.c.* Kaizuka (*J.c.* Torulosa), large bush or small tree, with spreading branches and bright green scale leaves; *J.c.* Obelisk, columnar habit, leaves awl-shaped, blue green, dense; *J.c.* Pfitzerana, see *J.* × *media; J.c. procumbens*, see *J. procumbens. J.c.* Variegata, conical habit, leaves awl-shaped, glaucous, some shoots white, slow-growing. *J. communis*, common juniper; N. Hemisphere; spreading shrub or small tree, to 4m (occasionally to 12m); leaves always awl-shaped, 6–15mm long, each with a central glaucous band above; berries purple-black with waxy white patina, round to oval, 6mm wide. *J.c. nana* (*J.c. montana*, *J.c. saxatilis*, *J. sibirica*), mat-forming; leaves less spreading than type, somewhat shorter and blunter (the mountain and arctic form). Many cultivars of *J. communis* occur in a variety of forms, some of the best-known being: *J.c.* Compressa, Noah's Ark juniper, dense, columnar, small leaves, very slow-growing (to 45cm tall in 20 years); *J.c.* Hibernica, Irish juniper, columnar, to 3m tall; *J.c.* Oblonga Pendula, main stems erect, branchlets pendulous, leaves to 2cm long; *J.c.* Repanda, semi-prostrate, mat-forming, leaves silvery beneath. *J. conferta*, Japan (sea-coast); widely mat-forming, to 20cm tall; leaves to 1·5cm long, awl-shaped, bright green. *J. coxii*, see *J. recurva*. *J. horizontalis* (*J. prostrata*, *J. sabina procumbens*), creeping juniper; N. America; prostrate, wide-spreading mat-forming, sometimes with erect branchlets to 60cm tall; leaves juvenile and adult, the former grey-green to glaucous in the cultivated forms; berries 6–15mm long, bluish. *J.h.* Bar Harbor, ground-hugging, leaves scale-like, steely-blue; *J.h.* Wiltonii (*J.h.* Blue Rug), ground-hugging, leaves scale-like, blue-grey. *J.* × *media* (*J. chinensis* × *J. sabina*), a collection of named clones blending the parental characters, some at least of which may have been collected in the wilds of N.E. Asia: *J.* × *m.* Blaauw, vigorous shrub to 1·5m tall, leaves mainly scale-like, grey-blue, in feathery sprays; *J.* × *m.* Pfitzerana, wide-spreading shrub with branches at a 45° angle, eventually to 2m or more tall, rather flat-topped, main leaves halfway between scale and awl, closely appressed, with sprays of true awl-shaped, glaucous foliage mixed together; *J.* × *m.* Pfitzerana Aurea, golden foliage in summer; *J.* × *m.* Pfitzerana Old Gold, more compact, bronze-gold, also in winter. *J. procumbens* (*J. chinensis procumbens*), Japan; spreading shrub forming low, wide hummocks, to 30cm or more tall; leaves awl-shaped, about 8mm long, prickly pointed, glaucous; berries rarely produced in cultivation. *J.p.* Nana (*J.p.* Bonin Isles), smaller and more compact than type. *J. prostrata*, see *J. horizontalis*. *J. recurva*, Himalayan juniper; E. Himalaya to Yunnan and Burma; tree, eventually to 15m or more, broadly conical habit with drooping branchlets; leaves awl-shaped, densely overlapping, to 6mm long, dull grey-green, pointed; berries purple-brown, ovoid, to 1cm long. *J.r. coxii* (*J. coxii*), more pendulous than type; leaves to 8mm, less closely overlapping. *J. sabina*, savin; S. and S.E. Europe to Caucasus; shrub 2–5m tall, usually stiff spreading; leaves juvenile and adult, the former 3–4mm long, unpleasantly aromatic when bruised, somewhat glaucous; berries globose to ovoid, 5–6mm wide; several cultivars are known, the best being: *J.s.* Blue Danube, wide, low-growing habit, leaves scale-like, grey-blue; *J.s. procumbens*, see *J. horizontalis*; *J.s.* Tamariscifolia, wide-spreading, low, flat-topped bush, leaves awl-shaped, bright green. *J. sibirica*, see *J. communis nana*. *J. squamata* (*J. recurva densa*, *J.r. squamata*), Himalaya to China; semi-prostrate shrub; leaves awl-shaped, to 5mm long, prickle-pointed, overlapping; berries ellipsoid, 6–8mm long, red-brown to black. *J.s.* Meyeri, erect shrub, eventually to 6m or more; leaves to 12mm long, bright glaucous. *J. virginiana*, pencil or red cedar; E. and C.N.America; tree to 20m or 50 (33m in the wild), conical habit; leaves juvenile and adult, the former 5–6mm long, prickle-pointed, glaucous above; fruit rounded to ovoid, 6mm long; many cultivars are known, some of the best being: *J.v.* Burkii, columnar, dense, slow-growing, leaves steely-blue, bronze-purple in winter; *J.v.* Grey Owl, wide-spreading, vigorous shrub, leaves silvery-grey, sometimes thought of hybrid origin with *J.* × *media* Pfitzerana; *J.v.* Skyrocket, narrowly columnar, fast-growing, leaves blue-grey.

Below: *Juniperus communis* Hibernica
Bottom: *Juniperus communis* berries
Right above: *Kalmia latifolia*
Right below: *Kerria japonica* Pleniflora

Kaffir lily – see *Clivia* and *Schizostylis*.

Kalmia

(for Pehr Kalm, 1715–79, Finnish pupil of Linnaeus who in 1748 was sent to N. America to report on natural resources there). American laurel. ERICACEAE. A genus of 6–8 species of mainly evergreen shrubs from N. America and Cuba. They have ovate to narrowly obovate or lanceolate, alternate or opposite leaves, and 5-lobed flowers in umbels or corymbs (rarely solitary). Each flower is saucer- or bowl-shaped with 10 stamens, each bent back with a bow, the tip held in a small pocket that shows as a neat projection on the outside. Visiting insects dislodge the stamens which spring up, discharging pollen. Grow in moisture-retentive but well-drained, lime-free, humus-rich soil in sun or light shade. Plant autumn or spring. Propagate by cuttings with a heel, late summer, layering suckers (where possible) and from seed in spring, the latter under glass.

Species cultivated: *K. angustifolia*, sheep or dwarf laurel; E. N.America; slender, erect, 60–90cm or more tall; leaves oblong to elliptic-lanceolate, 3–6·5cm long, in opposite pairs or 3s; flowers 8–13mm wide, rose-purple to crimson, in lateral corymbs, early summer. *K. latifolia*, mountain laurel, calico bush; E. USA; to 3m or more, sometimes a small tree; leaves elliptic, 4–10cm long, glossy deep green; flowers 1·5–2·5cm wide, clear rose-pink, in large terminal corymbs, early summer. *K.l.* Alba, white; *K.l.* Rubra, deep crimson. *K. polifolia*, bog laurel; Canada, N. USA; slender, erect, 30–60cm tall; leaves linear to lanceolate, 2–4cm long, lustrous above, glaucous white beneath, in pairs or 3s; flowers 1–2cm wide, rose-purple, early summer; a bog-dweller in the wild but does not need wet conditions to thrive.

Kansas gay feather – see *Liatris*.

Kentranthus – see *Centranthus*.

Kerria

(for William Kerr, died 1814, sent by Kew Gardens to collect in China, Java, Philippines, and introducer of *Lilium tigrinum* and *Nandina domestica* among others). Jew's mallow. ROSACEAE. A genus of 1 deciduous shrub from temperate E. Asia: *K. japonica*, suckering shrub with twiggy green stems; 1·5–2m tall; leaves alternate, 4–10cm long, ovate to lanceolate, doubly toothed; flowers 5-petalled, 3–4cm wide, golden-yellow, starting with young leaves, spring to summer; usually represented in gardens by *K.j.* Pleniflora (*K.j.* Flore Pleno), more

vigorous and erect, often to 2·5m tall, flowers double. *K.j.* Aureo-variegata, leaves yellow-edged; *K.j.* Picta (*K.j.* Variegata, *K.j.* Argenteo-variegata), leaves white-edged; *K.j.* Simplex, unnecessary name for the single-flowered wild type previously described. Grow in any well-drained but not dry soil in a sunny or shady site. Plant autumn to spring. Propagate by division or suckers at planting time, by layering shoots in spring, or cuttings of young shoots with a heel late summer.

Kingcup – see *Caltha palustris*.

Kirengeshoma

(Japanese vernacular name *ki*, yellow, *renge*, lotus blossom, and *shoma*, hat). SAXIFRAGACEAE (HYDRANGEACEAE, KIRENGESHOMACEAE). A genus of 1 or 2 species from Japan and Korea. *K. palmata*,

Japan; clump-forming herbaceous perennial, 60–120cm tall; stems erect; leaves to 20cm long, palmate, maple-like, with 7–10 toothed lobes; flowers pendant, bell-like, 3–4cm long, the 5 petals yellow and fleshy, in terminal leafy panicles, autumn. *K.p. koreana* (*K. koreana*), very similar to type, but leaves more ovate in outline; flowers longer, paler yellow, more upright. Grow in moisture-retentive, humus-rich soil in light shade. Plant spring or autumn just as the stems die down. Propagate either by careful division or from seed during spring.

Kniphofia

(for Johann Hieronymus Kniphof, 1704–63, German botanist and professor of medicine). Red-hot poker. LILIACEAE. A genus of 60–75 species of mainly evergreen perennials from E. and S. Africa, Malagasy. The mainly hardy S. African species described here are clump-forming or tufted from a short, trunk-like stem, leaves grassy to linear-

Left: *Kirengeshoma palmata*
Left below: *Kniphofia* Bees Lemon
Above: *Kniphofia galpinii*
Below: *Kochia scoparia trichophylla* Childissi in autumn
Above right: *Kniphofia sparsa*

lanceolate, tapered and often keeled, flowers pendant, tubular, 6-lobed, in dense terminal racemes atop leafless stems; frequently the buds and newly opened flowers are reddish, ageing to yellow. Grow in well-drained but moisture-retentive, preferably humus-rich soil in sun. In very cold areas plants may need protection, or even lifting, in winter. Plant spring. Propagate by division or from seed in spring. In addition to the species listed here are many hybrid cultivars combining the collective characters of some of the most garden-worthy. All are well worth trying, although the newer ones have yet to undergo the test of time.

Species cultivated: *K. alooides*, see *K. uvaria*. *K. caulescens*, tufted basal trunk almost woody, to 30cm tall; stems 1–1·5m tall; leaves to 90cm long, glaucous; flowers about 2·5cm long, light salmon-red ageing to yellowish, autumn. *K. galpinii*, clump-forming; stems to 80cm tall; leaves to 60cm or more, grassy; flowers to 2·5cm long, bright reddish-orange, well-spaced, autumn. *K. modesta* (of gardens), see *K. sparsa*. *K. northiae*, tufted from short trunk; stems 1·2m tall; leaves to 1·5m long by 15cm wide, not keeled, glaucous; flowers to 3cm long, red ageing pale yellow, early summer. *K pumila*, clump-forming; stems 45–60cm tall; leaves grassy, to 60cm long, glaucous; flowers orange-red, late summer. *K. sparsa* (*K. modesta*), clump-forming; stems 60cm tall; leaves grassy, 60–90cm long; flowers rose-red in bud, opening ivory white, autumn. *K. tuckii* (of gardens), similar to the next species but flowers sulphur-yellow from light pinkish-red buds. *K. uvaria*, clump-forming; stems 1·2–1·5m tall; leaves to 90cm long; flowers 3–4·5cm long, scarlet, ageing yellow, autumn. *K.u.* Nobilis (*K.u.* Grandiflora, *K. alooides* Maxima, *K. praecox*), stems to 1·8m tall, racemes longer, flowers red to orange.

Knotweed – see *Polygonum*.

Kochia

(for Wilhelm Daniel Josef Koch, 1771–1849, professor of botany at Erlangen, W. Germany).

CHENOPODIACEAE. A genus of 80–90 species of annuals, perennials and sub-shrubs from C. and S. Europe to W. Asia, Africa, Australia. 1 species is commonly cultivated: *K. scoparia*, summer cypress; S. Europe to Japan; half-hardy annual, to 1·5m tall, columnar or pyramidal in outline; leaves narrowly lanceolate to linear, 3–6cm long, bright pale green; flowers tiny, petalless, green, barely noticeable; generally represented in cultivation by *K.s. trichophylla* (not *K.s. trichophila*), burning bush, more compact, rarely above 60cm tall, leaves turning red in autumn; *K.s.t.* Childsii, generally neater, more uniform strain. Grow in fertile, well-drained soil in a sunny site. Sow seed in mid spring at a temperature of 16–18°C; prick off seedlings as soon as true leaves show, at 4–5cm apart each way into boxes of any commercial potting mixture, and harden off in early summer. Can also be sown *in situ* late spring to early summer.

Koelreuteria

(for Josef Gottlieb Koelreuter, 1773–1806, professor of natural history, Karlsruhe, W. Germany, an early investigator of plant hybridization). SAPINDACEAE. A genus of 4 species of deciduous trees from China, Taiwan, Korea, Fiji, 1 generally available: *K. paniculata*, golden rain tree, varnish tree; 8–15m tall or more, broad-headed; leaves pinnate, sometimes bipinnate, 30–45cm long, red-stalked leaflets ovate, lobed and toothed; flowers 1cm wide, deep yellow, 4-petalled in terminal panicles 30cm or more long, summer; fruit a somewhat conical, papery, bladder-like capsule containing hard, black, bead-like seed; usually needs a fine, warm summer to flower well and a good autumn for the leaves to turn bright yellow. Grow in any well-drained soil, preferably in a sunny site sheltered from strong winds. Plant autumn to spring. Propagate from seed when ripe, or by root cuttings during winter in a frame or cool greenhouse.

Kolkwitzia

(for Richard Kolkwitz, born 1873, German professor of botany). CAPRIFOLIACEAE. A genus of 1 species of deciduous shrub from C. China: *K. amabilis*, beauty bush; 2–4m tall, bushy when young, becoming gaunt with age; leaves in opposite pairs, broadly ovate, slender-pointed, sparsely hairy above, bristly beneath, 2·5–7·5cm long; flowers 1·5cm long, bell-shaped with 5 rounded lobes, the lowest one longest, soft pink with yellow throat in freely borne lateral corymbs, late spring to early summer. *K.a.* Pink Cloud and *K.a.* Rosea are similar clones with pink flowers brighter than type. Grow in any well-drained moderately fertile soil in a sunny site. Plant from autumn to spring. Propagate from seed sown in spring, by cuttings with a heel taken in late summer or early autumn and inserted into sandy soil in a cold frame.

+Laburnocytisus

Graft hybrid between *Cytisus purpureus* and *Laburnum anagyroides* arising as a chimaera at the union of stock and scion. +*L. adamii* is much like the *Laburnum*, forming a tree to 8m tall but with somewhat smaller leaves and flowers, the latter yellow, suffused purple. Here and there, shoots arise that are identical to both 'parents' creating a sight more curious than beautiful. Propagation by grafting onto seedlings of *Laburnum*.

Laburnum

(ancient Latin name). Golden rain. LEGUMINOSAE. A genus of 3 species of deciduous trees and shrubs from Europe to W. Asia. They have trifoliate leaves and racemes of pea-shaped flowers followed by slim, poisonous pods. Grow in any well-drained soil in a sunny site. Propagate from seed in autumn or spring, the cultivars by grafting onto species

seedlings in mid spring.

Species cultivated: *L. alpinum*, Scotch laburnum; C. E. Europe; tree to 8m or more tall; leaflets oval to obovate, 5–10cm long, somewhat downy beneath; flowers bright rich yellow, 2cm long in pendant racemes 24–35cm long, early summer; pods 5–7cm long, flattened, upper edge knife-like. *L.a.* Pendulum, slow-growing, weeping habit. *L. anagyroides* (*L. vulgare*), laburnum, golden chain, golden rain; tree to 8m tall or more; leaflets elliptic-obovate, downy beneath, 4–7cm long, rich yellow; racemes pendant, 10–25cm long, late spring; pods 4–7cm long, not flattened, upper edge thickened and keeled. *L.a.* Aureum, leaves soft yellow; *L.a.* Autumnale (*L(a.* Semperflorens), flowering again in late summer and autumn, but variable in this respect; *L.a.* Pendulum, smaller than type, weeping habit; *L.a.* Quercifolium, leaflets deep.y lobed. *L. vulgare*, see *L. anagyroides*. *L.* × *watereri* (*L. alpinum* × *L. anagyroides*), closer to first parent but leaves more hairy and fewer, often only partially developed pods; *L.* × *w.* Vossii, long racemes very freely produced.

Lady's mantle – see *Alchemilla*.

Lady's slipper orchid – see *Cypripedium calceolus*.

Lagerstroemia

(for Magnus von Lagerström, 1691–1759, Swedish merchant and friend of Linnaeus). LYTHRACEAE. A genus of 53 species of large shrubs or trees from

Far left: *Koelreuteria paniculata* in flower and fruit
Left: *Kolkwitzia amabilis*
Left below: +*Laburnocytisus adamii*
Below: *Laburnum* × *watereri* Vossii

tropical Asia to N. Australia and Pacific Is, 1 of which is half hardy: *L. indica*, crape myrtle; China; deciduous large shrub or small tree, to 8m or so; leaves alternate or almost opposite, oblong-elliptic to obovate, 3–7cm long; flowers in terminal panicles, to 20cm or more long, each bloom 5–7cm wide, of 6 curiously slender-stalked petals, the blade cordate, rounded, strongly waved, white, pink, purple, summer; several cultivars, including a dwarf strain which may be raised as an annual, are usually available. In mild areas may be grown outside on a sunny wall and worth trying elsewhere if protected in winter. Warm summers are needed for flowering and to ripen the new growth to withstand winter cold. Plant late spring, at the foot of a warm wall in fertile, well drained soil. May be trained flat or allowed to develop into a bush. Best pruned hard annually in spring, the previous season's stems cut back to a few centimetres. Apply liquid feed at fortnightly intervals in summer. Propagate by cuttings in summer, bottom heat 18°C or seed in spring at 20–25°C.

Lagurus

(Greek *lagos*, a hare, and *oura*, a tail – the flower-spikes are somewhat similar). GRAMINEAE. A genus of 1 species of annual grass from the Mediterranean: *L. ovatus*, hare's tail; tufted habit; stems to 30cm tall; leaves narrowly linear, grey-green, downy; flowering panicles 2–3cm long, very dense and woolly, ovoid, white, summer. Grow in any well-drained soil in a sunny site. Sow seed *in situ* in spring, or autumn in sheltered sites. In cold areas may be sown in boxes and over-wintered in a cold frame. In some gardens it comes regularly from self-sown seedlings.

Lamarckia

(for Chevalier Jean Baptiste de Monet Lamarck, 1744–1829, French botanist, naturalist and author whose work on evolution foreshadowed that of Darwin). GRAMINEAE. A genus of 1 species of annual grass from the Mediterranean: *L. aurea*, goldentop; tufted; stems erect, 10–30cm tall; leaves linear, 5–13cm long; panicles 3–7cm long, dense, oblong, spike-like, composed of tiny, straw-yellow or golden, sterile and fertile spikelets, the latter awned, summer. Grow in well-drained soil in sun. Sow late spring *in situ*, or autumn in pans or boxes in a cold frame, transplanting in spring when the coldest weather has passed.

Lamiastrum

(*lamium*, old Latin name for a dead-nettle, and *aster*, similar to). LABIATAE. A genus of 1 species from Europe, formerly classified in the genus *Lamium*: *L. galeobdolon* (*Galeobdolon luteum*, *Lamium galeobdolon*), yellow archangel; perennial, vegetative growth prostrate; flowering stems erect, leafy, 30–60cm tall; leaves ovate, 3–8cm long, coarsely crenate, hairy; flowers 2cm long, yellow, late spring to summer, represented in gardens by *L.g.* Variegatum (*L.g.* Florentinum), having leaves with 2 broad silver-mottled bands; useful, fast-growing ground cover for shade but apt to be invasive. For cultivation see next entry.

Lamium

(old Latin name for a dead-nettle). Dead-nettle. LABIATAE. A genus of 40–50 species of annuals and perennials from Europe, Asia, N. Africa. They are tufted to clump-forming, often spreading widely, with whorls of tubular flowers in the upper leaf-axils. Each flower is 2-lipped, the upper one hooded. Grow in any well-drained soil in sun or partial shade. Plant autumn to spring. Propagate by division at planting time or from seed in spring.

Species cultivated: *L. galeobdolon*, see *Lamiastrum*. *L. garganicum*, large red dead-nettle; S. Europe; clump-forming perennial; stems 30–40cm tall; leaves ovate-cordate, to 7cm long, crenate; flowers 2·5–4cm long, pink or red-purple, late spring to summer. *L. maculatum*, spotted dead-nettle, Europe; decumbent perennial forming wide patches; leaves triangular-cordate-ovate, 4–8cm, coarsely toothed with an irregular, central, silvery-white band; flowers pale red-purple on stems 20–40cm tall, early to late summer. *L.m.* Album, flowers white;

Far left: *Lagerstroemia indica*
Left: *Lagurus ovatus*
Bottom left: *Lamiastrum galeobdolon* Variegatum
Below: *Lamium maculatum*
Bottom: *Lamium maculatum* Aureum

L.m. Aureum, leaves bright greenish-yellow; *L.m.* Roseum, soft clear pink. *L. orvala*, N. Italy and W. Austria to Yugoslavia and Hungary; clump-forming perennial; stems 40–100cm tall; leaves triangular-ovate, coarsely toothed, 4–15cm long; flowers to 4·5cm long, light to deep red-purple, summer; needs humus-rich, moisture-retentive soil to do its best.

Lampranthus

(Greek *lampros*, shining, and *anthos*, flower – the petals have a satiny sheen). AIZOACEAE. A genus of 160 species of succulent perennials and sub-shrubs, formerly included in *Mesembryanthemum*, from S.Africa. They are prostrate to erect, with opposite pairs of cylindrical leaves and terminal, solitary or cymose clusters of many-petalled flowers, superficially resembling daisies. Greenhouse, or treated as a half-hardy annual, except in areas of mild winters where they can be grown outside in well-drained soil in sun. Under glass provide a minimum temperature of 5–7°C, sunny and well-ventilated. Grow in a good commercial potting mixture. Pot or repot spring, the trailing species being effective in hanging baskets. Plants to be grown outside should be planted late spring when fear of frost has passed. The same plants may be lifted in autumn, potted and over-wintered, or cuttings taken late summer and the young plants only over-wintered. Propagate by cuttings spring to late summer or from seed in spring at 16–18°C.

Species cultivated: *L.haworthii*, shrubby, stems more or less erect, 30–60cm tall; leaves 2·5–4cm long, semi-cylindrical, grey-green; flowers 5–7cm wide,

light purple, summer. *L. multiradiatus*, see next species. *L. roseus* (*L. multiradiatus*), shrubby, stems erect to spreading, 30–60cm tall; leaves 2–3cm long, triangular in cross-section, glaucous with translucent dots; flowers to 4cm wide, pale pink to light rose-purple, summer. *L. stipulaceus*, shrubby, to 40cm tall, stems with many short shoots from leaf-axils; leaves 4–5cm long, semi-cylindrical to almost triangular in cross-section, bright green with translucent dots; flowers 4cm wide, purple, summer.

Lantana

(old Latin name for a *Viburnum* that this genus somewhat resembles). VERBENACEAE. A genus of 150 species of evergreen shrubs and perennials from tropical America, W. Indies, tropical and W. Africa. The shrubby species cultivated have opposite pairs of ovate to oblong, toothed leaves and small, tubular, 5-lobed flowers in dense flattened heads, followed by berry-like, black drupes. Outside in warm areas or greenhouse, minimum temperature 7°C, sunny and well-ventilated. The plants may be stood or bedded outside from mid summer to mid autumn. Under glass, large specimens may be grown in a border, tub or large pot, or small plants grown annually from cuttings. Pot, repot or top-dress annually in spring, shortening back the previous season's stems to 8–19cm. Apply liquid feed at 2–3 weekly intervals to container-grown plants during the summer. Propagate by cuttings in late summer, bottom heat above 18°C, and pot when rooted into 7·5–9cm containers of sandy or seed-sowing soil mixture. Over-winter at 10–13°C. Pinch out stem tips 2–3 times to promote a bushy habit, and successively pot on into 13 or 15cm, and 18 or 20cm pots, using a richer or all purpose potting mixture. Plants may be flowered in 13–15cm pots with feeding, or hardened off and planted out. Seed may be sown at 16–18°C, and if this is done in early spring plants will flower same year.

Species cultivated: *L. camara*, yellow sage; tropical America, naturalized to weed proportions in some tropical countries; 1–2m tall; stems sometimes prickly; leaves 5–10cm long, rough-textured, dark green; flower-heads to 5cm wide, the central florets opening yellow or orange-yellow, then ageing red or white, late spring to autumn; the various forms and cultivars range from yellow to red, pink and white changing colour or tone as they age. *L.c. hybrida* covers a race of dwarf forms, usually the most commonly met in cultivation. *L. montevidensis* (*L. delicata*, *L. delicatissima*, *L. sellowiana*), S. America; prostrate; stems to 1m long; leaves to 3cm long; flower-heads 2–3cm wide, the florets rose-purple with yellow eyes; flowering into winter if minimum temperature of 13°C maintained; attractive in hanging baskets.

Lapageria

(for the Empress Josephine de la Pagerie). LILIACEAE. A genus of 1 species of evergreen climber from Chile and the national flower of that country: *L. rosea*, Chilean bell flower, copihue; stems twining, to 3m or more; leaves alternate, ovate-lanceolate, pointed, leathery, deep glossy green; flowers 6-tepalled, waxy-textured, rose to rose-crimson, faintly spotted within, to 7cm long, late summer to autumn; fruit a greenish, oblong-ovoid berry. *L.r. albiflora*, white; several other forms are sometimes available with larger and/or darker, sometimes striped flowers. Frost-free greenhouse or sheltered site outside in mild areas, preferably shaded from summer sun, in a soil containing abundant peat or leaf mould and well-drained. Best planted out but may be grown in pots of an all-peat mixture with ⅓-part coarse sand added. Pot or plant spring and provide strings or wires for support. Propagate by layering in spring or from seed sown when ripe. The latter must not be kept above 13°C and is slow to germinate and the seedlings take several years to flower.

Left: *Lampranthus aurantiacus*
Below: *Lantana camara*
Above right: *Lapageria rosea*
Below right: *Lapeirousia laxa*

Lapeirousia

(*Lapeyrousia*). (for Baron Philippe Picot de la Peyrouse, 1744–1818, Pyrenean botanist). IRIDACEAE. A genus of about 50 species of cormous plants from S. Africa, 1 of which is generally

available: *L. laxa* (*L. cruenta, Anomatheca c.*), leaves narrowly sword-shaped, to 20cm long, in fan-like tufts; stems slender, to 25cm tall, terminating in a short raceme of slender-tubed, carmine-crimson flowers each to 2·5cm long with 6 spreading lobes, the outer 3 bearing darker red basal blotches, late summer to autumn. *L.l.* Alba, flowers pure white. Frost-free greenhouse or a sheltered sunny site outside .Plant spring, those in pots in a good commercial potting mixture. In cold areas corms are best given protection or lifted in late autumn and stored cool but frost-free until spring. Propagate by separating cormlets when dormant or from seed in spring at about 15°C.

Larch – see *Larix*.

Larix

(ancient Latin name). Larch. PINACEAE. A genus of 10 species of coniferous trees from northern temperate zone. They much resemble *Cedrus* in essential characters but are deciduous and have smaller, persistent cones that do not break up when ripe. Flowers (strobili) with very young leaves, males rounded to ovoid, females like tiny versions of the mature cones, often pink or red. Culture as for *Cedrus*; ideally plant out 1–2 year old seedlings.

Species cultivated: *L. decidua* (*L. europaea*), common European larch; Alps, Carpathians to Poland and Ukraine, much planted elsewhere; to 45m tall; of conical outline, the main branches in whorls, drooping when old; bark brownish-grey; stems pale yellow; leaves 2–3cm or up to 6cm on vigorous leading stems, bright pale green when young; male strobili rounded, flattened, 5–10mm long, whitish then yellow with pollen, females red, same length; cones ovoid to 4cm long, ripening the first year. *L.* × *eurolepis* (*L.* × *henryana, L.* × *hybrida*), (hybrid between *L. decidua* × *L. kaempferi*), Dunkeld or hybrid larch; to 32m or more, vigorous and fast-growing; bark reddish-brown, otherwise intermediate between parents in other characters; however, seed from this hybrid shows a range of variation between the parents with a tendency towards *L. kaempferi*. *L. kaempferi* (*L. leptolepis*), Japanese larch; to 37m tall, broadly conical; bark reddish-brown; stems usually dark orange-red, sometimes dark brown or purplish; leaves greyish-green; male strobili broadly ovoid, 6mm long, female 8mm long, pink and cream or yellow; cones about 3 × 3cm, rosette-like, margins of scales reflexed.

Larkspur – see *Delphinium*.

Lathyrus

(Greek *lathyros*, for a pea). LEGUMINOSAE. A genus of 100–150 species of annual and perennial, erect and climbing plants from northern temperate zone, mountains of Africa and S. America. They have alternate, mainly pinnate leaves, the terminal leaflet of the climbers modified to a tendril, and axillary racemes of pea flowers followed by slender pods of hard, rounded seed. Grow in well-drained, humus-rich soil in a sunny site. For sweet peas on all but the richest soils, add 1–2 large buckets of well-decayed farmyard manure, garden compost or leaf mould and 120g bonemeal per sq m. Take out an equivalent amount of soil from the planting site (trench or bed), replace with the manure and fork in to a depth of 25cm. Plant perennials autumn to spring and propagate by division or from seed at the same time, the seed sown *in situ*, boxes or pots. Annuals may be sown in the same way. In colder areas sweet peas are best in a cold frame. Soak the seed in tepid water for

24 hours first, and then space-sow at 4–5cm apart each way in boxes of a good commercial potting mixture. For a good germination percentage, ensure that the temperature does not fall below 13°C. An autumn sowing will produce bigger and earlier-flowering plants. Ventilate the frame or cold greenhouse on all mild days and keep the compost just moist. When seedlings have 3 true leaves pinch out the growing tips to encourage strong basal shoots. As soon as basal shoots appear, pot singly into 7·5–9cm pots of potting mixture and provide supports. After hardening off for 2–3 weeks, plant out mid to late spring (earlier in mild areas or very sheltered sites, or if cloches can be used during cold spells). Tall pea sticks or canes and netting are suitable supports for garden display, the plants being allowed to climb naturally. For exhibition-type flowers a cordon system is used. The plants are thinned to 1 strong stem soon after planting out and this stem is tied to a stake at intervals, all tendrils and axillary shoots being removed when young. Remove spent blooms daily.

Species cultivated: *L. cyaneus* Albo-roseus (of gardens), see *L. vernus* Albo-roseus. *L. digitatus*, see *L. vernus* Albo-roseus. *L. latifolius*, everlasting pea; Europe, widely naturalized in USA; perennial climber, to 3m or so; leaflets 2, each ovate to lanceolate, 4–10cm long; racemes of 5–15, rose-purple or white, 2–3cm wide flowers, late summer. *L. odoratus*, sweet pea; S. Italy, Sicily; annual climber, to 2m tall; leaflets 2, each 2–6cm long, ovate-oblong to elliptic, somewhat glaucous-green; racemes of 3 or more fragrant purple flowers to 3·5cm wide, summer; breeding and selection from this species and its forms have resulted in 100s of cultivars with waved, self, bicoloured and picotee blooms to 4·5cm wide in practically every colour of the rainbow and including *L.o. nanellus*, a dwarf, non-climbing mutant typified by Little Sweetheart. *L. rotundifolius*, Persian everlasting pea; W. Asia, Crimea, C. USSR; perennial climber, to 80cm tall; leaflets 2, ovate-orbicular to elliptic, 2·5–6cm long; racemes of 3–8 rose flowers, each about 2cm wide, summer. *L. vernus* (*Orobus v.*), spring vetch; clump-forming, erect perennial about 30cm or more tall; leaflets 4–8, sometimes only 2, ovate to lanceolate; racemes of 3–10, red-purple and blue flowers, each 1·3–2cm long, spring. *L.v.* Albo-roseus, flowers pink and white – sometimes confused with *L. cyaneus* (*L. digitatus*), an allied species with linear leaflets.

Far left: *Larix decidua*
Left: *Lathyrus latifolius*
Left below: *Lathyrus odoratus* cultivars
Below: *Laurus nobilis*
Right: *Lavandula angustifolia* Nana Alba
Right below: *Lavandula angustifolia* Munstead
Right bottom: *Lavandula stoechas*

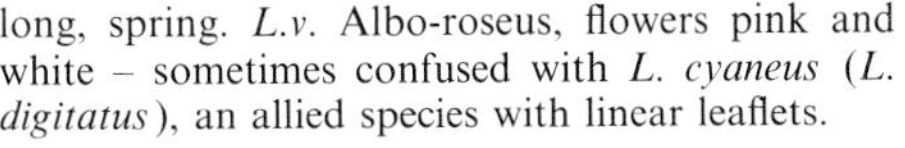

Laurel – see *Laurus* and *Aucuba*.

Laurestinus – see *Viburnum tinus*.

Laurus

(old Latin name for bay laurel). LAURACEAE. A genus of 2 species of evergreen trees from the Mediterranean, Canary Is to the Azores, 1 of which is commonly grown as a foliage plant and for flavouring: *L. nobilis*, bay laurel; Mediterranean; 10–20m tall in the wild or in a sheltered garden, easily kept as a bush of 2–3m; leaves narrowly oval to ovate, glossy deep green, leathery, aromatic; flowers unisexual, perianth greenish, 4–6 lobed, males with 8–12 yellowish stamens, in axillary clusters, spring; fruit a black, ovoid, berry-like drupe 1–1·5cm long. Grow in any moderately fertile soil, preferably in sun, although partial shade is tolerated. Plant spring. Propagate from seed sown when ripe and kept in a cold frame, or by cuttings in late summer, the seedlings and rooted cuttings best grown in pots for 1–2 years before planting out. May be grown permanently in large pots or tubs of J.I. potting compost No 2 or its equivalent; stands clipping well. Moderately frost hardy.

Lavandula

(Latin *lavo*, to wash – for its use in lavender water and other toiletries). Lavender. LABIATAE. A genus of about 20 species of evergreen shrubs and sub-

Above: *Lavatera olbia* Rosea
Top right: *Lavatera trimestris* Splendens Alba
Above right: *Lavatera trimestris* Loveliness
Far right: *Layia platyglossa*
Far right below: *Ledum groenlandicum*

shrubs from the Canary Is to the Azores, Mediterranean to Somalia and India. They have opposite pairs of linear to oblong-lanceolate, sometimes toothed or pinnately lobed leaves, and dense spikes of tubular, 2-lipped flowers. Grow in any well-drained soil in sun; some species need a sheltered site. Plant spring. Propagate by cuttings in late summer, from seed in spring under glass.

Species cultivated: *L. angustifolia* (*L. spica*, *L. officinalis*, *L. vera*), common or English lavender; Mediterranean; shrub 60–100cm or more tall; leaves linear, 2–5cm long, white-downy when young; flowers purple, about 1cm long, in spikes to 8cm long, terminating erect almost leafless stems to 30cm or more long, late summer; several cultivars are available, among them: *L.a.* Alba, flowers white; *L.a.* Hidcote (*L.a.* Nana Atropurpurea), compact, to 75cm tall, flowers violet; *L.a.* Loddon Pink, like *L.a.* Hidcote but flowers pale pink; *L.a.* Munstead, compact, to 75cm, leaves greener than type, flowers bright lavender-blue; *L.a.* Vera, Dutch lavender, robust, to 1·2m tall, leaves broad, somewhat oblanceolate, much grown as a source of lavender oil. *L. dentata*, S. and E. Spain, Balearic Is; shrub 30–90cm tall; leaves linear-oblong, toothed or pinnately cut into small, narrow lobes; flowers 8mm long, dark purple in spikes topped by purple bracts, late summer. *L. lanata*, mountains of S. Spain; like *L. angustifolia* but persistently white-woolly. *L. stoechas*, French lavender; Mediterranean, Portugal; shrub 30–90cm tall; leaves 1–4cm long, linear to oblong-lanceolate, greyish-green; flowers 6–8mm, dark purple, spikes 2–3cm long topped by a tuft of purple ovate bracts, on leafy stems.

Lavatera

(for J. R. Lavater, doctor and naturalist of Zurich in the 16th century). MALVACEAE. A genus of 20–25 species of annuals, biennials, perennials and shrubs from Canaries, Mediterranean, Europe (coasts), Asia, Australia, California. They are mainly erect, with alternate, ovate to palmately lobed leaves and leafy terminal racemes of 5-petalled flowers having obovate, often notched petals and 3–6 (rarely 9) bracts at their bases united to form a calyx-like structure. Grow in any fertile, well-drained soil in a sunny site. Plant perennials or shrubs autumn or spring, the annuals sown *in situ* in spring (autumn also in sheltered places). Propagate perennials by division or cuttings spring, biennials from seed spring, or cuttings late summer.

Species cultivated: *L. arborea*, tree mallow; Europe; biennial, 2–3m tall; forms a woody-based stem to 1m or so the first year; with palmate, 5–9 lobed, pubescent leaves, to 25cm wide, elongating to full height second summer, with smaller leaves and axillary racemes of 5cm wide, rose-purple, darker-veined flowers. *L. cachemiriana* (*L. kashmiriana*), Kashmir; herbaceous perennial 1·2–2·4m tall; lower leaves rounded, 5–7 lobed, 8–12cm long, upper ones smaller, 3–5 lobed; flowers to 7·5cm wide, petals bi-lobed at tip, pink, late summer. *L. olbia*, W. Mediterranean, Portugal; shrub to 2m tall; lower leaves ovate, 6–10cm long, 3–5 lobed, upper smaller, oblong-ovate to lanceolate, often slightly 3-lobed; flowers 7–9cm wide, reddish-purple, petals bi-lobed, summer to autumn. *L.o.* Rosea, bright lilac-pink. *L. trimestris*, Mediterranean, Portugal; annual, 60–120cm tall; leaves rounded, cordate, somewhat 3–7 lobed, 3–6cm long; flowers 6–8cm wide, bright pink, summer, autumn.

Lavender – see *Lavandula*.

Layia

(for George Tradescant Lay, died 1845, botanist and naturalist who accompanied Capt. F. W. Beechey's voyage of exploration to N. W. America 1825–28). COMPOSITAE. A genus of 15 species of annuals mainly from California, 1 of which is generally available: *L. platyglossa* (*L. elegans*), tidytips; hardy, erect to prostrate, to 30–45cm tall, well-branched; leaves narrowly oblong to linear, lower ones pinnatifid, glandular hairy, grey-green, aromatic; flower-heads daisy-like, 5cm wide, yellow, ray florets tipped cream, summer to autumn, freely produced. *L.p. campestris*, plant erect – the commonly grown form in gardens. Culture as for annual *Coreopsis*, although autumn-sown seedlings

may need cloche protection in cold areas. An easily grown plant.

Ledum

(Greek *ledon* for *Cistus*, taken over for this genus by Linnaeus). ERICACEAE. A genus of 4–10 species (depending on the classifier) of dwarf shrubs from the northern temperate and polar regions. They are similar to dwarf rhododendrons but the flowers open widely, composed of 5 separate white petals. Grow in acid, peaty, moist soil in cool sites but open to the sky. Plant autumn to spring. Propagate from seed, by layers, or by careful division in spring, or cuttings late summer in a cold frame.

Species cultivated: *L. groenlandicum* (*L. latifolium*), Labrador tea, N. N.America, Greenland; bushy, erect, 60–90cm tall; shoots rusty downy; leaves 1–4·5cm long, elliptic to narrowly oblong, dark green and somewhat hairy above, rusty downy beneath; flowers 1–1·5cm wide, with 5–8 stamens, in conspicuous umbels, spring to early summer. *L.g.* Compactum, dwarfer, with shorter, broader leaves.

L. palustre, N.Europe and Asia; similar to *L. groenlandicum*, but leaves linear to narrowly oblong and flowers with 10 stamens, summer.

Legousia

(for Legous de Gerland, founder of the Dijon Botanic Garden in 1773). CAMPANULACEAE. A genus of about 15 species of annuals from Europe, N.Africa, W.Asia, 2 of which are sometimes available. They are branched from the base with erect or shortly decumbent stems bearing oblong to obovate or spathulate leaves and 5-petalled flowers with tubular bases from the upper axils. Grow in any well-drained soil in sun. Sow seed *in situ* in spring, or autumn in mild areas if large plants are wanted.

Species cultivated: *L.hybrida* (*Specularia h.*), S. and W.Europe; 10–20cm or more tall; leaves to 2cm long, undulate, crenate; flowers in corymbose clusters, 1cm long, lilac blue to reddish-purple, with

prominent, awl-shaped, calyx lobes, summer. *L. speculum-veneris* (*Specularia s.-v.*) Venus's looking glass; S.W. and S.C. Europe, north to Holland; to 40cm tall; leaves to 4cm long; flowers often in panicle-like clusters, 1–2·5cm long, violet-blue or white, with prominent calyx lobes, summer.

Leiophyllum

(Greek *leios*, smooth, and *phyllon*, a leaf). ERICACEAE. A genus of 1 species of dwarf evergreen shrub from E. N.America: *L. buxifolium*, sand myrtle; 60–90cm tall, often less, densely branched and of rounded habit; leaves alternate, sometimes opposite, 3–13mm long, oval to oblong, leathery, lustrous; flowers small, 5-petalled, white, pink in bud, in dense umbel-like corymbs, early summer; *L.b. hugeri*, leaves longer, flowering pedicels glandular; *L.b. prostratum* (*L. lyonii*), loosely spreading prostrate habit, leaves mostly opposite. Grow in moisture-retentive, peaty, sandy, acid soil in sun, although light shade is tolerated. Plant autumn or spring. Propagate from seed or by layering in spring, cuttings late summer.

Lemna

(Greek name for an unspecified water weed, used by Linnaeus). Duckweed. LEMNACEAE. A genus of about 10 species of very small aquatic plants of cosmopolitan distribution. They are mainly floating and formed of tiny, oval, flattened, leaf-like stems (plant bodies or thalli), each with 1 to few trailing roots (but see *L. trisulca*). The minute, unisexual, petalless flowers are partially embedded in the sides of the stems, consisting of solitary or paired stamens and single pistils. Grow in ponds or aquaria in sun or partial shade. Plant by dropping into the water in spring or summer. Propagate by division at the same time. All species multiply quickly and can be very invasive, especially in mineral rich water, and a complete covering of the floating species will debilitate submerged aquatic plants growing beneath it.

Species cultivated: *L. gibba*, fat duckweed; cosmopolitan; plant bodies 3–5mm long, ovate, convex above and below with 1 root; finely dark and yellow-green mottled. *L. minor*, common duckweed; temperate regions; plant bodies 1·5–4mm long; the commonest and most rapidly colonizing species. *L. polyrhiza*, greater duckweed; almost cosmopolitan; plant bodies 5–8mm or more long, ovate to rounded, flat and glossy, often purplish beneath with several roots. *L. trisculca*, ivy-leaved duckweed; almost cosmopolitan; plant bodies submerged, in groups of 7 or more, 7–12mm long, oblong lanceolate, dark translucent green either with one root or with no roots at all.

Left: *Legousia speculum-veneris*
Left below: *Leiophyllum buxifolium*
Below: *Lemna minor* on pool surface
Right: *Leontopodium alpinum*

Lenten rose – see *Hellebor's.*

Leontopodium

(old Latin vernacular meaning the footprint of a little lion, originally alluding to flower-heads of the similar *Evax*, but transferred to this genus). Edelweiss. COMPOSITAE. A genus of perhaps 20–30 species of herbaceous perennials from the mountains of Europe, Asia, S. America. A taxonomically difficult genus with many of the species very similar and often listed under names of no botanical standing. They are mainly tufted to shortly mat-forming with narrowly lanceolate, or spathulate to linear leaves, and dense terminal clusters (cymes) of small flower-heads and radiating, somewhat petal-like, woolly bracts. Grow in well-drained but not dry soil in a sunny open site. Plant autumn or spring. Propagate from seed sown under the protection of cold glass in late winter, or by division of the clumps in spring, just as the new growth begins to show.

Species cultivated: *L. aloysiodorum* of gardens, see *L.haplophylloides*. *L. alpinum*, common edelweiss; Pyrenees, Alps, Carpathians; forming tufted mats; stems 15–25cm tall; leaves linear to oblong-lanceolate, white-woolly; head of bracts white, star-like, 3–10cm wide, summer. *L.a. krasense* (*crasense*, *crassense*, and wrongly as *L. crassum* in some lists), somewhat more slender and whiter than type. *L. haplophylloides*, C. China; tufted; stems to 30cm or more tall; leaves linear, grey-hairy, set with black glands, lemon-scented; head of bracts white, to 5cm

wide, summer. *L. souliei*, S. China; similar to *L. alpinum*, but stoloniferous; stems 30cm or more tall and heads of bracts spidery. *L. stracheyi*, Tibet, W. China; tufted; stems 30–50cm tall; leaves ovate-lanceolate, thinly hairy, set with brown glands above, white hairy beneath; head of bracts dense, white, to 6·5cm wide, summer.

Leopard's bane – see *Doronicum pardalianches*.

Leptosiphon – see *Linanthus*.

Leptospermum

(Greek *leptos*, slender, and *sperma*, seed – the seed is very narrow). MYRTACEAE. A genus of 40–50 species of evergreen trees and shrubs from Australasia and Malaysia. They are generally of bushy habit with slender stems, alternate, small, linear to rounded leaves, and 5-petalled, widely expanded flowers, solitary or in small clusters in the upper leaf-axils. With the exception of *L. humifusum*, the species described here need a frost-free, sunny and well-ventilated greenhouse, or sheltered, warm wall with protection in winter in all but the mildest areas. Pot or plant spring in well-drained soil or a good commercial potting mixture; limy soils should be well-laced with peat. Propagate by cuttings with a heel late summer, bottom heat 16–18°C, or from seed at about 15°C. spring.

Species cultivated: *L. cunninghamii*, see *L. lanigerum*. *L. flavescens*, E. Australia; shrub, to 3m or more tall; leaves linear to lanceolate, to 2cm long; flowers white or yellow tinted, 1–1·5cm wide, summer. *L.f. obovatum*, leaves obovate, to 1·5cm long, the commonest and hardiest form in Britain. *L. humifusum* (*L. rupestre*, *L. scoparium prostratum* of gardens), Tasmania; hardy prostrate shrub spreading to 1·5m or more, sometimes to 20cm or more high; leaves crowded, 5–8mm long, elliptic to obovate, round-tipped; flowers 1–1·5cm wide, white, early summer. *L. lanigerum*, woolly tea tree; S.E. Australia including Tasmania; 3–4m tall or eventually a small tree; leaves narrowly obovate to oblong, 8–18mm long, with silky silvery hair; flowers 1·5–2cm wide, white, summer; surprisingly hardy and well worth trying against a wall even in the colder areas. *L.l. cunninghamii*, leaves smaller and greyer than type, young growths pinkish-

Below: *Leptospermum scoparium* Keatleyi, **bottom:** *L. scoparium* Nanum, **right:** *L. lanigerum cunninghamii* and **below right:** *L. scoparium* Red Damask

brown, flowering late summer, equally hardy but may lose much of its foliage in a hard winter. *L. rupestre*, see *L. humifusum*. *L. scoparium*, manuka; New Zealand, Victoria, Tasmania; shrub 2–4m tall or small tree to 6m or more in mild areas; leaves 8–15mm long, narrowly oblong or elliptic to oblanceolate, prickly-pointed; flowers to 1·5cm wide, white, late spring; a very variable shrub in habit and leaf shape; among several cultivars known are *L.s.* Chapmanii, foliage flushed bronze, flowers rose-red; *L.s.* Keatleyi, young growth red-flushed, flowers large, soft pink, less hardy than some forms; *L.s.* Nanum, dense shrublet to 30cm tall, flowers pale pink with crimson eye, moderately hardy in sheltered sites; *L.s.* Nichollsii, leaves small, linear, flushed bronzy-purple, flowers carmine with darker eye; *L.s. prostratum*, see *L. humifusum*; *L.s.* Red Damask, flowers deep cherry-red, fully double.

Leptosyne – see *Coreopsis*.

Lespedeza

(for Vincente Manuel de Léspedes, Spanish governor of Florida about 1790). Bush clover. LEGUMINOSAE. A genus of about 100 species of shrubs, sub-shrubs, perennials and annuals from Himalaya to Japan, E. N.America and Australia, 1 species is widely available: *L. thunbergii* (*L. sieboldii, Desmodium t., D. penduliflorum*), N. China, Japan; sub-shrub 2–3m tall; stems herbaceous, dying back to a woody rootstock each winter; leaves trifoliate, leaflets elliptic, 4–5cm long; flowers pea-shaped, rose-purple, 1–1·5cm long, in clustered drooping racemes to 15cm long, autumn; pods small, 1-seeded; not at its best in cold, wet seasons. Grow in humus-rich, well-drained soil in sun. Plant spring. Propagate from seed or by division in spring.

Below: *Lespedeza thunbergii*
Top right: *Leucocoryne purpurea*
Right: *Leucogenes leontopodium*
Below right: *Leucogenes grandiceps*

Leucanthemum – see *Chrysanthemum*.

Leucocoryne

(Greek *leukos*, white, and *koryne*, a club – alluding to the sterile stamens). ALLIACEAE (AMARYLLIDACEAE, LILIACEAE). A genus of 5–6 species of half-hardy bulbous plants from Chile. They are allied to *Brodiaea*, with several linear, channelled basal leaves and erect, leafless stems topped by umbels of 6-tepalled, widely expanded flowers that open in late spring. Outdoors in the extreme south or greenhouse, minimum temperature 7°C, sunny and well-ventilated. Grow in pots of loam-based potting mixture. Pot in late autumn and keep barely moist until the leafy shoots are well up, then water regularly but allow to dry between applications. Liquid feed at fortnightly intervals when in full growth is beneficial. As much sun as possible is needed during growth to develop flower-buds. When flowers and leaves fade, dry off and store in the pots until autumn. Propagate by offsets at potting time or from seed sown in spring; plants from seed take several years to reach flowering size.
Species cultivated: *L. ixioides*, glory of the sun; stems 30–40cm tall or more; leaves 2–3, each 20–30cm long; flowers 3–4cm wide, pale blue, fragrant, 5–9 in each umbel. *L. purpurea*, as for *L. ixioides*, but flowers lilac-purple with a red-purple centre; often classified as a variety of *L. ixioides*.

Leucogenes

(Greek *leukos*, white, and *eugenes*, noble – an alternative version of edelweiss that this genus greatly resembles). COMPOSITAE. A genus of 2 species of dwarf, woody-based, evergreen alpine perennials from New Zealand. They are tufted, with slender decumbent stems forming loose to dense mats with crowded, obovate to oblong-lanceolate, usually silvery hairy leaves and edelweiss-like flower clusters, but with a neater head of shorter, woolly bracts. Grow in sheltered sunny screes, dry walls or pans in alpine house. Plant or pot spring – if the latter, preferably in equal parts grit and one of the peat composts. Propagate by careful division or from seed in spring, or by cuttings in sand late summer.
Species cultivated: *L. grandiceps*, S.Island edelweiss; forming loose mats to 15cm or so wide; leaves 5–10mm long, obovate-cuneate, usually silky white but sometimes buff hairy; stems to 10cm or more tall, topped by 5–15 small, groundsel-like heads surrounded by 8–15 white woolly bracts to 1cm long, summer. *L. leontopodium*, N.Island edelweiss; similar to *L. grandiceps* but usually more vigorous, forming larger, denser mats of 8–20mm long, oblong-lanceolate leaves and flower-head clusters with up to 20 woolly bracts to 2cm long.

Leucojum

(*leukon*, white, and *ion*, violet – Greek vernacular for several kinds of fragrant white flowers, used for this genus by Linnaeus). Snowflake. AMARYLLIDACEAE. A genus of 9 species of bulbous perennials from Portugal to the Caucasus and Morocco to Algeria. They have strap-shaped to filiform leaves and erect, leafless stems bearing 1 to several, 6-tepalled, nodding, snowdrop-like flowers, but with the 3 inner tepals the same size as the outer. *L. aestivum* and *L. vernum* should be grown in ordinary soil in sun or light shade, *L. autumnale* in well-drained soil in a sheltered, sunny site, the remaining species in a frost-free frame or greenhouse, although they can be grown outside in mild areas. Plant in early autumn (summer for *L. autumnale*) or immediately after flowering. Any commercial potting mixture is suitable for pot culture, the all-peat sorts mixed with ⅓-part grit or coarse sand. Propagate from seed when ripe or by offsets separated at planting time.
Species cultivated: *L. aestivum*, summer snowflake; C. and S. Europe to Caucasus; stems to 35cm tall; leaves strap-shaped, to 48cm long by 1–1·5cm wide, glossy rich green; flowers 2–5, each about 2·5cm long, tepals white, green-tipped, late spring, early summer; *L.a. pulchellum*, leaves paler than type, 6–10mm wide, flowers smaller, opening somewhat earlier. *L. autumnale*, autumn snowflake; N.W. Africa, Portugal, Spain, Sardinia, Sicily; stems 8–16cm tall, sometimes more; leaves filiform, about 16cm long; flowers 1–4, each 1–1·4cm long, white, pink-tinged at base, late summer, autumn before or with very young leaves. *L. hiemale*, see next species. *L. nicaeense* (*L. hiemale*), S. France; stems 4–13cm tall; leaves narrowly linear, to 15cm or more long; flowers usually solitary, white, 1–1·4cm long, spring; will grow outside in warm areas, otherwise under glass. *L. roseum* (*Acis rosea*), Corsica, Sardinia; like a smaller, pale pink version of *L. autumnale* with greyish leaves; needs greenhouse culture to thrive and flower. *L. vernum*, spring snowflake; C. Europe; stems 10–30cm tall; leaves strap-shaped, to 22cm long, deep glossy green; flowers usually solitary, about 2·5cm long, tepals green-tipped, spring, sometimes opening while stem and leaves are very short. *L.v. carpathicum*, often with 2 flowers per

Above left: *Leucojum vernum*
Left: *Leucojum aestivum*
Bottom left: *Leucothoe fontanesiana*
Above: *Lewisia cotyledon* hybrids
Right: *Lewisia cotyledon howellii*

stem, tepals tipped yellow or greenish-yellow; *L.v. vagneri*, robust, usually with 2 flowers; these 2 varieties are not always constant.

Leucothoe

(daughter of Orchamus and 1 of the loves of Apollo). ERICACEAE. A genus of about 45 species of deciduous and evergreen shrubs from E. Asia, N. and S. America, Malagasy. They are similar to *Gaultheria*, with alternate, lanceolate to ovate leaves, and axillary racemes of urn-shaped flowers followed by flattened, rounded, dry capsules. Culture as for *Gaultheria*, but more shade-tolerant.
Species cultivated: *L. catesbaei* (of gardens), see next species. *L. fontanesiana* (*Andromeda catesbaei*, *A. fontanesiana*, *L. catesbaei* in part, *L. editorum*), dog hobble, fetterbush; mountains of S.E. USA; evergreen, 1–2m tall; stems zia-zag; slender arching; leaves 7–13cm long, ovate-lanceolate, dark glossy green; flowers white, about 6mm long in racemes to 7·5cm, late spring. *L.f.* Rainbow, young leaves pink then variegated cream and white; *L.f.* Rollissonii, leaves smaller and narrower than type. *L. keiskei*, Japan; like a smaller version of the previous species, low, arching stems sometimes almost prostrate, flowers fewer per raceme but 1·2–1·5cm long.

Lewisia

(for Capt. Meriwether Lewis, 1774–1809, who – with Capt. W. Clark – led the first crossing of N. America from Saint Louis to the Pacific coast). Bitterroot. PORTULACACEAE. A genus of 16 species of perennials from W. N.America. They are tufted, rosette-forming, with fleshy roots and leaves, and usually spreading, 4–18 petalled flowers, solitary or in panicles. Grow in pots in a cold greenhouse using a neutral or lime-free potting mixture with $\frac{1}{3}$–2 part extra coarse sand or grit added, or grow outside in a scree, on a dry wall or in vertical crevices in a rock garden. Drainage around the neck of the plant must be good as most lewisias are prone to rotting during wet summers or winters. Plant spring. Propagate by division or from seed in spring. Seed stored in a refrigerator for 1 month before sowing is likely to germinate more freely and quickly.
Species cultivated: *L. brachycalyx*, S.W. USA; deciduous; leaves oblanceolate to spathulate, to 7cm long; flowers 4–5cm wide, petals 5–9, white, solitary on stems 2–5cm long, early summer; will thrive in a scree but generally rather short-lived. *L. columbiana*, N.W. N.America; evergreen; leaves narrowly oblanceolate, very fleshy, to 5cm or more long; flowers 3cm or more wide, petals 4–7, toothed, pink or white with red or pink veins, in panicles 12–30cm tall, early to late summer. *L. cotyledon*, N. California, S. Oregon; evergreen; leaves spathulate, 4–10cm long, sometimes undulate; flowers 2–3cm wide, petals 8–10, white, tinged pink to salmon, ageing rose-red, in panicles to 30cm or more tall, late spring to summer; a very variable species in foliage and flower colour, several variants having been described as species, notably *L.c. heckneri*, leaves broader, toothed, flowers larger, and *L.c. howellii*, leaves narrow, the margins often incurved and strongly waved or crisped, flowers larger, rose to apricot; many hybrids between these forms and other species have arisen and largely replace the original wildlings in gardens. *L. nevadensis*, W. USA; deciduous; leaves linear, 3–7cm long; flowers 2–3cm wide, petals 6–10, white, solitary on stems shorter than leaves, summer. *L. rediviva*, bitter root; N.W. N.America; roots edible but bitter-skinned, deciduous; leaves linear, glaucous, 4–5cm long; flowers 5cm wide, petals 12–18, rose, sometimes white, spring to summer; best under glass and kept almost dry while dormant (late autumn to early or mid spring). *L. tweedyi*, British Columbia, Washington State; evergreen; leaves obovate, 7–15cm long; flowers to 5cm wide, petals 10–12, usually salmon-pink varying to peach, yellow and

Above: *Leycesteria formosa*
Right: *Liatris spicata montana* Kobold
Bottom right: *Libertia formosa*

white, 1–3 on stems as long as, or just above leaves, late spring to summer.

Leycesteria

(for William Leycester, enthusiastic gardener and Chief Justice of Bengal c1820). CAPRIFOLIACEAE. A genus of 6 species of deciduous and evergreen shrubs from W. Himalaya, Tibet, China, 1 of which is generally cultivated: *L. formosa*, Himalaya honeysuckle; range of genus; deciduous, to 2m or more tall; stems hollow, green, mainly from ground level, erect, arching above; leaves in pairs, ovate-cordate to lanceolate, slender-pointed, 5–18cm long; flowers about 2cm long, funnel-shaped, 5-lobed, white, flushed purple, surrounded by purple bracts, in terminal, pendant spikes to 10cm long, summer to autumn; fruit a red-purple berry. Grow in any well-drained soil in sun or partial shade. Plant autumn to spring. Propagate by cuttings summer to autumn, or from seed in spring.

Liatris

(derivation unknown). Button snakeroot, blazing-star, Kansas gay-feather. COMPOSITAE. A genus of 40 species of herbaceous perennials from N. America. They are clump-forming, mainly from a cluster of rounded corms or tubers, with narrow leaves and spikes or racemes of cylindrical to bell-shaped flower-heads, each composed of slender disc florets opening from the top downwards. Grow in any well-drained but not dry soil, preferably humus-rich, in sun. Plant autumn to spring. Propagate by division at planting time or from seed in spring.

Species cultivated: *L. callilepis* (of gardens), see *L. spicata*. *L. pycnostachya*, C. to S.E. USA; to 1·5m tall; leaves linear, lowest to 15cm long; inflorescence spicate, dense, flower-heads to 1cm wide, rose-purple, summer to autumn. *L. scariosa*, E. USA; about 90cm tall; lower leaves lanceolate to narrowly obovate to 25cm long, upper smaller and narrower; inflorescence a raceme or cylindrical panicle, flower-heads rounded, 1·5–2·5cm wide, purple, late summer to autumn. *L.s.* Snowflake, a 45cm cultivar with white florets, is offered for this species. *L. spicata* (*L. callilepis*), S.E. USA; to 1·5m tall, lower leaves linear, to 16cm long; inflorescence spicate, dense, flower-heads cylindrical, about 1cm wide, rose-purple, late summer to autumn. *L.s. montana*, stems shorter than type, leaves broader; *L.s.m.* Kobold, stems stiffly erect, to 60cm.

Libertia

(for Marie A. Libert, 1782–1863, Belgian botanist). IRIDACEAE. A genus of about 12 species of evergreen perennials from Australasia, New Guinea, S. America. They have sword-shaped leaves in fan-like clusters and erect, wiry stems bearing panicles of 3-petalled flowers followed by yellow or orange-tinted seed capsules. Grow in well-drained but moisture-retentive, ideally humus-rich, neutral to acid soil in sun or light shade. Plant spring. Propagate by division after flowering or spring, or from seed when ripe or spring under glass. The species described are moderately hardy but are damaged in severe frosts and should be protected by covering with dry ferns, leaves or straw in winter.

Species cultivated: *L. formosa*, Chile; clump-forming; leaves to 45cm long; panicles narrow, 60–120cm tall, flowers about 2cm wide, white, freely borne, early summer. *L. grandiflora*, New Zealand; clump-forming; leaves to 50cm or more long; panicles diffuse, to 90cm tall, flowers 2–3cm wide, pure white, summer. *L. ixioides*, New Zealand; tufted to clump-forming, in 1 form stoloniferous; leaves 30–50cm long, often with a pale mid-rib and orange-brown basal margins; panicles narrow with leafy bracts, to 60cm tall, flowers 1·5–2·5cm wide, white above, yellowish below, summer.

Libocedrus – see *Calocedrus*.

Ligularia

(Latin *ligula*, a strap – referring to shape of the ray florets). COMPOSITAE. A genus of 80–150 species of herbaceous perennials from temperate Europe and Asia. Formerly included in *Senecio* and separated from it on small botanical details only, the ligularias are clump-forming with large, basal, palmate leaves and erect stems bearing racemes, panicles or cymes of daisy-like flower-heads. Grow in moisture-retentive soil in sun or partial shade. Plant autumn

to spring. Propagate by division at planting time or from seed in spring.
Species cultivated: *L. clivorum*, see next species. *L. dentata* (*L. clivorum, Senecio clivorum*), China, Japan; leaves rounded to kidney-shaped, cordate, to 30cm long; inflorescence corymbose, 90–120cm tall, flower-heads 6·5–12cm wide, ray florets bright orange-yellow, late summer. *L.d.* Desdemona, stems and undersides of leaves rich red-purple, flowers bright orange. *L. przewalskii* (pronounced jev-al-ski-eye), (*Senecio p.*), N. China; stems black-purple, to 1·5m tall; leaves 20–30cm wide, deeply palmately lobed, the lobes again lobed or jaggedly toothed; flower-heads in slender racemes, ray florets 1–2, yellow, disc florets 3, late summer. *L. stenocephala* (*Senecio s.*), China, Japan, Taiwan; stems dark purple, 1·5–2m tall; leaves triangular-cordate, coarsely toothed, to 35cm long; flower-heads in racemes, ray florets 1–3, yellow, disc florets 5–12, summer. *L.s.* The Rocket, the form most commonly met with in cultivation, formerly listed under *L. przewalskii*.

Ligustrum

(Latin vernacular for wild privet). OLEACEAE. A genus of about 50 species of deciduous and evergreen shrubs and small trees from Europe to Asia, Malaysia and N. Australia. They have opposite pairs of mainly ovate to oblong leaves, terminal panicles of small, tubular, 4-lobed, white flowers, and black-purple, berry-like fruit. Grow in any well-drained soil in sun or light shade. Plant autumn to spring. Propagate by semi-hardwood cuttings late summer, hardwood cuttings autumn or from seed when ripe.
Species cultivated: *L. ibota* (of gardens), see *L. obtusifolium*. *L. japonicum*, Japanese privet; Japan, Korea; bushy evergreen shrub 2–4m tall; young stems with minute brown down; leaves 5–8cm long, elliptic to ovate-elliptic, deep lustrous green; flowers 5–6mm long, tube slightly longer than lobes, in pyramidal panicles 5–12cm long, late summer to autumn. *L.j.* Rotundifolium (*L.j.* Coriaceum), slow-growing, leaves rounded, very dark. *L. lucidum*, Chinese or wax-leaf privet; China, Korea; large evergreen shrub or small tree, 3–10m or more tall; similar to *L. japonicum* but young shoots smooth; leaves ovate, somewhat acuminate; flowers 3–4mm long, tube slightly shorter than lobes, in panicles 10–18cm long. *L.l.* Excelsum Superbum, leaves margined and mottled yellow and white; *L.l.* Tricolor, leaves narrower than type, irregularly bordered white, tinted pink when young. *L. obtusifolium* (*L. ibota* of gardens, not the true, rarely cultivated species), Japan, Korea; deciduous shrub 2–3m tall, spreading, well-branched, graceful habit; leaves oblong-lanceolate to broadly oblanceolate, 2–6cm long; flowers 7–9mm long, tube $1\frac{1}{2}$–$2\frac{1}{2}$ times as long as lobes, in dense, downy panicles 2–3cm long, summer. *L. ovalifolium*, oval leaf privet; Japan; semi-evergreen, erect shrub 3–5m tall; leaves elliptic to ovate or obovate, thick-textured, glossy, 4–10cm long; flowers about 8mm long, tube longer than lobes, late summer; a most familiar hedging privet of gardens, but not reliably hardy in N. N. America where the hybrid with *L. obtusifolium* – *L.* × *ibolium* – is recommended. *L.o.* Argenteum, leaves margined creamy-white; *L.o.* Aureum, golden privet, leaves yellow or with a green centre. *L. sinense*, China; deciduous or semi-evergreen shrub 3–6m tall, of dense, spreading habit; twigs downy; leaves elliptic-oblong to lanceolate, 3–7cm long; flowers 5mm long in downy panicles 7–10cm long, summer; this species is probably the most floriferous and decorative of all the privets.

Left: *Ligularia dentata*
Below: *Ligularia stenocephala* The Rocket
Right above: *Ligustrum ovalifolium* Aureum

Lilac – see *Syringa*.

Lilium

(Latin form of the Greek *leirion* for the Madonna lily). Lily. LILIACEAE. A genus of about 80 species of bulbous plants from the N. Hemisphere. They have bulbs composed of separate overlapping scales, erect stems bearing usually narrow, alternate, scattered or whorled leaves, and terminal racemes of 6-tepalled funnel-, trumpet-, bowl-, star- and turban-shaped flowers. Grow in a well-drained but not dry, humus-rich soil in sun or partial shade, and screened from the hottest midday sun. Some species need acid soil and these are mentioned here. Many species produce roots from the base of the bulb and from the stem just above. Such species need to be planted 15cm or more deep, while the non-stem-rooters can be set at about 10cm. *L. candidum* is best planted shallowly, the tip of the bulb only 2–3cm beneath the surface. Plant autumn to early spring, making sure that the persistent basal roots are not unduly damaged. Many lilies make fine pot plants for the cold or cool greenhouse. If possible pot the bulbs in autumn using a peat based potting mixture with ⅓-part coarse sand added. Keep cool, ideally plunged in peat, sand or weathered ashes outside, or in a well-ventilated cold frame. Bring in to the greenhouse from late winter onwards and maintain 8–10°C until shoots are 10–15cm tall, and then increase to 15°C if earlier flowers are required. Ventilate freely on sunny days and provide shade from hot sun. Apply liquid feed at 10-day intervals from the time the buds are just visible until flowers fade. Propagate by dividing large clumps or separating bulblets when dormant, sowing stem bulbils in late summer or when they fall, taking bulb scales in winter or sowing seed in a cold frame as soon as ripe, under glass in late winter at 14–16°C, or outside in spring. The seed of some species germinates and forms tiny bulbs but these do not produce leaves for up to a year after sowing, eg *L. auratum*, *L. canadense*, *L. martagon*, *L. pardalinum*, *L. superbum*. This process can be speeded up by fairly simple means. Mix the seed with moist peat, sand or vermiculite and place in screw-cap jars or sealed plastic bags. Place in a minimum temperature of 18°C (in summer, no artificial heat is needed), and as soon as small bulbs are observed place in the bottom of a refrigerator or where the temperature does not rise above 6°C. After 6 weeks sow the tiny bulbs and place in a minimum temperature of 10–13°C; leaf growth

Above: *Ligustrum lucidum*

Below: *Lilium auratum*

Below: *Lilium canadense*

Left: *Lilium candidum*
Above: *Lilium henryi*
Above right: *Lilium longiflorum*
Right: *Lilium martagon*

should appear in a month or so.

Species cultivated (stem-rooting unless indicated by*): *L. amabile*, Korea; to 90cm tall; leaves lanceolate, to 9cm long; flowers nodding, tepals bright red, 5cm long, strongly reflexed, anthers chocolate, rather unpleasantly scented, summer. *L.a. luteum*, clear orange-yellow. *L. aurantiacum*, see *L. bulbiferum*. *L. auratum*, goldband or golden-rayed lily; Japan; 1–2m or more tall; leaves ovate to lanceolate, to 23cm long; flowers bowl-shaped, 20–30cm wide, each tepal white with central yellow band and crimson spots, late summer; needs sharply drained acid soil, plenty of moisture while growing and a sunny site to thrive; prone to virus infection; *L.a. rubro-vittatum* and *L.a. rubrum* have red-banded tepals. *L. bulbiferum* (*L. aurantiacum*), orange lily; S. Europe; 90–120cm tall; leaves lanceolate, to 10cm long; flowers cup-shaped, erect, to 8cm long, orange-red, in umbellate racemes, summer. *L.b. croceum*, tangerine-orange. *L. canadense**, meadow, Canada, or wild yellow lily; E. N.America; to 1·5m tall; leaves whorled, lanceolate to oblanceolate, to 15cm long; flowers bell-shaped, nodding, tepals 5–7·5cm long, orange-yellow to red, spotted purple-brown, flaring outwards with upturned tips. *L.c. flavum*, clear yellow, needs acid soil. *L. candidum**, Madonna lily; probably Balkan Peninsula but naturalized and cultivated around the Mediterranean; 90–150cm tall; basal leaves to 20cm or more long appearing in autumn, oblanceolate – stem leaves lanceolate, shorter; flowers widely bell-shaped, tepals pure white with curved tips, to 8cm long, summer. *L.c. salonikae*, Greece; probably the original wild type, having smaller, more wide open flowers. *L. chalcedonicum**, scarlet Turk's cap; Greece; to 1·3m tall; stem not rooting; leaves lanceolate to oblanceolate, to 11·5cm long; flowers pendant, 7cm wide, bright reddish-orange, tepals strongly recurved, summer. *L. columbianum*, Oregon lily; W. N.America; 60–150cm tall; stem non-rooting; leaves mostly in whorls, oblanceolate, to 10cm long; flowers nodding, bright orange-yellow, tepals 4–6cm long, strongly reflexed, late summer. *L. davidii*, W. China; 90–120cm tall; leaves linear, to 10cm long; flowers nodding, tepals 8cm long, orange-red, black-spotted, strongly reflexed, late summer. *L.d. willmottiae* (*L. sutchuenense*, *L. willmottiae*), C. and W. China; to 2m tall; flowers vivid orange in clusters of up to 40. *L. formosanum** (*L. longiflorum f.*, *L. philippinense f.*), Taiwan; to 1·5m or more tall; leaves linear, to 20cm long, dark green; flowers 13–20cm long, funnel-shaped, fragrant, white with chocolate or red-purple markings without, summer to autumn; not reliably hardy and best grown as a cool greenhouse plant; will flower from seed in 6–9 months if potted on regularly into a good commercial compost. *L. giganteum*, see *Cardiocrinum*. *L. hansonii*,* Korea, Japan (Hokkaido) and adjacent USSR; like a robust *L. martagon;* to 1·5cm tall; flowers orange-yellow, to 6·5cm wide, summer. *L. henryi*, C. China; 1–2·4m tall; stem often arching; leaves lanceolate, to 15cm long; flowers orange, spotted brown, papillose within, tepals to 8cm long, strongly recurved, late summer. *L.* × *hollandicum* (*L.* × *umbellatum*), complex hybrid strain derived from crossing *L. bulbiferum* and *L.b. croceum* with *L.* × *maculatum* (a group of long cultivated Japanese cultivars probably from *L. dauricum* × *L. concolor*); available cultivars rarely exceed 60cm tall with erect, cup-shaped flowers in shades of deep red to lemon-yellow in umbel-like clusters. *L. lancifolium*, see *L. speciosum* and *L. tigrinum*. *L. longiflorum**, Easter, or white trumpet lily; Japan; to 90cm tall; leaves to 18cm long, lanceolate to oblong-lanceolate, glossy green; flowers funnel-shaped, pure white, fragrant, 13–18cm long, summer to late summer; needs a warm, sheltered site outside, the shoots protected from frost; an excellent pot plant for a cool greenhouse. *L. longiflorum formosanum*, see *L. formosanum*. *L. martagon**, Europe, temperate Asia; 1–2m tall; leaves in whorls, usually oblanceolate, to 6·5cm long; flowers pendulous, tepals purple with black spots, strongly recurved, 3–3·5cm long, summer; several colour forms are known, ranging from pure white (*L.m. album*) to black-purple (*L.m. cattaniae*). *L. monadelphum**, Caucasian lily; N. Caucasus; 1–1·5m tall; leaves lanceolate to oblanceolate, to 13cm long; flowers fragrant, pendant, bell-shaped, tepals pale to deep yellow, to 9cm long, recurved, sometimes with a few purple spots at the base within and flushed reddish without, stamen filaments more or less fused at base to form a tube, anthers with yellow pollen, summer. *L.m. szovitsianum*, see *L. szovitsianum*. *L. pardalinum**, leopard or panther lily; Oregon, California; 1·2–2m tall; leaves usually in whorls, linear to lanceolate, to 18cm long; flowers nodding, to 10cm wide, tepals orange-red, tipped crimson, spotted maroon, strongly reflexed, summer. *L. philippinense formosanum*, see *L. formosanum*. *L. pumilum* (*L. tenuifolium*), coral lily; Korea, China, E. Siberia; to 45cm tall; leaves linear, to 10cm long; flowers bright waxy-scarlet, tepals 4cm long, strongly reflexed, summer. *L. pyreniacum*, Pyrenean or yellow Turk's cap lily; Pyrenees, S.W. France; 60–120cm tall; leaves linear-lanceolate, to 12cm long; flowers pendant, about 3·5cm wide, sulphur-yellow, tepals spotted purple-black, strongly reflexed, early summer. *L. regale*, regal lily; W. China; 75–180cm tall; leaves linear, to 12cm long, dark green; flowers fragrant, funnel-shaped, 12–15cm long, tepals white, flushed yellow at base within, red-purple without, in umbel-like clusters; of easy culture, usually flowering the second year from seed. *L. speciosum* (*L. lancifolium*), Japan, Taiwan, China; to 1·5m or so; leaves broadly lanceolate, to 18cm long; flowers nodding, fragrant, 10–15cm wide,

tepals white, suffused crimson, with darker papillae at base, waved and reflexed, late summer to autumn; requires acid soil; *L.s. album*, flowers white; *L.s. rubrum*, carmine, white-margined. *L. superbum**, Turk's cap or swamp lily; E. USA; to 2m or more tall; leaves whorled, lanceolate, to 15cm long; flowers pendant, tepals 6·5–10cm long, strongly recurved, orange shading to crimson tips, spotted maroon; yellow forms with and without spots are known. *L. sutchuenense*, see *L. davidii willmottiae*. *L. szovitsianum** (*L. monadelphum s.*), like *L. monadelphum* but stamens never united at base and anthers with reddish pollen. *L. tenuifolium*, see *L. pumilum*. *L.* × *testaceum* (*L. candidum* × *L. chalcedonicum*), nankeen lily; 1–1·8m tall; stem not rooting; leaves linear, to 10cm long at base, smaller upwards; flowers nodding, tepals 8cm long, maize or nankeen-yellow, often pink-flushed, reflexed, summer. *L. tigrinum* (now botanically known as *L. lancifolium*, but as this name is also a synonym of *L. speciosum*, the more familiar *L. tigrinum* is used here), tiger lily; China, Korea, Japan; 1–2m tall; stems purplish, cobwebby/hairy; leaves linear-lanceolate, to 19cm long, bearing black-purple bulbils in their axils; flowers nodding, tepals to 10cm long, bright orange-red, spotted black-purple, strongly reflexed, late summer to autumn; bulbs much used as food in E. Asia. *L.t. fortunei*, Korea, stem densely woolly, more floriferous than type, tepals salmon-orange, autumn; *L.t.* Giganteum, taller than type, more vigorous; *L.t. splendens*, Japan, flowers larger than type, rich red, more boldly spotted. *L.* × *umbellatum* of gardens, see *L.* × *hollandicum*. *L. willmottiae*, see *L. davidii w*.

Hybrids: during the past century, 100s of hybrid cultivars have been raised, much of the pioneer work being done in Britain. Most of the recent cultivars have come from the Oregon Bulb Farms in the USA, founded by Jan de Graaff and now the largest concern of its kind in the world. Many of the modern cultivars are easier to grow than the species, combining and re-combining in several ways the better habits, flower colours and shapes of the species in a bewildering way. To create order from the chaos of cultivars a 9-point classification has been devised, using the more outstanding features of the genus as points of reference: **Division 1** – Asiatic hybrids, **Sub-division 1A**, plants with erect or outwards-facing flowers, eg *L.* × *hollandicum* (see Species cultivated), Mid-Century group including Destiny, lemon-yellow, Enchantment, nasturtium-red, Harmony, bright orange; **1B**, flowers outwards-facing, eg Preston group; **1C**, flowers pendant, Turk's cap form, eg Citronella and Fiesta groups.

Far left top: *Lilium speciosum* hybrid
Far left: *Lilium regale*
Far bottom: *Lilium* Burbankii (Div. 4)
Left: *Lilium pardalinum*
Left bottom: *Lilium* Citronella (Div. 1C)
Below: *Lilium* × *testaceum*
Bottom: *Lilium* Enchantment (Div. 1A)

Top: *Lilium* Corsage (Div. 1B)
Left above: *Lilium* Damson (Div. 6A)
Left below: *Lilium* Imperial Silver (Div. 7C)
Above: *Lilium* Imperial Gold (Div. 7C)
Right: *Limnanthes douglasii*

Division 2 – Martagon hybrids, Turk's cap flowers, largely derived from *L. hansonii* or *L. martagon*, eg *L.* × Marhan J.S. Dijt, creamy-white, purple-spotted. **Division 3** – Candidum hybrids, Turk's cap flowers, derived from *L. candidum*, *L. chalcedonicum* and allied species but not *L. martagon*, eg *L.* × *testaceum* (see Species cultivated). **Division 4** – American hybrids, derived from American species only, eg Bellingham hybrids. **Division 5** – Longiflorum hybrids, trumpet lilies derived from *L. longiflorum* and *L. formosanum*, eg White Queen, Mt Everest. **Division 6** – Trumpet and Aurelian hybrids, derived from *L. henryi*, *L. sargentiae* and other Asiatic species but not *L. auratum*, *L. speciosum*, *L. japonicum* or *L. rubellum*; **Sub-division 6A**, Trumpet types, eg Aurelian group (*L. sargentiae* × *L. henryi* × *L. leucanthum*), Golden Clarion group, Black Dragon; **6B**, Bowl-shaped blooms, eg some of the Aurelian group; **6C**, Pendant blooms of various shapes; **6D**, Flat, star-shaped blooms. **Division 7** – Oriental hybrids, derived from the 4 species excluded from Division 6, plus *L. henryi* and others; **Sub-division 7A**, Trumpet types; **7B**, Bowl-shaped; **7C**, Flat star-shaped, eg Imperial Crimson, Imperial Gold, Imperial Silver. **Division 8** – all hybrids and cultivars not covered by the previous divisions. **Division 9** – all true species and their botanical varieties (see Species cultivated).

Lily – see *Lilium*.

Lily-of-the-valley – see *Convallaria*.

Lime tree – see *Tilia*.

Limnanthemum – see *Nymphoides*.

Limnanthes

(Greek *limne*, marsh, and *anthos*, a flower – the species grow in moist places in the wild). LIMNANTHACEAE. A genus of 7 species of annuals from W. N.America, 1 of which is commonly cultivated: *L. douglasii*, meadow foam; California, S. Oregon; spreading habit, branching from base; stems decumbent to erect; leaves 5–12cm long, pinnatifid to bipinnatifid, yellow-green; flowers 5-petalled, widely bowl-shaped, about 2·5cm wide, each petal yellow with a white-notched tip (all-white, all-yellow and pink-tinted forms are known in the wild) on stems to 15cm or more tall, spring to summer, a good bee flower. Grow in any moderately fertile soil in sun. Sow seed *in situ* spring or autumn.

Limonium

(Greek *leimon*, a meadow – alluding to the sea marsh habitat). Sea lavender. PLUMBAGINACEAE. A genus of 150–300 species (depending on classifier) of annuals, perennials and sub-shrubs of cosmopolitan distribution, especially Mediterranean. They are tufted or clump-forming with mostly basal, obovate to oblanceolate, often pinnately lobed leaves, and erect, wiry stems bearing stiff panicles composed of small spikelets of flowers, each bloom with a tubular, persistent, sometimes coloured calyx and 5-lobed corolla often of different colour. Grow in well-drained soil in sun. Plant perennials autumn or spring. Sow annuals *in situ* in late spring to early summer or under glass early to mid spring at 13–16°C, pricking off seedlings into J.I. compost No 2 or its equivalent, at 4cm apart each way when first true leaf well-developed, hardening off and planting out early summer. Plants may also be grown in pots from an autumn or early spring sowing for cold or cool greenhouse decoration. Propagate perennials from seed or by division in spring; *L. latifolium* also by root cuttings late winter.

Species cultivated: *L. bellidifolium*, shores of Europe to E. Asia; perennial, rootstock much branched, woody; leaves obovate to spathulate, 1·5–4cm long, usually fading before flowering ceases; flowers 5mm long, pale lilac, the panicles on decumbent stems, 7–30cm long, radiating outwards, late summer; allied species are sometimes offered under this name. *L. bonduellii*, Algeria; much like *L. sinuatum* with yellow flowers. *L. incanum* (*Goniolimon callicomum*, *Statice c.*), woody-based perennial; stems 30–60cm tall; leaves lanceolate to oblong-elliptic, about 5cm long; flowers violet-rose, calyx white, summer. *L.i. dumosum*, flowers pink. *L. latifolium* (*Statice l.*), S.E. Europe to USSR; evergreen perennial; stems 30–50cm tall; leaves oblong-elliptic, 25cm long; panicles large, flowers 6mm long, light violet-blue, late summer. *L.l.* Blue Cloud, lavender-blue; *L.l.* Violetta, violet. *L. sinuatum* (*Statice s.*), biennial or perennial but usually grown as an annual; stems winged; leaves to 10cm long, oblanceolate, deeply pinnately lobed and waved; flowers white, calyces funnel-shaped, 10–12mm long, purple, summer to autumn; several strains and cultivars are listed with calyces in shades of pink, red, orange, yellow, blue and lavender. *L. suworowii* (*Psylliostachys s.*, *Statice s.*), Caucasus, C. Asia, Iran; hardy annual; stems to 45cm; leaves oblanceolate, lobed and waved, 15–25cm long; panicle formed of dense-fingered spikes, flowers 4mm long, rose-pink, early summer to autumn if sown in succession for late winter; it makes a good pot plant.

Left above: *Limonium bonduellii*
Left below: *Limonium sinuatum*
Above: *Limonium suworowii*
Below: *Limonium latifolium* Violetta
Right above: *Linanthus androsaceus*

Linanthus

(Greek *linon*, flax, and *anthos*, flower). POLEMONIACEAE. A genus of about 35 species of mainly small annuals chiefly from W. N.America and Chile, closely allied to *Gilia*. 1 species is generally available: *L. androsaceus* (*Gilia a.*, *Gilia lutea*, *Leptosiphon a.*), California; erect, mainly branched from base, 10–20cm tall; leaves 1–3cm long, divided into 5–9 linear to oblanceolate segments; flowers slender-tubed, to 1·5cm long with 5 rounded lobes 5–8mm long, pink, lilac, yellow, summer to autumn; usually offered as *Leptosiphon hybridus* or French Hybrids. Grow in well-drained soil in sun. Sow *in situ* spring or early autumn in a sheltered site.

Linaria

(Greek *linon*, flax – alluding to the similarity of the foliage of some species to flax – *Linum*). Toadflax. SCROPHULARIACEAE. A genus of 100 or more species of annuals and perennials from northern temperate zone, mainly the Mediterranean region. They are erect to decumbent, with narrow, alternate or whorled leaves and racemes of flowers like those of *Antirrhinum* but with a basal spur. Grow in ordinary, well-drained soil in a sunny site. Plant perennials autumn or spring. Sow seed of annuals *in situ* in spring, or autumn in a sheltered site; may also be sown under glass in early spring and planted out in early summer. Propagate perennials by root cuttings during late winter, by cuttings and from seed in the spring, or by careful division at planting time.

Species cultivated: *L. alpina*, alpine toadflax; mountains of C. and S. Europe; tufted perennial; stems decumbent, 10–25cm long; leaves 5–15mm long, linear to oblong-lanceolate, glaucous; flowers 1·5–2cm long, violet usually with orange mouth, summer to autumn. *L. cymbalaria*, see *Cymbalaria muralis*. *L. dalmatica* (*L. genistifolia d.*), see next species. *L. genistifolia*, E.S. and C. Europe; erect perennial, 60–90cm tall; leaves alternate, amplexicaul, linear to ovate, 2–6cm long, thick-textured; flowers 2–5cm long, yellow with bearded orange mouth, summer to autumn; *L.g. dalmatica* (*L. dalmatica*, *L. macedonica*), leaves ovate, glaucous; flowers primrose-yellow, 4–5cm long (including spur). *L. maroccana*, Morocco; erect annual to 30cm or more tall; leaves linear, whorled in the lower part; flowers 2–3cm long (including spur), violet-purple with yellow mouth; generally represented in gardens by strains in shades of purple, blue, red, pink and yellow, probably of hybrid origin, eg *L.m.* Excelsior and the dwarf (23cm) *L.m.* Fairy Bouquet. *L. pallida*, see *Cymbalaria p. L. purpurea*, purple toadflax; C. and S. Italy, Sicily, naturalized elsewhere; slender, erect perennial 60–120cm tall; leaves linear, glaucous, 2–6cm long, whorled below; flowers about 1·5cm long, violet-purple, with bearded white mouth, summer to autumn. *L.p.* Canon Went, flowers pink, coming true from seed if parent plant isolated. *L. triornithophora*, three birds; W.N. and C. Spain, Portugal; erect, usually short-lived perennial 30–90cm tall; leaves lanceolate, somewhat glaucous, 2·5–7cm long in whorls; flowers in whorls of 3, purple with darker stripes and yellow mouth, about 4–5cm long, summer to autumn; not reliably hardy in cold areas. *L. tristis*, S. Spain and Portugal, N. Africa; decumbent perennial; stems 10–30cm long; leaves linear-oblong, 8–20mm long, usually glaucous; flowers yellow tinged brown with brown mouth. *L.t. lurida* (*L.t.* Toubkal), compact habit; leaves waxy blue-green; flowers jade-green and maroon, summer.

Linden – see *Tilia*.

Far left top: *Linaria triornithophora*
Far left above: *Linaria tristis*
Top: *Linaria maroccana* mixed strains
Left above: *Linaria genistifolia dalmatica*
Above: *Linum perenne alpinum*

Lindera

(for Johann Linder, 1676–1723, Swedish physician and botanist). LAURACEAE. A genus of 100 species of deciduous and evergreen trees and shrubs mainly from S. and E. Asia, 2 in E. N.America. 1 hardy species is usually available: *L. benzoin*, Benjamin or spicebush; E. N.America; deciduous shrub of rounded habit, 2–5m tall; leaves alternate, 5–13cm long, oblong-obovate, aromatic when bruised; flowers dioecious, about 6mm wide, petalless, calyx 6-lobed, yellow-green; fruit berry-like, ellipsoid, red, to 1cm long. Grow in moisture-retentive soil in partial shade or sun. Plant autumn to spring. Propagate from seed as soon as ripe, in a cold frame, by layering in spring, or cuttings in summer with bottom heat 16–18°C.

Ling – see *Calluna*.

Linnaea

(for Carl Linnaeus, 1707–78, Swedish botanist and naturalist, pioneer in systematic classification of all natural things). CAPRIFOLIACEAE. A genus of 1 species of prostrate shrub from N. Europe, N. N.America, N. Asia and mountains farther south: *L. borealis*, twinflower; evergreen, mat-forming when well-established; leaves in opposite pairs, rounded, crenate, 5–15mm long; flowers 8mm long, bell-shaped with 5 rounded lobes, pink, often darker within, in pairs on slender, erect stems 3–7cm tall. *L.b. americana*, more vigorous and satisfactory in cultivation than type; flowers to 12mm long, summer. Grow in any humus-rich, moist but not wet soil in shade. Plant spring. Propagate by careful division or separating naturally-rooted layers in spring; cuttings in late summer.

Linosyris–see *Aster linosyris.*

Linum

(ancient Latin name for flax). Flax. LINACEAE. A genus of 200–230 species of annuals, perennials and shrubs of cosmopolitan distribution, but especially the Mediterranean region. They are tufted, with erect to decumbent stems, alternate linear to lanceolate or spathulate leaves, and terminal clusters of 5-petalled, wide open flowers. Grow in well-drained soil in sun. Plant spring or autumn. Propagate from seed in spring, the annuals *in situ*, or cuttings of non-flowering shoots in summer. When rooted, the latter should be potted and over-

Above: *Linum* × Gemmell's Hybrid
Above right: *Linum flavum*
Right: *Linum grandiflorum*
Far right: *Linum narbonense*

wintered in a cold frame until spring.

Species cultivated: *L. alpinum*, see *L. perenne alpinum*. *L. arboreum*, tree flax; S. Aegean (Crete, Greece); shrub to 1m tall; leaves 1–2cm long, spathulate, thick-textured; inflorescence few-flowered, each bloom 2·5–4cm wide, yellow, summer; not fully hardy, needing sheltered nook and winter protection in cold areas. *L. extraaxillare*, see *L. perenne extraaxillare*. *L. flavum*, yellow flax; C. and S.E. Europe; woody-based perennial; stems 40–60cm tall; lower leaves 2–3·5cm long, spathulate, upper lanceolate, smaller; inflorescence well-branched, flowers 2–3cm wide, yellow, summer; variable in cultivation in stature, habit and deepness of colour of foliage and flower; sometimes offered as *L. paniculatum*. *L.f.* Compactum, plant shorter than type, denser habit. *L.* × Gemmell's Hybrid (*L. elegans* × *L. campanulatum* both closely allied to *L. flavum*), forming mounds of glaucous foliage to 15cm tall bearing deep yellow flowers in profusion. *L. grandiflorum*, N. Africa; hardy annual 30–50cm tall; leaves lanceolate, to 3cm long; flowers 3–4cm wide, shades of red, summer. *L.g.* Rubrum (*L. rubrum*), flowers bright red, the commonest form in gardens. *L. monogynum*, New Zealand; perennial, woody-based when old; stems to 40cm or more tall; leaves linear to lanceolate, to 2·5cm long; flowers 2–3cm wide, white sometimes bluish, summer; not reliably hardy and often rather short-lived. *L. narbonense*, beautiful flax; C. and W. Mediterranean to N.E. Portugal; like a robust *L. perenne* with leaves to 5mm or more wide and azure-blue flowers to 3cm wide. *L. perenne* (*L. sibiricum*), perennial flax; Europe, mainly C. and E.; woody-based perennial;

stems to 60cm tall; leaves linear to narrowly lanceolate, somewhat glaucous, to 2·5cm long × 2·5mm wide; flowers about 2·5cm wide, blue, in often well-branched panicles, summer; a variable species with several distinct sub-species; *L.p. alpinum* (*L. alpinum*), stems decumbent to ascending, 5–30cm long; *L.p. extraaxillare* (*L. extraaxillare*), stems ascending or erect, leaves to 4mm wide, confused in cultivation with *L.p. alpinum*. *L. rubrum*, see *L. grandiflorum* Rubrum. *L. salsoloides*, see *L. suffruticosum*. *L. sibiricum*, see *L. perenne*. *L. suffruticosum*, white flax; S.W. Europe; perennial, more or less woody-based; leaves linear, 1–1·5cm long, minutely toothed, sharp-pointed; stems prostrate, to 40cm long with erect inflorescences to 20cm tall; flowers 4–5cm wide, white, summer. *L.s. salsoloides* (Nanum of gardens), much smaller and flatter than type; leaves dense, 4–5mm long, blunt, glaucous above – probably the plant originally described as *L. ortegae* and deserving of specific rank under that name. *L. usitatissimum*, common flax (of ancient cultivation and not known wild, perhaps derived from the wild pale flax, *L. bienne*); annual to 1·2m tall; leaves lanceolate to linear, to 3cm or more long, somewhat glaucous; flowers 2–3cm wide, pale blue, summer; several cultivars have been selected for fibre (for linen-making) and linseed oil production, some with larger, deeper blue flowers.

Lippia

(for Augustin Lippi, 1678–1701, Italian botanist and naturalist killed while collecting in Abyssinia). VERBENACEAE. A genus of about 200 species of shrubs and perennials from N. and S. America, Africa. They may be prostrate or erect with opposite pairs or whorls of obovate to lanceolate leaves and axillary spikes or panicles of small, tubular, 4-lobed, 2-lipped flowers. Grow in well-drained soil in mild sunny areas or a frost-free greenhouse. In colder areas winter protection is needed or the plant maybe bedded out in early summer and over-wintered under glass. Propagate by cuttings in spring or summer, or from seed in spring under glass.

Species cultivated: *L. canescens* (*L. filiformis*, *L. repens*), S. America; mat-forming, somewhat woody perennial; leaves spathulate to lanceolate, hoary; flowers in dense, head-like spikes, lilac to pink with yellow eye, summer. *L. citriodora* (*Aloysia c.*, *Verbena c.*, *V. triphylla*; some botanists think the correct name to be *Aloysia triphylla*), lemon verbena; Argentina, Chile; deciduous shrub to 3m or more tall; leaves in 2s or 3s, lanceolate, 6–10cm long, strongly lemon-scented and yielding the verbena oil of commerce; flowers very small, white to palest purple in axillary spikes or terminal panicles, late summer; may be pruned hard annually in spring.

Liquidambar

(Latin *liquidus*, liquid, and *ambar*, amber – referring to the fragrant resin storax prepared from the inner bark). ALTINGIACEAE (HAMAMELIDACEAE). A genus of 4 species of deciduous trees from E. N.America and S.W. Turkey to China, 1 of which is generally available: *L. styraciflua*, sweet gum; E. USA, C. America; to 40m or less in some gardens; bark grey or brown, becoming rough and fissured into squares, head conical to ovoid, spreading with age; leaves alternate, usually 5–7 lobed, maple-like, 10–15cm wide, glossy rich green above, some trees turning red or yellow and purple in autumn; flowers unisexual, small, petalless, females in globular heads, males in short catkins; fruit a ball of 2-valved woody capsules. Grow in deep, moist, humus-rich soil in a sunny or partially shaded site. Plant autumn or spring; ve· y young plants may need frost protection in cold areas. Propagate by layering in spring, suckers in autumn or from seed when ripe, the latter sometimes taking 18 months to germinate.

Liriodendron

(Greek *leirion*, lily, and *dendron*, tree). Tulip tree. MAGNOLIACEAE. A genus of 2 species of deciduous trees from C. China and S.E. USA, 1 of which is generally available: *L. tulipifera*, tulip tree, tulip poplar whitewood, the wood known as yellow poplar;

Left: *Lippia citriodora*
Bottom and below: *Liquidambar styraciflua* in autumn colours

to 65m in the USA or less elsewhere; bark grey, shallowly ridged, head conical to columnar or narrowly domed; leaves 10–15cm long, somewhat wider, 4-lobed with saddle-shaped tip, turning yellow in autumn; flowers cup-shaped, to 5cm long, each of the 6 greenish-yellow petals having a basal, inverted, v-shaped orange mark, early summer – produced only on mature trees. *L.t.* Aureomarginatum, leaves yellow-edged. Grow in moist, humus-rich soil in sun. Plant early spring. Propagate from seed sown when ripe and kept in a cold frame. Seedlings best grown in deep pots and planted out when 2 years old.

Liriope

(Greek wood nymph, mother of Narcissus). Lily turf. LILIACEAE. A genus of 5 or 6 species of evergreen perennials from China, Japan, Vietnam. They are rhizomatous or clump-forming, with grassy, leathery leaves and racemes of 6-tepalled, bell-shaped flowers followed by berry-like black fruit. Grow in well-drained, humus-rich soil. Propagate by division in spring or seed when ripe. **Species cultivated:** *L. graminifolia*, China, Vietnam; leaves to 40cm long, arching to a height of 20cm; raceme stem violet-tinted, flowers pale violet. *L.g. minor*, plant smaller than type, fewer flowers per raceme. *L. graminifolia* is confused with *L. spicata*, a similar but rarely grown species having longer leaves and flowers with the tepals fused at the base to form a tube. *L.g. densiflora*, see *L. muscari*. *L. hy-*

Top left: *Liriodendron tulipifera* in autumn
Far left: *Liriodendron tulipifera* flowers
Left: *Liriodendron tulipifera* leaves in autumn
Above: *Liriope muscari*

acinthiflora, see *Reineckea carnea*. *L. muscari* (*L. platyphylla*, *L. graminifolia densiflora*), dense clump-forming; leaves 30–60cm long, narrowly strap-shaped, dark green, arching; racemes 30–40cm tall; flowers 5–10mm wide, lavender, in dense racemes, autumn. *L.m.* Majestic, robust, raceme tip-crested (fasciated), flowers violet – a common form. *L. platyphylla*, see *L. muscari*. *L. spicata*, see *L. graminifolia*.

Lithodora – see *Lithospermum*.

Lithospermum

(Greek *lithos*, a stone, and *sperma*, seed – alluding to the hard nutlets). BORAGINACEAE. A genus of 44 species of annuals, perennials and sub-shrubs from

the temperate regions of the world except Australasia. They are erect to prostrate, with alternate, lanceolate to elliptic or linear leaves, and terminal cymes of 5-lobed, tubular to funnel-shaped flowers; fruit a group of 4 nutlets. Botanists now classify the following list of species under *Lithodora*, but the more familiar *Lithospermum* is retained here for convenience. Grow in well-drained, preferably humus-rich soil in sun or very light shade. Plant autumn or spring. Not reliable in cold, wet areas. Propagate by seed in spring or cuttings in summer, pot up when rooted and plant out in spring.
Species cultivated: *L. diffusum* (*L. prostratum*, *Lithodora diffusa*), evergreen prostrate sub-shrub, 5–10cm tall, wide-spreading; leaves to 2cm long, linear-oblong, hispid, deep green; flowers funnel-shaped, to 1·5cm long, blue to blue-purple, early summer. *L.d.* Grace Ward, large deep blue flowers; *L.d.* Heavenly Blue, bright gentian-blue flowers in profusion – needs an acid soil to thrive. *L. doerfleri*, *L. graminifolium* and *L.* × *intermedium*, see *Moltkia*. *L. oleifolium* (*Lithodora o.*), sub-shrub; stems slender, decumbent to ascending, forming low mounds 10–15cm tall; leaves to 4cm long, obovate to oblong, silky white hairy below; flowers funnel-shaped, to 1·5cm long, at first pink, and then pale blue, in the summer.

Far left: *Lithospermum diffusum*
Far left below: *Lithospermum oleifolium*
Left above: *Lobelia siphilitica*
Left: *Lobelia cardinalis*
Left below: *Lobelia erinus* Cambridge Blue
Above: *Lobelia splendens* Jean

Lobelia

(for Mathias de l'Obel, 1538–1616, Belgian doctor to King James I of England, and a noted botanist). CAMPANULACEAE (LOBELIACEAE). A genus of about 375 species of annuals, perennials, shrubs and (rarely) trees of cosmopolitan distribution, mainly tropics. They have alternate, ovate to linear leaves, and racemes of tubular flowers, each basically 2-lipped, having 2 narrow lobes above and 3 shorter ones below. Grow the half-hardy species in well-drained, humus-rich soil in a sunny, sheltered site, the shrubby and perennial sorts requiring protection in winter in all but mild areas, or to be kept in a cool greenhouse. Grow hardy perennials in moisture-retentive soil in sun or partial shade. Plant spring, the tender bedding species when fear of frost has passed. Propagate from seed under glass in spring, cultivars of *L. erinus* in early spring at 13–16°C, pricking off groups of 2–4 seedlings when large enough to handle at 4cm apart each way into a soil based mixture or an all-peat equivalent. Perennials may be divided in spring and shrubby sorts by cuttings in spring or summer.
Species cultivated: *L. cardinalis*, cardinal flower; E. N.America; evergreen perennial, 60–90cm tall; leaves lanceolate, irregularly toothed, to 10cm long, often flushed red-purple; flowers scarlet, 3–4cm long, late summer. *L.c.* Alba, flowers white; *L.c.* Rosea, flowers pink; *L.c.* Queen Victoria, leaves beetroot-coloured – liable to rot off during mild, wet winters when premature foliage is produced, and it is recommended to over-winter at least some plants in a well-ventilated cold frame. *L. erinus*, S. Africa; half-hardy perennial grown as an annual; tufted, bushy; stems slender, to 15cm tall; leaves obovate to linear, 1–2·5cm long; flowers 1·2–2cm long, blue to violet with whitish or yellowish eye, summer; many cultivars are known, varying in habit and flower colour: *L.e.* Cambridge Blue, sky-blue, *L.e.* Crystal Palace (*L.e.* Dark Blue Improved), Oxford-blue, *L.e.* Mrs Clibran (*L.e.* Dwarf Royal Blue), deep violet, *L.e.* Rosamond, red, *L.e.* White Lady, white – all 10cm tall, *L.e.* Pendula, stems prostrate, good for hanging baskets, available in shades of light blue, violet-blue and purplish-red. *L. fulgens*, see *L. splendens*. *L.* × *gerardii* (*L.* × *vedrariensis*), (*L. cardinalis* × *L. siphilitica*), akin to latter parent, but 1–1·5m tall; flowers pinkish-violet to purple, to 4·5cm long. *L.* × *hybrida*, name of no botanical standing used for hybrids involving *L. cardinalis*, *L. splendens* and *L. siphilitica*, see *L.* × *gerardii*. *L. linnaeoides*, New Zealand; hardy, evergreen, mat-forming perennial; stems slender, prostrate, rooting, rarely more than 15cm long; leaves rounded, 4–8mm long; flowers 8–12mm long, white to pale blue, solitary on erect, thread-like stems, to 6cm, summer. *L. siphilitica* (*L. syphilitica*), blue cardinal flower; E. USA; hardy perennial, 60–90cm tall; leaves ovate, irregularly toothed, to 10cm long; flowers about 2·5cm long, bright blue, late summer to autumn. *L.s.* Alba, flowers white. *L. splendens* (*L. fulgens*), S. USA, Mexico; half-hardy perennial; similar to *L. cardinalis* but more slender; leaves narrowly lanceolate to linear, 5–18cm long. *L. tenuior*, W. Australia; half-hardy, spreading annual or perennial, to 30cm or more tall; lower leaves to 6·5cm long, linear, irregularly pinnately lobed, upper ones smaller; flowers about 2·5cm long, bright blue, throat yellow-spotted, late summer; best as a greenhouse pot plant or bedded out. *L.* × *vedrariensis*, see *L.* × *gerardii*.

Lobularia

(Latin *lobulus*, a small pod – the seed-pods are small, rounded and slightly inflated). CRUCIFERAE. A genus of 5 species of annuals and perennials from Canary Is to Azores, Mediterranean to Arabia, 1 of which is commonly grown: *L. maritima* (*Alyssum m.*), sweet alyssum; S. Europe, naturalized elsewhere; annual or short-lived perennial; stems much-branched, slender, spreading, 10–15cm tall, sometimes more; leaves linear to oblanceolate, usually hoary, 2–6cm long; flowers white, 4-petalled, about 6mm wide in

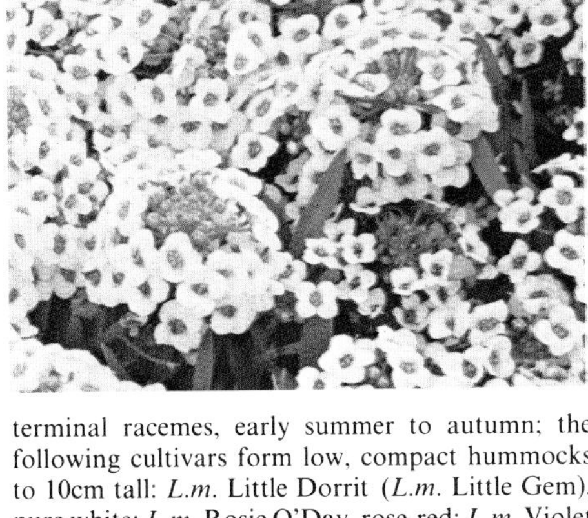

terminal racemes, early summer to autumn; the following cultivars form low, compact hummocks to 10cm tall: *L.m.* Little Dorrit (*L.m.* Little Gem), pure white; *L.m.* Rosie O'Day, rose-red; *L.m.* Violet Queen, violet-purple. *L.m. minimum* (*Alyssum benthamii*), almost prostrate, to 7·5cm tall. Grow in any well-drained soil in sun or partial shade. Sow *in situ* in spring, or for early flowering, under glass in early spring at 10–13°C, pricking off seedlings into boxes of any commercial potting mixture, hardening off and planting out late spring. These plants are often found in seed lists under the more familiar name of *Alyssum*.

Loiseleuria

(for Jean Louis Auguste Loiseleur-Deslongchamps, 1774–1849, French physician and botanist). ERICACEAE. A genus of 1 species of evergreen shrub from circumpolar regions and mountains farther south: *L. procumbens* (*Azalea* and *Rhododendron p.*), trailing or alpine azalea; mat-forming, to 30cm or more wide by 5–10cm or sometimes more high; leaves opposite, densely borne, 3–8mm long, elliptic to oblong, margins rolled under, deep glossy green; flowers 4–5cm across, widely bell-shaped, 5-lobed, pink, in terminal clusters of 1–5, early summer; needs a cool site and does not thrive well where summers are warm. Grow in peaty, moisture-retentive soil in a site open to the sky and facing north. Plant autumn to spring. Propagate by separating self-layered stems or from seed in spring, or by cuttings in summer.

Lomaria – see *Blechnum*.

Lomatia

(Greek *loma*, edge or margin – referring to the winged margins of the seed). PROTEACEAE. A genus of 12 species of evergreen trees and shrubs formerly classified as *Embothrium* from E.Australia, Tasmania and S.America. They have alternate or opposite, entire or pinnate leaves and white or yellow, embothrium-like flowers in axillary racemes. The species described are of borderline hardiness and need sheltered, ideally partially shaded sites and a moisture-retentive, neutral to acid soil. In cold areas grow in large pots or tubs in a frost-free greenhouse. Plant spring. Propagate from seed in spring at 16°C or by cuttings in summer, bottom heat 18–21°C.

Species cultivated: *L. ferruginea*, Chile, Argentina; large shrub or small tree to 15m tall in mild areas; stems covered with velvety red-brown hair; leaves 7–20cm or more long, pinnate to bipinnate, leaflets oblong to obovate, white to tawny downy; flowers 1–1·5mm long, yellow and red, summer. *L. hirsuta* (*L. obliqua*), Ecuador to Chile; large shrub or small tree to 7m, occasionally to 15m or more; leaves alternate, 4–10cm long, ovate, crenate, tawny downy when young, then deep glossy green; flowers 6–8mm long, white, early summer. *L. longifolia*, see next entry. *L. myricoides* (*L. longifolia*), S. E.Australia; shrub to 2m or more tall, often tree-like in the wild; leaves narrowly to oblong lanceolate, 7–15cm long, widely, coarsely toothed; flowers 1–1·5cm long, cream to pale yellow, summer. *L. silaifolia*, to 1m tall, wide-spreading; leaves 8–20cm long, usually bi- or tripinnate; flowers 1cm long, cream-white in terminal panicles or racemes; sometimes confused with the next species; almost hardy but needs a sunny, well-drained site. *L. tinctoria*, guitar plant; Tasmania; suckering shrub to 1m tall; leaves 4–8cm long, pinnate or bipinnate; flowers white or cream, 1cm long, late summer.

Lonas

(derivation not recorded). COMPOSITAE. A genus of 1 species of hardy annual from the Mediterranean: *L. annua* (*L. inodora*), African daisy; erect, well-branched from base, to 30cm tall; lower leaves 3-lobed, upper ones pinnatifid with linear lobes; individual flower-heads about 8mm wide, golden-yellow, grouped in flattened, terminal clusters, to 5cm wide, summer, autumn; involucral bracts chaffy and flower clusters dry well if cut in full bloom. Grow in well-drained, moderately fertile soil. Sow seed thinly *in situ* in spring; may also be raised under glass in early spring at 13–16°C for earlier flowering.

Far left: *Lobularia maritima* Royal Carpet
Far left below: *Lobularia maritima* Little Dorrit
Left: *Lomatia tinctoria*
Left below: *Lomatia hirsuta*
Below: *Lonas annua*

London pride – see *Saxifraga* × *urbium*.

Lonicera

(for Adam Lonitzer, 1528–86, German botanist). Honeysuckle, woodbine. CAPRIFOLIACEAE. A genus of about 200 species of shrubs and climbers from the N. Hemisphere. They have opposite pairs of ovate to elliptic or lanceolate leaves, and 5-lobed, tubular to bell-shaped flowers in terminal or axillary spikes or clusters. Within the inflorescence the flowers are borne in pairs, the ovaries of which may be wholly or partially fused; fruit a single or double berry. Grow in well-drained, moisture-retentive soil in sun or light shade, and support climbing forms. Plant autumn to spring. Propagate by cuttings in the late summer or autumn, or alternatively by seed when ripe.

Species cultivated: *L.* × *americana* (*L. grata*, *L. italica*), (*L. caprifolium* × *L. etrusca*), deciduous climbing to 9m in ideal conditions; similar to *L. caprifolium* but leaves more pointed and flowers in whorled spikes, yellow suffused red-purple. *L.* × *brownii*, deciduous or evergreen climber to 4m or more; leaves ovate to oblong, glaucous beneath, to 7·5cm long, those on floral shoots perfoliate; flowers 3–4cm long, orange-scarlet, late spring and late summer; *L.* × *b.* Fuchsioides is very similar. *L. caprifolium*, Europe, W. Asia; deciduous climbing to 8m or so; leaves elliptic to obovate, glaucous

beneath, 5–10cm long, those on floral shoots perfoliate; flowers white to deep cream, sometimes pink-tinted, 4–5cm long, strongly 2-lipped, late spring to early summer, berries orange. *L.c.* Pauciflora, flowers red-purple without. *L. etrusca*, Mediterranean; semi-evergreen climber, to 10m or so; leaves oval to obovate, glaucous beneath, 4–9cm long, those on floral shoots perfoliate; flowers cream, ageing yellow, fragrant, about 4cm long, summer. *L. flexuosa*, see *L. japonica repens*. *L. fragrantissima*, China; partially evergreen to deciduous shrub, to 2m tall; leaves ovate to elliptic, leathery, to 5cm long; flowers creamy-white, 1·5cm long, very sweetly fragrant, in axillary clusters, winter to spring. *L. grata*, see *L.* × *americana*. *L.* × *heckrottii* (perhaps *L.* × *americana* × *L. sempervirens*), deciduous, loose shrub or semi-climber; leaves elliptic, 4–6·5cm long, glaucous beneath, those on floral shoots perfoliate; flowers 4cm long in whorled spikes, yellow, flushed purple-pink without, late summer to autumn. *L.* × *h.* Goldflame, said to be a synonym, but plants under this name can have more richly coloured flowers, at least on some soils. *L. henryi*, W. China; evergreen climber, to 10m or more; leaves oblong-lanceolate to ovate, slender-pointed, 4–8cm long; flowers 2cm long, yellow, stained red, in terminal clusters, summer; berries black-purple. *L. involucrata* (including *L. ledebourii*), N. America, Mexico; deciduous shrub 2–3m tall; leaves ovate to oblong-lanceolate, to 10cm long, margins downy; flowers to 1·5cm long, in pairs, yellow, surrounded by 2, reddish, heart-shaped bracts, summer; berries black. *L.i. ledebourii*, flowers red-tinted, lower leaf surfaces downy. *L. italica*, see *L.* × *americana*. *L. japonica*, Japan, Korea, China; vigorous evergreen or partially evergreen climber, to 10m or more; leaves elliptic to ovate, sometimes lobed, 3–8cm long; flowers in pairs from upper leaf-axils, 4–5cm long, creamy-white, ageing yellow, sometimes purple-tinged, fragrant, summer; berry black. *L.j.* Aureoreticulata, leaves

Above left: *Lonicera japonica* Aureoreticulata
Left: *Lonicera sempervirens*
Below: *Lonicera japonica halliana*

Top: *Lonicera nitida* Baggesen's Gold
Above: *Lonicera pileata*
Right: *Lonicera × americana*

with a network of gold veins; *L.j. halliana*, flowers pure white, ageing yellow, very fragrant; *L.j. repens* (*L. flexuosa*), stems, leaves and outsides of flowers flushed red-purple. *L. ligustrina yunnanensis*, see *L. nitida* Fertilis. *L. nitida*, S.W. China; evergreen shrub, 1·5–3m or more; dense, twiggy habit; leaves ovate to rounded, 6–15mm long, dark lustrous green; flowers whitish, in axillary pairs, mostly hidden by leaves, about 6mm long; berries translucent-amethyst; much used for hedging, standing hard clipping well and suitable for low hedges of 1m or less. *L.n.* Baggesen's Gold, leaves yellow in summer; *L.n.* Ernest Wilson, lateral stems short, horizontal or drooping, leaves mostly narrowly ovate, bright green, sparsely flowering, formerly much grown for hedging but now largely superseded by *L.n.* Yunnan; *L.n.* Fertilis (*L. ligustrina yunnanensis* and *L. pileata y.*), lateral stems long, arching, leaf pairs well-spaced, in 2 parallel ranks, leaves elliptic to lanceolate, 7–13mm long, dark green, free-flowering and fruiting; *L.n.* Yunnan (*L. pileata yunnanensis* and *L. yunnanensis*), lateral stems erect, leaves broadly ovate to triangular-ovate, 4·5–11mm long, fairly free-flowering and fruiting, forms a firmer hedge than the preceding cultivars. *L. periclymenum*, honeysuckle or woodbine; Europe to W. Asia; deciduous climber, to 6m or more; leaves ovate to obovate, 4–5·6cm long, somewhat downy and glaucous beneath; flowers in whorled spikes, 4–5cm long, 2-lipped, creamy-white, deepending with age,

sometimes purplish without, sweetly fragrant, early summer to early autumn; berries red. *L.p.* Belgica, early Dutch honeysuckle, flowers red-purple without; *L.p.* Serotina, like *L.p.* Belgica but flowering later. *L. pileata*, W. China; evergreen shrub (or partially deciduous in hard winters), to 60cm (rarely 1m or more) tall; branches horizontal, wide-spreading; leaves ovate to oblong-lanceolate, 1–3cm long, bright lustrous green; flowers in axillary pairs, whitish, 6mm long, hidden by leaves; berries translucent-purple; good ground cover, especially in shade. *L.p. yunnanensis*, see *L. nitida*. *L.* × *purpusii* (*L. fragrantissima* × *L. standishii*), similar to *L. fragrantissima* and sometimes confused with it, but more compact in habit and with heavy, bristly hairs edging leaves. *L. sempervirens*, trumpet honeysuckle; E. USA; evergreen or partially so, bushy climber to 8m; leaves 4–7·5cm long, elliptic to obovate, blue-white beneath, those on floral shoots perfoliate; flowers 4–5cm long, not fragrant, slenderly trumpet-shaped, rich orange-scarlet without, yellow within, summer. *L. syringantha*, China, Tibet; deciduous shrub to 2m or more tall, broad, rounded habit; leaves sometimes in whorls of 3, oblong to elliptic, 1–2·5cm long, sea-green; flowers fragrant, in axillary pairs, soft lilac, 9–12mm long, early summer; berries red. *L. tatarica*, USSR – S. Russia to Turkestan; deciduous shrub, to 3m tall or so; well-branched; leaves oblong-ovate to lanceolate, 2–6·5cm long; flowers axillary, 2–2·5cm long, white or pink, early summer; berries red. *L. t.* Alba, flowers white; *L.t.* Hack's Red, flowers rose-red; *L.* × *tellmanniana* (*L. tragophylla* × *L. sempervirens*), similar to first parent, but with somewhat smaller leaves and flowers, the latter a

Top left: *Lonicera sempervirens*
Above: *Lonicera* × *tellmanniana*

rich coppery-yellow, red-flushed without and carried in large terminal clusters, summer; grows well in partial or full shade. *L. tragophylla*, W. China; bushy deciduous climber to 5m or so; leaves 5–12cm long, oblong, glaucous beneath, those on floral shoots perfoliate; flowers not scented, 6–9cm long, bright yellow, profusely borne in short dense spikes, summer; berries red; very shade-tolerant. *L. yunnanensis* (of gardens), see *L. nitida*; the true *L. yunnanensis*, a climbing plant, probably not cultivated.

Loosestrife – see *Lysimachia* and *Lythrum*.

Lopezia

(for Tomas Lopez, Spanish botanist who wrote about S.American plants circa 1540). ONAGRACEAE. A genus of 18 species of annuals, perennials and sub-shrubs from Mexico and C.America, 1 of which is usually available: *L. coronata*, crown jewels; S.Mexico, El Salvador; hardy annual 30–60cm tall, less in poor soil; stems erect, branched; leaves alternate, lanceolate to ovate, to 4cm long; flowers in terminal, leafy racemes. Each flower is 1·5–2cm wide, composed of 4 narrow red sepals, 4 spathulate lilac-pink petals, 2 very much larger than the others, and 2 stamens, 1 sterile and spoon-shaped, the other enclosing the fertile stamen. The anther is held in a state of tension and bursts when a visiting insect alights and pushes it down. Grow in any moderately fertile, well-drained soil in sun. Sow seed *in situ* late spring, or under glass at 13–16°C for earlier flowering.

Lords and ladies – see *Arum maculatum*.

Loropetalum

(Greek *loron*, strap or thong, and *petalon*, petal). HAMAMELIDACEAE. A genus of 1 or possibly 2 species of evergreen shrubs, closely allied to *Hamamelis*, from E.Asia. *L. chinense*, Assam, China, Japan; rounded habit, to 1·5m or more tall; stems slender, much-branched; leaves alternate, 2·5–6·5cm long, ovate, unequal at base and pointed-tipped; flowers like those of *Hamamelis*, petals white, to 2cm long, late winter to spring; not always reliably hardy. Grow in moisture-retentive but well-drained, neutral to acid soil in partial shade or sun at the foot of sheltered walls in all but the mildest areas. Protect outside specimens during severe winter weather. In cold areas grow in a frost-free greenhouse in pots, tubs or borders. A compost without lime should be chosen, particularly one of the all-peat types. Pot autumn to spring, plant outside spring only. Propagate from seed when ripe, by layering in spring and by cuttings late summer, ideally under mist or at least with bottom heat, 18–21°C.

Left: *Lonicera tatarica*
Left below: *Lopezia coronata*
Below: *Loropetalum chinense*
Right: *Lotus corniculatus*
Right below: *Lotus bertholetii*

Lotus

(Greek vernacular *lotos*, applied to several members of the pea family, including clovers and birdsfoot trefoil, taken up for this genus by Linnaeus). LEGUMINOSAE. A genus of about 100 species of perennials and sub-shrubs, mainly from temperate Africa, Europe, Asia. They have alternate, trifoliate or pinnate leaves and axillary umbels of pea flowers having distinctively beaked keels, followed by slender pods. Grow the hardy species described in any well-drained soil in sun; plant autumn to spring; propagate from seed or by careful division spring, cuttings late spring or late summer. Grow the tender species only in warm areas, otherwise elsewhere under glass or over-winter there, minimum temperature 5–7°C, sunny and well-ventilated. Pot spring. Propagate from seed in spring at a temperature of 18°C, or by cuttings late spring or summer, bottom heat 21°C.

Species cultivated: *L. bertholetii*, coral gem, parrots ear or pelicans beak (USA); Canary and Cape Verde Is; tender, silvery hairy sub-shrubs; stems low, arching or trailing, to 60cm long; leaves pinnate, leaflets 3–7, linear, 1–1·8cm long; flowers about 2·5cm long, scarlet, like slender gaping beaks, in umbels of 2–3 or more, summer; may be grown outside from early summer to autumn; makes an effective hanging basket plant. *L. corniculatus*, bird's-foot trefoil; Europe, Asia, mountains of N. and E.Africa; hardy, tufted perennials; stems slender, decumbent, 10–40cm long; leaves pinnate, leaflets 5, upper 3 obovate, lowest pair ovate to lanceolate, 3–10mm long; flowers about 1·5cm long, bright yellow, often tipped, streaked or flushed red, in long-stalked umbels of 2–6, summer to autumn; pods cylindrical, to 3cm long, often reddish. *L.c.* Plenus (*L.c.* Flore-pleno), flowers double.

Lotus flower, sacred lotus – see *Nelumbo*.

Love-in-a-mist – see *Nigella*.

Love-lies-bleeding – see *Amaranthus caudatus*.

Luetkia

(for Count Feodor P. Lutke, 1797–1882, captain, later admiral, of the 4th Russian expedition to circumnavigate the earth). ROSACEAE. A genus of 1 species of small, evergreen perennial from W. N.America: *L. pectinata* (*Saxifraga p.*), somewhat woody-based, rhizomatous and stoloniferous, forming mats like those of a mossy saxifrage; leaves tufted, 1–2cm long, bi- or triternately dissected into linear lobes; flowers 5-petalled, to 7mm wide, white, in racemes to 10cm or more tall, summer. Grow in moisture-retentive, preferably peaty, neutral to acid soil in a north-facing or partially shaded site. Plant autumn to spring. Propagate from seed or by division, spring, or cuttings late summer.

Lunaria

(Latin *luna*, the moon, alluding to the silvery membrane – septum – that divides each seed-pod). Honesty, satin-flower. CRUCIFERAE. A genus of 3 species of annuals and perennials from Europe, 1 of which is commonly grown: *L. annua* (*L. biennis*), honesty; S.E. Europe, naturalized elsewhere; usually biennial, sometimes an annual or short-lived perennial; main stem robust, to 90cm tall; leaves in opposite pairs, 8–15cm long, ovate-cordate, boldly toothed; flowers 4-petalled to 2cm wide, shades of red-purple or white, in terminal racemes, spring to summer; pods flat, broadly oval to rounded, 3–7cm long. *L.a.* Variegata, leaves irregularly margined creamy-white. *L. biennis*, see *L. annua*. *L. rediviva*, less common but similar to *L. annua* and sometimes confused with it; pods elliptic-lanceolate, usually tapered to each end. Grow in any well-drained soil in sun or shade. Sow seed *in situ*, or a nursery bed, in late spring to early summer; transplant if necessary in autumn.

Below and bottom left: *Lunaria annua*, white and purple flowered forms
Above: *Lunaria annua* immature seed pods
Above right: *Lupinus arboreus*
Below right: *Lupinus* Catherine of York
Far right: *Lupinus* Blue Jacket

Lupinus

(reputedly from Latin *lupus*, the wolf, because it was believed that lupins robbed the soil of fertility. It is now known that, like other legumes, the roots of lupins bear nitrogen-fixing nodules, and some species are used for green manuring). Lupin. LEGUMINOSAE. A genus of about 200 species of annuals, perennials and shrubs from N. and S. America, Mediterranean. They have alternate, digitate (compound palmate) leaves composed of 5–15 narrow leaflets, and terminal racemes of pea flowers followed by narrow, flattened pods. Grow in well-drained but moisture-retentive soil, preferably in full sun. Plant perennials autumn to spring. Sow annuals *in situ* in spring or mid autumn in a sheltered site for earlier blooming. Propagate perennials by division at planting time, cuttings of basal shoots with a heel in a cold frame spring, or from seed in a nursery row spring, thinning or transplanting seedlings 15cm apart and setting out in flowering positions in autumn.

Species cultivated: *L. arboreus*, tree lupin or lupine; California; evergreen shrub 1m or more tall; leaflets 5–12, oblanceolate, to 5·5cm long; racemes to 30cm long, flowers fragrant, 1·4–1·7cm long, usually yellow, sometimes lilac to blue, summer; tends to be short-lived but easily raised from seed. *L. hartwegii*, Mexico; annual, 60–90cm tall; leaflets 7–9, hairy; racemes 20–30cm long, flowers to 2cm long, blue to pinkish or reddish with white keel, summer to autumn; cultivar strains are available in a wider colour range, in particular the dwarf *L.h.* Pixie Delight, to 45cm tall. *L. polyphyllus*, California to British Columbia; clump-forming perennial to 1·5m tall; leaflets 10–17, oblanceolate, 7–15cm long; racemes 15–60cm long, flowers 1·2–1·4cm long, blue, purple or reddish, early summer; mainly represented in cultivation by hybrids with *L. arboreus* resulting, after many years of breeding and selection work, in the famous British Russell strain with all colours of the rainbow, including bi-coloured blooms. Russell lupins may be raised from seed as complete mixtures or more restricted colour selections, eg yellow shades, rose and white, blue and white, or obtained as named cultivar plants. They rarely exceed 90cm tall and the Monarch Dwarf Lulu are only 60cm, very sturdy and wind-resistant.

Luzula

(Italian *lucciola* or Latin *lucere*, to shine – alluding to the white flowers of some species). Woodrush. JUNCACEAE. A genus of 80 species of grassy-leaved perennials of cosmopolitan distribution, mainly from cold to temperate regions. They are tufted, sometimes stoloniferous, with arching, linear leaves and small, 6-tepalled flowers in few to many flowered cymes, sometimes dense and spike-like. Grow in any moderately fertile soil in sun or partial shade, particularly the latter as found in light woodland conditions. Plant autumn to spring. Propagate from seed when ripe or spring, or by division at planting time.

Species cultivated: *L. maxima*, see *L. sylvatica*. *L. nivea*, snowy woodrush; mountains of C. and W.Europe, 40–80cm tall; leaves to 30cm long, ciliate, particularly at junction with stem; flowers 1cm wide, white, in loose clusters, 4–6cm wide, summer. *L. sylvatica* (*L. maxima*), greater woodrush; most of Europe; densely leafy, spreading widely when established, to 30cm or more tall; leaves 10–30cm long by 6–12mm wide, leathery, glossy deep green; flowers 6–7mm wide, chestnut-brown, in loose, long-branched clusters to 10cm or more wide, early summer; a good ground cover for shady sites that do not get too dry. *L.s.* Marginata (*L.s.* Variegata), leaves with very narrow, creamy-yellow margins.

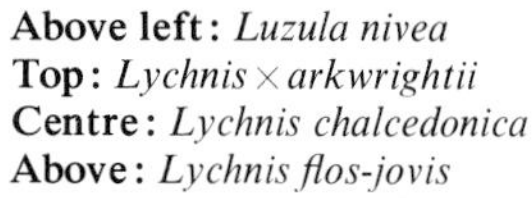

Above left: *Luzula nivea*
Top: *Lychnis × arkwrightii*
Centre: *Lychnis chalcedonica*
Above: *Lychnis flos-jovis*
Right above: *Lychnis coronaria* Abbotswood Rose

Lychnis

(probably Greek *lychnos*, a lamp – alluding either to the bright red flowers of some sorts, or use of woolly-leaved species as wicks for lamps). Catchfly. CARYOPHYLLACEAE. A genus of 12–35 species (depending on the classifier) of perennials and annuals from temperate Europe and Asia, closely allied to *Agrostemma* and *Silene*. They are tufted to clump-forming, with erect stems, opposite pairs of ovate to lanceolate or spathulate leaves, and 5-petalled flowers in tubular calyces borne in dense and head-like to loose and panicle-like cymes. Grow in any well-drained, fertile soil in sun. Plant perennials autumn to spring, sow annuals *in situ* in spring or early autumn. Propagate perennials by division at planting time or from seed sown in spring, growing them on in a nursery bed until autumn, when they can be transplanted to their permanent positions.

Species cultivated: *L. alpina* (*Viscaria a.*), alpine catchfly; N. Europe, mountains farther south; tufted perennial, 10–20cm tall; basal leaves linear to spathulate, to 5cm long, stem leaves in a few pairs, shorter and broader; flowers rose-purple or white, 6–12mm wide, smaller ones often female only, petals deeply bifid, in dense, terminal clusters, summer. *L. × arkwrightii* (*L. chalcedonica × L. × haageana*), about 30cm tall, midway between parents; flowers intense scarlet, about 4cm wide, in terminal clusters of 5–10, summer. *L. chalcedonica*, Maltese or Jerusalem cross; N. USSR; clump-forming herbaceous perennial, to 90cm tall; leaves 5–10cm long, ovate, hispid; flowers 1·5–2cm long, petals bright scarlet, deeply bifid, up to 50 in dense, flattened heads, summer. *L. coeli-rosa*, see *Silene c.-r.* *L. coronaria* (*Agrostemma c.*), rose campion, dusty miller; S.E. Europe; biennial or short-lived perennial, usually flowering first year from seed if sown early; whole plant white-woolly; stems to 60cm tall; leaves to 10cm long, ovate to lanceolate; flowers 3–4cm wide, purple-cerise or pure white, summer to autumn. *L. dioica*, see *Silene d.* *L. flos-jovis* (*Agrostemma f.-j.*), flower of Jove; Alps; white-woolly perennial, to 60cm tall; leaves lanceolate; flowers red-purple or white, to 1·5cm wide in terminal clusters, early summer. *L. f.-j.* Hort's Variety, flowers rose-pink. *L. fulgens*, see next species. *L. × haageana* (*L. fulgens*, similar to *L. chalcedonica*, × *L. coronata*, large-flowered Asiatic species), about 30cm or so tall; leaves ovate to lanceolate, sometimes purple-flushed; flowers 5cm wide, bright orange, scarlet or white, summer; short-lived and rather weak-stemmed but striking. *L. viscaria* (*L. vulgaris*, *Viscaria v.*, *Viscaria viscosa*), German catchfly; Europe; tufted perennial, to 50cm tall; like a very much larger *L. alpina*; stems with sticky zones beneath each leaf-pair; flowers 1·5–2cm wide, pinkish to dark red-purple or white in spike-like clusters, summer. *L.v.* Splendens Plena, flowers double. *L. vulgaris*, see *L. viscaria*.

Lycium

(Greek name for a thorny tree used medicinally, from Lycia in Turkey, and taken up for this genus by Linnaeus). Box thorn, matrimony vine. SOLANACEAE. A genus of 80–100 species of shrubs and semi-climbers from temperate and sub-tropical regions, particularly S.America. They have alternate, sometimes clustered, linear to obovate leaves, 5-lobed funnel- or salver-shaped flowers, solitary or clustered in the leaf-axils, and usually red berry fruit. Grow in well-drained soil in sun. Plant autumn to spring. Propagate by suckers or from seed in spring, cuttings in summer.

Species cultivated: *L. barbarum* (*L. chinense*, *L. europaeum* of gardens, *L. halimifolium*), Chinese box thorn, Duke of Argyll's tea plant, matrimony vine (USA); China, naturalized elsewhere; deciduous shrub to 2·5m tall; stems slender, sometimes spiny, arching to pendulous; leaves elliptic, to ovate lanceolate or rhomboid, 2·5–6·5cm long, bright to grey-green; flowers funnel-shaped, about 1cm long, rose-purple ageing brownish-yellow, usually in 2s or 3s, summer to autumn; fruit oblongoid to ovoid, 1–2cm long, scarlet; grows well near the sea; a very variable species, formerly – and by some botanists still – classified as 3 species (see synonyms given here); *L.b. chinense*, stems rarely spiny, leaves rhomboid to ovate, bright green; *L.b.c.* Carnosum, flowers pink; *L.b. halimifolium*, stems often spiny, leaves to 6cm long, lanceolate, grey-green. *L. chilense* (*L. grevilleanum*), Chile, Argentina; deciduous shrub 1·5–2m tall; stems arching, dense; leaves 1–5cm long, obovate to lanceolate, somewhat fleshy, grey-green in some forms; flowers solitary or in pairs, 9–12mm wide, purple and ivory-white, summer to autumn; fruit globular, 8mm orange-red. *L. chinense*, see *L. barbarum chinense*, *L. europeaeum* of gardens, see *L. barbarum*. *L. grevilleanum*, see *L. chilense*. *L. halimifolium*, see *L. barbarum h.*

Lycoris

(for the beautiful actress, mistress of Mark Antony). AMARYLLIDACEAE. A genus of about 10 species of bulbous plants allied to *Amaryllis* from E.Himalaya to Japan. They have strap-shaped basal leaves that die away just as, or before the erect, leafless, flowering stems arise; flowers in terminal umbels, 6-tepalled, funnel-shaped. Culture as for *Nerine*, but see also species descriptions below for individual requirements.

Species cultivated: *L. alba*, see *L. radiata*. *L. africana* (*L. aurea*), golden spider or hurricane lily (USA); Burma to China and Taiwan; stems to 30cm tall; flowers to 7·5cm long, tepals wavy-margined, golden-yellow, late summer; once thought to be a native of Africa, hence the confusing name; best grown at a minimum temperature of 16°C and watered throughout the year when it stays evergreen and flowers more readily. *L. albiflora*, Japan; like *L. africana* but flowers somewhat smaller, white. *L. aurea*, see *L. africana*. *L. incarnata*, C.China; stems 30–45cm tall; flowers 7–10cm wide, fragrant, pale rose, late summer; usually hardy outside at the foot of a sunny, sheltered wall. *L. radiata*, red spider lily; China; stems to 45cm tall; flowers 5–6cm wide, tepals reflexed, wavy, bright red, autumn; in USA confused with *Nerine sarniensis*. *L.r.* Alba, flowers white. *L. sanguinea*, Japan; stems 30–45cm tall; flowers 6–8cm wide, blood-red, late summer. *L. sprengeri*, C.China; much like *L. incarnata* and equally hardy; flowers pink with a bluish suffusion, late summer. *L. squamigera* (*Amaryllis hallii*), magic or resurrection lily (USA); Japan; stems 50–70cm tall; flowers 7·5cm wide, fragrant, pink to rose lilac, not unlike those of *Amaryllis belladonna*, autumn; the hardiest species but needs a warm summer to flower well.

Above and below: *Lycium barbarum*

Below: *Lycoris radiata*

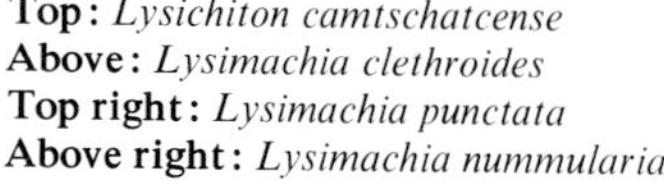

Top: *Lysichiton camtschatcense*
Above: *Lysimachia clethroides*
Top right: *Lysimachia punctata*
Above right: *Lysimachia nummularia*

Lyonia

(for John Lyon, died 1818, Scottish gardener and botanist who introduced many N.American plants into Britain). ERICACEAE. A genus of 40–50 species of evergreen and deciduous shrubs or small trees from E.Asia, N.America, and particularly the W.Indies. They have alternate, elliptic to ovate or obovate leaves and tubular to urn-shaped flowers in axillary clusters or terminal racemes, or panicles. Grow in acid, moist, preferably peaty soil in sun or partial shade. Plant autumn or spring. Propagate from seed or by layering in spring, cuttings late summer.

Species cultivated: *L. ligustrina*, male berry, he-hucklebury; E. USA; deciduous shrub eventually to 4m tall; leaves 3–7·5cm long, lanceolate, oblong-elliptic to obovate; flowers 4–6mm long, white, in terminal panicles, 5–15cm long, early summer. *L. lucida* (*Pieris lucida*), fetter bush; S.E. USA; evergreen shrub to 2m tall; stems sharply 3-angled; leaves 3–8cm long, lanceolate to oblong-ovate, leathery, rich lustrous green; flowers, 6–9mm long, narrowly urn-shaped, white or pink, in axillary clusters, early summer. *L. mariana*, stagger bush; E.USA; deciduous shrub eventually to 2m tall; leaves 2–7cm long, elliptic to obovate, red in autumn; flowers about 1cm long, broadly urn-shaped, white or pink-tinted in umbels or racemose clusters, early summer onwards. *L. ovalifolia*, E.Asia; deciduous shrub to 3m tall (sometimes a tree to 10m in the wild); leaves 5–13cm long, elliptic to ovate-oblong, leathery; flowers to 1cm long, narrowly bell-shaped, white, in terminal and axillary racemes 5–13cm long, early summer; *L.o. elliptica*, leaves elliptic, slender-pointed, bronze-flushed when young, slightly later-flowering, flower racemes shorter than in the type.

Lysichiton

(*Lysichitum*). (Greek *lysis*, loose, and *chiton*, a cloak or covering – alluding to the widely expanding floral spathe). ARACEAE. A genus of 2 species of herbaceous perennials from N.E. Asia and W. N. America. They are robust clump-forming, with thick rhizomes, large, oblanceolate leaves, and arum-like inflorescences. Grow in wet or permanently moist soil in sun or light shade. Plant autumn to spring. Propagate by division in spring or from seed sown as soon as ripe.

Species cultivated: *L. americanum*, yellow skunk cabbage; California to Alaska and Montana; leaves 60–150cm long, spadices thick, cylindrical, greenish; flowers tiny, petalless, spathes yellow, widely boat-shaped, to 18cm long, on stalks 30cm or more tall, before or with very young leaves, early spring. *L. camtschatcense*, N. Japan, Kamchatka, Sakhalin, Kuriles; similar to *L. americanum*, but somewhat smaller; leave glaucous-green; spathes white, opening a few weeks later.

Lysimachia

(reputedly for King Lysimachos of Thrace in Greece, his name from the Greek *lysimacheion*, 'ending strife'). Loosestrife. PRIMULACEAE. A genus of about 165 species of annuals, perennials and sub-shrubs of cosmopolitan distribution. Those in general cultivation are erect, decumbent or prostrate hardy perennials with alternate opposite pairs of rounded to narrowly lanceolate leaves, and either terminal racemes of, or solitary, 5-petalled flowers in the upper leaf-axils. Grow in moisture-retentive soil in sun or shade. Plant autumn to spring. Propagate by division at planting time or from seed in spring.

Species cultivated: *L. clethroides*, gooseneck loosestrife; China, Japan; rhizomatous, forming colonies; stems to 90cm tall; leaves opposite and alternate, ovate, 7–12cm long; flowers about 1cm wide, in dense, tapered, arching racemes, point bent forward and upwards, summer to autumn. *L. nummularia*, creeping jenny, moneywort; Europe; prostrate, mat-forming; stems to 60cm, branched; leaves opposite, rounded, to 2cm long; flowers solitary in leaf-axils, cup-shaped 1·5cm wide, bright yellow, summer. *L.n.* Aurea, leaves golden-green. *L. punctata*, E.C. and S. Europe; rhizomatous, forming colonies; stems to 90cm tall; leaves opposite or in whorls of 3–4, lanceolate to elliptic, downy, dotted with glands beneath, 4–7·5cm long; flowers yellow, about 1·5cm wide, in whorled racemes, summer; rather invasive; sometimes confused with *L. vulgaris*, common yellow loosestrife, but that plant has a branched, panicle-like inflorescence.

Lythrum

(Greek *lythron*, blood – from colour of the flowers). LYTHRACEAE. A genus of 30–35 species of perennials and shrubs from temperate regions of the world. 1 species and its hybrids is generally available: *L. salicaria*, purple loosestrife; Europe, N. Africa, W. and N. Asia, naturalized N. America; erect, woody-based herbaceous perennial 90–120cm tall; leaves opposite, lanceolate, 4–7cm long; flowers 5-petalled, rose-purple to magenta, 1–1·5cm wide in long, dense, tapered, spike-like inflorescences, summer; several cultivars with richer, brighter or pinker flowers are available, some of them probably hybrids with the shorter, more slender *L. virgatum*. Culture as for *Lysimachia*; particularly good for wet ground or by the waterside.

Macleaya

(for Alexander Macleay, 1767–1848, Secretary of the Linnean Society and Colonial Secretary for New

Above: *Lythrum virgatum* The Rocket
Top right: *Macleaya microcarpa*
Far right top: *Magnolia campbellii*
Far right above: *Magnolia sieboldii*
Far right: *Magnolia wilsoniana*

South Wales). PAPAVERACEAE. A genus of 2 species of herbaceous perennials from E. Asia, 1 commonly grown: *M. microcarpa* (*Bocconia m.*), plume poppy; C. China; to 2·4m tall, widely suckering; basal leaves rounded, deeply lobed, white downy beneath, to 25cm long, upper leaves smaller; flowers small, petalless with 2 buff-pink sepals and 8–12 stamens, many in large, handsome, terminal panicles, late summer; often grown as *M. cordata* (*Bocconia cordata*), but that Chinese and Japanese species has white sepals and 24–30 stamens to each flower. *M.m.* Coral Plume, coral-pink. Grow in moisture-retentive, fertile soil in sun or light shade. Plant autumn or spring. Propagate by root cuttings late winter, division spring, cuttings of non-flowering lower stem shoots or suckers, summer.

Madwort – see *Alyssum*.

Magnolia

(for Pierre Magnol, 1638–1715, Director of the Botanic Gardens and Professor of Botany at Montpellier, France). MAGNOLIACEAE. A genus of about 80 species of evergreen and deciduous trees and shrubs from Himalaya to Japan, Java, Borneo, E. N.America to C. America and Venezuela. They have alternate, ovate to oblanceolate leaves, and generally large, solitary, terminal, bowl to goblet-shaped, frost-tender flowers with 6–15 petals. Grow in sun or partial shade in fertile, well-drained but moisture-retentive soil, preferably neutral to acid, although some species tolerate some lime if the site is not hot and dry and there is plenty of humus. Plant spring. Propagate by layering in spring or from seed when ripe – this may take 18 months to germinate.
Species cultivated (deciduous unless otherwise stated): *M. campbellii*, Himalaya; to 20m or so (33m in the wild); leaves broadly elliptic, 15–25cm long, glaucous beneath; flowers to 25cm wide, erect, white, pink or crimson, before leaves, early spring; takes 15–20 years to flower from seed. *M.c.* Alba, flowers white. *M.c. mollicomata* (*M. mollicomata*), Yunnan, Burma; flowers mauve-pink, stalks downy, flowers in 9–12 years from seed; there are several good cultivars derived from crossing this with type *M. campbellii*. *M. conspicua*, see *M. denudata*. *M. delavayi*, W. China; evergreen tree, to 10m; leaves 13–20cm long, leathery, ovate, glaucous beneath; flowers 15–20cm wide, cream, fragrant, late summer to autumn; needs wall-protection in all but milder areas, tolerant of lime. *M. denudata* (*M. conspicua*, *M. heptapeta*, *M. yulan*), Yulan, China; large shrub or broad tree to 10m or more; leaves 7–15cm long, obovate; flowers fragrant, erect, 12–15cm wide, pure white, before leaves, spring; sometimes confused with white clones of *M.* × *soulangiana*. *M. discolor*, see *M. liliiflora*. *M. grandiflora*, bull bay; S.E. USA; evergreen tree to 33m but often less in gardens; leaves obovate-oblong, leathery, dark polished green above, rusty downy beneath; flowers creamy-white, fragrant, 15–25cm wide, summer to autumn; several lime-tolerant cultivars are available differing in flower size, leaf shape, habit, including *M.g.* Goliath, with flowers to 30cm wide and leaves almost devoid of rusty down. *M. halliana*, see *M. stellata*. *M. heptapeta*, see *M. denudata*. *M.* × *highdownensis*, see *M. sinensis*. *M. hypoleuca* (*M. obovata*), Japan, Kuriles; tree to 18m or more; leaves obovate, to 30cm long; flowers white, to 18cm wide, early summer. *M. kobus*, Japan; tree 10–12m tall or more, pyramidal when young; bark aromatic; leaves obovate, 7–15cm long; flowers white, starry, 7–10cm wide with about 6 petals, spring, before leaves; can be propagated by late summer cuttings. *M. liliiflora* (*M. discolor*, *M. quinquepeta*), China, much grown in Japan; shrub 3–4m tall, higher

trained on walls; leaves ovate to obovate, 7–20cm long; flowers erect, purple without, white within, 7–10cm wide, spring to summer. *M.l.* Nigra, flowers dark purple. *M.* × *loebneri* (*M. kobus* × *M. stellata*), like *M. kobus* but with somewhat narrower leaves and about 12 petals to each flower. *M.* × *l.*

Far left: *Magnolia liliiflora* Nigra
Left below: *Magnolia* × *soulangiana*
Left: *Magnolia stellata*
Above: *Magnolia grandiflora*

Leonard Messel, flowers lilac-pink. *M. mollicomata*, see *M. campbellii m. M. nicholsoniana*, see *M. wilsoniana. M. obovata*, see *M. hypoleuca. M. parviflora*, see *M. sieboldii. M. quinquepeta*, see *M. liliiflora. M. salicifolia*, Japan; much like *M. kobus*, but less tall; leaves narrower and flowers larger; bark lemon-scented on bruising. *M. sieboldii* (*M. parviflora*), Japan, Korea; large shrub or small tree 3–4m tall; leaves elliptic to obovate, glaucous beneath, 10–15cm long; flowers to 10cm wide, more or less nodding, fragrant, white with red stamens, late spring to late summer. *M. sinensis*, W. China; large shrub or small tree to 6m; leaves oval to obovate, 7–18cm long; white downy beneath and bright green above; flowers pendant, to 10cm wide, white with red stamens, summer; *M.* × *highdownensis* (reputedly a hybrid between this and *M. wilsonii*) is very similar but having leaves shaped like the latter, although somewhat larger with white hairs beneath, very lime-tolerant. *M.* × *soulangiana* (*M. denudata* × *M. liliiflora*), much like first parent but more vigorous and shapely, flowering a little later; flower colour ranges from pure white – *M.* × *s.* Alba Superba (*M.* × *s.* Alba) – to strongly flushed rose-purple (*M.* × *s.* Lennei); several good cultivars are available, very lime-tolerant. *M. sprengeri*, China; much like *M. denudata* but more tree-like, taller; leaves to 17cm long; flowers longer, white with purple base or pink. *M.s. diva*, leaves broadly ovate, flowers rose-pink, darker-lined; *M.s. elongata*, flowers white, leaves lanceolate to narrowly obovate. *M. stellata* (*M. halliana*), Japan; much-branched shrub 2–4m tall; leaves 6·5–10cm long, narrowly oblong to obovate; bark aromatic; flowers 6–8cm wide, white starry, of 12–18 narrow petals, spring, before leaves. *M.s.* Rosea, flowers flushed pink; *M.s.* Rubra, flushed purple-pink; breeding experiments more than suggest that *M. stellata* is a dwarf mutant of *M. kobus*, but it is convenient to retain the long familiar name and status. *M. taliensis*, see *M. wilsoniana. M. wilsoniana* (*M. taliensis*, *M. nicholsoniana*), W. China; much like *M. sinensis*, but leaves ovate-lanceolate, dull green above, pale velvety-brown beneath (although plants formerly classified as *M. taliensis* and *M. nicholsoniana* have leaves almost hairless beneath).

Mahonia

(for Bernard M'Mahon, 1775–1816, American horticulturalist). BERBERIDACEAE. A genus of 70–100 species of evergreen shrubs from Asia, N. and C. America. They were formerly included in, and are

Top left: *Mahonia aquifolium*
Above left: *Mahonia japonica* young leaves
Left: *Mahonia aquifolium* berries
Above: *Mahonia* × *media*
Below right: *Maianthemum bifolium*

closely allied to, *Berberis*, but primarily distinguished by spineless stems, pinnate prickle-toothed leaves and the racemes of flowers carried in terminal clusters (fascicles). Grow in humus-rich, well-drained but not dry soil in shade or sun. Plant autumn or spring. Propagate from seed when ripe and kept in a cold frame, stem tip cuttings in summer at 16–18°C, leaf-bud cuttings in autumn, division or suckers where possible and layering in spring.

Species cultivated: *M. aquifolium*, Oregon grape; N. W. N.America; suckering; stems erect, few-branched, 1–2m tall; leaves 15–30cm long of 5–9, ovate, lustrous, dark green leaflets; flowers golden-yellow in terminal and axillary racemes to 7cm long, late winter to spring; berries black with waxy-glaucous patina. *M.a.* Atropurpureum, leaves red-purple in winter; *M.a.* Moseri, leaves pale green, flushed pink to coppery-red. *M. bealei*, China; like *M. japonica* and for long confused with it in cultivation but differing in having flowers in the axils of small, scale-like bracts; racemes erect to spreading, and a large terminal leaflet to each leaf, although this latter character is not always reliable. *M.* × Charity, see *M.* × *media*. *M. japonica*, China, long cultivated in Japan; erect to somewhat spreading habit; stems robust, sparsely branched; leaves 30–45cm long of 13–19 leathery, lanceolate to oblong, glossy leaflets, the terminal one equalling, or smaller than, laterals; flowers yellow, fragrant, in the axils of bracts almost as long as flower-stalk, racemes to 20cm or more long, pendulous, late autumn to spring; hybridizes with *M. bealei*, adding to the confusion between the 2. *M. lomariifolia*, Burma, W. China, Taiwan; 2–4m or more tall, often with a single, erect trunk; 25–60cm long leaves in palm-like clusters at branch tips, leaflets 25–39, oblong-ovate to lanceolate, dark leathery-green; flowers fragrant, bright yellow, racemes erect, 10–20cm long, winter; liable to be cut back in severe frosts but usually regenerates from ground level. *M.* × *media* (*M. japonica* × *M. lomariifolia*), group of cultivars including those of a second generation, variously combining the parental characters; best-known to date are: *M.* × *m.* Charity, much like a more vigorous *M. japonica* but with 17–21 leaflets and erect to spreading racemes of lemon-yellow flowers; *M.* × *m.* Buckland, akin to *M. lomariifolia* in leaf, with long, lax, branched racemes; several others on a similar theme are available. *M. pinnata* (*M. fascicularis*), California, Oregon; allied to *M. aquifolium*, but usually taller (3m or more in cultivation); leaves to 12cm long, leaflets 5–9 (sometimes more), usually overlapping, ovate to oblong, wavy-margined; plants under this name in gardens are usually hybrids with *M. aquifolium* and perhaps also *M. repens* (dwarf species 30–60cm tall); best-known is *M.* × Undulata, like a robust *M. aquifolium* with strongly waved leaf margins; hybrids between *M. pinnata* and *M. aquifolium* are also known as *M.* × *wagneri*.

Maianthemum

(Greek *maios*, May, and *anthemon*, flower). May lily. LILIACEAE. A genus of 3 species of herbaceous perennials from the northern temperate zone, 1 of which is generally available: *M. bifolium*, Europe, Asia; slender, creeping rhizomes forming large colonies; stems erect, 10–20cm tall; leaves 1–3 (usually 2), stalked, broadly ovate-cordate, 3–7cm long; flowers 4-tepalled, about 4mm wide, white, in terminal, 5cm-long racemes, early summer; fruit a 6mm wide, globular berry, white to mauve, speckled red. *M.b. kamtschaticum*, E. Asia to W. N.America; to 35cm tall; leaves to 20cm long; now given specific rank as *M. dilatum* or *M. kamtschaticum*. *M. b. canadense*, N. N.America; like *M. bifolium* but leaves sessile, basal lobes close together; now given specific rank as *M. canadense*. Grow in humus-rich, moisture-retentive soil in shade. Plant autumn or spring. Propagation by division in spring.

Maidenhair tree – see *Ginkgo*.

Malcolmia

(*Malcomia*). (for William Malcolm, died 1820, and his son, also William, 1769–1835, London nurserymen). CRUCIFERAE. A genus of about 30 species of annuals and perennials from Mediterranean to C. Asia and Afghanistan, 1 of which is commonly cultivated: *M. maritima*, Virginian stock; S. and W. Greece, S. Albania, naturalized elsewhere; annual, to 20cm or more; leaves oblong to obovate; flowers 4-petalled, about 1·5cm wide, shades of pink, red, purple, white, in terminal racemes, spring to autumn. Grow in well-drained soil in sun. Sow seed *in situ* in autumn, spring or summer.

Mallow – see *Malva*.

Malope

(ancient Greek for kind of mallow). MALVACEAE. Genus of 3 annual species, Mediterranean, 1 generally available: *M. trifida* (*M. grandiflora*), erect to 60cm, branched; leaves rounded, often sharply 3-lobed; flowers 5–7cm wide, rose-purple, darker veins, summer, autumn; also white, pink and crimson forms. Needs sun, humus-rich, well-drained soil. Sow seed *in situ* spring.

Malus

(Latin name for apple). Apple, crab. ROSACEAE. A genus of 25–35 species of deciduous trees and shrubs from the northern temperate zone. They have alternate, rounded to lanceolate, toothed, rarely lobed leaves, umbel-like clusters of usually showy, 5-petalled flowers in spring, and fleshy fruit known as crab-apples. See Apple entry. Grow in any well-drained, fertile soil, preferably in sun, although light shade is tolerated. Plant autumn to spring. Propagate from seed when ripe, or sown soon after extraction from the fruit in late winter or spring. Named cultivars must be budded or grafted on to seedling domestic apples or 1 of the specially selected apple rootstocks such as Malling II or Malling-Merton III.

Species cultivated: *M.* × *aldenhamensis*, see *M.* × *purpurea*. *M.* × *atrosanguinea* (*M. halliana* × *M. sieboldii*), much like *M. floribunda* but with arching branches, dark glossy green leaves, and darker pink flowers. *M. baccata*, Siberian crab; Himalaya, E. Siberia and China to Korea; tree to 12m tall; leaves ovate, 4–9cm long; flowers white, 2·5–4cm wide; fruit globular, about 1cm wide, yellow to red. *M. coronaria*, American crab; E. N.America; tree to 8m or more tall; leaves 5–11cm long, ovate to elliptic, sometimes 3-lobed; flowers fragrant, white, tinted pink, 2·5–4cm wide; fruit rounded, to 4cm wide, yellow-green. *M.* × *domestica*, correct name for the orchard apple. *M.* × *eleyi* (*M.* × *purpurea eleyi*), (*M. niedzwetzkyana* × *M. spectabilis*), much like members of the *M.* × *purpurea* group, but generally smaller, leaves more richly purple-flushed and flowers darker, opening slightly later. *M. floribunda*, Japan; large shrub or small tree to 7m with dense, rounded head; leaves ovate, 4–7·5cm long; flowers 2·5–3cm wide, rose-red in bud, opening blush-pink in great profusion; fruit rounded, yellow, 2cm wide; plant cultivated as *M. floribunda* is now considered to be a hybrid, differing from the wild Japanese plant (now known as *M. spontanea*). *M.* Golden Hornet, see *M. prunifolia*. *M.* × *hillieri*, see *M.* × *scheideckeri*. *M. hupehensis* (*M. theifera*), C. and W. China; tree to 8m tall; leaves ovate with short, slender point, finely toothed, purplish when young, 5–10cm long; flowers white, tinged pink on opening, fragrant, to 4cm wide; fruit globose, yellow, flushed red, 8mm wide; an apomictic triploid species coming true from seed. *M.* × John Downie (perhaps derived from *M. prunifolia* or *M. sylvestris*, but parentage unspecified), flowers white; fruit conical, to 3cm long, bright orange and red, usually carried in profusion, sweet; perhaps the finest fruiting crab. *M.* × Lemoinei, see *M.* × *purpurea*. *M.* × Magdeburgensis (probably a *M.* × *domestica* cultivar × *M. sylvestris* or *M. spectabilis*), much like a culinary apple, forming a small, tree with large, flowers, deep rose-red in bud, pale rose-purple

Far left above: *Malcolmia maritima*
Far left: *Malope trifilda*
Left above: *Malus* × *eleyi*
Left: *Malus floribunda*
Above: *Malus* × John Downie fruit

within; fruit greenish or yellowish. *M. niedzwetzkyana* (*M. pumila n.*), S.W. Siberia, Turkestan; much like a domestic apple with all parts bearing red anthocyanin pigment; flowers to 4cm wide, deep purple-red; fruit conical, red-purple, 5cm long; probably only a colour variant of *M.* × *domestica* or 1 of its parents – perhaps *M. sieversii*. *M.* × Profusion (*M.* × *purpurea* Lemoinei × *M. sieboldii*), small tree; leaves purple when young, then bronze-green; flowers deep purple-red, later paling, to 4cm wide, carried in abundance; fruit 1cm long, very dark red. *M. prunifolia*, said to come from N.E. Asia, but not known truly wild; tree to 9m; leaves elliptic to ovate, 5–10cm long; flowers white, 3–4cm wide; fruit globular to ovoid, to 2·5cm long, yellow or red. *M.p. rinki* (*M. ringo*, *M. pumila rinki*), downy, pinkish flowers; fruit pleasant eating, the yellow form being 1 parent of *M.* × Golden Hornet, bearing heavy crops of egg-shaped, golden crab-apples that hang long after leaf-fall. *M. pumila*, name used to cover several entities, including *M.* × *domestica* and *M. sylvestris*, but in a strict

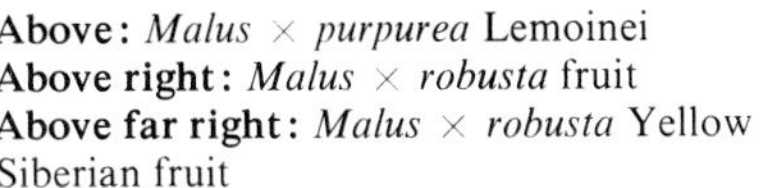

Above: *Malus* × *purpurea* Lemoinei
Above right: *Malus* × *robusta* fruit
Above far right: *Malus* × *robusta* Yellow Siberian fruit
Right: *Malus tschonoskii* autumn colour

sense belonging to the French paradise apple (from which some of the Malling rootstocks have been selected), although probably originally derived from *M. dasyphylla*, 1 of the putative parents of *M.* × *domestica*. *M.* × *purpurea* (*M. niedzwetzkyana* × *M.* × *atrosanguinea*), tree to 7m or so; leaves ovate, to 7cm or more long, coarsely toothed, sometimes with small lobes, purple-red, especially when young; flowers 2·5–3cm wide, ruby-red in bud, lighter on opening; fruit purple-red, globose, about 2·5cm long. *M.* × *p.* Aldenhamensis, at least some flowers semi-double, leaves often slightly lobed; *M.* × *p.* Eleyi, see *M.* × *eleyi*; *M.* × *p.* Lemoinei, flowers deep rosy-purple, leaves dark purple when young, fruit very dark. *M. ringo*, see *M. prunifolia*. *M.* × *robusta* (*M. baccata* × *M. prunifolia*), Siberian or cherry crab; vigorous shrub or small tree with spreading, arching branches; leaves elliptic; flowers pink or white, 2·5–4cm wide; fruit round to oval, 2·5cm long, red or yellow. *M.* × *r.* Red Siberian, fruit red; *M.* × *r.* Yellow Siberian, fruit yellow. *M. sargentii*, see *M. sieboldii*. *M.* × *scheideckeri* (*M. floribunda* × *M. prunifolia*), slow-growing shrub or small tree to 3m or more tall; leaves 5–11cm long, ovate; flowers pink, 4cm wide; fruit globose, yellow, 1·5cm wide; mainly represented in cultivation by *M.* × *s.* Hillieri, a vigorous clone with freely borne, semi-double flowers crimson in bud. *M. sieboldii* (*M. toringo*), Japan, Korea; shrub or small tree to 4m; branches arching to pendulous; leaves ovate to deeply 3-lobed, 2·5–6·5cm long, coarsely toothed, downy, especially beneath; flowers pink, to 2cm wide; fruit globose, red or brownish-yellow, 8mm wide. *M.s. sargentii* (*M. sargentii*), Japan; more bushy than type, usually under 2·5m tall; flowers white; fruit red. *M. spectabilis*, N. China, but not known in the wild; tree to 8m tall, erect habit when young; leaves elliptic to obovate to rounded, 5–9cm long; flowers red in bud, blush on opening, to 5cm wide; fruit globose, yellow, 2–2·5cm wide. *M.s.* Riversii (*M.s.* Rosea Plena), flowers semi-double. *M. sylvestris* (*M. pumila* in part, qv), common wild, or crab apple; Europe, S.W. Asia; shrub or tree to 10m or more tall; branchlets sometimes thorny; leaves elliptic to rounded, about 4cm long; flowers white, usually pink in bud; fruit 2–3cm wide, green-yellow, sometimes red-flushed; may be confused in the wild with self-sown *M.* × *domestica*, but easily distinguished by its thinner-textured, hairless leaves.

M. theifera, see *M. hupehensis*. *M. toringo*, see *M. sieboldii*. *M. tschonoskii*, Japan; tree 9–12m tall, of pyramidal habit; young stems with dense grey-white down; leaves broadly ovate to rounded, 5–10cm long, felted grey-white beneath, in autumn turning to shades of yellow, orange, red and purple; flowers 2·5–3cm wide, white; fruit globose, about 2·5cm wide, yellowish, flushed reddish.

Malva

(ancient Latin vernacular for mallow). Mallow. MALVACEAE. A genus of 30–40 species of annuals, biennials and perennials from Europe, N. Africa, Asia. Much like *Lavatera* in general appearance. Grow in fertile, well-drained soil in a sunny site. Plant perennials autumn or spring, annuals sown *in situ*, spring (autumn in sheltered places). Propagate perennials by division or cuttings, spring, biennials

from seed, spring, or by cuttings late summer. **Species cultivated:** *M. alcea*, Europe; erect, branched perennial to 1·25m; lower leaves rounded, cordate, often shallowly 3–5 lobed; flowers 5–7cm wide, pink to pale rose-purple, summer to autumn. *M.a.* Fastigiata, neater than type, lateral branches more erect – the commonest form in gardens. *M. moschata*, musk mallow; stems 60–80cm tall; leaves deeply 5–7 lobed, each lobe pinnatifid; flowers bright rose-purple, 5cm wide, summer to autumn. *M.m.* Alba, flowers pure white.

Mammoth tree – see *Sequoiadendron*.

Manna ash – see *Fraxinus ornus*.

Manzanita – see *Arctostaphylos manzanita*.

Maple – see *Acer*.

Marguerite – see *Chrysanthemum leucanthemum*.

Margyricarpus

(Greek *margarites*, a pearl, and *karpos*, a fruit – the fruit is white). ROSACEAE. A genus of 10 species of small, evergreen shrubs from the Andes, 1 of which is usually available: *M. pinnatus* (*M. setosus*), pearl berry or fruit; prostrate, sometimes to 30cm tall when old; stems almost covered by straw-coloured, papery stipules; leaves pinnate, to 2cm long, leaflets linear, deep green above; flowers tiny, petalless, green, summer; fruit berry-like, about 4mm long, each one formed of a single achene surrounded by a fleshy calyx tube, edible; liable to damage during severe winters. Grow in well-drained soil in a sunny, sheltered site or in a frost-free greenhouse. Plant spring. Propagate by seed or layering in spring, the former in a cold frame, or by cuttings in summer.

Left: *Malva moschata* Alba
Above: *Margyricarpus pinnatus*
Above right: *Matteuccia struthiopteris*
Right: *Matthiola* Brompton strain
Below right: *Matthiola* Excelsior strain

Marigold – see *Calendula* and *Tagetes*.

Marigold, Corn – see *Chrysanthemum segetum*.

Marigold, Marsh – see *Caltha*.

Marsh marigold – see *Caltha*.

Marvel of Peru – see *Mirabilis*.

Matricaria chamomilla – see *Chamaemelum nobile*; **M. eximia** – see *Chrysanthemum parthenium*.

Matteuccia

(for Carlo Matteuci, 1800–68, Italian scientist). ASPIDIACEAE (POLYPODIACEAE). A genus of 3 species of ferns from northern temperate regions, 1 of which is generally available: *M. struthiopteris* (*Onoclea s.*), ostrich fern; Europe, Asia; deciduous perennial spreading by far-creeping rhizomes, sterile fronds arching, slenderly elliptic to oblanceolate, deeply bipinnatifid, 60–120cm long, forming vase- or shuttlecock-shaped rosettes, fertile fronds very much smaller in the centres of the rosettes, pinnate, the pinnae rolled around the sporangia until they ripen. Grow in moist, humus-rich soil in sun or partial shade. Plant autumn to spring. Propagate by division or spores in spring.

Matthiola

(for Pierandrea Mattioli, 1500–77, Italian doctor and botanist). Stock. CRUCIFERAE. A genus of 55 species of annuals, biennials, perennials and sub-shrubs from Mediterranean, Canary Is to Azores, Europe to C. Asia. They have alternate or rosetted, oblong to linear, sometimes pinnatifid leaves covered with starry or branched hairs and erect racemes of 4-petalled flowers. Grow in well-drained, preferably alkaline soil in sun. Sow seed of hardy annuals *in situ* in spring. Sow seed of perennials/biennials grown as annuals under glass early spring at 13–15°C. Prick off seedlings at 4–5cm apart each way into a good commercial potting mixture, harden off and plant out late spring to early summer. All Double and Trysomic stocks should be grown at about 15°C until ready for pricking off. The temperature should then be dropped to 10°C and, in 2–3 days or so, the then

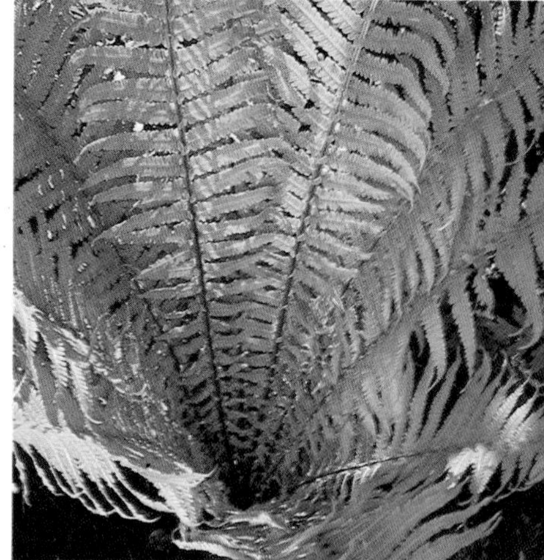

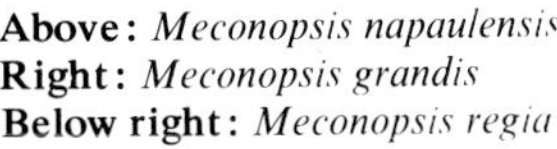

Above: *Meconopsis napaulensis*
Right: *Meconopsis grandis*
Below right: *Meconopsis regia*

greener single-flowered seedlings will stand out from the yellower doubles and can be discarded. For perennials/biennials grown to bloom winter to spring, sow outside in nursery rows in late summer. Prick off seedlings when 2–3 true leaves show, at 15cm apart each way. In early autumn lift carefully and transfer to 15cm pots and keep in a well-ventilated greenhouse, night temperature 5–7°C, day 10–15°C. Plants over-wintered in a barely frost-free frame or greenhouse will flower in early spring. In sheltered areas young plants may be over-wintered outside with or without cloche protection, for a spring display.

Species cultivated: *M. bicornis*, see *M. longipetala*. *M. incana*, stock; S.W. Europe – coasts; woody-based perennial usually grown as a biennial or annual; 30–80cm tall; leaves linear to oblong-lanceolate, with grey-white down or felt, 5–10cm long; flowers fragrant, 2–3cm wide, purple, pink or white in the wild, additionally purple-blue, red or yellow in cultivated strains; variable species in stature and form classified for convenience into the following groups: **1** 10 weeks, treated as annuals; plants listed under this name are about 30cm tall, branched and with single flowers; Trysomic with 85 per cent, and All Double with 100 per cent fully-double flowers are similar; Column or Excelsior stocks are unbranched, growing to 90cm tall – good for cutting and may be sown in spring for summer-flowering or late summer for the next spring. Giant Imperial at 60–75cm tall and Mammoth or Beauty at 45cm are similar and can be had in single-coloured cultivars. **2** Perpetual Flowering or All the Year Round, grown as annuals and biennials and in light soils will survive as short-lived perennials; they grow 35–40cm tall with greener leaves and white flowers. **3** Brompton, grown as biennials; plants under this name are 45cm tall, well-branched with single and double flowers; East Lothian are shorter – about 37cm – and may be grown as annuals or biennials. *M. longipetala bicornis* (*M. bicornis*), night scented stock; C. and S. Greece, Aegean; annual, 20–40cm tall; lower leaves narrowly lanceolate, sinuate-toothed to pinnatifid, upper ones smaller, narrower, few-toothed; flowers to 2cm wide, lilac-pink to purple, petals dull and drooping by day, opening and sweetly-scented at night, summer; best grown with *Malcolmia* to provide daytime colour.

May – see *Crataegus monogyna*.

May apple – see *Podophyllum*.

Mayflower – see *Epigaea repens*.

Meadow sweet – see *Filipendula ulmaria*.

Meconopsis

(Greek *mekon*, a poppy, and *opsis*, like). PAPAVERACEAE. A genus of 43 species of annuals, biennials and perennials, some monocarpic, from Himalaya to W. China, 1 in W. Europe. They much resemble the true poppies (*Papaver*), but have single-celled ovaries that taper to a short-stalked stigma. Grow in humus-rich, well-drained soil in partial shade protected from strong winds. Clay or close-textured soils should be liberally dressed with grit and leaf mould or peat forked into the top 20cm or so. Plant early autumn or spring. Propagate from seed when ripe or spring under glass. Young seedlings from a late summer sowing are best over-wintered in a well-ventilated frame or cold greenhouse. Perennial species may be carefully divided or offsets removed and planted out in spring. Provided these basic cultural requirements are met, meconopsis are much easier to grow than is often supposed.

Species cultivated: *M. baileyi*, see next species. *M. betonicifolia* (*M. baileyi*), blue poppy; China, Tibet, Upper Burma; stems to 1m or more tall; basal leaves long-stalked, oblong-ovate, to 15cm long; flowers several from upper leaf axils, 5–6cm wide, sky-blue on acid soil, lavender on alkaline soil, early summer; easily grown but tends to be biennial or monocarpic especially on over-rich soil – first year's flowering stem should be removed to promote offsets. *M. cambrica*, Welsh poppy; W. Europe; tufted perennial; stems slender, 45–60cm tall; leaves deeply pinnately lobed and toothed, to 20cm long; flowers to 4cm wide, yellow. *M.c. aurantiaca*, flowers rich orange, late spring, summer. *M. chelidonifolia*, W. China; perennial; stems to 1m tall; basal leaves long-stalked, deeply pinnately lobed; flowers 2·5cm wide, yellow, nodding, in loose panicled clusters, summer.

M. grandis, Himalaya; like a superior *M. betonicifolia*, leaves and flowers larger, the latter often with more than 4 petals, gentian-blue, or purple, early summer; usually reliably perennial; with *M. betonicifolia* has given rise to several cultivars under the collective name *M.* × *sheldonii*, the best ones with larger, vivid blue flowers, eg *M.* × *s.* Branklyn and *M.* × *s.* Crewdson Hybrid. *M. horridula* (*M. prattii*). Nepal to W. China; monocarpic, rosette leaves elliptic to oblanceolate, to 25cm long, sometimes lobed, spiny-bristly, stem and raceme to 1m or more; flowers light blue, purple or white, petals 4–8, each to 4·5cm long, best in sunnier sites, summer. *M. integrifolia*, lampshade poppy; Himalaya to W. China; monocarpic; stem 15–90cm tall; rosette leaves linear-lanceolate, to 20cm long, soft-hairy, flowers long-stalked, yellow, to 10cm wide with 6–8 rounded petals, best in sunnier sites. *M. napaulensis* (*M. wallichii*), satin poppy; E. Himalaya to W. China; monocarpic; rosette leaves narrowly oblong, deeply pinnately lobed, toothed, downy and hispid, to 50cm long; stem to 2m or more tall, the top ⅓ a broad ovoid panicle of long-stalked, nodding, 5–7·5cm wide flowers in shades of red, pink, purple, blue, rarely white, summer. *M. paniculata*, Himalaya; monocarpic; a yellow-flowered version of *M. napaulensis* with even larger or more handsome winter rosettes. *M. prattii*, see *M. horridula*. *M. quintuplinervia*, harebell poppy; China, Tibet; rhizomatous perennial forming small colonies of rosettes; leaves obovate to lanceolate, hairy, 15–25cm long; flowers lavender to purple-blue, 6–8cm wide, pendant, solitary on wiry stems to 30cm tall. *M. regia*, Nepal; monocarpic, of similar form to *M. napaulensis* but rosette leaves narrowly elliptic, densely silver-hairy (sometimes golden); stem to 1·5m; flowers about 7cm wide, yellow, summer. *M.* × *sheldonii*, see *M. grandis*. *M. superba*, Bhutan, Tibet; monocarpic; closely related to *M. regia* with attractive, silky white-hairy rosettes; stem to 1m tall; leaves oblanceolate, to 40cm long; flowers white, 6–7cm wide, summer. *M. wallichii*, see *M. napaulensis*.

Meehania

(for Thomas Meehan, 1826–1901, London-born nurseryman, botanist and writer who lived in Philadelphia). LABIATAE. A genus of 3 species of perennials from E.USA and Japan. They are tufted, 2 species producing long stolons, with opposite pairs of ovate leaves and leafy racemes of tubular, 2-lipped flowers. Grow in well-drained but moisture-retentive, moderately humus-rich soil in partial shade – although full sun is tolerated. Plant autumn to spring. Propagate by division at planting time, leaf-bud cuttings from trailing stems in summer, or from seed in spring.

Species cultivated: *M. cordata*, E.USA; stolons prostrate, forming quite dense mats; leaves 1·5–4cm long, broadly ovate-cordate, crenate; flowers 2–3·5cm long, pale purple, on stems to 15cm tall, late spring, summer. *M. urticifolia*, Japan; stolons arching then prostrate, particularly on well-established plants, deciduous, mat-forming but less dense than *M. cordata*; leaves 2–5cm long, triangular ovate-cordate, blunt-toothed; flowers 3·5–4cm long, blue-purple, lower lip with darker markings, sweetly aromatic from glands on the calyces, on stems 20–30cm tall, late spring.

Melandrium – see Silene.

Melia

(Greek vernacular for ash – *Fraxinus* – presumably because of its similar pinnate leaves). MELIACEAE. A genus of 2–15 species (depending on the classifier) of large shrubs or trees from tropical and subtropical Asia and Australia, 1 of which is sometimes cultivated: *M. azedarach*, bead tree, chinaberry, Persian lilac, pride of India; N. India, China, but grown elsewhere in mild climates; half-hardy

Far left: *Meehania urticifolia*
Top and above: *Melia azedarach* in flower and fruit
Top right: *Melianthus major*
Centre right: *Melittis melissophylum*
Far right: *Mentha suaveolens* Variegata

deciduous tree to 12m or more; leaves alternate, pinnate or bi-pinnate, 30–60cm long, leaflets 4–5cm long, ovate, slender-pointed, toothed; flowers 5-petalled, 2cm wide, lilac, fragrant, in loose axillary panicles 10–20cm long, summer; fruit yellow, berry-like drupes, ovoid, about 1cm long. Except in mildest areas grow in warm, sheltered sites against wall. In cold areas grow in greenhouse in large pots of potting mixture. Pot or plant spring. Propagate from seed under glass at 13–16°C as soon as ripe, or by cuttings, summer, bottom heat 18–21°C.

Melianthus

(Greek *meli*, honey, and *anthos*, a flower – the flowers produce plentiful nectar). MELIANTHACEAE. A genus of 6 species of shrubs or shrubby perennials from S.Africa and India, 1 species being usually available: *M. major*, honeybush or honey flower; S.Africa and India; half-hardy shrub to 3m tall; stems sparingly branched, hollow; leaves alternate, pinnate, 25–45cm long, leaflets 7–13, ovate, 5–13cm long, very coarsely toothed, glaucous; flowers in terminal racemes, to 30cm or more long, each bloom irregularly 5-petalled, brownish-red, about 2·5cm long, summer. Grow in well-drained, fertile soil in sun. In all but the mildest areas place against a sheltered wall and protect in winter. Also makes a handsome foliage plant for summer bedding, or a pot or tub plant for the cool greenhouse. Any commercial potting mixture is suitable for container culture. Pot or plant spring. Propagate by division or suckers when possible in spring, or cuttings in summer, bottom heat 18–20°C.

Melittis

(Greek *melitta* or *melissa*, a honey bee – the flowers are attractive to bees). LABIATAE. A genus of 1 perennial herbaceous species from C. and S. Europe: *M. melissophyllum*, bastard balm; clump-forming; stems 25–45cm tall; leaves in opposite pairs, ovate, crenate, 5–8cm long, pleasantly aromatic; flowers in whorls in upper leaf-axils, tubular, 2-lipped, 2·5–4cm long, usually creamy-white, spotted rose-purple, early to late summer; much more showy than common balm. Grow in humus-rich, well-drained soil in partial shade. Plant autumn or spring. Propagate by division or from seed in spring.

Mentha

(Latin *menta*, and Greek *minthe*, for mint). Mint. LABIATAE. A genus of about 25 species of aromatic perennials from the northern temperate zone, S.Africa and Australia. The culinary mints have long been used by man, possibly at least as far back as Neolithic times in S.Europe. Even the Latin and Greek names have probably been derived from an older and now extinct Mediterranean language. Most species are rhizomatous with erect stems, square in cross-section, simple leaves in opposite pairs, and terminal whorled spikes of tiny, tubular, 2-lipped flowers, summer to autumn. Grow in any moderately fertile, moisture-retentive soil in sun or partial shade. Plant autumn to spring. Propagate by division at planting time. Culinary mints are more productive if top-dressed with decayed compost or manure each spring and replanted every third year. If rust fungus is troublesome propagate by stem cuttings in spring or late summer. Rhizomes lifted and planted in trays of soil in autumn and brought at intervals into a greenhouse heated 10–15°C, will give fresh mint from winter to early spring.

Species cultivated: *M.* × *alopecuroides* and Bowles mint, see *M.* × *villosa*. *M. aquatica*, water mint; Europe, Asia, N. Africa; 20–90cm tall; leaves ovate to lanceolate, toothed, 3–9cm long, often purplish-flushed; flowers about 6mm long, lilac, in short, head-like spikes; strongly peppermint-smelling, rather invasive waterside plant with medicinal properties. *M. citrata*, see *M.* × *piperita*. *M. crispa*, a name given to several kinds of mint with the leaf margins variously waved, curled or deeply toothed. *M.* × *gentilis* (*M. arvensis* × *M. spicata*), ginger or Scotch mint; 30–90cm tall; leaves ovate-lanceolate to elliptic-oblong, 3–7cm or more long; flowers 5mm long, lilac, in interrupted leafy spikes, plant often red-tinged and smelling of spearmint. *M.* × *g.* Variegata, leaves with veins yellow-striped. *M. longifolia* (*M. sylvestris*), horse or long-leaved mint; Europe to W. Siberia; 45–120cm tall; stem white or grey downy; leaves 3–8cm long, lanceolate to oblong-lanceolate, hairy above, grey-felted beneath; flowers about 5mm in dense spikes to 10cm long; not unlike a downy *M. spicata* but usually with a pungent musty scent. *M. niliaca*, see *M.* × *rotundifolia*. *M.* × *piperita* (*M. aquatica* × *M. spicata*), peppermint; 40–90cm tall; leaves lanceolate, 4–8cm long; flowers lilac-pink, about 6mm long, sterile, in interrupted spikes to 8cm long; yields the world's supply of peppermint oil. *M.* × *p. citrata*, Eau de Cologne, orange, lemon or bergamot mint; to 50cm tall; more akin to *M. aquatica* in inflorescence, with

Far left: *Mentha × piperita* Citrata
Left: *Mentha × gentilis* Variegata
Top: *Mentzelia lindleyi*
Above: *Menyanthes trifoliata*

ovate, subcordate leaves often purple-tinged. *M. × p. officinalis*, white peppermint; more slender in habit than type, stems lighter, leaves narrower, paler, brighter green. *M. × p. piperita*, black peppermint; stems deep purple, to 60cm; leaves narrowly ovate, purple, tinged deep green (grown commercially in USA for peppermint oil). *M. pulegium*, pennyroyal; Europe, W. Asia; mat-forming; leaves oblong to elliptic, 8–20cm or more long; flowers mauve-lilac, 4–5mm long in interrupted leafy spikes 10–30cm tall; can be used for flavouring but grown mainly for its peppermint-like aroma and can be used to make small, fragrant lawns either by itself or combined with grass. *M.*

requienii, Corsica, Sardinia, naturalized in W. Europe; mat-forming; stems filiform, rooting; leaves rounded to ovate, 5–14mm long; flowers to 3mm long, pale lilac in interrupted leafy spikes 3–10cm tall; strongly peppermint-scented, sometimes called crème de menthe mint. *M. rotundifolia*, see *M. suaveolens*. *M. × rotundifolia* (*M. niliaca*), (*M. longifolia × M. suaveolens*), rarely cultivated, being much confused with *M. suaveolens* and *M. × villosa alopecuroides*. *M. spicata* (*M. viridis*), (possibly of hybrid origin between *M. longifolia* and *M. suaveolens*), spearmint; 30–90cm or more tall; leaves oblong-lanceolate to lanceolate, sharply toothed, downy or glabrous, 5–9cm long; flowers lilac, pink or white, 4–5mm long in slender, somewhat leafy spikes; the most popular mint although somewhat inferior in flavour to Bowles Variety (*M. × villosa*). *M. suaveolens* (*M. rotundifolia*), apple, round-leaved or woolly mint; S. and W. Europe; 40–100cm tall; stems with a dense to sparse white down; leaves ovate-oblong to rounded, to 4·5cm long, rugose, grey-white hairy above, almost woolly beneath, smelling of mint and apples; flowers pinkish or whitish, 4–5mm long, in dense spikes 4–9cm long. *M.s.* Variegata, pineapple mint; leaves irregularly splashed creamy-white. *M. × villosa* (*M. spicata × M. suaveolens*), very variable hybrid represented in cultivation by *M. × v. alopecuroides* Bowles Variety, French mint; resembling and confused with *M. suaveolens* in gardens, but more robust, smelling like spearmint and the leaves with spreading teeth (those of *M. suaveolens* often turned under); flowers pink. *M. viridis*, see *M. spicata*.

Mentzelia

(for Christian Mentzel, 1622–1701, German physician and botanist). LOASACEAE. A genus of about 60 species of annuals, biennials, perennials and shrubs from N. to S. America, 1 of which is generally available: *M. lindleyi* (*Bartonia aurea*), California; hardy annual 30–40cm tall or more; leaves alternate, sessile, 2–17cm long, pinnatifid, hispid; flowers axillary from upper leaves or in small, terminal clusters, 5-petalled, 5–6·5cm wide, glistening golden-yellow with orange-red eye, fragrant, summer. Sow seed *in situ* in well-drained, fertile soil in sun.

Menyanthes

(Greek *menanthos*, for the allied fringed water lily, *Nymphoides*, transferred to this genus). MENYANTHACEAE (GENTIANACEAE). A genus of 1 species of wet-land perennial from the northern temperate zone: *M. trifoliata*, bogbean, buckbean, marsh trefoil; rhizomatous, forming colonies; leaves trifoliate on stalks to 20cm long, leaflets elliptic to obovate, 4–8cm long; flowering stem 12–30cm tall bearing a short raceme of 10–20 flowers, each bloom pink in bud, white within, tubular, the 5 spreading lobes bearing long, bead-tipped hairs, late spring to summer. Grow in permanently moist or wet soil or in shallow water, in sun or very light shade. Plant autumn or spring. Propagate by division or separate lengths of rhizomes 15–20cm long, removing latter during spring.

Menziesia

(see Menziesii). ERICACEAE. A genus of 6 or 7 species of deciduous shrubs from E.Asia to N.America.

Left: *Mentha pulegium*
Below: *Menziesia ciliicalyx purpurea*

They have alternate, elliptic to obovate leaves, and terminal, umbel-like clusters of pendant, bell- or urn-shaped, 4–5 lobed flowers. Grow in well-drained but moisture-retentive, neutral to acid, preferably peaty soil in partial shade. Plant autumn to spring. Propagate by layering in spring, cuttings late summer, and from seed when ripe or spring in cold frame.

Species cultivated: *M.ciliicalyx*, Japan; erect habit, to 60cm tall; leaves 2–5cm long, ciliate; flowers 3–8, 1·3–1·7cm long, narrowly bell-shaped, pale yellow or greenish-yellow, 4- and 5-lobed, early summer. *M.c.multiflora* (*M.multiflora*), flowers purplish, calyx lobes narrowly lanceolate, 4–6mm long; *M.c.purpurea* (*M.lasiophylla*, *M.purpurea* of gardens), flowers rose-purple, calyx lobes 1–2mm long; not to be confused with the true *M.purpurea* of Maximowicz, a shrub to 2·5m tall, having broader, 4-lobed flowers with white, hairy ovaries. *M.ferruginea*; rusty leaf; W. N.America; to 2m tall, more in the wild; leaves 2–6·5cm long, finely toothed, rusty bristly hairy; flowers 2–5, tubular bell-shaped, 1cm long, yellowish-red, early summer. *M.lasiophylla* and *M.purpurea* (of gardens), see *M.ciliicalyx purpurea*.

Mertensia

(for Franz Carl Mertens, 1764–1831, Professor of botany at Bremen, Germany). BORAGINACEAE. A genus of about 45 species of herbaceous perennials from northern temperate zone south to Mexico and Afghanistan. They are tufted or small clump-forming with branched, erect to prostrate stems bearing alternate, lanceolate to ovate or spathulate leaves, and tubular, 5-lobed flowers in usually nodding, racemose or panicled cymes; fruit a cluster of 4 wrinkled nutlets. Grow in well-drained but moisture-retentive, humus-rich soil in sun or light shade. Plant autumn or spring. Propagate by careful division at planting time or from seed when ripe.

Species cultivated: *M. ciliata*, W. USA; stems to 60cm or more tall; leaves ovate to lanceolate, glaucous, to 15cm or more long; flowers pendant, pale blue, 1·5–2cm long, calyx ciliate, spring to summer. *M. echioides*, Himalaya; leaves oblong to spathulate, downy beneath; flowers deep blue, about 1cm long, summer. *M. virginica*, Virginia cowslip or bluebells; Kansas to New York and Alabama; stems 40–60cm tall; leaves elliptic to ovate, glaucous, the basal ones 20cm long; flowers pendant, 2–2·5cm long, violet-blue, spring; best in shade of trees – dies down in summer.

Mesembryanthemum criniflorum – see *Dorotheanthus*.

Below: *Mertensia virginica*
Right: *Metasequoia glyptostroboides*

Metasequoia

(Greek *meta*, with or sharing, and *Sequoia*, qv, referring to the relationship). TAXODIACEAE. A genus of 1 deciduous coniferous tree from China: *M. glyptostroboides*, dawn redwood, water fir; about 20m tall in cultivation (to date), up to 35m in the wild; narrowly conical habit, branches ascending; bark orange to red-brown, stringy; young stems pale orange-brown; leaves linear, 2–4cm long, often purple-tinted when expanding, glaucous beneath, in opposite pairs arranged in 2 parallel ranks, turning to shades of yellow, pink and red, male flowers (strobili) catkin-like, small, ovoid, not yet seen in some gardens, females globular, green, developing into long-stalked cones 1·2–2·5cm long; similar to – and sometimes confused with – *Taxodium*, but that tree has alternate leaves. The genus *Metasequoia* was founded in 1941 on fossil specimens and 3 species recognized. Amazingly in 1945 a fourth, living species was discovered in N.E. Szechuan and Hupeh, and seed reached the USA and Europe in 1948. Grow in moisture-retentive, fertile soil in sun or light shade, ideally sheltered from strong, drying winds. Plant autumn to spring. Propagate by cuttings with a heel, late summer to autumn.

Meum

(Greek vernacular for this plant). UMBELLIFERAE. A genus of 1 species of herbaceous perennial from the mountains of Europe: *M.athamanticum*, spignel, baldmoney; tufted, 20–60cm tall; leaves aromatic, long-stalked, mainly basal, bipinnate, the leaflets

thread-like; flowers tiny, 5-petalled, white or purplish, in terminal compound umbels 3–6cm wide, summer. Grow in any moist soil, in sun or partial shade. Plant autumn to spring. Propagate from seed when ripe, or by division at planting time.

Mexican giant hyssop – see *Agastache mexicana*.

Mexican orange blossom – see *Choisya ternata*.

Michaelmas daisy – see *Aster*.

Michelia

(for Pietro Antonio Micheli, 1679–1737, Italian botanist). MAGNOLIACEAE. A genus of about 50 species of evergreen trees and shrubs from tropical and temperate Asia. They are closely allied to *Magnolia*, but the flowers are axillary and bear the carpels on a stalk above the ring of stamens. Grow in well-drained but moisture-retentive, neutral to acid, humus-rich soil in sun or partial shade. Suited only to areas where frosts are not severe, or on south or west walls with winter protection (but see *M.compressa*). In cold areas grow under glass, minimum temperature 7°C, with good ventilation and light shade in summer. Plants in pots or tubs can be stood outside from early summer to autumn. Plant or pot spring. Propagate by layering in spring, cuttings late summer, bottom heat 18–21°C.

Species cultivated: *M.compressa*, Japan, Taiwan; a rounded shrub to 3m or more, or a tree to 15m or more; leaves 5–10cm long, ovate-oblong to obovate, lustrous; flowers 3cm wide, white to pale yellow with red-purple centre, fragrant, late spring; at least some clones of this species are hardy in sheltered sites. *M.doltsopa*, E.Himalaya to W. China; tree rarely to 16m in gardens, to 30m tall in the wild; leaves 7–18cm long, oblong-elliptic, lustrous deep green above, pale beneath; flowers 7–10cm wide, soft light yellow to white, fragrant, spring. *M.figo* (*M.fuscata*), banana-shrub; shrub eventually to 3m or more, but slow-growing; leaves 4–10cm long, elliptic to oblong-obovate, deep glossy green; flower-buds covered with brown hairs, opening 3–4cm wide, creamy-yellow, edged or flushed purple, strongly fragrant of bananas or pear drops, spring to summer; makes an interest pot plant, starting to flower while small.

Far left above: *Meum athamanticum*
Above: *Michelia doltsopa* in bud
Left: *Microcachrys tetragona*

Microcachrys

(Greek *mikros*, small, and *kachrys*, a cone). PODOCARPACEAE. A genus of 1 species of small coniferous shrub from Tasmania: *M.tetragona*, prostrate; stems sinuous; leaves evergreen, 4-ranked, scale-like and overlapping, giving the stems a 4-angled appearance; flower clusters small, ovoid, cone-shaped, dioecious; female cones 6–8mm long when mature, the ripe seed partially embedded in the scales, that become fleshy and red. Grow in well-drained but not dry soil in a sheltered, sunny site. Despite a reputation for tenderness, this alpine shrub stands moderate frost or makes an interesting pot plant for the alpine house. Plant autumn or spring. Propagate by cuttings in late summer or from seed when available, when ripe, or spring.

Microglossa – see *Aster albescens*.

Micromeria

(Greek *mikros*, small, and *meris*, a part – alluding to the small flowers and leaves). LABIATAE. A genus of 70–100 species of small shrubs and perennials of almost world-wide distribution but mainly Mediterranean. They have opposite pairs of ovate to linear leaves and whorls of tubular, 2-lipped flowers in upper leaf-axils, sometimes forming spikes. Grow in well-drained soil in sun. Plant autumn or spring. Propagate by cuttings late summer, from seed or by division spring.

Species cultivated: *M. corsica* (of gardens), see *Teucrium marum*. *M. rupestris*, see next species. *M. thymifolia* (*M.rupestris*, *Satureja r.*), Balkan Peninsula, north to mountains of Hungary, Italy; woody-based perennial; stems 20–50cm tall, mainly erect; leaves 5–15mm or more long, elliptic to ovate, often remotely crenate-toothed, glabrous; flowers 5–9mm long, white and purple, summer.

Mignonette – see *Reseda odorata*.

Milium

(ancient Latin name for millet). Millet. GRAMINEAE. A genus of 6 species of annual and perennial grasses

from northern temperate zone, the yellow-leaved form of 1 being generally available: *M. effusum* Aureum, golden wood millet; Europe, Asia. N.E. N. America; tufted perennial; stems 60–150cm tall; leaves arching, linear, 10–30cm long by 5–15mm wide; panicles loose, ovate in outline, nodding, spikelets 3–4mm long, early to late summer. Grow in well-drained but not dry soil, preferably in shade. Plant autumn to spring. Propagate by division or from seed in spring.

Milk vetch – see *Astragalus* and *Oxytropis*.

Milkwort – see *Polygala*.

Millet, wood – see *Milium*.

Mimulus

(Latin *mimos*, a mimic actor – the flowers of 1 species fancifully resemble a monkey's face). Monkey musk. SCROPHULARIACEAE. A genus of 100–150 species of annuals, perennials and shrubs from S. Africa, Asia, Australia and the Americas. They have opposite pairs of ovate-linear-lanceolate leaves and showy, tubular, 5-lobed flowers that may be solitary or several from upper leaf-axils. Grow perennials in fertile, moisture-retentive soil, particularly by the waterside, in sun or light shade. Grow shrubs in well-drained soil in a sunny, sheltered site or in a frost-free greenhouse. Plant in spring, those raised from seed in early summer after hardening off. Propagate from seed under glass (early spring at 13–16°C for a reliable flowering same year), by cuttings or division in spring, the shrubs also by late summer cuttings, bottom heat about 18°C.

Species cultivated: *M. aurantiacus* (*M. glutinosus*, *Diplacus aurantiacus*, *D. glutinosus*), California, Oregon; half-hardy evergreen shrub to 1m or more; leaves narrowly to oblong lanceolate, about 5cm long, somewhat sticky glandular; flowers from upper leaf-axils, to 4cm long, yellow, orange or buff,

Left above: *Milium effusum* Aureum
Above: *Mimulus aurantiacus*
Right: *Mimulus variegatus* Queens Prize
Right: below: *Mimulus luteus*

late spring to autumn; see *M. puniceus*; needs winter protection except in mild areas. *M.* × *bartonianus* (*M. cardinalis* × *M. lewisii*), similar to latter parent; flowers rose-red with brown-red throat spotted yellow. *M. cardinalis*, S.W. USA, N. Mexico; herbaceous perennial, to 90cm or more tall; leaves oblong to obovate, to 10cm long; flowers in leafy racemes, 5cm long, scarlet, summer to autumn; will stand drier soil than most perennials, best in a sheltered site; some forms tend to sprawl especially after rain and wind. *M. cupreus*, S. Chile; similar to *M. luteus*, but more compact and often only of annual duration; flowers yellow, changing to bright coppery-orange; several redder cultivars are known. *M. glutinosus*, see *M. aurantiacus*. *M. guttatus* (*M. langsdorfii*), monkey flower or musk; W. N. America, N. Mexico; similar to *M. luteus* but often taller; stems to 60cm; leaves larger, irregularly toothed; flowers to 5cm long, yellow, usually with red-spotted throat, calyx bell-shaped. *M.* × *hybridus* (*M. luteus* × *M. guttatus*), blends parental characters in various ways. *M. langsdorfii*, see *M. guttatus*. *M. lewisii*, W. N. America; herbaceous perennial, to 75cm tall, whole plant with a sticky down; leaves sessile, oblong-elliptic, to 7cm long; flowers in leafy racemes, to 5·5cm long, rose-purple, summer to autumn. *M. luteus*, monkey musk or flower; Chile; perennial, forming mats or colonies of decumbent stems up to 30cm or more tall in flower; leaves to 7cm long, broadly ovate, with a few regular teeth; flowers to 4·5cm long, yellow with small red spots in throat, large spots on lobes, summer to autumn. *M. moschatus*, musk; N.W. N. America, naturalized elsewhere; sticky downy perennial spreading by rhizomes; stems 10–40cm long; leaves ovate or elliptic, 1–4cm long; flowers to 2cm long, yellow, sometimes dotted red-brown, summer, autumn; formerly widely grown for its musk scent, but plants in gardens rarely have this, although still reported

of some plants in the wild. *M. puniceus* (*M. glutinosus puniceus*), California; much like *M. aurantiacus* but flowers to 4·5cm long, red; plants listed as *M. aurantiacus* with red or reddish flowers are either this species or hybrids from it. *M. radicans*, see *Mazus r. M. ringens*, lavender water musk; E. N. America west to Colorado; aquatic perennial, to 90cm or more tall; leaves oblong, elliptic or oblanceolate, toothed, to 10cm long;

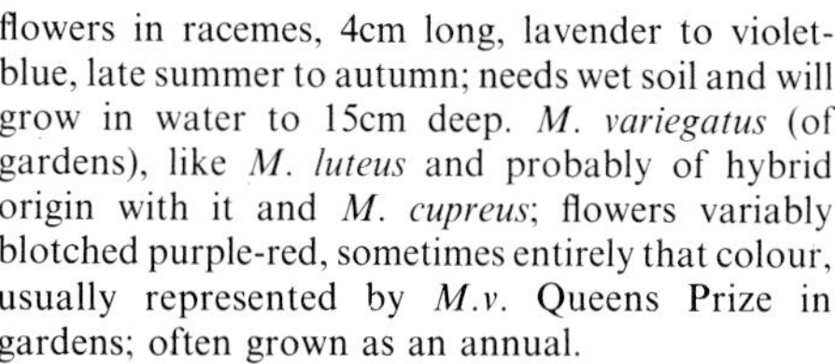

flowers in racemes, 4cm long, lavender to violet-blue, late summer to autumn; needs wet soil and will grow in water to 15cm deep. *M. variegatus* (of gardens), like *M. luteus* and probably of hybrid origin with it and *M. cupreus*; flowers variably blotched purple-red, sometimes entirely that colour, usually represented by *M.v.* Queens Prize in gardens; often grown as an annual.

Mirabilis

(Latin for wonderful). NYCTAGINACEAE. A genus of about 60 species of annuals and perennials mainly from the warmer parts of N. and S. America, 1 from Himalaya. 1 species is widely grown: *M. jalapa*, 4 o'clock, marvel of Peru; tropical America; tender, tuberous-rooted perennial often grown as a half-hardy annual; stems erect, branched, 60–90cm tall; leaves ovate-lanceolate; flowers fragrant, formed of a tubular coloured calyx, to 5cm long, expanded to a rotate mouth, in clusters from upper leaf-axils, summer; blooms vary from white, yellow, red, pink to striped, opening late afternoon until the following morning. Grow in humus-rich soil in a sunny sheltered site or in pots of any commercial mixture under glass, minimum temperature 10°C. Sow seed early spring at 18–20°C, ideally singly in 6·5–7·5cm containers. Pot on young plants into 12·5cm containers, harden off in early summer and plant out when fear of frost has gone. Alternatively grow on in pots, finishing off in 20cm containers. Plants bedded outside that form good tubers can be treated as dahlias but may not over-winter well.

Miscanthus

(Greek *miskos*, a stem, and *anthos*, a flower – presumably referring to the stalked spikelets). GRAMINEAE. A genus of about 20 species of tall perennial grasses from Asia. The species generally grown in gardens are hardy, forming bold clumps of broad grassy leaves topped by feathery panicles of paired, awned spikelets. Grow in moisture-retentive soil in sun or partial shade. Plant in autumn or spring. Propagate by division in spring.

Species cultivated: *M. sacchariflorus* (*Imperata s.*), Amur silver grass; rhizomes thick, spreading, forming colonies; stems to 3m or more tall; leaves to 2cm wide; spikelets grey-brown, almost awnless, surrounded by longer silky hairs; sometimes wrongly listed as *M. saccharifolius* and often confused with next species. *M. sinensis* (*Eulalia japonica*), rhizomes thick, short, dense, clump-forming; stems to 3m tall; leaves to 1cm wide, mid-rib whitish; spikelets awned, surrounded by hairs of the same length, or just shorter, in panicles to 20cm or more long, late summer to autumn. *M.s.* Gracillimus, much smaller, leaves to 6mm wide; *M.s.* Variegatus, leaves with central cream stripe; *M.s.* Zebrinus, leaves horizontally banded creamy-yellow.

Mitchella

(for Dr John Mitchell, 1676–1768, American physician and botanist who lived in Virginia and corresponded with Linnaeus). RUBIACEAE. A genus of 2 species of evergreen perennials from N. America, Japan and Korea, 1 of which is usually available: *M. repens*, partridge berry, twin berry, squaw berry; E. N.America; stems prostrate, mat-forming; leaves in pairs, broadly ovate to rounded, 1–2cm long, dark lustrous green above, often with a pale or whitish vein pattern; flowers fragrant, 1cm long, tubular, with 4 spreading lobes, white, often pink-tinted, in axillary and terminal pairs, the ovaries united, spring; fruit are berry-like double drupes, scarlet, rarely white, edible but almost tasteless. Grow in moisture-retentive but well-drained, humus-rich, neutral to acid soil in partial shade. Plant autumn to spring. Propagate by careful division or separating self layers at planting time, or cuttings late summer.

Mitella

(Greek diminutive *mitra*, a cap – referring to the shape of the young fruit). Mitrewort

Far left top: *Mimulus × bartonianus*
Far left: *Mimulus moschatus*
Left top: *Mirabilis jalapa*
Left: *Miscanthus sinensis* Zebrinus
Below: *Mitella breweri*

SAXIFRAGACEAE. A genus of 12 species of perennials from N. America and N.E. Asia. They are tufted or clump-forming with mainly basal, rounded to ovate, often more or less lobed and cordate leaves and slender, erect racemes of tiny flowers having 5 deeply pinnately cut petals. Grow in moisture-retentive, ideally humus-rich soil in shade, although sun is tolerated. Plant autumn or spring. Propagate by division at planting time, or seed when ripe, or in spring.

Species cultivated: *M. breweri*, N.W. N.America; leaves shallowly lobed, kidney-shaped, to 5cm wide or so; flowers 5mm wide, petals greenish-yellow, with 5–7 slender lobes, in leafless racemes to 20cm tall, early summer. *M. caulescens*, N.W. N.America; similar to previous species but racemes to 30cm tall with 1–3 leaves. *M.nuda*, N. N.America to E. Asia; tufted, with long runners; leaves to 2·5cm wide, doubly round-toothed; flowers to 1cm wide, petals yellow-green cut into 8 slender lobes, racemes few-flowered, to 20cm tall.

Mitraria

(Greek *mitra*, a cap or mitre – alluding to the shape of the seed capsules). GESNERIACEAE. A genus of 1 species of evergreen shrub from S. Chile: *M. coccinea*, root climber to 2m or more or small, free-standing shrub; leaves in opposite pairs, ovate, toothed, glossy deep green, 1–2cm long; flowers pendant, to 3cm long, tubular, slightly inflated with 5 short lobes, scarlet, solitary from upper leaf-axils, early summer to autumn. Frost-free greenhouse or

sheltered, shaded site outside in mild areas. Grow in a well-drained but moisture-retentive, humus-rich soil; for pot culture an all-peat compost or loam type mixed with $\frac{1}{3}$-part sphagnum moss or leaf mould. Requires shade and humidity and a moss stick or bark support to climb successfully. Plant or pot spring. Propagate by cuttings of non-flowering shoots from late spring to autumn, or division when possible in spring.

Mitrewort – see *Mitella*.

Moccasin flower – see *Cypripedium acaule*.

Mock orange – see *Philadelphus*.

Mocker nut – see *Carya tomentosa*.

Top left: *Mitraria coccinea*
Left: *Molinia caerulea* Variegata
Above: *Moltkia petraea*

Molinia

(for Juan Ignacio Molina, 1740–1829, natural historian of Chile). GRAMINEAE. A genus of 5 species of perennial grasses from Europe and Asia. They are clump-forming, with narrow, arching leaves, and slender panicles with small, 2–5 flowered spikelets. Grow in moisture-retentive soil in sun, although partial shade is tolerated. Plant spring or autumn. Propagate by division or from seed in spring.
Species cultivated: *M. arundinacea altissima* (*M. altissima*, *M.litoralis*), range of genus; like the text species but larger; stems 1·4–1·8m tall; panicles 30–50cm long. *M. caerulea*, purple moor grass; Europe, Asia; densely clump-forming, deciduous; stems 45–75cm tall; leaves to 20cm × 4–7mm; panicles 12–20cm long, purplish, late summer; often represented by *M.c.* Variegata, leaves striped creamy-white, often pink-tinted when young.

Moltkia

(for Count Joachim Gadoke Moltke, 1746–1818, Danish statesman). BORAGINACEAE. A genus of 6 species of hairy perennials and sub-shrubs from E.Europe and S.W.Asia. Formerly included in *Lithospermum*, they differ only in small details, eg throat of corolla not crested, lobes erect, and stamens exserted. Culture as for *Lithospermum*.

Species cultivated: *M. doerfleri* (*Lithospermum d.*), mountains of N.E.Albania; rhizomatous perennial; stems erect, 30–50cm tall; leaves lanceolate, ciliate, lower ones not developing fully; flowers 2–2·5cm long, deep purple, summer. *M.* × *froebelii*, see *M.* × *intermedia* Froebelii. *M.* × *intermedia* (*Lithospermum* × *intermedium*), (*M. petraea* × *M.suffruticosa*), intermediate between parents but of more vigorous constitution; 20–25cm tall; leaves dark green; flowers rich blue. *M.* × *i.* Froebelii *M.* × *froebelii*), 15–20cm tall; flowers azure-blue. *M. petraea*, mountains of Yugoslavia to Greece; sub-shrub to 20cm or more tall; leaves 1–5cm long, linear to oblong-oblanceolate, whitish hairy beneath; flowers in dense cymes, 6–10mm long, deep violet-blue, early summer. *M. suffruticosa* (*Lithospermum graminifolium*), mountains of N.Italy; much-branched sub-shrub to 30cm or more tall in bloom; leaves linear, 5–10cm or more long, whitish beneath; flowers 1·3–1·7cm long, soft blue, in dense cymes, summer.

Moluccella

(derivation uncertain, but reputedly Molucca Is, Indonesia, from whence 1 species was supposed to come). LABIATAE. A genus of 4 species of annuals and perennials from Mediterranean to N.W. India, 1 of which is generally cultivated: *M. laevis*, bells of Ireland, shell flower; Turkey to Syria; annual, to 50cm or so tall; leaves in opposite pairs, long-stalked, boldly crenate, rounded to triangular-ovate, to 5cm long; flowers white, tubular, 2-lipped, about 1cm long, calyces 2–3cm wide, bowl-shaped or shell-like, in terminal spikes, late summer to autumn. Grow in any well-drained fertile soil in sun. Sow seed *in situ* late spring, or sow earlier under glass at 13–15°C, pricking off into boxes of a standard potting compost, hardening off and planting out in early summer.

Monarda

(for Nicholas Monardes, 1493–1588, Spanish physician and botanist who wrote an account of products from America as then known). LABIATAE. A genus of about 12 species of annuals and perennials from N. America and Mexico. Those described here are clump-forming, erect herbaceous perennials, with opposite, ovate to lanceolate, usually toothed leaves, and dense terminal clusters of slender, tubular, 2-lipped flowers attractive to bees. Grow in any moisture-retentive soil in sun or partial shade. Plant autumn to spring. Propagate by division at planting time or from seed in spring.

Species cultivated: *M. didyma*, bee balm, bergamot, oswego tea; E. USA; 60–90cm tall; leaves ovate, slender-pointed, sparsely hairy, 5–10cm long; flowers to 3cm long, bright scarlet, in solitary terminal heads or with a second cluster from the uppermost leaf pair, summer to autumn; several cultivars varying in flower colour are grown, including: *M.d.* Cambridge Scarlet, crimson-scarlet; *M.d.* Croftway Pink, pink; *M.d.* Mahogany, brownish-red; *M.d.* Snow Queen, white; *M.d.* Violet Queen, violet-purple. *M. fistulosa*, E. N. America; similar to *M. didyma*, but leaves ovate-lanceolate, generally short-hairy; flower-heads usually solitary, flowers lavender-purple; will thrive in drier soils than *M. didyma*; confused in gardens with *M. didyma* and some cultivars under that name may belong here or be of hybrid origin.

Mondo jaburan – see *Ophiopogon jaburan*.

Moneywort – see *Lysimachia nummularia*.

Monkey flower – see *Mimulus luteus*, *M. guttatus*.

Monkey puzzle – see *Araucaria araucana*.

Monkshood – see *Aconitum*.

Far left below: *Moluccella laevis*
Left: *Monarda didyma* Cambridge Scarlet
Left below: *Monarda didyma* Croftway Pink
Below: *Montia perfoliata*
Bottom: *Moraea spathulata*

Montia

(for Guiseppe Monti, 1682–1760, Italian professor of botany at Bologna). PORTULACACEAE. A genus of 35–50 species of annuals and perennials from N. Hemisphere and Australasia. They may be tufted and erect or mat-forming, with somewhat fleshy, spathulate to lanceolate or ovate leaves, 2–6 petalled flowers usually in axillary or terminal racemes. Grow in moisture-retentive, but not wet, soil in sun or partial shade. Plant autumn or spring. Propagate from seed when ripe, division in spring.

Species cultivated: *M. australasica*, white purslane; temperate Australia, New Zealand; mat-forming perennial; stems prostrate, rooting, sometimes underground; leaves linear to oblanceolate, 2–8cm long; flowers 5-petalled, white, 1–1·5cm wide, in terminal clusters of 1–4, summer; usually represented in gardens by a form with glaucous leaves. *M. parvifolia* (*Claytonia p.*), W. N. America; tufted perennial, rootstock fleshy; main or basal leaves in rosettes, 1–3cm long, obovate to lanceolate; lateral

stems or stolons arching to prostrate; flowers white or pink, 5-petalled, 1cm or more wide, in racemes, summer; often represented in cultivation by *M.p. flagellaris*, a plant densely stoloniferous with larger, usually pink flowers and abundant bulbil-like plantlets, invasive in some gardens. *M. perfoliata* (*Claytonia p.*), miners' lettuce, spring beauty; W. N. America; over-wintering annual, 10–30cm tall; leaves long-stalked, ovate to elliptic-obovate, 5–20cm long; flowers 5-petalled, white, about 1cm wide, in clusters surrounded by a disc-like pair of fused bracts giving the effect of an old-fashioned posy, spring to summer; can be invasive. *M. sibirica* (*Claytonia s.*), pink purslane; Siberia, W. N. America; annual, similar to *M. perfoliata*, but floral bracts ovate and separate; flowers white or pink.

Moonflower – see *Ipomoea bona-nox*.

Moosewood – see *Acer pensylvanicum*.

Moraea

(for Robert More, 1703–80, British amateur botanist). Butterfly iris. IRIDACEAE. A genus of about 100 species of cormous perennials from tropical to S. Africa. They superficially resemble *Iris* but the flowers lack a perianth tube and the rootstock is a corm. The species described are half-hardy and succeed outside only in mild areas in well-drained soil and sun. Alternatively, greenhouse, minimum temperature 5–7°C, well-ventilated, in borders or pots of a good potting mixture. Plant after flowering or early autumn; keep pots barely moist until growth recommences. Propagate by division at planting or from seed in spring at 15–18°C.

Species cultivated: *M. neopavonia* (*M. pavonia*, *Iris p.*), peacock iris; S. Africa; stem to 60cm tall, usually branched; leaves linear, downy, 1 per corm; flowers to 6cm wide, bright orange-red, each of the falls with an iridescent bluish or greenish-black spot; early summer. *M. pavonia* see *M. neopavonia*. *M. ramosa*, see next species. *M. ramosissima* (*M. ramosa*). S. Africa; stems 60–90cm tall, much-branched; leaves linear, to 75cm long, several; flowers 5cm wide, fragrant, bright yellow, the falls with brownish or greyish basal spot, early summer. *M. spathacea*, see next species. *M. spathulata* (*M. spathacea*), S. Africa; leaves solitary, sword-shaped, to 60cm tall; stems 60–120cm tall; flowers fragrant, bright yellow, about 5cm wide; sometimes confused with an unspecified species of *Dietes*, perhaps *D. vegeta*, but that genus has a rhizomatous rootstock.

Morina

(for Louis Pierre Morin, 1635–1715, French botanist). MORINACEAE (DIPSACACEAE). A genus of about 10 species of herbaceous perennials from S.E. Europe to C. Asia, 1 of which is generally available: *M. longifolia*, whorlflower; Himalaya; clump-forming, evergreen, 60–90cm tall; leaves basal and in pairs on the stems, narrowly oblong, to 30cm long, pinnatifid, margins undulate and spine-toothed, dark green; flowers to 4cm long, tubular, 5-lobed, opening white, ageing crimson, in whorls from the axils of spiny leafy bracts, summer. Grow in fertile, well-drained soil in sun or partial shade, ideally sheltered from cold winds. Plant autumn or spring. Propagate from seed in spring or by divisison after flowering, or spring.

Above: *Morina longifolia*
Top right: *Morisia monanthus*
Above right: *Morus nigra*

Morisia

(for Giuseppe Giacinto Moris, 1796–1869, professor of botany at Turin, Italy, who wrote a flora of Sardinia). CRUCIFERAE. A genus of 1 small evergreen perennial from Corsica and Sardinia: *M. monanthos* (*M. hypogaea*), tufted, stemless; leaves 2–7cm long, lanceolate, pinnately cut into triangular lobes; flowers 4-petalled, to 1·5cm wide, bright yellow, borne on short stalks in the rosette centres, spring; the short, 2-jointed pods are pushed underground by the elongating flower-stalk, but are seldom produced on cultivated specimens. Grow in gritty or sharply-drained soil in sun. Plant spring or autumn. Propagate by root cuttings early spring in a cold frame, or by careful division of congested plants after flowering, or spring.

Morning glory – see *Ipomoea*.

Morus

(the Latin vernacular name). Mulberry. MORACEAE. A genus of about 10 species of deciduous trees from

N. and S. America, Africa, Asia. They have alternate, ovate, sometimes lobed leaves; tiny, unisexual, greenish flowers in short catkins. The somewhat loganberry-like fruit is botanically a syncarp – that is, a tight cluster of individual fruitlets; the fleshy part is formed of persistent, much swollen calyces. Grow in any well-drained but moisture-retentive, fertile soil in sun. Plant autumn to spring. Propagate by hardwood cuttings in autumn, or from ripe seed kept in cold frame.

Species cultivated: *M. alba*, white or silkworm mulberry; S. and E. China; 12–15m tall, sometimes

Top left: *Morus alba* Pendula
Top: *Muehlenbeckia axillaris*
Centre: *Muscari latifolium*
Above: *Muscari moschatum ambrosiacum*

to 24m; leaves to 10cm or more long, ovate, cordate, often 3-lobed, toothed, glossy above; fruit 2·5–5cm long, whitish or pinkish to black-purple, sweet; several cultivars grown for fruiting are sometimes available *M.a.* Pendula, a weeping form. *M. nigra*, common or black mulberry; W. Asia; to 10m tall, broad-headed; leaves broadly ovate-cordate, toothed, sometimes lobed; fruit 2–3cm long, black-red, juicy, sub-acid; the best fruiting mulberry, but often grown for ornamental purposes.

Mother of thousands – see *Saxifraga stolonifera*.

Mountain ash – see *Sorbus aucuparia*.

Mountain everlasting – see *Antennaria*.

Mountain laurel – see *Kalmia latifolia*.

Muehlenbeckia

(for Henri Gustave Muehlenbeck, 1798–1845, French doctor and botanist). POLYGONACEAE. A genus of 20 species of climbing and prostrate shrubs from S. America and Australasia. They have tough, wiry stems, alternate leaves, sometimes reduced to scales, and tiny, greenish or whitish flowers in axillary clusters. Each blossom has a 5-lobed perianth that persists and becomes swollen and fleshy when the seed (nutlet) ripens. Grow in any well-drained soil in sun, preferably in a sheltered site. Plant or pot spring or autumn. Propagate from seed when ripe or by cuttings in summer.
Species cultivated: *M. axillaris*, New Zealand; prostrate, forming tangled mats, sometimes to 1m wide; stems very slender, rooting at nodes; leaves deciduous, 3–10mm long, ovate-oblong to rounded; fruiting perianths white, forming a 5-lobed cup. *M. complexa*, New Zealand; dioecious, climbing to 6m tall, but forming intertwined, shrub-like plants without support; stems wiry, dark purple-brown; leaves variable, mainly rounded or notched on either side, 5–10mm or more long, often purple-brown margined; fruiting perianths white, but only if both sexes are present. *M. platyclados* (*Homalocladium p.*), Solomon Is; curious shrubby species with flattened, ribbon-like green stems; sometimes grown as a house or greenhouse plant, needs minimum temperature of 13°C.

Mukdenia

(after Mukden – Shen-Yang – the nearest town to the area in N.China – Manchuria – where this genus was first collected). SAXIFRAGACEAE. A genus of 1 species of herbaceous perennial from Korea and S.Manchuria, formerly classified as *Aceriphyllum* and *Saxifraga* and much like a member of the latter genus: *M. rossii*, shortly rhizomatous and clump-forming; leaves almost basal, long-stalked, almost orbicular, to 10cm wide, palmately 5–7 lobed, irregularly toothed; flowers small, bell-shaped, white, in panicles 25–35cm tall, summer. Grow in well-drained but moisture-retentive, humus-rich soil in partial shade. Plant autumn to spring. Propagate from seed or by division spring.

Mulberry – see *Morus*.
Mullein – see *Verbascum*.

Muscari

(Turkish for the sweetly aromatic scent of the flowers of *M. racemosum*, in turn derived from Persian *mushk*, testicle, musk being extracted from a pod-like gland of the musk deer). Grape hyacinth. LILIACEAE. A genus of 40–60 species of bulbous plants from Mediterranean and S.W. Asia. They have tufts of linear, often channelled, somewhat fleshy leaves; erect, leafless stems topped by racemes of rounded, bell- or urn-shaped flowers, with 6 small lobes, opening in spring. In some species, the uppermost flowers of each raceme are sterile, smaller and paler. Grow in any well-drained soil in sun. Plant in autumn. Propagate by offsets or bulblets removed when dormant, or from seed when ripe, or spring.
Species cultivated: *M. ambrosiacum*, see *M. moschatum ambrosiacum*. *M.* Argaei Album, catalogue name for a plant of uncertain affinities not unlike a white-flowered *M. neglectum*. *M. armeniacum*, N.E. Turkey; stems 20–30cm tall; leaves 6–8, to 30cm long, appearing in autumn; flowers ovoid, bright violet-blue, to 8mm long. *M.a.* Blue Spike, flowers double, soft blue; *M.a.* Cantab, single, sky-blue. *M. atlanticum*, see *M. neglectum*. *M. azureum*, see *Hyacinthus a. M. botryoides*, C. and S. Europe to Caucasus; stems to 15cm or more; leaves 2–4, to

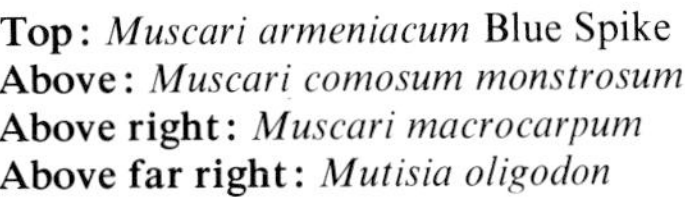

Top: *Muscari armeniacum* Blue Spike
Above: *Muscari comosum monstrosum*
Above right: *Muscari macrocarpum*
Above far right: *Mutisia oligodon*

30cm long; flowers globose, about 5mm long, deep blue; *M.b.* Album, flowers white. *M. comosum*, tassel hyacinth; S. Europe, N. Africa; stems 30cm or more tall; leaves 3–4, to 45cm long; upper flowers erect, sterile, bell-shaped, pale purple-blue, lower flowers larger, to 8mm long, bluish-olive-brown, horizontal to pendant. *M.c. monstrosum* (*M.c. plumosum*), flowers all sterile, reduced to a feathery mass of filaments. *M. latifolium*, Turkey; stems 30cm or more tall; leaves solitary, rarely 2, narrowly oblanceolate, with hooded tip; flowers about 6mm long, rich blue-violet, in long dense racemes; perhaps the finest species. *M. macrocarpum* (*M. moschatum flavum*), like *M. moschatum*, but flowers yellow. *M. moschatum* (*Muscarimia m.*), musk hyacinth; Turkey; stems 20–25cm tall; leaves 5–6, to 30cm long; flowers broadly ovoid, purplish, ageing to yellow, tinged violet-brown, musk-scented. *M.m. ambrosiacum*, flowers pale lavender, ageing pearly-white. *M. m. flavum*, see *M. macrocarpum*. *M. neglectum* (*M. atlanticum*, *M. racemosum*), Mediterranean north to Britain; stems 10–25cm tall; leaves about 5, sometimes less or more, 15–30cm long; flowers ovoid, 3–5mm long, dark purple-blue; confused with *M. armeniacum* in gardens. *M. paradoxum*, Caucasus; stems 20–25cm tall; leaves 3–4, to 40cm long by 2cm wide; flowers bell-shaped, deep slate-blue, in dense conical racemes. *M. racemosum*, see *M. neglectum*. *M. tubergenianum*, Oxford and Cambridge grape hyacinth; N.W. Iran; stems to 15cm or more tall; leaves 2–3, to 25cm long; flowers ellipsoid, to 5mm long, rich blue, the upper sterile ones much paler.

Muscarimia – see *Muscari macrocarpum* and *M. moschatum*.

Musk – see *Mimulus*.

Musk mallow – see *Malva moschata*.

Musk rose – see *Rosa moschata*.

Mutisia

(for José Celestino Mutis, 1732–1809, Spanish doctor and botanist who lived in Bogota, Colombia, and sent specimens to Linnaeus). COMPOSITAE. A genus of 60 species of mainly evergreen climbers and shrubs from S. America. They have alternate linear to oblong-ovate or rarely pinnate leaves, and terminal, solitary, daisy-like flower-heads opening from distinctive cylindrical or cigar-shaped buds. Several climbing species are offered from time to time, all unreliably hardy in areas with cold winters. Grow in well-drained soil in a sheltered, sunny site preferably among low shrubs. Plant spring, providing a support of twiggy sticks or trellis. Propagate from seed under glass in spring, growing singly in pots for the first year, by cuttings in summer or suckers where possible in spring.

Species cultivated: *M. ilicifolia*, Chile; stems to 5m bearing toothed wings; leaves to 6cm long, ovate, sessile, boldly spiny toothed, a slender tendril arising from the notched apex; flower-heads to 6·5cm wide with 8–12, arching, pink to mauve rays, usually summer to autumn. *M. oligodon*, Chile to Argentina; semi-climbing to prostrate; stems suckering, to 1m or more; leaves 2·5–4cm long, narrowly oblong, boldly toothed with terminal tendril; flower-heads 5–7·5cm wide with 6–12 satiny pink to salmon rays, summer to autumn; top may be killed back in winter but regenerates from base and usually long-lived once established.

Myosotidium

(related to *Myosotis*). Chatham Island lily, forget-me-not. BORAGINACEAE. A genus of 1 species of evergreen perennial from the Chatham Islands: *M. hortensia* (*M. nobile*), clump-forming; leaves mostly basal, long-stalked, broadly ovate, boldly veined, lustrous rich green, to 30cm or more long; flowers bright blue, 5-lobed, 1·2–1·5cm wide, in dense cymes 10–15cm wide just above the leaves, spring. Half-hardy, grow outside in mild maritime or cool areas, in well-drained but not dry, preferably neutral to acid soil in a sunny site, ideally mulched with rotted seaweed. Alternatively grow in a frost-free, well-ventilated greenhouse in a good potting mixture. Propagate from seed sown under glass in spring.

Below: *Myosotidium hortensia*
Right below: *Myosotis sylvatica* Blue Ball
Right bottom: *Myosotis australis*
Far right below: *Myrica gale fruit*

Myosotis

(Greek *mus*, mouse, and *ous* or *otos*, an ear; ancient vernacular name for several plants with short, pointed, hairy leaves, but used by Linnaeus for this genus). Forget-me-not. BORAGINACEAE. A genus of at least 50 species of annuals and perennials from the temperate regions, particularly Europe, Asia, Australasia. They are tufted, erect or creeping, with hairy, alternate, oblong to spathulate leaves and branched scorpioid cymes of solitary, tubular flowers having 5, spreading, rounded lobes; fruit a group of 4, small, usually polished, black or brown nutlets. Grow in moisture-retentive but well-drained soil in sun or partial shade. Plant autumn or spring. Propagate from seed in spring (summer for those grown as biennial bedding plants), careful division after flowering or spring, or cuttings of non-flowering shoots, summer.

Species cultivated: *M. alpestris* (*M. rupicola*, *M. sylvatica alpestris*), alpine forget-me-not; rhizomatous, variable in habit, from low cushion-forming to erect, and 15cm or more tall; leaves usually oblong-lanceolate to spathulate, hoary-green; flowers 6–10mm wide, bright to deep blue, spring to summer; plants listed as *M. rupicola*, with a tight cushion habit, belong here, and the small, mat-forming *M. alpina* is closely related; several cultivars grown as bedding plants are listed as *M. alpestris*, but most are referable to *M. sylvatica*. *M. alpina*, see previous entry. *M. australis*, temperate Australia including Tasmania, New Zealand; annual or short-lived perennial, 20–30cm tall; leaves 2–6cm long, spathulate to oblanceolate, hispid, often flushed coppery-brown; flowers 3–5mm wide, white or yellow from New Zealand and Tasmania, white or blue from Australia, summer. *M. colensoi* (*M. decora*), New Zealand; mat-forming, to 30cm wide; leaves 2–3cm long, lanceolate; flowers 8mm wide, white with yellow eye, solitary or in small clusters, summer. *M. explanata*, Arthur's Pass forget-me-not; South Island, New Zealand; tufted perennial, to 20cm tall; leaves 3–7cm long, obovate to spathulate; flowers 1–1·5cm wide, white with yellow eye, rarely blue, summer. *M. oblongata*, see *M. sylvatica*. *M. palustris*, see *M. scorpioides*. *M. rupicola*, see *M. alpestris*. *M. scorpioides* (*M. palustris*), water forget-me-not; northern temperate zone, S. to N. Africa; rhizomatous and often stoloniferous perennial 15–45cm tall; leaves up to 7cm long, oblong-lanceolate; flowers 5–10mm wide, sky-blue in branched cymes, early summer to autumn. *M.s. semperflorens*, more compact than type, 10–20cm tall. *M. sylvatica*, wood or garden forget-me-not; Europe, Asia; biennial or short-lived perennial, tufted; leaves to 8cm long, broadly to narrowly ovate or elliptic; flowers 6–10mm wide, bright blue, in branched cymes, late spring to summer; several cultivars are listed, some of compact growth, eg *M.s.* Blue Ball, or with white or pink flowers; some of these may be hybrids with *M. alpestris* but the 2 species are closely allied and intermediates occur in the wild.

Myrica

(Greek *myrike* for tamarisk, and used by Linnaeus for this genus). MYRICACEAE. A genus of 50–60 species of deciduous and evergreen shrubs and trees of almost cosmopolitan distribution. They have alternate, often oblanceolate leaves, and tiny, unisexual, petalless flowers in short, catkin-like spikes; fruit a berry-like drupe or nut. Grow in moist soil in sun; ideal for waterside or bog garden. Plant autumn to spring. Propagate from seed when ripe, suckers removed at planting time or layering in spring.

Species cultivated: *M. asplenifolia* (now correctly *Comptonia peregrina asplenifolia*, but previous name retained here for convenience), sweet fern; E. N.America; slender deciduous shrub 60–120cm tall; leaves 5–10cm long, linear-lanceolate, pinnatifid, sweetly aromatic when bruised; fruit like small soft burrs. *M. caroliniensis*, see *M. pensylvanica*. *M. gale*, bog myrtle, sweet gale; northern temperate zone; deciduous suckering shrub 60–250cm tall; leaves 2–6cm long, oblanceolate, usually toothed at apex, greyish-green, aromatic; fruit a tiny winged resinous nut. *M. pensylvanica* (*M. caroliniensis* in part), bayberry, candleberry, wax myrtle; E. N.America; deciduous erect shrub 2–3m tall; leaves to 10cm

long, elliptic or oblong to oblanceolate, downy above, aromatic; fruit 3–5mm wide, globular, coated with whitish wax.

Myriophyllum

(Greek *myrios*, many, and *phyllon*, a leaf – alluding to the many, often dissected leaves). Water milfoil. HALORAGIDACEAE. A genus of 45 species of submerged aquatic and bog plants of cosmopolitan distribution. They have slender, flexible stems, alternate, narrow, opposite or whorled leaves, and minute 4-petalled or petalless flowers in terminal spikes, or from upper leaf-axils, borne above the water. The following species are all aquatic with whorled leaves. Grow hardy species in ponds or cold water aquaria with moderate light; tender species in warm water aquaria or heated greenhouse pools, minimum temperature 13–16°C, shaded in summer. Grow and propagate by securing 3–4 shoots in a lead clip and pushing into the sand base of an aquarium. Alternatively and for more vigorous growth, pot into containers of a standard compost or good loam, surface with shingle or gravel and sink in a pond or aquarium.

Species cultivated: *M. aquaticum* (*M. brasiliense, M. proserpinacoides*), water or parrot's feather; Brazil, Argentina, Chile; stems to 2m long, usually less, the tips above water; leaves 2–3cm long, pinnatifid, 4–6 per whorl, those above water glistening blue-green; half-hardy and best in warm water, although sometimes surviving outside in mild areas. *M. brasiliense*, see *M. aquaticum*. *M. hippuroides*, western or red water milfoil; California to Washington State; stems to 60cm long, tips above water; leaves 1·5–3cm long, pinnatifid, the aerial ones smaller, pectinate, 4–6 per whorl; almost hardy. *M. proserpinacoides*, see *M. aquaticum*. *M. spicatum*, spiked water milfoil; Europe, Asia, N. America, N. Africa; stems 50–250cm long; leaves 1·5–3cm long, pinnate, usually 4 per whorl; hardy. *M. verticillatum*, whorled water milfoil or myriad leaf; northern temperate zone, N. Africa, S. America; stems 50–300cm long; leaves 2·5–4·5cm long, pinnate, usually 5 per whorl; hardy – produces detached over-wintering resting buds (turions) that provide an alternate means of propagation.

Below left: *Myriophyllum aquaticum*
Bottom left: *Myriophyllum spicatum*
Below: *Myrrhis odorata*

Myrrhis

(Greek vernacular for this plant and true myrrh). Myrrh. UMBELLIFERAE. A genus of 1 species of herbaceous perennial from Europe, mainly the mountains: *M. odorata*, sweet cicely; clump-forming, 60–100cm tall; basal leaves long-stalked, to 30cm long, bi- to tripinnate, leaflets oblong-ovate, pinnatisect, sweetly aromatic; flowers white, 2–4mm wide, 5-petalled, in compound umbels, early summer; fruit (seed) slender, 2–2·5cm long, sharply ribbed, black. Grow in any well-drained but not dry soil in sun or partial shade. Plant autumn to spring. Propagate from seed when ripe, preferably *in situ* or by division, spring.

Myrsine

(Greek vernacular for myrtle taken up by Linnaeus for this genus). MYRSINACEAE. A genus of 5–7 species of evergreen shrubs and trees from Azores and Africa to China. They have alternate, elliptic to obovate leaves, tiny, 4–5 lobed flowers in axillary clusters, and berry-like drupes. Grow in warm climates in well-drained, fertile soil, or in a frost-free greenhouse using any commercial potting compost. Pot or plant spring. Propagate from seed when ripe or by cuttings late summer.
Species cultivated: *M. africana*, Cape myrtle, African boxwood (USA); shrub to 2m or, in a mild climate, a small tree; leaves 6–25mm long, mainly elliptic to ovate but variable, aromatic; flowers dioecious, 4-lobed, pale brown, early summer; fruit globular, about 6mm wide, pale to deep blue-purple; some forms or clones are much hardier than others. *M. australis* (*Suttonia australis*), mapou; New Zealand; shrub or small tree to 6m tall in the wild, often less in gardens; twigs dark orange-red; leaves 3–6cm long, oblong to obovate or broadly elliptic, strongly waved; flowers unisexual, whitish, each with 4 separate petals; fruit 2–3mm wide, brown to black; best under glass in cold areas. *M. nummularia* (*Rapanea* and *Suttonia n.*), creeping matipo; New Zealand; prostrate; stems to 50cm long, red-brown; leaves 4–10mm long, obovate to oblong or almost orbicular; flowers 4-petalled; fruit 5–6mm wide, blue-purple; the hardiest species, being sub-alpine in the wild.

Myrtle – see *Myrica* and *Myrtus*.

Myrtus

(Greek vernacular name). Myrtle. MYRTACEAE. A genus of 100 species of evergreen shrubs and trees from the tropics and subtropics. Some authorities have re-classified all but 16 of these species in other genera. They have opposite pairs of lanceolate to obovate leaves, small cymes of, or solitary, 4–5 petalled flowers followed by fleshy, often edible berries. The species described are half-hardy and need well-drained soil at the foot of a sunny, sheltered wall, but see *M. nummularia*. In cold areas they are best grown, or at least over-wintered, in a frost-free greenhouse. Pot or plant spring. Propagate from seed in spring at 15–18°C, or cuttings with a heel in summer, bottom heat 18°C.
Species cultivated: *M. apiculata*, see *M. luma*. *M. bullata* (*Lophomyrtus b.*), ramarama; New Zealand; shrub or small tree 3–5m, usually erect when young; leaves broadly ovate, 2–3cm long, prominently bullate, purplish to reddish tinged; flowers 4-petalled, solitary, white, to 1·5cm wide, summer; berries ovoid, dark red to black, 4–8mm long, not always produced. *M. chequen* (*M. cheken, Myrceugenella chequen, Luma c.*), Chile; shrub or small tree to 5m or more; leaves dense, broadly elliptic to ovate or obovate, 7–28mm long; flowers usually 4-petalled, solitary or in 3s, white, 8–12mm wide, summer to autumn; berries globose, black, 6mm wide; moderately hardy. *M. communis*, common myrtle; probably W. Asia, but now much naturalized S. and E. Europe; shrub 2–4m tall; leaves lanceolate to ovate, 2·5–5cm long, glossy rich green; flowers solitary, white, 2cm wide, summer; berries broadly oblong, 9–12mm long, purplish to bluish-black. *M.c.* Flore Pleno, flowers double; *M.c.* Microphylla, dwarf habit, leaves less than 2·5cm long; *M.c. tarentina* (*M.c.* Jenny Reitenbach), narrow leaves about 2cm long, berries white, somewhat hardier; *M.c.* Variegata, leaves margined creamy-white. *M. lechlerana* (*M. luma* in part, *Amomyrtus luma*), Chile; shrub or small tree to 5m or more tall; leaves ovate to broadly elliptic, 1·5–3cm long, coppery when young, dark green and glossy later; flowers in clusters of 4–10, creamy-white, to 12mm wide, spring; berries globose, red to glossy black, 6–8mm wide; sometimes confused with the next species but flowers with 5 petals and trunk lacking the attractive bark. *M. luma* (*M. apiculata, Myrceugenia a., Luma a.*), Argentina, Chile; shrub or tree 3–15m or more tall; leaves elliptic, 2–3cm long; flowers 4-petalled, usually solitary, 1·5–2cm wide, late summer to autumn; berries globose, red to purple-black, 1cm wide, sweet; distinctive with its cinnamon bark flaking to reveal cream patches. *M. nummularia* (*Myrteola n.*), S. S. America; prostrate, mat-forming, to 60cm or more wide; stems red; leaves oval to rounded, 4–8mm long; flowers solitary, 4–5 petalled, white, 4–6mm wide, early

summer, sometimes later; berries oblong-ovoid, 6mm long, white flushed pink; needs a moist peaty soil; hardy in moderate frosts. *M. obcordata* (*Lophomyrtus o.*), New Zealand; shrub 3–5m tall; leaves inverted heart-shaped, 5–12mm long; flowers solitary, 4-petalled, white, about 6mm wide; berries broadly ovoid, bright to dark red, or violet, 6–7mm long. *M. ugni* (*Eugenia u.*, *Ugni molinae*), Chilean myrtle; Chile; shrub 1–2m tall, usually erect; leaves lanceolate to ovate, 2–2·5cm long; flowers 5-petalled, broadly bell-shaped, nodding, waxy-white to pink, fragrant, 8mm wide, early summer; berries globular, mahogany-red, to 1cm wide, sweet.

Nandina

(Latinized form of the Japanese vernacular *nanten*). NANDINACEAE (BERBERIDACEAE). A genus of 1 species of evergreen shrub from India to E. Asia: *N. domestica*, heavenly or sacred bamboo; slender, little-branched, erect shrub to 2m or more; leaves alternate, bi- to tripinnate, 30–45cm long, leaflets lanceolate, 3–7cm long, well-spaced, flushed coppery-red when young and tinted red to purple in autumn; flowers about 6mm long, formed of several whorls of tepals, upper ones petal-like, in airy terminal panicles, 20–35cm long, summer; fruit a 2-seeded globular red berry 6–8mm wide; white and purple fruited and dwarf cultivars to 60cm tall are sometimes listed. Grow in well-drained but moisture-retentive, humus-rich, preferably neutral to acid soil in sun or partial shade sheltered from cold winds. Plant autumn or spring. Propagate from seed when ripe in a cold frame or cuttings with a heel, bottom heat 18°C in late summer.

Left: *Myrtus communis*
Below left: *Myrtus ugni*
Below: *Nandina domestica*

Narcissus

(ancient Greek name of the youth obsessed by his own beautiful reflection and turned by the gods into a flower). AMARYLLIDACEAE. A genus of 26–60 or more species (depending on the classifier) of bulbous perennials from Europe, N. Africa and Asia, but mainly W. Europe. They have strap-shaped or rush-like leaves and leafless erect stems bearing an umbel of, or solitary, flowers surrounded by a sheath or spathe in bud. Each flower has a tubular base becoming funnel-shaped at the top and terminating in 6 tepals. In the centre is a cup- or trumpet-shaped structure known as a corona, formed of a flange of tissue at the junction of the tube and lobes. The fruit is an ovoid capsule containing polished black seed. Grow in well-drained soil that is well supplied with water during the growing season, in sun and partial shade. Plant early autumn. Propagate by offsets when dormant or from seed when ripe, the latter taking 3–5 years to flower. Both species and cultivars make good pot plants for the cool greenhouse or home. Grow the dwarf species in pans with drainage holes, the large cultivars in pots or bulb bowls. Ideally, use a standard potting mixture. Although bulb fibre is adequate for the large, vigorous cultivars, they are weakened afterwards and need a year or so in the garden to flower again. In a potting mixture, with feeding, they will flower the next year. Pot bulbs as soon as available, placing the larger ones with the necks just above the mixture; dwarf species, 2–4cm deep at least. For a good display, the large cultivars should be touching, ie about 5 in a 13–14cm container. Place the potted bulbs in a cool spot outside, ideally covered with peat, sand or weathered boiler ash; alternatively, they can go in a cool room or cellar. *Narcissus* Paper White should be kept in a cool dining room window or placed in a cool greenhouse directly. In early winter, or when shoots are about 5–6cm long, bring into home or greenhouse where the temperature does not rise above 10–13°C. Once the leaves are green and growing well the temperature can rise then to 16°C by day, but preferably not above 7–10°C at night. Make sure the mixture is moist but do not overwater. A combination of too high a temperature and too much wetness or dryness at the roots is the primary cause of failure to flower. Popular spring flowers in gardens for at least 400 years, narcissi have been much hybridized and 1000s of cultivars have been named. In an endeavour to bring order to such a vast assemblage of cultivars and their derivative species, a horticultural system has been devised by the Royal Horticultural Society, London, and used by all interested. Choosing cultivars from the several 100s currently available is a personal matter and specialist bulb catalogues should be consulted. However, the examples given under each group of the following classification can be recommended: Division **1** – Daffodils or trumpet narcissi; 1 flower per stem, the corona as long or longer than the tepals. **1A**, tepals and corona the same colour or tepals paler, eg Dutch Master, Golden Harvest. **1B**, tepals white, corona coloured, eg Queen of Bicolours, Spring Glory. **1C**, tepals and corona white (sometimes cream or yellow in bud), eg Beersheba, Mount Hood. Division **2** – Large-cupped narcissi; 1 flower per stem, the corona more than ⅓ the length of the tepals. **2A**, tepals in shades of yellow, orange, red, the cup usually darker, eg Carlton (yellow cup), Armada (orange cup), Scarlet Elegance (red cup). **2B**, tepals white, cup coloured, eg Flower Record (cup bright orange), Green Island (cup green-white and yellow), **2C**, tepals white, cup white or cream, eg Castella (cup lemon, ageing cream). Division **3** – Small-cupped narcissi; 1 flower per stem, corona less than ⅓ the length of the tepals. **3A**, tepals and cup coloured, eg Edward Buxton (yellow and orange). **3B**, tepals white, cup coloured, eg Verger (cup yellow, bordered bright orange). **3C**, tepals and cup white, eg Verona. Division **4**–Double-flowered narcissi; 1 per flower per stem, eg Golden Ducat (deep yellow), Irene Copeland (white and yellow), Texas (yellow and orange-red). Division **5** – Triandrus narcissi; several nodding flowers per stem with reflexed or recurved tepals. **5A**, cup not less than ⅔ length of

Top right: *Narcissus* Dutch Master (Div. 1A)
Right: *Narcissus* Fortune (Div. 2A)

Top: *Narcissus* Duke of Windsor (Div. 2B)
Above: *Narcissus* Ardour (Div. 3A)
Top right: *Narcissus* Texas (Div. 4)
Right: *Narcissus* Actaea (Div. 9)
Top far right: *Narcissus* Bartley (Div. 6)

tepals, eg Thalia. **5B**, cup less than ⅔ length of tepals, eg April Tears (yellow). Division **6** – Cyclamineus narcissi; 1 nodding flower per stem with recurved tepals. **6A**, cup not less than ⅔ length of tepals, eg March Sunshine. **6B**, cup less than ⅔ length of tepals, eg Beryl (cream and orange). Division **7** – Jonquil narcissi; several small flowers per stem and often deep green very narrow leaves. **7A**, cup not less than ⅔ length of tepals, eg Sweetness (pale and deep yellow). **7B**, cup not less than ⅔ length of tepals, eg Trevithian. Division **8** – Tazetta narcissi; several flowers per stem having a basic resemblance to *N. tazetta*, eg Paper White, an unreliably hardy sort used for bowl cultivation. Also included are hybrids with *N. poeticus*, known as poetaz, having fewer larger flowers per stem, later flowering and hardy, eg Geranium (white and orange-yellow). Division **9** – Poeticus narcissi; 1 flower per stem, very small cup;

all cultivars of the wild species, eg Actaea (white tepals, cup yellow, red-edged). Division **10** – all true wild species, forms and hybrids, see Species cultivated. Division **11** – Miscellaneous narcissi that do not fit the previous classification, in particular the Collar and Split Corona groups that have divided, petal-like coronas, eg Evolution (white and yellow), Golden Orchid (pale and deep yellow).

Species cultivated (flowers solitary unless stated otherwise): *N. asturiensis* (*N. minimus*), Spain, Portugal; stems to 10cm tall; leaves grey-green; flowers 2–2·5cm long, corona and tepals about the same length, deep yellow; a perfect miniature daffodil but not always very permanent outside, good for the cold greenhouse in pans. *N. bulbocodium*, hoop petticoat daffodil; France, Spain, Portugal, N.W. Africa; stems 10–15cm tall, sometimes more or less; leaves green, filiform; flowers 2–3·5cm long, the corona large and generally funnel-shaped, tepals very small, narrow and pointed, pale to deep yellow; a variable species in size, shape and colouring of corona and height of stem. *N.b. cantabricus*, see *N. cantabricus*; *N.b. conspicuus*, generally more robust than type, flowers deep yellow; *N.b. monophyllus*, see *N. cantabricus monophyllus*; *N.b. nivalis*, 6–8cm tall, flowers about 2·5cm long, the corona narrower, pale yellow; *N.b obesus*, Portugal, leaves prostrate, corona larger, to 3·5cm wide, deep yellow; *N.b. romieuxii*, see *N. romieuxii*; *N.b.* Tenuifolius, to 8cm tall, corona narrowly funnel-shaped. *N. campernellii*, see *N.* × *odorus*. *N. canaliculatus*, see *N. tazetta*. *N. cantabricus* (*N. clusii*, *N. bulbocodium cantabricus*), S. Spain, N.W. Africa; much like *N. bulbocodium* but having white flowers. *N.c. monophyllus* (*N. bulbocodium monophyllus*), 1 leaf per bulb; *N.c. foliosus*, 3–8 leaves per bulb. *N. clusii*, see *N. cantabricus*. *N. cyclamineus*, cyclamen-flowered daffodil; Spain, Portugal; stems to 20cm tall; leaves bright rich green, linear; flowers 4·5cm long, corona and sharply reflexed tepals about same length, deep yellow; best in a moist soil in partial shade. *N. gayi*, see *N. pseudo-narcissus*. *N. jonquilla*, jonquil; S. Europe, Algeria; stems to 30cm tall; leaves rush-like, deep green; flowers in umbels of 2–6, each 3–4cm wide, corona 4mm long, rich yellow, very sweetly fragrant. *N. juncifolius*, N. Spain, Portugal, S.W. France; a miniature jonquil to

Top: *Narcissus* Sweetness (Div. 7A)
Top centre: *Narcissus bulbocodium*
Centre right: *Narcissus* × *odorus* Rugulosus
Right: *Narcissus cyclamineus*
Top far right: *Narcissus rupicola*
Bottom far right: *Narcissus pseudo-narcissus*

long, white, tepals reflexed, corona about 1cm long. *N.t. concolor*, flowers pale golden-yellow. *N. viridiflorus*, Morocco, Gibraltar, S. Spain; leaves dark green, rush-like, 1 per bulb; stems like leaves and usually replacing them in flowering specimens, to 25cm tall at flowering time, elongating later; flowers 2–6, each olive-green, 1·5–3cm wide, corona very small, 6-lobed, autumn; shy flowering and reputedly best under glass with a summer baking, but opinions vary. *N. watieri*, Morocco – Atlas Mountains; like a pure white *N. rupicola*; leaves grey-green, narrowly linear, about 3mm wide; best in an alpine house.

Nasturtium – see *Tropaeolum*.

Neillia

(for Patrick Neill, 1776–1851, Scottish printer and Secretary of the Caledonian Horticultural Society).

Left: *Narcissus poeticus*
Below: *Neillia longiracemosa*
Bottom: *Nelumbo nucifera*

15cm tall; flowers 1–5, each 2–2·5cm wide. *N. juncifolius rupicola*, see *N. rupicola*. *N. lobularis*, see *N. obvallaris*. *N. minimus*, see *N. asturiensis*. *N. minor*, see *N. nanus*. *N. moschatus*, probably Pyrenees; like *N. pseudo-narcissus*, but flowers almost pendant, creamy-white. *N. nanus*, Europe; stems to 15cm or more; leaves grey-green; flowers to 3·5cm long, corona deep yellow, almost as long as soft yellow tepals; *N. minor* is similar but smaller. *N. obvallaris* (*N. lobularis*), Tenby daffodil; Britain (Wales) and perhaps Europe; similar to *N. pseudo-narcissus*, but flower deep yellow, borne horizontally or inclined upwards, tepals flat, somewhat overlapping; corona as long as or longer than tepals. *N.* × *odorus* (*N. campernellii*), (*N. jonquilla* × *N. pseudo-narcissus*), similar to *N. jonquilla*, but leaves flattened, to 6mm wide; flowers slightly larger with corona 1–1·5cm long, fragrant. *N.* × *o.* Rugulosus, tepals shorter, broader, overlapping; *N.* × *o.* Rugulosus Flore Pleno, corona double. *N. poeticus*, poet's or pheasant's eye narcissus; Spain to Greece; stems 30–36cm tall; leaves narrowly strap-shaped; flowers 4·5–7cm wide, fragrant, tepals pure white, often somewhat reflexed, corona a very short, flared cup, orange-red or yellow-edged crimson; the latest species to flower, some forms opening early to mid summer; an important parent of the small and large-cupped narcissus cultivars. *N. pseudo-narcissus*, wild daffodil; Europe; stems 20–35cm tall; leaves 1·5cm wide, grey-green; flowers somewhat nodding, 5–7cm long, tepals pale yellow, wavy or twisted, corona deep yellow, almost straight-sided, sometimes flared at mouth, about as long as tepals. *N.p. gayi* (*N. gayi*), more robust than type, with larger flowers. *N. romieuxii* (*N. bulbocodium romieuxii*), tetraploid species probably derived as a hybrid between *N. bulbocodium* and *N. cantabricus*; like the former with sulphur-yellow flowers. *N. rupicola* (*N. juncifolius rupicola*), Portugal, Spain; similar to *N. juncifolius*, but leaves grey-green and flowers solitary. *N. scaberulus*, Portugal; a smaller form of *N. rupicola*; to 10cm tall; flowers 1 or 2 per stem, deep orange-yellow, about 1cm wide; needs plenty of moisture when growing and to be almost dry when dormant – a good pan plant. *N. tazetta*, polyanthus narcissus; Portugal to Japan; stems 30–45cm tall; leaves green, 1–2cm wide; flowers 4–8, fragrant, each 2·5–4cm wide, tepals white, corona a short cup, white or yellow; winter-flowering and not reliably hardy, best in the home or under glass. *N.t. canaliculatus*, hardy miniature version, to 20cm tall, flowering in spring, needs a site that gets warm and dry in summer to flower well. *N. triandrus*, angel's tears; Portugal, W. Spain; stems to 15cm or more tall; leaves grey-green, linear; flowers 1–3 or more, each nodding, to 3cm

ROSACEAE. A genus of 10–13 species of deciduous shrubs from Himalaya to Korea and S.E. Asia, 1 being generally available: *N. longiracemosa*, China; 2–3m tall, spreading habit; leaves alternate, ovate, slender-pointed, sharply toothed, 5–10cm long; flowers tubular, 5-lobed, to 8mm long, pink, in terminal simple or branched racemes to 15cm long, early summer and sometimes a smaller display in autumn. *N. opulifolia*, see *Physocarpus o.* Culture as for *Spiraea*.

Nelumbium – see *Nelumbo*.

Nelumbo

(Sinhalese vernacular name). Lotus. NELUMBONACEAE (NYMPHAEACEAE). A genus of 2 species of aquatic perennials from Asia and N. America. They are rhizomatous with large peltate leaves on stalks above the water, and solitary, water-lily-like, many-petalled flowers, each followed by a cluster of 1-seeded fruit embedded in a large, ornamental, top-shaped receptacle. Grow in wet, humus-rich soil, or tubs or pools of water in sun. If covered with 30cm or more of water or grown where the rhizomes will not get frozen, they can be grown in a sheltered pool outside. In most northern temperate areas, however, they are best grown either permanently under glass, or over-wintered there. A mixture of equal parts heavy loam and well-rooted manure is recommended. Pot or replant annually in spring in large pots, chicken wire containers or a commercial water-lily basket, ideally at least 45cm wide or larger. If over-wintered under glass, put outside when fear of frost has passed, usually last week or so of early summer, and bring in mid to late autumn or immediately after the first frost. Propagate by division of rhizomes or from seed in spring, the latter sown singly in sandy soil in pots covered by water at 18–24°C and growing under glass the first year. Seed takes less time to germinate if filed or nicked before sowing.

Species cultivated: *N. flavescens*, see *N. lutea* Flavescens. *N. lutea* (*N. pentapetala*, *Nelumbium l.*), American lotus, water chinquapin; E.USA; leaf-stalks 1–2m tall, blades circular, somewhat cupped, blue-green, 30–60cm wide; flowers above leaves, cup-shaped, to 25cm wide, yellow, fragrant, summer. *N.l.* Flavescens (*N. flavescens*), flowers more freely produced but smaller; hardier than *N. nucifera*, especially if obtained from the northern area of its native habitat. *N. nucifera* (*N. speciosa*, *Nelumbium nelumbo*), sacred or East Indian lotus; Asia; similar in overall appearance and size to *N. lutea*, but flowers pink and leaves more grey-green; several cultivars are known ranging from carmine to white, and double. *N. pentapetala*, see *N. lutea*, *N. speciosa*, see *N. nucifera*.

Nemesia

(ancient Greek vernacular for a plant of similar appearance). SCROPHULARIACEAE. A genus of 50 species of annuals, perennials and sub-shrubs from S. Africa, 1 of which is widely grown: *N. strumosa*, half-hardy annual, 30–50cm tall; leaves in opposite pairs, lanceolate, coarsely toothed, pale green; flowers 2cm wide, white, yellow or purple, shortly tubular, broadly 2-lipped and 5-lobed, in terminal racemes, summer; represented in gardens by several single and mixed coloured cultivars, mostly ranging from 20–30cm tall with larger flowers, eg *N.s.* Suttonii, shades of white, orange, pink, red, blue, purple. Grow in humus-rich, well-drained soil in sun. Sow seed under glass at 16°C in spring. Prick off seedlings when true leaves show at 4cm apart each way into boxes of any commercial potting mixture. Harden in early summer and plant out when fear of frost has passed.

Above: *Nemesia strumosa* Triumph Mixed
Below: *Nelumbo nucifera* flower

Nemophila

(Greek *nemos*, a wooded pasture or grove, and *phileo*, to love – some species grow in open pine forest). California bluebell. HYDROPHYLLACEAE. A genus of 11 species of annuals from N.America. They are slender-stemmed, erect to decumbent, leaves alternate or opposite, narrow, toothed or pinnately lobed, flowers 5-petalled, cup-shaped or rotate, solitary on long stalks from upper leaf-axils. Grow the following species in well-drained soil in sun. Sow seed *in situ* in spring, or in a sheltered site in autumn; may also be sown under glass in autumn and grown in pots for flowering in a cold greenhouse late spring.

Species cultivated: *N. insignis*, see *N. menziesii*. *N. maculata*, fivespot; California; stems erect to decumbent, about 15cm tall; leaves 1–3cm long, oblong to oval, deeply 5–9 lobed; flowers bowl-shaped, about 2·5cm wide, petals white, with purple veins and blotched tips, summer. *N. menziesii*, baby blue-eyes; California; stems decumbent, vaguely

winged or angled, to 20cm tall; leaves 2–5cm long, oblong, deeply 9–11 lobed, sometimes silvery-spotted; flowers bowl-shaped, about 3cm wide, sky-blue, with white centres, summer; a form with black-purple veins and spots is sometimes seen.

Neopanax – see *Pseudopanax*.

Nepeta

(ancient Latin name for catmint or catnip). Catmint. LABIATAE. A genus of 250 species of perennials and, rarely, annuals from Asia, Europe, N. Africa and tropical African mountains. They are usually clump-forming, erect to prostrate with opposite pairs of lanceolate to ovate leaves and terminal spikes of tubular, 2-lipped flowers. Grow in any well-drained soil in sun. Plant autumn to spring. Propagate from seed, by cuttings or division in spring.

Species cultivated: *N.* Blue Beauty, see *N.* Souvenir d'André Chaudron. *N. cataria*, catmint, catnip; Europe, Asia; aromatic, erect perennial 60–90cm tall; leaves ovate, crenate or serrate, with grey down, 3–7cm long; flowers about 1–2cm long, white with pale purple spots, late summer to autumn; attractive to cats. *N.* × *faassenii* (*N. mussinii* × *N. nepetella*), perennial; stems branched, erect to decumbent, to 45cm tall; leaves lanceolate to oblong-ovate, and grey downy, 1·5–3cm long; flowers about 1·5cm long, violet-blue, early summer, autumn; often confused with *N. mussinii*, but superior as a garden plant and sterile. *N. glechoma* and *N. hederacea*, see *Glechoma*. *N. macrantha*, see *Dracocephalum sibiricum*. *N. mussinii*, Caucasus, Iran; decumbent to prostrate, forming mats up to 30cm tall; leaves 2·5–4cm long, bluntly triangular-ovate, cordate, prominently toothed, greyish, somewhat rankly aromatic; flowers lavender-blue, about 1·5cm long, summer to autumn; seeds freely on the lighter soils and sometimes invasive; see also *N.* × *faassenii*. *N. nervosa*, Kashmir; perennial, to 60cm tall; leaves narrowly lanceolate, to 10cm long; flowers about 1cm long, usually blue, sometimes yellow, in dense spikes to 13cm long. *N. sibirica*, see *Dracocephalum sibiricum*. *N.* Six Hills Giant, not unlike a giant *N.* × *faassenii*, to 90cm tall, sometimes listed under *N. gigantea* (of gardens) but almost certainly of hybrid origin. *N.* Souvenir d'André Chaudron (*N.* Blue Beauty), probably a hybrid of *Dracocephalum sibiricum* and like a more compact form of it.

Nerine

(for the Greek water nymph, *Nereis*, alluding to the history of the first described species, *N. sarniensis*, reputedly washed ashore from a shipwreck on Guernsey, although evidence now shows that bulbs

were brought ashore by sailors from a stranded vessel). AMARYLLIDACEAE. A genus of 20–30 species of bulbous plants from S. Africa. They have tufts of usually deciduous, narrowly strap-shaped, arching leaves and erect, leafless stems bearing umbels of 6-tepalled flowers in autumn, like spidery lilies. Mainly greenhouse, minimum temperature 10°C, sunny and well-ventilated. A few species, eg *N. bowdenii*, are almost hardy and thrive outside in a sheltered site. Pot or plant late summer, repotting every 3–5 years. Use 9cm pots for single bulbs,

Top far left: *Nemophila menziesii*
Top left: *Nepeta* Souvenir d'André Chaudron
Left: *Nepeta* Six Hills Giant
Below left: *Nepeta* × *faassenii*
Above: *Nerine bowdenii*

13–15cm for 3–4 bulbs; a pot 3–4cm wider than the bulb is adequate as over-potting tends to inhibit flowering. Use a loam-based commercial potting mixture, setting each bulb with the neck above the soil. Bulbs outside should be covered with at least 5cm of soil, deeper in frosty areas as they seldom survive being frozen solid. Begin watering potted bulbs when either flowering stems or leaves appear. Water regularly but allow the compost almost to dry out each time. Apply liquid feed to well-established plants at fortnightly intervals while in full growth. Withhold water when leaves yellow and keep dry until growth recommences. Propagate from seed sown when ripe (they are soft and fleshy and do not store) or by offsets removed at potting time.

Species cultivated: *N. bowdenii*, stems about 45cm; leaves about 30cm long, glossy, usually present at flowering time; flowers 6–12, tepals waved, pink, to 7cm long. *N.b.* Fenwick's Variety, more vigorous than type, taller; flowers deep pink. *N. corusca*, see under *N. sarniensis*. *N. crispa*, see *N. undulata*. *N. curvifolia*, see under *N. sarniensis*. *N. filifolia*, stems 20–30cm tall; leaves narrowly linear, grass-like, 15–20cm long; flowers 6–10, tepals rose-red, 2·5cm long. *N. flexuosa*, similar to *N. bowdenii*, but stems 60–90cm tall; flowers 10–20, tepals pink with crisped margins. *N.f.* Alba, flowers white. *N. fothergillii*, see under *N. sarniensis*. *N. masonorum*, stems 20–25cm tall; leaves filiform, 25–35cm long; flowers 9–11 or fewer, tepals undulate, rose-pink with darker zone, 1–1·5cm long. *N. sarniensis*, Guernsey lily; stems 25–50cm tall; leaves to 30cm long by 2cm wide, green or glaucous; flowers 4–8, tepals 3–4cm long, recurved and sometimes undulate, crimson to scarlet, sometimes pink; a variable species, in the past several of the variants have been species names, eg *N. curvifolia* (*N. fothergillii*), leaves glaucous, flowers scarlet, *N. corusca*, more robust with up to 30, larger, bright salmon-red flowers; these and other forms of *N. sarniensis* have been intercrossed and used with other species to provide many fine cultivars. *N. undulata* (*N. crispa* of gardens), stems 20–40cm tall; leaves 25–45cm long; flowers 10–15, tepals strongly undulate, pink, to 2·5cm long.

Nerium

(ancient Greek vernacular for oleander). Oleander. APOCYNACEAE. A genus of 2 species of evergreen shrubs from Mediterranean to Japan, 1 of which is commonly cultivated: *N. oleander*, common oleander or rose bay; range of genus; 2–5m or more tall, usually erect, at least when young; leaves 6–20cm

long, linear-lanceolate, in opposite pairs or whorls of 3 or more; flowers funnel-shaped with 5 broad lobes, 3–5cm wide, in terminal cymes, summer to autumn; usually in shades of pink, red or purple-red, but variable: *N.o.* Album Plenum, double white, *N.o.* Luteum Plenum, double creamy-yellow, *N.o.* Roseum Plenum, double pink, *N.o.* Variegatum, leaves margined cream, flowers pink. Greenhouse, minimum temperature 7°C, sunny and well-ventilated. Can be stood outside from early summer to mid autumn and grown outside against a wall in mild areas. Pot or plant in spring, using any medium strength standard potting mixture. Water freely in summer, sparingly in winter. Apply liquid fertilizer at fortnightly intervals to well-established plants during the summer. Large pots or tubs will be needed for good-sized, free-flowering specimens. Propagate by cuttings in summer, bottom heat about 18°C, or from seed in spring at 16–18°C.

Nertera

(Greek *nerteros*, lowly – referring to the growth habit). Bead plant. RUBIACEAE. A genus of 12 species of small evergreen perennials from Pacific Is and adjacent mainland. They have filiform, creeping stems forming mats or low hummocks, tiny, ovate leaves in pairs, minute, funnel-shaped, 4–5 lobed, greenish or whitish flowers in the leaf-axils and orange or red, 2-seeded, berry-like drupes. Frost-free greenhouse or sheltered, damp, shady site outside. Grow in any standard potting mixture kept just moist at all times. Pot or plant spring. Avoid sites which get direct sunshine in summer that can scorch the delicate growths. Propagate by careful division or from seed, spring, at 13–15°C.

Species cultivated: *N. balfouriana*, New Zealand; stems forming dense mats to 25cm wide; leaves 2–4mm long, broadly ovate to oblong or obovate; fruit broadly pear-shaped, 7–9mm long, yellow to light orange. *N. depressa* (of gardens), see next species. *N. granadensis*, Mexico and C. America; stems forming low, mossy cushions to 25cm wide; leaves broadly ovate, 4–5mm long; fruit globose, about 6mm wide, bright orange; best under glass; often considered synonymous with *N. depressa* from New Zealand, but plants under that name are hardier, often more vigorous, flatter-growing and with bright to dark red fruit about 4mm wide.

Top left: *Nerium oleander* Variegatum
Above left: *Nerium oleander* Roseum Plenum
Above: *Nerium oleander*
Right: *Nertera granadensis*

Neviusia

(for the discoverer, Rev. Ruben Denton Nevius, 1827–1913, of Alabama). ROSACEAE. A genus of 1 species of deciduous shrub from S.E. USA: *N. alabamensis*, snow wreath; to 2m tall, of spreading habit; leaves alternate 2·5–9cm long, ovate-oblong, finely double-toothed; flowers in small clusters terminating short, lateral, leafy shoots, petalless, each 2cm wide, with 5 whitish sepals and a conspicuous bunch of white stamens, late spring; often rather greenish-white in Britain and sometimes flowering poorly. Grow in well-drained fertile soil in sun. Plant autumn to spring. Propagate by soft cuttings in summer, bottom heat 18–21°C, or from seed when ripe or spring.

Nicandra

(for Nikander, about 150AD, a poet of ancient Greek city, Colophon, in Turkey, who wrote about plants and their uses). SOLANACEAE. A genus of 1 annual species from Peru: *N. physalodes*, shoo-fly, apple of Peru; stems erect, branched, 60–150cm tall; leaves alternate, ovate, 10–20cm or more long, irregularly sinuate-toothed or shallow-lobed; flowers solitary from upper leaf-axils, nodding, widely bell-shaped with 5 broad lobes, blue, 2·5–4cm wide; fruit a dryish, globose berry enclosed in the enlarged, lantern-shaped calyx. Grow in fertile, well-drained soil in sun or as a pot plant. Sow seed *in situ* in spring or under glass in mid spring at 16°C for earlier flowering.

Nicotiana

(for Jean Nicot, 1530–1600, ambassador to Portugal who introduced tobacco to France). Tobacco. SOLANACEAE. A genus of 66 species of annuals, perennials, rarely shrubs, from warm temperate to tropical N. and S. America, Polynesia and Australasia. They have generally ovate to lanceolate leaves in a basal tuft or rosette, erect-branched stems with smaller alternate leaves, and terminal racemes of long-tubed, 5-lobed flowers, often only expanding fully at dusk. The species described here, including the perennials, are mostly grown as half-hardy annuals, but may be grown as pot plants under glass. Grow in humus-rich, well-drained soil in sun, in frost free areas. Sow seed under glass early to mid spring at about 18°C. Sow thinly on the surface of the compost but do not cover. Prick off seedlings as soon as they are large enough to handle into boxes of potting mixture, at 4–5cm apart each way. Harden off and plant out post-frosts in early summer. For pot culture under glass use 15–18cm containers.

Species cultivated: *N. affinis*, see *N. alata* Grandiflora. *N. alata*, flowering tobacco: S. America; sticky hairy perennial to 90cm or more tall; basal leaves ovate, 10–25cm long; flowers 6–10cm long, white within, green-tinted without, summer-opening, and fragrant at dusk. *N.a.* Grandiflora (*N. affinis*), flowers larger than type, yellowish without, sometimes survives mild winters (see *N.* × *sanderae* for cultivars with red flowers). *N. forgetiana*, see *N.* × *sanderae*. *N. glauca*, tree tobacco; S. Bolivia to N. Argentina, naturalized in many warm countries; shrub or small tree 3–10m tall in mild climates; often grown as an annual for its smooth, glaucous, ovate leaves, to 25cm long; flowers 3–4·5cm long, yellow, summer. *N. rustica*, wild or Turkish tobacco; Ecuador to Bolivia; sticky, downy annual, 45–90cm tall; leaves elliptic to ovate cordate, to 20cm long; flowers to 2cm long, greenish-yellow; seldom grown for ornament, but the original tobacco plant and first to be introduced to Europe; still much grown as a source of nicotine for insecticides etc. *N.* × *sanderae* (*N. alata* × *N. forgetiana*), similar to *N. alata*, but flowers in shades of red inherited from *N. forgetiana*, a Brazilian species with small, red blooms that remain open by day; several cultivar strains are available in shades of white, pink and red, some of which open by day. *N. suaveolens*, S.E. Australia; annual, 60–100cm tall; leaves lanceolate to oblanceolate, 10–25cm long with winged stalk; flowers nodding, to 3cm long by 4cm wide, purple-veined cream without, white within, fragrant at night. *N. sylvestris*, Argentina; similar to *N. alata* Grandiflora, but more robust, to 1·5m or more tall; flowers longer, the tube somewhat inflated in the middle, summer; a short-lived perennial in mild areas or if protected. *N. tabacum*, tobacco; tropical America, but not known as a truly wild species; sticky hairy annual or short-lived

New Jersey tea – see *Ceanothus americanus*.

New Zealand bur – see *Acaena*.

New Zealand flax – see *Phormium*.

New Zealand laburnum – see *Sophora microphylla*.

Above: *Nicandra physalodes*
Below: *Nicotiana alata* Sensation Mixed
Far right: *Nicotiana tabacum*

type, compact habit: almost hardy and survives outside in sheltered sites. *N. repens* (*N. rivularis*), white cup; Uruguay, Argentina, Chile; stems slender, creeping just under the soil and forming mats; leaves erect, oblong to spathulate, 3cm long; flowers above the leaves, cup-shaped, white, 3–5cm wide, summer. *N. rivularis*, see *N. repens*. *N. scoparia* (*N. frutescens*), Uruguay, Argentina; akin to *N. hippomanica*, but 45–90cm tall; leaves 2cm long; flowers 3–4cm wide, light blue with white margins, summer to autumn or much of the year as a greenhouse pot plant. *N.s. atroviolacea*, deep violet.

perennial to 2m or more tall; leaves lanceolate to ovate, to 40cm long; flowers 4–5·5cm long, usually pink, sometimes red or greenish-white; several cultivars specially bred for tobacco production are usually available, needing a rich, moisture-retentive soil in a sunny, sheltered site, or a warm area, to do really well.

Nierembergia

(for Juan Eusebio Nieremberg, 1595–1658, Spanish Jesuit and natural historian). SOLANACEAE. A genus of 30–35 species of perennials and sub-shrubs from Mexico to S. S.America. They are prostrate or erect, with linear to spathulate leaves and either terminal cymes or solitary, rotate or cup-shaped, 5-lobed flowers. *N. repens* is the hardiest, the others being grown as half-hardy annuals or as pot plants for a cool greenhouse. Grow in well-drained soil in sun. Plant spring. Propagate by cuttings in early autumn or from seed in spring at 16°C; *N. repens* is best divided in spring.

Species cultivated: *N. caerulea*, see *N. hippomanica violacea*. *N. frutescens*, see *N. scoparia*. *N. hippomanica*, Argentina; sub-shrub, 15–30cm or more tall; stems slender, much-branched; leaves linear-spathulate to 1·5cm long; flowers cup-shaped, 2cm wide, lavender with yellow throat, profusely borne, summer to autumn; usually represented in gardens by *N.h. violacea* (*N. caerulea*), with leaves linear-lanceolate, to 2·5cm long; flowers 3–4cm wide, violet-blue. *N.h.v.* Purple Robe, darker flowers than

Top left: *Nicotiana sylvestris*
Above left: *Nicotiana* Crimson Rocket
Top: *Nierembergia repens*
Above: *Nierembergia hippomanica violacea*

Nigella

(diminutive form of Latin *niger*, black – the colour of the seed). RANUNCULACEAE. A genus of 20 species of annuals from the Mediterranean to C. Asia, 1 of which is commonly cultivated: *N. damascena*, love-in-a-mist, devil-in-the-bush; N. Africa, S. Europe; erect, branched, wiry-stemmed, to 45cm or more tall; leaves cut into filament-like segments; flowers solitary, terminal, to 4cm wide, partially enclosed by

Above: *Nigella damascena* Persian Jewels Mixed

ruffs of filamentous bracts, sepals 5, petal-like, light blue, petals modified to nectaries, summer; fruit inflated globular capsules; several cultivars and mixed strains are available in shades of pale to deep blue, mauve, purple and pink. Grow in fertile, well-drained soil in sun. Propagate by seed sown *in situ* in spring or autumn, the latter sowing giving the larger plants.

Noble fir – see *Abies procera.*

Nolana

(Latin *nola*, a small bell – alluding to the flower shape). Chilean bellflower. NOLANACEAE. A genus of about 60 species of mainly fleshy-leaved perennials and sub-shrubs from Peru, Chile, Argentina, a few of which are sometimes available. They are prostrate, decumbent or ascending, with alternate or

Above: *Nolana paradoxa*

opposite, linear to oblong-ovate or spathulate leaves, and wide-spreading, bell- or funnel-shaped flowers. Fruit is a somewhat woody, deeply lobed capsule that breaks into 1–8 seeded sections when ripe. The species described are usually grown as half-hardy annuals, although in mild areas they may grow for a few years. Grow in sharply drained, moderately fertile soil in sun. Propagate from seed in spring at 13–16°C, pricking off seedlings into boxes of any standard potting mixture, the all-peat types mixed with ⅓-part coarse sand. Harden off young plants and set outside in early summer when fear of frost has passed.

Species cultivated: *N. acuminata* (*N. lanceolata*), Chile; prostrate to decumbent, to 10cm tall; leaves opposite, to 7cm or more long, narrowly lanceolate, downy; flowers to 4cm wide, deep blue with a white or pale yellow centre, summer. *N. atriplicifolia* and *N. grandiflora*, see *N. paradoxa*. *N. humifusa* (*N. prostrata*), Peru; similar to *N. paradoxa*, but leaves ovate to bluntly diamond-shaped, to 2·5cm long; flowers about 3cm wide. *N. lanceolata*, see *N. acuminata*. *N. paradoxa* (*N. atriplicifolia*, *N. grandiflora*), Chile; decumbent, to 15cm or sometimes more tall; leaves alternate, to 5cm long, ovate, downy; flowers 4–5cm wide, blue to purple-blue, with white or pale yellow throat, summer; the commonest species in cultivation. *N. prostrata*, see *N. humifusa*.

Nomocharis

(Greek *nomos*, meadow, and *charis*, grace or loveliness). LILIACEAE. A genus of about 15 species of bulbous-rooted perennials from E. Himalaya to W. China. They basically resemble *Lilium* and are closely related, but in most species the flowers open widely, saucer-shaped to almost flat, the inner tepals often much broader and sometimes fringed. Culture as for hardy *Lilium* species. Propagation mainly

Top: *Nomocharis aperta*
Above: *Nomocharis pardanthina*

from seed or by scales.

Species cultivated (all summer-flowering): *N. aperta*, W. China; 45–65cm tall; leaves lanceolate, 5–10cm long; flowers to 10cm wide, pink to light rose-purple, spotted and blotched crimson within. *N. farreri*, N.E. Burma; 60–90cm tall; leaves narrowly lanceolate, to 4cm long, whorled; flowers to 7·5cm wide, pink with a few red spots at base of inner 3 tepals. *N.* × *finlayorum* (*N.* × *hybrida*), race of hybrids derived from *N. farreri*, *N. mairei* and *N. pardanthina*, blending the parental characters in various ways. *N.* × *hybrida*, see *N.* × *finlayorum*. *N. mairei*, W. China; to 60cm or more tall; leaves

7–10cm long, ovate to lanceolate, often whorled; flowers almost flat, to 10cm wide, white, sometimes flushed purple without, rose-purple within. *N. oxypetala* (*Fritillaria o.*, *Lilium oxypetalum*), N.W. Himalaya; 20–25cm tall; leaves linear to lanceolate, 5–7cm long; flowers solitary, nodding, bell-shaped, greenish-yellow, 4–5cm long. *N. pardanthina*, S.W. China; 40–75cm or more tall; leaves ovate to lanceolate, 5cm long, in whorls; flowers to 7cm wide, almost flat, nodding, pink, basal ⅓ of inner tepals spotted purple-brown. *N. saluenensis*, N. Burma, W. China, S.E. Tibet; 60–90cm tall; leaves lanceolate to 7·5cm long; flowers to 9cm wide, pale pink or yellow, purple-spotted.

Nothofagus

(Greek *nothos*, false, *Fagus*, beech; S.Hemisphere equivalent of N.Hemisphere beech). FAGACEAE. A genus of 35–40 species (only 20 according to some

Top: *Nomocharis saluenensis*
Above: *Nothofagus procera* autumn colour

authorities) of trees from S. America, New Zealand, Australia, New Guinea, New Caledonia. They have a basic resemblance to *Fagus*, but in general the leaves are smaller, in many species evergreen, and the flower clusters and fruiting capsules or husks are smaller with nuts in 3s. Culture is much the same as for *Fagus* for the hardy, or almost hardy, species mentioned here, but shelter from cold winds is an advantage and necessary for the less hardy sorts and the soil must be neutral to acid. Propagation, while usually from seed, can also be by layering and several species can be grown from cuttings, especially when using a mist unit and rooting hormones.

Species cultivated: *N. antarctica*, Antarctic beech; Chile, Argentina; 15–30m or so tall; deciduous; leaves to about 2·5cm long, broadly ovate or somewhat triangular, often cordate at base, irregularly and minutely toothed, occasionally slightly lobed; fruiting husk 6–7mm long. *N.a.* Prostrata, branches low, arching to prostrate. *N. cunninghamii*, S.E. Australia, Tasmania; to 60m, usually much less, evergreen; leaves triangular to broadly ovate, irregularly toothed, glossy, 6–15mm long; fruiting husk about 6mm long, bristly. *N. dombeyi*, Chile, Argentina; to 25m tall but usually less; evergreen leaves ovate-lanceolate to broadly wedge-shaped or rounded, pointed, 2–4cm long, dark lustrous green above, paler beneath; almost deciduous in hard winters. *N. menziesii*, silver beech; New Zealand; to 20–30m tall, often much less and shrub-like; similar to *N. cunninghamii* but leaves doubly toothed and with small, hairy pits (domatia) in basal vein axils; fruiting husks 6–7mm long, with gland-tipped appendages. *N. obliqua*, roblé; Chile, Argentina; to 30m in gardens or more in the wild; deciduous; leaves ovate to oblong, asymmetric, usually shallowly lobed, finely toothed, 4–7·5cm long, often somewhat glaucous beneath; fruiting husk bristly, about 1cm long; one of the easiest and hardiest species. *N. procera*, rauli; Chile, Argentina; to 24m tall; deciduous; leaves oblong to narrowly oval, very finely toothed, 4–10cm long, often colouring well in autumn; fruiting husks about 1cm long bearing fringed appendages; this and *N. obliqua* are now grown for timber in Britain.

Below: *Nothofagus dombeyi*
Right below: *Notholirion campanulatum*
Right bottom: *Notholirion thompsonianum*

Notholirion

(Greek *nothus*, false, and *leirion*, lily). LILIACEAE. A genus of 4 species of bulbous plants from Asia. They are allied to *Lilium* and *Fritillaria* with a general resemblance to the former genus but differ in having monocarpic bulbs with a papery, outer tunic, basal leaves that appear in autumn, and stigmas cleft into 3 narrow branches (those of *Fritillaria*, *Lilium* and *Cardiocrinum* are thickened and somewhat 3-lobed). Culture as for *Lilium* and will thrive in limy soils. The winter leaves can be damaged by frosts and gales and the bulb subsequently weakened, so grow in a sheltered site or under glass. Plant bulbs shallowly. Porpagation is easy by detaching after flowering and planting out the usually numerous bulblets produced by flowered bulbs; these die after blooming.

Species cultivated: *N. bulbiferum* (*N. hyacinthinum*), W. China and S. Tibet to Nepal; stems 60–100cm tall; basal leaves 30–45cm long; flowers 7–30, carried horizontally, about 2·5cm long, tepals broad, wide-

spreading, pale lavender-blue, green-tipped. *N. campanulatum*, S.W. China, N. Burma and adjacent Tibet; stems 90–120cm tall; basal leaves to 30cm long; flowers in long raceme, nodding, 4–5cm long, dark red, tipped green, summer. *N. hyacinthinum*, see *N. bulbiferum*. *N. thompsonianum* (*Fritillaria* and

Right: *Notospartium carmichaeliae*
Below right: *Nuphar lutea*

Lilium t.), W. Himalaya to Afghanistan; stems 60–90cm tall; basal leaves up to 45cm long by 2–3cm wide; flowers 10–30, fragrant, carried horizontally, to 6·5cm long, the tepals very narrow, pale rose-purple, mid summer; the easiest species to cultivate and most readily obtainable.

Nothopanax — see *Pseudopanax*.

Notospartium

(Greek *notos*, southern, and *Spartium*, weaver's or Spanish broom – the genus is a S.Hemisphere counterpart of the European broom). Southern broom. LEGUMINOSAE. A genus of 3 species of trees and shrubs from S.Island, New Zealand. They bear alternate, simple leaves in the seedling and young plant stages, but thereafter are largely leafless, having slender, slightly flattened, drooping green stems and lateral racemes of small pea flowers. The pods do not split explosively but break up into 1-seeded sections. Grow in well-drained soil in sunny, sheltered sites, against a south or west wall in colder parts or in a frost-free greenhouse. Plant autumn or spring. Propagate from seed when ripe or spring in a cold frame, or by cuttings late summer, bottom heat about 18°C and over-wintering the young plants in a frame until the following summer.
Species cultivated: *N. carmichaeliae*, pink broom; 2–4m tall; stems flattened, 2·5–3·5mm wide; racemes to 5cm long, flowers crowded, 8mm long, pink to lilac-pink with darker veins, summer. *N. glabrescens*, to 4m or more tall, to 10m in the wild; similar to *N. carmichaeliae* but racemes looser, flowers pinkish-purple, to 12mm long, early summer.

Nuphar

(from *naufar*, the Arabic vernacular for water-lily). NYMPHAEACEAE. A genus of about 25 species of aquatics from N. Hemisphere. They have thick, creeping rhizomes, heart-shaped, submerged, floating or aerial leaves on flexible stalks, and rounded flowers formed of 4–6 petaloid sepals and numerous, narrow petals followed by squat, bottle-shaped, berry-like capsules. Grow in water up to 1m deep in sun or light shade. Ideally grow in natural mud bottom, although plants may be invasive, otherwise set in baskets of humus-rich soil, eg equal parts heavy loam and well-decayed manure or compost surfaced with pebbles. Plant spring as growth starts. Propagate by division at planting time or from seed when ripe in pots just submerged in tanks of water, ideally in a cold frame.
Species cultivated: *N. advena*, yellow pond-lily, common spatterdock; E. and C. USA; leaves oblong to rounded, to 40cm long, usually above the water; flowers 3–4cm above water, 6–10cm wide, yellow, summer; will grow in slow-moving and brackish water. *N. lutea*, yellow water-lily, brandy-bottle; Europe, N. Africa, N. Asia; similar to *N. advena*, but leaves rarely more than 30cm long, mainly floating, some submerged; flowers about 6cm wide, bright yellow, summer. *N. minima*, see next entry. *N. pumila* (*N. minima* of gardens); N. and C. Europe, N. Asia; like a small version of *N. lutea*; leaves 10–14cm long, floating and submerged; flowers to 3·5cm wide, summer; a form in cultivation in gardens has orange-yellow flowers.

Nymphaea

(for Nymphe, one of the Greek water nymphs). NYMPHAEACEAE. A genus of 30–50 species of aqua-

Above: *Nymphaea* Escarboucle
Right: *Nymphaea* × *chromatella*

tics of almost cosmopolitan distribution. They have thick, sometimes tuberous rhizomes, rounded floating leaves on flexible stalks and cup-shaped, floating flowers with many petals, followed by a spongy, berry-like capsule. Culture of hardy species as for *Nuphar*. Tropical species need greenhouse treatment, tanks at least 1m sq, water temperature about 20°C. Plant tubers early summer and cover with 10cm of water. When several leaves have formed, fill tank gradually over a period of days. In autumn, when growth ceases, gradually reduce water level, then allow the layer or basket of compost almost to dry out. Finally store the tubers in sealed jars of barely moist sand at about 10°C. Propagate by dividing or separating the tubers. Some tropical species and hybrids produce plantlets at the junction of leaf-blade and stalk and these may be detached from the parent plant and potted when each has 3–4 leaves.

Species cultivated (hardy unless stated otherwise; all summer-flowering): *N. alba*, white water-lily, platter dock; Europe, Asia, N. Africa; leaves to 30cm wide, red when young; flowers 10–13cm wide, white. *N.a.* Froebeli, flowers deep red, fragrant; *N.a.* Gladstoniana, flowers to 25cm wide, white, fragrant, probably of hybrid origin; *N.a. rubra*, flowers rosy-pink. *N. caerulea*, N. and C.Africa; very similar to *N. stellata*, but leaves only wavy-margined; greenhouse. *N. capensis*, S. and E.Africa and Malagasy; similar to *N. stellata*, but leaves to 40cm wide and flowers with more petals. *N.* × *chromatella* (*N.* × *marliacea chromatella*), probably a hybrid between *N. mexicana* and *N. alba* or *N. tuberosa*; similar to the first parent; flowers canary-yellow, to 20cm wide. *N.* Escarboucle, flowers to 18cm wide, glowing ruby-red; best with water depth to 45cm. *N. flava*, see *N. mexicana*. *N.* Gladstoniana and *N.*

Above: *Nymphaea* × *marliacea* Carnea
Left: *Nymphaea* × Henry Shaw

Froebeli, see *N. alba*. *N.* Graziella, small, neat growth; leaves flecked red-brown; flowers 5cm wide, reddish-copper; suitable for tub culture, water depth not above 30cm. *N.* × *helvola* (*N. pygmaea helvola*), (*N. tetragona* × *N. mexicana*), similar to *N. tetragona*, but leaves blotched purple-brown; flowers sulphur-yellow. *N.* James Brydon, strong-growing; leaves purple-tinted; flowers 13–15cm wide, peony-shaped, deep rose-crimson with yellow stamens; water depth 30–60cm. *N.* × *laydekeri*, probably *N. alba rubra* × *N. tetragona*; similar to *N. alba* but smaller; leaves flecked red-brown; flowers 6·5–7·5cm wide. *N.* × *l.* Lilacea, flowers rosy-lilac; *N.* × *l.* Purpurata, rich wine-red, orange-red stamens, water depth not above 30cm. *N.* × *marliacea*, probably *N. alba* × *N. odorata rosea*; similar to first parent but more vigorous, flowers standing just above water. *N.* × *m.* Albida, flowers pure white, to 18cm wide; *N.* × *m.* Carnea, blush-white to pink, to 20cm wide; *N.* × *m.* Chromatella, see *N.* × *chromatella*. *N. mexicana* (*N. flava*). S. USA, Mexico; not fully hardy, except in warm areas; rhizome erect, tuber-like, spreading by runners; leaves 10–20cm wide, blotched red-brown above, suffused dull crimson beneath; flowers 10cm wide, bright yellow. *N.* × *moorei*, almost certainly *N. alba* × *N. mexicana* and very much like *N.* × *chromatella*. *N.* Mrs Richmond, vigorous growth, free-blooming; flowers to 25cm wide, pale to deep pink. *N. odorata*, N. and tropical America; similar to *N. alba*, but leaves duller green; flowers fragrant, opening in the mornings only. *N.o.* Alba, flowers pure white. *N.o.* Minor, plant less than half-sized; flowers white, 5–7cm wide; good for tubs or shallow pools, water depth 15–30cm. *N.o.* Sulphurea, flowers soft sulphur-yellow (not to be confused with

Left: *Nymphaea* Sunrise
Left below: *Nymphoides peltata*
Above: *Nymphaea* × *marliacea* Albida

the tender, deeper yellow-flowered *N. sulphurea* from Angola). *N.o.* Turicensis (*N. turicensis*), with soft rose, very fragrant flowers, probably belongs here. *N. pygmaea* (of gardens), probably *N. tetragona* × *N. alba*; similar to first parent but slightly larger; flowers sterile; see also *N. tetragona*. *N.p.* Alba, flowers white; *N.p.* Rubra, rose to wine-red, see also *N.* × *helvola*. *N.* × *robinsonii*, probably *N. alba rubra* × *N. mexicana*, but flowers yellow, overlaid rose to vermillion; hardy. *N. stellata*, blue lotus; S. and E. Asia; leaves to 30cm wide, irregularly sinuate-toothed, purple beneath; flowers 7·5–10cm or more wide, sky blue, fragrant; best under glass, needing frost-free conditions in winter. *N.* Sunrise, similar to *N. alba*, but larger; leaf- and flower-stalks hairy; flowers 20cm or more wide, deep primrose-yellow. *N. sulphurea*, see *N. odorata*. *N. tetragona* (*N. pygmaea*), Siberia to N. America; leaves 7–10cm wide, reddish beneath, blotched above when young; flowers white, 4–6·5cm wide, opening in the afternoon only; ideal for shallow pools, tubs, aquaria; water depth 15–30cm. *N. tuberosa*, magnolia water-lily; N. America; rhizomes bearing short, tuber-like, detachable branches; leaves to 38cm wide; flowers pure white, magnolia-like, 10–22cm wide; open in the morning. *N.t.* Richardsonii, flowers with extra petals. *N. turicensis*, see *N. odorata* Turicensis. The following tropical cultivars are sometimes available – in general they have large flowers standing well above the water and leaves variably mottled red-brown: Blue Beauty, deep blue flowers, attractive leaves; Emily Grant Hutchings, amaranth-red; General Pershing, pink, to 25cm wide; Henry Shaw, vigorous, free-flowering, large, bright blue; Juno, pure white; Director G. T. Moore, deep purple, smallish flowers but freely produced; Missouri, white, very large, opening at night, to 35cm wide; St. Louis, soft yellow, to 25cm wide.

Nymphoides

(*Limnanthemum*). (*Nymphaea*, and *oides*, like). Floating heart. MENYANTHACEAE (GENTIANACEAE). A genus of 20 species of aquatic perennials from tropical and temperate regions, 1 of which is generally available: *N. peltata* (*N. nymphaeoides*, *Limnanthemum nymphoides*, *L. peltatum*), fringed water lily, water fringe; Europe, Asia, naturalized elsewhere; rhizomatous, bottom-rooting, with vigorous, slender runners floating below the surface; leaves orbicular, deeply cordate, to 10cm wide on the surface; flowers 5-petalled, 3cm wide, yellow-fringed, in clusters from upper leaf-axils, opening well above water, summer to autumn. Ideally grow in shallow water over a mud bottom, or plant in baskets of loam or a proprietary compost with an anchoring layer of grit. Plant spring or summer. Propagate by cuttings of runners inserted *in situ*, baskets or pots in summer.

Nyssa

(for *Nysa* or *Nyssa*, one of the Greek water nymphs). Tupelo. NYSSACEAE. A genus of about 6 species of deciduous trees from N. America and Asia, 1 of which is widely available: *N. sylvatica*, black or sour gum, tupelo; E. USA; to 33m but often less in cultivation; leaves alternate, obovate to elliptic, 5–12cm long, usually glossy; flowers unisexual, very small, 5-petalled, greenish-white, the males in stalked, umbel-like clusters, the females in groups of 2–3 or more, early summer; fruit blue-black, berry-like drupes, 1–1·5cm long, autumn; cultivated primarily for autumn colour, the leaves turning bright scarlet to deep red and yellow. *N. aquatica*, cotton gum; S.E. USA; of similar height to *N. sylvatica*, leaves to 25cm long, fruit purple. Suited to wetter swampy areas but less commonly found outside the USA. Grow in moisture-retentive, humus-rich, neutral to acid soil in a sunny site sheltered from strong winds. Plant autumn to spring. Propagate from seed when ripe in a cold frame, pricking off seedlings individually into pots, or by layering into pots in spring. Young plants resent root disturbance and should therefore be set out in permanent sites as soon as the seedlings are big enough.

Oak – see *Quercus*.

Oenothera

(Greek vernacular *oinotheros* or *onotheros*, probably for a species of willow-herb, transferred to this genus by Linnaeus). Evening primrose. ONAGRACEAE. A genus of 80 species mainly of annuals and perennials from N. and S.America. They have alternate, obovate to linear, sometimes

Left: *Nyssa sylvatica*
Below: *Oenothera tetragona fraseri*

pinnatifid leaves and 4-petalled, often large, cup-shaped flowers in spikes, or solitary in upper leaf axils; fruit an ovoid to cylindrical capsule, with corky ribs or wings in some semi-desert species, eg *O. acaulis*, opening only when wet. Grow in well-drained soil in sun, the marginally hardy sorts in sheltered sites. Plant hardy species autumn to spring, the others in spring. Propagate all species from seed in spring, preferably under glass, the hardy clump-forming ones also by division at planting time, or cuttings of young shoots early summer.

Species cultivated: *O. acaulis* (*O. taraxacifolia*), Chile; tufted perennial, usually short-lived; leaves oblanceolate, 10–20cm long, pinnatifid with very large, lobed, terminal leaflet, usually red-spotted; flowers sessile, 5–7cm wide on slender corolla tube, 5–10cm long, pure white ageing pale rose-purple, opening late afternoon or evening; not reliably hardy but can be grown as an annual if sown under glass. *O.a.* Aurea, flowers yellow. *O. albicaulis nuttallii*, see *O. nuttallii*. *O. berlandieri*, see *O. speciosa childsii*. *O. biennis*, common evening primrose; N. America; usually biennial, with fleshy edible root; rosette leaves narrowly oblanceolate, 10–30cm long; stems 50–100cm tall with smaller lanceolate leaves; flowers about 4cm wide, yellow, summer to autumn. *O. caespitosa*, W. N.America; much like *O. acaulis* but leaves linear-lanceolate, sinuate-pinnatifid. *O. cinaeus*, see *O. tetragona fraseri*. *O. × erythrosepala* (*O. lamarckiana*), probably *O. biennis* × *O. hookeri* and very similar to latter parent but with broadly lanceolate leaves, red-striped sepals and always yellow petals. *O. flava*, W. USA; similar to *O. caespitosa* but leaves with a long, tapered point, and short, narrow lobes in lower part; flowers pale yellow, 2·5–4cm wide. *O. fruticosa*, E. USA; hardy perennial – not shrubby despite its name – basal leaves ovate to spathulate, 2·5–7·5cm long; stems 30–60cm tall with smaller, lanceolate leaves; flowers 3–5cm wide, deep yellow, summer; seed capsule club-shaped, tapered to base; in general, plants listed in the trade under this name belong to the allied *O. tetragona*. *O.f. fraseri*, see *O.t. fraseri*. *O.f. youngii*, see *O. tetragona*. *O. glaber* of gardens, see *O. tetragona* Glaber. *O. glauca*, see *O. tetragona fraseri*. *O. hookeri*, W. USA; biennial or short-lived perennial; stems to 1·2m tall; basal rosette leaves lanceolate to elliptic-oblanceolate, sinuate-toothed, more or less wrinkled, 10–18cm long; flowers 5–6cm wide, yellow, ageing orange-red, summer to autumn. *O. lamarckiana*, see *O.* × *erythrosepala*. *O. macrocarpa*, see next entry. *O. missouriensis* (*O. macrocarpa*), Missouri and Kansas to Texas; tufted perennial; stems decumbent, to 40cm long; leaves lanceolate, 3–10cm long; flowers to 8cm wide, bright yellow, often ageing reddish, summer to autumn. *O. nuttallii* (*O. albicaulis nuttallii*), N.W. N.America; rhizomatous perennial 40–100cm tall; leaves linear to oblong lanceolate, 2–10cm long; flowers white, ageing pink, 4–5cm wide, summer; for the dwarf, yellow-flowered plant also named *nuttallii*, see *O. tanacetifolia*. *O. odorata*, see *O. stricta*. *O. pallida*, W. USA; similar to *O. nuttallii*, 20–50cm tall; leaves to 5cm long. *O.p. trichocalyx* (*O. trichocalyx*), leaves grey-green, usually wavy-toothed. *O. perennis* (*O. pumila*), E. N.America; perennial, 20–60cm tall; basal leaves oblanceolate to spathulate, 2·5–5cm long; stems erect, slender, with smaller linear-lanceolate leaves; flowers yellow, 1·5–2cm wide, sepals often reddish, summer. *O. pumila*, see *O. perennis*. *O. riparia*, see *O. tetragona riparia*. *O. speciosa*, S. USA, Mexico; perennial, to 60cm tall, superficially like *O. nuttallii* but leaves sometimes pinnately lobed and flowers more widely expanded. *O.s. childsii* (*O. berlandieri* of some authorities), stems slender, to 15cm tall; flowers smaller, rose-red. *O. stricta* (*O. odorata*, *O. sulphurea* of gardens), Chile; erect to decumbent, usually short-lived perennial, 60–90cm tall; basal leaves linear-lanceolate, to 10cm long, with well-spaced, sharp teeth; stems slender, reddish, bearing shorter, broader leaves; flowers 2·5–4·5cm wide, pale yellow, ageing red, summer to autumn. *O. sulphurea*, see *O. stricta*. *O. tanacetifolia* (*O. nuttallii* in part), similar to, and sometimes confused in cultivation with, *O. flava*, but leaves deeply pinnatifid throughout and with a short, blunter tip; flowers yellow ageing red. *O. taraxacifolia*, see *O. acaulis*. *O. tetragona* (*O. fruticosa youngii*, *O. youngii* of gardens), E. USA; much like *O. fruticosa*, but with gland-tipped hairs on calyx and seed capsule, the latter oblongoid, angular, abruptly tapered to base. *O.t. fraseri* (*O. cinaeus*, *O. fruticosa fraseri*, *O. glauca*), plant hairless, leaves oval to broadly ovate, wavy-toothed, glaucous beneath; *O.t.f.* Fyrverkeri (*O.t.f.* Fireworks), to 45cm, flower-buds waxy-red; *O.t.* Glaber, about 45cm tall, leaves mahogany-flushed; *O.t. riparia* (*O. riparia*), stems well-branched, forming low bushes to 23cm tall. *O. trichocalyx*, see *O. pallida t.* *O. youngii*, see *O. tetragona*.

Top left: *Oenothera caespitosa*
Left: *Oenothera missouriensis*
Above: *Olea europaea*

Old man – see *Artemisia abrotanum*.

Old man's beard – see *Clematis vitalba*.

Olea

(ancient Latin vernacular for olive). OLEACEAE. A genus of 20 species of evergreen trees and shrubs from the E.Hemisphere, 1 of which is generally available: *O. europaea*, olive; Mediterranean; large shrub or tree, 5–14m tall; leaves in opposite pairs, 2–8cm long, lanceolate to narrowly obovate, dark greyish-green above, densely scaly and pale grey beneath; flowers 5mm wide, white, shortly tubular, 4-lobed, in axillary panicles, late summer; fruit plum-like, 1–3·5cm long, glossy black when ripe and yielding the olive oil of commerce. This description refers to the cultivated olive, *O.e. europaea* (*O.e. communis*, *O.e. sativa*); the wild olive, *O.e. sylvestris* (*O.e. oleaster*), has inedible fruit and angular, spiny stems. Frost-free greenhouse or a sheltered, sunny site outside in mild areas. Grow in any standard potting mixture or well-drained soil. Pot or plant spring. Propagate by cuttings with a heel late summer, bottom heat 18–20°C, or from seed in spring at similar temperature.

Oleander – see *Nerium*.

Olearia

(for *Olearius*, the Latin pseudonym of Adam Olschlager, 1603–71, a German botanist; also said to derive from *Olea* – olive – alluding to the likeness of some species). Daisy bush. COMPOSITAE. A genus of 100–130 species of evergreen shrubs or small trees from Australasia. They have mainly alternate (rarely opposite), leathery, ovate to linear leaves, and axillary and terminal clusters (rarely solitary) of mainly white, small, daisy-like flower-heads. The genus has a reputation for tenderness but a number of species are hardier than often thought and may be grown where frosts are regular but light; none will survive a severe winter. All thrive near the sea, standing strong winds and salt spray well and many are tolerant of regular clipping, making good hedges. Grow in any well-drained, fairly moisture-retentive soil in sun. Plant spring. Propagate by heel cuttings late summer, seed when ripe, or spring, under glass.

Species cultivated (all from New Zealand unless otherwise stated): *O. albida*, shrub 2–3m tall (tree to 8m in wild); leaves 5–10cm long, ovate-oblong, undulate, white-felted beneath; flower-heads 7mm long, in panicles, late summer; rarely seen in gardens, the plant under this name often being the somewhat hardier *O. avicenniifolia*, see next species. *O. avicenniifolia*, similar to *O. albida*, but leaves elliptic to oblong-lanceolate, felted buff or off-white beneath; individual flower-heads with 2–3 florets only (*O. albida* 3–10). *O. chatamica* see *O. semidentata*. *O. erubescens*, Tasmania, Victoria; shrub to 1m or more; leaves 1·5–4cm long, oblanceolate to obovate, irregularly and sharply toothed, dark lustrous green above, silky red-brown downy beneath; flower-heads in clusters of 3–5, each about 2·5cm wide, ray florets white or pale pinkish-purple, mid summer; often represented in gardens by *O. e. ilicifolia* with larger leaves and flower-heads; needs sheltered wall. *O. forsteri*, see *O. paniculata*, *O. frostii* (*Aster f.*, *O. stellulata f.*), Bogong daisy bush; Victoria Range; shrub to 1·5m tall, downy throughout; leaves 1·5–3cm long, deep sage-green; flower-heads 1–3, about 3cm wide, ray florets mauve to lilac, summer to autumn; a comparative newcomer

Far left: *Olearia macrodonta*
Bottom left: *Olearia ilicifolia*
Left: *Olearia semidentata*

to gardens and probably hardier than sometimes stated. *O. gunniana*, see *O. phlogopappa*. *O.* × *haastii* (*O. avicenniifolia* × *O. moschata*, originally collected in the wild), dense, rounded shrub to 2m (rarely to 3m) tall; leaves 1·5–2·5cm long, leathery, deep green above, white-felted beneath; flower-heads 6–8mm long in profusely borne clusters, early autumn. *O. ilicifolia*, mountain holly; compact shrub to 2m (rarely to 5m) tall; leaves 5–10cm long, narrowly oblong to lanceolate, strongly undulate with almost spiny teeth, smooth whitish-felted beneath; flower-heads about 8mm long, fragrant, in large terminal corymbs, summer. *O. insignis* (*Pachystegia i.*), spreading shrub rarely above 1m tall in gardens (to 2m in wild); stems robust, white-felted; leaves 7–16cm long, oblong-obovate to obovate, lustrous above, thickly white- or buff-felted below; flower-heads 5–7·5cm wide on long stalks from upper leaf-axils, summer to autumn. *O.i. minor*, smaller than type in all its parts, to about 30cm tall; flower-heads to 4·5cm wide; needs a sheltered site, but generally hardier than stated. *O. lirata*, see *O. scillonensis*. *O. macrodonta*, large shrub or small tree 3–6m tall; leaves 5–10cm long, ovate to oblong, undulate with coarse, firm teeth, lustrous above, silvery-white-felted beneath; flower-heads 6–8mm long in large terminal corymbs, summer. *O.m.* Major, larger leaves and inflorescences than type; *O.m.* Minor, dwarf form to 1·5m tall, with smaller leaves. *O.* × *mollis* Zennorensis (*O. ilicifolia* × *O. lacunosa*), shrub to 2m tall; leaves linear-lanceolate, to 10cm long, saw-toothed, somewhat lustrous olive-green above, whitish beneath, shy flowering but a handsome foliage plant, probably hardier than stated; for the *O.* × *mollis* of gardens, see in next entry. *O. moschata*, dense, rounded shrub to 2m tall; leaves 8–15mm long, oblong to obovate, closely white-felted and musk-scented; flower-heads 6–7mm long, in axillary corymbs, summer. *O.m.* × *ilicifolia*, generally but incorrectly known as *O.* × *mollis*, is similar to type, but has elliptic, blunt-pointed, waved and crinkly-toothed leaves to 4·5cm long; see also under *O.* × *mollis*. *O. nummulariifolia*, shrub of dense erect habit, 1–3m tall; leaves dense, 5–10mm long, broadly obovate to rounded, margins recurved, whitish- or buff-felted beneath, deep yellow-green above; flower-heads solitary, 8–10mm long, fragrant, summer. *O.n. cymbifolia*, leaves more strongly rolled than type and appearing narrower. *O.* × *oleifolia* (perhaps *O. avicenniifolia* × *O. odorata*), slow-growing shrub to 1·5m or so, somewhat resembling *O.* × *haasti*, but leaves matt grey-green above, broadly lanceolate, some to 8cm long; *O.* × *o.* Waikariensis, leaves lanceolate, somewhat glossy above, buff beneath; the plant grown under this name is like *O.* × *oleifolia* with leaves rarely above 5–6cm long (sometimes misspelt Waikensis). *O. paniculata* (*O. forsteri*), shrub or small tree to 6m tall; leaves 3–10cm long, elliptic to ovate-oblong, undulate, lustrous above, buff- or white-felted beneath; flower-heads 4–5mm long, in axillary corymbs, fragrant, autumn to winter; suitable only for mild areas where it makes a good hedge. *O. phlogopappa* (*Aster p.*, *O. gunniana*, *O. stellulata* in part – of gardens), S.E. Australia, Tasmania; erect shrub, 1–2m tall; stems white-felted; leaves oblong to elliptic or oblanceolate, 1–5cm long, deep matt-green above, toothed, white or grey-white beneath; flower-heads about 2cm wide, early summer; a variable species. *O.p.* Splendens, a grex name covering forms with flowers in shades of pink, mauve, purple, blue, generally with smaller leaves and less vigour – best pruned after flowering. *O.* × *scillonensis*, a hybrid between *O. phlogopappa* and the allied and similar *O. lirata*, is much like *O. phlogopappa* but more vigorous and floriferous and is now the most commonly seen of this type. *O.*

Above: *Oleria phlogopappa* Splendens
Right: *Omphalodes cappadocica* Anthea Bloom
Right above: *Omphalodes cappadocica*

semidentata, Chatham Is; rounded shrub to 1m or more tall; stems white-felted; leaves 3·5–7cm long, narrowly lanceolate, toothed in upper half, glossy deep green above, white-felted beneath; flower-heads solitary, to 3·5cm wide, ray florets purple, summer; the plant in Britain under this name has flower-heads 4–5cm wide with pale purple florets and leaves toothed to near the base, and is most probably a hybrid with the allied *O. chatamica*; requires cool, moist summers and no more than light frosts in winter to thrive. *O. solandri*, shrub 2–4m tall, much-branched and heath-like; twigs yellowish, downy; leaves in opposite clusters, on young plants to 1·5cm long, linear-spathulate, on mature plants 5–10mm, linear-obovate; flowers to 1cm long, solitary, fragrant, late summer to mid autumn. *O. stellulata*, Tasmania, S.E. Australia; similar to *O. phlogopappa*, but leaves to 9cm long by 2cm wide, clothed with starry, yellowish hairs beneath; most plants under this name are referable to *O. phlogopappa*. *O.s. frostii*, see *O. frostii*. *O.s.* Splendens, see *O. phlogopappa*. *O. traversii*, Chatham Is; large shrub or small tree, 5–7m tall; stems 4-angled, silvery-whitish; leaves 4–6·5cm long, in opposite pairs, oblong to obovate, with closely pressed, silky white hairs beneath; flower-heads 6–7mm long in axillary panicles, summer; good for exposed sites near the sea. *O. virgata*, much-branched shrub 2–3m tall; stems slender, 4-angled; leaves in opposite clusters, 6–12mm long, linear-obovate; flowers solitary, in small clusters, 4–5mm long, summer; usually represented in cultivation by *O.v. lineata*, to 5m tall, branchlets drooping, leaves linear, 2–2·5cm long. *O.* × *zennorensis*, see *O.* × *mollis* Zennorensis.

Olive – see *Olea*.

Omphalodes

(Greek *omphalos*, a navel: the cupped seed – nutlet – is likened to a human navel). BORAGINACEAE. A genus of 24–28 species of annuals and perennials from Europe, Asia, Mexico. They are basically similar to *Cynoglossum*, though often smaller and with relatively larger flowers; fruit of 4 nutlets in at least 1 species with inrolled margins and appearing cupped. Culture as for *Cynoglossum*, but mostly more shade-tolerant. The annual *O. linifolia* may be sown *in situ* in spring.

Species cultivated: *O. cappadocica*, Turkey; rhizomatous perennial, forming colonies; leaves tufted, long-stalked, ovate-cordate, 5–9cm long; flowers to 8mm wide, deep blue with white eye, in loose cymes, 15–25cm tall, early summer. *O.c.* Anthea Bloom, flowers sky-blue, leaves greyish. *O. linifolia* (*Cynoglossum l.*), Venus's navelwort; S.W. Europe; erect annual to 30cm tall; leaves glaucous, spathulate to lanceolate, 1–5cm long; flowers to 1cm wide, white or blue-tinted, summer. *O. luciliae*, Greece, Turkey; tufted perennial; leaves bright glaucous, ovate, elliptic to oblong, to 5cm or more; flowers 1cm wide, soft blue from pink buds, summer; needs well-drained limy soil in sun. *O. verna*, C.S. Europe; stoloniferous perennial forming

mats; leaves ovate to ovate-cordate, 5–20cm long; flowers 8–10mm wide, deep clear blue, spring; best in light shade. *O.v.* Alba, flowers white.

Onoclea

(Greek *onos*, a vessel, and *kleio*, to close – alluding to the closely-rolled fertile fronds). ASPIDIACEAE (POLYPODIACEAE). A genus of 1 species of fern from temperate regions in both hemispheres: *O. sensibilis*, sensitive fern; rhizomatous, sterile fronds solitary, to 60cm or more tall, long-stalked, the blade triangular-ovate, deeply pinnatipartite, the pinnae wavy-toothed; fertile fronds much smaller, bipinnate, the pinnae erect and pinnules rolled around the sori, dark brown to blackish when mature; the vernacular name refers to the sensitivity of the fronds to the first frosts of autumn. Grow in any moisture-retentive soil in sun or shade. Plant and propagate by division or spores in spring. Illustrated overleaf.

Ononis

(Greek vernacular for some species – used by Linnaeus for whole genus). LEGUMINOSAE. A genus of about 75 species of annuals, perennials, subshrubs from Canary Is, Mediterranean, Europe to C.Asia. They have alternate, trifoliate or unifoliate, rarely pinnate leaves and pea-shaped flowers from the upper axils, sometimes forming leafy racemes or panicles. Grow in well-drained soil in sun. Plant autumn or spring. Propagate perennials by basal cuttings in late spring, shrubs by cuttings late summer, seed in spring — annuals *in situ*.

Species cultivated: *O.aragonensis*, Pyrenees, E. and C.Spain; shrub 15–30cm tall; stems often contorted; leaves trifoliate, leaflets 4–10mm long, elliptic to rounded, obtuse or notched-tipped; flowers

1·2–1·8cm long, yellow, in loose panicles, summer. *O. cenisia*, see next species. *O. cristata* (*O. cenisia*), mountains of E.Spain, Apennines, S.W.Alps; rhizomatous perennial 10–25cm tall; stems glandular downy; leaves trifoliate, leaflets 5–10mm long, oblong to oblanceolate, toothed; flowers 1–1·4cm long, pink in raceme-like clusters, summer. *O. fruiticosa*, shrubby restharrow; mountains of Spain and S.E.France; erect shrub, 25–60cm or more tall; leaves mostly trifoliate, leaflets 7–25mm long, oblong-lanceolate; flowers 1–2cm long, in raceme-like clusters, pink to rose-purple, summer. *O. natrix*, large yellow restharrow; S. and W.Europe; bushy erect shrub 20–60cm tall; stems sticky glandular hairy; leaves trifoliate, the lower ones rarely pinnate, leaflets 1–2cm long, narrowly oblong to ovate; flowers 1·2–2cm long, yellow, usually with red or purple veins, in leafy panicles, early to late summer. *O. rotundifolia*, round-leaved restharrow; mountains of S.E.Spain to Austria and C.Italy; shrub 35–50cm tall; leaves trifoliate, leaflets 2·5cm long, elliptic to orbicular, coarsely toothed; flowers 1·5–2cm long, pale to deep pink, the standard with red veins, summer.

Onopordum

(*Onopordon*). (Greek *onos*, an ass, and *porde*, fart). COMPOSITAE. A genus of about 25 species of biennial or monocarpic plants from Europe, N. Africa, W. Asia. They form large rosettes of oblong-lanceolate, often lobed and spiny margined basal leaves the first year (sometimes 2 or 3 years), and then a tall, branched, leafy and winged stem bearing several large, thistle-like flower-heads. Grow in any well-drained, moderately fertile soil in sun. Propagate by seed ideally sown *in situ* in spring; alternatively, sow in a nursery bed, transplant following autumn, retaining as much of the root system as possible. Plants may also be raised in containers.

Species cultivated: *O. acanthium*, cotton or Scotch thistle; Europe, Asia; whole plant cottony white hairy; basal leaves lobed, spiny, 35–60cm or more long; stem 2–3m tall; flower-heads to 5cm wide, florets pale purple, summer. *O. arabicum*, see next entry. *O. nervosum* (*O. arabicum*), S. and C. Spain and Portugal; similar in overall appearance to *O. acanthium*, but lacking the dense, white hairs; leaves green with pale veins; flowers pink.

Onosma

(Greek *onos*, an ass, and *osme*, a smell – the roots of some species reputedly have an animal odour). BORAGINACEAE. A genus of about 130 species of

Far left top: *Ononis natrix*
Left: *Onoclea sensibilis*
Top left: *Ononis rotundifolia*
Below: *Onopordum acanthium*

hispid annuals, perennials and sub-shrubs from the Mediterranean, Himalaya, China. They have a tufted habit, alternate, oblong to linear leaves, and scorpioid cymes of nodding, tubular, 5-lobed flowers from the upper leaf-axils. Grow in well-drained soil in sun, those species disliking winter wet in a dry wall or in pans in an alpine house. Propagate from seed under glass in spring, or by cuttings of small, unflowered shoots in summer.
Species cultivated: *O. alboroseum* (*O. albopilosum* of gardens), Turkey; low-growing, sub-shrubby perennial to 20cm tall; leaves oblong-spathulate, white starry hairy; flowers about 2·5cm long, opening white, ageing to deep rose from the mouth downwards, summer; best in dry wall or alpine house. *O. echioides*, Italy, Sicily, W. Balkan Peninsula; woody-based perennial, 15–30cm tall; leaves 2–6cm long, narrowly oblong, with dense to sparse starry hairs; flowers 2–2·5cm long, pale yellow, summer. *O. stellulatum*, W. Yugoslavia; woody-based perennial, to 25cm tall; leaves 4–10cm or more long, oblong-spathulate, downy and starry-bristly; flowers 2cm long, pale yellow, summer. *O. tauricum*, S.E. Europe; similar to *O. stellulatum*, but flowers to 3cm long, calyx 10–13mm long (*O. stellulatum* 7–9mm) and individual flower-stalks about 2mm (*O. stellulatum* 6–14mm).

Ophiopogon

(Greek *ophis*, snake, and *pogon*, beard, based on a translation from the Japanese vernacular *ja-no-hige*, beard of serpents; perhaps a fanciful allusion to the shape of the opening flower-buds). Lilyturf. LILIACEAE. A genus of 10 or more species of evergreen perennials from Himalaya to Japan and Philippines. They are tufted, often stoloniferous or rhizomatous, with leathery, grassy leaves and racemes of small, 6-tepalled, bell-shaped, nodding flowers followed by berry-like seed. *Ophiopogon* may be confused with the allied *Liriope* but that genus has the individual flowers facing outwards or upwards on straight stalks. Grow in well-drained, preferably humus-rich soil in shade. The species described are fairly hardy in all but the severest winters, the tenderest being the variegated forms of *O. jaburan*. This species makes a good and easy pot plant for the cool greenhouse or room. Plant or pot spring. Propagate by division at planting time and from seed when ripe.
Species cultivated: *O. arabicus*, see *O. planiscapus* Nigrescens. *O. jaburan* (*Mondo j.*), Japan; tufted to clump-forming; leaves linear, to 60cm or more long, lustrous deep green; racemes 30–50cm tall, flowers

Left: *Onopordum acanthium*
Bottom left: *Onosma echioides*
Below: *Ophiopogon planiscapus* Nigrescens
Bottom: *Ophiopogon jaburan Viltatus*

7–8mm long, white to pale purple, summer; fruit oblongoid, violet-blue; sometimes confused in gardens with *Liriope muscari*. *O.j.* Vittatus (*O.j.* Variegatus of gardens), young leaves white-striped, gradually becoming totally green. *O. japonicus*, Japan; tufted, with underground stolons, mat-forming; leaves 10–20cm long, grassy, dark green; racemes 7–12cm tall, flowers 4–5mm long, lilac to white, summer; fruit pea-sized, deep blue. *O.j. wallichianus*, see *O. planiscapus*. *O. planiscapus* (*O. japonicus wallichianus*), similar in habit to *O. japonicus* but less dense in growth; leaves 30–50cm long; racemes 20–30cm tall, flowers 6–7mm long, white or pale purple, late summer; usually represented in cultivation by *O.p.* Nigrescens (*O. arabicus* of gardens) with purple-black leaves to 25cm long; racemes to 12cm tall and whitish flowers flushed violet; slow-growing and possibly not fully hardy.

Orache – see *Atriplex*.

Origanum

(ancient Greek vernacular *origanon* for marjoram). LABIATAE. A genus of 15–20 species of perennials and sub-shrubs from Europe, Mediterranean to C. Asia. They are generally erect with opposite pairs of ovate leaves and small, tubular, 2-lipped flowers, often in crowded spikelets that in turn are usually borne in terminal leafy panicles. Some species are aromatic. Grow in well-drained soil in sun, unreliably hardy ones in shelter. Plant spring, autumn. Propagate by division at planting, seed, preferably under glass, spring, cuttings late spring. **Species cultivated:** *O. amanum*, Turkey; low, bushy perennial to 10cm tall; leaves 5–13mm long, ovate, cordate, ciliate; flowers pink with a slender tube to 4cm long, in the axils of red-purple bracts, late summer; needs a sheltered site in sharply drained

soil and often short-lived. *O. dictamnus*, Cretan dittany; Greece, Crete; sub-shrub 20–30cm tall; leaves ovate to rounded, white woolly, 1·3–2·5cm long; flowers 9–12mm long, pink from hop-like spikelets of rose-red bracts, summer; needs alpine house treatment or sheltered scree. *O. hybridum* (*O. sipyleum*, *Amaracus s.*), Turkey; herbaceous perennial similar to *O. dictamnus* but leaves smooth or almost so. *O. laevigatum*, Syria, Turkey; forming wide clump, 30–40cm or more tall; leaves ovate, grey-green, lower ones to 2·5cm long, upper much smaller; flowers red-purple, about 8mm long (in the wild some forms to 14mm), autumn. *O. pulchrum*, see *O. scabrum pulchrum*. *O. rotundifolium*, N.E. Turkey; rhizomatous, woody-based perennial forming wide clumps; stems 10–20cm tall; leaves orbicular, bluish-grey, 2–3cm long; flowers pale pink, about 5mm long, almost hidden by bright pale green bracts 3–4cm long in nodding clusters, late summer. *O. scabrum*, mountains of Greece; rhizomatous, clump-forming; stems 30–45cm tall; leaves 1–3cm long, ovate to rounded, cordate; flowers pink, from ovoid, hop-like, nodding spikelets of purple, 8–19mm long bracts, summer. *O.s. pulchrum* (*O. pulchrum*), in cultivation represented by a compact plant 15–20cm tall, *O. sipyleum*, see *O. hybridum*. *O. tournefortii*, dittany of Amorgos; Crete, Greece; allied and similar to *O. dictamnus*, but leaves 1·5–3cm long, more densely borne, the clone in cultivation being glaucous and hairy (can be woolly or hairless in the wild); flowers longer, the tubes somewhat inflated.

Ornithogalum

(Greek *ornis*, a bird, and *gala*, milk – an unfortunate reference to the colour of the flowers, and birds' – doves' – excreta). LILIACEAE. A genus of 100–130

species of bulbous perennials from Europe, Asia, Africa. They have basal tufts of strap-shaped to linear, often channelled leaves, and leafless, erect, elongated or umbel-like racemes of starry, 6-tepalled flowers. Grow in any well-drained soil in sun, the tender species in warm, sheltered sites or lifted and stored frost-free during the winter. All may be grown in pots or pans of a standard potting mixture for flowering in a cool greenhouse. Plant or pot autumn, the tender species in spring. Propagate by offsets or division of congested clumps while dormant, or from seed when ripe or in spring. **Species cultivated:** *O. arabicum*, Mediterranean; leaves glaucous, narrowly strap-shaped, to 60cm long; racemes elongated, 40–60cm tall, flowers 5cm wide, pearly-white with black-green pistil, early summer; not reliably hardy, although will withstand some frost; not very free-flowering. *O. balansae*, N.E. Turkey, adjacent USSR; leaves broadly linear, channelled, to 8cm long; racemes few-flowered, to 10cm tall, flowers comparatively large, sometimes opening before the stem reaches full height, 2·5cm wide, white within, green without, early spring. *O. miniatum*, see *O. thyrsoides aureum*. *O. nutans*, drooping star of Bethlehem; Europe to W. Turkey; leaves linear, 30–45cm long; racemes elongated, 20–50cm tall, flowers nodding, 2–3cm long, silvery-white within, green without, not opening widely as in most other species, late spring. *O. pyramidale*, Mediterranean; leaves linear, somewhat fleshy, to 45cm long, withering during flowering; racemes elongated, 40–60cm tall, flowers 2·5cm wide, white, the segments green-striped without, late spring. *O. saundersiae*, giant chincherinchee; S. Africa; like a much taller version of *O. arabicum*; 1–2m tall; flowers cream with green-black pistil, summer; best under glass, or lifted in autumn in all the mildest areas. *O. thyrsoides*, chincherinchee, wonder flower;

Far left above: *Origanum amanum*
Left top: *Origanum hybridum*
Left above: *Origanum rotundifolium*
Top: *Origanum dictamnus*
Above: *Ornithogalum umbellatum*

S. Africa; leaves linear to lanceolate, to 30cm long, somewhat fleshy; racemes elongated, to 45cm tall, sometimes more, flowers 3–4cm wide, creamy-white, very long-lasting; best under glass or stored for the winter. *O.t. aureum* (*O. miniatum*), flowers yellow or orange. *O. umbellatum*, star of Bethlehem; Europe, N. Africa; leaves linear, 15–30cm long with silvery-white mid-rib; racemes umbel-like, 10–30cm tall, flowers 3–4cm wide, glistening white within, broad green stripe on each segment without, spring to early summer; produces numerous offsets and bulblets, and can become a weed on light soils.

Orobus vernus – see *Lathyrus vernus.*

Orontium

(Greek vernacular *orontion*, for a plant not now identifiable that grew in the River Orontes, Syria; name given to this plant by Linnaeus). Golden club. ARACEAE. A genus of 1 aquatic perennial from S.E. USA: *O. aquaticum*, leaves from a thick rhizome, in rosettes or tufts, blade somewhat glaucous, oblong-elliptic, to 30cm long, long-stalked and floating in deep water, standing above in shallow water; flowers tiny, 6-tepalled, in dense, spike-like spadix, 5–10cm long, above the water, early summer. Grow in water, ideally about 30cm deep but may range from 15–60cm. Plant spring in containers of equal parts clay-loam and decayed manure or compost, or else in the mud bottom of a natural pond. Propagate by division in spring or from seed when ripe in pans of compost covered with a few centimetres of water.

Orpine – see *Sedum telephium.*

Osier – see *Salix.*

Osmanthus

(Greek *osme*, fragrance, and *anthos*, flower). OLEACEAE. A genus of 30–40 species of evergreen trees and shrubs from E. Asia, Mexico, E. USA and Pacific Is. They have opposite pairs of ovate to lanceolate, often leathery leaves, and usually axillary clusters of tubular, 4-lobed flowers; fruit is a berry-like drupe seldom produced in cultivation. The species described are moderately hardy but likely to suffer some damage in moderate to severe winters; generally they do not survive the prolonged

Top left: *Ornithogalum nutans*
Left: *Orontium aquaticum*
Above: *Osmanthus heterophyllus* Aureomarginatus

cold of continental winters. Grow in humus-rich, moisture-retentive but well-drained soil in sheltered sites in sun or partial shade. Plant autumn or spring. Propagate by cuttings with a heel late summer, bottom heat about 18°C.

Species cultivated: *O. aquifolium*, see *O. heterophyllus*. *O. armatus*, W. China; shrub or small tree 2·5–5m tall; leaves 7–15cm long, oblong-lanceolate with triangular, hard-pointed teeth, rich matt green; flowers fragrant, 6mm long, creamy-white; thrives in sun or shade and hardier than sometimes stated. *O.* × *burkwoodii* (*O. delavayi* × *O. decorus*), bushy, spreading shrub to 3m tall; leaves ovate, 2·5–5cm

Below: *Osmanthus* × *burkwoodii*
Bottom: *Osmaronia cerasiformis*
Right: *Osmanthus delavayi*

long, slightly toothed, somewhat lustrous; flowers fragrant, white, 8–9mm long, in clusters of 6–7, spring; a useful hedging plant better known as × *Osmarea b. O. decorus* (*Phillyrea decora*), W. Asia (USSR); rounded shrub to 3m tall, often wider; leaves ovate-lanceolate, 5–13cm long, glossy deep green; flowers white, about 8mm long, in dense clusters, spring; fruit not infrequent, ovoid, black-purple, 1cm long; one of the hardiest species formerly and still best-known as a *Phillyrea. O. delavayi* (*Siphonosmanthus d.*), W. China; wide-spreading shrub to about 2m tall, occasionally much more; leaves ovate, 1–3cm long, toothed, glossy deep green; flowers fragrant, pure white, 9–12mm long, in axillary and terminal clusters of 4–8, spring. *O. heterophyllus* (*O. aquifolium, O. ilicifolius*), Japan; rounded shrub or small tree 2·5–6m tall; leaves holly-like, 4–7cm long, elliptic to oblong, with triangular, spine-tipped teeth; on mature plants the upper shoots may have leaves with few or no teeth and plants propagated from these growths retain the toothless foliage; flowers fragrant, white, 5mm long in clusters of 4–5, autumn; fruit oblongoid, 1–5cm long, blue-black; forms a distinctive hedge. *O.h.* Aureomarginatus (*O.h.* Aureovariegatus, *O.h.* Aureus), leaves yellow-margined; *O.h.* Myrtifolius, more slow-growing and compact habit, leaves toothless; *O.h.* Purpureus, young leaves black-purple, ageing purplish-green, hardier than the green-leaved species and cultivars; *O.h.* Variegatus (*O.h.* Argenteomarginatus), leaves white-margined. *O. ilicifolius*, see *O. heterophyllus*.

× **Osmarea** – see *Osmanthus* × *burkwoodii*.

Osmaronia

(Greek *osme*, fragrance, and the genus *Aronia* – alluding to the resemblances, plus scent). ROSACEAE. A genus of 1 species of deciduous shrub from W. N.America: *O. cerasiformis* (*Oemleria c.*, *Nuttallia c.*), Indian plum or oso berry; California to British Columbia; suckering, forming thickets of erect stems to 2·5m, sometimes more; leaves alternate, 5–9cm long, oblong-lanceolate, greyish beneath; flowers fragrant, usually dioecious, 5-petalled, white, about 6mm wide in stiffly pendant racemes to 5cm long, spring; fruit blue-black bitter drupe to 1cm long; breaks into fresh green young leaf in late winter, providing a foretaste of spring. Grow in any moisture-retentive but well-drained, fertile soil in sun or shade. Plant autumn to spring. Propagate by suckers detached from the parent plant from autumn to late winter or early spring.

Osmunda

(derivation in question: perhaps Latin *os*, mouth, and *mundare*, to purify, or for Asmund – Osmundus – an 11th century Scandinavian writer instrumental in preparing the way for Christianity to be accepted in Sweden). OSMUNDACEAE. A genus of 10–12 species of ferns of almost world-wide distribution (not in Australasia). They are clump-forming with bipinnate fronds, the fertile pinnules of which are much reduced and bear marginal sporangia. Grow in moisture-retentive, humus-rich soil, preferably in partial shade, although *O. regalis* will grow in sun. Propagate by division or spores in spring.

Species cultivated (all deciduous): *O. cinnamomea*, cinnamon fern, fiddleheads; N. and S. America, E. Asia; sterile fronds to 1m or more tall, lanceolate in outline, rusty downy when young; fertile fronds bright green, maturing lustrous cinnamon-brown. *O. claytoniana*, interrupted fern; N. America; fronds to 1m tall, lanceolate to oblong-ovate in outline, either entirely sterile or with a middle section of fertile pinnae that ripen dark brown and wither by mid summer, giving an interrupted appearance; will

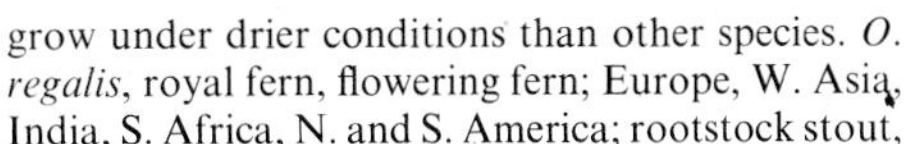
grow under drier conditions than other species. *O. regalis*, royal fern, flowering fern; Europe, W. Asia, India, S. Africa, N. and S. America; rootstock stout,

Top: *Osmunda regalis*
Centre left: *Osmunda regalis* fronds unfurling
Above left: *Osmunda claytoniana*
Above: *Osmunda regalis* fronds with ripening sporangia

erect, with abundant black roots often forming a mound or trunk-like base above the soil when grown in wet sites; fronds 1–3m tall, oblong-ovate in outline, either entirely sterile or with the topmost pinnae fertile, ripening light brown; the roots provide the osmunda fibre of commerce much used by orchid growers.

Osteospermum – see *Dimorphotheca*.

Ostrich fern – see *Matteuccia*.

Ostrya

(Greek vernacular *ostrys*). Hop hornbeam. CARPINACEAE (BETULACEAE). A genus of 10 species of deciduous trees from the N. Hemisphere. The species described much resemble hornbeam (*Carpinus*) but the nutlets are enclosed in green, bladder-like involucres, the fruiting catkins having a hop-like appearance. Culture as for hornbeam.
Species cultivated: *O. carpinifolia* (*O. vulgaris*), S.Europe, Asia Minor; to 19m tall, trunk fissured, oak-like in mature specimens; crown rounded or broadly conical; leaves 5–12cm long, sharply double-toothed, usually lustrous deep green; fruiting catkins pendant, 5cm long. *O. virginiana*, American hop hornbeam, leverwood, ironwood; E. N.America; similar to previous species.

Above: *Ostrya japonica* fruiting catkin
Above right: *Ostrya carpinifolia* in spring
Right: *Othonnopsis cheirifolia*

Oswego tea – see *Monarda*.

Othonnopsis

(*Othonna*, a genus of succulent plants, and Greek *opsis*, like). COMPOSITAE. A genus of about 12 species of shrubby evergreen perennials mainly from S. Africa with a few N. Africa to W. Asia. 1 species is generally available: *O. cheirifolia* (*Othonna c.*, *Hertia c.*), Algeria; decumbent shrub 20–30cm tall; leaves about 5cm long, broadly paddle-shaped, glaucous, in 2 alternate facing ranks; flower-heads solitary or a few together, terminal, 3–4cm wide, ray florets rich yellow, summer. Not reliably hardy during hard frost but survives most winters in milder areas. Grow in well-drained soil in sun. Plant spring. Propagate by cuttings in summer, over-wintering the young plants in a cold frame or greenhouse.

Ourisia

(for Governor Ouris of the Falkland Is). SCROPHULARIACEAE. A genus of 24 species of mainly evergreen perennials from S. S.America, New Zealand, Tasmania. They may be rhizomatous, forming wide clumps or colonies, prostrate and mat-forming or tufted, with long-stalked, ovate to sessile, oblong or spathulate leaves. The flowers are tubular, 5-lobed, in some species 2-lipped with the 3 lower lobes larger, arranged in racemes, corymbs, whorls, or sometimes solitary. Grow in well-drained but moisture-retentive, neutral to acid, humus-rich soil in partial shade, although full sun is tolerated provided the substrate never dries out. Most species do well in peat beds. Plant spring. Propagate by division or from seed in spring.
Species cultivated: *O. caespitosa*, New Zealand; stems slender, prostrate, much-branched, rooting at nodes; leaves to 1cm long, crowded, broadly to narrowly spathulate with a few notch-like teeth; flowers in pairs, white, yellow-eyed, about 2cm wide, summer. *O.c. gracilis*, leaves to 6mm long, toothless or with 2 notches; flowers often larger, solitary. *O. coccinea*, Chile, Argentina; rhizomatous; leaves

broadly ovate to oblong, often cordate, irregularly toothed, 3–6cm long; flowers slender, nodding, long-tubed, about 2·5cm long, bright scarlet, in several whorls of 3 on stems to 20cm or more tall, late spring to autumn. *O. macrocarpa*, mountain foxglove; New Zealand; rhizomatous; leaves in erect tufts, long-stalked, the blades 4–10cm or more long, broadly ovate, regularly crenate-toothed, thick-textured; flowers 2–3cm wide, white, yellow-eyed, in several close-set whorls on stems to 50cm or more tall, summer. *O. macrophylla*, mountain foxglove; New Zealand; similar appearance to previous species, but flowers 1·5–2cm wide, the tube hairy without.

Oxalis

(Greek *oxys*, acid or sharp – alluding to the taste of the leaves). OXALIDACEAE. A genus of about 850 species of annuals, perennials and shrubs, some bulbous or tuberous-rooted, others succulents, of cosmopolitan distribution. They have long-stalked, mainly trifoliate leaves (some species have up to 20 leaflets), closing at night, and 5-petalled flowers in umbel-like cymes, or solitary from leaf-axils. The seed is enclosed in an elastic aril that turns inside out when ripe or touched, ejecting the seed from the capsule to considerable distances. Grow hardy plants in any well-drained soil in sun or shade according to individual requirements. Plant autumn to spring. Propagate by division at planting time, from seed in spring or by cuttings in summer of the shrubby and succulent sorts. For any other cultural requirements see species descriptions.

Species cultivated (leaves trifoliate, and hardy unless stated otherwise): *O. acetosella*, common wood sorrel; Europe to Japan; rhizomatous, stemless perennial, 5–10cm tall; leaflets obcordate, 1–2cm long; flowers solitary, to 1·5cm long, white with lilac to purple veins. *O.a.* Rosea, flowers pink, purple-veined, spring. *O. adenophylla*, Chile, Argentina; bulbous perennial, 10–15cm tall, leaflets usually about 12, sometimes to 22, obcordate, glaucous, to 1·2cm long; flowers solitary or sometimes in umbels of 2–3, lilac-pink, to 2·5cm long, late spring; needs a warm site. *O. articulata* (*O. floribunda*), Brazil to Argentina; clump-forming perennial from short, thick, tuber-like rhizomes, 10–20cm tall; leaflets 1–3cm long, obcordate; flowers in large umbels, 1–1·5cm long, deep bright pink, late spring to autumn; the familiar cottage garden species, sometimes white-flowered. *O. bowiei* (*O. purpurata b.*), S. Africa; bulbous perennial, 20–30cm tall; leaflets rounded to broadly obovate, to 5cm long; flowers in umbels of 3–12, pink to rose-purple, 2·5–4cm long, summer; hardy in mild areas. *O. brasiliensis*, Brazil; tender bulbous perennial, 15–25cm tall; leaflets obcordate, 2·5cm long; flowers

Far left top: *Ourisia macrocarpa*
Far left above: *Ourisia macrophylla*
Left top: *Oxalis chrysantha*
Left above: *Oxalis adenophylla*
Top: *Oxalis depressa*
Centre: *Oxalis pes-caprae*
Above: *Oxalis laciniata*

in umbels of 1–3, vivid purple-red, 3cm long, summer; plant spring, lift autumn in all but the mildest areas and store; makes a good pot plant. *O. cernua*, see *O. pes-caprae*. *O. chrysantha*, Brazil; tender, mat-forming perennial to 5cm tall; stems almost woody, creeping and rooting; leaflets triangular-obcordate, about 8mm long; flowers solitary, 1–2cm long, yellow, funnel-shaped, summer, often a small flush again in autumn; best under glass in frosty areas. *O. deppei*, lucky clover, good luck plant; Mexico; bulbous perennial to about 30cm tall; leaflets 4, broadly obovate, to 4cm long; flowers in umbels of 5–12, red or violet-purple, 2cm long, summer; a white-flowered form is known; tubers edible. *O. depressa* (*O. inops*), S. Africa; bulbous and rhizomatous perennial 6–10cm tall; leaflets grey-green, rounded to triangular-obovate, 6–10mm long; flowers solitary, about 2cm long, usually bright rosy-pink, but white to violet forms are known, early summer; can become invasive in mild areas and light soils. *O. drummondii*, see under *O. vespertilionis*. *O. enneaphylla*, S. S.America including Falkland Is; similar to *O. adenophylla* but leaflets usually about 9 (to 20) and flowers always solitary, fragrant, white or pink with lavender veins. *O. floribunda*, see *O. articulata*. *O. inops*, see *O. depressa*. *O. laciniata*, S. Argentina, Chile; scaly rhizomatous perennial forming tufted patches, but otherwise akin to *O. enneaphylla*, to 5mc tall; flowers fragrant, pink to maroon-purple (usually light purple-blue in cultivation) with darker veins, early summer; hardy but must be well-drained, especially in winter. *O. lasiandra*, Mexico; bulbous, stemless perennial 15–30cm tall; leaflets 5–10, narrowly oblong, to 5cm long; flowers in umbels of up to 15, purple-crimson, 2cm long, summer; best lifted in cold areas. *O. lobata*, temperate S. America; bulbous, stemless perennial to 6cm tall; lea£ets very broadly obcordate, to 1cm long; flowers bright yellow, 1·5–2cm long; produces spring leaves, dies down in summer, then leaves again and flowers in autumn; needs a sheltered site or alpine house treatment in cold areas. *O. magellanica*, temperate S. America; mat-forming perennial to 5cm tall; stems creeping and rooting; leaves obcordate, about 6mm long, red-tinged; flowers solitary, white, 8–10mm long, summer to autumn; best in peaty soil. *O. obtusa*, S. Africa; bulbous, stemless perennial 6–10cm tall; leaflets obovate, grey-green; flowers solitary, 3cm long, with red veins and yellow eye, early summer; sheltered site or greenhouse. *O. oregana*, redwood sorrel; N. California to Washington State; essentially a robust *O. acetosella* but rhizomatous; leaflets 2–3cm long; flowers white to deep pink, 1·3–2cm long. *O. pes-caprae* (*O. cernua*), Bermuda buttercup; S. Africa but widely naturalized around the world; tender, bulbous perennial to 30cm tall; leaflets deeply obcordate, 2cm long; flowers in umbels of 3–8, drooping, bright lemon-yellow, 2–2·5cm long, spring to summer; best under glass in frosty areas but likely to become a serious weed elsewhere. *O. purpurata bowiei*, see *O. bowiei*. *O. rosea*, Chile; seldom cultivated annual, to 45cm tall, with rose-pink flowers, but plants under this name in gardens are often *O. articulata*. *O. vespertilionis*, Mexico; bulbous, stemless perennial to 20cm or more tall; leaflets v-shaped with 2 linear lobes to 3cm long; flowers in umbels of 3–10, purple, 2cm long; confused with *O. drummondii* (Texas), having leaflet lobes lanceolate to ovate, and violet flowers.

Oxlip – see *Primula elatior*.

Oxycoccus

(Greek *oxys*, acid or sharp, and *kokkos*, a berry). Cranberry. ERICACEAE. A genus of 3 species of evergreen shrubs from northern temperate and arctic zones. They form mats of prostrate, interlacing, wiry stems bearing ovate, alternate leaves and nodding flowers with 4, slender, much-reflexed corolla lobes; fruit a comparatively large globose berry. Grow in acid, peaty, semi-boggy or permanently moist soil in sun. Plant autumn to spring. Propagate by layers or careful division in spring, or from seed when ripe.

Species cultivated: *O. macrocarpus* (*Vaccinium macrocarpon*), large or American cranberry; E. N.America; eventually 60–90cm wide; leaves 1–2cm long, glaucous beneath; flowers pink, lobes about 8mm long, summer; fruit globose, 1·2–2cm wide, red; much grown commercially in USA and several cultivars are known. *O. palustris* (*O. quadripetalus*, *Vaccinium oxycoccus*), small or European cranberry; range of genus; leaves 6–10mm long, very glaucous beneath; flowers pink, lobes 6mm long, summer; fruit 6–10mm wide, whitish and freckled, then red all over.

Oxydendrum

(Greek *oxys*, acid or sharp, and *dendron*, a tree – the leaves are pleasantly acid-tasting). ERICACEAE. A genus of 1 species of deciduous tree from S.E. USA: *O. arboreum*, sorrel tree or sourwood; to 26m or so tall, but slow growing and often less; leaves alternate, oblong-elliptic to lanceolate, 10–20cm long, deep lustrous green, turning scarlet in autumn; flowers white, 6–8mm long, narrowly urn-shaped, in

Above: *Oxycoccus palustris*
Below: *Oxydendrum arboreum*

Above: *Oxypetalum caeruleum*

drooping panicles to 25cm long, late summer to autumn in Britain; a good bee plant. Grow in acid, humus-rich, moisture-retentive soil in partial shade or sun, preferably sheltered from strong winds. Plant autumn, spring. Propagate by cuttings taken during late summer, layering or from seed in spring, the latter under glass.

Oxypetalum

(Greek *oxys*, sharp, and botanical Latin *petalum*, a petal). ASCLEPIADACEAE. A genus of 125–150 species of perennials and sub-shrubs from Mexico to Brazil, 1 of which is usually available: *O. caeruleum* (*Tweedia c.*), Brazil, Uruguay; tender sub-shrub, stems weakly twining to 1m or more; leaves in opposite pairs, oblong-lanceolate, cordate, to 10cm long, hairy; flowers 2·5cm wide, sky-blue, ageing purple and lilac, shortly tubular with 5 spreading lobes, in loose axillary cymes, summer. Greenhouse, minimum temperature 10°C, well-ventilated in summer, or grown as a half-hardy annual. Propagate by cuttings late spring or summer, bottom heat 18–20°C, or from seed in spring at not less than 16°C. If grown as a half-hardy annual, sow early to mid spring, prick off into small pots of a commercial potting mixture, harden off in early summer and plant out. If treated as a greenhouse perennial, repot annually and prune back flowered stems to 2 pairs of buds in spring.

Oxytropis

(Greek *oxys*, sharp, and *tropis*, a keel – referring to the flowers). LEGUMINOSAE. A genus of about 300 species of mainly low-growing perennials from N.Hemisphere. They are tufted, either stemless or with decumbent to erect stems, mainly basal pinnate leaves, and pea-shaped flowers in short, dense, axillary racemes; seed-pods are often somewhat inflated. Grow in well-drained soil in sun. Plant autumn to spring. Propagate from seed in spring, ideally sown *in situ* as *Oxytropis* do not transplant well, or by careful division at planting time.

Species cultivated: *O. campestris*, meadow milk vetch; northern temperate zone, mainly on mountains; similar to *O. halleri* but larger; leaves to 15cm long, leaflets 1–2cm long, narrowly oblong; flowers yellow, tinted purple, summer. *O. halleri* (*O. sericea*, *O. uralensis*), silky milkvetch; Pyrenees, Alps, Carpathians; stems very short; leaves to 10cm long, leaflets 5–8mm long, elliptic, softly hairy; flowers about 2cm long, pale purple, the keel tipped darker, racemes as long as – or a little shorter than – leaves, summer. *O. lambertii*, locoweed, purple loco (USA); W. N.America; stemless; leaves to 20cm long, leaflets ovate to linear, often silky grey hairy; flowers 2–3cm long, purple to rose-purple or white, in racemes overtopping leaves, summer. *O. pilosa*, woolly milkvetch; C. and E.Europe; stems erect to sprawling, to 20cm or more long, softly long hairy; leaflets 19–27, narrowly oblong to lanceolate; flowers 1·5cm long, light yellow, summer to early autumn. *O. sericea* and *O. uralensis*, see *O. halleri*.

Pachysandra

(Greek *pachys*, thick, and *andros*, man or male – the stamens have thick, fleshy filaments). BUXACEAE. A genus of 4–5 species of soft sub-shrubs or perennials from S.E. USA and E. Asia. They have alternate, ovate to obovate leaves, mainly crowded towards the tips of the stems, and terminal or basal spikes of petalless, unisexual flowers, the males rendered conspicuous by the 4 thick white stamens. Grow in humus-rich soil, shade. Plant autumn, spring. Propagate by division, spring, cuttings late summer.

Species cultivated: *P. axillaris*, S.W. China; evergreen, 15–30cm tall; leaves 5–10cm long, ovate, coarsely toothed; flower-spikes to 3cm long, spring. *P. procumbens*, Alleghany spurge; S.E. USA; evergreen, to 30cm tall; leaves to 7·5cm long, broadly ovate, coarsely toothed in top half, often with pale marbling; flower-spikes about 5cm long from near base of stems, spring to early summer. *P. terminalis*, Japan; evergreen, semi-woody at base, to 30cm tall; leaves 5–8cm long, obovate, the top half toothed; flower-spikes 2–3cm long, spring; very useful ground cover in deep shade. *P.t.* Variegata, leaves margined white.

Pachystegia insignis – see *Olearia insignis*.

Paeonia

(reputedly for the Greek physician Paeon, changed into the plant by Pluto in gratitude for his many cures). Peony. PAEONIACEAE (RANUNCULACEAE). A genus of 33 species of herbaceous perennials and deciduous shrubs from temperate Europe, Asia, N.W. N.America. The herbaceous species are tuberous-rooted and clump-forming, some of the shrubs rhizomatous, both with alternate, pinnately cut leaves; flowers above the leaves, usually large, bowl-shaped to almost flat, with 5–10 petals. Fruit is cluster of 2–8 pod-like follicles, usually red within; fertile seed is large, glossy, blue to black, sterile seed small, often red. Grow in well-drained but moisture-retentive, humus-rich soil in sun or partial shade, the shrubs in sheltered sites where late spring frosts do not occur or are minimal. Plant early autumn to

Left below: *Pachysandra terminalis*
Below: *Paeonia delavayi*
Bottom: *Paeonia lactiflora* Mons. Jules Elie

Top: *Paeonia officinalis* Rubra Plena
Centre: *Paeonia mlokosewitschii*
Above: *Paeonia suffruticosa*
Centre right: *Paeonia* × *lemoinei* Souvenir de Maxime Cornu

spring. Propagate from seed when ripe or by careful division of large or congested clumps, the shrubs also by layering in spring or by wedge or cleft grafting onto tubers of herbaceous sorts late summer, potting and over-wintering in a cold frame. Cuttings can be taken in early autumn, inserted outside or in a frame, but rooting is often unreliable even with hormone treatment. Seedlings take several years to flower and only species come true. **Species cultivated** (all herbaceous unless otherwise stated): *P. albiflora*, see *P. lactiflora*. *P. arietina*, see *P. mascula arietina*. *P. cambessedesii*, Balearic Is; 30–45cm tall; leaves biternate, purple beneath, leaflets ovate to lanceolate, to 10cm long; flowers 6·5–10cm wide, deep rose-pink, pistils purple, spring; not reliably hardy in frosty areas unless sited against a sunny wall or protected with a layer of bracken, bark chips or sand. *P. corallina*, see *P. mascula*. *P. decora*, see *P. peregrina*. *P. delavayi*, S.W. China; shrub 1·5–2m or more tall; leaves 20–30cm long, biternate, leaflets oblong-elliptic; flowers 7–9cm across, maroon-red, opening widely, early summer. *P. delavayi angustiloba*, see *P. potaninii*; *P. delavayi lutea*, see *P. lutea*. *P. emodii*, Himalaya – Kashmir; allied to *P. lactiflora*, but flowers 7·5–13cm wide, always white, usually with 1 pistil, summer; best grown among sheltering shrubs. *P. lactiflora* (*P. albiflora*), Chinese peony; Tibet, Siberia, China; 60–90cm tall; leaves biternate, leaflets elliptic to lanceolate, sometimes lobed; flowers 7–10cm wide, usually white, sometimes pink or red, fragrant, summer; many cultivars are listed under this name, some of mutant – others hybrid – origin; choice is largely a personal matter but the following can be recommended for garden worthiness: Balliol, single, maroon-red; Bowl of Beauty, mallow-purple, filled with pale yellow staminodes; Duchess de Nemours, double, pure white; Felix Crausse, double, rose-red; Festiva Maxima, double, white, flecked red-purple; Lady Alexandra Duff, large double, pale pink, ageing white; Mons. Jules Elie, double, silvery lilac-pink; Sarah Bernhardt, rose-purple, edged pink; Solange, double, waxy-white, flushed yellow to buff-salmon in centre; Shirley Temple, double, pale pink, ageing white; The Moor, single, deep maroon-crimson; Whitleyi Major (*P. whittleyi*), single, pure white. *P.* × *lemoinei* (*P. lutea* × *P. suffruticosa*), large race of cultivars blending the characters of the parents in several ways, the flowers often in shades of yellow: *P.* × *l.* Aurore, semi-double, coppery-terracotta; *P.* × *l.* Alice Harding, double, canary-yellow; *P.* × *l.* Chromatella, very large double, sulphur-yellow; *P.* × *l.* Souvenir de Maxime Cornu, large fully double, deep yellow, edged and shaded salmon-carmine. *P. lobata*, see *P. peregrina*. *P. lutea* (*P. delavayi lutea*), S.W. China; much like *P. delavayi*, but flowers cup-shaped, 5–8cm wide, yellow. *P.l. ludlowii*, Tibet; to 3m tall; flowers 7·5–13cm wide – now the most widely grown form in Britain. *P. mascula* (*P. corallina*), S. and E. Europe; 60–90cm tall; leaves biternate, leaflets narrowly to broadly elliptic, sometimes with 2–3 narrow lobes; flowers 7–13cm wide, rose-red, early summer. *P.m. arietina* (*P. arietina*), S.E. Europe, Turkey; leaves downy beneath, the lower ones with 12–15 leaflets. *P. mlokosewitschii*, Caucasus; 60cm tall or more; leaves biternate, grey-green, leaflets to 10cm long, ovate to oblong or obovate; flowers 7·5–12cm wide, lemon-yellow, spring. *P. moutan*, see *P. suffruticosa*. *P. obovata*, China to Japan and Sakhalin; 45–50cm tall; leaves biternate, terminal leaflets obovate, to 15cm long, grey-green, tinted copper when young; flowers 7cm across, opening widely, rose-purple to white, early summer. *P. officinalis*, France to Albania; to 60cm tall; leaves biternate, leaflets pinnatipartite, downy beneath; flowers 7·5–13cm wide, red, petals spreading, early summer. *P.o.* Alba Plena, double white; *P.o.* Anemoniflora, deep pink with crimson and yellow petaloids; *P.o.* J. C. Weguelin, crimson; *P.o.* China Rose, salmon-red, orange-yellow stamens; *P.o.* Rubra Plena, double, deep red, the old cottage garden favourite. *P. peregrina* (*P. decora*, *P. lobata*), Italy, Balkan Peninsula, Romania; 60cm tall; leaves mostly biternate, leaflets elliptic, some deeply lobed; flowers rounded, cup-shaped, 7–12cm wide, intense red, early summer. *P.p.* Sunshine, salmon-red with orange patina. *P. potaninii* (*P. delavayi angustiloba*), S.W. China; similar to a dwarf *P. delavayi*, the woody stems 60–90cm or more tall; spreading by rhizomes and forming colonies; flowers 5–6cm wide, maroon-red, early summer. *P.p. trollioides*, flowers yellow, cup-shaped. *P. suffruticosa* (*P. moutan*), tree peony, moutan; Bhutan, Tibet, China; 1–2m tall; leaves bipinnate, leaflets 5–10cm long, toothed or lobed; flowers bowl-shaped, 15–20cm wide, pink to white, each petal blotched magenta at base, early summer; many cultivars have been raised both in China, Japan and the West; a few of the more garden-worthy are: *P.s.* Beni Tsukasa (*P.s.* Scarlet Leader), semi-double, cherry-red; *P.s.* Comtesse de Tudor, double, salmon-red; *P.s.* Godaishu (*P.s.* Large Globe), semi to double, white with yellow centre; *P.s.* Kumagai (*P.s.* Bears Valley), deep pink, ageing purple-red; *P.s.* Osiris, double, velvet-red;

P.s. Reine Elizabeth (*P.s.* Queen Elizabeth), double, deep salmon-pink; *P.s.* Yachiyo-tsubaki (*P.s.* Eternal Camellias), semi to double, coral-pink. *P. tenuifolia*, S.E. Europe to Caucasus; about 45cm tall; leaves dense, finely cut into linear segments, creating a fern-like effect; flowers 6–7·5cm wide, deep crimson, cup-shaped, early summer. *P. veitchii*, S.W. China; about 30cm tall; leaves biternate, the leaflets deeply cut and lobed; flowers 6–10cm wide, rose-purple, nodding, early summer. *P.v. woodwardii*, rose-pink, *P. whittleyi*, see *P. lactiflora*. *P. woodwardii*, see *P. veitchii woodwardii*.

Pagoda tree – see *Sophora japonica*.

Paliurus

(old Greek vernacular for Christ's thorn). RHAMNACEAE. A genus of 6–8 species of spiny shrubs from S.Europe to E.Asia, 1 of which is usually available: *P. spina-christi* (*P. aculeata*), Christ's thorn; S.Europe to N.China; large shrub or occasionally a small tree, 2·5–6m tall; stems slender, at each node bearing a pair of spines, 1 short and curved, the other longer and straight; leaves alternate, 2·5–4cm long, broadly ovate, prominently 3-veined; flowers small, greenish-yellow, 5-petalled, in rounded, axillary cymes; fruit 2–3cm wide, composed of a disk-like wing with a central, 3-seeded capsule. Grow in well-drained, fertile soil in sheltered, sunny sites. Plant autumn to spring. Propagate from seed sown when ripe or earlier in a cold frame, by root cuttings planted late winter or layering in spring.

Above: *Paliurus spina-christi*
Top right: *Pancratium illyricum*
Above right: *Panicum miliaceum*
Above far right: *Papaver orientale* King George

Pancratium

(Greek vernacular for a bulbous plant of uncertain identity, applied to this genus by Linnaeus). AMARYLLIDACEAE. A genus of about 15 species of bulbous perennials from the Mediterranean to tropical Africa and Asia. They have basal, strap-shaped leaves and erect, leafless stems bearing umbels of white, somewhat daffodil-like flowers. Each bloom has a funnel-shaped base, 6 narrow, radiating, petal-like lobes, and a central corona or cup formed of flange-like outgrowths from the stamen filaments. The species described may be grown outside in warm, mild areas at the base of a wall, but in cold areas need a frost-free greenhouse. Pot or plant after flowering to early autumn, those outside, 15cm deep in sharply drained but fertile soil. Any commercial potting mix is suitable for pot culture, although the all-peat types are best with added sand or grit. Keep barely moist until the leaves are 10cm tall, then water regularly until mid summer. Liquid feed may be given at 10–14 day intervals when in full growth. Dry off potted bulbs when leaves start to yellow in summer; plants outside may be covered with cloches during a wet season. Propagate by separating offsets at planting time, or from seed when ripe or in spring.

Species cultivated: *P. illyricum*, Spain, Corsica, Sardinia; similar to the more common *P. maritimum* but hardier, the flowers to 8cm long with a small, starry corona. *P. maritimum*, sea daffodil; Mediterranean – maritime sands; stems 30–60cm tall, flattened (those of *P. illyricum* are terete); leaves 60cm or longer, glaucous; flowers 3–15, each 12cm long with a deep, cup-shaped corona, summer.

Panicum

(Latin vernacular for one of the millets, *P. miliaceum*). GRAMINEAE. A genus of 500–600 species of annual and perennial grasses of almost cosmopolitan distribution, particularly the tropics. They may be tufted or clump-forming, some of the perennials with rhizomes or stolons and bearing terminal, graceful panicles of tiny, 2-flowered spikelets. Grow in any well-drained soil in sun. Plant or sow *in situ* in spring. Propagate perennials by division during spring.

Species cultivated: *P. miliaceum*, common, hog or broom corn millet; probably Asia; annual, usually branched from base, 30–120cm tall depending on soil fertility; leaf-sheaths hairy, blades 15–30cm long by 1–2cm wide; panicles 10–30cm long, usually nodding, spikelets green or purple, late summer; a form with leaves and spikelets purple-tinted is sometimes offered as *P. violaceum*. *P. variegatum*, see *Oplismenus hirtellus*. *P. virgatum*, switch grass; N. and C. America; tufted rhizomatous perennial 1–2m tall; leaves hairless, blades linear, 15–60cm long; panicles 50cm long, in cultivated forms to 25cm wide, spikelets with conspicuous purple anthers, late summer.

Pansy – see *Viola tricolor*, and *V.* × *wittrockiana*.

Papaver

(Latin vernacular for a poppy – probably *P. somniferum*). PAPAVERACEAE. A genus of at least 50 species (some authorities optimistically state 100) of annuals and perennials from Europe, Asia, W. N.America, S. Africa and Australia. They are tufted to clump-forming, with long, basal leaves in rosettes and erect, usually sparingly leafy stems bearing terminal, 4-petalled, bowl-shaped flowers. Each bloom has a crown of many stamens and a central, cylindrical to barrel-shaped pistil with a roof-like ribbed stigma. Grow in well-drained soil in sun. Plant autumn or spring. Propagate annuals from seed sown *in situ* autumn or spring, perennials ideally the same way, but alternatively either under glass or in nursery rows, by division in spring, or by root cuttings in sandy soil in a frame or cool greenhouse early to mid spring.

Species cultivated: *P. alpinum*, alpine poppy; mountains of Europe, north to Arctic; tufted perennial; stems 10–20cm tall; leaves all basal, pinnate to bi- or tripinnatisect, hairy, glaucous; flowers solitary, 2·5–4cm wide, white, yellow, red; a very variable plant now split up into several separate species, the following sometimes available: *P. burseri* (*P. alpinum alpinum*), leaves bi-tripinnate, flowers white, 3–4cm wide, stigma ribs 4; *P. kerneri*, like *P. burseri* but flowers yellow, stigma ribs 5; *P. radicatum*, leaves 3–6cm long, pinnatisect to pinnatifid, flowers usually yellow, stigma ribs 5; *P. rhaeticum* (*P. alpinum r.*, *P. pyrenaicum r.* – the original *P. alpinum* of Linnaeus), leaves pinnate or bipinnate, flowers 4–5cm wide, golden-yellow, rarely red or white, stigma ribs 5–7; *P. sendtneri* (*P. alpinum s.*), similar to *P. burseri* but leaves pinnate to bipinnate, stigma ribs 5. *P. atlanticum*, Morocco; much like, and closely allied to, *P. rupifragum*, but silky hairy throughout; flowers pale orange-red, summer; can be invasive on light soils. *P. burseri*, see *P. alpinum*. *P. heldreichii*, see *P. spicatum*. *P. kerneri*, see *P. alpinum*. *P. miyabeanum*, Kurile Is; small, neat edition of *P. nudicaule* and formerly classified as a sub-species of it; leaves hairy, forming hummocks with bristly stems 10–15cm tall; flowers yellow, summer to autumn; in the past wrongly spelt *moyabenum*, *tokewokii* and *takedake*, sometimes in combination and with other spelling aberrations, arising out of the addition of the authors' names, Dr

M. Tatewaki and Dr K. Miyabe. *P. nudicaule*, Iceland poppy; Arctic regions, south to USA and Asia; tufted perennial; stems 30–45cm tall; leaves all basal, 10–15cm long, pinnatifid, hairy; flowers solitary, 4·5–6·5cm wide, white, yellow, orange, red, fragrant, summer to autumn; several cultivars are available with larger, sometimes double flowers on stems to 60cm or more. *P. orientale*, oriental poppy; S.W. Asia; clump-forming, hispid perennial; stems sparsely leafy, about 1m tall; basal leaves to 25cm long, pinnatipartite, dark green; flowers 10cm or more wide, red with a basal black blotch to each petal, early summer; among well-tried cultivars are: *P.o.* Marcus Perry, orange-scarlet, very large flowers; *P.o.* Mrs Perry, clear pink; *P.o.* Perry's White, chalk-white; *P.o.* Salmon Glow, double, salmon-pink. *P. pyrenaicum*, see *P. rhaeticum* under *P. alpinum*. *P. radicatum* and *P. rhaeticum*, see *P. alpinum*. *P. rhoeas*, common field or corn poppy; Europe, Asia, introduced elsewhere; hairy annual, 60–90cm tall; basal leaves usually bipinnatisect, the lobes cut or deeply toothed; flowers rich scarlet, 7–10cm wide, summer; represented in gardens by *P.r.* The Shirley, a mixed strain in shades of red, pink and white, often with picotee margins; double-flowered strains are also available. *P. rupifragum*, S. Spain; somewhat woody-based, tufted perennial; stems to 50cm tall; leaves pinnatisect, hispid on mid-ribs and stalks only; flowers 4–5cm wide, brick-red, summer; seeds freely on light soils. *P. sendtneri*, see *P. alpinum*. *P. somniferum*, opium poppy; S.E. Europe, W. Asia; robust, glaucous annual to 1m or more tall; leaves 7–12cm long, ovate-oblong, lobed, stem-clasping; flowers 7–10cm wide, red, purple, white, with blackish spot at base of each petal; several cultivar strains are available in a wider range of shades, often double. *P. spicatum* (*P. heldreichii*), Turkey; tufted, densely white, hairy perennial; leaves oblong to narrowly elliptic, toothed; flowers 3cm or more wide, orange-red, 6 or more in spike-like racemes, summer.

Parahebe

(Greek *para*, near or close to, and the genus *Hebe*). SCROPHULARIACEAE. A genus of 11 species of sub-shrubs or shrubs from New Zealand. They differ from *Hebe* in being always prostrate or decumbent, the slender stems rooting at the nodes, with long-stalked racemes and flattened seed capsules having a partition across the narrowest diameter (in *Hebe* this partition is usually across the widest diameter). Culture as for *Hebe*.

Top left: *Papaver rhoeas* The Shirley
Left: *Papaver nudicaule* Meadhouse
Below left: *Papaver somniferum* Pink Chiffon
Below: *Parahebe canescens*
Bottom: *Parahebe catarractae*
Below right: *Paraquilegia grandiflora*

Species cultivated: *P.* × *bidwillii*, see *P. decora*. *P. canescens* (*Veronica lilliputiana*), atypical of genus in being a deciduous, totally prostrate perennial; stems thread-like forming matted patches; leaves broadly ovate, 1–2·5mm long, hoary with sparse white hairs; flowers usually solitary, blue, 5–6mm long, summer. *P. catarractae*, decumbent, usually about 15cm tall but sometimes to 30cm or more; leaves 1–4cm long, elliptic to lanceolate or linear, toothed, leathery, whitish-green beneath; flowers 1–1·5cm wide, white, veined pink or purple, summer to autumn; very variable in height, spread, leaf length and degree of veining in the petals; several named forms are sometimes cultivated, including *P.c.* Delight, flowers lilac, veined red-purple; *P.c.* Diffusa, dense, mat-forming, leaves small, ovate, similar to *P. lyallii*. *P. decora*, prostrate, mat-forming; stems wiry, interlaced; leaves 1·5–4mm long, broadly ovate to orbicular, deep glossy green; racemes erect, to 10cm or more tall, flowers 1cm wide, white, often veined or flushed pink, summer; the garden clone of *P.* × *bidwillii* (*P. decora* × *P. lyallii*) is much like *P. decora* but usually more compact, the leaves having 2–4 teeth. *P. hookeriana*, decumbent, forming mounds 5–10cm tall; leaves densely borne, 5–12mm long, ovate to almost orbicular, toothed, often lightly to densely white hairy; flowers to 1cm wide, white to lavender, summer. *P. lyallii*, decumbent, forming loose mounds 10–15cm tall; leaves 5–10mm long, ovate to ovate-oblong, sometimes broader or narrower, deeply crenate-toothed, glossy above, pale beneath; flowers about 1cm wide, white, veined and/or flushed pink to red-purple, summer; more robust forms with larger leaves, very pale green beneath, are probably hybrids with *P. catarractae*. *P. perfoliata*, see *Veronica perfoliata*.

Paraquilegia

(Greek *para*, near or close to, and the genus *Aquilegia*). RANUNCULACEAE. A genus of about 8 species of small, tufted perennials from Afghanistan to C. Asia, 1 of which is usually obtainable: *P.*

grandiflora (*P. anemonoides*), C. Asia; densely tufted, 10–15cm tall; leaves glaucous, triternate, the leaflets deeply lobed; flowers solitary, 2·5–3cm wide, nodding to erect, 5-petalled, anemone-like, delicate mauve-blue or white, spring. Grow in moist scree in sun, or pans of peaty, gritty soil in an alpine house or frame. Plant spring. Propagate by careful division early spring, or from seed when ripe.

Paris

(Latin *par*, equal, referring to the regular number of leaves and floral parts of the first described species, *P. quadrifolia*). TRILLIACEAE (LILIACEAE). A genus of 6–20 species (depending on the classifier) of rhizomatous herbaceous perennials from Europe and temperate Asia. They have erect, naked stems, each one topped by a single whorl of linear to obovate leaves and a solitary, 4–6 petalled flower followed by a fleshy, berry-like fruit. Grow in

humus-rich, moisture-retentive soil in partial shade. Plant autumn to spring. Propagate from seed when ripe – it may take 18 months or more to germinate and several years to flower – or by division at planting time.
Species cultivated: *P. polyphylla*, Himalaya; rhizomes short and thick; stems 40–90cm tall; leaves 5–9, narrowly to broadly oblong-lanceolate, 7–15cm long; flowers 6–10cm wide, sepals 4–6, leaf-like, ovate-lanceolate, greenish, petals 4–6, thread-like, yellow, stamens yellow, pistil violet, early to late summer; fruit red. *P. quadrifolia*, herb paris; Europe to Siberia; rhizomes comparatively long and slender; stems 15–40cm tall; leaves 4, obovate, 6–12cm long; flowers 5–7cm wide, sepals 4, lanceolate, greenish, petals 4, filiform, yellow-green, early summer; fruit black.

Parochetus

(Greek *para*, near or close to, and *ochetos*, a brook – the plant frequents moist places in the wild). LEGUMINOSAE. A genus of 1 species of evergreen perennial from the mountains of Africa, Asia: *P. communis*, shamrock pea, blue oxalis; prostrate, mat-forming; leaves alternate, long-stalked, trifoliate, leaflets obcordate, 2cm long; flowers

1·5–2cm long, pea-like, bright blue, usually solitary in leaf-axils, summer to autumn; not hardy in frosty areas and often killed back to the root but usually regenerating later; makes an attractive, cool, greenhouse pot plant. Grow in humus-rich soil, moist but not wet, in sheltered, sunny or partially shady sites. Plant spring. Propagate by careful division or from seed under glass, spring, by cuttings in summer.

Paronychia

(Greek *para*, near, and *onyx*, a nail – alluding to the plant's supposed cure for whitlows). CARYOPHYLLACEAE. A genus of 45–50 species of small annuals and perennials of cosmopolitan distribution. They are tufted, often mat-forming, the slender stems bearing whorls or opposite pairs of small, lanceolate to obovate leaves, papery stipules, and terminal clusters of tiny, petalless flowers

surrounded by petal-like, papery-white or silvery bracts. Grow in any well-drained soil in sun. Plant autumn or spring. Propagate from seed or by division in spring or by cuttings in summer.
Species cultivated: *P. argentea*, S. Europe; mat-forming, to 30–60cm wide; leaves 4–8mm long, ovate-lanceolate; floral bracts ovate, 4–6mm long, silvery-white, summer. *P. capitata* (*P. nivea*), S. Europe; mat-forming, up to 30cm wide; leaves 3–6mm long, oblong to linear-lanceolate, downy and ciliate, grey-green; floral bracts 6–10mm long, silvery-white, summer. *P. kapela*, S. Europe, north to Austria; similar to *P. capitata*, but floral bracts 3–5mm long. *P.k. serpyllifolia* (*P. serpyllifolia*), leaves elliptic to ovate, 1·5–3·5mm long, densely crowded, flattened in one plane. *P. nivea*, see *P. capitata*. *P. serpyllifolia*, see *P. kapela serpyllifolia*.

Parrotia

(for F. W. Parrot, 1792–1841, German traveller and naturalist, and in 1834, the first ever to climb Mount Ararat). HAMAMELIDACEAE. A genus of 1 species of deciduous tree from N. Iran and adjacent USSR: *P. persica*, Persian ironwood; 8–15m tall, sometimes bushy from the base like a large shrub; bark smooth, greyish, flaking in squares to reveal yellow to rosy-

Far left below: *Parochetus communis*
Far left bottom: *Paronychia argentea*
Below and bottom: *Parrotia persica* autumn colours

buff inner bark; leaves alternate, 6–13cm long, obovate to oblong or ovate, unevenly wavy-toothed at apex, boldly-veined, turning yellow, orange and crimson in autumn; flowers small, petalless, with prominent red stamens, borne in small clusters amid velvety-brown bracts before the leaves, spring. Grow in fertile, well-drained, moisture-retentive soil in sun or partial shade, ideally sheltered from strong winds to preserve autumn colour. Hardy to light frost. Plant autumn to spring. Propagate by layering in spring, cuttings in summer under mist, or from seed sown as soon as possible in a cold frame.

Parthenocissus

(Greek *parthenos*, virgin, and *kissos*, ivy, a translation of the French *vigne-vierge* and English Virginia creeper; the state of Virginia was named after the Virgin Queen – Elizabeth I). VITIDACEAE (VITACEAE). A genus of 15 species of woody deciduous climbing plants from temperate Asia and N.America. They have alternate, palmate or digitate leaves and branched tendrils, in some species bearing sucker tips enabling the plant to climb flat, vertical surfaces; flowers are small, greenish, 5-petalled, in branched cymes, followed by small, grape-like, blue-black to blue berries. Grow in fertile, well-drained but moisture-retentive soil in sun or partial shade. Plant autumn to spring. Propagate by cuttings in summer in a frame, hardwood cuttings *in situ* in autumn, layering in spring or from seed when ripe.

Species cultivated: *P. henryana* (*Vitis h.*), C.China; 5–10m tall; stems sharply 4-angled, self-clinging; leaves long-stalked, 5–13cm long, leaflets 3–5, oblanceolate to obovate, slender-pointed, toothed, deep velvety-green with a silvery vein pattern, turning red in autumn; fruit dark blue; best on a sheltered, partially shaded wall. *P. himalayana* (*Ampelopsis h.*), Himalaya; of similar general appearance to *P. quinquefolia*, but leaflets 3, to 15cm long; fruit deep blue. *P. inserta* (*P. quinquefolia vitacea*, *P. vitacea*), Virginia creeper, woodbine (USA); N.America – Quebec to Arizona; like *P. quinquefolia*, but tendrils twining, without sucker tips, leaves somewhat larger, glossy green beneath. *P. quinquefolia*, Virginia creeper, American ivy, woodbine (USA); N.E.USA to Mexico; vigorous, self-clinging, to 20m or more high; leaves digitate, leaflets 5, elliptic to obovate, slender-tipped, coarsely toothed, dull, somewhat glaucous beneath, 4–15cm long, turning crimson in autumn; fruit blue-black. *P. semicordata*, closely allied to *P. himalayana*, but smaller leaves, bristly hairy beneath. *P. tricuspidata* (*Ampelopsis t.*, *Vitis inconstans*), Boston ivy or creeper, Japanese ivy or creeper; China, Korea, Japan; self-clinging, to 20m or more high; leaves 5–20cm wide, mainly broadly ovate, 3-lobed, toothed, but on young plants may lack the lobes or be cut into 3 leaflets, bright crimson in autumn; fruit dark blue with waxy patina. *P.t.* Veitchii (*Ampelopsis veitchii*), leaves a little smaller than type, purple when young; *P.t.* Lowii, leaves small, 3–7 lobed, curiously crimped. Over the years, *P. tricuspidata* has sometimes been planted instead of true Virginia creeper in gardens, and as they superficially resemble each other both are known under the name of the latter; the digitate, 5-leaflet leaves clearly distinguish the true plant.

Partridge berry – see *Mitchella*.

Pasque flower – see *Pulsatilla*.

Top right: *Parthenocissus semicordata*
Right: *Parthenocissus inserta*
Top far right: *Parthenocissus henryana*
Far right: *Parthenocissus tricuspidata*

Passiflora

(Latin *passio*, passion, and *flos*, flower: a missionary name, Christ's crucifixion being seen as symbolized in the floral organs, eg 3 knobbed styles the 3 nails, 5 anthers the 5 wounds, and the corona the crown of thorns). Passion flower. PASSIFLORACEAE. A genus of at least 400 species mainly of evergreen woody or herbaceous climbers principally from the Americas – a few in Asia and Australia. They have alternate, ovate, often 3–5 lobed leaves, twining tendrils, and generally solitary flowers from the upper leaf-axils followed by globular to ovoid berries, in some species large and edible. The flower has a unique structure: the base is tubular – in some species (formerly classified as *Tacsonia*) it is longer than the 10 tepals that arise from the top and may spread flat or overlap to form a bowl-shape; the ovary and 5 large stamens are borne together on a central stalk (androphore) surrounded at the base by 1 to several rows of fleshy, short to long filaments (the corona). Grow in borders, large pots or tubs of any standard potting mixture, particularly soil based ones. Pot or plant spring, providing strings, wires or sticks for support. Prune congested or overgrown plants in spring by thinning out the main stems and cutting back laterals on those that remain to 15cm. Propagate by cuttings in summer, bottom heat 18°C, seed when ripe or in spring at 21°C.

Species cultivated: *P. caerulea*, common or blue passion flower; C. and W. S.America; to 10m tall; stems slender, grooved; leaves deeply 5–9 lobed, 10–15cm wide; flowers 6–10cm wide, tepals white or orange; one of the hardiest species, surviving light winter frosts in sheltered sites provided the base is protected. *P.c.* Constance Elliott, flowers entirely white.

Passion flower or **fruit** – see *Passiflora*.

Patrinia

(for Eugene L.M. Patrin, 1724–1815, French mineralogist and amateur botanist who collected in E.Asia). VALERIANACEAE. A genus of 15–20 species of herbaceous perennials from C. to E.Asia, 1 of which is generally available: *P. triloba* (*P. palmata*), Japan; shortly rhizomatous and stoloniferous; stems 30–60cm tall; leaves in opposite pairs, palmate, 3–5 lobed, toothed, 4–8cm wide, lustrous, turning red in autumn; flowers shortly tubular, 5-lobed, spurred at base, 7–8mm wide, golden-yellow, fragrant, in large, terminal, much-branched, panicle-like cymes, late summer. Several similar species with ovate or pinnate leaves are sometimes listed, eg *P. gibbosa*, *P. scabiosaefolia*, *P. sibirica* and *P. villosa* (white-flowered). Grow in any well-drained, humus-rich soil in sun or partial shade. Plant autumn to spring. Propagate by division or rooted stolons at planting time, from seed when ripe, or spring in a cold frame.

Left: *Patrinia triloba*
Top: *Passiflora caerulea*
Above: *Paulownia tomentosa*

Paulownia

(for Princess Anna Paulowna, 1795–1865, daughter of the Russian Tsar Paul I). SCROPHULARIACEAE. A genus of 6 species (17 according to some authorities) of deciduous trees from E.Asia, sometimes classified in BIGNONIACEAE. They have ovate, long-stalked leaves in opposite pairs and terminal panicles or axillary cymes of tubular, somewhat foxglove-like flowers followed by ovoid capsules bearing small, winged seed. Grow in any well-drained, fertile soil in sheltered, sunny sites. Plant autumn to spring. Propagate by root cuttings late winter or from seed in spring under glass, by leaf cuttings when blades about 3cm wide, or stem cuttings late summer.

Species cultivated: *P. fargesii* of gardens, see *P. lilacina*. *P. imperialis*, see *P. tomentosa*. *P. lilacina*, W. China; 10–20m tall; leaves broadly ovate-cordate, slender-pointed, 15–30cm long; flowers in terminal panicles, pale lilac with large yellow throat blotch, to 7·5cm long by 6cm wide, late spring; the true *P. fargesii* for long confused with this species is rarely if ever seen in gardens. *P. tomentosa* (*P. imperialis*), princess tree; China; 10–15m tall; leaves broadly ovate, entire or 3-lobed to 25cm long, dark grey-green above, greyish woolly beneath; flowers blue-purple, fragrant, 4–5cm long, in terminal panicles to 30cm long, late spring; the flower-buds form in autumn and do not always survive the fitful winters of Britain; can be grown purely as a foliage plant by cutting to ground level every spring; robust stems and massive leaves then develop.

Pelargonium

(Greek *pelargos*, a stork – alluding to the slender beaked fruit like a stork's bill). Storksbill. GERANIACEAE. A genus of 250–280 species of perennials and shrubs from Africa (mainly south), adjacent Atlantic Is and E. Mediterranean to S. Arabia, S. India and Australasia. They have paired or alternate, ovate to palmate, sometimes deeply lobed leaves, long-stalked, axillary umbels of 5-petalled flowers, each with a small nectary spur united to the pedicel, and beaked fruit that splits suddenly into 5 sections each with a hairy, tail-like sliver of the enlarged style. Bedding, greenhouse or home, sunny and well-ventilated, minimum temperature 7–10°C. Grow in pots of soil or peat based potting mixture. Pot or repot spring. Water regularly during the main growing season but keep on the dry side in winter if temperatures drop below 10°C. Apply liquid feed at 10-day intervals in summer. The popular *P.* × *hortorum* (so-called zonal geranium) and *P. peltatum* (ivy geranium) cultivars are the geraniums most usually grown or bedded outside in summer when fear of frost has passed. To keep them, they should be cut back by half in autumn, potted and over-wintered under glass. Cuttings may also be taken in late summer and over-wintered as young plants; they provide the best way of increasing favourite varieties. Propagate from seed in spring, that of the *P.* × *hortorum* cultivars specially bred to be raised as annuals, in early spring, 16–18°C. Prick off seedlings into potting mixture, either in boxes or 6·5–7·5cm pots, when first true leaf shows. As soon as roots mesh on the pot-ball, move on into 10–13cm containers. Harden off in early summer prior to planting out or pot on into 15–18cm containers for home or greenhouse display. Most of the shrubby species and cultivars are propagated by cuttings taken in late summer or spring at a temperature of about 18°C. Pot up singly when rooted.

Species cultivated (S. African and summer-flowering unless stated otherwise): *P. abrotanifolium*, southernwood geranium; shrubby, to 1m tall; leaves small, 3-lobed, each lobe deeply cut, velvety-grey downy, aromatic; flowers 2cm wide, white or pink, veined red. *P. capitatum*, rose-scented geranium; shrubby, usually somewhat decumbent, 30–60cm tall; leaves shortly 3–5 lobed and toothed, to 5cm wide, softly hairy; flowers pink, veined red-purple, 2cm long, in tight umbles; sometimes confused with *P. karooense*, a more erect plant having deeply lobed leaves. *P. citriodorum*, a synonym of *P. acerifolium*, but material offered is usually *P.* × *citrosum*, a hybrid of *P. crispum* with larger, lemon-scented leaves. *P. crispum*, lemon geranium; erect, much-branched shrub to 1m tall; leaves crowded, in 2 ranks, shallowly 3-lobed, crisp or somewhat curled or cupped, 2–3cm wide, lemon-scented; flowers 2–2·5cm long, white to pink, purple-veined, solitary or in 2s or 3s. *P.c.* Variegatum, leaves edged cream and white. *P. cucullatum*, shrubby, to 2m tall; leaves kidney-shaped, somewhat cupped, crenate, long hairy, to 6·5cm wide; flowers purple-red, darker-veined, 4–5cm wide but petals narrow; a pale purple form or hybrid is sometimes offered under this name. *P. denticulatum*, shrubby, to 1m tall; leaves bipinnate-partite, lobes slender, basal ones longer, giving a palmate appearance, balsam-scented; flowers 1·5–2cm wide, lilac or pink, purple-blotched. *P.d.* Filicifolium, leaves more finely dissected and ferny. *P.* × *domesticum*, regal, fancy or show geraniums; a complex group of cultivars involving crosses between *P. cucullatum*, *P. angulosum*, *P. grandiflorum*, *P. fulgidum* and others; shrubby, usually stiff and compact, growth 40–60cm tall; leaves 5–10cm wide, toothed, usually shallowly lobed or deeper; flowers 4–5cm wide, shades of white, pink, red, purple, often darker-blotched, bicoloured or picotee-edged, the petals of many cultivars waved or ruffled; many cultivars are available, the following selection having stood the test of time and more recent competition: *P.* × *d.* Carisbrooke, rose-pink, maroon blotch; *P.* × *d.* Doris Frith, veined creamy-white and blotched garnet-purple; *P.* × *d.* Grandma Fischer, salmon-

Far left below: *Pelargonium crispum* Variegatum
Far left bottom: *Pelargonium* L'Elegante
Left below: *Pelargonium* × *hortorum* Caroline Schmidt
Left bottom: *Pelargonium* × *hortorum* Mrs Henry Cox
Below: *Pelargonium* × *fragrans*
Bottom: *Pelargonium* × *hortorum* Irene Cal

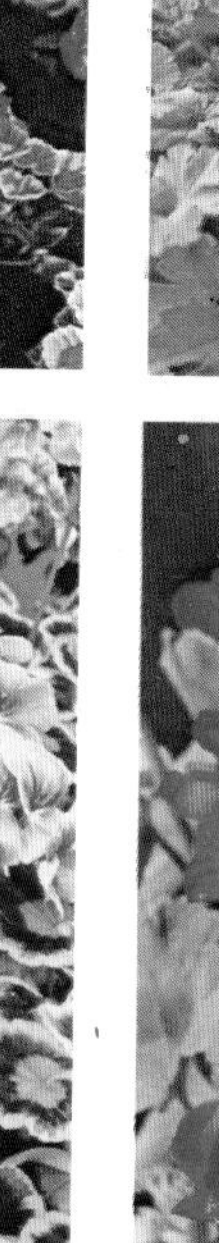

orange, blotched black on each petal; *P.* × *d.* Grand Slam, rose-red, shaded violet; *P.* × *d.* Marie Rober, black-purple overlaying a wine-red base; *P.* × *d.* Princess of Wales, strawberry-pink, white centre, strongly ruffled; *P.* × *d.* South American Bronze, bronze, white picotee; several miniature cultivars are now available. *P. endlicherianum*, Turkey; herbaceous perennial from short, thick rhizome; basal leaves long-stalked, ovate-cordate, shallowly 5-lobed, 4–6cm wide; stems 35–40cm tall with a few, smaller, deeper-lobed leaves; flowers rose-pink, carmine-veined, curiously asymmetrical with the 2 erect upper petals 2·5–3cm long, the lower 3 minute; hardy in areas of light frost. *P. filicifolium*, see *P. denticulatum* Filicifolium. *P.* × *fragrans* (*P. exstipulatum* × *P. odoratissimum*), similar to latter parent but leaves more or less 3-lobed, variously described as nutmeg, pine or lemon-scented. *P. fulgidum*, sub-shrubby, to 60cm or more tall; leaves 7cm long, pinnately lobed, silvery-hairy; flowers bright scarlet, to 4cm wide. *P. graveolens* (*P. terebinthinaceum*), rose geranium; shrubby, to 1m tall; leaves grey-green, palmatipartite with 5 deeply lobed, toothed segments; flowers 3–4cm wide, veined rose-pink and spotted purple; at least some plants listed under this name are hybrids with *P. radens*; the source of commercial geranium oil; *P.* Clorinda, larger, more robust, with basically 3-lobed leaves, is a hybrid of this species. *P.* × *hortorum*, the familiar pot plant and bedding zonal geranium derived from *P. inquinans*, *P. zonale* and several allied species; to 1·5m tall or more; leaves 6–13cm wide, rounded to kidney-shaped, scalloped and crenate, often but not invariably with a brown or bronze horseshoe mark; flowers 2–5cm wide in many shades of red, pink, white, purple, sometimes bicoloured, picotee-edged, double or quilled; several have variegated leaves in shades of white, yellow, red and bronze; of the 100s of cultivars available and that are added to annually, the following have stood the test of time or are currently popular. Single-flowered: *P.* × *h.* Dot Slade, salmon-pink, darker-veined, full, rounded bloom; *P.* × *h.* Golden Lyon, pale orange; *P.* × *h.* Maloja, brilliant orange-red; *P.* × *h.* Perfect, large, crimson, white eye; *P.* × *h.* Venus, pure white; *P.* × *h.* White Bird's Egg, white, spotted-purple. Double and semi-double flowered: *P.* × *h.* A. M. Mayne, magenta; *P.* × *h.* Irene, rich crimson; *P.* × *h.* Irene Cal, soft salmon-pink; *P.* × *h.* Hermione, white. Miniature cultivars (rarely exceeding 20m tall): *P.* × *h.* Fleurette, double, deep salmon-red, dark foliage; *P.* × *h.* Grace Wells, single, fuchsia-pink, dark foliage; *P.* × *h.* Red Black Vesuvius, single, bright red, black-green foliage; *P.* × *h.* Snowbaby, double, large white. Variegated-leaved: *P.* × *h.* Caroline Schmidt, grey-green, edged cream, flowers double, red; *P.* × *h.* Marechal MacMahon, rich green leaves with broad brown zone, flowers single, vermilion; *P.* × *h.* Mr (Mrs) Henry Cox, coppery-red and green to black-green with yellow border, variable in pattern, flowers single, pale pink. *P. inquinans*, shrubby, to 1m tall; leaves cordate, rounded, shallowly 5-7 lobed; flowers 3–4cm wide, pink to vermilion. *P. karooense*, see under *P. capitatum*. *P. odoratissimum*, apple geranium; shrubby; stems sprawling, 25–45cm long; leaves ovate-cordate, 2–3cm wide, ruffled and velvety hairy, sweetly apple-scented; flowers to 2cm wide, white, dotted and veined red. *P. peltatum*, ivy-leaved geranium; stems slender, trailing, to 1m or more long; leaves 5–7cm wide, 5-angled or -lobed, ivy-like but somewhat peltate and fleshy; flowers 3–4cm wide, white to carmine; several cultivars, some of hybrid origin, are available: *P.* Abel Carrière, semi-double, soft red-purple; *P.* Galilee, double, rose-pink; *P.* L'Elégante, leaves variegated cream, tinted rose-purple, flowers white, veined purple; *P.* Mrs W. A. R. Clifton, fully double, scarlet; *P.* White Mesh, leaves with cream vein pattern, flowers salmon-pink. *P. quercifolium* (*P. terebinthinaceum*), oak-leaved geranium; shrubby, 60–120cm tall; leaves ovate in outline, deeply lobed, waved and toothed, often blotched brown, sweetly but pungently aromatic; flowers rosy-mauve, blotched and veined deep purple, about 3cm wide. *P. radens* (*P. radula*), shrubby, to 1m tall; leaves aromatic, 4–7cm long, bipalmatipartite, lobes slender, margins rolled, bristly hairy; flowers about 3cm wide, rose, blotched red-purple. *P. terebinthinaceum*, see *P. graveolens* and *P. quercifolium*; material listed under this name is usually the latter or a cultivar. *P. tetragonum*, shrubby succulent to 1m tall; stems 4-sided, fleshy; leaves 5-lobed to 4cm wide, glaucous; flowers 2·5–3·5cm wide, petals 4, the upper 2 longer, rose-purple, darker-feathered. *P. tomentosum*, peppermint geranium; shrubby, sprawling or trailing; stems to 1m or more long; leaves triangular-ovate, shallowly 5-lobed, densely downy, strongly peppermint-scented; flowers about 1cm wide, white and red. *P. zonale*, shrubby, to 2m tall; leaves orbicular-cordate, crenate, usually with a light to dark, horseshoe-shaped zone; flowers to 4cm wide, pink to red or petunia-purple, petals narrow but equal; rarely seen, but described as a parent of the *P.* × *hortorum* group.

Top: *Peltiphyllum peltatum* autumn colour
Above: *Peltiphyllum peltatum* flower heads
Top right: *Pennisetum villosum*
Above right: *Pennisetum alopecuroides*

Peltiphyllum

(having peltate leaves). SAXIFRAGACEAE. A genus of 1 species of herbaceous perennial from California and Oregon: *P. peltatum* (*Saxifraga p.*), umbrella plant; rhizomatous, forming wide colonies; leaves peltate, 15–25cm wide, orbicular, shallowly 6–10 lobed, somewhat lustrous, bright red in autumn, on erect stalks to 1·5m or more; flowers 5-petalled, pink or white, 1–1·5cm wide in dense, long-stemmed corymbs, spring before the leaves. Grow in moisture-retentive soil or by the waterside in sun or partial shade. Plant autumn or spring. Propagate by division at planting or seed, spring, in cold frame.

Peltoboykinia – see *Boykinia*.

Pennisetum

(Latin *penna*, a feather, and *seta*, a bristle – the foxtail flower-spikes bear many long, often plumose hairs or bristles). GRAMINEAE. A genus of 130–150 species of annual and perennial grasses from tropical to warm temperate regions. The species cultivated are densely tufted or clump-forming perennials sometimes grown as annuals. All are unreliably hardy where severe winters, but in well-drained soil in sunny, moderately sheltered sites they will persist for several to many years. Propagate from seed or by division in spring, seed ideally under glass at about 13–15°C, seedlings hardened and not planted out until fear of frost has passed.

Species cultivated: *P. alopecuroides*, E. Asia to E. Australia; stems to 1·5m tall; leaves very narrow, slender-pointed, 30–60cm long; flower-spikes oblongoid to cylindrical, 10–20cm long, yellow, purple or greenish, bristles numerous but not plumed, summer. *P. longistylum*, see *P. villosum*. *P. orientale*, S.W. to C. Asia and N.W. India; clump-forming, shortly rhizomatous; leaves very slender, arching, 30–60cm long; stems erect to arching, 30–90cm tall; flower-spikes 7–13cm long, usually tinted rosy or purple, bristles silky hairy, summer to autumn. *P. ruppellianum* and *P. ruppellii*, see next species. *P. setaceum* (*P. ruppellianum*, *P. ruppellii*), fountain grass; N. and N.E. tropical Africa, S.W. Asia, Arabia; similar to *P. orientale*, but stems more stiffly erect, usually taller; flower-spikes 10–30cm long; less hardy as a perennial. *P. villosum*, feather top; mountains of N.E. tropical Africa; similar to *P. orientale*, but with denser, tawny to whitish flower-spikes; often cultivated under the incorrect name *P. longistylum*.

Pennyroyal – see *Mentha pulegium*.

Penstemon

(*Pentstemon*). (Greek *pente*, 5, and *stemon*, a stamen: the flowers have 5 stamens – 1 sterile –

distinguishing them from allied genera with 4). SCROPHULARIACEAE. A genus of 250 species of perennials and sub-shrubs from Canada to C. America, 1 in N.E. Asia. They are tufted, erect or decumbent; leaves are in opposite pairs, ovate to linear; flowers are tubular, 5-lobed, generally 2-lipped, in terminal racemes or narrow panicles. Grow in well-drained soil. Not all are fully hardy. Plant autumn to spring. Propagate by cuttings late spring to late summer, division where possible and from seed in spring, the latter under glass.

Species cultivated (summer-flowering): *P. barbatus* (*Chelone b.*), Utah to Mexico; perennial, to 1m or more tall; leaves oblong to linear, 3–8cm long; flowers 2·5cm long, scarlet, the lower lip yellow-bearded. *P.b.* Carnea, light pink. *P. campanulatus* (*P. pulchellus*), Mexico, Guatemala; perennial, 40–60cm tall; leaves linear to lanceolate, sharply toothed, to 10cm long; flowers 2·5cm long, pink, purple or violet; often represented in gardens as hybrid cultivars, eg *P.* × Garnet, wine-red, summer to autumn. *P. confertus*, see *P. procerus*. *P. crassifolius*, see *P. fruticosus*. *P. cristatus*, see *P. eriantherus*. *P. davidsonii* (*P. menziesii d.*), British Columbia to Oregon; mat-forming sub-shrub to 15cm tall; leaves entire, elliptic or broadly obovate to orbicular, about 1cm long; flowers 3–4cm long, violet-purple. *P.d. menziesii* (*P. menziesii*), leaves elliptic to ovate, obscurely to obviously toothed. *P. eriantherus* (*P. cristatus*), British Columbia and Washington State, east to Nebraska; perennial, to 40cm tall; leaves lanceolate to ovate, glandular-downy; flowers 2·5cm long, violet-purple to lavender. *P.e. reductus*, 10–20cm tall, leaves lanceolate. *P. fruticosus* (*P. crassifolius*, *P. menziesii douglasii*), Oregon to British Columbia; erect sub-shrub, 20–40cm tall; leaves lanceolate to oblanceolate, 3–5cm long, entire to sharply toothed; flowers 3–4·5cm long, lavender to light purple. *P.f. scouleri* (*P. scouleri*), leaves linear-lanceolate, always finely toothed. *P.f.s.* Alba, flowers white. *P.* × Garnet, see *P. campanulatus*. *P. gentianoides*, see *P. hartwegii*. *P. glaber* (*P. gordonii*), N. Dakota to Nebraska and Wyoming; perennial 30–60cm tall; leaves lanceolate to oblanceolate, 5–15cm long; flowers 3cm long, blue-purple; a hybrid seed strain with stems 30cm tall and flowers in shades of purple, blue, pink and red is offered under this name. *P.* × *gloxinioides* a name of no botanical standing covering hybrids between *P. cobaea* and *P. hartwegii*, the several cultivars of which comprise the familiar, somewhat half-hardy garden penstemons with broad, 5cm-long, foxglove-like flowers in shades of crimson, scarlet, pink, white and bicolours, eg *P.* × Pennington Gem, cerise, white throat; *P.* × Schonholzeri (*P.* × Firebird), vigorous and free-flowering, scarlet. *P. gordonii*, see *P. glaber*. *P. hartwegii* (*P. gentianoides*), Mexico; perennial, to 60cm tall; leaves lanceolate to narrowly ovate, to 10cm long; flowers 5cm long, scarlet to deep red; the main parent of *P.* × *gloxinioides*. *P. heterophyllus*, California; sub-shrub, 30–60cm or more tall; leaves linear to lanceolate, to 5cm long, sometimes glaucous; flowers purple to bright blue, to 4cm long. *P.h.* Blue Gem, flowers blue. *P. isophyllus*, Mexico; sub-shrub, 60–90cm tall; leaves elliptic-ovate, 3–6·5cm long; flowers about 4·5cm long, crimson-scarlet; not reliably hardy in severe winters. *P. laetus*, California; sub-shrub 30–60cm tall, whitish downy; leaves linear to lanceolate, to 10cm long; flowers 2·5cm long, blue-violet to lavender. *P.l. roezlii*, flowers 2cm. *P. menziesii*, see *P. davidsonii* and *P. fruticosus*. *P. micranthus*, see *P. procerus*. *P. newberryi*, mountain pride; N. California, Nevada;

Far left top: *Penstemon isophyllus*
Far left above: *Penstemon fruticosus*
Left top: *Penstemon* × Six Hills
Left above: *Penstemon* × Pennington Gem
Top: *Penstemon hartwegii*
Above: *Penstemon fruticosus scouleri* Alba

sub-shrub to 30cm or more tall; stems decumbent; leaves elliptic to ovate, toothed, 2–4cm long; flowers to 3cm long, cerise-crimson; confused in gardens with *P. laetus roezlii*. *P. newberryi rupicola*, see *P. rupicola*. *P. pinifolius*, S.W. New Mexico, adjacent Arizona, Mexico; mat-forming sub-shrub, 10–30cm tall; leaves stiff linear, needle-like, 2cm long; flowers scarlet, 2·5–3·5cm long. *P. procerus* (*P. micranthus*), Alaska and Yukon to Colorado; perennial, to 45cm tall; leaves lanceolate to oblanceolate, to 7·5cm long; flowers 1·2cm long, purple-blue; the similar *P. confertus* has pale yellow flowers. *P. pulchellus*, see *P. campanulatus*. *P. roezlii*, see *P. laetus r.* *P. rupicola* (*P. newberryi r.*), N. California to Washington State; mat-forming sub-shrub to 10cm; leaves elliptic to rounded, to 2cm, usually glaucous; flowers to 3cm, carmine; confused with *P. davidsonii*. *P. scouleri*, see *P. fruticosus s.* *P.* × Six Hills (*P. rupicola* × *P. eriantherus*), midway between parents; 25cm tall; flowers lilac, foliage glaucous.

Pentstemon – see *Penstemon*.

Peony – see *Paeonia*.

Pepper tree – see *Drimys*.

Peppermint – see *Mentha* × *piperita*.

Perilla

(derivation not known, perhaps Latin *pera*, a bag – alluding to the shape of the fruiting calyx). LABIATAE. A genus of 5 or 6 species of annuals from India to Japan, 1 of which is generally available: *P. frutescens* (*P. ocymoides*), Himalaya to E.Asia; half-hardy, 60–90cm tall; stems erect; leaves in pairs, broadly ovate, more or less pointed and toothed; flowers small, insignificant, tubular, 5-lobed, white. *P.f.* Atropurpurea, leaves dark purple; *P.f.* Crispa (*P.f. nankinensis*, *P. laciniata*), leaves deeply cut, bronze to purple – often listed as *P.f.* Foliis Atropurpureis Laciniatus. Grow in light, fertile but not dry soil, in sun. Sow seed in early spring at 18°C; prick off seedlings when true leaves show at 4–5cm apart in boxes of any commercial potting mixture; harden off in early summer and plant out when fear of frost has passed. Can also be grown as a foliage pot plant for the cool or warm greenhouse.

Periwinkle – see *Vinca*.

Pernettya

(for Antoine Joseph Pernetty, 1716–1801, who sailed with the explorer Bougainville, visiting S.America and Falkland Is, and later wrote about it). ERICACEAE. A genus of 20–25 species of evergreen shrubs from Mexico to temperate S.America, Falkland Is, New Zealand, Tasmania. They resemble *Gaultheria* and are so closely related that they will probably be included under that genus eventually. Culture as for *Gaultheria*.

Species cultivated: *P. ciliata* (*Gaultheria c.*, *P. buxifolia*, *P. hirsuta*, *P pilosa*, *P. mexicana*), Mexico – mountains; like *P. prostrata* but in some forms branchlets densely bristly and leaves ciliate. *P. empetrifolia*, see *P. pumila*. *P. mucronata*, S.Chile and Argentina to Straits of Magellan; densely branched, 60–100cm tall; leaves dense, ovate to oblong-lanceolate, toothed and mucronate, 8–20mm long; flowers 6mm long, nodding, from upper leaf-axils, early summer; fruit globose, 8–12mm wide, white, pink, red, lilac-purple, often in profusion and long-lasting; partially dioecious and best planted in small groups with at least 1 pollen-producing clone, eg *P.m.* Thymifolia. *P.m.* Bell's Seedling is a good hermaphrodite clone with large, dark red fruit. *P prostrata*, Costa Rica to Chile – mountains; mat-forming, prostrate or to 30cm tall; young stems downy and sparsely bristly; leaves ovate, bristly toothed, to 1·5cm long; flowers solitary in leaf-axils, nodding, white, about 8mm long, summer; more commonly represented in cultivation by *P.p. pentlandii*, with longer, oblong leaves; fruit blue-purple, 6–9mm wide. *P. pumila* (*P. empetrifolia*), southern tip S.America, Falkland Is; resembles a prostrate *P. mucronata*, but leaves lack pointed tip and rarely above 6mm long; flowers and fruit 4·5mm long; usually dioecious, and male and female plants are needed to obtain the edible fruit. *P. tasmanica*, Tasmania; prostrate, mat-forming; stems wiry; leaves narrowly elliptic, 3–6mm long, sometimes obscurely toothed; flowers solitary, 3–4mm long, white; fruit rounded, 6–8mm wide, red, sometimes cream or white (*P.t.* Alba).

Perovskia

(*Perowskia*). (for V. A. Perovski, 1794–1857, Russian general and provincial governor). LABIATAE. A genus of 7 species of aromatic, woody-based, shrub-like perennials from E.Iran to N.W.India. They have erect stems, square in cross-section, opposite pairs of ovate to oblong leaves, the upper ones sometimes pinnately lobed, and branched spikes of tubular, 2-lipped flowers. Grow in any well-drained soil in sun. Plant autumn to spring. Propagate from seed in spring or when ripe, or by cuttings of non-flowering shoots in summer in a cold frame, over-wintering young plants in the frame until spring.

Top left: *Perilla frutescens* Atropurpurea
Left: *Pernettya mucronata* Pink Pearl
Above: *Perovskia atriplocifolia*
Top right: *Petasites japonicus*
Above right: *Petasites fragrans*

Species cultivated: *P. abrotanoides*, USSR (Turkmenia, Tianshan), Iran, Baluchistan; 60–120cm tall, more or less covered with a thin coating of grey-white, starry hairs; leaves 2·5–5cm long, narrowly oblong, pinnatisect, lobes sometimes deeply cut; flowers violet-blue, 8mm long, late summer; often confused with forms of following: *P. atriplicifolia*, W.Himalaya, Afghanistan; similar to *P. abrotanoides* but more robust and prominently white downy; leaves oblong to slightly obovate, coarsely toothed or pinnatifid. *P.a.* Blue Haze, leaves entire or almost so; *P.a.* Blue Spire, lower leaves pinnatipartite, lobes sometimes pinnatifid.

Persian lilac – see *Melia*.

Petasites

(Greek *petasos*, a hat with a broad brim – alluding to the large leaves of some species). Butterbur. COMPOSITAE. A genus of 15 species of perennials

from Europe, Asia, N.America, several of which are rhizomatous and highly invasive. They have long-stalked, palmate leaves from ground level and racemes of large, groundsel-like flower-heads often before or with young leaves. Grow in any moderately moisture-retentive soil in sun or partial shade; *P. japonicus* is best in wet soil. Plant autumn to spring. Propagate by division at planting.

Species cultivated: *P. fragrans*, winter heliotrope; W.Mediterranean; rhizomatous, evergreen; leaves rounded-cordate, 10–20cm wide; flowering stems to 25cm tall, bearing 5–10 tubular, lilac, vanilla-scented heads, winter; very invasive. *P. japonicus*, Japanese butterbur; Korea, China, Ryukyus; rhizomatous, herbaceous; leaves rounded to kidney-shaped, to 30cm wide; flowering stems 15–20cm tall, enveloped in broad, 5–6·5cm long, lime-green bracts, flower-heads white, in terminal clusters, before the leaves, early spring. *P.j. giganteus*, N.Japan, Sakhalin, Kuriles; leaves larger than type, to 1·5m wide on stems to 2m tall; invasive in wet soil; leaf-stalks used as a vegetable, or candied.

Petrophytum

(Greek *petros*, rock, *phyton*, a plant – the species inhabit rocky places). ROSACEAE. A genus of about 4 species of mat- or cushion-forming perennials from mountains of W. N.America, 1 species usually being available: *P. hendersonii* (*Spiraea h.*), Washington, Olympic mountains; hummock mat-forming evergreen shrub; leaves oblanceolate, bluish-green, purple-tinted in winter, 2cm long; flowers tiny, many-stamened, creamy-white, in fluffy racemes

4–7·5cm long, well above the leaves, early summer. Grow in well-drained, neutral to acid soil in partial shade, ideally the north side of a rock outcrop or boulder, or alternatively as a pot plant in an alpine house. Plant or pot autumn or spring. Propagate by cuttings taken immediately the flowers fade or from seed when ripe or spring under glass.

Petunia

(Brazilian vernacular *petun*, for tobacco in Latin form – the genus is allied to *Nicotiana*). SOLANACEAE. A genus of about 40 species of half-hardy annuals and perennials from S.USA to S.America. They are tufted, erect to decumbent, often sticky glandular hairy, with alternate, spathulate to lanceolate or ovate leaves, and solitary, funnel- or salver-shaped flowers in the upper leaf-axils. Grow in fertile, well-drained soil in sun or in 13–18cm pots of any commercial potting mixture for greenhouse decoration. Sow seed thinly in mid spring at 16–21°C, barely covering with soil; prick out seedlings when large enough to handle into boxes at 4cm apart, minimum temperature 15°C. Harden off early summer and plant out post-frost.
Species cultivated: *P. axillaris*, large white petunia; S. Brazil to Argentina; erect to decumbent; stems 30–60cm long; leaves ovate to lanceolate, 5–11cm long; flowers funnel-shaped, 6·5cm long by 5cm wide, white, fragrant at night; seldom available but the primary parent of the following: *P.* × *hybrida*, a large complex group of hybrid cultivars derived from *P. axillaris* and the allied and similar *P. inflata* and *P. violacea* (red to violet flowered). This group has mutated freely and plants may be compact or elongate with flowers frilled to heavily crested, single to double, in a vast range of red, purple, yellow, white shades, the largest ones to 13cm wide. The many cultivars available may be grouped as follows, those given as examples being recommended, although always likely to be superceded by the continuing flow of new ones: **1** Multiflora, plants bushy, 15–30cm tall, flowers single or double, 5cm wide, very freely borne, weather-resistant; *P* × *h.* Snowdrift, pure white; *P.* × *h.* Summer Sun, yellow; *P.* × *h.* Red Satin, scarlet; *P.* × *h.* Plum Blue, soft clear blue. **2** Grandiflora, plants similar to Multiflora but flowers fewer and larger – to 10cm or more wide: *P.* × *h.* Miss Blanche, white; *P.* × *h.* Mariner, deep blue; *P.* × *h.* Polynesia, coral-salmon; *P.* × *h.* Happiness, rose-pink. **3** Nana compacta, plants low-growing, not above 15cm tall: *P.* × *h.* Dwarf Resisto, blue, red, pink; *P.* × *h.* Dwarf Giants of California, large waved blooms in mixed colours – good for pot culture. **4** Pendula, plants with long, trailing stems, ideal for hanging baskets or summer ground cover: *P.* × *h.* Avalanche, mixed colours.

Phacelia

(Greek *phacelos*, a bundle – the first described species had bunched flowers). HYDROPHYLLACEAE. A genus of about 200 species of annuals and perennials from N. and S.America, especially California. They are mainly tufted, erect to decumbent, with alternate, ovate to linear, sometimes lobed leaves, and 5-lobed, tubular to rotate flowers in scorpiod cymes often in panicles. Culture of annual species as *Nemophila*.
Species cultivated: *P. campanularia*, California bluebell; S.California; annual, 20–30cm tall; stems erect, branching from base; leaves elliptic to broadly ovate, coarsely toothed or angular, 2–7cm long; flowers tubular bell-shaped, 1·5–3cm long, rich bright blue, in loose, raceme-like cymes, summer. *P. tanacetifolia*, S.W.USA, Mexico; annual, 45–90cm tall; stems erect, branched; leaves to 10cm or more long, pinnate or bipinnately lobed; flowers broadly bell-shaped, 6–9mm long, blue to lavender.

Top: *Petunia* × *hybrida* Brilliant Mixed
Centre top: *Petunia* × *hybrida* double flowered cultivars
Centre above: *Petunia* × *hybrida* Summer Sun
Above: *Phacelia campanularia*

Phalaris

(Greek vernacular for a grass, probably of this genus). GRAMINEAE. A genus of about 15 species of annual and perennial grasses from northern and southern temperate regions. They are tufted or rhizomatous with linear leaves and dense, spike-like panicles composed of flattened, 1-flowered spikelets. Grow in any ordinary garden soil in sun, although most of the perennials will stand partial shade. Plant perennials autumn to spring. Propagate perennials by division at planting time, annuals from seed sown *in situ* in spring.
Species cultivated: *P. arundinacea*, reed canary grass; northern temperate zone, S.Africa; rhizomatous, forming extensive colonies; stems 60–180cm tall; leaves arching, 10–35cm long; panicles oblongoid, lobed, 6–25cm long, purplish or whitish-green; invasive, especially on moist soils; usually represented in gardens by *P.a.* Picta (*P.a.* Variegata), gardener's garters, ribbon grass; leaves white-striped; *P.a.* Luteopicta, leaves yellow-striped. *P. canariensis*, Canary grass; W.Mediterranean; annual, to 60cm or more tall; leaves finely pointed, to 25cm long, rough; panicles ovoid, very dense, 2–6cm long, whitish-green, yellowish when ripe; much grown commercially for its polished grain that is used as bird seed.

Above: *Phalaris arundinacea* Picta

Pharbitis – see *Ipomoea*.

Pheasant's eye – see *Adonis annua*.

Philadelphus

(said to be for Ptolemy Philadelphus, 283–247BC, king of ancient Egypt). Mock orange, 'syringa'. PHILADELPHACEAE (SAXIFRAGACEAE). A genus of about 65 species of deciduous shrubs from the northern temperate zone. They are densely branched, usually suckering freely from the base, with opposite pairs of ovate to lanceolate leaves and white, 4-petalled flowers in racemes (occasionally solitary) opening in summer from buds of the previous year. Grow in any well-drained, moderately fertile soil in sun, although partial shade is tolerated. Plant autumn to spring. Propagate by suckers at planting time, semi-hardwood cuttings rooted in a cold frame late summer, or hardwood cuttings taken in autumn. Seed may be sown in spring but seldom comes true to type if collected from garden plants.
Species cultivated: *P.* Avalanche, see *P.* × *lemoinei*. *P.* Beauclerc and *P.* Belle Etoile, see *P.* × *purpureo-maculatus*. *P.* Bouquet Blanc, see *P.* × *cymosus*. *P.* Burfordensis, see *P.* × *virginalis*. *P. coronarius*,

Left: *Philadelphus* × *lemoinei* Avalanche
Far left below: ***Philadelphus*** **×** ***purpureomaculatus*** Belle Etoile
Left below: *Philadelphus* × *virginalis* Virginal
Above: *Philadelphus coronarius* Aureus
Below: *Philesia magellanica*

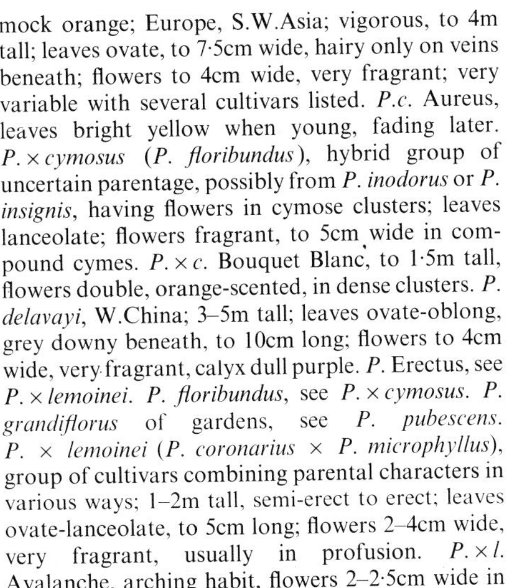

mock orange; Europe, S.W.Asia; vigorous, to 4m tall; leaves ovate, to 7·5cm wide, hairy only on veins beneath; flowers to 4cm wide, very fragrant; very variable with several cultivars listed. *P.c.* Aureus, leaves bright yellow when young, fading later. *P.* × *cymosus* (*P. floribundus*), hybrid group of uncertain parentage, possibly from *P. inodorus* or *P. insignis*, having flowers in cymose clusters; leaves lanceolate; flowers fragrant, to 5cm wide in compound cymes. *P.* × *c.* Bouquet Blanc, to 1·5m tall, flowers double, orange-scented, in dense clusters. *P. delavayi*, W.China; 3–5m tall; leaves ovate-oblong, grey downy beneath, to 10cm long; flowers to 4cm wide, very fragrant, calyx dull purple. *P.* Erectus, see *P.* × *lemoinei*. *P. floribundus*, see *P.* × *cymosus*. *P. grandiflorus* of gardens, see *P. pubescens*. *P.* × *lemoinei* (*P. coronarius* × *P. microphyllus*), group of cultivars combining parental characters in various ways; 1–2m tall, semi-erect to erect; leaves ovate-lanceolate, to 5cm long; flowers 2–4cm wide, very fragrant, usually in profusion. *P.* × *l.* Avalanche, arching habit, flowers 2–2·5cm wide in 7-blossomed racemes; *P.* × *l.* Erectus, confused with *P.* × *l.* Avalanche, but flowers in 3–5 blossomed racemes and of erect habit at least in the early years; *P.* × *l.* Manteau d'Hermine, compact habit to 1·2m tall, flowers double creamy-white. *P. microphyllus*, S.W.USA to Mexico; dense habit to 1·5m tall; leaves ovate to lanceolate, 1–3cm long; flowers usually solitary, fragrant, 2–2·5cm wide. *P. pubescens* (*P. grandiflorus* of gardens), S.E.USA; to 3m or more tall; leaves ovate, to 10cm long, sparsely toothed, grey downy beneath; flowers in racemes of 5–9, each one 4cm wide, calyx downy. *P.* × *purpureomaculatus* (*P. coulteri* × *P.* × *lemoinei*), group of cultivars, 1·5–2m tall, characterized by flowers flushed purple in the centre. *P.* × *p.* Belle Etoile, flowers to 3cm wide in compound cymes, very sweetly scented; *P.* × *p.* Sybille, flowers to 4cm wide, solitary or in groups of 2–3, the basal half of each petal stained rose-purple, the tip fringed. *P.* Virginal, see next entry. *P.* × *virginalis*, group of hybrid cultivars of uncertain origin, possibly *P.* × *lemoinei* crossed by *P.* × *nivalis* (*P. coronarius* × *P. pubescens*); best known is *P.* × *v.* Virginal, 2·5–3m tall, rather sparse habit when old; leaves ovate, 4–9cm long, coarsely toothed on non-flowering stems; flowers semi-double, 4–5cm wide, calyx densely downy; one of the oldest cultivars.

× **Philageria** – see next entry.

Philesia

(Greek *phileo*, to love–alluding to the beauty of the flowers). PHILESIACEAE (LILIACEAE). A genus of 1 species of dwarf evergreen shrub from S.Chile: *P. magellanica* (*P. buxifolia*), suckering, forming colonies of wiry stems, 30–120cm tall (usually shorter in cultivation); leaves alternate, 3–4cm long, narrowly oblong, with rolled margins, stiff, dark glossy green above, glaucous beneath; flowers terminal, solitary, nodding, rose-crimson, the 3 petals forming a slender bell 5–6·5cm wide; closely allied to

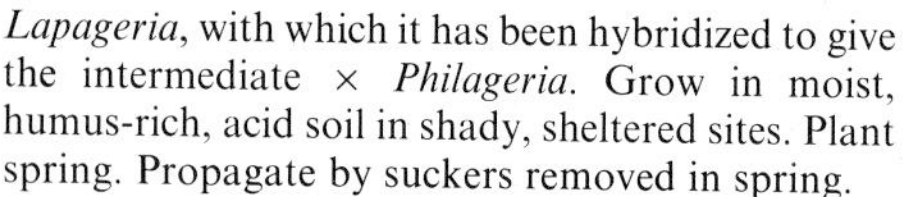

Lapageria, with which it has been hybridized to give the intermediate × *Philageria*. Grow in moist, humus-rich, acid soil in shady, sheltered sites. Plant spring. Propagate by suckers removed in spring.

Phillyrea

(Greek vernacular name, although apparently derived from another language). OLEACEAE. A genus of 4 species of evergreen shrubs or trees from S.W. Asia, Mediterranean, Madeira. They have opposite pairs of leathery, linear to ovate leaves, short, axillary racemes of small, tubular, 4-lobed, white flowers and black, berry-like drupes. Grow in any well-drained, fertile soil, in mild areas and sun. Plant autumn or spring. Propagate by cuttings in a cold frame late summer or from seed when ripe.
Species cultivated: *P. angustifolia*, Portugal and Mediterranean to Turkey; dense, rounded shrub to 3m or more tall; leaves linear-oblong or lanceolate, 2·5–6cm long, rarely toothed, deep matt-green; flowers 6mm wide, greenish-white, fragrant, in racemes 1–1·5cm long, early summer; fruit blue-black, ovoid, 6mm long. *P. decora*, see *Osmanthus decorus*. *P. latifolia* (*P. media*), Mediterranean to Turkey; rounded or spreading shrub or tree, 5–10m tall; leaves ovate, elliptic to lanceolate, usually toothed, 5–6·5cm long, deep glossy green; flowers 5mm wide, greenish-white, late spring, early summer; fruit globose, 6mm wide. *P. media*, see *P. latifolia*.

Phlomis

(Greek vernacular, probably not for any member of this genus, used by Linnaeus). LABIATAE. A genus of about 100 species of perennials and evergreen shrubs from Mediterranean to China. The perennials are clump-forming with long-stalked basal leaves, the shrubs with opposite pairs of narrowly to broadly oblong or ovate leaves, both having tubular, 2-lipped, hooded flowers in the upper leaf-axils forming spike-like inflorescences. Grow in any well-drained site in sun, in mild areas and sheltered from strong, icy winds. Plant autumn or spring. Propagate perennials by division at planting time, shrubs by cuttings in late summer, all species from seed in spring, preferably under glass.
Species cultivated: *P. chrysophylla*, E.Mediterranean, adjacent S.W.Asia; shrub 60–90cm tall; leaves oblong to elliptic to ovate, 4–6cm long, densely starry hairy on both sides, golden-tinted especially when young; flowers 2–3cm long, golden-yellow, summer. *P. fruticosa*, Jerusalem sage; Mediterranean, west to Sardinia; shrub to 1·3m tall; leaves elliptic, lanceolate or narrowly ovate, truncate at base, starry hairy, denser and whiter beneath; flowers 2·5–3·5cm long, deep yellow, late spring to late summer. *P. italica*, Balearic Is (despite its name); shrub 1–2m tall; leaves oblong to oblong-lanceolate, crenate, 4–9cm long, starry white hairy on both sides; flowers pink to purple, 2cm long, each in the axil of a tiny bract (bracteole) to 2mm wide, summer. *P. purpurea*, S.Spain, S.Portugal; much like *P. italica* but leaves very shortly starry, downy above; flowers about 2·5cm long and bracteoles 2–4mm wide. *P. russeliana* (*P. viscosa* of gardens, not the true sub-shrubby *P. viscosa* described by Poiret), Turkey; perennial; stems leafy, 90–120cm tall; basal leaves 15–30cm long, finely wrinkled, sage-green above, starry hairy beneath; flowers about 3cm long, yellow, summer. *P. samia*, Greece, S.Yugoslavia; perennial; stems leafy, to 1m tall; basal leaves 8–18cm long, lanceolate-ovate, cordate or sagittate at base, crenate or serrate, white starry downy, particularly beneath; flowers 2·5–3·5cm long, purple, summer.

Phlox

(Greek vernacular for a plant, not of this genus, with flame-coloured flowers, used by Linnaeus). POLEMONIACEAE. A genus of about 60 species of annuals, perennials and sub-shrubs, mainly from N.America (1 only in Siberia). They are erect, decumbent or prostrate, with opposite pairs of linear to ovate leaves, and 5-lobed, tubular flowers in terminal cymes or panicles, sometimes solitary. Grow clump-forming perennials in moisture-retentive, humus-rich soil in partial shade, and annuals and alpines in well-drained soil in sun, but see also species descriptions for special requirements. Plant autumn or spring. Propagate by division at planting time, stem cuttings after flowering, root cuttings and from seed in spring.
Species cultivated: *P. adsurgens*, California, Oregon; stems prostrate or ascending, to 15cm or more tall, from creeping underground rootstock; leaves evergreen, ovate to elliptic, 1–3cm long; flowers 1·5–2cm wide, bright pink to purple and white, early summer; best in light shade and peaty soil. *P.a.* Wagon Wheel, flowers large, deep pink. *P. amoena* of gardens, see *P.* × *procumbens*. *P.* × *arendsii*, a name of no botanical validity for hybrids between *P. paniculata* and *P. divaricata*, similar in impact to the first parent, but 30–60cm tall, flowering early summer onwards: *P.* × *a.* Anja, red-purple; *P.* × *a.* Hilda, lavender; *P.* × *a.* Susanne, white, red eye. *P. austromontana* (*P. douglasii a.*), W.USA – mountains; mat- or low hummock-forming, 5–10cm tall in bloom; leaves evergreen, linear, firm-pointed, 8–20mm long, hairy; flowers 1·2–1·8cm wide, usually solitary but borne in abundance, white, rarely lavender or pink, early summer; several cultivars are listed, those with red

Far left top: *Phlomis fruticosa*
Top left: *Phlomis purpurea*
Top: *Phlomis russeliana*
Above: *Phlox paniculata* Brigadier

Top: *Phlox borealis*
Centre: *Phlox bifida*
Above: *Phlox drummondii* Beauty Mixed
Top right: *Phlox maculata* Omega foreground
Centre right: *Phlox adsurgens*
Above right: *Phlox subulata* White Delight

to crimson flowers probably of hybrid origin with *P. subulata*. *P. bifida*, sand phlox; west and south of Gt Lakes; tufted, from creeping rhizomes; stems slender, decumbent to erect, to 20cm tall; leaves 2·5–5cm long, linear to lanceolate, pointed; flowers about 2cm wide, the lavender to white petals deeply cleft, early summer; best in peaty, sandy soil. *P. borealis* of some gardens, stems prostrate, mat-forming; leaves evergreen, linear, to 2cm long; flowers to 2cm wide, deep pink with ring-like darker eye, late spring; possibly a *P. subulata* hybrid. *P. brittonii*, see *P. subulata*. *P. caespitosa* (*P. douglasii*), Oregon and Montana to New Mexico; tufted, hummock-forming to 13cm high; leaves linear, 5–12mm long; flowers white to lilac, 1·5cm wide; plants grown in gardens under this name may be the flatter-growing *P. austromontana*. *P. canadensis*, see next entry. *P. divaricata*, E. N.America; non-flowering stems prostrate, rooting, flowering stems erect, 15–25cm or more tall; leaves to 5cm long, elliptic to oblong; flowers 3–4cm wide, lobes notched, lavender to pale violet, late spring; best in peaty soil and partial shade. *P.d. laphamii* (*P. canadensis l.*), petal-lobes un-notched, deep blue-violet; *P.d.* Chattahoochee, hybrid with *P. pilosa* having bright mauve-blue flowers with a cerise eye. *P. douglasii* of gardens, see *P. austromontana*; for the true species see *P. caespitosa*. *P. drummondii*, annual phlox; Texas; half-hardy annual, 30–50cm tall; leaves to 7cm long, ovate to lanceolate, sessile, partially stem-clasping; flowers to 2·5cm wide, in shades of purple, red, pink, buff and white, summer to autumn; best sown under glass at 13–16°C, pricked off into boxes and hardened off for early summer planting; many cultivars and mixed strains are available that can be classified into 3 groups: Grandiflora, having larger flowers; Cuspidata (star phlox), petals slender-pointed, sometimes fringed; and Nana Compacta, dwarf bushy habit to 23cm. *P. hoodii*, N.W. N.America; cushion-forming, to 5cm high; leaves grey-green, linear, 4–10mm long, usually long hairy; flowers 1·3–1·6cm wide, white to lilac; plants with non-hairy leaves, 1–1·5cm long and slightly larger, lilac to pink flowers are likely to be *P. diffusa* (California, Oregon). *P. kelseyi*, E.Montana to Wyoming; tufted, forming loose cushions 10–15cm tall; leaves linear-lanceolate, 1–2·5cm long, somewhat succulent and often hairy; flowers 2cm wide, white to lavender; very doubtfully in cultivation in gardens, forms or hybrids of *P. austromontana* or allied species masquerading in its place. *P. maculata*, wild sweet William (USA); E.C.USA; clump-forming; stems erect, usually purple-spotted (except in white or pale-flowered cultivars), 1m or more tall; leaves 8–13cm long, linear to lanceolate on lower part, ovate above; flowers fragrant, 1·5–2cm wide, purple, violet-pink to white, in cylindrical panicles, summer. *P.m.* Alpha, flowers pink; *P.m.* Omega, white, tinted violet. *P. nivalis*, see *P. subulata*. *P. paniculata* (*P. decussata*), border or fall phlox; E.USA, from New York south; clump-forming; stems erect, 1–1·5m tall; leaves 10cm or more long, elliptic to ovate; flowers fragrant, about 2·5cm wide, rose-purple to white, in pyramidal panicles, late summer to autumn; represented in gardens by dozens of cultivars, some of which are probably hybrids with *P. maculata*: Brigadier, orange-red, 1–2m; Dorothy Hanbury Forbes, clear pink, 1m; Fairy's Petticoat, pale mauve, dark eye; Harlequin, leaves boldly variegated cream, flowers purple-violet; Leo Schlageter, bright deep scarlet; Mia Ruys, pure white, only 50cm tall; Vintage Wine, purplish-red, 80cm; White Admiral, white, 1m. *P.* × *procumbens* (*P. amoena* of gardens), (*P. stolonifera* × *P. subulata*), stems decumbent, 15–30cm tall; leaves evergreen, oblanceolate to elliptic, to 2·5cm long; flowers 2cm wide, bright purple, early summer. *P.*×*p.* Folio-Variegata, leaves cream-variegated; *P.*×*p.* Millstream, vigorous, clear pink, red and white eye, needs humus-rich soil and partial shade. *P. stolonifera*, creeping phlox; S.E.USA; non-flowering stems prostrate, forming loose mats, flowering stems erect, 15–30cm tall; leaves evergreen, spathulate to obovate or ovate, 3–7cm long; flowers 2–3cm wide, violet or purple, late spring; needs humus-rich soil in light shade. *P.s.* Blue Ridge, clear lavender-blue; best in light shade. *P. subulata*, moss or mountain phlox; N.E.USA; mat-forming, to 1m wide; stems prostrate; leaves evergreen, linear, 1–2·5cm long; flowers to 2cm wide, lobes shallowly notched, red to violet-purple, pink or rarely white, late spring; several cultivars are available, some of them strictly belonging to the similar but glandular hairy *P. nivalis*: *P.s.* Alexander's Surprise, large flowers, bright salmon-pink; *P.s.* Oakington Blue Eyes, sky-blue; *P.s.* G.F. Wilson, soft lavender-blue, starry; *P.s.* Red Wings, flowers large, scarlet, dark-eyed; *P.s.* Temiskaming, magenta; *P.s.* White Delight, snow-white.

Phormium

(Greek *phormion*, a mat – the strong leaf fibres are woven to make cloth, mats, baskets, rope etc). New Zealand flax. AGAVACEAE (LILIACEAE). A genus of 2 species of evergreen perennials from New Zealand and adjacent islands. They are clump-forming with leathery, sword-shaped leaves and stiff panicles of 6-tepalled, tubular flowers followed by cylindrical capsules and flattened, satiny black seed. Grow in fertile, moisture-retentive soil in sun, although partial shade is tolerated. Generally much hardier than often stated but liable to damage in severe winters, and in areas of moderate frost best against walls. Plant spring. Propagate from seed in spring under glass, or by division at the same time.

Species cultivated: *P. cookianum* (*P. colensoi*), mountain flax; leaves 1–1·5m, sometimes 2m long, arching or drooping when mature, usually glossy; flowering stems to 2m tall, flowers greenish to orange or yellowish, 2·5–4cm long; capsules pendulous, almost cylindrical, twisted, to 10cm or more long; several cultivars, some of hybrid origin with the species *P. tenax* are available: *P.c.* Purpureum, leaves dark purple; *P.c.* Tricolor, leaves striped creamy-yellow and margined red; *P.c.* Aurora, bronze, striped pink, red, burnt-orange; *P.c.* Bronze Baby (*P.c.* Baby Bronze), leaves bronze, somewhat glaucous beneath; plants under this name in Britain

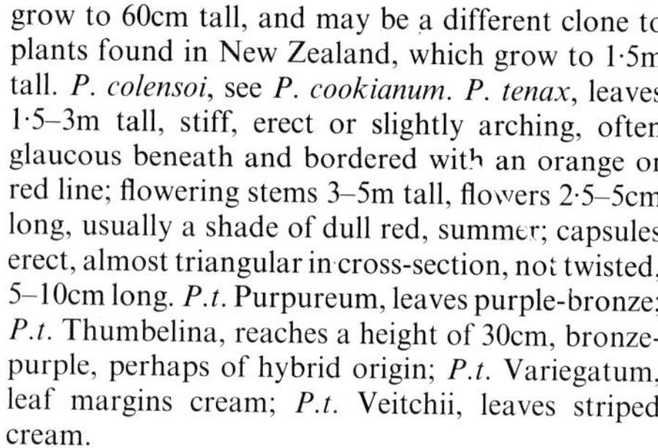

grow to 60cm tall, and may be a different clone to plants found in New Zealand, which grow to 1·5m tall. *P. colensoi*, see *P. cookianum*. *P. tenax*, leaves 1·5–3m tall, stiff, erect or slightly arching, often glaucous beneath and bordered with an orange or red line; flowering stems 3–5m tall, flowers 2·5–5cm long, usually a shade of dull red, summer; capsules erect, almost triangular in cross-section, not twisted, 5–10cm long. *P.t.* Purpureum, leaves purple-bronze; *P.t.* Thumbelina, reaches a height of 30cm, bronze-purple, perhaps of hybrid origin; *P.t.* Variegatum, leaf margins cream; *P.t.* Veitchii, leaves striped cream.

Photinia

(Greek *photos* or *phos*, light – alluding to the often shining leaves). ROSACEAE. A genus of about 40 species of shrubs and trees from E. and S.Asia. They have alternate, ovate to oblong or lanceolate, toothed leaves – often red-flushed in spring or autumn – corymbs or panicles of mainly small, white, 5-petalled flowers, and red, berry-like fruit. Grow in well-drained but moisture-retentive, preferably humus-rich soil in sun or partial shade. Hardy to light frost. Plant autumn or spring. Propagate by cuttings in late summer, bottom heat 16–18°C, or from seed sown when ripe and kept in a cold frame until large enough to transplant.

Species cultivated: *P.* × *fraseri* (*P. glabra* × *P. serrulata*), hybrid intermediate in character between the parents, generally more robust with brightly coloured young leaves and thriving on chalky soils. *P.* × *f.* Birmingham, young growth bronze-red; *P.* × *f.* Red Robin, bright red young leaves, equal to *Pieris formosa forrestii*; *P.* × *f.* Robusta, strong-growing and hardiest of this group, leaves bright coppery-red. *P. glabra*, Japan, China; to 3m tall; leaves evergreen, 4–9cm long, elliptic to narrowly obovate, bronze when young, then deep glossy green; flowers about 8mm wide, white, tinted-pink, summer; fruit to 6mm wide, red then black, a useful hedging plant in sheltered sites. *P.g.* Rubens, young leaves waxy-red. *P. serrulata*, China; shrub or tree to 10m or more; leaves evergreen, oblong, 8–15cm long, bright coppery-red when young, deep glossy green when mature; flowers 8–10mm wide, white, in large corymbose panicles, late spring; fruit red; one of the finest evergreens for chalky soils – see also *P.* × *fraseri*. *P. sinica*, see *P. villosa sinica*. *P. variabilis*, see next species. *P. villosa* (*P. variabilis*), Japan, China, Korea; shrub or small tree to 5m tall; leaves deciduous, 4–9cm long, ovate-lanceolate to obovate, slender-pointed, turning scarlet and yellow in autumn; flowers about 1cm wide, white, in small corymbs, early summer; fruit ellipsoid, red, to 8mm long; needs neutral to acid soil to thrive.

Phuopsis

(Greek vernacular *phou*, for a sort of valerian, presumably referring to the vague similarity of the flowers). RUBIACEAE. A genus of 1 perennial from the Caucasus, E.Turkey, N.W.Iran: *P. stylosa*, clump-forming and rhizomatous; stems prostrate to decumbent, forming thick, pungently smelling mats 1–2m wide, sometimes much more; leaves in whorls of 6–7, narrowly elliptic, sharply pointed, 1·5–2·5cm long; flowers in dense terminal heads, each bloom 1·5–2cm long, slenderly tubular, expanding to 5 pink lobes, summer to autumn. Grow in any well-drained soil in sun. Plant autumn to spring. Propagate by division at planting time or cuttings of non-flowering shoots in summer.

Phygelius

(Greek *phyge*, avoidance or flight – referring, according to Sir W. J. Hooker, to its 'having so long escaped the researches of botanists'). SCROPHULARIACEAE. A genus of 2 species of sub-shrubs from S.Africa. They have erect stems, opposite pairs of ovate, toothed leaves, and terminal panicles of pendant, tubular, 5-lobed flowers. Grow in well-drained but not dry, humus-rich soil in sun or partial shade. On sheltered walls or with winter protection the stems become woody and may be trained as for wall shrubs, but the plants are not hardy, except in mild areas, and when frosted behave as herbaceous perennials. Plant spring. Propagate from seed under glass in spring, or by cuttings of non-flowering lateral shoots late summer, ideally with bottom heat 16–18°C.

Species cultivated: *P. aequalis*, to 1m tall as a

Far left top: *Phormium cookianum* Tricolor
Far left above: *Phormium tenax*
Left: *Photinia* × *fraseri* Robusta
Top: *Photinia glabra* Rubens
Above: *Phygelius capensis*
Below: *Phuopsis stylosa*

herbaceous perennial; stems 4-angled or narrowly winged; leaves 5–10cm long; flowers almost straight-sided, 3–4·5cm long, soft coral-red with yellow throat and dark lower lobes, summer to autumn. *P. capensis*, Cape figwort, Cape fuchsia; like previous species, but flowers strongly curved, bright red.

Phyllitis scolopendrium – see *Asplenium scolopendrium*.

Phyllodoce

(for a Greek sea nymph of that name). Mountain heath. ERICACEAE. A genus of 8 species of small, evergreen, heath-like shrubs from the northern temperate and circumpolar zones. They have crowded, alternate, linear almost needle-like leaves and terminal umbels of nodding, urn or bell-shaped flowers. Grow in moist, acid-peaty soil in partial shade; in warm areas best with a north exposure to ensure cool conditions in summer. Plant autumn to spring. Propagate from seed when ripe or spring, by cuttings late summer and layering spring.

Species cultivated: *P. aleutica*, E.Asia to Alaska; 15–25cm tall; leaves about 1cm long, yellow-green with a white line beneath; flowers urn-shaped, 7–8mm long, whitish to bright pale yellow-green, early summer. *P. caerulea* (*P. taxifolia*), circumpolar and mountains farther south; to 15cm tall; leaves 6–12mm long, dark glossy green; flowers urn-shaped, 7–8mm long, purple, fading bluish, summer. *P. empetriformis*, Alaska to California; to 30cm or more tall, spreading, eventually forming large mats; leaves 5–15mm long; flowers bell-shaped, purple-rose, 7mm long, spring to summer, sometimes later. *P. glanduliflora*, W. N.America, including Alaska; 10–20cm tall; leaves 6–12mm long, dark

Left: *Phyllodoce empetriformis*
Above: *Phyllostachys nigra* Henonis
Right below: *Physalis alkekengi*

green above, white-lined beneath; flowers urn-shaped, 6–7mm long, sulphur-yellow to greenish-white, glandular downy, late spring. *P.* × *intermedia* (*P. empetriformis* × *P. glanduliflora*), group of natural hybrids, the clone most commonly seen being like *P. empetriformis* but with urn-shaped, glabrous-pink flowers; the easiest phyllodoce to grow. *P. nipponica*, Japan; 10–25cm or more tall; leaves 6–10mm long, darkish glossy green above, white-lined beneath; flowers bell-shaped, 6–7mm long, white, tinted pink, late spring. *P. taxifolia*, see *P. caerulea*.

Phyllostachys

(Greek *phyllon*, a leaf, and *stachys*, a spike – the flowering panicles are leafy). GRAMINEAE. A genus of 30–40 species of hardy bamboos from Himalaya and temperate E.Asia. They are rhizomatous, forming large clumps or small thickets of rather zig-zag stems, the internodes of which are alternately flattened and grooved; lateral branches 2 from each node; leaves lanceolate; flowers greenish, typically grass-like, spikelets 2–4 flowered, not regularly produced. All species are attractive, with edible young shoots. Grow in humus-rich, moisture-retentive soil in sun or partial shade. Plant autumn or spring. Propagate by division, spring, cuttings of young rhizomes in cold frame late winter.

Species cultivated: *P. aurea*, golden or fishpole bamboo; China, long cultivated in Japan; clump-forming, canes to 6m or less in cool areas nodes with a swollen band beneath, giving a unique, articulated appearance, the basal ones very crowded, bright green, maturing yellow-green to yellow; leaves 5–11·5cm long, linear. *P. bambusoides* (*P. quilioi*), China, long cultivated in Japan; clump-forming; canes to 24m tall but only to 6m in cool areas, glossy deep green; leaves linear to lanceolate, to 15cm or more long, bright green above, glaucous beneath. *P.b.* Allgold (*P. sulphurea*), canes maturing deep yellow. *P. boryana*, see *P. nigra* Boryana. *P. flexuosa*, China; thicket-forming; canes bright to deep green, to 9m or less in cool areas; leaves to 15cm long, dark green above, glaucous beneath. *P. henonis*, see *P. nigra* Henonis. *P. nigra*, black bamboo; China; clump-forming; canes to 8m tall, less in cool areas; green at first, gradually maturing to deep purple-black; leaves to 9cm long, dark above, glaucous beneath. *P.n.* Boryana (*P.n.* Bory), mature canes yellow, mottled purple; *P.n.* Henonis (*P.n.* Henon), mature canes brownish-yellow. *P. quilioi*, see *P. bambusoides*. *P. sulphurea*, see *P. bambusoides* Allgold.

x Phyllothamnus

(*Phyllodoce* × *Rhodothamnus*). ERICACEAE. A hybrid genus containing 1 clone: ×*P. erectus* (*Rhodothamnus chamaecistus* × *Phyllodoce empetriformis*), evergreen shrublet 20–35cm or more tall; leaves linear, 1–1·5cm long; flowers in terminal, umbel-like clusters, each one broadly funnel-shaped, pink, 1·2–1·4cm wide, late spring. Culture as for *Phyllodoce*, but propagation by layering or cuttings only.

Physalis

(Greek *physa*, a bladder – alluding to the inflated fruiting calyces). SOLANACEAE. A genus of 80–100 species of annuals and perennials of cosmopolitan distribution. They have alternate, lanceolate to ovate leaves, solitary, nodding, widely bell-shaped to rotate flowers with 5 lobes, and berry fruit enclosed in the enlarged, lantern-like calyces. Grow hardy species in any well-drained, moderately fertile soil in sun or partial shade. Plant and propagate by division autumn to spring. Grow the half-hardy annuals in humus-rich soil in sunny, sheltered sites. Sow seed under glass at about 18°C in mid spring; prick off seedlings into boxes at 5cm apart each way

or into 6·5cm pots of good commercial potting mixture and when well-established place in 10cm pots; harden off in early summer and plant out when fear of frost has passed. Supports may be needed in windy areas.

Species cultivated: *P. alkekengi* (*P. bunyardii*, *P. franchetii*), bladder, winter or ground cherry, Chinese or Japanese lanterns; S.E. Europe to Japan; rhizomatous perennial; stems erect, unbranched, 40–60cm tall; leaves broadly to triangular ovate, 6–9cm long; flowers off-white, 1·5–2·5cm wide, summer; fruiting calyces orange to coral red, 3–5cm long, berry globose, red, edible. *P. bunyardii*, see *P. alkekengi*. *P. franchetii*, see *P. alkekengi*. *P. ixocarpa*, tomatillo, jamberry; Mexico; half-hardy, almost hairless annual, 60–120cm tall, usually well-branched; leaves ovate to lanceolate, toothed or entire, to 7·5cm long; flowers about 2·5cm wide, yellow, with 5 basal purple-brown blotches; fruiting calyces globose, yellowish, purple-veined, berry purplish to yellowish-green, 3–5cm wide or more, often bursting the calyx. *P. peruviana*, cape gooseberry, strawberry tomato; tropical S. America; much like *P. ixocarpa* but glandular downy; leaves cordate, toothed; fruit smaller, yellow, seldom bursting calyx; cultivars listed under this name generally belong to *P. ixocarpa*, eg *P.i.* Golden Nugget. *P. pruinosa*, dwarf Cape gooseberry, strawberry tomato; E. N.America; similar to *P. peruviana*, but stems weak, reclining to decumbent; leaves hoary-downy; fruiting calyces 2–3cm long; the common 'husk tomato' of E.USA.

Physocarpus

(Greek *physa*, a bladder, and *karpos*, a fruit – the follicles are inflated when mature). ROSACEAE. A genus of 10 species of deciduous shrubs from N.America and N.E.Asia. They have alternate, often rounded, palmately veined or lobed and toothed leaves, and umbel-like corymbs of small, 5-petalled, spiraea-like flowers followed by clusters of small, bladder-shaped fruit (follicles). Grow in any moderately fertile, well-drained soil in sun or partial shade. Plant autumn to spring. Propagate from seed when ripe or spring, semi-hardwood cuttings late summer or hardwood cuttings in autumn.

Species cultivated: *P. malvaceus*, W. N.America; erect habit, 1–2m tall; leaves 4–7·5cm long, broadly oval, 3-, or rarely 5-lobed; flowers white, 8–10mm wide, summer. *P. opulifolius* (*Spiraea o.*), nine bark; E. N.America; spreading or bushy habit, 1–3m tall; leaves 4–7·5cm long, broadly ovate, usually 3-lobed; flowers white, tinted pink, about 8mm wide, summer; fruit reddish or purple-tinged. *P.o. intermedius*, fruit downy; *P.o.* Luteus, leaves golden-yellow when young.

Physoplexis – see *Phyteuma comosum*.

Physostegia

(Greek *physa*, a bladder, and *stege*, a covering – alluding to the fruiting calyces that are somewhat enlarged). False dragonhead. LABIATAE. A genus of 15 species of perennials from N.America, 1 of which is readily available: *P. virginiana* (including *P. speciosa*), obedient plant; E.USA, S.E. Canada; herbaceous, rhizomatous perennial forming clumps and colonies; stems to 1·2m tall, erect, branching, if at all, near the top; leaves in opposite pairs, lanceolate, sharply toothed, 4–12cm long; flowers in simple or branched spikes, tubular-funnel shaped, 2-lipped, to 3cm long, rose-purple, summer to autumn; each flower has a short, hinge-like stalk and will stay put when pushed to the left or right. *P.v.* Summer Snow, flowers pure white; *P.v.* Summer Spire, rose-pink, both 75cm tall; *P.v. speciosa*, coarser, with larger, broadly lanceolate, sharply toothed leaves, represented in cultivation by *P.v.s.* Rose Bouquet, soft pink, to 90cm tall, and *P.v.s.* Vivid, bright, deep lilac-pink, 45–60cm tall.

Phyteuma

(Greek vernacular for a species of *Reseda*, used for this genus by Linnaeus). Horned rampion. CAMPANULACEAE. A genus of about 40 species of perennials from Mediterranean, Europe, Asia. They are akin to *Campanula*, but the small flowers are borne in tight heads or spikes, each with 5 slender petals that remain united until the pollen is shed, then open out. Grow in well-drained soil in sun, *P. comosum* in scree, rock crevice or alpine house. Plant autumn or spring. Propagate from seed when ripe or in spring in a cold frame, or by division in spring.

Species cultivated: *P. comosum* (*Physoplexis c.*), S. Alps; tufted; stems 5–15cm long, decumbent; leaves kidney-shaped, deeply sharply toothed, to 5cm long; flowers bottle-shaped, 1·5–2cm long, pale pinkish-lilac, tipped blackish-violet, early summer; distinct from other phyteumas in having the corolla tips permanently fused and each flower with a pedicel 2–5mm long, for which reasons some botanists give it separate generic status; very prone to attack by slugs. *P. scheuchzeri*, S. Alps, N. Appenines; tufted or small clump-forming; stems 25–45cm long, erect to decumbent; leaves linear to broadly lanceolate, toothed, long-stalked, 5–10cm long; flowers deep

Far left below: *Physalis peruviana*
Far left bottom: *Physocarpus opulifolius* Luteus
Left below: *Physostegia virginiana*
Left bottom: *Phyteuma comosum*
Below: *Phytolacca clavigera* flowers
Bottom: *Phytolacca clavigera* fruits

blue in dense, globose heads, 2–3cm wide, early summer. *P. spicatum*, spiked rampion; Europe; clump-forming; stems 30–80cm or more tall; leaves ovate-cordate, toothed, long-stalked, 3–5cm long; flowers white to pale yellow-green or blue, in dense spikes to 8cm or more long, late summer.

Phytolacca

(Greek *phyton*, a plant, and the modern Latin version of the Hindi *lakh*, the dye extracted from the lac insect; the berries have similar staining qualities). Pokeweed or pokeberry. PHYTOLACCACEAE. A genus of about 25 species of herbaceous perennials, shrubs and trees from the tropics to temperate regions. Only the hardy perennials are generally available. They are clump-forming, robust, erect, with alternate, ovate to lanceolate leaves, racemes of small, 5-petalled flowers, and glossy, berry-like fruit formed of several, closely pressed or partially united, fleshy, 1-seeded carpels. Grow in fertile, moisture-retentive soil in sun or partial shade. Plant autumn or spring. Propagate by division spring, seed when ripe.

Species cultivated: *P. acinosa*, China, Japan, naturalized in India; 1–1·5m tall; leaves edible when cooked, elliptic to ovate or lanceolate, to 25cm long; racemes erect, to 15cm long, flowers 7mm wide, green and white, summer. *P. americana* (*P. decandra*), Virginian pokeweed or poke, scoke, red ink plant; E.USA to Mexico; 1·5–3m tall; leaves oblong to narrowly ovate, 15–35cm long; racemes lax, to 15cm or more long, flowers white or purple-tinted, 6–8mm wide, late summer. *P. clavigera*, China; similar to *P. americana*, but racemes denser, flowers rose-purple and stems bright rhubarb-red in the autumn.

Picea

(Latin *picis*, *pix*, for pitch – *P. abies* yields the resin known as Burgundy pitch). Spruce or spruce fir. PINACEAE. A genus of about 45 species of evergreen trees from the northern temperate zone, particularly E.Asia. They have erect main trunks or stems with tiered whorls of much smaller lateral branches, creating trees of conical or columnar appearance; leaves are short, needle-like, borne on short, peg-like projections in dense spirals; flowering spikes (strobili) catkin-like, the females like soft, miniature cones; mature cones are cylindrical or cigar-shaped, pendulous, falling intact when seed is shed – see *Abies* for the same characters that enable the 2 genera to be separated easily. The genus is important for timber, several species yielding resin and turpentine; many are of imposing appearance. Grow in well-drained, moisture-retentive, preferably humus-rich soil in sun or partial shade. Plant autumn or spring. Propagate from seed when ripe or spring, preferably in a cold frame; the cultivars by cuttings with a heel late summer to autumn.

Species cultivated: *P. abies* (*P. excelsa*), common or Norway spruce; C. and N.Europe; eventually to 45m or more tall; leaves 1–2cm long, 4-angled, glossy dark green; cones 10–18cm long, purplish when young. *P.a.* Nidiformis, slow-growing, dense, rounded, flat-topped bush growing about 2cm a year. *P. albertiana*, see *P. glauca albertiana*. *P. brewerana*, Brewer's spruce; N.California, S. Oregon; to 30m tall in the wild, or less in gardens, branches arching down, laterals hanging vertically, curtain-like; leaves flattened, 2–3·5cm long, deep green above, white-lined beneath; cones 10–12cm long, purple when young. *P.engelmannii*, Engelmann or mountain spruce; British Columbia to New Mexico; spire-like, to 50m in the wild, or less in cultivation, leaves similar to *P. abies* but grey-green to blue-grey, sharp-pointed; cones 4–7·5cm long. *P.e. glauca*, a good blue-grey leaved form. *P. excelsa*, see *P. abies*. *P. glauca*, white spruce; N.N.America; to 28m or more tall, branchlets drooping; leaves 4-angled, 1·2–1·4cm long, grey or pale green, white-lined; cones 5–6·5cm long, coppery or orange-brown when mature. *P.g. albertiana*, Alberta spruce, W.N.America, leaves more crowded, blue-green, cones 4cm long; *P.g.a.* Conica, dense conical bush to 2m tall or more, leaves bright green. *P. jezoensis*, Hondo spruce; Korea, Manchuria, Japan; to 50m in the wild, often less in gardens; conical to spire-like; leaves flat, 1·5cm long, sharp-pointed, glossy deep green above with 2 broad white bands beneath; young shoots and female catkins red; cones 5–7·5cm long. *P. mariana*, black spruce; Canada, N.USA; to 20m tall; conical, often broadly so, densely branched; leaves 1–1·5cm long, dark above, banded blue white beneath,

Top: *Picea englemannii glauca*
Left above: *Picea mariana* Nana
Above: *Picea pungens* Globosa
Left: *Picea glauca albertiana* Conica

Far left: *Picea brewerana*
Left above: *Pieris japonica*
Left: *Pieris japonica* Variegata
Above: *Pieris* Forest Flame

appearing overall blue-grey from a distance; cones in bunches, ovoid, 3–4cm long, purple when young, glossy brown at maturity. *P.m.* Nana, slow-growing dense globular bush. *P. omorika*, Serbian spruce; Yugoslavia; to 28m or more tall; slender columnar habit, lateral branches short, down-curving; leaves 1·2–1·8cm long, keeled, pointed when young, blue-tipped on mature trees, deep green above, white-banded beneath; cones 4–6cm long, blue-black when young. *P. orientalis*, oriental or Caucasian spruce; N.E. Turkey, Caucasus; to 33m tall (60m in the wild), conical; leaves 6–8mm long, almost square in cross-section, glossy dark green; cones to 7cm long. *P. pungens*, Colorado spruce; S.W.USA; to 33m in the wild or less in gardens, conical; leaves 2–3cm long, 4-angled, bluish-green; cones about 10cm long, purplish-brown when immature. *P.p. glauca*, blue spruce; a name covering the naturally occurring glaucous-leaved forms and their garden-raised seedlings: *P.p.g.* Koster (*P.p.g.* Kosteriana), smaller-growing, leaves intense silvery-blue; *P.p.* Globosa, slow-growing, dense, rounded, flat-topped bush with glaucous leaves. *P. sitchensis*, Sitka spruce; Alaska to California; to 60m or more in the wild or less in gardens, conical; leaves 2–3cm long, flattened, keeled, sharp-pointed, bright green above with 2 blue-white bands beneath; trees appear a curiously fuzzy dark blue-grey from a distance; cones 5–10cm long, maturing whitish. *P. smithiana*, W. Himalayan or morinda spruce; Himalaya – Afghanistan to Nepal; to 65m in the wild or less in gardens; branches more or less horizontal, the tips upturned, laterals hanging vertically; leaves 3–4cm long, rounded to angular in cross-section, slender, sharp-pointed, glossy dark green; cones 12–18cm long.

Pickaback plant – see *Tolmiea menziesii*.

Pickerel weed – see *Pontederia*.

Pieris

(from Pierides, the group name of the Greek muses). ERICACEAE. A genus of 8 species of evergreen shrubs from E.Asia and N.America. They have alternate, lanceolate to obovate, leathery leaves and axillary racemes or terminal panicles of mainly white, urn-shaped, pendant flowers. Grow in neutral to acid, preferably peaty, moisture-retentive soil in sun or partial shade, sheltered from strong, cold winds. Not always hardy. Plant autumn or spring. Propagate from seed when ripe or spring, or by cuttings in late summer, both in a cold frame.

Species cultivated: *P. floribunda*, S.E.USA; to 2m tall, habit dense; leaves 4–7·5cm long, ovate to oblong-lanceolate, bristly ciliate; flowers 6mm long in erect, terminal panicles, spring. *P.f.* Elongata, larger panicles, the branches of which can reach 20cm long. *P. formosa*, Nepal to China; 2·5–4m tall, sometimes a small tree to 6m; leaves 7–15cm long, oblong to lanceolate or elliptic, finely toothed, usually glossy deep green, reddish when young; flowers 6–7mm long with green sepals, in large panicles, late spring, early summer. *P.f. forrestii*, somewhat pendant habit; leaves red when young; flowers rounder with whitish sepals; represented in gardens by: *P.f.f.* Wakehurst, young leaves bright red, flowers 9mm long; *P.f.f.* Charles Michael, largest flowers in genus – 1–2cm long; *P.f.f.* Jermyns, flower-stalks and sepals as well ss young leaves vinous-red; young growth of all these prone to late frost damage. Very similar is *P.* Forest Flame, a seedling deduced to be *P.f.f.* Wakehurst × *P. japonica;* young leaves less brilliant but earlier and hardier, habit more elegant. *P. japonica*, Japan; similar to *P. floribunda*, but leaves glossy deep green, coppery when young, and drooping panicles. *P.j.* Bert Chandler (*P.j.* Chandleri), young leaves salmon-pink, ageing white then green; *P.j.* Daisen, flowers pink, deeper in bud; *P.j.* Christmas Cheer, flowers flushed pink at the mouth, some opening during mild winters; *P.j.* Variegata, leaves edged cream, often flushed pink when young. *P. nana*, the currently correct name for *Arcterica nana*. *P. taiwanensis*, Taiwan; closely allied to *P. japonica* but leaves to 10cm and flowers to 9cm long in larger, more erect panicles, at least in cultivation; drooping panicles do occur in some seed-raised plants.

Pileostegia

(Greek *pilos*, felt, and *stege*, a roof – referring to the form of the flower). HYDRANGEACEAE (SAXIFRAGACEAE). A genus of 3 species of evergreen climbers closely allied to *Schizophragma*, and by some botanists included in that genus, from Himalaya to Taiwan. 1 species is generally available: *P. viburnoides*, range of genus; self-clinging, like ivy,

Below: *Pileostegia viburnoides*

to 8m or more high; leaves in opposite pairs, 7–15cm long, narrowly oblong to elliptic or obovate, dark green, leathery; flowers white, 4–5 petalled, about 9mm wide in terminal panicles 10–20cm wide, autumn. Grow in well-drained, humus-rich soil in sun or partial shade. Plant autumn, spring. Propagate by layering spring, cuttings late summer.

Pimelea

(Greek *pimele*, fat – the seed is oily). Rice flower. THYMELAEACEAE. A genus of 80 species of evergreen shrubs from Australasia, New Guinea to Philippines, 1 of which is generally available: *P. prostrata* (*P. coarctata* of gardens), New Zealand; mat-forming, eventually to 1m wide; leaves dense, ovate to elliptic-oblong, 3–6mm long; flowers 3–4mm long, white, with 4 spreading lobes, in terminal heads of 3–10, summer; fruit berry-like, ovoid, red or white; the form grown in British gardens has glaucous leaves, white fruit, and is hardy in all but the severest winters. Grow in well-drained but moisture-retentive soil, sun. Plant autumn, spring. Propagate by cuttings late summer, self-layered branchlets carefully severed spring.

Pimpernel – see *Anagallis*.

Pincushion flower – see *Scabiosa*.

Pine – see *Pinus*.

Pineapple flower – see *Eucomis*.

Pinguicula

(Latin *pinguis*, fat – the slippery, glossy leaves have a greasy appearance). Butterwort. LENTIBULARIACEAE. A genus of 45 species of carnivorous perennials of wide distribution mainly in temperate climates. They have rosettes of linear to broadly ovate leaves, the upper surfaces of which bear glands producing a sticky, muscilaginous fluid that attracts and traps small insects. When an insect is caught and dies, the leaf margins roll inwards, the glands secreting an enzyme that digests the soft parts and absorbs nitrogenous and other substances. In the wild these plants often inhabit areas deficient in soil nutrients. The flowers are solitary, somewhat violet-like with long spurs. Grow hardy species outside in a bog garden in a sunny site, the tender sorts in a greenhouse, minimum temperature 7–10°C, well-ventilated and lightly shaded in summer. The hardy species make interesting pan plants for a cold greenhouse. Grow in pans of an all-peat mixture with 2 parts sphagnum moss added, ideally topping with living moss tips. Pot or repot spring as growth commences, standing the pans in permanent saucers of water. Propagate by division at potting time, from seed when ripe, or spring, sowing on surface of potting mixture, or leaf cuttings in summer.

Species cultivated: *P. bakerana*, see *P. caudata*. *P. caudata* (*P. bakerana*), bog violet; Mexico; tender; rosettes loose; leaves obovate to rounded, to 10cm long; flowers among the largest of the genus, very long-spurred, violet-purple to rich carmine, on stems to 18cm tall, autumn; in winter the plant shows as a dense rosette less than 5cm wide of narrow, fleshy leaves; best kept on the dry side in winter. *P. grandiflora*, large-flowered or greater butterwort; W.Europe; hardy; rosettes loose; leaves 2–8cm long, ovate-oblong; flowers about 2cm wide with longer spur, violet-purple, summer, on stems 8–20cm tall; over-winters as a rootless bud. *P. gypsicola*, Mexico; tender; rosettes dense; leaves linear, widening at the base, 5–6cm long; flowers 2·5cm wide, long-spurred, rosy-violet, on stems 10cm or more tall; in winter the plant shows as a small, dense, sempervivum-like rosette of spathulate leaves. *P. vulgaris*, common butterwort; northern arctic and temperate zones; hardy; similar to *P. grandiflora* but flowers smaller, 1–1·5cm wide, on stems 5–15cm tall.

Far left top: *Pimelia prostrata*
Far left above: *Pinguicula grandiflora*
Above: *Pinus ayacahuite*

Pinks – see *Dianthus*.

Pinus

(Latin vernacular for pine, originally mainly for *P. pinea*, but used for this genus by Linnaeus). PINACEAE. A genus of 80 species of evergreen coniferous trees from N. Hemipshere and mountains farther south. In general, and particularly when young, they have a conical outline with erect main stems and regular whorls of smaller branches, although with age some become flat-topped. They have long and short shoots, the former extending the height and spread of the tree, the latter never more than tiny, leaf-bearing pegs. Depending on the species, the slender, needle-like leaves are carried in pairs, 3s or 5s on each short shoot; seedlings do not show this character immediately, starting with a dense spiral of solitary leaves. The flowers (strobili) are catkin-like, monoecious; males cylindrical, females smaller and barrel-shaped, later developing into the familiar top-shaped or cylindrical cones, bearing nut-like seed that is usually winged. Apart from their ornamental value, pines are very important timber trees, also yielding resins, pitch, tar oils, turpentine, etc, plus pine leaf oil used for medical purposes. The seed of some species is a source of food at least in localized areas. Grow in well-drained, moderately fertile soil, in sun or a site open to the sky. Plant autumn or spring. Propagate from seed in spring in a cold frame or outside.

Species cultivated: *P. aristata*, hickory or bristlecone pine; S.W.USA; shrub or small tree from 3–13m. slow-growing but vigorous; leaves in 5s, 2–4cm long, dark green, blue-white on inner surface, spine-tipped; cones 5–7·5cm long, each scale with a bristle-like spine; formerly considered to be the oldest living tree, specimens of 5000 years old being found, but now known to be the closely related but rarely cultivated *P. longaeva*, *P. armandii*, David's pine; W. China, Taiwan, Japan; to 18m in gardens (30m in the wild); leaves in 5s, 10–15cm long, pendulous, bright green; cones barrel-shaped, orange to purple-brown, 8–15cm long. *P. austriaca*, see *P. nigra*. *P. ayacahuite*, Mexican white pine; Mexico; similar to the more commonly planted *P. wallichiana*, but young shoots orange downy (those of *P. wallichiana* smooth and glaucous). *P. banksiana*, jack pine; E.Canada, N.E.USA; to 30m but usually much less in cultivation, leaves in pairs, 2–4cm long, curved or twisted, olive-green; cones 3–6cm long. *P. cembra*, arolla or Swiss stone pine; Alps, Carpathians; 17–27m tall; columnar habit, branching from near ground level; leaves in 5s, lying close together, 7–9cm long, dark green; cones shortly cylindrical, to 8cm long, tinted blue-violet, ripening red-brown. *P. contorta*, shore or beach pine; Alaska to N.California; usually a bush or small tree to 10m in the wild but often taller in gardens; leaves in pairs, 2·5–7cm long, twisted, dark to yellow-green; cones about 5cm long. *P.c. latifolia*, lodgepole pine, more vigorous, to 45m, with straighter trunk, broader leaves and larger cones. *P. densiflora*, Japanese red pine; Japan; to 15m tall, similar to *P. sylvestris* but leaves 8–12cm long, deep green. *P. excelsa*, see *P. wallichiana*. *P. halepensis*, Aleppo pine; Mediterranean region; to 16m tall, narrowly conical when young, becoming round-headed with maturity; leaves in pairs, curved and twisted, 5–9cm long, bright green; cones 5–11cm long, red-brown; somewhat tender when young; seed should be collected from most northern provenances. *P. griffithii*, see *P. wallichiana*. *P. insignis*, see *P. radiata*. *P. jeffreyi*, Jeffrey or black pine; Oregon, California, N.Mexico; much like *P. ponderosa* and sometimes considered a variety of it, but shoots and leaves glaucous, usually in 3s. *P. lambertiana*, sugar pine; California to mid-Oregon; the largest species of pine, to 80m tall in the wild; leaves in 5s, 7–10cm long, spirally twisted, deep green outside, blue-white inside; cones (only on mature trees) 30–45cm long, cylindrical; similar to *P. strobus*, but young shoots red-brown downy all over, lemon-scented when broken; prone to rust disease. *P. laricio*, see *P. nigra maritima*. *P. montezumae*, rough-barked Mexican pine; Mexico; to 20m tall in gardens, 30m or more in the wild; with a broad-domed head and knobbly-ridged, grey bark; leaves in 5s, sometimes 3–8, stiff but slender, blue-grey, 20–30cm long; cones 6–10cm long, barrel-shaped, brown to purple-brown; not reliably hardy, often represented in cool areas by *P.m. hartwegii*, having leaves 13–18cm long, often in 3s–5s, and orange-brown cones. *P. mugo* (*P. montana*, *P. mughus*), dwarf or Swiss mountain pine; broad, bushy shrub or small tree to 10m tall; leaves in pairs, 4–7cm long, rich bright green; cones 2·5–5cm long. *P. m. mugo* (*P. mughus*), prostrate to decumbent; *P.m. pumilio*, bushy with erect branches to 2m; *P.m.* Gnom, small, condensed, globular bush, leaves dark green; *P.m. rostrata*, the tree form to 20m, now classified as *P. uncinata* (rarely obtainable); *P.m.* Slavinii, similar to *P.m. pumilio* but more compact, leaves bluish-green. *P. muricata*, bishop pine; California; to 29m tall, usually less in gardens, narrowly conical to broadly domed or flattened; leaves in pairs, 7–15cm long, curved, dark blue-grey to grey-green; cones to 8cm long, hard and heavy; good for exposed sites but not on chalky soils. *P. nigra*, Europe to Turkey; a variable species with several geographical varieties, the following frequently cultivated: *P.n. maritima* (*P. laricio*), Corsican pine; S.Italy, Corsica, Sicily; more sparsely branched than *P.n. nigra*, leaves less dense and more flexible; much used for forestry in Europe, thriving on all soils, including sand, chalk and peat. *P.n. nigra* (*P. austriaca*), Austrian pine; C.S.Europe; to 33m or more tall, broad-headed; leaves in dense pairs, stiff, dark green, 10–15cm long; cones 5–8cm long. *P. parviflora*, Japanese white pine; Japan; 6–20m tall, conical to columnar, often becoming flat-headed with layered branches; leaves in 5s, 5–8cm long, twisted, blue-green with white lines; cones 5–6·5cm long, orange-brown to purple-brown. *P. pinaster*, maritime or cluster pine; Mediterranean Europe, Greece to Portugal; to 30m tall sometimes more in the wild; flat-topped when mature, with long, bare, handsomely reddish-plated bole; leaves in pairs, stout, rigid, 15–20cm long, horny-pointed, pale grey-green; cones 10–15cm or more long, glossy brown. *P. pinea*, stone or umbrella pine; Mediterranean to Portugal; to 22m tall or more, with a rounded to umbrella-shaped crown; leaves in pairs, 10–15cm long, often somewhat twisted, dark grey-green; cones almost globose, 10–15cm long. *P. ponderosa*, western yellow pine; British Columbia to Texas and Mexico; to 70m in the wild but usually less; concial crown even when old; leaves in 3s, sometimes mixed with 2s and 5s, 13–25cm long, dark grey-green; cones 7–10cm long, occasionally larger, each scale with a tiny spine. *P.*

Left below: *Pinus pinea*
Below: *Pinus strobus*
Bottom: *Pinus pinaster*

radiata (*P. insignis*), Monterey pine; California; to 44m tall, usually less than 30m in gardens; conical when young, domed at maturity; leaves in 3s, slender, dense, bright green, 7–15cm long; cones very asymmetrical at base, 10–15cm long, glossy brown; rapid-growing when young, thriving near the sea and in poor, sandy soils. *P. rigida*, northern pitch pine; E. N.America; to 20m or more tall, usually with a domed head; leaves in 3s, 8–12cm long, somewhat curved and twisted, thick, dull grey-green; cones 3–7cm long, scale tips yellow-brown with small, curved prickle. *P. strobus*, Weymouth or white pine; E. N.America; to 50m or more tall, usually less in gardens, with narrowly conical habit broadening with age; young stems green to green-brown, bearing minute hairs below the bases of the leaf clusters; leaves in 5s, 7–12cm long, bluish to grey-green; cones cylindrical, to 15cm or more long, often curved; prone to rust disease. *P. sylvestris*, Scots pine or fir; Europe, Asia; to 35m or more, conical, maturing flat-topped, upper trunk red-flushed; leaves in pairs, 5–7cm long, more on vigorous young trees, stiff, twisted, grey-green; cones 3–7cm long; important timber tree yielding deal and whitewood *P.s.* Argentea, leaves silvery blue-green; *P.s.* Aurea, small, slow-growing, leaves bright yellow in winter; *P.s.* Beuvronensis, miniature dome-shaped shrublet; *P.s.* Fastigiata, narrowly columnar habit; *P.s.* Pumila, see next entry; *P.s.* Watereri (*P.s.* Pumila), slow-growing, broadly conical bush, leaves blue-green. *P. thunbergii* (*P. thunbergiana*), Japanese black pine; Korea, Japan; from 20–40m in height; conical to columnar, becoming irregular with age; leaves in dense pairs, 7–10cm long, rigid, thick, twisted, sharply pointed, grey-green; cones to 6cm long. *P. wallichiana* (*P. excelsa*, *P. griffithii*), Bhutan or Himalayan white pine; Himalaya; from 35–50m in height; conical, with heavy, lateral-drooping branches at maturity; leaves in 5s, 12–20cm long, drooping, blue-grey-green; cones cylindrical, 15–30cm, resin-encrusted.

Top: *Piptanthus nepalensis*
Above: *Pittosporum tenuifolium* Garnettii
Top right: *Pittosporum crassifolium*
Right: *Pittosporum tobira*

Piptanthus

(Greek *pipto*, to fall, and *anthos*, flower – alluding to the way that both corolla and calyx fall after pollination). LEGUMINOSAE. A genus of 8 deciduous and evergreen shrubs from Asia, 1 of which is generally available: *P. nepalensis* (*P. laburnifolius*), Himalaya; deciduous or partially evergreen shrub to 3m or more tall; leaves trifoliate, leaflets lanceolate to oblanceolate, 6–12cm long, dark green above, glaucous beneath; flowers pea-shaped, to 4cm long, bright yellow, in erect racemes, to 7·5cm long, early summer; reputedly somewhat tender, but if sited in a sheltered, sunny spot in well-drained, fertile soil survives where frost is light. Plant spring. Propagate from seed in spring under glass, growing seedlings in pots until ready for permanent planting, as root disturbance severely checks growth.

Piripiri – see *Acaena*.

Pittosporum

(Greek *pitta*, pitch, and *spora*, a seed – the seed has a sticky coating). PITTOSPORACEAE. A genus of 150 species of evergreen trees and shrubs mainly from E.Asia, Australasia and Pacific Is. They have alternate, ovate to oblong or linear to obovate leaves, and clustered or solitary, 5-petalled flowers often with shortly tubular bases; fruit rounded to ovoid capsules with the seed surrounded by a sticky, muscilage like bird lime. Grow in well-drained but not dry, moderately fertile soil in sheltered, sunny sites, in the colder, frosty areas, against walls or in frost-free greenhouses; see notes on hardiness under Species cultivated. Plant or pot late spring. Propagate from seed under glass in spring at a temperature of 13–15°C, or by cuttings taken in late summer, bottom heat about 18°C. Grow rooted cuttings and seedlings in pots until ready for planting out.

Species cultivated: *P. crassifolium*, New Zealand; erect shrub or small tree to 9m or more; twigs white downy; leaves 5–7cm long, obovate, white woolly beneath; flowers about 1cm wide, dark purple-red, in terminal umbels; one of the hardiest species and excellent as a wind-break by the sea. *P. dallii*, New Zealand; spreading shrub to 3m tall (small tree to 6m in the wild); leaves usually crowded towards stem tips, 5–10cm long, elliptic to oblong, coarsely toothed; flowers 1·5cm wide, white, fragrant, in terminal umbels but not always produced; one of the hardiest shrubs. *P. eugenioides*, New Zealand; spreading shrub or tree to 12m tall; leaves 5–10cm or more long, elliptic-oblong, lustrous, sweetly aromatic, margins undulate; flowers 5–7mm wide, yellow, honey-scented, in compound umbels. *P.e.* Variegatum, leaves margined creamy-white; needs a cool greenhouse in all but the mildest areas. *P. tenuifolium* (*P. mayi*), New Zealand; erect shrub or tree to 10m tall; twigs purple-black; leaves 2·5–6·5cm long, oblong to elliptic-ovate, pale lustrous green, more or less undulate; flowers about 1cm wide, chocolate-purple, fragrant, in small cymes; one of the hardiest species, suffering only during hard winters; grown commercially for cut foliage for florists and a good hedge or wind-break in mild areas; the following cultivars are less hardy: *P.t.* Atropurpureum, leaves dark purple; *P.t.* Garnettii, leaves variegated white, flushed pink; *P.t.* Golden King and *P.t.* Warnham Gold, leaves golden-yellow, particularly in winter; *P.t.* Silver Queen, leaves suffused silvery-grey. *P. tobira*, China, Japan; rounded shrub or tree to 6m tall but slow-growing; leaves obovate; 5–10cm long, lustrous deep green; flowers about 1cm wide, white to pale yellow, fragrant, in umbellate clusters; *P.t.* Variegatum, leaves suffused grey, blotched and margined white; not fully hardy, grow in sheltered areas. *P. undulatum*, S.E.Australia; shrub or tree to 6m tall (14m in the wild); leaves 6–12cm long, oblong to lanceolate, pointed, somewhat undulate; flowers about 1cm wide, white, sweetly fragrant, in umbellate clusters; fruit berry-like, orange; greenhouse or sheltered wall in mild areas.

Plagianthus lyallii – see *Hoheria lyallii*.

Plane – see *Platanus*.

Plantago

(Latin vernacular for at least 1 species, used for this genus by Linnaeus). Plantain. PLANTAGINACEAE. A genus of about 250 species of perennials, annuals and sub-shrubs of cosmopolitan distribution. Several species are world-wide weeds, eg ribwort plantain or ribgrass (*P. lanceolata*), and few are really garden-worthy. Most species are rosette-forming with ovate to lanceolate leaves and spikes of tiny, 4-lobed flowers, in some cases with conspicuous stamens. Several species have muscilaginous seed that when wet is easily transported from place to place. Grow in well-drained soil in sun. Plant autumn to spring. Propagate from seed when ripe or spring, or by division at planting time.

Species cultivated: *P. argentea*, S. and S.E.Europe;

perennial; leaves narrowly lanceolate, 10–30cm long, silvery hairy; flowers and anthers white, in spikes to 2cm long, summer. *P. major*, greater or common plantain; Europe; herbaceous perennial; leaves long-stalked, ovate to elliptic, very prominently veined; flowers green, in tapered spikes; a familiar lawn and waste ground weed, the following mutants of which are interesting or decorative: *P.m.* Rosularis, 'green rose', flower-spike reduced to a dense rosette of petal-like green bracts; *P.m.* Rosularis Rubrifolia, leaves red-purple; *P.m.* Atropurpurea, leaves bronze-purple. *P. nivalis*, Spain – Sierra Nevada; perennial; leaves 3–7cm long, densely silvery-white hairy; flowers brownish, anthers yellow in 1cm globular heads.

Plantain – see *Plantago*.

Plantain lily – see *Hosta*.

Platanus

(Greek vernacular for *P. orientalis*, taken up for whole genus by Linnaeus). Plane. PLATANACEAE. A genus of 8 species of deciduous trees from S.E.Europe to S.E.Asia, N.America, Mexico. Except for the atypical and tender *P. kerrii* from Vietnam, they have alternate, palmately lobed leaves and small, unisexual, greenish flowers with

Below: *Platanus orientalis* seed balls
Bottom: *Platanus* × *hispanica* bark
Right: *Platanus orientalis*
Right below: *Platanus* × *hispanica*

rudimentary corollas in dense, spherical heads that develop into the familiar brown seed balls on long, pendant stalks. Grow in moist, humus-rich soil in sun, although light shade is tolerated. Plant autumn to spring. Propagate from seed or by layering in spring, hardwood cuttings in cold frame, autumn.
Species cultivated: *P.* × *hispanica* (*P.* × *acerifolia*, *P.* × *hybrida*), (*P. occidentalis* × *P. orientalis*), London plane; tall, fast-growing, eventually to 40m tall; trunk smooth, bark flaking, revealing creamy patches; leaves very variable, from small and broadly ovate to 5- or sometimes 7-lobed, 10–25cm wide; lobes deep to shallow, entire to prominently toothed; seed balls 2–2·5cm wide, 2–4 on each stalk; early history not known with certainty, but probably arose in S.France or Spain about 1650; a small percentage of seeds are fertile and trees raised from them vary, seeming quite often to favour the buttonwood. *P. occidentalis*, buttonwood, western plane, eastern sycamore, American plane: E.USA; much like *P.* × *hispanica* in general appearance, to 45m tall with more flaking bark, leaves shallowly 3–5 lobed, the gaps between filled with large, well-spaced teeth; seed balls usually 1 per stalk; does not thrive in all areas as prone to spring frosts and disease. *P. orientalis*, oriental plane: S.E.Europe, W.Asia, much planted elsewhere since ancient times; to 30m tall, trunk shorter and more rugged than London plane, less obviously flaking, especially when mature, branches widespreading; leaves deeply 3–5 lobed, sometimes with a few teeth, seed balls 3–6 per stalk; very long-lived tree.

Platycodon

(Greek *platys*, broad, and *codon*, a bell). Balloon flower. CAMPANULACEAE. A genus of 1 species of herbaceous perennial from E.Asia: *P. grandiflorus*, tufted to small clump-forming; stems erect, to 60cm or more; leaves alternate, often whorled in the lower part, ovate to lanceolate, toothed, glaucous beneath, to 7cm long; flowers balloon-shaped in bud, expanding to widely bell-shaped, 5–7·5cm across, deep to pale purple-blue, solitary or in small loose clusters, summer. *P.g.* Apoyama (*P.g.* Apoyensis of some lists), dwarf, 15–23cm tall; *P.g.* Mariesii, to 45cm, flowers more nearly blue and slightly earlier; *P.g.* Mariesii Album, flowers white; *P.g.* Mother of Pearl, soft pink; *P.g.* Snowflake, semi-double white. Grow in well-drained, humus-rich soil in sun. Plant autumn to spring. Propagate from seed under glass and by division in spring.

Below: *Platycodon grandiflorus* Mariesii
Right: *Platystemon californicus*
Right below: *Pleione bulbocodioides* Blush of Dawn
Far right: *Pleione bulbocodioides* Limprichtii
Far right below: *Pleione yunnanensis*

Platystemon

(Greek *platys*, broad, and *stemon*, stamen – alluding to the expanded stamen filaments). PAPAVERACEAE. A genus of 1 species of annual from California, adjacent Arizona and Mexico: *P. californicus*, cream cups; 20–30cm tall, branching from the base, lower stems decumbent; leaves narrowly oblong, hairy, grey-green, 2–7cm long; flowers solitary from upper leaf-axils, 6-petalled, bowl-shaped, cream to pale yellow, 2–3cm wide, late spring to autumn; variable in the wild, some with flowers tipped pink or more definitely yellow. Grow in any well-drained soil in sun, although partial shade is tolerated. Sow seed in spring or autumn in sheltered sites; plants can often be maintained from self-sown seedlings unless winters are severe.

Pleioblastus simonii, P. viridistratus – see *Arundinaria*.

Pleione

(Greek mother of the 7 Pleiades). ORCHIDACEAE. A genus of 10 species of orchids from India to S.E.Asia and Taiwan. They are allied to, and were once included in, *Coelogyne*, but have tightly clustered pseudobulbs of annual duration, solitary flowers and deciduous, elliptic, somewhat pleated leaves. Most species come from fairly high mountain forests where they live as semi-epiphytes on moss-covered rocks, banks, tree trunks. Greenhouse, minimum temperature 7°C and give them light shade in summer. Grow in shallow pans of any potting mixture ideally mixed with $\frac{1}{3}$-part sphagnum moss; all peat mixtures give good results if not allowed to become over wet. Outside, plant in peat beds or sheltered pockets on the rock garden. Plant or repot spring after flowering and just as new roots start to form. In all areas where frosts occur the pseudobulbs should be protected with about 5cm of peat, pulverized bark or chopped bracken. In light, peaty soils it is a good idea to bury the pseudobulbs a few centimetres when planting. Subsequent pseudobulbs will push to the surface but may be replanted deeper when dividing. In pans, set the bulbs with the lower $\frac{1}{3}$ in the soil. Water sparingly until the leaves unfold, then water regularly until foliage yellows in late autumn, then keep dry. Liquid fertilizer is beneficial applied during the summer at fortnightly intervals. Propagate by division of clumps when repotting or by the tiny pseudobulblets that often form on the top of the larger ones.
Species cultivated: *P. bulbocodioides* (*P. delavayi*, *P. formosana*, *P. limprichtii*, *P. pogonioides*, *P. pricei*), Tibet, China, Taiwan; pseudobulbs subglobose, green, sometimes black-purple, 2–3cm wide; leaves 3–6·5cm wide; flowers 7–10cm wide, pale or deep mauve to rosy-magenta, labellum fringed paler or white, blotched red, purple or yellow, spring, with young leaves. *P.b.* Blush of Dawn (*P. formosana*), tepals pale lilac-rose, labellum white or faintly tinged lilac; *P.b.* Limprichtii, tepals phlox-purple, labellum paler, thickly spotted and streaked red; *P.b.* Oriental Grace, pseudobulbs globular, black-purple, tepals light violet, labellum white, flushed lilac at base without; sometimes grown as *P. pricei*; *P.b.* Oriental Jewel, pseudobulbs black-purple, flowers deep pink; *P.b.* Oriental Splendour, pseudobulbs flask-shaped with conical tip, black-purple, tepals pale violet, labellum white with fine apricot lines at base, the clone long known as *P. pricei*; *P.b.* Polar Sun, flowers pure white; all the cultivars of *P. bulbocodioides*, with the possible exception of *P.b.* Polar Sun, are surprisingly hardy if treated as here described. *P. delavayi*, see *P. bulbocodioides*. *P.*

Top left: *Podocarpus nivalis* fruit
Left: *Podocarpus alpinus*
Above: *Podocarpus macrophyllus maki*
Top right: *Polemonium viscosum*
Right: *Polemonium foliosissimum*
Below right: *Podophyllum hexandrum*

formosana, see *P. bulbocodioides* Blush of Dawn. *P. limprichtii*, see *P. bulbocodioides*. *P. pogonioides*, see *P. bulbocodioides*. *P. priceri*, see *P. bulbocodioides* Oriental Splendour and *P. bulbocodioides* Oriental Grace. *P. reichenbachiana wallichiana*, see *P. praecox*. *P. yunnanensis*, E.Himalaya, Burma, W.China; flowers 7cm wide, bright rose-magenta, labellum paler, blotched deep purple or carmine, late winter, spring; reasonably hardy.

Plum-fruited yew – see *Cephalotaxus* and *Podocarpus*.

Podocarpus

(Greek *podos*, a foot, and *karpos*, a fruit – alluding to the way the fruit of some species is carried on the end of a swollen stalk, or what appears to be one). PODOCARPACEAE. A genus of 75–100 species of evergreen trees and shrubs from the S.Hemisphere north to tropical and E.Asia. They are dioecious conifers (qv) with linear, spirally arranged leaves, and catkin-like male inflorescences. The females are small, consisting of a few scales and ovules, only 1 of the latter developing into an exposed, hard, ovoid seed. As the seed develops, the scales fuse and unite with the stalk, swelling and often turning red. In a few anomalous species the scales do not swell but the seed coat becomes fleshy, creating a plum-like fruit. The species described here are hardy or almost so unless otherwise stated. Grow in well-drained but moisture-retentive, fertile soil in sun, although the tree species will stand partial shade. Plant autumn or spring. Propagate from seed sown when ripe or by cuttings of young shoots late summer, in a cold frame.

Species cultivated: *P. alpinus*, Tasmania, S.E. Australia; much-branched shrub to 3m in the wild but often half this in gardens; leaves crowded, 6–12mm long; fruit red with exposed seed. *P. andinus* (*Prumnopitys elegans*), plum-fruited yew; Chile, Argentina to Andes; tree to 20m tall, usually less in gardens and slow-growing, somewhat yew-like but less dense; leaves deep green and spine-tipped on juvenile plants, to 2cm long, somewhat bluish-green, to 5cm on mature trees; fruit plum-like, yellowish-white, to 2cm long, edible, with grape-like flavour; needs a site sheltered from cold winds. *P. macrophyllus*, China, Japan; shrub or small tree to 6m tall, but slow-growing; branches horizontal, leaves 10–18cm long, lustrous deep green above, yellowish below; fruit dark red with exposed, 1cm-long, greenish seed. *P.m. maki*, China, much cultivated in Japan; dwarfer and more compact than type; branches more erect, leaves 4–8cm long; variegated forms are sometimes available; both *P. macrophyllus* and *P.m. maki* need sheltered sites but are reasonably hardy. *P. nivalis*, alpine or mountain totara; New Zealand; much-branched, spreading shrub to about 1m (sometimes to 3m in the wild); leaves 6–15mm long, usually bright to yellow-green; fruit bright red with exposed greenish seed.

Podophyllum

(abbreviated version of *Anapodophyllum*, Latin *anas*, duck, Greek *podos*, foot, and *phyllon*, leaf). PODOPHYLLACEAE (BERBERIDACEAE). A genus of 5–10 species of herbaceous perennials mainly from Himalaya and E.Asia – 1 in E. N.America. They are shortly rhizomatous, forming clumps of erect stems bearing pairs of rounded leaves and solitary, 6–9 petalled flowers; some species have several flowers in umbels and all have solitary leaves on the non-flowering stems; fruit is a large, fleshy berry. Grow in moist, humus-rich soil in partial shade; under glass in cold areas. Plant autumn to spring. Propagate from seed when ripe or by division in spring.
Species cultivated: *P. emodi*, see next species. *P. hexandrum* (*P. emodi*), Himalayan may apple; Himalaya; to 45cm tall, often less at flowering time; leaves to 25cm wide, deeply 3–5 lobed, often marbled purple-brown; flowers white or pink, 2·5–4cm wide, erect to nodding, rather fugitive, spring; berry to 5cm long, ellipsoid, red, edible. *P. peltatum*, may apple, American mandrake; E. N.America; to 45cm tall, less at flowering time; leaves 5–9 lobed, to 30cm wide; flowers white, bowl-shaped, nodding, 3·5–5cm wide, spring; berry yellowish or reddish, to 5cm long, edible.

Pokeweed – see *Phytolacca*.

Polemonium

(Greek *polemonion*, derived from a medicinal plant associated with Polemon of Cappadocia, used for this genus by Linnaeus). POLEMONIACEAE. A genus of 20–50 species (depending on the botanical authority) of annuals and perennials mainly from northern temperate zone, chiefly W. N.America. They are tufted to clump-forming with pinnate leaves and racemose or corymbose cymes, sometimes dense, of tubular, 5-lobed flowers. Grow in fertile, moisture-retentive but well-drained soil in sun or partial shade; some of the alpine species thrive best in a scree. Plant autumn to spring. Propagate from seed when ripe or spring, and by division at planting time.

Species cultivated (all summer-flowering): *P. archibaldae*, see *P. foliosissimum*. *P. caeruleum*, Jacob's ladder; N.Hemisphere; to 60cm, sometimes to 90cm tall; leaflets 19–27, lanceolate to elliptic, 7–40mm long, terminal one separate; flowers to 2·5cm wide, blue or white, in corymbose cymes; a very variable species. *P.c.* Cashmirianum (*P. cashmirianum* of gardens), flowers brighter than type, paler blue, somewhat larger. *P.c. occidentale* (*P. occidentale*), Yukon to Nevada; inflorescence narrow, flowers less than 1·5cm wide. *P.c.* Richardsonii, see *P.* × *jacobaea*. *P. carneum* (*P. luteum*), Washington State to California; stems 40–80cm long, erect to spreading, forming large mounds to 45cm tall; leaflets 13–21, ovate to oblong-lanceolate, to 4cm long; flowers widely bell-shaped, to 2·5cm wide, pink, purple or yellow – the latter coloured form formerly known as *P. luteum* (of Howell, not Greene). *P. confertum*, see *P. viscosum*, *P. delicatum*, Colorado, Arizona, Utah, New Mexico mountains; tufted, to 20cm tall; leaflets 11–23, ovate-lanceolate to elliptic, 3–15mm long, terminal one separate; flowers blue, somewhat bell-shaped, 5–11mm long. *P. filicinum*, see next species. *P. foliosissimum* (*P. archibaldae*, *P. filicinum*), Rocky Mountains south to Arizona; to 80cm or more tall, much like a robust *P. caeruleum*; leaflets 11–25, elliptic to narrowly lanceolate, 1–3·5cm long, the terminal 4 decurrent onto the midrib; flowers densely borne, 1·5cm wide, usually deep violet to purple-blue in cultivation, but can be white, cream or blue; will flower into autumn if spent flower-heads are removed; the plant listed in catalogues as *P. archibaldae* is only 45cm tall. *P.* × *jacobaea* Richardsonii (*P. caeruleum* × *P. reptans*), the only clone of this putative parentage, basically resembling a more compact, richly-coloured *P. caeruleum*; listed in catalogues as *P. richardsonii*, but this name is a synonym of the dwarf, softly hairy *P. boreale* (to 23cm tall). *P. luteum*, see *P. carneum*. *P. occidentale*, see *P. caeruleum occidentale*. *P. pauciflorum*, N.Mexico to Arizona and Texas; sticky glandular hairy perennial or annual, 25–55cm tall; leaflets 11–25, narrowly lanceolate, 1–2·5cm long; flowers slenderly funnel-shaped, 3–4cm long, soft yellow, tinged red; flowers the first year from spring-sown seed. *P. pulcherrimum*, Alaska to California and Nevada mountains; tufted, 10–30cm tall; leaflets 11–23, ovate to orbicular, sometimes elliptic, 5–15mm long; flowers bell-shaped, 5–8mm long, blue, yellowish at base; varies greatly according to soil fertility and site; neatest and smallest in scree. *P. viscosum* (*P. confertum*), W. N.America; tufted to 15cm or more tall; leaflets with 3–5 elliptic to spathulate lobes to 1cm long, arranged in whorls around the leaf-stalk, sticky glandular downy; flowers 1·7–3·5cm long, narrowly funnel-shaped with rounded lobes, blue, late spring; very variable, the best forms with dense, head-like flower clusters of clear blue.

Polyanthus – see *Primula* × *tommasinii*.

Polygala

(Greek *polys*, much, and *gala*, milk – certain species were reputed to aid milk secretion in cattle). Milkwort. POLYGALACEAE. A genus of 500–600 species of annuals, perennials, shrubs and trees of

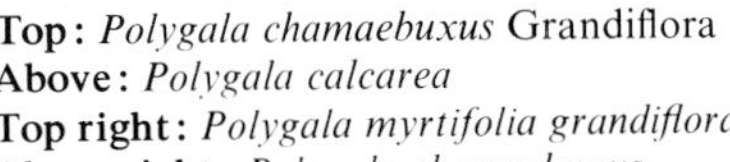

Top: *Polygala chamaebuxus* Grandiflora
Above: *Polygala calcarea*
Top right: *Polygala myrtifolia grandiflora*
Above right: *Polygala chamaebuxus*

cosmopolitan distribution, excepting New Zealand and Polynesia. They have alternate, opposite or whorled, generally narrow, simple leaves, and flowers in axillary or terminal racemes, sometimes solitary or in 2s or 3s. Individual blooms superficially resemble those of the pea family (LEGUMINOSAE), but are more complicated; 2 of the 5 sepals are large and petaloid (wings), and only 3 of the potentially 5 petals are fully developed or present, the lowest 1 folded to form a keel, sometimes with a brush-like tip. Grow hardy species in any well-drained soil in sun or partial shade. Grow tender species under glass, the one described here – *P. myrtifolia* – at minimum temperature of 5–7°C, well-ventilated and lightly shaded in summer. Plant or pot spring, the hardy species also in autumn. Grow the tender species in pots of a good commercial potting mixture and shorten back any leggy or overlong growths by ½–⅔ at the same time. Water regularly, less during winter. Propagate by cuttings late spring or summer, the greenhouse species at 16–18°C, perennial sorts also by division at planting time, all species from seed in spring under glass.

Species cultivated: *P. calcarea*, W.Europe including S.England; evergreen perennial forming tufted mats; basal leaves spathulate to obovate, 5–20mm long; flowering stem erect, with linear leaves and racemes of deep blue, 6–7mm long flowers, early to late summer. *P. chamaebuxus*, W. C.Europe to Germany and Yugoslavia; evergreen shrublet, 5–10cm or more tall; leaves alternate, to 3cm long, lanceolate to ovate-oblong, dark green, leathery; flowers solitary or in pairs from upper leaf-axils, 1·5cm long, wing sepals white, keel yellow, ageing brownish-crimson, early autumn to the following summer. *P.c.* Grandiflora, (*P.c.* Purpurea, *P.c.* Atropurpurea), wings purple, mainly spring to summer. *P. myrtifolia*, S.Africa; evergreen erect shrub, eventually to 2m or more tall; leaves 2–3cm long, alternate, elliptic oblong to obovate; flowers 2cm long, whitish, veined purple, in short racemes, spring to autumn; represented in cultivation in Britain by *P.m. grandiflora* with larger, richer purple flowers. *P. vayredae*, E.Pyrenees; much like and formerly classified as a variety of *P. chamaebuxus*, but leaves linear to linear-lanceolate, and wings and petals except the keel, rosy-purple; confused with *P. chamaebuxus* Grandiflora in gardens.

Polygonatum

(Greek *polys*, many, and *gony*, knee joint – alluding to the prominently many-jointed rhizomes). Solomon's seal. LILIACEAE. A genus of about 30 species of rhizomatous herbaceous perennials from the N. Hemisphere. They have erect stems, often arching at the tips, bearing either whorls of narrow leaves or alternate or opposite broader ones in 2 ranks. Tubular, bell-shaped, pendant flowers of 6 tepals are borne in the upper leaf-axils, followed by globose, blue-black or red berries. Grow in moisture-retentive, preferably humus-rich soil in partial shade, although sun is tolerated. Plant autumn to late winter. Propagate from seed when ripe, which takes several years to reach flowering size, or by division at planting time.

Species cultivated: *P. commutatum* (*P. canaliculatum*), great Solomon's seal; E. N.America; 1–2m tall; leaves alternate, ovate, 9–18cm long, yellowish-green to greenish-white, in clusters of 2–10, early summer. *P. falcatum*, Japan, Korea; 50–80cm tall; leaves alternate, 8–13cm long, lanceolate; flowers greenish-white, to 2cm long, in clusters of 3–5, early summer; the dwarf plant listed under this name is probably *P. pumilum*. *P. hookeri*, Tibet, W.China, Sikkim; 5–10cm tall; leaves alternate, ovate, to 2cm long; flowers 1–1·5cm long, lilac-pink, solitary, but clustered on young shoots and opening just above the soil, late spring. *P.* × *hybridum* (*P. multiflorum* × *P. odoratum*), common Solomon's seal; to 90cm tall; stems ridged to a variable degree; leaves elliptic oblong to ovate, 5–15cm long; flowers 1·8–2·2cm long, somewhat contracted in the middle, greenish-

Above: *Polygonatum × hybridum*
Above right: *Polygonum campanulatum*
Below right: *Polygonum aubertii*
Above far right: *Polygonum amplexicaule* Atrosanguineum

white in clusters of 2–4, largely sterile, summer; one of the commonest Solomon's seals in gardens, usually under *P. multiflorum. P. × h.* Striatum, leaves white-striped. *P. japonicum,* see *P. odoratum thunbergii. P. multiflorum,* Europe to Japan; to 60cm tall, sometimes more; much like a less robust *P. × hybridum,* but stems smooth, leaves rarely more than 10cm long; flowers 1–1·5cm long, distinctly contracted in the middle, in clusters of 2–5, early summer. *P. odoratum,* angular Solomon's seal; Europe to Japan; 20–45cm tall, sometimes more; stems ridged or angled; leaves alternate, 5–10cm long; flowers to 2cm long, greenish-white, fragrant, solitary or in pairs, summer. *P.o. thunbergii* (*P. japonicum, P. thunbergii*), more robust than type, 50–100cm tall; leaves 8–15cm long; flowers to 2·5cm long, white, tipped green. *P.o.t.* Variegatum, rarely above 60cm tall; leaves cream-tipped and striped, confused with *P. × hybridum* Striatum. *P. pumilum,* China; to 15cm tall; leaves few, ovate, about 4cm long; flowers white, tipped green, 1–1·5cm long, solitary or in pairs, late spring. *P. thunbergii,* see *P. odoratum thunbergii. P. verticillatum,* whorled Solomon's seal; Europe, Caucasus, Himalaya; 30–80cm or more tall; stems slender; leaves linear-lanceolate, 5–12cm long in whorls of 3–6; flowers 6–8mm long, greenish-white in clusters of 1–4, summer; fruit 6mm, red.

Polygonum

(Greek *polys,* many, and either *gonos,* offspring – some species multiply freely – or *gony,* knee joint: many species have prominent nodes). Knotweed. POLYGONACEAE. A genus of 150–300 species (depending on the classifier) of annuals, perennials and sub-shrubs of cosmopolitan distribution. They may be erect to prostrate; leaves alternate, ovate to linear with prominent membraneous stipules forming a collar around each node; flowers small, petalless, the calyx bell- to funnel-shaped, 5-lobed, each one giving rise to a triangular achene. Grow in any moderately rich soil in sun, but see species descriptions for any special requirements. Plant autumn to spring. Propagate from seed in spring or by division at planting time, trailing species also by cuttings spring to late summer.

Species cultivated: *P. affine,* Himalaya; mat-forming perennial to 60cm or more across; leaves tufted, erect, oblanceolate, 6–10cm long, bronze in winter; flowers rosy-red in cylindrical spikes 20–30cm tall, autumn. *P.a.* Darjeeling Red, flowers deep crimson; *P.a.* Donald Lowndes (*P.a.* Lowndes Variety), foliage rusty-brown in autumn, flowers rose-pink. *P. amplexicaule,* Himalaya; clump-forming perennial, 90–120cm tall; basal leaves lanceolate to ovate, slender-pointed, to 20cm or more long, stem leaves smaller, amplexicaul; flowers red, in dense, slender spikes, 5–15cm long, summer to autumn. *P.a.* Atrosanguineum, flowers rich crimson; *P.a.* Firetail, similar but brighter shade in larger spikes. *P. aubertii* (*Bilderdykia a.*), silver lace vine; W.China, Tibet; much like *P. baldschuanicum* but flowers always white or greenish-tinted, panicles narrower and stiffer with stalks and pedicels scabrid. *P. baldschuanicum* (*Bilderdykia b.*), Russian vine; S.Tadzhikstan, USSR; woody, twining climber, to 15m or more high; leaves ovate to lanceolate, 4–10cm long; flowers pink or white, pink-tinted in

broad, fluffy panicles, the stalks and pedicels of which are quite smooth, summer, autumn; rampantly vigorous and best over an old tree or unsightly shed; confused with *P. aubertii*. *P. bistorta*, bistort, Easter ledges, snakeroot, snakeweed (USA); Europe to C.Asia; rhizomatous perennial, to 50cm tall; basal leaves 5–10cm long, broadly ovate, the top of the long petioles winged, edible when young; flowers pink, in dense spikes, 5cm long; represented in gardens by *P.b.* Superbum, larger than type, to 75cm tall, early summer. *P. campanulatum*, Himalaya; rhizomatous perennial forming wide clumps or colonies, to 90cm tall; leaves 6–15cm long, elliptic to ovate, prominently veined, hairy; flowers pale pink, bell-shaped, in spreading, terminal panicles, summer to autumn. *P. capitatum*, Himalaya; half-hardy, evergreen, mat-forming perennial; stems slender, rooting at nodes; leaves ovate to elliptic, to 5cm long, each with a v-shaped, bronze to purple-brown zone; flowers pink, in tight, globular heads, 1–2cm wide, summer; needs a sheltered site and best in a frost-free greenhouse, at least in winter; good for hanging baskets. *P. cuspidatum* (*Reynoutria japonica*), Japanese knotweed, Mexican bamboo; Japan; herbaceous, woody-based, rhizomatous perennial, 2–3m tall, forming extensive colonies; leaves elliptic to broadly ovate, cuspidate, truncate at base, to 15cm long; flowers white, in branched spikes from upper leaf-axils, late summer to autumn; very invasive and not recommended for garden planting; the following are more garden-worthy and somewhat less invasive: *P.c. compactum* (*Reynoutria compacta*), to 1·2m tall, more compact; *P.c.c.* Pink Cloud, 80–100cm tall, flowers deep pink, fruit crimson; *P.c.* Variegatum (*Reynoutria japonica* Variegata), leaves splashed creamy-yellow and pink. *P. equisetiforme*, Mediterranean; woody-based perennial, to 45cm tall; stems wiry, ephedra-like; leaves linear to oblong, 2–4cm long, often falling early; flowers white or pink, in axillary clusters from upper stems, forming long panicles, autumn; needs a sunny, sheltered site. *P. filiforme* (*P. virginianum f.*, *Tovara v.f.*), Japan; rhizomatous perennial to 80cm tall; leaves 7–15cm long, elliptic to oblong, deep green, sometimes with dark v marking or blotches; flowers pink, in short spikes from upper leaf-axils, late summer. *P.f.* Variegata, leaves heavily splashed yellow and brownish-orange; flowers white; often listed as *Tovara virginiana* Variegata, and possibly 2 similar clones are involved. *P. macrophyllum* (*P. sphaerostachyum*), Himalaya, China; clump-forming perennial akin to *P. bistorta*; leaves oblong-lanceolate, to 23cm long, margins crenate and waved; flowers deep rose-red in spikes to 10cm long, summer. *P. milletii*, Himalaya to W.China; akin to *P. bistorta*, to 45cm tall; leaves oblong-lanceolate, long-stalked; flowers deep pink or crimson, in dense, cylindrical spikes, to 8cm long, summer. *P. molle* (*P. rude*, *P. paniculatum*), N.India to W.China, Indonesia; bushy perennial, to 1·5m tall; leaves lanceolate, silky hairy beneath; flowers white, in large terminal panicles, summer. *P. paniculatum*, see *P. molle*. *P. reynoutria*, see *P. cuspidatum*. *P. sphaerostachyum*, see *P. macrophyllum*. *P. tenuicaule*, Japan; tufted, rhizomatous perennial forming leafy mats to 10cm tall; leaves ovate-elliptic, 3–8cm long; flowers white, forming fluffy spikes to 3·5cm tall with unfolding foliage, spring; best in partial shade in moist soil. *P. vacciniifolium*, Himalaya; prostrate deciduous shrub; stems wiry; leaves ovate, 1–1·5cm long; flowers bright pink, erect in tapered spikes, 5–7cm long, autumn. *P. virginianum* of gardens, see *P. filiforme*.

Polypodium

(Greek *polys*, many, and *pous*, a foot – alluding to the branched and often wide-spreading rhizomes). POLYPODIACEAE. A genus of 75 species of ferns (formerly over 1000 before reclassification by Copeland and Ching) of cosmopolitan distribution. 1 species and its cultivars are generally available: *P. vulgare*, common polypody or wall fern; N.Hemisphere, S.Africa, Kerguelen; epiphytic and terrestrial evergreen, rhizomes densely brown scaly, usually creeping on the surface, forming mats or colonies; fronds solitary, ovate to linear-lanceolate or oblong in outline, pinnatisect or pinnatipartite, 10–30cm or more long; fertile pinnae with large, rounded, yellow to brown sori in single rows between mid-rib and margin; a variable species with many geographic forms and mutant cultivars: *P.v.* Bifidum Cristatum, pinnae forked and frond-tip broadly crested; *P.v.* Cambricum, fronds broad, 30–50cm long, pinnae cut into many narrow lobes; *P.v.* Cornubiensis, fronds variously tri- and quadripinnate, sometimes reverting to the normal pinnate state – such fronds should be removed; *P.v.* Longicaudatum, similar to species, but frond tips much elongated; *P.v.* Pulcherrimum, fronds tripinnatipartite. Grow in well-drained, humus-rich soil in shade, either beneath trees on banks, or in dry walls. Once established, the plants shouldn't be disturbed. Makes a durable plant for cold or cool greenhouse in pans or baskets of an all-peat compost. Pot or plant autumn or spring; propagate by division same time.

Top left: *Polygonum affine* Donald Lowndes
Above left: *Polygonum capitatum*
Above: *Polypodium vulgare* Pulcherrimum
Top right: *Polystichum lonchitis*
Above right: *Polystichum setiferum* Diversilobum Densum

Polystichum

(Greek *polys*, many, and *stichos*, row – the arrangement of the sori on the fronds). Shield fern, holly fern. ASPIDIACEAE (POLYPODIACEAE). A genus of 120–135 species of ferns of cosmopolitan distribution. They have thick, erect rhizomes and terminal rosettes of pinnate or bipinnate fronds, the fertile pinnae or pinnules with 2 rows of sporangia beneath. Grow in moisture-retentive but not wet soil in shade. Plant autumn to spring. Propagate by spores or division in spring.

Species cultivated: *P. acrostichoides* (*Asplenium a.*), Christmas fern, dagger fern; E. N.America; evergreen; fronds to 60cm long, pinnate, pinnae lanceolate, eared or lobed at base, the fertile ones towards the tips and markedly smaller, lustrous deep green; hardy, but often more satisfactory in a cold or cool greenhouse; mutants with forked, twisted or crested pinnae are sometimes available. *P. aculeatum*, hard or prickly shield fern; Europe, Asia and S.America; evergreen; fronds to 1m long, lanceolate in outline, bipinnate, rigid, somewhat leathery, pinnules toothed, bristle-spine tipped, dark, somewhat lustrous green; confused with, and often sold as, *P. setiferum*. *P. falcatum*, see *Cyrtomium f. P. lonchitis*, mountain holly fern; arctic and northern temperate zone, mountains farther south; evergreen, fronds 15–60cm long, linear or narrowly lanceolate in outline, pinnate, pinnae 1–3cm long, often overlapping, ovate-lanceolate, unequal at base, sharply bristle-spine toothed, somewhat lustrous; hardy but not always easy to please, needing a cool humid environment and often best in a shaded cold greenhouse. *P. setiferum* (*P. angulare*), soft shield or hedge fern; temperate climates, N. and S.hemispheres; similar to *P. aculeatum*, but fronds rather soft, arching or drooping, the pinnules having fewer, larger teeth. *P.s.* Acutilobum (*P.s.* Proliferum), plume fern, fronds bearing numerous tiny plantlets, particularly along the mid-rib, pinnules narrower but dense, very hardy and garden-worthy; *P.s.* Divisilobum Densum, fronds tri- and quadripinnate, densely plumose; several similar cultivars are available.

Pomegranate – see *Punica*.

Poncirus

(French for a kind of citron – *Citrus*). RUTACEAE. A genus of 1 deciduous shrub from N.China, Korea. *P. trifoliata* (*Citrus t.*, *Aegle sepiaria*), Japanese bitter orange; shrub or small tree 6m tall, often 2–3m in gardens; stems green, bearing sharp, stout spines, 2–5cm long; leaves rather sparse, usually trifoliate, leaflets obovate, to 4cm long; flowers 5-petalled, white, fragrant, 4–5cm wide, stamens pink, not united as in *Citrus*, early summer; fruit to 4cm wide, like tiny orange, bitter and acrid unless candied. Grow in mild areas in well-drained, humus-rich soil in sun. Plant autumn to spring. Propagate from seed when ripe in a cold frame or by cuttings late summer, bottom heat about 18°C.

Pondweed – see *Potamogeton*.

Pontederia

(for Giulio Pontedera, 1688–1757, Italian professor of botany at Padua). PONTEDERIACEAE. A genus of 4 species of aquatic perennials from N. and S.America, 1 of which is generally available: *P. cordata*, pickerel weed; E. N.America; rhizomatous, forming colonies; stems to 60cm or more tall; leaves 7–20cm long, narrowly ovate, cordate, rich glossy green; flowers funnel-shaped, 6-lobed, somewhat 2-lipped with the upper 3 lobes fused, blue with 2 yellow spots. Grow in bogs, or water to 30cm deep, in sun. Plant spring or autumn, either into a natural mud bottom, or containers of equal parts loam and decayed manure or compost. Propagate by division at planting time.

Poplar – see *Populus*.

Poppy – see *Papaver*.

Populus

(Latin vernacular name for poplar). Poplar, aspen, cottonwood. SALICACEAE. A genus of about 35 species of deciduous trees from the northern temperate zone. They have alternate, triangular to broadly ovate leaves, often on flattened petioles, and tiny, dioecious, petalless flowers in pendant catkins before the leaves, the males with red stamens. The seed is minute, bearing long white hairs for wind dispersal; when shed in summer it appears like masses of cotton wool, hence the American vernacular name. Grow in moisture-retentive soil in sun. Plant autumn to spring. Propagate by hardwood cuttings in autumn or soft tips under mist in summer. Seed must be sown as soon as ripe, on the surface of compost kept continually moist until seedlings appear. Poplars are important timber trees and of handsome appearance, but fast-growing; roots can invade drains and foundations.

Species cultivated: *P. alba*, white poplar, abele; Asia, Europe, N.Africa; to 30m tall, but sometimes half this in gardens; leaves to 5cm long, rounded to heart-shaped, irregularly wavy-margined on mature trees or branches, to 13cm long and palmately 3–5 lobed on young trees or sucker shoots, always white woolly beneath; catkins 5–8cm long. *P.a.* Pyramidalis (*P.a.* Bolleana), narrowly pyramidal habit. *P. balsamifera* (*P. tacamahacca*), balsam poplar, tacamahac; N. N.America; to 25m or more tall; leaves 7–12cm long, ovate to ovate-lanceolate, whitish beneath, balsam-scented, particularly when young. *P.* × *berolinensis* (*P. laurifolia* × *P. nigra* Italica), columnar habit, to 20m or more; leaves to 10cm long, slender-pointed, margins translucent. *P.* × *canadensis* (*P.* × *euramericana*), (*P. nigra* × *P. deltoides*), a group of mainly very vigorous hybrid clones combining the parental characters in various ways, but leaves usually ciliate, at least when young, and with the 2 glands at junction of blade and petiole typical of *P. deltoides*. *P.* × *c.* Eugenei, Carolina poplar; columnar habit; leaves broadly triangular, to 8cm or more wide, coppery when young; male. *P.* × *c.* Gelrica, similar to *P.* × *c.* Serotina in habit; leaves brownish-red when young, maturing pale green; a male and female clone are known. *P.* × *c.* Robusta, very vigorous, branches ascending; leaves to 13cm long, triangular-ovate, teeth rounded, widely spaced at base, reddish-bronze when young; male. *P.* × *c.* Serotina, Canadian poplar; perhaps the oldest of this hybrid group; to 45m tall, with wide-spreading ascending branches; leaves broadly triangular-ovate, somewhat grey-green, 5–15cm wide, with red petioles; male. *P.* × *c.* Serotina Aurea, leaves yellow when young, maturing yellow-green. *P.* × *candicans*, see *P.* × *gileadensis*. *P.* × *canescens* (*P. alba* × *P. tremula*), grey poplar; much like *P. alba* but leaves entirely lacking the long lobes, the margins only with large, irregular, blunt teeth and a thickened margin; vigorous shoots have the pair of glands at the junction of each leaf-stalk and blade, characteristic of *P. tremula*. *P. deltoides* (*P. monilifera*), cottonwood, necklace poplar; E. N.America; to 30m or more tall, with a short trunk and broad head; leaves 7–13cm long, triangular to broadly ovate, slender-pointed, balsam-scented, 2 small, yellowish glands at junction of leaf-stalk and blade. *P.* × Eugenei, *P.* × *euramericana* and *P.* × Gelrica, see *P.* × *canadensis*. *P.* × *generosa* (*P. deltoides* × *P. trichocarpa*), extremely vigorous,

Far left below: *Poncirus trifoliata*
Left: *Pontederia cordata*
Below: *Populus* × *gileadensis* Aurora

sometimes 2m per year but much prone to canker and wind breakage; leaves to 30cm long on young trees, triangular-ovate, grey beneath, balsam-scented; male and female clones are known. *P.×gileadensis* (*P. candicans*), balm of Gilead, Ontario poplar; probably *P. deltoides* × *P. balsamifera*, but by some authorities considered to be a distinctive female clone of *P. balsamifera subcordata*; much like the latter but broad-headed, usually with cordate-based leaves, densely downy on veins beneath. *P.×g.* Aurora (*P. candicans* Aurora), young leaves almost wholly white, pink-tinted, gradually maturing green; best grown stooled or pollarded for the largest, most colourful leaves. *P. lasiocarpa*, Chinese necklace poplar; C.China; to 23m tall in gardens; spreading, rather gaunt habit; young stems stout, downy; leaves ovate, 15–35cm long, finely toothed, bright green, petiole and veins red, downy beneath; best propagated by tip cuttings under a mist unit. *P. monilifera*, see *P. deltoides*. *P. nigra*, black poplar; Europe, Asia; to 30m or more, trunk blackish, usually with large, distinctive burrs when mature; broad-headed, the lower branches arching down

with ascending laterals; leaves 5–8cm long; without glands. *P.n. betulifolia* (*P.* 'Wilsonii' of some catalogues), Manchester poplar, N. and W.Europe, including Britain; leaves pubescent when young; now seldom planted, being largely replaced by *P.×canadensis* clones, and often confused with *P.* Serotina. *P.n.* Italica, Lombardy poplar; male clone of narrowly fastigiate habit, frequently planted; confused with it is the wider and bushier *P.n.* Plantierensis, with downy young shoots and occurring as male and female clones, and the female *P.n.* Afghanica having whitish bark. *P.* Robusta and *P.* Serotina, see *P. canadensis*. *P. tacamahacca*, see *P. balsamifera*. *P. tremula*, aspen; Europe, N.Africa, N.Asia; to 16m or so tall, conical when young, broadening later; bark smooth, greenish-grey; leaves 4–6cm long, orbicular to broadly ovate, with rounded, curved teeth, deep, somewhat grey, green above, paler beneath, the petiole much-flattened, clear yellow in autumn; not easily rooted from hardwood cuttings but reasonably successful as tip cuttings in summer under a mist propagation unit. *P. tremuloides*, American or quaking aspen; Alaska and Canada to N.W.Mexico; to 30m or more in the wild, sometimes half this in gardens; similar to *P. tremula*, but leaves finely and evenly toothed, ciliate when young, and yellowish bark. *P. trichocarpa*, western balsam poplar, black cottonwood; Alaska to California and adjacent Mexico; to 60m but often less in gardens, erect habit, rather untidy when

Above: *Populus alba* catkins
Right: *Populus alba* bark

old; leaves 10–30cm long, oblong to broadly ovate, thick-textured, dark green above, white beneath, balsam-scented, turning yellow in autumn. *P. wilsonii*, W. and C.China; to 25m tall in the wild, less in cultivation, pyramidal habit, at least when young; leaves 8–23cm long, ovate-cordate, finely toothed, sea-green above, greyish beneath; similar to *P. lasiocarpa*, reputedly distinguished by red petioles and leaf veins, but these do not appear to be reliable characters; propagate by summer cuttings under mist; confused with *P. nigra betulifolia*.

Portuguese laurel – see *Prunus lusitanicus*.

Portulaca

(Latin vernacular name for common purslane). PORTULACACEAE. A genus of 100–200 species (depending on the classifier) of annuals and perennials from the tropics to warm temperate regions, particularly the Americas. They have alternate to almost opposite, often fleshy, ovate to linear leaves, and terminal flowers with 5 spreading petals that only open in sun. Grow hardy and half-hardy species mentioned here in well-drained soil in sun. Sow hardy purslane seed thinly in shallow drills 25–30cm apart in spring, thinning seedlings in stages to 20–25cm apart. The thinnings may be eaten. Sow seed of *P. grandiflora* under glass in spring at 16–18°C. Prick off seedlings into boxes of a good commercial potting mixture when 2–3 true leaves are showing; space them 4cm apart each way, harden off and plant out post-frost; sow *in situ* in late spring, early summer.

Species cultivated: *P. grandiflora*, sun plant, rose moss; Brazil, Uruguay, Argentina; tufted habit to 15cm or more tall; stem prostrate to ascending; leaves to 2·5cm long, fleshy, cylindrical; flowers opening widely, 2–3cm across, red, pink, yellow, purple, white, with a boss of yellow stamens, summer to autumn; several strains are available, usually in mixed colours, some doubles. *P. oleracea*, common purslane; probably from India but now worldwide as a weed; mat-forming; stems prostrate to decumbent; leaves 2–3cm long, oblong-obovate to spathulate, sometimes sub-opposite, fleshy; flowers to 1·5cm wide, yellow, summer. *P.o. sativa*, larger and more fleshy in all its parts, sometimes grown as a salad plant or pot herb. *P.o. sativa* Gigantea, has double blooms to 2·5cm wide.

Potamogeton

(Greek *potomos*, river, and *geiton*, neighbour). POTAMOGETONACEAE. A genus of 80–100 species of aquatic perennials of cosmopolitan distribution. They are mainly rhizomatous, rooted in the bottoms of ponds and lakes; leaves linear to ovate, either translucent and totally submerged, or some opaque and floating; flowers small, insignificant, with 4, green or brownish perianth segments, borne in axillary or terminal spikes, usually above but sometimes below the surface – then pollinated by water currents. Grow in ponds or aquaria, planted in pots or containers of a loam-based mixture surfaced with grit, or into a natural mud bottom. Plant spring or summer. Propagate by cuttings, 2 or 3 secured together by a lead clip and pushed into the mud or potted and anchored by pebbles. Some species produce turions that can be collected or dredged in winter and either broadcast in the water or kept in containers of water until they start to grow, then potted.

Species cultivated: *P. crispus*, curled pondweed; Europe, Asia, naturalized in USA; stems 30–120cm long, more or less 4-angled; leaves all submerged, 3–9cm long, lanceolate, usually rounded or blunt-tipped, toothed and strongly waved; turions leafy, 1–5cm long. *P. densus* (now reclassified as *Groenlandia densa* but retained here for convenience), frog's lettuce; Europe, Asia; stems much-branched, 10–30cm long; leaves dense, in opposite pairs or whorls, all submerged, 1·5–2·5cm long, ovate-triangular to lanceolate, minutely serrate. *P. lucens*, shining pondweed; Europe, W.Asia; stems 0·5–2m or more long; leaves all submerged, 10–20cm long, oblong-lanceolate, minutely toothed, pale, shining green. *P. pectinatus*, fennel pondweed; almost cosmopolitan; stems very slender, usually much-branched; leaves all submerged, 5–20cm long, linear to hair-like, dark green; usually over-winters as tuber-like buds on the rhizomes. *P. polygonifolius*, bog pondweed; Europe, N.W.Africa, E. N.America; stems to 20cm or more long; submerged leaves long-stalked, 8–20cm long, narrowly lanceolate, floating leaves 2–6cm long, broadly elliptic to lanceolate, dark green; best in shallow acid water.

Left below: *Portulaca* Improved Double Mixed
Below: *Potamogeton polygonifolius*
Right: *Potentilla* William Rollison
Right below: *Potentilla* × *tonguei*

Potentilla

(Latin *potens*, powerful – alluding to the medicinal properties formerly accorded to certain species). Cinquefoil. ROSACEAE. A genus of 500 species of annuals, perennials and shrubs of almost cosmopolitan distribution, but mainly N.Hemisphere. They have tufted, often long-stalked, pinnate, trifoliate or digitate leaves, and 5-petalled, wide open flowers that are characterized by an epicalyx (sepal-like bracts alternating with the true sepals). Grow in well-drained, moderately fertile soil in sun. Plant autumn to spring. Propagate from seed in spring, by division at planting time and cuttings of the shrubs taken in late summer in a cold frame or in autumn outside.

Species cultivated: *P. alba*, C. E.Europe to Caucasus; tufted, spreading perennial to 15cm tall; leaves digitate, leaflets 5, oblong to obovate-lanceolate, 2–4cm long, silvery silky beneath; flowers about 2cm wide, white, spring to autumn. *P. alpestris*, see *P. crantzii*. *P. ambigua* (*P. cuneata* of gardens), Himalaya; tufted perennial; stems prostrate to ascending, 7–10cm tall; leaves trifoliate, leaflets obovate, 1cm long; flowers to 2·5cm wide, golden-yellow, summer. *P. arbuscula* (*P. fruticosa a.*, *P. rigida*), Himalaya, S.E.Tibet, W. China; much like *P. fruticosa* but rarely above 90cm tall; stems with large, prominent, dark-brown, papery stipules; leaves pinnate to trifoliate, leaflets elliptic, silky-hairy, grey-green; flowers to 4·5cm wide, golden-yellow, summer to late autumn; see also *P.* × Elizabeth. *P. argyrophylla*, Himalaya; tufted to clump-forming perennial; 45cm or more tall; leaves trifoliate, leaflets elliptic to obovate, sharply toothed, white hairy beneath; flowers 2–3cm wide, yellow, in panicled cymes, early summer to autumn. *P. atrosanguinea*, Himalaya; a dark velvety-red flowered version of *P. argyrophylla*; these 2 species and probably *P. nepalensis* have been hybridized together to create a race of larger-flowered, often double or semi-double cultivars, eg *P.* Gibson's Scarlet, bright scarlet; *P.* Gloire de Nancy, coral-red and orange-brown, semi-double; *P.* Monsieur Rouillard, mahogany-crimson; *P.* William Rollison, orange-red and yellow; *P.* Yellow Queen, bright yellow, red eye. *P. aurea*, C. and S.Europe; tufted, rootstock somewhat woody; stems erect to sprawling, often forming loose mats, 10–15cm tall;

Top left: *Potentilla × Elizabeth*
Left: *Potentilla fruticosa* Manchu
Top: *Potentilla fruticosa* Red Ace
Top right: *Potentilla aurea*
Right: *Potentilla ambigua*

basal leaves digitate, leaflets 5, oblong, silvery-ciliate, sharply toothed; flowers 1·5–2cm wide, golden-yellow, darker eye. *P.a. chrysocraspeda* (*P. ternata*), leaves trifoliate with blunt teeth; *P.a.* Plena, flowers double. *P. cinerea* (*P. tommasiniana*), S.E. and C.Europe; mat-forming; stems somewhat woody, prostrate, rooting; leaves trifoliate or digitate, leaflets 3–5, oblong to broadly obovate, toothed, 5–20mm long, grey-green with starry and simple hairs; flowers 1–2cm wide, pale yellow, in clusters of 3–5 above the leaves, early to late summer. *P. crantzii* (*P. alpestris*), alpine cinquefoil; tufted, rootstock woody; stems to 20cm or more tall; leaves digitate, leaflets 5 (sometimes 3), 8–20mm long, oblanceolate to broadly obovate, blunt-toothed and hairy; flowers 1·5–2·5cm wide, yellow, each petal often with a basal orange blotch, summer. *P. cuneata* (of gardens), see *P. ambigua*. *P.* × Elizabeth (*P. arbuscula* of some catalogues), (*P. arbuscula* × *P. fruticosa mandschurica*), dense domed habit to 1m tall, and somewhat broader; flowers 4·5cm wide, rich canary-yellow, in dense cymes. *P. eriocarpa* of gardens, Himalaya; mat-forming, to 30cm or more wide by 5cm high: leaves trifoliate, leaflets cuneate, toothed in upper half, grey hairy; flowers 2–3cm wide, bright yellow, summer; best in a scree. *P. fragiformis*, N.E.Asia; tufted, from short, thick rhizomes, 10–25cm tall; leaves trifoliate, leaflets elliptic to obovate, coarsely toothed, silky hairy; flowers several in loose, corymb-like clusters, each 2–3cm wide, golden-yellow, summer. *P.f. megalantha*, see *P. megalantha*. *P. fruticosa*, shrubby cinquefoil; northern temperate zone and mountains farther south; much-branched, twiggy, deciduous shrub to 1m or more tall; leaves pinnate, leaflets 3–7, usually 5, oblong-lanceolate, 1–2cm long; flowers 1·5–2·5cm wide, yellow, solitary or in small cymes, summer to early autumn; very variable in habit, hairiness, flower size and shade – among many cultivars the following are worthy of note: *P.f.* Arbuscula, see *P. arbuscula*; *P.f.* Berlin Beauty or *P.f.* Friedrichsenii, to 2m tall, leaves grey-green, flowers light yellow; *P.f.* Katherine Dykes, to 2m tall, flowers primrose-yellow, abundantly borne; *P.f.* Klondyke, to 60cm tall, bright golden-yellow, to 4cm wide; *P.f.* Longacre, spreading habit, to about 40cm tall, pale yellow; *P.f.* Manchu (*P.f. mandschurica*), spreading habit, to about 50cm tall, leaves grey-green, flowers white; *P.f.* Red Ace, flowers yellow in bud, opening vermilion – a very new cultivar largely untried, mentioned only because of its startling colour; *P.f.* Sunset, orange to brick-red but fading in hot weather; *P.f.* Tangerine, dwarf, wide-spreading, flowers coppery-yellow, soon fading, especially in sun; *P.f.* Veitchii, 1m tall, arching habit, flowers white; *P.f.* Vilmoriniana, erect, to 2m tall, leaves silvery hairy, flowers cream; *P.f.* William Purdom (*P.f. purdomii*), semi-erect, to 1·5m, flowers light yellow, in abundance. *P. megalantha* (*P. fragiformis m.*), Japan; much like *P. fragiformis* but more silky hairy; thicker-textured leaves and more loosely borne flowers 3–4cm wide; often grown as *P. fragiformis*. *P. nepalensis*, Himalaya; tufted, to 45cm or more tall; leaves digitate, leaflets 5, obovate to oblanceolate, 2·5–6·5cm long, coarsely toothed, hairy; flowers 2·5cm wide, rose-red, summer. *P.n.* Miss Willmott, 30cm tall; flowers rose-crimson. *P. nitida*, Alps and Appenines; tufted and mat-forming, to 5cm tall; leaves trifoliate, leaflets 5–10mm long, obovate to oblanceolate, silvery silky grey hairy; flowers solitary or in pairs, 2–3cm wide, apple-blossom pink or rarely white, late summer; not free-flowering and best in a limestone scree. *P. recta*, C.E. and S.Europe; tufted, 30–60cm tall; leaves digitate, leaflets 5–7, oblong to obovate, toothed to pinnatisect, 2–10cm long; densely downy, often grey-green; flowers 1·5–2·4cm wide, yellow, profusely carried in loose cymes, summer. *P.r.* Warrenii (misspelt Warrensii, *P. warrenii* of gardens), flowers to 3cm wide, bright yellow. *P. rupestris*, rock cinquefoil; Europe to C.Asia; tufted, 20–50cm tall; basal leaves pinnate, leaflets 5–9, ovate, doubly toothed, 2–6cm long; stem leaves trifoliate, smaller; flowers 1·5–3cm wide, white, in loose, leafy corymbs; usually represented in gardens by *P.r. pygmaea* to 10cm tall with more numerous, prostrate to ascending stems and smaller flowers. *P. tabernaemontani* (*P. verna* in part), spring cinquefoil; Europe to Bylo Russia; mat-forming, with numerous, prostrate, rooting stems; leaves digitate, leaflets 5–7, oblanceolate to obovate, toothed, 1–4cm long; flowers about 1·5cm wide, yellow, spring to summer. *P.t.* Nana, smaller and neater than type; leaves darker green. *P. ternata*, see *P. aurea chrysocraspeda*. *P. tommasiniana*, see *P. cinerea*. *P.* × *tonguei* (*P.* × *tormentillo-formosa*), a name of no botanical validity for *P. anglica* × *P. nepalensis*; prostrate to ascending, forming loose mats to 10cm tall; leaves trifoliate or 5 digitate, leaflets obovate, coarsely toothed, to 2·5cm long; flowers about 2cm wide, yellow to apricot with red base to each petal forming crimson eye, summer. *P. verna*, see *P. tabernaemontani*. *P. warrenii*, see *P. recta* Warrenii.

Poterium – see *Sanguisorba*.

Pratia

(for C. L. Prat-Bernon, French Naval Officer who died in 1817 at the outset of one of Freycinet's voyages of exploration to the Pacific).

Far left top: *Pratia angulata*
Far left above: *Pratia angulata* Treadwellii
Left top: *Primula allionii* (2)
Left above: *Primula auricula* (2)
Top: *Primula marginata* (2)
Above centre: *Primula pulverulenta* (4)
Above: *Primula japonica* Posrford White (4)

CAMPANULACEAE (LOBELIACEAE). A genus of 25–35 evergreen perennials closely allied to *Lobelia* from Australasia, S.America, tropical Africa and Asia. They are mostly prostrate, a few ascending to erect, with alternate, toothed, often orbicular to ovate leaves, irregular, tubular, 5-lobed flowers, the tubes of which are split nearly to the base on the upper side, and globose to obovoid berries. The species described here are generally hardy in Britain. Grow in moisture-retentive but well-drained soil in sheltered, partially shaded or sunny sites. Plant spring. Propagate from seed in a cold frame, by division in spring or cuttings in summer.

Species cultivated: *P. angulata*, New Zealand; mat-forming; stems prostrate and rooting; leaves to 1cm or more long, broadly ovate to rounded, with large, shallow teeth; flowers 8–16mm wide, white with purplish veins, solitary from leaf-axils, summer; berries 7–12mm long, purple-red. *P.a.* Treadwellii, plant more robust than type, flowers larger. *P. macrodon*, New Zealand; mat-forming; stems prostrate; leaves 5–10mm long, broadly ovate, prominently sharply toothed; flowers 1·2–1·8cm long, white or very pale yellow with yellowish throat, summer; berries 6–9mm wide, glossy red-purple.

Prickly ash – see *Zanthoxylum*.

Pride of India – see *Melia*.

Primrose – see *Primula vulgaris*.

Primula

(indirectly derived from Latin *primus*, first, attached to the early names of several sorts of early-flowering plants, used for this genus by Linnaeus). PRIMULACEAE. A genus of about 400 species of evergreen and deciduous perennials mainly from the N. Hemisphere. They are tufted to clump-forming, having basal rosettes of oblanceolate to orbicular leaves and leafless scapes bearing umbels of tubular flowers with 5 broad lobes. These lobes are characteristically but not invariably obovate with notched tips. See also Pin-eyed. Although there are strong basic resemblances from species to species, the genus as a whole displays a wide range of growth forms, from the low, dense cushions of *P. allionii* to the lush leafy clump and robust scapes of *P. florindae*. Botanists have grouped the species with characters in common into 30 named sections:

1 AMETHYSTINA	2 AURICULA
3 BULLATAE	4 CANDELABRA
5 CAPITATAE	6 CAROLINELLA
7 CORTUSOIDES	8 CUNEIFOLIA
9 DENTICULATA	10 DRYADIFOLIA
11 FARINOSAE	12 FLORIBUNDAE
13 GRANDIS	14 MALACOIDES
15 MALVACEAE	16 MINUTISSIMAE
17 MUSCARIOIDES	18 NIVALES
19 OBCONICA	20 PARRYI
21 PETIOLARES	22 PINNATAE
23 PYCNOLOBA	24 REINII
25 ROTUNDIFOLIA	26 SIKKIMENSIS
27 SINENSIS	28 SOLDANELLOIDEAE
29 SOULIEI	30 VERNALES

Some sections also indicate cultural requirements: CANDELABRA and SIKKIMENSIS grow best by the waterside or in a bog; AURICULA needs well-drained soil and a fair amount of sun to flower well; CORTUSOIDES likes shade and a humus-rich soil, being a native of woodland. Most primulas are hardy (see culture details), but a few tender species are important greenhouse pot plants, eg *P.* × *kewensis*, *P. malacoides*, *P. obconica* and *P. sinensis*. Although short-lived perennials, these are grown as annuals, minimum temperature 7°C, well-ventilated and lightly shaded in summer. Sow seed thinly and barely cover, using a standard seed sowing mixture at 16°C from spring to mid summer. Cover with glass or plastic and keep shaded until germination. Prick off seedlings when the first true leaf is well developed at 4cm apart each way into a good potting soil or all peat equivalent. When the leaves of the young plants start to overlap, plant up singly into 9cm pots. Plants from spring sowings may now be placed in partially shaded cold frames with the tops removed in summer. When plants from this spring sowing have filled the pots with roots, pot on into 13 or 15cm containers for flowering. Plants sown in mid summer can be flowered in the 9cm pots if desired,

Top: *Primula helodoxa* (4)
Above centre: *Primula beesiana* (4)
Above: *Primula rosea* (11)
Right top: *Primula capitata* (5)
Right above: *Primula sieboldii* Geisha Girl (7)
Far right top: *Primula denticulata* Alba (9)
Far right above: *Primula frondosa* (11)

particularly if given liquid feed at 7-day intervals. *P. obconica* can be divided after flowering and grown on as a perennial, but generally plants are finer and more floriferous the first year from seed. For the most part, hardy species need humus-rich, moisture-retentive soil in partial shade, but full sun is tolerated by the majority; see also previous comments. Many species are suitable for, and grow best by, the waterside or in a bog garden, while others require good drainage; see individual descriptions for extra cultural requirements. Plant late summer to spring or after flowering. Propagate from seed ideally as soon as ripe when it germinates abundantly, or in spring in a cold frame; also by division at planting time.

Species cultivated (the number after each species indicates the botanical section to which it belongs, as listed above): *P. acaulis*, see *P. vulgaris*. *P. allionii* (**2**), Maritime and Ligurian Alps; low cushion-forming with crowded rosettes; leaves 1·5–4·5cm long, oblanceolate to rounded, sometimes finely toothed, densely sticky downy; scapes very short, flowers to 2·5cm wide, clear pink to red-purple, just above leaves, spring; best grown in a vertical crevice in the rock garden or in the alpine house. *P. alpicola* (*P. microdonta a.*) (**26**), S.E.Tibet, Bhutan; leaves to 15cm long, elliptic to oblong, crenate; scapes 30–50cm tall, sometimes with 2 superimposed umbels, flowers to 2·5cm wide, pendulous, yellow, fragrant, early summer. *P.a. violacea*, flowers purple to violet. *P. altaica*, name given to several pink primroses but most commonly to the next species. *P. amoena* (**30**), Caucasus, N.E.Turkey; leaves oblong-spathulate, to 7·5cm long, densely white woolly beneath; scapes to 15cm tall, flowers primrose-like, about 2·5cm wide, violet to lavender-blue with yellow eye, spring. *P. aurantiaca* (**4**), W.China; leaves oblanceolate to obovate, to 20cm long; scapes to 30cm tall, flowers about 1·2cm wide, reddish-orange, in 2–6 whorls, summer; suitable for bog or waterside. *P. auricula* (**2**), auricula; Alps, Carpathians, Appenines; tufted, forming short, gnarled trunks or stems when old; leaves 2–12cm long, usually obovate but varying from lanceolate to rounded, sometimes irregularly toothed; scapes 5–15cm tall, flowers 1·5–2cm wide, deep yellow, fragrant, spring; a variable species that has given rise to many hybrids in a wide range of colours and shades, some of them with bold eye markings and green-grey or white picotee margins. *P. beesiana* (**4**), W.China; leaves ovate-lanceolate, to 20cm or more long; scapes to 60cm tall, flowers 2cm wide, rose-carmine with yellow eye, in 2–8 whorls, summer; best in bog or at waterside. *P. bhutanica* (**21**), Himalaya; leaves to 10cm long, oblong-spathulate; scapes 6–10cm tall, flowers 2·5cm wide, pale blue with brownish-yellow eye, each lobe 3-toothed, spring. *P.* × *bilekii*, see *P.* × *steinii*. *P. bracteosa* (**21**), Himalaya; leaves 5cm long, oblong-ovate, farinose; scapes very short, flowers 2–2·5cm wide, lilac with yellow eye, lobes 2–3 toothed, spring. *P. bulleyana* (**4**), W.China; leaves 13–30cm long, ovate-lanceolate; scapes to 60cm or more tall, flowers 2–2·5cm wide, orange-yellow, in 5–7 whorls, summer; best in bog or waterside. *P. burmanica* (**4**), Upper Burma, W.China; leaves 20–30cm long, oblanceolate; scapes to 60cm tall, flowers to 2cm wide, red-purple, with golden eye, summer. *P. capitata* (**5**), Himalaya; leaves 7–15cm long, oblong-lanceolate, farinose beneath; scapes 30–45cm tall, flowers 1cm wide, purple-blue, in dense, head-like umbels, summer. *P.c. mooreana*, more robust than type; leaves pure white farinose beneath; often flowers until autumn. *P. chionantha* (**18**), W.China; leaves 15–25cm long, oblanceolate, yellow farinose beneath; scapes 40–60cm tall, flowers 2·5cm wide, creamy-white, fragrant, in 1–4 whorls, early summer; the most easily grown NIVALES primula but must have moist soil. *P. chungensis* (**4**), Bhutan, Assam, W.China; leaves 10–30cm long, oblong-obovate; scapes to 60cm tall, flowers 1·5–2cm wide, tube red, lobes pale orange, in 2–5 whorls, summer; bog or waterside. *P. clarkei* (**11**), Kashmir; leaves 2–5cm long, broadly ovate to rounded, cordate; scapes very short, flowers to 2cm wide, lobes rose-pink, tube yellow, spring. *P. cockburniana* (**4**), W.China; leaves to 15cm long, oblong-obovate, faintly small-lobed; scapes to 30cm tall, slender, flowers 1·5cm wide, deep orange-red, in 1–3 whorls, summer. *P. concholoba* (**17**), Himalaya; leaves to 7cm long, oblanceolate, hairy; scapes to 10cm or more tall, flowers 1–1·5cm wide, violet, white farinose without, in compact umbels, late spring. *P. cortusoides* (**7**), W.Siberia; leaves long-stalked, to 7cm long, oblong-ovate, cordate with small crenate lobes, downy; scapes to 30cm or more tall, flowers 2cm wide, rose, late spring. *P. denticulata* (**9**), Himalaya; leaves to 30cm long, oblong-obovate to oblanceolate; scapes 10–30cm tall, flowers 1–1·5cm wide, lilac to red or blue-purple with yellow eye, in dense globular heads, early spring to early summer; variable in colour, and several cultivars are listed including the white *P.d.* Alba. *P. edgeworthii* (*P. winteri*) (**21**), W.Himalaya; spring leaves to 7cm long, spathulate, irregularly toothed or small-lobed, undulate, summer leaves to 15cm long, triangular-ovate; scapes very short, flowers to 2cm wide, pale mauve with white eye, spring to summer; needs well-drained but humus-rich soil and protection from excessive winter rain, eg a pane of glass. *P.e.* Alba, flowers white. *P. elatior* (**30**), oxlip; S.W. and C.Europe, to C.Asia; leaves 5–20cm long, elliptic-oblong to almost orbicular, usually grey-green and hairy beneath; scapes 10–30cm tall, flowers 1·5–2·5cm wide, sulphur-yellow, nodding, in 1-sided umbels, winter to spring; variable in hairiness and leaf shape. *P.e. pallasii*, leaves obovate-oblong, hairless. *P. farinosa* (**11**), bird's-eye primrose; Europe, Asia; leaves 2–10cm long, oblanceolate to elliptic, usually farinose beneath; scapes 5–20cm tall, flowers 8–16mm wide, rosy-lilac with yellow eye, spring. *P. florindae* (**26**), giant cowslip; S.E.Tibet; leaves broadly ovate-cordate, to 20cm long including long, reddish stalks; scapes to 1m or more tall, flowers 2cm wide, bright yellow, pendant, in dense umbels, fragrant, summer to autumn; bog or waterside. *P. forrestii* (**3**), W.China; forming woody, rhizome-like stems when old; leaves long-stalked, blades ovate-elliptic, to 10cm long, finely wrinkled, glandular hairy; scapes 25–40cm or more tall, flowers 2cm wide, yellow with orange eye, fragrant, summer; alpine house or scree sheltered from winter wet. *P. frondosa* (**11**), C.Bulgaria; leaves 3–9cm long, spathulate to obovate, usually densely farinose; scapes 5–12cm tall, flowers 1–1·5cm wide, rosy-lilac to red-purple with yellow eye, spring. *P. geraniifolia* (**7**), E.Himalaya to W.China; leaves long-stalked, blades 4cm long, orbicular-cordate with small, rounded lobes, hairy; scapes 15–25cm tall, flowers 2cm wide, pale purple, late spring. *P. glaucescens* (**2**), S.Alps; leaves 2–7cm long, broadly lanceolate to obovate, leathery, glossy; scapes 3–12cm tall, flowers about 2·5cm wide, rose to pale purple, spring. *P. gracilipes* (**21**), Sikkim, Himalaya; leaves 10cm long, broadly spathulate to elliptic, coarsely and irregularly toothed, wavy-margined; scapes very short, flowers 2·5–3cm wide, rich pink with dark greenish-yellow-white ringed eye, lobes toothed, winter to spring; the easiest PETIOLARES primula. *P. halleri* (*P. longiflora*) (**11**), Alps, Carpathians, mountains of Balkan Peninsula; leaves 2–8cm long, oblong-obovate to oblanceolate, densely yellow farinose beneath; scapes 8–18cm tall, flowers 1·5–2cm wide, longer-tubed, lilac to pale violet, spring. *P. helodoxa* (**4**), W.China, Burma; leaves broadly lanceolate to obovate, 20–35cm long; scapes to 90cm tall, flowers 2·5cm wide, bright rich yellow, fragrant, in 4–6 whorls, summer; bog or waterside. *P. heucherifolia* (**7**), Tibet, W.China; rhizomatous; leaves long-stalked, blades to 7·5cm long, almost orbicular with several broadly triangular, toothed lobes; scapes 20–30cm tall, flowers 2–2·5cm wide, lilac-pink to purple, late spring. *P. hirsuta* (*P. rubra*, *P. viscosa*) (**2**), C.Pyrenees, Alps; leaves 2–9cm long, ovate, obovate or rounded, finely or coarsely toothed, sticky with yellowish or reddish glands; scapes 2–7cm tall, flowers 2–2·5cm wide, lilac to deep purple-red, usually with a white eye, spring. *P. inayatii* (**11**), N.W.Himalaya; leaves 10–15cm long, narrowly oblanceolate; scapes to 13cm tall, flowers 2cm wide, blue-purple with yellow eye, spring. *P. integrifolia* (**2**), Alps, Pyrenees; leaves 1–4cm long, lanceolate to obovate; scapes 0·5–5cm tall, flowers 2cm wide, rosy-lilac to red-purple, early summer. *P.* × Inverewe (probably *P.* × Ravenglass Vermilion), (parentage almost certainly *P. cockburniana* × *P. pulverulenta*) (**4**), similar to *P. pulverulenta* but somewhat shorter; flowers bright brick-red; a sterile clone needing to be divided regularly to maintain vigour. *P. involucrata* (**11**), Himalaya; leaves ovate to oblong, 5–15cm long; scapes 15–30cm tall, flowers 2cm wide, white with yellow eye, early summer. *P.i. wardii*, see *P. yargongensis*. *P. ioessa* (**26**), S.E.Tibet; leaves to 20cm long, oblanceolate; scapes to 30cm tall, flowers 2–2·5cm wide, nodding, rosy-mauve to violet, summer. *P. japonica* (**4**), Japan; leaves to 30cm long, oblong-obovate; scapes to 60cm or more tall, flowers 2–2·5cm wide, red-purple, in 2–6 whorls, summer; variable in colour, several cultivars being available, eg Miller's Crimson, Postford White. *P. juliae* (**30**), Caucasus; rhizomatous, eventually forming mat-like colonies; leaves long-stalked, blades 2–4cm long, rounded, coarsely toothed; scapes very short, flowers 2·5cm wide, bright purple, tube yellow, spring. *P.* × *juliana*, see *P.* × *pruhoniciana*. *P.* × *kewensis* (*P. floribunda* × *P. verticillata*) (**12**), leaves to 20cm long, obovate, toothed and waved, lightly farinose; scapes 30cm or more tall, flowers 2cm wide, buttercup-yellow, in 2–5 whorls with leafy bracts, late winter to spring; cool greenhouse. *P. lichiangensis*, see *P. polyneura*. *P. lichiangensis wardii*, see *P. yargongensis*. *P. littoniana*, see *P. vialii*. *P. longiflora*, see *P. halleri*. *P. macrophylla* (**18**), Himalaya; leaves 10–13cm long, lanceolate to oblanceolate, white farinose beneath; scapes 12–25cm tall, flowers 2cm wide, purple or rarely white, summer. *P. marginata* (**2**) S.W. Alps; leaves 3–9cm long, lanceolate to obovate, toothed, margins white-farinose; scapes 5–10cm tall, flowers 2–2·5cm wide, blue-lilac with white farinose eye, spring; needs well-drained soil, ideally a rock crevice or dry wall. *P.m.* Alba, flowers white. *P. microdonta*, see *P. sikkimensis*. *P.m. alpicola*, see *P. alpicola*. *P. minima* (**2**), E.C. and S.E.Europe; tufted; longest leaves 5–30mm long, wedge-shaped, the tips truncated and deeply toothed; scapes very short or up to 4cm tall, flowers 1 or 2, each 1·5–3cm wide, the bright pink lobes deeply cleft, summer. *P. muscarioides* (**17**), W.China, S.E.Tibet; leaves 10–20cm long, obovate to elliptic or oblong, crenate; scapes 30–40cm tall, flowers narrowly bell-shaped, 5–7mm wide, pendant, deep purple-blue, fragrant, in short spikes, summer. *P. nutans* (of gardens) (**28**), W.China; leaves to 20cm long, elliptic to oblanceolate, softly hairy; scapes 30–40cm or more tall, flowers widely funnel-shaped, nodding, lavender to violet, farinose, in compact clusters, summer; the name *nutans* rightly belongs to a different species from N.USSR and the well-known

Left: *Primula farinosa* (11)
Below left: *Primula* × *kewensis* (12)
Bottom left: *Primula vialii* (17)
Below: *Primula edgeworthii* (21)
Bottom: *Primula bhutancia* (21)

species described here has now been renamed *P. flaccida*. *P. parryi* (**20**), Rocky Mountains, W.USA; leaves 15–30cm long, oblanceolate to obovate; scapes 20–45cm tall, flowers 2–2·5cm wide, bright red-purple, early summer. *P. petiolaris* (**21**), Himalaya – Nepal, Bhutan; leaves to 7cm long, oblong-spathulate, pointed-toothed; scapes very short, flowers 2–3cm wide, deep pink with white eye, spring; hybrids and other species are known to masquerade under this name. *P. poissonii* (**4**), W.China; leaves to 25cm long, oblong-obovate, toothed, glaucous; scapes to 45cm tall, flowers 2·5cm wide, deep magenta with yellow eye, in 2–6 whorls, summer; bog or waterside. *P. polyantha*, see *P.* × *tommasinii*. *P. polyneura* (*P. lichiangensis, P. veitchii*) (**7**), W. China, S.E.Tibet; leaves long-stalked, blades to 10cm long, triangular-ovate to rounded with small lobes, cordate; scapes 20–40cm tall, flowers 2·5cm wide, rose-red to crimson or purple with yellow eye, early summer. *P. prolifera*, see *P. smithiana*. *P.* × *pruhoniciana* (*P.* × *juliana*), (*P. juliae* × other species in section VERNALES, mainly *P. elatior, P. veris, P. vulgaris*) (**30**), a varied group of cultivars more robust and tufted than *P. juliae*, with either very short scapes or pronounced ones to 10cm or more tall, generally with flowers in shades of purple or red; best-known are: *P.* × *p.* Garryarde Guinevere, leaves flushed bronze-purple, scapes 10–15cm tall, flowers pink; *P.* × *p.* Wanda, like a dwarf primrose with claret-crimson flowers. *P.* × *pubescens* (*P. auricula* × *P. rubra*) (**2**), a group of cultivars blending the parental characters in various ways, usually with farinose leaves and flowers in some shade of rose-crimson or purple with a white eye; best-known are: *P.* × *p.* Falconside, scapes 10–15cm tall, flowers rich crimson; *P.* × *p.* Mrs J.H.Wilson, flowers violet, large; *P.* × *p.* Rufus, scapes to 20cm or more, flowers brick-red. *P. pudibunda*, see *P. sikkimensis pudibunda*. *P. pulverulenta* (**4**), W.China; leaves to 30cm long, obovate to oblanceolate, toothed; scapes to 90cm tall, white farinose, flowers about 2·5cm wide,

Far top left: *Primula florindae* (26)
Far left above: *Primula nutans* (28)
Left top: *Primula vulgaris* (30)
Centre: *Primula juliae* (30)
Above left: *Primula elatior* (30)
Top: *Primula amoena* (30)
Above: *Primula veris* (30)

dark red with deeper eye, in several whorls, summer. *P.p.* Bartley Strain, flowers in shades of pink. *P. reidii* (**28**), N.W.Himalaya; leaves 7–20cm long, oblong to lanceolate, crenate or with small, rounded lobes; scapes 5–15cm tall, flowers 2cm wide, bell-shaped, ivory-white, early summer; not easy to grow and best in a moist scree or, preferably, an alpine house. *P. rosea* (**11**), leaves to 20cm long, obovate to oblanceolate, toothed; scapes 3–13cm tall, flowers 2cm wide, bright pink with yellow eye, spring, with unfurling foliage. *P.r.* Grandiflora, flowers larger than type. *P. rubra*, see *P. hirsuta*. *P. scotica* (**11**), N.Scotland; leaves 1–5cm long, elliptic, oblong or spathulate; scapes 2–10cm tall, flowers 5–8mm wide, dark purple with yellow throat, summer. *P. secundiflora* (**26**), W.China; leaves 15–30cm long, oblong to oblanceolate, finely crenate, yellowish farinose when young; scapes to 60cm tall, white farinose, flowers, 2cm wide, funnel-shaped, pendant, crimson-rose to purple-red, slightly fragrant, robust stems sometimes with 2 superimposed umbels, summer. *P. sieboldii* (**7**), Japan; leaves long-stalked, blades to 7cm long, oblong-ovate, cordate, with numerous small-toothed lobes; scapes 15–25cm tall, flowers 2·5–3cm wide, pink, purple or white with white eyes, late spring to summer; popular in Japan, where many cultivars have arisen with often larger, sometimes fringed flowers in a wider colour range, eg *P.s.* Geisha Girl, deep pink, very large flowers with deeply cleft petals; *P.s.* Snowflakes, pure white. *P. sikkimensis* (*P. microdonta*), (**26**), Himalaya; leaves to 30cm or more long, elliptic to oblong-lanceolate; scapes to 60cm tall, sometimes more, flowers 2·5cm wide, funnel-shaped, pendant, yellow, early summer. *P.s. hopeana*, more slender than type, with creamy-white flowers; *P.s. pudibunda* (*P. pudibunda*), alpine variety with smaller flowers. *P. sinoplantaginea* (**18**), W.China; leaves to 10cm long, narrowly lanceolate, yellow farinose beneath: scapes 15–20cm tall, flowers 2cm wide, deep purple with grey eye, fragrant, early summer. *P. sinopurpurea* (**18**), W.China; similar to *P. sinoplantaginea* but more robust, leaves oblanceolate, flowers violet, 2–3cm wide. *P. smithiana* (*P. prolifera*) (**4**), Tibet, Bhutan; leaves to 20cm long, oblanceolate; scapes to 60cm tall, flowers to 2cm wide, pale yellow, in 1–4 whorls, summer. *P. sonchifolia* (**21**), W.China, S.E.Tibet, W.Burma; leaves to 30cm long, oblong-obovate, irregularly lobed and toothed; scapes to 7cm, flowers 2–5cm wide, varying shades of purple-blue with dark yellow-white ringed eye, early spring with expanding leaves. *P.* × *steinii* (*P.* × *bilekii*), (*P. minima* × *P. hirsuta*) (**2**), similar to, but larger than, *P. minima*, with umbels of 2–5 deep pink flowers, spring. *P. suffrutescens* (**8**), Sierra primrose; mountains of California; somewhat shrubby, with woody, prostrate, branching stems tipped by rosettes; leaves to 4cm long, cuneate-spathulate; scapes 4–10cm tall, flowers 1·5–2cm wide, magenta with yellow eye and tube, summer. *P.* × *tommasinii* (*P.* × *variabilis*, *P.* × *polyantha*), (*P. veris* × *P. vulgaris*) (**30**), false oxlip, polyanthus; intermediate between parents in foliage with generally rather primrose-shaped but darker flowers on scapes to 15cm or more. Early forms of polyanthus arose from crosses between the coloured forms of cowslip and primrose common to E.Europe and W.Asia. They were usually in shades of red, although mutants with golden picotee petals soon arose. Later, in the 1880s, backcrosses with the primrose occurred naturally, resulting in larger flowers, including shades of yellow. Since then plant breeders have produced many single-coloured and mixed cultivars with flowers to 5cm or more wide. Recommended names to look for in catalogues are: Pacific, Crescendo and Giant, that cover shades of purple, blue, red, yellow, pink and white. *P.* × *variabilis*, see *P.* × *tommasinii*. *P. veitchii*, see *P. polyneura*. *P. veris* (**30**), cowslip; Europe, W.Asia; leaves 5–15cm long, ovate-oblong, often pubescent above and grey or white tomentose beneath; scapes 10–30cm tall, flowers 1–1·5cm wide, deep yellow with orange spots at base of lobes, sometimes wholly orange or red, somewhat nodding, fragrant, spring; variable species in leaf, and in flower size and colour. *P. vialii* (*P. littoniana*) (**17**), W.China; leaves 20–30cm long, lanceolate to oblong, toothed, hairy; scapes 40–60cm tall, flowers about 1cm wide, bell-shaped, blue-violet, calyces globose, scarlet, fragrant, in dense, poker-like spikes, summer; probably the most distinctive of all primulas. *P. viscosa*, see *P. hirsuta*. *P.* × *vochinensis* (*P. minima* × *P. wulfeniana*) (**2**), similar to latter parent but leaves toothed and flowers deep red. *P. vulgaris* (*P. acaulis*) (**30**), common primrose (English primrose in USA); Europe, W.Asia; leaves to 25cm long, oblanceolate to obovate, wrinkled, usually downy beneath; scapes very short, flowers 2–3cm wide, pale yellow, sometimes white, with darker eye, fragrant, winter to spring; a variable species. *P.v. sibthorpii*, Balkan Peninsula, naturalized elsewhere; leaves less hairy than on type species; flowers pink, red, purple shades; several double-flowered cultivars of this and ordinary *P. vulgaris* have arisen, the following usually being available: Alba Plena, white; Lilacina Plena, lavender. Common and Sibthorp's primrose have been crossed together, and with *P. juliae* and *P.* × *tommasinii* (modern polyanthus cultivars), to create several strains of multicoloured, large-flowered primroses, eg Biedermeier, Europa, Colour Magic, Dean's Hybrids. *P. waltonii* (**26**), W.China, Tibet, Bhutan; leaves to 20cm or more long, oblanceolate, sharply toothed; scapes to 60cm tall, flowers 2–3cm wide, funnel-shaped, nodding, pink to wine-purple, early summer. *P. wanda*, see *P.* × *pruhoniciana*. *P. wardii*, see *P. yargongensis*. *P. warshenewskiana* (**11**), Afghanistan; similar to *P. rosea*, but spreading by stolons to form mats; leaves to 7cm long, oblanceolate, pale green; scapes up to 5cm tall, flowers 1·5cm wide, bright rose-pink with yellow eye, spring. *P. winteri*, see *P. edgeworthii*. *P. wulfeniana* (**2**), S.E.Alps to S.Carpathians; leaves 1·5–4cm long, oblanceolate to obovate, glossy margin toothless, horny, densely glandular hairy; scapes 1–7cm tall, flowers 2–2·5cm wide, deep pink to lilac, spring; needs well-drained soil in sunny site. *P. yargongensis* (*P. involucrata wardii*, *P. wardii*, *P. lichiangensis w.*) (**11**), W.China; leaves to 10cm long, sometimes more, oblong-lanceolate to ovate, irregularly toothed; scapes 20–30cm tall, flowers 2cm wide, mauve-pink or purple with white eye, late summer.

Prince Albert's yew – see *Saxegothaea*.

Prince's feather – see *Amaranthus hypochondriacus*.

Privet – see *Ligustrum*.

Proboscidea

(Greek *proboskis*, elephant's trunk – alluding to the curved, tapered tips of the fruit). MARTYNIACEAE. A genus of 9 species of annuals and perennials from N. and S.America, 1 of which is usually available: *P. louisianica* (*Martynia l.*, *M. proboscidea*), common unicorn plant, ram's-horn, proboscis flower; S.USA; annual; stems robust, somewhat fleshy, often decumbent, to 60cm or more long, but much less grown as a pot plant; leaves alternate, 10–30cm long, ovate to orbicular, wavy-margined, sticky glandular hairy; flowers in short, terminal racemes, each about 5cm long, bell-shaped with 5 unequal lobes, white to violet or pale red, summer; fruit 10–15cm or more long, ovoid with a tapered beak of equal length; when ripe it splits longitudinally and the fleshy coat sloughs off, revealing a gaping, woody capsule with 2, slender, tusk-like projections. Greenhouse, minimum temperature 13°C, lightly shaded in summer, or humus-rich soil in a sheltered, sunny site outside. Sow seed in spring at 18°C, ideally singly in 7·5cm pots of a standard potting compost such as J.I. No 1. When well-rooted, pot on into 13cm containers of J.I. No 2 or 3. Harden off and plant out in early summer when fear of frost has passed, or move on into 18–20cm containers for flowering and fruiting under glass. The fruit can be gathered when young and pickled. After fruiting discard the plants.

Prosartes – see *Disporum*.

Above: *Prostanthera rotundifolia*

Prostanthera

(Greek *prosthema*, an appendage, and *anthera*, anther – the anthers bear spur-like outgrowths). Mint-bush. LABIATAE. A genus of 50 species of aromatic evergreen shrubs from Australia. They have opposite pairs of linear to orbicular leaves and axillary racemes or leafy panicles of tubular, 5-lobed, 2-lipped flowers. Greenhouse, minimum temperature 5–7°C, well-ventilated and very lightly shaded in summer. Some species, see following descriptions, can be grown in mild areas or in sheltered, sunny corners in well-drained soil. Grow in any good potting mixture, particularly a soil based one. Pot or repot autumn or spring, or plant out spring after fear of frost has passed. Propagate from seed in spring at 16–18°C, or cuttings in summer, bottom heat 18–21°C.

Species cultivated: *P. cuneata*, alpine mint-bush; New South Wales, Victoria, Tasmania; about 1m tall, habit compact and spreading; leaves mint-scented, 5–10mm long, orbicular, often with dwarf, leafy shoots in their axils and appearing clustered; flowers 1–1·5cm long, white or palest mauve with purple markings in throat, in leafy racemes, summer; probably the hardiest species but not as yet widely tested outside in gardens. *P. rotundifolia*, round-leaved mint-bush; S.E.Australia, Tasmania; bushy habit, to 2m tall, twice this in the wild; leaves 5–10mm long, rounded, crenate or smooth-edged; flowers about 1cm long, purple-blue to lilac, in dense terminal racemes, late spring; suitable for mild areas and sheltered walls.

Prumnopitys – see *Podocarpus andinus*.

Prunella

(German *brunella*, perhaps from *braune*, meaning quinsy – which self-heal was supposed to cure – or Latin *prunum*, purple, referring to the flower colour). LABIATAE. A genus of 7 species of evergreen perennials from Asia, N.America, Europe and N.W.Africa. They form low, wide clumps of erect to decumbent shoots, bearing opposite pairs of ovate to oblong, sometimes deeply lobed leaves, and erect flowering stems bearing whorled spikes of tubular, 2-lipped flowers. Grow in moisture-retentive, moderately fertile soil in partial shade or sun. Plant autumn to spring. Propagate by division at planting time or from seed in spring.

Species cultivated: *P. grandiflora*, Europe; about 30cm tall; leaves 5–9cm long, ovate to broadly lanceolate; flowers 2–3cm long, deep violet, summer. *P.g.* Alba and *P.g.* Rosea, white- and pink-

flowered respectively. *P.g. pyrenaica* (*P. hastifolia*), leaves somewhat shorter than type, hastate. *P.g. webbiana* (*P. webbiana* of gardens), several cultivars derived from crosses between *P. grandiflora* and *P.g. pyrenaica*; the following are sometimes listed under *P. grandiflora*: *P.g.w.* Loveliness, pale violet; *P.g.w.* Pink Loveliness, clear pink; *P.g.w.* White Loveliness, flowers large, white. *P. incisa*, see next species. *P. vulgaris* (*P. incisa*), self-heal, heal-all; Europe, Asia; 10–15cm or more tall; leaves 4–5cm long, ovate to diamond-shaped; flowers 1–1·5cm long, violet-blue, sometimes white or pink, summer to autumn. *P.v.* Rubra (*P. incisa* Rubra), to 23cm tall; leaves deeply lobed; flowers violet-purple; probably a hybrid with *P. laciniata*, an allied white-flowered species with pinnatifid leaves. *P. webbiana*, see *P. grandiflora*.

Prunus

(old Latin vernacular for plum – used for whole genus by Linnaeus). ROSACEAE. A genus of 400 to 430 species of trees and shrubs in the broad sense, but split up by some botanists into several smaller genera, eg *Amygdalus* (peaches, almonds), *Cerasus* (cherries), *Padus* (bird cherries), *Laurocerasus* (cherry laurels), and *Prunus* (plums, apricots). The broad sense is used here. They are native to the N.Hemisphere, mainly temperate regions, with a few in S.America. They have alternate, generally deciduous (a few are evergreen), lanceolate to broadly ovate toothed leaves, 5-petalled, white to red or purplish flowers in umbel-like clusters or racemes, and sometimes solitary and fleshy, 1-seeded fruit (drupes). The genus contains the important stone fruits: cherry, plum, peach, the almond nut and many ornamental species, eg Japanese cherries and flowering peaches. Grow in fertile, well-drained but moisture-retentive soil in sun. Plant autumn to spring. Propagate from seed when ripe, by semi-hardwood cuttings in late summer, bottom heat 18–21°C, by hardwood cuttings in autumn (not successful for all species), and by grafting or budding in summer on common plum, cherry plum or seedling peach (for flowering peach cultivars), and on seedling cherries (for all Japanese and any other double-flowered or sterile cultivars).

Species cultivated (all spring-flowering unless otherwise stated): *P.* Accolade (*P. sargentii* × *P. subhirtella*), tree 5m or more tall, blending characters of parents, with spreading habit and pendant clusters of 4cm-wide, semi-double, rich pink flowers. *P.* × *amygdalo-persica* (*P. dulcis* × *persica*), tree 6–9m tall, much like *P. dulcis* but with larger flowers and fruit halfway between a peach and almond; is usually represented in gardens by *P.* × *a.-p.* Pollardii, flowers bright pink. *P. amygdalus*, see *P. dulcsi*. *P. avium*, gean, mazzard, wild cherry; Europe, Asia; tree to 20m or more tall, broadly pyramidal until middle-aged; leaves 7–13cm long, ovate-acuminate; flowers 2·5cm wide, pure white, in umbels. *P.a.* Plena (*P.a.* Multiplex), flowers larger and double. *P.* × *blireana* (*P. cerasifera* Pissardii × *P. mume* Alphandii), large shrub or small tree to 5m; similar to *P. cerasifera* Pissardii but of denser habit; leaves bronze-red, ageing deep green; flowers 3cm wide, double, rose-pink, before or with unfurling leaves. *P.* × *b.* Moseri, flowers smaller than type, paler pink. *P. cerasifera*, cherry plum, myrobalan; not known truly wild and now considered to be derived from the similar but seldom cultivated *P. divaricata*; tree to 10m or more tall, round-headed; leaves 4–6·5cm

Top left: *Prunella grandiflora webbiana* Pink Loveliness
Below: *Prunus* Hokusai
Top right: *Prunus serrula* bark
Right: *Prunus padus* fruit
Below right: *Prunus laurocerasus*

Above left: *Prunus subhirtella* Pendula Rubra
Left: *Prunus* × *yedoensis* Pink Shell
Above: *Prunus spinosa* fruit

long, ovate to obovate; flowers 2–2·5cm wide, pure white, solitary or in small clusters, before the leaves, often in profusion; fruit 2–3cm wide, globose, yellow and red. *P.c.* Nigra, leaves very dark purple, flowers opening pink, possibly a clone of *P.c.* Pissardii. *P.c.* Pissardii (*P.c.* Atropurpurea), young leaves red, ageing purple; flowers pink in bud. *P. cerasus*, sour cherry; S.W.Asia, Europe, but not known truly wild; large shrub or small, rounded tree to 5m or so tall, suckering freely and sometimes forming thickets; leaves 4–7·5cm long, ovate, abruptly pointed, somewhat lustrous; flowers 2–2·5cm wide, pure white, in clusters. *P.c. austera*, Morello cherry; habit somewhat pendulous; fruit dark to black-red. *P.c.* Rhexii, flowers larger than type, fully double. *P.* Cistena (*P. cerasifera* Pissardii × *P. pumila*), similar to first parent but dwarf and dense, to 2m tall; leaves smaller, brighter red; flowers smaller, white; makes a distinctive and dense hedge. *P. communis*, see *P. dulcis*. *P. davidiana*, David's peach; China; much like *P. persica* but more slender, with smaller, profusely borne, pale pink flowers, late winter. *P.d.* Alba, leaves bright green, flowers pure white; fruit not always produced, 3cm wide, yellowish with thin flesh. *P. domestica*, and its subspecies are the main parents of the plum, greengage, damson and bullace, and not dealt with here. *P. dulcis* (*P. amygdalus, P. communis*), almond; S.W.Asia, S.E.Europe, perhaps N.Africa, much naturalized in the Mediterranean; tree 6–19m tall, erect when young, later spreading; leaves 7·5–13cm long, lanceolate, long-pointed; flowers 3–4cm wide, pink, singly or in pairs before leaves, often in profusion; the fruit rarely matures in cool climates. *P.d.* Alba, flowers white. *P. glandulosa*, Chinese bush cherry, flowering almond (USA); China, Korea, long cultivated in Japan; shrub to 1·5m or so, rounded habit; leaves 3–6·5cm long, ovate-lanceolate; flowers 1–1·3cm wide, pink or white, often very numerous; fruit 8–10mm wide, bright dark red, showy when freely produced. *P.g.* Alboplena, flowers double white; *P.g.* Sinensis (*P. japonica* Flore Roseoplena), double pink. *P.* Hally Jolivette (*P. subhirtella* × *P.* × *yedoensis*), similar to the former parent but more graceful, with larger, 3cm-wide, blush-white, pink-budded flowers. *P.* × *hillieri* (*P. sargentii* × *P. incisa* as stated by Hillier & Sons the introducer, but the latter parent is doubted by some authorities, who suggest *P.* × *yedoensis*), tree eventually to 10m tall, of spreading habit; botanically similar to *P.* × *yedoensis*; leaves bronze when young, colouring well in autumn; flowers larger, blush-pink, freely borne. *P.* × *h.* Spire, of conical habit to 8m tall by 3m wide. *P. incisa*, Fuji cherry; Japan; large shrub or tree 6–10m tall; leaves 2·5–6·5cm long, ovate to obovate, slender-pointed, colouring in autumn; flowers 1·2–2cm wide, petals notched, white or pale pink, usually very freely borne in early spring. *P. ivesii*, see *P.* × *yedoensis* Ivesii. *P. lannesiana*, a synonym of the seldom grown *P. serrulata* and *P. speciosa* (not described), and sometimes used as an umbrella name to cover all the hybrid Japanese cultivars; see cultivar section at end of Species cultivated. *P. laurocerasus*, cherry laurel; E.Europe, S.W.Asia; evergreen, large, spreading shrub or small tree to 6m or so; leaves 10–15cm long, oblong to oblanceolate, leathery, glossy green; flowers 8mm wide, cream to dull white in erect, axillary racemes; fruit conical, 1cm long, red to black. *P.l.* Otto Luyken, low, compact habit, to 1m tall, leaves shorter and narrower than type; *P.l.* Rotundifolia, leaves shorter and broader ($\frac{1}{2}$ as long as broad); *P.l.* Schipkaensis (of gardens), leaves small, 5–10cm long by 2–4cm wide, very hardy; *P.l.* Variegata, leaves splashed and mottled white; *P.l.* Zabeliana, horizontal habit and wide-spreading, usually under 1m tall, leaves like those of *P.l.* Schipkaensis. *P. lusitanica*, Portugal laurel; Spain, Portugal; evergreen, large shrub or small tree, 3–6m or more tall, compact habit; leaves 6–13cm long, ovate, leathery, lustrous deep green; flowers 8–10mm wide, white, in axillary racemes, early summer; fruit conical, 8mm long, deep purple. *P.l. azorica*, Azores, leaves larger and brighter than type, racemes fewer-flowered; *P.l.* Variegata, leaves white-margined, sometimes pink-tinted in winter. *P. mume*, Japanese apricot; S.W.China, Korea, long cultivated in Japan; tree 6–10m tall, of rounded habit; leaves 6–10cm long, broadly ovate, slender-pointed; flowers 2·5–3cm wide, singly or in pairs, pale pink, almond-scented, before the leaves; fruit globose, to 3cm wide, yellowish; dried or salted in native country and eaten as a pickle. *P.m.* Beni-shidon, madder-pink, very fragrant; *P.m.* O-moi-no-wac, white, semi-double. *P. nana*, see *P. tenella*. *P.* × Okame (*P. campanulata* × *P. incisa*; sometimes listed as *P.* × *incam*), similar to *P. incisa* but neater and more bushy; flowers carmine-rose, usually in abundance. *P. padus*, bird cherry; Europe, Asia; tree 10–15m tall; leaves 7–13cm long, elliptic to obovate, acuminate; flowers 8–12mm wide in pendant to arching racemes, 7–15cm long. *P.p.* Albertii, growth erect, racemes shorter than type but very freely borne; *P.p.* Colorata, shoots and young leaves coppery-purple, flowers pale pink; *P.p.* Watereri, vigorous growth, racemes to 20cm long. *P.* Pandora (*P. subhirtella* Ascendens Rosea × *P.* × *yedoensis*), similar to latter parent but with ascending branches forming a vase-shaped crown; flowers to 3cm wide, the pale pink petals with a darker edge; leaves often colour well in autumn. *P. persica*, peach; China; possibly derived from *P. davidiana* many 100s of years ago; tree 5–7m tall, spreading and bushy habit; leaves 7–15cm long, lanceolate; flowers 2·5–4cm wide, usually solitary, pale pink, before leaves, usually in abundance; several ornamental cultivars are known, among them: *P.p.* Foliis Rubris, leaves red-purple when young, ageing bronze-green; *P.p.* Iceberg, flowers semi-double, white; *P.p.* Klara Mayer (incorrectly Clara), double, true peach-pink; *P.p.* Russell's Red, double crimson *P.* × *pollardii*, see *P.* × *amygdalo-persica*. *P. prostrata*, mountain or rock cherry; E.Europe, W.Asia, N.Africa; shrub

Below: *Prunus* Shimidsu Sakura
Centre: *Prunus triloba* Multiplex
Bottom: *Prunus* Kanzan

spreading, almost prostrate habit, eventually to 2m wide by 60cm tall; leaves 2–4cm long, narrowly oblong to obovate; flowers 1·2–2cm wide, bright pink, singly or in pairs. *P. sargentii*, Sargent cherry; Japan, Sakhalin; tree to 10m in cool areas, 20m in the wild, round-headed when mature; leaves 5–10cm long, slender-pointed and sometimes almost cordate, reddish when young, bright reds and yellows in autumn; flowers 3–4cm wide, deep blush-pink; fruit like a small, black cherry. *P.* × *schmittii* (*P. avium* × *P. canescens*), narrowly conical habit to 10cm; foliage similar to *P. avium*; flowers pale pink. *P. serotina*, wild rum or black cherry (USA); E. N.America to Mexico and Guatemala; large shrub or small tree to 10m in cool areas, 25m or more in the wild; leaves 5–15cm long, lanceolate to oblong-ovate or obovate, glossy; flowers 8mm wide, white, in racemes, early summer. *P. serrula*, W.China; tree to 10m tall, grown mainly for its attractive, highly-polished and peeling, red-brown trunk; leaves 5–10cm long, lanceolate, slender-pointed; flowers 1·5cm wide, whites in 2s or 3s, mainly hidden by leaves; sometimes listed as *P.s. tibetica*. *P. serrulata*, hill cherry; China, Korea, Japan; sparingly branched tree, 10–20m tall; leaves 6–13cm long, ovate to broadly lanceolate, slender-pointed; flowers to 4cm wide, in stalked clusters of 3–5, white or pink; the originally described specimen was a double-flowered Chinese cultivar; several different wild and mutant forms are known but seldom grown in gardens, and some authorities place all the Japanese cherries here; see cultivar section following. *P. spinosa*, blackthorn, sloe; Europe, Asia; suckering spiny shrub or small tree 3–6m tall; leaves 2–4·5cm long, ovate to obovate; flowers 1·2–2cm wide, singly or in pairs, pure white, before the leaves, often in profusion. *P.s.* Purpurea, leaves purple-red, darkening with age. *P. subhirtella*, spring, higan or rosebud cherry; Japan; tree, erect habit, 5–8m tall; leaves 4–7·5cm long, slender-pointed; flowers 2cm wide, soft pink, before or with young leaves. *P.s. ascendens*, the truly wild progenitor of the various garden forms that were originally described by botanists; leaves to 13cm long and relatively narrower. *P.s.* Autumnalis, of more spreading habit than type, with semi-double, pinkish-budded white flowers opening from autumn to spring. *P.s.* Autumnalis Rosea, small tree of weeping habit with rich pink buds and paler flowers; *P.s.* Pendula Rubra, like preceding but buds carmine, flowers deep pink. *P. tenella* (*P. nana*), dwarf Russian almond; S.E.Europe, S.W.USSR; suckering to 1m or more, but usually about 60cm tall; leaves 4–8cm long, oblong to obovate; flowers 1–1·5cm wide, bright pink. *P.t.* Fire Hill, flowers rose-red. *P. triloba* Multiplex, China; shrub or small tree 3–5m tall; leaves 3–6·5cm long, ovate to obovate; flowers 3–4cm wide, fully double, light rose-pink; the single, smaller-flowered, wild type, *P.t. simplex*, was described at a later date and is rarely grown. *P.* × *yedoensis* (*P. yoshino*), Yoshino cherry; Japan, but unknown in the wild and considered to be a natural hybrid between *P. speciosa* and *P. subhirtella*; tree 10–15m tall with arching branches; leaves 6–11cm long, broadly ovate to obovate; flowers about 3cm wide, pale pink or white, lightly fragrant, in stalked clusters of 4 or more. *P.* × *y.* Ivesii, small weeping tree, flowers white; *P.* × *y.* Shidare Yoshino, branches low-arching to pendant, flowers pale pink.
Japanese cherry cultivars: several 100s of flowering cherries have been selected from the wild or purposefully hybridized mainly in Japan but also in the West. In Japan they are collectively known as Sato Zakura (domestic cherries), and are largely derived from *P. speciosa* and *P. serrulata*, with a lesser part played by other species. They have basic resemblance to *P. serrulata*, with red- or purple-tinted young leaves and scentless flowers, but some have the greener leaves and fragrant flowers of *P. speciosa*. The following is a recommended selection of easily obtainable cultivars: *P.* Amanogawa (*P. serrulata erecta*), like a small, very narrow

Lombardy poplar with fragrant, pale pink flowers; *P.* Cheal's Weeping (*P.* Kiku-shidare Sakura of some gardens), weeping habit with vertically pendulous branchlets, and pink, fully double flowers; *P.* Fudanzakura (*P. serrulata semperflorens*), round-headed tree producing pink-budded white flowers during mild spells late autumn to spring; *P.* Fugenzo (*P. serrulata fugenzo*), similar to *P.* Kanzan but a broader, smaller tree, with double, rose-pink flowers, late spring; *P.* Hisakura, small tree with single, deep pink flowers sometimes with a few extra petals, formerly confused with *P.* Kanzan, a very different cultivar; *P.* Kanzan, vigorous tree with steeply ascending branches forming an inverted triangular head, and double, magenta-pink flowers; *P.* Kiku-shidare Sakura, see *P.* Cheal's Weeping; *P.* Ojochin, stiff habit, large leaves and single, white-flushed pink flowers; *P.* Oku Miyako, see *P.* Shimidsu Sakura; *P.* Pink Perfection (*P.* Shimidsu Sakura, probably pollinated by *P.* Kanzan), midway between parents but more akin to *P.* Kanzan, with rose-pink flowers; *P.* Shimidsu Sakura, small tree with broad-flattened crown, and double flowers, pink-tinted in bud, petals fimbriated pure white, sometimes wrongly called *P.* Oku Miyako; *P.* Shirofugen (*P. serrulata alborosea*), spreading tree to 10m tall, flowers purplish in bud, opening white, then ageing magenta-pink; *P.* Shirotae (*P. serrulata albida*, *P.* Mount Fuji, *P.* Kojima), small tree with horizontal or arching branches, and large, single or semi-double, fragrant, pure white flowers; *P.* Tai Haku, great white cherry, to 12m tall, with single, glistening white flowers; *P.* Taoyama Zakura (*P.* Tao-Yoma), small, slow-growing tree of spreading habit, with semi-double, pale pink, fragrant flowers; *P.* Ukon (*P. serrulata grandiflora*, *P.s. luteovirens*), robust tree, somewhat spreading, with semi-double, palest greenish-cream or yellow, sometimes pink-tinted flowers; *P.* Yoshiro, see *P.* × *yedoensis*.

Pseudolarix

(Greek *pseudo*, false, and the genus *Larix*). PINACEAE. A genus of 1 species of deciduous coniferous tree closely allied to *Larix*, from E.China: *P. amabilis* (*P. kaempferi*), golden larch; broadly conical tree to 40m in the wild but often less, much like larch in general appearance but stems more robust, the short shoots or spurs slowly elongating over the years and somewhat club-like; leaves 3–7cm long, pale green, turning gold in autumn; cones 4–6cm long, with triangular leathery scales, rather like a small globe artichoke, breaking up when ripe. Rather slow-growing in regions where the young tips are killed by severe frost. Grow in well-drained but moisture-retentive, humus-rich soil in sun, although partial shade is tolerated; in colder areas place in sites sheltered from spring frosts. Propagate from seed when ripe.

Below left: *Pseudolarix amabilis* cones
Above: *Pseudolarix amabilis* in autumn
Above right: *Pseudopanax colensoi montanum*

Pseudomuscari

(Greek *pseudo*, false, and the genus *Muscari*). LILIACEAE. A genus of about 7 species of small, bulbous plants formerly included in *Muscari* and *Hyacinthus*, 1 of which is commonly available: *P. azureum* (*Hyacinthella a.*, *Hyacinthus a.*, *Muscari a.*), E.Turkey to Caucasus; leaves 2–4, narrowly oblanceolate, channelled, to 15cm long; scapes leafless, 10–15cm tall bearing terminal, dense spikes 2–3cm long, flowers 6-tepalled, 5mm long, bell-shaped (not constricted at the mouth as in *Muscari*), pale blue, each tepal with a darker central stripe, spring. Grow in well-drained soil in sun. Plant autumn. Propagate by offsets when dormant or at planting time, or from seed when ripe or in spring.

Pseudopanax

(Greek *pseudo*, false, and the genus *Panax*). ARALIACEAE. A genus of about 20 species of evergreen trees and shrubs from China, Chile, New Caledonia, Tasmania and New Zealand. Several species, notably *P. crassifolium* and *P. ferox*, have a very pronounced juvenile phase with leaves totally unlike those when adult. Seedlings produce tall, unbranched stems with spirally arranged, deflexed, linear, toothed or lobed leaves. Eventually branches develop at the top of the stem bearing much smaller, sometimes digitate leaves of 3–5 leaflets. The small, 5-petalled, yellowish, greenish or purplish-brown flowers are carried in small, rounded, irregularly compound umbels followed by berry-like, purple-black fruit. Grow in well-drained, moisture-retentive, humus-rich soil in sheltered, partially shaded or sunny sites. Most species are of borderline hardiness and in cold areas are best in a frost-free greenhouse. Plant or pot spring. Propagate from seed when ripe, in a frame or greenhouse.

Species cultivated (all but 1 from New Zealand): *P. arboreum* (*Neopanax a.*, *Nothopanax a.*), large shrub or small tree 3–5m tall; twigs robust; leaves long-stalked, digitate with 3–7 leaflets, the latter also stalked, 8–20cm long, obovate-oblong to oblong-elliptic, coarsely toothed, leathery, glossy rich green; flowers in large terminal clusters; fruit purple-black; makes a handsome tub specimen for a cool greenhouse. *P. colensoi* (*Nothopanax c.* and *Neopanax c.*), similar to *P. arboreum*, but a more compact habit and 3–5 leaflets relatively broader and sessile. *P.c. montanum*, shrub 1–2m tall; leaves trifoliate; an almost hardy plant but seldom seen. *P. crassifolium*, tree to 5m tall, to 15m in the wild; juvenile phase to 3m or more; leaves to 1m long, distinctly sharply-toothed with prominent pale midribs; adult leaves on branching stems, 10–20cm long, entire or digitate with 3–5 leaflets, the latter lanceolate to narrowly oblanceolate; flowers greenish; fruit black; hybrids with *P. arboreum* occur in the wild and are sometimes cultivated. *P. davidii* (*Nothopanax d.*, *Panax d.*), W. and C.China; tree 3–6m tall; leaves simple or with 2–3 leaflets, 7–15cm long, narrowly lanceolate, deep glossy green; flowers yellow-green, the umbels carried in terminal panicles; fruit black. *P. ferox*, akin to *P. crassifolium* but juvenile leaves to 50cm long, with distant, irregular, small, somewhat hooked lobes; adult leaves always simple, 5–15cm long, linear-oblong to narrowly oblanceolate; male flowers in terminal racemes, females in umbels; somewhat less hardy than *P. crassifolium*. *P. laetum* (*Neopanax l.*, *Nothopanax l.*), similar to *P. arboreum*, but leaf-stalks purple-red, leaflets 10–25cm long, obovate. *P. lessonii*, shrub to 3m tall, or a tree to 6m in the wild; leaves long-stalked, with 3–5 leaflets, those of adult plants 5–10cm long, obovate to oblong-lanceolate, entire or widely toothed, those of juveniles much longer and relatively narrower, irregularly coarsely toothed; juvenile plants make distinctive pot plants for a cool greenhouse or room.

Pseudosasa japonica – see *Arundinaria japonica*.

Pseudotsuga

(Greek *pseudo*, false, and the genus *Tsuga*). PINACEAE. A genus of 5 or 6 evergreen coniferous trees from W. N.America, Mexico, E.Asia, 1 of which is widely grown: *P. menziesii* (*P. douglasii*, *P. taxifolia*), Douglas fir; W. N.America to Mexico; to 90m in the wild but usually less in cultivation; conical in habit until old, branches whorled, upper ones ascending, lower horizontal with pendulous branchlets; leaves needle-like, crowded, 2–2·5cm long, dark to yellow-green above, white-banded beneath, sweetly aromatic when crushed; female flowers (strobili) often pale to deep pink when young, developing into pendant, ovoid, light brown cones. The latter are 5–8cm long, composed of thin scales from which protrude 3-pronged bracts like snake's tongues. *P.m. glauca*, blue or Colorado Douglas fir; smaller than type at maturity, leaves bright glaucous. Grow in well-drained but moisture-retentive, humus-rich soil in sun, although partial shade is tolerated. Plant autumn to spring. Propagate from seed in spring. Spruce adelgids can be damaging to this tree, causing yellowing of leaves, premature leaf-fall and disfiguring galls. Spray with malathion as soon as the waxy white woolly aphids are seen.

Pseudowintera – see *Drimys colorata*.

Ptelea

(Greek vernacular for an elm tree, presumably because of the similar circular winged fruit). RUTACEAE. A genus of 3 species of deciduous shrubs or small trees from N.America and Mexico, 1 of which is generally available: *P. trifoliata*, hop tree, stinking ash (USA); E. N.America; large, spreading shrub or small tree 3–7m tall; leaves long-stalked, trifoliate, leaflets 5–10cm long, lanceolate or ovate to obovate, dotted with tiny, translucent oil glands responsible for the aromatic odour; flowers to 1cm wide, 4–5 petalled, greenish-white, in corymbs 5–7cm wide, summer; fruit disc-like, winged, 2–2·5cm wide. *P.t.* Aurea, leaves bright yellow when young, later turning pale green. Grow in any well-drained but reasonably moisture-retentive soil in partial shade or sun. Plant autumn to spring.

Left: *Pseudotsuga menziesii*
Above: *Ptelea trifoliata* fruit
Below: *Pterocarya fraxinifolia*

Propagate from seed when ripe in a cold frame, or by layering in spring.

Pterocarya

(Greek *pteron*, a wing, and *karyon*, a nut – the fruit is a small winged nutlet). JUGLANDACEAE. A genus of 10 species of deciduous trees from the Caucasus to Japan, 1 of which is generally available: *P. fraxinifolia* (*P. caucasica*), Caucasian wingnut; Caucasus to Iran; to 25m tall, sometimes more, branching low and wide-spreading: bark deeply

furrowed; leaves alternate, pinnate, to 45cm long, leaflets 11–27, each one ovate-oblong to lanceolate, toothed, 5–10cm long; flowers unisexual, small, petalless, in pendulous catkins, the females 30–50cm long, greenish, males shorter; nutlets with semi-circular wings, to 2cm wide. Grow in moisture-retentive, humus-rich soil in sun. Plant autumn to spring. Propagate from ripe seed in cold frame, suckers at planting time, layering in spring.

Pterocephalus

(Greek *pteron*, a wing, and *kephale*, a head – alluding to the feathery seed-heads). DIPSACACEAE. A genus of 20–25 species of annuals, perennials and sub-shrubs from the Mediterranean to C.Asia, Himalaya to W.China and tropical Africa, 1 of which is generally available: *P. perennis* (*P.*

parnassi, *Scabiosa pterocephala*), mountains of Albania and Greece; somewhat woody-based perennial forming dense, low cushions; leaves 2–5cm long, oblong-spathulate to lyrate, usually crenate and densely grey downy; flower-heads scabious-like, 2·5–4cm wide, florets small, tubular, 5-lobed, pink to rosy-purple, solitary, just above the foliage, summer. Grow in any well-drained soil in sun, particularly in screes, rock crevices or dry walls. Plant spring or autumn. Propagate from seed or by careful division in spring, cuttings in summer.

Ptilotrichum – see *Alyssum spinosum.*

Pulmonaria

(Latin *pulmo*, lung – the species with white-spotted leaves were formerly considered to be a remedy for lung diseases). Lungwort. BORAGINACEAE. A genus of 10–13 species of perennials from Europe. They have thickened, creeping rhizomes forming wide clumps or colonies with mainly basal, ovate-cordate to lanceolate leaves, the summer ones larger and more distinctive than the over-wintering ones, and funnel-shaped, 5-lobed flowers in forked cymes on shortly leafy stems in spring. Grow in moisture-retentive, humus-rich soil in partial shade, although full sun is tolerated, particularly by *P. angustifolia.* Plant autumn to spring. Propagate by division at planting time, or from seed when ripe or spring.

Species cultivated: *P. angustifolia* (*P. azurea*), blue cowslip; stems 20–30cm tall; summer leaves oblong to narrowly lanceolate, to 40cm long, unspotted; flowers about 2cm long, bright blue. *P.a.* Munstead Blue, intense blue. *P. azurea*, see *P. angustifolia. P. longifolia*, stems to 30cm tall; summer leaves to

Left above: *Pterocephalus perennis*
Left below: *Pulmonaria saccharata*
Above: *Pulmonaria angustifolia*
Right above: *Pulsatilla alpina apiifolia*
Right: *Pulsatilla vulgaris* Rubra
Right below: *Pulsatilla vulgaris* Alba

50cm long, narrowly lanceolate, bristly hairy, white-spotted; flowers 2cm long, violet to blue-violet from pinkish buds; unspotted-leaved forms are confused with *P. angustifolia. P. maculata*, see next species. *P. officinalis* (*P. maculata*), Jerusalem cowslip or sage; stems 20–30cm tall; summer leaves to 16cm long, ovate-cordate, bristly hairy, white-spotted; flowers 2cm long, reddish to bluish-violet. *P. rubra*, summer leaves to 15cm long, oblong-ovate, softly hairy, unspotted; flowers 2cm long, brick-red. *P.r.* Bowles Red, light red, winter to spring, leaves faintly spotted. *P. saccharata*, Bethlehem sage; stems to 30cm or more tall; summer leaves to 27cm long, narrowly ovate to elliptic, bristly hairy, white-spotted; flowers 2–2·5cm long, reddish, then violet to blue. *P.s.* Argentea, leaves almost entirely silvery-white, possibly of hybrid origin; *P.s.* Cambridge Blue, flowers pink and blue; *P.s.* Pink Dawn, flowers pink; *P.s.* White Wings, flowers white.

Pulsatilla

(presumably from Latin *pulsus*, impulse, pulse, beat or stroke, either from the way the flowers pulsate in the wind, or because the plant is toxic and can cause palpitations of the heart). RANUNCULACEAE. A genus of about 12 species of perennials from Europe, Asia, N.America. They are tufted, fibrous-rooted, with solitary flowers, otherwise much like *Anemone*, in which genus some botanists classify the species following. The only real point of difference between the 2 genera is the slender, hairy style that elongates after flowering to provide an organ of wind dispersal as in *Clematis.* Grow in well-drained, fertile soil in sun. Plant autumn or spring. Propagate from seed as soon as ripe, or the following autumn; older or thoroughly dried seed often germinates erratically and poorly.

Species cultivated: *P. albana* (*P. caucasica* and *P. vulgaris c.* of gardens), Caucasus, Iran; similar to *P. pratensis*, but leaves bi- or tripinnatisect and flowers clear pale yellow. *P.a. armena* (*P.a. violacea*), violet-blue. *P. alpina*, alpine anemone; mountains of C. and S.Europe; leaves long-stalked, to 15cm or more long, bipinnate, downy; scapes 15–35cm tall, involucre leafy, flowers 4–6cm wide, white, often backed bluish-purple or red. *P.a. apiifolia* (*P.a. sulphurea*), flowers sulphur-yellow, spring. *P. caucasica*, see *P. albana. P. halleri*, Alps, W.Carpathians, Balkan Peninsula; similar to *P. vulgaris* but leaves simply pinnate and usually densely woolly; leaflets linear, pinnatifid; flowers deep violet. *P. pratensis* (*P. nigricans*), C. and E.Europe to Scandinavia and N.Yugoslavia; leaves tripinnate, the segments cut into narrow lobes, silky

downy; scapes 10–30cm tall, flowers 3–4cm wide, bell-shaped, nodding, bright deep purple in best forms but varying to pale violet and greenish-yellow, spring. *P. vernalis*, mountains of Europe; leaves pinnate to pinnatipartite, lobes or leaflets 3–5 lobed or toothed, deep green; scapes 5–15cm tall, yellow hairy, involucre of linear hairy segments, flowers 4–6cm wide, cup-shaped, nodding, then erect, white within, flushed bluish, purplish or pink without, spring. *P. vulgaris*, pasque flower; Europe, eastwards to Ukraine; leaves pinnate, the linear leaflets bi- or tripinnatisect, silky hairy when young;

Far left above: *Pulsatilla vulgaris*
Far left: *Pulsatilla vulgaris* Letchworth
Left above: *Punica granatum nana* fruiting
Left: ***Punica granatum nana***
Above: *Puschkinia scilloides*
Below: *Puya alpestris*

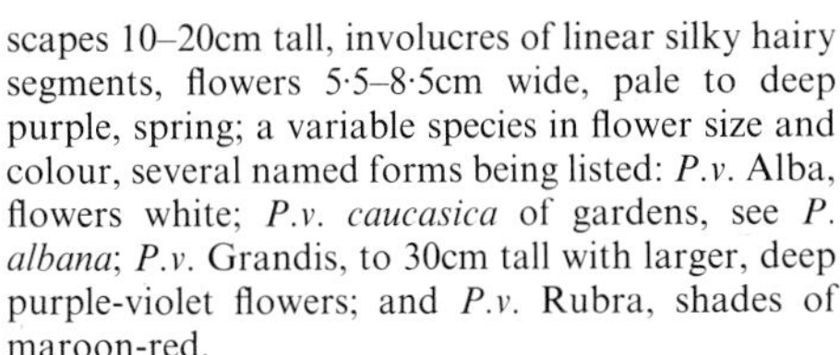

scapes 10–20cm tall, involucres of linear silky hairy segments, flowers 5·5–8·5cm wide, pale to deep purple, spring; a variable species in flower size and colour, several named forms being listed: *P.v.* Alba, flowers white; *P.v. caucasica* of gardens, see *P. albana*; *P.v.* Grandis, to 30cm tall with larger, deep purple-violet flowers; and *P.v.* Rubra, shades of maroon-red.

Punica

(Latin *punicum malum*, Carthaginian purple). PUNICACEAE. A genus of 2 species of shrubs from S.E.Europe to Himalaya and Socotra, 1 generally available: *P. granatum*, pomegranate; S.E.Europe to Himalaya, much grown elsewhere; deciduous, 3–5m tall, sometimes tree-like and larger, twigs angled, sometimes spiny; leaves 2–7·5cm long, in opposite pairs, oblong to lanceolate, glossy; flowers to 4cm wide, cup-shaped, of 5–7, somewhat crinkled, orange-red petals, summer to autumn; fruit globose, 6·5–10cm wide, brownish-yellow, flushed purple-red, the leathery rind or skin containing many small, woody seeds each surrounded by a layer of very juicy pulp. *P.g.* Flore Pleno, flowers double red; *P.g.* Legrellei (*P.g.* Mme Legrelle, *P.g.* Variegata), flowers double, orange-red, streaked whitish; *P.g. nana*, dwarf pomegranate; smaller than type in all its parts, usually semi-evergreen, flowering when under 30cm tall, less hardy and making a good pot plant for home and greenhouse. The common pomegranate rarely develops ripe fruit in cool climates, but has attractive flowers over a long period. Grow in fertile, well-drained soil against a sunny, sheltered wall. In cooler, less sunny areas grow under glass, minimum temperature 5°C, sunny and well-ventilated. Grow in any standard potting mixture, particularly the loam-based ones if available. Pot autumn to spring; plant out spring only. Propagate from seed, layering spring, softwood cuttings summer.

Purslane – see *Portulaca oleracea.*

Puschkinia

(for Count Apollos Apollasovič Mussin-Puschkin, died 1805, Russian chemist who collected plants in the Caucasus and Ararat). LILIACEAE. A genus of 2 species of small, bulbous plants, allied to *Scilla*, and from W.Asia. 1 is generally available: *P. scilloides* (*P. libanotica*), striped squill; Caucasus, E.Turkey to Lebanon; leaves all basal, linear to oblanceolate, channelled, 10–15cm long; scapes 10–15cm tall, flowers in racemes, 6-tepalled, 1·5cm wide, opening widely, pale to bright blue or white, each tepal with a central darker line, early spring; distinguished from *Scilla* by the short corona surrounding the bases of the stamens and by the bases of the tepals being united into a short tube. Grow in well-drained but not dry soil in sun. Plant autumn or after flowering. Makes a good alpine house plant.

Puya

(Chilean Spanish vernacular name). BROMELIACEAE. A genus of about 120 species of evergreen, often woody-based perennials from the drier parts of S.America. They have dense rosettes of hard, linear-tapered, spiny-margined leaves, either sessile or terminating short trunks. The somewhat bell-shaped flowers are carried in spikes, racemes or panicles well above the leaves. Except in mild areas the species described need greenhouse culture, minimum temperature 5–7°C, sunny and well-ventilated (but see *P. alpestris* in Species cultivated). Grow in pots, tubs or borders of any well-drained soil. Pot or plant out spring. Propagate from seed in spring, 18–21°C, or by offsets at potting time. The spines on the leaf margins are very sharp and often hooked, and the plants should be handled with care.

Species cultivated (all from Chile): *P. alpestris*, leaves to 60cm long by 1–2·5cm wide at base, bright green above, densely pale scaly beneath; flowers 5cm long, metallic greenish-blue, in open, short, branched panicles, 1–1·5m tall, early summer; the hardiest *Puya*, surviving in areas of moderate frost and thriving outside at the base of a sunny wall or out in the open in mild coastal areas. *P. berteroniana*, leaves 1m long by about 5cm wide at base, densely greyish scaly beneath, thinly above; flowers 5–6cm long, blue-green, in dense, oblong panicles 3–4m tall. The tips of the panicle branches bear a few small bracts only, and these are reputedly used as perches for pollinating humming birds. *P. chilensis*, similar to *P. berteroniana* in general appearance, but leaves glaucous and flowers soft yellow. *P. venusta*, leaves 60–90cm long, silvery-grey scaly on both surfaces; flowers deep violet-red in open panicles to 1·5m tall.

Pyracantha

(Greek *pyr*, fire, and *akantha*, a thorn – an apt allusion to the profuse, glowing masses of fruit borne on spiny twigs). Firethorn. ROSACEAE. A genus of about 6–8 species of more or less spiny evergreen shrubs from S.E.Europe and Asia. They have alternate, narrowly oblong to obovate leaves, small, white, 5-petalled flowers in corymbs in early

summer, and globose, berry-like fruit resembling miniature apples and botanically of the same structure. Grow in any well-drained but moisture-retentive fertile soil. Plant autumn or spring. Propagate from seed when ripe in a cold frame or by cuttings with a heel in late summer, bottom heat 18–21°C. Rooted cuttings should be over-wintered in a cold frame and grown in pots until placed in permanent sites. In some areas pyracantha scab disease can be a nuisance, causing a felty, olive-brown to blackish coating on leaves and fruit; later, leaves yellow and fall prematurely. Severe attacks can check growth, cause dieback, and make the plants unsightly. To control, spray with Captan at 10–14 day intervals from spring to mid summer. Alternatively, grow some of the more recent hybrid cultivars selected for their disease resistance, eg *P.* Orange Glow, *P.* Orange Charmer and *P.* Shawnee. **Species cultivated:** *P. angustifolia*, S.W.China; 2–4m tall, bushy habit; leaves 1·5–5·5cm long, narrowly oblong to lightly obovate, dark green above, grey-felted beneath; flowers 6mm wide in corymbs 5cm wide; fruit 6–9mm wide, bright orange-yellow, grey downy at first. *P. atalantoides* (*P. gibbsii*), C.China; large shrub or small tree 4–7m tall; stems often spineless; leaves 2·5–7·5cm long, oblong-oval to obovate, glossy rich green; flowers 8–12mm wide in

corymbs 4–5cm wide; fruit 5–6mm wide, scarlet. *P.a.* Aurea (*P.a.* Flava), fruit yellow. *P.* × Buttercup, similar to *P. atalantoides* Aurea but of more spreading habit and richer yellow fruit. *P. coccinea*, S.Europe, W.Asia; shrub or small tree to 5m tall, densely leafy, spiny; leaves 2·5–6·5cm long, narrowly obovate to elliptic, toothed, pointed, glossy rich green; flowers 8mm wide in corymbs to 5cm wide; fruit 6mm wide, coral-red. *P.c.* Lalandei, more vigorous than type, broader leaves, bright orange fruit; one of the best-known of all the firethorns. *P. crenatoserrata* (*P. fortuneana, P. gibbsii yunnanensis, P. yunnanensis*), W.China; similar to *P. atalantoides* but leaves obovate-oblong, usually coarsely toothed, 3–7·5cm long; retains its profusely borne red fruit throughout the winter, birds permitting. *P. crenulata*, Himalaya; closely allied to *P. coccinea* but leaves rounded-tipped, fruit orange-yellow; slower-growing but somewhat tender. *P. fortuneana*, see *P. crenatoserrata*. *P. gibbsii*, see *P. atalantoides*. *P.* × Orange Glow, a hybrid probably derived from *P. coccinea* × *P. crenatoserrata* and similar to the latter parent but more vigorous; fruit to 1cm wide, orange-red; reputedly scab-resistant. *P.* × Orange Charmer (probably *P. rogersiana* × *P. coccinea*), similar to first parent with oblong-elliptic leaves and orange-red fruit. *P.* × Golden Charmer, same parentage as *P.* × Orange Charmer, but with orange-yellow fruit; both hybrids are claimed to be scab-resistant. *P. rogersiana* (*P. crenulata r.*), W.China; 2·5–3·5m tall, habit dense, almost pyramidal when young; leaves 1–4cm long, oblanceolate to narrowly obovate, bright green above; flowers 6–7mm wide, in corymbs to 3cm wide; fruit 6mm wide, orange-red. *P.r.* Flava, fruit yellow. *P.* × Shawnee (*P. crenatoserrata* × *P. koidzumii*), vigorous, wide-spreading shrub favouring the first parent; fruit light orange in abundance, colouring early; claimed to be resistant to fireblight and scab diseases. *P.* × *watereri* (*P. atalantoides* × *P. rogersiana*), midway between parents; vigorous, dense habit, to 2·5m tall; fruit bright red, in profusion. *P. yunnanensis*, see *P. crenatoserrata*.

Pyrethrum

(Greek *pyr*, fire – alluding to the use of *Anacyclus pyrethrum* as a remedy for fevers; name taken up for this genus by Zinn). COMPOSITAE. This genus is now generally amalgamated with *Chrysanthemum*, but the 1 familiar species is retained here for convenience: *P. roseum* (now *Chrysanthemum coccineum*), S.W.Asia; herbaceous clump-forming perennial to 60cm tall; leaves pinnatifid or bipinnatifid, divided into many linear segments; flower-heads terminal, to 7·5cm wide, daisy-like, disc yellow, rays pink or red, early summer; the dried

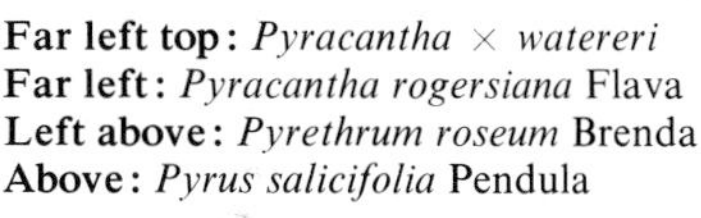

Far left top: *Pyracantha* × *watereri*
Far left: *Pyracantha rogersiana* Flava
Left above: *Pyrethrum roseum* Brenda
Above: *Pyrus salicifolia* Pendula

heads are a source of the insecticide pyrethrum. *P.r.* Avalanche, pure white; *P.r.* Brenda, bright cerise; *P.r.* Bressingham Red, deep red; *P.r.* Eileen May Robinson, salmon-pink, large; *P.r.* Evenglow, salmon-red; *P.r.* Kelways Glorious, rich scarlet, early; *P.r.* Madeleine, double pale pink, large; *P.r.* Progression, double soft pink, early; *P.r.* Silver Challenger, white, blushed pink, large. Grow in well-drained but moisture-retentive, humus-rich soil in sun. Plant autumn to spring. Propagate from seed in spring or by division at planting time. For *Pyrethrum ptarmiciflorum* (*P. ptarmicaefolium* of some catalogues), see *Tanacetum p.*

Pyrus

(ancient Latin name for pear). ROSACEAE. A genus of about 20 species of deciduous trees and shrubs, from Europe and temperate Asia, and including the fruiting pears (qv). They have alternate, orbicular to lanceolate leaves, 5-petalled white flowers in small corymbs that open in spring with the expanding leaves, and rounded to typically pear-shaped fruit. The latter is botanically of the same structure as an apple, the main fleshy part of the fruit being an enlarged hollow receptacle. Grow in any well-drained, fertile soil in sun. Plant autumn to spring. Propagate species from seed sown when ripe, preferably in a cold frame; all cultivars or selected clones need to be budded and grafted on to pear or quince rootstocks as they do not come true from seed. **Species cultivated:** *P. amygdaliformis*, S.Europe; large shrub or small tree to 7m or more tall; stems sometimes spiny; leaves 4–6·5cm long, elliptic to ovate or obovate, silvery hairy when young, then sage-green and somewhat glossy; flowers 2·5cm wide in corymbs of 8–12; fruit rounded, 2–2·5cm wide, yellowish-brown, not edible. *P. calleryana*, C. and S.China; tree eventually to 10m or more tall; leaves 4–7·5cm long, ovate to broadly so, turning red in autumn; flowers 2cm wide, in small clusters; represented in cultivation mainly by 2 cultivars: *P.c.* Bradford, vigorous, round-headed, to 15m or more tall; *P.c.* Chanticleer, smaller and narrowly conical, a good street tree or where space is limited; both cultivars are resistant to fire blight disease. *P. communis*, common pear; see Pear. *P. pashia*, Afghanistan through Himalaya to W.China; tree to 12m or more tall, round-headed; leaves 5–10cm long, oblong to ovate; flowers 2cm wide, pink-tinted in bud, opening white with red anthers; fruit almost

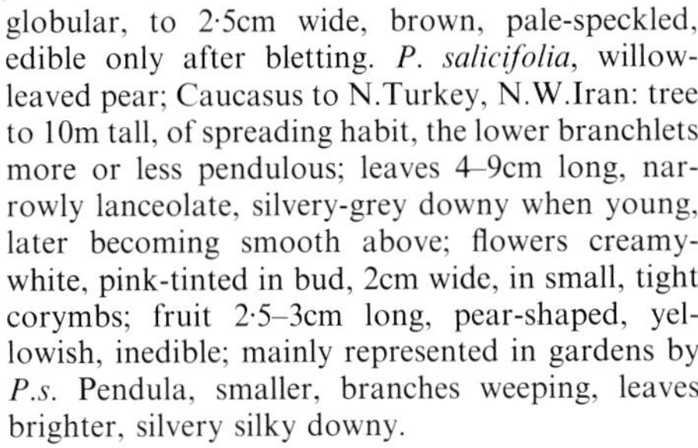

globular, to 2·5cm wide, brown, pale-speckled, edible only after bletting. *P. salicifolia*, willow-leaved pear; Caucasus to N.Turkey, N.W.Iran: tree to 10m tall, of spreading habit, the lower branchlets more or less pendulous; leaves 4–9cm long, narrowly lanceolate, silvery-grey downy when young, later becoming smooth above; flowers creamy-white, pink-tinted in bud, 2cm wide, in small, tight corymbs; fruit 2·5–3cm long, pear-shaped, yellowish, inedible; mainly represented in gardens by *P.s.* Pendula, smaller, branches weeping, leaves brighter, silvery silky downy.

Quamoclit – see *Ipomoea*.

Quercus

(old Latin name for oak). FAGACEAE. A genus of 450 species of trees and a few shrubs from the northern temperate zone and on mountains farther south. They are deciduous to evergreen, with alternate, entire to deeply lobed, elliptic or lanceolate to ovate and obovate leaves, and tiny, petalless, unisexual flowers, the males in pendant loose catkins, the females 1 to several in short spikes. The fruit or acorn is a solitary nut borne like an egg in a cup-shaped structure of small, fused bracts. Grow in well-drained but moisture-retentive, preferably humus-rich soil in sun or partial shade. Plant autumn to spring. Propagate from seed sown as soon as ripe, preferably singly in deep pots in a cold frame protected from mice; cultivars must be budded or grafted onto seedlings of the parent species.

Species cultivated: *Q. borealis*, see *Q. rubra*. *Q. canariensis* (*Q. mirbeckii*), Algerian oak; N.Africa, Spain, Portugal (not the Canary Is); deciduous to semi-evergreen tree, conical to ovoid, 20–30m or more tall; winter buds surrounded by whiskery scales; leaves 9–15cm long, ovate-oblong to obovate, coarsely toothed or lobed, cordate, dark green and lustrous above, glaucous beneath; acorn 2·5cm long enclosed in cup $\frac{1}{3}$ as deep. *Q. cerris*, Turkey oak; S.Europe, W.Asia; deciduous tree to 38m or more tall; leaves 9–12cm long, lanceolate to oblong-obovate, pinnatifid lobes triangular; acorn 2·5–3cm long in mossy cup 1cm deep; vigorous young trees or suckers from cut back trees may have much larger, more coarsely lobed leaves. *Q.c.* Variegata, leaves white-margined. *Q. coccinea*, scarlet oak; E. N.America; deciduous tree to 26m tall; winter buds reddish, downy; leaves 7–15cm long, usually broadly elliptic, oblong or obovate in outline with 6, deep, widely spaced lateral lobes, each irregularly shallowly lobed and pointed-toothed, lustrous deep green above, bright red in autumn; acorn 1·3–2·5cm long in cup $\frac{1}{3}$–$\frac{1}{2}$ as deep; sometimes confused with *Q. rubra*, qv. *Q.* × *hispanica* (*Q. lucombeana*), Spanish or Lucombe oak; a group of hybrids between *Q. cerris* and *Q. suber*, 20–30m tall, blending parental characters in various ways, second generation seedlings often strongly favouring 1 parent; best-known is *Q.* × *h.* Lucombeana; the original tree has pale grey bark, an open, tall-domed head of comparatively few branches, and almost evergreen leaves 10–12cm long, oblong-elliptic with triangular lobes – in hard winters they fall by mid spring. A seedling of this tree is also offered under the same name, but differs greatly in being lower-growing with dark grey bark and a dense, domed head of branches bearing more persistent leaves. *Q. ilex*, holm, holly or evergreen oak; evergreen tree 15–28m tall with a dense, broad-domed head; leaves 4–7·5cm long, entire on mature specimens, often toothed or lobed on young ones, dark glossy green above, greyish downy beneath; acorn 1·5–2cm long in cup $\frac{1}{3}$–$\frac{1}{2}$ as deep. *Q. imbricaria*, shingle or laurel oak; E.USA; deciduous tree 15–20m tall, sometimes to 26m, with broad-domed head; leaves 13–18cm long,

Far left top: *Quercus coccinea* autumn colour
Far left above: *Quercus cerris* acorns
Top: *Quercus* × *hispanica* Lucombeana
Above: *Quercus robur* Fastigiata in autumn

oblong-lanceolate, wavy-margined, deep glossy green above, pale downy below; acorn 1–2cm long, almost as broad, in cup $\frac{1}{3}$ as deep. *Q. macranthera*, Caucasus to N.Iran; deciduous tree to 20m or more, with narrow-domed head; winter buds dark, glossy red; leaves 10–23cm long, obovate, with 6–10 pairs of shallow lobes; acorn 2–2·5cm long in cup $\frac{1}{2}$ as deep, covered with erect, downy, lanceolate scales. *Q. palustris*, pin or Spanish oak; E.USA; deciduous tree to 25m or more tall; similar to, and sometimes confused with, *Q. coccinea*, but of more elegant habit with slender twigs bearing smooth winter buds and somewhat smaller, more deeply lobed leaves, the undersides with brown tufts of hairs in the vein axils (scarcely visible or non-existent in *Q. coccinea*); acorn 1–1·5cm long and wide, in cup to $\frac{1}{3}$ as deep. *Q. pedunculata*, see *Q. robur*. *Q. petraea*, sessile or durmast oak; Europe, W.Asia; similar to *Q. robur*, but with radiating, more even-sized branches; leaves somewhat smaller, less prominently lobed, with cuneate to shallowly cordate bases on petioles 1cm or more long and acorns on very short stalks or stalkless; hybrids with *Q. robur* often occur and can be difficult to classify, see *Q.* × *rosacea*. *Q. phellos*, willow oak; S.E.USA; deciduous tree to 25m or more tall, with domed head; leaves 5–10cm long, oblong to lanceolate, entire; acorn 1cm long, globose, in cup to $\frac{1}{4}$ as deep. *Q. pontica*, Armenian oak; Turkey, Caucasus; deciduous large shrub or small tree 3–7m tall; stems robust, ribbed; leaves 10–16cm long, broadly elliptic to obovate, boldly veined and irregularly coarsely toothed, smooth above, glaucous beneath; acorn in cup to $\frac{1}{2}$ as deep. *Q. robur* (*Q. pedunculata*), common or English oak; Europe to N.E.USSR and S.W.Asia, N.Africa; deciduous tree to 37m tall but usually much less, with a wide, irregularly domed head, usually with several massive branches when old; leaves 5–12cm long, obovate-oblong with 3–6 pairs of irregularly rounded lobes, base cordate and auricled (eared), on short stalks or stalkless; acorn on long stalk, 2–4cm long, in cup to $\frac{1}{3}$ as deep. *Q.r.* Atropurpurea, slow-growing, leaves red-purple when young, ageing to greenish-grey-purple; *Q.r.* Fastigiata, columnar habit; *Q.r.* Filicifolia, see *Q.* × *rosacea*; *Q.r.* Pendula, weeping oak, small-growing, with pendulous branches. *Q.* × *rosacea* (*Q. petraea* × *Q. robur*), very variable natural hybrid occurring wherever the 2 species grow together, involving back-crossing to the parents and further generations; the characters are blended in various ways and some individuals closely resemble 1 of the parent species. *Q.* × *r.* Filicifolia (*Q.r.* Filicifolia), fern-leaved oak; leaves cut into slender lobes almost to the mid-rib. *Q. rubra* (*Q. borealis*), red oak; N.E. N.America; deciduous tree, 25–35m tall, conical when young, becoming broad-domed; leaves 10–22cm long, oblong-elliptic in outline, deeply 7–9 lobed, the lobes with few to several whisker-tipped teeth, usually turning deep red in autumn; acorn 2–3cm long, flat-based, in cup $\frac{1}{4}$–$\frac{1}{3}$ as deep. *Q.r.* Aurea, smaller-growing than type, leaves bright yellow when young, ageing to mid-green. *Q. suber*, cork oak; S.Europe, N.Africa; evergreen tree occasionally to 20m tall, but usually less, with broad-domed head; trunk bearing widely fissured and finely ridged, dull grey or pale brown cork bark when mature, yielding the cork of commerce; leaves 4–7cm long, ovate, with spine-tipped teeth or shallow lobes, glossy deep green above, grey or glaucous and downy beneath; acorn 1·5–3cm long in cup $\frac{1}{2}$ as deep; not hardy.

Ramonda

(for Baron Louis François Ramond de Carbonnières, 1753–1827, French botanist and traveller in the Pyrenees). GESNERIACEAE. A genus of 3 species of evergreen perennials from the Pyrenees and S.E.Europe. They form flattened rosettes of wrinkled, ovate to orbicular leaves in the centres of which arise several erect stems bearing shortly tubular, 4–5 petalled, slightly 2-lipped flowers in late spring. Grow in steeply inclined to vertical rock crevices, dry walls or screes preferably with a northerly aspect. Alternatively, grow in pots in an alpine house using a mixture of equal parts leaf mould, peat and grit. Pot or plant autumn or spring. Propagate from seed or by careful division in spring, leaf cuttings in summer. The dust-like seed is best mixed with sand before sowing; the seedlings are minute and slow-growing and must not be allowed to become too wet.

Species cultivated: *R. myconi* (*R. pyrenaica*), C. and E.Pyrenees and adjacent mountains of N.E.Spain; leaves 2–6cm long, ovate to rhombic-orbicular, crenate, deep green; scapes 6–12cm tall, flowers 1–6, each usually 5-petalled, 3–4cm wide, deep violet with yellow centre. *R.m.* Alba, flowers white.

Above: *Ramonda myconi* Rosea
Top right: *Ranunculus calandrinioides*
Above right: *Ranunculus gramineus*
Right: *Ranunculus asiaticus*
Bottom right: *Ranunculus lyallii*

R.m. Rosea, flowers pink. *R. nathaliae*, N.Yugoslavia, N.Greece; leaves 3–5cm long, ovate to rounded, entire or faintly crenate, deep green; scapes 6–8cm tall, flowers 1–3, each usually 4-petalled, 3–3·5cm wide, lilac to violet with orange-yellow centre. *R.n.* Alba, flowers pure white. *R. pyrenaica*, see *R. myconi*. *R. serbica*, Albania, S.Yugoslavia, N.W.Bulgaria, N.W. Greece; leaves 3–5cm long, narrowly obovate, irregularly crenate or dentate; scapes 6–8cm tall, flowers 1–3, each 5-petalled, 2·5–3cm wide, much like *R. myconi* but more cup-shaped, lilac-blue.

Ranunculus

(Latin diminutive of *rana*, a frog – some species are aquatic). Crowfoot, buttercup. RANUNCULACEAE. A genus of about 400 species of annuals and perennials from temperate regions of both hemispheres. They may be tufted or clump-forming, sometimes tuberous-rooted or stoloniferous, with simple or compound, often long-stalked leaves and solitary, cup or bowl-shaped flowers formed of 5–15 petals. Most species thrive in ordinary garden soil in sun, but alpines need a gritty, humus-rich mixture and the aquatics must be grown in at least 10–15cm of water, ideally with a mud bottom or planted in containers of a loam-based mixture. Plant autumn to spring; the aquatics best in spring. Propagate from seed when ripe or by division at planting time.

Species cultivated (all perennials): *R. aconitifolius*, fair maids of France, fair maids of Kent; Europe, C.Spain to C.Yugoslavia; clump-forming, to 50cm tall; leaves palmate, 3–5 lobed, deeply toothed; stems branched, with smaller, sessile leaves; flowers 2cm wide, pure white, reddish in bud, early summer. *R.a.* Flore Pleno, white bachelors' buttons, flowers fully double. *R. acris*, meadow buttercup; Europe, Asia; clump-forming, 50–90cm tall; stems branched; leaves palmate, 5–7 lobed, each lobe toothed or again pointed-lobed; flowers to 2·5cm wide, golden-yellow; represented in gardens by *R.a.* Flore Pleno, bachelors' buttons, flowers fully double, early summer. *R. alpestris*, alpine buttercup; mountains of Europe; tufted perennial to 12cm tall; leaves palmate, 3–5 lobed, deeply crenate, lustrous; flowers

2cm wide, white, spring to summer. *R. amplexicaulis*, Pyrenees, mountains of N.Spain; tufted or clump-forming, to 30cm tall; basal leaves ovate-lanceolate, glaucous; stem leaves smaller, amplexicaul; flowers 2cm wide, white, late spring. *R. aquatilis*, water buttercup or water crowfoot; Europe; aquatic annual or perennial; stems 30–60cm long; submerged leaves cut into many thread-like segments, floating leaves rounded, deeply lobed or cut into several segments; flowers above the water, 1·2–1·8cm wide, white, with a tiny, circular nectary at the base of each petal, early summer; *R.a. submersus*, without floating leaves; a variable species and often confused with the allied *R. peltatus* (qv). *R. asiaticus*, Persian buttercup (USA); S.W.Asia, Crete; tufted to clump-forming, tuberous-rooted perennial, 30–45cm tall; leaves trifoliate to deeply 3-lobed, the lobes or leaflets deeply toothed to pinnatisect; flowers 3–5cm wide, white, red, yellow, purple, summer; mainly represented in cultivation by fully double forms, often listed as Turban ranunculus. *R. bulbosus*, bulbous buttercup; tufted to clump-forming perennial to 40cm tall, with rounded, corm-like stem tubers; leaves ovate in outline, 3-lobed, middle lobe stalked, all lobes cleft and toothed; flowers 1·5–2·5cm wide, golden-yellow, late spring to summer; represented in gardens by *R.b.* Pleniflorus (*R.b.* Flore Pleno, *R.b.* Speciosus Plenus), flowers fully double. *R. calandrinioides*, Morocco; tufted perennial 10–15cm tall; leaves lanceolate to narrowly ovate, glaucous, wavy-margined; flowers 4–5·5cm wide, white, flushed pink, spring; best in an alpine house. *R. crenatus*, Alps, Apennines, Carpathians, Balkan Peninsula; tufted alpine 4–10cm tall; leaves rounded, shallowly cordate, crenate; flowers 2–2·5cm wide, white, summer. *R. ficaria*, lesser celandine, pilewort, ficaria; Europe, W.Asia; tufted, tuberous-rooted perennial 10–25cm tall; leaves broadly ovate-cordate, bluntly angled, glossy; flowers 2·5–5cm wide, golden-yellow, fading whitish, spring; represented in gardens by mutant forms. *R.f.* Albus, flowers white; *R.f.* Cupreus, coppery-yellow; *R.f.* Majus (*R.f.* Grandiflorus), much larger flowers on robust plants; *R.f.* Pictons Double, clear yellow with double anemone centre; *R.f.* Primrose, large creamy-yellow blooms. *R. flammula*, lesser spearwort; Europe, temperate Asia; tufted, stoloniferous perennial 30–50cm tall; lower leaves ovate, upper sessile, lanceolate; flowers about 2cm wide, glossy pale yellow, summer; a bog or wet ground plant suitable for pond margins. *R. glacialis*, glacier buttercup or glacier crowfoot; mountains of Europe; tufted alpine perennial 8–15cm tall; leaves trifoliate, leaflets deeply lobed, to 2·5cm wide, white, sometimes tinted purple or pink, summer. *R. gouanii*, Pyrenees; shortly rhizomatous, clump-forming perennial closely related to *R. montanus*; 20–30cm tall; flowers 2·5–4cm wide, golden-yellow, early summer; distinguished from *R. montanus* by semi-amplexicaul stem leaves and 3–4mm hairs at tips of rhizomes. *R. gramineus*, S.Europe; clump-forming perennial 30–50cm tall; leaves lanceolate to narrowly so, glaucous; flowers 2·5–3cm wide, bright yellow, late spring to summer. *R. lingua*, greater spearwort; Europe to Siberia; much like a larger, more robust version of *R. flammula*, 60–120cm tall; basal leaves broader; flowers to 5cm wide, bright glossy yellow. *R.l.* Grandiflorus, flowers larger and finer than type. *R. lyallii*, giant buttercup, Mount Cook lily; New Zealand; tufted alpine perennial to 1·2m tall, often less in gardens, leaves 10–30cm wide, orbicular, crenate, somewhat fleshy; flowers 5–7·5cm wide, white, summer; 1 of the most spectacular species but difficult to grow to maturity; needs cool conditions and plenty of moisture. *R. montanus*, mountain buttercup; Alps to mountains of Yugoslavia; rhizomatous, clump-forming perennial about 15cm tall; leaves rounded in outline, 3–5 lobed and toothed; flowers 2–4cm wide, golden-yellow, early summer; sometimes confused with several closely allied species, particularly *R. gouanii*. *R.m.* Molten Gold, vigorous and free-flowering. *R. peltatus*, pond crowfoot; similar to *R. aquatilis*, but floating leaf-blades generally broader than long, fan- to kidney-shaped, and nectary at base of each petal pear-shaped. *R. "speciosus plenus"*, see *R.bulbosus* Pleniflorus.

Raoulia

(for Edouard Raoul, 1815–1852, French naval surgeon who collected plants in New Zealand). COMPOSITAE. A genus of about 25 species of evergreen perennials from New Zealand and mountains of New Guinea. They are mat- or cushion-forming, some of the latter with woody stems, having densely borne, often rosetted, hairy, linear to ovate or spathulate leaves and small, sessile, solitary flower-heads composed entirely of tiny disc florets. Grow in moist but sharply drained soil or screes in sun. The large cushion-forming species, eg *R. eximia* (vegetable sheep), are not easy to grow and must be protected from winter wet with either a pane of glass, or grown in pots in an alpine house. A mixture of $\frac{2}{3}$ grit and $\frac{1}{3}$ all-peat potting medium has proved successful for pot culture. Plant or pot spring. Propagate by division, removing rooted pieces from the periphery of mature plants, or from seed. The latter, which should be sown when ripe or in spring usually germinates poorly or not at all.

Species cultivated (all from New Zealand and summer-flowering): *R. australis*, scabweed; flat mat-forming, to 1m or more wide; leaves 2mm long, spathulate, the tips silvery-grey downy; flower-heads 4–5mm wide, yellow. *R. glabra*, loosely mat-forming, up to 30cm wide; leaves 3–5mm long, narrowly ovate to oblong, pale green, often with tuft of hairs near tips; flower-heads 7–9mm wide, white. *R. haastii*, green mat daisy; stems creeping and rooting and ascending, forming wide cushions to 10cm or more tall; leaves 2mm long, linear, silky hairy, bright green in summer, bronze-grey in winter; flower-heads to 5mm wide, straw-yellow. *R. hectori*, mat-forming; leaves 3–4mm long, broadly ovate, upper part silvery woolly; flower-heads 4mm wide, straw-coloured. *R. hookeri*, mat-forming, to 30cm or more wide; leaves 2mm long, narrowly obovate, spathulate, upper parts white to buff, woolly; flower-heads 5–7mm wide, whitish to straw-coloured; *R. hookeri* of some gardens does not tally with this description and is probably confused with *R. parkii*. *R.h. apice-nigra*, mats looser than type; leaves 3mm long, spathulate, almost completely white woolly with dark brown to black tips. *R. parkii*, mat-forming; leaves to 5mm long, obovate spathulate to cuneate, broadly rounded or flat-tipped, densely white to buff, woolly; flower-heads 4–7mm wide, yellow. *R. tenuicaulis*, tutahuna; densely mat-forming, to 60cm or more wide; leaves to 5mm long, narrowly lanceolate, sparsely white-woolly at tips, appearing grey-green; flower-heads to 6mm wide, white.

Rapanea – see *Myrsine nummularia*

Raphiolepis – see *Rhaphiolepis*.

Red-hot poker – see *Kniphofia*.

Reed canary grass – see *Phalaris arundinacea*.

Reed grass, reed meadow grass – see *Glyceria maxima*.

Reed mace – see *Typha*.

Rehderodendron

(for Alfred Rehder, 1863–1949, German botanist). STYRACACEAE. A genus of 9 species of deciduous trees from S. and W.China, 1 of which is usually available: *R. macrocarpum*, W. China; eventually 8–10m tall; leaves alternate, 7–13cm long, elliptic to oblong-lanceolate or ovate, finely toothed, red-stalked; flowers to 2cm long, 5-petalled, white, in cymose racemes or panicles just before or with young leaves, late spring, early summer; fruit 5–7cm long, ellipsoid to oblongoid, red on sunny side. Grow in humus-rich, moisture retentive, neutral to acid soil in sheltered, sunny, or partially shaded sites. Plant autumn or spring. Propagate from seed when ripe, in a cold frame or cuttings in late summer, bottom heat 18–21°C.

Top: *Raoulia glabra*
Centre: *Raoulia australis*
Above: *Raoulia parkii*

Reineckea

(for Johann Heinrich Julius Reinecke, 1799–1871, German horticulturist). LILIACEAE. A genus of 1 species of evergreen perennial from E.Asia: *R.*

carnea (*Liriope hyacinthiflora*), rhizomatous, eventually forming wide clumps or colonies; leaves all basal, 10–40cm long, linear to lanceolate and narrowly oblanceolate; flowers 8–12mm long, bell-shaped with 6 reflexed lobes, pale pink, fragrant, in spikes to 8cm long, late summer; fruit berry-like, red. Grow in humus-rich soil in shade. Plant autumn or spring. Propagate by division at planting time or from seed when ripe in a cold frame.

Reseda

(Latin *resedo*, to heal – certain species were formerly used to treat bruises). RESEDACEAE. A genus of about 60 species of annuals, biennials and perennials from the Mediterranean to C.Asia, 1 of which is generally available: *R. odorata*, mignonette; N.Africa; short-lived perennial or annual, 25–38cm tall, branching from the base; leaves alternate, to 7·5cm long, oblanceolate to spathulate, entire or 3-lobed; flowers in terminal racemes, petals 6-lobed, yellowish-white, stamens many, prominent, orange-yellow, strongly sweetly scented, summer, autumn. *R.o.* Crimson Giant, flowers red; *R.o.* Golden Goliath, golden-yellow. Grow in well-drained, fertile soil in sun. Sow seed *in situ* in spring, thinning seedlings to at least 15cm each way.

Reynoutria japonica – see *Polygonum cuspidatum*.

Rhamnus

(Greek vernacular for various spiny shrubs, taken up by Linnaeus for this genus). Buckthorn. RHAMNACEAE. A genus of 110–150 species of deciduous and evergreen shrubs and small trees from the northern temperate regions, S.Africa, S.America. They have alternate, sometimes opposite, ovate to oblong-lanceolate leaves, axillary clusters of small, greenish or yellowish, 4–5 petalled flowers, and berry-like, black to purple-black drupes. Grow in any moderately fertile, well-drained but moisture-retentive soil in sun or partial shade. Plant autumn to spring. Propagate from seed when ripe or by cuttings in late summer.

Species cultivated: *R. alaternus*, Italian buckthorn; S.Europe; evergreen shrub or small tree of bushy habit, 3–6m tall; leaves 2–5cm long, narrowly to broadly oblong-ovate to obovate, more or less toothed, dark glossy green; flowers 3mm wide, yellow-green in small, umbel-like racemes, spring. *R.a.* Angustifolia, smaller and more compact, with lanceolate, prominently toothed leaves; *R.a.* Argenteovariegata (*R.a.* Variegata), leaves marbled grey and bordered creamy-white, somewhat less hardy than type. *R. cathartica*, common buckthorn; Europe, W.Asia, N.Africa; deciduous shrub or small tree, 4–6m tall; stems thorny; leaves 3–6cm long, ovate to elliptic, prominently veined, toothed; flowers 4mm wide, 4-petalled, pale green, early summer; both bark and berries are purgative. *R. frangula* (*Frangula alnus*), alder buckthorn; Europe to Siberia, N.Africa; deciduous shrub, or more rarely a small tree 3–5m tall, erect when young; stems green, becoming grey-brown, spineless; leaves 2–7cm long, obovate, prominently veined; flowers 3mm wide, 5-petalled, yellow-green, summer; fruit turns red then purple-black, purgative; grows well in wet or swampy soils. *R.f.* Asplenifolia, leaves thread-like. *R. imeretina*, W.Caucasus, N.E.Turkey; deciduous shrub to 3m tall; stems stout; leaves 10–25cm or more long, oblong to ovate, subcordate at base, slender-pointed, boldly veined, dark green, bronze-purple in autumn; flowers small, green; the most garden-worthy of the deciduous buckthorns.

Rhaphiolepis

(*Raphiolepis*). (Greek *raphis*, needle, and *lĕpis*, scale – alluding to the narrow, pointed bracts at the bases of the inflorescences). ROSACEAE. A genus of about 14 species of evergreen shrubs from subtropical

Far left: *Rhamnus alternus* Argenteovariegata
Far left below: *Rhamnus frangula*
Far left bottom: *Rhamnus cathartica*
Left: *Reseda odorata*
Below: *Rhaphiolepis indica*

E.Asia. They have alternate, leathery, generally glossy, dark, oblong-lanceolate to obovate leaves, and terminal racemes or panicles of 5-petalled flowers followed by berry-like fruit. Grow in well-drained, fertile soil in sheltered sunny sites. In cold areas *R. indica* is best in a frost-free greenhouse in large pots or tubs of a good commercial potting mixture. Plant or pot autumn or spring. Propagate from seed when ripe or by cuttings late summer, bottom heat 18–21°C.

Species cultivated: *R.* × *delacourii* (*R. indica* × *R. umbellata*), to 2m or more, of rounded habit; leaves 4–9cm long, obovate, toothed in upper half; flowers in pyramidal panicles to 10cm long, each 1·3–2cm wide, rose-pink, late winter to late summer. *R. indica*, Indian hawthorn (USA); S.China; 1–1·5m tall, rounded habit; leaves 5–7·5cm long, oblong-lanceolate, toothed; flowers in terminal racemes to 7·5cm long, each 1·5cm wide, white, flushed pink with darker stamens, late winter to autumn. *R. umbellata*, Korea, Japan; to 3m or more tall, rounded habit; leaves 4–9cm long, broadly elliptic to obovate, shallowly toothed in upper ½; flowers in stiff racemes or panicles, 7–10cm long, each 2cm wide, white, fragrant, summer; fruit about 1cm long, pear-shaped, blue-black; the hardiest species.

Rhazya

(for Abu Bekr-el-Rasi – also known as Rhazes – who died about 932, and was an Arabian physician and compiler of a medical encyclopedia). APOCYNACEAE. A genus of 2 species of herbaceous perennials from Greece to Turkey, and Arabia to N.W.India, 1 of which is generally available: *R. orientalis*, Greece to N.W.Turkey; woody-based, clump-forming; stems 30–50cm tall; leaves alternate, to 4cm long, lanceolate, ciliate; flowers 1cm wide, tubular with 5 pointed lobes, blue to violet, in terminal corymbs, late summer; sometimes confused with *Amsonia*. Grow in moisture-retentive, fertile soil in sun or partial shade. Plant autumn to spring. Propagate from seed or by division in spring.

Rheum

(Greek vernacular *rheon* or *rha*, giving rise to *rhaponticum* – *rha* of the Pontus, and *rhabarbarum* – *rha* of the barbarians or foreigners). Rhubarb. POLYGONACEAE. A genus of about 25 species of herbaceous perennials from temperate to subtropical Asia. They are clump-forming with thick, fleshy roots, large, long-stalked, basal, ovate leaves, and robust, erect stems terminating in broad, spike-like inflorescences composed of short, axillary panicles of small, 6-tepalled flowers, sometimes sheltered by broad white bracts. Grow in humus-rich, moisture-retentive soil in sun or partial shade. Plant autumn to spring. Propagate from seed in spring or by division at planting time.

Species cultivated: *R. alexandrae*, Himalaya; 60–120cm tall; basal leaves 15–30cm long, ovate-oblong, cordate; stem leaves progressively smaller, turning into reflexed, cream-coloured bracts where the flowers begin, early summer. *R. nobile*, Himalaya; 90–120cm tall; basal leaves 30–40cm long, ovate-oblong; stem leaves smaller, changing from palest green to broad, overlapping, straw-coloured bracts often with pink margins, completely covering small green flowers, summer. *R. officinale*, W.China, Tibet; 2–3m tall; basal leaves rounded, to 90cm wide; stem leaves much smaller; flowers pale greenish to creamy-white, densely borne, early summer; formerly grown as a medicinal plant. *R. palmatum*, N.E.Asia; 2m tall; basal leaves rounded, cordate, palmately lobed, the lobes again sometimes cut; flowers red, early summer. *R.p.* Atrosanguineum and *R.p.* Bowles Crimson, leaves more deeply lobed, bright red when young, flowers cerise-red; *R.p. tanguticum*, leaves less deeply lobed, usually purple-flushed. *R. rhabarbarum* and *R. rhaponticum*, rhubarb, are not dealt with here.

Rhodanthe – see *Helipterum*.

Rhododendron

(Greek vernacular for the pink-flowered oleander, from *rhodon*, rose, and *dendron*, a tree – adapted for this genus by Linnaeus). ERICACEAE. A genus of about 800 species of evergreen and deciduous shrubs and trees from temperate regions of N.Hemisphere, particularly Himalaya, S.E.Asia, mountains of Malaysia with 1 species in N.E.Australia. Ranging from prostrate mats to large trees, they have leathery, linear to ovate leaves, mainly aggregated towards the tips of the stems, and terminal, umbel-like clusters of – or sometimes solitary – tubular, funnel- or bell-shaped, 5–8 lobed flowers, often in profusion. Grow the hardy species and cultivars in humus-rich, moisture-retentive, well-drained, acid soil, the small-leaved sorts in sun or light shade, the large-leaved species in partial shade sheltered from strong, cold winds. Half-hardy species need a frost-free greenhouse or warm area, tender species a minimum temperature of 7°C and moist atmosphere. For pot culture, use a proprietary all-peat acid mix or loam based type made up with neutral to acid loam and without chalk in the fertilizer. Pot or plant autumn or spring. Propagate from seed at either 13–16°C in late winter or without artificial heat in a frame or greenhouse in spring. Sow thinly on the surface of an all-peat mixture or plain moss peat and avoid overwatering when the tiny seedlings show. Prick off when 2–3 true leaves are visible into pans or boxes of all-peat mixture and grow on in well-ventilated, lightly shaded frames. Early-sown plants can be lined out in nursery rows in autumn, spring-sown ones a year later. Several years, usually 4–10 or more, will elapse before the plants flower. Layering in spring is an easier and quicker means of

Far left top: *Rhaphiolepis umbellata*
Left top: *Rhazya orientalis*
Top: *Rheum officinale*
Centre: *Rheum alexandrae*
Above: *Rheum palmatum*

propagation, and cuttings of many species can be taken in late summer and autumn. Cuttings of hardy, small-leaved species can be rooted in a cold frame in autumn; the remainder are best with bottom heat about 18°C. Saddle- and side-grafting in late winter may also be used to increase rhododendrons, using *R. ponticum* seedlings of pencil-thickness and 1-year-old shoots as scions. After the grafts have been made and tied, they are plunged in peat in a propagating frame at 18°C. Grafting, however, is best left to the skilled propagator and seed or cuttings are to be preferred.

This large and varied genus has had much attention from botanists endeavouring to classify the many dissimilar species and put them into some sort of useful and logical order. Several systems have been devised. Best-known and still extensively used generally by gardeners and botanists alike is the series system, whereby all species that have characters in common are grouped under the name of the best-known or most representative species; 43 of these series are recognized, many of them with several smaller sub-series. Other classifiers maintain that the series do not always represent clearly defined groups, and have split up *Rhododendron* into 8 sub-genera, each with 1 or more sections that is comparable to the series. This system is followed in 'Hortus Third', the most authoritative gardening encyclopedia in the USA (1976). The most sensible approach at the present time is taken in 'Trees and Shrubs Hardy in the British Isles' Vol 3, 8th edition, where the series are retained for convenience but are grouped in 4 categories based on characters of essential difference. **1** LEPIDOTE. All species bear glandular hairs known as scales (lepida). Each hair has a very short stalk and a disc-like, multicellular head with a central boss or umbo. The edges of these shield-like hairs may be entire, crenate or deeply lobed. Many lepidote rhododendrons also have normal, simple hairs but these are never branched, unlike those in the next category. The following series are covered in this category: *Anthopogon*, *Boothii*, *Camelliiflorum*, *Campylogynum*, *Carolinianum*, *Cinnabarinum*, *Dauricum*, *Edgeworthii*, *Ferrugineum*, *Glaucophyllum*, *Heliolepis*, *Lapponicum*, *Lepidotum*, *Maddenii*, *Micranthum*, *Moupinense*, *Saluenense*, *Scabrifolium*, *Trichocladum*, *Triflorum*, *Uniflorum*, *Vaccinioides* and *Virgatum*. Under the Hortus Third treatment, these series are covered by sub-genera *Rhododendron*, *Pseudazalea*, *Rhodorastrum* and *Pseudorhodorastrum*. **2** ELEPIDOTE. None of the species bear scales and they are further distinguished by often-branched hairs that in some species densely coat the leaf undersides. If glandular hairs are present they are of the simple pin-head structure. A number of species, notably in series *Grande* and *Falconeri*, have 8-lobed flowers, while those in *Fortunei* have 7 lobes; there are other exceptions. The seed is more or less winged and the cotyledons of the seedlings are ciliate. The series are: *Arboreum*, *Auriculatum*, *Barbatum*, *Campanulatum*, *Falconeri*, *Fortunei*, *Fulvum*, *Grande*, *Griersonianum*, *Irroratum*, *Lacteum*, *Neriiflorum*, *Ponticum*, *Taliense* and *Thomsonii*. In Hortus Third these are covered by sub-genus *Hymenanthes* with a number of sub-sections. **3** AZALEA. None of the species bears scales or branched hairs, and most are deciduous. The few evergreen species are technically semi-evergreen, losing the older lower leaves but retaining the upper ones through the winter, eg *R. obtusum*. Linnaeus founded his genus, *Azalea*, on species with 5 stamens to each flower, eg *R. luteum*, *R. viscosum*, *R. indicum*, but it was realized early on that this character is too unreliable to delimit at the generic level. **4** AZALEASTRUM. A rather mixed group, resembling AZALEA in lacking scales and branched hairs, but mainly characterized by bearing lateral flower clusters from leaf-axils, not terminal as in most rhododendrons.

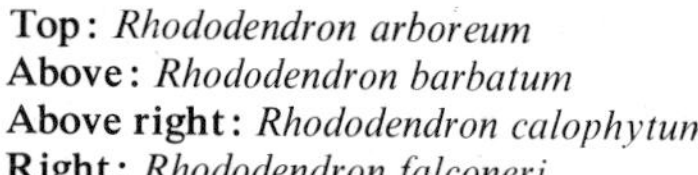

Top: *Rhododendron arboreum*
Above: *Rhododendron barbatum*
Above right: *Rhododendron calophytum*
Right: *Rhododendron falconeri*

Species cultivated (all of comparatively bushy, evergreen habit and flowering in spring unless otherwise stated; the numbers 1–4 after each species name refer to the broad categories already outlined): *R. albrechtii* **3,** Japan; deciduous, to 2m tall, often of rather thin, loose habit; leaves in clusters of 5, each 5–12cm long, obovate, grey downy beneath; flowers with 10 stamens, 4–5cm wide, rose-purple, green-spotted within; sometimes confused with *R. vaseyi*, but that species has 5 stamens and is paler. *R. arboreum* **2,** Himalaya; large shrub or small tree to 6m tall (more than twice this in the wild); leaves 10–20cm long, oblong-lanceolate to oblanceolate, silvery to brown hairy beneath; flowers 5cm long, narrowly bell-shaped, blood-red, sometimes starting to open late winter; a variable species, some forms less hardy than others, in shades of pink, red and white. *R. artosquameum*, see *R. oreotrephes*. *R. augustinii* **1,** C. and W.China; to 3m or more tall; leaves 4–10cm long, oblong-lanceolate, minutely wrinkled, finely downy; flowers 5–6·5cm wide, broadly funnel-shaped, lavender to violet in the best forms, but often pinkish, spotted yellow, olive-green or brown within. *R.a.* Electra, bright violet-blue. *R. auriculatum* **2** W.China; large shrub 3–4m tall; leaves 15–30cm long, narrowly oblong, auriculate, rusty downy beneath; flowers funnel-shaped, 7–10cm wide, white or pink, summer. *R. barbatum* **2,** Himalaya; large shrub to 5m tall (to 15m or more in wild); leaves 10–23cm long, elliptic-lanceolate to oblong, petioles prominently bristly hairy; flowers 4cm wide, bell-shaped, deep red. *R. beanianum* **2,** N.Burma, S.E.Tibet; shrub of open habit, to 2m tall; young shoots 6·5–9·5cm long, oblong-obovate, glossy above, red-brown downy beneath; flowers 4cm long, narrowly bell-shaped, crimson, sometimes carmine to pink. *R. brachycarpum* **2,** Japan, Korea; 2–3m tall; leaves 10–13cm long, narrowly oblong, usually felted beneath; flowers 5cm wide, funnel-shaped, cream, flushed pink; very hardy. *R. bullatum*, see *R. edgeworthii*. *R. caeruleum*, see *R. rigidum*. *R. calendulaceum* **3,** flame azalea; S.E.USA; deciduous shrub to 3m tall; leaves to 7·5cm long, elliptic to obovate, downy beneath; flowers 5cm wide, funnel-shaped, orange-yellow to scarlet; the main source of scarlet and orange in the deciduous azalea hybrids. *R. calophytum* **2,** shrub or tree to 5m tall (to 15m in the wild); leaves 20–30cm long, oblong-lanceolate; flowers 6·5–7·5cm wide, broadly bell-shaped, white to rose-pink with deep crimson basal blotch. *R. calostrotum* **1,** dwarf shrub to 60cm tall; leaves 2·5cm long, elliptic to obovate, densely scaly; flowers 4cm wide, very widely funnel-shaped, bright red-purple, usually in pairs. *R.campanulatum* **2,** Himalaya; spreading shrub 2–3m tall; leaves 7–15cm long, broadly elliptic, glossy above, rusty-brown or fawn-felted beneath; flowers 5cm wide, broadly bell-shaped, white or shades of rose-purple, darker-spotted within. *R. campylocarpum* **2,** Himalaya; shrub 1–3m tall; leaves 5–8cm long, ovate to elliptic, glossy dark green above, glaucous-green beneath; flowers 6–7cm wide, bell-shaped, pale to bright yellow, sometimes with a red basal blotch and red-flushed in bud; 1 of the best yellow-flowered species. *R. campylogynum* **1,** W.China; generally a low, wide shrub 30–60cm tall, but occasionally to 2m; leaves to 2·5cm long, obovate, margins recurved and crenulate; flowers 2cm wide, bell-shaped, rose to black-purple, long-stalked, in clusters of 1–4. *R.c. myrtilloides* (*R. myrtilloides*), lower-growing shrublet than type, with plum-purple flowers. *R. cerasinum* **2,** S.E.Tibet; 2–3m tall; leaves 5–7·5cm long, oblong-elliptic, undersides somewhat glaucous; flowers 5cm wide, white, edged cherry-red or entirely scarlet. *R. chryseum* **1,** shrub 45–75cm tall; leaves 1–1·5cm long, ovate-elliptic, densely scaly, aromatic; flowers 2·5cm wide, funnel-shaped, bright yellow. *R. ciliatum* **1,** Himalaya; 1–1·5m tall; young stems and leaves setose, the latter 4–9cm long, elliptic to oblong; flowers 6–7cm wide, broadly bell-shaped, pink in bud, ageing white. *R.cinnabarinum* **1,** Himalaya; to 2m tall; leaves 5–10cm long, elliptic, somewhat metallic grey-green, particularly when young; flowers 3–5cm long, slenderly bell-shaped, cinnabar-red, pendant. *R.c. blandfordiiflorum*, flowers orange-red without, yellowish or greenish within. *R.c. roylei*, leaves more glaucous than type; flowers shorter, rich rose-red. *R. concatenans* **1,** S.E.Tibet; much like *R. cinnabarinum* but leaves to 6cm long, flowers to 4cm long, apricot, tinted purple outside. *R. dauricum* **1,** Siberia, China, Korea, Japan; 1·5–2m tall; deciduous or partially evergreen; leaves 2–4cm long, elliptic, dark green above, densely scaly below; flowers 2·5–4cm wide, widely funnel-shaped, bright rose-purple, solitary winter to spring, depending on the season. *R.d.* Midwinter, evergreen; flowers phlox-purple. *R. dauricum mucronulatum*, see *R. mucronulatum*. *R.*

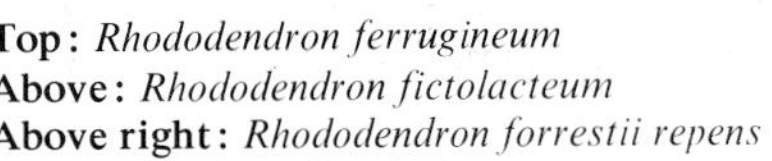

Top: *Rhododendron ferrugineum*
Above: *Rhododendron fictolacteum*
Above right: *Rhododendron forrestii repens*
Right: *Rhododendron luteum*

davidsonianum **1,** W.China; to 3m tall, often of leggy habit; leaves 4–5·5cm long, narrowly lanceolate to oblanceolate, densely scaly beneath; flowers 4–5cm wide, funnel-shaped, pink, spotted red. *R. decorum* **2,** W.China; shrub to 3m tall, sometimes much more; leaves to 15cm long, oblong-ovate to obovate, glaucous beneath; flowers 5–7cm wide, widely funnel-shaped, white or shell-pink, fragrant. *R. desquamatum* **1,** W.China, N.Burma, S.E.Tibet; large shrub or small tree, 3–8m tall; leaves 8–10cm long, oblong-elliptic to lanceolate, densely scaly beneath, aromatic; flowers 5·5–7cm wide, broadly funnel-shaped, mauve, spotted crimson. *R. edgeworthii* (*R. bullatum*) **1,** Himalaya; 2–3m tall, of rather straggling habit, often epiphytic in the wild; leaves 4–14cm long, ovate, dark green, somewhat bullate above, thickly tawny-felted beneath; flowers 6·5–11cm wide, fleshy, waxy-white, flushed pink without, yellow-stained within, strongly fragrant; half-hardy and needs a frost-free greenhouse in all but the mildest areas. *R. exquisitum*, see *R. oreotrephes*. *R. falconeri* **2,** Himalaya; eventually a tree 10–16m tall, but rarely above 5m in Britain; stems robust, rather sparse, brown woolly when young; leaves 15–30cm long, elliptic to obovate, rusty downy beneath; flowers 5cm wide, bell-shaped, 8-lobed, cream to pale yellow with basal purple blotch. *R. fargesii* **2,** W.China; shrub or small tree to 3m or more in Britain; leaves 5–9cm long, oblong-ovate, sub-cordate at base, glaucous beneath; flowers 6cm wide, widely funnel-shaped, 7-lobed, pale pink or palest purple, often darker-spotted within. *R. fastigiatum* **1,** small, twiggy, mound-forming shrub, 60–90cm tall; leaves 1cm long, elliptic to oblanceolate, densely scaly, sea-green when young, darkening with age but remaining hoary; flowers 2–2·5cm across, funnel-shaped, purple to blue-purple; confused with *R. impeditum* (qv). *R. ferrugineum* **1,** alpine rose; mts of C. Europe; small shrub 90–120cm tall; leaves 2·5–4·5cm long, elliptic to oblanceolate, thickly rusty scaly beneath; flowers to 2cm wide, funnel-shaped, scarlet to rose-red. *R.f. album*, flowers white. *R. fictolacteum* **2,** W.China, S.E.Tibet; large shrub or tree to 15m in the wild, often much less in gardens; leaves 13–30cm long, elliptic to oblanceolate, dark green above, densely brown-felted beneath; flowers 4·5–6·5cm wide, bell-shaped, 7–8 lobed, creamy-white, sometimes rose-tinted, with a deep crimson basal blotch. *R. forrestii* **2,** S.E.Tibet, W.China, N.Burma; low hummock to mat-forming, sometimes to 30cm tall; leaves to 4cm long, rounded to obovate, dark glossy green above, purple-flushed beneath; flowers 3·5cm long, narrowly bell-shaped, deep crimson, usually singly or in pairs, often shy-flowering. *R.f. repens*, always prostrate with leaf undersides pale to glaucous. *R. fortunei* **2,** E.China; wide-spreading shrub, 3–4m tall; leaves 10–20cm long, oblong, glaucous beneath; flowers 6–7·5cm wide, pale lilac-pink, fragrant; probably first of the hardy Chinese species to be introduced to the west. *R. fulvum* **2,** W.China, S.E.Tibet; shrub or small tree, 3–6m tall; young stems yellow-brown, woolly; leaves 10–20cm long, oblong-obovate to lanceolate, thickly cinnamon to fawn-felted beneath; flowers 4cm long, narrowly bell-shaped, 5–6 lobed, white, flushed pink to deep rose, sometimes with a crimson basal blotch. *R. glaucophyllum* **1,** Himalaya; 1–2m tall; leaves 2·5–7cm long, elliptic to lanceolate or oblanceolate, deep dull green above, bright glaucous beneath; flowers 2–3cm wide, rose-purple to pale rose-red. *R. griersonianum* **2,** W.China; shrub of open habit, 1–2m tall; young stems bristly and glandular; leaves 10–18cm long, lanceolate, buff woolly beneath; flowers trumpet-shaped, to 7cm wide, rosy-scarlet with darker spots and lines within; needs a sheltered and fairly sunny site to succeed; it has been used extensively in hybridizing, many of its progeny receiving awards. *R. haematodes* **2,** W.China; shrub of dense habit, 90–120cm tall in cultivation, but 2–3m in the wild; young stems densely brown woolly; leaves 4–9cm long, obovate, deep glossy green above, red-brown-felted beneath; flowers about 4cm wide, funnel-shaped, scarlet to blood-red with a red calyx. *R. hippophaeoides* **1,** W.China; twiggy bush, 1–1·5m, erect when young; leaves 2–4cm long, oblong to elliptic, dark green above, grey beneath, acridly aromatic when bruised; flowers 2–2·5cm wide, almost saucer-shaped, lilac to lavender, sometimes pinkish or blue-purple. *R. hirsutum* **1,** hairy alpen rose; C. and E.Alps; mountains of N.W.Yugoslavia; similar to *R. ferrugineum* but shoots and leaves bristly hairy, the latter less scaly beneath; will grow on slightly limy soils. *R.h.* Album, flowers white. *R. impeditum* **2,** W.China; much like *R. fastigiatum* and formerly considered to be that species, but differing most obviously in the dark green leaves and mauve flowers. *R. indicum* (*Azalea indica*) **3,** Indian azalea; S.Japan; 1–2m tall, dense habit; leaves 2·5–4cm long, lanceolate to oblanceolate, somewhat lustrous deep green above, paler beneath, bearing appressed reddish bristly hairs; flowers 4–5cm wide, broadly funnel-shaped, with 5 stamens, in shades of red, solitary or in pairs; not reliably hardy and usually needs a sheltered, fairly sunny site; much confused with the allied Chinese *R. simsii* (qv), the many cultivars of which now provide the Indian azaleas of commerce. *R.i.* Balsaminiflorum, rarely above 30cm tall; flowers fully double, salmon-pink. *R. japonicum* **3,** Japan; deciduous, 1–2m tall; leaves 5–10cm long, elliptic to obovate, hairy, somewhat glaucous beneath; flowers 6·5–8·5cm wide, funnel-shaped, rose, salmon or orange-red; a parent of the Mollis azaleas. *R. johnstoneanum* **1,** Assam, Manipur; to 2m tall; young stems scaly and bristly; leaves 5–10cm long; elliptic to obovate, densely scaly beneath, ciliate when young; flowers to 7·5cm wide, funnel-shaped, highly fragrant, white, with or without a rose-purple flush along the centres of the lobes, and a yellow throat patch. *R.j.* Rubeotinctum, corolla lobes striped pink and yellow, and pink throat patch; barely hardy, needing a sheltered site outside or a frost-free greenhouse. *R. kaempferi* (*R. obtusum k.*, *R. indicum k.*) **3,** Japan; rounded, twiggy, semi-deciduous to evergreen bush, eventually to 2m or more, but slow-growing; leaves of 2 types, those formed in spring 3–5cm long, ovate or elliptic to lanceolate, those developing in the summer at the tips of the stems smaller, elliptic to obovate, all with scattered bristly brown hairs, dark and somewhat glossy above; flowers 4–5cm across, funnel-shaped, in various shades of red and pink; best in dappled shade; a parent of the Kurume azaleas. *R.k.* Daimio, salmon-pink, and *R.k.* Mikado, salmon-apricot, both summer-flowering. *R. keleticum* **1,** E.Tibet, N.Burma, W.China; prostrate or forming mounds to 30cm tall; leaves 7–20mm long, oblong-elliptic, glossy above, densely brown scaly beneath, sometimes ciliate; flowers to 4cm wide, broadly funnel-shaped, purplish-crimson with darker markings, solitary or in 2s and 3s, early summer. *R. kiusianum* **3,** Japan; low, dense, semi-evergreen shrub, 60–100cm tall and much wider; leaves of 2 types, those formed in spring to 2cm long, broadly elliptic to obovate, summer ones oblanceolate to elliptic, persisting through winter; flowers 2·5cm wide, funnel-shaped, shades of mauve to magenta, sometimes pinkish or white, early summer; a parent of the Kurume azaleas. *R.k.*

Above: *Rhododendron yunnanense*
Right: *Rhododendron neriiflorum*

Amoenum (*R. obtusum* Amoenum, *R. indicum* Amoenum, *Azalea amoena*), 1·5–2m tall; flowers with petaloid calyx (hose-in-hose), appearing semi-double, bright rose-purple, possibly of hybrid origin with *R. kaempferi*. *R.k.* Amoenum Coccineum, flowers carmine-rose; tends to revert to type. *R. lepidostylum* **1,** W.China; 30–60cm or more tall by 60cm or more wide; leaves to 4cm long, ovate to obovate, intensely glaucous; flowers 4cm wide, funnel-shaped, pale to greenish-yellow, solitary or in pairs, summer; grown primarily for its luminous foliage. *R. lepidotum* **1,** N.W.Himalaya to W.China; 1–1·5m tall; leaves 2·5–4cm long, lanceolate to obovate, densely scaly, sometimes almost deciduous; flowers 2·5cm wide, almost flat, ranging from white, greenish-yellow and yellow, to pink, red and purple, singly or a few together. *R. leucaspis* **1,** Tibet; to 60cm tall; leaves 4–7cm long, elliptic to obovate, sparsely bristly and lustrous green above, glaucous and yellow scaly beneath; flowers 5cm wide, almost flat, white with 10 chocolate-brown anthers, usually in pairs, late winter to early spring; best in a sheltered site because of its early flowering. *R. lutescens* **1,** W.China; 2–3·5m tall, rather loose habit; leaves 4–9cm long, lanceolate, slender-pointed, scaly; flowers 2·5–4cm wide, broadly funnel-shaped, lemon to primrose-yellow, singly or in pairs, winter to early spring; best in a sheltered, fairly sunny site because of its early flowering. *R. luteum* (*Azalea pontica*) **3,** E.Europe, Caucasus; deciduous, eventually to 3m or more tall; leaves 6–13cm long, narrowly oblong to oblanceolate with hairy mid-ribs and margins; flowers 5cm across, funnel-shaped, deep bright yellow, fragrant; an important parent of the Ghent azaleas. *R. macabeanum* **2,** Assam, Manipur; large shrub to 5m tall (a tree to 15m in the wild); leaves 15–30cm long, oblong-elliptic, grey-white woolly beneath, dark green above; flowers 7·5cm long by 5·5cm wide, narrowly bell-shaped, 8-lobed, ivory-white to sulphur or deep yellow, in large umbels. *R. maximum* **1,** great laurel, rosebay (USA); E.USA; shrub or small tree 4–10m tall; leaves 10–25cm long, oblong to narrowly obovate, dark green above, paler and hairy beneath; flowers to 4cm across, widely bell-shaped, rose-pink to purplish-pink, white-centred and green-spotted; important as a parent of many early hybrids, but now seldom cultivated. *R. molle* (*Azalea mollis*), **3,** Chinese azalea; E. to C.China; much like *R.japonicum*, but leaf undersides densely felted, calyx lobes shorter and less bristly and flowers always a shade of yellow; a weak grower and seldom grown, but important as a parent of several of the azalea cultivar groups. *R. moupinense* **1,** W.China; 60–120cm tall; leaves 2–4cm long, elliptic to obovate, somewhat convex; flowers 3–4cm wide, broadly funnel-shaped, white or pink, sometimes spotted red or purple, fragrant, singly or 2–3 together, later winter to spring; an epiphyte in the wild on trees and mossy rocks; a parent of several award-winning cultivars. *R. mucronatum* **3,** Japan; 1–2m tall; young stems bristly hairy; leaves 4–9cm long, lanceolate to oblong, hairy; flowers to 6·5cm wide, broadly funnel-shaped, pure white; now considered by several authorities to be of hybrid origin involving *R. macrosepalum*, *R. ripense*, and perhaps others. *R.m.* Bulstrode, flowers larger than type, with faint yellow-green patch within; *R.m.* Lilacinum, pale lilac-mauve. *R. mucronulatum* (*R. dauricum m.*) **1,** N.E.Asia; deciduous, to 2m or more tall, of somewhat open habit; leaves 4–8cm long, lanceolate, slender-pointed; flowers 4–5cm wide, broadly funnel-shaped, rose-purple, with darker anthers, solitary, winter to spring; best in a sheltered site to protect the early flowers. *R. myrtilloides*, see *R. campylogynum myrtilloides*. *R. neriiflorum* **2,** E.Himalaya, N.Burma, W.China; shrub 2–3m, in the wild a tree to 8m tall; leaves 5–10cm long, oblong to narrowly obovate, dark green above, glaucous beneath; flowers 4cm wide, narrowly bell-shaped, deep scarlet to crimson. *R. niveum* **2,** Himalaya – Sikkim; large shrub 3–5m tall; leaves 7–18cm long, narrowly oblong to oblanceolate, white to pale brown-felted beneath, dark green above; flowers 3–5cm long, narrowly bell-shaped, plum-purple to magenta, in very dense umbels. *R. occidentale* **3,** western azalea; mountains of Oregon and California; deciduous shrub to 3m tall; leaves to 10cm long, elliptic to obovate, ciliate and downy; flowers 6–7cm wide, funnel-shaped, white or pink-tinted with yellow blotch, fragrant, summer. *R.* Obtusum (*R. obtusum*), now known to be a hybrid of *R. kempferi*, probably with *R. kiusianum* and 1 or more other species; with spreading, compact habit, to 1m tall; leaves and flowers smaller; for *R. obtusum* Amoenum, see *R. kiusianum*. *R. orbiculare* **2,** W.China; 2–3m tall; leaves 5–10cm long, broadly ovate to orbicular, cordate, dark green above, glaucous beneath; flowers 5cm wide, broadly bell-shaped, 7-lobed, rose-pink to pale magenta-pink. *R. oreotrephes* (*R. timeteum*, *R. artosquameum*, *R. exquisitum*) **1,** W.China, N.Burma, S.E.Tibet; shrub or small tree to 3m or more tall; leaves 3–8cm long, oblong to elliptic or rounded, green to grey-green above, more or less glaucous beneath; flowers 5–5·5cm wide, funnel- to bell-shaped, in shades of pink to rosy-lavender; sometimes marked with reddish-crimson spots. *R.o. exquisitum*, mauve-pink with crimson spots; *R.o. timeteum*, rosy-purple. *R. pemakoense* **1,** Tibet; hummock-forming, sometimes suckering, 30–45cm tall; leaves 1·2–2·8cm long, oblong to obovate, dark green above, glaucous and brown scaly beneath; flowers solitary, sometimes in pairs, 4–5cm across, widely funnel-shaped, pinkish-purple. *R. pentaphyllum* **3,** Japan; deciduous shrub to 3m or more; stems slender, much-branched; leaves 3–6·5cm long, elliptic-lanceolate, pointed, toothed and ciliate, borne in whorls of 5 at stem tips, orange and red in autumn; flowers solitary or in pairs, 5cm wide, bright rose-pink; best in woodland. *R. ponticum* **2,** W. and E.Europe, W.Asia; large shrub or small tree to 5m or more; leaves 10–20m long, elliptic to oblanceolate; flowers 5cm wide, funnel-shaped, rose-purple to magenta; a parent of the first hardy hybrid cultivars, particularly with the American *R. maximum*; useful as a rootstock for grafting and attractive *en masse*, but very invasive in woodland and has become a forester's weed; some of the naturalized colonies in Britain's woods and heaths show signs of hybridity and probably started life as game coverts planted from garden seedlings. *R. praevernum*, see *R. suchuenense*. *R. racemosum* **1,** W.China; 1–2m tall, variable in habit and often rather leggy; leaves to 5cm long, elliptic to oblong, glaucous and scaly beneath; flowers 2·5cm wide, broadly funnel-shaped, shades of pink to red, in clusters of 1–6 in upper leaf-axils, forming raceme-like clusters. *R.r.* Forrest's Dwarf, compact, low-growing habit; stems red, flowers bright pink. *R. radicans* **1,** Tibet; mat-forming, to 15cm tall; closely allied to *R. keleticum* but of flatter growth; leaves narrower, oblanceolate; flowers smaller, purple. *R. reticulatum* **3,** Japan; deciduous, to 2m or more tall; leaves 2·5–6·5cm long, diamond to broadly ovate, hairy when young; flowers solitary or in pairs, 4–5cm wide, broadly funnel-shaped, purple, before the leaves; somewhat variable in the wild, several variants having been given specific rank; the species as described here is usually seen in Britain and tallies with *R. wadanum* of Japanese botanists. *R. rex* **2,** W.China; much like *R. fictolacteum*, but leaves generally larger, grey to buff-felted beneath; flowers rose-red to white with crimson spots and basal blotch. *R. rigidum* (*R. caeruleum*) **1,** W.China; closely allied to *R. yunnanense*, but leaves bluish-green above, glaucous beneath; flowers white to lilac or rose-pink. *R. rubiginosum* **1,** W.China, S.E.Tibet; 2–6m tall, rather stiff habit; leaves 4–8cm long, elliptic-

Above: *Rhododendron sinogrande*

lanceolate, rusty scaly beneath, aromatic; flowers 4–5cm wide, funnel-shaped, mauve, spotted crimson-brown. *R.r.* Album, flowers white; said to grow in slightly limy soils. *R. russatum* **1,** W.China; compact, leafy habit, eventually to 1m or more tall but slow-growing; leaves 2–4·5cm long, elliptic to ovate, scaly, rusty-yellow beneath, dark green above; flowers 2·5cm wide, broadly funnel-shaped, deep purple-blue to violet with white-haired centre. *R.saluenense* **1,** W.China, S.E.Tibet; 45–120cm tall; leaves 2–2·5cm long, oblong to elliptic, scaly, dark green above, paler beneath; flowers 4–4·5cm wide, pinkish to crimson-purple, in pairs or 3s. *R. sargentianum* **1,** W.China; dwarf, dense, twiggy shrub, eventually to 60cm tall by 1m wide, but slow-growing; leaves 8–15mm long, elliptic, glossy above, scaly beneath, aromatic; flowers to 1·5cm wide, funnel-shaped, lemon-yellow; not always very free-flowering and best in a sunny site. *R. schlippenbachii* **3,** Korea, N.E.China and adjacent USSR; deciduous, 3–5m tall, rounded habit; leaves 6·5–13cm long, obovate to diamond-shaped, generally in whorls of 5 at stem tips; flowers 7·5–9cm wide, broadly funnel-shaped, pale rose-pink, sometimes darker, or white, spotted red-brown, before or with young leaves; not suitable for areas prone to spring frosts. *R. scintillans* **1,** W.China; to 1m tall, dense twiggy habit; leaves 6–20mm long, oblong-lanceolate to oblanceolate, very scaly, dark above, greyish beneath; flowers 2–2·5cm across, widely funnel-shaped, lavender to purple-blue; deep violet in the RHS First Class Certificate clone. *R. simsii* (*R. indicum* in part, *R.i. simsii, Azalea indica*) **3,** Indian azalea; S.C. and S.W.China, Taiwan, Burma, Thailand; evergreen or semi-deciduous, 60–100cm tall (to 2m in the wild); akin to *R. indicum* and similar, but with leaves of 2 sorts as in *R. kaempferi*, spring ones to 5cm long, elliptic-oblong, summer leaves to 4cm long, obovate to oblanceolate; flowers to 5cm wide, broadly funnel-shaped, with 10 stamens, in shades of red with darker markings; half-hardy and best under glass in all but the mildest areas; the primary parent of the many Indian azalea cultivars so popular as winter-flowering pot plants. *R. sinogrande* **2,** W.China, N.Burma and S.E.Tibet; large shrub or tree 4–10m tall; stems robust, silvery-grey; leaves 25–50cm long, rarely to 75cm, dark green above, silvery beneath; flowers 5cm wide, bell-shaped, 8–10 lobed, creamy-white to soft yellow with basal red blotches; almost hardy but best grown under woodland conditions for wind shelter. *R. sutchuenense* (*R. praevernum*) **2,** W.China; large shrub or small tree 3–6m tall; young stems very robust; leaves 15–25cm long, oblong-elliptic to oblanceolate; flowers to 6·5cm wide, bell-shaped, rosy-lilac, purple-spotted, sometimes with a basal blotch, early spring. *R. thomsonii* **2,** Himalaya; to 4m or more tall and wide; leaves 5–10cm long, ovate or orbicular, cordate, glossy dark green above, glaucous beneath; flowers 5–7cm wide, bell-shaped, glowing deep blood-red; best in sheltered sites as young growth and buds prone to spring

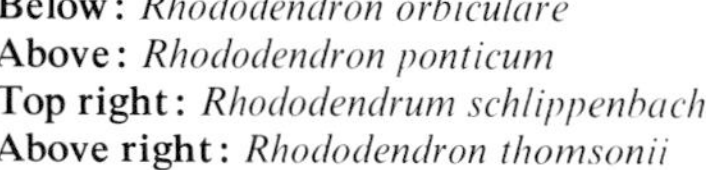

Below: *Rhododendron orbiculare*
Above: *Rhododendron ponticum*
Top right: *Rhododendrum schlippenbachii*
Above right: *Rhododendron thomsonii*
Right: *Rhododendron wardii*
Below right: *Rhododendron williamsianum*

Above left: *Rhododendron yakushimanum*
Above: *Rhododendrum* Yellow Hammer

frosts. *R. timeteum*, see *R. oreotrephes*. *R. vaseyi* **3**, pink shell azalea; N.Carolina, USA; deciduous, 3–5m tall, bushy habit; leaves 5–12cm long, elliptic to oblong; flowers 4cm across, widely bell-shaped, almost 2-lipped, bright pale pink, before the leaves. *R. viscosum* **3**, swamp honeysuckle; E.USA; deciduous, to 2m tall; leaves 3–6·5cm long, obovate to oblong-lanceolate, bristly ciliate; flowers 2·5–4cm long, slenderly funnel-shaped, white or pink, fragrant, summer; thrives in boggy ground, but not essential for success. *R. wadanum*, see *R. reticulatum*. *R. wardii* **2**, W.China, S.E.Tibet; 2–3m tall (6m or more in the wild); leaves 4–12cm long, oblong-elliptic to almost orbicular, more or less cordate, somewhat glaucous beneath; flowers 5cm or more wide, saucer to shallowly cup-shaped, bright yellow, sometimes with a basal crimson blotch. *R. williamsianum* **2**, W.China; dome-shaped, to 1·5m tall; leaves 3–5·5cm long, ovate to orbicular, cordate, bronze when young, then dark glossy green above, glaucous below; flowers 5cm wide, bell-shaped, shell to deep pink, usually in pairs, sometimes 1–4. *R. xanthocodon* **1**, S.E.Tibet, Bhutan; to 3m or more tall; allied and similar to *R. cinnabarinum* but flowers creamy to soft yellow and leaves densely scaly beneath. *R. yakushimanum* **2**, Japan; to 1·5m tall, compact, dome-shaped; leaves to 7·5cm long, narrowly oblong to oblanceolate, white to buff-felted when young, somewhat convex with rolled margins, later dark green above; flowers 5cm wide, bell-shaped pink in bud, ageing white; much used in recent years to create a race of dwarf, floriferous, hardy cultivars. *R. yunnanense* **1**, W.China, S.E.Tibet, N.Burma; semi-evergreen to almost deciduous, 2–4m tall, of rather open habit; leaves 4–7·5cm long, narrowly elliptic to oblanceolate; flowers 4–5cm wide, broadly funnel-shaped, white or pale shades of pink or lavender with a patch of brown, crimson or yellow-green spots.

HYBRID GROUPS AND CULTIVARS: rhododendrons are easily hybridized and yield interesting and sometimes highly garden-worthy progeny. As a result, 1000s of crosses have been made and almost as many cultivars named, although comparatively few have attained general popularity. They can be grouped under 3 main headings: evergreen hybrids, the largest of the 3 groups and containing all crosses between species in categories **1** and **2** already discussed; azaleas (hybrid and evergreen), all crosses between species in category **3**; and azaleodendrons, mainly crosses between deciduous azaleas and evergreen rhododendrons in categories **1** and **2**.

Evergreen hybrids: *R.* Alison Johnstone (*R. concatenans* × *R. yunnanense*), flowers tubular with flared mouth to 4cm wide, apricot to amber-pink. *R.* Blue Diamond (*R. augustinii* × *R. fastigiatum* × *R. intricatum*), flowers almost flat, to 4·5cm wide, deep violet-blue. *R.* Blue Tit (*R. augustinii* × *R. impeditum*), flowers to 4cm wide, broadly funnel-shaped, pale lavender-blue; sometimes flowers rather irregularly. *R.* Bo-Peep (*R.lutescens* × *R. moupinense*), flowers 5cm across, widely funnel-shaped, pale yellow with 2 lines of dark speckles, solitary or in pairs. *R.* Carmen (*R. forrestii* × *R. sanguineum didymum*), flowers to 4cm wide, bell-shaped, dark blood-red; to 60cm tall. *R.* Cilpinense (*R. ciliatum* × *R. moupinense*), similar to first parent; flowers pale pink with darker edges and lines of crimson dots. *R.* Elizabeth (*R. forrestii* × *R. griersonianum*), flowers to 7cm wide, obliquely funnel-shaped, scarlet with black anthers; often considered to be one of the best – if not the best – of the smaller hybrids. *R.* Fabia (*R. dichroathum* × *R. griersonianum*), flowers 6·5–7·5cm wide, funnel-shaped, scarlet, shaded orange, brown-speckled within, calyx petaloid; several sister seedlings of this cross have separate names, eg *R.* Tangerine, vermilion, pink, orange. *R.* Hawk (*R. campylocarpum* × *R. discolor* × *R. wardii*), flowers to 7·5cm wide, broadly funnel-shaped, yellow; best known by the sister seedlings *R.* Jervis Bay, primrose-yellow with deep red eye, and the more famous *R.* Crest, flowers to 10cm wide, 7-lobed and lacking the red eye (actually the best seedling, from a repeat of the original cross). *R.* Humming Bird (*R. haematodes* × *R. williamsianum*), flowers to 5·5cm across, widely bell-shaped with petaloid calyx, carmine-pink. *R.* Lady Rosebery (*R. cinnabarinum* × *R.c. roylei* × *R. maddennii*), much like the first parent, flowers crimson, shading pink on the lobes. *R.* May Day (*R. griersonianum* × *R. haematodes*), flowers drooping, 7cm wide, narrowly bell-shaped, calyx sometimes petaloid, scarlet with black anthers. *R.* Praecox (*R. ciliatum* × *R. dauricum*), flowers 4–4·5cm across, widely funnel-shaped, rose-purple, winter to early spring. *R.* Purple Splendour, parentage not fully documented but probably *R. ponticum* × *R. maximum* × *R. catawbiense* and others; flowers 7·5cm across, widely funnel-shaped, wavy-edged, deep purple, about 15 in a domed cluster. *R.* Songbird (*R.* Blue Tit × *R. russatum*), flowers almost flat, 2·8cm wide, hairy-throated, deep violet-blue; dwarf habit. *R.* Yellow Hammer (*R. flavidum* × *R. sulfureum*), of compact habit, growing 1·5–2cm tall; leaves 4cm long, dark green above, scaly beneath; flowers 2cm wide, narrowly bell-shaped, soft yellow, often flowers during spring and again later in the year.

Hybrid azaleas: unlike the previous group, comparatively few species have been crossed and those that have, have been combined and re-combined to form grexes of similar appearance but with a wide colour range. There are 6 main grexes recognized: **1** Ghent (*R.* × *gandavense*), originating in Belgium, the parentage not fully documented, but it is known that *R. luteum* and the American *R. calendulaceum*, *R. periclymenoides* (*R. nudiflorum*), *R. roseum* and *R. viscosum* are involved; the plants grow 1·8–2·5m tall, with freely produced, long-tubed flowers in late spring; the foliage usually colours well in autumn. Among cultivars available are the following: *R.* Corneille, double, cream, flushed deep pink; *R.* Gloria Mundi, bright orange with yellow flare, frilled; *R.* Nancy Waterer, bright golden-yellow; *R.* Narcissiflorum, double pale yellow, darker in centre, fragrant; *R.* Pucella (*R.* Fanny), deep rose-magenta with orange centre, paling with age. **2** Knap Hill, the largest and most colourful group derived by the 2 Anthony Waterers, father and son, of Knap Hill Nursery, England, from Ghent cultivars crossed back to some American species, eg *R. calendulaceum*, *R. arborescens*, and also with the Chinese *R. molle*. The plants are similar to Ghent azaleas but have larger flowers – to 7·5cm wide – in vivid shades of crimson, scarlet, orange, yellow, pink and white. The Exbury strain of Knap Hill azaleas was bred by Lionel de Rothschild from *R.* George Reynolds (qv), *R. molle* and various unnamed Knap Hill seedlings. Among cultivars available are: *R.* Avon, straw-yellow, golden-yellow flare; *R.* Cam, deep pink with frilled margins and yellow blotch; *R.* Devon, orange-red; *R.* Frome, saffron-yellow, orange-red in the throat, wavy-margined; *R.* George Reynolds, butter-yellow with chrome and green spotting; *R.* Golden Oriole, golden-yellow with orange flare, young leaves bronze-flushed; *R.* Homebush, semi-double, rose-madder with paler shading; *R.* Medway, pale pink with darker margins and orange flash. *R.* Orwell, geranium-red; *R.* Thames, rose, darker-veined, with apricot blotch and frilled margins. **3** Mollis, originating in Belgium, started as selections of *R. japonicum* that were later crossed with *R. molle* producing similar plants but having larger flowers with more varied and intense colouring. Cultivars include: *R.* Hollandia, yellow with orange flare; *R.* Koster's Brilliant Red, glowing orange-red; *R.* Salmon Queen, apricot-yellow, edged pink, ageing salmon-pink; *R.* Snowdrift, white with yellow flash, ageing orange; *R.* Spek's Orange, orange, late flowering for a Mollis azalea; *R.* Sunbeam, large bright yellow with orange blotch. **4** Occidentale, originated by the elder Anthony Waterer of Knap Hill Nursery, has the stamp of *R. occidentale* with long-tubed, fragrant flowers in pastel shades opening in summer. The plants were produced by crossing a good form of *R. occidentale* with various Ghent azaleas and *R.* Albicans (*R. occidentale* × *R. molle*). Cultivars include: *R.* Exquisetum, flesh pink, flushed deep pink, with orange flare and frilled margins; *R.* Irene Koster, cream-striped and flushed pink with yellow flare; *R.* Superbum, pink with apricot blotch, petals frilled. **5** Rustica, double-flowered cultivars derived from crossing double Ghent azaleas with *R. japonicum;* cultivars include: *R.* Byron, white, pink-tinted; *R.* Freya, pale pink, flushed salmon-orange; *R.* Norma, rose-red; *R.* Phidias, reddish in bud, expanding cream-flushed pink. **6** Evergreen azaleas, these are hybrids between *R. obtusum* and allied species in category **3**, series *Azalea* (or sub-genus *Tsutsia*), in particular *R. kaempferi*, *R. kiusianum*, *R. indicum* and *R. simsii*. There are 2 main groups with several smaller, more modern ones developed from them: **a** Indian, blending the characters of *R.indicum* and *R. simsii*. The plants are best-known as small, bushy, pot plants forced under glass for Christmas or winter-flowering; cultivars include: *R.* Hexe (*R.* Firefly), hose-in-hose, crimson; *R.* Purple Queen, hose-in-hose, fuchsia-purple with frilled margins; and *R.* Satsuki, pink with dark blotch, **b** Kurume, a hardy group derived from *R. kaempferi*, *R. kiusianum* and *R. obtusum*, and blending the characters of all 3. They are compact, slow-growing, floriferous plants with flowers 2·5–3·5cm wide, and arose originally as seedlings from selected wild forms of the first 2 parents collected from Mount Kirishima, and grown at Kurume, Kyushu, Japan. Further selection work in Japan resulted in most of the cultivars grown there today, 50 of which E. H. Wilson took to the USA in 1918 where further cultivars have been raised; popular cultivars include: *R.* Azuma-

Top right: *Rhododendron* Blue Diamond
Above right: *Rhododendron* Elizabeth
Right: *Rhododendron* Lady Rosebery
Above far right: *Rhododendron* Freya
Far right: *Rhododendron* May Day

Above left: *Rhododendron* Spek's Orange
Below left: *Rhodohypoxis baurii* cultivars
Top: *Rhodothamnus chamaecistus*
Above: *Rhodotypos scandens*

kagami, hose-in-hose, phlox-pink with darker markings, tall-growing, eventually to 1·8m; *R.* Hatsugiri, crimson-purple, dwarf; *R.* Hinodegiri, bright crimson; *R.* Ino-hayama, white, margined pale lavender; *R.* Kirin, hose-in-hose, deep rose with silvery shading; *R.* Kure-no-yuki (*R.* Snowflake), hose-in-hose, white, dwarf; *R.* Roselind, hose-in-hose, rose-pink, low-spreading habit; *R.* Surprise, light orange-red; *R.* Ukamuse, hose-in-hose, pale salmon-rose with darker flash. Other evergreen azalea groups include the Vuyk, raised by the Dutch nurseryman of that name and involving *R. kaempferi* and allied species reputedly crossed with the *Mollis* azalea J.C.van Tol. No characters of this latter parent appear, however, and it is now considered that seed arose by apomixis (parthogenesis). Best-known are *R.* Palestrina, white, and *R.* Beethoven, orchid-purple with fringed margins. Several other evergreen azaleas raised by Vuyk do not involve the supposed apomictic origin. Sander hybrids result from crosses between Indian and Kurume azaleas. Satsuki hybrids are mainly *R. indicum* × *R. simsii* cultivars, and Wada hybrids are of mixed evergreen parentage. Oldhamii hybrids are *R. kaempferi* × *R. oldhamii* cultivars, the latter parent being a larger-leaved version of *R. simsii* from Taiwan. Glen Dale hybrids developed at the United States Dept. of Agriculture station of that name in Maryland are of very mixed origin, but Kurume types feature largely. Gable hybrids were raised at Stewartstown, Pennsylvania by J.B.Gable largely from *R. kaempferi* × *R. poukhanense*, the latter a small, hardy, deciduous, rose-purple flowered species, plus several other species and cultivars. **Azaleadendrons:** under this heading are several cultivars that have arisen from crosses between members of categories **2** and **3** and **1** and **3**. The latter combination is difficult to achieve and only the Hardijzer group of cultivars, derived from *R. racemosum* and a Kurume cultivar, represent it. Among azaleodendrons in the **2** × **3** category are: *R.* Broughtonii Aureum (*R.* Norbitonense Broughtonianum), (*R. maximum* × *R. ponticum* × *R. molle*), semi-evergreen, to 2m tall, leaves 5–15cm long, narrowly obovate, flowers 6cm wide, soft primrose-yellow with red-brown spots, pink in bud, early summer, and *R.* Glory of Littleworth, semi-evergreen, small azalea-like shrub of erect habit, leaves oblong-lanceolate, flowers 5cm wide, slender-tubed, cream to milky-white, with a flare of coppery-orange spots, fragrant, early summer.

Rhodohypoxis

(Greek *rhodo*, red, and the closely allied genus *Hypoxis*). HYPOXIDACEAE. A genus of 2 species of small, rhizomatous perennials from S.Africa, 1 of which is generally available: *R.baurii*, rhizomes ovoid, corm-like, clump-forming; leaves all basal, 5cm long or more, linear, pointed, white hairy; flowering stems slender, as long as or shorter than the leaves; flowers about 2cm wide, solitary, shortly tubular with 6 spreading tepals in shades of red and pink. *R.b. platypetala*, flowers white or pink-tinted, summer to autumn. Several cultivars are usually available, among them: *R.b.* Albrighton Red, deep red; *R.b.* Dawn, pale pink; *R.b.* Fred Broome, creamy-pink; *R.b.* Garnet, deep crimson; all these have larger flowers than the wild species. Grow in well-drained soil in sheltered, sunny rock gardens or screes, in wet areas with a pane of glass overhead during winter, or alternatively, in pots or pans in an alpine house or cool greenhouse in any good potting mix, particularly loam based. Plant or pot spring. Water those in containers sparingly until leaves show, then regularly, but do not overwater. Dry off when leaves yellow in late autumn and keep dry over winter. Propagate by separating the rhizomes at potting time or from seed in spring under glass.

Rhodothamnus

(Greek *rhodon*, a rose, and *thamnos*, a shrub). ERICACEAE. A genus of 2 species of evergreen shrubs from the Alps and N.E.Turkey, 1 of which is usually available: *R.chamaecistus* (*Rhododendron c.*), Alps; erect to semi-prostrate, 20–30cm tall; leaves alternate, 6–12mm long, elliptic to oblong-obovate; flowers 2·5cm wide, saucer-shaped with 5 broad lobes, pink or pale rose-purple, borne in small, terminal clusters, summer. Culture as for *Rhododendron.*

Rhodotypos

(Greek *rhodon*, a rose, and *typos*, a type – the flowers are like those of a species rose). ROSACEAE. A genus of 1 species of deciduous shrub allied to *Kerria* from

China, Korea, Japan: *R. scandens* (*R. kerrioides*), to 2m tall, often suckering; stems slender, greenish; leaves opposite, 4–6cm long, ovate, slender-pointed, doubly-toothed; flowers solitary, terminal, 3–4cm wide, 5-petalled, white, late spring to summer; fruit of 1–4 glossy black achenes in clusters, each 7–8mm long. Culture as for *Kerria*; propagation also from seed sown when ripe in a cold frame.

Rhus

(Greek vernacular for 1 European species – used for the whole genus by Linnaeus). Sumach. ANACARDIACEAE. A genus of 150–250 species (depending on the botanical authority) of evergreen and deciduous trees, shrubs and climbers from temperate and subtropical regions of both hemispheres. Most are poisonous to a greater or lesser extent, some species yielding wax, lacquer, dyes and tannin. They have alternate, either simple, trifoliate or pinnate leaves, and tiny, 4–6 petalled flowers in axillary or terminal panicles. Fruit is a small, hard, dry drupe, sometimes coloured. Grow in any moderately fertile soil in sun, although partial shade is tolerated. Plant autumn to spring. Propagate by rooted suckers removed at planting time, root cuttings late winter in a cold frame, stem cuttings late summer – preferably with bottom heat 18–21°C, but not suitable for all species – and from seed when ripe in spring in a frame or greenhouse.

Species cultivated: *R. americanus* and *R. cotinoides*, see *Cotinus obovatus*. *R. cotinus*, see *Cotinus coggygria*. *R. glabra*, smooth sumach; E. N.America; like *R. typhina*, to 6m tall but often only half that; twigs smooth and leaves glaucous beneath. *R.g.* Laciniata, leaflets deeply cut, creating a ferny effect. *R. potaninii*, W.China; round-headed, deciduous tree to 10m tall; leaves pinnate, 25–40cm long, leaflets 6–13cm long, oblong-lanceolate, slender-pointed, colouring red in autumn; flowers greenish-white in terminal panicles, summer; fruit rich red, downy, in pendant panicles not always produced in gardens. *R. trilobata*, skunk-bush; W.USA, Mexico; deciduous shrub to 2m tall; leaves trifoliate, leaflets 1–2·5cm long, centre 1 fan-shaped, laterals broadly ovate, all coarsely toothed or with small lobes; smelling curiously unpleasant when bruised and hence the curious vernacular name; flowers yellow-green in rounded panicles to 2cm wide before or with expanding leaves in spring; fruit like small, hairy redcurrants. *R. typhina*, stag's horn sumach; E. N. America; large deciduous shrub or small tree to 8m or more tall, frequently suckering; stems robust, comparatively sparsely branched, antler-like and covered with dense, brown, velvety hairs; leaves pinnate 30–60cm, leaflets 5–11cm long, oblong-lanceolate, slender-pointed, toothed, hairy when young, red, yellow and orange in autumn; flowers dioecious, greenish in dense, erect, pyramidal panicles, summer; fruit crimson, hairy. *R.t.* Dissecta (*R.t.* Laciniata of gardens), leaflets deeply cut: may be stooled annually in spring to obtain vigorous stems and very large, handsome leaves.

Rhynchelytrum

(Greek *rhynchos*, a beak, and *elytron*, a scale – referring to the beak-like appearance of the upper glume and lower lemma). GRAMINEAE. A genus of about 35 species of annual and perennial grasses from Africa, Malagasy, Arabia and India, 1 of which is generally available: *R. repens* (*R. rosea*), Natal grass; tropical and S.Africa; short-lived, tender perennial grown as a half-hardy annual; tufted, 50–90cm tall; leaves linear to 30cm long, pointed; panicles up to 20cm long, terminal, ovoid, of light, fluffy appearance formed of many, tiny, red, purple or white, hairy spikelets, summer to autumn. Grow in fertile, well-drained but moisture-retentive soil in sun, preferably sheltered from strong winds. Sow seed in spring at about 16°C and when seedlings have 2–3 leaves, prick off into boxes of any standard potting mixture at 4–5cm apart each way. Harden off and plant out when fear of frost has passed. Seed may also be sown *in situ* in late spring but the plants are often rather small and flower late if the summer is a cool one.

Ribes

(probably from Arabic or Persian *ribas*, acid-tasting). GROSSULARIACEAE (SAXIFRAGACEAE). A genus of about 150 species of deciduous and evergreen shrubs from the northern temperate regions and cooler parts of S.America. The genus is best-known in the fruit garden (see Currants, Gooseberry), but also contains some valuable ornamentals. They have alternate, ovate, often palmately lobed leaves, smooth or prickly and spiny stems, and pendant or erect racemes of somewhat bell-shaped to tubular flowers with 5 petals and 5

Far left below: *Rhus typhina*
Far left bottom: *Rhus typhina* in autumn
Left below: *Ribes sanguineum*
Below: *Ribes laurifolium*
Bottom: *Ribes sanguineum glutinosum* Albidum

often petaloid sepals. They are followed by fleshy berry-fruits. Grow in any moderately fertile, well-drained but moisture-retentive soil in sun or partial shade. Plant autumn to spring. Propagate from seed when ripe, semi-hardwood cuttings late summer in cold frame, hardwood cuttings autumn.

Species cultivated: *R. alpinum*, mountain or alpine currant; C. and N.Europe; 1–2m tall, dense, rounded, twiggy habit; leaves 2–6cm long, broadly ovate, deeply 3–5 lobed, coarsely toothed; flowers dioecious, small, greenish, in erect racemes, spring; fruit scarlet, insipid; very shade-tolerant and makes a good low hedge. *R.a.* Aureum, leaves yellow when young; *R.a.* Pumilum, up to 1m tall, usually wider than high. *R. aureum*, golden or buffalo currant; W.USA; deciduous, to 2m or more tall, erect when young, then spreading; leaves 2–5cm wide, rounded, prominently 3-lobed, toothed; racemes pendant, to 5cm long, flowers about 1cm long, tubular with petaloid calyx lobes, bright golden-yellow, spicily fragrant, spring; fruit 6–8mm wide, black, edible; confused with *R. odoratum* in gardens, but flowers a little shorter, the tube less than twice as long as the sepal-lobes. *R.* × *gordonianum* (*R. odoratum* × *R. sanguineum*), midway between the parents in all characters, the flowers reddish without and yellow within. *R. grossularia* and *R. hirtellum*, see Gooseberry. *R. laurifolium*, W.China; evergreen shrub usually under 60cm tall in gardens, but 1–2m in the wild; leaves 7–13cm long, ovate to elliptic, coarsely toothed; racemes pendant, 4–6·5cm long, flowers dioecious, bright greenish-yellow, about 8mm long and wide, early spring; fruit about 1cm wide, purple-black; best in a sheltered site because of its early blooming; makes an interesting pot plant for the alpine house. *R. nigrum*, see Currants (black). *R. odoratum*, buffalo currant; C.USA; like *R. aureum* but flowers longer and more fragrant, the tube about twice as long or more than the sepal-lobes. *R. petraeum* and *R. rubrum*, see Currants (red). *R. sanguineum*, flowering currant; W.USA, British Columbia to California; large, deciduous shrub to 3m or more tall; leaves 5–10cm wide, rounded, palmately 3–5 lobed, cordate, toothed, downy beneath, curiously aromatic; racemes pendant, 5–10cm long; flowers 1cm long, bell-shaped, rose-red, spring; fruit 6–8mm wide, purple-black, thickly waxy-glaucous. *R.s.* Albescens, flowers white, tinted pink (confused with the very similar *R.s. glutinosum* Albidum, but this has sticky glandular leaves and flowers about 2 weeks earlier); *R.s.* Album, flowers white; *R.s.* Atrorubens (*R.s.* Atrosanguinea), deep crimson; *R.s.* Brocklebankii, leaves golden-yellow, flowers pink, smaller-growing than type; *R.s.* Carneum (*R.s.* Grandiflorum), flowers deep pink; *R.s.* King Edward VII, intense crimson, smaller-growing and more compact than type; *R.s.* Pulborough Scarlet, deep red. *R. speciosum*, fuchsia-flowered currant or gooseberry; California; large deciduous shrub 2–4m tall; stems spiny; leaves 2–3cm long, rounded, 3–5 lobed, sparsely toothed; racemes short, bearing 2–4, fuchsia-shaped, pendant, crimson flowers, each 1cm long, red stamens to 2cm, spring; best against a wall in cold areas as it breaks into young leaf in late winter. *R. spicatum* and *R. sylvestre*, are currants (red), and *R. uva crispa*, is the gooseberry.

Below: *Ribes sanguineum* Brocklebankii
Bottom: *Ribes speciosum*
Right below: *Ribes aureum*
Centre right below: *Ricinus communis* cultivars
Right bottom: *Robinia pseudoacacia*

Ricinus

(Latin for a tick – alluding fancifully to the shape and colour of the seed). Castor-oil plant. EUPHORBIACEAE. A genus of 1 tender evergreen shrub from E. and N.Africa, but now extensively grown in all warm countries and often naturalized: *R. communis*, as a shrub or small tree, eventually to 5m or more, but in temperate countries usually grown as a half-hardy annual for its handsome foliage; leaves alternate, long-stalked, the blades 15–50cm long, palmately 5–11 lobed, often bronze- to red-tinted, particularly when young, lustrous; flowers unisexual, petalless, in terminal panicles, the lowest flowers male with many yellow stamens, the upper ones female, comprising an ovoid ovary with many soft green or reddish bristles and 3 feathery stigmas. Fruit is a woody capsule that explodes when ripe to release the 3 glossy, brown-mottled, beetle-like seeds. In the drier parts of the tropics and subtropics this is an important crop plant, the seed yielding the medicinal purgative castor oil that is also widely used in the manufacture of soaps, dyes, paints, varnishes, high-grade lubricants, plastics and cosmetics. Several cultivars are grown as ornamentals: *R.c.* Cambodgensis (*R.c.* Black Beauty), leaves very dark purple; *R.c.* Gibsonii, small-growing, leaves metallic dark red; and *R.c.* Zanzibarensis, leaves bright green with whitish veins. Grow in humus-rich soil in sheltered, sunny sites. Sow seed in spring at 16–18°C, ideally singly in 7·5cm pots of any standard potting compost. When the young plants are well-rooted, pot on into 13–15cm pots and later harden off for planting out in early summer, after fear of frost has passed.

Robinia

(for Jean Robin, 1550–1629, gardener and herbalist to the French kings Henri IV and Louis XIII). False acacia or locust. LEGUMINOSAE. A genus of 20 species of deciduous trees and shrubs from N.America and Mexico. They have alternate pinnate leaves – each often with a pair of stipules modified to spines – racemes of pea-shaped flowers in summer, and flattened seed-pods (legumes). Grow in well-drained, moderately fertile soil in sun. In rich soils they tend to make very vigorous stems that are prone to wind damage. Plant autumn to spring. Propagate from seed in spring in a cold frame, by suckers at planting time (making sure that the plant is not grafted onto *R. pseudoacacia*, as is sometimes done in nurseries), or by root cuttings in late winter in a frame or cool greenhouse.

Species cultivated: *R. hispida*, rose acacia, moss locust (USA); S.E.USA; suckering shrub to 2m tall;

stems brown, glandular bristly but without stipular spines; leaves 15–23cm long, leaflets 7–13, oblong to orbicular, 2–5cm long; racemes 3–8 flowered, each 2·5–3cm long, rose-purple; needs a sheltered site. *R.h. macrophylla*, stems without or with very few bristles, flowers larger than type. *R. kelseyi*, N.Carolina, USA; similar to *R. hispida* but with stipular spines and lacking the bristles; flowers 2cm long, bright lilac-pink. *R. luxurians*, S.W.USA; large shrub or small tree 6–10m tall; stems glandular downy, spiny; leaves 15–30cm long, leaflets 15–21, oblong to ovate, 2·5–4·5cm long; racemes 5–7·5cm long, dense, flowers 2–2·5cm long, pale pink to almost white. *R. pseudoacacia*, false acacia, black locust; E. and C.USA, S.E.Canada; suckering tree 20–30m tall; stems spiny; leaves 15–30cm long, leaflets 9–21, elliptic to ovate, 2·5–4·5cm long, silky hairy when young; racemes 7–15cm long, flowers

2cm long, white, fragrant. *R.p.* Bessoniana, small, oval-headed tree, sometimes confused with *R.p.* Umbraculifera, a slightly smaller, densely round-headed tree with spineless twigs; *R.p.* Fastigiata, see *R.p.* Pyramidalis; *R.p.* Frisia, small- to medium-sized tree with rich yellow foliage all summer; *R.p.* Inermis, small, mop-headed tree without spines, often planted in parks and as a street tree, rarely flowers; *R.p.* Pyramidalis, columnar habit, rather like a narrow Lombardy poplar, stems spineless.

Rocket – see *Hesperis*.

Rockfoil – see *Saxifraga*.

Rock rose – see *Helianthemum*.

Rodgersia

(for Rear-Admiral John Rodgers, 1812–82, of the American navy, who, from 1852–56, led an expedition of exploration during which time this genus was discovered). SAXIFRAGACEAE. A genus of 5–6 species of robust herbaceous perennials from E.Asia. They are rhizomatous, clump- to colony-forming, with long-stalked, pinnate, digitate or entire leaves, and large, terminal panicles of small, 5-petalled flowers in summer. Grow in humus-rich, moisture-retentive soil in sunny or partially shaded sites sheltered from strong winds. Plant autumn to spring. Propagate by division at planting time or from seed in spring in a cold frame.

Species cultivated: *R. aesculifolia*, China; 1–2m tall; leaves digitate, leaflets about 7, obovate, coarsely toothed, 15–25cm long; panicles 40–60cm long, pyramidal, the white flowers in dissected tiers. *R. pinnata*, China; 1–1·2m tall; leaves pinnate, leaflets 5–9, oblanceolate, 15–20cm long; panicles formed of rounded clusters, flowers red without, white within. *R.p.* Superba, taller than type; leaves bronze-flushed; flowers pink. *R. podophylla*, China, Japan; 1–1·5m tall; leaves digitate, leaflets 5, obovate to oblanceolate, sharply toothed, 15–25cm long; panicles large, the branches arching to nodding, flowers cream. *R. sambucifolia*, China; to 1m tall; leaves pinnate, leaflets 3–7 or more, oblong-lanceolate; panicles small, flat-topped, flowers

white. *R. tabularis*, N.China, Korea; to 1m tall; leaves orbicular, peltate, 30–60cm wide, many tooth-like lobes; panicles astilbe-like, flowers white.

Romanzoffia

(for Prince Nicholas Romanzoff, originator and financer of a round-the-world expedition 1816–17). HYDROPHYLLACEAE. A genus of 4 species of small perennials akin to *Saxifraga* from W. N.America. They have either clusters of small root tubers, or the bases of the leaves are flattened, swollen and overlapping, forming a bulb-like base; leaves are long-stalked, rounded; flowers are in raceme-like cymes above the leaves, bell- to funnel-shaped with 5 spreading lobes. Grow in humus-rich, particularly peaty, moisture-retentive soil in partial shade. Plant autumn to spring. Propagate by careful division at planting time, or from seed in spring.

Species cultivated: *R. sitchensis*, Alaska to Californian mountains; bulbous; 10–20cm tall; leaves 1–2·5cm wide, round to reniform, crenately toothed or lobed, smooth or white hairy; flowers funnel-shaped, about 8mm long, white, each on a long, slender pedicel, spring. *R. unalaschensis*, E.Siberia to W.Canada, Alaska; bulbous, 5–15cm tall; similar to *R. sitchensis* but dark hairy and flowers pale purple to almost white.

Romneya

(for Thomas Romney Robinson, 1792–1882, Irish astronomer and friend of the discoverer, Thomas Coulter). PAPAVERACEAE. A genus of 1 species of woody-based perennial from California: *R. coulteri*, California tree or matilija poppy; roots white, spreading, sending up suckers and eventually forming clumps or colonies; stems robust, 2–2·6m

Far left top: *Robinia hispida*
Left top: *Rodgersia aesculifolia*
Left above: *Rodgersia podophylla*
Left: *Rodgersia pinnata* Superba
Above: *Romneya* × White Cloud

tall, branched; leaves to 15cm or more long; pinnatisect to pinnatipartite, the 5–9 ovate to lanceolate leaflets 1–2cm wide, toothed or cleft, glaucous; flower-buds somewhat beaked, smooth; flowers 10–15cm wide, solitary, poppy-like, but 6-petalled, white, fragrant, late summer to autumn; seed capsule oblong-ovoid, bristly hairy, seed dark brown with microscopic papillae. *R.c. trichocalyx* (*R. trichocalyx*), often treated as a separate species but differing only in the following small characters: stems somewhat more slender, tending to branch lower down; leaves mostly to 10cm long with narrower lobes (to 1cm wide), often continuing in a reduced form right up to the flowers; buds rounded with appressed bristly hairs; seed straw-coloured to brown, smooth. These differences are rather blurred in the hybrids between the 2 that often represent the species in cultivation; generally, the hybrids are more sstisfactory in gardens, the best named being White Cloud, having larger, more shapely flowers, and bolder, round-lobed leaves. Grow in fertile, well-drained soil in sunny, sheltered sites. Plant spring. Propagate by root cuttings or from seed in spring in a frame or cool greenhouse, or by careful division at planting time. Young plants from root cuttings and particularly divisions take 1–2 growing seasons to get established before growing and flowering properly.

Romulea

(for Romulus, legendary founder and King of Rome). IRIDACEAE. A genus of 75–90 species of cormous-rooted perennials from Europe, Mediterranean to S.Africa. They resemble crocus but the flowers are mostly carried well above the ground on a true stem and the leaves lack the distinctive central white line. European and Mediterranean species should be grown in well-drained soil in sunny, sheltered sites. The S.African species are only successful outside in areas of little or no frost, and elsewhere require a frost-free greenhouse. Plant in autumn, those under glass in pots or pans of any standard commercial potting mixture. Water sparingly until leaves appear, then water regularly but allow the mixture partially to dry out between applications. When the leaves start to yellow, dry off. Propagate by offsets at planting time or from seed in spring under glass.

Species cultivated: *R. bulbocodioides*, S.Africa; stems 6–10cm tall; leaves 2, eventually to 30cm long; flowers about 2·5cm wide, bright to greenish-yellow, spring. *R. bulbocodium*, Mediterranean, W.France; stems 5–7cm tall; leaves about 4, almost cylindrical,

5–8cm long; flowers 3cm wide, bluish-lilac with yellow or white throat, spring. *R. longituba* (*Syringodea luteo-nigra*), S.Africa; leaves filiform; flowers about 3cm wide by 5cm tall, yellow, sometimes with creamy tip and purple shading without, late summer; the only species to have long-tubed flowers with the ovary underground as in crocus. *R.l. alticola*, pure yellow, can be grown outside in Britain in sheltered nooks. *R. requienii*, Corsica, Sardinia; stems to 10cm tall; leaves 10–15cm long; flowers 1·5–2cm wide, deep purple, spring; best under glass. *R. rosea* (*R. longifolia*), S.Africa; stems 5–7·5cm tall; leaves about 4, to 30cm long; flowers 3–4cm wide, pink to cerise, yellow-centred, sometimes purple-veined, early summer.

Rosa

(ancient Latin name for a rose). ROSACEAE. A genus of 100–250 species (depending on the botanical authority, but nearer to the first number seems more realistic) of shrubs and woody climbers from the northern temperate zone and mountains farther south. They have alternate, pinnate, toothed leaves, bristly to hooked-prickly stems, and clusters of widely expanded, 5-petalled flowers. The globular to ovoid fruit, known as a hip or hep, is a hollow receptacle filled with nutlet-like achenes. Grow in well-drained but moisture-retentive soil in sun, although the climbers are shade-tolerant and may be grown up trees or on shady walls. Plant autumn to spring. All roses, but more especially the hybrid tea, floribunda, miniature and rambler groups, need regular feeding and/or mulching. An annual mulch of decayed manure or well-made garden compost in spring is ideal. Alternatively, moss or sedge peat or shredded bark can be used with a general fertilizer at about 90g per sq m, or a specially compounded rose fertilizer applied to maker's instructions. Propagate from seed when ripe, outside or in a cold frame, or by hardwood cuttings in autumn; soft and semi-hardwood cuttings may also be taken in late spring or summer in a propagating case or under mist. The many cultivars of hybrid tea, floribunda and some of the weaker-growing shrub roses are usually budded on to *Rosa canina* or *R. multiflora* stocks, 1-year seedlings or rooted cuttings in summer. In general, the species roses require little if any pruning except to keep them within bounds. Most cultivar groups need regularly pruning to keep the plants vigorous and producing blooms of good quality. Pruning may be carried out at any time from autumn to spring, but most rose specialists favour early spring just as the buds are starting to grow out. Whenever pruning is done, choose mild weather and sharp secateurs. The amount of pruning varies with the cultivar groups and the following is a guide: **1** hybrid teas; cut back all the main strong stems of newly planted bushes to 3–4 buds, choosing an outwards-pointing bud each time. Remove weak stems. The following year prune the new stems in the same way and repeat annually thereafter. Once the bush is 4–5 years old, remove 1 of the older branches annually and thin out parts of any others that are congested. **2** floribundas and polyanthas; cut back newly planted bushes as for hybrid teas. The following year, remove the top ⅓ only of all strong stems and cut the remainder back hard to 1 or 2 buds. The third spring, cut back flowered stems to 5–7cm and tip all the strong, 1-year, basal growths as before. Continue annually. **3** miniatures; prune the really small cultivars as for hybrid teas, the more vigorous ones (30cm or more tall) as for floribundas. **4** climbers (excluding species); cut back the main stem or stems of newly planted specimens by ½ and remove very thin or weak ones entirely. In the following years, remove the soft, thin tips of the leading stems and cut back the laterals to 2 buds. As branches become congested, remove entirely those that are weak or very twiggy and not producing much blossom. **5** ramblers; also sometimes listed as Wichuraiana ramblers, these too are climbers but they flower best on the previous season's strong stems. The aim of pruning is the production of as many strong, 1-year-old stems as possible. After planting, cut back all stems to 30cm. The following spring there will be nothing to do, but after the last bloom has fallen, cut out all the flowered stems to near ground level and continue this procedure annually. Some ramblers produce young stems 30cm or so up from the ground on the flowering stems, and if there are only a few right from ground level these should be retained, cutting just above the point where they arise. Some so-called ramblers are midway between climbers and true ramblers, eg Alberic Barbier. They tend to produce fewer new

Above left: *Romulea bulbocodium*
Top right: *Rosa bracteata*
Top centre right: *Rosa californica* Plena
Above right: *Rosa fedtschenkoana*
Right: *Rosa chinensis* Minima

basal stems each year, but flower the third year from the bases of the previous year's laterals. To prune, remove some of the 2- and 3-year-old stems annually. **6** standards; these are usually hybrid teas and floribundas or polyanthas budded 60–120cm above the ground onto *Rosa rugosa* or *R. canina* stems, and the pruning of the head of the branches is as for those groups when bushes – see instructions already given.

With the exception of ramblers and some climbers, all the aforementioned groups are budded onto species, usually *R. canina*. Suckers of this stock are always likely to occur and should be watched out for and promptly removed by scraping the soil away at the base and pulling off with a twist and a tug downwards. They are green-stemmed, small-leaved, and bear prominent, down-hooked prickles.

Left: *Rosa chinensis* Viridiflora
Below: *Rosa foetida*

Species cultivated (all deciduous and summer-flowering unless stated otherwise; cultivar groups are dealt with separately): *R.* × *alba* (probably *R. damascena* × *R.canina*), white rose of York, Jacobite rose; shrub 1·5–2·5m tall; prickles more or less hooked and of various sizes; leaflets 5–7, oblong to ovate, 2·5–6·5cm long, grey-green, finely wrinkled; flowers 6·5–9cm wide, white, fragrant; hips 2cm long, oblong, bright red; the type species of the Alba group of cultivars (old shrub roses). *R.* × Andersonii, see *R.* × *collina*. *R. arvensis*, field rose; W. and S.Europe; mound-forming shrub, sometimes semi-climbing; stems slender, interlacing, often purple-tinted and somewhat glaucous, bearing hooked prickles; leaflets 5–7, ovate to elliptic, 1–3·5cm long; flowers 3–5cm wide, white; hips about 1cm long, globose to ovoid, dark red; parent of several hybrid cultivars. *R. banksiae*, Banksian or Lady Banks' rose; China; semi-evergreen climber to 7m or more; stems without prickles; leaflets 3–5, oblong-lanceolate, 2·5–6cm long; flowers 3cm wide, fragrant; hips small, globose, red. *R.b.* Alba Plena, double white; *R.b.* Lutea, double yellow; *R.b.* Lutescens, single yellow; *R.b. normalis*, single white, the original wild species from C. and W.China discovered after the cultivars were named. *R. bracteata*, Macartney rose; China; evergreen scrambling shrub to 6m on walls; stems with bristles and hooked prickles; leaflets 5–9, narrowly obovate, rich glossy green above, downy beneath, 2–4cm long; flowers solitary, 7–9cm wide, white, fragrant; hips globose, 2–3cm wide, orange; best on a warm, sheltered wall. *R. brunonii* (*R. moschata* of gardens), Himalayan musk rose; Himalaya; vigorous climber 8–12m tall; stems hairy and glandular with hooked prickles; leaflets 5–7, elliptic-lanceolate, 2·5–5cm long, downy, somewhat bluish-green; flowers to 5cm wide, white, strongly fragrant; hips ovoid, 8mm long, brownish; needs a warm, sheltered site. *R.b.* La Mortola, leaves larger than type, more greyish-green; flower clusters larger; hardier. *R. californica*, California to British Columbia; shrub 1·5–2·5m tall; stems hooked, prickly; leaflets 5–7, elliptic, 1·5–4cm long, downy; flowers 3–4cm wide, pink; hips globose to pear-shaped, red, 1·5–2cm long; usually represented in gardens by *R.c.* Plena, semi-double, deep pink. *R. canina*, dog rose; Europe, S.W.Asia, N.Africa, naturalized elsewhere; shrub to 3m; stems with strongly hooked prickles; leaflets 5–7, ovate to elliptic or obovate, 1·5–4cm long; flowers 3–4cm wide, deep pink to white, fragrant; hips ovoid to globose, 1·5–2cm long, scarlet; very variable species with many named botanical varieties and forms; seldom cultivated as a shrub but important as a rootstock. *R.* × *centifolia*, cabbage or Provence rose; ancient rose of hybrid origin involving *R. canina*, *R. gallica*, *R. moschata* and *R. phoenicea*; shrub to 2m tall; stems erect, prickly; leaflets 3–7, broadly elliptic to ovate; flowers double with broad, overlapping petals, red, fragrant; it is the type species for many old-fashioned shrub rose cultivars. *R.* × *c.* Cristata (*R.* × *c.* Crested Moss), crested cabbage or crested moss rose; sepals elaborately crested, petals pink; *R.* × *c.* Muscosa, moss rose; stems, flower-stalks and calyces covered with a sticky, glandular, bristly, moss-like outgrowth having a balsam odour; flowers pink; the progenitor of the moss rose cultivars. *R. chinensis* (*R. mutabilis*, *R. indica*), China or monthly rose; C.China; shrub or semi-scrambler 2–3m or more tall; stems smooth or slightly prickly; leaflets 3–5, ovate, 2·5–6·5cm long, lustrous; flowers 5cm wide, crimson, pink or white; hips 1·2–2cm long, obovoid, scarlet; probably the most important parent of all the modern cultivars. *R.c.* Minima (*R. roulettii*), 15–30cm tall, flowers double, the main parent of the miniature roses. *R.c.* Mutabilis, shrub 1–2m tall, young stems purple, foliage coppery, flower-buds orange, opening buff, flushed carmine to crimson, tea-scented; *R.c.* Viridiflora, flowers double, small, ragged, green or brownish-green – a curiosity only. *R.* × *collina* (probably *R. canina* × *R. gallica*), shrub to 1·5m tall;

Above: *Rosa gallica* Versicolor
Right: *Rosa moyesii*
Below right: *Rosa hugonis*
Below far right: *Rosa × harisonii*

stems with hooked prickles; leaflets 5, long-pointed; represented in British gardens by *R.* × *c.* Andersonii, having flowers 5–7·5cm wide, clear rose-pink, fragrant; hips like those of *R. canina*. *R. damascena*, damask rose; Turkey; probably of hybrid origin between *R. gallica*, *R. moschata* and *R. phoenicea*; shrub to 2m or more tall; stems erect, bearing many straight bristles and stouter, hooked prickles; leaflets 5, ovate, grey-green, 3–6·5cm long; flowers 6–8cm wide, double, pink to red; hips to 2·5cm long, pear-shaped, red, bristly. *R.d.* Trigintipetala, flowers smaller than type, loosely double, soft pink, very fragrant, extensively grown in Bulgaria for attar of roses; *R.d.* Versicolor, York and Lancaster rose, flowers white, flecked or blotched pink and red – often confused with *R. gallica* Versicolor. *R.* × *dupontii* (*R. moschata nivea*), (probably *R. gallica* × *R. moschata* or 1 of its old hybrids), shrub 2–2·5m tall, of open habit; stems robust, prickles few and small; leaflets 5, elliptic to ovate, to 5cm long; flowers 7·5cm wide, blush, ageing creamy-white, fragrant. *R.ecae*, Afghanistan; to 1m or more tall, densely branched, very prickly; leaflets 5–11, ovate to almost orbicular, 5–7mm long; flowers solitary, 2·5cm wide, rich yellow, late spring to early summer; hips globose, 6mm wide, glossy red; but best in a warm, sunny site. *R. eglanteria*, see *R. rubiginosa*. *R. elegantula* (*R. farreri*), W.China; to 1·5m tall, suckering; young stems densely red bristly; leaflets 7–11, elliptic to ovate, 8–20mm long; flowers 2·5cm wide, pink, usually represented in gardens by *R.e. persetosa*, threepenny-bit rose; leaflets and flowers smaller than type, the flowers coral-red in bud, opening deeper pink. *R. farreri*, see *R. elegantula*. *R. fedtschenkoana*, Turkestan; shrub 1·5–2·5m tall; stems with slender, straight prickles or bristles; leaflets 5–7, elliptic, to 2·5cm long, pale glaucous-green; flowers 5cm wide, white; hips pear-shaped, red, to 2cm long. *R. filipes*, W.China; climber to 6m or more tall; stems with hooked prickles; leaflets 5–7, ovate-lanceolate, 5–7cm long; flowers 2·5cm wide, cream to white, sometimes pink-tinted, fragrant, in large, hanging panicles; hips 1cm wide, globose; best grown through a tree and cascading down. *R.f.* Kiftsgate, more vigorous than type, young leaves copper-flushed, panicles larger. *R. foetida* (*R. lutea*), Austrian briar; S.W.Asia, for long naturalized in C. and S.Europe; shrub to 1·5m or more tall; stems chestnut-brown with straight prickles; leaflets 5–9, elliptic to obovate, 2–4cm long; flowers solitary or in pairs, 5–6cm wide, deep yellow; hips globose, red, 1cm wide, not commonly produced; 1 of the parents of modern rose cultivars, providing the yellow flower colour; needs a sunny, warm site. *R.f.* Bicolor, Austrian copper, yellow and bright coppery-red; *R.f.* Persiana, double yellow, the form most used for hybridizing. *R. forrestiana*,

S.W.China; shrub to 2m tall; stems erect, arching, prickly; leaflets 5–7, orbicular to broadly elliptic, to 1·2cm long; flowers 2–3cm wide, rose-crimson to pink, fragrant; hips 1cm long, ovoid, red. *R. gallica* (*R. rubra*), French rose; S.Europe, W.Asia; shrub 1–1·5m tall; stems erect, bearing slender, straight or curved prickles; leaflets 3–7, broadly ovate to elliptic, rugose above, downy beneath, 2·5–7cm long; flowers 5–6·5cm wide, usually solitary, dark red to pink, fragrant; hips round to pear-shaped, dark dull red, 8–12mm long, the parent of many important rose hybrids and cultivars. *R.g.* Officinalis, apothecary's rose, red rose of Lancaster or old red damask, flowers semi-double, crimson, strongly fragrant; *R.g.* Versicolor (*R.g.* Rosa Mundi), semi-double, crimson, striped white, sometimes entirely red. *R. glauca*, see *R. rubrifolia*. *R. gymnocarpa*, W. N.America; shrub to 2m or more; stems slender, with or without slender, straight prickles; leaflets 5–7, elliptic to rounded, 1·5–4cm long; flowers usually solitary, 2·5–3cm, wide, rose-pink; hips globose to ellipsoid, 6–8mm long, red. *R.* × *harisonii* (*R. lutea hoggi*), (*R. foetida* × *R. spinosissima*), shrub 1–2m tall, blending the characters of the parents, commonly represented by *R.* Harison's Yellow, with solitary, brilliant yellow, semi-double flowers; often misspelt Harrison's in catalogues. *R. helenae*, W.China; climber or scrambler, 4–6m tall, not unlike *R. filipes* in general appearance; leaflets 3–9, ovate-oblong, 2–6·5cm long; flowers to 4cm wide, white, fragrant; hips egg-shaped, orange-red, about 1cm long. *R.* × *highdownensis*, much like *R. moyesii* and perhaps a distinct form of that species, although often considered of hybrid origin; flowers 4–6·5cm wide, carmine with a white centre; hips flask-shaped, scarlet; very free-flowering and fruiting. *R. hugonis*, China; shrub to 2m or more tall; stems arching, bearing straight, flattened spines and bristles; leaflets 5–11, elliptic to obovate, 7–20mm long; flowers solitary, 5cm wide, bright yellow, late spring; hips 1–1·5cm wide, globose, black-red; elegant and 1 of the very few late-spring blooming roses. *R. indica*, see *R. chinensis*. *R. lutea*, see *R. foetida*. *R.l. hoggii*, see *R.* × *harisonii*. *R. macrophylla*, Himalaya; large, erect shrub 3–5m tall; stems dark red to purple, prickles straight, few; leaflets 5–11, elliptic-ovate, 2·5–4cm long; flowers singly or in small clusters, 5–7·5cm wide, bright cerise-pink; hips pear-shaped, 2–4cm long, bright red, glandular bristly; forms with glaucous leaves and larger fruit are sometimes available. *R. microphylla*, see *R. roxburghii*. *R.moschata* of gardens (not the similar but more shrubby smooth-leaved species that is not so readily available), see *R. brunonii*. *R. moyesii*, W.China; shrub to 3m tall, of open habit; stems red-brown with straight prickles and bristles; leaflets 7–13, elliptic-ovate, 1·5–4cm long, pale to somewhat glaucous beneath; flowers 5–6·5cm wide, blood-red; hips flask-shaped, 3cm long, crimson to orange-red. *R.m.* Geranium, slightly more compact habit than type, flowers geranium-red. *R. multiflora* (*R. polyantha*), N.China, Korea, Japan; climber or scrambler 3–6m tall; stems with slender, scattered prickles; leaflets 5–11, obovate to lanceolate, 2–5cm long; flowers 2·5cm wide, white in large panicles; hips 6mm long, ovoid to round, red; the main parent of the polyantha cultivar group. *R.m.* Platyphylla, seven sisters rose; flowers double, cerise-purple, ageing to white. *R. nitida*, N.E. N.America; suckering, dwarf shrub 45–60cm tall; stems erect, prickly bristly; leaflets 5–9, narrowly elliptic, deep lustrous green, 1–3cm long; flowers usually solitary, 4–6cm wide, rose-red; hips 8mm wide, globose-scarlet, somewhat bristly. *R.* × *odorata* (*R. chinensis* × *R. gigantea*), tea rose; semi-evergreen, partly climbing, leaflets 5–7, elliptic, glossy; flowers 5–7·5cm wide, double or semi-double, pink, white or

Top: *Rosa omeiensis pteracantha*
Far left: *Rosa pimpinellifolia altaica*
Left: *Rosa macrophylla* Master Hugh

Above and above right: *Rosa rubrifolia*
Left: *Rosea × paulii*
Left below: *Rosa rubinosa*
Right: *Rosa rugosa*
Right below: *Rosa rugosa* Blanc Double de Coubert

yellow; a group of old cultivars raised in China, important as parents of the modern hybrid tea group. *R. omeiensis*, Mount Omei rose; W.China; shrub 2·5–4m tall, usually of dense habit; stems with bristles and flattened prickles; leaflets 7–13 or more, oblong to elliptic, 1–3cm long; flowers solitary, 2·5–4cm wide, white, usually 4-petalled and very distinctive for this reason, early summer; hips 1·2–2·5cm long, pear-shaped, red and yellow, falling when ripe. *R.o. pteracantha* (*R. sericea p.*), prickles large, flattened, blade- or wing-like, translucent blood-red when young, gradually ageing to brown and grey by the second year; should be pruned like a rambler rose if plenty of vigorous young shoots, that bear the largest prickles, are required. *R. × paulii*, (*R. arvensis × R. rugosa*), stems 2–4m long, forming mats or low mounds, prickly; leaves and flowers similar to *R. rugosa*, the latter white and faintly clove-scented. *R. pendulina* (*R. alpina*), alpine rose; mountains of C. and S.Europe; shrub to 1·2m tall; stems smooth or with a few prickles; leaflets 5–9, elliptic to ovate, 2·5–6cm long; flowers 3·5–5cm wide, often solitary and somewhat nodding, magenta-pink; hips 2cm long, flask-shaped, bright red. *R.p. oxyodon* (*R. oxyodon*), Caucasus, taller than type, flowers deep pink, hips dark red. *R. persica* (*R. berberifolia*, *Hulthemia persica*), Iran, Afghanistan; wiry shrublet 30–60cm tall; stems prickly; leaves 1–2·5cm long, grey to bluish-green, simple; flowers solitary, 2·5cm wide, rich yellow with red eye; fruit globose, prickly, green; unique among roses with its simple leaves and red-eyed flowers; difficult to grow and obtain, best in a frost-free,

sunny greenhouse. *R. pimpinellifolia* (*R. spinosissima*), burnet, scotch rose; Europe to N.Asia; suckering, bushy shrub to 1m or more tall; stems erect, thickly set with straight prickles and bristles; leaflets 5–9, rounded to broadly obovate, 6–15mm long; flowers 2–4cm wide, creamy-white, sometimes pale pink; hips flattened, globose 1·5–2cm wide, glossy purple-black; a very variable species in stature, flower size and colour. *R.p. altaica*, Siberia, 2m or more tall, flowers 5–6cm wide; *R.p.* Lutea, sparsely prickly, flowers bright yellow, 5cm wide, probably a hybrid with *R. foetida*. *R. polyantha*, see *R. multiflora*. *R. pomifera*, see *R. villosa*. *R. primula*, Turkestan to N.China; bushy shrub, 2–3m tall; stems red-brown, prickly; leaflets 7–13, elliptic to oblong, to 1·2cm long, aromatic when bruised; flowers to 4cm wide, primrose-yellow, ageing to near white; hips globose, dark red, about 1cm long; sometimes confused with *R. ecae*. *R. roxburghii* (*R. microphylla*), burr or chestnut rose; China, Japan; shrub to 2m or more tall; stems with slightly hooked prickles, later with flaking, papery bark; leaflets 7–15, elliptic to lanceolate, 1–2·5cm long; flowers 6–7·5cm wide, pale pink, fragrant; hips globular, flattened, 2·5–3cm wide, green to orange-yellow, densely prickly. *R. rubiginosa* (*R. eglanteria*), eglantine, sweet briar; Europe to N.W.India; shrub to 2m or more tall, not unlike *R. canina* in general appearance; stems erect, arching, bearing hooked prickles and stout bristles; leaflets 5–9, broadly elliptic to rounded, 1–2·5cm long, glandular beneath and sweetly aromatic; flowers 3·5–4·5cm wide, pale pink, 1–3 together; hips 1–1·5cm long, globose to ovoid, scarlet; a parent of the shrub rose cultivars known as Penzance briars.

Left: *Rosa primula*
Far left below: *Rosa rugosa* Rubra
Left below: *Rosa rugosa* Frau Dagmar Hastrup
Below: *Rosa virginiana* in autumn
Right: *Rosa willmottiae*

Above: *Rosa woodsii fendleri*
Below: *Rosa villosa* Duplex
Right: *Rosa webbiana*
Right below: *Rosa xanthina* Canary Bird (6)

R. rubra, see *R. gallica*. *R. rubrifolia* (*R. glauca*), C.Europe, mainly in the mountains; shrub 1·5–2·5 cm tall; stems with waxy, purple patina, prickles few, straight or curved; leaflets 5–9, ovate to elliptic, 2–4cm long, flushed purple-red and grey; flowers 3–4cm wide, deep pink to purple-red; hips 9–12mm long, almost globular. *R. rugosa*, Japanese or ramanas rose; China, Korea, Japan; shrub to 2m tall; stems densely prickly and bristly; leaflets 5–9, elliptic, leathery; finely wrinkled and glossy above, downy beneath; flowers 6–9cm wide, shades of rose-purple, solitary or in small clusters; hips globose, flattened, 2–3cm wide, glossy bright red; parent of several garden-worthy shrub rose cultivars. *R.r.* Alba, flowers white; *R.r.* Blanc Double de Coubert, flowers semi-double, white; *R.r.* Frau Dagmar Hastrup, more compact habit, light rose-pink and freely borne, bright crimson hips; *R.r.* Rubra, wine-crimson; *R.r.* Scabrosa, flowers up to 14cm wide, violet-crimson, hips large. *R. sericea*, Himalaya; much like *R. omeiensis* but leaflets 7–11, flowers with 4–5 cream to pale yellow petals. *R.s. pteracantha*, see

R. omeiensis p. R. setipoda, W.China; shrub 2–3m tall; stems erect, robust, with or without straight prickles; leaflets 3–9, lanceolate or elliptic to ovate, 2·5–7·5cm long, sweetly aromatic like sweet briar when bruised; flowers 5–6·5cm wide, pink to purplish-pink; hips to 2·5cm long, flask-shaped, red, glandular bristly. *R. soulieana*, W.China; large shrub or scrambler to 4m tall; stems robust, vigorous, with pale, hooked spines; leaflets 5–9, elliptic to obovate, 1–2·5cm long, bright grey-green; flowers 3–4cm wide, white to cream; hips 1cm long, ovoid, orange-red; the most brightly grey-leaved of all roses. *R. spinosissima*, see *R. pimpinellifolia*. *R. villosa* (*R. pomifera*), apple rose; Europe, W.Asia; shrub 1–2m tall; stems erect, slender with straight prickles; leaflets 5–9, elliptic to ovate, 2·5–8·5cm long, downy greyish-green, aromatic; flowers 4–6·5cm wide, deep pink; hips 2·5–4cm long, ovoid to rounded, bristly hairy, dark red. *R.v.* Duplex, Wolley-Dod's rose, flowers semi-double, clear pink. *R. virginiana* (*R. lucida*), E. N.America; suckering shrub 1–2m tall; stems erect, forming thickets, bearing straight to curved, bristly prickles; leaflets 5–11, elliptic to ovate, 2·5–5cm long, leathery, lustrous deep green; flowers solitary or in small groups, 5–6cm wide, crimson-pink; hips 1cm long, rounded, red, glandular hairy. *R.v.* Alba, white flowers. *R.v.* Plena, double, pink flowers. *R. webbiana*, Himalaya; shrub 1·2–2m tall; stems slender, arching, glaucous when young, with a few straight prickles; leaflets 5–9, broadly elliptic to rounded, 6–20mm long; flowers mainly solitary, 4–5cm wide, clear, pale pink; hips 1–2cm long, flask-shaped, sealing-wax red. *R. wichuraiana*, memorial rose (USA); E.Asia; semi-evergreen climber or trailer to 4m or more long; stems with scattered, curved prickles; leaflets 5–9, broadly ovate to almost orbicular, 6–25mm long, deep lustrous green; flowers 4–5cm wide, white, strongly fragrant; hips 1cm long, ovoid, dark red; the main parent of several well-known climbing and rambler rose cultivars, eg *R.w.* Alberic Barbier and *R.w.* Dorothy Perkins. *R.*

Far left top: *Rosa* Mme Hardy (1)
Above left: *Rosa* William Lobb (1)
Far left: *Rosa* La Reine Victoria (2)
Below left: *Rosa* Zéphirine Drouhin (2)
Top left: *Rosa* Koenigin von Danemark (1)
Left: *Rosa* Reine des Violettes (2)
Below: *Rosa* Perle d'Or (4)

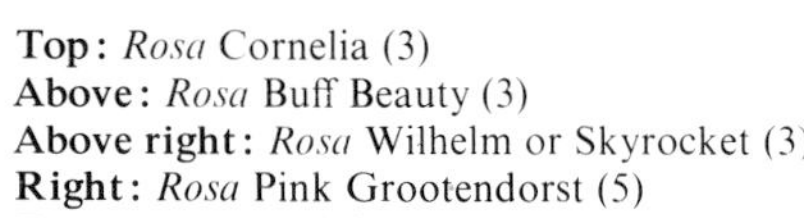

Top: *Rosa* Cornelia (3)
Above: *Rosa* Buff Beauty (3)
Above right: *Rosa* Wilhelm or Skyrocket (3)
Right: *Rosa* Pink Grootendorst (5)
Far right: *Rosa* Schneezwerg (5)

willmottiae, W.China; shrub 1·5–3m tall, densely branched; stems glaucous when young, bearing straight prickles; leaflets 7–9, elliptic to obovate or almost orbicular, 6–12mm long, sea-green, aromatic when bruised; flowers solitary, about 3m wide, rose-purple; hips to 1·5cm long, ovoid to pear-shaped, orange-red. *R. woodsii*, W. N. America, N. Mexico; shrub 1·5–2m tall; stems erect with straight to somewhat curved prickles; leaflets 5–7, obovate to oblong, to 3cm long; flowers solitary or in small clusters, 3–4cm wide, lilac-pink; hips 1cm long, globose to ovoid, red. *R.w. fendleri*, leaves glandular, flowers strongly scented and hips more brightly coloured than type. *R. xanthina*, China; shrub 2–4m tall; stems arching, prickly; leaflets 7–13, elliptic to almost orbicular, 8–20mm long; flowers about 4cm wide, semi-double, golden-yellow; an ancient Chinese cultivar named before the original wild species was discovered. *R. xanthina spontanea*, N.China, Korea; leaves pale glaucous-green; flowers single; hips 1–1·5cm wide, globose, dark red; the wild species and allied to *R. hugonis*. Canary Bird (see **6** below), formerly confused with *R.x.s.*, is probably a hybrid with *R.x.* as one parent.

Hybrid groups and cultivars: over the centuries, various rose species have combined naturally, in the wild and in gardens, and have been intentionally crossed, producing the several hybrid groups and countless cultivars grown today. The selections of cultivars included here are representative only, and have been chosen for their availability and continuing popularity. For a wider selection, particularly of the very popular hybrid tea and floribunda groups, numbers of which come and go with great regu-

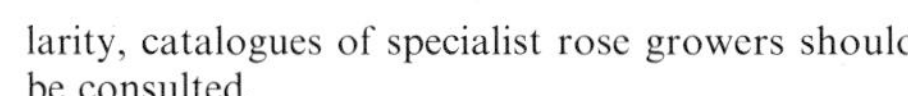

larity, catalogues of specialist rose growers should be consulted.

1 Old shrub roses. These are derived from *R. × alba*, *R. × centifolia*, *R. damascena* and *R. gallica*, their hybrids, mutants and forms. Those described as 'moss' have the mossy stalks and buds characteristic of *R. × centifolia* Muscosa. Apart from a few exceptions, they flower in summer only, have double flowers and are very fragrant: *R.* Belle de Creçy (*R. gallica*), 1·2m tall, neat mauve flowers with button-like centre; *R.* Blanche Moreau (moss), 2m tall, flowers cupped to flat, white, summer to autumn; *R.* Cardinal de Richelieu (*R. gallica*), 1·5m tall, velvety maroon flowers with rolled petals; *R.* Céleste (*R.* Celestial), (*R. × alba*), 2m tall, greyish leaves, clear pink flowers; *R.* Complicata (*R. gallica*), 1·5m tall, sometimes semi-climbing, bright pink flowers with white eye; *R.* Crested Moss, see *R. × centifolia* Cristata; *R.* Fantin-Latour (*R. × centifolia*), 2m tall, flat, full-petalled, blush-pink flowers; *R.* Henri Martin (moss), 1·5m tall, broad-petalled, crimson flowers; *R.* Koenigin von Danemark (*R.* Queen of Denmark), (*R. × alba*), 1·5m tall, open habit, shapely crimson-pink flowers, ageing soft pink; *R.* Maiden's Blush (*R.* Great Maiden's Blush), (*R. × alba*), 1·5m tall, grey-green leaves and flat, blush-pink flowers; *R.* Mme Hardy (*R. damascena*), 2m tall, cupped white flowers, pink-tinted on opening; *R.* Nuits de Young (moss), 1·5m tall, small, neat, maroon flowers; *R.* Queen of Denmark, see *R.*

Koenigin von Danemark; *R.* Tour de Malakoff (*R.* × *centifolia*), 2m tall, lax habit needing support, cerise-magenta to violet and mauve flowers; *R.* William Lobb (*R.* Old Velvet Moss), (moss), 2m tall, gaunt habit when mature, crimson-purple, to grey-lavender on ageing.

2 Bourbons and Hybrid Perpetuals. These are old shrub roses crossed with *R. chinensis* that brings in a remontant or perpetual-blooming habit and rich crimson colouring, plus, in some cultivars, a lessening of fragrance. They form a transition group to the popular hybrid teas: *R.* Boule de Neige (Bourbon), 2m tall, white, round-petalled flowers from crimson-tinted buds; *R.* Emperor de Maroc (h.p.), 90cm tall, maroon-crimson flowers; *R.* La Reine Victoria (Bourbon), 2m tall, full, cup-shaped, bright pink, richly fragrant flowers; *R.* Madame Isaac Perrière (Bourbon), 2·1m tall as a bush, 4–5m trained up a wall, flowers deep madder-pink with raspberry fragrance; *R.* Mrs John Laing (h.p.), 1·2m tall, fully double, rich pink flowers; *R.* Reine de Violettes (h.p.), 1·5m tall, flowers rose, ageing violet-purple; *R.* Souvenir de la Malmaison (Bourbon), 1·2m tall, bushy habit, flat, creamy-blush flowers; *R.* Zéphirine Drouhin (Bourbon), thornless shrub or climber 4–5m tall, cerise-pink flowers with raspberry fragrance.

3 Hybrid Musks. Shrubs with *R. chinensis*, *R. moschata*, *R. multiflora* and some of the old shrub roses in their ancestry. They are vigorous and make dense masses of stems carrying large clusters of usually very fragrant flowers from summer to autumn: *R.* Buff Beauty, 2m tall, flowers of hybrid tea shape, apricot-yellow; *R.* Cornelia, 1·5m tall,

Far top left: *Rosa* Constance Spry (6)
Far left: *Rosa* Frühlingsmorgen (6)
Far left below: *Rosa* Frühlingsgold (6)
Far left bottom: *Rosa* Nevada (6)
Left: *Rosa* Dorothy Perkins (7)
Below: *Rosa* Albertine (7)

rosette-like flowers of coppery-pink; *R.* Moonlight, 2m tall, stems mahogany, leaves very dark green, flowers creamy-white, semi-double; *R.* Wilhelm or Skyrocket, 2m tall, crimson flowers with a hint of purple, good red hips; *R.* Will Scarlet, sport from from the previous rose, flowers scarlet, white-eyed.

4 China roses. This group includes early hybrids of *R. chinensis* or those that show its influence strongly: *R.* Bloomfield Abundance, like *R.* Cécile Brunner and often confused with it, but up to 2·4m tall and calyx lobes with 'leafy' tips; *R.* Cécile Brunner, 1m tall, flowers shell-pink, small but elegantly shaped from pointed buds; *R.* Jenny Wren, 1·2m tall, flowers similar but larger than *R.* Cécile Brunner, coral-red; *R.* Old Blush, monthly or blush monthly rose, 2·4m tall, usually less, flowers semi-double, soft pink from crimson-tinted buds; *R.* Perle d'Or, 1·2m tall, flowers as *R.* Cécile Brunner, fatter, yolk-yellow.

5 Rugosa roses. Under this heading are grouped hybrids and forms of *R. rugosa.* For straight cultivars see under the *R. rugosa* species description; the following are all of hybrid origin: *R.* Conrad F. Meyer, 2·4m tall, flowers of hybrid tea form, silvery-pink, rather gaunt habit when mature; *R.* F. J. Grootendorst, 2m tall, flowers in panicles, fringed-petalled, like small, crimson carnations; *R.* Pink Grootendorst, a clear pink flowered sport of *R.* F. J. Grootendorst; *R.* Schneezwerg (*R.* Snow Dwarf), 2m tall, bushy, flowers semi-double, pure white.

6 Modern shrub roses. Varied and miscellaneous group of cultivars mostly with the remontant or perpetual blooming character of *R. chinensis.* Many arose incidentally as rose breeders sought (and still seek) to produce free-flowering, trouble-free shrubs with hybrid tea or floribunda type blooms: *R.* Canary Bird, 2m tall, much like *R. xanthina spontanea* but with larger, brighter yellow flowers; *R.* Constance Spry, 2·1m tall, vigorous, leaves coppery when young, flowers cupped, fully double, clear rose-pink; *R.* Frühlingsgold, 2–2·5m tall similar to *R. pimpinellifolia altaica* but with larger, creamy-yellow flowers, *R.* Frühlingsmorgen, 2m tall, similar shrub to *R.* Frühlingsgold, but flowers pink with yellow eye and maroon stamens; *R.* Golden Wings, 1·2m tall, compact habit, flowers very large, single yellow with light mahogany stamens; *R.* Kassel, 2m tall as shrub, near double this as a climber, dark glossy leaves and cinnabar and cherry-red flowers; *R.* Maigold, to 5m tall on a wall, leaves dark, glossy, flowers semi-double, deep yellow, richly scented; *R.* Marguerite Hilling, 2·1m tall, a pink-flowered sport of the next cultivar; *R.* Nevada, 2–2·5m tall, dense habit, stems arching, almost without prickles, flowers large, creamy-white, single with a few extra petals, profusely borne; *R.* Scarlet Fire (*R.* Scharlachglut), 2·1m tall, arching habit, suitable as a shrub or low climber, flowers single, brilliant velvety scarlet.

7 Ramblers. Climbing roses of limited height that continually produce new flowering stems from the base (see pruning details): *R.* Albéric Barbier, half-way between a true rambler and a climber (see special pruning details), to 8m tall, glossy foliage and creamy-yellow, apple-scented flowers; *R.* Albertine, another semi-rambler of bushy growth, glossy leaves, salmon and carmine-pink flowers; *R.* Dorothy Perkins, 3m tall, flowers small, double,

Far left below: *Rosa* Mermaid (8)
Far left bottom: *Rosa* Pink Perpétue (8)
Above: *Rosa* Iceberg (11)
Left below: *Rosa* Baby Masquerade (10)
Below: *Rosa* Elizabeth of Glamis (11)
Bottom: *Rosa* Blue Moon (12)

Top: *Rosa* Peace (12)
Above: *Rosa* Super Star (12)
Below right: *Roscoea purpurea*
Top far right: *Roscoea cautleoides*

bright pink; *R.* Sanders White, 3m tall, glossy foliage, profusely borne, small, double white flowers; *R.* Violette, to 5m tall, vigorous, pale glossy leaves and double, deep crimson-purple flowers ageing maroon.

8 Climbing roses. Here are grouped climbing hybrids and cultivars not dealt with under a species name, including climbing sports of hybrid teas and floribundas: *R.* Danse de Feu, 3m tall, dark foliage and large, double, vivid red flowers; *R.* Golden Showers, 2·5m tall, flowers double, bright golden-yellow, carried in profusion; *R.* Handel, 3–5m tall, large but neat, semi-double white flowers each petal having a cerise picotee edging; *R.* Mermaid, to 10m tall, vigorous evergreen growth similar to its *R. bracteata* parent, flowers single, yellow with reddish-amber stamens; *R.* Mrs Sam McGredy (climbing sport), 3m tall, hybrid tea flowers of deep rose and gold; *R.* Pink Perpêtue, 2·5m tall, semi-double, bright coral-pink flowers; *R.* The New Dawn, 12m tall, dark glossy leaves and fragrant, double, silvery-pink flowers in both small and large clusters.

9 Polyantha roses. Derived from China rose hybrids, this group was the forerunner of the popular floribundas. The cultivars vary in stature but are usually smaller than floribundas with freely borne, smaller flowers: *R.* Conchita, shell-pink; *R.* Fireglow, orange-scarlet; *R.* Paul Crampel, scarlet.

10 Miniature and dwarf polyanthas. These include the true miniature cultivars derived from *Rosa chinensis* Minima and crosses between them, polyanthas and floribundas: *R.* Baby Faurax, 30cm tall, lavender-purple flowers; *R.* Baby Masquerade, 30–45cm tall, pink and buff-orange, ageing yellow; *R.* Coralin, 30cm tall, salmon-red; *R.* Little Flirt, 30–40cm tall, bearing bi-coloured blooms, each petal red within, golden-yellow without; *R.* Sneezy, bright soft pink.

11 Floribundas. A large and popular group of showy, but often scentless, cultivars derived from crossing polyanthas with hybrid teas. They are vigorous plants 75–150cm tall if regularly pruned, bearing large panicles of single to double blooms: *R.* Allgold, 75cm tall, dark glossy foliage and shapely, double, bright yellow flowers; *R.* Dearest, 90cm tall, glossy, red-tinted foliage and bright pink, salmon-tinted flowers; *R.* Elizabeth of Glamis, a unique shade of clear salmon-orange, but not very vigorous and prone to mildew; *R.* Evelyn Fison, 90cm tall, bushy habit, flowers bright crimson; *R.* Iceberg, 1·2m tall, almost double, pure white blooms from shapely, pink-tinted buds; *R.* The Queen Elizabeth, 1·5m or up to 2·1m if lightly pruned, very vigorous with bright pink, hybrid tea sized flowers. This is one of the several large-flowered floribundas that blur the distinction between this group and the next one and for which some rose specialists propose the intermediate category Grandiflora.

12 Hybrid teas. The largest and most popular group of modern roses developed from crosses between hybrid perpetual and tea-scented cultivars. They have large, shapely, generally double flowers either solitary or in small clusters, with or without fragrance (single-flowered cultivars do exist, but very few are commercially available): *R.* Blue Moon, 75cm tall, erect, sparse habit, flowers pink in bud, blue-lilac and scented when expanded; *R.* Ernest H. Morse, 1m tall, dark foliage and fragrant, bright crimson flowers; *R.* Fragrant Cloud, 90cm tall, full-petalled, fragrant, orange-red blooms, vigorous and disease-resistant; *R.* King's Ransom, 90cm tall, shapely, full-petalled, clear bright yellow blooms; *R.* Pascali, 90cm tall, fragrant, pearly-white flowers with a central amber flush; *R.* Peace, 1·5m, sometimes more, vigorous, large glossy leaves, golden-yellow, full-petalled flowers with pink flush, slight scent, the best-known of all hybrid tea roses; *R.* Piccadilly, 75cm tall, neat, vigorous growth, flowers flame-red and gold, becoming pink on ageing; *R.* Super Star, 1m or more tall, erect, vigorous habit with clusters of intense, vermilion flowers; *R.* Wendy Cussons, 90cm tall, vigorous, flowers sweetly scented, deep rose-pink; *R.* Whisky Mac, 75cm tall, young, crimson-purple foliage, flowers fragrant, amber-orange.

Roscoea

(for William Roscoe, 1753–1831, a founder of the Liverpool Botanic Garden, historian, promoter of the arts and opponent of the slave trade). ZINGIBERACEAE. A genus of about 15 species of fleshy or tuberous-rooted perennials from Himalaya and W.China. They are tufted to small clump-forming with narrow leaves and short, terminal spikes of orchid-like flowers borne either low down with developing leaves or at the top of leafy stems. Each

flower has a slender tube, 3 petal-like lobes, the upper one larger and erect or hooded, and a broad, petal-like staminode equivalent to the labellum of an orchid. Grow in humus-rich, moisture-retentive soil in partial shade or sun. Plant autumn to spring. Propagate from seed sown as soon as ripe in a cold frame, or by careful division in spring when shoots are visible; some species do not show until late spring or early summer. Not always hardy.

Species cultivated (summer-flowering): *R. alpina*, Himalaya; 10–20cm tall; leaves oblong-lanceolate, to 10cm long; flowers 2·5–3cm long, tube white, lobes light rose-purple, sometimes confused with the next species. *R. capitata*, Himalaya; similar to *R. alpina* but larger; to 30cm tall; leaves to 15cm or more; flowers to 4cm long, blue-purple. *R. cautleoides*, China; 30cm tall, slender; leaves to 15cm long, lanceolate; flowers to 7cm long, primrose-yellow. *R. humeana*, China; to 20cm tall, robust; leaves 10–20cm long, ovate-lanceolate, only partly grown at flowering time; flowers violet-purple, the tube to 10cm or so long, lobes 3–5cm long. *R. procera*, see *R. purpurea procera*. *R. purpurea*, Himalaya; to 30cm tall; leaves 15cm long, narrowly lanceolate; flowers blue-purple, similar to those of *R. humeana* but smaller and shorter-tubed. *R.p. procera*, flowers white-marked, larger than type.

Rose – see *Rosa*.

Rose of Sharon – see *Hypericum calycinum*.

Rosmarinus

(the old Latin name for rosemary – derived from *ros*, dew, and *maritimus*, maritime). Rosemary. LABIATEAE. A genus of 3 evergreen shrubs from the Mediterranean. They have opposite pairs of linear, sweetly aromatic leaves with rolled margins and tubular, 2-lipped flowers from the upper leaf-axils. Grow in well-drained soil in a sunny site, sheltered in cold areas. *R. lavandulaceus* is only suitable for mild areas. Plant autumn or spring. Propagate by cuttings late summer in a cold frame or 2–3 year old stems with the tops trimmed back, inserted *in situ* in autumn.

Species cultivated: *R. lavandulaceus* (*R. officinalis prostratus*), prostrate, mat-forming, 1–2m wide; leaves 1–1·5cm long; flowers 2–3cm long, violet-blue, in small, dense clusters, spring to summer. *R. officinalis*, erect or semi-erect, to 2m or more tall, but usually less than this in gardens: leaves 2–5cm long, white-felted beneath; flowers to 2cm long, pale violet-blue to white, in clusters of 2–3, spring to summer, sometimes also in autumn. *R.o.* Benenden Blue, smaller-growing than type, leaves very narrow, dark green, flowers bright blue, less hardy; *R.o.* Fastigiatus (*R.o.* Miss Jessup's Variety or *R.o.* Jessup's Upright), stiff, erect habit; *R.o.* Prostratus, see *R. lavandulaceus*; *R.o.* Pyramidalis, similar to *R.o.* Fastigiatus; *R.o.* Roseus, flowers lilac-pink; *R.o.* Severn Sea, dwarf habit, arching branches, flowers bright blue; *R.o.* Tuscan Blue, small-

growing, leaves broader, flowers brighter.

Rowan – see *Sorbus*.

Rubus

(old Latin name for raspberry, used for the whole genus by Linnaeus). ROSACEAE. A genus of about 250 species in the broad sense or about 3000 in the narrow sense (many species are apomiects developing viable seed without fertilization; every minor variant can breed true from seed, meriting the rank of a species or microspecies in the eyes of botanists). *Rubus* is of cosmopolitan distribution but mainly from the N. Hemisphere. Its members are deciduous and evergreen, often prickly shrubs and scramblers, sometimes herbaceous perennials with pinnate, digitate or simple leaves and panicles or few-flowered clusters of 5-petalled flowers. The edible, rounded to cylindrical aggregate fruit is composed of many single-seeded drupelets. Grow in well-drained, moderately fertile soil in sun or partial shade. Plant autumn to spring. Propagate by division, suckers at planting time, tip-layering in summer or from seed when ripe, preferably in a cold frame. Species with the raspberry habit of growth, eg *R. biflorus* and *R. cockburnianus*, are best pruned as for that fruit in order to encourage plenty of young decorative basal stems.

Species cultivated: *R. arcticus*, arctic bramble; N. Hemisphere; herbaceous, rhizomatous perennial; stems erect, 10–20cm tall; leaves trifoliate, leaflets 2–5cm long; flowers solitary to 2cm wide, pink, summer; fruit rounded, dark red. *R. bambusarum*,

Above: *Rosmarinus officinalis*

Left below: *Rubus deliciosus*
Above: *Rubus phoenicolasius*
Below: *Rubus thibetanus*

see *R. henryi b. R. biflorus*, Himalaya; deciduous shrub 2–3m tall, with erect, raspberry-like stems covered with a bright, waxy-white coating; leaves pinnate, leaflets 3–5, ovate, 3–5cm long; flowers in small clusters to 2cm wide, white, summer; fruit rounded, yellow. *R. calycinoides* (*R. fockeanus* of gardens), Taiwan; small, mat-forming, evergreen shrub; stems rooting to 90cm long; leaves 1·5–4cm wide, broadly ovate, 3-lobed, finely wrinkled and glossy above, grey-felted beneath; flowers usually solitary, to 1·5cm wide, white, summer, often rather hidden by the leaves; fruit 1·5cm long, scarlet; a useful, small, ground-cover plant often confused with the very similar but seldom cultivated *R. fockeanus* from China. *R. cockburnianus* (*R. giraldianus*), N. and C.China; deciduous shrub, in overall appearance similar to *R. biflorus*, but branches pendulous and leaves with 7–9 leaflets, each 4–6·5cm long; flowers smaller, purplish; fruit black. *R. deliciosus*, Rocky Mountains, Colorado, USA; deciduous shrub 2m or more tall, of spreading, arching habit; leaves to 7·5cm long, rounded to kidney-shaped with 3–5 broad lobes; flowers mostly solitary, to 5cm wide, white, like small, single roses; fruit 1·2cm wide, dark purple or red but dry and flavourless. *R. fockeanus* of gardens, see *R. calycinoides*. *R. fruticosus*, forms cultivated for blackberries. *R. giraldianus*, see *R. cockburnianus*. *R. henryi*, C. and W.China; semi-climbing evergreen shrub; stems 3–6m long, slender, slightly prickly; leaves 10–15cm long, deeply 3 (sometimes 5) lobed, smooth above, whitish-felted beneath; flowers to 2cm wide, pinkish, summer; fruit 1cm wide, glossy black. *R.h. bambusarum* (*R. bambusarum*), leaves composed of 3 separate leaflets. *R. idaeus*, forms cultivated for raspberries. *R. illecebrosus*, strawberry-raspberry; Japan; herbaceous perennial or sub-shrub with creeping rhizomes and erect, slightly prickly stems, 30–60cm tall; leaves pinnate, leaflets 3–7, lanceolate, 3–8cm long; flowers 2·5–4cm wide, white, solitary or in small clusters; fruit 3cm long, oblongoid to ellipsoid, red, juicy and sweetish but flavourless; inclined to be invasive on richer soils. *R. laciniatus* (*R. fruticosus laciniatus*), cut- or fern-leaved blackberry; provenance unknown but probably of mutant origin coming true from seed apomictically; semi-evergreen shrub forming mounds to 2m tall and more wide, or scrambling; stems robust, bearing sharp, hooked prickles; leaves digitate, the 3–5 leaflets cut into narrow lobes or further leaflets; flowers 2–3cm wide, palest pink, in large panicles, summer; fruit rounded, to 2cm long, glossy black, of good flavour. *R. occidentalis*, cultivated for raspberries. *R. odoratus*, flowering raspberry, thimbleberry; E.USA; deciduous suckering shrub to 2m or more tall; stems without prickles, the bark peeling and papery; leaves palmate, 10–25cm or more wide with 5, irregularly toothed lobes, velvety hairy; flowers 4–5cm wide, rose-purple, fragrant, late summer; fruit red, small, flat, dry. *R. phoenicolasius*, wineberry; China, Korea, Japan; deciduous shrub of scrambling habit; stems to 3m or more long, densely covered with gland-tipped, reddish bristles; leaves trifoliate, leaflets 5–10cm long, broadly ovate, lateral ones somewhat oblique; flowers 4cm wide across the slender, reddish, glandular sepals, petals 6mm long, pink; fruit 2cm long, conical, red, sweet and juicy, but rather insipid. *R. spectabilis*, salmon berry; Alaska to California east to Idaho; deciduous, suckering shrub 1·2–1·8m tall; stems erect, bearing fine prickles; leaves trifoliate, leaflets to 10cm long, ovate; flowers 2·4–4cm wide, purple-red, solitary or in small clusters, summer; fruit ovoid to 2cm long, salmon-red to orange-yellow; grows well beneath trees but can be invasive in moist, fertile soil. *R. thibetanus* (*R. veitchii*), W.China; deciduous shrub to 2m tall of raspberry-like growth; stems semi-erect, purple-brown with waxy-white patina and slender, straight prickles; leaves pinnate, leaflets 13, ovate, 2–5cm long, deep, somewhat glossy green above, whitish-felted beneath; flowers 1cm wide, purple, summer; fruit rounded, 1·5cm long, black with waxy patina. *R. tricolor*, W.China; evergreen, prostrate, mat-forming or scrambling into nearby shrubs, to 1m or more high; stems yellow-brown bristly; leaves ovate-cordate, 6–10cm long, deep lustrous green above, whitish-felted beneath; flowers to 2cm wide, white, summer; fruit bright red, of good flavour. *R.* × *tridel* Benenden (*R. deliciosus* × *R. trilobus*), much like *R. deliciosus* but more vigorous and free-flowering, individual flowers up to 7cm wide. *R. ulmifolius*, elm-leaved blackberry; Europe, N.W.Africa; semi-evergreen, shrub-forming tangled mounds or semi-climbing to 1·5m tall; stems furrowed with curved prickles and light waxy, whitish patina when young; leaves digitate, leaflets 3–5, obovate, 4–7·5cm long, dark green above, white-felted beneath; flowers 2cm wide, purplish-pink, late summer; fruit rounded, glossy black; a true non-apomictic blackberry species very common in Europe, represented in gardens by *R.u.* Bellidiflorus, flowers very fully double, pink. *R. veitchii*, see *R. thibetanus*.

Rudbeckia

(for Olof Rudbeck, 1630–1702, Swedish anatomist, botanist and antiquarian, and his son of the same name, 1660–1740, both professors at Uppsala University – the son befriended Linnaeus, who later named the genus in their honour). Coneflower, gloriosa daisy. COMPOSITAE. A genus of 25 species of annuals, biennials and perennials from N.America. They are mostly sturdy, erect plants with simple to pinnate leaves and daisy-like flower-heads, the central disks of which vary from hemispherical to cone-shaped. Grow in any moderately fertile soil in sun or partial shade. Plant autumn to spring. Propagate by division at planting time or from seed in spring.

Species cultivated: *R. bicolor*, see *R. hirta pulcherrima*. *R. deamii*, now considered a variety of the next species. *R. fulgida*, E.USA; rhizomatous perennial to 60cm or more tall; stems with sessile leaves, branched basal leaves 5–12cm long, long-stalked, narrowly lanceolate to oblanceolate, toothed or not; flower-heads solitary, to 6cm wide, ray florets bright yellow, disks shortly conical, brown-purple, summer, autumn. *R.f. deamii* (*R. deamii*), leaves broadly elliptic to ovate, those on the stem of even size. *R.f. speciosa* (*R. newmannii* and *R. speciosa* of gardens), basal leaves with smooth or obscurely crenate margins, stem leaves coarsely serrate or with tooth-like lobes; *R.f. sullivantii* (*R. sullivantii*, *R. speciosa s.*), like *R.f. deamii* but stem leaves successively reduced in size, the uppermost ones merely large bracts, flowers often somewhat larger than type, the most frequently cultivated variety,

Left below: *Rudbeckia nitida* Goldquelle
Left bottom: *Rudbeckia hirta* Rustic Dwarfs
Above: *Rudbeckia fulgida sullivantii* Goldsturm

R.f.s. Goldsturm being an improved selection from it. *R. hirta*, black-eyed Susan; E.USA; annual, biennial or short-lived perennial 60–90cm tall; stems bristly hairy, branched; basal leaves 7–10cm long, broadly ovate, abruptly narrowed to base, coarsely toothed, roughly hairy; flower-heads to 10cm wide, ray florets orange-yellow, disks conical, purple-brown, summer to autumn. *R.h. pulcherrima* (*R. bicolor*, *R. serotina*), mid-W.USA; leaves oblanceolate, smooth-edged or finely toothed; flower-heads sometimes larger with rays banded or suffused maroon; it has given rise to *R.h.p.* Gloriosa and *R.h.p.* Double Gloriosa (both tetraploid) with flowers to 18cm wide, and to the smaller, yellow and maroon *R.h.p.* Superba. *R. laciniata*, N.America; clump-forming perennial 2–3m tall, lowest leaves pinnate with 5–7, often deeply lobed leaflets, upper leaves 3–5 lobed or entire; flower-heads with olive-green, hemispherical to conical disks and yellow, reflexed ray florets 4–6·5cm long, late summer; see also *R. nitida*. *R.l.* Soleil d'Or, ray florets broader than type; *R.l.* Hortensia (*R.l.* Golden Glow), double bright yellow. *R. maxima*, C. and S.USA; clump-forming perennial 1·2–2m tall; leaves to 30cm or more long, elliptic, glaucous; flower-heads with very prominent, greenish-black, cylindrical-conical disks 4–8cm long and golden ray florets 4–5cm long, summer. *R. newmannii*, see *R. fulgida speciosa*. *R. nitida*, S.E.USA; similar to *R. laciniata* and confused with it but rarely above 1·2m tall with simple leaves that are ovate to lanceolate. *R.n.* Goldquelle (*R. laciniata* Goldquelle of catalogues), flowers double, brassy-yellow. *R. purpurea*, see *Echinacea p.* *R. serotina*, see *R. hirta pulcherrima*. *R. speciosa* of gardens, see *R. fulgida s.* *R. speciosa sullivantii*, see *R. fulgida s.* *R. sullivantii*, see *R. fulgida s.*

Rue – see *Ruta*.

Ruscus

(Latin vernacular for butcher's broom). Butcher's

broom. RUSCACEAE (LILIACEAE). A genus of 3–7 species of evergreen, dioecious shrubs from Atlantic Is, W. and C.Europe, Mediterranean to Iran and Caucasus. They are clump-forming or tufted from underground rhizomes, with green stems and leaf-like cladodes (cladophylls) that carry small, starry, 6-tepalled flowers in the axils of the scale leaves; fruit red or yellow berries with 1 or 2 bony seeds. Grow in humus-rich soil in shade or partial shade. Plant autumn to spring. Propagate by division in spring or from seed when ripe.

Species cultivated: *R. aculeatus*, butcher's broom; W.Europe to Iran; rhizomatous, tufted to clump-forming, 40–90cm tall; stems erect, stiff, dark green, branched, cladodes 2–4cm long, ovate, spine-tipped, rigid, dark green; flowers solitary or paired, 6mm wide, whitish-green, from upper centre of cladode, winter, spring; fruit glossy red or occasionally yellow, about 1cm long. *R.a.* Hermaphroditus, male and female flowers on the same plant. *R. hypoglossum*, S.Europe; clump-forming, suckering, 8–40cm tall; stems arching,

flexible, branched; cladodes 5–11cm long, elliptic to oblanceolate, glossy; flowers in clusters of 3–5, in the axil of a small true leaf, each one greenish-yellow, 7–10mm wide, spring; fruit scarlet, 1–2cm long.

Ruta

(Greek and Latin name for the plant; Latin vernacular for rue, meaning bitter). RUTACEAE. A

genus of 7–40 species (depending on the botanical treatment) of evergreen perennials, sub-shrubs and shrubs from Atlantic Is, Mediterranean and S.W.Asia. 1 shrubby species is generally available: *R. graveolens*, common rue, herb of grace; S.Europe; 60–90cm tall, bushy habit; leaves 4–8cm long, pinnate or pinnatipartite, glaucous, acridly aromatic; flowers 1·5–2cm wide with 4 or 5 cupped yellow petals in open terminal corymbs, summer to autumn. *R.g.* Jackman's Blue, leaves more richly glaucous than type; *R.g.* Variegata, leaves white-bordered. Sometimes used as a flavouring herb for salads, sandwiches, fish and egg dishes, but strong-flavoured and needed only in small quantities. Grow in well-drained soil in sun. Plant autumn to spring. Propagate from seed in spring, preferably under glass, or by cuttings late summer in a cold frame.

Saffron – see *Crocus sativus*.

Saffron, meadow – see *Colchicum autumnale*.

Sagina

(Latin for fodder, from the sheep-feeding uses of spurrey – *Spergula arvensis* – a species originally included in this genus). Pearlwort. CARYOPHYLLACEAE. A genus of 20–30 species of mainly weedy annuals and perennials from the N.Hemisphere and mountains of Africa, S.America and New Guinea. The golden-leaved mutant of 1

Left above: *Ruscus aculeatus*
Left below: *Ruta graveolens*
Above: *Sagina subulata* Aurea
Right above: *Sagittaria sagittifolia*

species is available and used in carpet bedding: *S. subulata* Aurea (*S. glabra* and *S. pilifera* Aurea of gardens), heath pearlwort; W. and C.Europe; stems slender, much-branched, mat-forming; leaves 6–15mm long, bristle-like; flowers 5-petalled, about 5mm long, white, on thread-like stalks 2–4cm high, summer; cultivated for its golden-green foliage. Grow in well-drained soil in sun. Plant autumn to spring. Propagate by division in autumn and spring. May be grown in pots and over-wintered in a cold frame ready for summer bedding.

Sagittaria

(Latin *sagitta*, an arrowhead – the shape of the leaf-blades). Arrowhead. ALISMATACEAE. A genus of 20 species of aquatic and bog-dwelling perennials of cosmopolitan distribution. They are stoloniferous, often tuber-bearing, with tufts or clumps of linear to sagittate, submerged or aerial leaves and whorled racemes or panicles of 3-petalled, often unisexual white flowers. Grow in shallow water in a rich, loamy soil or in bogs or wet soil in sun. Plant spring. Propagate by division or separating tuber at planting time. Seed may be sown when ripe or in spring in pots or trays of soil stood in water, but development is slow.

Species cultivated: *S. japonica*, see *S. sagittifolia* Flore-pleno. *S. latifolia*, duck potato; N.America; tuberous, to 1m or more tall; leaves to 20cm long, ovate-sagittate with long, barb-like lobes; flowers about 3–4cm wide, summer to autumn. *S. natans*, see *S. subulata*. *S. sagittifolia*, common arrowhead, swamp potato; Europe, Asia; similar to *S. latifolia* but smaller with linear, submerged, translucent leaves and sagittate aerial ones; flowers 2cm wide, each petal with a basal violet blotch; will grow in water 30–45cm deep. *S.s.* Flore-pleno (*S. japonica* of gardens), flowers double. *S. subulata* (*S. natans* of gardens), S.E.USA; leaves reduced to linear phyllodes, submerged, to 1m or more long; flowers about 2cm wide, usually in a single whorl, late summer to autumn; mainly represented in gardens by a small form with phyllodes to 30cm long and grown as an aquarium plant.

Saint Bernard's lily – see *Anthericum liliago*.

Saint Dabeoc's heath – see *Daboecia*.

Saint John's wort – see *Hypericum*.

Saint Patrick's cabbage – see *Saxifraga spathularis*.

Salix

(Latin vernacular for willow). Sallow, willow. SALICACEAE. A genus of 300–500 species (depending on the botanical classifier) of trees and shrubs mainly from the N.Hemisphere. They are deciduous with alternate, linear to ovate, simple leaves and tiny, petalless, dioecious flowers packed into ovoid to cylindrical catkins. The seed is minute, and bears long, silky, tangled hairs for wind-dispersal. Some of the more vigorous species, mainly large shrub and tree species, are known as osiers and regularly stooled or pollarded for the production of long 1-year-old stems (osiers or withies) for basket-making. Grow in moderately fertile, moisture-retentive soil in sun or partial shade. Plant autumn to spring. Propagate by softwood cuttings under mist in summer or hardwood cuttings outside in autumn. Seed must be sown within a few days of ripening as it is very short-lived.

Species cultivated: *S. alba*, white willow; Europe, N.Asia, N.Africa; tree to 25m tall, having a rather narrow crown of pendulous-tipped branches; leaves 5–10cm long, lanceolate-acuminate, covered with silky-white appressed hairs; catkins with the young leaves, 2·5–5cm long, straw-yellow, best by the waterside. *S.a.* Britzensis, see *S.a.* Chermesina; *S.a. caerulea*, see *S.* × *rubens*; *S.a.* Chermesina, scarlet willow, winter twigs glossy orange-red, best grown annually stooled or pollarded to produce as many vigorous young stems as possible; *S.a.* Tristis, and *S.a.* Ramulis Aureis, see *S.* × *chrysocoma*; *S.a.* Vitellina (*S. vitellina*), winter twigs deep yellow, best stooled or pollarded; *S.a.* Vitellina Pendula, see *S.* × *chrysocoma*. *S. apoda*, Caucasus; prostrate shrublet to 60cm or more wide; leaves oval, to 3cm long, glossy above; catkins erect, the males to 2·5cm long, anthers yellow, before the leaves. *S. arbuscula*, N.Europe, N.USSR; twiggy shrub 30–60cm tall,

prostrate to ascending; leaves 5–20mm long, ovate to elliptic, lanceolate, glossy above, somewhat glaucous beneath; catkins with young leaves, to 1·5cm long. *S. babylonica*, weeping willow; China, but long cultivated in W.Asia, E.Europe and N.Africa; weeping tree 10–18m tall; stems brown; leaves 10–15cm long, narrowly lanceolate, glaucous beneath; catkins with young leaves 2·5–4cm long; often confused with other similar weeping willows, particularly with the yellow-twigged *S.* × *chrysocoma; S.b.* Annularis, leaves spirally curled. *S. basfordiana*, see *S.* × *rubens* Basfordiana. *S. bockii*, China; shrub eventually to 3m tall but of spreading habit and slow-growing; leaves oblong to obovate, to 2cm long; deep bright green above, glaucous and silky hairy beneath; catkins 2·5–4cm long, late summer to autumn; the only willow in

Top left: *Salix* × *chrysocoma*
Far left: *Salix daphnoides*
Above left: *Salix gracilistyla* Melanostachys
Left: *Salix hastata* Wehrhahnii
Top: *Salix lanata*
Above: *Salix myrsinites* in fruit

general cultivation to flower at this time of the year. *S.* × *boydii* (*S. lapponum* × *S. reticulata* or a mutant form of *S. lapponum*), Scotland; gnarled, erect, very slow-growing shrublet to 90cm tall; leaves about 2cm long, nearly orbicular to broadly obovate, prominently veined, grey-white downy; catkins 1–2cm long, females only are known and are rarely produced. *S. caerulea*, see *S.* × *rubens*. *S. caprea*, sallow, goat or pussy willow; Europe, S.W.Asia; large shrub or small tree 3–10m tall; leaves 5–10cm long, elliptic to obovate, dark green above when mature, grey woolly beneath; catkins before leaves 2–3·5cm long, the males showy when covered with yellow anthers. *S.c.* Pendula, Kilmarnock willow, stiffly pendulous habit, usually female. *S.* × *chrysocoma* (*S. alba* Vitellina Pendula, *S.a.* Tristis), (*S. alba* Vitellina × *S. babylonica*), tree to 20m tall with spreading crown and vertically pendulous branchlets; twigs yellow; leaves to 10cm long, slender-pointed, bright green above, glaucous beneath and somewhat silky hairy; catkins with the young leaves, to 5cm or more long; the best-known and most frequently seen weeping willow in Britain. *S.* × *c.* Sepulcralis (*S.* × *salamonii*, *S. sepulcralis*), (*S. alba* × *S. babylonica*), less vertically pendulous habit than type; twigs brownish, much confused with *S. babylonica*. *S. daphnoides*, violet willow; N.Europe, C.Asia, Himalaya; large shrub or small tree to 12m; young stems purple-brown overlaid with waxy-white patina; leaves to 10cm or more long, lanceolate, glaucous beneath; catkins before the leaves, to 5cm long, the males showy with yellow stamens; best pollarded or stooled if plenty of long white stems are wanted. *S. elaeagnos* (*S. incana* in part, *S. rosmarinifolia* of gardens), hoary willow; mountains of C. and S.Europe, Turkey; shrub 3–6m tall, spreading and bushy, or a small tree to 14m; leaves to 12cm long by 1–2cm wide, linear-lanceolate, green above, white-felted beneath when mature catkins with young leaves 2·5–4cm long. *S.e. angustifolia*, leaves narrowly linear, 5–10mm wide. *S. fargesii*, C.China; wide-spreading shrub eventually 2–3m tall; stems robust, polished reddish-brown in their second year, winter buds sealing-wax red; leaves 7–18cm long, elliptic to oblong, finely wrinkled and deep lustrous green above, silky hairy beneath; catkins erect, 10–15cm long with young leaves; much confused in gardens with the almost identical *S. moupinensis*, but that species has smooth leaf undersides. *S. fragilis*, crack willow; Europe to N.Russia, W.Siberia and Iran; tree 10–25m tall, with a broad crown of wide-spreading branches; twigs olive-brown, very fragile at the junctions; leaves 6–15cm long, lanceolate, slender-pointed, bright green above, glaucous beneath; catkins with the leaves, drooping, 2·5–7cm long; see also *S.* × *rubens*. *S. gracilistyla*, China, Korea, Japan; shrub 2–3m tall, usually of spreading habit; shoots grey-downy; leaves 5–10cm long, oblong-elliptic to narrowly ovate, grey-green above, glaucous and silky hairy beneath; catkins 2·5–4cm long, males reddish, before the leaves. *S.g.* Melanostachys, a male clone with almost black catkins having red stamens that burst to show yellow pollen. *S. hastata*, mountains of S.C.Europe to N.E.Asia and Kashmir; shrub to 1·5m tall; leaves 3–10cm long, broadly elliptic to obovate; catkins before or with very young leaves,

Left: *Salix alba* Chermesina
Above: *Salix matsudana* Tortuosa
Below: *Salix reticulata*

4–7cm long. *S.h.* Wehrhahnii, 1–1·2m tall, male catkins intense silvery hairy, then bright yellow with pollen and more decorative than the type species. *S.herbacea*, dwarf or least willow; N. polar regions and mountain tops of the northern temperate zone; mat-forming, rhizomatous shrublet rarely above 5cm tall to 30cm or more wide; leaves 6–20mm long, broadly ovate to obovate or orbicular, glossy above; catkins with the leaves, erect, 5–15mm long; a true dwarf shrub and not herbaceous in the accepted sense. *S. incana*, see *S. elaeagnos*. *S. irrorata*, S.W.USA; shrub to 3m tall, of erect habit; young stems brown-purple with waxy-white patina; leaves 5–10cm long, oblong to narrowly lanceolate, glossy above, glaucous beneath; catkins before leaves to 2·5cm long, of similar value to *S. daphnoides* and best stooled or pollarded for winter effect. *S. lanata*, woolly willow; arctic and subarctic Europe and Asia; shrub 60–120cm tall; stems robust, grey woolly; leaves 2·5–6·5cm long, ovate to obovate, silky downy above at first, persistently so beneath; catkins with leaves, males to 5cm long, females to 8cm, silky yellow hairy. *S. magnifica*, W.China; shrub or small tree to 6m tall, of sparse habit; stems robust, reddish or purplish-brown, buds red; leaves to 20cm or more long, magnolia-like, elliptic to obovate, greyish-green above, somewhat glaucous beneath; catkins with leaves, males to 18cm long, females to 30cm. *S. matsudana*, Pekin willow; China; tree 12–16m tall, of pyramidal habit; leaves 5–10cm long, narrowly lanceolate, glaucous beneath; catkins with leaves, 1·5–2·5cm long. *S.m.* Pendula, similar to *S. babylonica* and disease-resistant; *S.m.* Tortuosa, branches and young catkins curiously contorted. *S. melanostachys*, see *S. gracilistyla* Melanostachys. *S. moupinensis*, see comments under *S. fargesii*. *S. myrsinites*, whortle-leaved willow; N.Europe, N.Asia; shrub 10–40cm tall; stems decumbent, often loosely mat-forming; leaves 1·5–3cm long, ovate to elliptic, bright glossy green; catkins usually with the young leaves, 2–5cm long. *S. purpurea*, purple osier or willow; Europe to Siberia and Japan, south to N.Africa and Turkey; shrub to 3m tall; leaves 4–10cm long, obovate-oblong to narrowly lanceolate, often in opposite pairs; catkins before the leaves, 2–3·5cm long; a very distinctive species with its opposite leaves. *S.p.* Eugenei, to 5m or more tall, often of small tree form, catkins grey-pink, freely borne; *S.p.* Gracilis, dwarf, compact habit; *S.p.* Pendula, small stature, weeping habit. *S. repens*, creeping willow; Europe to C.Asia and Siberia; usually prostrate to decumbent, mat-forming shrub to about 30cm tall by 2–3m wide, but in some forms almost erect, to 2m or so tall; leaves 1–4cm long, lanceolate to elliptic or oblong, silvery silky hairy beneath, and usually also above when young; catkins before the leaves, 5–25mm long. *S.r. argentea*, leaves persistently silvery hairy on both sides. *S. reticulata*, net-leaved willow; arctic and subarctic regions and mountains farther south; mat-forming shrublet 10–15cm tall by 60cm or more wide; leaves 1–3cm long, broadly elliptic to orbicular, cordate, prominently net-veined and finely rugose above, glaucous beneath; catkins with the well-developed leaves, 1·2–3cm long. *S. rosmarinifolia* of gardens, see *S. elaeagnos*. *S.* × *rubens* (*S.* × *viridis*), (*S. alba* × *S. fragilis*), range of hybrid forms combining parental characters in varying ways, in gardens often mistaken for *S. fragilis*. *S.* × *r.* Coerulea (*S. alba caerulea*), cricket-bat willow; similar to *S. alba* but leaves almost hairless, bluish-green above and glaucous beneath. *S.*×*r.* Basfordiana (*S. fragilis basfordiana*, *S. basfordiana*), similar to *S. fragilis*, a male clone with orange-red winter stems. *S. sachalinensis*, Japan, Sakhalin Is; tree to 10m tall; leaves 6–10cm long, lanceolate, dark green above, somewhat glaucous and slightly downy beneath; catkins before the leaves, 2–5cm long, the males conspicuous. *S.s.* Sekka (*S.s.* Setsuka), a percentage of the stems always fasciated. *S.* × *salamonii* and *S. sepulcralis*, see *S.* × *chrysocoma* Sepulcralis. *S.* × *smithiana* (*S. cinerea* × *S. viminalis*), small group of hybrids combining the parental characters in various ways, usually a tree to 6m or more tall; leaves 7–15cm long, oblong-lanceolate, dark green above, glaucous and downy beneath; catkins before the leaves 2·5–5cm long, males with yellow stamens, and borne in abundance; one of the most handsome of the flowering willows. *S. triandra*, almond willow; large shrub or small tree 4–10m tall, with smooth, flaking bark; leaves 5–10cm long, oblong-ovate to lanceolate, rich lustrous green above, glaucous beneath; catkins with leaves 2·5–5cm long, males with yellow stamens and fragrant; sometimes flowers a second time late summer; much grown, especially in Europe as an osier. *S. viminalis*, common osier; Europe to Caucasus, Himalaya, Japan; large shrub or small tree to 5m or more tall; stems densely downy when young; leaves 10–25cm long, linear-lanceolate, gradually tapered to a slender point, undulate, dark green above, white silky downy beneath; catkins before the leaves, 2·5–6cm long, males with yellow anthers; much grown for basket-making. *S. vitellina*, see *S. alba* Vitellina. *S. wehrhahnii*, see *S. hastata* Wehrhahnii.

Sallow – see *Salix caprea*.

Salmon berry – see *Rubus spectabilis*.

Salpiglossis

(Greek *salpinx*, a trumpet, and *glossa*, a tongue – alluding to the clarinet-shaped style). SOLANACEAE. A genus of 5–18 species (depending upon the botanical authority) of annuals, biennials and perennials allied to *Petunia* from S.America, 1 of which is commonly cultivated: *S. sinuata* (the following 10 synonyms are all sometimes listed: *S. atropurpurea*, *S. barclayana*, *S. coccinea*, *S. flava*, *S. gloxiniiflora*, *S. grandiflora*, *S. picta*, *S. staminea*, *S. superbissima*, *S. variabilis*), painted tongue (USA); Chile; almost hardy annual 60–90cm tall, branching in the lower part; leaves alternate, up to 10cm long at base, elliptic, pinnatifid or sinuately toothed, sticky downy; flowers in terminal racemes, funnel-shaped, 5-lobed, to 6·5cm long by 5cm wide, in many shades of red, purple, blue, yellow, often striped or with a

Above: *Salpiglossis sinuata*
Right: *Salvia haematodes*

contrasting vein pattern, summer, autumn; several horticultural strains are listed under cultivar names, most of them with larger flowers in a wider range of colours and shades. Grow in humus rich soil in sun. Sow seed in spring at 18°C. Prick off seedlings when 1–2 true leaves show, at 4–5cm apart each way into boxes of a standard potting mixture. Harden off and plant out when fear of frost has passed. Seed may also be sown *in situ* in late spring. *Salpiglossis* make attractive pot plants for a cool greenhouse and can be had in bloom in winter and spring from a late summer to early autumn sowing, provided a winter minimum temperature of about 16°C can be maintained.

Salvia

(Latin *salvus*, safe or well – from the reputed medicinal qualities of several species). LABIATAE. A genus of 700–750 species of annuals, biennials perennials, sub-shrubs and shrubs of world-wide distribution. They are often of erect habit with stems square in cross-section, linear to obovate – sometimes pinnately cut – leaves in opposite pairs, and tubular, 2-lipped flowers in whorls from the upper leaf-axils forming spike-like inflorescences. Grow hardy and half-hardy species in well-drained, fertile soil in sun, the latter in warm, sheltered sites or in a frost-free greenhouse. See also individual species descriptions for any additional cultural comments. Plant spring, the hardy perennials also in autumn. Propagate all species from seed in spring, half-hardy ones under glass at about 16°C, perennials by division at planting time and sub-shrubs and shrubs by cuttings late spring to late summer.

Species cultivated (all summer-flowering): *S. ambigens*, see *S. guaranitica*. *S. argentea*, silver sage (USA); S.Europe; herbaceous or semi-evergreen perennial 75–90cm tall; leaves mostly basal, to 20cm long, ovate to oblong, irregularly shallowly lobed or toothed, white woolly, particularly when young; flowers to 5cm long, white- or pink-tinged, in branched, panicle-like clusters; needs a well-drained site, but hardier than sometimes suggested. *S. coerulea*, see *S. guaranitica*. *S. elegans* (*S. rutilans*), pineapple-scented sage; Mexico; sub-shrub to 1m tall; leaves 5–10cm long, ovate-cordate, downy, toothed, aromatically pineapple-scented; flowers to 4cm long, scarlet; needs a sheltered site and winter protection in all but the mildest areas. *S. farinacea*, Texas, New Mexico; almost hardy perennial 60–90cm tall; leaves 4–7·5cm long, ovate to lanceolate, coarsely, irregularly toothed; flowers 1–1·5cm long, violet-blue in woolly white calyces often purple-tinted; usually grown as a half-hardy annual. *S. grahamii*, Mexico; almost hardy shrub 1–1·2m tall; leaves 2–7cm long, ovate, somewhat downy; flowers to 2cm long, deep red, ageing magenta; hardy in moderate frosts in sheltered sites. *S. guaranitica* (*S. ambigens*, *S. coerulea*), S.E.Brazil to N.Argentina; half-hardy, woody-based perennial or sub-shrub 1–1·5m tall; leaves 5–13cm long, ovate, hairy; flowers 4–5cm long, dark blue to violet, sometimes lilac and with a white base; can be grown as a half-hardy annual. *S. haematodes*, Greece; biennial or short-lived perennial to 90cm or more tall; basal leaves long-stalked, 20–25cm long, ovate-cordate, crenate, rugose, hairy beneath; flowers 1·5cm long, blue-violet in large, pyramidal, panicle-like clusters. *S. horminum*, see *S. viridis*. *S. involucrata*, rosy leaf sage (USA); Mexico, C.America; near hardy sub-shrub 90–120cm tall; leaves 5–10cm long, ovate, crenate; flowers 4–5cm long, pink to red, covered by conspicuous, pink to reddish bracts when in bud; late summer to autumn; needs a mild area. *S.i.* Bethellii, more robust than type, leaves and floral bracts larger. *S. neurepia*, Mexico; sub-shrub to 2m; leaves about 5cm long, ovate, softly hairy, yellow-green, aromatic; flowers 2–3cm long, carmine; best against a sheltered wall. *S. officinalis*, sage; S.Europe; hardy evergreen shrub to 60cm or more; leaves 2·5–6·5cm long, oblong, grey-green, finely wrinkled; flowers light violet-blue, pink or white *S.o.* Alba, flowers white; *S.o.* Icterina, leaves gold-variegated; *S.o.* Purpurascens, leaves purple-flushed; *S.o.* Tricolor, leaves splashed creamy-white with tints of pink and purple; all have sage flavours. *S. patens*, mountains of Mexico; tuberous-rooted, almost hardy perennial 60–90cm tall; leaves 6–13cm long, triangular to oblong-ovate, cordate or with 2 basal lobes, crenate, hairy; flowers 5–7cm long, gentian-blue; will survive even cold winters provided the crowns are protected. *S. rutilans*, see *S. elegans*. *S. sclarea*, clary; S.Europe; biennial or short-lived perennial to 1m tall; basal leaves 12–23cm long, broadly ovate-cordate, downy, wrinkled; flowers 2·5cm long, pale blue to lilac, surrounded by white, pink or lilac-tinted bracts, borne in narrowly pyramidal, panicle-like clusters. *S.s. turkestanica*, usually more robust than type, flowers white, pink-tinted with larger, more conspicuous bracts. *S. splendens*, scarlet sage; S.Brazil; tender sub-shrub 1–2m tall but grown as a half-hardy annual 30–50cm tall in cool climates; leaves to 9cm long, ovate-acuminate, toothed; flowers to 4cm long, surrounded by bracts in bud, both bright scarlet; several cultivars are readily available in various shades of scarlet, ranging from 25–40cm tall when grown as an annual; purple- and white-flowered and taller selections are sometimes available. *S.* × *superba* (*S. virgata nemorosa*), (probably *S. nemorosa* × *S. pratensis* × *S. villicaulis*), herbaceous perennial

Left below: *Salvia* × *superba*
Left: *Salvia officinalis* Purpurascens
Above: *Salvia splendens*
Below: *Salvia viridis*
Bottom: *Salvia argentea*

90cm or more tall; leaves 3–7·5cm long, ovate-oblong, toothed, finely wrinkled; flowers 1cm long, violet-purple, surrounded by red-purple bracts in dense spikes. *S. uliginosa*, bog sage (USA); S.Brazil to Argentina; almost hardy herbaceous perennial to 1·5m tall; leaves up to 10cm long, oblong-lanceolate, deeply toothed; flowers 1·5–2cm long, azure-blue; needs a moist soil and a sheltered site or winter protection in cold areas. *S. virgata nemorosa*, see *S.* × *superba*. *S. viridis* (*S. horminum*), S.E.Europe; branched hardy annual to 45cm tall; leaves 2·5–6·5cm long, elliptic to ovate-oblong, crenate, hairy; flowers 1cm long, pale lilac to purple, not showy, in spikes crowned by a tuft of large, scarlet, crimson, purple, blue or white bracts with darker veins; this species is often wrongly and confusingly listed as clary in catalogues – see *S. sclarea*.

Above: *Salvia officinalis* Icterina
Below: *Salvia neurepia*

Sambucus

(old Latin vernacular for elder). Elder. SAMBUCACEAE (CAPRIFOLIACEAE). A genus of about 20 species of deciduous shrubs or small trees of almost cosmopolitan distribution. They have hollow, pith-filled stems, opposite pairs of pinnate leaves and compound umbel- or panicle-like cymes of small, white, rotate flowers with 5 lobes. The small, globular, fleshy fruit is a berry-like drupe, edible in some species, poisonous in others. Grow in any fairly moisture-retentive but well-drained soil in sun or partial shade. Plant autumn to spring. Propagate from seed when ripe, by semi-hardwood cuttings in summer, hardwood cuttings outside in autumn or division where possible at planting time.

Species cultivated: *S. canadensis*, American or sweet elder; E. N.America; shrub 2·5–4m tall; leaflets usually 7, elliptic to lanceolate, up to 14cm long; umbel-like cymes to 25cm wide, summer; fruit purple-black, edible. *S.c.* Aurea, leaves golden-yellow, fruit red. *S.c.* Maxima, more robust than type, cymes to 35cm wide. *S.c.* Rubra, fruit red. *S.c.* Scotia and *S.c.* York, both selected for quality and yield of fruit – other cultivars grown for fruit are available in USA. *S. nigra*, common or European elder; Europe, N.Africa, W.Asia; large shrub or small tree 4–10m tall; leaflets 5–7, ovate-lanceolate to elliptic, to 9cm long; umbel-like cymes to 15cm or more wide, summer; fruit glossy black, edible. *S.n.* Albovariegata (*S.n.* Marginata, *S.n.* Argenteomarginata), leaflets with irregularly cream-white margins; *S.n.* Aurea, golden elder, leaves golden-yellow. *S.n.* Laciniata, fern-leaved elder, leaves divided into thread-like segments; *S.n.* Purpurea, leaves flushed purple. *S. racemosa*, red-berried elder; Europe, W.Asia; shrub to 4m tall; leaflets 5–7, ovate to elliptic, 4–8cm long; cymes panicle-like, ovoid, to 7cm long, late spring; fruit scarlet. *S.r.* Plumosa Aurea, leaflets golden-yellow, deeply cut with slender segments. *S.r.* Tenuifolia, small shrub with slender stems and deeply divided leaflets like a Japanese maple cultivar.

Sand myrtle – see *Leiophyllum*.

Sandwort – see *Arenaria*.

Sanguinaria

(Latin *sanguis*, blood – all parts of the plant, in particular the roots, exude a reddish sap when injured). PAPAVERACEAE. A genus of 1 species of rhizomatous perennial from E. N.America: *S. canadensis*, bloodroot, red puccoon; plant is a stout-branched fleshy, rhizome that gives rise to solitary, long-stalked leaves 15–30cm tall when fully developed; leaf-blades to 15cm or more wide, rounded, cordate, with overlapping, rounded lobes and a scalloped margin, blue-grey and prominently veined; flowers to 4cm wide, solitary, 8–16 petalled; spring, with unfurling young leaves. *S.c.* Multiplex (*S.c.* Plena, *S.c.* Flore Plena), flowers fully double. Grow in humus-rich, moisture-retentive soil in dappled or partial shade. Plant when dormant, preferably autumn, or immediately after flowering. Propagate by division at planting time or from seed when ripe, the latter germinating irregularly up to 1½ years later and slow to reach maturity.

Sanguisorba

(Latin *sanguis*, blood, and *sorbeo*, to soak up – some species were reputed to have styptic qualities). Blood root, burnet. ROSACEAE. A genus of 3–30 species, depending on the botanical authority, of herbaceous perennials from the northern temperate zone. They are clump-forming with long-stalked, pinnate leaves and almost globular to cylindrical spikes of petalless flowers with prominent stamens and brush-like stigmas. Grow in fertile, well-drained, but not dry soil in sun. Plant autumn to spring. Propagate by division at planting time or from seed in spring, preferably in a cold frame.

Species cultivated (all formerly included in the genus *Poterium*): *S. canadensis*, E. N.America; 1·2–2m tall; stems branched; leaflets 7–17, narrowly oblong to ovate, 2·5–9cm long; flower-spikes 5–20cm long, white, summer. *S. minor* (*P. sanguisorba*), salad burnet; Europe, Asia; 40–60cm tall; leaflets 9–21, rounded to oblong, 5–10mm long; flower-spikes globular to shortly cylindrical, 1·5cm long, green, purple-tinted, styles purple-red, summer. *S. obtusa*

Left above: *Sambucus racemosa* Plumosa Aurea
Left bottom: *Sanguinaria canadensis* Multiplex
Below: *Sanguisorba canadensis*
Bottom: *Sanguisorba obtusa*

(*P. obtusa* and *P. obtusatum* of gardens), Japan; about 1·2m tall, leaflets 5–16, ovate to elliptic, 4–6·5cm long, glaucous beneath; flower-spikes 5–9cm long, rose-purple, summer. *S. officinalis*, great burnet; Europe, Asia; similar to *S. canadensis*, but spikes shorter, deep reddish to purplish; young leaves can be used for flavouring salads etc. *S. tenuifolia*, Asia; to 1·2m or more tall; stems slender; leaflets 13–21, narrowly oblong, 3–7cm long; flower-spikes 5cm long, pink or red, summer. *S.t.* Alba, flowers white.

Santolina

(Latin *sanctum linum*, holy flax – used for 1 species). COMPOSITAE. A genus of 8–10 species of small, aromatic, evergreen shrubs from the Mediterranean region. They have alternate, narrow, usually toothed or pinnate leaves, and button-like flower-heads without any ray florets. Grow in well-drained soil in sun. Plant autumn to spring. Propagate by semi-hardwood cuttings in late summer in a cold frame or hardwood cuttings in autumn *in situ*. May be sheared over annually to maintain a neat, compact habit.

Species cultivated: *S. chamaecyparissus* (*S. incana*), lavender cotton; W. to C.Mediterranean; 40–60cm tall, hummock-forming, whole plant densely grey-white downy; leaves 2–4cm long, leaflets to 2mm long, bluntly cylindrical, arranged in 4 ranks at right angles to the mid-rib; flower-heads to 1cm wide, lemon-yellow on almost leafless stems, late summer. *S.c. insularis* (*S. neapolitana*), C.Mediterranean, usually of somewhat taller, looser habit, with longer, more feathery leaves having leaflets 2·5mm or more long; *S.c.i.* Sulphurea, leaves grey-green, flowers primrose-yellow; *S.c.* Nana (*S.c.* Compacta, *S.c.* Corsica), dwarfer, denser habit than type; *S.c. tomentosa* (*S. pinnata*), Pyrenees to C.Italy, leaves hairless or almost so, green, flowers off-white. *S. incana*, see *S. chamaecyparissus*. *S. neapolitana*, see *S. chamaecyparissus insularis*. *S. pectinata*, see *S. rosmarinifolia*. *S. pinnata*, see *S. chamaecyparissus tomentosa*. *S. rosmarinifolia* (*S. pectinata*, *S. virens*, *S. viridis*), Spain, Portugal, S.France; to 45cm or more tall; leaves 2–5cm long, narrowly linear with closely appressed teeth, bright green; flower-heads 7–12mm wide, bright yellow. *S.r.* Primrose Gem, flowers pale yellow. *S. virens*, see *S. rosmarinifolia*. *S. viridis*, see *S. rosmarinifolia*.

Sanvitalia

(for Professor Federico Sanvitali, 1704–1761, Italian botanist). COMPOSITAE. A genus of 7 species of annuals, perennials and shrubs from S.W.USA, Mexico, C.America and Bolivia to Argentina, 1 of which is generally available: *S. procumbens*, creeping zinnia; Mexico, Guatemala; hardy, decumbent annual forming wide mounds to 15cm tall; leaves in opposite pairs, to 6·5cm long, ovate to lanceolate, strigose; flower-heads daisy-like, 2·5cm, with broad black-purple centres and short, broad, ray florets, summer to autumn. Grow in fertile, well-drained soil in sun. Sow seed *in situ* autumn or spring, or early spring under glass at 13–16°C, pricking off seedlings when first pair of true leaves shows and planting out in late spring to early summer.

Saponaria

(Latin *sapo*, soap – the roots of *S. officinalis* lather when crushed and were once used as a soap substitute). CARYOPHYLLACEAE. A genus of 30 species of annuals, biennials and perennials from Europe and Asia, but mainly the Mediterranean. They are tufted or rhizomatous, erect to decumbent, with terminal cymes of 5-petalled flowers with tubular calyces. At the eye of each flower is a ring of 5 scales forming a minute corona. Grow in any moderately fertile soil in sun. Plant autumn to spring. Propagate by division at planting time, cuttings of non-flowering stems late spring or late summer or from seed in spring.

Species cultivated: *S.* × Bressingham, hybrid of unspecified parentage but with the habit of *S. pumilio*; flowers 1·2cm wide, rich pink with rounded petals. *S. caespitosa*, Pyrenees (Spain, France); perennial, densely tufted, 5–10cm tall; leaves linear-lanceolate, about 2·5cm long; flowers in head-like terminal clusters, each bloom 1–1·5cm wide, rose-purple, summer; needs a sheltered site outside or an alpine house. *S. ocymoides*, S.W. and S.C.Europe; perennial, tufted, mat-forming, to 15cm tall by 60–100cm wide; leaves 1·5–2·5cm wide, ovate-lanceolate to elliptic or almost spathulate; flowers in loose cymes, each about 1cm wide, rose-purple, summer. *S.o.* Alba, flowers white; *S.o.* Rubra, flowers deep red; *S.o.* Rubra Compacta, smaller than type, compact habit; *S.o.* Splendens, flowers larger than type, deeper rose-purple. *S. officinalis*, bouncing Bet, soapwort; Europe, Asia, naturalized USA; rhizomatous perennial forming colonies, to 90cm tall; leaves 5–10cm long, ovate to lanceolate;

Far left: *Santolina chamaecyparissus* Nana
Left above: *Sanvitalia procumbens*
Above: *Saponaria ocymoides*

Far left below: *Santolina chamaecyparissus insularis*
Left below: *Saponaria officinalis* Roseo Plena
Below: *Saponaria ocymoides* Rubra Compacta

flowers clustered in panicle-like inflorescences, each bloom 2·5–4cm wide, pink or white. *S.o.* Alba Plena, *S.o.* Roseo Plena and *S.o.* Rubro Plena are all double-flowered, white, pink and red respectively; rather invasive, especially on rich soils. *S.* × *olivana* (*S. pumilio* × *S. caespitosa*), blending parental characters and similar in general effect to the former, but easier to grow and flowering more freely. *S. pumilio* (*Silene pumila*), E.Alps, S.E.Carpathians; densely tufted, forming small, flat mats; leaves 1·2–2·5cm long, linear, somewhat fleshy, bright green; flowers almost sessile; about 2cm wide, petals deeply cleft, bright rose, summer; not easy to grow and must have acid soil.

Sarana – see *Fritillaria.*

Sarcococca

(Greek *sarkos*, flesh, and *kokkos*, a berry – alluding to the plants' close relationship to box, but having fleshy, not dry fruit). BUXACEAE. A genus of about 14 species of evergreen shrubs from Himalaya, W.China and S.E.Asia. They have alternate to almost opposite pairs of ovate to lanceolate leaves, axillary clusters of unisexual, petalless, often fragrant flowers, the males having conspicuous

white stamen-filaments, and black or red berries. Grow in any well-drained but moisture-retentive soil, preferably humus-rich, in partial shade, sheltered from cold winds. Plant autumn or spring. Propagate by cuttings in late summer in a cold frame or seed when ripe. Unless otherwise stated, the species are fairly hardy and flower in winter.

Species cultivated: *S. confusa*, probably China; eventually to 2m tall, of dense, spreading habit; leaves elliptic, 3–5cm or more long, smooth dark green above; male flowers cream, female flowers with 2–3 stigmas; fruit black. *S. hookeriana*, W.China; to 2m tall, of suckering habit; leaves 4–8cm long, oblong to lanceolate, slender-pointed; male flowers white, sometimes pink-tinted, females with 3 stigmas; fruit black; not reliably hardy in severe winters; usually represented in gardens by *S.h. digyna*, somewhat dwarfer and more slender, stems purplish in some forms, female flowers with 2 stigmas, hardy. *S.h. humilis* (*S. humilis*), rarely above 60cm tall, upper leaves often in opposite pairs, male flowers pink, female flowers with 2 stigmas. *S. humilis*, see *S. hookeriana humilis*. *S. ruscifolia*, sweet box; C.China; similar to *S. confusa* but 60–120cm tall; leaves broadly ovate, deep lustrous green above, paler beneath; male flowers milky-white; fruit red; often represented in gardens by *S.r. chinensis*, more vigorous, to 2m tall, leaves longer and narrower, much more like *S. confusa* than the type but distinguished by female flowers always with 3 stigmas and red fruit.

Sarothamnus scoparius – see *Cytisus scoparius.*

Sassafras

(derived from the local Indian name through the French settlers in Florida). LAURACEAE. A genus of 3 species of deciduous, spicily aromatic trees, 1 each in N.America, China and Taiwan, 1 of which is generally available: *S. albidum* (*S. officinale*, *S. variifolium*), sassafras; E. N.America; to 18m but often a large, bushy shrub 6–10m tall in gardens; leaves alternate, 6–13cm long, usually with 3, broad, forward-pointing lobes, but often with 1 or both lobes reduced or missing, glossy above, glaucous beneath, red and orange in autumn; flowers dioecious, 6mm wide, with 6 greenish-yellow perianth segments, borne in short racemes; fruit 1cm long, ovoid, dark blue. Grow in humus-rich, moisture-retentive soil in sun or partial shade. Plant

Above left: *Sarcococca confusa*
Above: *Sassafras albidum* autumn colour

autumn to spring. Propagate by suckers at planting time, root cuttings late winter in a cold frame, and from seed when ripe.

Satureja

(*Satureia*). (Latin vernacular name for savory). Savory. LABIATAE. A genus of about 30 species of aromatic annuals, perennials and sub-shrubs from temperate and warm regions, mainly the Mediterranean. They have opposite pairs of linear to ovate leaves and tubular, 2-lipped flowers in whorled spikes or spike-like panicles formed of several stalked, axillary cymes. Grow in well-drained soil in sun. Plant autumn or spring. Propagate by cuttings in late spring, division at planting time, or from seed *in situ* in spring.

Species cultivated: *S. hortensis*, summer savory; Mediterranean region; a slender, erect annual, 15–30cm tall, with linear leaves and small, tubular, pale purple to almost white flowers in the upper leaf axils. *S. montana*, winter savory; S. Europe, N.Africa; semi-evergreen sub-shrub, 15–30cm tall; leaves 1–3cm long, linear to oblanceolate; flowers 8–14mm long, usually pale purple, in rather loose, leafy spikes, summer; a very variable species, some forms grown as ornamentals, eg *S.m.* Caerulea, with purple-blue flowers and *S.m. illyrica* (*S. subspicata*), flowers in dense spikes. *S. repanda*, a name of no botanical standing, used in gardens for *S. spicigera*. *S. rupestris*, see *Micromeria thymifolia*. *S. spicigera* (*S. repanda* of gardens), Turkey and

Below: *Satureja hortensis*

Above: *Satureja montana*

adjacent USSR; prostrate, mat-forming sub-shrub to 5cm high by 60cm or more wide; leaves 1–2cm long, linear to narrowly lanceolate; flowers about 8mm long, white, in stalked cymes forming spike-like panicles to 10cm or more long, late summer to autumn. *S. subspicata*, see *S. montana illyrica*.

Savory – see *Satureja.*

Saxegothaea

(for Prince Albert of Saxe-Coburg-Gotha, 1819–1861, Consort of Queen Victoria and a patron of horticulture). PODOCARPACEAE. A genus of 1 species of coniferous evergreen tree from S.Chile and adjacent Argentina: *S. conspicua*, Prince Albert's Yew; eventually to 15m tall but slow-growing; rather yew-like but with scaly bark; leaves spirally arranged, 1–2cm long, linear, dark green above, glaucous beneath; male and female flowers (strobili) on the same tree, the males small, ovoid, in the upper leaf-axils; cones 8–12mm wide, rounded but angular with fleshy, grooved scales; not totally hardy in severe winters. Grow in well-drained but moisture-retentive soil in sheltered, sunny or partially shaded sites. Plant spring. Propagate from seed in a cold frame in spring or by cuttings in a frost-free greenhouse or frame in late summer.

Saxifraga

(Latin *saxum*, a rock, *frango*, to break – alluding to the supposed ability of the plants to break rocks, from the habit of some species found growing in rock crevices). Rockfoil or saxifrage. SAXIFRAGACEAE. A genus of about 350 species of mainly small perennials and a few annuals from mountains and rocky places in the northern temperate zone and S. America. They are largely of tufted habit with linear to orbicular leaves in rosettes that are often arranged in mats or cushions. Some species have leaves with a marginal white or silvery encrustation of lime that adds to their attraction. The 5-petalled flowers are borne in racemes, panicles or cymes, the scapes with few or much reduced leaves. Grow in well-drained soil in sun or partial shade, although some species will grow in full shade, eg *S. × urbium* and *S. umbrosa*. Plant autumn or spring or later if pot-grown. Propagate from seed when ripe or in spring, by division at planting time or after flowering and by cuttings of single rosettes summer to autumn.

Species cultivated (spring-flowering unless stated otherwise); *S. aizoon* see *S. paniculata*. *S. × apiculata* (*S. juniperifolia sancta × S. marginata rocheliana*), low cushion- to mat-forming, to 30cm wide or more; leaves about 1cm long, linear-oblong, sharp-pointed; flowering stems 6–10cm tall, flowers several, 1cm wide, primrose-yellow. *S. × a.* Alba, flowers white. *S. × borisii (S. ferdinandi-coburgii × S. marginata)*, blends characters of parents, with yellow flowers. *S. boryi*, see *S. marginata*. *S. burseriana*, E.Alps; small cushion- to mat-forming; leaves 5–12mm long, linear, glaucous; flowers solitary, white, about 2cm wide, on reddish, 2–5cm stalks. *S.b.* Crenata, petals crimped; *S.b.* Gloria, flowers to 3cm wide; *S.b.* Major, more robust than type, large flowers. *S. caesia*, Pyrenees to Alps, W. Carpathians and Appennines; dense, small cushion-forming; leaves 3–6mm long, oblong-spathulate to elliptic, glaucous and encrusted; flowering scapes 4–10cm tall, flowers several, 1–1·5cm wide, white. *S. callosa* (*S. lingulata*), Appennines, Sicily, Maritime Alps; low cushion- to mat-forming; leaves 2·5–9cm long, linear to oblanceolate, glaucous and lime-encrusted, often red at base; panicles 30–45cm tall, columnar to narrowly pyramidal, arching, flowers 1·3–1·8cm wide, white, often crimson-dotted, early summer. *S.c. catalaunica* (*S. catalaunica*), leaves 1·5–3cm long, oblanceolate, panicles smaller. *S. × canis-dalmatica* (*S. paniculata × S. cotyledon*), midway between parents; flowering stems to 30cm tall, flowers white, heavily purple-spotted. *S. cochlearis*, Maritime Alps; rosettes in hummock-like tufts; leaves 1–4cm long, narrowly spathulate with thickened, reflexed tips, densely encrusted; flowering stems to 15cm or more, flowers in panicles, about 1·5cm wide, white, usually red-dotted. *S.c.* Minor, miniature form with rosettes to 1·5cm wide. *S. cotyledon* (*S. pyramidalis*), S.Alps, C.Pyrenees, Iceland, Scandinavia; rosettes large, clustered; leaves tongue-shaped with broad tips, 3–7cm long, encrusted; panicles pyramidal, to 50cm or more tall, flowers numerous, to 2cm wide, white, fragrant, summer; best in lime-free soil; several larger forms are sometimes available, including *S.c.* Caterhamensis, having red-dotted flowers. *S. crustata*, E.Alps to Yugoslavia; densely cushion- or mat-forming; leaves 1·5–6cm long, linear, glaucous and encrusted; panicles 12–30cm tall, flowers about 1·5cm wide, white, summer. *S. cuneifolia*, mountains of N. Spain to N.W.Yugoslavia; mat-forming; rosettes flattened; leaves broadly spathulate, 2–4cm long, fleshy-leathery, dark green; panicles 15–20cm or more tall, flowers 6–8mm wide, white, yellow at the base, late spring; grows best in shade. *S. × elizabethae* (*S. burseriana × S. juniperifolia sancta*), blends characters of parents, forming vigorous, blue-green mats with head-like clusters of yellow flowers. *S. ferdinandi-coburgii*, mountains of Bulgaria and Greece; rosettes columnar, closely packed to form hard cushions; leaves 5–7mm long, linear-oblong, prickle-tipped, glaucous; flowering stems 3–7cm tall, flowers in fairly compact cymes, 1–1·5cm wide, bright yellow. *S. fortunei*, China, Japan; small clump-forming, deciduous; leaves long-stalked, blades 5–15cm wide, rounded to kidney-shaped, palmately lobed and toothed, somewhat fleshy, often purplish beneath; panicles loose and graceful, to 40cm tall, flowers white, about 1cm wide with 1 or 2 pendulous lower petals to 1·5cm long, autumn; best in humus-rich soil in shade. *S.f.* Wada's Form, leaves flushed deep wine-purple. *S. × geum* (*S. hirsuta × S. umbrosa*), blends characters of parents; leaf-blades like *S. umbrosa* with narrow, hairy leaf-stalks and flowers of *S. hirsuta*, often confused in cultivation with the true *S. hirsuta* (qv). *S. granulata*, meadow saxifrage, fair maids of France; Europe; tufted to narrowly clump-forming; leaves deciduous, long-stalked, blades 1–3cm wide, kidney-shaped, crenate, white glandular-hairy; flowering stems 10–30cm tall, flowers in cymes, about 2cm wide, pure white; the plant over-winters as a cluster of small bulbils just below soil level: these afford an easy means of propagation. *S.g.* Flore-Pleno (*S.g.* Plena), flowers larger than type, fully double; *S. grisebachii*, Balkan Peninsula; rosettes forming irregular hummocks or cushions; leaves 1–3cm long, oblanceolate to spathulate, silvery-grey; inflorescence spike-like, 10–18cm tall, the stem and bract-like leaves covered with a plush of purple-red glandular hairs; flowers 4–5mm wide with pale

Far left below: *Saxifraga × apiculata*
Far left bottom: *Saxifraga ×* Jenkinsae
Left below: *Saxifraga juniperifolia* Macedonica
Left bottom: *Saxifraga longifolia*
Below: *Saxifraga marginata*
Bottom: *Saxifraga cotyledon*

purple or pink petals partly concealed by the inflated, red hairy calyces. *S.g.* Wisley, stem leaves and calyces more richly coloured than type. *S. hirsuta*, kidney saxifrage; Pyrenees, S.W.Ireland; sometimes naturalized elsewhere; mat-forming; leaves long-stalked, blades 1–4cm long, orbicular to ovate-oblong, crenate, hispid, often reddish beneath; flowering stems 12–30cm tall, glandular hairy, panicles diffuse, flowers 7–10mm wide, white, yellow in centre, with or without crimson dots, summer; seldom available but included because of its confusion with *S.* × *geum*. *S. hypnoides*, mossy saxifrage, Dovedale moss; N.W.Europe; mat-forming, composed of creeping leafy stems and rosettes; leaves linear or 3–5 lobed, 1–2cm long; flowering stems 10–20cm tall, flowers few, 1–2cm wide, white; seldom cultivated, being represented in gardens by forms and hybrids, eg *S.h.* Kingii, compact habit, leaves turning red in winter. *S.* × Irvingii (probably *S. burseriana* × *S. lilacina*), cushion-forming; leaves glaucous; flowers pale lilac-pink, early spring. *S.* × Jenkinsae, probably the same parentage as *S.* × Irvingii and very similar to that plant but somewhat more robust with flowers of a richer, pinker hue. *S. juniperifolia*, Bulgaria, Caucasus; similar in habit to *S. burseriana*, but leaves 1–1·4cm long and neither glaucous nor lime-encrusted; flowering stems 2–4cm tall, bearing ovoid, head-like cymes of 6–11 flowers, each 1–1·5cm wide, bright yellow. *S.j.* Macedonica (*S. macedonica*), flowers deep yellow; *S.j. sancta* (*S. sancta*), Greece, leaves 7–11mm long, flowers 3–7, in rounded, almost corymbose clusters. *S.* × *kellereri* (*S. burseriana* × *S. stribrnyi* or the similar *S. sempervivum*), much favouring the latter parent; leaves 2–2·5cm long, silvery; flowers pale pink on deep pink stems, winter to spring. *S. lilacina*, W.Himalaya; plant similar to *S. caesia* but flowers solitary, amethyst, to 1·2cm wide; best in acid soil and light shade. *S. lingulata*, see *S. callosa*. *S. longifolia*, E.Spain and Pyrenees; rosettes solitary or in small groups; leaves dense, 3–8cm long, narrowly spathulate, lime-encrusted; panicles 30–60cm long, narrowly pyramidal to columnar, arching, flowers numerous, 1–1·4cm wide, white, sometimes red-dotted, summer; best in vertical rock crevices or dry walls; rosette dies after flowering, but usually first produces offsets. *S. macedonica*, see *S. juniperifolia macedonica*. *S. marginata*, Balkan Peninsula, S.Carpathians, and C. and S.Italy; cushion- to mat-forming, rosettes dense, sometimes columnar; leaves 5–12mm long, linear-oblong to obovate-spathulate, somewhat fleshy, encrusted; flowering stems 5–9cm tall, flowers 1·5–2·5cm wide, white or pale pink in clusters of up to 8. *S.m. coriophylla*, rosettes columnar, flowers in pairs; *S.m.* Lutea, flowers primrose-yellow; *S.m. rocheliana*, rosettes flat, flowers pink in bud. *S. moschata*, S.W.Spain to Italy and Balkan Peninsula, low cushion- or thick mat-forming; leaves 5–15mm long, fan-shaped, deeply 3-, sometimes 5-lobed, glandular hairy; flowering stems to 10cm tall, flowers few, to 1cm wide, usually dull yellow to cream, but sometimes pure white or red; the wild species is seldom grown but several pink and red cultivars represent it in cultivation, some of which may be hybrids with allied species. *S.m.* Cloth of Gold, leaves golden-bronze, flowers white; *S.m.* Triumph, flowers scarlet. *S. oppositifolia*, purple saxifrage; arctic and subarctic Europe and mountains south to Spain, Italy, Bulgaria; loosely mat-forming with long, jointed, creeping stems and short, erect laterals; leaves in opposite pairs, crowded on the laterals, to 6mm long, obovate to rounded, ciliate, dark green with 1–5 white lime glands; flowers solitary, almost sessile, 1–2·5cm wide, pink to rich purple. *S.o.* Ruth Draper, vigorous, with large, rich red flowers in profusion; *S.o.* Splendens, flowers bright red-purple. *S. paniculata* (*S. aizoon*), mountains of Europe from Spain, Italy and Greece to Norway; rosettes with short runners forming low hummocks; leaves to 4cm or more long, narrowly oblong to obovate, the tips upturned, encrusted; panicles 15–30cm tall, flowers 1–1·5cm wide, white to cream, sometimes red-dotted, summer. *S.p. baldensis*, rosettes smaller than type, thicker, broader grey leaves; *S.p.* Lutea, flowers soft yellow; *S.p.* Pectinata, leaves toothed, silvery-encrusted, flowers cream, possibly a hybrid with *S. crustata; S.p.* Rosea, flowers pink. *S.* × *paulinae* (*S. burseriana* × *S. ferdinandi-coburgii*), combining parental characters though favouring the latter somewhat more; flowers pale yellow. *S. pectinata*, see *Luetkea pectinata*. *S.* × *petraschii* (*S. marginata* × *S. tombeanensis*), intermediate between parents; flowers to 2·5cm wide, white in small clusters. *S. porophylla*, C. and S.Italy; similar to *S. grisebachii* but smaller; leaves 6–15mm long, oblanceolate; infloresecence 5–8cm tall of 6–12 flowers only (*S. grisebachii* has 15–25). *S.p. thessalica*, see *S. sempervivum*. *S.* × Primulaize (*S. umbrosa primuloides* × *S. aizoides*), much like a tiny London pride (see *S.* × *urbium*) with panicles to 8cm tall and bright carmine flowers in summer. *S. primuloides*, see *S. umbrosa primuloides*. *S. retusa*, C.Pyrenees, Alps, Carpathians; similar to a smaller, compact *S. oppositifolia* with recurved leaves 2–4mm long and 1cm-wide flowers in clusters of 2–5, sometimes solitary. *S. rossii*, see *Mukdenia rossii*. *S. sancta*, see *S. juniperifolia sancta*. *S. sarmentosa*, see *S. stolonifera*. *S. scardica*, Balkan Peninsula; similar to *S. marginata*, with somewhat larger, keeled, often toothed leaves and larger cymes with up to 12 flowers. *S. sempervivum* (*S. media porophylla* in

Far left below: *Saxifraga fortunei*
Far left bottom: *Saxifraga oppositifolia*
Left below: *Saxifraga stolonifera* Tricolor
Left bottom: *Saxifraga* × *urbium*
Below: *Saxifraga porophylla*
Bottom: *Saxifraga umbrosa* Variegata

part, *S. porophylla thessalica*), Balkan Peninsula; similar to *S. grisebachii* in general appearance, leaves 8–15mm long, linear; flowering stems 8–14cm tall with 7–20 flowers. *S. spathularis*, St Patrick's cabbage; N.W.Spain, N.Portugal, Ireland; similar to *S. umbrosa*; leaves spathulate to obovate or orbicular, coarsely toothed, stalks longer than the blades, sparsely ciliate; seldom cultivated but noteworthy as the other parent of the common London pride – *S.* × *urbium*. *S. stolonifera* (*S. sarmentosa*), mother of thousands, strawberry geranium; E.Asia; mat-forming, producing a web of long, slender, much-branched, red stolons bearing numerous plantlets; leaves in rosettes, long-stalked, the blades to 10cm wide, orbicular, coarsely toothed, silvery-veined above, reddish beneath; panicles 30–60cm tall, flowers about 2cm wide with 1 or 2 petals longer than the rest, white, late summer; a popular house plant suitable for unheated rooms; may be grown outside in sheltered, shaded sites, but not fully hardy. *S.s.* Tricolor, leaves smaller than type, splashed white, flushed pink. *S. stribrnyi*, Bulgaria, N.Greece; akin to *S. grisebachii* in overall appearance but inflorescence a narrow panicle of 10–30 flowers. *S.* × *stuartii* (*S. stribrnyi* × *S. aretioides*), similar to first parent but with the yellow flowers of the latter. *S.* × *suendermannii* (*S. burseriana* × *S. marginata*), intermediate between parents with large white flowers solitary on red, 5cm-tall stems. *S. tombeanensis*, Italian Alps; rosettes elongated, forming firm cushions; leaves 3–5mm long, lanceolate to rhombic, ciliate, somewhat glaucous; flowering stems 3–7cm tall bearing 2–6 white flowers, each to 2·5cm wide. *S. umbrosa*, London pride; W. and C.Pyrenees; low hummock- or mat-forming; leaves to 6cm long, obovate-oblong, broadly crenate, leathery and deep green, borne on slightly shorter, broad, flattened and ciliate stalks; panicles 30–45cm tall, flowers 8mm wide, white with red dots, early summer; best in humus-rich soil in shade; uncommon in cultivation, the familiar London pride being *S.* × *urbium*. *S.u.* Primuloides, a miniature plant with stems to 15cm tall and pink petals; *S.u.* Variegata, leaves blotched cream. *S.* × *urbium* (*S. spathularis* × *S. umbrosa*), London pride; midway between parents, more vigorous than either; will grow in sites that never receive direct sunlight. *S.* × *zimmeteri* (*S. paniculata* × *S. cuneifolia*), blends parental characters, favouring *S. cuneifolia* in stature, but leaves margined grey; flowers white with orange anthers.

Below: *Saxifraga scardica*
Below right: *Scabiosa ochroleuca*
Bottom right: *Scabiosa graminifolia*
Far right: *Scabiosa atropurpurea*
Far right below: *Scabiosa caucasia* Clive Greaves

Scabiosa

(Latin *scabies*, a disease that certain members of the genus were once supposed to cure). Pincushion flower. DIPSACACEAE. A genus of 80–100 species of annuals and perennials from Europe, Africa and Asia, but particularly from the Mediterranean region. They are tufted to clump-forming, with opposite pairs of entire or pinnately dissected leaves and cushion-like flower-heads with the same basic formation as a daisy (see Composite). Each floret is tubular to funnel-shaped, 4–5 lobed, the outer ones usually much longer than the rest like ray florets. The sepals are bristle-like. At the base of each floret is a ribbed, funnel-shaped structure called an epicalyx or involucel that has an expanded, membraneous margin. After flowering, the involucel enlarges with the 1-seeded fruit within and becomes the seed used for propagation. In each species the involucel is differently formed, developing pits and grooves and a larger membraneous margin to aid dispersal by wind. The fruit form is used by botanists to classify the species. Grow in well-drained, moderately fertile soil in sun. Plant perennials autumn to spring; sow annuals *in situ* in spring. Propagate perennials by division autumn or spring, or from seed in spring.

Species cultivated: *S. alpina* of gardens, see *S. columbaria*; the name is also a synonym of the seldom-cultivated *Cephalaria alpina*, a tall, yellow-flowered plant similar to *C. gigantea*. *S. atropurpurea*, sweet scabious; S.Europe to Turkey; biennial to short-lived perennial grown as an annual; to 60cm or more tall; stems branched; lower leaves ovate-lanceolate, lyrate, upper leaves pinnate; flower-heads 3–5cm wide, lilac to red and deep purple, summer to autumn; several improved strains are available from seedsmen, including more compact, shorter-growing sorts 38–45cm tall. *S.caucasia*, N.Iran, Caucasus, C. and N.Russia; perennial to 55–75cm tall or more; lower leaves lanceolate, the upper pinnately divided, glaucous; flower-heads to 6cm or more wide, lavender-blue, early to late summer. *S.c.* Bressingham White, white; *S.c.* Clive Greaves, rich lavender; *S.c.* Loddon White, creamy-white; *S.c.* Moorheim Blue, deep lavender-blue. *S. columbaria*, small scabious; Europe, W.Asia, Siberia, N.Africa; tufted perennial 15–70cm tall; basal leaves obovate to oblanceolate, simple and crenate to lyrate-pinnatifid, upper leaves pinnate with linear leaflets or segments, hispid; flower-heads 1·5–3·5cm wide, lavender to lilac, summer to autumn; mainly represented in gardens by dwarf forms – to 15cm tall – under the names '*S. alpina*' and '*S.a. nana*', names that have no botanical validity. *S. graminifolia*, S.Europe; tufted, usually short-lived perennial to 30cm or more tall; leaves dense, mainly basal pinnate or bipinnate with grey-green, linear to narrowly lanceolate leaflets; flower-heads often solitary, 2·5–4cm wide, mauve to pink, summer. *S.g.* Pinkushion, flowers clear pink. *S. lucida*, mountains of C. and S.Europe; much like *S. columbaria* but usually shorter with smooth leaves and rose-lilac to light red-purple flowers; the bases of the bristle-like calyx segments on the fruit (seed) are winged. *S. ochroleuca*, E.C. and S.E.Europe; almost identical with *S. columbaria* but flowers pale yellow. *S. pterocephala*, see *Pterocephalus perennis*.

Schisandra

(*Schizandra*). (Greek *schizo*, to divide or split, and *aner* or *andros*, male – alluding to the widely separated anther lobes). SCHISANDRACEAE (MAGNOLIACEA). A genus of 25 species of woody climbing plants from E.Asia and E.N.America, 1

of which is most decorative: *S. grandiflora*, Himalaya; to 6m or more; stems twining; leaves alternate, 6–13cm long, obovate, pointed, toothed; flowers unisexual, solitary in the leaf-axils, 2·5–3cm wide, bowl-shaped, pale pink on slender, nodding pedicels, early summer; fruit rounded red berries in dense spikes. *S.g. cathayensis*, W.China, leaves smaller than type, flowers rose-pink; *S.g. rubriflora* (*S. rubriflora*), W.China, flowers deep crimson, berries scarlet. Grow in humus-rich soil in sun or partial shade. Plant autumn to spring, providing support for the twining stems. Propagate from seed when ripe in a cold frame, by layering in spring or cuttings in summer, bottom heat at a temperature of about 18°C.

Above: *Schisandra grandiflora rubriflora*
Below: *Schizanthus pinnatus*
Right: *Schizanthus* cultivar
Far right: *Schizophragma hydrangeoides*
Far right bpttom: *Schizostylis coccinea* Major

Schizanthus

(Greek *schizo*, to divide or split, and *anthos*, a flower – the corolla is deeply cleft). Poor man's orchid. SOLANACEAE. A genus of 10–15 species of annuals, biennials and short-lived perennials from Chile. They have erect, branched stems, alternate, pinnatifid to pinnate leaves, and terminal racemes of more or less 2-lipped, superficially orchid-like flowers. Usually grown as a spring-flowering pot plant for greenhouse or conservatory, minimum temperature 7–10°C, well-ventilated and sunny. May also be grown as a half-hardy annual sown in spring at 16°C, the young plants subsequently hardened off and planted out when fear of frost has passed. For winter-flowering, sow seed thinly in late summer in a cold frame. Prick off seedlings when the first true leaf can be seen, putting into a good commercial potting mixture, at 4–5cm apart each way. When the young plants begin to overlap, pot singly into 9cm containers and provide a thin cane for support. When the weather cools, provide the minimum temperature. Pot on into 15cm pots in late winter. Liquid feed at 10-day intervals is advantageous once the flower-spikes are just visible.

Species cultivated: *S. pinnatus*, butterfly flower; 60–90cm or more tall; leaves pinnate or bipinnate; flowers 2·5–4cm wide, in shades of deep pink to purple-red, often pale or white in the centre, middle upper lobe at least partly yellow with purple markings. Modern strains and selections embrace a wider range of colours and shades, often with the whole central part of the flower yellow or white, spotted or streaked purple; the following are mixed colour strains: *S.p.* Dwarf Bouquet, 30cm tall; *S.p.* Giant Hybrid, 90–120cm tall; *S.p.* Hit Parade, 30cm tall, very compact, with a wide colour range; *S.p.*

Pansy flowered, 50–90cm tall, flowers in a wide range of self-colours. *S.* × *wisetonensis* (reputedly *S. pinnatus* × *S. retusus grahamii*), now doubtfully grown in its original form, plants under this name being indistinguishable from the modern strains and cultivars listed under *S. pinnatus*.

Schizophragma

(Greek *schizo*, to divide or split, and *phragma*, a fence or screen – alluding to the way the ripe seed capsules are split between the ribs). HYDRANGEACEAE (SAXIFRAGACEAE). A genus of 4 species of woody-stemmed climbers from Himalaya to E.Asia, 1 of which is generally available: *S. hydrangeoides*, Japan, Korea; to 10m or more tall; stems clinging by aerial roots like those of ivy; leaves in opposite pairs, long-stalked, the blades 5–12cm long, broadly ovate to rounded, coarsely and sharply toothed, glaucous beneath; flowers tiny, 5-petalled, whitish, in flattened, corymbose panicles to 10cm wide, the main stalks tipped by a sterile flower, 1 sepal of which is greatly enlarged and bract-like, ovate, 2–3cm long, summer; sometimes confused with the climbing *Hydrangea anomala petiolaris* but the sterile florets are quite distinct. *S.h.* Roseum, bract-like sepals, pink-flushed; the closely allied *S. integrifolium* from C.China has almost or completely toothless leaves, larger inflorescences and larger, bract-like sepals. Grow in humus-rich, well-drained but moisture-retentive soil in sun or partial shade. They are particularly effective growing into old trees or over tall stumps. *S. integrifolium* is best on a sheltered wall in cold areas. Plant autumn to spring. Propagate from seed when ripe in spring in a cold frame or greenhouse, by layering in spring or cuttings late summer, ideally with bottom heat about 18°C.

Schizostylis

(Greek *schizo*, to divide or split, and *stylis*, a column or style – the styles are divided into 3). IRIDACEAE. A genus of 2 species of evergreen, rhizomatous perennials from S.Africa, 1 of which is generally available: *S. coccinea*, Kaffir lily, crimson flag; clump- or colony-forming, to 60cm or more tall; leaves 30–40cm long, narrowly sword-shaped in fan-like tufts; flowers 6-tepalled, crocus-like, 5cm wide, crimson, borne in 2 opposite ranks forming a flattened, terminal spike, autumn to early winter; hardy in warm areas, otherwise best protected in winter against severe frost; may also be grown in a

frost-free greenhouse or deep frame for winter-flowering. *S.c.* Gigantea (*S.c.* Grandiflora) and *S.c.* Major, flowers larger than type; *S.c.* Mrs Hegarty, clear pink; *S.c.* Rosalie, salmon-pink. Grow in humus-rich, moisture-retentive soil in sun. Plant and propagate by division in spring.

Sciadopitys

(Greek *skias* or *skiados*, an umbel, and *pitys*, a fir or pine – the leaves are arranged like the ribs of an umbrella). TAXODIACEAE. A genus of 1 species of

evergreen, coniferous tree from Japan: *S. verticillata*, Japanese umbrella pine; 15–20m in gardens but to 35m in the wild; typically conical in outline, sometimes narrowly so, but quite often a many-stemmed, erect bush, always slow-growing; leaves of 2 kinds – triangular and scale-like, 3–6mm long in whorls of 10–30, and needle-like, 5–13cm long, deep glossy green with 2 longitudinal grooves, carried in the axils of the scale-leaves; each leaf is considered to be a fused pair borne on a minute, undeveloped spur shoot. The male flowers (strobili) are globose to ovoid catkins 6–9mm long, carried in compact, terminal clusters; females are solitary, small, developing into ovoid cones 6·5–10cm long, brown when ripe. Grow in humus-rich, moisture-retentive but well-drained soil, in sun or partial shade, preferably with shelter from strong winds. Plant autumn or spring. Propagate from seed when ripe or in spring in a cold frame.

Scilla

(Greek vernacular *skilla* for sea squill – *Urginea maritima* – formerly an original member of this genus as named by Linnaeus). Squill. LILIACEAE. A genus of about 80 species of bulbous plants mainly from temperate Europe and Asia, some in tropical and S.Africa. They have basal tufts of linear to strap-shaped leaves and leafless scapes bearing racemes of 6-tepalled, bell to star-shaped flowers. Grow in well-drained, moderately humus-rich soil in sun or partial shade. The half-hardy species require a minimum temperature of 5°C and are best in pots in a frame or greenhouse. Plant or pot autumn. Propagate from seed when ripe or as soon afterwards as possible, ideally in a cold frame, or by offsets separated when dormant or at planting time. At least some species may be increased by leaf-cuttings in summer.

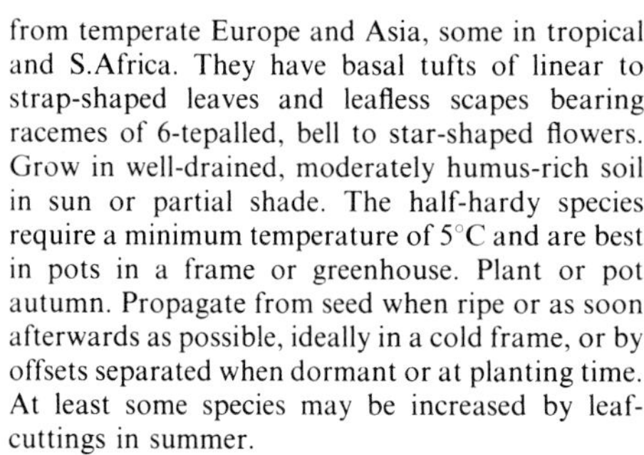

Species cultivated: *S. adlamii*, S.Africa; half-hardy; bulbs stoloniferous; leaves linear-lanceolate, to 20cm or more long, fleshy, brownish-green with darker stripes; scapes shorter than leaves, flowers very small, 3mm long, bell-shaped, mauve-purple, spring; a new generic name, *Ledebouria*, has been proposed for this and other S.African species. *S. bifolia*, S.Europe to Turkey; leaves usually 2, linear-lanceolate, channelled, hooded at tip; scapes 8–15cm tall, flowers starry, 1·5cm wide, mauve-blue; spring. *S.b. rosea*, flowers pink. *S. campanulata*, see *Endymion hispanicus*. *S. mischtschenkoana*, see *S. tubergeniana*. *S. monophylla*, Spain, Portugal, Morocco; leaves solitary, 15–23cm long; scapes 10–20cm tall, flowers starry, 1cm wide, bright blue,

Far left top: *Schizostylis coccinea* Mrs Hegarty
Far left and above: *Sciadopitys verticillata*
Below: *Scilla sibirica* Taurica

Top: *Scilla peruviana* Alba
Above: *Scilla tubergeniana*
Above right: *Scirpus tabernaemontani* Albescens

late spring; needs a sheltered, sunny site. *S. natalensis*, S.Africa; half-hardy; leaves strap-shaped, to 30cm long; scapes 60–90cm tall, flowers 2cm wide, starry, deep to lilac blue, early autumn; can be grown outside in mild areas but best under glass elsewhere. *S. non-scriptus* and *S. nutans*, see *Endymion non-scriptus*. *S. peruviana*, Cuban lily; Portugal, Spain, Italy; leaves in rosettes, to 30cm or more long by 3cm wide, somewhat fleshy; scapes to 25cm tall, racemes very dense, broadly conical, flowers starry, 2–2·5cm wide, violet-blue to purple, early summer; the botanist Clusius, who named this species, was under the mistaken impression that the plant came from Peru, hence the anomalous name. *S.p.* Alba, flowers white. *S. sibirica*, Siberian squill; Turkey, Iran, Caucasus; leaves 2–5, strap-shaped, to 15cm long when mature, glossy; scapes 10–15cm tall, flowers bell-shaped, to 2cm wide, nodding, brilliant deep blue, spring; often starts to flower when only a few centimetres tall, elongating later. *S.s.* Alba, flowers white; *S.s.* Spring Beauty, vigorous and somewhat earlier than type; *S.s.* Taurica, flowers light blue, each tepal with a darker mid-vein. *S. tubergeniana* (*S. mischtschenkoana*), N.Iran, S.Caucasus; much like *S. sibirica* but flowering as soon as the shoot pierces the ground in late winter, elongating later; flowers opening somewhat more widely, palest blue, each tepal with a deeper mid-vein. *S. violacea*, S.Africa; half-hardy; bulbs at, or above, soil level forming clumps; leaves 5–8cm long, ovate to lanceolate, purple beneath and silvery-green, blotched purple above; scapes to 10cm, flowers very small, bell-shaped, nodding, green edged white, purplish stamens, summer to autumn: the name *Ledebouria socialis* is now proposed for this plant.

Scirpus

(old Latin name for a rush). Clubrush. CYPERACEAE. A genus of 250–300 species of rushes from wet places throughout the world. They are tufted, often rhizomatous and forming colonies, with leaves grass-like or reduced to basal sheaths and green, leaf-like stems rounded or triangular in cross-section. The tiny flowers are petalless, forming compact, ovoid spikelets that may be borne in terminal panicles or sessile clusters. Grow in permanently moist soil or ponds – if the latter,

placed in submerged containers of a rich, loamy compost. Plant or pot spring or autumn. Propagate by division at planting time.

Species cultivated: *S. cernuus* (*Isolepis gracilis* of gardens), W. and S.Europe, N.Africa; densely tufted evergreen, to 15cm tall; leaves and stems filiform, the latter taller and bearing solitary, 5mm long, greenish or red-brown tinted spikelets in summer; formerly much grown as a small pot plant for edging greenhouse benches, but hardy outside. *S. lacustris* (*Schoenoplectus l.*), bulrush, common clubrush; world-wide; rhizomatous, to 1m or more tall; stems round in cross-section, deep green; leaves short or reduced to sheaths but sometimes well-developed under water; spikelets 5–8mm long, red-brown in panicles, summer; can be invasive in ponds with natural mud bottoms. *S. tabernaemontani* (*Schoenoplectus t.*), grey or glaucous bulrush or clubrush; Europe, temperate Asia; similar to *S. lacustris*, but usually shorter, the stems glaucous; if not grown in water the rhizomes are best protected in winter in cold areas. *S.t.* Albescens, stems yellowish-white with longitudinal green stripes; *S.t.* Zebrinus, zebra rush, stems cross-banded white.

Scolopendrium – see *Asplenium scolopendrium*.

Scrophularia

(Latin *scrofula*, a disease that some of these plants were supposed to cure). SCROPHULARIACEAE. A

genus of about 200 species of biennials, perennials and sub-shrubs from Europe, Asia, N. and tropical America, 1 of which is grown for its striking foliage: *S. auriculata*, water figwort; Europe, N.Africa; clump-forming perennial to 1m tall; stems robust, 4-winged; leaves 6–12cm long, ovate, crenate; flowers to 1cm long, almost globular with 5 small lobes at the mouth, purple-brown, in terminal cymose panicles, summer to autumn; represented in gardens by *S.a.* Variegata (misidentified as a form of *S. nodosa* and sometimes listed under that name); leaves boldly cream-margined. Grow in fertile, moisture-retentive soil in sun or partial shade. Plant from autumn to spring. Propagate by division at planting time or cuttings of basal shoots late spring to summer.

Scutellaria

(Latin *scutella*, a small shield – referring to the form of the fruiting calyces). LABIATAE. A genus of about 300 species of annuals, perennials and sub-shrubs of almost cosmopolitan distribution. They have opposite pairs of linear to ovate leaves, tubular, 2-lipped, hooded flowers in the upper leaf-axils or in dense terminal racemes. Grow the hardy species described here in well-drained but moisture-retentive, fertile soil in sun. Plant autumn to spring.

Above: *Scrophularia auriculata* Variegata
Below: *Scutellaria alpina*

Propagate by division at planting time, from seed in spring in a cold frame.
Species cultivated: *S. alpina*, mountains of S.Europe to S.C.USSR; rhizomatous; stems to 25cm or more tall; leaves 1·5–3cm long, ovate, toothed; flowers 2–2·5cm long, purple in dense racemes, late summer. *S.a.* Alba, flowers white. *S. baicalensis*, E.Asia; stems decumbent, to 30cm tall; leaves sessile, lanceolate-ciliate; flowers 2·5cm long, blue-purple in 1-sided racemes, late summer. *S. hastifolia* (*S. hastata* of catalogues), Europe; rhizomatous; stems more or less erect, to 15cm or so tall; leaves to 2·5cm long, lanceolate to ovate-hastate; flowers in axillary pairs 1·5–2cm long, violet-blue, summer. *S. indica*, China, Japan; tufted; stem decumbent, to 15cm tall; leaves up to 2·5cm long, ovate-crenate, downy, grey-green; flowers 2·5cm long, blue-purple in short, dense, terminal racemes, summer. *S.i. parvifolia*, Japan, plant smaller and more compact than type, leaves about 1cm long, sometimes confused in cultivation with *S. laeteviolacea* (*S.i. humilis*), but that species has triangular-ovate leaves 1–2cm long and strongly hooded flowers. *S. scordiifolia*, Korea; rhizomes narrowly tuber-like, far-creeping; stems to 20cm tall, sometimes more; leaves 2–4cm long, elliptic to oblong; flowers 1·5–2cm long, deep purple-blue, summer. Invasive on light soils.

Top far left: *Scutellaria scordiifolia*
Top left: *Sedum caeruleum*
Above left: *Sedum kamtschaticum ellacombianum*
Top: *Sedum hispanicum*
Above: *Sedum rosea*

Sea buckthorn – see *Hippophae*.

Sea heath – see *Frankenia*.

Sea holly – see *Eryngium maritimum*.

Sea lavender – see *Limonium*.

Sea pink – see *Armeria*.

Sea poppy – see *Glaucium flavum*.

Sedge – see *Carex*.

Sedum

(Latin *sedo*, to sit – alluding to the way some species grow on walls and rocks). Stonecrop. CRASSULACEAE. A genus of 500–600 species of succulent perennials and sub-shrubs, including a few annuals, biennials and monocarps, from the N.Hemisphere. They are prostrate to erect with often crowded, alternate to opposite, linear to orbicular or cylindrical to ovoid, succulent leaves and terminal cymes of starry, 5-petalled flowers. Grow hardy species in well-drained soil in sun, the half-hardy or tender species under glass or in the home, minimum temperature 5–7°C, well-ventilated and bright. Pot or plant spring to autumn. Propagate from seed in spring under glass or by stem-cuttings in summer; those species with large, readily detachable leaves may also be increased by leaf-cuttings.
Species cultivated (summer-flowering unless stated otherwise): *S. acre*, common or biting stonecrop, golden carpet (USA), wall pepper; Europe, W.Asia, N.Africa; mat-forming, to 5cm tall; leaves 4–5mm long, triangular-ovate; flowers 1cm wide, bright yellow. *S.a.* Variegatum, young leaves creamy-yellow, especially in spring. *S. aizoon*, Siberia, China, Japan; tufted or clump-forming herbaceous perennial; stems erect, 30–45cm tall; leaves 5–7·5cm long, linear-lanceolate to ovate, coarsely toothed; flowers 1cm wide, yellow to orange in compact clusters. *S. album*, white stonecrop; Europe, W.Asia, N.Africa; mat-forming, 7–10cm tall; leaves 5–10mm, linear-oblong, almost cylindrical; flowers 8–10mm wide, white. *S. altissimum*, see *S. sediforme*. *S. anacampseros*, S.Europe; stems creeping, upturned at the tips, to 15cm tall; leaves 1–2·5cm long, obovate to rounded, glaucous; flowers not opening widely, to 6mm across, purple; in dense clusters. *S. anglicum*, English stonecrop; W.Europe; small, mat-forming, 2–2·5cm tall; leaves 3–4·5mm long, elliptic, very thick and often red-tinged; flowers 1cm wide, white, flushed pink; seed capsules red. *S. caeruleum*, islands of W.Mediterranean, naturalized elsewhere; branched annual to 10cm or more tall; leaves 1–2cm long, ovoid to oblongoid, reddish in dry, sunny sites; flowers 6mm wide, 7–9 petalled, sky-blue, white at base. *S. cauticolum*, N.Japan; tufted, loosely mat-forming, dying back to a thickened rootstock; leaves 2–2·5cm long, opposite or alternate, orbicular-spathulate, glaucous; flowers 1cm wide, rose-purple in flattened heads, autumn. *S. cyaneum* of gardens, see *S. ewersii*. *S. dasyphyllum*, S.Europe, N.Africa; small, tufted, 2·5–5cm tall; leaves opposite, 3–4·5mm long, egg-shaped, glandular-downy, often pinkish grey-green; flowers 6mm wide, white, pinkish in bud. *S. divergens*, W. N.America; similar in habit to *S. album*, but leaves opposite, 6mm long, obovate, thick, often red-flushed; flowers to 2cm wide, yellow. *S. ellacombianum*, see *S. kamtschaticum ellacombianum*. *S. ewersii* (*S. cyaneum* of gardens), Himalaya to Mongolia; herbaceous, dying back to a twiggy, much-branched rootstock; stems 15–30cm tall; leaves opposite or almost so, sessile, 2cm long, ovate to orbicular, the upper ones cordate and stem-clasping, glaucous; flowers about 1cm wide, purplish-pink in compact heads, early autumn. *S. floriferum*, N.E.China; tufted, from woody rootstock; stems ascending to decumbent, about 15cm long; leaves to 4cm long, sessile, oblanceolate, coarsely toothed in upper part; flowers about 1cm

wide, yellow, in profuse cymes, late summer. *S. forsteranum* (*S. rupestre*), rock stonecrop; W.Europe; mat-forming, 15–30cm tall; leaves 8–20mm long, linear, flat on upper surface and not very fleshy, usually bright glaucous and densely borne; flowers 9–12mm wide, sometimes with 6–8 petals, bright yellow. *S. glaucum*, see next species. *S. hispanicum* (*S. glaucum*), S.E.Europe; usually annual but sometimes biennial or short-lived perennial, bushy, 7–15cm tall; leaves 7–18mm long, linear, semi-cylindrical, glaucous; flowers 6–9 petalled, 7–12mm wide, white; very variable in stature and leaf length. *S. kamtschaticum*, E.Asia; rootstock woody and much-branched; stems 15–23cm tall; leaves to 5cm long, sessile, spathulate to obovate, toothed in upper $\frac{1}{3}$; flowers to 2cm wide, orange-yellow, summer to autumn. *S.k. ellacombianum* (*S. ellacombianum*), stems shorter than type, leaves more spathulate and boldly toothed, flowers smaller, clear yellow, in more compact clusters; *S.k. middendorffianum* (*S. middendorffianum*), leaves linear, flowers yellow in branched leafy cymes. *S. lydium*, Turkey; small mat-forming, 5–10cm tall in bloom; leaves dense, 6mm long, cylindrical, bright green, often red-tinted; flowers 6mm wide, white, in flat, compact clusters. *S. maximum*, see *S. telephium maximum*. *S. middendorffianum*, see *S. kamtschaticum middendorffianum*. *S. morganianum*, burro's or donkey's-tail; probably Mexico; tender; stems to 60cm or more long, prostrate or pendulous; leaves overlapping, to 2·5cm long, almost cylindrical, tapered to a point and curved inwards, glaucous-white; flowers about 1cm long, red, in small clusters, spring; probably epiphytic and an ideal hanging basket plant. *S. obtusatum* (*S. rubroglaucum*), California, Nevada; similar to *S. oreganum*, but leaves glaucous and petals 6–9mm long, rather more spreading, lemon-yellow fading buff or pinkish. *S. oreganum*, W.N.America; low hummock- to mat-forming, 15cm tall; leaves alternate or opposite, about 2cm long, spathulate, glossy green, often red-tinted, the basal ones in rosettes; flowers about 1·2cm long – the slender-pointed, yellow, sometimes red-tinted petals erect or spreading at tips only, late summer. *S. palmeri*, Mexico; half-hardy; stems decumbent, rising 15–23cm tall; leaves about 2·5cm long, spathulate, somewhat reflexed, glaucous; flowers 1·5cm wide, orange, in arching cymes, spring in a greenhouse, minimum temperature 10°C, early summer in a cold frame or sheltered site outside; needs winter protection outside in all but mildest areas. *S. pluricaule*, Sakhalin Is, Japan; herbaceous, dying back to almost woody twiggy base; stems 5–7cm long in compact clusters; leaves 1cm long, ovate to rounded, glaucous; flowers to 5mm wide, purple, in rounded clusters. *S. populifolium*, W.Siberia; sub-shrub to 30cm or more tall; leaves long-stalked, the blades 2cm long, ovate-cordate, coarsely and irregularly toothed; flowers to 1cm or more wide, pink or white, fragrant, in loose cymes, late summer. *S. pulchellum*, E.USA; tufted, 10–30cm tall; leaves crowded, 1·5cm long, cylindrical, bright green; flowers 4-petalled, 1cm wide, rose-purple, in long, arching cymes; best in moist soils. *S. reflexum*, reflexed stonecrop; Europe; loosely mat-forming, up to 30cm tall in bloom; leaves crowded, 1cm long, cylindrical, tapered to a point, green or glaucous; flowers 5–7 petalled, 1–1·5cm wide, yellow in compact cymes. *S.r.* Cristatum, stems fasciated, fan-shaped, the leaves congested towards the top. *S. rosea* (*S. rhodiola*, *Rhodiola rosea*), roseroot; circumpolar and mountains farther south; herbaceous, rootstock thick, branched and partially above ground; stems 15–30cm tall; leaves numerous, 4cm long, lanceolate to obovate, more or less toothed at tip, glaucous; flowers dioecious, 4-petalled, yellow or greenish-yellow in compact clusters, late spring to summer; the dried roots are fragrant. *S. rubroglaucum*, see *S. obtusatum*. *S.* × *rubrotinctum* (parentage unknown), Christmas cheer; tender sub-shrub to 20cm or more tall; stems erect; leaves crowded, 1·5–2cm long, oblongoid to club-shaped, lustrous green, often diffused red; flowers 9–12mm wide, bright yellow in branched cymes. *S. rupestre*, see *S. forsteranum*. *S. sediforme* (*S. altissimum*), S.Europe and Mediterranean; tufted, somewhat woody-based, 25–60cm tall; leaves 1–2cm long, semi-cylindrical, flattened above, apiculate or mucronate, glaucous; flowers 1–1·5cm wide, 5–8 petalled, greenish-white to straw-coloured, rarely yellow. *S. sempervivioides* (*S. sempervivum*), Turkey to Caucasus; biennial or monocarpic, forming sempervivum-like rosettes that elongate to 15cm or more when in bloom; leaves to 3cm long, oblong-spathulate, finely downy, grey-green with reddish margins; flowers about 1cm wide, having crimson petals and fleshy red sepals in large terminal compound cymes. *S. sexangulare*, Europe to S.W.Asia; mat-forming, to 10cm tall; leaves crowded, arranged in 6 spiralling ranks, 3–6mm long, cylindrical, blunt at tip, spurred at base; flowers 8–10mm wide, yellow. *S. sieboldii*, October plant; Japan; herbaceous; tufted from a rootstock bearing small, carrot-like tubers; stems low, arching to semi-prostrate, 15–25cm long; leaves in whorls of 3, sessile, 1–2cm long, nearly orbicular, glaucous; flowers about 1cm wide, pink, in compact, leafy cymes, autumn. *S.s.* Medio-variegatum, leaves with central yellow splash. *S. spathulifolium*, British Columbia to California; low hummock- to mat-

Top left: *Sedum spectabile* Autumn Joy
Above left: *Sedum sieboldii* Medio-variegatum
Top: *Sedum spathulifolium* Purpureum
Above: *Sedum spathulifolium* Cape Blanco
Top right: *Sedum spurium* Schorbusser Blut

forming, to 10cm tall; leaves in rosettes increasing by offsets, 1·5–2·5cm long, spathulate, glaucous, often red-tinged; flowers 1·2–1·5cm wide, bright yellow, early summer. *S.s.* Cape Blanco, leaves almost white when young; *S.s.* Purpureum, leaves purple with waxy-white patina. *S. spectabile*, ice-plant (Britain); China, Korea, long cultivated in Japan; herbaceous, clump-forming, 35–45cm tall; stems erect, robust; leaves opposite, sometimes in 3s, 5–7·5cm long, obovate, bright pale glaucous; flowers 1–1·2cm wide, pink in flattened heads 10–15cm wide, early autumn. *S.s.* Autumn Joy, 60cm tall, salmon-pink; *S.s.* Brilliant, 35cm tall, deep rose-pink; *S.s.* Iceberg, 30cm tall, white; *S.s.* September Ruby, 30cm tall, dark rose-pink. *S. spurium*, Caucasus; mat-forming, 30–60cm wide; stems creeping and decumbent, to 15cm tall; leaves opposite, 2cm long, obovate-cuneate, bluntly toothed in upper half, ciliate; flowers 1·2cm long, the petals semi-erect, pink in flat, dense heads; sometimes confused with *S. stoloniferum* (qv). *S.s.* Coccineum, ruby-red; *S.s.* Erdblut, carmine; *S.s.* Greenmantle, bright green leaves, fast-growing, rarely if ever flowers but makes good ground cover; *S.s.* Roseum, flowers rose-pink; *S.s.* Ruby Glow, rose-red; *S.s.* Schorbusser Blut, bronze leaves, dark red flowers. *S. stoloniferum*, Caucasus, Turkey, Iran; much like, and formerly confused with, *S. spurium*, but easily separated on the following characters: stems red, leaves toothless or only vaguely crenate, flowers with widely spreading petals. *S. tartarinowii*, N.China; herbaceous, tufted to clump-forming, rootstock tuberous; stems to 15cm tall; leaves 1–2·5cm long, linear-lanceolate with a few large teeth; flowers about 1cm wide, pale pink. *S. telephioides*, see next species. *S. telephium*, live-forever, live-long, orpine; Europe, Asia (represented in N. America by the similar *S. telephoides*); herbaceous, clump-forming to 60cm tall; leaves 2·5–7·5cm long, ovate-oblong, irregularly toothed, sometimes glaucous; flowers tl 1·5cm wide, purple-red, late summer; a variable species, including: *S.t. maximum* (*S. maximum*), more robust, to 80cm tall, leaves 4–10cm long, flowers greenish- to yellowish-white; *S.t.m.* Atropurpureum, leaves dark red-purple, flowers pinkish; *S.t.* Variegatum, leaves with cream markings. *S. ternatum*, E.USA; tufted, forming small, loose mats 7–10cm or more tall; stems decumbent to ascending; leaves in whorls of 3, obovate, 1–2·5cm long, pale green; flowers 4-petalled, 1cm wide, white, in widely branched cymes, late spring; best in partial shade.

Self-heal – see *Prunella vulgaris*.

Sellieria

(for François Noel Sellier, 1737 to about 1800, French engraver who worked for the botanists Cavanilles and Desfontaines). GOODENIACEAE. A genus of 2 species of creeping perennials from Australasia and S.America, 1 of which is usually available: *S. radicans*, Australia, Tasmania, New Zealand, Chile; mat-forming; stems prostrate, rooting, to 30cm long; leaves long-stalked, solitary, at each alternate node, or in clusters of 2–4, narrowly spathulate, obovate-spathulate or linear, the blades 7–15mm or more long, somewhat fleshy, glossy; flowers solitary or paired in axils, 7–10mm wide, tubular, 5-lobed, the tube oblique and split down the back, white to very pale blue, summer; fruit 6–10mm long, obovoid, fleshy; confused with *Hypsela*, but the flower tube of that genus is not split. Culture as for *Hypsela*.

Sempervivum

(Latin *semper*, always, and *vivus*, alive – the plants are evergreen and very tenacious of life). Houseleek. CRASSULACEAE. A genus of 25–40 species of perennial succulents from the mountains of Europe, W.Asia and N.Africa. They form hummocks or mats of dense rosettes composed of fleshy, oblong to obovate leaves often tinted or flushed red or purple. Each rosette is monocarpic, living 1 to several years before flowering, but producing offsets annually during its life. At flowering time, the rosette elongates to an erect, leafy stem bearing branched cymes of narrow-petalled, 1–2cm wide flowers in summer. Depending on the botanical authority, *Sempervivum* is divided into either 2 sections or 2 separate genera, ie *Sempervivum* and *Jovibarba*. In *Sempervivum* true, the flowers have 9–20 petals that open out flat; in *Jovibarba* there are 6–7 petals that are fringed and stay erect. Although the flowers are attractive, they are not always freely produced and the interest lies in the variously shaped and coloured rosettes. Grow in well-drained soil in sun, ideally in screes, rock crevices, dry walls or sink gardens. Plant autumn or spring. Propagate by division at planting time or by separating well-grown offsets late summer.

Species cultivated: *S. allionii* (*Jovibarba a.*), S.Alps; rosettes 2–3cm wide, globular, downy and ciliate, yellow-green, sometimes with red-flushed tips; flowers greenish-white. *S. andreanum*, N.Spain; rosettes 2–3cm wide, blue-green with dark tips; stems 10–12cm tall; flowers pale pink, deeper at the base. *S. arachnoideum*, cobweb houseleek; Pyrenees, Alps, Apennines, Carpathians; rosettes 1·5–2cm wide, green or red-flushed, the leaf tips spun together with long, white, cobwebby hairs; stems 8–13cm tall; flowers rose-red; several forms and hybrids are sometimes available. *S. arenarium* (*Jovibarba a.*), E.Alps; rosettes 5–20mm wide, globular, ciliate; stems 7–12cm tall; flowers greenish-white. *S. ballsii*, N.W.Greece; rosettes about 3cm wide, bronze to red-tinted on outer leaves; flowers matt-pink; offsets rather sparingly produced. *S. calcareum* (*S. tectorum c.*), French Alps; like *S. tectorum*, but rosettes grey-green with large, purple-brown tips; flowers seldom produced. *S. ciliosum*, Bulgaria, Yugoslavia, N.W.Greece; rosettes 3·5–5cm wide, downy and ciliate, somewhat hoary, the outer leaves red-flushed; stems 10cm tall; flowers greenish-yellow. *S.* × Commander Hay (*S.*

Far left above: *Sedum telephium maximum* Atropurpureum
Left above: *Sedum spurium*
Above: *Sempervivum calcareum*

Left below: *Sempervivum grandiflorum*
Below: *Sempervivum* × Commander Hay

tectorum giganteum × *S. tectorum* × *S. marmoreum* Rubrifolium), rosettes large, deep red, green-tipped. *S.* × *funckii* (probably *S. arachnoideum* × *S. montanum* × *S. tectorum*), rosettes to 4cm wide, glandular downy and ciliate; flowers purple-rose; sometimes confused with *S. calcareum*. *S. globiferum*, see next species. *S. grandiflorum* (*S. globiferum*), S.Switzerland, N.Italy; rosettes variable in size, 2–10cm wide, sticky glandular downy, dull green, somewhat pungently and unpleasantly aromatic; stems 15–30cm tall; flowers large, greenish-yellow. *S. giuseppii*, N.W.Spain; rosettes 2·5–4cm

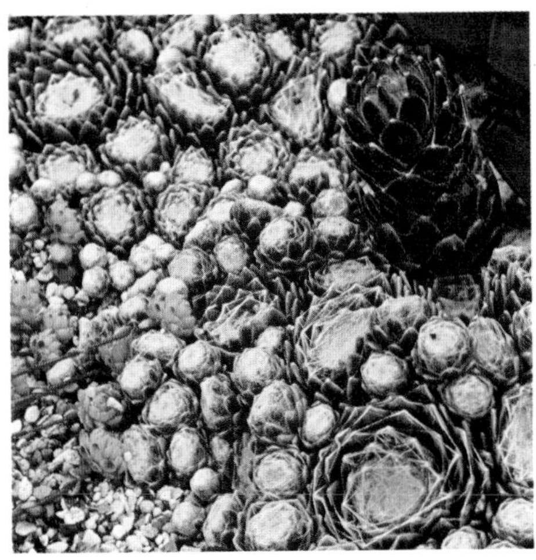

wide, densely downy and stiffly ciliate, pale green with brown tips; stems 12–15cm tall; flowers rose-red. *S. hirtum* (*Jovibarba h.*), E.Alps, Carpathians to N.Balkan Peninsula; rosettes 2·5–7cm wide, ciliate, green to yellow-green, in some forms red-flushed in sunny, dry sites; stems 10–20cm tall; flowers pale yellow to greenish-white. *S. kosaninii*, S.W.Yugoslavia; rosettes 4–8cm wide, glandular hairy, ciliate, dark green, red-tipped; stems 15–20cm tall; flowers green and white with red anthers. *S. marmoreum* (*S. schlehanii*), E.Europe, Balkans; a variable species much like *S. tectorum*, but with at least young leaves hairy; some forms and cultivars, eg *S.m.* Brunneifolium and *S.m.* Rubrifolium (*S.m.* Rubicundum) have red-brown to red leaves. *S. montanum*, Pyrenees, Corsica, Alps, Carpathians; rosettes 2–4·5cm wide, glandular hairy, wholly dull green; stems to 10cm or more tall; flowers violet-purple; a variable species and parent of many hybrids. *S.m. stiriacum*, rosettes to 8cm wide with deep red-brown tips. *S. nevadense*, Sierra Nevada, Spain; rosettes 2·5–3·5cm wide, ciliate, pinkish-bronze in summer, scarlet in winter; stems 8–13cm tall; flowers deep pink. *S. octopodes*, S.W.Yugoslavia; closely allied to *S. ciliosum*; rosettes 1–2cm wide, densely glandular downy, ciliate, tipped red-brown; stems to 9cm tall; flowers yellow, spotted red at the base, sepals red-purple; distinctive in bearing offsets on thread-like stolons to 7cm long; not one of the easiest to grow, disliking both excessive wetness and dryness. *S.o. apetalum*, rosettes to 3cm wide, flowers without petals and stamens, easily grown. *S. schlehanii*, see *S. marmoreum*. *S. soboliferum* (*Jovibarba s.*), hen and chickens houseleek; N.Europe to C.USSR; rosettes 2–3cm wide, bright green, often with coppery-red tints; stems 10–20cm tall; flowers greenish-yellow, rarely produced; offsets globular, very freely produced on top of the rosettes, and easily detached. *S. tectorum*, common or roof houseleek; Pyrenees to Balkan Peninsula; widespread; rosettes to 18cm wide, usually dark green, often purple-brown tipped, white ciliate; stems 30–50cm tall; flowers pink or purplish-red, anthers orange-brown, very variable. *S.t. alpinum*, rosettes to 6cm wide with or without dark tips; *S.t.* Atropurpureum, rosettes deep violet; *S.t. calcareum*, see *S. calcareum*; *S.t. glaucum*, rosettes to 10cm wide, glaucous; *S.t.* Nigrum, prominent red-purple leaf tips.

Senecio

(Latin *senex*, an old man, an oblique reference to the hoary pappus). COMPOSITAE. A genus variously estimated at between 2000 and 3000 species of cosmopolitan distribution. The largest genus of flowering plants, it includes annuals, perennials (including succulents), shrubs, sub-shrubs, small trees and climbers. They have alternate leaves in a wide variety of forms and generally terminal clusters of daisy-like flower-heads, sometimes without any ray florets. As a generalization, grow the hardy species, whatever their growth form, in fertile, well-drained soil in sun; half-hardy to tender species need a frost-free climate, minimum 5–7°C, sunny and well-ventilated except in summer when the non-succulent species need light shade. For more specific requirements, see individual species descriptions. Plant hardy perennials and shrubs autumn to spring. Pot or repot greenhouse species in spring using a good commercial potting mixture. Propagate perennials by division at planting time or basal cuttings in spring, shrubs and trees by cuttings in late summer, succulents by cuttings in summer. All species may be grown from seed in spring, ideally under glass, the half-hardy annuals at 13–16°C, setting out the young plants in their flowering sites when fear of frost has passed. *S. elegans* may also be sown *in situ* in late spring, early summer. For *S.* × *hybridus*, the following culture is recommended: sow seed as for half-hardy annuals, in spring for winter flowering, summer for blooming the following late spring to early summer. Prick off the seedlings when the first true leaf is well-developed at 4–5cm apart in boxes of weak potting mixture. When the young plants overlap each other, pot into 9cm containers of richer potting mixture and place in a cold frame when fear of frost has passed. The summer sowing and subsequent potting can be done entirely in a cold frame. Ventilate freely on warm days and remove lights entirely during the summer unless it is very cool and windy. Provide light shade from hot sun. Pot on into 13–15cm containers when well-grown and about 4 weeks later apply liquid feed at 7–10 day intervals. In autumn, either take into a greenhouse or provide a winter minimum temperature of 8–10°C, or up to

Far left above: *Sempervivum arachnoideum*
Far left below: *Sempervivum arachnoideum* in flower
Left below: *Senecio bicolor cineraria*
Above: *Senecio* × *hybridus*
Below: *Senecio elegans*

15°C if earlier blooms are required. The plants are best discarded after flowering, but special ones can be cut back and grown on or the basal shoots taken as cuttings.

Species cultivated: *S. abrotanifolius*, S. and E.Alps, Carpathians, Balkan Peninsula; hardy, rhizomatous perennial 15–30cm tall; leaves 2·5–7cm long, bi- or tri-pinnatisect, the ultimate division linear; flower-heads 2cm wide, solitary or a few together, the rays yellow to orange-red with brownish stripes, summer to autumn. *S. articulatus* (*Kleinia a.*), candle plant; S.Africa; tender, erect, succulent shrub 30–60cm tall; stems 1·5–2cm thick, cylindrical, jointed, grey-green; leaves long-stalked, the blades to 5cm long, deeply 3–5 lobed, on young stems only, mainly during the winter; flower-heads about 1·5cm long, yellowish-white, groundsel-like; often sheds stem sections that can be used for propagation. *S. bicolor cineraria* (*S. cineraria*, *S. maritimus*, *Cineraria m.*), dusty miller; W. and C.Mediterranean; evergreen

half-hardy shrub, 50–100cm tall; leaves 4–10cm or more long, ovate to lanceolate in outline, deeply toothed to pinnatisect, densely white woolly; flower-heads to 1·5cm wide in compound corymbs, rays yellow, summer; usually listed as *S.* Silverdust or *S.* White Diamond. *S. cineraria*, see *S. bicolor c. S. clivorum*, see *Ligularia dentata*. *S. compactus*, New Zealand; almost hardy, similar to *S. greyi*, but leaves 2–4cm long, obovate, margins usually finely crenate and waved, dull green above; flower-heads to 3cm wide, rays yellow, solitary or in small racemes, late summer; a parent of the Dunedin Hybrids (qv). *S. cruentus* of gardens, see *S.* × *hybridus*. *S* × Dunedin Hybrids (*S. greyi*, *S. laxifolius* × *S. compactus*), group of hybrids that have long masqueraded in gardens as *S. greyi* and *S. laxifolius* – only 1 clone is commonly met with, now named Sunshine; to 1m tall by 1·5–2m wide, rounded habit; stems white-felted; leaves 3–6cm long by 1·5–3cm wide, ovate to elliptic, entire to slightly wavy margined, smooth to thinly downy above, densely white-felted beneath; flower-heads 2–3cm wide, yellow, in large, spreading corymbs with stalked, leaf-like bracts; reasonably hardy, but sometimes damaged in severe winters. *S. elegans*, S.Africa; half-hardy annual 40-60cm tall; leaves 5–8cm long, sessile, stem-clasping, shallowly to deeply pinnately lobed and toothed; flower-heads 3–4cm wide, rays bright rose-purple to rose-lilac in large terminal corymbs, late summer to autumn; white and double-flowered forms are known. *S. grandifolius*, S.Mexico; greenhouse shrub to 2m or more tall; stems purple, very robust; leaves 20–45cm long, ovate, usually with large, shallow, well-spaced teeth, tawny hairy beneath; flower-heads small, 5-rayed, yellow in dense terminal corymbose cymes to 30cm or more wide, winter; can be grown annually from spring cuttings or as a shrub in large pots or tubs. *S. greyi*, New Zealand; almost hardy shrub to 2m tall, spreading habit; stems white-felted; leaves well-spaced, 4–8cm long, by 2·5–4·5cm wide, oblong to ovate-oblong, blunt to rounded-tipped, entire to shallowly sinuate, when mature glossy green above with white-felted margins and undersides; flower-heads 2–3cm wide, yellow, the stalks and involucral bracts (phyllaries) glandular pubescent, in large corymbs, summer to autumn; see also *S.* × Dunedin Hybrids and *S. laxifolius*. *S. heritieri*, Canary Is (Tenerife); tender, tufted sub-shrubby perennial to 30cm tall by 60cm wide; stems slender, somewhat zigzag; leaves long-stalked, the blades rounded, cordate, shallowly 5–7 lobed, cobwebby hairy above, white-felted beneath; flower-heads in small, long-stalked clusters, 3·5–5cm wide, rays glistening light purple, white at base, discs dark purple, mainly autumn to spring; almost half-hardy and surviving outdoors in sheltered sites in mild areas. *S.* × *hybridus* (*S. cruentus* of gardens, not the original species), a name covering the florists' cinerarias, a group of hybrid cultivars largely derived from *S. cruentus* × *S. heritieri*, probably also with other allied Canary Is species; short-lived perennial 30–90cm tall; leaves 10–20cm long, rounded-

Below: *Senecio* × Dunedin Hybrids Sunshine
Right: *Sequoia sempervirens*

cordate, toothed and shallowly lobed, downy beneath; flower-heads 3–8cm wide in shades of pink, red, mauve, purple, lavender and white, often bicoloured; 3 main strains are available: *S.* × *h.* Multiflora Nana (*S.* × *h.* Grandiflora Nana) covers plants about 30cm tall with very compact, rounded heads of bloom, *S.* × *h.* Multiflora is similar but grows 40–50cm tall, *S.* × *h.* Stellata grows 50–75cm tall, bearing looser clusters of more starry flowers. All 3 groups contain several self- and mixed-coloured cultivars, all good in their separate ways but basically very similar. *S. laxifolius*, New Zealand; similar to *S. greyi*, but differs in being hardier and having more closely set leaves 2–6cm long by 1–2cm wide, elliptic to lanceolate-oblong, somewhat pointed, entire to lightly crenate, and flower-heads to 2cm wide, the phyllaries downy but not glandular; these are the extreme differences, but in the wild there are many intermediates and recent botanical study suggests that both are forms of 1 species – both species are rare to uncommon in gardens, the plants grown under these names being *S.* × Dunedin Hybrids. *S. leucostachys*, see *S. vira-vira*. *S. maritimus*, see *S. bicolor*. *S. monroi*, New Zealand; hardy, evergreen shrub to 1m tall, often less in gardens, of much-branched, spreading habit; leaves 2–4cm long, by 5–15mm wide, narrowly obovate-oblong, blunt-tipped, leathery, the margins crenate and finely waved, dark, sometimes almost brownish-green above, white-felted beneath; flower-heads 2cm wide in dense corymbose clusters, summer. *S. przewalskii*, see *Ligularia p.* *S. reinoldii* (*S. rotundifolius*), New Zealand; half hardy, evergreen shrub 2–3m tall, usually of compact, rounded habit in gardens, but often a small, rather leggy tree to 6m in the wild; leaves 6–12cm long or more, rounded to broadly oblong, stiffly leathery, glossy above, pale buff- to whitish-felted beneath and on the margins; flower-heads 1cm wide, bell-shaped, buff to whitish-woolly, without rays, in panicles; excellent seaside foliage shrub, standing gale force winds and salt spray. *S. rotundifolius*, see previous species. *S. stenocephala*, see *Ligularia s.* *S. tanguticus*, China; hardy herbaceous rhizomatous perennial to 1·5m or more tall, forming large clumps or colonies; leaves to 20cm long, broadly ovate in outline, deeply pinnately lobed and toothed; flower-heads to 2cm wide, rays 3–4, yellow, in plume-like terminal panicles 15–30cm long, autumn; needs moisture-retentive soil but apt to be invasive. *S. vira-vira* (*S. leucostachys*, *Cineraria candidissima*), Argentina; evergreen shrub or sub-shrub to 60cm or more tall; much like *S. bicolor cineraria* and sometimes confused with it, but leaves more finely dissected and flower-heads without ray florets.

Sequoia

(for George Gist, 1770–1843, better known under his nickname Sequoyah – a Cherokee Indian name for the opossum – and a half-breed, inventor of the Cherokee alphabet). TAXODIACEAE. A genus of 1 species of giant evergreen coniferous tree from California and S.W.Oregon: *S. sempervirens*, redwood or coast redwood; the tallest known tree species often topping 100m in the wild, at least 1 specimen known to be 113m when measured some years ago, but more usually rarely above 40m; pyramidal or columnar with a buttressed trunk and thick, stringy, cinnamon bark; leaves 1·2–2·5cm long, linear in 2 parallel ranks forming flat sprays; flowers (strobili) unisexual, the males 2mm long, rounded, the females developing into globose to ovoid cones about 2cm long. *S.s.* Adpressa, less vigorous than type, shoot tips creamy-white; *S.s.* Prostrata (*S.s.* Nana Pendula), prostrate habit with broad, glaucous leaves, sometimes produces erect, reversion shoots that should be cut out. Grow in moist but well-drained, humus-rich soil in sun or partial shade, ideally sheltered from strong, cold winds. Plant autumn or spring. Propagate from seed in spring or by cuttings late summer to early autumn, in a cold frame.

Sequoiadendron

(the genus *Sequoia* and Greek *dendron*, a tree – a close ally of *Sequoia* and formerly classified in it). TAXODIACEAE. A genus of 1 species of giant, evergreen, coniferous tree from Sierra Nevada, California: *S. giganteum* (*Sequoia g.*, *Wellingtonia g.*), big tree, giant redwood, mammoth tree, Wellingtonia; similar to *Sequoia sempervirens*, but less tall in the wild, although to 50m in Britain, more massive and with darker, spongy bark; leaves 4–8mm long, scale- to needle-like, glaucous when young, dark green later; male strobili 6–8mm long, mature cones ovoid, 5–8cm long. Culture as for *Sequoia*, although it stands more exposure, particularly when young.

Far left below: *Senecio vira-vira*
Below: *Sequoiadendron giganteum* young tree

Service tree – see *Sorbus domestica*.

Shadbush – see *Amelanchier*.

Shamrock – see *Oxalis acetosella* (wood sorrel), *Medicago lupulina* (black medick), *Trifolium repens* (white clover).

Sheep-laurel – see *Kalmia angustifolia*.

Shell flower – see *Molucella*.

Shibataea kumasasa – see *Phyllostachys ruscifolia*.

Shooting star – see *Dodecatheon*.

Shortia

(for Dr Charles W. Short, 1794–1863, American botanist). DIAPENSIACEAE. A genus of 7–8 species of evergreen perennials including those formerly listed under *Schizocodon*, from E.Asia and S.E.USA. They are tufted, sometimes small, mat-forming, with long-stalked, evergreen leaves, the blades rounded, leathery and glossy; flowers solitary or in racemes, somewhat bell-shaped, the 5 petals notched or fringed. Grow in moisture-retentive but well-drained, humus-rich soil in partial shade. Plant spring or autumn. Propagate by careful division at planting, seed in shaded cold frame, spring.

Species cultivated: *S. galacifolia*, Oconee bells; N. and S.Carolina; to 15cm tall; leaf-blades 4–7·5cm long, ovate to orbicular, rounded-toothed, glossy, bronze-red in autumn; flowers about 2·5cm wide, solitary, nodding, white, often ageing pink, toothed, spring to early summer. *S. soldanelloides* (*Schizocodon s.*), fringe-bell or galax (USA); Japan; similar to *S. galacifolia* in general appearance but leaves more highly polished and flowers fringed, pink or white, in short racemes, early summer. *S. uniflora* (*Schizocodon u.*), Japan; much like *S. galacifolia* but more vigorous and likely to form mats when well-suited; flowers to 3cm wide, pink, spring. *S.u.* Grandiflora, flowers somewhat larger than type and more freely produced.

Sidalcea

(from the closely allied genera *Sida* and *Alcea*). MALVACEAE. A genus of 22–25 species of annuals and perennials from W. N.America, 1 of which is widely available: *S. malviflora* (*S. malvaeflora*), Oregon, California and adjacent Mexico; clump-forming perennial 90–120cm tall; leaves long-stalked, the blades of the basal ones 5–8cm wide, rounded, crenately notched to shallowly 7–9 lobed; stem leaves smaller with fewer, deeper lobes; flowers about 5cm wide with 5, spreading, notched, pink petals. *S.m.* Croftway Red, deep red, 1m tall; *S.m.* Loveliness, shell-pink, 80cm tall; *S.m.* Sussex Beauty, large, clear pink, 1·3m tall; *S.m.* William Smith, large, salmon-red, 1m tall. Grow in moisture-retentive, well-drained, fertile soil in sun. Plant autumn to spring. Propagate by division at planting time or from seed in spring, though seedlings from cultivars do not come true to type.

Silene

(old Greek name for sticky or German catchfly, *Lychnis viscaria*, used for this allied genus by Linnaeus). Catchfly, campion. CARYOPHYLLACEAE. A genus of about 500 species of annuals, perennials and sub-shrubs from the N.Hemisphere. They are tufted to clump-forming, prostrate to erect, with opposite pairs of narrow leaves and terminal cymes of 5-petalled flowers with tubular to inflated calyces. Grow the species described here in well-drained, moderately fertile soil in sun. Plant autumn to spring. Propagate by division at planting time, basal cuttings in spring, or from seed when ripe or spring.

Species cultivated: *S. acaulis*, moss campion, cushion pink; circumpolar and mountains farther south; tufted perennial, low hummock- or mat-forming, to 30cm or more wide; leaves 6–12mm long, linear, stiffly ciliate; flowers solitary, 9–12mm wide, deep pink, just above the leaves, summer; shy flowering and best in a scree or poor, gritty soil. *S.a. elongata* (*S. longiscapa*, *S. pedunculata*), flowers on stems to 5cm tall. *S. alpestris* (*S. quadrifolia* in part, *Heliosperma alpestre*), tufted perennial rather woody-based; stems 15–30cm long, slender, erect to ascending, branched; leaves grassy, linear to oblanceolate; flowers 1cm or more wide, each petal 4–6 toothed, white, summer. *S.a.* Plena, flowers double. *S. armeria*, sweet William catchfly; Europe; branched annual 30–40cm tall; leaves to 7·5cm long, spathulate to ovate, stem-clasping, glaucous; flowers 1·5–2cm wide, pink or white in dense terminal clusters, summer to autumn. *S. coeli-rosa* (*Lychnis c.-r.*, *Viscaria elegans*), rose of heaven; S.Europe; slender, erect annual 30–50cm tall; leaves 4–7cm long, linear-lanceolate; flowers 2–3cm wide, rose-purple, summer to autumn. *S.c.-r.* Blue Pearl, lavender-blue; *S.c.-r.* Cardinalis, crimson; *S.c.-r.* Love, rose-pink; *S.c.-r.* Oculata, mixed colours but

Far left: *Shortia soldanelloides*
Far left below: *Shortia uniflora*
Left above: *Sidalcea malviflora* William Smith
Left below: *Silene acaulis*
Above: *Silene schafta*
Below: *Silene maritima*

flowers dark-eyed; several mixed strains are available in shades of the above colours and white. *S. dioica* (*Melandrium d.*, *M. rubrum*, *Lychnis r.*), red campion; Europe, W.Asia and N.Africa; clump-forming, 40–70cm tall; leaves 4–10cm long, obovate to oblong; flowers unisexual to 2·5cm wide, bright pink, the females with inflated calyces, late spring and summer. *S.d.* Flore Pleno, flowers fully double, rose-red. *S. maritima*, sea campion; coastal areas Norway to Spain; mat-forming, to 90cm wide; leaves 2–3cm long, lanceolate to ovate, glaucous; flowers 2–2·5cm wide, white, on stem to 10cm tall; usually represented in gardens by *S.m.* Flore-pleno, with flowers larger than type, double. *S. pendula*, nodding catchfly; S.Mediterranean to Caucasus and S.USSR; annual 20–40cm tall; stems branched, decumbent; leaves 2–5cm long, ovate to lanceolate,

Above: *Silene armeria*

downy; flowers 2cm wide, bright rose, summer to autumn. *S.p.* Compacta, compact, cushion-forming habit, 20–30cm high and wide; *S.p.* Compacta Double Salmon Rose, flowers double salmon-pink; *S.p.* Ruberrima, to 40cm tall, flowers ruby-red. *S. schafta*, Caucasus; tufted perennial to 15cm tall; stems ascending to decumbent, slender, usually unbranched; leaves 1–2cm long, ovate to obovate; flowers 2–2·5cm wide, pink to rose-magenta, mid summer to late autumn; long-lived in sharply drained soils, good in dry walls.

Silky oak – *Grevillea robusta.*

Silphium

(old Greek name for a local resin-producing plant taken up by Linnaeus for this genus). Compass plant. COMPOSITAE. A genus of about 20 species of herbaceous perennials from E. N.America, 1 of which is commonly cultivated: *S. laciniatum*, compass plant; Ohio to S.Dakota and Texas; clump-forming, to 2m tall; stems robust; basal leaves 30–50cm long, ovate, pinnatipartite; flower-heads terminal, daisy-like, to 12cm or more wide, yellow, late summer to autumn; the lower leaves are held vertically and in the wild reputedly align the blades north–south, hence the vernacular name. Grow in fertile, moisture-retentive but well-drained soil in sun. Plant autumn to spring. Propagate by division at planting time or from seed in spring.

Silver bell tree – see *Halesia.*

Silverberry – see *Elaeagnus commutata.*

Silybum

(Greek *silybon* for a thistle-like plant). COMPOSITAE. A genus of 2 species from the Mediterranean, 1 being generally available: *S. marianum*, milk, blessed, holy, Our Lady's or St Mary's thistle; biennial; 60–120cm tall, depending on soil fertility; stems robust, simple or with a few branches; basal leaves 30–60cm long, oblong, sinuately lobed to pinnatifid, spiny-margined, glossy with a bold pattern of white veins; flower-heads about 5cm wide, erect to more or less nodding, involucral bracts spine-tipped, florets tubular, red-purple, summer. Grow in well-drained, fertile soil in sun. Propagate from seed sown *in situ* in spring.

Sinoarundinaria murielae, S. nitida – see *Arundinaria.*

Sisyrinchium

(ancient Greek name for a plant now unknown, but probably related to *Iris*, taken up by Linnaeus for this genus). IRIDACEAE. A genus of about 75 species of perennials from N. and S.America. They are tufted to clump-forming, with mostly basal, grassy to sword-shaped leaves and often winged stems bearing paired, leaf-like bracts (spathes), from which 6-tepalled, starry or sometimes bell-shaped flowers emerge. The flowers only last a day, but several from the same bract open in succession. Grow in moisture-retentive but well-drained, preferably moderately fertile soil in sun. Plant autumn or spring. Propagate by division at planting time or from seed in spring.

Species cultivated (summer-flowering unless otherwise stated): *S. angustifolium* (*S. gramineum*), blue-eyed grass; N.America; loosely tufted, spreading to erect, 30–50cm long, sometimes less; stems winged, branched; leaves 2–6mm wide; spathes 1·5–2cm long, stalked, flowers 1–1·3cm wide, blue, ageing violet; sometimes confused in gardens with *S. bermudiana* and *S. montanum crebrum*. *S. bermudiana* (*S. iridioides*), Bermuda; tufted, 30cm or more tall, more erect than *S. angustifolium*; stems broadly winged; leaves 6mm wide; spathes stalked, flowers 2cm wide, nodding, violet-blue with yellow eye; not fully hardy in severe winters. *S. boreale* and *S. brachypus*, now included under the next species. *S. californicum* (including *S. boreale* and *S. brachypus*), golden-eyed grass; California to Vancouver Is; tufted, 15–60cm tall; leaves to 6mm wide, often somewhat glaucous, outer bract of spathe longer than inner, 2–5cm long; flowers 2–2·5cm wide, bright yellow; plants under *S. brachypus* in gardens are generally less than 15cm tall with relatively shorter, broader leaves *S. douglasii* (*S. grandiflorum*), spring bell, purple-eyed grass; California to British Columbia; sparsely tufted; stems slightly flattened, not winged; leaves narrowly linear, semi-cylindrical; outer bract of spathe 5–12cm long, leaf-like, inner one much shorter, flowers pendant, bell-shaped, to 2cm long, violet to reddish-purple, spring. *S. filifolium*, Falkland Is; similar habit to *S. douglasii*, but flowers more or less erect, white with a delicate red-purple vein pattern, late spring. *S. grandiflorum*, see *S. douglasii*. *S. iridioides*, see *S. bermudiana*. *S. montanum*, N.America; tufted, 30–60cm tall; stems slender, narrowly winged, mostly simple; leaves 1–3mm wide, pale green; spathes sessile, the outer one 2–8cm long, its basal margins united, flowers 2cm wide, blue-violet. *S.m. crebrum* (*S. angustifolium* in part), distinguished from true *S. angustifolium* by its mostly unbranched stem and sessile spathes, leaves deeper green, spathes often purple-tinged. *S. odoratissimum*, S. S.America; similar to *S. filifolium*, but flowers more funnel-shaped, nodding, white with brown-purple veins, fragrant; best in an alpine or cool greenhouse; now classified by some botanists as *Phaiophleps biflora*. *S. striatum*, S.Chile, clump-forming, robust, to 60cm tall; stems with

Left above: *Sisyrinchium californicum*
Left: *Silybum marianum*
Above: *Sisyrinchium striatum*

many crowded spathes forming a long, spike-like inflorescence; leaves sword-shaped in iris-like fans, to 30cm long, somewhat glaucous; flowers 2–2·5cm wide, pale yellow with dark veining, summer to autumn. *S.s.* Variegatum, leaves boldly white-margined.

Top: *Sisyrinchium striatum* Variegatum
Above: *Sisyrinchium bermudiana*

Top: *Skimmia japonica*
Above left: *Skimmia japonica* Rubella
Above: *Skimmia laureola*

Skimmia

(from *shikimi*, the Japanese vernacular name, in Latin form). RUTACEAE. A genus of 7–9 species of evergreen shrubs from Himalaya to Japan and Philippines. They have alternate, leathery, oblong-ovate to lanceolate leaves, aromatic when bruised, terminal panicles of small, dioecious or bisexual, fragrant, 4–5 petalled flowers in spring followed by berry-like red drupes with 2–4 white nutlets. Grow in humus-rich soil in sun or partial shade, the less hardy species in sheltered sites. Plant autumn or spring. Propagate by cuttings in late summer, with or without bottom heat, layering in spring, or from seed when ripe in a cold frame.

Species cultivated: *S.* × *foremanii*, see *S. japonica* Foremanii. *S. japonica*, Japan; 1–1·5m tall, of rounded, usually bushy habit; leaves 7–10cm long, narrowly elliptic to obovate; flowers mainly dioecious, 4-petalled, white in panicles to 8cm long; fruit 8mm wide, bright red. *S.j.* Foremanii (*S.j.* Veitchii), more vigorous than type, flowers female, fruit in larger clusters provided a pollinator is nearby; *S.j.* Fragrans, male flowers freely and densely borne, strongly fragrant; *S.j.* Rogersii, compact dwarf habit, leaves somewhat twisted, flowers female; *S.j.* Rogersii Nana, even smaller than *S.j.* Rogersii, flowers male; *S.j.* Rubella, flowers male, red-budded, in large panicles; *S.j.* Veitchii, see *S.j.* Foremanii. *S. laureola*, Himalaya; to 1m or more tall, of dense habit; leaves 7–15cm long, lanceolate to oblong or obovate, curiously pungent when bruised; flowers dioecious, pale greenish-yellow, fragrant; fruit bright red; reasonably hardy but best in sheltered sites. *S. reevesiana* (*S. fortunei*), China, Taiwan, Philippines (mountains); 60–90cm tall, occasionally to 2m tall in warm, sheltered sites; leaves 6–10cm long, oblong-lanceolate to narrowly elliptic; flowers 5-petalled, hermaphrodite, white; fruit matt crimson, long lasting; not reliably hardy, best in neutral to acid soils.

Skunk cabbage – see *Lysichiton*.

Slipper flower – see *Calceolaria*.

Sloe – see *Prunus spinosa*.

Smilacina

(diminutive of *Smilax*, although there is no obvious close similarity). False Solomon's seal. LILIACEAE. A genus of 25 species of rhizomatous perennials from N.America and Asia. They are similar to Solomon's seal (*Polygonatum*) in habit and foliage, but each

stem terminates in a raceme or panicles of small, 6-tepalled, rather starry flowers. Fruit is a globular, few-seeded berry. Grow in humus-rich, moisture-retentive but not wet soil in partial shade. Plant autumn to spring. Propagate by careful division at planting time or from seed when ripe; seedlings take several years to flower.

Species cultivated: *S. racemosa*, false spikenard; N.America; 60–90cm tall; leaves 8–15cm long, lanceolate to ovate-oblong, slender-pointed, downy beneath; flowers white in plume-like panicles, to 15cm long, late spring; fruit red, sometimes purple-spotted. *S. stellata*, star-flowered lily-of-the-valley; W.N.America; to 60cm tall; leaves 5–15cm long, oblong to lanceolate, long-pointed; flowers white, in dense racemes to 5cm long, late spring; fruit green with blackish stripes then dark red.

Smoke tree – see *Cotinus*.

Snake's beard – see *Ophiopogon*.

Snake's head – see *Fritillaria meleagris*.

Snakeweed – see *Polygonum bistorta*.

Snapdragon – see *Antirrhinum*.

Sneezewort – see *Achillea ptarmica*.

Snowball tree – see *Viburnum opulus* Sterile.

Snowberry – see *Symphoricarpos*.

Snowdrop – see *Galanthus*.

Snowdrop tree – see *Halesia*.

Snowflake – see *Leucojum*.

Snow-in-summer – see *Cerastium tomentosum*.

Soapwort – see *Saponaria officinalis*.

Solanum

(old Latin name, probably for black nightshade, used for the whole genus by Linnaeus). SOLANACEAE. A genus of about 1700 species of annuals, perennials, shrubs and climbers of cosmopolitan distribution. They have alternate, simple to pinnate leaves and

solitary or cymose clusters of flowers that appear to be lateral but do not arise in leaf-axils and are actually terminal with an axillary stem growing beyond. The corolla of each flower is fused at the base with 5 long to short spreading lobes and the stamens form a central yellow cone. The fruit is a rounded berry, often poisonous but in some cases edible, as the aubergine. The species described are

Far left below: *Smilacina racemosa*
Left below: *Solanum crispum* Glasnevin
Above: *Solanum jasminoides* Album

tender or half-hardy, needing sheltered, sunny sites outside or a frost-free greenhouse in cold areas. Any moderately fertile, well-drained soil is suitable. *S. capsicastrum* is frost-tender and must at least be over-wintered under glass or in the home, preferably at minimum temperature of 7–10°C. Plant half-hardy species in spring and propagate by cuttings from summer to late summer, over-wintering the young plants under glass. The climbers described here are vigorous and are best pruned annually in spring, cutting out all weak stems completely and spurring back the remainder to 10–15cm. Sow seed of *S. capsicastrum* and *S. pseudocapsicum* in early spring at 16–18°C. Prick off seedlings when first true leaves develop at 4cm apart each way in boxes of a good potting mixture. When the young plants overlap each other place singly in 9cm containers and put in a cold frame when fear of frost has passed. Leave the tops off the frames during the summer. When the pots are full of roots move the plants into 13–15cm pots. Seed may also be sown late spring or early summer for small fruiting plants, in 10cm pots. Once the plants are established in their final pots, liquid fertilizer at 7–10 day intervals is beneficial. Cover the plants at night in early autumn and provide heat, or take into a greenhouse as soon as frosts are likely. The plants can be cut back by ½ – ⅔ in spring, repotted and grown on, but are best raised annually from seed.

Species cultivated: *S. aviculare*, kangaroo apple; New Zealand, S.E.Australia; shrub or small tree to 3m tall, usually less in cool areas; stems robust; leaves 15–30cm long, lanceolate to narrowly so, entire or irregularly pinnatifid on same plant; flowers solitary or in cymes, 2–3·5cm wide, lavender to pale violet, summer to autumn; berries ovoid, 2–2·5cm long, yellowish; needs a sheltered site against a wall in frosty regions and best in a greenhouse in cold areas; often behaves as an herbaceous perennial if the root and stem bases are protected in winter. *S. capsicastrum*, false Jerusalem cherry, winter cherry; Brazil; evergreen shrub to 60cm or more tall, but rarely above 30cm grown as an annual; leaves 4–7cm long, oblong-lanceolate to obovate, bearing short, branched hairs, each main leaf with a smaller one at its base; flowers solitary or in 2s or 3s, about 1cm wide, white; berries ovoid, pointed, 1·5–2mm long, scarlet; much confused with *S. pseudocapsicum*. *S.c.* Nanum and *S.c.* Pattersonii, see *S. pseudocapsicum* Nanum and *S.p.* Pattersonii. *S. crispum*, Chile; scrambling shrub to 4m or more tall, usually evergreen, but almost deciduous in hard winters; leaves 6–10cm long, ovate-lanceolate, often crisped; flowers 2cm wide, blue-purple in dense clusters, late summer to autumn; berries small, rounded, yellowish-white; comparatively hardy on walls in all but the worst winters. *S.c.* Glasnevin (*S.c.* Autumnale), a good, free-flowering form with a longer season than type. *S. jasminoides*, potato vine; Brazil; semi-twining woody climber to 5m tall; stems slender; leaves 3–7cm long, entire or irregularly pinnately lobed; flowers to 2·5cm wide, broadly lobed, bluish-white in branched cymes, summer to autumn. *S.j.* Album, flowers pure white, needs a very sheltered wall to survive outside in all but the milder areas. *S. laciniatum*, S.E.Australia, New Zealand; much like *S. aviculare* but somewhat more robust, with purplish stems and blue-purple flowers to 5cm wide; now considered to be a tetraploid form of *S. aviculare* and placed under that species by some botanists. *S. pseudocapsicum*, Jerusalem cherry; E.S.America, naturalized in many parts of tropics and subtropics; erect shrub to 1m or more tall; leaves 5–10cm long, oblong to lanceolate, somewhat glossy, smooth, often in unequal pairs; flowers 1·5cm wide, solitary or in 2s and 3s; berries globose,

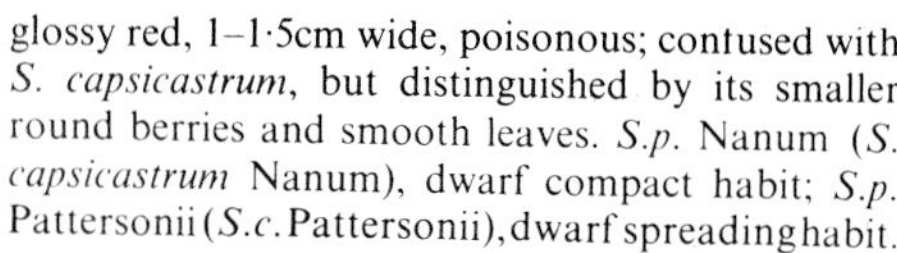

glossy red, 1–1·5cm wide, poisonous; confused with *S. capsicastrum*, but distinguished by its smaller round berries and smooth leaves. *S.p.* Nanum (*S. capsicastrum* Nanum), dwarf compact habit; *S.p.* Pattersonii (*S.c.* Pattersonii), dwarf spreading habit.

Above left: *Solanum capsicastrum*
Top: *Soldanella montana*
Above: *Soldanella villosa*
Top right: *Soleirolia soleirolii*
Right: *Solidago* Lemore

Soldanella

(reputedly the diminutive of Italian *soldo*, a coin – from the shape of the leaves). Snowbell. PRIMULACEAE. A genus of 10 species of small evergreen perennials from the mountains of S. and C.Europe. They are clump- to mat-forming with comparatively long-stalked, orbicular, leathery, dark green leaves and 5-petalled, fringed, nodding, bell-shaped flowers on slender, leafless scapes in spring. Grow in moisture-retentive but well-drained, preferably gritty, humus-rich soil in sun or partial shade. In southern and warm areas they need as cool a site as possible, ideally facing north and away from overhanging trees. A sheet of glass overhead is advantageous in wet winters. Plant autumn or spring. Propagate by careful division at planting time or from seed when ripe or as soon afterwards as possible, and ideally placed where it can become frozen in winter.

Species cultivated: *S. alpina*, common or alpine snowbell; mountains of Europe; leaves to 4cm wide, rounded to kidney-shaped, usually cordate, dark green on both sides; scapes 5–15cm tall, flowers 2–4, each 8–13mm long with a flared fringe to halfway, violet to blue. *S. carpatica*, W.Carpathians; similar to *S. alpina*, but leaves to 5cm wide, narrowly cleft, usually purplish beneath; flowers 2–5, more deeply fringed. *S. minima*, least snowbell; E.Alps, Appennines: leaves to 1cm wide, often longer than wide, rarely cordate; scapes 2–10cm tall, flowers usually solitary, 8–15mm long, fringed $\frac{1}{4}$ – $\frac{1}{5}$, pale violet to almost white. *S. montana*, mountain tassel; C.Europe to Italian Alps and Bulgaria; leaves to 6cm wide, orbicular, sometimes obscurely toothed or crenate, bright green, often purplish beneath; scapes 10–25cm tall, flowers 5–8, each 1·5cm long with a flared fringe $\frac{3}{5}$ or $\frac{3}{4}$, violet. *S.m. villosa*, see *S. villosa*. *S. pindicola*, N.W.Greece; like *S. carpatica* but leaves widely cleft at base and glaucous beneath. *S. villosa* (*S. montana v.*), W.Pyrenees; like *S. montana* but leaves to 7cm wide, pale green, not purplish beneath; scapes to 30cm tall, densely hairy, flowers 3–4, each to 1·6cm long, fringed $\frac{2}{3}$ – $\frac{4}{5}$.

Soleirolia

(for Joseph François Soleirol, d. 1863, who collected extensively in Corsica). Mind-your-own-business, baby's tears. URTICACEAE. A genus of 1, half-hardy, evergreen, mat-forming perennial from Corsica and Sardinia, naturalized elsewhere: *S. soleirolii* (*Helxine s.*), stems filiform, interlacing, forming dense, mossy, invasive mats to 60cm or more; leaves alternate, 2–6mm long, obliquely rounded, sparsely hairy; flowers petalless, minute, unisexual, solitary in leaf-axils; golden-leaved and variegated forms are sometimes available. Grow in moisture-retentive but well-drained soil in partial shade or sun in sheltered sites. Alternatively grow in pots or pans or as ground cover under greenhouse benches. Pot or plant spring to autumn. Propagate by division at almost any time.

Solidago

(Latin *solido*, to make whole or sound, to strengthen – alluding to reputed healing properties of some species). Goldenrod. COMPOSITAE. A genus of 100–130 species of perennials, mainly from N.America, with a few in S.America, Europe, Asia. They are clump-forming with long to short rhizomes, mainly narrow, simple, alternate leaves, and terminal racemes or panicles of tiny, yellow flower-heads – each with a few disc and short ray florets. Grow in any moisture-retentive but not wet soil in sun, although partial shade is tolerated. Plant autumn to spring. Propagate by division at planting time or from seed in spring in a cold frame. The

cultivars do not come true from seed and must be divided.

Species cultivated: *S. brachystachys* of gardens, see *S. virgaurea*. *S. canadensis*, N. N.America east of Rocky Mountains; to 1·5m tall; leaves crowded, 6–13cm long, linear-lanceolate with 3 main veins, sharply toothed, pubescent beneath; flower-heads 3mm long in broadly pyramidal panicles 10–40cm long, late summer to autumn; a main parent of the garden cultivars, see below. *S. virgaurea*, Europe, Asia, N.Africa; 30–75cm tall; leaves to 10cm long, oblanceolate to obovate with a single main vein, toothless or obscurely toothed; flower-heads 6–10mm long in erect leafy panicles to 20cm or more long, summer to autumn; a variable species including several dwarf forms: *S.v.* Brachystachys (*S. brachystachys* of gardens), stems downy, 20–25cm

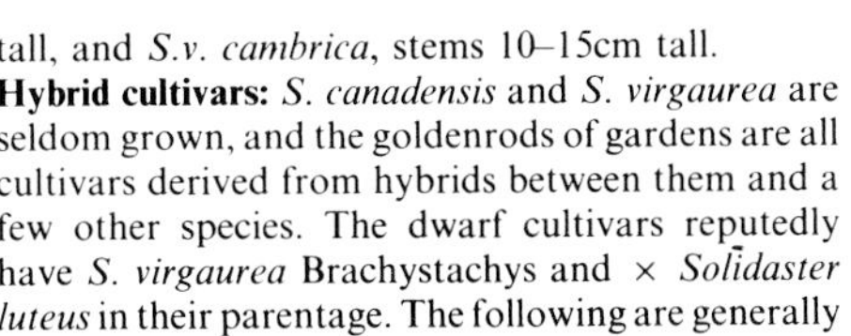

tall, and *S.v. cambrica*, stems 10–15cm tall.
Hybrid cultivars: *S. canadensis* and *S. virgaurea* are seldom grown, and the goldenrods of gardens are all cultivars derived from hybrids between them and a few other species. The dwarf cultivars reputedly have *S. virgaurea* Brachystachys and × *Solidaster luteus* in their parentage. The following are generally

available and recommended: *S.* Cloth of Gold, 45cm tall, vigorous and sturdy, deep yellow; *S.* Crown of Rays, 60cm tall, panicles with wide-spreading lateral branches, bright yellow; *S.* Golden Thumb (*S.* Queenie, *S.* Tom Thumb), 30cm tall, bushy and neat, yellow-tinted foliage and yellow flowers; *S.* Goldenmosa, 75cm tall, compact and bushy, panicles mimosa-like, with yellow stalks and bright yellow flowers; *S.* Lemore, 75cm tall, sturdy habit, lemon to primrose-yellow flowers in wide panicles.

× Solidaster

(bigeneric hybrid between *Solidago* and *Aster*). COMPOSITAE. Intermediate between parent genera

but favouring *Aster* in general appearance. 1 hybrid species (clone) is available: × *S. luteus* (*Aster hybridus luteus* of gardens), 60–75cm tall; leaves 8–15cm long, lanceolate with 3 main veins; flower-heads to 1cm wide, yellow, the rays ageing creamy-yellow, in corymb-like panicles; reputedly derived from the linear-leaved, white-flowered *A. ptarmicoides* and an unknown *Solidago*, perhaps *S. canadensis*. Culture as for *Solidago*.

Solomon's seal – see *Polygonatum*.

Sophora

(said by Linnaeus to be the ancient name of an allied plant – according to some authorities of Arabic

derivation). LEGUMINOSAE. A genus of about 50 species of shrubs and trees mainly from tropical to warm temperate regions. They have alternate, pinnate leaves and racemes or panicles of pea-shaped flowers followed by narrow pods that are often abruptly constricted between the seeds. Grow in well-drained, fertile soil in sunny, sheltered sites. In all but the mildest areas *S. microphylla* and *S. tetraptera* need the protection of a wall. Plant *S. japonica* and *S. davidii* autumn to spring, the others in spring only. Propagate from seed in spring under glass or cuttings late summer, bottom heat 18°C and

Far left: *Solidago* Crown of Rays
Far left below: *Solidago virgaurea cambrica*
Above left: × *Solidaster luteus*
Below: *Sophora japonica*
Above: *Sophora microphylla*

hormone treatment, ideally under mist.
Species cultivated: *S. davidii* (*S. viciifolia*), W. and C.China; deciduous shrub of rounded habit, 2–3m tall; leaves 4–6·5cm long, leaflets 13–19, elliptic, 6–9mm long; flowers to 2cm long, blue-white to white, in racemes, summer; the easiest species to root from cuttings. *S. japonica*, Japanese pagoda or Chinese scholar tree; China, Korea, long cultivated in Japan; deciduous tree 15–25m tall, generally of rounded habit; leaves 15–25cm long, leaflets 7–17, ovate to elliptic, glaucous beneath, 2·5–5cm long; flowers to 1·2cm long, creamy-white in large terminal panicles, late summer, autumn. *S. microphylla* (*S. tetraptera m.*, *Edwardsia m.*), kowhai; New Zealand; large shrub or small tree 3–10m tall, usually evergreen, but losing many leaves in cold winters; leaves to 15cm or more long, leaflets 41–81, obovate-oblong, silky hairy when young, then dark green above, 5–9mm long; flowers 3·5–4·5cm long, all petals pointing forwards, lemon-yellow, in short racemes, late spring, early summer; the hardiest New Zealand species, surviving in the open where winters are mild; plants from seed may pass through a low, dense, twiggy juvenile stage. *S. tetraptera* (*Edwardsia t.*), kowhai; New Zealand, Chile; large shrub or smallish tree 5–12m tall; leaves to 15cm long, leaflets 21–41, ovate to elliptic-oblong, 1·5–3·5cm long, with appressed silky hairs; flowers to 5cm long, all petals pointing forwards, golden-yellow, in short racemes, late spring, early summer; needs a sheltered wall, or a frost-free greenhouse in cold areas. *S.t. microphylla*, see *S. microphylla*.

Sorbaria

(Latin for resembling the genus *Sorbus*). False spiraea. ROSACEAE. A genus of about 10 species of deciduous shrubs formerly classified under *Spiraea* from E. and C.Asia. They are of vigorous, suckering growth with alternate, pinnate leaves and terminal, plume-like panicles of tiny, white, 5-petalled flowers. Grow in moisture-retentive but well-drained, moderately fertile soil in sun, although partial shade is tolerated. Plant autumn to spring. Propagate by suckers at planting, semi-hardwood cuttings late summer, hardwood autumn.
Species cultivated: *S. aitchisonii* (*Spiraea a.*), Afghanistan, Kashmir; 3–4m tall, graceful spreading habit; leaves 20–38cm long, leaflets 11–23, lanceolate, sharply toothed, 4–10cm long; panicles 30–45cm long, late summer. *S. arborea*, C. and W.China; similar to *S. aitchisonii*, but to 5m tall; leaflets 13–17, downy. *S. sorbifolia* (*Spiraea s.*), N.Asia to Japan; to 2m tall, often profusely suckering; stems erect; leaves 20–30cm long, leaflets 13–25, lanceolate, toothed, 5–9cm long; panicles 15–25cm long, erect, late summer.

Sorbus

(Latin *sorbum*, the fruit of the service tree – *Sorbus domestica*). ROSACEAE. A genus of 85–100 species of deciduous trees and shrubs from the N.Hemisphere. They have alternate, pinnate or simple, toothed leaves, often colouring well in autumn, small, usually white to cream, 5-petalled flowers in terminal corymbose panicles, and colourful, berry-like fruit. Grow in fertile, well-drained but not dry soil in sun, although light shade is tolerated. Plant autumn to spring. Propagate from seed when ripe, ideally in a cold frame, cultivars and selected forms by layering or grafting on to the type species, *S. americana* or *S. aucuparia*.
Species cultivated (all with pinnate leaves to 20cm or more long and flowering in summer, unless otherwise stated): *S. americana*, American mountain ash; E. N.America; tree to 10m tall; winter buds red and sticky; leaflets 11–17, lanceolate, 4–10cm long; panicles to 20cm wide; fruit 6mm wide, bright red. *S.a. decora*, see *S. decora*. *S. aria*, whitebeam; Europe; tree 15–25m tall, forming a wide, dense head; leaves simple, to 12cm long, usually ovate, sometimes shallowly lobed, densely white-felted beneath; panicles to 10cm wide; fruit ovoid, 8–15mm long, scarlet. *S.a.* Decaisneana (*S.a.* Majestica), leaves elliptic, to 15cm long, fruit larger than type; *S.a.* Lutescens, leaves creamy-downy above, ageing to grey-green by late summer. *S. aucuparia*, rowan, mountain ash; Europe to N.Africa and N.Turkey; tree to 15m or more tall, usually with a comparatively narrow head; leaflets mainly 13–15, oblong, 3–6cm long; panicles 10–13cm wide; fruit 6–9mm wide, scarlet. *S.a.*

Below: *Sophora microphylla* fruit
Bottom: *Sorbaria aitchisonii*
Right: *Sorbus aucuparia*

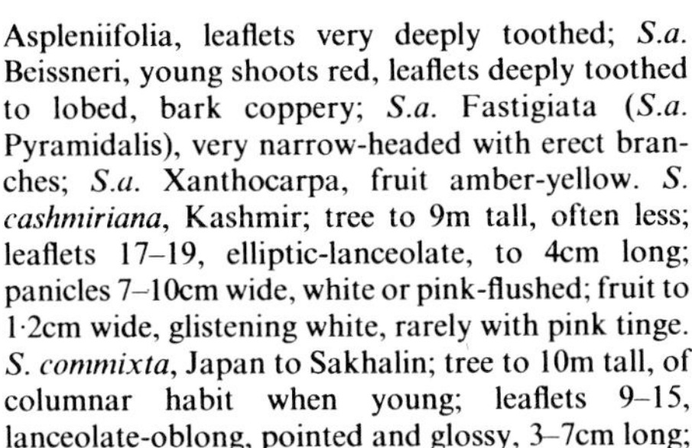

Aspleniifolia, leaflets very deeply toothed; *S.a.* Beissneri, young shoots red, leaflets deeply toothed to lobed, bark coppery; *S.a.* Fastigiata (*S.a.* Pyramidalis), very narrow-headed with erect branches; *S.a.* Xanthocarpa, fruit amber-yellow. *S. cashmiriana*, Kashmir; tree to 9m tall, often less; leaflets 17–19, elliptic-lanceolate, to 4cm long; panicles 7–10cm wide, white or pink-flushed; fruit to 1·2cm wide, glistening white, rarely with pink tinge. *S. commixta*, Japan to Sakhalin; tree to 10m tall, of columnar habit when young; leaflets 9–15, lanceolate-oblong, pointed and glossy, 3–7cm long; panicles 5–10cm wide; fruit 5cm wide, scarlet; recommended for its bright leaf colour in autumn. *S. conradinae* of gardens, see *S. pohuashanensis*. *S. decora* (*S. americana d.*), N.E. N.America; like *S. americana*, but leaflets usually shorter and broader, attractively blue-green above, whitish beneath; panicles to 16cm wide, looser; fruit glaucous, 6–12mm long; for *S. decora* of gardens and *S.d. nana*, see *S. scopulina*. *S. discolor* of gardens, see *S.* Embley. *S. domestica*, service tree; S.Europe to Turkey, N.Africa; similar to *S. aucuparia* in general appearance, but taller with more-spreading branches; winter buds sticky; fruit 2–3cm long, green to brown, red-flushed on sunny side, edible when bletted as for medlars. *S.d. maliformis*, fruit apple-shaped; *S.d. pyriformis*, fruit pear-shaped; *S.* Embley (*S. discolor* of gardens), similar to *S. commixta*, but with glistening orange fruit and glowing red autumn leaves colouring later and lasting longer. *S. fennica*, see *S. hybrida*. *S. hupehensis*, W.China; tree to 10m or more tall; leaflets 11–17, narrowly oblong, 4–7cm long, abruptly pointed, somewhat bluish-green; panicles 5–10cm wide, loose; fruit 6mm wide, white or pink-flushed. *S.h. obtusa*, leaflets blunt, fruit pink. *S. hybrida* (*S. fennica*), Scandinavia, Finland; tree to 12m tall, of compact habit; leaves 7–10cm long, pinnate at the base, with 1–2 pairs of leaflets, variously lobed towards the tip, bluish-green above, grey-white downy beneath; panicles 5–10cm wide; fruit 1–1·2cm wide, red; according to some authorities a natural hybrid between *S. aucuparia* and *S. rupicola* (a shrubby species closely allied to *S. aria*), sometimes confused with *S.* × *thuringiaca*. *S.* × *hybrida* of gardens, see *S.* × *thuringiaca*. *S.* Joseph Rock, China; tree to 10m or more tall; leaflets 15–19, narrowly oblong, turning to shades of orange-red, flushed copper and purple in autumn, 4cm long; fruit 8mm wide, amber-yellow; introduced from China as Rock 23657, and considered by some authorities to be a natural hybrid from *S. serotina* (a species similar to *S. commixta*) and by others an unnamed true species. *S. majestica*, see *S. aria* Decaisneana. *S. pohuashanensis* (*S. conradinae* of gardens), N.China; tree to 11m or more tall; leaflets 11–15, oblong to elliptic, pointed, grey downy beneath; panicles 10cm wide; fruit 6mm wide, orange-red. *S. reducta*, N.Burma, W.China; suckering, thicket-forming shrub, 30–60cm tall; leaflets 9–15, ovate to elliptic, 2–2·5cm long, dark lustrous green above; panicles small; fruit 6mm wide, white, tinted pink. *S. sargentiana*, W.China; tree 8–10m tall; stems robust; winter buds large and sticky; leaves to 30cm long, leaflets 7–11, oblong-lanceolate, slender-pointed, 7–13cm long, rich red in autumn; panicles 12–15cm wide; fruit 5–6mm wide, scarlet, densely borne, late-ripening; among the most handsome species for leaf and fruit. *S. scalaris*, W.China; large shrub or small tree to 6m tall; leaflets 21–33, narrowly oblong, grey hairy beneath, 2–4cm long; panicles 10–12cm wide, bright red. *S. scopulina* (*S. americana nana*, *S. decora* of gardens), W. N.America; shrub or small tree to 6m tall; columnar habit, slow-growing; leaflets 11–15, oblong, 2·5–6·5cm long, dark green; panicles 5–10cm wide; fruit to 8mm wide, orange to scarlet, glossy; at least some of the plants in cultivation under this name are probably of hybrid origin. *S.* × *thuringiaca* (*S.* × *hybrida* of gardens), (*S. aria* × *S. aucuparia*), similar to, and often confused with, *S. hybrida*, but head of branches more compact and erect, somewhat larger and narrower leaves with smaller elliptic leaflets. *S. vilmorinii*, W.China; large, wide-spreading shrub or small tree, 3–6m tall; leaflets 11–31, elliptic, to 2cm long, grey beneath; panicles to 7·5cm wide; fruit 6–8mm wide, red to white flushed pink.

Top: *Sorbus hybrida*
Below: *Sorbus aucuparia* Beissneri
Top right: *Sorbus cashmiriana*
Below right: *Sorbus aria*
Top far right: *Sorbus aucuparia* Xanthocarpa

Sorrel tree – see *Oxydendrum*.

Sour gum – see *Nyssa*.

Southern beech – see *Nothofagus*.

Southernwood – see *Artemisia abrotanum*.

Sparaxis

(Greek *sparasso*, to tear – alluding to the papery bracts, beneath the flowers, that appear as if torn). IRIDACEAE. A genus of about 5 species of cormous

Above left: *Sparaxis tricolor*
Above: *Spartium junceum*
Below right: *Spiraea* × *vanhouttei*
Bottom right: *Spiraea japonica* Anthony Waterer

perennials from S.Africa. Each corm produces a narrow fan of sword-shaped leaves and a taller, wiry, sometimes branched stem bearing terminal, 6-tepalled flowers rather like widely expanded crocuses. 1 species is generally available: *S. tricolor*, harlequin flower; 30–45cm tall; leaves linear, to 30cm long; flowers to 5cm wide in shades of red, yellow, purple, white, usually with yellow, black-bordered throat, summer, earlier under glass. Culture as for *Ixia*.

Spartium

(Greek *sparton*, esparto grass – alluding to the uses of the stems for weaving into mats, etc). LEGUMINOSAE. A genus of 1 species of broom-like shrub from S.W.Europe, Mediterranean; distinguished from *Genista* and *Cytisus* by the 1-lipped, spathe-like calyx: *S. junceum* (*Genista j.*), Spanish or weaver's broom; 3–4m tall, erect and bushy; stems deep glaucous green; leaves 1–3cm long, narrowly oblong to lanceolate, sparse and short-lived; flowers 2–2·5cm long, pea-shaped, rich bright yellow, in terminal racemes, summer to autumn; not reliably hardy in severe winters but survives in most moderate frost. Plant spring or summer. Propagate from seed in frame or greenhouse early spring, ideally 2 seeds in 9–10cm pots, thinning later to strongest seedling. Plant out when 30–40cm tall, or in cold areas sow late spring and over-winter plants in frost-free greenhouse, planting out following spring.

Spearmint – see *Mentha*.

Spearwort – see *Ranunculus flammula* and *R. lingua*.

Specularia – see *Legousia*.

Speedwell – see *Veronica*.

Spicebush – see *Lindera*.

Spider flower – see *Cleome*.

Spider-lily – see *Lycoris*.

Spiderwort – see *Tradescantia*.

Spignel – see *Meum*.

Spindle – see *Euonymus*.

Spiraea

(Greek *speiraira*, a plant used in making garlands). ROSACEAE. A genus of about 100 species of deciduous shrubs from the northern temperate zone, South Mexico and Himalaya. They have alternate, usually toothed or lobed, narrowly lanceolate to ovate leaves, and small, 5-petalled flowers in corymbs or panicles. The latter are borne either on short lateral shoots from the previous season's stems or terminal on current season's growth. Species with terminal inflorescences may be cut back near to ground level each late winter to produce strong stems and large inflorescences. The remaining may be pruned after flowering, cutting out weak stems and thinning the remainder if necessary. Alternatively, all species may be left unpruned if large specimens are required, merely removing dead stems and flower-heads if unsightly. Plant autumn to spring. Propagate by semi-hardwood cuttings late summer, hardwood cuttings late autumn, suckers removed at planting time, or layering in spring.

Species cultivated: *S. aitchisonii*, see *Sorbaria a. S. albiflora*, see *S. japonica* and *S.j.* Albiflora. *S.* × *arguta* (*S. crenata* × *S. hypericifolia* × *S. thunbergii*), to 2m tall, of dense but graceful habit; stems slender; leaves 2–4cm long, oblanceolate; flowers 7mm wide, pure white in numerous small lateral umbels, spring, before or with tiny leaves. *S. ariaefolia*, see *Holodiscus discolor*. *S. bella*, Himalaya; 1–1·5m tall; stems angular; leaves 2·5–6·5cm long, ovate, slender-pointed; flowers 6mm wide, bright rose, in corymbs, summer. *S.* × *billiardii* (*S. douglasii* × *S. salicifolia*), 2–3m tall; similar to *S. douglasii*, but leaves pointed and grey downy beneath; flowers bright pink, in narrow terminal panicles, to 20cm long, summer to early autumn. *S.* × *b.* Triumphans (*S. menziesii* Triumphans), flowers purplish-rose, in dense, conical panicles. *S. bullata*, see *S. japonica* Bullata. *S.* × *bumalda*, see *S. japonica*. *S. crispifolia*, see *S. japonica* Bullata. *S. digitata*, see *Filipendula purpurea*. *S. discolor*, see *Holodiscus d. S. douglasii*, W. N.America; suckering shrub 1·5–2·5m tall; stems erect, reddish, downy when young; leaves 3–9cm long, elliptic to oblong, blunt-tipped, toothed in upper half, grey-white felted beneath; flowers small, purplish-rose, in dense, narrowly pyramidal panicles 10–20cm long, summer; does not thrive in dry chalky soils. *S. filipendula*, see *Filipendula vulgaris*. *S. gigantea*, see *Filipendula kamtschatica*. *S. japonica* (*S. albiflora*, *S.* × *bumalda*), Japan, Korea, China, E.Himalaya; twiggy shrub 1–1·5m tall (60–90cm tall if pruned annually to near ground level); leaves 5–10cm long, ovate to lanceolate, pale to glaucous beneath; flowers 3–6mm wide, pale pink to rose, in flattened, terminal corymbs 10–30cm wide (largest on annually pruned plants), late summer. *S.j.* Albiflora (*S.j.* Alba, *S. albiflora*), smaller in all its parts and less vigorous, flowers white; *S.j.* Alpina (*S.j.* Nana), dense, mound-forming habit 50–60cm tall, the outer stems decumbent to prostrate, leaves and flowers smaller than type, rose-pink – *S.j.* Little Princess and *S.j.* Nyewoods are similar but dwarfer, with rose-crimson flowers; *S.j.* Anthony Waterer (*S.* × *bumalda* Anthony Waterer), like *S.j.*Bumalda, but somewhat taller, bearing scattered, pink and cream, variegated shoots and crimson flowers; *S.j.* Bullata (*S. bullata*, *S. crispifolia*), curious but attractive mutant, to 25cm tall, leaves small, broadly ovate, crinkled and bullate, dark green, flower-heads small, crimson; *S.j.* Bumalda (*S.* × *bumalda*), reputedly a hybrid between a form of the type species and *S.j.* Albiflora, about 60cm tall if pruned annually, flowers carmine. *S. kamtschatica*, see *Filipendula k. S. lobata*, see *Filipendula nigra rubra*. *S. menziesii*, W. N.America; like *S. douglasii*, but stems brown, leaves glabrous or almost so and somewhat smaller. *S.m.* Triumphans, see *S.* × *billiardii* Triumphans. *S. opulifolis*, see *Physocarpus o. S. prunifolia*, E.Asia; to 1·8m tall; stem erect, then arching; leaves 2·5–4cm long, ovate-elliptic, finely toothed, somewhat glossy above, downy beneath; flowers about 1cm wide, white, fully double, in small clusters, spring, early summer; sometimes known as *S.p.* Plena, but the double garden form was described first and this cultivar name is unnecessary.

Left: *Spiraea thunbergii*
Below far left: *Spiraea japonica* Little Princess
Bottom far left: *Spiraea* × *billiardii*
Above: *Stachys grandiflora*
Below: *Stachys byzantina* Silver Carpet

S.p. simpliciflora, the original single-flowered wild species, rarely seen in gardens. *S. salicifolia*, Europe to N.E.Asia, to 2m tall; of dense, suckering habit; similar to *S. menziesii*, but leaves pointed, more sharply and sometimes doubly toothed; flowers pink, in panicles to 10cm long, summer. *S. sorbifolia*, see *Sorbaria s. S. thunbergii*, China, much grown and naturalized in Japan; to 1·5m tall; of dense, spreading habit; stems slender and wiry; leaves 1–3cm long, linear-lanceolate, toothed, pale green; flowers 6mm wide, pure glistening white, in small umbels all along the stems, before or with developing leaves, spring; the earliest and purest white of all spiraeas. *S. ulmaria*, see *Filipendula u. S.* × *vanhouttei* (*S. cantoniensis* × *S. trilobata*), to 2m tall; stems erect to arching; leaves 2–4cm long, obovate to rhombic, usually shallowly 3–5 lobed, toothed, dark green above, glaucous beneath; flowers 7mm wide, pure white, in corymbs 2·5–5 cm wide, summer. *S. venusta*, see *Filipendula rubra*.

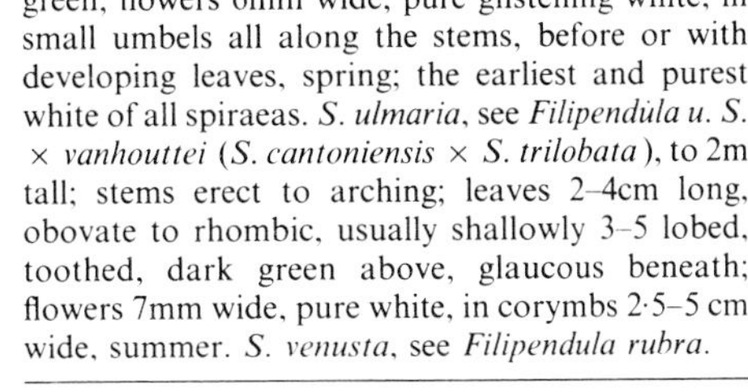

Spleenwort – see *Asplenium*.

Spruce fir – see *Picea*, particularly *P. abies*.

Spurge – see *Euphorbia*.

Spurge laurel – *see Daphne laureola*.

Squill – see *Scilla*.

Stachys

(Greek vernacular for a spike and used for several members of the dead nettle family). Woundwort. LABIATAE. A genus of about 300 species of annuals, perennials and sub-shrubs from temperate and subtropical regions and tropical mountains. They are erect to spreading with the stems square in cross-section, bearing opposite pairs of lanceolate to ovate leaves and tubular, 2-lipped flowers in whorled spikes. Grow the species described here in well-drained soil in sun. Plant autumn to spring. Propagate by division at planting time, cuttings in spring or late summer, or from seed in spring in a cold frame.

Species cultivated: *S. affinis* (*S. tuberifera*), Chinese artichoke; grown as a vegetable for its edible tubers. *S. betonica*, see *S. officinalis*. *S. byzantina* (*S. lanata*, *S. olympica*), S.W. Asia to European Turkey; bunnies' ears, lambs' ears, lambs' lugs, lambs' tongue; mat-forming perennial with erect flowering stems 30–45cm tall; leaves 3–10cm long, oblong-spathulate to elliptic, thickly white woolly; flowers 1·5–2·5cm long, purple, summer; grown primarily for its silvery-white basal leaves. *S.b.* Silver Carpet, non-flowering clone, excellent ground cover. *S. discolor* (*S. nivea* of gardens), Caucasus; mat-forming, woody based perennial; flowering stems 20–30cm tall; leaves 2·5–4cm long, oblong-lanceolate, deeply crenate, wrinkled dark green above, white-felted beneath; flowers rose or (rarely) cream, summer; see also true *S. nivea*. *S. grandiflora* (*Betonica g.*, *B. macrantha*), Caucasus; clump-forming, 45–60cm tall; leaves 5–7cm long, ovate, coarsely crenate; flowers 3–4cm long, mauve-purple, summer. *S.g.* Robusta, more vigorous with richer-toned flowers. *S. lantana* see *S. byzantina*. *S. macrantha*, see previous species. *S. nivea*, Syria; woody-based perennial 20–30cm tall; leaves to 4cm long, obovate to oblong, densely white wooly; flowers 1–1·5cm long, white, summer; confused in gardens with *S. discolor*. *S. officinalis* (*S. betonica*, *Betonica officinalis*), betony; Europe to Caucasus and N.Africa; clump-forming, 40–60cm tall; leaves 3–7cm long, oblong to ovate, coarsely crenate; flowers to 1·5cm long, red-purple, summer. *S.o.* Alba, flowers white; *S.o.* Rosea, clear pink. *S. olympica*, see *S. byzantina*. *S. sieboldii*. *S. tuberifera*, see *S. affinis*.

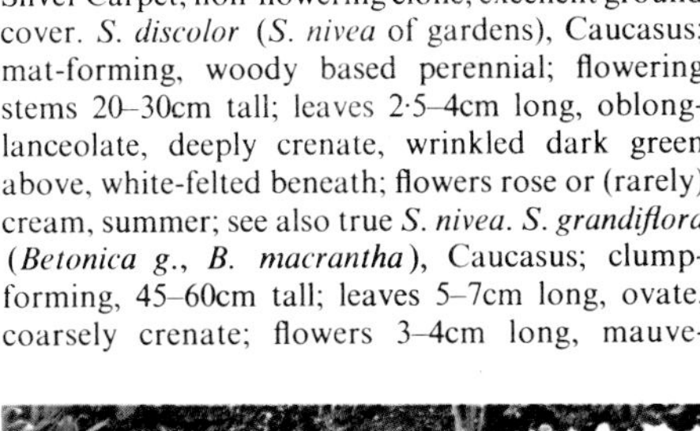

Stachyurus

(Greek *stachys*, a spike, and *oura*, a tail – alluding to the form of the inflorescences). STACHYURACEAE. A genus of 10 species of deciduous shrubs from E.Asia, 1 of which is generally available: *S. praecox*, Japan; 2–3m tall, of spreading habit; leaves alternate, 6–15cm long, ovate to lanceolate, slender-pointed; flowers 6–8mm wide, cup-shaped, pale yellow, in stiff, pendant spikes to 7cm long, late winter, early spring, before the leaves. The very similar, but difficult to obtain Chinese *S. chinensis* has narrower, longer-pointed leaves, and racemes

10–13cm long opening 2 weeks later. Grow in humus-rich soil in sun or partial shade, preferably sheltered from strong wind and frost. Plant autumn to spring. Propagate by layering in spring, or cuttings late summer, bottom heat at about 18°C.

Stag's-horn sumach – see *Rhus typhina*.

Staphylea

(Greek *staphyle*, a cluster – alluding to the compact panicles). Bladder nut. STAPHYLEACEAE. A genus of 10 species of deciduous shrubs and small trees from the northern temperate zone. They have opposite pairs of trifoliate or pinnate leaves, and terminal or axillary panicles of 5-petalled flowers followed by bladder-like capsules containing a few hard, polished, nut-like seeds. Plant autumn to spring. Propagate from seed when ripe, by layering in spring, softwood cuttings at 18°C late spring to early summer, or semi-hardwood cuttings late summer.

Species cultivated: *S. colchica*, Caucasus; 2·5–4m tall; branches erect; leaves pinnate, leaflets 3–5, ovate-oblong, 6–9cm long, glossy green; flowers to 2cm long, white, in erect panicles to 13cm long, late spring. *S. holocarpa*, China; large shrub or small tree, 3–10m tall, of spreading habit; leaves trifoliate, leaflets oblong-lanceolate, 6–10cm long, dark glossy green above; flowers 1·2cm long, pink in bud, opening white, in drooping axillary panicles, late spring. *S.h.* Rosea, flowers soft pink, young leaves bronze-tinted. *S. pinnata*, common bladder nut; Europe, Turkey; large shrub to 4m or more tall; leaves pinnate, leaflets 5–7, ovate, 5–10cm long; flowers 1·2cm long, white, in terminal, pendant panicles, 6–12cm long, late spring, early summer.

Star of Bethlehem – see *Ornithogalum umbellatum*.

Statice – see *Limonium*.

Stephanandra

(Greek *stephanos*, a crown, and *aner*, a man – male – the stamens persist in a crown-like tuft). ROSACEAE. A genus of 4 species of deciduous shrubs from E.Asia. They are related to *Spiraea*, with alternate, ovate, often lobed, sharply toothed leaves and panicles of tiny, 5-petalled, whitish flowers. Culture as for *Spiraea*. Primarily grown for elegant foliage and winter stems. Protect in cold areas.

Species cultivated: *S. flexuosa*, see next species. *S.*

incisa (*S. flexuosa*), Japan, Korea; 1·5–2m tall, bushy arching habit; stems slender, zig-zag, bright brown; leaves 4–6·5cm long, broadly ovate, deeply lobed; flowers 4–5mm wide, greenish-white in lateral panicles to 7cm long, summer. *S.i.* Crispa (*S.i.* Prostrata), dwarf habit, forming low mounds of arching stems to 90cm or more. *S. tanakae*, Japan; to 2m tall, arching habit; stems rich bright brown; leaves 5–12cm long, broadly ovate, shallowly 3–5 lobed, downy beneath, colouring orange in autumn; flowers 5mm wide, dull white, in panicles to 10cm long, summer.

Sternbergia

(for Count Kaspar von Sternberg, 1761–1838, Austrian botanist and founder of the Bohemian National Museum, Prague). AMARYLLIDACEAE. A genus of 6–8 species of bulbous plants from E.Mediterranean to Caucasus and Iran. They have strap-shaped leaves and yellow, 6-tepalled flowers somewhat like crocuses but shorter-tubed and usually carried on short scapes. Grow in well-drained soil in sheltered, sunny sites. Plant late summer, early autumn. Propagate by separating offsets at planting time, or from seed when ripe. Seedlings take several years to reach maturity.

Species cultivated: *S. clusiana* (*S. macrantha*), Turkey to Israel and Iran; leaves linear, 5–20mm wide, greyish-green; flowers before leaves, to 7cm long with the ovary at ground level, mid to late autumn. *S. fischeriana*, Caucasus, Iran; similar to *S. lutea*, but leaves to 1cm wide, greyish-green;

Far left top: *Stachyurus praecox*
Far left: *Staphylea pinnata*
Left above: *Stephanandra tanakae*
Top: *Sternbergia lutea*
Above: *Sternbergia clusiana*

flowering in spring. *S. lutea*, Mediterranean Europe to Turkey, Iran and Algeria; leaves linear, 5–15mm wide, dark green; flowers 4–5cm long, bright yellow, on scapes 10cm or so tall, mid to late autumn; needs a really sunny site to flower freely. *S. macrantha*, see *S. clusiana*.

Stewartia

(*Stuartia*). (for John Stuart, 3rd Earl of Bute, 1713–92, British Prime Minister and enthusiastic patron of botany and horticulture). THEACEAE. A genus of 10 species of deciduous shrubs and trees from E.Asia and E.USA. They have smooth, often attractively flaking bark, alternate, toothed, ovate to obovate leaves often colouring in autumn, and solitary, white, 5-petalled, flat to bowl-shaped flowers from the upper leaf-axils in late summer.

Grow in humus-rich, well-drained but moisture-retentive, neutral to acid soil, preferably in partial shade. Plant autumn to spring. Propagate from seed when ripe or spring in a cold frame, by layering in spring or cuttings late summer, bottom heat about 18°C.

Species cultivated: *S. koreana* (*S. pseudocamellia k.*), Korea; tree 9–18m tall; bark flaking; leaves to 10cm long, elliptic, usually downy beneath, orange-red in autumn; flowers flat, to 6·5cm wide. *S. ovata* (*S. pentagyna*), mountain camellia; S.E.USA; shrub 3–5m tall; leaves to 13cm long, ovate; flowers to 7·5cm wide, bowl-shaped with orange anthers. *S. pseudocamellia*, Japan; tree eventually to 18m; bark flaking; leaves 5–9cm long, ovate to obovate, yellow and red in autumn; flowers bowl-shaped, 5–6cm wide, petals downy beneath. *S.p. koreana*, see *S. koreana*. *S. sinensis*, China; large shrub or small tree, 5–10m tall; bark flaking; leaves 5–10cm long, elliptic to obovate-oblong, crimson in autumn; flowers 4–5cm wide, bowl-shaped, fragrant.

Stipa

(Greek *stuppe*, tow – the fluffy broken fibres of flax or hemp – alluding to the feathery inflorescences). Feather grasses. GRAMINEAE. Depending on the botanical authority, a genus of 150–300 species of perennial grasses of widespread distribution. They are tufted to clump-forming with slender, linear leaves and terminal panicles of 1-flowered spikelets each with a twisted, long to very long, sometimes feathery awn. Grow the species described in well-drained soil in sun. Plant autumn or spring. Propagate by division or from seed in spring.

Species cultivated: *S. calamagrostis* (*Achnatherum c.*), C. and E.Europe; to 1m tall; leaves stiff, usually rolled and rush-like, particularly in dry weather; panicles 12–25cm long, loose, semi-nodding, spikelets 8–10mm long, silky silvery hairy, awns 1–1·5cm long, often tinted violet to russet, summer. *S. gigantea*, Spain, Portugal, Morocco; 1·5–2m tall; leaves to 70cm long, rolled when dry; panicles spike-like, to 50cm long, spikelets 3cm long, yellowish, awns 15–20cm long, finely hairy, summer. *S. pennata*, common feather grass; C. to S.E.Europe; 60–90cm tall; leaves very slender, rolled; panicles spike-like, spikelets to 2·5cm long, awns to 35cm long, silvery-silky feathery, summer.

Far left: *Stewartia pseudocamellia*
Left below: *Stewartia sinensis* showing bark
Left: *Stewartia pseudocamellia* autumn colours
Below: *Stipa gigantea*

Stokesia

(for Dr Jonathan Stokes, 1755–1831, British botanical author). COMPOSITAE. A genus of 1 species of evergreen perennial from S.E.USA: *S. laevis* (*S. cyanea*), Stokes' aster; clump-forming, to 60cm tall; basal leaves 10–20cm long, oblong-spathulate, softly spiny toothed at base, stem leaves smaller, clasping; flower-heads solitary or in small corymbs, 6–10cm wide, somewhat cornflower-like, with 5-

lobed ray florets, lavender-blue, summer to autumn; cultivars with white, creamy-yellow, blue or purple flowers are sometimes available. Grow in fertile, well-drained soil in sun. Plant autumn to spring. Propagate from seed or by division in spring, the former preferably in a cold frame.

Stonecrop – see *Sedum*.

Stranvaesia

(for William Thomas Horner Fox-Strangways, 1795–1865, 4th Earl of Ilchester, British diplomat and botanist). ROSACEAE. A genus of 4–5 species of evergreen shrubs and small trees from Himalaya to China, Taiwan and Philippines, 1 of which is readily available: *S. davidiana*, W. China; large shrub or sometimes a small tree 3–10m tall; leaves alternate, 6–13cm long, oblong-lanceolate, some turning red in autumn; flowers 5-petalled, 8mm wide, in loose, corymbose panicles, summer; fruit like that of *Cotoneaster*, globose, 8mm wide, crimson; fairly hardy but liable to damage in severe winters. *S.d. salicifolia* (*S. salicifolia*), of more erect habit than type, leaves narrower and with more veins; *S.d. undulata* (*S. undulata*), spreading shrub to 3m tall, often wider than high, leaves wavy-margined; *S.d.u.* Fructuluteo, fruit bright yellow. Culture as *Cotoneaster*; tolerant of light shade.

Stratiotes

(Greek for soldier, presumably because of the sword-shaped leaves, although the name was once used for *Pistia*). Water soldier or aloe. HYDROCHARITACEAE. A genus of 1 species of submerged aquatic perennial from Europe and N.W.Asia: *S. aloides*, stoloniferous, rosette-forming, not unlike an aloe or agave but not fleshy; leaves 15–50cm long, linear-lanceolate, spiny margined; flowers usually dioecious, 3–4cm wide, 3-petalled, white, just above the water in summer. The plants live at the bottom of ponds and lakes for much of the year but rise to the surface in summer. If only one clone is grown, they will not set seed, increase being by offsets and detached winter resting buds (turions). Grow in still, clear water to 60cm deep, ideally with gravelly muddy bottom. Plant autumn or spring, dropping the plants into the water, as they do not root into the bottom. Propagate by detaching well-grown offsets from late summer to spring or by collecting the turions.

Strawberry raspberry – see *Rubus illecebrosus*.

Strawberry tomato – see *Physalis peruviana*.

Strawberry tree – see *Arbutus*.

Stuartia – see *Stewartia*.

Stylophorum

(Greek *stylos*, style, and *phorus*, bearing – a reference to the prominent style). PAPAVERACEAE. A genus of 3 species of herbaceous perennials from E.Asia and N.America, 1 of which is usually available: *S. diphyllum*, celandine poppy; E. N.America; tufted habit, to 30cm or more tall; leaves mostly basal, long-stalked, the blades pinnatisect with 5–7 oblong toothed lobes; peduncles equalling the leaves, usually with 5 small leaves near the top; flowers 3–5cm wide, 4-petalled, cup-shaped, deep yellow, solitary or in small terminal umbels, late spring, early summer. Grow in moisture-retentive, humus-rich soil in partial shade. Plant autumn to spring. Propagate from seed when ripe or spring, or by division in spring.

Left above: *Stokesia laevis*
Left below: *Stranvaesia davidiana*
Above: *Stratiotes aloides*
Below: *Stylophorum diphyllum*
Right: *Styrax hemsleyana*

Styrax

(ancient Greek derived from the Semitic name for storax – *S. officinalis* – rarely grown in Britain). Storax. STYRACACEAE. A genus of about 130 species of evergreen and deciduous trees and shrubs mainly from tropical to warm temperate regions in the N.Hemisphere. They have alternate, simple, ovate to obovate or lanceolate leaves and nodding, white, solitary or clustered, 5-petalled flowers. The fruit are small, plum-like. The species mentioned are generally hardy. Grow in moisture-retentive, fertile, neutral to acid soil in sun or partial shade, ideally protected from strong, cold winds. Plant autumn to spring. Propagate from seed when ripe in a cold frame, by layering in spring or cuttings late summer, bottom heat about 18°C.

Species cultivated: *S. hemsleyana*, C. and W.China; deciduous tree to 10m tall; leaves 10–13cm long, obliquely ovate to obovate, sparsely starry hairy beneath; flowers about 2·5cm wide, in racemes 10–15cm long, summer. *S. japonica*, Japanese snowbell (USA); Korea, Japan; large, deciduous shrub or small tree, 3–8m tall; leaves 5–9cm long, with tufts of hairs in the vein axils beneath; flowers to 2cm wide, in short but freely borne racemes, summer. *S. obassia*, fragrant snowbell (USA); Japan; large deciduous shrub or small, round-headed tree, 4–10m tall; leaves 10–20cm long,

broadly ovate to almost orbicular, densely downy beneath; flowers about 2·5cm wide, fragrant, in racemes 15–20cm long, summer.

Succisa

(Latin *succido*, to cut from below – alluding to the abruptly truncated rootstock). DIPSACACEAE. A genus of 3 species of herbaceous perennials from Europe to W.Siberia, Africa, south to Cameroun Mountains, 1 of which is usually available: *S. pratensis* (*Scabiosa succisa*), Devil's-bit scabious; Europe to W.Siberia and Caucasus, N.Africa; clump-forming, 40–60cm or more tall; basal leaves 5–15cm long, in rosettes, obovate-lanceolate to narrowly elliptic, sparsely hairy, sometimes toothed; stems with opposite pairs of branches and smaller leaves; flower-heads solitary, to 2·5cm wide, florets 4–7mm long, 4-lobed, mauve to deep purple, summer to autumn; a dwarf form, 10–15cm tall, is sometimes listed. Grow in any moisture-retentive, reasonably fertile soil in sun. Plant autumn to spring. Propagate by division or from seed, spring.

Sumach – see *Rhus*.

Sundew – see *Drosera*.

Sunflower – see *Helianthus*.

Sunrose – see *Cistus* and *Helianthemum*.

Suttonia – see *Myrsine*.

Sweet alyssum – see *Lobularia maritima*.

Sweet briar – see *Rosa rubiginosa*.

Sweet cicely – see *Myrrhis*.

Sweet corn – see *Zea mays*.

Sweet flag – see *Acorus calamus*.

Sweet gale – see *Myrica gale*.

Sweet gum – see *Liquidambar*.

Sweet pea – see *Lathyrus odoratus*.

Sweet rocket – see *Hesperis matronalis*.

Sweet sultan – see *Centaurea moschatus*.

Sweet William – see *Dianthus barbatus*.

Sweet woodruff – see *Galium odoratum*.

Sycamore – see *Acer pseudoplatanus* and *Platanus occidentalis*.

Sycopsis

(Greek *sykon*, fig, and *opsis*, appearance – meaning is obscure). HAMAMELIDACEAE. A genus of 6 species of evergreen shrubs and small trees from Himalaya to China and Philippines, 1 of which is generally available: *S. sinensis*, C.China; large shrub or small tree, 3–6m tall; leaves alternate, 5–12cm long, elliptic-lanceolate, sometimes slightly toothed, boldly veined, leathery deep green; flowers petalless,

unisexual, the males with reddish anthers, in small clusters surrounded by velvety-brown bracts, early spring. Culture as for *Hamamelis*.

Symphoricarpos

(Greek *symphorein*, bear together, and *karpos*, a fruit – the fruit are carried in clusters). Snowberry. CAPRIFOLIACEAE. A genus of 18 species of deciduous, suckering shrubs, all but 1 from N.America, the other in China. They have slender, twiggy stems, mostly ovate to rounded leaves in opposite pairs and small, bell-shaped, 4–5 lobed flowers in terminal clusters followed by pink or white berries. Grow in any moderately moisture-retentive soil in sun or shade. Plant autumn to spring. Propagate by division or suckers at planting time, cuttings in late summer or autumn, or from seed when ripe.

Species cultivated: *S. albus* (*S. racemosus*), common snowberry, N.America, east of Continental Divide; to 1m tall; leaves to 3cm or more long, broadly elliptic to rounded, those on vigorous young stems sometimes lobed; flowers 5–6mm long, pink, summer to autumn; fruit 8mm wide, white; confused with *S. rivularis* in some gardens. *S.a. laevigatus*, see *S. rivularis*. *S.* × *chenaultii* (probably *S. microphyllus* × *S. orbiculatus*), to 1m tall, erect habit; leaves to 2cm long, elliptic, downy beneath; flowers in spikes, pinkish; fruit pinkish-white,

Left below: *Sycopsis sinensis*
Above: *Symphoricarpos orbiculatus*
Below: *Symphoricarpos rivularis*
Right above: *Symphyandra hofmannii*
Right below: *Symphytum* × *uplandicum* Variegatum

flushed red-purple on sunny side. *S.* × *c.* Hancock spreading to prostrate habit. *S.* × *doorenbosii* (*S.* × *chenaultii* × *S. rivularis*), group of hybrid cultivars of vigorous growth, 1–1·5m tall, combining the parental characters in various ways. *S.* × *d.* Magic Berry, bushy, spreading habit, berries rose-pink; *S.* × *d.* Mother of Pearl, dense habit, berries white, rose-flushed, borne in profusion; *S.* × *d.* White Hedge, erect, compact habit, berries white. *S. orbiculatus*, coral berry, Indian currant; New York to Colorado, south to Texas; 2m tall, bushy habit; leaves 2·5–4cm long, broadly elliptic to rounded, downy and somewhat glaucous beneath; flowers 3–4mm long, greenish-white, pink-tinted; berries 5–7mm long, ellipsoid, purple to coral pink. *S.o.* Variegatus, leaves irregularly yellow-margined. *S. racemosus*, see *S. albus*. *S. rivularis* (*S. albus laevigatus*), snowberry; Alaska to Montana and California; 1·5–3m tall, forming dense thickets; similar to *S. albus*, but leaves somewhat larger, particularly those on sucker shoots; flowers pink to white; berries larger, 1–1·5cm wide, in larger clusters; one of the commonest snowberries in gardens and formerly planted as game converts.

Symphyandra

(Greek *symphuio*, to grow together, and *aner*, male – the anthers are joined). Ring bellflower (USA). CAMPANULACEAE. A genus of 8–10 species of herbaceous perennials from E.Mediterranean to Caucasus and C.Asia. They are closely allied to, and superficially resemble, *Campanula*, but the anthers

are joined in a ring and the seed capsules open at the top (those of *Campanula* open at the base). Culture as for *Campanula*.

Species cultivated: *S. armena*, Caucasus; 30–60cm tall; stems sprawling to erect; basal leaves long-stalked, the blades to 10cm long, ovate-cordate, deeply irregularly toothed; flowers 2cm long, blue or white, velvety downy, erect, summer. *S. hofmannii*, Yugoslavia; usually biennial, 30–60cm tall; leaves 5–10cm long, ovate to lanceolate, coarsely toothed, basal ones with winged petioles; flowers 2–3cm long, cream, pendant, in leafy panicles, summer. *S. wanneri*, Bulgaria, Romania, Yugoslavia; 20–45cm tall; leaves 3–11cm long, linear-oblong to lanceolate, toothed, basal ones with winged petioles; flowers 2·5–3·5cm long, violet, in panicles, summer; does well in partial shade.

Symphytum

(ancient Greek name for a plant that heals wounds). Comfrey. BORAGINACEAE. A genus of 25 species of perennials from Europe and W.Asia. They are clump-forming or rhizomatous, sometimes tuberous, with ovate to lanceolate, often rough-textured leaves and tubular to funnel-shaped, 5-

lobed flowers in pendant cymes from the upper leaf-axils. Grow in any reasonably fertile, moisture-retentive soil in sun or partial shade. Plant autumn to spring. Propagate by division at planting time or from seed in spring.

Species cultivated: *S. caucasicum*, Caucasus; to 60cm tall; softly hairy throughout; leaves to 20cm long, ovate-oblong to lanceolate; flowers 2cm long, red-purple, maturing sky-blue. *S. grandiflorum*, Caucasus; slender, rhizomatous, forming leafy mats or colonies; flowering stems unbranched, 20–30cm tall; basal leaves long-stalked, blades 5–10cm long, ovate to elliptic, hispid; flowers 1–1·5cm long, cream, spring, then off and on until summer; a useful ground cover beneath trees where not too dry. *S. officinale*, common comfrey; Europe to W.Siberia and Turkey; roots narrowly tuberous; stems 50–120cm tall, bearing long, deflexed hairs; lower leaves 15–25cm long, ovate-lanceolate, upper ones smaller, sessile, decurrent; flowers 1·5–1·7cm long, white, cream, purple or pink, early summer. *S. rubrum* of gardens, possibly a hybrid between a red-flowered form of *S. officinale* and *S. grandiflorum*; 45cm tall, more or less midway between supposed parents in appearance and spreading habit; flowers crimson, early summer. *S.* × *uplandicum* (*S. asperum* × *S. officinale*), a varied assemblage of hybrids, similar in overall appearance to *S. officinale* but combining the non-decurrent leaf, hooked bristle, and blue flower characters of *S. asperum*; flowers usually in shades of blue and purple, summer. *S.* × *u.* Variegatum, leaves greyish-green, boldly cream-margined.

Symplocos

(*Symplocus*). (Greek *symploke*, connection – the stamens are joined at their bases). Sweetleaf. SYMPLOCACEAE. A genus of 290–350 species (depending on botanical authority) of evergreen and deciduous trees and shrubs from Asia, Australia, Polynesia, America, mainly the warmer areas. 1 hardy species is usually available: *S. paniculata* (*S. crataegoides*), sapphire berry, Asiatic sweetleaf; Himalaya to China, Japan; deciduous shrub or small tree 4–10m or more tall, of dense habit; leaves alternate, 2–9cm long, elliptic to obovate, finely toothed, tawny-downy beneath; flowers 5-petalled, 7–8mm wide, white, fragrant, in panicles 6–8cm long, early summer; fruit berry-like, globose to ellipsoid, 6–8mm long, bright blue; often fruits poorly and usually needs 2 or more distinct individuals (not the same clone) to achieve cross-pollination. Grow in humus-rich, well-drained but moisture-retentive soil, ideally in sheltered, sunny sites. Plant autumn to spring. Propagate by layering in spring, cuttings late summer, bottom heat about 18°C, or from seed when ripe, in a cold frame.

Left: *Symphytum caucasicum*
Bottom left: *Symplocos paniculata*
Above: *Synthyris reniformis*
Below: *Syringa vulgaris* Souvenir de Louis Spaeth

Synthyris

(Greek *syn*, together, and *thyris*, a small door – referring to the valves of the seed capsules). SCROPHULARIACEAE. A genus of about 15 species of mostly small perennials from the mountains of N.W. N.America, 1 of which is usually available: *S. reniformis* (*S. rotundifolia*), Washington State to N.California; clump-forming, to 10cm or more tall; leaves evergreen, all basal, 2–5cm wide, orbicular to kidney-shaped, crenate, sometimes hairy, deep green; flowers narrowly bell-shaped, 4-lobed, purple-blue, in short racemes, spring. Grow in humus-rich, well-drained but not dry soil, in partial shade. Plant autumn or spring. Propagate from seed in spring, preferably in shaded cold frame, or by careful division at planting time.

Syringa

(Greek *syrinx*, a tube or pipe – referring to the young, hollow stems when originally applied to what is now *Philadelphus*). Lilac. OLEACEAE. A genus of about 30 species of deciduous shrubs and small trees from S.E.Europe, Himalaya, E.Asia. They have opposite pairs of lanceolate to ovate, sometimes pinnate leaves and terminal panicles or thyrses of tubular, often fragrant flowers with 4 spreading petal lobes. Grow in fertile, moisture-retentive soil in sun or partial shade. Plant autumn to spring. Propagate by suckers at planting time (but

not the grafted cultivars of *S. vulgaris*), layering in spring, cuttings in a propagating frame late summer, or hardwood cuttings outside in autumn. Seed may also be sown in spring, preferably in a cold frame, but takes several years to reach flowering size, and cultivars do not come true to type.

Species cultivated (all flowering early summer): *S. afghanica*, Afghanistan; 1–1·5m tall; leaves to 7cm long, pinnately lobed; flowers 8–9mm long, lilac, in slender panicles. *S. emodii*, Himalayan lilac; Himalaya; large shrub or small tree 3–5m tall; stems robust, warty; leaves 10–20cm long, ovate to obovate, whitish beneath; flowers 7–8mm long, pale lilac, ageing white, in erect panicles to 15cm long. *S.e.* Aureovariegata, leaves blotched yellow. *S.* × *hyacinthiflora* (*S. oblata* × *S. vulgaris*), group of hybrid cultivars combining parental characters but with the overall appearance of *S. vulgaris*. *S.* × *h.* Clarke's Giant, large flowers in panicles, lilac-blue, rosy-mauve in bud; *S.* × *h.* Lamartine, blue-lilac, young leaves flushed bronze. *S.* × *josiflexa* (*S. josikaea* × *S. reflexa*), group of hybrid cultivars combining parental characters in various ways, best known being *S.* × *j.* Bellicent, large, arching panicles of clear rose-pink. *S. josikaea*, Hungarian lilac; C. and E.Europe; large shrub, to 4m tall; leaves 5–13cm long, elliptic, glossy above, glaucous beneath; flowers 9–12mm long, violet-mauve, fragrant, in erect panicles to 18cm long. *S. microphylla*, N. and W.China; shrub to 1·5m or more tall, bushy habit; leaves 1–5cm long, broadly ovate; flowers 7–8mm long, rosy-lilac, fragrant, in small panicles, early summer with a smaller display in autumn. *S.m.* Superba, flowers rosy-pink, flowering intermittently early summer to autumn. *S. palibiniana*, see next species. *S. patula* (*S. palibiniana*, *S. velutina*), Korean lilac; China, Korea; to 3m tall; leaves 5–10cm long, elliptic to ovate-oblong, pubescent on both surfaces; flowers 7–8mm long, lilac to lilac-pink, in elegant panicles, to 13cm long. *S.* × *persica* (*S. afghanica* × *S. laciniata*), Persian lilac; shrub to 2m or more tall, bushy habit; leaves 3–6·5cm long, lanceolate; flowers 7–8mm long, lilac, fragrant, in panicles to 7·5cm long. *S.* × *prestoniae* (*S. reflexa* × *S. villosa*), group of hybrid cultivars combining parental characters in various ways; among the best are: *S.* × *p.* Elinor, flowers purple-red in bud, opening pale lavender, carried in erect panicles; *S.* × *p.* Isabella, mallow-purple, in rather erect panicles. *S. reflexa*, C.China; shrub 3–4m tall; stems robust, angular, warty; leaves 7–15cm long, elliptic-oblong to lanceolate or obovate; flowers 8mm long, pink, white within, borne in dense, cylindrical, arching to pendulous panicles 15–18cm long. *S. sweginzowii*, W.China; shrub to 3m tall; leaves 5–10cm long, ovate to lanceolate; flowers 7–8mm long, rosy-lilac to pink, fragrant, in loose panicles, to 20cm long. *S. velutina*, see *S. patula*. *S. villosa*, N.China; 3–4m tall; leaves 5–15cm long, elliptic to oblong, flowers 9–12mm long, lilac-pink, in compact, erect panicles to 30cm long. *S. vulgaris*, common lilac; E.Europe, naturalized elsewhere; large shrub or small tree 3–6m tall; leaves 5–13cm long, ovate, often cordate, pointed; flowers 8mm or more long, lilac or white, fragrant, in erect, pyramidal panicles 15–25cm long; usually in terminal pairs; among the many cultivars available, the following are recommended. Single-flowered: *S.v.* Clarke's Giant, now considered a cultivar of *S.* × *hyacinthiflora* (qv). *S.v.* Firmament, lilac-blue; *S.v.* Maud Notcutt, pure white; *S.v.* Night, dark purple; *S.v.* Primrose, pale primrose; *S.v.* Sensation, purple-red, edged white; *S.v.* Souvenir de Louis Spaeth, wine-red. Double-flowered: *S.v.* Charles Joly, dark purple-red; *S.v.* Katherine Havemeyer, lavender-purple fading lilac-pink; *S.v.* Madame Lemoine, pure white, creamy-yellow in bud.

Far left: *Syringa* × *persica*
Far left bottom: *Syringa vulgaris* Primrose
Left: *Syringa microphylla* Superba
Left bottom: *Syringa vulgaris* Maud Notcutt
Above: *Syringa* × *prestoniae*

Syringodea luteo-nigra – see *Romulea longituba*.

Tagetes

(for the Etruscan god Tages). African and French marigolds. COMPOSITAE. A genus of 30–50 species of half-hardy and tender annuals and perennials from S.USA to Argentina. The annuals mentioned here are erect, often much-branched, with alternate, pinnately lobed leaves and terminal flower-heads. The latter are composed of a bell-shaped involucre and a ring of broad ray florets surrounding several tubular florets. Grow in any well-drained, moderately fertile soil in sun. Sow seed in spring at 18°C. Prick off seedlings as soon as first true leaf is visible, setting them 4–5cm apart in boxes of good commercial potting mixture. Harden off and plant out when fear of frost has passed. Seed may also be sown *in situ* in early summer.

Species cultivated: *T. erecta*, African or Aztec marigold; Mexico, C.America, long naturalized in many warm countries; to 1m tall, branched but not bushy; leaves pinnate; flower-heads 5–13cm wide, yellow to orange; represented in gardens by many semi-double and double-flowered cultivars, often with crimped, quilled or 2-lipped florets, the shorter more bushy sorts of hybrid origin with *T. patula*. *T. minuta*, Brazil, Peru, Argentina, Chile; 1–1·5m tall; leaves pinnate; flower-heads 4–5mm wide, pale yellow, in dense corymbs; not ornamental but occasionally grown for seasoning and medicinal purposes; in addition, the roots exude a substance inimical to eel worms (nematodes) and the plant is sometimes recommended as biological control. *T. patula*, French marigold; Mexico, Guatemala; 15–45cm tall, bushy; leaves pinnate; flower-heads up to 5cm wide, yellow to orange, often marked or suffused red-brown, sometimes strikingly bi-coloured; represented in gardens by many cultivars, some double, the larger ones of hybrid origin with *T. erecta*. *T. signata*, see next species. *T. tenuifolia* (*T. signata*), signet or striped marigold; Mexico, C.America; up to 60cm tall; stems slender, much-branched; leaves pinnate; flower-heads about 2·5cm wide, bright yellow, profusely borne; represented in gardens by *T.t. pumila* that covers several cultivars up to 30cm tall.

Tamarix

(the ancient Latin name). Tamarisk. TAMARICACEAE. A genus of 54 species of deciduous shrubs and small trees from Europe, Africa, Asia, often from deserts or salty ground. They are slender-stemmed with alternate, scale-like leaves and tiny, 4–5-petalled flowers in racemes or panicles. Grow in well-drained soil in sun. Plant autumn to spring. Propagate by semi-hardwood cuttings in late summer, or hardwood cuttings in late autumn either in a nursery bed or *in situ*.

Species cultivated: *T. aestivalis* of gardens, see *T. ramosissima*. *T. anglica*, see next species. *T. gallica* (*T. anglica*), common tamarisk; S.W.Europe; large shrub or small tree 3–4m tall; stems deep purple-brown; leaves lanceolate, glaucous-green; flowers 5-petalled, pink, in racemes to 5cm long, summer. *T. hispida* of gardens and *T. pallasii*, see *T. ramosissima*. *T. parviflora* (*T. tetrandra purpurea*), S.E.Europe, Crete, Turkey; shrub or tree 3–9m tall; stems purple to brown; leaves ovate, bright green; flowers 4-petalled, deep pink, in racemes to 4cm long, early summer. *T. pentandra*, see next species. *T. ramosissima* (*T. pallasii*, *T. pentandra*; *T. aestivalis* and *T. hispida* of gardens – not the true *T. hispida*, a densely hispid-downy shrub seldom cultivated), E.Europe to E.Asia; large shrub or small tree 3–6m tall; stems reddish-brown; leaves lanceolate; flowers 5-petalled, pink, in slender racemes 2–7cm long, early to late summer. *T. tetrandra*, E.Balkan Peninsula; large shrub of open, spreading habit, to 3m or more tall; stems blackish; leaves lanceolate; flowers 4-, sometimes 5-petalled, white to palest pink, in racemes 3–6cm long, freely borne, early summer; sometimes confused with the deep pink *T. parviflora*. *T.t. purpurea*, see *T. parviflora*.

Top left: *Tagetes erecta* Lemon Lady
Left: *Tagetes patula* Gypsy Dancer
Below left: *Tagetes tenuifolia* Orange Gem
Below: *Tamarix tetrandra*
Right: *Tanacetum haradjanii*
Below right: *Tanacetum vulgare*

Tanacetum

(medieval Latin *tanazita* for tansy). COMPOSITAE. A genus of about 50 species of annuals and perennials, the latter sometimes sub-shrubby, from the N.Hemisphere, mainly Europe and Asia. They are closely allied to *Chrysanthemum*, and some species are difficult to distinguish from that genus; leaves often more deeply dissected, to bi- or tripinnate, flower-heads often in corymbs and sometimes without ray florets. Grow in moderately fertile, well-drained soil in sun. Plant autumn to spring. Propagate by division at planting time, from seed

and by basal cuttings spring, the latter also in late summer when non-flowering stems are available.
Species cultivated: *T. argenteum* (*Chrysanthemum a.*), Turkey; tufted, mat-forming; leaves 2–7cm long, narrowly pinnatisect or bipinnatisect, white woolly; flower-heads to 5mm wide, rayless, yellow, in dense terminal corymbs to 15cm tall, summer, autumn. *T. balsamita*, see *Chrysanthemum b. T. corymbosum* (*Chrysanthemum c.*), Europe to Caucasus; clump-forming perennial, to 90cm tall; leaves 3–4cm long, pinnatisect to pinnatipartite; flower-heads 3–5cm wide, daisy-like with a yellow disc and white rays, summer. *T. densum* (*Chrysanthemum d.*), Turkey, Syria; rhizomatous perennial forming mats 60–90cm wide; leaves 5cm long, closely bipinnate, feathery, silvery white-woolly; flower-heads 8–14mm wide, both rays and discs yellow, in sparse to dense corymbs, summer; not free-flowering but a fine silver-foliage plant. *T.d. amanum* of gardens, see next species. *T. haradjanii* (*T. densum amanum* and *Chrysanthemum h.*), Turkey; tufted; stems more or less erect, 23–36cm tall; leaves 4–7cm long, bi- or tripinnatisect, silvery grey-woolly; flower-heads 3–4mm wide, rayless, in terminal corymbs, late summer. *T. herderi*, Turkestan; tufted, hummock-forming, to 20cm or more tall by 30cm wide; leaves bi- or tripinnatifid, silvery hairy; flower-heads small, yellow, rayless, in corymbs; mainly grown as silver foliage plant, best in a scree. *T. parthenium*, see *Chrysanthemum p. T. praeteritum* (*Chrysanthemum p.*), Turkey; much like *T. densum*, but flower-heads solitary with white rays. *T. ptarmaciflorum* (*Cineraria candicans*, *C. candidissima*, *Chrysanthemum p.*, *Pyrethrum p.*), dusty miller, silver lace (USA); Canary Is; sub-shrub to 50cm, leaves 5–10cm long, bi- or tripinnatisect, ferny, silvery grey-woolly; flower-heads 2–3cm wide, with yellow discs and white rays, in terminal corymbs; half-hardy, sometimes used as a silver-leaved bedding plant; needs over-wintering under frost-free glass in all but the mildest areas. *T. vulgare* (*Chrysanthemum v.*), tansy; Europe, Turkey to Siberia; clump-forming perennial 60–100cm tall; basal leaves 15–25cm long, bipinnate, the segments toothed, dark green, ferny; flower-heads 7–12mm wide, button-like, yellow, in dense, terminal, flattish corymbs, late summer, autumn; whole plant sweetly aromatic; formerly grown as a medicinal and pot herb.

Tansy – see *Tanacetum vulgare*.

Tarragon – see *Artemisia dracunculus*.

Taxodium

(Latin *Taxus*, yew, and Greek *eidos*, resemblance – alluding to the leaf-shape and formation). Swamp cypress. TAXODIACEAE. A genus of 2 species of deciduous and evergreen coniferous trees from E.USA and mountains of Mexico, 1 of which is generally available: *T. distichum*, bald cypress; E.USA; deciduous tree, to 35m or more tall, pyramidal when young, becoming broad-headed with age; leaves 8–20mm long, linear, those on the short shoots (secondary branchlets) in 2 parallel ranks, those on long (extension) shoots spirally arranged; in autumn all the short shoots and their leaves are shed; male strobili slender, dull yellow catkins, 8–10cm long, cones globular, to 3cm long, bright green, ripening purplish-brown. *T.d. nutans* (*T. ascendens*), pond cypress; S.E.USA; smaller, leaves shorter, usually appressed to stem. A swamp or waterside tree in the wild, often growing in standing water and then producing many erect breathing roots known as 'knees' or pneumatophores. Grow in fertile, moisture-retentive soil in sheltered, sunny or partially shaded sites. Plant autumn to spring. Propagate from seed in cold frame in spring or when ripe, cuttings late summer in a cold frame.

Taxus

(old Latin vernacular for yew). Yew. TAXACEAE. A genus of 8–10 species of evergreen coniferous trees from the N.Hemisphere, south to Himalaya, Philippines, Mexico. They have linear, leathery leaves arranged in 2 ranks on the short shoots, spirally on the long shoots; strobili dioecious, males globose to ovoid catkins, females very small consisting of several scales and a solitary ovule; after fertilization a fleshy-red, cup-shaped aril forms around the hard seed. With the exception of the aril, all parts of the yew are poisonous. Plant autumn or spring. Propagate from seed when ripe, at least some of which may take 18 months to germinate, or by cuttings in a cold frame late summer, early autumn.
Species cultivated: *T. baccata*, common yew; Europe, S.W.Asia, N.Africa; 10–25m tall, broadly conical to spreading, often branching from the base; bark reddish-brown; leaves 2–4cm long, pointed, dark, somewhat lustrous green; fruit about 1cm long, autumn; of many cultivars, the following are available: *T.b.* Adpressa, to 10m tall, usually less, wide-spreading, leaves 6–12mm long; *T.b.* Fastigiata, Irish yew, erect, columnar habit with all leaves spirally arranged, mainly represented by a female clone; *T.b.* Fastigiata Aureomarginata, golden Irish yew, leaves yellow-margined; *T.b.* Repandens, wide-spreading, semi-prostrate bush, good as

Left: *Taxodium distichum*
Below: *Taxus baccata*
Above: *Taxus baccata* Standishii

ground cover in sun or shade; *T.b.* Repens Aurea, spreading, prostrate habit, leaves yellow when

young; *T.b.* Standishii, slow-growing, like a dwarf golden Irish yew. *T. cuspidata*, Japanese yew; to 15m in the wild, often only makes a large shrub in gardens; similar to *T. baccata*, but leaves 2–3·5cm long, dark matt green, almost spine-tipped; fruit glossy scarlet; seed-raised plants tend to grow taller more quickly. *T.* × *media* (*T. baccata* × *T. cuspidata*), small group of cultivars intermediate between the parents; mainly represented in gardens by *T.* × *m.* Hatfieldii, erect, dense habit with spirally arranged leaves, good for hedging. *T.* × *m.* Hicksii, broadly columnar, rather like Irish yew.

Tea – see *Camellia sinensis*.

Tecoma grandiflora, T. radicans – see *Campsis*.

Tecophilaea

(for Tecophila Billotti, botanical artist daughter of Luigi Colla, 1766–1848, Italian botanist). Chilean crocus. AMARYLLIDACEAE. A genus of 2 species of cormous-rooted plants from Chile, 1 of which is generally available: *T. cyanocrocus*, 10–15cm tall; leaves basal only, usually 2–3, linear, 7–12cm long; flowers solitary, sometimes 2 or 3, somewhat crocus-like, 6-tepalled, 3–4cm long, deep gentian-blue with white eye, spring. *T.c. leichtlinii*, paler blue than type with larger white eye; *T.c. violacea*, blue-purple, not fully hardy and needs a greenhouse in cold areas. Grow in sharply drained but fertile soil in sunny, sheltered sites, in mild areas ideally at the foot of a south wall. Alternatively, grow in pots or pans of a good commercial potting mixture, in a frost-free to cool greenhouse. Plant or pot autumn, those in containers kept barely moist until growth starts, then watered regularly until the leaves yellow when they should be dried off. Plants outside benefit from cloche protection in wet summers. Propagate from seed under glass in spring, or by offsets removed at potting time.

Top: *Taxus baccata* Repens Aurea
Below: *Tecophilaea cyanocrocus*

Telekia speciosum – see *Bupthalmum speciosum*.

Teline canariensis – see *Cytisus canariensis*.

Tellima

(anagram of *Mitella*, a closely allied genus). SAXIFRAGACEAE. A genus of 1 species of evergreen perennial from Alaska to California: *T. grandiflora* (*T. odorata*), fringecup; clump-forming, to 60cm tall; basal leaves long-stalked, blades to 10cm long, broadly ovate-cordate, toothed, hairy; flowering stems with 2–4 smaller leaves; flowers 1–1·5cm wide, urn-shaped at the base, with 5, pinnatifid, fringed, reflexed petals, greenish-white, flushing red with age, late spring, summer. *T.g.* Purpurea (*T.g.* Rubra), leaves purple-red in winter, flowers flushed pink. Grow in moisture-retentive but well-drained soil in sun or shade; good ground cover, particularly beneath trees. Plant autumn to spring. Propagate by division at planting time, or from seed when ripe or spring.

Above: *Tellima grandiflora*
Above right: *Teucrium polium*
Right: *Teucrium chamaedrys*

Teucrium

(Greek for germander, perhaps derived from King Teucer of Troy who reputedly used the plants medicinally). Germander. LABIATAE. A genus of about 300 species of evergreen perennials, sub-shrubs and shrubs of cosmopolitan distribution but mainly from the Mediterranean. They have opposite pairs of ovate to lanceolate, sometimes lobed or cut leaves, and tubular, obliquely 5-lobed and somewhat 2-lipped flowers in terminal whorls. Grow in well-drained soil in sun (*T. scorodonia* will also thrive in partial shade). Plant autumn to spring. Propagate by division or from seed in spring, or cuttings in summer.

Species cultivated: *T. aroanium*, mountains of S.Greece; prostrate, twiggy shrub to 30cm wide; leaves 6–15mm long, ovate-oblong to obovate, white woolly beneath; flowers 1·5–2cm long, soft blue-purple, summer. *T. chamaedrys*, Europe, S.W.Asia; rhizomatous sub-shrub to 30cm or more; leaves to 2cm long, ovate-oblong, toothed, glossy deep green above; flowers 9–16mm long, pale to deep rosy-purple, late summer. *T. fruticans*, tree germander; W.Mediterranean and Portugal; shrub to 2·5m, especially if wall-trained; stems white woolly; leaves to 3cm long, ovate to lanceolate, white or sometimes reddish woolly beneath; flowers to 2·5cm long, lavender-blue or lilac, summer; needs a warm, sheltered wall in all but the mildest areas or regions. *T. marum* (*Micromeria corsica* of many gardens), cat thyme; islands of W.Mediterranean and Murter, Yugoslavia; brittle, twiggy, aromatic shrub, eventually to 30cm tall; stems thinly white woolly; leaves to 1cm long, rhombic to lanceolate, grey-white woolly beneath; flowers 9–12mm long, pinkish-purple, summer; attractive to cats, who often roll on it or tear it to pieces. *T. polium*, S.Europe, S.W.Asia; soft shrub 20–45cm tall; stems erect to sprawling, grey-white or yellowish downy; leaves 1–2cm long, narrowly oblong to obovate with rolled, boldly crenate margins, grey or white downy; flowers about 8mm long, whitish or reddish, in head-like clusters, summer. *T. pyrenaicum*, N.Spain, S.W.France; white, hairy, usually prostrate sub-shrub; stems to 20cm or so long; leaves 1–2·5cm long, almost orbicular, crenate; flowers to 2cm long, white or purple and white, summer to early autumn. *T. scorodonia*, wood sage; S.W. and C.Europe; rhizomatous sub-shrub, 20–50cm tall; leaves 3–7cm long, ovate to triangular-ovate, cordate, finely wrinkled, crenate; flowers 12–15mm long, pale yellow-green, late summer; mainly represented in gardens by *T.s.* Crispum, with attractive leaf margins waved and crested, purple-tinted in winter – sometimes erroneously listed under *T. scordium*, the wild water germander, with oblong leaves and purple flowers; *T.s.* Crispum Marginatum, as *T.s.* Crispum, but margins also whitish, pink-flushed when young. *T. subspinosum*, Balearic Is; similar in its characters to *T. marum*, but rarely more than 10cm tall by up to approximately 30cm wide, the lateral branches slender and spine-tipped; flowers about 8mm long, purple-red.

Thalictrum

(Greek vernacular name, probably referring to a member of this genus, used by Linnaeus). Meadow rue. RANUNCULACEAE. A genus of 100–150 species of perennials, mainly from the N.Hemisphere with a few on mountains in the S.Hemisphere. They are clump-forming, sometimes rhizomatous and forming colonies, with mainly compound leaves like *Adiantum* or *Aquilegia*, a few species trifoliate or unifoliate. The generally small flowers are petalless with numerous stamens, although in some species the 4–5 sepals are persistent, petaloid and showy. They are carried in airy, terminal panicles. Grow in humus-rich, moisture-retentive but well-drained soil in sun or partial shade. Plant autumn to spring. Propagate from seed when ripe or in spring, or by division at planting time; basal cuttings may also be rooted in a frame in spring.

Species cultivated: *T. aquilegifolium*, E. and C.Europe, N.Asia; 60–90cm tall; leaves bi- or triternate; leaflets obovate, toothed; panicles much-branched, corymbose, flowers with small white sepals and lilac, purple, pink or white stamens, early summer. *T. chelidonii*, Himalaya; 1–1·5m tall; leaves several times ternate or pinnate; leaflets rounded, lobed or toothed; panicles much-branched, flowers 1·5–1·8cm wide, sepals large, lilac, stamens drooping, yellow, summer; needs a cool, moist site to thrive. *T. delavayi*, W.China; 75–150cm tall; leaves several times biternate; leaflets 3-lobed; panicles well-branched, flowers 1·5–2·5cm wide, sepals large, mauve to lilac, stamens yellow, summer; fruit (seed) 9–10mm long, not winged or only very slightly so. *T.d.* Hewitt's Double (*T. dipterocarpum* Hewitt's Double), flowers fully double; often confused in cultivation with *T. dipterocarpum*. *T. diffusiflorum* (*T. diffusiforme* of gardens), S.E.Tibet; to 1m or more tall; similar to *T. chelidonii*, but leaflets smaller and more numerous; panicles smaller, flowers larger, bell-like, 2–2·5cm wide, mauve to violet; also needs cool, moist conditions. *T. dipterocarpum*, W.China; almost indistinguishable from *T. delavayi*, but fruit about 5mm long, with distinct but narrow, marginal wings. *T.d.* Hewitt's Double, see *T. delavayi* Hewitt's Double. *T. flavum*, common meadow rue; Europe, temperate Asia; 1–1·5m tall, rhizomatous, forming colonies; leaves bi- or tripinnate; leaflets obovate to oblong-lanceolate, 3–4 lobed, dark green above, pale beneath; panicles compact, well-branched, flowers with 4 whitish sepals 4–6mm long and bright yellow stamens 7–8mm long, late summer. *T.f. glaucum* (*T.f. speciosum*, *T. glaucum*, *T. speciosissimum*), plant more clump-forming and robust than type; leaves glaucous, panicles larger. *T. kiusianum*, Kyushu, Japan; stoloniferous, forming small patches 10–15cm tall; leaves trifoliate or biternate, leaflets lobed; flowers 6–8mm wide, sepals 2–3mm long, purple, stamens pinkish or pale purple, late summer to autumn. *T. minus*, lesser meadow rue; Europe, N.Asia; very variable species, 15–150cm tall, tufted or vigorously rhizomatous, forming wide colonies; leaves several (3–4) times ternate, leaflets rounded, irregularly toothed or lobed; panicles loose, well-branched, flowers with tiny, yellowish or purplish-

Far left: *Thalictrum aquilegifolium*
Above left: *Thalictrum flavum glaucum*
Left: *Thalictrum dipterocarpum*
Above: *Thalictrum rochebrunianum*

green sepals and yellow stamens 5–7mm long; an elegant foliage plant but often invasive. *T.m. arenarium*, 15–20cm tall, leaves often glaucous, fast-spreading. *T. rochebrunianum* (*T. rocquebrunianum* of some catalogues), Japan; 70–100cm tall; leaves several (3–4) times ternate, leaflets obovate, often 2–3 lobed; panicles large and well-branched; flowers 1·2–1·6cm wide, sepals large, pale purple, late summer. *T. speciosissimum*, see *T. flavum glaucum*.

Thea sinensis – see *Camellia sinensis*.

Thelypteris

(Greek *thelys*, female, and *pteris*, a fern). THELYPTERIDACEAE (POLYPODIACEAE). A genus of about 4 species (or 500, depending on the botanical treatment) of ferns of cosmopolitan distribution. They are rhizomatous, with fronds in rosettes, tufted or solitary, with small, rounded sori near the margins of the leaf segments. Grow in humus-rich, moisture-retentive but well-drained soil in shade or

Above: *Thelypteris phegopteris*

partial shade. Plant autumn or spring. Propagate by division at planting time or spores in spring.
Species cultivated: *T. oreopteris* (*T. limbosperma*), mountain fern or mountain wood fern; scattered in the N.Hemisphere south to Madeira; rhizomes short and thick, ascending; fronds in rosettes, deciduous, 30–90cm long, lanceolate in outline, bipinnate, firm-textured, yellow-green, fragrant of lemons when bruised; sori ½mm or less wide. *T. phegopteris*, beech fern; scattered in N.Hemisphere, south to Virginia, USA; rhizomes slender, creeping below ground; fronds solitary, deciduous, long-stalked, the blades to 20cm or so long, triangular-ovate in outline, carried at almost right angles to the stalk; pinnate, the pinnae deeply lobed, sori ½mm or less wide.

Thermopsis

(Greek *thermos*, a lupin, and *opsis*, like). LEGUMINOSAE. A genus of 20–30 species of herbaceous perennials from C. to N.E.Asia and N.America. They are rhizomatous, with erect stems bearing alternate or opposite trifoliate leaves with prominent basal stipules, and terminal racemes of lupin-like flowers. Grow in fertile, well-drained soil in sun. Plant autumn or spring. Propagate by division when planting or seed under glass in spring.
Species cultivated: *T. caroliniana*, E.USA; 1–1·5m tall, sparsely branched if at all; leaflets 5–7·5cm long, ovate to obovate, glaucous, stipules leaflet-like; flowers to 5cm long, yellow, in racemes to 25cm long, summer. *T. mollis*, E.USA; to 60cm tall; stems branched, softly hairy; leaflets 2–4cm long, elliptic to ovate, tawny hairy beneath, stipules similar; flowers 2–3cm long, yellow, in flexuous racemes to 15cm long, summer. *T. montana*, N.W.USA; to 60cm tall; leaflets 3–7cm long, linear-lanceolate, stipules similar, to 2·5cm long; flowers 1·3–2cm long, golden-yellow, in compact racemes 10–20cm long, summer.

Thistles – see *Carlina, Cirsium, Onopordum* and *Silybum.*

Thlaspi

(Greek for a kind of cress). Penny-cress. CRUCIFERAE. A genus of about 60 species of annuals and perennials mostly from the N.Hemisphere with a few in S.America. The perennial species mentioned here are tufted, with mainly basal, obovate to elliptic leaves in rosettes, and racemes of 4-petalled flowers. Grow in well-drained soil in sun. Plant autumn to spring. Propagate from seed, by division or basal cuttings, spring.
Species cultivated: *T. alpinum*, alpine penny-cress; Alps; tufted, often small mat-forming, 10–15cm tall; basal leaves long-stalked, blades 1–2·5cm long; stem leaves amplexicaul; flowers 5–9mm wide, white, spring to summer. *T. bulbosum*, Greece; roots tuberous, tufted, 5–10cm tall; basal leaves long-stalked, blades to 2cm long, broadly ovate, purple-flushed; stem leaves sessile, basally lobed; flowers 7–10mm wide, dark violet, spring to summer; prefers partial shade. *T. limosellifolium*, see next species. *T. rotundifolium*, mountains of E.France to Italy and N.Yugoslavia; tufted and stoloniferous, forming small mats to 10cm or more tall; basal leaves long-stalked, the blades about 1cm wide, broadly ovate to orbicular; stem leaves amplexicaul; flowers 5–8mm wide, purple to rosy-lilac, spring. *T.r. limosellifolium* (*T. limosellifolium*), plant smaller, more compact than type, leaves spathulate.

Thrift – see *Armeria.*
Throatwort – see *Trachelium.*

Left: *Thermopsis caroliniana*
Above: *Thlaspi rotundifolium limosellifolium*
Right: *Thuja occidentalis* Rheingold

Thuja

(*Thuya*). (Greek name for a kind of juniper, used for this genus by Linnaeus). Arbor-vitae. CUPRESSACEAE. A genus of 5 evergreen coniferous trees from E.Asia and N.America. They basically resemble *Chamaecyparis*, but have somewhat larger scale leaves and ovoid to cylindrical cones composed of oblong scales sometimes hooked at the tips. Cultural directions are the same as for species of *Chamaecyparis*.
Species cultivated: *T. lobbii*, see *T. plicata*. *T. occidentalis*, American arbor-vitae, white cedar; N.E. N.America; to 20m tall, bark reddish to orange-brown, scaling and shredding; usually of rather openly conical habit, branches horizontal, turning up at tips; leaves 2·5–4·5mm long, blunt to pointed, usually somewhat yellowish-green, aromatic; cones 8–12mm long, oblongoid, yellowish and erect until ripe, then pendant and brown; the following cultivars are available and garden worthy: *T.o.* Danica, dense, globular bush to 45cm or more tall, flattened leaf sprays vertical; *T.o.* Hetz Midget, slow-growing, globular, dark green bush to 30cm tall; *T.o.* Holmstrup, slow-growing, narrowly conical habit to 1·5m or more; *T.o.* Lutea Nana, broadly pyramidal, 1·5–2m tall, foliage golden all year; *T.o.* Rheingold, slow-growing, conical habit, 1–1·5m or more tall, foliage old gold shaded bronze, producing longer, awl-shaped juvenile leaves when small (then sometimes known as *T.o.* Ellwangerana Pygmaea Aurea). *T. orientalis* (*Platycladus o.*, *Biota o.*), Chinese arbor-vitae; N. and W.China; large shrub or small tree 5–12m or more tall; dense habit, ovoid to conical when young, irregularly rounded with age; foliage sprays flattened, held vertically; leaves to 2mm long, triangular, having a resinous smell when bruised; cones ovoid, the thick scales with prominently hooked tips, glaucous until mature, then brown; among the most popular cultivars are: *T.o.* Aurea Nana, dense, globose to ovoid bush, eventually to 75cm or more tall, foliage golden-green; *T.o.* Conspicua, compact, conical habit to 2m or more, foliage golden-yellow; *T.o.* Elegantissima, columnar habit, 2–3m tall, foliage yellow in summer, bronze in winter; *T.o.* Meldensis, dense globular habit, to 45cm or more, foliage semi-juvenile, sea-green in summer, purplish in winter; *T.o.* Minima Glauca, dense, globular bushlet to 30cm or more, foliage semi-juvenile, sea-green in summer, brownish-yellow in winter; *T.o.* Rosedalis, dense, ovoid habit to 80cm or so, foliage juvenile, sea-green in summer, brownish-purple in winter, bright yellow in spring. *T. plicata* (*T. lobbii*), western red cedar, giant arbor-vitae; Alaska to

California; to 50–60m tall, often less in gardens; bark cinnamon to purplish red-brown, thick and soft; conical habit, lower branches sweeping up at the tips; leaves 3–6mm long, bluntly to long-pointed, rich lustrous green, strongly and sweetly aromatic when bruised; cones 9–12mm long, ovoid, erect until mature; fewer cultivars are known in this species, the most readily available being: *T.p.* Aureovariegata, see *T.p.* Zebrina; *T.p.* Rogersii, slow-growing, compact, conical bush – to 1·2m in 30 years, foliage bronze and gold; *T.p.* Stoneham Gold, slow-growing, dense, conical bush to 60cm or more tall, foliage deep olive-green tipped bronze-gold; *T.p.* Zebrina (*T.p.* Aureovariegata), like the type species in habit and vigour but the foliage sprays are yellow-banded.

Thujopsis

(genus *Thuja*, and Greek *opsis*, like). CUPRESSACEAE. A genus of 1 species of evergreen coniferous tree, at one time classified under *Thuja*, from Japan (culture as for *Chamaecyparis*): *T. dolabrata*, 15–25m tall, often less in gardens; bark dark red-brown, stringy and shredding, either columnar and single-stemmed with short, lateral branches, or broadly conical with several erect stems; leaves to 7mm long, broadly triangular, somewhat concave and waxy-white below, lustrous rich to yellowish-green above; cones 1–2cm long, ovoid, scales wedge-shaped with a triangular, pointed or hooked boss. *T.d.* Aurea, leaves gold tinted; *T.d. hondae*, the northern form of the species, to 30m in the wild, leaves smaller and more crowded; *T.d.* Nana, compact, flat-topped bush to 60cm tall; *T.d.* Variegata, foliage irregularly splashed creamy-white.

Thunbergia

(for Carl Peter Thunberg, 1743–1828, Dutch botanist, doctor and student of Linnaeus, who travelled and collected in S.Africa and Japan; later professor of botany at Uppsala). THUNBERGIACEAE (ACANTHACEAE). A genus of between 100 and 200 species of annuals and perennials, often climbing, from C. and S.Africa, Malagasy, S.Asia. They have erect or twining stems, opposite pairs of ovate to lanceolate leaves, and tubular, irregularly 5-lobed flowers either in racemes or solitary from upper leaf-axils. Greenhouse, minimum temperature 10°C, humidity and light shade in summer, the annual sites. Grow in greenhouse borders, or pots of a good commercial potting mixture. Water regularly but less in winter. Plants in pots require liquid-feed during the summer at 7–10 day intervals. Pot or repot perennials in spring. Propagate all species from seed in spring at about 18°C, perennials also by cuttings in early summer, bottom heat 18–21°C.

Top left: *Thuja plicata*
Top: *Thujopsis dolabrata*
Above: *Thuja orientalis* Rosedalis
Right: *Thunbergia alata*

Species cultivated (all climbing): *T. alata*, black-eyed Susan; tropical Africa, naturalized elsewhere; perennial, to 3m long; leaf-stalks winged, blades to 7·5cm long, triangular-ovate; flowers in leaf-axils,

4cm long, white, cream to orange-yellow with chocolate-purple centre, summer; often grown as an annual. *T. gibsonii*, see *T. gregorii*. *T. grandiflora*, blue trumpet vine (USA); N.India; woody-stemmed, to 6m or more long; leaves 10–20cm long, ovate, angular-toothed, rough-textured; flowers to 7cm long and wide, blue, in pendulous racemes, summer. *T. gregorii* (*T. gibsonii*), tropical Africa; similar to *T. alata*, but leaves ovate and flowers 4·5cm long, orange throughout.

Thymus

(the ancient Greek name for thyme). LABIATAE. A genus of 300–400 species of shrubs and sub-shrubs from Europe and Asia. They have wiry, erect to prostrate stems, aromatic, linear to ovate leaves in opposite pairs, and small, tubular, 2-lipped flowers in terminal, whorled spikes or heads, sometimes with coloured bracts. Grow in any well-drained soil in sun. Plant autumn to spring. Propagate by division or from seed in spring, or by cuttings early or late summer, the latter usually successful inserted *in situ* if not allowed to dry out during rooting.

Species cultivated (mainly summer-flowering): *T. azoricus*, see next species. *T. caespititius* (*T. azoricus*, *T. micans*), Spain, Portugal, Azores; low hummock- to mat-forming; leaves 8mm long, narrowly spathulate, ciliate at base; flowers 6mm or more long, purplish-pink to almost white. *T. carnosus* (*T. erectus* of gardens), S.Portugal; erect, Irish yew-like bushlet 15–40cm tall; leaves 5–7mm long, ovate-lanceolate, somewhat fleshy; flowers about 6mm long, whitish; sometimes confused in gardens with *T. richardii nitidus*. *T. cilicicus*, Turkey; compact bushlet 7–18cm tall; leaves 9–12mm long, linear, ciliate; flowers 7mm long, lilac or mauve *T.* × *citriodorus* (*T. pulegioides* × *T. vulgaris*), lemon-scented thyme; spreading bush 10–30cm tall, similar to *T. vulgaris* but with flat, broader, smooth, lemon-scented leaves. *T.* × *c.* Argenteus (*T. vulgaris* Argenteus), leaves white-variegated; *T.* × *c.* Aureus (*T. vulgaris* Aureus), leaves yellow. *T. coccineus*, see *T. praecox arcticus* Coccineus. *T. doefleri*, N.E.Albania, much like *T. praecox*, but leaves 8–14mm long, narrowly spathulate, densely covered with long and short hairs. *T. drucei*, see *T. praecox arcticus*. *T. erectus*, a name of no botanical validity, see *T. carnosus*. *T. herba-barona*, caraway thyme; Corsica, Sardinia; mat-forming, 5–10cm tall; leaves 6–9mm long, elliptic to rhombic-ovate, ciliate at base; flowers to 9mm long, pale purple. *T. lanuginosus*, in gardens a name applied to several prostrate, hairy thymes, see *T. pseudolanuginosus*. *T. leucotrichus*, mountains of C. and S.Greece; mat-forming, to 10cm tall; leaves 6–10mm long, linear-lanceolate, covered with long and short hairs; bracts beneath the flowers purplish; flowers 7–10mm long, pinkish-purple. *T. micans*, see *T. caespititius*. *T. nitidus*, see *T. richardii n.* *T. praecox*, Europe; mat-forming, 5–10cm tall; leaves 5–14mm long, obovate to almost orbicular, ciliate at base; flowers to 8mm long in shades of purple, often in great profusion; very variable species divided into 5 sub-species, only 1 of which is commonly cultivated: *T.p. arcticus* (*T. drucei*, *T. serpyllum* of gardens, not the true species of Linnaeus), wild, or mother of thyme; leaves obovate, 5–8mm long; flowers about 6mm long, variable in colour. *T.p.a.* Albus, pale foliage, white flowers; *T.p.a.* Annie Hall, flesh-pink; *T.p.a.* Coccineus (*T. coccineus*), dark foliage, crimson flowers; *T.p.a.* Pink Chintz, salmon-pink. *T. pseudolanuginosus* (*T. lanuginosus* of gardens), provenance unknown; mat-forming, to 5cm tall, much like *T. praecox arcticus*, but leaves smaller, broadly elliptic, with long, white hairs; flowers 4–5mm long, pink. *T. richardii*, Balearic Is, Sicily, W.Yugoslavia; mat-forming with prostrate to low arching stems, to 12cm tall; leaves 7–12mm long, ovate to elliptic; flowers 7–9mm long, purple; usually represented in gardens by *T.r. nitidus* (*T. nitidus*), Sicily, leaves more than twice as long as wide, calyces densely glandular, the upper teeth with long hairs. *T. serpyllum* of gardens, see *T. praecox arcticus*. *T. vulgaris*, common or garden thyme; W. Mediterranean; spreading shrub to 30cm tall; leaves 3–8mm long, linear to elliptic, margins rolled, finely grey-hairy, usually with a cluster of smaller leaves in the axils; flowers about 5mm long, whitish to pale purple. *T.v.* Aureus and *T.v.* Argenteus, see *T.* × *citriodorus*.

Tiarella

(diminutive of Greek *tiara*, an ancient Persian head-dress – alluding to the form of the fruit). SAXIFRAGACEAE. A genus of 6 species of evergreen perennials, 1 in E.Asia, the rest in N.America. They are rhizomatous, sometimes also stoloniferous, forming clumps or mats of ovate, long-stalked, simple or compound leaves, and erect racemes or panicles of tiny, narrowly petalled flowers. The curious fruits are narrow capsules formed of 2 loosely fitting valves of unequal size. Grow in humus-rich, moisture-retentive but well-drained soil in partial shade. Plant autumn to spring. Propagate by division or from seed in spring.

Species cultivated: *T. collina*, see *T. wherryi*. *T. cordifolia*, foamflower; rhizomatous and stoloniferous, forming wide mats; leaf-blades 6–10cm long, ovate-cordate, shallowly 5–7 lobed, toothed,

Far left: *Thymus praecox*
Far left below: *Thymus* × *citriodorus* Argenteus
Left: *Thymus* × *citriodorus* Aureus
Left below: *Thymus praecox arcticus* Coccineus
Below: *Tiarella cordifolia*

hispid, often flecked deep maroon, flushed reddish-bronze in winter; scapes 15–30cm tall, flowers 2·5–5mm long, in racemes, white or pink-tinted; excellent ground cover between trees and shrubs. *T.c. collina*, see *T. wherryi*. *T. polyphylla*, Himalaya to Japan and Taiwan; clump-forming, rhizomatous; leaf-blades 5–7cm long, broadly ovate to rounded, shallowly 3–5 lobed, toothed; scapes 30–45cm tall, flowers 2–4mm long in racemes, nodding, white. *T. trifoliata*, N.W. N.America; clump-forming; leaf-blades cut into 3 leaflets, central one to 4cm or more long, laterals shorter, asymmetrically bilobed, hairy; scapes 20–50cm tall, flowers 2·5–4mm long, in cylindrical panicles, white, pink-tinted in bud. *T. wherryii* (*T. collina*, *T. cordifolia c.*), S.E.USA; like *T. cordifolia*; clump-forming, lacking stolons; leaves distinctly maroon-flecked, racemes more slender.

Tidy tips – see *Layia platyglossa*.

Tiger flower – see *Tigridia*.

Tiger lily – see *Lilium tigrinum*.

Tigridia

(Latin *tigris*, a tiger, from the patterning on the flowers; in this case, spotted like a jaguar which the early Spanish naturalists in S.America confused with the Asiatic tiger). Tiger or shell-flower. IRIDACEAE. A genus of about 27 species of bulbous plants from Mexico to Chile, 1 of which is generally available: *T. pavonia*, peacock or tiger flower; Mexico, Guatemala: 40–60cm tall: leaves in fan-like tufts, 30–45cm long, narrowly lanceolate, pleated; flowers 8–15cm wide, 6-tepalled, the outer 3 forming a bowl-shaped base, then spreading widely, the inner 3 much smaller and partially folded, red, the centre yellow heavily spotted purple, late summer to autumn; several cultivars are known but seldom available by name, usually sold as a mixture and including shades of white, red, red-purple and yellow. Grow in fertile, well-drained soil in sunny, sheltered sites. Plant at least 10cm deep in spring. In areas of hard winter frosts, lift in autumn when leaves killed by first frost, remove all foliage and store in dry peat at 7–10°C. Propagate from seed in spring, under glass the first year, or by offsets removed at planting time. May also be grown in pots in a sunny, cold or cool greenhouse.

Tilia

(ancient Latin name for lime or linden tree). Lime tree, linden. TILIACEAE. A genus of 30–50 species of deciduous trees from N.Hemisphere, south to the mountains of Mexico and Vietnam. They have alternate, toothed, usually broadly ovate, obliquely cordate leaves, and small, fragrant, 5-petalled flowers in long-stalked, pendant cymes from the axils of wing-like bracts in summer. When the small, woody seed capsules are ripe the whole cluster attached to its bract breaks away and is distributed by wind. Grow in fertile, moisture-retentive but not wet soil in sun or partial shade. Plant autumn to spring. Propagate from seed when ripe, but seed from garden trees often has a low viability and may be hybrid if other species are nearby. Layering in late winter is the usual means of increase, also tip-cuttings in summer under a mist unit.

Species cultivated: *T. americana*, American linden, basswood; New Brunswick to Virginia and Texas; to 40m in the wild often less in gardens, of domed habit; bark rich brown, deeply furrowed; leaves 10–20cm long, yellow-green above and below; flowers yellowish-white; does not always grow successfully elsewhere. *T. cordata*, small-leaved lime; Europe to Caucasus and Siberia; to 30m tall, narrowly irregularly domed habit; bark smooth, grey, cracked into shallow plates when old; leaves 4–7cm long, glossy rich green above, paler, somewhat glaucous beneath; flowers whitish; a good bee tree. *T.* × *euchlora* (probably *T. cordata* × *T. dasystyla*), Crimean lime; to 20m tall but often less in gardens; tall, untidily domed habit, bark

Far left below and bottom: *Tigridia pavonia*, two colour forms

Below: *Tilia* × *europaea*

smooth grey; leaves 5–10cm or more long, deep glossy green above, pale beneath, at least some turning gold in autumn; flowers yellowish, nectar has narcotic effect on bees; useful in parks and streets in being free of aphids. *T.* × *europaea* (*T. vulgaris*), (*T. cordata* × *T. platyphyllos*), common lime; to 40m or more tall, of domed habit, with arching, eventually massive lower branches; trunk with smooth to finely fissured grey bark, often burred and covered with congested masses of sucker shoots or 'sprouts'; leaves 6–10cm long, dark green above, pale beneath; flowers yellowish-white. *T. petiolaris*, pendant silver lime; provenance not known for sure, probably Caucasus or derived from *T. tomentosa*; to 30m or more tall, narrowly domed habit with the outer branchlets pendulous; leaves very long-stalked, blades 6–12cm long, dark green above, thinly white-felted beneath; flowers pale

yellow, very fragrant, but narcotic to bees. *T. platyphyllos*, large-leaved lime; Europe to Turkey and Caucasus; to 30m or more tall, narrowly domed habit; bark dark grey and fissured; leaves 6–15cm long, downy, dark green above, pale beneath; flowers yellowish; a good bee tree. *T.p.* Rubra, winter twigs dark red, generally more broadly domed in habit. *T. tomentosa*, silver lime; S.E.Europe, S.W.Asia; to 30m, but often only 25m in gardens; broadly domed habit; leaves 6–12cm long, dark green above, silvery-felted beneath; flowers pale yellow, with golden anthers, late summer.

Toad lily – see *Tricyrtis*.

Toadflax – see *Linaria* and *Cymbalaria muralis*.

Tobacco – see *Nicotiana*.

Tolmiea

(for Dr William Fraser Tolmie, 1812–1886, surgeon for Hudson Bay Company at Fort Vancouver).

SAXIFRAGACEAE. A genus of 1 species of evergreen perennial from W. N.America: *T. menziesii*, pick-aback plant, youth-on-age; clump-forming, 40–60cm tall in bloom; leaves long-stalked, blades 4–10cm long, broadly ovate-cordate, shallowly palmately lobed, toothed, hairy; at the junction of the stalk and blade a plantlet arises that roots and forms a new plant when the leaf touches the soil; flowers in slender racemes, each 1·2–2cm long, tubular but split almost to base on one side, with 5, greenish-purple, petal-like calyx lobes and 4, thread-like, chocolate-purple petals, summer. Grow in any moderately fertile, moisture-retentive but well-drained soil in partial shade. It also makes an intriguing and very adaptable house plant, thriving in cold and warm conditions and in poor light. Pot or plant autumn to spring. Propagate by division at planting time or the leaf plantlets in late summer to autumn – the latter may be either pegged down to the soil *in situ*, or detached when they have several leaves and treated as cuttings.

Tomatillo – see *Physalis ixocarpa*.

Toothache tree – see *Zanthozylum americana*.

Torenia

(for the Reverend Olaf Toren, 1718–1753, Chaplain to the Swedish East India Company in India and China). SCROPHULARIACEAE. A genus of 40–50 species of annuals and perennials from tropical and subtropical Asia and Africa, 1 of which is usually available: *T. fournieri*, blue wings (USA), wishbone flower; Vietnam; bushy, erect annual to 30cm tall; leaves in opposite pairs, 3–5cm long, ovate to narrowly so, toothed; flowers in short, terminal racemes, each 3–4cm long, tubular, 4-lobed, upper lobe largest, like a standard, pale violet to blue with the 3 lower lobes deep velvety blue-purple, summer to autumn. *T.f.* Grandiflora, flowers somewhat larger. Greenhouse, or as a half-hardy annual outside in fertile, moisture-retentive but well-drained soil in sheltered, partial shade. Sow seed in spring at 18°C, scattering thinly and barely covering. Prick off seedlings when large enough to handle at 4cm apart each way into boxes of a commercial potting mixture. Harden off and plant out in early summer when fear of frost has passed. Alternatively, when the young plants are growing well and start to overlap each other, place singly into 9cm pots, moving later into 13–15cm containers for flowering in a cold or cool greenhouse. Lightly shade under glass; liquid-feed every 10 days when buds show.

Far left above: *Tilia platyphyllos*
Far left: *Tilia petiolaris*
Left above: *Tolmeia menziesii*
Above: *Torenia fournieri*
Below: *Trachelium caeruleum*

Tovara virginiana – see *Polygonum filiforme*.

Trachelium

(Greek *trachelos*, a neck – *T. caeruleum* was formerly used medicinally for infections of the

throat). Throatwort. CAMPANULACEAE. A genus of about 7 species of usually somewhat woody-based perennials from the Mediterranean. They have alternate, obovate to ovate or elliptic leaves and small, slenderly tubular, 5-lobed flowers in corymbs or corymbose panicles. Grow in sharply drained, moderately fertile soil in sunny, sheltered sites. *T. caeruleum* is not reliably hardy and is often grown as a pot plant or as a half-hardy annual. Plant, pot or repot spring. Propagate from seed at 16–18°C in spring, or by basal cuttings late spring or late summer.

Species cultivated: *T. caeruleum*, W. and C.Mediterranean; 60–120cm tall; leaves 3–7cm long, ovate, toothed; flowers 6mm long, violet-blue, in corymbose panicles, late summer. *T. jacquinii rumelianum* (*T. rumelianum, Diosphaera r.* and *D. dubia*), Bulgaria, Greece; 15–30cm tall; stems rather

Above: *Trachelium jacquinii rumelianum*
Below: *Trachelospermum jasminoides*

sprawling; leaves 2–5cm long, ovate to oblong, sparsely toothed; flowers to 5mm long, blue or lilac, in dense, head-like corymbs, late summer; best in a limestone dry wall, sheltered rock garden, crevice or alpine house.

Trachelospermum

(Greek *trachelos*, a neck, and *sperma*, a seed). APOCYNACEAE. A genus of 10–30 species, depending on the botanical authority, of woody evergreen climbers mainly from E.Asia, 1 in S.USA. They have

twining stems – sometimes also with aerial-clinging roots like those of ivy – opposite pairs of leathery, elliptic to lanceolate leaves, and tubular, 5-lobed, fragrant, somewhat jasmine-like flowers in small cymes during late summer. Grow in humus-rich, moisture-retentive but well-drained soil at the foot of sunny or partially shaded walls. In cold areas, *T. jasminoides* is best in a frost-free greenhouse, particularly on the wall of a lean-to or conservatory. Plant autumn or spring, providing support for the twining stems. Propagate by layering in spring or cuttings late summer, bottom heat 18°C.

Species cultivated: *T. asiaticum* (*Rhynchospermum a.*), Japan, Korea; to 6m tall; leaves elliptic, 2·5–5cm long, lustrous deep green; flowers 2·5cm wide, white, ageing creamy-yellow, with erect to spreading calyx lobes; the hardiest species which can also be grown up trees in sheltered areas. *T. jasminoides* (*Rhynchospermum j.*), star jasmine (USA); China; to 7m tall, but comparatively slow-growing; stems with aerial roots; leaves 4–7·5cm long, elliptic to oblanceolate, deep lustrous green; flowers 2·5cm wide, white, ageing cream, with very long, reflexed calyx lobes.

Trachycarpus

(Greek *trachys*, rough, and *karpos*, a fruit). PALMAE. A genus of 6–8 species of palms from Himalaya to E.Asia, 1 of which is generally available: *T. fortunei* (*T. excelsus, Chamaerops excelsa* of catalogues), Chusan palm; Himalaya (Burma) to E.China; to 10m or more tall; stems solitary, covered with thick, brown, fibrous leaf bases; leaves in terminal rosettes, long-stalked, blades 60–120cm or more long, almost orbicular, fan-shaped, pleated, divided to the middle or more into many narrow lobes; flowers usually dioecious, small, 3-petalled, yellowish, in arching panicles to 60cm long; fruit globose, blue-black, about 1cm wide, single-seeded; the hardiest known palm, individuals having survived at least –15°C where the climate is suitable. Grow in humus-rich soil in sun or partial shade. Plant autumn or spring. Propagate from seed under glass in spring at 18–21°C, growing the young plants in pots for 2–3 years protected in winter, before planting in permanent sites.

Trachymene

(*Didiscus*). (Greek *trachys*, rough, and *meninx*, a membrane – alluding to the fruit of some species). HYDROCOTYLACEAE (UMBELLIFERAE). A genus of 12–40 species, depending on botanical authority, of annuals and perennials from Australia and S.E.Asia Is, 1 of which is usually available: *T. coerulea* (*Didiscus c.*), blue lace flower; W.Australia; annual to 60cm tall; stems erect, branched; leaves deeply ternately or biternately divided into narrow, toothed lobes; flowers tiny, unequally 5-petalled, light blue, in long-stalked umbels, 4–7cm wide, summer. Grow plants in well-drained, moderately humus-rich soil in sun. Sow seed *in situ* in spring. Also makes an attractive pot plant for the frost-free or cool greenhouse if sown in autumn, the seedlings placed singly into 13cm pots of good commercial potting mixture; plants will then flower in spring.

Tradescantia

(for John Tradescant, 1608–1662, gardener to King Charles I). Spiderwort. COMMELINACEAE. A genus of 20–60 species, depending on botanical authority, of perennials from N. and S.America. They range from erect, hardy, herbaceous perennials to tender, decumbent or trailing evergreens; leaves are alternate, lanceolate to ovate, somewhat fleshy; flowers 3-petalled with bearded stamens, emerging in succession from paired terminal leaf or spathe-like bracts. Grow hardy species in fertile, well-drained but moisture-retentive soil in sun or partial shade. Plant autumn to spring. Propagate by division at planting time or from seed in spring.

Species cultivated: *T.* × *andersoniana* (*T. virginiana* of gardens), species of hardy cultivars combining the 3 similar N.American species, *T. ohiensis, T. subaspera* and *T. virginiana*; clump-forming, erect, to 60cm tall; leaves narrowly lanceolate, somewhat grassy; flowers 2·5–3·5cm wide in shades of velvety blue to red-purple and white, summer to autumn: *T.* × *a.* J. C. Weguelin, 45cm, azure-blue; *T.* × *a.* Osprey, 60cm, white with blue-bearded stamens; *T.* × *a.* Purple Dome, 45cm, rich purple; *T.* × *a.* Rubra, 45cm, deep rose-red. *T. blossfeldiana*, Argentina; tender, decumbent to semi-erect, to 20cm tall; stems purple; leaves elliptic, 5–10cm long, dark green above, purple-flushed and

Above: *Tradescantia* × *andersoniana* Osprey
Below: *Tradescantia* × *andersoniana* Isis

Left: *Tradescantia* × *andersoniana* hybrid
Above: *Tricyrtis hirta*
Above right: *Trifolium repens* Purpurascens
Below right: *Trillium sessile*

hairy beneath; flowers 1cm wide, purple-rose with white centres, spring, in many-flowered umbels. *T. brevicaulis*, old name of ambiguous application for plants now considered dwarf forms of *T. virginiana*. *T. virginiana* (*T. virginica* of some catalogues), common spiderwort; E.USA; hardy, clump-forming, to 35cm tall; leaves to 30cm long, linear-lanceolate, grassy; flowers 2–3cm wide, blue, purple or pinkish, summer; plants listed under this name are usually *T.* × *andersoniana*.

Travellers' joy – see *Clematis vitalba*.
Tree mallow – see *Lavatera arborea*.
Tree of heaven – see *Ailanthus altissima*.
Tree poppy – see *Romneya*.
Trefoil – see *Trifolium*.
Tricuspidaria – see *Crinodendron*.

Tricyrtis

(Greek *tri*, 3, and *kyrtos*, humped – alluding to the 3 nectary swellings at the base of the flowers). Toad lily. LILIACEAE. A genus of 15 species of herbaceous perennials from Himalaya to Japan and Taiwan. They are rhizomatous, forming clumps or colonies of erect stems bearing alternate, often sessile, clasping, elliptic to obovate leaves, and terminal cymes or solitary, erect or nodding, somewhat bell-shaped flowers in early autumn. Each flower is composed of 6 tepals forming a tube at the base, then flaring out, usually densely spotted. Grow in humus-rich, well-drained but moisture-retentive soil in sun or partial shade, preferably sheltered from cold winds. Not fully hardy. Plant autumn or spring. Propagate by division at planting time or from seed in spring in a cold frame.

Species cultivated: *T. bakeri* of gardens, see *T. latifolia*. *T. formosana*, Taiwan; 60–90cm tall; leaves to 13cm long, oblanceolate, glossy deep green; flowers erect, in loose, terminal cymes, 2·5–3cm long, almost white to pale mauve with darker spots, yellow at the throat. *T.f. stolonifera* (*T. stolonifera*), usually vigorously stoloniferous, leaves lanceolate to oblanceolate. *T. hirta*, Japan; to 90cm tall; stems hairy; leaves 8–15cm long, ovate-oblong to lanceolate; flowers erect in small cymes, or solitary, terminal and from upper leaf-axils, 2·5–3cm long, white with purple spots. *T. hirta* Alba, white with pink stigma and stamens. *T. latifolia* (*T. bakeri* of gardens), Japan; 50–90cm tall; leaves 8–15cm long, obovate; flowers erect in cymes, 2–2·5cm long, yellow, purple-spotted. *T. macrantha*, Japan; 50–75cm tall; stems coarsely pale brown hairy; leaves to 10cm long, ovate-oblong to lanceolate; flowers pendulous in small cymes or solitary from upper axils, 3–4cm long, yellow, spotted purple-brown, basal nectaries shortly spurred. *T. macropoda*, Japan; 60–90cm tall; leaves 8–13cm long, ovate to oblong; flowers erect in cymes, to 2cm long, white, spotted purple. *T. stolonifera*, see *T. formosana s.*

Trifolium

(Latin *tri*, 3, and *folium*, a leaf). Clover, trefoil. LEGUMINOSAE. A genus of about 300 species of annuals and perennials widely distributed in temperate and subtropical countries. They are tufted to mat-forming with trifoliolate leaves and tiny, pea-shaped flowers usually arranged in dense, globular, ovoid or cylindrical heads from the upper leaf-axils. Grow in any moderately fertile, well-drained soil in sun. Plant autumn to spring. Propagate by division or from seed in spring.

Species cultivated: *T. incarnatum*, crimson clover; Mediterranean; erect annual to 50cm tall, leaflets 1–3cm long, obovate, downy; flower-heads 4–7cm long, cylindrical, usually crimson, but pink and cream forms are known, summer, autumn. *T. pannonicum*, Hungarian clover; S.E.Europe, Turkey; rhizomatous, erect perennial to 90cm tall; leaflets 1·2cm long, oblong-lanceolate to obovate; flower-heads 3–5cm long, ovoid to oblong, white or creamy-yellow, summer. *T. repens*, white or Dutch clover; Europe, N. and W.Asia, N.Africa; mat-forming; stems to 50cm long, rooting at nodes; leaflets 1–2cm or more long, obovate to obcordate; flower-heads 1·5–2cm long, globular, white, often ageing pink, sometimes entirely pinkish or purplish, summer to autumn; a common constituent of grassland, vigorous strains sown as forage or for green manuring; in gardens usually represented by *T.r.* Purpurascens, leaves bronze-purple; *T.r.* Purpurascens Quadriphyllum, leaves bronze-purple, composed of 3–5 or more leaflets.

Trillium

(Latin *tri*, 3 – the plants have leaves and floral parts in 3s). Wake-robin, birth-root, wood-lily. TRILLIACEAE (LILIACEAE). A genus of about 30 species of herbaceous perennials from N.America, Himalaya to E.Asia. They are shortly rhizomatous, forming small to large clumps, each stem bearing 3 elliptic to ovate leaves at the top and solitary, 3-petalled, sometimes sessile flowers in spring to early summer, followed by a 3-lobed, reddish berry. Grow in moisture-retentive, but well-drained, humus-rich soil in partial shade. Plant when dormant (late summer/autumn to late winter). Propagate by division at planting time or from ripe seed. This takes 1½–2½ years to germinate, more to flower.

Species cultivated: *T. californicum*, see *T. ovatum*. *T. catesbaei* (*T. nervosum*, *T. stylosum*), S.E.USA; 30–45cm tall; leaves to 10cm long, elliptic to ovate; flowers nodding, to 5cm long, pale to deep pink. *T. cernuum*, E. N.America; 30–45cm tall; leaves 5–15cm long, rhombic-ovate; flowers nodding, partly hidden beneath leaves, to 2·5cm long, white or pink-flushed. *T. chloropetalum* (*T. sessile californicum*), Washington State to C.California; 30–60cm tall; leaves 10–15cm long, broadly to rhombic-

Above: *Trillium grandiflorum*
Below: *Trillium ovatum*
Bottom: *Trillium catesbaei*
Above right: *Tripteris hyoseroides*

ovate, often with a darker mottling; flowers sessile, 5–9cm long, greenish-yellow to white, or purplish. *T.c. giganteum*, California, petals maroon to pinkish-lilac; *T.c.* Rubrum of gardens is the maroon form. *T. erectum*, birthroot, squawroot, stinking Benjamin; E. N.America; 30–45cm tall; leaves 5–18cm long, rounded to rhombic-ovate; flowers erect to inclined, 2·5–5cm long, crimson to purple, brown, sometimes white (*T.e.* Album) or greenish. *T.e.* Flavum (*T.e. luteum* of gardens, *T. flavum*), flowers yellow. *T. grandiflorum*, wake-robin, common wood lily; E. N.America; 30–45cm tall, robust; leaves to 15cm long, rounded to rhombic-ovate; flowers to·5cm or more long, white, ageing pink; very prone to mutate, many aberrant forms having been described, including several with double flowers and from 2 to 4 or more leaves and petals. *T.g.* Plenum, flowers double, of shapely form; *T.g.* Variegatum, petals green-striped. *T. luteum*, see *T. viride l. T. nervosum*, see *T. catesbaei*. *T. nivale*, dwarf white, wood lily; S.E.USA; 8–15cm tall; leaves 2·5–5cm long, elliptic to ovate; flowers 1·5–3cm long, white, sometimes pink-striped or spotted at base. *T. ovatum* (*T. californicum*), 20–30cm or more tall; leaves 5–15cm long, rhombic-ovate; flowers 2·5–5·5cm long, white, ageing pinkish. *T. recurvatum*, prairie or purple wake-robin; E. N.America; 30cm or more tall; leaves 5–11cm long, obovate to lanceolate; flowers to 4·5cm long, maroon to greenish-yellow. *T. rivale*, California, Oregon; similar to *T. nivale*, but to 25cm tall; leaves to 7cm long; flowers to 5cm long, usually eventually nodding, white, marked rose-carmine within. *T. sessile*, toadshade, wake-robin; E. N.America; 20–30cm tall; leaves to 10cm long, ovate or elliptic, often broadly so, and with a mottled pattern of pale and dark green; flowers sessile, to 4cm long, maroon to yellow-green. *T.s. californicum*, see *T. chloropetalum*; *T.s. luteum*; see *T. viride l*; *T.s.* Rubrum, red-purple. *T. stylosum*, see *T. catesbaei*. *T. undulatum*, painted wood-lily; E. N.America; to 30cm tall, sometimes more; leaves 7–17cm long, ovate, acuminate; flowers 3–4cm long, petals waved, white with a basal horseshoe of reddish-purple. *T. viride*, S.E.USA; much like *T. sessile*, but more robust; stem often hairy and flowers greenish. *T.v. luteum* (*T. luteum*, *T. sessile l.*), flowers yellow.

Tripteris

(Greek *tri*, 3, *pteron*, wing – the fruit, or seed, has 3 membraneous wings). COMPOSITAE. A genus of 40 species of annuals and perennials from S.Africa to Arabia, 1 of which is usually available: *T. hyoseroides* (*Osteospermum h.*), S.Africa; bushy, erect, aromatic annual to 60cm tall, stems slender; leaves alternate, to 13cm long, narrowly oblong to oblanceolate, waved and toothed; flower-heads daisy-like, about 5cm wide, discs blue-black, rays brilliant yellow-orange, summer to autumn. Grow in any reasonably fertile, well-drained soil in sun.

Sow seed *in situ* late spring or when fear of worst frost has passed. For an earlier display sow under glass mid spring at 16–18°C and prick off at 5cm apart into boxes of a good potting mixture, hardening off and planting out late spring.

Tristagma uniflora – see *Ipheion uniflora*.

Triteleia – see *Brodiaea* and *Ipheion*.

Tritoma – see *Kniphofia*.

Tritonia

(Greek *triton*, in the sense of a weathercock – alluding to the variable directions of the stamens). IRIDACEAE. A genus of about 50 species of cormous perennials from tropical and S.Africa. They have flattened, fan-shaped tufts of sword-shaped or falcate leaves and short spikes of showy flowers, the 6 tepals of which are united into a funnel-shaped base. Culture as for *Sparaxis*.

Species cultivated: *T. aurea*, see *Crocosmia a. T. crocata*, S.Africa; 30–45cm tall; leaves to 20cm long, curved; flowers 5–6cm wide, bright tawny-yellow, summer. *T.c. miniata*, flowers smaller than type, bright red. *T. rosea*, see next species. *T. rubrolucens* (*T. rosea*), S.Africa; 40–60cm tall; leaves to 30cm long, linear; flowers about 5cm wide, rose-red with 3 basal spots, borne in branched spikes.

Trollius

(from Swiss-German for globe flower, *trollblume*). Globe flower. RANUNCULACEAE. A genus of 20–25 species of herbaceous perennials from N.Hemisphere. They are clump-forming, with long-stalked, palmately lobed leaves, and terminal flowers like large buttercups but generally more rounded and formed of 5–15, yellow, petal-like sepals. Grow in fertile, moist soil or preferably a bog garden in sun, although partial shade is tolerated. Plant autumn to early spring. Propagate by division at planting time or from seed sown as soon as ripe. Can take up to 2 years to germinate.

Species cultivated (all summer-flowering): *T. acaulis*, Himalaya; to 15cm or more tall; leaves 5–7 lobed, cleft to the base, each division 3-lobed; flowers to 5cm wide, 9-sepalled, deep yellow, opening out flat. *T.* × *cultorum* (*T.* × *hybridus* of catalogues), group of garden cultivars mainly derived from *T. europaeus*, the similar but smaller *T. asiaticus*, and the more robust *T. chinensis*; they resemble *T. europaeus* in general appearance, but generally have larger flowers and are more robust; among the best are: *T.* × *c.* Alabaster, pale primrose; *T.* × *c.* Canary Bird, large lemon-yellow; *T.* × *c.* Commander-in-Chief, very large deep orange; *T.* × *c.* Earliest of All, lemon-yellow, late spring; *T.* × *c.* Golden Queen (*T. ledebourii* Golden Queen), golden-orange with protruding petaloids; *T.* × *c.* Orange Princess, orange-yellow, early summer; *T.* × *c.* Salamanda, deep orange. *T. europaeus*, Europe to Caucasus and Canada; to 60cm tall; leaves 3–5 lobed, usually to the base, lobes deeply cut and toothed; flowers to 3cm wide, sepals about 10, pale yellow. *T.e.* Superbus, to 75cm, clear lemon-yellow. *T.* × *hybridus*, see *T.* × *cultorum*. *T. ledebourii* of gardens (not the true species which appears not to be in cultivation), see *T.* × *cultorum* Golden Queen. *T. pumilus*, Himalaya; 15–25cm tall; leaves mostly basal, small, 2–5cm wide, 5–7 lobed and laciniate; flowers 2·5cm wide, 5–7 sepalled, buttercup-yellow, opening widely. *T.p. yunnanensis*, see next entry. *T. yunnanensis* (*T. pumilus y.*), W. China; to 60cm tall; leaves to 10cm wide, 3–5 lobed, broadly and sharply toothed; flowers 4–5cm or more wide, 5-tepalled, golden-yellow, opening flat.

Tropaeolum

(Latin *tropaeum*, Greek *tropaion*, trophy, a plant of *T. majus* reminded Linnaeus of a trophy pillar set upon a battlefield by the victors and hung with shields – the round leaves – and bloody helmets – the red flowers – of the vanquished). Nasturtium (not to be confused with the genus *Nasturtium*, see Watercress). TROPAEOLACEAE. A genus of 50–90 species depending on the botanical authority, of annual and perennial climbers and trailers from Mexico to S. S.America. They are often tuberous-rooted, with slender stems and alternate, peltate to digitate leaves, the long stalks of which wind around supports like tendrils. The flowers arise singly from the upper leaf-axils, sometimes in terminal leafy racemes. Each bloom has 5, sometimes coloured, sepals, the uppermost with a long nectary spur, and 5, broad, often spreading petals. The 3-lobed fruit splits into 3 triangular-ovoid sections ('seeds') often with a dry, somewhat pithy coat. Grow tender species under glass, minimum temperature 7°C. Pot or repot tubers in autumn, using a good commercial potting mixture and provide twiggy sticks for support. Water very sparingly until the shoots are 10–15cm long, then water regularly until the last flowers fade. Apply liquid feed at 10-day intervals once the flower-buds show and until the flowers fade. When the leaves start to yellow, dry off until autumn. Grow hardy perennials in humus-rich, well-drained soil in sun, with the exception of *T. speciosum* which needs a moister, but not wet, acid soil and partial shade, ideally growing up through an evergreen shrub such as holly or yew. The annual species will grow in any moderately fertile soil in sun. Propagate the perennials from seed when ripe or spring, by offsets or division where possible, or by cuttings of basal shoots removed close to the tuber in spring, bottom heat about 18°C, annuals by seed *in situ* when fear of frost has passed, or singly in small pots under glass in mid spring, hardening off and planting out later.

Left: *Trollius yunnanensis*
Below left: *Trollius* × *cultorum* Earliest of All
Bottom left: *Trollius europaeus* Superbus
Below: *Tropaeolum* Dwarf Double Jewel
Bottom: *Tropaeolum majus* Alaska
Below right: *Tropaeolum polyphyllum*
Bottom right: *Tropaeolum peregrinum*

Species cultivated: *T. aduncum* and *T. canariense*, see *T. peregrinum*. *T. lobbianum*, see *T. peltophorum*. *T. majus*, garden nasturtium or Indian cress; Peru; vigorous annual climber 3–4m or more long; leaves 5–15cm wide, orbicular, peltate, glabrous; flowers 5–6·5cm wide, long-spurred, shades of red, orange, yellow, summer to autumn; several cultivars and strains are available, some of hybrid origin with *T. minus* (itself rarely available), that can be grouped according to habit. **1** Nanum, Dwarf or Tom Thumb: bushy plants with small leaves, rarely above 25cm tall, semi-double and single-flowered. **2** Gleam: semi-trailing habit, semi-double flowers. **3** Tall: like the type species, climbing or trailing, single flowers. **4** Fully double: small group of cultivars with fully double flowers and a trailing habit that do not set seed and must be grown regularly from cuttings and over-wintered under glass, eg *T.* Burpeei and *T.* Hermine Grasshof. *T. peltophorum* (*T. lobbianum*), Colombia, Ecuador; annual, similar to *T. majus* with which it is sometimes confused, but stems and leaf undersurfaces downy, and petals toothed and basally fringed. *T. peregrinum* (*T. aduncum*, *T. canariense*), Canary creeper; Peru to Ecuador; annual (or short-lived perennial under glass); stems climbing, 4–5m long; leaves deeply 5–7 lobed; flowers 2–2·5cm wide, upper 2 petals much longer than the rest, bright yellow and fringed, summer to autumn; reputedly introduced to the Canary Is by the Spanish and from there to Britain, hence its name. *T. polyphyllum*, mountain screes of

Chile; hardy, tuberous-rooted, herbaceous perennial, mat-forming when well-established; stems to 2m or more long, usually less in gardens; leaves digitate, the 5–7 leaflets obovate, folded and glaucous; flowers in dense, leafy racemes 3cm wide, petals notched, waved, yellow to orange, sometimes crimson-veined, summer; needs a mild area and very well-drained soil. *T. speciosum*, flame nasturtium; Chile; hardy herbaceous perennial from a fleshy, tuber-like rhizome; stems slender, climbing, to 4m or more long; leaves digitate; leaflets 6, obovate; flowers to 4cm wide, petals rounded, very

Above: *Tropaeolum speciosum*

slender-stalked, vermilion-scarlet, late summer; seed blue. *T. tricolorum*, Chile, Bolivia; tender, tuberous-rooted; stems very slender, climbing, 60–90cm long; leaves small, digitate, leaflets 5–7, obovate; flowers 2–3cm long, sepals and spur crimson, petals short, yellow, usually edged maroon, spring; needs a sunny greenhouse to flower well. *T. tuberosum*, Bolivia, Peru; half-hardy, tuberous-rooted; stems climbing, to 3m or more long; leaves peltate, 5-lobed, somewhat glaucous; flowers 2–3cm wide, petals orange-yellow, sepals 2cm long, spur scarlet, late summer to autumn; the somewhat pear-shaped, yellow, crimson-splashed tubers are edible but insipid; they are produced near the soil surface and in cold gardens the site should be mounded with peat, sand or pulverized bark in autumn, or the tubers replanted about 10–15cm deep to protect from frost; alternatively, lift and store in dry peat in a frost-free place.

Tsuga

(the Japanese vernacular name). Hemlock, hemlock spruce. PINACEAE. A genus of 9–10 species of evergreen coniferous trees from N.America and E.Asia. They are conical in habit, with a central trunk and whorls of lateral branches; leaves in 2, flattened, parallel ranks or spirally arranged, linear with 2 white bands of stomata beneath; male flowers (strobili) small, globular to ovoid catkins; cones small, ovoid, pendulous. Culture as *Pseudotsuga*.
Species cultivated: *T. canadensis*, Canadian or eastern hemlock, E. N.America; to 30m or more tall, irregularly conical in habit; leaves 1–1·2cm long in 2 ranks with a central row along the stem showing white undersurface; cones ovoid, to 1·5cm long. *T. heterophylla*, western hemlock; S.W.Alaska to California; regularly conical in habit; leaves of greatly varying sizes together, 5–18mm long in 2 ranks; cones bluntly ovoid, 2–3cm long; stands clipping well and makes a dense, quick hedge.

Above: *Tsuga heterophylla*

Tulip tree – see *Liriodendron*.

Tulipa

(Arabic for turban, in Latin guise). Tulip. LILIACEAE. A genus of about 100 species – although different botanical authorities give from 50 to 150 – of bulbous plants from Europe and Asia, particularly the steppes of C.Asia. Typically, each plant consists of an erect stem bearing a few sessile, linear to ovate leaves and a terminal, usually erect, 6-tepalled, cup-shaped flower opening out widely with age. Several species have all or most leaves basal and several flowers per stem. Fruit is of large, triangular-ovoid capsules with disc-like seed. Each bulb is of annual duration, new ones being formed at the base of the stem each year. They are enclosed in a coat or tunic that may be papery or shell-like, in some species lined with woolly hairs. Grow in any moderately fertile, well-drained soil in sun. Plant mid to late autumn, ideally lifting and replanting annually, and not longer than every 2–3 years. Propagate by separating offsets when replanting or from seed when ripe in a cold frame – the latter take 4–7 years to flower. Both species and cultivars make good pot plants for the alpine or cool greenhouse or home. Potting and subsequent treatment is as for *Narcissus*. The specially-treated bulbs of cultivars recommended in catalogues for forcing will, however, stand warmer conditions than those given for narcissi.

Tulips were first cultivated in Turkey; they were probably introduced to Europe about 1572 and to Britain a few years later. In the 17th century the tulip became an extravagant cult in Holland, becoming known to historians as Tulipomania; single bulbs of new cultivars changed hands for vast sums of money. Popularity has been maintained over the centuries with Holland still the main centre of new cultivar production, although vast numbers of bulbs

Top: *Tulipa* Pink Beauty (Div. 1)
Above: *Tulipa* Orange Nassau (Div. 2)

are now grown commercially in Britain and N.W.USA. Garden cultivars number several 100s, although literally 1000s have been produced in the past 200 years. Those available today are mainly the results of extensive breeding work by specialist growers and scientists. In an endeavour to bring order to such a large assemblage of varied cultivars the following system of classification was devized by the Royal General Dutch Bulb Growers' Society with the Royal Horticultural Society of London. Initially, the classification ran to 23 divisions, but further study has reduced it to 15. Choosing cultivars from the many available is a personal matter and specialist bulb catalogues should be consulted; the examples given under each of the following divisions can be recommended. **1** Single early, 15–38cm tall, flowering spring, or early spring under glass or in the home: Brilliant Star, bright scarlet, black and yellow centre; Pink Beauty, carmine-pink and white; Ursa Minor, golden-yellow; all suitable for forcing and growing outside. **2** Double early, 25–35cm tall, as for single early but flowers double, often very fully so: Madame Testout, deep rose-pink; Orange Nassau, orange-brown; Schoonoord (Purity), snow-white. **3** Mendel (hybrids between single early and Darwin), 40–50cm tall, flowering late spring to early summer outside, earlier under glass: Athlete, pure white; Krelege's Triumph, dark geranium-red; Sulphur Triumph, sulphur-yellow. **4** Triumph, similar to Darwin in flower shape but only to 50cm tall and blooming 10 days earlier: Crater, bright red; Dutch Princess, buff-orange and gold; Garden Party, white, edged carmine. **5** Darwin Hybrids (hybrids between Darwin and *T. fosteriana*), 50–70cm tall, the largest-flowered of all tulips, to 18cm wide when fully expanded, flowering late spring to early summer: Apeldoorn, orange-scarlet, black and yellow centre; Golden Springtime (Santiago), deep golden-yellow; Tender Beauty, white with broad pink margins. **6** Darwin, flowers deeply cup-shaped until fully blown, with a broad almost square base, 55–75cm

tall, flowering early to mid summer: Dreamland, bright rose, white base; Golden Niphetos, deep yellow; Queen of Night, black-purple; Scarlett O'Hara, brilliant scarlet with black and yellow centre; The Bishop, blue-purple; White Giant, pure white, tepals thick-textured. **7** Lily-flowered, flowers slender, tepals with pointed, flared tips, 45–60cm tall, flowering mid to late spring: Aladdin, orange-red and yellow within, scarlet with cream edge without; Dyanito, bright red; Mariette, rose-pink; White Triumphator, pure white. **8** Cottage or Single late, similar to Darwin but with more ovoid blooms, 35–65cm tall, flowering early summer: Advance, cerise-scarlet with blue base; Artist, salmon-pink and green within, purple and pink without; Golden Harvest, deep lemon-yellow. **9** Rembrandt, Darwin tulips with colour-breaking virus, creating blooms splashed or irregularly striped with other colours or shades: May Blossom, purple and cream; Zomerschoon, salmon-pink and cream. **10** Parrot, mainly mutants from other divisions, in particular Darwin, with the tepals irregularly fringed, waved and twisted, sometimes with the colour-breaking virus, 40–60cm tall, flowering late spring to early summer: Black Parrot, black-purple; Blue Parrot, bluish-heliotrope; Fantasy, soft pink, salmon and white; Texas Gold, yellow with narrow red margin. **11** Double late, flowers double, often fully so and resembling double peonies, 40–70cm tall, flowering late spring: Mount Tacoma, pure white, large; Orange Triumph, soft orange and brown; Symphonia, carmine-red. **12** Cultivars mainly derived from *T. kaufmanniana*, basically resembling that species but with flowers of different colours: César Franck, yellow within, carmine-red, edged yellow, without; Lady Rose, soft pink; The First, white, banded red. **13** Cultivars derived mainly from *T. fosteriana*, basically resembling that species but with flowers of varying shades and colours: Easter Parade, yellow, with a black, red-rimmed base; Purissima (White Empress), pure white; Red Emperor (Mme LeFeber), a selected large form of the wild species, to 45cm tall. **14** Cultivars derived mainly from *T. greigii*, basically resembling that species in always having a purple-maroon to brown mottling or striping on the leaves, but with flowers of different colours: Oriental Beauty, vermilion-red, deep brown base; Oriental Splendour, 30–35cm tall, lemon-yellow with a green, red-ringed base; Perlina,

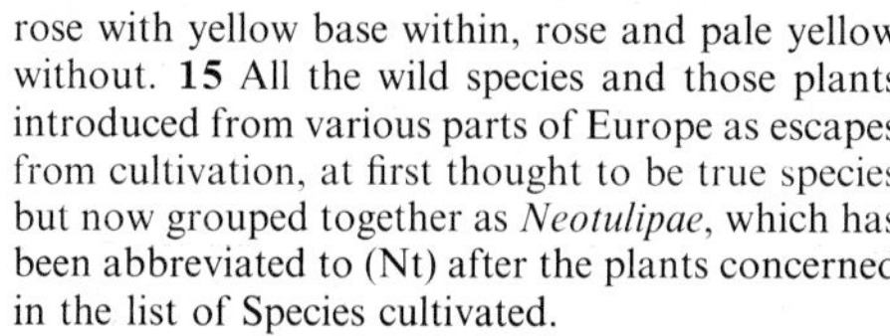

rose with yellow base within, rose and pale yellow without. **15** All the wild species and those plants introduced from various parts of Europe as escapes from cultivation, at first thought to be true species but now grouped together as *Neotulipae*, which has been abbreviated to (Nt) after the plants concerned in the list of Species cultivated.

Top left: *Tulipa* Golden Harvest (Div. 8)
Centre left: *Tulipa* May Blossom (Div. 9)
Above left: *Tulipa* Texas Gold (Div. 10)
Top: *Tulipa* Apeldoorn (Div. 5)
Centre top: *Tulipa* Aladdin (Div. 7)
Centre bottom: *Tulipa* The Bishop (Div. 6)
Above: *Tulipa* Dutch Princess (Div. 4)

Top: *Tulipa* Mount Tacoma (Div. 11)
Centre top: *Tulipa* The First (Div. 12)
Centre bottom: *Tulipa* Purissima (Div. 13)
Above: *Tulipa* Oriental Splendour (Div. 14)

Species cultivated (flowering mid to late spring unless stated otherwise): *T. acuminata* (*T. cornuta*) (Nt), horned tulip; form of *T. gesneriana* with narrow, pointed and twisted, red and yellow tepals. *T. aitchisonii*, Kashmir; 7–10cm tall; leaves linear, 7–10cm long; flowers sometimes in pairs, to 4cm long, white, crimson-flushed without; best in a sheltered site or alpine house. *T. aucherana*, see under *T. humilis*. *T. batalinii*, Turkestan; like a creamy-yellow version of *T. linifolia* with more glaucous leaves and perhaps an albino of that species; often represented by hybrids between the 2 in shades of yellow to bronze, flushed apricot or orange, eg *T.b.* Bright Gem, *T.b.* Bronze Charm. *T. biflora*, Caucasus, S.USSR; 10–15cm tall; leaves linear, about as long; flowers 2–5, about 4cm long, white, yellow-centred within, flushed green and pinkish without; needs lifting and replanting annually or soon dies out. *T.b. turkestanica*, see *T. turkestanica*. *T. chrysantha*, see *T. clusiana chrysantha*. *T. clusiana*, lady tulip; Iran, Afghanistan to W.Pakistan; 20–30cm tall; leaves to 25cm long, linear, channelled, greyish-green, often red-edged; flowers to 5cm long, white, crimson-centred within, stained crimson-pink without. *T.c. chrysantha* (*T. chrysantha*), yellow and red; *T.c. stellata*, like type species but yellow-centred within. *T. cornuta*, see *T. acuminata*. *T. dasystemon* of gardens, see *T. tarda*. *T. eichleri*, Iran to Tadjikistan; 20–30cm tall; leaves to 20cm long, broadly lanceolate, glaucous; flowers to 7cm long, brilliant scarlet with black, yellow-margined basal blotch within. *T. fosteriana*, Uzbekistan to Tadzhkistan, USSR; 25–45cm tall; leaves to 20cm long, ovate, glaucous; flowers to 10cm long, brilliant scarlet with black, yellow-margined, basal blotch within. *T.f.* Princeps, sturdy, to 20cm tall, best for exposed, windy sites. *T. gesneriana* (Nt), Turkey; to 60cm tall; leaves to 15cm long, lanceolate-ovate, glaucous; flowers to 7cm long, dull crimson-scarlet with yellow-margined, blackish to olive, basal blotch within; this is considered to be the basic species from which most of the garden cultivars have arisen, although it is not known truly wild and is found in varied forms, some white or yellow. *T. greigii*, Turkestan; to 25cm tall; similar to *T. fosteriana* but leaves boldly streaked and mottled dark purple. *T. hageri*, Greece, W.Iran; to 30cm tall; leaves to 20cm long, lanceolate; flowers 1–4, about 4·5cm long, soft red, with greenish-black, yellow-margined centre and green markings without. *T. humilis*, Iran; to 10cm tall; leaves mainly basal, to 10cm long, linear; flowers to 3·5cm long, greenish-red without, purple and yellow within, early to mid spring; the following species are very closely allied and by some authorities considered to be varieties of it: *T. pulchella*, *T. violacea* (*T. pulchella v.*), shades of violet-purple; *T. aucheriana*, pink, greenish-yellow striped without. *T. kaufmanniana*, water-lily tulip; Turkestan; to 20cm tall; leaves of similar length, broadly oblong; flowers to 7·5cm long, cream to yellow, outer tepals flushed pink or red, early to mid spring; many hybrid cultivars are available, see division **12** above. *T. linifolia*, Turkestan; to 15cm tall; leaves mostly basal, to 13cm long, linear, slightly glaucous and wavy; flowers to 5cm long, tepals pointed, dull red without, glossy scarlet within. *T. marjolettii* (Nt), 45–60cm tall; leaves lanceolate; flowers 4–5cm long, pale yellow, ageing almost white, tinted purple-red without; probably another form or hybrid of *T. gesneriana*. *T. maximowiczii*, Afghanistan, Uzbek, USSR; very much like *T. linifolia* but with the leaves arranged up the stem and flowering slightly earlier. *T. orphanidea*, Greece; about 20cm tall; allied to *T. hageri* but smaller and more slender in all its parts; flowers somewhat bronze-tinted. *T.o.* Flava, flowers yellow, tinted orange and green. *T. praestans*, C.Asia; to 30cm tall; leaves to 25cm long, narrowly lanceolate, channelled; flowers 1–4, about 5·5cm long, bright vermilion-scarlet. *T. pulchella*, see under *T. humilis*. *T. saxatilis*, Crete; 20–30cm tall, occasionally more; leaves to 20cm long, ovate to

Top: *Tulipa tarda*
Centre top: *Tulipa humilis* Magenta Queen
Centre bottom: *Tulipa batalinii*
Above: *Tulipa praestans*

lanceolate, glossy; flowers 1–3, to about 5cm long, bright lilac-pink with deep yellow centre, anthers dark purple, fragrant; rather shy-flowering unless in a hot dry site; 1 of a small group of stoloniferous tulips that spread to form extensive colonies. *T. stellata*, see *T. clusiana stellata*. *T. sylvestris*, Europe to Iran; stoloniferous; to 30cm tall; leaves to 25cm long, lanceolate, somewhat glaucous; flowers 1–2, nodding, at least in bud, to 6cm long, tepals pointed, soft bright yellow within, greenish-yellow without, usually fragrant. *T. tarda* (*T. dasystemon* of gardens), E.Turkestan; 10–15cm tall; leaves mainly basal, 15–23cm long, linear to lanceolate; flowers 3–7, to 4cm long, white, suffused yellow-green and reddish without, yellow within, outer ⅓ of each tepal white. *T. turkestanica* (*T. biflora t.*), Turkestan; 20–30cm tall; like a more vigorous, larger-flowered *T. biflora* with up to 7 blooms per stem; a much better garden plant that can be left *in situ*. *T. urumiensis*, N.W.Iran; of similar appearance to *T. tarda*, but flowers olive-red without and entirely buttercup-yellow within. *T. violacea*, see under *T. humilis*. *T. whittallii*, W.Turkey; to 30cm tall, allied to, and much like, a more robust *T. hageri* with more orange-hued flowers.

Tupelo – see *Nyssa*.

Turtlehead – see *Chelone*.

Tutsan – see *Hypericum androsaemum*.

Tweedia caeruleum – see *Oxypetalum*.

Twin berry – see *Mitchella repens*.

Twinflower – see *Linnaea borealis*.

Typha

(ancient Greek vernacular for reed-mace). Reed-mace, cat-tail, bulrush. TYPHACEAE. A genus of 9–10 species of herbaceous perennials from wet places throughout the world. They are rhizomatous, often

rampantly so, forming extensive colonies with tufts of slender, linear leaves and erect, unbranched stems bearing ovoid to cylindrical, velvety-brown, mace-like flower-heads. The flowers are tiny, unisexual, petalless, very densely borne in spikes or spadices, the males above the females, sometimes just touching or with a short length of stem between. Grow in water or wet ground in sun or partial shade. In garden ponds the larger species should be confined to containers or they will take over if there is a continuous mud bottom. Plant autumn or spring. Propagate by division in spring.

Species cultivated: *T. angustifolia*, lesser reed-mace, narrow-leaved cat-tail; N.America, Europe, Asia; 1–3m tall; leaves 4–10mm wide, convex on the back; flower-spikes long, cylindrical, male and female 1–9cm apart, light brown. *T. latifolia*, great reed-mace, common cat-tail, often erroneously known as bulrush, a name more correctly applied to *Scirpus lacustris*; widely dispersed in the N.Hemisphere, less so in the Southern; 1·5–2·5m tall; leaves 1–2cm wide, somewhat glaucous; flower-spikes long, cylindrical, male and female contiguous, dark brown. *T. minima*, Europe, Caucasus to E.Asia; 35–75cm tall; leaves to 3mm wide, grassy; flower-spikes ovoid to shortly cylindrical, male and female usually 1–2·5cm apart, rusty-brown; the best species for small pools.

Ulex

(ancient Latin name for gorse). Gorse. LEGUMINOSAE. A genus of about 20 species of densely spiny shrubs from W.Europe and N.W.Africa, 1 of which is grown in gardens: *U. europaeus*, furze, gorse, whin; W.Europe to S.W.Scandinavia; 1·5–2m or more tall, bushy habit; all stems and shoots spine-tipped, younger ones green; leaves reduced to scales or spines on adult plants but seedlings start with soft, trifoliate ones; flowers 1·5cm long, pea-shaped, rich bright yellow, fragrant, often crowded on the spine-tipped lateral shoots at the ends of the stems, mainly spring and summer but also sporadically during mild winters. The small, hairy, black-brown

pods explode when ripe. Usually represented in gardens by *U.e.* Plenus (erroneously *U.e.* Flore Pleno in some catalogues), flowers double. Grow in well-drained, sandy or chalky soil in full sun; in the moister, richer soils it tends to grow rankly and flower poorly. Plant autumn to spring. Propagate from seed in spring, either *in situ* or singly in small pots to avoid root damage at transplanting time, *U.e.* Plenus only from cuttings in late summer in a cold propagating frame, potting carefully as soon as the young roots are 2–3cm long.

Ulmus

(ancient Latin name for elm). Elm. ULMACEAE. A genus of 18–45 species, depending on the botanical authority, of deciduous trees from the northern temperate zone. They have alternate, asymmetrically elliptic to ovate or obovate, doubly toothed leaves and tiny, petalless flowers in axillary, bud-like clusters mainly before the leaves in early spring, sometimes in autumn. Fruit (samaras) of soft, ovoid nutlets, each nutlet surrounded by disc-like membraneous wing, ripening early summer. Grow in at least moderately fertile, moisture-retentive but not wet soil in sun, although some shade is tolerated. Propagate the species from seed when ripe or by suckers at planting time, all species, forms and cultivars by layering in autumn or softwood tip cuttings 10–13cm long, in mid to late summer, hormone-treated, bottom heat 21°C under mist; hardwood cuttings in autumn may also be tried, ideally hormone-treated and calloused in warmth, but results are usually very poor. In recent years the bark beetle transmitted fungus, *Ceratocystus ulmi* – better known as Dutch elm disease – has become a major threat in some countries. It usually starts showing as yellowing leaves on isolated branches that then die. Sometimes the tree becomes totally infected soon after and dies, other times there is partial recovery or a more gradual decline. If possible, the branch showing first symptoms should be removed immediately and the wound sealed with white lead paint or a proprietary sealing compound; although this will not necessarily cure the tree, it will help contain the disease. Totally infected trees should be removed and burned or at least have their bark removed to discourage breeding of bark beetle.

Species cultivated: *U. americana*, white or American elm; N.America from east coast to Rocky Mountains; to 25m tall in Britain, to 40m in the wild; bark coarsely ridged; branches wide-spreading, forming a domed head; leaves to 15cm long, obovate-lanceolate, scabrous but glossy. *U.a.* Aurea, see *U. glabra* Lutescens. *U. angustifolia cornubiensis*, see *U. carpinifolia cornubiensis*. *U. campestris*, see *U. procera* and next species. *U. carpinifolia* (*U. nitens*, formerly confused with *U. campestris* before that species was reclassified), Europe, S.W.Asia, N.Africa; 20–30m tall; bark thickly ridged with vertical fissures; of comparatively narrow habit with ascending and arching branches; leaves 6–8cm long, typically more or less elliptic but very variable, glossy above. *U.c. cornubiensis* (*U. angustifolia c.*, *U. stricta*), Cornish elm; S.W.England; of conical outline when young, becoming domed or spreading with age. *U.c.* Dampieri, see *U.* × *hollandica* Dampieri. *U.c. sarniensis* (*U.* × *sarniensis*, *U. procera* Wheatleyi, *U. wheatleyi*), conical until old, then narrowly domed at the top; often confused with *U. cornubiensis* when young; stated to be of hybrid origin with *U.* × *hollandica* as the other parent, but difficult to verify and opinions are varied. *U. glabra* (*U. montana*, *U. scabra*), wych elm, Scotch elm, Europe

Far left top: *Tulipa saxatilis*
Far left below: *Typha latifolia*
Left: *Ulex europaeus*
Below: *Ulmus carpinofolia* fruit

Left: *Ulmus procera*
Left below: *Ulmus glabra* Camperdownii
Above: *Ulmus americana* autumn colours
Below: *Umbellularia californica*

to Siberia to 30m tall or more; bark smooth and grey on youngish trees, then browner and ridged; branches spreading, forming an irregularly domed head; leaves 10–18cm long, obovate, sometimes with 1 or 2 pointed lobes. *U.g.* Camperdownii, branches and branchlets pendulous, forming a rounded, weeping head; *U.g.* Exoniensis (*U.g.* Fastigiata), Exeter elm, to 17m tall, narrowly columnar when young, broadening with age; *U.g.* Lutescens (*U. americana* Aurea), leaves creamy-yellow when young, ageing yellow-green; *U.g.* Pendula, weeping wych elm, rarely to 9m tall, flat-topped with long, pendulous branches. *U.* × *hollandica* (*U. carpinifolia* × *U. glabra*), Dutch elm; to 35m or more tall; main branches strongly ascending, laterals spreading to form a shallowly domed head; leaves 12–15cm long, elliptic to obovate, often puckered. *U.* × *h.* Vegeta (*U.* × *vegeta*), Huntingdon or Chichester elm, narrower domed habit than type, leaves 10–13cm long, smooth, deep glossy green; *U.* × *h.* Commelin, similar to *U.* × *h.* Vegeta but more narrowly domed and smaller-leaved, resistant to some strains of Dutch elm disease; *U.* × *h.* Dampieri (*U. carpinifolia* Dampieri), narrowly conical habit. *U. montana*, see *U. glabra*. *U. nitens*, see *U. carpinifolia*. *U. parvifolia*, Chinese elm; China, Korea, Japan; to 18m tall, often less in gardens; bark cracked and flaking, red-brown to dark grey, densely domed habit; leaves 3–4cm or more long, elliptic to oblanceolate, semi-evergreen, at least in mild winters; flowers in autumn; apparently resistant to Dutch elm disease; a graceful species deserving to be more widely planted. *U. procera* (*U. campestris*), English elm; England, possibly S.E.France; to 36m tall; bark deeply cracked into small squares, dark brown to blackish; of conical habit when young, then developing a billowing, domed head; leaves mainly ovate to orbicular, 4–10cm long, dark green; largely sterile, spreading by root suckers. *U.p.* Louis van Houtte (*U.p.* Van Houttei), leaves yellow; *U.p.* Wheatleyi, see *U. carpinifolia sarniensis*. *U.* × *sarniensis*, see *U. carpinifolia s.* *U. scabra*, see *U. glabra*. *U. stricta*, see *U. carpinifolia cornubiensis*. *U.* × *vegeta*, see *U.* × *hollandica* Vegeta. *U. wheatleyi*, see *U. carpinifolia sarniensis*.

Umbellularia

(having flowers in umbels). LAURACEAE. A genus of 1 evergreen tree from California and Oregon: *U. californica*, California laurel, bay or olive; to 25m tall in the wild, often less in gardens; leaves alternate, 6–12cm long, oblong-lanceolate with a narrow but rounded tip, somewhat lustrous, strongly aromatic; flowers small, petalless, yel-

lowish, in umbels from upper leaf-axils; fruit to 2·5cm long, obovoid, plum-like, dark purple drupes. Grow in fertile, moisture-retentive but not wet soil in sheltered, sunny sites. Plant spring. Propagate from ripe seed in cold frame, by layering spring.

Umbrella pine – see *Sciadopitys verticillata*.

Umbrella plant – see *Peltiphyllum peltatum*.

Unicorn plant – see *Proboscidea louisianica*.

Ursinia

(for Johannes Heinrich Ursinus, 1608–67, German botanist and author). COMPOSITAE. A genus of 40–80 species, depending on botanical authority, of annuals, perennials, sub-shrubs and shrubs from S.Africa. They are mainly of slender growth with leaves pinnately cut into linear or thread-like segments and terminal, daisy-like flower-heads in summer. Grow in well-drained soil in sunny, sheltered sites or as pot plants in a sunny, well-ventilated greenhouse. Plant or sow when fear of frost has passed in late spring. Propagate annuals and perennials from seed at 18°C, perennials also by basal shoot cuttings spring, late summer.

Species cultivated: *U. anethoides*, shrub to 60cm tall; leaves to 4cm long, dissected into filiform, semi-cylindrical segments, often hairy; flower-heads to 5cm wide, rays orange with purple base; usually grown as an annual from seed sown under glass. *U. calenduliflora*, annual to 35cm tall; leaves to 6·5cm long, pinnate; flower-heads about 6cm wide, rays deep yellow, discs purple. *U. speciosa*, annual 30–40cm tall; leaves to 5cm long, bipinnate; flower-heads 5cm wide, rays deep yellow to orange, sometimes white, discs deep yellow.

Above: *Ursinia speciosa*

Utricularia

(Latin *utriculus*, a little bottle – alluding to the bladders). Bladderwort. LENTIBULARIACEAE. A genus of about 200 species of carnivorous, mainly aquatic or wet-land plants, some also epiphytic, of world-wide distribution. They have linear to rounded leaves, those of the aquatic species divided into thread-like segments. The land species usually live in moist moss and the epiphytes have swollen, water-storing branches. All bear tiny bladders on the leaves, each with a door that only opens inwards. When any tiny creature comes close enough to touch the sensitive trigger mechanism it is sucked into the bladder that shuts behind it. Enzymes break down the body, providing the plant with an additional food source. The flowers are strongly 2-lipped and spurred, solitary or in racemes. Only a few of the hardy aquatic species are sometimes available. Grow in ponds or aquaria. Species that dwell partly in the mud should be anchored to the bottom of pots or trays of loam or potting mix. Floating species should be dropped into the water. Plant spring or summer. Propagate by division at planting time.

Species cultivated: *U. intermedia*, N.Hemisphere, but local; stems 10–25cm long, some with green leaves with few or no bladders, others colourless, buried in the mud and bearing bladders; leaves 4–12mm long, palmately lobed, bristly; bladders 3mm long; flowers 8–12mm long, bright yellow with red-brown lines, in short racemes above the water, late summer; best in acid water. *U. minor*, lesser bladderwort; N.Hemisphere; stems 7–25cm long, similar to *U. intermedia* but smaller; leaf segments branched, smooth; flowers 6–8mm long, pale yellow, summer. *U. vulgaris*, greater or common bladderwort; N.Hemisphere; stems 15–45cm long, free-floating, all bearing green leaves with many bladders; leaves 2–2·5cm long, pinnate, segments with bristly teeth; bladders 3mm long; flowers 1·2–1·8cm long, bright yellow.

Above: *Utricularia vulgaris*

Uvularia

(anatomical term *uvula* for the lobe hanging at the top of the throat in man, a not very apt allusion to the pendant flowers). Bellwort, merrybells (USA). LILIACEAE. A genus of 4–5 species of herbaceous perennials from E. N.America. They are rhizomatous, eventually forming colonies of erect to arching stems with alternate, sessile or perfoliate leaves, and pendant, 6-tepalled, bell-like flowers. Grow in moisture-retentive but not wet, humus-rich soil in partial shade. Plant autumn to early spring. Propagate by division at planting time or, from seed.

Species cultivated: *U. grandiflora*, stems 35–60cm tall, usually branched; leaves 6–13cm long, perfoliate, oblong to narrowly ovate, downy beneath; flowers to 5cm long, lemon-yellow, early summer. *U. perfoliata*, similar to *U. grandiflora*, with which it is often confused, but less robust; leaves glabrous beneath; flowers to 4cm long, pale yellow.

Below: *Uvularia grandiflora*

Vaccinium

(probably Latin *vaccinus*, of cows). Blueberry, bilberry. ERICACEAE. A genus of 150–400 species, depending on botanical authority, of evergreen and deciduous shrubs, rarely small trees, from temperate regions of the world including tropical mountains. They have alternate, obovate or ovate to linear leaves, nodding, bell- to urn-shaped, 4–5 lobed flowers, and edible, globular, fleshy, berry-fruit. Culture as for × *Gaulnettya*; propagation also from seed when ripe, or spring.

Species cultivated: *V. angustifolium*, lowbush blueberry; rhizomatous, deciduous, twiggy shrub to 30cm tall; leaves 7–20mm long, narrowly lanceolate; flowers 5–6mm long, urn-shaped, white or tinged pink, in short racemes, late spring; berries to 8mm wide, blue with waxy white patina. *V. corymbosum*, highbush or swamp blueberry; E. N.America; deciduous shrub to 2m or more tall; leaves 4–8cm long, elliptic to ovate, turning scarlet and bronze in autumn; flowers 6–12mm long, narrowly urn-shaped, white or pale pink, early summer; berries to 1cm or more wide, blue-black with waxy patina; several cultivars have been raised for their fruit quality and are grown commercially, particularly in USA; the following are usually available in Europe and USA (ideally, 2 different cultivars should be grown together for cross-pollination; a moist, acid, peaty soil is essential): *V.c.* Early Blue (*V.c.* Earliblue), early; *V.c.* Grover, mid-season; *V.c.* Jersey and *V.c.* Pemberton, late. *V. delavayi*, W.China; evergreen shrub to 1·5m or more, but slow-growing; compact habit; leaves to 1·2cm long, ovate to obovate, notched at tip; flowers 4mm long, broadly urn-shaped, white, tinted pink, early summer; berries 4mm wide, red to purplish. *V. floribundum* (*V. mortinia*), mountains of Ecuador; evergreen shrub to 1m or more tall; spreading widely when established; leaves 1–1·5cm long, ovate to rounded, dark green above, red-purple when young; flowers 4–6mm long, narrowly urn-shaped, pink, in

Above: *Vaccinium vitis-idaea*

Below: *Vaccinium nummularia*

racemes, summer; fruit 5mm wide, glaucous-red to purple. *V. glaucoalbum*, Himalaya; suckering, evergreen shrub 1–1·8m tall; leaves 4–6·5cm long, elliptic to oblong-obovate, leathery, vivid glaucous beneath; flowers to 6mm long, almost cylindrical, white, flushed pink, in racemes with glaucous bracts, early summer; berries 5–8mm wide, glaucous-black; not fully hardy in severe winters. *V. macrocarpum*, see *Oxycoccus m. V. mortinia*, see *V. floribundum. V. moupinense*, W.China; evergreen shrub to 60cm tall; neat, compact habit; leaves 1–1·5cm long, elliptic to obovate; flowers 4–5mm long, urn-shaped, red to mahogany, early summer; fruit 6mm wide, purple-black. *V. myrtillus*, bilberry, blueberry, whortleberry; Europe, N.Asia; in general appearance much like *V. angustifolium* but leaves 1–3cm long, ovate, and berries black with a waxy white patina. *V. nummularia*, Himalaya; evergreen shrub to 45cm tall; compact habit; stems arching, brown-bristly; leaves 1·2–2·5cm long, orbicular-ovate, dark glossy green; flowers 5mm long, cylindrical, pink to rose-red, in racemes, early summer; berries 6mm long,

Above: *Vaccinium corymbosum* autumn colour

ovoid, black; 1 of the most attractive species but not fully hardy and in cold areas best in an alpine house. *V. ovatum*, California huckleberry; W. N.America; evergreen shrub to 3m tall, of compact habit; leaves 2–4cm long, ovate to oblong-lanceolate, toothed, lustrous above; flowers 6mm long, bell-shaped, white to pink, summer; berries 6–8mm wide, red, ripening black; the pleasing foliage is used by florists in USA. *V. oxycoccus*, see *Oxycoccus palustris. V. vitis-idaea*, cowberry; Asia, Europe; creeping evergreen rhizomatous shrub 10–30cm tall; leaves 1–3cm long, obovate, dark lustrous green above, paler beneath; flowers 4mm long, bell-shaped, white, tinged pink, in short racemes, summer; berries 8–10mm wide, red. *V.v.-i. minus*, mountain cranberry, N.America, dwarf, mat-forming, leaves 1–2cm long, flowers pink to red.

Valerian – see *Valeriana.*

Valeriana

(medieval Latin name, perhaps from *valere*, to be healthy – alluding to the medicinal properties of some species). Valerian. VALERIANACEAE. A genus of about 200 species of perennials, sub-shrubs and shrubs of wide distribution in both hemispheres. They have opposite pairs of simple or pinnate leaves and small, tubular, 5-lobed flowers in terminal, often paniculate cymes. Fruits are tiny, ovoid nuts with a feathery pappus. Needs fertile, well-drained soil, sun, partial shade. Plant autumn to spring. Propagate spring by division, basal cuttings, seed.
Species cultivated: *V. arizonica*, Colorado and Utah to Mexico; rhizomatous, mat-forming with flowering stems to 10cm tall (up to 30cm in the wild); leaves 2–6cm long, ovate to rounded, sometimes pinnately divided; flowers about 1cm long, pink, sometimes white, in head-like clusters, spring, summer. *V. montana*, mountain valerian; Pyrenees, Alps, Apennines; rhizomatous, 12–50cm tall; leaves to 4cm long, elliptic-ovate to orbicular; flowers 3–5mm long, pink or white, in clustered cymes, spring, summer; represented in British gardens by a dwarf, broad-leaved form, 7–10cm tall. *V. officinalis*, common or cat's valerian; Europe, temperate Asia; clump-forming, 1–1·5m tall; leaves to 20cm long, pinnate, leaflets lanceolate, sometimes irregularly toothed; flowers 5mm long, pale pink, lavender or white, fragrant, in panicles, summer. *V. phu*, Caucasus; clump-forming, to 90cm tall; leaves oblong-elliptic, 7–15cm long; flowers tiny, white, in panicles, late summer; represented in gardens mainly by *V.p.* Aurea with bright yellow young foliage. *V. saxatilis*, rock valerian; N.Apennines, C. and E.Alps; rhizomatous, mat-forming, 7–30cm tall; leaves to 3cm or more long, elliptic to oblanceolate; flowers 1–2mm long, white, in small, long-stalked clusters, summer; seldom cultivated,

Top: *Valeriana montana*
Above: *Valeriana phu* Aurea

but confused with *V. montana* and other small, pink-flowered species. *V. supina*, dwarf valerian; E. and E.C.Alps; rhizomatous, mat-forming, 2–12cm tall; leaves to 2cm long, spathulate or orbicular; flowers 3–4mm long, deep pink, in dense, head-like clusters, throughout summer.

Vallisneria

(for Antonio Vallisnieri, 1661–1730, professor of botany at Padua, Italy). Eel or tape grass. HYDROCHARITACEAE. A genus of 8–10 species of aquatic perennials of wide distribution in both hemispheres. They are tufted, often spreading by runners, with slender, strap-shaped, semi-translucent leaves and tiny, 3-petalled, dioecious flowers. The female flowers are solitary on very slender stems just above the water, the males in short, ovoid spikes that break off and float to the surface where they open and discharge pollen. After fertilization the female stems coil up, drawing the developing fruit to the bottom. Grow in sheltered ponds or aquaria, planted in a natural mud bottom or in pots or pans of loam or potting mix. Plant spring. Propagate by division spring or early summer. In cold areas plants are best over-wintered in tanks in a frost-free greenhouse.
Species cultivated: *V. gigantea*, S.E.Asia to Australia; leaves to 1m long if grown in rich compost or mud, to 2cm wide, deep green with longitudinal black and brown lines. *V.g. minor*, smaller than type, leaves very pale green; *V.g.* Rubrifolia (*V. rubra* of gardens), leaves bronzy-crimson, lined purple. *V. spiralis*, S.E.Europe, W.Asia; leaves to 60cm or more long by 5–12mm wide, bright green. *V.s.* Torta, leaves twisted in corkscrew fashion.

Above: *Vallisneria spiralis*

Vancouveria

(for Captain George Vancouver, R.N., 1758–98, British explorer, particularly of the N.W. coast of N.America, 1791–5, see also *Menziesii*). BERBERIDACEAE. A genus of 3 species of evergreen and deciduous perennials from N.W.America, basically resembling *Epimedium*. 1 species is generally available: *V. hexandra*, deciduous, rhizomatous, 20–40cm tall, forming colonies; leaves long-stalked, 10–30cm long, biternate, or partially triternate, leaflets ovate-cordate, 3-lobed; flowers in open panicles, nodding, sepals and petals reflexed, the latter white, 5–8mm long, early summer. Culture as for *Epimedium*.

Below: *Vancouveria hexandra*

× Venidio-arctotis

(hybrids between species of *Venidium* and *Arctotis*). COMPOSITAE. A group of cultivars derived from crossing *Arctotis breviscapa* and *A. grandis* with *Venidium fastuosum*, blending the parental characters in various ways. They are erect, well-branched plants to 50cm tall with oblong-lanceolate, lobed leaves, white-felted beneath, and a profusion of 6·5–7·5cm wide, daisy-like flowers in summer and autumn. The following cultivars are sometimes available: × *V.-a.* Aurora, chestnut-bronze; × *V.-a.* Bacchus, wine-purple; × *V.-a.* China Rose, rose-pink; × *V.-a.* Sunshine, buff-yellow with crimson zone; × *V.-a.* Tangerine, orange-yellow; × *V.-a.* Terra-cotta, rich brownish-red. The plants are sterile and half-hardy and must be over-wintered in a frost-free greenhouse. Grow in fertile, well-drained soil in sun. Plant early summer or when fear

of frost has passed. Propagate by cuttings late summer or spring, bottom heat 16–18°C.

Venidium

(Latin *vena*, a vein – alluding to the ribbed fruit, or seed). COMPOSITAE. A genus of 20–30 species of half-hardy perennials and annuals from S.Africa, 1 of which is usually available: *V. fastuosum*, monarch of the veldt; annual; 60–90cm tall, branched from the base; leaves 10–15cm long, irregularly pinnately lobed, grey-hairy; flowers solitary, 10–15cm wide, rays golden-yellow to bright orange with purple-brown basal blotch, summer to autumn, only opening in sunshine. A so-called hybrid strain, *V.f.* Art Shades, is available with flowers in shades of

orange, yellow, ivory, cream and white. Grow in moderately fertile soil in sun. Sow seed under glass in spring at 16–18°C; prick off seedlings when first true leaf shows, either at 5cm apart each way in boxes, or singly into 7·5–9cm pots of a good commercial potting mixture. Harden off and plant out during early summer or when any possibility of frost has passed.

Venus's looking glass – see *Legousia speculum-veneris*.

Veratrum

(Latin vernacular, from *vere*, truly, and *ater* or *atratum*, black or darkened, from the poisonous black roots). False hellebore or helleborine.

LILIACEAE. A genus of 25 species of mainly robust herbaceous perennials from the northern temperate zone. They are shortly rhizomatous, clump-forming, with alternate or whorled, boldly ribbed and pleated, ovate to lanceolate leaves, and generally large, dense panicles of small, 6-tepalled flowers in summer. Grow in moisture-retentive, humus-rich soil in sun or partial shade. Plant autumn to spring. Propagate from seed in spring, which takes several years to flower, or by careful division in late winter.

Species cultivated: *V. album*, white false hellebore; Europe, temperate Asia; to 2m tall; basal leaves to 30cm long, oblong to elliptic, stem leaves many, smaller, in whorls of 3, hairy beneath; flowers 1·5cm wide, palest green, almost white within, in panicles 30–60cm long. *V. nigrum*, black false hellebore; C. and S.E.Europe, N.Asia; 1·2–2m tall; basal leaves to 30cm long, broadly elliptic, stem leaves few, smaller and narrower, smooth beneath; flowers 1cm wide,

Far left above: × *Venidio-arctotis* China Rose
Far left below: *Venidium fastuosum*
Above and top: *Veratrum album* in flower and spring foliage

maroon. *V. viride*, Indian poke, American white hellebore; E. N.America; 1·2–2m tall; basal leaves 20–30cm long, elliptic to ovate, stem leaves many, smaller; flowers 2–2·5cm wide, yellow-green, in panicles 30–60cm long.

Verbascum

(Latin vernacular name for mullein). Mullein. SCROPHULARIACEAE. A genus of 250–360 species, depending on botanical authority, of biennials, perennials and sub-shrubs from Europe and Asia, mainly Mediterranean, several species naturalized world-wide. The biennials and perennials are rosette-forming, the latter developing into clumps, with ovate to lanceolate, usually hairy leaves and long, simple or branched flowering spikes or racemes. The sub-shrubs are twiggy, with smaller alternate leaves and short racemes. Flowers rotate with 5 broad lobes and woolly stamen filaments mainly in summer. Grow in any well-drained soil in sun. Plant perennials and sub-shrubs autumn or spring. Propagate all species from seed in spring, perennials by division and sub-shrubs, cuttings of roots in late winter or basal non-flowering shoots in late summer. Biennials may be sown *in situ* or grown on in nursery rows and planted in permanent sites in autumn.

Species cultivated: *V. arcturus* (*Celsia a.*), Crete; sub-shrub 30–70cm tall; lower leaves 8–15cm long, lyrate, terminal lobe ovate-oblong, upper leaves smaller; flowers 2·5–3cm wide, yellow, anthers violet woolly; not reliably hardy and needs sheltered site and cloche protection in all but the mildest areas; makes an effective plant for the cool greenhouse. *V. bombyciferum* (*V. broussa* of gardens), Turkey; biennial to 2m tall; basal leaves to 40cm long, ovate to obovate, silky white-felted; flowers to 4cm wide, bright yellow. *V. broussa* of gardens, see *V. bombyciferum*. *V. chaixii* (also see *V. vernale*), S.C. and E.Europe including N.E.Spain; perennial 50–90cm tall; basal leaves 10–30cm long, ovate-oblong, crenate, sometimes slightly lobed at the base, grey hairy; flowers 1·5–2·2cm or more wide, yellow, anthers purple woolly. *V.c.* Album, flowers white. *V. densiflorum* (*V. thapsiforme*), Europe; biennial, to 1·5m tall; basal leaves to 30cm long, sometimes more, oblong-elliptic, stem leaves smaller, long decurrent, yellow to white woolly; flowers 2·5–5cm wide, yellow. *V. dumulosum*, S.W.Turkey; sub-shrub 15–30cm tall; leaves elliptic to oblong, woolly; flowers to 2·5cm wide, lemon-yellow, anthers purple woolly; not fully hardy and needs sheltered, sunny site; makes an excellent alpine house plant. *V.* × Letitia (*V. dumulosum* × *V. spinosum*), sub-shrub to 25cm tall and wide, intermediate between parents; leaves oblong-lanceolate, to 5cm long, silvery-white woolly; flowers 2·5cm wide, bright yellow, freely produced; hardier than *V. dumulosum* but needs a sheltered site. *V. olympicum* of gardens, reputedly from Greece; biennial or perennial 1·5–2·5m tall; basal leaves to 30cm or more long, lanceolate, white woolly; flowers 2·5–3cm wide, bright rich yellow. *V. phoeniceum*, purple mullein; E.C. and S.E.Europe, Asia; perennial 90–120cm tall; basal leaves to 18cm long, ovate, usually dark green above; flowers 2·5–3·5cm wide, shades of purple, rarely yellow; many cultivars are recorded, some of hybrid origin, the following available: *V.p.* Bridal Bouquet, white; *V.p.* Cotswold Beauty, biscuit, anthers lilac woolly; *V.p.* Cotswold Queen, terracotta; *V.p.* Gainsborough, primrose-yellow, to 1·35m tall; *V.p.* Hartleyi, biscuit-yellow, suffused plum-purple. *V. thapsiforme*, see *V. densiflorum*. *V. thapsus*, common mullein, flannel plant; Europe, Asia; biennial 1·2–2m tall; basal leaves 20–50cm long, elliptic to oblong-obovate, grey or white woolly; flowers 2–3·5cm wide, yellow. *V. vernale* of gardens, botanically a synonym of *V. chaixii* and other species but distinct as a garden plant; perennial to 2m tall; stem freely branching; leaves to 30cm or more long; flowers vivid yellow.

Above: *Verbascum phoeniceum* Gainsborough
Left: *Verbascum bombyciferum*
Top right: *Verbascum* × Letitia
Above right: *Verbascum vernale*

Verbena

(old Latin name for vervain – *V. officinalis* – a herb credited with medicinal and magical properties). VERBENACEAE. A genus of about 250 species of annuals, perennials, sub-shrubs and shrubs mainly from N. and S.America, a few in Europe, Asia. They are prostrate to erect, with opposite pairs or whorls of 3, linear to ovate, usually toothed or lobed leaves, and terminal spikes, corymbs or panicles of small, tubular, 5-lobed, somewhat 2-lipped flowers. Grow in fertile, well-drained soil in sun, half-hardy sorts planted out as soon as fear of frost has passed and either over-wintered under glass or discarded and grown annually from seed. Plant hardy species in spring. Propagate from seed in spring under glass, half-hardy sorts at 18–20°C; hardy species also by division in spring; all species by cuttings late spring or late summer.

Species cultivated: *V. aubletia*, see *V. canadensis*. *V.*

Top: *Verbena tenera* Mahonettii
Above: *Verbena rigida*
Top right: *Verbena peruviana*
Above right: *Verbena* × *hybrida* Sparkle

bonariensis, Brazil, Paraguay, Argentina; perennial, hardy or almost so, 1–1·5m tall; stems 4-angled; leaves 4–10cm long, oblong-lanceolate, rugose, dark green; flowers 3mm wide, lavender-blue in several short dense spikes forming head-like clusters, summer to autumn. *V. canadensis* (*V. aubletia*), rose verbena; E. N.America west to Colorado and Mexico; hardy perennial to 45cm tall; stems decumbent or ascending; leaves 3–9cm long, ovate-oblong, pinnately lobed or cleft; flowers about 1·5cm wide, red-purple to lilac, pink or white; several cultivars are available. *V. chamaedrifolia* and *V. chamaedryoides*, see *V. peruviana*. *V. corymbosa*, Chile; hardy perennial much like *V. rigida*, but to 90cm tall and with leaves having 2 small, often toothed, basal lobes. *V.* × *hortensis*, see next entry. *V.* × *hybrida*, garden or florists' verbena; exact origin unknown but probably *V. peruviana* is the primary parent crossed with the more tender and seldom grown *V. incisa*, *V. phlogiflora* and *V. platensis*; tender perennial usually grown as a half-hardy annual; stems procumbent to ascending, 20–30cm tall; leaves 5–10cm long, oblong-lanceolate to ovate, usually with lobe-like teeth; flowers 1–2cm wide, in dense, head-like spikes, scarlet, purple, lavender, creamy-yellow and white, fragrant, summer to autumn; several mixed strains and single-colour cultivars are available, eg *V.* × *h.* Amethyst, mid blue; *V.* × *h.* Blaze, bright scarlet; *V.* × *h.* Delight, coral-pink; *V.* × *h.* Sparkle, scarlet with white eye; *V.* × *h.* White Ball, pure white. *V. peruviana* (*V. chamaedrifolia* and *V. chamaedryoides* of gardens), S.Brazil to Argentina; half-hardy perennial usually grown as an annual; stems prostrate, tips ascending to 10cm tall; leaves to 5cm long, oblong-lanceolate to ovate; flowers 1cm wide in head-like spikes, bright scarlet, summer to autumn; can be over-wintered outside in mild areas or under a cloche. *V. pulchella*, see *V. tenera*. *V. rigida* (*V. venosa*), S.Brazil to Argentina; almost hardy, erect tuberous-rooted perennial 30–60cm tall; leaves 5–7·5cm long, oblong, rigid and harsh-textured; flowers 5mm wide in dense spikes, purple to magenta, usually borne in groups of 3, summer. *V. tenera* (*V. pulchella*), S.Brazil; mat-forming, almost hardy perennial to 15cm tall; leaves to 2·5cm long, usually trilobed, each lobe pinnatisect; flowers 1·5cm wide, rose-violet, in short, dense spikes, summer; usually represented in gardens as *V.t.* Mahonettii (*V. alpina* of gardens), having white-margined petals. *V. venosa*, see *V. rigida*.

Veronica

(for St Veronica). Speedwell. SCROPHULARIACEAE. A genus of about 300 species of annuals, perennials and sub-shrubs mainly from the northern temperate zone. For the shrubby species formerly included, see *Hebe* and *Parahebe*. They have opposite pairs of linear to ovate, sometimes lobed leaves, and axillary or terminal racemes or spikes of irregular flowers – the latter have tubular bases and basically 5 lobes often of varying sizes but frequently appearing as 4 owing to the fusion of the 2 upper ones. Grow the species described here in fertile, well-drained soil in sun, but see also species descriptions for special requirements. The genus also contains aquatic species, eg *V. beccabunga*, that require wet soil or shallow water over mud to thrive. Plant autumn to spring. Propagate by division at planting time or from seed in spring, the sub-shrubs and evergreen perennials also by cuttings in summer.

Species cultivated: *V. austriaca* (*V. latifolia*), Europe; clump-forming perennial 25–50cm tall; stems erect to ascending; leaves 2–5cm long, narrowly lanceolate to rounded in outline, pinnatisect or bipinnatisect; flowers 1–1·3cm wide, blue, in racemes from upper leaf-axils, early summer; a variable plant with several sub-species, usually represented in cultivation by: *V.a. teucrium* (*V. teucrium*), 30–100cm tall; leaves to 7cm long, deeply toothed or cleft or merely crenate; flowers rich blue. *V.a.t.* Crater Lake Blue, 30cm tall, deep blue; *V. a.t.* Pavane, 60cm tall, pink; *V.a.t.* Shirley Blue, 20cm tall, brilliant blue; *V.a.t.* Trehane, 20cm tall, golden-green foliage, deep blue flowers. *V. balfouriana* of gardens, a confusing name, having been used for a hybrid *Hebe* and a more robust form or hybrid of *V. fruticans*. *V. beccabunga*, brooklime; Europe to Japan, N.Africa; aquatic evergreen perennial 20–30cm or more tall; stem creeping and rooting, decumbent; leaves 3–6cm long, elliptic-oblong; flowers 7–8mm wide, blue, in axillary racemes, early summer to autumn; does not need standing water but soil must be wet. *V. bombycina*, Lebanon; tufted, mat-forming perennial a few centimetres tall; leaves 3–4mm long, ovate to spathulate, silky white woolly; flowers about 5mm wide, pale blue or reddish, summer; needs a sheltered scree or an alpine house. *V. cinerea*, Turkey; mat-forming, evergreen perennial 10–15cm tall; leaves lanceolate to linear, margins inrolled, grey-white downy; flowers 5–7mm wide, pale blue, in spikes, summer. *V. exaltata*, see *V. longifolia exaltata*. *V. filiformis*, Turkey, Caucasus; densely mat-forming perennial spreading widely; leaves about 5mm long, rounded, crenate; flowers solitary from the crowded upper leaf-axils, 1–1·3cm wide, mauve-blue with darker stripes, spring to summer; although undeniably attractive, this species soon becomes an invasive weed of lawns and borders and its planting is not recommended. *V. fruticans* (*V. saxatilis*), rock speedwell; Greenland, Iceland, arctic Europe and mountains farther south; sub-shrubby, evergreen perennial to 15cm tall, usually much-branched; leaves 8–20mm long, obovate to narrowly oblong, entire or slightly crenate; flowers 1·1–1·5cm wide, deep blue with reddish centres, in short racemes, late summer. *V. fruticulosa*, higher mountains of W. and S.C.Europe; much like *V. fruticans* but a little smaller and with pink flowers 9–12mm wide. *V. gentianoides*, Crimea, Caucasus; rhizomatous perennial 30–40cm tall; leaves in tufts or rosettes, 3–8cm long, lanceolate to broadly obovate, dark green; flowers 1cm wide, palest blue with darker veins, in terminal racemes, early summer. *V.g. variegata*, leaves spashed white. *V. incana*, see *V. spicata incana*. *V. latifolia*, see *V austriaca*. *V. longifolia*, N.E. and C.Europe, Asia; herbaceous

Below: *Veronica longifolia* Foerster's Blue

perennial 60–120cm tall; leaves 3–12cm long, lanceolate to narrowly so, doubly toothed, slender-pointed; flowers 6–8mm wide, lilac or blue, in long, terminal racemes, summer. *V.l. exaltata*, Siberia, 1·2m tall, leaves more deeply toothed, flowers clear pale blue, the most distinctive and graceful form of *V. longifolia*; *V.l.* Foerster's Blue, 60cm tall, flowers deep blue. *V. nummularia*, Pyrenees; mat-forming, woody-based perennial 5–10cm tall; leaves 4–5mm long, broadly elliptic to rounded; flowers 6mm wide,

Top left: *Veronica austriaca teucrium* Trehane
Above left: *Veronica cinerea*
Below left: *Veronica austriaca teucrium* Shirley Blue
Top: *Veronica virginica* Rosea
Above: *Veronica pectinata* Rosea

blue or pink, in short, head-like spikes, summer. *V. pectinata*, Turkey; mat-forming, to 5cm tall; leaves 1–2·5cm long, obovate to elliptic, deeply toothed, white hairy; flowers to 1cm wide, deep blue, in racemes. *V.p.* Rosea, flowers bright pink. *V. perfoliata*, digger speedwell; S.E.Australia; evergreen, almost sub-shrubby, rhizomatous perennial to 60cm or more tall; leaves 3–6·5cm long, sessile, each pair united at their bases; flowers about 1cm wide, blue-violet, in nodding-tipped racemes from upper leaf-axils, summer to autumn; classified by some authorities in *Parahebe* but not generally accepted. *V. prostrata* (*V. rupestris* of gardens), Europe; mat-forming perennial to 10cm tall; leaves 8–25mm long, narrowly oblong to ovate, downy; flowers 6–8mm wide, pale blue, in lateral racemes near stem tips, early summer. *V.p. scheereri*, W. and W.C.Europe, leaves narrowly oblong to lanceolate, sparsely shortly downy, flowers 8–14mm wide, deep bright blue – the commonest variety in cultivation. *V. rupestris* of gardens, see *V. prostrata*. *V. saturejoides*, Balkan Peninsula; mat-forming perennial 5–8cm tall; leaves 6–10mm long, oblanceolate to rounded, entire, somewhat fleshy, ciliate; flowers 7mm wide, bright blue, late spring to early summer. *V. saxatilis*, see *V. fruticans*. *V. selleri*, Japan; a diminutive, dark blue flowered *V. spicata* to 15cm tall. *V. spicata*, spiked speedwell; Europe, Asia; herbaceous perennial 30–60cm tall; stems erect; leaves 2–8cm long, lanceolate to ovate, crenate, more or less hairy; flowers 5–8mm wide, blue, in terminal spikes, late summer; a variable species in stature, hairiness, spike-length and colour. *V.s.* Barcarolle, 45cm tall, flowers rich pink; *V.s.* Blue Fox, 40cm tall, bright lavender-blue; *V.s. incana* (*V. incana*), 30cm tall, leaves silvery-white hairy, flowers deep blue; *V.s.* Red Fox, flowers crimson; *V.s.* Snow White, flowers pure white. *V. teucrium*, see *V. austriaca teucrium*. *V. virginica* (*Veronicastrum v.*), Culver's root, blackroot (USA); E.USA; herbaceous perennial 1·2–2m tall; stem erect, clump-forming; leaves in whorls of about 5, each to 15cm long, lanceolate, slender-pointed; flowers 3–4mm wide, palest blue or lilac-pink, late summer to autumn. *V.v.* Alba, like type, but with white flowers.

Veronicastrum – see *Veronica virginica*.
Vervain – see *Verbena*.

Viburnum

(old Latin name for *Viburnum lantana*, the wayfaring tree). CAPRIFOLIACEAE. A genus of about 200

species of evergreen and deciduous shrubs and occasionally small trees, mainly from N.Hemisphere but also S.America and Java. They have opposite pairs of lanceolate to orbicular leaves, and terminal, often flattish, umbel-like cymes or panicles of small, tubular, 5-lobed, mainly white flowers followed by often showy, berry-like, 1-

Above: *Viburnum lantana*
Below: *Viburnum davidii*

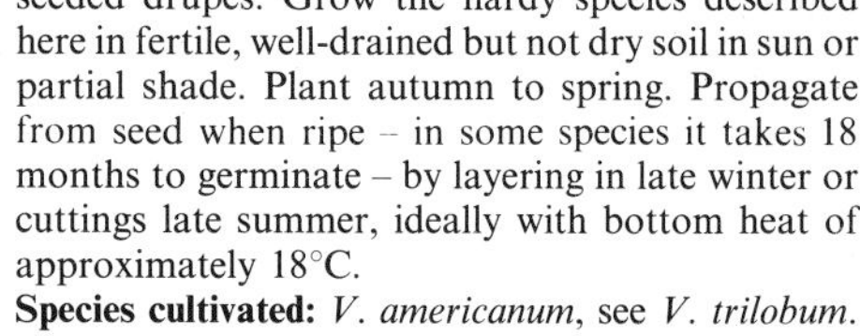

seeded drupes. Grow the hardy species described here in fertile, well-drained but not dry soil in sun or partial shade. Plant autumn to spring. Propagate from seed when ripe – in some species it takes 18 months to germinate – by layering in late winter or cuttings late summer, ideally with bottom heat of approximately 18°C.

Species cultivated: *V. americanum*, see *V. trilobum*. *V. betulifolium*, China; 3–4m tall, erect habit; leaves deciduous, 5–8cm long, ovate to rhombic, coarsely toothed; flowers 5mm wide, in flattened cymes, summer; fruit to 6mm long, almost translucent bright red, sometimes in abundance and then among the finest of berrying shrubs; ideally, several different individuals (not the same clone) should be planted together for cross-pollination. *V.* × *bodnantense* (*V. farreri* × *V. grandiflorum*), several hybrid cultivars blending the characters of the parents, generally like *V. farreri* but with larger flowers. *V.* × *b.* Dawn, leaves similar to *V. grandiflorum*, flowers white, tinted pink, very freely borne, autumn to spring; *V.* × *b.* Deben, flowers pink in bud, opening white. *V. buddleifolium*, China; 2–3m tall; leaves almost evergreen, 10–20cm long, lanceolate to obovate, pale green, downy above, grey-felted beneath; flowers 8mm wide, in clusters 7·5cm wide, summer; fruit ovoid, 8mm long, red, turning black. *V.* × *burkwoodii* (*V. carlesii* × *V. utile*), to 2m high, taller if trained on a wall; leaves evergreen or semi-evergreen, 4–10cm long, ovate, dark glossy green above, downy beneath; flowers 7–10mm wide, pink in bud, very fragrant, in flattish clusters to 9cm wide, late winter to spring; a good wall shrub; several similar clones are available, eg *V.* × *b.* Chenaultii, *V.* × *b.* Park Farm Hybrid. *V.* × *carlcephalum* (*V. carlesii* × *V. macrocephalum*), similar to the first

Left: *Viburnum plicatum*
Below left: *Viburnum opulus* Compactus
Below: *Viburnum carlesii* Aurora

parent, but more robust and with pink-tinted flowers in clusters to 13cm wide. *V. carlesii*, Korea; to 1·5m or more tall, rounded habit; leaves deciduous, 5–9cm long, ovate to elliptic, downy matt green above, greyish beneath, often colouring in autumn; flowers to 1cm wide, waxy white, pink in bud, strongly fragrant, in cymes to 7cm wide, spring. *V. cinnamomifolium*, China; to 3m or more tall; leaves evergreen, to 13cm long, elliptic-oblong, boldly veined, dark glossy green; flowers 5mm wide, in flattish clusters 10–15cm wide, summer; fruit ovoid, 5mm long, glossy blue-black; needs a sheltered site and thrives in partial shade. *V. davidii*, W.China; 1–1·5m tall, compact and wide-spreading, otherwise like *V. cinnamomifolium* but with bright blue fruit; some plants tend to be largely male or female and several clones should be planted together if a good crop of fruit is required. *V. farreri* (*V. fragrans*), N.China; shrub to 3m; leaves deciduous, 4–8cm long, elliptic to obovate, toothed, conspicuously veined, bronze-flushed when young; flowers to 1cm or more long, white or pink-flushed, fragrant, in small, panicled cymes, late autumn to spring. *V.f.* Candidissimum, flowers pure white; *V.f.* Nanum (*V.f.* Compactum), dwarf, dense habit, but not flowering very freely. *V. furcatum*, Japan, Korea; 3–4m tall; leaves deciduous, 9–15cm long, broadly ovate-cordate, crimson in autumn; fertile flowers 4–5mm wide in flat clusters to 10cm wide surrounded by several large, sterile flowers like those of a lacecap hydrangea, early summer; fruit 8mm long, red, finally black; needs shade and moist, acid soil to thrive. *V. grandiflorum* (*V. nervosum*), Himalaya; similar to *V. farreri*, but of more erect habit; leaves and flowers a little larger, the latter carmine in bud and often in nodding clusters, mainly late winter to spring. *V. henryi*, C.China;

Below: *Viburnum tinus*
Right: *Viburnum plicatum tomentosum* Pink Beauty

2–3m tall, of erect but open habit; leaves evergreen, 5–13cm long, narrowly elliptic to obovate, somewhat toothed and lustrous; flowers to 6mm wide in pyramidal panicles to 10cm long and wide, summer; fruit to 8mm long, bright red then black. *V. hupehense*, C.China; to 2m tall; leaves deciduous, 5–7·5cm long, broadly ov te, slender-pointed, coarsely toothed; flowers a out 5mm wide, in clusters to 5cm wide, early summer; fruit ovoid, 8–15mm long, orange-yellow to red. *V.* × *juddii* (*V. bitchiuense* × *V. carlesii*), much like latter parent but more vigorous and usually freer-flowering. *V. lantana*, wayfaring tree; Europe to Turkey and Caucasus, Algeria; 2–4m tall; leaves deciduous, 5–10cm long, elliptic, ovate to obovate, rugose above, densely downy beneath; flowers 6mm wide in dense cymes 6–10cm wide, early summer; fruit elliptic, flattened, 8mm long, red, finally black. *V. nervosum*, see *V. grandiflorum*. *V. opulus*, guelder rose; Europe, W. and N.Asia, Algeria; 2–4m tall; leaves 5–8cm long, 3–5 lobed, irregularly toothed, rather maple-like, usually turning red in autumn, leaf-stalks with disc-like glands; fertile flowers 6mm wide, in cymes 5–10cm wide, surrounded by several, much larger, sterile flowers, summer; fruit rounded, 8mm long, bright translucent red. *V.o.* Aureum, compact habit, leaves bright yellow, best in partial shade; *V.o.* Compactum, small, 1–1·5m tall, compact habit; *V.o.* Fructuluteo, fruit chrome-yellow, tinted pink; *V.o.* Notcutts, larger flowers and fruit than type; *V.o.* Roseum (*V. o.* Sterile), snowball tree, all flowers sterile, in mop-like heads becoming pink-tinged with age; *V.o.* Sterile, see *V.o.* Roseum; *V.o.* Xanthocarpum, fruit golden-yellow, translucent on maturity. *V. plicatum* (*V. tomentosum* Plicatum, *V.t. sterile*), Japanese snowball tree; China, Japan; to 3m or more tall, wide-spreading, horizontal branches creating a tiered effect; leaves deciduous, 5–10cm long, elliptic to ovate, more or less downy, usually colouring in autumn; flowers all sterile in globular heads, 5–7·5cm wide, early summer; long cultivated in China and Japan and described before the wild species was known to Western botanists. *V.p. tomentosum* (*V. tomentosum*), the original wild species, with flattened cymes of 5–6mm wide fertile flowers, surrounded by a few larger sterile ones; fruit small, red, then black. *V.p.t.* Lanarth, strong-growing with a less obviously tiered habit of growth; *V.p.t.* Mariesii, strongly tiered habit, very free-flowering; *V.p.t.* Pink Beauty, sterile flowers, mature pink; *V.p.t.* Rowallane, similar to *V.p.t.* Lanarth, but less vigorous and sterile flowers larger, more freely fruiting than other forms of *V.p. tomentosum*. *V.* × *rhytidophylloides* (*V. lantana* × *V. rhytidophyllum*), much like latter parent but more vigorous and often to 5m or more high and wide; leaves evergreen, broader and less rugose. *V. rhytidophyllum*, C. and W.China; 4–5m or more high and wide; leaves evergreen, 10–20cm long, oblong-elliptic, rugose and deep, lustrous green above, grey-felted beneath; flowers about 6mm wide, yellowish-white, in cymes to 15cm or more wide, early summer; fruit ovoid, 8mm long, red, then black. *V. tinus*, laurustinus; S.E.Europe; 3–5m tall, sometimes tree-like; leaves 4–9cm long, ovate-oblong, dark, somewhat glossy green; flowers 5–6mm wide, pink in bud, in flattened cymes 5–10cm wide, late autumn to spring, depending on mildness of winter; fruit ovoid, 6mm long, deep blue but usually rather hidden by the foliage. *V.t.* Eve Price, very dense habit, leaves smaller than type, flowers carmine in bud; *V.t. hirtulum* (*V.t. hirtum*), leaves larger, bristly hairy, less hardy than type; *V.t. lucidum*, larger glossier leaves than type, cymes wider, flowering in spring; *V.t.* Variegatum, leaves marked creamy-yellow. *V. tomentosum*, see under *V. plicatum*. *V. trilobum* (*V. americanum*), cranberry bush, highbush cranberry, squawbush (USA); N. N.America; virtually identical to *V. opulus* but leaf-stalks with small glands. *V. utile*, C.China; 2m or more tall, open, graceful habit; leaves evergreen, 3–7·5cm long, narrowly ovate to oblong, glossy deep green above, white downy beneath; flowers 5–8mm wide, fragrant, in dense rounded clusters 7cm wide, early summer.

Vinca

(Latin *vincio*, to bind up – alluding to the use of the wiry stems in wreath-making). Periwinkle. APOCYNACEAE. A genus of 5 species of evergreen perennials or sub-shrubs from Europe, W.Asia, N.Africa. They have opposite pairs of lanceolate to elliptic or ovate, leathery, glossy leaves, tubular flowers with 5, somewhat asymmetrical lobes, solitary from the leaf-axils, and fruit of a pair of cylindrical capsules joined at the base. Grow in any well-drained soil in sun or shade. Plant autumn to spring. Propagate by division or separating rooted stems at planting, cuttings in cold frame late summer.

Top right: *Viburnum opulus* Xanthocarpum
Above right: *Viburnum rhytidophyllum* unripe fruit
Right: *Viburnum* × *rhytidophylloides*
Above far right: *Vinca major*
Far right: *Vinca minor* Atropurpurea

Vine – see *Vitis.*

Vine, Russian – see *Polygonum baldschuanicum.*

Viola

(Latin name for various fragrant flowers, including violets – used for this genus by Linnaeus). Pansy, violet. VIOLACEAE. A genus of 500 species of annuals, perennials and sub-shrubs of cosmopolitan distribution, but mainly the northern temperate zone and Andes. They are mostly clump-forming, sometimes stoloniferous, with cordate, linear to orbicular leaves, although some species are semi-climbers and many of the almost uncultivatable Andean species mimic houseleeks. The horizontally-borne or nodding flowers have 5 petals, the upper 2 often longer and erect, the lower 1 usually broader and with a nectary spur. Many species also produce tiny cleistogamic flowers that never open and produce seed by self-fertilization. From a gardener's point of view, the group of species and hybrids with flat-faced flowers and prominent, leafy, lobed stipules are known as pansies. They are distinguished in the descriptions below by a (p) after the species' names. When ripe, the ovoid seed capsules split into 3 sections or valves. Each valve then folds upwards squeezing the smooth seeds, like an orange pip between thumb and forefinger, shooting them away to considerable distances. Grow in at least moderately humus-rich soil, well-drained but not dry, in partial shade or sun, the latter ideally for the pansies. Plant autumn to spring. Propagate from seed or by division in spring, or by basal cuttings late summer in a cold frame. For winter- and spring-flowering pansies, sow seed late summer in nursery rows or boxes and plant out the young plants into permanent sites in late autumn. For summer blooming, sow seed under glass in early spring at 13–16°C, setting out the young plants in flowering quarters late spring.

Species cultivated: *V. acutifolia*, see next species. *V. difformis* (*V. acutifolia*), W.Mediterranean; much like *V. major* but completely hairless, with pale lilac-blue flowers having rhomboid lobes, autumn to early winter only; evergreen only in mild areas. *V. major*, greater periwinkle; C. and S.Europe, N.Africa; evergreen perennial, to 30cm or more tall; stems slender, ascending then arching over and trailing and rooting, soon forming mat-like colonies to 2m wide or so; leaves to 5cm long, ovate, sometimes heart-shaped, ciliate; flowers to 4cm wide, bright purple-blue, early spring to summer, sometimes later. *V.m.* Elegantissima, see *V.m.* Variegata; *V.m. hirsuta*, see next entry; *V.m. pubescens* (*V.m. hirsuta*), leaves narrower than type, downy, flowers with narrower, pointed, rich purple lobes; *V.m.* Variegata, leaves blotched and margined creamy-white. *V. minor*, lesser periwinkle, running myrtle; Europe, W.Asia; evergreen perennial; stems wiry, prostrate, mat-forming; leaves 2·5–4cm long, elliptic to ovate; flowers about 2·5cm wide, purple-blue, spring to summer, then off and on to autumn. *V.m.* Alba, flowers white; *V.m.* Atropurpurea, deep plum-purple; *V.m.* Azurea Flore Pleno, double blue; *V.m.* Bowles Variety (*V.m.* Bowlesii), flowers larger than type, blue; *V.m.* Multiplex, double, plum-purple; *V.m.* Variegata, leaves marked creamy-white, flowers as type.

Species cultivated (all perennials): *V. aetolica* (*V. saxatilis a.*) (p), Balkan Peninsula; similar and allied to *V. tricolor*, but more prostrate and to 10cm tall;

Top left: *Vinca minor* Aureo-variegata Alba
Above left: *Vinca difformis*
Above: *Viola hederacea*
Top right: *Viola gracilis*
Above right: *Viola labradorica* Purpurea
Right: *Viola tricolor*

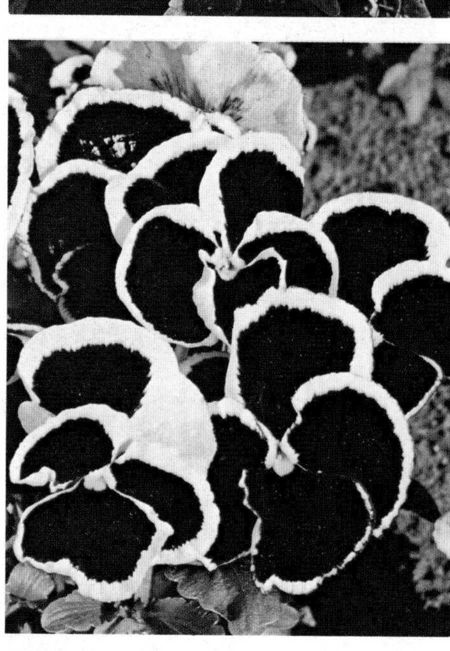

leaves about 2cm long, ovate to lanceolate, ciliate, greyish-green; flowers 1·5–2cm wide, bright yellow. *V. cornuta* (p), Pyrenees; rhizomatous and small clump-forming, to 15cm or more tall; stems ascending to decumbent; leaves 2–5cm long, ovate, crenate, hairy beneath; flowers 2–3cm or more wide, with slender spur 1–1·5cm long, fragrant, violet-purple to lilac, summer. *V.c.* Alba, flowers white; *V.c. minor*, plant smaller and neater than type, see also *V.* × *williamsii*. *V. cucculata*, E. N.America; deciduous, from thick fleshy rhizomes, 7–10cm tall; leaves 5–9cm wide, broadly ovate-cordate to kidney-shaped, crenate; flowers about 2cm wide, violet-purple, spring to summer. *V.c. albiflora*, white, confused with *V. sororia* in some gardens. *V. elatior*, Europe, W.Asia; deciduous, tufted or forming small clumps, 30–50cm tall; stems erect; leaves 4–7·5cm long, lanceolate to narrowly ovate, shortly hairy; flowers 2–2·5cm wide, pale blue, early summer. *V. gracilis* (p), Balkan Peninsula; mat-forming, 10–15cm tall; stems decumbent; leaves 2–3cm long, broadly ovate to oblong; flowers 2–3cm wide, yellow or violet; often represented in gardens by more robust forms or hybrids. *V.g.* Major, flowers deep purple; *V.g.* Moonlight, pale yellow. *V. hederacea*, ivy-leaf violet; S.E.Australia; stoloniferous, mat-forming, about 10cm tall; leaves 2·5–4cm wide, kidney-shaped, wavy, pale green; flowers well above leaves, to 2cm wide, petals violet-purple with white tips, mainly spring to summer, but off and on all year; not winter-hardy in the colder areas but easily over-wintered with a cloche or in a frost-free greenhouse; makes a good pot plant for a cool room. *V.* × *hortensis*, see *V.* × *wittrockiana*, *V. labradorica*, N. N.America to Greenland; mat-forming to 10cm tall; leaves 1·5–3cm long, broadly ovate to orbicular, cordate; flowers 1–1·5cm wide, light purple-blue, spring. *V.l.* Purpurea, leaves suffused deep purple. *V. lyallii*, New Zealand; tufted, to 10cm or more tall; leaves 1–3cm long, broadly ovate to rounded, cordate; flowers 1–2cm wide, white, streaked lilac and yellow, summer. *V. odorata*, sweet violet; Europe, N.Africa, Asia; stoloniferous, mat-forming, to 10cm or more tall; leaves 4–7cm long, orbicular to kidney-shaped, cordate; flowers 1·5–2cm wide, violet-purple, fragrant, early spring to summer; a variable species and many cultivars have been recorded in shades of violet, purple and lilac, some much larger and double. *V.o.* Alba, flowers white; *V.o.* Coeur d'Alsace, carmine-pink; *V.o.* Czar, large deep violet-purple flowers; *V.o.* Sulphurea, apricot-yellow within, purple-tinted without. *V. papilionacea*, see *V. sororia p. V. pedata*, bird's foot or pansy violet; E.USA; tufted or small clump-forming, to 15 cm tall; leaves 5–10cm long, palmately cleft into 3–5 lobes, each lobe again divided; flowers to 3cm wide with broad, flat lobes, entirely lilac-purple or with upper lobes much darker, stamens orange, spring to summer; best in free draining soil in a sunny site.

Top far left: *Viola odorata* Coeur d'Alsace; **above far left:** *V. riviniana;* **top left:** *V.* × *wittrockiana* Monarch Mixed; **above left:** *V.* × *wittrockiana* Arkwright Red; **top:** *V.* × *wittrockiana* Monch; **above:** *V.* × *wittrockiana* Gemini; **right:** *V.* × *williamsii* Blue Heaven

V. riviniana, common dog violet; Europe including Iceland, N.Africa, Madeira; tufted, producing colonies from sucker shoots, to 15cm tall, usually less; leaves 2–8cm long, ovate-orbicular, cordate; flowers 1·5–2cm wide, blue-violet, spring to summer; confused with *V. odorata*, but flowers scentless and plant lacking stolons. *V. rupestris*, N. Hemisphere; 2–4cm tall; leaves 5–10mm long; flowers 1–1·5cm wide, pale blue-purple, early summer; pink, white and reddish-purple flowered forms are known; much like a diminutive *V. riviniana*. *V. saxatilis aetolica*, see *V. aetolica*. *V. septentrionalis*, N.E. N.America; similar to *V. sororia* but smaller, the leaves generally narrower and more prominently toothed; flowers deep violet-purple to lilac or white, all petals downy. *V. sororia* (*V. papilionacea*), E. N.America; deciduous, from thick fleshy rhizomes, to 10cm tall; leaves broadly ovate, wider than long, toothed, softly hairy beneath; flowers to 3cm wide, rich violet with white eye, sometimes light blue or reddish, late spring to summer. *V.s.* Albiflora, white with blue-purple

Top: *Viola cornuta* Alba
Above: *Viola* × *wittrockiana* Jungfrau

veining and suffusion in the centre, confused with *V. cucculata albiflora* in gardens; *V.s. papilionacea* (*V. papilionacea*), leaves hairless. *V. tricolor* (p), heartsease, wild pansy; Europe, Asia; annual or short-lived tufted perennial; to 15cm or more tall; stems ascending to decumbent; leaves to 5cm long, ovate to lanceolate, crenate but sometimes cordate; flowers 1–2·5cm or more wide, blue-violet or yellow, often bi-coloured, spring to autumn; most cultivars listed under this name belong to *V.* × *wittrockiana*. *V.t.* Bowles Black, flowers black-purple. *V. verecunda yakusimana* (*V. yakusimana*), Yakushima, Japan; tufted, 2–3cm tall; leaves to 6mm long, reniform, cordate, shallowly toothed; flowers 7–8mm wide, white, lower lobes purple-veined, early summer; the tiniest violet. *V.* × *williamsii* (p), group name covering the several sorts of tufted pansies or so-called garden or bedding violas, derived from crossing *V.* × *wittrockiana* and *V. cornuta*; habit of latter parent and sound perennials but with round, pansy-like flowers usually in self colours; normally propagated by division or summer cuttings; cultivars available include: *V.* × *w.* Admiration, deep blue-purple; *V.* × *w.* Irish Molly, copper-yellow; *V.* × *w.* Maggie Mott, silvery-mauve; *V.* × *w.* Norah Leigh, lavender-blue; *V.* × *w.* Primrose Dame, light yellow; *V.* × *w.* White Swan, pure white. *V.* × *wittrockiana* (*V.* × *hortensis*), garden pansy; a varied group of cultivars and strains of the familiar pansy, derived from crossing *V. lutea*, *V. tricolor* and *V. altaica*; short-lived perennials much like *V. tricolor*, but more robust and having larger flowers 4–12cm across in a wide range of colours usually with a black mask-like blotch in the centre; among the many cultivars and strains offered by seedsmen the following are recommended – Hiemalis or winter-flowering: *V.* × *w.* Celestial Queen, light blue; *V.* × *w.* Claret, wine-red; *V.* × *w.* Helios, golden-yellow; *V.* × *w.* Ice King, white with dark eye; *V.* × *w.* Mars, deep blue; *V.* × *w.* Winter Sun, yellow with dark eye. Spring to early summer flowering: *V.* × *w.* Azure Blue, bright blue; *V.* × *w.* Majestic Giants, mixed colours, including red, yellow, blue, white; *V.* × *w.* Sunny Boy, golden-yellow, black blotch. Summer-flowering: *V.* × *w.* Clear Crystals, mixed self-colours; *V.* × *w.* Engelman's Giant, mixed; *V.* × *w.* Roggli Swiss Giants, as a mixture or named single colour shades, eg *V.* × *w.* Berna, deep violet; *V.* × *w.* Brunig, mahogany-red; *V.* × *w.* Jungfrau, creamy-white; *V.* × *w.* Monch, yellow; see also *V.* × *williamsii*. *V. yakusimana*, see *V. verecunda y.*

Violet – see *Viola.*

Virginia creeper – see *Parthenocissus.*

Virginian stock – see *Malcolmia maritima.*

Virgin's bower – see *Clematis viticella.*

Viscaria alpina, V. vulgaris – see *Lychnis.*

Viscaria elegans – see *Silene coeli-rosa.*

Vitaliana – see *Douglasia.*

Vitex

(Latin name for the chaste tree). VERBENACEAE. A genus of 250 species of shrubs and trees mainly from tropical to warm temperate regions. 1 species is usually available: *V. agnus-castus*, chaste or hemp tree; S.Europe; aromatic shrub or small tree 3–6m tall, of spreading habit; leaves in opposite pairs, digitate, leaflets 5–7, lanceolate to elliptic, 5–12cm long, grey downy beneath; flowers to 8mm long, tubular, 5-lobed and somewhat 2-lipped, pale violet, fragrant, in terminal racemes to 18cm long, late summer to autumn. *V. a.-c.* Alba, flowers white; *V.a.-c.* Latifolia, more vigorous, with broader leaflets. Grow in moderately fertile, well-drained soil in sun, preferably against a south wall. Plant autumn or spring. Propagate by cuttings late summer, bottom heat 18–21°C.

Vitis

(Latin name for grape vine). VITIDACEAE (VITACEAE). A genus of 60–70 woody climbers from N.Hemisphere. They have branched, modified stem tendrils that may twine or produce sucker-like tips, alternate, generally palmate leaves, small, insignificant flowers with petals that fall as a cap on opening, and edible berry-fruit. Grow in humus-rich, moisture-retentive but well-drained soil in sun or partial shade. Plant autumn to spring. Propagate from seed when ripe in a cold frame, or by eye cuttings in late winter or hardwood cuttings *in situ* in autumn.

Species cultivated: *V. aconitifolia*, see *Ampelopsis a.* *V.* × Brant (*V. vinifera* Brant), (*V. labrusca* × *V. riparia* × *V. vinifera*), similar to *V. vinifera* but

Top right: *Vitis vinifera* Purpurea
Centre right: *Vitis* × Brant autumn colour
Right: *Vitis coignetiae* autumn colour

robust, the deeply 3–5 lobed leaves turning shades of dark red to purple with yellow veins in autumn; fruit like that of a small black common grape, having a sweet, somewhat aromatic flavour. *V. brevipedunculata*, see *Ampelopsis b. V. capensis*, see *Rhoicissus c. V. coignetiae*, crimson glory vine; Japan, Korea, Sakhalin; to 20m or more high; leaves to 30cm long, orbicular-cordate, sometimes shallowly lobed, grey to rusty-downy beneath, turning to shades of crimson and scarlet in autumn; berries about 1cm long, black with a glaucous bloom, barely edible. *V. elegans*, see *Ampelopsis brevipedunculata* Elegans. *V. henryana*, see *Parthenocissus h. V. heterophylla*, see *Ampelopsis brevipedunculata. V. inconstans*, see *Parthenocissus tricuspidata. V. quinquefolia*, see *Parthenocissus q. V. vinifera*, grape vine; in addition to the fruiting cultivars of this species there are several with ornamental foliage: *V.v.* Apiifolia (*V.v.* Laciniosa), parsley vine, leaves deeply dissected; *V.v.* Brant, see *V.* × Brant; *V.v.* Purpurea, Teinturier grape, leaves claret-red when young, ageing red-purple.

Wahlenbergia

(for George Wahlenberg, 1780–1851, Swedish botanist and professor at Uppsala). CAMPANULACEAE. A genus of about 150 species of annuals, perennials and sub-shrubs of wide distribution but mainly temperate S. Hemisphere. They have the same basic characters as *Campanula*, differing only in the way the seed capsules open by pores at the top within the persistent sepals (in *Campanula* they open at the base or sides beneath the sepals). Culture as for *Campanula*.
Species cultivated: *W. albomarginata*, New Zealand bluebell; S.Island, New Zealand; rhizomatous, tufted perennial forming mat-like colonies to 10cm tall or more; leaves 1–3cm or more long, elliptic to lanceolate or spathulate; flowers usually solitary, nodding, 1·5–2·5cm wide, pale blue to white; a variable species and growing longer in rich soil. *W. congesta* (*W. saxicola c.*), New Zealand; rhizomatous perennial forming low, dense mats to 10cm or more wide by 5cm high; leaves 8–25mm long, rounded to oblong or elliptic-spathulate, glossy; flowers solitary, to 1·2cm wide, pale blue or white, summer. *W. graminifolius*, see *Edraianthus g. W. pumilio*, see *Edraianthus p. W. saxicola congesta*, see *W. congesta. W. serpyllifolius*, see *Edraianthus s.*

Wake-robin – see *Trillium*.

Waldsteinia

(for Count Franz Adam Waldstein-Wartenburg, 1759–1823, Austrian botanist and author). ROSACEAE. A genus of 5–6 species of mat-forming perennials, akin to *Potentilla* and *Fragaria*, and from the northern temperate zone, 1 of of which is generally available: *W. ternata*, C.Europe to Siberia and Japan; evergreen; forming mats to 1m or so wide by 10cm tall; leaves trifoliate, leaflets 1–3cm long, ovate, irregularly toothed; flowers in stalked clusters of 2–7, 5-petalled, to 2cm wide, yellow, spring to early summer; a good ground cover plant for sun or shade. Grow in any well-drained but not dry soil. Plant autumn to spring. Propagate by division at planting time.

Wallflower – see *Cheiranthus cheiri*.

Wall-rue – see *Asplenium ruta-muraria*.

Walnut – see *Juglans*.

Wand flower – see *Dierama*.

Water avens – see *Geum rivale*.

Water crowfoot – see *Ranunculus aquatilis*.

Water fern – see *Azolla*.

Water hawthorn – see *Aponogeton*.

Water milfoil – see *Myriophyllum*.

Water plantain – see *Alisma*.

Water soldier – see *Stratiotes*.

Water-lily – see *Nuphar* and *Nymphaea*.

Watsonia

(for Sir William Watson, 1715–87, British physician and scientist). Bugle lily. IRIDACEAE. A genus of 60–70 species of cormous perennials mainly from S.Africa. They are clump-forming, each corm producing a fan of sword-shaped leaves and a slender spike, sometimes branched, of 6-lobed flowers, each with a slender curved tube. Grow in moderately fertile, well-drained soil in sun. The species described here are half-hardy and outside need warm areas and with some protection in winter where frost is slight. In cold areas they are best in a frost-free greenhouse in either a border, or large pots of a good commercial potting mixture. Plant or pot in spring, or the deciduous species in late summer. Propagate by division of clumps at potting or planting time, or from seed under glass in spring, growing on in pots for the first year until good-sized corms have formed.
Species cultivated: *W. ardernei*, 1–1·5m tall; leaves deciduous, 60cm long; spikes branched, flowers about 4cm long, white, early summer. *W. beatricis*, 1–1·2m tall; leaves evergreen, 60–75cm long; flowers 5cm long, orange-red, late summer to autumn. *W. marginata*, 1–1·5m tall; leaves deciduous, to 75cm long; flowers 3–4·5cm long, rose-pink, fragrant, early summer. *W. versfeldii*, to 1·5m tall; leaves deciduous, to 90cm long; flowers to 5cm or more long, rose, early summer.

Wayfaring tree – see *Viburnum lantana*.

Top: *Waldsteinia ternata*
Below left: *Watsonia ardernii*
Below: *Watsonia beatricis*

Weigela

(for Christian Ehrenfried Weigel, 1748–1831, German professor of botany). CAPRIFOLIACEAE. A genus of 10–12 species of deciduous shrubs from E.Asia. They have opposite pairs of elliptic to ovate leaves and small, lateral clusters of funnel-shaped, 5-lobed flowers in early summer. Grow in any moderately fertile soil that does not dry out, preferably in sun, although partial shade is tolerated. Plant autumn to spring. More shapely and floriferous specimens can be had by annually removing the flowered stems once the last blossom has faded, cutting back to a healthy shoot below the lowest truss of faded or fallen flowers. Propagation by semi-hardwood cuttings in late summer, by hardwood cuttings outside in autumn, or from seed in spring, the latter not coming true to type from cultivars.

Species cultivated: *W. florida* (*W. rosea*, *Diervilla f.*, *Diervilla r.*), N.China, Korea; 2–3m tall if not regularly pruned; leaves 5–10cm long, ovate-oblong to obovate, acuminate; flowers 3cm long, rose-pink without, paler within; several cultivars are available, some of them probably of hybrid origin with the allied, hairy-leaved *W. floribunda*: *W.* Abel Carrière, flowers large, rose-carmine; *W.* Avalanche, white; *W.* Bristol Ruby, erect habit, flowers ruby-red; *W.* Conquête, flowers to 5cm long, deep rose-pink; *W.* Eva Rathke, bright crimson, long-flowering; *W.* Fleur de Mai, flowers salmon-rose within, marbled rose-purple without; *W.* Foliis Purpureis, leaves purple-flushed, flowers pink; *W.* Looymansii Aurea, leaves yellow, flowers pink; *W.* Newport Red, like *W.* Eva Rathke, but more erect habit and larger, brighter red flowers; *W.* Variegata, compact habit, leaves margined creamy-white, flowers pink. *W. middendorffiana*, N.China, Japan; to 1·5m tall; leaves 5–8cm long; ovate; flowers about 3cm long, almost bell-shaped, sulphur-yellow with dark orange markings on lower lobes; thrives best in a sheltered, partially shaded position. *W. rosea*, see *W. florida*.

Wellingtonia – see *Sequoiadendron*.

Whitebeam – see *Sorbus aria*.

Whortleberry – see *Vaccinium myrtillus*.

Willow – see *Salix*.

Willow herb – see *Epilobium*.

Wineberry – see *Rubus*.

Winter cherry – see *Physalis alkekengi*.

Winter heliotrope – see *Petasites fragrans*.

Wintergreen – see *Gaultheria procumbens*.

Winter's bark – see *Drimys winteri*.

Wintersweet – see *Chimonanthus*.

Wisteria

(*Wistaria*). (for Caspar Wistar, 1761–1818, professor of anatomy at the University of Pennsylvania, USA). LEGUMINOSAE. A genus of 9–10 species of woody climbers from E.Asia and E.USA. They have alternate pinnate leaves, and pendant racemes of often fragrant pea-flowers, sometimes followed by quite large, bean-shaped pods that explode when ripe. Grow in humus-rich, well-drained but moisture-retentive soil in sun, providing support for the vigorous twining stems. Plant autumn or spring. Propagate from seed under glass and by layering in spring, or by cuttings late summer – bottom heat about 18°C. Plants may be allowed to grow

Below left: *Weigela* Variegata
Bottom left: *Weigela* Newport Red
Below: *Weigela florida*

naturally if there is adequate space; however, they are amenable to pruning – ideally all young twining stems should be cut back to 2–3 basal leaves during late summer, with the same treatment being afforded to any stems that grow subsequently in winter.

Species cultivated: *W. brachybotrys*, see next species. *W. floribunda* (*W. brachybotrys*), Japan; stems to 10m or more long; leaflets 13–19, ovate, 3–8cm long, racemes 13–25cm long; flowers to 2cm long, violet to purple-blue, summer. *W.f.* Alba (*W. multijuga* Alba), flowers white, tinted lilac; *W.f.* Macrobotrys (*W. multijuga*), racemes 30–90cm long, sometimes more, flowers lilac, tinted blue-purple. *W. multijuga*, see *W. floribunda* Macrobotrys and *W.floribunda* Alba. *W. sinensis*, China; stems 18–20m long; leaflets 9–13, elliptic to oblong, 4–7·5cm long; racemes 20–30cm long, flowers about 2·5cm long, mauve to deep lilac, opening just before or with young leaves, late spring to early summer. *W.s.* Alba, flowers white; *W. s.* Black Dragon, double, deep purple; *W.s.* Plena, double, rosetted, lilac.

Witch hazel – see *Hamamelis*.

Wolf's bane – see *Aconitum vulparia*.

Wood anemone – see *Anemone nemorosa*.

Wood lily – see *Trillium*.

Wood sorrel – see *Oxalis acetosella*.

Woodbine – see *Lonicera periclymenum*.

Woodwardia

(for Thomas Jenkinson Woodward, 1745–1820, British botanist). Chain fern. BLECHNACEAE (POLYPODIACEAE). A genus of about 12 species of ferns, mainly from the N.Hemisphere, 1 of which is usually available: *W. virginica*, N.America; rootstock a far-creeping robust rhizome; fronds solitary along the rhizome or in small clusters, to 1m or more tall with blades to 60cm long, pinnate, the pinnae narrowly oblong, deeply and regularly lobed; sori in 2 chain-like rows along the middle of each lobe. Grow in humus-rich, moisture-retentive or wet soil in partial shade; thrives well in the bog garden and even in shallow water at the edge of a pond. Plant autumn or spring. Propagate by division in spring.

Below: *Wisteria floribunda* Alba
Right: *Woodwardia radicans*
Below right: *Wisteria sinensis*
Bottom right: *Wisteria floribunda* Macrobotrys

Xeranthemum

(Greek *xeros*, dry, and *anthos*, a flower – alluding to the petal-like involucral bracts that surround the flower-heads). COMPOSITAE. A genus of 6 species of annuals from the Mediterranean to S.W.Asia, 1 of which is usually available: *X. annuum*, immortelle; S.E. and E. C.Europe; erect annual, branching from the base, to 60cm tall; leaves 2–6cm long, linear to oblong, densely white downy beneath, more sparsely above; flower-heads solitary, 3–5cm wide, the petal-like bracts spreading, bright pink, lilac, purple and white, florets all tubular, purple or white, summer; a useful everlasting, keeping its colour well if cut and dried when in full bloom. *X.a.* Ligulosum (*X. imperiale, X. superbissimum*), flower-heads double to semi-double. Grow in fertile, well-drained soil in sun. Sow seed *in situ* in spring.

Yarrow – see *Achillea millefolium.*

Yellow archangel – see *Lamiastrum galeobdolon.*

Yew – see *Taxus.*

Youth and age – see *Zinnia elegans.*

Yucca

(from the Carib Indian name for manihot or cassava, a member of the spurge family EUPHORBIACEAE, unfortunately chosen for this genus by Linnaeus). Adam's needle, Spanish bayonet. AGAVACEAE (LILIACEAE). A genus of about 40 species of evergreen trees and shrubs from S.USA, Mexico and W.Indies. They may be stemless, or almost so, or have erect, robust stems, sometimes sparingly branched, bearing terminal rosettes of linear, pointed leaves and large panicles of 6-tepalled, bell-shaped, white to cream flowers. In the wild the flowers are uniquely pollinated by the small *Pronuba* moth that gathers a ball of pollen from 1 flower, flies to another, lays eggs in the ovary, and then presses the pollen onto the stigma. The moth larvae feed on some of the developing seed, but there are plenty left to mature. Grow the hardy species mentioned here in well-drained soil in sunny, preferably sheltered sites. Plant autumn or spring. Propagate from seed when available, under glass, or by separating suckers in spring.

Species cultivated: *Y. filamentosa*, S.E.USA; almost stemless, forming clumps, 2–5m tall in bloom; leaves 35–75cm long, oblong-lanceolate to oblanceolate, slightly glaucous, with numerous margined curly threads; flowers white, 5cm long, late summer; confused with *Y. flaccida* and the narrower-leaved *Y. smalliana*. *Y. flaccida*, S.E. USA; much like *Y. filamentosa*, but with less rigid, more-tapered leaves having straight, marginal threads. *Y. glauca*, S.Dakota to N.Mexico, USA; clump-forming, to

Top far left: *Xeranthemum annuum*
Top: *Yucca glauca*
Left: *Yucca recurvifolia*
Above: *Yucca filamentosa* Variegata

1m tall in bloom; leaves to 60cm or more long by 1–1·5cm wide, linear, margins white with a few threads; flowers to 6·5cm long, greenish-cream, often tinged red-brown, summer. *Y. gloriosa*, Spanish dagger, palm lily (USA); to 2m or more tall; leaves to 75cm long, rigid, dark green; panicles 1–2m tall, flowers 6–10cm long, white, often tinged red, late summer to autumn. *Y. recurvifolia*, S.E.USA; similar habit to *Y. gloriosa*, but leaves softer, recurved; panicles looser and more branched. *Y.r.* Variegata, leaves with central yellow stripe.

Zantedeschia

(*Richardia*). (for Francesco Zantedeschi, born 1797, Italian botanist). Calla lily (USA), arum lily. ARACEAE. A genus of about 6 species of rhizomatous perennials from tropical to S.Africa. They have short, thick, fleshy, tuber-like rhizomes, tufts of long-stalked, sagittate to lanceolate leaves, and small, petalless flowers in spadices surrounded by broad, often coloured and showy spathes in summer. Greenhouse, but see also under *Z. aethiopica*; minimum temperature about 10°C, although *Z. aethiopica* will survive at 5–7°C, and *Z. elliottiana* is best at 12–15°C. Grow in pots of a standard compost such as J.I. No 2 or 3. Pot early spring and give 1 good watering, applying no more until shoots are several centimetres high. Water regularly thereafter and apply liquid feed at 7–10 day intervals once the young spathes show. *Z. aethiopica* is best kept just moist at all times, but the other species should be dried off once the leaves start to yellow after flowering. Propagation by offsets separated at potting time, or from seed in spring at 16–18°C.

Species cultivated: *Z. aethiopica* (*Z. africana* and *Richardia a.*), common calla or arum lily; S.Africa, naturalized in many frost-free areas of the world; to 1m tall; leafy blades sagittate, 25–45cm long, lustrous deep green; spathes 13–25cm long, white to creamy, surrounding bright yellow spadix; as a pot plant, best stood outside in summer; may be grown outside in sheltered moist sites, mounded over with peat, sand, pulverized bark, in late autumn; also thrives in water to 30cm deep, and in such situations survives moderate frost. *Z.a.* Crowborough, more compact-growing than type and reputedly hardier. *Z. albomaculata* (*Richardia a.* and *Z. melanoleuca*), S.Africa to Zambia; to 60cm tall; leaf-blades 20–45cm long, narrowly triangular, translucent white-spotted; spathes to 10cm or more long, whitish to pale yellow, red-purple at base within, rarely pink. *Z. elliottiana* (*Richardia e.*), golden or yellow calla or arum lily; S.Africa; 60–90cm tall; leaf-blades 15–30cm long, ovate-cordate, translucent whitish-spotted; spathes to 15cm long, bright yellow within, green-tinted without. *Z. melanoleuca*, see *Z. albomaculata*. *Z. rehmannii* (*Richardia r.*), pink or red calla or arum lily; S.Africa; 40–60cm tall; leaf-blades 15–30cm long, lanceolate, slender-pointed; spathes 7–13cm long, rosy-purple with white to pink margins but variable, some clones varying from bright pink to violet-red. Hybrids between this and other species are sometimes offered.

Zanthoxylum

(*Xanthoxylum*). (Greek *xanthos*, yellow, and *xylon*, wood – referring to the colour of the heart wood of some species). Prickly ash. RUTACEAE. A genus of about 200 species of deciduous and evergreen trees with pinnate leaves, from N. and S.America, Africa, Asia and Australia, 1 of which is usually available: *Z. americana*, northern prickly ash, toothache tree; E. N.America; deciduous large shrub or small tree 3–7m tall; stems spiny; leaves alternate, pinnate, leaflets 5–11, oblong to ovate, 4–6·5cm long, aromatic; flowers very small with 4–5 yellow-green petals in axillary, umbel-like clusters, spring; fruit berry-like, jet-black; the dried bark has medicinal uses. Grow in ordinary, well-drained soil in sun or partial shade. Plant autumn to spring. Propagate by suckers removed at planting time, from seed when ripe, and by root cuttings in late winter in a cold frame.

Zauschneria

(for Johann Baptist Zauschner, 1737–99, Bohemian professor of natural history). California fuchsia. ONAGRACEAE. A genus of 4 species of somewhat woody-based rhizomatous perennials from W.USA to Mexico. They have opposite pairs of linear to ovate leaves and terminal racemes of tubular, somewhat fuchsia-like flowers having 4 sepal-lobes and 4 petal-lobes. Grow in well-drained soil in sunny, sheltered sites. Plant autumn or spring. Propagate by cuttings of basal non-flowering sideshoots in late summer, or by division in spring. In cold areas cover with a cloche late autumn or propagate by cuttings which should be over-wintered in a frost-free place.

Left: *Zantedeschia aethiopica*
Below: *Zauschneria cana*

Species cultivated: *Z. californica* (*Z. mexicana*), California, Mexico; sub-shrubby at base, 30cm or more tall; stems branched; leaves crowded, linear, 1–4cm long, 2–6mm wide, grey-downy; flowers 2·5–4cm long, summer to autumn. *Z.c. canescens*, see next entry; *Z.c. latifolia* (*Z.c. canescens*), herbaceous, leaves broader than type, 7–17mm wide. *Z. cana* (*Z. microphylla*), California; sub-shrubby at base; similar to *Z. californica* but leaves narrowly linear to 2mm wide; whole plant more downy grey-hairy. *Z. canescens*, see *Z. californica latifolia*. *Z. mexicana*, see *Z. californica*. *Z. microphylla*, see *Z. cana*.

Zea

(Greek name for a food grass, probably a primitive type of wheat called spelt). GRAMINEAE. A genus of 3 species of annual and perennial grasses from tropical America, 1 of which is widely grown: *Z. mays*, sweet corn, maize, Indian corn, mealies. Of ancient origin. Not found wild; arose in Mexico and possibly Peru. Many cultivars are grown for 'corn on the cob' but several cultivars are grown primarily for ornamental purposes: *Z.m.* Gracillima, dwarf, leaves very narrow; *Z.m.* Gracillima Variegata, leaves white-striped; *Z.m.* Japonica Variegata and *Z.m.* Japonica Quadricolor, leaves striped yellow and white, often flushed pink. There are also mutant forms with grains red, purple and almost black, sometimes all in 1 cob.

Zelkova

(from the Caucasian vernacular name *zelkoua* or *tselkwa*). ULMACEAE. A genus of 5–7 species of deciduous trees from Crete to Japan. They are elm-like in general appearance but have small, rounded fruit technically classified as drupes. Culture as for *Ulmus*. May be propagated by grafting on to elm.
Species cultivated: *Z. carpinifolia* (*Z. crenata*), Caucasian elm; to 35m tall, rarely above 25m in Britain; of unique habit, a great sheaf of branches radiating from the top of a short, smooth trunk; leaves 5–9cm long, elliptic, prominently crenate; fruit about 5mm wide. *Z. crenatae*, see *Z. carpinifolia*. *Z. serrata*, saw-leaf zelkova or keaki; Japan; to 30m or more in the wild but rarely above 20m in Britain; widely domed habit with spreading branches; leaves 5–12cm long, ovate, coarsely sharp-toothed, colouring well in autumn; fruit 3mm wide.

Zenobia

(named after Zenobia, Queen of Palmyra, Syria, about AD266). ERICACEAE. A genus of 1 species of semi-evergreen shrub from S.E. USA: *Z. pulverulenta* (*Z. speciosa*), to 2m tall, of loose habit; leaves alternate, 3–7cm long, oblong to elliptic, entire or slightly toothed, bright glaucous particularly while young; flowers about 1cm long, bell-shaped, 5-lobed, waxy-white, fragrant, in lateral, pendulous umbels, summer. *Z.p. nitida* (*Z.p. nuda*), leaves non-glaucous. Grow in moisture-retentive, peaty, acid soil, preferably in partial shade. Plant autumn to spring. Propagate from seed or by layering in spring, by cuttings late summer, and suckers when available at planting time.

Top far left: *Zauschneria californica latifolia*
Left: *Zea mays* Gracillima Variegata
Top left: *Zea mays* Japonica Quadricolor
Above: *Zea mays* coloured grain cultivar

Zephyranthes

(Greek *zephryros*, the west wind, and *anthos*, a flower – alluding to plants' W.Hemisphere origin). Zephyr or rain lily. AMARYLLIDACEAE. A genus of

about 40 species of bulbous perennials from the warmer parts of N. and S.America, W.Indies. They have tufts of all-basal, linear to filiform, evergreen or deciduous leaves and solitary, 6-tepalled, tubular-based flowers. Grow hardy or half-hardy

Left: *Zelkova carpinifolia*
Below left: *Zenobia pulverulenta*
Above: *Zephyranthes candida*
Below: *Zephyranthes grandiflora*

species in well-drained, moderately fertile soil in sunny, sheltered sites, protecting the half-hardies in cold areas. Frost-free greenhouse or home for the tender species, in pots of J.I. potting compost No 1 or 2. Pot, repot or plant, spring. Potted specimens seem to flower more freely if they are left in the same container for several years (until congested, in fact). During the growing season liquid feed should be applied at 10-day intervals. Watering should be done with care, allowing the compost almost to dry out between applications. Little or no water is required in winter. Plants outdoors in wet areas benefit from a cloche in winter to keep off excess water. Propagation by separating offsets or dividing clumps at planting or potting time, or from seed in spring under glass.

Species cultivated: *Z. candida*, Argentina, Uruguay; hardy, evergreen except in severe winters; leaves rush-like, 20–30cm long; scapes 10–20cm tall, flowers crocus-like, 3·5–5cm long, white, autumn. *Z. carinata*, see *Z. grandiflora*. *Z. citrina*, S.America; tender; leaves to 30cm long, narrowly linear, channelled; scapes 15–25cm tall, flowers 3·5–4·5cm

Above: *Zigadenus elegans*
Above: right: *Zinnia elegans* Pink Ruffles
Right: *Zinnia elegans* Envy
Above far right: *Zinnia haageana* Persian Carpet
Far right: *Zinnia elegans* Scarlet Ruffles

long, bright yellow, summer to autumn. *Z. grandiflora* (*Z. carinata*, *Z. rosea* of gardens, not the much smaller-flowered true species), S.Mexico, Guatemala; half-hardy; leaves 25–40cm long by up to 8mm wide; scapes to 20cm or more tall, flowers 7–10cm long, opening widely, late summer to autumn; best under glass in cold areas. *Z. robusta*, see *Z. tubispatha*. *Z. rosea* of gardens, see *Z. grandiflora*. *Z. tubispatha* (*Z. robusta*, *Habranthus r.*), Argentina, Uruguay; half-hardy; leaves to 30cm or so long, linear, greyish; scapes 15–25cm tall, flowers 6–9cm long and wide, bright pink, late summer after leaves have died down; classified by some botanists under *Habranthus*.

Zigadenus

(*Zygadenus*). (Greek *zygon*, a yoke, and *aden*, a gland – referring to the paired glands at the base of the tepals of the first described species). LILIACEAE. A genus of 15 species of bulbous or rhizomatous perennials mainly from N.America (with 1 in E.Asia), 1 of which is generally available: *Z. elegans* (*Z. glaucus*), white camass, alkali grass; C.USA to N.Mexico and Alaska; bulbous, clump-forming, to 60cm or more tall; leaves 15–30cm long, linear, glaucous; flowers 6-tepalled, 1·5–2cm wide, each tepal greenish without, whitish within, bearing a conspicuous bilobed gland, in racemes or panicles, summer. Grow in moisture-retentive but not wet, neutral to acid, preferably peaty soil. Plant autumn to spring. Propagate by division or seed, spring.

Zinnia

(for Johann Gottfried Zinn, 1727–1759, German professor of botany at Gottingen). COMPOSITAE. A genus of 17–20 species of annuals, perennials and shrubs from S.W.USA and Mexico to Chile. They are mainly erect, with opposite pairs of linear to ovate leaves and solitary flower-heads with tubular to bell-shaped involucres and 1 to several rows of ray florets. Grow the annuals described here in at least moderately humus-rich soil in full sun and, ideally, sheltered from strong winds. Sow seed in spring at 21°C, if possible dressed with orthocide captan to minimize damping off. For best results space-sow in boxes at 4–5cm apart, or sow singly into 5cm pots. If seedlings are to be pricked off, do this within 4–5 days of germination to avoid root breakage. Seedlings in small pots are best potted on into 7–9cm containers of a good commercial potting mixture, when well-rooted. Harden off and plant out in early summer or when fear of frost has passed.

Species cultivated: *Z. angustifolia*, see comments under *Z. haageana*. *Z. elegans*, youth and age; Mexico; to 60cm or more tall; leaves 7–13cm long, sessile, lanceolate to ovate-oblong; flower-heads to 10cm or more wide, basically red but also in shades of purple-pink, orange, buff and white, summer to autumn. Many cultivars and mixed strains are available, varying greatly in stature, flower size and doubleness, the ray florets often elongated, or broader, or quilled. California Giant type: *Z.e.* Dahlia-flowered, very large heads; *Z.e.* State Fair, vigorous, good in poor summers; *Z.e.* Super Giants, florets quilled. Ruffles group, very fully double, freely branching and vigorous in single colours, eg *Z.e.* Cherry Ruffles, *Z.e.* White Ruffles, *Z.e.* Yellow Ruffles, or mixed; *Z.e.* Envy, chartreuse-green; *Z.e.* Peter Pan, to 30cm tall, very weather-resistant, good colour range. *Z. haageana* (*Z. angustifolia* of gardens, not the true species, with linear leaves and flower-heads to 4cm; *Z. mexicana*), Mexico; to 45cm or more tall; leaves 4–7·5cm long, lanceolate; flower-heads to 5cm wide, rays orange, or red and yellow or orange bi-coloured, summer to autumn; several cultivars are available with double flower-heads in a wide colour range, eg *Z.h.* Old Mexico, 30cm tall, flowers larger than type; *Z.h.* Persian Carpet, 30–37cm tall, many miniature flowers including bright bicolors.

Zizania

(Greek name for an unspecified wild grain, used by Linnaeus for this genus). Wild rice, water oats, Canada rice. GRAMINEAE. A genus of 3 species of annual and perennial aquatic grasses from N.E. N.America, E.Asia. They are of tufted or rhizomatous habit with broad but typically grass-like, linear leaves and terminal panicles of 1-flowered spikelets followed by large, cylindrical grains with a high nutritive value and greatly liked by water fowl. Grow in containers of rich loamy compost submerged in water 30–60cm deep, or plant directly into a natural mud bottom. Plant spring. Propagate perennials by division at planting time, the annuals from seed sown in spring, ideally in pots of compost stood in trays of water under glass, planting out when each plant has 3–4 leaves.

Species cultivated: *Z. aquatica*, annual wild or Indian rice; E. N.America; to 3m tall; leaves 2–4cm wide; panicles to 30cm or more long, female spikelets and subsequent grain to 2cm long, late summer to autumn. *Z. latifolia*, Manchurian wild rice; E.Asia; rhizomatous perennial 1·5–2·5m tall; leaves glaucous-green, 50–150cm long by 2–3cm wide; panicles 40–60cm long, female spikelets 1·8–2·5cm long, summer, when produced; grown mainly for its long, arching, densely-borne leaves.

Glossary

ACUMINATE	tapering to a slender point
ACUTE	sharply pointed but not tapering
AMPLEXICAUL	stem clasping, as a leaf base might
AXIL	junction between leaves, leaf stems, bracts, lateral flower buds, and the stem from which they arise
BI-	2, thus bipinnate is 2-pinnate
BRACT	a modified leaf below flowers, or clusters of flowers, and sometimes as showy as petals may be, as in many spurges, *Euphorbia*
CALYX	the outer whorl of modified leaves that protect the flower organs, sometimes persisting and showy, as in anemones, sometimes being shed when the flower opens, as in poppies
CLADODE	a flattened leaf like stem, as in butcher's broom, *Ruscus*
CORDATE	heart shaped with 2 rounded lobes at the base on either side of a stalk
CORYMB	a flat topped inflorescence made by the lower flower stalks being longer than those higher, as in candytuft, *Iberis*
CULTIVAR	short for cultivated variety and referring to a distinct variant of a species or hybrid maintained in cultivation
CYME	an inflorescence formed by repeated branching of each successive flowering stem, as in campion, *Silene* and in forget-me-not, *Myosotis*
DIGITATE	fingered leaves composed of more than 3 leaflets radiating from the same point at the top of a stalk, as in horse chestnut, *Aesculus*
DIOECIOUS	having male and female flowers on separate plants, as in holly, *Ilex*
DRUPE	a fleshy fruit with, usually, 1 hard, stony walled, seed, as in plums and cherries; small drupes, druplets, or drupels, form fruits such as of the raspberries and blackberries, *Rubus*
FILIFORM	thread like
GLANDULAR	with glands – small secretory organs often terminating in hairs or like minute pores
GLOBOSE	spherical, ball like
GLUME	a small bract with an axillary flower, as in grasses
HASTATE	triangular as a spear head
IMPARIPINNATE	see PINNATE
INFLORESCENCE	the flower bearing part of a plant formed of one or more flowers and arranged in various ways, such as a corymb or cyme for instance
INVOLUCRE	a ring of bracts surrounding a flower cluster, as the daisy, *Bellis*
LABELLUM	a specially modified tepal or petal, usually of an orchid flower, also called a lip
LANCEOLATE	lance or spear head shaped, 3–6 times as long as wide, broadest below the middle, with curving, tapered sides
LINEAR	leaves, petals and other organs with parallel sides for much of their length and at least 12 times as long as wide
MONOECIOUS	having separate male and female flowers on the same plant, as in hazel, *Corylus*
OB-	usually a prefix meaning inverted, as in oblanceolate or obovate with the broadest parts above the middle instead of below
ORBICULAR	disc shaped
OVATE	egg shaped in outline, from twice as long to as long as broad, widest below the middle and rounded to point tipped
OVOID	a solid, egg-shaped object
PALMATE	hand shaped, often fingered or lobed, as in maples, *Acer*
PANICLE	branched flower cluster of corymbs or racemes
PAPPUS	the modified calyx of members of the daisy family, the Compositae
PARIPINNATE	see PINNATE
PEDATE	shaped or lobed as a (bird's) foot
PETALOID	petal like
PHYLLOCLADE	a cladode

PINNATE — compound leaves with opposite pairs of separate leaflets, as in ash, *Fraxinus*. Pinnate leaves ending with an odd terminal leaflet are imparipinnate; those ending with a pair of leaflets paripinnate

PINNATIFID — leaves pinnately cut, the lobes extending less than halfway to the midrib; leaves with lobes extending more than halfway are pinnatipartite and those with lobes extending to the midrib pinnatisect

PINNATIPARTITE — see PINNATIFID

PINNATISECT — see PINNATIFID

PINNULE — leaflet of a bipinnate leaf, particularly applied to ferns

PSEUDOBULB — the bulb like swollen stems of orchids which store food and water

RACEME — inflorescence with a central stem bearing alternate or spirally arranged flowers each on a separate stalk

SAGITTATE — shaped like an arrowhead

SEPAL — one of the outer of the perianth segments, sometimes petal like as in the tulip, but usually green and often leaf like

SESSILE — without stalk

SORI — groups of sporangia, the spore containing bodies of ferns, often oval or circular, found on the under surface of the leaves

SPADIX — a flower spike the central stem of which is fleshy with the flowers embedded in it, as in cuckoo pint, *Arum*

SPATHE — the protective bract, or hood, ensheathing flowers. In cuckoo pint, *Arum*, and other similar flowers, it is large, showy and may be coloured while in other plants such as the daffodil, *Narcissus*, it forms a papery membrane

SPATHULATE — spoon or spatula shaped

STAMINODE — a stamen

STELLATE — star shaped

STIPULE — outgrowths, usually paired, at the base of the leaf stalks in some plants and taking various forms such as scale like and protecting the young leaves, then falling, in oak, *Quercus*, or spine like in false acacia, *Robinia*, and in many plants leaf like

STROBILI — cone, also the bud and catkin like inflorescence of conifers

TEPAL — tepals are the combined sepals and petals of a flower when they are similar as in the tulip

TERNATE — in threes, biternate therefore with 3 further divided into 3

TRI- — 3, thus trifoliate – leaves in groups of 3 or leaves cut into 3 leaflets

UMBEL — an inflorescence the stalks of which arise from one point, usually the terminal one

WHORL — a ring of leaves, bracts, flowers or other parts, radiating out from the same level on a stem similarly to the spokes of a wheel

ZYGOMORPHIC — applied to irregular flowers (e.g. pansies, peas and snapdragons) which can be cut into mirror halves in one plane only

Bibliography

The Concise Encyclopedia concentrates on describing the best of the hardy plants and the bedding plants commercially available, and also covers their basic cultivation. For further reading therefore, the *Reader's Digest Illustrated Guide to Gardening* (Reader's Digest, London) is recommended for its fuller approach to the practical aspects of cultivation, for the various groups of garden plants including those grown for indoor decoration and those grown for culinary purposes. It is mainly illustrated with black and white drawings and diagrams though a most useful section on pests and diseases is illustrated in colour.

Also to be recommended for those who wish to extend their knowledge of the huge range of plants available in cultivation is the one volume *Hortus Third* (by the staff of the L. H. Bailey Hortorium, Cornell University; Macmillan, New York) which is unparalleled. It is a large, not inexpensive but good value, dictionary of plants which in covering the plants in cultivation in the United States incidentally covers most of those available in Europe, including Britain. The few illustrations are black and white diagrams showing family characteristics.

A fuller version of the same sort of information but with the addition of more cultural details is *The New York Botanical Garden Encyclopedia of Gardening* (Garland Publishing, New York and London), which is written in an easily accessible style.

Further identification pictures of plants are to be found in the book published as the *Color Dictionary of Garden Plants* (McGraw Hill) in the United States and as the *Dictionary of Garden Plants in Colour* (Michael Joseph) in Britain. Though now old in origin it has been reprinted regularly and has over 2000 colour photographs.

The Royal Horticultural Society's *Dictionary of Gardening* (Oxford University Press) in four volumes with a supplement, although published some years ago, is still an indispensable reference work for the serious gardener.

For specialist subjects, books dealing with a single group or genus of plants, there is a flood of new writing constantly appearing. There is also a large number of possible subjects and the best plan is to get advice from the appropriate specialist society or association dealing with your particular interest. Your local gardening group or national horticultural society should be able to supply you with the right information and will almost certainly be delighted to do so.

Acknowledgments

Photographs were supplied by A-Z Botanical Collection, B. Alfieri, Heather Angel, K. A. & G. Beckett, Pat Brindley, R. J. Corbin, John K. B. Cowley, Valerie Finnis, Brian Furner, S. Hamilton, Iris Hardwick Library, Anthony Huxley, G. E. Hyde, Archivio IGDA, Tania Midgely, Ray Proctor, G. Rodway, Kenneth Scowen, Donald Smith, Harry Smith Horticultural Photographic Collection, Peter Stiles, Michael Warren.